Human
Adjustment

Human
Adjustment

second edition

Jane S. Halonen
Alverno College

John W. Santrock
University of Texas at Dallas

Brown & Benchmark
PUBLISHERS

Madison, WI Dubuque Guilford, CT Chicago Toronto London
Mexico City Caracas Buenos Aires Madrid Bogotá Sydney

Book Team

Executive Publisher *Edgar J. Laube*
Acquisitions Editor *Steven Yetter*
Developmental Editor *Linda Falkenstein*
Production Editor *Kristine Queck*
Proofreading Coordinator *Carrie Barker*
Designer *Jeff Storm*
Art Editor *Miriam Hoffman*
Photo Editor *Carol Judge*
Permissions Coordinator *Karen L. Storlie*
Production Manager *Beth Kundert*
Production/Costing Manager *Sherry Padden*
Design and New Media Development Manager *Linda Meehan Avenarius*
Marketing Manager *Carla Aspelmeier*
Copywriter *Jennifer Smith*
Proofreader *Mary Svetlik Anderson*

Basal Text *10/12 Minion*
Display Type *Minion*
Typesetting System *Macintosh® QuarkXPress®*
Paper Stock *50# Mirror Matte*

PUBLISHERS

President and Chief Executive Officer *Bob McLaughlin*
Vice President, Business Manager *Russ Domeyer*
Vice President of Production and New Media Development *Vickie Putman*
National Sales Manager *Phil Rudder*
National Telesales Manager *John Finn*

A Times Mirror Company

The credits section for this book begins on page C–1 and is
considered an extension of the copyright page.

Cover design by *LuAnn Schrandt*

Cover image © John Kelly/Image Bank Texas

Copyedited by *Wendy Nelson;* proofread by *Sarah Greer Bush*

Library of Congress Catalog Card Number: 95–83923

ISBN 0–697–23571–8

Printed in the United States of America by Times Mirror Higher Education Group, Inc.,
2460 Kerper Boulevard, Dubuque, IA 52001

10 9 8 7 6 5 4 3 2 1

Brief Contents

CONTENTS

CHAPTER EIGHT

Gender 166

CHAPTER NINE

Human Sexuality 194

CHAPTER TEN

Caring and Close Relationships 224

CHAPTER ELEVEN

Adult Lifestyles 248

CHAPTER TWELVE

Careers and Work   276

CHAPTER THIRTEEN

Adult Development and Aging   304

CHAPTER FOURTEEN

Abnormal Psychology   332

SOCIOCULTURAL WORLDS OF ADJUSTMENT

CRITICAL THINKING

SELF-ASSESSMENT

PREFACE

This preface especially highlights what is new to the second edition of *Human Adjustment* and the book's extensive, extremely effective learning system.

NEW TO THE SECOND EDITION

The second edition of *Human Adjustment* underwent an extensive, substantive revision. The changes include the addition of critical thinking as a major theme, a new coauthor, a fine-tuning of the sociocultural approach, an extensive overhaul of the content, and the inclusion of a new chapter.

Critical Thinking as a Major Theme

An important change in the second edition is the dramatic increase in emphasis on **critical thinking.** Some textbooks on adjustment have begun to include critical thinking, but we believe that the way critical thinking has been infused into *Human Adjustment,* second edition, is truly a unique system of challenging students to stretch their minds.

New Coauthor Jane Halonen

The addition of critical thinking as a new major theme of *Human Adjustment* was made possible by the contributions of new coauthor Jane Halonen. We emphasize various intellectual skills or outcomes that should be enhanced in an introductory course on adjustment. This emphasis promotes active engagement with the concepts and principles of human adjustment used throughout the text.

Modification of Sociocultural Contexts Material

The first edition of *Human Adjustment* was a unique departure from the standard adjustment text. How the sociocultural contexts in which we live influence the way we adjust in our lives was woven throughout the book. The emphasis on **sociocultural contexts**—culture, ethnicity, and gender—has been retained in the second edition of *Human Adjustment.* We have carefully considered how and where sociocultural material is presented, with the help of extensive feedback from reviewers, adopters, and students.

Overhaul of Content and Readability

In addition to the major changes in material on critical thinking and sociocultural contexts, *Human Adjustment* also underwent a substantial overhaul in content and readability. We left virtually no stone unturned in our effort to create a truly readable, up-to-date rendering of human adjustment. Every section, paragraph, sentence, figure, table, and legend went under a microscope and, whenever necessary, was amplified, trimmed, clarified, or tweaked with regard to content and readability.

New Chapter

Our effort to make *Human Adjustment* the very best text for students led to the creation of a new chapter—chapter 17, "Values and Religion." We believe that the important topics of values and religion have been underrepresented in texts on adjustment. Yet when we talk with people from many different walks of life about their adjustment, the topics of values and religion often crop up. We are indebted to Dr. Raymond Paloutzian of Westmont College, one of the world's leading experts on the psychology of religion, for his outstanding contributions to this chapter.

THE LEARNING SYSTEM IN *HUMAN ADJUSTMENT,* SECOND EDITION

Human Adjustment, second edition, has the most extensive learning system of any adjustment text. It is both very effective and very challenging.

Critical Thinking

Extremely important to the learning system in the book's second edition are the well-orchestrated critical-thinking components. The critical-thinking system includes the following:

- A major new section in chapter 1, called "Critical Thinking and Adjustment," that outlines the key features of the system
- Critical-thinking boxes in each chapter to encourage students to practice and enhance their abilities in critical thinking
- More extensive "Critical Thinking About Adjustment" end-of-chapter pieces that focus on topics related to the chapter's contents
- Picture and graphics legends t^{h} encourage active learning b^{y} pushing students to thin^{k} the implications of th^{e} illustrated in the ar^{t}

Pedagogical System

We want not only to encourage students to think critically about human adjustment but also to help them learn. The pedagogical system begins with the Visual Student Preface (following this Preface); the Visual Student Preface portrays how the student can effectively learn from the text. A chapter outline at the beginning of each chapter reveals the organization of the material.

We believe that human adjustment can best be understood by combining scientific research with human stories. We implement this belief in two ways. First, following the outline is an easy-to-read, high-interest introduction to the chapter called "The Story of. . . ." The Preview section links the story to the chapter's contents. Second, quotations also are sprinkled through the text to embellish the chapter contents with human voices from many different backgrounds and traditions.

Key terms appear in the text in bold-faced type; their definitions follow immediately in italics. This important pedagogical feature provides students with a very clear understanding of important adjustment concepts. The key terms also are defined in a book-ending Glossary.

Another key dimension of the learning system is the Review sections, which appear two to five times in each chapter. We designed reviews to activate students' memory and comprehension of main topics or important related ideas that have been discussed. This allows students to get a handle on complex concepts before they reach the end of the chapter. The review sections serve as a cognitive framework for organizing the most important information in that part of the book.

Figures, tables, photographs, and cartoons were carefully chosen for *Human Adjustment,* second edition. The unique visual figures combine a description of important content information with one or more photographs to illustrate the content. Some of the visual figures present summaries or reviews of salient issues that have been discussed in the text. The visual figures enhance students' retention and make the book a more attractive one to study.

Two other boxed features appear in every chapter. First, Sociocultural Worlds of Adjustment gives special attention to the cultural, ethnic, and gender dimensions of adjustment. Second, the Self-Assessment feature presents carefully selected self-tests for students to complete. Instructions on how to score and interpret them are found at the end of every chapter.

A number of pedagogical features appear at the end of each chapter. The chapter-ending material begins with the section Critical Thinking About Adjustment, which highlights an aspect of critical thinking related to a particular dimension of the chapter's material. Next is an Overview section with two parts: a cognitive map of the chapter's main topics, and a brief summary of the chapter's contents. Key Terms are then listed, page-referenced.

A practical, applied component concludes each chapter. The Practical Knowledge About Adjustment feature consists of book reviews (including photographs of the book covers) designed to encourage students to read further about the chapter's contents.

ANCILLARY MATERIALS FOR THE INSTRUCTOR

We've tried to combine a student-oriented textbook with an integrated ancillary package designed to meet the unique needs of instructors and students. Our goal has been to create a teaching package that is as enjoyable to teach with as it is to study from.

The *Instructor's Manual and Test Item File* (ISBN 0–697–23572–6) provides many useful tools to enhance your teaching. In the instructor's manual, by Terri Pettijohn of Ohio State University, learning objectives, an extended chapter outline, suggestions for teaching, lecture/discussion suggestions, video and film suggestions, classroom activities, and handout forms are provided for each chapter. The Test Items were written by Gregory Cutler of Bay de Noc Community College. There are over 50 questions per chapter.

The questions in the test item file are also available on *MicroTest III,* a powerful but easy-to-use test-generating program by Chariot Software Group. MicroTest is available for your use in DOS (3.5 [ISBN 0–697–23577–7]), Windows (ISBN 0–697–23579–3), and Macintosh (ISBN 0–697–23581–5) versions. With MicroTest, instructors can easily select questions from the Test Item File and print tests and answer keys. Instructors can also customize questions, headings, and instructions; add or import their own questions; and print tests in a choice of printer-supported fonts.

Or take advantage of Brown & Benchmark's free call-in **Testing Service.** With 48 hours notice, our Educational Resources department will prepare your test and fax you the questions and the answer key. Simply select your questions in advance and call 1–800–338–5371 and our educational resources representatives will be glad to help you.

The Brown & Benchmark *Introductory Psychology Activities Handbook* offers additional activities, in-class and out-of-class projects, and discussion questions. The activities handbook will help you get your students actively engaged and thinking critically.

The *Student Study Guide* (ISBN 0–697–23573–4) provides students with learning objectives, a detailed outline of each chapter, a guided review of terms and concepts, and multiple-choice practice tests.

A large selection of *videotapes* is also available to adopters based on the number of textbooks ordered. Consult your Brown & Benchmark Sales Representative for ordering policies.

A new supplement, *Resources for Improving Human Adjustment,* includes a wide array of valuable resources that can be used to improve human adjustment. This practical book includes lists of agencies, phone numbers, and booklets, covering many areas of human adjustment, that students can refer to. This supplement mirrors the organization of *Human Adjustment,* second edition, and can be packaged with the text at no additional cost.

B&B CourseKits™

B&B CourseKits™ are course-specific collections of for-sale educational materials, custom packaged for maximum convenience and value. CourseKits offer you the flexibility of customizing and combining Brown & Benchmark course materials (B&B CourseKits™, Annual Editions®, Taking Sides®, etc.) with your own or other material. Each CourseKit contains two or more instructor-selected items conveniently packaged and priced for your students. For more information on B&B CourseKits™, please contact your local Brown & Benchmark Sales Representative.

Annual Editions®

Magazines, newspapers, and journals can provide current, first-rate, relevant educational information. *Annual Editions* provides convenient, inexpensive access to a wide range of current, carefully selected articles from magazines, newspapers, and journals. Written by psychologists, researchers, and educators, *Annual Editions: Personal Growth and Behavior* provides useful perspectives on important and timely topics. *Annual Editions* is updated yearly, and includes a number of features designed to make it particularly useful, including a topic guide, annotated table of contents, and unit overviews. For the professor using Annual Editions in the classroom, an Instructor's Resource Guide with test questions is available. Consult your Brown & Benchmark Sales Representative for more details.

CourseMedia™

As educational needs and methods change, Brown & Benchmark adds innovative, contemporary student materials for the computer, audio, and video devices of the 1990s and beyond. These include:

· Stand-alone materials
· Study guides
· Software simulations
· Tutorials
· Exercises

CourseWorks

CourseWorks (formerly Kinko's Course-Works in the U.S.) is the Brown & Benchmark custom publishing service. With its own printing and distribution facility, CourseWorks gives you the flexibility to add current material to your course at any time. CourseWorks provides you with a unique set of options:

· Customizing Brown & Benchmark CourseBooks
· Publishing your own material
· Including any previously published material for which we can secure permissions
· Adding photos
· Performing copyediting
· Creating custom covers

ACKNOWLEDGMENTS

No textbook of this size or scope is possible without the efforts and scrutiny of a number of thoughtful, conscientious reviewers. Many thanks go to the following reviewers:

Pearleen Breshears
Southwest Baptist University
Melanie Lesar
Oakland Community College
Harriette B. Ritchie
American River College
Jeanne M. Slattery
Clarion College
Dr. Floyd S. Tesmer
Strayer College

Sharon Thomas
Miami-Dade Community College–Kendall Campus
Kristin Vermillion
Rose State College
Lois J. Willoughby
Miami-Dade Community College

We also benefited considerably from the reviews of the first edition of *Human Adjustment.* Many thanks also go to these individuals:

Gary G. Ford
Stephen F. Austin State University
Lawrence L. Galant
Gaston College
William J. Gnagy
Illinois State University
Richard E. Miller
Navarro College
Thomas Eckle
Modesto Junior College
Donald L. Fischer
Southwest Missouri State University
Peter Gram
Pensacola Junior College
Edward Moriarity
Springfield Technical Community College
Norm Presse
Dalton College
Donald M. Stanley
North Harris College
Margaret Theobold
Southeast Missouri State University

We also owe special thanks to our editor, Steven Yetter, and our developmental editor, Linda Falkenstein, for their excellent guidance on this project. Thanks also go to Terri Pettijohn of Ohio State University, who prepared a very useful instructor's course planner and student study guide, and to Gregory Cutler of Bay de Noc Community College, who prepared a new test item file.

A final note of thanks goes to our spouses—Brian Halonen and Mary Jo Santrock—for their enthusiastic support of our work, for their patient tolerance of our single-minded work habits, and for their companionship and unfailing humor.

VISUAL STUDENT PREFACE

How the Learning System Works

his book contains an extensive and very effective learning system that will both challenge you to think critically and help you to learn the material more competently.

CRITICAL THINKING

Critical Thinking Boxes

These boxes are inserted periodically in each chapter to encourage you to stretch your mind about a topic in that particular section of the chapter.

CRITICAL THINKING

Evaluating Stereotypes About the Elderly

Because of ageism, older adults might be shunned socially because they are perceived as senile or boring. Their children might edge them out of their lives. In these circumstances, a social network of friendships becomes an important support system for older adults. Researchers have found that close attachment to one or more individuals, whether friends or family, is associated with greater life satisfaction.

How are the elderly portrayed on television and in magazines? Are they stereotyped as tired, ugly, helpless, sick, lonely, and ready to die? Sometimes they are portrayed more positively—as wise and kind—which also can be stereotypes. Analyze how elderly are portrayed today in a variety of magazines, such as *Time, Ladies' Home Journal,* and other popular magazines. Then go to the library and find some magazines from earlier decades in this century. Compare the earlier portrayals with today's portrayals. Have images of the elderly become less stereotyped, less negative, or have they remained about the same? By comparing the media images of the elderly in different decades, you are learning to think critically about development *by examining the influence of context and culture on behavior.*

ageism and racism (Tran, Wright, & Chatters, 1991). Both wealth and health decrease more rapidly for the ethnic minority elderly than for elderly White Americans. The ethnic minority elderly are more likely to become ill but less likely to receive treatment. They are also more likely to have a history of less education, unemployment, worse housing conditions, and shorter life expectancies than their elderly White American counterparts. Many ethnic minority workers never enjoy the Social Security and Medicare benefits to which their earnings contribute, because they die before reaching the age of eligibility for benefits.

A possible double jeopardy also faces many women—the burden of *both* ageism and sexism (Harrison, 1991; Kogan & Black, in press; Lopata, 1995). The poverty rate for elderly women is almost double that of elderly men. According to Congresswoman Mary Rose Oakar, the number one priority for midlife and older women should be economic security. She predicts that 25 percent of all women working today can expect to be poor in old age. Only recently has scientific and political interest in aging women developed. For many years, aging women were virtually invisible in aging research and in protests involving rights for the elderly. An important research and political agenda for the 1990s is increased interest in the aging and rights of elderly women (Markson, 1995).

Not only is it important to be concerned about the double jeopardy of ageism and sexism involving older women, but special attention also needs to be devoted to the elderly who are female ethnic minority individuals. They face what could be described as triple jeopardy—ageism, sexism, and racism (Stoller & Gibson, 1994). Income is a special problem for these women. For example, more than one-third of all older African American women have incomes below the poverty level (compared to less than one-fourth of all older African American men and approximately 13 percent of older White American women). One-fourth of all older Latina women have incomes below the poverty level (compared to 19 percent of Latino men) (U.S. Bureau of the Census, 1990). More information about being female, ethnic, and old appears in Sociocultural Worlds of Adjustment.

American women living alone, the figure is 55 percent. Almost one-fourth of all elderly Latinos are below the poverty line. Only 10 percent of elderly White Americans fall below the poverty line.

Comparative information about African Americans, Latinos, and White Americans indicates a possible double jeopardy for elderly ethnic minority individuals, who face problems related to *both*

Critical Thinking About Adjustment

This section appears at the end of each chapter and usually involves a more elaborate exploration of critical thinking than the boxed inserts.

CRITICAL THINKING ABOUT ADJUSTMENT
Labeling and Justice

When you began this chapter, you constructed a list of characteristics that you thought captured your personality. We challenged you to think about whether the traits you selected were representative, enduring, consistent, and realistic. We questioned whether others would describe you in the same way.

Compassion could have been one of the traits you selected. Suppose we wanted to develop a simple self-report inventory similar to the self-assessments you completed in this chapter, that would allow the measurement of some aspects of compassion. Walter Mischel suggests that traits interact with situations. Suppose, to measure your compassion, we asked you which of the following acts you would perform:

* Agreeing to a request to sponsor a child in a technologically disadvantaged country
* Intervening in a friend's drug or alcohol problem
* Offering money to the homeless when they confront you personally
* Taking in stray animals
* Sacrificing your own plans to help a friend
* Volunteering assistance to a driver with a disabled car
* Alerting a friend who has some lunch stuck between his teeth
* Letting a sick friend copy your homework
* Giving away all your possessions to a needy organization

As you can see, measuring the trait of compassion with this inventory would be extremely difficult. The actions listed in this self-report checklist could all be compassionate in some circumstances, but it would certainly be difficult to evaluate a person's compassion using responses to this list. For example, you could endlessly adopt stray animals, but there are practical constraints on how much compassion you could show using this behavior. You could let a friend copy your homework in the compassion of the moment, but that judgment might be far from compassionate in the long run because your friend will be unlikely to learn something that could be useful in the future. Could we rule out your having any compassion if you indicated you wouldn't perform any of the actions on the list? Probably not. Although our compassion self-report checklist has face validity (that is, each item relates to compassion), it is unlikely that we could use it as it stands to conduct valid research on the trait.

Making judgments about traits is difficult not only in research situations; it can be surprisingly challenging in life. Although we regularly make trait attributions to help us understand situations, we might not sufficiently capture the complexity of the situation. The use of traits to explain behavior can help us be efficient processors of reality, but it is doubtful that it helps us make accurate or fair-minded interpretations. Sometimes the labels lead us to make premature

judgments and turn our attention elsewhere—we assign a trait as the reason for an action and move on.

How can this knowledge help us to be more effective critical thinkers in relation to judgments about personality? We should be able to *apply psychological concepts to enhance personal adaptation* by incorporating the following skills:

1. **Reserve judgment, particularly when making negative attributions.**
   How important is it to resolve a behavioral question by attributing someone's actions to a trait? In many situations, labeling requires making a judgment that we may later regret. In the tradition of Skinner, it may be more helpful to think about and describe specific behaviors involved in the situation than dispense with the situation by assigning dysfunctional traits as the cause. For example, marriage therapists often help couples learn to describe the behaviors that are upsetting to them rather than continue to use hurtful and unhelpful labeling (such as "You are inconsiderate and insecure").

2. **Recognize the boundaries of labels.**
   When we feel compelled to make trait judgments, it is still helpful to remember the context in which the behavior occurred and confine the judgment to that circumstance. For example, if you think of your father as "mean," it will be useful to identify the circumstances in which he is mean. He might be mean when he has not gotten enough sleep or when he is trying to watch his weight. This restricted use of the label recognizes that there are likely to be many circumstances in which he is not mean, which brings into question the fairness of the use of the term.

3. **Abandon expectations about consistency.**
   As you read in this chapter, many other cultures may be less intense about defining, categorizing, and judging personality features. This attitude may be a function of living in collectivistic cultures where there is no particular advantage in labeling others' traits. Richard Brislin (1993) believes that enduring relationships in collectivistic cultures may show greater tolerance about inconsistencies in human behavior. Even if we don't live in a collectivistic culture, we can save some frustration if, like collectivists, we do not expect human beings to be consistent across all situations.

The very purpose of existence is to reconcile the glowing opinion we hold of ourselves with the appalling things that other people think about us.

—Quentin Crisp

PEDAGOGICAL SYSTEM

Not only do we want to challenge you to think critically about psychology but we also want to help you learn the material. The following representation of the pedagogical system is organized by beginning, interior, and ending of chapter.

Beginning of Chapter

Chapter Outline

Each chapter begins with an outline that reveals the organization of topics. The outline gives you an overview of the arrangement and structure of the chapter.

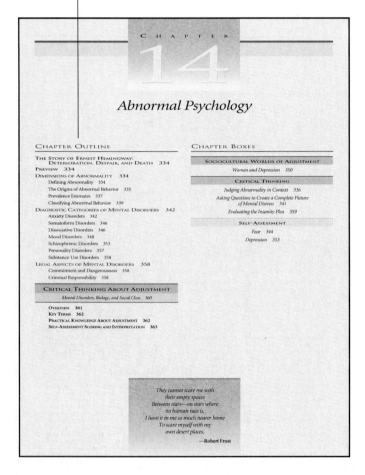

C H A P T E R

14

Abnormal Psychology

They cannot scare me with
their empty spaces
Between stars—on stars where
no human race is.
I have it in me so much nearer home
To scare myself with my
own desert places.

—Robert Frost

The Story of . . .

This easy-to-read, high-interest piece introduces you to some aspect of the chapter's contents.

THE STORY OF ALICE WALKER: DISADVANTAGE AND TRIUMPH

In the summer of 1966, Alice Walker, who would later win a Pulitzer Prize for *The Color Purple*, spent her days battling racism in Mississippi. She had recently won her first writing fellowship and could have chosen to follow her dream of moving to Senegal, Africa, but instead she put herself in the heart and heat of the civil rights movement. Walker grew up knowing the brutal effects of poverty and racism. Born in 1944, she was the eighth child of Georgia sharecroppers who earned about $300 a year. When she was 8, her brother accidentally shot her in the left eye with a BB gun. By the time her parents got her to the hospital a week later (they had no car), she was blind in that eye and it had developed a disfiguring layer of scar tissue. Despite the counts against her, Walker has become an essayist, poet, award-winning novelist, short-story writer, and social activist, who, like her characters (especially the women), has overcome pain and anger to celebrate the human spirit. As Walker puts it, she writes about people who "make it, who come out of nothing. People who triumph."

Alice Walker won the Pulitzer Prize for her book *The Color Purple*. Like the characters in her book (especially the women), Walker overcame pain and anger to triumph and celebrate the human spirit.

PREVIEW

What leads one person, so full of promise, to cope poorly with life's problems while another turns poverty and trauma into a rich harvest of adjustment? How can we explain why one person can pick up the pieces of a life shattered by tragedy, such as a loved one's death, while another seems to come unhinged by life's minor hassles? Why is it that some people are real whirlwinds—successful at work, maintaining good relationships with their friends and family, and active participants in community organizations—while others hang out on the sidelines, mere spectators in life? Understanding these individual differences is an important goal of the psychology of adjustment. We will begin this chapter by exploring the nature of adjustment, then encourage you to think critically about adjustment. Next we will distinguish psychology from pseudopsychology, and finally we will encourage you to become a wise consumer of psychological knowledge.

Preview

This section tells you what the chapter's contents are.

WHAT IS ADJUSTMENT?

It isn't your imagination—it is getting tougher to cope in this world. We are exposed to overwhelming amounts of information daily. For example, one day's edition of the *New York Times* is packed with more information than a person who lived in the Middle Ages acquired during a lifetime.

Experts estimate that information doubles at a rate too rapid to calculate (Sternberg, 1996). However, information overload is not the only challenge in contemporary life. We also must deal with changes caused by the United States' diminishing role as an undisputed industrial giant. As the need to both import and export goods increases, so does global interdependence and the need to understand other cultures in order to effectively cope with our world. We live in a nation where the workforce is increasingly diverse. By the year 2000 a full five-sixths of new workers entering the job market will be women and ethnic minorities (Ickovics, 1991). Even the increasing knowledge gathered by psychologists and other scientists makes our daily decisions more complex as we

try to choose lifestyles that will help us cope better with the world and live longer, healthier lives.

These challenges raise questions that are extremely important to the future of any society. By better understanding the nature of adjustment, we can reduce conflict and meet the challenges that lie ahead by seeking answers to questions like these: How can we cope with the increased overload of information that we have to digest each day? How can people from different ethnic and cultural backgrounds get along better with each other? How can women and men successfully adapt to the

4   *Halonen/Santrock: Human Adjustment*

While the roommate might agree that the request is reasonable, he might fail to comply because he doesn't like the unstated implication that he is being given orders in this relationship. Similar situations occur in couple relationships, as when one member buys something, makes plans for the weekend, or invites a guest to dinner without first asking the other member.

Finally, interpersonal communication is **transactional,** *which means that communication is an ongoing process between sender and receiver that unfolds across time, and that it is not unusual for information to be communicated almost simultaneously between the participants.* Much of interpersonal communication is not a one-time, brief interaction that lasts several seconds. Rather, most of our interpersonal communication involves an ongoing volley or parley of verbal and nonverbal actions between the sender and the receiver. Initially person A may be the sender, person B the receiver; then after 15 seconds, person A may become the receiver and person B the sender; and so on, back and forth, over a period of time. At the same time as person A is sending a message verbally, person B may be sending a message nonverbally.

Let's consider an example of how these transactional characteristics of interpersonal communication might work. Jay comes in from work and asks his wife, Jan, "How come dinner isn't ready yet?" Jan responds, "I got home late from work myself. It's going to be about an hour before it is ready." Already, in this brief social communication that has taken only about 10 seconds, both individuals have served as senders and receivers of messages. When Jay got to the word *dinner* in his sentence, Jan had begun to give him a blank stare, and by the time he spoke the word *yet,* the stare had a tone of anger as well. Further, by the time Jan got to the words *an hour before it's ready,* Jay was displaying an angry grimace. Thus, in this interchange, Jay and Jan were sending and receiving messages simultaneously.

Social communication always occurs in a *context,* the environment in which messages are sent and received. The context influences the form and content of social communication. In today's world,

FIGURE 7.1

Some Important Components of Interpersonal Communication

the sociocultural dimensions of context are especially important for understanding interpersonal communication. For example, when people from different cultural and ethnic groups interact, they might follow different rules of communication. This can produce confusion, unintentional insults, inaccurate perceptions, and other miscommunications.

The importance of paying attention to cultural context has sometimes escaped manufacturers trying to capture a world market (Petras & Petras, 1994). For example, the brand name *Coca-Cola* translates to the Chinese consumer as "Bite the wax tadpole." Japanese beverages have been marketed in the West with the names *Kolic, Ucc, Mucos,* and *Pocari*

Sweat. Obviously, successful international marketing requires attention to the rich dimensions of language.

Now that we have examined the main components and characteristics of interpersonal communication, we can define it. **Interpersonal communication** *is a transactional process that is ongoing over time. This process involves at least two individuals, each of whom acts as both sender and receiver, encoding and decoding messages, sometimes simultaneously. These messages are sent through verbal or nonverbal channels. Noise can limit the accuracy of a message. Communication always takes place in a context.* (See figure 7.1 for a visual depiction of these important components of interpersonal communication.)

Halonen/Santrock: *Human Adjustment*

Interior of Chapter

Visual Figures

Visual figures combine a description of important content information with one or more photographs to illustrate the content. Some of the visual figures present summaries of key ideas in the text to enhance your retention.

Key Terms

Key terms appear in the text in boldfaced type, with their definitions following immediately within the text in italics.

Review

The review sections are a key dimension of the learning system. They appear two to five times in each chapter and are designed to activate your memory and comprehension of main topics or important ideas that have been discussed to that point. This allows you to get a handle on key concepts before you reach the end of the chapter.

Quotations

Quotations are sprinkled through each chapter to stimulate further thought about a topic.

REVIEW

Psychodynamic and Humanistic Therapies

Psychodynamic therapies stress the importance of the unconscious mind, early family experiences, and extensive interpretation by the therapist. Psychoanalysis is Freud's technique for analyzing an individual's unconscious thought. Free association, catharsis, interpretation, dream analysis, transference, and resistance are techniques used in psychoanalytic therapy. Although psychodynamic therapy has changed, many contemporary psychodynamic therapists still probe the unconscious mind for early family experiences that might provide clues to the client's current problems. The development of the self in social contexts is an important theme in Kohut's contemporary approach.

In the humanistic therapies, clients are encouraged to understand themselves and to grow personally. The humanistic therapies emphasize conscious thoughts, the present, and growth and fulfillment. Person-centered therapy, developed by Rogers, emphasizes that the therapist should provide a warm and supportive atmosphere to improve the client's self-image and to encourage the client to gain insight into problems. The therapist replaces conditions of worth with unconditional positive regard and uses genuineness, accurate empathy, and active listening to raise the client's self-esteem. Gestalt therapy, developed by Fritz Perls, emphasizes that the therapist should question and challenge clients in order to help them become more aware of their feelings and face their problems. Gestalt therapy is more directive than is the nondirective approach of person-centered therapy.

---

to understand their true selves, to develop a sense of freedom, and to look at what they are doing with their lives.

Now that we have studied the insight therapies, we will turn our attention to therapies that take a very different approach to working with individuals to reduce their problems and improve their adjustment—the behavior therapies.

> *Every new adjustment is a crisis in self-esteem.*
>
> —Eric Hoffer

Behavior Therapies

Behavior therapies *use principles of learning to reduce or eliminate maladaptive behavior.* Behavior therapies are based on the behavioral theory of learning and personality described in chapter 2. Behavior therapists do not search for unconscious conflicts, like psychodynamic therapists, or encourage individuals to develop accurate perceptions of their feelings and self, like humanistic therapists. Insight and self-awareness are not the keys to helping individuals develop more adaptive behavior patterns, say the behavior therapists. The insight therapies—psychodynamic and humanistic—treat maladaptive symptoms as signs of underlying, internal problems. Behavior therapists, however, assume that the overt maladaptive symptoms are

the problem. Individuals can become aware of why they are depressed and still be depressed, say the behavior therapists. A behavior therapist tries to eliminate the depressed symptoms or behaviors themselves rather than try to get individuals to gain insight or awareness about why they are depressed (O'Donahue & Krasner, 1995).

Behavior therapists initially based their interventions almost exclusively on the learning principles of classical and operant conditioning, but behavior therapies have become more diverse in recent years. As cognitive social learning theory grew in popularity and the cognitive approach became more prominent in psychology, behavior therapists increasingly included cognitive factors in their therapy. First we will discuss the classical and operant conditioning approaches; then we will turn to the cognitive therapies.

Classical Conditioning Approaches

We acquire, or learn, some behaviors, especially fears, through classical conditioning. These behaviors can be unlearned, or extinguished. If an individual has learned to fear snakes or heights through classical conditioning, perhaps the individual could unlearn the fear. Two procedures based on classical conditioning that are used in behavior therapy are systematic desensitization and aversive conditioning.

Systematic Desensitization System**atic desensitization** *is a method of behavior therapy that treats anxiety by associating deep relaxation with successive visualizations of increasingly intense anxiety-producing situations; this technique is based on classical conditioning* (Wolpe, 1963). Consider the common fear of taking a test. Using systematic desensitization, a behavior therapist first asks the client which aspects of the fearful situation—in this case, taking a test—are the most and least frightening. Then, the behavior therapist arranges these circumstances in order from most to least frightening. An example of this type of desensitization hierarchy is shown in figure 15.4.

The next step is to teach individuals to relax. Behavior therapists teach clients to recognize the presence of muscular contractions, or tensions, in various parts of their bodies and then to contract and relax different muscles. Once individuals are relaxed, the therapist asks them to imagine the least fearful stimulus in the hierarchy. Subsequently the therapist moves up the list of items from least to most fearful while the clients remain relaxed. Eventually individuals are able to imagine the most fearful circumstance without being afraid—in our example, on the way to the university the day of an exam. In this manner, individuals learn to relax while thinking about the exam instead of feeling anxious.

Chapter 15: Therapies 375

Visual Student Preface

SOCIOCULTURAL WORLDS OF ADJUSTMENT

The Extended Family System in African American and Mexican American Families

In the 1985 Children's Defense Fund study "Black and White Children in America: Key Facts" (Edelman, 1987), African American children were three times as likely as White children to be poor, live with a parent who has separated from a spouse, and die of child abuse; five times as likely to be dependent on welfare; and twelve times as likely to live with a parent who never married. Nonetheless, it is important to keep in mind that millions of African American families are not on welfare; have children who stay in school and out of trouble; and, if they experience difficult times, find a way to cope with and overcome their problems. In 1967 Martin Luther King, Jr., reflected on the African American family and gave the following caution: As public awareness of the predicament of the African American family increases, there will be opportunity and danger. The opportunity will be to deal fully rather than haphazardly with the problem as a whole, as a social catastrophe brought on by many years of oppression. The danger is that the problems will be attributed to innate African American weaknesses and will be used to justify further neglect and to rationalize continued oppression. In today's world, Dr. King's words still ring true.

The African American cultural tradition of an extended family household—in which one or several grandparents, uncles, aunts, siblings, or cousins either live together or provide support—has helped many African American parents cope with adverse social conditions such as economic impoverishment (McAdoo, 1993). African American extended families can be traced to the African heritage of many African Americans, in which a newly married couple does not move away from relatives. Instead, the extended family assists its members with basic family functions. Researchers have found that African American extended families help reduce the stress of poverty and single parenting through emotional support, the sharing of income and economic responsibility, and surrogate parenting (McLoyd & Wilson, 1990; Wakschlag, Chase-Lansdale, & Brooks-Gunn, 1996). The presence of grandmothers in the households of many African American adolescents and their infants has been an important support system for both the teenage mothers and the infants (Stevens, 1984). Active and involved extended family support systems also help a parent or parents from other ethnic minority groups cope with poverty and its related stress.

A basic value in Mexico is represented by the saying "As long as our family stays together, we are strong." Mexican children are brought up to stay close to their families, often playing with siblings rather than with schoolmates or neighborhood children, as American children usually do. Unlike the father in many American families, Mexican fathers are the undisputed authority on all family matters and are usually obeyed without question. Mothers are revered as the primary source of affection and care. This emphasis on family attachment leads the Mexicans to say, "I will achieve mainly because of my family, and for my family, rather than myself." By contrast, a self-reliant American would say, "I will achieve mainly because of my ability and initiative and for myself rather than for my family." Unlike most Americans, families in Mexico tend to stretch out in a network of relatives that often runs to scores of individuals.

Both cultures—Mexican and American—have undergone considerable change in recent decades. It is difficult to predict whether Mexican children will gradually take on the characteristics of American children, or American children will shift closer to Mexican children. The cultures of both countries will probably move to a new order more in keeping with future demands, retaining some common features of the old while establishing new priorities and values.

The extended family plays an important role in the adjustment of ethnic minority individuals.

Mexican American children often grow up in families with a network of relatives that runs into scores of individuals.

Sociocultural Worlds of Adjustment

This boxed feature gives special attention to the cultural, ethnic, and gender dimensions of psychology.

Self-Assessment

These boxed inserts, which appear one or more times in each chapter, present carefully selected self-tests for you to complete. Instructions on how to score and interpret your responses can be found at the end of each chapter.

SELF-ASSESSMENT

Attitudes Toward Women

Instructions

The statements listed to the right describe attitudes toward the role of women in society that different people have. There are no right or wrong answers, only opinions. Express your feeling about each statement by indicating whether you (A) agree strongly, (B) agree mildly, (C) disagree mildly, or (D) disagree strongly.

To score and interpret your responses, please turn to the end of this chapter.

Items	Agree Strongly	Agree Mildly	Disagree Mildly	Disagree Strongly
1. Swearing and obscenity are more repulsive in the speech of a woman than of a man.	A	B	C	D
2. Women should take increasing responsibility for leadership in solving the intellectual and social problems of the day.	A	B	C	D
3. Both husband and wife should be allowed the same grounds for divorce.	A	B	C	D
4. Telling dirty jokes should be mostly a masculine prerogative.	A	B	C	D
5. Intoxication among women is worse than intoxication among men.	A	B	C	D
6. Under modern economic conditions with women being active outside the home, men should share in household tasks such as washing dishes and doing the laundry.	A	B	C	D
7. It is insulting to women to have the "obey" clause remain in the marriage service.	A	B	C	D
8. There should be a strict merit system in job appointment and promotion without regard to sex.	A	B	C	D
9. A woman should be as free as a man to propose marriage.	A	B	C	D
10. Women should worry less about their rights and more about becoming good wives and mothers.	A	B	C	D
11. Women earning as much as their dates should bear equally the expense when they go out together.	A	B	C	D
12. Women should assume their rightful place in business and all the professions along with men.	A	B	C	D
13. A woman should not expect to go to exactly the same places or to have quite the same freedom of action as a man.	A	B	C	D
14. Sons in a family should be given more encouragement to go to college than daughters.	A	B	C	D
15. It is ridiculous for a woman to run a locomotive and for a man to darn socks.	A	B	C	D
16. In general, the father should have greater authority than the mother in the bringing up of children.	A	B	C	D
17. Women should be encouraged not to become sexually intimate with anyone before marriage, even their fiancés.	A	B	C	D
18. The husband should not be favored by law over the wife in the disposal of family property or income.	A	B	C	D
19. Women should be concerned with their duties of childbearing and house tending, rather than with desires for professional and business careers.	A	B	C	D
20. The intellectual leadership of a community should be largely in the hands of men.	A	B	C	D
21. Economic and social freedom is worth far more to women than acceptance of the ideal of femininity that has been set up by men.	A	B	C	D
22. On the average, women should be regarded as less capable of contributing to economic production than men.	A	B	C	D
23. There are many jobs in which men should be given preference over women in being hired or promoted.	A	B	C	D
24. Women should be given equal opportunity with men for apprenticeship in the various trades.	A	B	C	D
25. The modern girl is entitled to the same freedom from regulation and control that is given to the modern boy.	A	B	C	D

End of Chapter

Overview

The overview section consists of two parts: (1) a cognitive map that provides you with a visual organization of the chapter's main topics and (2) a brief summary of the chapter's main contents.

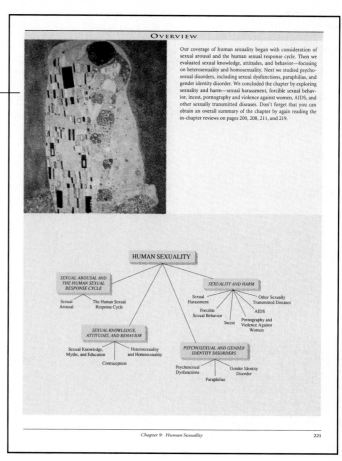

Our coverage of human sexuality began with consideration of sexual arousal and the human sexual response cycle. Then we evaluated sexual knowledge, attitudes, and behavior—focusing on heterosexuality and homosexuality. Next we studied psychosexual disorders, including sexual dysfunctions, paraphilias, and gender identity disorder. We concluded the chapter by exploring sexuality and harm—sexual harassment, forcible sexual behavior, incest, pornography and violence against women, AIDS, and other sexually transmitted diseases. Don't forget that you can obtain an overall summary of the chapter by again reading the in-chapter reviews on pages 200, 208, 211, and 219.

HUMAN SEXUALITY

SEXUAL AROUSAL AND THE HUMAN SEXUAL RESPONSE CYCLE
- Sexual Arousal
- The Human Sexual Response Cycle

SEXUALITY AND HARM
- Sexual Harassment
- Forcible Sexual Behavior
- Incest
- Pornography and Violence Against Women
- AIDS
- Other Sexually Transmitted Diseases

SEXUAL KNOWLEDGE, ATTITUDES, AND BEHAVIOR
- Sexual Knowledge, Myths, and Education
- Contraception
- Heterosexuality and Homosexuality

PSYCHOSEXUAL AND GENDER IDENTITY DISORDERS
- Psychosexual Dysfunctions
- Paraphilias
- Gender Identity Disorder

Key Terms

KEY TERMS

social perception   123
primacy effect   123
social comparison   123
impression management   123
ingratiation   124
self-promotion   124
intimidation   124
exemplification   124

supplication   124
self-monitoring   124
attribution theory   125
fundamental attribution error   125
attitudes   125
cognitive dissonance   126
self-perception theory   127
obedience   131

norms   134
roles   134
great person theory   134
situational theory of leadership   135
conformity   136
groupthink   138
deindividuation   138

Key terms are listed in the order in which they appeared in the chapter and are page-referenced.

Practical Knowledge About Adjustment

PRACTICAL KNOWLEDGE ABOUT ADJUSTMENT

This section consists of practical book reviews (including a photograph of the book). We hope that some of the books will interest you and that you will be motivated to read further about some of psychology's topics.

INFLUENCE

(1993, rev. ed.) by Robert Cialdini. New York: Quill.

This highly acclaimed book by a well-known social psychologist explores how influence works in today's marketplace. Cialdini provides valuable suggestions for persuading other people and understanding how others try to persuade us. He also covers how power works, the role of reciprocity in influence, the importance of commitment and consistency, how to say no, scarcity, relationships with others, advertising, sales techniques, and instant influence.

SHYNESS

(1987) by Philip Zimbardo. Reading, MA: Addison-Wesley.

According to Zimbardo, shyness is a widespread social problem that affects as many as four out of every five people at one time or another in their lives. He explores how and why people become shy and examines the roles that parents, teachers, spouses, and culture play in creating shy individuals. What does Zimbardo say shy people can do about their situations? First, you have to analyze your shyness and figure out how you got this way. Possible reasons include negative evaluations, fear of being rejected, fear of intimacy, or lack of adequate social skills. Second, you need to build up your self-esteem. To help you do this, Zimbardo spells out fifteen steps to becoming more confident. And third, you need to improve your social skills. Zimbardo describes several behavior modification strategies, tells you to set realistic goals, and advocates working hard toward achieving these goals. This is an excellent self-help book for shy individuals. It dispenses sound advice, is free of psychobabble, and is easy to read.

Self-Assessment Scoring and Interpretation

SELF-ASSESSMENT SCORING AND INTERPRETATION

This end-of-chapter feature tells you how to interpret your scores on the chapter's Self-Assessments.

SELF-MONITORING

Scoring

Give yourself one point for each of questions 1, 5, and 7 that you answered F. Give yourself one point for each of the remaining questions that you answered T. Add up your points.

Interpretation

If you are a good judge of yourself and scored 7 or above, you are probably a high-self-monitoring individual; 3 or below, you are probably a low-self-monitoring individual.

End of Book

Glossary

Key terms are defined alphabetically in a book-ending glossary, along with their page references.

GLOSSARY

A

abnormal behavior Behavior that is maladaptive, harmful, statistically unusual, personally distressing, and/or designated abnormal by the culture. 335

acceptance Kübler-Ross' fifth stage of dying, in which the dying person develops a sense of peace, an acceptance of fate, and, in many cases, a desire to be left alone. 326

acculturation Cultural change that results from continuous, firsthand contact between two distinct cultural groups. 92

acculturative stress The negative consequences of acculturation. 92

accurate empathy Rogers' term for the therapist's ability to identify with the client. 374

action therapy Therapy that promotes direct changes in behavior; insight is not essential for change to occur. 369

active listening Rogers' term for the ability to listen to another person with total attention to what the person says and means. 374

active-behavioral strategies Coping responses in which individuals take some type of action to improve their problem situation. 101

active-cognitive strategies Coping responses in which individuals actively think about a situation in an effort to adjust more effectively. 101

activity disorder An intense, driven, compulsive exercise pattern often combined with rigid dietary restrictions that can damage a person's body. 403

activity theory The theory that the more active and involved older people are, the more satisfied they will be with their lives and the more likely it is that they will stay healthy. 319

actor-observer hypothesis The hypothesis that differences in interpretations of motives are based on points of view. 125

actual self An individual's representation of the attributes she or he believes her- or himself to actually possess. 55

addiction Physical dependence on a drug. 414

adjustment The psychological process of adapting to, coping with, and managing the problems, challenges, and demands of everyday life. 6

adolescence The developmental period of transition from childhood to early adulthood, entered at approximately 10 to 12 and ending at about 18 to 22 years of age. 307

adrenal glands Glands located just above the kidneys that play an important role in our moods, energy levels, and ability to cope with stress. 80

aerobic exercise Sustained exercise—jogging, swimming, or cycling, for example—that stimulates heart and lung activity. 402

affectionate love Also called companionate love, this type of love occurs when individuals desire to have the other person near and have a deep, caring affection for the person. 230

ageism Prejudice against people based on their age. 319

aggressive behavior Hostile, often angry, behavior that involves deprecating others, and enhancing oneself at the expense of others. 113

agoraphobia The fear of entering unfamiliar situations, especially open or public spaces; the most common phobic disorder. 343

AIDS A sexually transmitted disease that is caused by the human immuno-deficiency virus (HIV), which destroys the body's immune system. 214

alternation model The model according to which individuals can develop bicultural competence without choosing one culture over another or diminishing their own subgroup identification. 92

altruism An unselfish interest in helping someone else. 226

Alzheimer's disease A progressive, irreversible brain disorder involving gradual deterioration of memory, reasoning, language, and eventually physical function. 323

anal stage Freud's second stage of development, occurring between 1½ and 3 years of age, in which the child's greatest pleasure involves the anus or the eliminative functions associated with it. 28

androgens The main class of male sex hormones. 181

androgyny The presence of desirable masculine and feminine characteristics in the same individual. 174

anger Kübler-Ross' second stage of dying, in which the dying person realizes that denial can no longer be maintained; the dying person often then feels anger, resentment, rage, and envy. 325

anorexia nervosa An eating disorder that involves the relentless pursuit of thinness through starvation. 406

antianxiety drugs Drugs that are commonly known as tranquilizers and reduce anxiety by making individuals less excitable and more tranquil. 392

antidepressant drugs Drugs that regulate mood. The three main classes of antidepressant drugs are tricyclics, such as Elavil; MAO inhibitors, such as Nardil; and SSRI inhibitors, such as Prozac. 392

G-1

Visual Student Preface

Human
Adjustment

Michio Takayama
Inner Peace, detail

The Nature of Adjustment

*What is needed is not the will to believe,
but the wish to find out.*

—Bertrand Russell

THE STORY OF ALICE WALKER: DISADVANTAGE AND TRIUMPH

I n the summer of 1966, Alice Walker, who would later win a Pulitzer Prize for *The Color Purple,* spent her days battling racism in Mississippi. She had recently won her first writing fellowship and could have chosen to follow her dream of moving to Senegal, Africa, but instead she put herself in the heart and heat of the civil rights movement. Walker grew up knowing the brutal effects of poverty and racism. Born in 1944, she was the eighth child of Georgia sharecroppers who earned about $300 a year. When she was 8, her brother accidentally shot her in the left eye with a BB gun. By the time her parents got her to the hospital a week later (they had no car), she was blind in that eye and it had developed a disfiguring layer of scar tissue. Despite the counts against her, Walker has become an essayist, poet, award-winning novelist, short-story writer, and social activist, who, like her characters (especially the women), has overcome pain and anger to celebrate the human spirit. As Walker puts it, she writes about people who "make it, who come out of nothing. People who triumph."

Alice Walker won the Pulitzer Prize for her book *The Color Purple.* Like the characters in her book (especially the women), Walker overcame pain and anger to triumph and celebrate the human spirit.

PREVIEW

What leads one person, so full of promise, to cope poorly with life's problems while another turns poverty and trauma into a rich harvest of adjustment? How can we explain why one person can pick up the pieces of a life shattered by tragedy, such as a loved one's death, while another seems to come unhinged by life's minor hassles? Why is it that some people are real whirlwinds—successful at work, maintaining good relationships with their friends and family, and active participants in community organizations—while others hang out on the sidelines, mere spectators in life? Understanding these individual differences is an important goal of the psychology of adjustment. We will begin this chapter by exploring the nature of adjustment, then encourage you to think critically about adjustment. Next we will distinguish psychology from pseudopsychology, and finally we will encourage you to become a wise consumer of psychological knowledge.

WHAT IS ADJUSTMENT?

It isn't your imagination—it is getting tougher to cope in this world. We are exposed to overwhelming amounts of information daily. For example, one day's edition of the *New York Times* is packed with more information than a person who lived in the Middle Ages acquired during a lifetime.

Experts estimate that information doubles at a rate too rapid to calculate (Sternberg, 1996). However, information overload is not the only challenge in contemporary life. We also must deal with changes caused by the United States' diminishing role as an undisputed industrial giant. As the need to both import and export goods increases, so does global interdependence and the need to understand other cultures in order to effectively cope with our world. We live in a nation where the workforce is increasingly diverse. By the year 2000 a full five-sixths of new workers entering the job market will be women and ethnic minorities (Ickovics, 1991). Even the increasing knowledge gathered by psychologists and other scientists makes our daily decisions more complex as we try to choose lifestyles that will help us cope better with the world and live longer, healthier lives.

These challenges raise questions that are extremely important to the future of any society. By better understanding the nature of adjustment, we can reduce conflict and meet the challenges that lie ahead by seeking answers to questions like these: How can we cope with the increased overload of information that we have to digest each day? How can people from different ethnic and cultural backgrounds get along better with each other? How can women and men successfully adapt to the changing gender roles they are experiencing? What roles do exercise and nutrition play in physical and mental health?

Meeting the challenges of today's world and developing strengths to cope with future challenges require knowledge of the adjustment process. This book is about that knowledge and about application of that knowledge. Although good adjustment requires a lot of work, we all have the capacity to understand ourselves better, use better strategies to solve our personal problems, and think more clearly about how to adapt to stressful circumstances or overcome them. Therefore, we hope that upon finishing this book you won't even consider burying your head in the sand to avoid dealing with conflicts in your life, but rather you will use your acquired information about effective coping to modify aspects of your life. After all, what effort is more worthwhile than improving your own future?

Our discussion of adjustment will be based primarily on the field of science known as psychology. Psychology is not a cure-all for every knotty problem, and it doesn't reveal *the* meaning of life. It does, however, contribute enormously to our knowledge about why people are the way they are, why they think and act the way they do, and how they can cope more effectively with their lives. The study of psychology shows significant potential to improve our lives as we approach the twenty-first century.

> *My friend, care for your psyche. Make it as good as possible. Know thyself, for once we know ourselves, we may learn how to care for ourselves, otherwise we never will.*
>
> **—Socrates**

Defining Psychology

Which finding would you predict to be true?

Finding 1: Couples who live together before marriage have a better chance of making the marriage last.
Finding 2: Couples who do not live together before marriage tend to have a lower divorce rate.

Even though the commonsense notion that "practice makes perfect" suggests

that the first finding is the more likely, researchers have found a higher marriage success rate for couples who legally marry initially rather than live together before marriage (Teachman & Polonko, 1990). As you can see, psychology doesn't accept assumptions about human nature at face value, however reasonable they sound. It is a rigorous discipline that tests assumptions and gathers evidence to support explanations of behavior.

Psychology *is the scientific study of behavior and mental processes in contexts.* Psychology emphasizes observing, describing, explaining, and predicting behavior. There are four aspects of this definition that need elaboration: behavior, mental processes, science, and contexts. Let's examine behavior first.

Behavior *is everything we do that can be directly observed*—such as two people *kissing*, a baby *crying*, a student *studying*. Psychologists strive to distinguish behavior from inferences we draw about behavior. Behaviors are usually described using verb forms that communicate observable actions. In contrast, **inferences** *are conclusions that we draw from observing behavior.*

Mental processes are trickier to define and describe than behavior is. They *encompass thoughts, feelings, and motives that each of us experiences privately but that cannot be observed directly.* Although we cannot directly observe and describe thoughts and feelings, they are no less real because of that. For example, mental processes include *thoughts* about kissing someone, *feelings* a baby experiences when its mother leaves the room, and *memories* a college student has about a fine afternoon on a motorcycle.

Because we can't observe these processes directly in others, we often *infer* the mental processes that support observable behavior. For example, what would you infer Alice Walker might have felt when she won the Pulitzer Prize? If we had been with her when she received the good news, we might have observed her *smiling* or *crying*, but we would have had to infer her mental processes. Would she have been overjoyed? stunned? relieved? thinking about how long it had taken to receive the recognition? planning on calling her loved ones? We would infer the impact of the news on her from our

observations of her behavior. To further evaluate the interpretation of behavior, turn to the Critical Thinking box.

Describing behavior is a relatively straightforward process; drawing inferences about unobservable mental processes is not. Our inferences can be right or wrong. Inferences can also vary from person to person. We can usually reach agreement about how to describe behavior we observe, but our inferences often reflect wide variations in how we each experience and interpret behavior.

As a **science,** *psychology uses systematic methods to observe, describe, explain, and predict behavior and mental processes.* Psychology's methods are not casual, but rather consist of careful, precise plans and conduct. When psychologists systematically evaluate or analyze the collected data, they also want to *explain* what their observations suggest. Another goal of psychology is to *predict* behavior. For example, researchers might construct a questionnaire on race relations, in order to describe patterns of prejudice, and give it to 500 college students (Halonen & Santrock, 1996). The results of the survey might indicate that college students today are less tolerant of other races than college students were a decade ago. The researchers might also try to predict the levels of college students' racial intolerance based on factors such as their conservative or liberal religious attitudes, or whether their background is rural, suburban, or urban.

Psychology, of course, is not all pure science and research. It has an applied, practical side as well. While many psychologists conduct research that is relevant to understanding adjustment, the careers of other psychologists center on helping individuals cope with their problems. For example, **clinical and counseling psychology,** *the most widely practiced specialization in psychology, involves evaluating and treating people with psychological problems.* The work of clinical psychologists and counseling psychologists is similar, although counseling psychologists are more apt to work with people experiencing fewer serious problems. In some instances, counseling psychologists work with students, advising them about personal problems and career planning.

Describe the behaviors you see in these photographs. What verbs accurately describe them? What kinds of inferences can we draw about the meanings of these behaviors? Did you observe the behaviors closely by taking into account the contexts in which they are occurring? This example illustrates the fact that interpreting behavior involves three steps: (1) *making accurate observations*, (2) *describing the behavior*, and (3) *drawing inferences about the behavior that reflect the contexts in which the behavior occurs.*

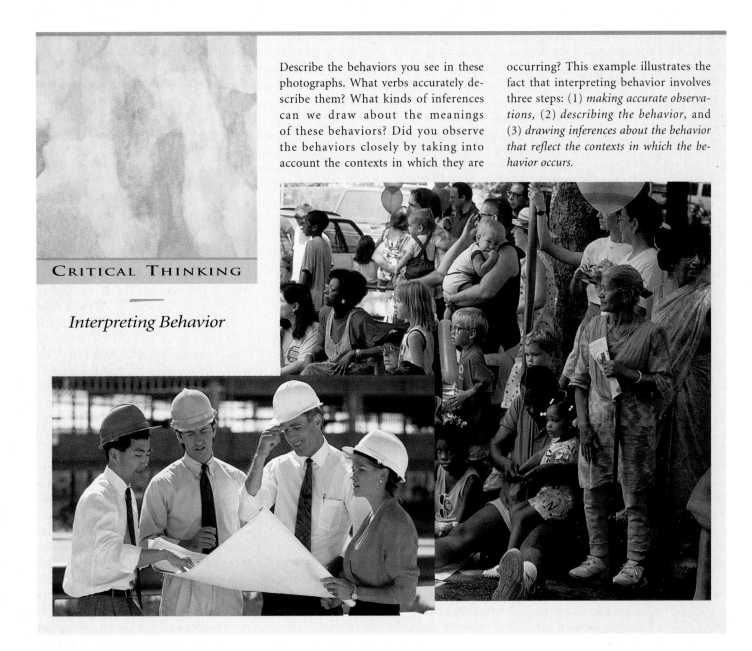

It is also important to know that counseling and clinical psychologists are different from psychiatrists. Typically, a psychologist has spent 3 or 4 years in graduate school to get a doctorate degree and then does a 1-year internship in a mental health facility. On the other hand, **psychiatry** *is a branch of medicine practiced by physicians who have specialized in abnormal behavior and psychotherapy.* Counseling psychologists, clinical psychologists, and psychiatrists are all interested in improving the lives of people with mental health problems. Because psychiatrists are medical doctors, however, they take a medical approach to problems and often prescribe drugs, whereas clinical and counseling psychologists cannot.

The last key aspect of our definition of psychology is contexts. **Contexts** *refer to the historical, economic, social, and cultural factors that influence mental processes and behavior.* People do not act, or react, in a vacuum. Everything we think, say or do is colored by where we come from, who we have spent time with, and what has happened to us. All human behavior occurs in a cultural context. These contexts—or settings—include homes, schools, churches, cities, neighborhoods, communities, and colleges, as well as nations with important and unique historical, economic, social, and cultural legacies.

Defining Adjustment in a Sociocultural Context

We have already mentioned the concept of adjustment a number of times, but have yet to define it. **Adjustment** *is the psychological process of adapting to, coping with, and managing the problems, challenges, and demands of everyday life.* Adjustment is involved when a student develops better study habits, when an employee learns to get along better with co-workers, when a person redefines life following a divorce, when a person

Context is an important dimension of psychology. *Contexts* are settings, which are influenced by historical, economic, social and cultural factors. Without reference to context, the racial tolerance of the college students shown here cannot be fully understood.

remains calm enough to help family members after a hurricane disaster, when a workaholic executive adopts a more balanced and relaxed lifestyle, when a depressed individual begins to face troubles rather than avoid them, when a person in an ethnic conflict tries to view the problem from the other person's perspective, and when a self-centered adult learns how to be nurturant and sensitive to another's feelings. As you can see, adjustment is a broad concept that affects many areas of human lives.

Adjustment increasingly involves an understanding of sociocultural contexts and issues (Bowser & Hunt, 1996). A **sociocultural approach** *emphasizes that culture, ethnicity, and gender are essential to understanding adjustment and behavior.* **Culture** *refers to the behavior patterns, beliefs, and other products of a particular group of people—including their values, work patterns, music, dress, diet, and ceremonies—that are passed on from generation to generation.* A cultural group can be as large and diverse as the United States, or it can be as small and unified as an African hunter-gatherer tribe, but whatever its size and complexity, the group's culture influences the identity, learning, social behavior, and adjustment

of its members (Kagitcibasi, 1996; Matsumoto, 1996; Triandis, 1994, 1996.)

Ethnicity *(the word* ethnic *comes from the Greek word for "nation") is based on cultural heritage, nationality characteristics, race, religion, and language. Ethnicity involves descent from common ancestors, usually in a specifiable part of the world.* Sometimes culture and ethnicity are identical, such as being Irish and living in Ireland. Often the terms indicate different aspects of one's identity, such as being Irish American—a person's culture is the United States and a person's ethnicity is Irish.

Ethnicity is central to the development of an **ethnic identity,** *a sense of membership in an ethnic group based upon shared language, religion, customs, values, history, and race.* All of us have ethnicity, but only some of us have a strong ethnic identity and use our ethnicity to define our individual identities. Without distinguishing between ethnicity and ethnic identity, we fail to understand the nature of people who have an ethnicity but who do not identify with or have much feelings about this fact. For example, when a person says, "I'm Jewish," the person might be stating a simple fact about a

geographical origin, making a statement about a religious belief, or speaking about a strong ethnic identity with full identification with the Jewish culture. Similarly, some Polish Americans, Italian Americans, and Mexican Americans have strong ethnic identities and others do not. Consider a college student who doesn't know much about her ancestors from Europe and who shows little interest in her European descent (her ethnicity); instead, she identifies herself as a fifth-generation Texan and is proud of it—her Texan roots are her ethnic identity.

Given the descent of individuals from common ancestors, people often make inferences about another's ethnicity based on physical features they believe to be typical of an ethnic group. For example, one of the downed American flyers in the recent Gulf war had features that would be considered "Arab." This flyer was treated worse by his captors than the other prisoners of war were. As this example illustrates, ethnicity is also a factor in how we are evaluated and how we interact with other persons, including how our own feelings about our ethnic identity differ from others' feelings about our ethnic identity. At times these evaluations are wrong and unfair.

So far we have discussed two aspects of sociocultural contexts—culture and ethnicity. A third important aspect is gender. Psychologists use the terms *sex* and *gender* in different ways. **Sex** *refers to the biological dimension of being female or male,* focusing on anatomical, reproductive, hormonal, and genetic aspects of being female or male. **Gender** *is the sociocultural dimension of being female or male,* emphasizing how we learn to think and behave as females and males (Gilligan, 1996; Rollins, 1996; Unger & Crawford, 1992). Few aspects of our existence are more central to our identity and to our social relationships than our sex and gender. Our gender-related attitudes and behavior seem to be changing, but how much change has actually occurred? How much change is desirable? Is there a limit to society's influence on what is considered appropriate behavior for males and females? A related concern of many feminist psychologists is that through much of its history, psychology has portrayed human behavior with a "male dominant theme," with the result that psychology has less knowledge about the female experience than about the male experience (Denmark, 1994; McLoyd & Ceballos, 1995; Paludi, 1995).

The sociocultural approach is one of psychology's newest lenses for examining behavior and adjustment. With the growing contact between people from quite different cultural backgrounds, a sociocultural approach is especially needed to make the psychology of adjustment a relevant discipline in the twenty-first century. See Sociocultural Worlds of Adjustment for an exploration of the growing diversity in American culture.

A special concern, from the sociocultural standpoint, is the prejudice and discrimination that many cultural and ethnic groups face. Persistent prejudice and discrimination are in many of life's domains, including the media, interpersonal interactions, and the workplace (Sue, 1990). Discrimination, of course, is not confined to cultural and ethnic groups. The aged, the physically and cognitively different, gays and lesbians, women, and advocates of religions and political stances also experience discrimination. When psychologists address adjustment issues from the standpoint of sociocultural influences, psychology becomes more meaningful and relevant for culturally diverse people rather than only for the White American males that once received nearly all of the research and theoretical attention (Kagiticibasi, 1995).

We will weave discussions of sociocultural issues throughout the remainder of this book. Each chapter includes material on sociocultural dimensions of adjustment and contains Sociocultural Worlds boxes that highlight such issues. Each chapter also includes other features that enhance your involvement as a reader and should improve your ability to apply the adjustment concepts you are learning to situations beyond the classroom.

CRITICAL THINKING AND ADJUSTMENT

There are two ways to slide easily through life; to believe everything or doubt everything. Both ways save us from thinking.

—**Alfred Korzybski**

What exactly is *critical thinking?* In the context of adjustment, **critical thinking** *is making appropriate decisions and developing competent strategies about what to do or believe about your own, and other people's, well-being* (Halonen, 1995). We have identified nine critical-thinking strategies for adjustment and growth (see figure 1.1). These strategies will be woven throughout this book to encourage you to think critically about adjustment.

Describing and Interpreting Behavior Carefully

Psychologists strive to observe and describe behavior with accuracy. However, this goal is rarely easy to accomplish. One of the reasons is that we often substitute interpretations when a behavioral description would work better. For example, suppose you have just had a fight with your roommate. If someone else asked you what was wrong, chances are good you would offer interpretations of the event rather than a description of behavior itself. "Casey's really crazy!" you might say, instead of saying, "Casey leaves books all over the apartment." The first statement is an interpretation, or an *inference*. The second statement is a behavioral description.

Accurate behavioral description emphasizes verbs—action words. Most people can agree on the actions involved in any sample of behavior, but they might not agree on the interpretation of the behavior. Interpretations tend to emphasize motivations (Why does Casey leave books around the apartment?) and promote the use of judgments and labels ("Casey must be crazy to engage in that behavior").

Good critical thinkers are precise in their descriptions of behavior and cautious in their interpretations of behavior. They recognize that broad interpretations leave plenty of room for error and miscommunication. They concentrate on being accurate in their descriptions and cautious in how they interpret the behavior of others, because they realize that they might not be aware of all the factors that would give rise to the behavior.

Identifying Values and Challenging Assumptions About Behavior

We learn values that govern our behavior from a variety of influences—our parents, our peers, our schools, and the media, among others. **Values** *are ideals*

R E V I E W

The Nature of Adjustment

The field of adjustment draws heavily from psychology. Psychology is the scientific study of behavior and mental processes in contexts. Behavior is everything we do that can be directly observed. Mental processes are the thoughts, feelings, and motives that we experience privately but cannot be directly observed. As a science, psychology seeks to describe, explain, and predict behavior. Contexts are the settings in which mental processes and behavior occur, settings that are influenced by historical, economic, social, and cultural factors. Psychology, of course, is not all pure science and research—it has an applied, practical side as well. Although many psychologists conduct research that is relevant to understanding adjustment, others spend their day helping individuals cope with problems. Clinical and counseling psychology is the most widely practiced specialty in psychology.

The sociocultural approach emphasizes that culture, ethnicity, and gender are essential to understanding adjustment and behavior. If the psychology of adjustment is to be a relevant discipline in the twenty-first century, increased attention needs to be given to sociocultural issues.

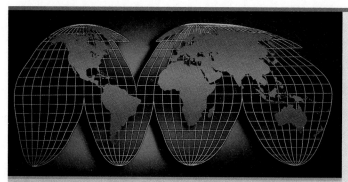

SOCIOCULTURAL WORLDS OF ADJUSTMENT

The Changing Tapestry of American Culture

In 1989 one-fifth of all children and adolescents in the United States under the age of 17 were members of ethnic minority groups—African American, Latino, Native Americans (American Indians), and Asians. By the year 2000, one-third of all U.S. school-age children will fall into this category. This changing demographic tapestry promises national diversity, but it also carries the challenge of extending the American dream to people of all ethnic and minority groups. Historically ethnic minorities have found themselves at the bottom of the economic and social order. They have been disproportionately among the poor and the inadequately educated (McLoyd, 1996; Taylor & Wang, 1996). Today, for instance, half of all African American children and one-third of all Latino children live in poverty, and the school dropout rate for minority youths is as high as 60 percent in some urban areas. Our social institutions can play an enormous part in helping correct these discrepancies. By becoming more sensitive to ethnic issues and by improving services to people of ethnic minority and low-income backgrounds, schools, colleges, social services, health and mental health agencies, and the courts can help bring minorities into the mainstream of American life (Jones, 1994; Lee & Hall, 1994; Marín, 1994; Taylor, 1996).

An especially important factor for social planners to keep in mind is the tremendous diversity within each ethnic group (Cauce, 1996). We're accustomed to thinking of American society as a melting pot of cultures—Whites, African Americans, Latinos, Native Americans, Asian Americans, Italian Americans, Polish Americans, and so on. However, just as there are no cultural characteristics common *across* all American ethnic groups, there is no cultural characteristic common to all African Americans or all Latinos, for instance.

African Americans make up the largest ethnic minority group in the United States. Latinos are distributed throughout the social class structure, although a disproportionate number are poor.

Latinos also are a diverse group of individuals. Not all Latinos are Catholic; many are, but some are not. Not all Latinos have a Mexican heritage. Many do, but others have cultural ties with South American countries, with Puerto Rico or other Caribbean countries, or with Spain.

Native Americans, with 511 distinct tribal units, also are an extremely diverse and complicated ethnic group (Trimble & Fleming, 1989). So are Asian Americans, with more then 30 distinct groups under this designation (Wong, 1982). Within each of these 511 Native American tribes and 30 Asian American groups, there is considerable diversity and individual variation.

America has embraced many cultures, and, in the process, the cultures have often mixed their beliefs and identities. Some elements of the cultures of origin are retained, some are lost, and some are mixed with the American culture. As the number of ethnic minority groups continues to increase rapidly in the next decade, one of psychology's most important agenda items is to understand better the role that culture and ethnicity play in the ways we think and act (Reid, 1996; Scott-Jones, 1996).

The tapestry of American culture has changed dramatically in recent years. Nowhere is the change more noticeable than in the increasing ethnic diversity of America's citizens. Ethnic minority groups—African American, Latino, Native American, and Asian American, for example—will make up approximately one-third of all individuals under the age of 17 in the United States by the year 2000. Two of psychology's challenges are to become more sensitive to race and ethnic origin and to provide improved services to ethnic minority individuals.

Good critical thinkers explore how differing values contribute to varying perceptions and preferred resolutions when trying to solve problems.

Examining the Influence of Context and Culture on Behavior

Contexts and cultures also influence behavior. For example, you might notice that you don't behave the same in all contexts. Do you act the same in the company of your best friends as you do when you are with your grandparents? Do you act the same at a circus as you would at a funeral? Our culture dictates that some behaviors are appropriate in certain contexts while others are not.

I seem to have an awful lot of people inside me.

—**Edith Evans**

Tourists sometimes discover the power of cultural influences when they fail to adapt to the cultural practices of the country they are visiting. For example, Jack was surprised when he admired the watch of his Japanese host. In keeping with the culture's custom, the host offered the watch to Jack—who refused it due to his own values, his discomfort at accepting such an expensive gift. By refusing the present, Jack offended his host and set back their relationship.

Good critical thinkers recognize that many behaviors can be more easily understood when the sociocultural context is taken into account. Sensitivity to context and culture enhances the critical thinker's ability to understand the behavior that occurs in a given context.

Evaluating the Validity of Claims About Behavior

Headlines in tabloid newspapers routinely make outrageous claims about how to change behavior. Want to increase your intelligence? Eat cauliflower every day. Want to enhance your sexual appeal? Check your horoscope. Feel out of sorts? Buy some crystals. Not all claims about behavior should be believed, because not all claims are *valid* or *truthful*. We will

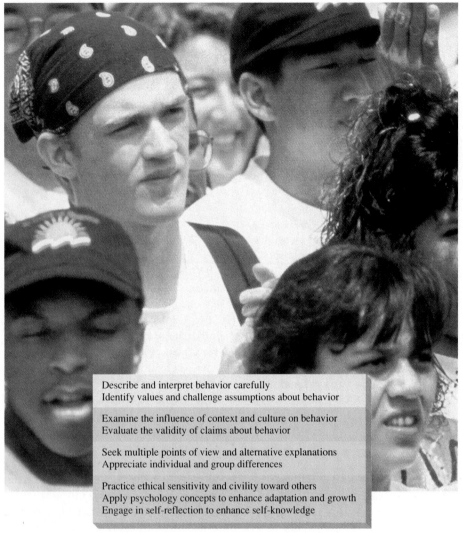

Describe and interpret behavior carefully
Identify values and challenge assumptions about behavior

Examine the influence of context and culture on behavior
Evaluate the validity of claims about behavior

Seek multiple points of view and alternative explanations
Appreciate individual and group differences

Practice ethical sensitivity and civility toward others
Apply psychology concepts to enhance adaptation and growth
Engage in self-reflection to enhance self-knowledge

FIGURE 1.1

Nine Critical-Thinking Strategies for Adjustment and Growth

that motivate our beliefs and choices. Values and assumptions sometimes can be acquired without conscious awareness. Consider Mary Kay's practice of preparing a roast. Mary Kay was taught by her mother to slice off the small end of her roast before placing it in the oven. Not until a dinner guest questioned her about this practice did she realize that she couldn't explain this step in the recipe. When she questioned her mother, she discovered the practice was a family tradition handed down from her grandmother, who didn't own a pan large enough to accommodate a roast. The tradition survived because no one thought to question the practice.

Good critical thinkers conscientiously examine the role that values and assumptions can play in influencing behavior. They question motives and actively challenge assumptions in order to understand behavior. They also avoid assuming that specific values automatically imply specific behaviors. For example, many Americans claim to be patriotic, yet a disappointingly small percentage of Americans turn out to vote.

Where we share the values of others, behavior may be easier to comprehend. However, when values differ, understanding behavior becomes more complicated. A **value conflict** *is a clash of beliefs about a problem that people are trying to solve.*

examine the nature of nonscientific claims about behavior in the next section.

When confronted with a claim about behavior, good critical thinkers tend to show **skepticism,** *a reluctance to believe expressed in a questioning stance.* They show a strong preference for believing claims that are supported by objective evidence from behavioral research. They also build their own arguments about behavior using objective evidence to support their point of view. They are especially careful about recognizing the limits of personal experience as the basis for persuasive evidence.

Seeking Multiple Points of View and Alternative Explanations

Have you ever had the experience of disagreeing with someone about the "facts" of an event? Both of you might vigorously defend your points of view. Although you both may have shared the event, your "realities" were different, shaped by your past experiences, your biases, and your information-processing skills.

Good critical thinkers recognize that their own perspectives might be imperfect renditions of reality. Seeking multiple perspectives is a hallmark of good critical thinkers. They recognize that the tendency to explain behavior from one individual's viewpoint produces a subjective bias that might not offer an accurate explanation. Conscientiously pursuing different points of view provides more information and can promote more effective problem solving.

Critical thinkers also carefully consider alternative explanations to enhance the depth of any behavioral explanation. For example, some people believe in a "full-moon effect" as the cause of a variety of unusual occurrences, from acting out in classrooms to increased crimes. Crime rates might be higher during the full moon, but it is unlikely that this is directly due to any lunar influence. A plausible alternative explanation is that better lighting conditions enhance both criminal activity and success in police captures.

Remaining open to multiple interpretations obviously helps good critical thinkers in interpersonal conflicts. They recognize that they can understand conflicts only from their own point of view. They actively seek to understand the other person's perspective in order to resolve interpersonal problems.

> *I've always felt that a person's intelligence is directly reflected by the number of conflicting points of view he can entertain simultaneously on the same topic.*
>
> —**Lisa Alther**

Appreciating Individual and Group Differences

Humans are alike in their basic anatomy and general genetic structure, yet their differences can be remarkable. Many people are surprised to discover how different other humans can be. They might discover this in the pages of a novel, in tourism, in other neighborhoods, or even at play in their own back yards, or on the streets.

Critical thinkers are exhilarated by the differences among people. They become excited about the possibilities for learning from those with different life experiences and points of view. They welcome opportunities to explore these differences.

Practicing Ethical Sensitivity and Civility Toward Others

> *We are healthy only to the extent that our ideas are humane.*
>
> —**Kurt Vonnegut**

As you will see in later chapters, psychology has not always been conducted with either ethical sensitivity or civility. Many early social experiments demonstrated questionable regard for the welfare of the subjects in the study. However, the American Psychological Association developed procedures to protect research participants by requiring researchers to undergo a review process before their research plans can be sanctioned.

One important element in the profile of the good critical thinker is humane concern for the well-being of others. This concern is expressed by enacting appropriate ethical standards of behavior toward others, including behaving with integrity, honesty, compassion, and civility.

Civility *is the practice of respectful behavior toward others.* Civility is not a simple matter, because different people and groups have different ideas about which behaviors are respectful. For example, many Americans believe that it is respectful to look another person in the eye when they speak to you (Axtell, 1992). However, Native Americans believe it is respectful to avoid eye contact. We will examine other examples of respect in cross-cultural contexts in chapter 3. A civil approach requires understanding how to show respect to those with whom you interact.

Applying Psychological Concepts to Enhance Adaptation and Growth

Many of the concepts explored in the pages that follow are useful in coping with *hassles,* the small, everyday life events to which you must adjust. Hassles include being rudely awakened by the alarm, having to decide which television show to watch, getting a parking ticket, and missing the bus. However, we will also explore how you can use psychology to adjust to larger, more complex events, such as the death of a loved one, an illness, or the end of a long-term relationship.

Sometimes the term *adjustment* is used with a pejorative (negative) tone. Adjustment can imply a passive acceptance of conditions and behavioral changes that allow the *status quo,* or current conditions, to be maintained. In some circumstances, we probably should not adjust to conditions but foster more dramatic changes in the circumstances themselves. Adjustment without growth is likely to be a hollow achievement. We think the concepts and principles presented in this book will facilitate both adjustment and growth.

Engaging in Self-Reflection to Enhance Self-Knowledge

> *Learn what you are, and be such.*
>
> —**Pindar**

In taking this course, you are embarking on a journey that will give you many opportunities to understand yourself better.

Each chapter contains self-assessments that will give you some insight into your motives, values, preferences, and eccentricities. We hope you will find these exercises to be fulfilling adventures that help you integrate your learning about adjustment with your daily-life concerns.

Next we will explore some topics for which critical-thinking skills can be useful: pseudoscientific explanations of personality, and how to evaluate research claims.

PSYCHOLOGY AND PSEUDOPSYCHOLOGY

In May of 1988, the topic of astrology made the front page of every newspaper and every national newscast. *Time* magazine even made astrology its cover story. The big news was that Nancy Reagan used astrologers to schedule President Reagan's political appointments. Suddenly, astrology was both the focus of serious scientific examination and the butt of many jokes.

At the beginning of this chapter we defined psychology as the *scientific study of behavior and mental processes in contexts*. We said that, as a science, psychology uses systematic observations to describe, explain, and predict behavior; these observations are carefully and precisely planned and conducted. We also said that these observations are often *verified* to check their accuracy. Astrology is not psychology, nor is it a separate *science*. Instead, astrology is a **pseudopsychology**—*a nonscientific system that only superficially resembles psychology. Pseudopsychologies lack a scientific base. Their descriptions, explanations, and predictions either cannot be directly tested or, when tested, turn out to be unfounded.* To determine how much you believe in pseudopsychological "psychic" phenomena, see the Self-Assessment.

Current popular pseudopsychologies include astrology and graphology. **Astrology** *is the pseudopsychology that uses the position of the stars and planets at the time of a person's birth to describe, explain, and predict their behavior. Scientific researchers have repeatedly demonstrated that astrology has no scientific merit.*

Astrological predictions are successful only when they are so vague that they are virtually guaranteed to be

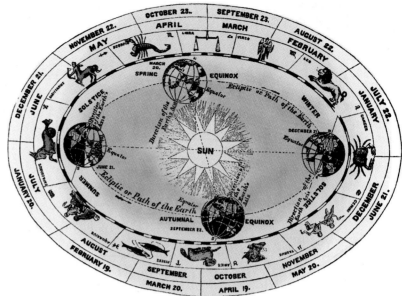

The Constellations, Seasons, Equinoxes, &c.

Why does the science of psychology urge you to be skeptical of astrology?

fulfilled (for example, "Money is likely to be a source of concern for you this month," or "A tragic plane crash will occur in the southern United States this winter.") Astrologers' more specific predictions ("You will have excess money during October and another shortage in the first week of December") rarely hold up. In spite of their lack of success, even unlikely astrological predictions may be played up in the press ("An unidentified flying object will land on the field during the halftime of the ABC Monday Night Football game on October 23, 1998") and yet uncritically dismissed after their failure.

Graphology *is the pseudopsychology of using handwriting analysis to describe, explain, and predict a person's behavior.* There has been a dramatic increase in the use of graphology as a measure to select employees for jobs and to assess an individual's personality and adjustment or job competence (Hines, 1988).

Individuals in the **New Age movement** *express a distrust of science while engaging in a search for new levels of spiritual awareness. These proponents maintain that there are hidden "spiritual dimensions" to reality that cannot be discovered by science's experimental strategies.* Although science is mistrusted, New Age followers readily and unquestioningly accept such pseudopsychologies as

astrology, crystal power (the use of quartz crystals for healing), channeling (the ability to enter a trance state and communicate with someone in another place and time, even centuries ago), and past life regressions (going back to vividly remember one of one's own previous human existences). While many New Age beliefs are fanciful and intriguing, such as actress Shirley MacLaine's claim that she lived one of her lives as a prostitute during the French Revolution and was beheaded, there is no scientific evidence to support them.

Scientology *is a pseudopsychology developed by L. Ron Hubbard in the 1950s. Scientology states that people become socially programmed and respond too automatically to their world. Scientology offers to free people from the shackles of their conditioning and deliver wondrous insights.* Scientology requires years of training for participants, is very expensive, and no documentation of scientology's success has ever been shown. Hubbard (1989) says that we have developed automatic behavior patterns (which he calls "engrams") that cause our problems. Hubbard and his scientology leaders claim that they can "clear" your mind of such automatic programming—after relieving you of substantial sums of money, of course. Do not be fooled by scientology's fancy words and

SELF-ASSESSMENT

—

Belief in Psychic Phenomena

For each of the following items, please indicate whether it is something you believe in, something you are not sure about, or something you do not believe in.

Please turn to the end of the chapter for an interpretation of your responses.

	Believe	Not Sure	Do Not Believe
In déjà vu, or the feeling that you have been somewhere or done something before			
In the Devil			
In ESP, or extrasensory perception			
That people on this Earth are sometimes possessed by the Devil			
In psychic or spiritual healing or the power of the human mind to heal the body			
In telepathy, or communication between minds without using the traditional five senses			
That houses can be haunted			
That extraterrestrial beings have visited Earth at some time in the past			
In clairvoyance, or the power of the mind to know the past and predict the future			
In astrology, or that the position of the stars and planets can affect people's lives			
In ghosts, or that spirits of dead people can come back in certain places and situations			
In reincarnation, that is, the rebirth of the soul in a new body after death			
That people can hear from or communicate mentally with someone who has died			
In telekinesis, or the ability of the mind to move or bend objects using just mental energy			
In witches			
In channeling, or allowing a "spirit being" to temporarily assume control of a human body during a trance			
That pyramids have a special healing power			
That rock crystals have a special healing power			

widely enthusiastic claims that by adopting its approach all things will be wonderful in your life. Neither scientology, nor other pseudopsychologies, will lead you to the promised land.

Be skeptical of astrology, the New Age movement, and scientology, or of anything else that claims access to wondrous powers and supernatural forces

(Ward & Grashai, 1995). Figure 1.2 explores the lure of graphology and why we should be suspicious of this pseudoscience. Might there even be a possible danger in following the advice of the pseudopsychologies? Yes—there is a *clear* danger because the pseudopsychologies divert people from coping with their lives in a rational and realistic way.

For most people who dabble in the pseudopsychologies, all that will be lost is some time and money for whatever brief comfort was gained, but for people with serious problems or who are in real distress, following the advice of astrologers, "mystics," and scientologists can prevent them from solving their problems and living productive lives.

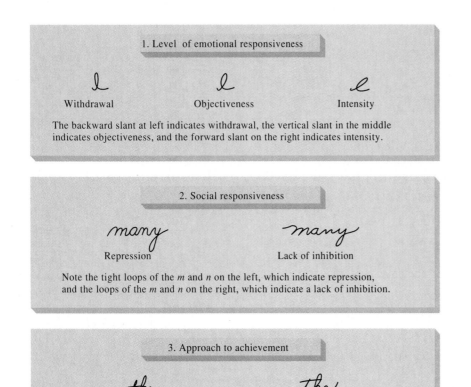

FIGURE 1.2

Graphology

At least 3,000 firms in the United States use graphology when hiring individuals. In other countries, such as Israel and Japan, the use of graphological analysis is even more widespread. Shown above are examples of the type of analysis graphologists use. If the research investigation of graphological claims is so negative, why is graphology so widely used and accepted? Graphological analysis has a mysterious, powerful ring to it. People are easily impressed by so-called experts and assume they know what they are talking about. Positive, unscientific reports of graphologists' abilities frequently appear in magazines and business commentaries. People are fascinated by graphology and want to believe that their handwriting, because it is highly individual, reveals something about themselves. Also, graphologists' predictions, like those of palmists and astrologers, are usually very general and difficult to disprove.

Outrageous claims are not the province solely of pseudopsychologies. Many research reports and advertisements also make unjustifiable claims. We will explore ways to identify and challenge such claims in the next section.

BEING A WISE CONSUMER OF PSYCHOLOGICAL KNOWLEDGE

Headlines and promotional announcements proclaim a variety of new insights about human behavior that are likely to be of interest to the general public. But how do you sort through the barrage of findings to distinguish believable claims from those that should be rejected and perhaps even ridiculed?

Not all psychological information presented for public consumption comes from professionals with excellent credentials and reputations at colleges, universities, and applied mental health settings. For journalists, television reporters, and other personnel in media who are not trained in psychology, it is not an easy task to make sound decisions about the best information to present to the public.

Unfortunately, the media often focus on sensationalist and dramatic psychological findings. Members of the media want you to read what they have written or stay tuned to their program.

They hope to capture and keep your attention by presenting dramatic, sensationalist, and surprising information. As a consequence, media presentations of psychological information tend to misrepresent researchers' conclusions.

Even when the popular media present high-quality research findings to the public, it can be difficult for them to inform people adequately about the findings and the implications these findings have for their lives. They do not have the luxury of time and space to specify in detail the limitations of research findings. They might have only a few minutes or a few lines, and they will focus on making maximum impact rather than on elucidating the complexity of a study's findings.

> *Science is always profound. It is only the half-truths that are dangerous.*
> —**George Bernard Shaw,**
> ***The Doctor's Dilemma*, 1913**

Some Guidelines

You can take several steps to improve your skills as a shrewd consumer by familiarizing yourself with typical problems that appear in popular press treatments of psychological knowledge. We detail these for you in the following sections.

Don't Predict Individual Performance from Research Results Based on Groups

Most psychological research is conducted at the level of the group. Individual variations in how subjects respond is often not a major focus of the research. For example, researchers interested in the effects of divorce on stress management might find that divorced women as a group cope more poorly with stress than married women do. This finding applies to divorced women as a group. In this particular study, some of the divorced women were probably coping better with stress than were some of their married counterparts—not as many, but some. Indeed, it is entirely possible that of the 100 women in the study, the 2 or 3 women who were coping the best with stress might have been well-adjusted divorced women. It would still be accurate to report the findings as showing that divorced women (as a group) cope more poorly with stress than married women (as a group) do.

As a consumer of psychological information, you want to know what the information means for you *individually,* not necessarily what it means for a group of people. The failure of the media to distinguish adequately between group research and individual application is not entirely their fault—researchers have not adequately done this either. Researchers too often fail to examine the overlap between groups and present only the differences between groups. When those differences are reported, too often they are stated as if there is no overlap between the groups being compared, when in reality there is a substantial overlap. If you read a research treatment in the popular press that divorced women coped more poorly with stress than married women did, it does not mean that all divorced women coped more poorly than did all married women. It simply means that, as a group, married women coped better—it would not mean that you, if you are a divorced woman, cope less well than married women do.

Don't Overgeneralize from a Small Sample

Often there isn't space or time in media presentations of psychological information to go into details about the nature of the sample. Sometimes you will get basic information about the sample's size—whether it is based on 10 subjects, 50 subjects, or 200 subjects, for example. In many cases, small or very small samples require that caution be exercised in generalizing to a larger population.

For example, if a study of divorced women is based on only 10 or 20 divorced women, the findings might not generalize to all divorced women, because the sample investigated might have some unique characteristics. The women in the sample might all have a high income, be White American, be childless, live in a small southern town, and be undergoing psychotherapy. In this study, then, we clearly would be making unwarranted generalizations if we thought

the findings might automatically characterize divorced women who have moderate to low incomes, are from other ethnic backgrounds, have children, are living in different contexts, and are not undergoing psychotherapy.

Don't Accept Results Based on a Single Study

The popular press might claim about an interesting piece of research or a clinical finding that it is something phenomenal with far-reaching implications. Although such studies and findings do occur, it is rare for a single study to provide earth-shattering and conclusive answers, especially answers that apply to all people. In fact, in most psychological domains, where there are many investigations, finding conflicting results about a particular topic or issue is common. Answers to questions in research usually emerge after many scientists have conducted similar investigations and have drawn similar conclusions. Thus, a report of one research study should not be taken as the absolute, final answer on an issue.

Don't Assume Causality When It Is Not Warranted

Drawing causal conclusions from studies that do not warrant them is one of the most common mistakes made in the media. Causal interpretations are not justified when two or more factors are simply correlated with each other. We are not justified in saying that one of the factors causes another unless strictly controlled research has established causality (McBurney, 1996).

For example, a headline about a study of divorce might read, "Low Income Causes Divorced Women to Have a High Degree of Stress." We read the article and find that it is discussing the results of a research study. However, if the research did not include adequate control procedures, it cannot be concluded that low income *causes* stress in divorced women. It might be that some of the women were already experiencing stress and that this hurt their chances of having a higher income. Their stress would also likely be related to other factors besides income, such as inadequate societal supports, a history of criticism from an ex-husband, and so on.

Don't Assume Credibility from Questionable Sources

Studies conducted by psychologists and mental health professionals are not automatically accepted by the research and clinical community. Psychological research submitted to a research or clinical journal will be reviewed by other psychologists in that specialized area, who make a decision about the value of publishing the findings. The quality of research and clinical findings published in journals is not uniform, but in most cases these studies have undergone far greater scrutiny than much of the work that is reported in the media. Within the media, though, a distinction can usually be drawn between what is presented in respected newspapers, such as the *New York Times* and the *Washington Post,* as well as credible magazines, such as *Time* and *Newsweek,* and much less respected and less credible periodicals such as tabloids, like the *National Inquirer* and *Star.* To further evaluate sources of information about adjustment, turn to the Critical Thinking box.

Evaluating Self-Help Books

Self-help books have become an important source of psychological advice for millions of Americans. Whether you want to improve your marital life, control your anger, gain self-fulfillment, raise your self-esteem, become a better parent, lose weight, solve a sexual problem, cope with stress, recover from an addiction, or any of myriad other possibilities, a self-help book has probably been written on the topic.

Our preoccupation with self-help books is nothing new. It's been around since the Bible. Although not exactly known as a self-help author, Benjamin Franklin dispensed self-improvement advice in *Poor Richard's Almanac*—"Early to bed, early to rise, makes a man healthy, wealthy, and wise," for example. In the nineteenth century, homemakers read *Married Ladies' Companion* for help in managing their house and family. In the early twentieth century, Sigmund Freud wrote a self-help book on interpreting dreams, and in the 1930s, Dale Carnegie's *How to Win Friends and Influence People* made him the aspiring entrepreneur's guru (Stark, 1989).

Carrots and Sex

Suppose you see a headline in a tabloid newspaper that "Scientists Find Eating Carrots Daily Improves Sex Life." In the next few days the story makes headlines in the evening news and major daily papers. Would the amount of coverage this research report is getting automatically make it more credible? Your answer addresses your ability to *evaluate the validity of claims about behavior.* The answer is no. Expanded coverage doesn't guarantee truth. Your questions would have to do with the credibility of the research design and the researcher, and the degree to which the claims might have been exaggerated in order to capture public attention.

The interest in understanding the human psyche and how to improve it heated up in the 1960s and 1970s, and with the interest came an increase in self-help books. *I'm O.K., You're O.K.* and *Your Erogenous Zones* were read by millions of Americans and made millions for their authors. Their popularity spawned unprecedented interest in the self-help movement.

The self-help book market has mushroomed into a bewildering array of choices that overwhelms the consumer. Some self-help books have been written by professionals with masterful insights about who we are, what we are all about, and how we can improve our lives. Others, to put it mildly, leave a lot to be desired, or as one concerned therapist commented, "Some self-help books are not worth the paper they are printed on."

Guidelines for Selecting a Self-Help Book

Are there some guidelines to help people pick the best self-help book for them? We offer nine suggestions.

1. Don't select a self-help book because of its cover, its title, its glitzy advertising, or because it's this year's so-called "breakthrough" book. The old saying "You can't tell a book by its cover" probably applies to self-help books more than any other type of book. The self-help book business has become big business.

Publishers spend huge sums of money creating splashy covers with sensationalist titles, put together glitzy Madison Avenue advertising campaigns, and, year after year, proclaim each year's new self-help books as "phenomenal breakthroughs" in understanding problems. Some good self-help books do have fancy covers and catchy titles, but so do the bad ones. The same is true with expensive ads—the bad books are just as likely to get huge advertising outlays as the good books.

Be an intelligent consumer of psychological knowledge and advice by going beyond the cover, the fancy ads, the hot author that's on every talk show, the bookstore's elaborate display, and believing everything the publicity campaign concocts for the book. Instead, make your choices based on the next eight keys.

2. Select a book that makes realistic recommendations, not grandiose claims. If you have a problem, you want to cope with it as effectively and painlessly as possible. The more quickly you can fix the problem, the better. Unfortunately, books that make extravagant claims are the most alluring and sell better than books that are more realistic. Most problems do not arise overnight and most can't be solved overnight. Avoid books that promise you magical, wondrous insights that can easily solve your problem. Coping effectively with a problem takes much

more effort and work than many self-help books lead you to believe.

3. Examine the evidence reported in the book. Unfortunately, many self-help books are based not on reliable scientific or clinical evidence, but rather on the author's anecdotal experiences. Too much of what you read in self-help books is based on intuitions that are highly speculative. The best self-help books are supported by some form of reliable evidence.

4. Select a self-help book that recognizes that a problem is caused by a number of factors and has alternative solutions. It's not just your imagination—you are a complex human being, living in a complex world. Your problems are not so simple that they have a single cause and a single solution, yet the human mind is biased toward simple answers to complex problems. After all, if there is one simple solution, then solving your problem is easier than if a number of factors have to be changed. The better books recognize that to solve a problem the best strategy is to change several factors in our lives, not just a single factor.

5. A self-help book that focuses on a particular problem is better than one that is a general approach to solving all of your problems. The best self-help books focus on how to solve a particular problem rather than promising to cure all of life's ills with several simple ideas. Books that try to solve all of life's problems are shallow and lack the specific, detailed solutions needed to solve a particular problem.

6. Don't be conned by psychobabble and slick writing. In 1977, R. D. Rosen wrote *Psychobabble,* a sizzling attack on the psychological jargon that fills the space between covers of many self-help books. Unfortunately, almost two decades later, psychobabble is alive and well. *Psychobabble* is self-improvement jargon—"hip" and vague language that is not going to help people cope effectively with their problems. Too often self-help book authors write in psychobabble like this: "You've got to get in touch with your feelings"; "Get with the program"; "Be the real you"; "You can do anything you want and it's o.k."; "You are sending off the wrong vibes"; and on and on.

Not all bad self-help books are infected with psychobabble. Some are

Self-help books are available on virtually every imaginable topic. What makes a good self-help book?

NOW IN PAPERBACK!

The Brave and Revealing Bestseller

CATS WHO LOVE WOMEN
WHO LOVE TOO MUCH

Courtesy of Suzy Becker, Widget Factory Cards.

that provide little additional knowledge. Such books lack the extensive, detailed recommendations and sound strategies needed to cope with life's ills.

The books characterized by psychobabble and slick writing frequently regress into motivational and inspirational cheerleading, which initially gets you pumped up to solve your problem. What happens all too often, though, is that you just get "pumped up" and "psychologically buzzed" without ever learning any precise strategies for solving your problem. After a few weeks or months, the "buzz" wears off because the author's recommendations lacked depth.

We are not against good, interesting writing, but it takes a lot more than slick language to help you cope with a problem. The best books are clearly written in a language that you can understand and include detailed recommendations for how to cope with a specific problem.

7. Check out the author's educational credentials. Not all authors of self-help books are mental health professionals who have gone through rigorous training at respected universities and spent years helping people solve problems. Just about anyone can write a self-help book if they can convince the publisher the book will make money. In most cases, the best self-help books are written by *legitimate* mental health professionals.

There are a lot of *charlatans*—so-called experts who claim to have knowledge and insights that they really don't have. Some of the charlatans write self-help books, even best-sellers! Legitimate experts who dispense wisdom about self-help often come with one or more titles attached to their name. If self-help authors only have *Dr.* preceding their names, be suspicious. Some people have phoney doctorates they purchase through the mail or get from diploma mills that are unaccredited. They might even be awarded by some religious cult that has no university affiliation. While the location of Ph.D., M.D., Ed.D., or Psy.D after authors' names is no guarantee the advice they give will help you, the vast majority of good self-help books are written by individuals with such credentials.

8. Be wary of authors who complain about or reject the conventional knowledge of mental health experts. Mental health

smoothly written and disguise their inadequacies with slick writing that is so friendly you get the feeling the authors are talking personally to you. After you have read just a few pages, you say to yourself, "Wow! They are talking about me. This book can really help me." All too often such slick books offer little more than one or two basic ideas that could be communicated in two or three pages. The rest of the book's 200–300 pages are filled with polished writing and colorful examples professionals—such as psychologists and psychiatrists—don't have the answers to all of life's problems. Indeed, some of the best psychologists and psychiatrists tell you that they don't have all of the answers, and they are simply being intellectually honest.

Some self-help book authors—especially those advocating New Age and Scientology ideas—attack the mental health professions as too conservative and too concerned with having scientific evidence to support claims for how to solve a problem. Consider such attacks as a red flag and avoid such authors. These antiestablishment, antiscience mavericks tell you they are ahead of their time. They say it will take years for mental health professionals to catch up with their avant-garde ideas.

There is nothing wrong with new ideas. Mental health professionals welcome new ideas, but the ideas have to be supported by reliable evidence. The self-help authors who condemn the mental health establishment have not written books that will help you.

9. Don't rely only on self-help books for coping advice. Throughout this book we will recommend well-regarded self-help books on particular topics. Most of these recommendations are based on a recent national survey of mental health professionals' recommendations. But remember that textbooks like this and local mental health professionals can also provide helpful resources to facilitate adjustment.

National Survey of Mental Health Professionals' Self-Help Book Recommendations

Recently, one of your authors—John Santrock—conducted a national survey of clinical and counseling psychologists' ratings of self-help books (Santrock, Minnett, & Campbell, 1994). All were members of the clinical and/or counseling psychology divisions of the American Psychological Association. To be a member of these divisions, the mental health professionals had to have obtained a doctorate from an accredited university and have been recommended for membership by their fellow colleagues. More

T	## TABLE 1.1
	The 25 Best Self-Help Books as Rated by Clinical and Counseling Psychologists in a Recent National Survey

1. *The Courage to Heal* by Ellen Bass and Laura Davis
2. *Feeling Good* by David Burns
3. *Infants and Mothers* by T. Berry Brazelton
4. *What Every Baby Knows* by T. Berry Brazelton
5. *Dr. Spock's Baby and Child Care* by Benjamin Spock and Michael Rothenberg
6. *How to Survive the Loss of a Love* by Melba Cosgrove & others
7. *To Listen to a Child* by T. Berry Brazelton
8. *The Boys and Girls Book About Divorce* by Richard Gardner
9. *The Dance of Anger* by Harriet Lerner
10. *The Feeling Good Workbook* by David Burns
11. *Toddlers and Parents* by T. Berry Brazelton
12. *Your Perfect Right* by Robert Alberti and Michael Emmons
13. *Between Parent and Teenager* by Haim Ginott
14. *The First Three Years of Life* by Burton White
15. *What Color Is Your Parachute?* by Robert Bolles
16. *Between Parent and Child* by Haim Ginott
17. *The Relaxation Response* by Herbert Benson
18. *The New Aerobics* by Kenneth Cooper
19. *Learned Optimism* by Martin Seligman
20. *Man's Search for Meaning* by Viktor Frankl
21. *Children: The Challenge* by Rudolf Dreikurs
22. *You Just Don't Understand* by Deborah Tannen
23. *The Dance of Intimacy* by Harriet Lerner
24. *Beyond the Relaxation Response* by Herbert Benson
25. *The Battered Woman* by Lenore Walker

than 500 clinical and counseling psychologists completed the ratings.

They were asked to rate books in 33 categories, such as addiction and recovery, child development and parenting, divorce, love and intimacy, positive thinking, self-esteem, self-improvement, sexual issues and problems, stress, and women's issues. Based on the mental health professionals' ratings, a list of the 25 best self-help books was generated (see table 1.1). In most instances, the keys for selecting a self-help book we outlined earlier were good predictors of the types of books that were on the best list. Most of the books on the best list will be profiled, along with many others, at the end of various chapters throughout *Human Adjustment*.

Critical Thinking About Adjustment, Psychology and Pseudopsychology, and Being a Wise Consumer of Psychological Knowledge

In the context of adjustment, critical thinking refers to making appropriate decisions and developing competent strategies to promote your own, or other people's, well-being. We identified nine critical-thinking strategies related to adjustment and growth: describing and interpreting behavior carefully, identifying values and challenging assumptions about behavior, evaluating the validity of claims about behavior, seeking multiple points of view and alternative explanations, appreciating individual and group differences, practicing ethical sensitivity and civility toward others, applying psychological concepts to enhance adaptation and growth, and engaging in self-reflection to enhance self-knowledge.

A pseudopsychology is a non-scientific system that resembles psychology. Pseudopsychologies, like astrology, graphology, the New Age movement, and Scientology, lack a scientific base. Their descriptions, explanations, and predictions either cannot be directly tested or, when tested, turn out to be unfounded. There is a clear danger in following the advice of pseudopsychologies—people can become diverted from coping with their lives in a rational and realistic manner.

It is important to be a wise consumer of psychological knowledge. The quality of research and clinical findings varies considerably. Being a wise consumer of psychological knowledge involves not predicting individual performance from research results based on groups, not overgeneralizing from a small sample, not accepting results based on a single study, not assuming causality when it is not warranted, and not assuming credibility from questionable resources.

Self-help books are written for the lay public to help people cope with problems and live more effective lives. They have become an important source of coping advice for millions of people. Among the criteria for effectively evaluating self-help books are not selecting a book based on its glitzy advertising appeal, selecting a book that makes realistic claims, examining the evidence in the book, selecting a book that recognizes that problems may have multiple causes, selecting a book that focuses on a particular problem, not being conned by slick writing and psychobabble, checking out the author's credentials, being wary of authors who reject the conventional wisdom of mental health professionals, and not relying solely on self-help books for advice.

CRITICAL THINKING ABOUT ADJUSTMENT

Where You've Been and Where You're Going

There is no royal road to anything.
One thing at a time, and all things in succession.
That which grows slowly endures.

—J. B. Holland

The only way round is through.

—Robert Frost

Before you registered for this course, you might not have given much thought to the idea of adjustment. Yet every day you have probably faced situations that placed some new demands on you. Sometimes those pressures come from family and interpersonal relationships. Sometimes work and school become a challenge. Sometimes the challenges we face are spiritual in nature. Life can be experienced as an endless demand for change, adjustment, and growth.

How have you fared on your distinctive journey so far? Are you usually unerring in your instincts about what to do and what direction to take? Do you generally rise to the occasion, overcome any obstacles, and respond to the challenges with vigor? Or do you often struggle to find the right path? Do you sometimes feel overwhelmed and discouraged? Most people experience all of those feelings at different times in their lives.

Your authors believe that if you gain insight into your own patterns of adjustment, this can reduce the strain you feel in living your complex life. Self-knowledge can enhance your ability to recognize and solve problems in a way that should lead to a more fulfilling existence for you. Of course, the study of adjustment is not a simple journey. Greater self-knowledge can be a source of pain. Examining your life more carefully may flood you with emotions that surprise you. Likely, much about your life is pleasant, even joyous, but most lives contain some shame, grief, frustration, regret, and turmoil. This might be one of the truly common ties that bind us to other human beings, all of whom are trying to figure out their own unique directions.

How enthused are you about what lies ahead for you in this course? What kinds of life experiences may have influenced your attitude—whether excited or guarded—about an intensive experience that explores and exposes such intimate aspects of your being? Your judgment will demonstrate your ability *to engage in self-reflection to enhance self-knowledge.* As partners in this journey, your authors hope that you will find this to be a very worthwhile exploration.

In this first chapter we explored what adjustment is, defining both psychology and adjustment as part of our discussion. Our coverage of critical thinking and adjustment focused on nine strategies—ranging from describing and interpreting behavior carefully to engaging in self-reflection to enhance self-knowledge. We also examined distinctions between psychology and some pseudopsychologies. And we discussed the importance of becoming a wise consumer of psychological knowledge, including following a number of guidelines and being able to effectively evaluate the quality of self-help books. Don't forget that you can obtain an overall summary of the chapter by again reading the in-chapter reviews on pages 8 and 19.

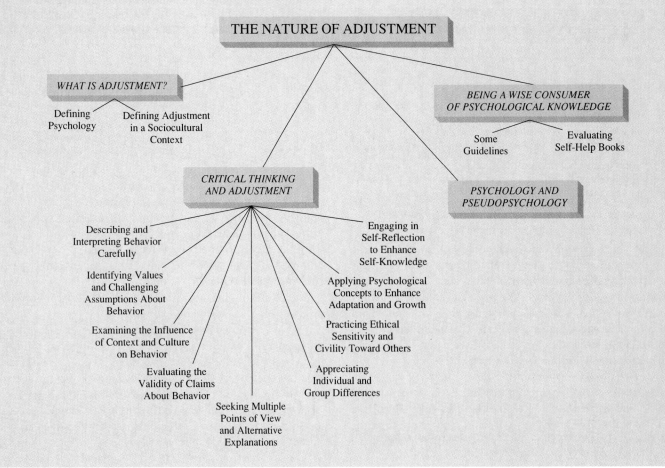

THE NATURE OF ADJUSTMENT

WHAT IS ADJUSTMENT?

Defining Psychology

Defining Adjustment in a Sociocultural Context

BEING A WISE CONSUMER OF PSYCHOLOGICAL KNOWLEDGE

Some Guidelines

Evaluating Self-Help Books

CRITICAL THINKING AND ADJUSTMENT

Describing and Interpreting Behavior Carefully

Identifying Values and Challenging Assumptions About Behavior

Examining the Influence of Context and Culture on Behavior

Evaluating the Validity of Claims About Behavior

Seeking Multiple Points of View and Alternative Explanations

Engaging in Self-Reflection to Enhance Self-Knowledge

Applying Psychological Concepts to Enhance Adaptation and Growth

Practicing Ethical Sensitivity and Civility Toward Others

Appreciating Individual and Group Differences

PSYCHOLOGY AND PSEUDOPSYCHOLOGY

psychology 5
behavior 5
inferences 5
mental processes 5
science 5
clinical and counseling psychology 5
psychiatry 6
contexts 6
adjustment 6

sociocultural approach 7
culture 7
ethnicity 7
ethnic identity 7
sex 7
gender 7
critical thinking 8
values 8

value conflicts 10
skepticism 11
civility 11
pseudopsychology 12
astrology 12
graphology 12
New Age movement 12
scientology 12

PRACTICAL KNOWLEDGE ABOUT ADJUSTMENT

THE AUTHORITATIVE GUIDE TO SELF-HELP BOOKS

(1994) by John Santrock, Ann Minnett, & Barbara Campbell. New York: Guilford.

This book presents the results of a national survey of more than 500 mental health experts who rated more than 1,000 self-help books. Covering the full range of self-help topics, the authors evaluate books in 32 categories, including abuse, addiction, anger, anxiety, depression, divorce, love, self-improvement, sexuality, and women's issues. Robert Alberti, author of *Your Perfect Right,* said that *The Authoritative Guide to Self-Help Books* is a monumental, comprehensive evaluation of the good, the bad, and the ugly in this field. A leading clinical psychologist from the University of Michigan, Neal Kalter, commented that *The Guide* is a "must" for people in search of expert advice.

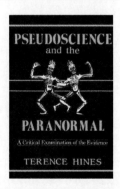

PSEUDOSCIENCE AND THE PARANORMAL

(1988) by Terence Hines. Buffalo, NY: Prometheus Books.

There are many pseudopsychologies that can attract people's attention, including ESP, astrology, the New Age movement, graphology, and Scientology. Author Terrence Hines tackles these and many other pseudopsychologies, debunking many myths about them. He explains how the promoters of the pseudopsychologies can easily persuade you that they can help you become happier and better adjusted. This book carefully guides you on a critical-thinking journey through the broad landscape of pseudopsychologies. If you believe in any pseudopsychologies, or are curious to learn more about them, *Pseudoscience and the Paranormal* is an excellent resource.

SELF-ASSESSMENT SCORING AND INTERPRETATION

BELIEF IN PSYCHIC PHENOMENA

Go back to the Self-Assessment to compare your beliefs in psychic phenomena with a random sample of Americans in a 1990s Gallup poll (Gallup & Newport, 1991). In the national poll of 1,236 adults:

- More than one-half said they believe in déjà vu.
- More than one-half said they believe in the Devil.
- Almost one-half said they believe in ESP.
- Almost one-half said they believe that people on this earth are sometimes possessed by the Devil.
- More than 40 percent said they believe in psychic or spiritual healing.
- More than one-third said they believe in telepathy.
- About 30 percent said they believe that houses can be haunted.
- More than one-fourth said they believe that extraterrestrial beings have visited Earth.
- About one-fourth said they believe in clairvoyance.
- One-fourth said they believe in astrology.
- One-fourth said they believe in ghosts.

- About 20 percent said they believe in reincarnation.
- Almost 20 percent said they can hear from or communicate mentally with someone who has died.
- Almost 20 percent said they believe in telekinesis.
- 14 percent said they believe in witches.
- 11 percent said they believe in channeling.
- Only 7 percent said they believe that pyramids have a special healing power.
- Only 4 percent said that rock crystals have a special healing power.

Only 7 percent of Americans denied believing in any of the 18 psychic experiences. Almost one-half said they believe in 5 or more of them.

How did you compare with the average American's belief in psychic experiences? If, after reading our critique of pseudopsychologies, you still responded that you believe in a number of these psychic phenomena, we encourage you to read Terence Hines's (1988) book *Pseudoscience and the Paranormal,* or read some articles in the journal *Skeptical Inquirer,* which should stimulate you to think critically about such phenomena.

C H A P T E R 2

Personality

*Every person cries out
to be read differently.*

—Simone Weil

I n the fall of 1890, Mark Twain decided to visit his publisher, George Putnam. According to Twain, the book clerk took one look at his clothes and formed some negative impressions about him that prompted the clerk to inform Twain somewhat harshly that Mr. Putnam "wasn't in." Twain knew it was a falsehood, so he decided to transact some unusual business with the clerk. He asked for a preferred volume, which the clerk retrieved. The clerk announced a price of three dollars for the transaction.

Then Twain identified himself as a publisher and requested that the clerk allow him the typical publisher's discount of 60 percent. The clerk appeared to be unmoved. Next Twain claimed that he was also an author and requested the discount of 30 percent reserved for authors. Twain observed that

Author Mark Twain's encounter with a bookseller illustrates the hazards of judging personality.

the clerk lost the color from his face. Finally Twain claimed that he also maintained his membership in the human species and suggested that the typical

discount for such membership was 10 percent. Without a word, the severe-looking clerk deliberated for a moment and announced that he would have to refund fifteen cents to Twain because the publisher also offered a discount to seriously shy people.

This story about one of the legendary characters in American literature illustrates several principles related to the key ideas in this chapter on personality. We almost relentlessly form judgments about other people's personalities based on how they look, how they dress, and how they behave. And it is quite easy to be wrong, as both Twain and the clerk so deftly illustrated—the clerk misjudging Twain's commercial potential due to his unimpressive dress, and Twain misjudging the clerk as humorless due to his severe manner.

PREVIEW

In this chapter we will examine the formal systems of explanation that have evolved in Western cultures to describe personality. You will see that psychologists believe that personality is a property of the individual but disagree about the nature of personality. We will explore three general perspectives on personality: psychoanalytic, the learning approaches, and humanistic. We will also explore various trait-based approaches and evaluate the influence of contexts on personality.

THE NATURE OF PERSONALITY

Capturing your uniqueness as a person is not an easy task. Most of us believe that we have some enduring personality characteristics. Psychologists define **personality** *as enduring, distinctive thoughts, emotions, and behaviors that characterize*

the way an individual adapts to the world. To think about your own personality, see the Critical Thinking box.

> *People have one thing in common; they are all different.*
> —**Robert Zend**

THEORIES OF PERSONALITY

Historically, psychologists have honored three theoretical perspectives—psychoanalytic, the learning approaches, and humanistic—as the dominant explanations for personality development. Each perspective offers distinctive insights.

What Are You Really *Like*?

Try to come up with five or six characteristics that you think are an enduring part of your makeup as a person. As you look at this list, consider the following about your self-reflection:

- Do you always behave in ways that are consistent with these traits?
- Would your closest friends agree with your characterization?
- How would those who don't like you describe you?
- Were your descriptions realistic or idealistic?

This exercise encourages you to *pursue multiple perspectives and alternative explanations to understand adjustment.*

The diversity of theories makes understanding personality a challenge (Maddi, 1996). Just when you think one theory has the correct explanation of personality, another theory will make you rethink your earlier conclusion. To keep from getting frustrated, remember that personality is a complex, multifaceted topic and no single theory has been able to account for all its aspects; each theory has contributed an important piece to the personality puzzle. In fact, many pieces of information in different personality theories are *complementary* rather than contradictory. Together they let us see the total landscape of personality in all its richness (Mayer & Sutton, 1996).

Psychoanalytic Perspectives

For psychoanalytic theorists, personality is unconscious—that is, beyond awareness—and heavily colored by emotion. Psychoanalytic theorists believe that behavior is merely a surface characteristic and that, to understand someone's personality, we have to look at the symbolic meanings of behavior and the deep inner workings of the mind. Psychoanalytic theorists also believe that early experiences with our parents extensively shape our personalities. These characteristics of personality were described by the original psychoanalytic theorist, Sigmund Freud.

Sigmund Freud, the founder of psychoanalytic psychology.

Freud's Theory

Loved and hated, respected and despised—Sigmund Freud, whether right or wrong in his views, has been one of the most influential thinkers of the twentieth century. Freud was a medical doctor who specialized in neurology and developed his ideas about psychoanalytic theory from his work with neurotic patients. He was born in Austria in 1856, and he died in London in 1939 at the age of 83. Freud spent most of his life in Vienna, but he left that city near the end of his career to escape Nazi anti-Semitism. To consider sociohistorical influences on Freud's theory, turn to the Critical Thinking box on Freud and Schwarzenneger

As the eldest child, Freud was regarded as a genius by his brothers and sisters and doted on by his mother. Later we will see that one aspect of Freud's theory emphasizes that young boys are sexually attracted to their mothers; it is possible that he derived this belief from his own romantic attachment to his mother, who was beautiful and about 20 years younger than Freud's father.

In Freud's view, much more of the mind is unconscious than conscious. He envisioned the mind as a huge iceberg, with the massive part below the surface of the water being the unconscious part. Freud said that each of our lives is filled with tension and conflict; to reduce this tension and conflict, we keep information locked in the unconscious mind. For Freud, the unconscious mind holds the key to understanding behavior. Freud believed that even trivial behaviors have special significance when the unconscious forces behind them are revealed. A twitch, a doodle, a joke, a smile, each may have an unconscious reason for appearing. They often slip into our lives without our awareness. For example, Allison is kissing and hugging Tyler, whom she is to marry in several weeks. She says, "Oh, *Jeff*, I love you so much." Tyler pushes her away and says, "Why did you call me Jeff? I thought you didn't think about him anymore. We need to have a talk!" You probably can think of times when such *Freudian slips* have tumbled out of your own mouth.

The Structure of Personality Freud (1917) believed that personality has three structures: the id, the ego, and the superego. One way to understand the three structures is to imagine them as three rulers of a country (Singer, 1984). The id is king or queen, the ego is prime minister, and the superego is high priest. The id is an absolute monarch, owed complete obedience; it is spoiled, willful, and self-centered. The id wants what it wants right now, not later. The ego, as prime minister, has the job of getting things done; it is tuned into reality and is responsive to society's demands. The superego, as high priest, is concerned with right and wrong;

the id might be greedy and needs to be told that nobler purposes should be pursued. It is important to think of these as processes and forces, however, not as concrete entities.

The **id** *is the Freudian structure of personality that consists of instincts, which are the individual's reservoir of psychic energy.* In Freud's view, the id is unconscious; it has no contact with reality. The id works according to the **pleasure principle,** *the Freudian concept that the id always seeks pleasure and avoids pain.*

It would be a dangerous and scary world if our personalities were all id. As young children mature, for example, they learn they cannot slug other children in the face. They also learn they have to use the toilet instead of their diaper. As children experience the demands and constraints of reality, a new structure of personality is formed—the **ego,** *the Freudian structure of personality that deals with the demands of reality. The ego is called the executive branch of personality because it makes decisions based on rationality.* Whereas the id is completely unconscious, the ego is partly conscious. It houses our higher mental functions—reasoning, problem solving, and decision making, for example. The ego abides by the **reality principle,** *the Freudian concept that the ego tries to make the pursuit of individual pleasure conform to the norms of society.* Few of us are cold-blooded killers or wild wheeler-dealers; we take into account the obstacles to our satisfaction that exist in our world. We recognize that our sexual and aggressive impulses cannot go unrestrained. The ego helps us test reality, to see how far we can go without getting into trouble and hurting ourselves.

> *If it were possible to talk to the unborn, one could never explain to them how it feels to be alive, for life is washed in the speechless real.*
>
> **—Jacques Barzun,**
> ***The House of Intellect, 1959***

The id and ego have no morality. They do not take into account whether something is right or wrong. In contrast, the **superego** *is the Freudian structure of personality that is the moral branch of*

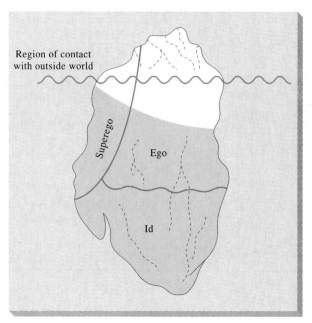

FIGURE 2.1

Conscious and Unconscious Processes: The Iceberg Analogy
This rather odd-looking diagram illustrates Freud's belief that most of the important personality processes occur below the level of conscious awareness. In examining people's conscious thoughts and their behaviors, we can see some reflections of the ego and the superego. Whereas the ego and superego are partly conscious and partly unconscious, the primitive id is the unconscious, totally submerged part of the iceberg.

personality. The superego takes into account whether something is right or wrong. The superego is what we often refer to as the "conscience." Like the id, the superego does not consider reality; it doesn't deal with what is realistic, only with whether the id's sexual and aggressive impulses can be satisfied in moral terms. You probably are beginning to sense that both the id and the superego make life rough for the ego. Your ego might say, "I will have sex only occasionally and be sure to use an effective form of protection against pregnancy and sexually transmitted diseases." However, your id is saying, "I want to be satisfied; sex feels so good." Your superego is also at work: "I feel guilty about having sex."

Remember that Freud considered personality to be like an iceberg; most of our personality exists below the level of awareness, just as the massive part of an iceberg is beneath the surface of the water. Figure 2.1 illustrates this analogy and the extent of the unconscious part of our mind, in Freud's view.

Defense Mechanisms The ego calls on a number of strategies to resolve the

conflict among its demands for reality, the wishes of the id, and the constraints of the superego. Through **defense mechanisms,** *the psychoanalytic term for unconscious methods of dealing with conflict, the ego distorts reality, thereby protecting itself from anxiety.* For example, when a person's ego blocks the pleasurable pursuits of the id, that person feels frustration. A diffuse state of distress ensues when the ego senses that the id is going to cause harm. This anxiety alerts the ego to resolve the conflict by means of defense mechanisms.

Repression *is the most powerful and pervasive defense mechanism, according to Freud; it works to push unacceptable id impulses and traumatic memories out of awareness and back into the unconscious mind.* Repression is the foundation from which all other defense mechanisms work; the goal of every psychological defense is to *repress* threatening impulses, or push them out of awareness. Freud said that our early childhood experiences, many of which he believed are sexually laden, are too threatening and stressful for us to deal with consciously. We reduce the anxiety of this conflict through repression.

CRITICAL THINKING

Freud and Schwarzenegger

Arnold Schwarzenegger's most popular films usually include high levels of violence and sexuality. *How would Freud explain his popularity?*

If Sigmund Freud were alive today, what reactions do you think he might have to the level of violence and sexuality in contemporary action films? Your consideration of this question sensitizes you to the importance of *identifying underlying values that influence behavior.* Conversely, how do you think Arnold might have fared in Freud's Viennese Victorian context?

Among the other defense mechanisms we use to protect the ego and reduce anxiety are rationalization, displacement, sublimation, projection, reaction formation, and regression. **Rationalization** *is the psychoanalytic defense mechanism that occurs when the ego does not accept the real motive for the individual's behavior and replaces it with a sort of cover motive.* For example, you are studying hard for tomorrow's exam. You are really getting into the material when a friend calls and says he is having a party in an hour. He tells you that a certain person you find attractive will be there. You know that if you don't stay in your room and study, you will do poorly on tomorrow's exam, but you tell yourself, "I did well on the first test in this class and I have been studying hard all semester; it's time I have some fun," so you go to the party. The real motive is wanting to go to the party, to have fun, and to see the attractive person. However, that reason wouldn't justify doing poorly on the exam, so you think you should stay home and study. Your ego now steps in and comes up with a better motive. Your ego says that you have worked hard all semester and you need to unwind, and that you will probably do better on the exam if you relax a little—a rationale that is more acceptable than just going to have fun and meet the desirable other person.

Displacement *is the psychoanalytic defense mechanism that occurs when an individual shifts unacceptable feelings from one object to another more acceptable object.* For example, a woman is harassed by her boss. She gets angry but she doesn't feel she can take the anger out on the boss because she might get fired. When she gets home that evening, she yells at her husband, thus transferring her feelings toward her boss to her husband.

Sublimation *is the psychoanalytic defense mechanism that occurs when the ego replaces an unacceptable impulse with a socially approved course of action.* Sublimation is actually a type of displacement. For example, an individual with strong sexual urges might turn them into socially approved behavior by becoming an artist who paints nudes.

Projection *is the psychoanalytic defense mechanism that occurs when we* *attribute our own shortcomings, problems, and faults to others.* For example, a man who has a strong desire to have an extramarital affair keeps accusing his wife of flirting with other men. A manipulative businesswoman who takes advantage of everyone to shove her way up the corporate ladder tells her associate, "Everybody around here is so manipulative; they never consider my feelings." When we can't face our own unwanted feelings, we *project* them onto others and see others as having the undesirable traits.

Reaction formation *is the psychoanalytic defense mechanism that occurs when we express an unacceptable impulse by transforming it into its opposite.* For example, an individual who is attracted to the brutality of war becomes a peace activist, or a person who fears his sexual urges becomes a religious zealot.

Regression *is the psychoanalytic defense mechanism that occurs when we behave in a way characteristic of a previous developmental level.* When anxiety becomes too great for us, we revert to an earlier behavior that gave us pleasure. For example, a husband and wife might each

TABLE 2.1

Possible Links Between Adult Personality Characteristics and Fixation at Oral, Anal, and Phallic Stages

Stage	Adult extensions	Sublimations	Reaction formations
Oral	Smoking, eating, kissing, oral hygiene, drinking, chewing gum	Seeking knowledge, humor, wit, sarcasm, being a food or wine expert	Speech purist, food faddist, prohibitionist, dislike of milk
Anal	Notable interest in one's bowel movements, love of bathroom humor, extreme messiness	Interest in painting or sculpture, being over generous, great interest in statistics	Extreme disgust with feces, fear of dirt, prudishness, irritability
Phallic	Heavy reliance on masturbation, flirtatiousness, expressions of virility	Interest in poetry, love of love, interest in acting, striving for success	Puritanical attitude toward sex, excessive modesty

From *Introduction to Personality* by E. Jerry Phares. Copyright © 1984 by Bell & Howell Company. Reprinted by permission of HarperCollins Publishers, Inc.

run home to their mothers every time they have a big argument.

Two final points about defense mechanisms need to be understood. First, defense mechanisms are unconscious; we are not aware that we are calling on them to protect the ego and reduce anxiety. Second, when used in moderation or on a temporary basis, defense mechanisms are not necessarily unhealthy. For example, defense mechanisms, such as denial, can help a person cope with difficult circumstances, such as impending death. Under some circumstances therapists might strengthen their clients' defenses to make them less vulnerable to anxiety. For the most part, though, we should not let defense mechanisms dominate our behavior and prevent us from facing life's demands directly.

Life is the art of being well-deceived.
—**William Hazlitt (1778–1830)**

The Development of Personality   As Freud listened to, probed, and analyzed his patients, he became convinced that their problems were the result of experiences early in life. Freud believed that we go through five stages of psychosexual development and that, at each stage of development, we experience pleasure in one part of the body more than others. **Erogenous zones** *are those parts of the body that, at each stage of development,*

according to Freud's theory, have especially strong pleasure-giving qualities.

Freud thought that adult personality is determined by the way we resolve conflicts among these early sources of pleasure—the mouth, the anus, and then the genitals—and the demands of reality. When these conflicts are not resolved, the individual may become fixated at a particular stage of development. **Fixation** *is the psychoanalytic defense mechanism that occurs when the individual remains locked in an earlier developmental stage because her or his needs are under- or overgratified.* For example, a parent may wean a child too early, be too strict in toilet training, punish the child for masturbation, or "smother" the child with too much attention. We will return to the idea of fixation and how it may show up in an adult's personality, but first we need to learn more about the early stages of personality development.

The **oral stage** *is the term Freud used to describe development during the first 18 months of life, in which the infant's pleasure centers on the mouth.* Chewing, sucking, and biting are chief sources of pleasure, and they help reduce tension.

The **anal stage** *is Freud's second stage of development, occurring between 1½ and 3 years of age, in which the child's greatest pleasure involves the anus or the elimination functions associated with it.* In Freud's view, the exercise of anal muscles reduces tension and provides pleasure.

The **phallic stage,** *Freud's third stage of development, occurs between the ages of 3 and 6; its name comes from the Latin word* phallus, *which means "penis." During the phallic stage, pleasure focuses on the genitals as the child discovers that self-stimulation is enjoyable.* In Freud's view, the phallic stage has a special importance in personality development because this period triggers the Oedipus complex. This name comes from Greek mythology, in which Oedipus, the son of the King of Thebes, unwittingly kills his father and marries his mother. The **Oedipus complex,** *in Freud's theory, involves the young child developing an intense desire to replace the parent of the same sex and to enjoy the affections of the opposite-sex parent.* The Oedipus complex, like many other aspects of Freud's theory, was not as universal as Freud believed; his concept was heavily influenced by the sociohistorical, cultural context of turn-of-the-century Vienna. Table 2.1 summarizes the impact of fixations in the first three Freudian stages on personality development.

At about 5 to 6 years of age, children recognize that their same-sex parent might punish them for their incestuous wishes. To reduce this conflict, the child identifies with the same-sex parent, striving to be like him or her. If the conflict is not resolved, the individual may become fixated at the phallic stage.

The **latency stage** *is the fourth Freudian stage of development, occurring approximately between 6 years of age and*

Oral stage

Anal stage

Phallic stage

Latency stage

Genital stage

FIGURE 2.2

Freudian Psychosexual Stages
Freud said we go through five stages of psychosexual development. In the oral stage, pleasure centers around the mouth. In the anal stage, pleasure focuses on the anus—the nature of toilet training is important here. In the phallic stage, pleasure involves the genitals—the opposite-sex parent becomes a love object. In the latency stage, a child represses sexual urges—same-sex friendship is prominent. In the genital stage, sexual reawakening takes place—the source of pleasure now becomes someone outside the family.

puberty; the child represses all interest in sexuality and develops social and intellectual skills. This activity channels much of the child's energy into emotionally safe areas and aids the child in forgetting the highly stressful conflicts of the phallic stage.

The **genital stage** *is the fifth and final Freudian stage of development, occurring from puberty on. The genital stage is the time of sexual reawakening; the source of sexual pleasure now becomes someone outside of the family.* Freud believed that unresolved conflicts with parents reemerge during adolescence. Once the conflicts are resolved, Freud believed, the individual becomes capable of developing a mature love relationship and of functioning independently as an adult. Figure 2.2 summarizes Freud's psychosexual stages.

Psychoanalytic Revisionists and Dissenters

Freud was among the first theorists to explore many new and uncharted regions of personality and is credited with founding psychoanalysis. As others joined him in this new medical frontier, neo-Freudians discovered that they had to update and revise Freud's ideas. Although they honored many of his concepts, they rejected some aspects of Freudian theory altogether. In particular, Freud's critics have said his ideas about sexuality, early experience, social factors, and the unconscious mind were misguided (Adler, 1927; Erikson, 1968; Fromm, 1947; Horney, 1945; Jung, 1917; Sullivan, 1953). The critics stressed several points:

- Sexuality is not the pervasive underlying force behind personality that Freud believed it to be.
- The first 5 years of life are not as powerful in shaping adult personality as Freud thought; later experiences deserve more attention than they have been given.
- The ego and conscious thought processes play more dominant roles in our personality than Freud gave them credit for; we are not wed forever to the id and its instinctual, unconscious clutches. The ego has a line of development separate from the id; viewed in this way, achievement, thinking, and reasoning are not always tied to sexual impulses, as Freud thought.
- Sociocultural factors are much more important than Freud believed. Freud placed more emphasis on the biological basis of personality by stressing the id's dominance.

Let's examine three theories by dissenters and revisionists of Freud's theory in greater detail—Horney's, Jung's, and Adler's.

Horney's Sociocultural Modification
Although she agreed with much of Freud's theory of personality development, Karen Horney (1885–1952) rejected the classical psychoanalytic concept that anatomy determines behavior in favor of an approach that emphasizes the importance of sociocultural factors in development. She cautioned that such ideas as penis envy are only hypotheses. She insisted that these hypotheses should be supported with observable data before they are accepted as fact.

Horney pointed out that previous research about how women function was

(a)   (b)

(*a*) Karen Horney developed the first feminist-based criticism of Freud's theory, creating a model of women with positive qualities and self-valuation. (*b*) Nancy Chodorow has developed an important contemporary feminist revision of psychoanalytic theory that emphasizes the meaningfulness of emotions for women.

limited by the fact that those who described women, who influenced and represented the culture, and who determined the standards for suitable growth and development were men. She countered the notion of penis envy with the hypothesis that both sexes envy the attributes of the other and that men covet women's reproductive capacities. She also argued that women who feel penis envy are desirous only of the status that men have in most societies, not of their anatomy (Westkott, 1986).

Freud, living at a time when women were proving their heads were no different from men's, substituted the penis for the head as the organ of male superiority, an organ women could never prove they had.

—**Una Stannard**

Horney also believed that the need for security, not for sex or aggression, is the prime motive in human existence. Horney reasoned that a person whose needs for security have been met should be able to develop his or her capacities to the fullest extent. She also suggested that people usually develop one of three strategies in their effort to cope with anxiety. First, individuals may *move toward* people, seeking love and support. Second, individuals may *move away*

from people, becoming more independent. Third, individuals may *move against* people, becoming competitive and domineering. A secure individual uses these three ways of coping in moderation and balance, whereas an insecure individual often uses one or more of these strategies in an exaggerated fashion, becoming too dependent, too independent, or too aggressive.

Psychologists continue to revise psychoanalytic theory. Nancy Chodorow's (1989) feminist revision of psychoanalytic theory, for example, emphasizes that many more women than men define themselves in terms of their relationships, that many men use denial as a defense mechanism in regard to their relationships with others, and that emotions tend to play a more prominent role in women's lives.

Psychoanalysis is the creation of a male genius, and almost all those who have developed these ideas have been men. It is only right and reasonable that they should evolve more easily a masculine psychology and understand more of the development of men than of women.

—**Karen Horney**

Jung's Depth Psychology
Freud's contemporary, Carl Jung (1875–1961),

FIGURE 2.3

Mandalas
Carl Jung (*right*) believed that mandalas (*left*) were so widely used to represent the self at different points in history that they were an archetype for the self.

shared an interest in the unconscious; however, he believed that Freud underplayed the unconscious mind's role in personality. Jung suspected that the roots of personality go back to the dawn of human existence. The **collective unconscious** *is the impersonal, deepest layer of the unconscious mind, which is shared by all human beings because of their common ancestral past.* These common experiences have made a deep, permanent impression on the human mind (Harris, 1996). **Archetypes** *are the primordial influences in every individual's collective unconscious that filter our perceptions and experiences.* Jung's psychoanalytic theory is often referred to as "depth psychology" because archetypes reside deep within the unconscious mind, far deeper than what Freud described as our personal unconscious.

Two common archetypes are *anima* (woman) and *animus* (man). Jung believed that each of us has a passive "feminine" side and an assertive "masculine" side. We also have an archetype for self, which often is expressed in art. For example, the mandala, a figure within a circle, has been used so often that Jung took it to represent the self (see figure 2.3). Another archetype is the shadow, our darker self, which is evil and immoral. The shadow appears in many evil and immoral figures—Satan, Dracula, Mr. Hyde (of Jekyll and Hyde), and Darth Vader (of the *Star Wars* movies) (Peterson, 1988).

> *I have never seen a greater monster or miracle in the world than myself.*
> —**Montaigne**

Adler's Individual Psychology

Alfred Adler (1870–1937) was another contemporary of Freud. **Individual psychology** *is the name Adler gave to his theory of psychology to emphasize the uniqueness of every individual.* To evaluate your own need for uniqueness, turn to the Self-Assessment. Unlike Freud's belief in the power of the unconscious mind, Adler argued that we have the conscious ability to monitor and direct our lives; he also believed that social factors are more important in shaping our personality than is sexual motivation.

Adler thought that everyone strives for superiority. Adler's concept of **striving for superiority** *emphasizes the human motivation to adapt to, improve, and master the environment.* Striving for superiority is our response to the feelings of inferiority that we all experience as infants and young children when we interact with people who are bigger and more powerful. We strive to overcome these feelings of inferiority because they are uncomfortable. **Compensation** *is Adler's term for the individual's attempt to overcome imagined or real inferiorities or weaknesses by developing her or his abilities.* Adler believed that compensation

is normal. He said we often make up for a weakness in one ability by excelling in a different ability. For example, one person may be a mediocre student but compensate for this by excelling in athletics. **Overcompensation** *is Adler's term for the individual's attempt to deny rather than acknowledge a real situation or the individual's exaggerated efforts to conceal a weakness.* Adler described two patterns of overcompensation. **Inferiority complex** *is the name Adler gave to exaggerated feelings of inadequacy.* **Superiority complex** *is his concept of exaggerated self-importance that is designed to mask feelings of inferiority.*

In summary, Adler's theory emphasizes that people are striving toward a positive being and that they create their own goals. Their adaptation is enhanced by developing social interests and reducing feelings of inferiority. Like Jung, Adler has a number of disciples today.

Evaluating the Psychoanalytic Perspectives

Although psychoanalytic theories have diverged, they do share some core principles. Psychoanalytic theorists assert that personality is determined both by current experiences and by those from early in life. Some principles of psychoanalytic theory have withstood the test of time. For example, early experiences do shape our personality to a degree, and personality can be better understood by examining it developmentally.

Another belief that continues to receive considerable attention is that we mentally transform, and sometimes distort, environmental experiences. Psychologists also recognize that the mind is not all consciousness; unconscious motives lie behind some of our puzzling behavior. Psychoanalytic theorists' emphasis on conflict and anxiety leads us to consider the dark side of our existence, not just its bright side. Adjustment is not always an easy task; the individual's inner world often conflicts with the outer demands of reality. Finally, psychoanalytic theories continue to force psychologists to study more than the experimental, laboratory topics of sensation, perception, and learning; personality and adjustment are rightful and important topics of psychological inquiry as well.

Need for Uniqueness

Instructions

The following statements concern your perceptions about yourself in a variety of situations. Your task is to indicate the strength of your agreement with each statement, utilizing a scale in which 1 denotes strong disagreement, 5 denotes strong agreement, and 2, 3, and 4, represent intermediate judgments. In the blank preceding each statement, place your number from 1 to 5. *There are no "right" or "wrong" answers, so select the number that most clearly reflects you on each statement.*

Turn to the end of the chapter to interpret your responses.

____ **1.** When I am in a group of strangers, I am not reluctant to express my opinion openly.

____ **2.** I find that criticism affects my self-esteem.

____ **3.** I sometimes hesitate to use my own ideas for fear they might be impractical.

____ **4.** I think society should let reason lead it to new customs and throw aside old habits or mere traditions.

____ **5.** People frequently succeed in changing my mind.

____ **6.** I find it sometimes amusing to upset the dignity of teachers, judges, and "cultured" people.

____ **7.** I like wearing a uniform because it makes me proud to be a member of the organization it represents.

____ **8.** People have sometimes called me "stuck-up."

____ **9.** Others' disagreements make me uncomfortable.

____ **10.** I do not always need to live by the rules and standards of society.

____ **11.** I am unable to express my feelings if they result in undesirable consequences.

____ **12.** Being a success in one's career means making a contribution that no one else has made.

____ **13.** It bothers me if people think I am being too unconventional.

____ **14.** I always try to follow rules.

____ **15.** If I disagree with a superior on his or her views, I usually do not keep it to myself.

____ **16.** I speak up in meetings in order to oppose those whom I feel are wrong.

____ **17.** Feeling "different" in a crowd of people makes me feel uncomfortable.

____ **18.** If I must die, let it be an unusual death rather than an ordinary death in bed.

____ **19.** I would rather be just like everyone else than be called a "freak."

____ **20.** I must admit I find it hard to work under strict rules and regulations.

____ **21.** I would rather be known for always trying new ideas than for employing well-trusted methods.

____ **22.** It is better always to agree with the opinions of others than to be considered a disagreeable person.

____ **23.** I do not like to say unusual things to people.

____ **24.** I tend to express my opinions publicly, regardless of what others say.

____ **25.** As a rule, I strongly defend my own opinions.

____ **26.** I do not like to go my own way.

____ **27.** When I am with a group of people, I agree with their ideas so that no arguments will arise.

____ **28.** I tend to keep quiet in the presence of persons of higher rank, experience, etc.

____ **29.** I have been quite independent and free from family rule.

____ **30.** Whenever I take part in group activities, I am somewhat of a nonconformist.

____ **31.** In most things in life, I believe in playing it safe rather than taking a gamble.

____ **32.** It is better to break rules than always to conform with an impersonal society.

The main concepts of psychoanalytic theories have been difficult to test; they are largely matters of inference and interpretation. Researchers have not, for example, successfully investigated such key concepts as repression in the laboratory.

Much of the data used to support psychoanalytic theories have come from clinicians' subjective evaluations of clients; in such cases, it is easy for each clinician to see what she expects because of the theory she holds. Other data come from patients' recollections of the distant past (especially those from early childhood) and are of dubious accuracy. Also, critics believe that psychoanalytic theories place too much weight on the ability of these early experiences within the family to shape personality, and that we retain the capacity for change and adaptation throughout our lives.

Some psychologists object that Freud overemphasized the role of sexuality in personality and that Freud and Jung placed too much faith in the unconscious mind's ability to control behavior. Others object that the psychoanalytic perspectives provide a model of a person that is too negative and pessimistic. We are not born into the world with only a bundle of sexual and aggressive instincts. The demands of reality do not always conflict with our biological needs.

Many psychoanalytic theories of personality, especially Freud's, have a male bias. Although Horney's theory helped correct this bias, psychoanalytic theory continues to be revised today.

At this point, you should have a sense of what personalty is and a basic understanding of the themes of psychoanalytic theories. Next, we will explore two views of personality that are very different from the psychoanalytic theories.

Learning Perspectives

Roy and Ann are engaged. We would probably informally describe them both as having warm, friendly personalities, from our observations of how much they appear to enjoy being with each other. Psychoanalytic theorists would say that their personalities are derived from long-standing relationships with their parents, especially their early childhood experiences. They also would argue that the reason for their attraction is unconscious; they are unaware of how their biological heritage and early life experiences have been carried forward to influence their adult personalities and behaviors.

In contrast, behaviorists (who hold a learning perspective) would observe Roy and Ann and infer something quite different. Behaviorists would examine their experiences, especially their most recent ones, to identify the reasons for their mutual pursuit of each other's company. For example, behaviorists might focus on

REVIEW

The Nature of Personality and Psychoanalytic Theories

Personality refers to our enduring thoughts, emotions, and behaviors that characterize the way we adapt. A key question is why individuals respond to a situation in different ways.

Freud was one of the most influential thinkers in the twentieth century. He was a medical doctor who believed that most of the mind is unconscious. Freud said that personality has three structures: id, ego, and superego. The id is the reservoir of psychic energy that tries to satisfy our basic needs; it is unconscious and operates according to the pleasure principle. The ego tries to provide pleasure by operating within the boundaries of reality. The superego is the moral branch of personality. The conflicting demands of personality structures produce anxiety; defense mechanisms protect the ego and reduce this anxiety. Repression, the most pervasive defense mechanism, pushes unacceptable id impulses back into the unconscious mind. Other defense mechanisms include rationalization, displacement, sublimation, projection, reaction formation, and regression. Freud was convinced that problems develop because of childhood experiences. He said we go through five psychosexual stages of development: oral, anal, phallic, latency, and genital. He believed that, if our needs are under- or overgratified at a particular stage, we can become fixated at that stage. During the phallic stage, the Oedipus complex is a major source of conflict.

The psychoanalytic dissenters and revisionists have argued that Freud placed too much emphasis on sexuality and the first 5 years of life

and too little emphasis on the ego and conscious thought processes, as well as sociocultural factors. Karen Horney rejected the classical psychoanalytic concept that anatomy determines behavior, advocated by Freud, in favor of a sociocultural approach. She especially emphasized that Freud's theory is male biased. Horney said that the need for security, not sex or aggression, is the prime motive in human existence. She also theorized that individuals usually develop one of three strategies to cope with anxiety—moving toward people, moving away from people, or moving against people. The rectification of male bias in psychoanalytic theory continues today through the efforts of such individuals as Nancy Chodorow. Jung thought Freud underplayed the role of the unconscious mind. He developed the concept of the collective unconscious, and his theory is often called depth psychology. Alfred Adler's theory is called individual psychology; it stresses every individual's uniqueness. Adler said people are striving toward a positive being and that they create their own goals. Their adaptation is enhanced by developing social interests and reducing feelings of inferiority.

The strengths of the psychoanalytic perspectives include an emphasis on the past, the developmental course of personality, mental representations of the environment, the concept of the unconscious mind, an emphasis on conflict, and their influence on psychology as a discipline. Their weaknesses include the difficulty in testing the main concepts, a lack of empirical data and an overreliance on reports of the past, too much emphasis on sexuality and the unconscious mind, a negative view of human nature, too much power given to early experience, and a male bias.

how Ann rewards Roy's attentiveness, and vice versa. They would avoid making references to unconscious thoughts, the Oedipus complex, and defense mechanisms and refer instead to behaviors and their consequences.

At approximately the same time as Freud was interpreting his patients' unconscious minds through their early childhood recollections, behaviorists Ivan Pavlov and John B. Watson were conducting detailed observations of behavior under controlled laboratory conditions. Each conducted research that evolved into distinctive therapies, which will be discussed in chapter 15. Pavlov's work led to classical conditioning interventions. Watson's research founded operant conditioning procedures.

Out of the learning tradition grew the belief that personality is the sum of observable behaviors, learned through experiences with the environment (Staats, 1996). We should examine only what can be directly observed and measured. This emphasis discourages exploring and explaining the origins of behavior. Instead, behaviorism encourages careful definition and precise measurement of behavior. Behavioral explanations shift the emphasis to the functions of behavior and how behavior can be modified.

In this section we will study several learning perspectives: Ivan Pavlov's classical conditioning, B. F. Skinner's operant conditioning, and cognitive social learning theory.

Classical Conditioning

It is a nice spring day. A father takes his baby out for a walk. The baby reaches over to touch a pink flower and is stung by a bumblebee sitting on the petals. The next day, the baby's mother brings home some pink flowers. She removes a flower from the arrangement and takes it over for her baby to smell. The baby cries loudly as soon as she sees the pink flower. The baby's panic at the sight of the pink flower illustrates the learning process of **classical conditioning,** *in which a neutral stimulus becomes associated with a meaningful stimulus and acquires the capacity to elicit a similar response.*

How Classical Conditioning Works

In the early 1900s, Russian physiologist Ivan Pavlov investigated the way the body digests food. As part of his experiments, he routinely placed meat powder in a dog's mouth, causing the dog to salivate. Pavlov began to notice that the meat powder was not the only stimulus that caused the dog to salivate. The dog also salivated in response to a number of stimuli associated with the food, such as the sight of the food dish, the sight of the individual who brought the food into the room, and the sound of the door closing when the food arrived. Pavlov recognized that the dog's association of these sights and sounds with the food was an important type of learning (which came to be called classical conditioning).

Pavlov wanted to know *why* the dog salivated to various sights and sounds before eating the meat powder. Pavlov observed that the dog's behavior included both learned and unlearned components. The unlearned part of classical conditioning is based on the fact that some stimuli automatically produce certain responses apart from any prior learning; in other words, the responses are inborn, or innate. **Reflexes** *are automatic stimulus-response connections that are "hardwired" into the brain.* They include salivation in response to food, nausea in response to bad food, shivering in response to low temperature, coughing in response to the throat's being clogged, pupil constriction in response to light, and withdrawal in response to a blow, burns, or pain, among others. An **unconditioned stimulus (US)** *is a stimulus that produces a response without prior learning;* food was the US in Pavlov's experiments. An **unconditioned response (UR)** *is an unlearned response that is automatically associated with the US.* In Pavlov's experiments, the saliva that flowed from the dog's mouth was the UR in response to the food, which was the US. In the case of the baby and her pink flower, the baby did not have to learn to cry when the bee stung her. Pain reactions are reflexive, or unlearned; a child's crying occurs automatically in response to the pain of a bee sting. In this example, the bee's sting is the US and the crying is the UR.

In classical conditioning, the **conditioned stimulus (CS)** *is a previously neutral stimulus that elicits the conditioned response after being associated with the unconditioned stimulus.* The **conditioned response (CR)** *is the learned response to the conditioned stimulus that occurs after CS-US association* (Pavlov, 1927). While he was conducting studies on digestive processes in dogs, Pavlov observed that striking a tone on a tuning fork before giving meat powder to a dog stimulated the dog's saliva flow. Prior to its association with food, the tone had no particular effect on the dog; the tone was a neutral stimulus. Once the dog began to associate the sound of the tone with the arrival of the food, the dog salivated when it heard the tone. The tone became a conditioned (learned) stimulus (CS) and the salivation a conditioned response (CR). Before conditioning (or learning), the tone and the food were not related. After the association, the conditioned stimulus (the tone) elicited a conditioned response (salivation). For the unhappy baby, the flower was the CS and the crying was the CR after the baby associated the flower with the sting (US). A summary of how classical conditioning works is shown in figure 2.4.

Classical Conditioning in Humans

Since Pavlov's experiments with dogs, psychologists have conditioned people to respond to the sound of a buzzer, a glimpse of light, or the touch of a hand. Outside of the laboratory setting, classical conditioning has a great deal of survival value for humans. Because of classical conditioning, we jerk our hands away before they are burned by fire, and we move out of the way of a rapidly approaching truck before it hits us. Classical conditioning is at work in words that serve as important signals. Walk into an abandoned house with a friend and yell "Snake!" Your friend will probably bolt out the door. Describe a peaceful, tranquil scene—an abandoned beach with waves lapping onto the sand—and the harried executive may relax as if she were actually lying on the beach.

Certain physical complaints—asthma, headaches, ulcers, and high blood pressure, for example—may be the products of classical conditioning. We usually say that such health problems are caused by stress, but often what happens is that certain stimuli, such as a boss' critical attitude or a spouse's threat of divorce, are conditioned stimuli for physiological responses. Over time, the frequent presence of the physiological responses may produce a health problem or disorder. A boss' persistent criticism may

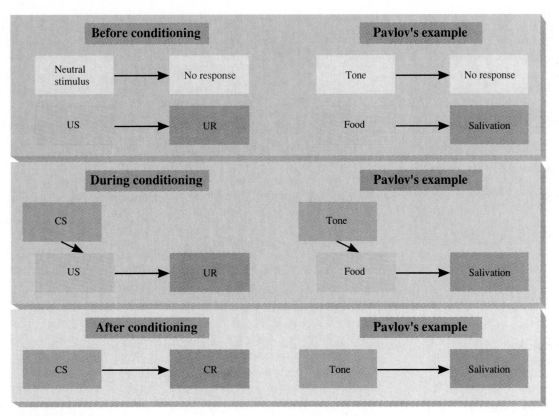

FIGURE 2.4

Classical Conditioning Procedure

At the start of conditioning, the US (food) will evoke the UR (salivation), but the bell, initially a neutral stimulus, does not. During conditioning, the tone becomes a CS through pairing with the US; the tone precedes the food presentation, which reliably elicits salivation. With repeated pairings, conditioning is achieved; the CS eventually elicits the CR (salivation) when presented alone.

cause an employee to develop muscle tension, headaches, or high blood pressure. Moreover, anything associated with the critical boss, such as work tasks themselves, can then trigger this stress response in the employee.

Classical conditioning also explains how prejudices develop and spread. For example, young children might regularly hear bigoted adults use negative nouns or adjectives—such as *stingy, lazy, alcoholic,* or *stupid*—to describe particular groups (such as Native Americans, Whites, or Jews). Eventually the child might associate those negative connotations with the groups themselves, and these negative evaluations of the groups might remain with the child into adulthood.

Classical conditioning is not restricted to unpleasant emotions. The things in our lives that produce pleasure because they have become conditioned might be the sight of a rainbow, a sunny

day, or a sentimental holiday song. If you have had a positive romantic experience, the location of that experience can become a conditioned stimulus, the result of the pairing of the place (CS) with the event (US). Sometimes, though, classical conditioning involves an experience that is both pleasant and deviant from the norm. Consider a fetishist who becomes sexually aroused by the sight and touch of certain clothing, such as pointed shoes. The fetish likely developed when the fetish object (the pointed shoes) was present during sexual arousal, probably during youth. Because of this pairing, the fetish object becomes a conditioned stimulus that can produce sexual arousal by itself (Chance, 1979).

Operant Conditioning

Although psychologists regard John B. Watson as the father of behaviorism, B. F.

Skinner's ideas dominated mainstream thinking about behavior for many decades. B. F. Skinner (1904–1990) concluded that personality is an individual's *behavior,* which is determined by the *external environment.* Skinner believed that psychologists do not have to resort to biological or cognitive processes to explain personality (behavior). Some psychologists say that including Skinner among personality theorists is like inviting a wolf to a party of lambs, because he took the "person" out of personality (Phares, 1984).

Behaviorists counter that you cannot pinpoint where personality is or how it is determined. In Skinner's view, personality simply consists of a collection of a person's observed, overt behaviors; it does not include internal traits or thoughts. For example, observations of Sam reveal that his behavior is shy, achievement-oriented, and caring. In short, these behaviors *are* his personality. According to Skinner,

B. F. Skinner, the prominent American behaviorist.

Sam is this way because the rewards and punishments in Sam's environment have shaped him into a shy, achievement-oriented, and caring person. Because of interactions with family members, friends, teachers, and others, Sam has *learned* to behave in this fashion.

Skinner believed that emphasizing mentalistic concepts prevented the development of a truly scientific approach to behavior. Thoughts and feelings should have no role in the analysis of behavior because they are covert events; they are neither directly observable nor necessary in accounting for behavior. Skinner characterized personality as a superfluous, mentalistic notion. He was satisfied with characterizing individuals according to the behaviors they use to operate in the environment. Psychologists who continue to support this reductionistic viewpoint are sometimes referred to as **radical behaviorists,** *psychologists who emphasize only observable behavior and reject its cognitive dimensions.*

Behaviorists who support Skinner's view would say that Sam's shy, achievement-oriented, and caring behavior might not be consistent and enduring. For example, Sam is uninhibited on Saturday night with friends at a bar, unmotivated to excel in English class, and occasionally nasty to his sister. In addition, Skinnerians believe that consistency in behavior comes from consistency in environmental experiences. If Sam's shy, achievement-oriented, and caring

behavior is consistently rewarded, his pattern of behavior is likely to be consistent. However, Skinner stressed that our behavior always has the capacity for change if new experiences are encountered. The issue of consistency in personality is an important one. We will return to it on several occasions later in the chapter.

Operant conditioning (instrumental conditioning) *is a form of learning in which the consequences of behavior produce changes in the probability of the behavior's occurrence.* In Skinner's (1938) operant conditioning, the person operates on the environment to increase the likelihood of some consequence.

The consequences—reinforcement or punishment—are contingent on the individual's behavior. **Reinforcement (reward)** *is a consequence that increases the probability a behavior will occur.* If someone smiles at you and the two of you continue talking for awhile, the smile has reinforced your talking. By contrast, **punishment** *is a consequence that decreases the probability a behavior will occur.* If someone frowns at you and the two of you stop talking, the frown has punished your talking with the individual.

The Cognitive Social Learning Perspective

Social learning theorists say that we are not mindless robots, responding mechanically to others in the environment. Nor do we respond like weather vanes, moving in response to the prevailing winds. Rather, we think, reason, imagine, plan, expect, interpret, believe, value, and compare. When others try to influence us, our values and beliefs allow us to evaluate their intentions and to resist or comply.

In the 1970s, social learning theory became more cognitive through the contributions of Walter Mischel (1973) and Albert Bandura (1977). They crafted **cognitive social learning theory,** *the contemporary version of social learning theory that stresses the importance of cognition, behavior, and environment in determining personality.*

Reciprocal determinism *is Bandura's social learning model, in which behavior, cognitive and other personal factors, and environmental influences operate*

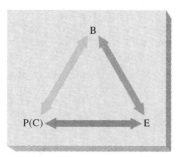

FIGURE 2.5

Bandura's Model of Reciprocal Influences
The arrows reflect how relations between behavior (B), person and cognitive factors (P(C)), and environment (E) are reciprocal rather than unidirectional. Examples of person factors include intelligence, skills, and self-control.

interactively. Behavior influences cognition, and cognition influences behavior; the person's cognitive activities influence the environment; environmental experiences change the person's thought. Likewise, one's behavior and environment influence each other (see figure 2.5).

Bandura also believes that we learn extensively by observing what others do. **Observational learning,** *also called modeling, is learning that occurs when a person observes and then repeats someone else's behavior.* The capacity to learn behavior patterns by observation eliminates tedious trial-and-error learning. Indeed, many of our successful adjustments involve our exposure to competent models who display appropriate behavior in solving problems and coping with the world.

As each of us grew up, we observed countless numbers of models engaged in many different behaviors including parents, teachers, friends, and people on television. Today, we continue to be exposed to many different models, some serving as positive models of adjustment, others as negative ones. What are some of the factors that influence whether we will imitate the behavior of a model? We especially tend to model the behavior of models we perceive to be attractive and powerful. Thus, we may adopt the behavioral mannerisms of famous movie stars and television personalities, athletes, and wealthy individuals. For example, some people who observe Shirley MacLaine

Albert Bandura (1925–   ), a pioneer cognitive social learning theorist.

ecstatically describe her New Age experiences in channeling may try to imitate her behavior, and overweight individuals who watched Oprah Winfrey tell about her diet program might adopt it for their own weight loss strategy. Some youths are drawn into drug use and drug dealing by observing successful drug dealers flaunt their money, power, and status.

Many educators and psychologists believe that if our nation's youths had better role models, they would be better adjusted and less likely to use drugs, commit delinquent acts, and drop out of school. For example, adolescents whose parents and best friends do not use drugs are themselves less likely to use drugs (Kandel, 1991). One way troubled youths can be helped to cope better and solve problems is to use **mentoring,** *in which a more experienced person agrees to develop a one-to-one relationship with a less experienced person and serve as a competent role model.* Mentors are often successful adults in the community, who provide young people with a concrete image of who a younger person can become while lending guidance and support to enable the youth to move toward better goals.

Recently, Bandura (1991, 1994) has addressed the importance of self-efficacy in personal adjustment and behavior change. **Self-efficacy** *is the belief that one can master a situation and produce*

positive outcomes. Bandura believes that self-efficacy is the key to improving our coping skills. As we face a personal problem and try to solve it, at each step of the way, we need to bolster our confidence by telling ourselves, "I can do this," "I'm going to make it," "I'm getting better," and so on. As people gain confidence and engage in more adaptive behavior, their success becomes intrinsically rewarding. Before long individuals will persist with considerable effort in solving their problems because of the pleasurable outcomes that were set in motion by self-efficacy.

Evaluating the Learning Perspectives

The behavioral and cognitive social learning theories emphasize that environmental experiences and situations influence behavior patterns referred to as personality. These approaches have fostered a scientific climate for understanding personality that highlights the observation of behavior. Cognitive social learning theory emphasizes both environmental influences and the cognitions of the human mind to explain personality; this theory also suggests that people have the ability to control their environment.

Critics of both behavioral and cognitive social learning perspectives have several bones to pick. Both approaches have been labeled "reductionistic," which means they try to explain the complex concept of personality in terms of one or two factors. Both approaches have been described as being too concerned with change and situational influences on personality and not paying adequate tribute to the enduring qualities of personality. Both views are said to ignore the role biology plays in personality. The behavioral view is criticized for ignoring the importance of cognition in personality. In other words, critics charge that the behavioral and cognitive social learning views are too mechanical, missing the most exciting, rich dimensions of personality. This latter criticism—that the creative, spontaneous, human dimensions of personality are missing from the behavioral and cognitive social learning perspectives—has been made on numerous occasions by humanistic psychologists, whose perspective we consider next.

Humanistic Perspectives

Remember our example of the engaged couple, Roy and Ann, who were described as having warm, friendly personalities. Phenomenological and humanistic psychologists would say that Roy and Ann's warm, friendly personalities are a reflection of their inner selves; these psychologists would emphasize that a key to understanding their mutual attraction is their positive perceptions of each other. Roy and Ann are not viewed as controlling each other or each other's behavior; rather, each has determined a course of action and has freely chosen to marry. No recourse to biological instincts or unconscious thoughts as reasons for their attraction is necessary in the phenomenological and humanistic perspectives. This explanation represents a **phenomenological worldview,** *which stresses the importance of our perceptions of ourselves and of our world in understanding personality; this worldview emphasizes that, for each individual, reality is what that individual perceives.*

The **humanistic perspective** *is the most widely adopted phenomenological approach to personality. The humanistic perspective stresses a person's capacity for personal growth, freedom to choose one's own destiny, and positive qualities.* Humanistic psychologists believe that each of us has the ability to cope with stress, to control our lives, and to achieve what we desire. Each of us has the ability to break through and understand ourselves and our world.

We carry with us the wonders we seek without us.
—**Sir Thomas Browne, 1642**

You probably sense that the phenomenological and humanistic perspectives provide stark contrasts to the psychoanalytic perspective, which is based on conflict, destructive drives, and little faith in human nature, and to the behavioral perspective, which, at worst, seems to reduce human beings to mere puppets on the strings of rewards and punishments. Carl Rogers and Abraham Maslow were two of the leading architects of the humanistic perspective (Engler, 1995).

Carl Rogers (1902–1987), a pioneer in the development of the humanistic perspective.

Carl Rogers' Approach

Like Freud, Carl Rogers (1902–1987) began his inquiry into human nature with people who were troubled. In the knotted, anxious, and defensive verbal stream of his clients, Rogers (1961) examined the nature of their world that kept them from having positive self-concepts and reaching their full potential as human beings. He proposed several concepts to explain the humanistic point of view.

Our Conditioned, Controlling World

Rogers believed that most people have considerable difficulty accepting their own feelings, which are innately positive. As we grow up, people who are central to our lives condition us to move away from these positive feelings. Our parents, siblings, teachers, and peers place constraints and contingencies on our behavior; too often we hear, "Don't do that," "You didn't do that right," and "How can you be so stupid?" When we don't do something right, we often get punished; parents might even threaten to take away their love. **Conditional positive regard** *is Rogers' term for making the bestowal of love or praise conditional on the individual's conforming to parental or social standards.* The result is low self-esteem.

These constraints and negative feedback continue during our adult lives. The result tends to be that our relationships either carry the dark cloud of conflict or we conform to what others want. As we struggle to live up to society's standards, we distort and devalue our true selves. By constantly acting according to other people's standards, we might even completely lose our sense of our self.

The Self   Through an individual's experiences with the world, a self emerges—the "I" or "me" of our existence. Rogers did not believe that all aspects of the self are conscious, but he did believe they are all accessible to consciousness. The self is a whole, consisting of one's self-perceptions (how attractive I am, how well I get along with others, how good an athlete I am) and the values we attach to these perceptions (good-bad, worthy-unworthy, for example). **Self-concept,** *a central theme for humanists, refers to our overall thoughts and feelings about ourselves.* According to Rogers, a person who has a poor self-concept is likely to think, feel, and act negatively. Some psychologists are turning their interest to the differences and similarities among the self-concepts of individuals from different ethnic backgrounds.

> *There's a period of life when we swallow a knowledge of ourselves and it becomes either good or sour inside.*
> **—Pearl Bailey**

In discussing self-concept, Rogers distinguished between the *real* self—that is, the self as it really is as a result of our experiences—and the *ideal* self, which is the self we would like to be. The greater the discrepancy between the real self and the ideal self, said Rogers, the more maladjusted we will be. To improve our adjustment, we can develop more positive perceptions of our real self, not worry so much about what others want, and increase our positive experiences in the world.

Unconditional Positive Regard, Empathy, and Genuineness

Rogers stressed that we can help a person develop a more positive self-concept through unconditional positive regard, empathy, and genuineness. Rogers said that we need to be accepted by others, regardless of what we do. **Unconditional positive regard** *is Rogers' term for accepting, valuing, and being positive toward another person regardless of the person's behavior.* Rogers recognized that, when a person's behavior is below acceptable standards, inappropriate, or even obnoxious, the person still needs the respect, comfort, and love of others. Rogers strongly believed that unconditional positive regard elevates a person's self-worth. However, Rogers (1974) distinguished between unconditional positive regard directed at an individual as a person of worth and dignity and unconditional positive regard directed at the individual's behavior. A Rogerian therapist creates supportive conditions in which the individual can come to terms with undesirable behavior.

Rogers also said we can help other people develop a more positive self-concept if we are *empathic* and *genuine.* Being empathic means being a sensitive listener and understanding another's true feelings. Being genuine means being open with our feelings and dropping our pretenses and facades. For Rogers, unconditional positive regard, empathy, and genuineness are three key ingredients of human relations. We can use these techniques to help other people to feel good about themselves, and the techniques also help us get along better with others.

The Fully Functioning Person

Rogers stressed the importance of becoming a fully functioning person—someone who is open to experience, is not very defensive, is aware of and sensitive to the self and the external world, and for the most part has a harmonious relationship with others. A discrepancy between the real self and the ideal self may occur, others may try to control us, and our world may have too little unconditional positive regard. However, Rogers believed that human beings are highly resilient and capable of becoming fully functioning.

Our self-actualizing tendency is reflected in Rogers' comparison of persons with a plant he once observed on the coastline of northern California. As Rogers looked out at the waves beating furiously against the jagged rocks and shooting mountains of spray into the air, he noticed the breakers pounding a sea palm (a kind of seaweed that looks like a 2- to 3-foot-high palm tree). The plant seemed fragile and top-heavy. The waves crashed against the plant, bending its slender trunk almost flat and whipping its leaves in a torrent of spray, yet the moment the wave passed the plant was erect, tough, and resilient again. It was incredible that the plant could take this incessant pounding hour after hour, week after week, possibly even year after year, all the time nourishing itself, maintaining its position, and growing. In this palmlike seaweed, Rogers saw the tenacity and forward thrust of life and the ability of a living thing to push into a hostile environment and not only hold its own but adapt, develop, and become itself. So is the potential with each of us, according to Rogers (1963).

> *The living self has one purpose only: to come into its own fullness of being, as a tree comes into full blossom, or a bird into spring beauty, or a tiger into lustre.*
>
> —**D. H. Lawrence**

Abraham Maslow's Approach

Another theorist who made self-actualization the centerpiece of his humanistic philosophy was Abraham Maslow (1908–1970). Maslow was one of the most powerful forces behind the humanistic movement in psychology. He called the humanistic approach the "third force" in psychology—that is, an important alternative to the psychoanalytic and behavioral forces. Maslow pointed out that psychoanalytic theories place too much emphasis on disordered individuals and their conflicts. Behaviorists ignore the person all together, he said.

Is it more important to get an A in this class or to go have a delicious meal? Is your own safety more important than risking your life to save a close family member? Is it more important to develop your own fashion style, or do you choose your clothing by what's popular with your friends? Is it more important to have a career or an intimate relationship? Is your paycheck more important than how interesting your work is? Throughout life, you must make choices between needs. How do you decide what is most important? According to Abraham Maslow (1954, 1971), a general guideline is that "basic" needs must be satisfied (or at least partially satisfied) before "higher" needs. As shown in figure 2.6, seven main groups of needs form a hierarchy from "must" or "basic" needs to "fulfilling" or "higher" needs. The **hierarchy of needs** *is Maslow's conception of the main kinds of needs that each individual must satisfy, in this sequence: physiological needs, safety needs, needs for love and belongingness, the need for esteem, cognitive needs, aesthetic needs, and the need for self-actualization.* Based on Maslow's hierarchy of needs, people need to eat before they can achieve, and they must satisfy their needs for safety before their needs for love.

It is the need for self-actualization that Maslow has described in the greatest detail. The need for **self-actualization,** *the highest and most elusive of Maslow's needs, is the motivation to develop one's full potential as a human being.* According to Maslow, self-actualization is possible only after the other needs in the hierarchy are met. Maslow cautions that most people stop maturing after they have developed a high level of self-esteem and thus fail to become self-actualized. Many of Maslow's writings focus on how people can reach the elusive motivational state of self-actualization.

Another way in which Maslow divided needs was into deficiency needs and metaneeds. **Deficiency needs** *is Maslow's term for essential requirements—physiological (such as food, shelter, comfort) and psychological (such as affection, security, self-esteem)—that must be met or else individuals will try to make up for their absence.* **Metaneeds (growth needs),** *according to Maslow, are higher needs involved in self-actualization; these include needs for truth, goodness, beauty, wholeness, vitality, uniqueness, perfection, justice, inner wealth, and playfulness.* Until lower needs are sufficiently met, metaneeds cannot be satisfied. Metaneeds are also different from deficiency needs in that metaneeds do not come in a universal hierarchy. For example, although the need for belongingness must be satisfied as a prerequisite for satisfying the need for self-esteem, the need for goodness does not necessarily come before the need for vitality. Still, fulfillment of metaneeds is important in the goal of being well-adjusted. For example, unfulfilled metaneeds may cause individuals to become alienated, weak, or cynical.

Maslow developed psychological profiles of famous people that he thought achieved a high level of self-actualization. He included such persons as Eleanor Roosevelt, Albert Einstein, Abraham Lincoln, Walt Whitman, William James, and Ludwig van Beethoven in this group. Table 2.2 provides Maslow's descriptions of the characteristics shared by these and other self-actualized individuals.

Evaluating Humanistic Perspectives

Humanistic perspectives have made psychologists aware that the way we perceive ourselves and the world around us is a key element of personality. Humanistic psychologists also have reminded us that we need to consider the whole person and the positive bent of human nature. Their emphasis on conscious experience has given us the view that personality contains a "well of potential" that can be developed to its fullest.

A weakness of the humanistic perspective is that its key concepts are difficult to test. Self-actualization, for example, is not clearly defined. Psychologists are not certain how to study this concept empirically. Some humanists

FIGURE 2.6

Maslow's Hierarchy of Needs

Abraham Maslow developed the hierarchy of human needs to show how we have to satisfy certain basic needs before we can satisfy higher needs. In the diagram, lower-level needs are shown toward the base of the pyramid, higher-level needs toward the peak. The lowest needs (those that must be satisfied first) are physiological—hunger, thirst, and sleep, for example. The next needs that must be satisfied are safety needs, which ensure our survival—we have to protect ourselves from crime and war, for example. Then we must satisfy love and belongingness needs—we need the security, affection, and attention of others for example. Then, esteem needs have to be met—we need to feel good about ourselves, for example. Next in the hierarchy are cognitive needs, which involve a motivation for knowledge and understanding. Near the top of the hierarchy are aesthetic needs, which can involve order and beauty, for instance. Finally, at the top of the pyramid and the highest of Maslow's needs are self-actualization needs, which involve the realization of one's potential.

Self-actualization

Aesthetic

Cognitive

Esteem

Love and belongingness

Safety

Physiological

TABLE 2.2

Maslow's Characteristics of Self-Actualized Individuals

Realistic orientation

Self-acceptance and acceptance of others and the natural world as they are

Spontaneity

Problem-centered rather than self-centered

Air of detachment and need for privacy

Autonomous and independent

Fresh rather than stereotyped appreciation of people and things

Generally have had profound mystical or spiritual, though not necessarily religious, experiences

Identification with humankind and a strong social interest

Tendency to have strong intimate relationships with a few special, loved people rather than superficial relationships with many people

Democratic values and attitudes

No confusion of means with ends

Philosophical rather than hostile sense of humor

High degree of creativity

Resistance to cultural conformity

Transcendence of environment rather than always coping with it

Source: Data from A. H. Maslow, *The Farther Reaches of Human Nature,* Viking Press, 1971, pp. 153–174.

even scorn the experimental approach, preferring clinical interpretation as a data base. Verification of humanistic concepts has come mainly from clinical experiences rather than controlled, experimental studies. Some critics also believe that humanistic psychologists are too optimistic about human nature, overestimating the freedom and rationality of humans. Some critics say the humanists encourage self-love and narcissism.

OTHER PERSPECTIVES: TRAITS AND CONTEXTS

It is relatively easy for us to characterize human beings using descriptive terms denoting **traits**, *broad dispositions that lead to characteristic responses.* Different explanations based on traits or types have emerged over time, with variable levels of acceptance, popularity, and durability. In this section, we will explore the historical basis and the current status of type- and trait-based explanations, as well as the important influence of the contexts in which personality develops.

REVIEW

The Behavioral/Cognitive Social Learning and Humanistic Perspectives

Pavlov developed the concept of classical conditioning, which occurs when a neutral stimulus acquires the ability to produce a response originally produced by another stimulus. Some of the behaviors we associate with health problems or mental disorders may be the products of classical conditioning. In Skinner's behaviorism, cognition is unimportant in understanding personality. Rather, personality is observed behavior, which is influenced by the rewards and punishments in the environment. Personality varies according to the situation, in the behavioral view.

The cognitive social learning perspective on personality grew out of social learning theory. In the 1970s, Mischel and Bandura crafted social learning theory's contemporary version, cognitive social learning theory,

which stresses the importance of cognition, behavior, and environment in understanding personality.

Strengths of both the behavioral and cognitive social learning perspectives include emphases on environmental determinants of behavior and a scientific climate for investigating personality, as well as the focus on cognitive processes and self-control in the cognitive social learning approach. The behavioral view has been criticized for taking the person out of personality and for ignoring cognition. These approaches have not given adequate attention to enduring individual differences and to personality as a whole.

The phenomenological worldview emphasizes our perceptions of ourselves and our world and centers on the belief that reality is what is perceived. The humanistic perspective is the most widely known phenomenological approach. In Carl Rogers' approach, each of us is a victim of

conditional positive regard. The result is that our real self is not valued. The self is the core of personality; it includes both the real and the ideal self. Rogers said we can help others develop a more positive self-concept in three ways: unconditional positive regard, empathy, and genuineness. Rogers also stressed that each of us has the innate, inner capacity to become a fully functioning person. Maslow called the humanistic movement the "third force" in psychology. Each of us has a self-actualizing tendency, according to Maslow. He distinguishes between deficiency needs and self-actualization needs, or metaneeds. The phenomenological and humanistic approaches sensitized psychologists to the importance of subjective experience, consciousness, self-concept, the whole person, and our innate, positive nature. Their weaknesses are the absence of an empirical orientation, a tendency to be too optimistic, and an inclination to encourage self-love.

Endomorph
Chef Paul Prudhomme

Mesomorph
Actor Sylvester Stallone

Ectomorph
Former U.N. Ambassador Jeanne Kirkpatrick

FIGURE 2.7

Sheldon's Body Types
Although these famous individuals fit the body types described by Sheldon, their personalities might not fit Sheldon's predictions.

Personality Type Theories

As early as 400 B.C., Hippocrates classified people's personalities according to their body types. Hippocrates thought that people with more yellow bile than others, for example, were "choleric" (easily angered) whereas others, with an excess of blood, were more "sanguine" (cheerful and buoyant). He linked temperament to physical makeup. Psychologists regard his explanation as historically interesting but inaccurate.

William Sheldon (1954) proposed a theory of body types and personality. **Somatotype theory** *is Sheldon's theory that precise charts reveal distinct body types, which in turn are associated with certain personality characteristics.* He concluded that individuals basically are one of three types (see figure 2.7). **Endomorph** *is Sheldon's term for a soft, round, large-stomached person who is relaxed, gregarious, and fun loving.* **Mesomorph** *is Sheldon's term for a strong, athletic, and muscular person who is energetic, assertive, and courageous.* **Ectomorph** *is Sheldon's term for a tall, thin, fragile person who is fearful, introverted, and restrained.*

Appealing as it was, somatotyping ran aground. For starters, research revealed

CRITICAL THINKING

The Fall of Type Theory

that there is no significant relation between body type and personality (Cortes & Gatti, 1970). Many people simply do not fit into a neatly packaged category. In addition, using one, two, or three categories to describe individuals ignores the rich diversity and complexity of human characteristics. Thus, somatotype theory is not popular today. To

Sheldon's approach to personality was an interesting one that has some intuitive appeal. You probably know some overweight people who are fun-loving, some muscular people who are athletic, and some thin people who are tentative and quiet. Can you imagine some of the difficulties you might encounter if you were to put Sheldon's theory to the test? Describe one problem you would have in demonstrating the validity of Sheldon's theory; this gives you an opportunity to *evaluate the validity of conclusions about behavior.*

further evaluate type theory, see the Critical Thinking box.

Trait Theories

Trait theories *propose that people have broad dispositions that are reflected in the basic ways they behave, such as whether they are outgoing and friendly or whether they are dominant and assertive.* People

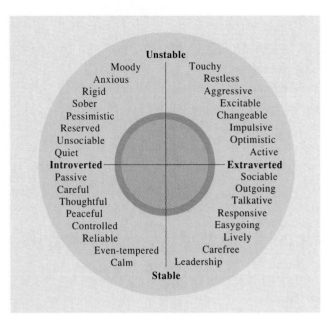

FIGURE 2.8

Eysenck's Dimensions of Personality
On the basis of his factor analytic studies, Eysenck concluded that personality consists of two basic dimensions: (1) stability-instability and (2) introversion-extraversion.

who have a strong tendency to behave in certain ways are described as high on the traits; those who have a weak tendency to behave in these ways are described as low on the traits. Although trait theorists sometimes differ on which traits make up personality, they all agree that traits are the fundamental building blocks of personality (Cloninger, 1996).

Early Trait Psychology

Trying to pigeonhole the traits that make up personality is a herculean task. Gordon Allport and H. S. Odbert (1936), for example, combed the dictionary and counted almost 18,000 words that could be used to describe people. Allport said that several overarching categories could be used to reduce the vast number of words used to describe traits. One of Allport's trait categories was *individual traits,* which refers to an individual's unique way of dealing with the world.

Hans Eysenck (1967) also tackled the task of determining the basic traits of personality. He gave personality tests to large numbers of people and analyzed each person's response. Eysenck consistently

found the traits of stability-instability and introversion-extraversion when he assessed the personalities of large numbers of individuals and suggested that these dimensions could be related. For example, he characterized an *introverted stable* personality as careful, even-tempered, and calm. He characterized an *extraverted unstable* personality as aggressive, excitable, and impulsive. The basic elements of Eysenck's theory have survived in modern views of trait psychology (see figure 2.8).

Contemporary Trait Psychology

Many contemporary trait psychologists are encouraged by evidence from a number of studies that reveals five basic dimensions of personality (Costa & McCrae, 1995; Hogan, 1987). Called the *big five factors in personality,* they are

- extraversion-introversion
- friendliness versus hostility
- neuroticism versus emotional stability
- conscientiousness
- intellect, imagination, or openness to experience

Extraversion-introversion focuses on assertiveness, gregariousness, and shyness; friendliness versus hostility involves a spectrum from love and friendship to enduring problems of aggression and lawlessness; emotional stability refers to relative freedom from moods and anxieties that interfere with functioning; conscientiousness emphasizes achievement motivation; and intellect includes intelligence and creativity. Turn to the Self-Assessment to evaluate your own extraversion.

> . . . *And I'm working all day and I'm*
>   *working all night*
> *To be good-looking, healthy, and wise.*
> *And adored.*
> *And contented.*
> *And brave.*
> *And well-read.*
> *And a marvelous hostess,*
> *Fantastic in bed,*
> *And bilingual,*
> *Athletic,*
> *Artistic . . .*
> *Won't someone please stop me?*
>
> —Judith Viorst,
> ***Self-Improvement Program***

Trait-Situation Interaction

In his landmark book *Personality and Assessment,* Walter Mischel (1968) criticized the trait view of personality as well as the psychoanalytic approach, both of which emphasize the internal organization of personality. Rather than viewing personality as consisting of broad, internal traits that are consistent across situations and time, Mischel said that personality often changes according to a given situation.

Mischel reviewed an array of studies and concluded that trait measures do a poor job of predicting actual behavior. For example, let's say Anne is described as an aggressive person. But when we observe her behavior, we find that she is more or less aggressive depending on the situation—she may be aggressive with her boyfriend but almost submissive with her new boss. Mischel's view was called **situationism,** *which means that an individual's personality can vary considerably from one*

Extraversion

Instructions

For each of the following 20 questions, answer either *yes* (if it is generally true for you) or *no* (if it is generally not true for you).

To interpret your responses, turn to the end of the chapter.

1. Do you often long for excitement?
2. Are you usually carefree?
3. Do you stop and think things over before doing anything?
4. Would you do almost anything for a dare?
5. Do you often do things on the spur of the moment?
6. Generally, do you prefer reading to meeting people?
7. Do you prefer to have few but special friends?
8. When people shout at you do you shout back?
9. Do other people think of you as very lively?
10. Are you mostly quiet when you are with people?
11. If there is something you want to know about, would you rather look it up in a book than talk to someone about it?
12. Do you like the kind of work that you need to pay close attention to?
13. Do you hate being with a crowd who plays jokes on one another?
14. Do you like doing things in which you have to act quickly?
15. Are you slow and unhurried in the way you move?
16. Do you like talking to people so much that you never miss a chance of talking to a stranger?
17. Would you be unhappy if you could not see lots of people most of the time?
18. Do you find it hard to enjoy yourself at a lively party?
19. Would you say that you were fairly self-confident?
20. Do you like playing pranks on others?

context to another. Mischel's argument was an important one, but many psychologists were not willing to abandon altogether the trait concept.

Today, most psychologists in the field of personality, including Mischel, are interactionists. They believe both trait (person) and situation variables are necessary to understand personality. They also agree that the degree of consistency in personality depends on the kind of persons, situations, and behaviors sampled (Mischel, 1995; Pervin, 1993).

> *Consistency requires you to be as ignorant today as you were a year ago.*
> —Bernard Berenson

Suppose you want to assess the happiness of Jahmal, an introvert, and Amy, an extrovert. According to trait-situation interaction theory, we cannot predict who will be happier unless we know something about the situations they are in. Imagine you get the opportunity to observe them in two situations, at a party and in a library. As described in figure 2.9, considering both the traits of the individuals and the settings they are in improves our ability to predict their happiness.

One outcome of the trait/situation controversy is that the link between traits and situations has been more precisely specified. For example, researchers have found that (1) the narrower and more limited a trait is, the more likely it will predict behavior; (2) some people are consistent on some traits and other people are consistent on other traits; and (3) personality traits exert a stronger influence on an individual's behavior when situational influences are less powerful.

The Sociocultural Perspective

Walter Mischel's attack on the adequacy of trait explanations prompted a closer examination of personality's contextual basis. In

the same vein, the sociocultural perspective also emphasizes the contextual basis of personality, although usually at a more global level than Mischel's (Katigbak, Church, & Akamine, 1996). From the sociocultural perspective, we will examine two related issues: the dichotomy of individualism versus collectivism, and the cross-cultural challenges to the study of personality.

Individualism Versus Collectivism

In America, "the squeaky wheel gets the grease." In Japan, "the nail that stands out gets pounded down." Such anecdotes suggest that people in Japan and America have very different views of self and other (Markus & Kitayama, 1991).

In cross-cultural research, the search for basic traits has been extended to a search for characteristics that are common to whole nations. In recent years, the most elaborate search for traits common to the inhabitants of a particular

Halonen/Santrock: Human Adjustment

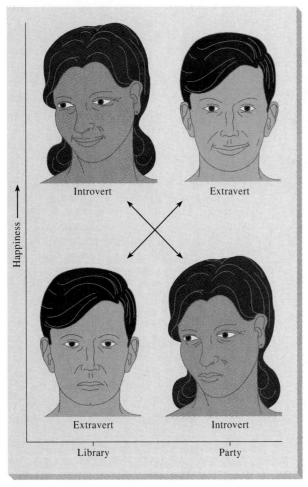

FIGURE 2.9

Trait-Situation Interaction
Who is happier, an introvert or an extravert? According to the concept of trait-situation interaction, we have to know the nature of the situation in which the introvert and extravert are behaving. At a party, the extravert probably will be happier than the introvert; at a library, the introvert probably will be happier than the extravert (Peterson, 1988).

country has focused on the dichotomy of individualism/collectivism (Triandis, 1994). **Individualism** *involves giving priority to personal goals rather than to group goals; it emphasizes values that serve the self, such as feeling good, personal achievement and distinction, and independence.* **Collectivism** *emphasizes values that serve the group by subordinating personal goals to preserve group integrity, the interdependence of members, and harmonious relationships.* Cross-cultural psychologists describe the cultures in many non-Western countries such as Russia, Japan, and India as more collectivistic than individualistic (Kagitcibasi, 1995; Triandis,

1994). To read about how collectivists and individualists can interact more effectively, turn to Sociocultural Worlds of Adjustment.

As with other attempts to explain personality, the individualism/collectivism dichotomy also has its detractors. They argue that describing entire nations of people as having a basic personality obscures the extensive diversity and individual variation that characterizes any nation's people. Also, certain values, such as wisdom, mature love, and tolerance, serve both individual and collective interests (Schwartz, 1990). We are unlikely to find significant differences in some values and

behaviors when we make cross-cultural comparisons between individualistic and collectivistic cultures.

Individualistic societies might promote the use of traits to describe personality, because there might be adaptive advantages to labeling systems that promote quick judgments about the actions of others in these contexts (Brislin, 1993). In contrast, collectivists are likely to maintain enduring relationships with individuals over a long period of time. Collectivists are far more likely to make subtle judgments about the behavior of others as a function of the setting or phase of life in which the behavior occurs.

Personality as a Cross-Cultural Construct

Cross-cultural psychologists believe that both the immediate setting and the broader cultural context are important in understanding personality. However, some challenge whether the concept of personality is useful in some cultural contexts.

As is true of a great deal of psychology's basic tenets, many of the assumptions about personality developed in Western cultures emphasize the individual or self (Lonner, 1988). Psychological terms related to personality often include the word *self*—for example, *self-actualization, self-awareness, self-concept, self-efficacy, self-reinforcement, self-criticism, self-doubt,* and *self-control.* Most therapies in Western cultures emphasize interventions that focus on changing the self rather than modifying the systems or contexts in which the individual participates. Some social scientists believe that many of our problems, such as anxiety, depression, and shyness, are intensified by the emphasis on the self and independence in American culture (Munroe & Munroe, 1975). Critics of Western culture argue that our emphasis on individualism may undermine the basic need our species has for relatedness (Kagitcibasi, 1995). Regardless of their cultural background, people need a positive sense of self *and* connectedness to others to develop fully as human beings.

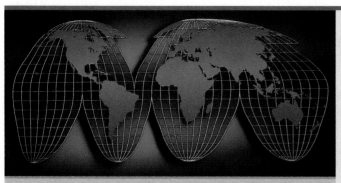

How Collectivists and Individualists Can Interact More Effectively

If you come from a collectivist culture and you are about to interact with someone from an individualist culture, are there ways you can communicate with the other person more effectively? Similarly, if you are from an individualist culture and are about to interact with someone from a collectivist culture, are there ways you can communicate with the person more effectively? Cross-cultural psychologists Harry Triandis, Richard Brislin, and C. Harry Hui (1988) think so. Some of their recommendations follow. First are the suggestions for collectivists interacting with individualists:

1. Do not expect the individualists' compliance with group norms to be as high as it is in a collectivist culture.

2. A person from an individualist culture is likely to be very proud of his or her accomplishments. Compliment the individualist more than you are used to in your collectivist culture.

3. Expect individualists to be more emotionally detached from events that occur in their ingroup than is likely in your collectivist culture.

4. Do not feel threatened if individualists act competitively; learn to expect individualists to be more competitive than collectivists.

5. It is all right for you, as a collectivist, to talk about your accomplishments. You do not have to be modest but, at the same time, do not boast.

6. Expect a person from an individualist culture to be less strongly attached to the extended family than is the case in your collectivist culture. For example, family obligations are less likely to be accepted by an individualist as an excuse for failing to complete an assignment.

7. If you try to change an individualist's opinions, do not expect that you will be as persuasive as you are in your own collectivist culture when you use arguments that stress cooperation, harmony, or avoidance of confrontation.

8. A person from an individualist culture is more likely to define status in terms of individual accomplishments rather than on the basis of ascribed attributes (sex, age, family name, and so on) than is the case in a collectivist culture.

Following are some suggestions for individualists interacting with collectivists:

1. Learn to pay attention to group memberships. Collectivists' behavior often depends on the norms of the ingroups that are important in their lives.

2. Take into account the attitudes of a collectivist person's ingroup authorities. A collectivist person's attitudes and behaviors will probably reflect them.

3. When a collectivist person's group membership changes, his or her attitudes and even personality probably will change to reflect the different group.

4. Spend some time finding out about a collectivist person's ingroups. What events occur in them? What duties are specified? A collectivist person is more likely to do what these norms specify than an individualist is used to seeing.

5. Do not use yourself as a yardstick of involvement in activities that involve ingroups. A collectivist is much more likely to be involved with groups than is an individualist.

6. A collectivist will probably be less comfortable in competitive circumstances than an individualist will be.

7. If you have to criticize, do so carefully and only in private. In your collectivist culture, people usually do not say no or criticize.

8. Cultivate long-term relationships. Be patient. People in collectivist cultures value dealing with "old friends."

Some social scientists believe that many of Americans' problems, such as anxiety, depression, and shyness, are intensified by the emphasis on the self and independence in the American culture. In many Eastern cultures, such as China, there is a much stronger emphasis on connectedness with others and group behavior. Similarly, pressures in collectivist cultures to conform may be experienced by some members as restricting freedom of choice.

R E V I E W

Other Perspectives: Traits and Contexts

Different explanations of types and traits have emerged over time. Personality type theory involves classifying individuals according to particular types; Sheldon's somatotype theory is an example. This view is heavily criticized. Trait theories emphasize that personality involves the organization of traits within the individual; these traits are believed to be enduring.

Allport stressed the individuality of traits; Eysenck sought the traits common to all of us. The search for trait dimensions continues; one contemporary view stresses that we have five basic traits.

Mischel's book *Personality and Assessment* ushered in an attack on trait theory; basically, Mischel argued that personality varies according to the situation considerably more than trait theorists acknowledge. Today most psychologists are interactionists; they believe personality is determined by a

combination of both traits (or person variables) and the situation.

The sociocultural perspective in personality emphasizes both the dichotomy between individualism and collectivism, and the cross-cultural challenge to personality theory. Cross-cultural psychologists believe that both the immediate setting and the broader cultural context are important determinants of personality. In Western cultures, many assumptions about personality emphasize the individual and self.

When you began this chapter, you constructed a list of characteristics that you thought captured your personality. We challenged you to think about whether the traits you selected were representative, enduring, consistent, and realistic. We questioned whether others would describe you in the same way.

Compassion could have been one of the traits you selected. Suppose we wanted to develop a simple self-report inventory similar to the self-assessments you completed in this chapter, that would allow the measurement of some aspects of compassion. Walter Mischel suggests that traits interact with situations. Suppose, to measure your compassion, we asked you which of the following acts you would perform:

- Agreeing to a request to sponsor a child in a technologically disadvantaged country
- Intervening in a friend's drug or alcohol problem
- Offering money to the homeless when they confront your personally
- Taking in stray animals
- Sacrificing your own plans to help a friend
- Volunteering assistance to a driver with a disabled car
- Alerting a friend who has some lunch stuck between his teeth
- Letting a sick friend copy your homework
- Giving away all your possessions to a needy organization

As you can see, measuring the trait of compassion with this inventory would be extremely difficult. The actions listed in this self-report checklist could all be compassionate in some circumstances, but it would certainly be difficult to evaluate a person's compassion using responses to this list. For example, you could endlessly adopt stray animals, but there are practical constraints on how much compassion you could show using this behavior. You could let a friend copy your homework in the compassion of the moment, but that judgment might be far from compassionate in the long run because your friend will be unlikely to learn something that could be useful in the future. Could we rule out your having any compassion if you indicated you wouldn't perform any of the actions on the list? Probably not. Although our compassion self-report checklist has face validity (that is, each item relates to compassion), it is unlikely that we could use it as it stands to conduct valid research on the trait.

Making judgments about traits is difficult not only in research situations; it can be surprisingly challenging in life. Although we regularly make trait attributions to help us understand situations, we might not sufficiently capture the complexity of the situation. The use of traits to explain behavior can help us be efficient processors of reality, but it is doubtful that it helps us make accurate or fair-minded interpretations. Sometimes the labels lead us to make premature judgments and turn our attention elsewhere—we assign a trait as the reason for an action and move on.

How can this knowledge help us to be more effective critical thinkers in relation to judgments about personality? We should be able to *apply psychological concepts to enhance personal adaptation* by incorporating the following skills:

1. **Reserve judgment, particularly when making negative attributions.**
   How important is it to resolve a behavioral question by attributing someone's actions to a trait? In many situations, labeling requires making a judgment that we may later regret. In the tradition of Skinner, it may be more helpful to think about and describe specific behaviors involved in the situation than dispense with the situation by assigning dysfunctional traits as the cause. For example, marriage therapists often help couples learn to describe the behaviors that are upsetting to them rather than continue to use hurtful and unhelpful labeling (such as "You are inconsiderate and insecure").

2. **Recognize the boundaries of labels.**
   When we feel compelled to make trait judgments, it is still helpful to remember the context in which the behavior occurred and confine the judgment to that circumstance. For example, if you think of your father as "mean," it will be useful to identify the circumstances in which he is mean. He might be mean when he has not gotten enough sleep or when he is trying to watch his weight. This restricted use of the label recognizes that there are likely to be many circumstances in which he is not mean, which brings into question the fairness of the use of the term.

3. **Abandon expectations about consistency.**
   As you read in this chapter, many other cultures may be less intense about defining, categorizing, and judging personality features. This attitude may be a function of living in collectivistic cultures where there is no particular advantage in labeling others' traits. Richard Brislin (1993) believes that enduring relationships in collectivistic cultures may show greater tolerance about inconsistencies in human behavior. Even if we don't live in a collectivistic culture, we can save some frustration if, like collectivists, we do not expect human beings to be consistent across all situations.

The very purpose of existence is to reconcile the glowing opinion we hold of ourselves with the appalling things that other people think about us.

—Quentin Crisp

OVERVIEW

We began this chapter by evaluating the nature of personality. We spent considerable time exploring personality theories—psychoanalytic, learning, and humanistic. We also studied other perspectives—type theory, trait theory, trait-situation interaction, and the sociocultural perspective. Remember that you can obtain an overall summary of the chapter by again studying the in-chapter reviews on pages 33, 41, and 47.

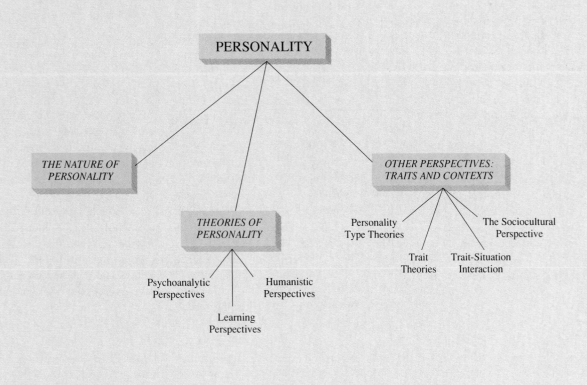

PERSONALITY

THE NATURE OF PERSONALITY

THEORIES OF PERSONALITY

Psychoanalytic Perspectives

Learning Perspectives

Humanistic Perspectives

OTHER PERSPECTIVES: TRAITS AND CONTEXTS

Personality Type Theories

Trait Theories

Trait-Situation Interaction

The Sociocultural Perspective

PRACTICAL KNOWLEDGE ABOUT ADJUSTMENT

CONTROL YOUR DEPRESSION (REVISED)

(1992) by Peter Lewinsohn, Ricardo Muñoz, Mary Youngren, and Antonnete Zeiss.
New York, NY: Fireside.

Control Your Depression tells you how to reduce your depression by learning self-control techniques, relaxation training, pleasant activities, planning ahead, modifying self-defeating thinking patterns, and other behavioral/cognitive strategies. Dozens of examples illustrate how to gauge your progress, maintain the gains you make, and also determine whether you need further help. Easy to follow step-by-step methods take you through a number of strategies for controlling depression.

GENTLE ROADS TO SURVIVAL

(1991) by Andre Auw.
Lower Lake, CA: Aslan.

In *Gentle Roads to Survival,* Auw presents a guide to making self-healing choices in difficult circumstances. Auw, a psychologist who was a close associate of Carl Rogers, tells you how to become a survivor. He believes that while some people may be born to be survivors, most of us have to learn survival skills. Auw addresses personal crises in religion, morality, agonizing parenting and marital breakups, the pain of cross-cultural adaptation, and many other highly stressful circumstances. He especially advocates that each person has to discover his or her own unique path of adaptation and coping.

Auw teaches readers the spirit of respect and caring in human relationships. Auw's approach is warm, sensitive, and compassionate. Before his death, Carl Rogers said that Andrew Auw's ideas contain a great deal of wisdom.

NEED FOR UNIQUENESS

Scoring

Reverse score on items 2, 3, 5, 7, 9, 11, 13, 14, 17, 19, 22, 23, 26, 27, 28, and 31. On these items, a 5 = 1, 4 = 2, 3 = 3, 2 = 4, and 1 = 5. Then add the score for all 32 items.

Interpretation

The *higher* the score, the greater the *need for uniqueness*. The scale does not necessarily tell how different one actually is. Of 1,400 students at the University of Kansas and Purdue University, a score of 100 was the 50th percentile.

EXTRAVERSION

Scoring

To arrive at your score for extraversion, give one point for each of the following items answered *yes:* #1, 2, 4, 5, 8, 9, 14, 16, 17, 19, and 20. Then, give yourself one point for each of the following items answered *no:* #3, 6, 7, 10, 11, 12, 13, 15, 18. Add up all the points to arrive at a total score.

Interpretation

Your total score should be between 0 and 20 inclusive. The higher your score, the higher your extraversion (and, of course, the lower your introversion). Therefore, high scores suggest extraversion and low scores suggest introversion.

Picasso
Young Boy with Dog, detail

C H A P T E R

3

The Self and Identity

CHAPTER OUTLINE

CRITICAL THINKING ABOUT ADJUSTMENT

CHAPTER BOXES

*The living self has one purpose only: to
come into its own fullness of being, as a
tree comes into full blossom, or a bird into
spring beauty, or a tiger into lustre.*

—D. H. Lawrence

T he Caterpillar and Alice looked at each other for some time in silence. At last the Caterpillar took the hookah out of its mouth, and addressed her in a languid, sleepy voice.

"Who are *you?*" said the Caterpillar.

This was not an encouraging opening for a conversation. Alice replied, rather shyly, "I—I hardly know, Sir, just at present—at least I know who I *was* when I got up this morning, but I think I must have changed several times since then."

"What do you mean by that?" said the Caterpillar, sternly. "Explain yourself!"

"I can't explain *myself,* I'm afraid, Sir," said Alice, "because I'm not myself, you see."

"I don't see," said the Caterpillar.

"I'm afraid I can't put it more clearly," Alice replied, very politely, "for I can't understand it myself, to begin with; and being so many different sizes in a day is very confusing."

"It isn't," said the Caterpillar.

Alice meets the Caterpillar.

"Well, perhaps you haven't found it so yet," said Alice, "but when you have to turn into a chrysalis—you will some day, you know—and then after that into a butterfly, I should think you'll feel it a little queer, won't you?"

"Not a bit," said the Caterpillar.

"Well, perhaps your feelings may be different," said Alice. "All I know is, it would feel very queer to *me.*"

"You!" said the Caterpillar contemptuously. "Who are *you?*"

—Lewis Caroll
Alice's Adventures in Wonderland (1916)

PREVIEW

The problem of understanding identity can sometimes feel as mystifying as the meeting between Alice and the Caterpillar. Many psychologists, especially humanists, consider the concept of self to be the central component of personality. In this chapter, we will explore the dimensions of and challenges to self-development. We will also examine sociocultural influences on self-awareness and self-definition. Erik Erikson's work on identity serves as the second emphasis in the chapter. We will compare his theory with ideas put forth by current theorists who study the self and ethnic identity.

THE SELF

"Who are you?" Your answers to that question reveal the perceptions you have about your **self,** *your sense of who you are and what makes you different from others.* When you think of who you are, do you start with your physical characteristics— how tall you are? how much you weigh? what your hair color is? Perhaps your description begins with your gender or ethnicity, or your status in your family, work, or school; or your goals and dreams. Although no facet is unique to you, the combination of your characteristics defines your individuality. Most human beings have a sense of their own distinctiveness, and this sense of self and the formation of identity are important parts of their existence. A person's developing sense of self is a motivating force in life.

Dimensions of the Self

Psychologists have conceptualized the self in a number of different ways. We will begin with the basic ideas of self-understanding and self-concept. We will also explore other frameworks for understanding the self, including the conscious and unconscious self, self-congruence, and possible selves. We will conclude this section by looking at self-esteem.

Self-Understanding and Self-Concept

Self-understanding *is the individual's cognitive representation of their self, the substance and content of the person's beliefs about their self and its operation.* Contrast these two examples: A 20-year-old describes himself as a student, a male, a lead guitarist in a band, a hacker, and a hot-line volunteer; a 26-year-old describes herself as an executive in training for a corporation, a mother, an African American, a tennis player, and a mystery reader. Though not the whole of personality identity, self-understanding provides identity's rational underpinnings (Damon & Hart, 1988).

> *We don't see things as they are, we see them as we are.*
> —**Anais Nin**

As we grow up, our self-understanding becomes more interiorized and self-reflective, but self-understanding is never completely cut off from the external world. Rather, self-understanding is a social cognitive construction, influenced by the sociocultural contexts in which we live—our family experiences, our relationships with friends, our ethnic, cultural, and gender experiences, and so on.

Related to self-understanding is a **self-concept** (*sometimes called self-understanding*), *which refers to our overall thoughts and feelings about ourselves*. However, the notion of self-concept often implies a fixed construction of the self, emphasizing the stable aspects of the self that might not show much variation over time. In contrast, self-understanding emphasizes self-perception as a process. Self-understanding provides for variability over time.

> *Today I am a small blue thing*
> *Like a marble or an eye.*
> —**Suzanne Vega**

Self-understanding and self-concept are complex. In the following sections we will examine a number of frameworks for how scholars have organized their observations about the self.

Conscious and Unconscious Selves

Early in the development of his psycho-analytic theory, Sigmund Freund conducted an intense analysis of his own psychological makeup. He looked into the meaning of his dreams, thought about his interactions with others, and reflected on his own childhood. Psychoanalytic theory is based upon Freud's self-analysis. Despite his vigorous pursuit of conscious awareness of his self, Freud believed that the self is primarily unconscious, beyond the individual's awareness.

Psychologists vary in their views about how extensively the self is conscious or accessible to awareness. For example, Jung also believed that unconscious forces strongly influence the self. By comparison, Skinner, Maslow, and Rogers downplayed the role of the unconscious mind's influence on behavior. Many contemporary psychologists believe that unconscious influences might be more easily understood as cognitive limitations on accessing information (Nisbett & Wilson, 1977). This approach suggests that we defensively avoid painful self-knowledge.

Psychologists agree that wide individual differences in self-awareness and self-understanding exist. Many individuals do not adequately examine why they are the way they are—they do not strive to be as consciously aware of themselves as possible. If we are not aware of what makes us win or lose, succeed or fail, be liked or hated by others, and so on, adjustment can be a rocky road for us.

Self-Congruence

Humanist Carl Rogers believed that adjustment is more likely to occur when various aspects of the self are *congruent*—when they fit together and feel smoothly integrated into the self-concept. Rogers emphasized congruence between the *idealized* and *real* selves as the key to adjustment.

> *You were born God's original. Try not to beome someone's copy.*
> —**Marian Wright Edelman**

E. Tory Higgins (1987) expanded on Rogers' ideas by describing the self as having three domains: the *actual* self, the *ideal* self, and the *ought* self. The **actual self** *is an individual's representation of the attributes she or he believes her- or himself to actually possess*. The **ideal self** *is an individual's representation of the attributes that she or he would ideally like to possess—that is, a representation of the person's hopes, aspirations, or wishes*. The **ought self** *is an individual's representation of the attributes he or she believes he or she should possess—that is, a representation of the person's duties, obligations, and responsibilities*. Each of these three domains of the self can be seen from either the individual's view or the view of a significant other in the individual's life, such as a parent, spouse, or friend.

Possible Selves

Another recent framework for understanding the self is called **possible selves,** *what individuals might become, including what they would like to become and what they are afraid of becoming* (Markus & Nurius, 1986). Our possible selves reflect both the outcomes that we hope for and the ones that we dread. The presence of both dreaded and hoped-for selves is psychologically healthy, providing a balance between positive, expected selves and negative, feared selves (Harter, 1990). The attributes of future possible selves (such as getting into a good graduate school, being admired, having a successful career) can direct future positive states, while attributes of negative possible selves (such as being unemployed, being lonely, not getting into graduate school) can frame what is to be avoided in the future.

Each possible self is a personalized construction that may be articulated in considerable detail by the person (McAdams, 1990). For example, if one of a person's possible selves is the *unemployed self,* the person might have developed a painfully clear picture of what this self might be like. The person might lose confidence in her ability to support herself and family members, envisioning herself as being unable to make mortgage payments, struggling to get by on food stamps, living in an overpriced and undersized apartment in a "bad part" of town, spending long hours with nothing much to do, applying for menial jobs, being humiliated in front of others, resenting peers who have good jobs, and gradually sinking into hopelessness and despair. In contrast, if the unemployed self is an important *feared* possible self within the individual's overall self, then the person is likely to go to great lengths to avoid its realization.

An important function of possible selves is *self-evaluation*. Possible selves provide frameworks in which we can evaluate how well or how poorly our lives are going. Thus, possible selves are powerful structures for determining the meaning of certain events. For example, suppose a college student who wants to become a doctor evaluates her current standing with regard to this possible self in very negative terms because she currently has a low grade-point average. This pre-med student's best friend also has low grades, but because her most cherished possible self involves raising a large family in a more traditional lifestyle and she has just accepted a marriage proposal, her equally low grade-point average has less influence on her self-evaluation.

Unfortunately, we sometimes engage in self-defeating behavior patterns that keep us from becoming one or more of our positive possible selves (Baumeister, 1991). Thus, some people persist in losing endeavors, with the result that they end up losing more. They may "choke" under pressure, make poor decisions, and seek immediate gratifications rather than work toward future larger rewards. In short, some individuals are vulnerable to various judgment errors that lead to maladaptive approaches in pursuing their positive possible selves.

In the case of the pre-med student with the low grade-point average, a critical evaluation needs to occur. She can make becoming a doctor a much less dominant possible self and choose a different career goal that does not require a high grade-point average. If she retains becoming a doctor as her dominant possible self, she needs to make some changes in her life that will help her get better grades. She might enroll in a study skills program to improve her study strategies. She might use time management techniques to learn to use her time better. Along with other changes, she can do things so that she can keep and achieve this dominant possible self. To further explore the concept of possible selves, see the Critical Thinking box.

Self-Esteem

Self-esteem *is the evaluative and affective dimension of self-concept. Self-esteem is also referred to as self-worth or self-image.* For instance, a person may perceive that she is not merely a student, but a *good* student. Another person may perceive

Exploring the Possibilities

In this exercise you need to recruit two friends to help. Conduct a conversation in which the three of you each shares two of your possible future selves. What do you envision will make you happiest about the self that you aspire to become? What prospect about a potential negative possibility in the future fills you with dread? To *appreciate individual differences,* try to determine in what ways your visions of the future are alike and in what ways they are different.

General feelings of self-worth and overall self-concept			
General competence	Moral self-approval	Power	Love worthiness

FIGURE 3.1

Four Main Areas of Self-Esteem: Epstein's Hierarchical Model

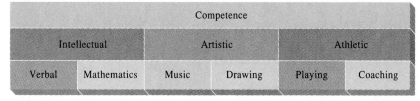

Competence					
Intellectual		Artistic		Athletic	
Verbal	Mathematics	Music	Drawing	Playing	Coaching

FIGURE 3.2

The Complexity of Self-Esteem: Further Hierarchical Differentiation

that he is not merely a guitar player, but a *good* guitar player. Therefore, the good student feels proud that she just received an A on an exam, and the good guitar player feels elated about his standing ovation at the club where he played last night. Of course, not all self-evaluations are positive. A person may feel sad that she is not a good student. Another person may feel ashamed that he is a poor reader. Both positive and negative judgments about one's self-esteem can be made.

Self-esteem is a complex concept that can be viewed as a hierarchy (Epstein, 1973). General feelings of self-worth and an individual's overall self-concept are at the summit of the hierarchy. Below this general level are more specific self-perceptions pertaining to four domains of the self: general competence, moral self-approval, power, and love worthiness (see figure 3.1). Within each of these four areas are even more specific self-evaluations. For example, in the area of competence, level of self-esteem might vary across intellectual, artistic, and athletic domains (see figure 3.2). Even further differentiation within these subareas

SELF-ASSESSMENT

Self-Esteem

To interpret your responses, turn to the end of this chapter.

Instructions

The statements below have been used by people to describe themselves. Please read each one carefully, and circle the number that best describes how much of a problem each has been for you in the past month, including today. Use the following scale for your answers:

a = Strongly agree
b = Agree
c = Disagree
d = Strongly disagree

1. I feel that I'm a person of worth, at least on an equal basis with others.   a b c d
2. I feel that I have a number of good qualities.   a b c d
3. All in all, I am inclined to feel that I am a failure.   a b c d
4. I am able to do things as well as most people.   a b c d
5. I feel I do not have much to be proud of.   a b c d
6. I take a positive attitude toward myself.   a b c d
7. On the whole, I am satisfied with myself.   a b c d
8. I wish I could have more respect for myself.   a b c d
9. I certainly feel useless at times.   a b c d
10. At times I think I am no good at all.   a b c d

---

is possible—mathematical and verbal competence within the domain of intellectual competence, for example. To evaluate aspects of your own self-esteem, see the Self-Assessment.

Perhaps no one who shares our cultural context manages stress-free development of the self. Even those who appear completely confident may have underlying struggles in self-definition. We will explore challenges in self-development in the next section.

Problems in Self-Development

Several kinds of challenges can hinder self-development. We will explore self-discrepancy, self-esteem concerns, narcissistic style, and multiple personality disorder as problem areas in self-development.

Self-Discrepancy

In Higgins' **self-discrepancy theory,** *problems occur when various selves in different domains or from different views are inconsistent, or discrepant, with each other.* Two types of discrepancies are especially problematic. Discrepancies between the actual and ideal selves lead the person to experience dejection-related emotions, such as sadness, disappointment, and shame. In such instances, people often believe that they have been

unable to reach their hopes, dreams, and aspirations that either they have set for themselves or that others have set for them. If parents set unrealistic goals for their children, such as wanting them to be professional athletes or musical performers when their children don't have the necessary talents, the children may feel dejected and depressed. Secondly, discrepancies between the actual self and the ought self can produce agitated emotions, such as anxiety, fear, and guilt. In these instances, people believe that they have failed to live up to standards (established by the self or other) for good, dutiful, and responsible behavior. The agitated emotions emerge because people feel they are being punished (by themselves or by others) for not doing what they ought to do.

I cannot see myself as I once was;
I would not see myself as I am now.
—**Aline Murray Kilmer**

In one study, college students were asked to list traits or attributes that described their actual, ideal, and ought selves (Higgins, 1984). Then matches and mismatches in traits across the three self domains were coded. For example, as

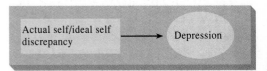

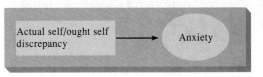

FIGURE 3.3

The Relation of Discrepancies in Actual, Ideal, and Ought Selves to Depression and Anxiety

part of a self-description a person might evaluate the actual self as "friendly," "sincere," and "hot-tempered," and the ought self as "friendly," "sincere," and "calm." In this example, there are two matches (friendly and sincere) and one mismatch (hot-tempered and calm). In this study, researchers also measured the college students' levels of depression (which involves dejection-related emotions) and anxiety (which involves agitated-related emotions). As predicted, actual self/ideal self discrepancies were associated with depression (but not anxiety) and actual self/ought self discrepancies were associated with anxiety (but not depression) (see figure 3.3).

Identify causes of
low self-esteem

Define domains
of competence

Demonstrate
achievement

Actively cope
with challenge

Promote social
support and approval

FIGURE 3.4

Five Key Aspects of Improving Self-Esteem

The Diminished Self

Many individuals suffer from low self-esteem. In this case, they have lower self-regard than others might think they should have. Self-esteem concerns are so common in our culture that self-esteem has come to be regarded as a major personality concern for this decade.

> *Every new adjustment is a crisis in self-esteem.*
>
> **—Eric Hoffer**

As illustrated in figure 3.4, five important aspects of improving low self-esteem are identifying the causes of low self-esteem, defining important domains of competence, demonstrating achievement, actively coping with the challenges to self-esteem, and promoting social support and approval.

Identifying the person's sources of self-esteem, that is, competence in domains important to the self—as well as social support—is critical to improving

Shown here is Jaime Escalante, a Latino high school teacher whose commitment to his students was portrayed in *Stand and Deliver.* Escalante believed that his Latino students' self-esteem suffered from chronic academic failure. He identified calculus as an important domain of skill and spent many evenings and weekends helping them achieve mastery. His commitment allowed them to face the challenge directly. Because of his unwavering support, many of his students obtained college scholarships and passed advanced placement tests in calculus.

self-esteem. Self-esteem researcher Susan Harter (1990) points out the self-esteem enhancement programs of the 1960s—in which self-esteem itself was the target and individuals were simply encouraged to feel good about themselves—were ineffective. Rather, Harter believes, interventions should target the *causes* of self-esteem.

> *I'm nobody. Who are you?*
> *Are you nobody too?*
> —**Emily Dickinson**

Individuals have the highest self-esteem when they perform competently in domains that are important to them. Therefore, programs that encourage individuals to identify and value their areas of competence should be promoted. One strategy is to encourage social recognition of the positive benefits of competence in many different domains, not just academic competence. Another strategy is to understand that education is the primary means for achieving success, and to provide individuals with poor academic skills and low self-esteem better support and more individualized attention. Insisting that high school and college athletes maintain a respectable grade point average is a policy that endorses the importance of academic achievement and competence in other domains, as is the requirement that students maintain respectable grades to participate in jobs programs (Harter, 1990). More about the self-esteem of ethnic minority individuals appears in Sociocultural Worlds of Adjustment.

Achievement also can improve an individual's self-esteem (Bednar & Peterson, 1995). For example, self-esteem can be enhanced by the straightforward teaching of skills to individuals. Individuals develop higher self-esteem because they know the important tasks to accomplish goals, and they have experienced performing them or similar behaviors. Our emphasis on the importance of achievement in improving self-esteem has much in common with Bandura's cognitive social learning concept of *self-efficacy,* which we discussed in chapter 2, and to which we will return when we describe the nature of coping in chapter 5.

CRITICAL THINKING

Advertising and Self-Enhancement

Watch television during two periods of the day—daytime television and prime time. Carefully evaluate the commercials. How many promote purchases or services that supposedly will enhance individual self-esteem? What appears to be the difference in esteem-enhancing commercials during those two periods? What might these differences imply about the perceived nature of the audiences during these two periods? Your analysis of commercials for their appeal to self-esteem will demonstrate your ability to *make careful observations and interpretations of behavior.*

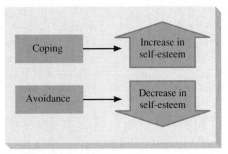

FIGURE 3.5

Coping and Avoidance: Strategies That Influence Self-Esteem

Self-esteem also is often increased when individuals face a problem and try to cope with it rather than avoid it (Bednar & Peterson, 1995) (see figure 3.5). When coping prevails, the individual often faces problems realistically, honestly, and nondefensively, leading to favorable self-evaluative thoughts, which lead to the self-generated approval and higher self-esteem. The converse is true of low self-esteem. Unfavorable self-evaluations trigger denial, deception, and avoidance in an attempt to disavow that which has already been glimpsed as true. This process leads to self-generated disapproval as a form of feedback to the self about personal adequacy.

Emotional support and social approval in the form of confirmation from others is a powerful influence on a person's self-esteem. Some individuals, however, experience little emotional support from their conflicted families or within their hostile marriages. Others receive negative feedback from teachers or from superiors at work. As a result, some people have low self-esteem. In some cases, alternative sources of emotional support can improve the person's self-esteem. Quality friendships can compensate for other shortcomings in emotional support, or individuals might seek counseling to improve their communication in marriage, thereby improving their self-esteem. One recent study found that both parental and peer support were related to the adolescent's self-esteem (Robinson, 1995). An accepting, supportive relationship is well-established as an important component of many approaches to psychotherapy, especially the humanistic approach, which we will discuss further in chapter 15. To further evaluate self-esteem, see the Critical Thinking box.

The Narcissistic Self

Some individuals don't seem to suffer any lack of self-esteem. In fact, they seem so self-involved that their style could be described as **narcissism,** *a self-centered and self-concerned approach in dealing with others.* Narcissus was a character in Greek

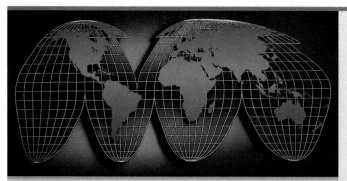

SOCIOCULTURAL WORLDS OF ADJUSTMENT

Self-Esteem in Ethnic Minority Individuals

Many of the early attempts to assess the nature of self-esteem and self-concept in different ethnic groups compared African Americans and White individuals (Clark & Clark, 1939; Coopersmith, 1967). These reports indicated that African Americans, especially African American children, had more negative self-concepts than White Americans did. More recent research suggests, however, that African Americans and Latinos have equally positive self-concepts and perhaps even higher self-esteem than White Americans (Allen & Majidi-Ahi, 1989; Powell & Fuller, 1972).

"Ethnic pride" was one of the positive movements to spring out of the social turmoil of the sixties. Its emphasis on the richness and diversity of various cultures appears to have improved the self-esteem of ethnic minority groups, especially when comparisons are made between groups that are similar in terms of social class (Garbarino, 1985). However, ethnic pride has both costs and benefits for individuals. One obvious benefit is a sense

of cultural identity (such as African American, Latino, or Native American) with clearly defined cultural roles as to what is expected of a competent person. Also, ethnic neighborhoods are often tight-knit and supportive. It's somewhat easier for a person to develop a positive sense of self in neighborhoods where people lend one another a hand and offer strategies for coping with problems. In addition, minority members who live in their ethnic neighborhoods can gain a sense of rootedness and acceptance.

There is no indication, however, that acceptance within an ethnic group translates into prestige within mainstream American society (Rosenberg, 1965). Even though a person has a secure sense of self as a member of an ethnic minority, he or she must also come to terms with prejudice beyond the ethnic neighborhood. When the values, morals, and behaviors of the ethnic neighborhood differ from society as a whole, a secure ethnic minority member may still find it difficult to develop a sense of competence in mainstream society. At the same time, belonging to a group in which one is highly valued can serve as a buffer against racial prejudice from other groups.

Discussions of ethnicity, self, and self-concept still boil down to a fundamental issue—"What kind of people does the world need?" (Garbarino, 1985). To enhance the quality of life, we must develop more harmonious, cooperative relationships. Society needs to foster individuals who define themselves in new ways that deemphasize competition, achievement, and materialism in favor of cooperation, connectedness with others, empathy, and spiritual development. We need to ask whether we are socializing children to develop the kind of self-concepts that encourage a competent, caring, sustainable society.

Mamie and Kenneth Clark conducted pioneering research on African American children's self-concepts and identity.

A generation of ethnic awareness and pride appears to have advanced the self-esteem of ethnic minority groups. A discussion of ethnicity and self-esteem raises the question of what kind of people the world needs. There is a growing desire to have a world of individuals who develop more harmonious, cooperative relationships.

mythology who so admired himself that a curse was placed on him. The gods caused him to fall in love with his own reflection. So absorbed was he in his own image that when he reached into the pool to touch his reflection, he fell in and drowned.

> She wanted to be the reason for everything and so was the cause of nothing.
>
> —Djuna Barnes

Typically, narcissistic individuals are unaware of their actual self and how others perceive them. This lack of awareness contributes to their adjustment problems (Westin, 1991). Narcissists are excessively self-centered and self-congratulatory, viewing their own needs and desires as paramount. As a result, narcissistic individuals rarely show any empathy toward others (Kohut, 1977). In fact, narcissistic individuals often devalue people around them to protect their own precarious self-esteem, yet they often respond with rage and shame when others do not admire them and treat them in accordance with their grandiose fantasies about themselves. Narcissistic persons are at their most grandiose when their self-esteem is threatened. Narcissists may fly into a frenzy if they have given an unsatisfactory performance.

Narcissistic individuals often make far-reaching claims about themselves without ever engaging in the important self-evaluative process of reflecting on how their behavior will be perceived and reacted to by others. One narcissistic individual spoke of the special awards he gets because his work is "greater than great." Another person unselfconsciously stated that he was perfect, then corrected this to: "No, not really perfect, but I could be."

A narcissist's conscious representation of self as extraordinary is a defensive transformation of their view of themself that is active unconsciously—namely, the self as worthless. Even people who are reasonably well-adjusted make use of similar defenses to ward off perceived insults or threats to their self-esteem, but they do so in greater contact with reality than narcissists. To learn more about the characteristics of narcissism, turn to the Self-Assessment.

The Crowded Self

When psychologists first observed multiple personality, they assumed that individuals with such problems were quite rare (Suinn, 1984). Recent estimates suggest that multiple personality disorder may be substantially more serious and widespread than originally suspected (Braun, 1988). Persons with **multiple personality disorder** *have two or more distinct personalities or selves.* Multiple personality disorder has been portrayed in films such as *The Three Faces of Eve* and *Sybil*.

Although controversial in diagnosis and treatment, multiple personality disorder has been found to be strongly linked with severe abuse or trauma in early childhood (Ludolph, 1982). Some psychologists believe that the creation of alternate selves, or "alters," may serve to protect the child against the horror of those experiences. The alter personalities can become distinctive entities with abilities, preferences, and lifestyles dramatically unlike those of the host personality, who might be unaware of the existence of the alters (Thigpen & Cleckley, 1957).

We will return to this disorder in a later chapter on mental health. Next we will explore the influence of sociocultural contexts on the self's development.

The Self in Sociocultural Context

Individualistic and collectivistic societies view the self differently. Western cultures tend to favor sharply defined selves and honor values that enhance the individual. Assertive self-management earns admiration in our culture. In contrast, non-Western cultures revere characteristics that strengthen the collective. As a result of increased exposure to the lifestyles of other cultures, some social critics have begun to wonder about the consequences of emphasizing individuality over the collective good.

Non-Western Zen Buddhism offers a negative perspective on the Western preoccupation with individuality. Alan Watts (1973) argued that Western societies place too much emphasis on the concepts of past and future when considering the self. By spending so much time thinking about their memories and worrying about the future, individuals neglect to live their lives in the present.

Living in the present moment by fully attending to the task at hand might have beneficial effects on our value system (Reynolds, 1984). In this perspective, your goal should be to do what needs to be done, whether it is trivial or substantial, whether it is pleasant or not. This approach—of doing what needs to be done rather than seeking only pleasurable activity, and experiencing the task fully—is what is involved in morita tasks. A therapy based on Japanese Zen Buddhism, **morita therapy** *emphasizes accepting feelings, knowing one's purposes, and, most importantly, doing what needs to be done.* Morita exercises not only teach you to do constructive work with full attention, they also decrease your sense of ego and self-consciousness (Reynolds, 1976).

Roy Baumeister (1991) suggests that Americans are over concerned with self-fulfillment and personal identity, so much so that these have become burdens for many people. Because of the high priority we place on developing, maintaining, and enhancing a positive self-image in both our personal and our career lives, many of us are too self-critical, too pushed toward change, and too stressed.

The pressures of seeking self-fulfillment can sometimes feel overwhelming. Some people avoid these pressures by turning to activities that diminish self-preoccupation. Some turn on the television or read science fiction books. Others meditate or listen to classical music. Some people lose themselves in dance, others in a pitcher of beer. Society offers and endorses many ways to forget ourselves for awhile. Unfortunately, many forms of escape have high costs. Some people develop substance-abuse problems, attempt suicide, or join radical cults. Escaping the burden of maintaining a personal identity can create even more serious challenges to the integrity of the self.

We indicated earlier in the chapter that self-understanding is an important aspect of an individual's identity, our next topic to explore.

Narcissism

Instructions

The statements to the right describe characteristics of persons. Answer each statement True or False as it applies to you.

Leadership/Authority

1. I see myself as a good leader.
2. I would prefer to be a leader.
3. I really like to be the center of attention.
4. I like having authority over other people.
5. I would be willing to describe myself as a strong personality.
6. I have a natural talent for influencing people.
7. I like to be the center of attention.
8. I am assertive.
9. People always seem to recognize my authority.

Self-Absorption/Self-Admiration

10. I like to look at my body.
11. I like to look at myself in the mirror.
12. I am an extraordinary person.
13. I like to display my body.
14. I have good taste when it comes to beauty.
15. I think I am a special person.
16. I like to be complimented.
17. I am going to be a great person.
18. I know that I am good because everyone keeps telling me so.

Superiority/Arrogance

19. Everybody likes to hear my stories.
20. I usually dominate any conversation.
21. I can make anybody believe anything.
22. I am a born leader.
23. I can read people like a book.
24. I am apt to show off if I get the chance.
25. People can learn a great deal from me.
26. I always know what I am doing.
27. I can usually talk my way out of anything.
28. Superiority is something you are born with.
29. I could do almost anything on a dare.

Exploitiveness/Entitlement

30. I expect a great deal from other people.
31. I am envious of other people's good fortune.
32. I insist upon getting the respect that is due me.
33. I will never be satisfied until I get all that I deserve.
34. I have a strong will to power.
35. I get upset when people don't notice how I look when I go out in public.
36. I find it easy to manipulate people.
37. I am more capable than other people.

Turn to the end of the chapter to interpret your responses.

R E V I E W

The Self

Self refers to a sense of who you are and what makes you different from others. Psychologists have conceptualized the self in a number of different ways—including self-understanding or self-concept. *Self-concept* refers to all of our thoughts and feelings about ourselves. Other frameworks for conceptualizing the self include conscious and unconscious selves, self-congruence, possible selves, and self-esteem (the evaluative and affective dimension of self-concept, also referred to as self-worth or self-image).

Several kinds of challenges can hinder self-development, including self-discrepancy, the diminished self (low self-esteem), narcissism, and the crowded self (multiple personality disorder).

To understand the self fully, it is important to consider the self in sociocultural contexts. Individualistic and collectivistic societies view the self differently.

IDENTITY

By far the most comprehensive story of identity development has been told by Erik Erikson. To begin, we will outline his eight stages of the human life span, then elaborate on his views of identity. Subsequently, we will study other aspects of identity, including its gender, cultural, and ethnic aspects.

Erikson's Eight Stages of the Life Span

Erik Erikson (1902–1994) spent his childhood and adolescence in Europe. After working as a young adult under Freud's direction, Erikson came to the United States in 1933. He became a U.S. citizen and taught at Harvard University. Erikson's ideas were influenced by the strain he experienced from having been born out of wedlock. One of his major interests was the development of identity.

Erikson recognized Freud's contributions but he believed Freud misjudged some important dimensions of human development. For one, Erikson (1968) said, we develop in *psychosocial stages,* in contrast to Freud's psychosexual stages. For another, Erikson emphasized developmental change throughout the human life span, whereas Freud argued that our basic personality is shaped in the first 5 years of our life. The **epigenetic principle** *is Erikson's term for the process that guides development through the life span. The epigenetic principle states that anything that grows has a blueprint, each part having a special time of ascendancy, until all of the parts have arisen to form a functioning whole.* In Erikson's theory, eight stages of development unfold as we go through the life span. Each stage consists of a unique developmental task that confronts the individual with a crisis that must be faced. For Erikson, this crisis is not a catastrophe, but a turning point of increased vulnerability and enhanced potential. The more the individual resolves the crises successfully, the healthier development will be.

Trust versus mistrust *is Erikson's first psychosocial stage, which is experienced in the first year of life. A sense of trust requires a feeling of physical comfort and a minimal amount of fear and*

Erik Erikson (*right*) with his wife, Joan.

apprehension about the future. Trust in infancy sets the stage for a lifelong expectation that the world will be a good and pleasant place to live.

Autonomy versus shame and doubt *is Erikson's second stage of development, occurring in late infancy and toddlerhood (1 to 3 years). After gaining trust in their caregiver(s), infants and toddlers begin to discover that their behavior is their own.* They start to assert their sense of independence, or autonomy. They realize their will. If infants and toddlers are restrained too much or punished too harshly, they are likely to develop a sense of shame and doubt.

Initiative versus guilt *is Erikson's third stage of development, occurring during the preschool years (3–5 years of age).*

As preschool children encounter a widening social world, they are challenged more than they were as infants. Active, purposeful behavior is needed to cope with these challenges. Children are asked to assume responsibility for their body, their behavior, their toys, and their pets. Developing a sense of responsibility increases initiative. Uncomfortable guilt feelings may arise, though, if the child is irresponsible and is made to feel too anxious. Erikson has a positive outlook on this stage. He believes most guilt is quickly compensated for by a sense of accomplishment.

Industry versus inferiority *is Erikson's fourth developmental stage, occurring approximately during the elementary school years (6–11 years of age). Children's initiative brings them in contact with a wealth of* new experiences. *As they move into middle and late childhood, they direct their energy toward mastering knowledge and intellectual skills.* At no other time is the child more enthusiastic about learning than at the end of early childhood's period of expansive imagination. The danger during the elementary school years is a sense of inferiority—of feeling incompetent and unproductive. Erikson believes teachers have a special responsibility for children's development of industry. They should "mildly but firmly coerce children into the adventure of finding out that one can learn to accomplish things which one would never have thought of by oneself" (Erikson, 1968, p. 127).

Identity versus identity confusion *is Erikson's fifth developmental stage, experienced by individuals during the adolescent years. At this time, individuals are faced with finding out who they are, what they are all about, and where they are going in life.* Adolescents are confronted with many new roles and adult statuses—vocational and romantic, for example. Parents need to allow adolescents to explore many different roles and different paths within a particular role. If the adolescent explores these roles in a healthy manner and arrives at a positive path to follow, then a positive identity will be achieved. If an identity is pushed on the adolescent by parents, if the adolescent does not adequately explore many roles, and if a positive future path is not defined, then identity confusion reigns.

Intimacy versus isolation *is Erikson's sixth developmental stage, experienced by individuals during the early adulthood years. At this time, individuals face the developmental task of forming intimate relationships with others.* Erikson described intimacy as finding yet losing oneself in another. If the young adult forms healthy friendships and an intimate close relationship with another individual, intimacy will be achieved; if not, isolation will result.

Generativity versus stagnation *is Erikson's seventh developmental stage, experienced by individuals during middle adulthood. A chief concern is to assist the younger generation in developing and leading useful lives; this is what Erikson* meant by generativity. The feeling of having done nothing to help the next generation is stagnation.

Integrity versus despair *is Erikson's eighth and final developmental stage, experienced by individuals during late adulthood, when they review their life* *and evaluate it as having been either primarily positive or primarily negative.* Through many different routes the older person may have developed a positive outlook in most or all of the previous stages of development. If so, the retrospective glances will reveal a picture

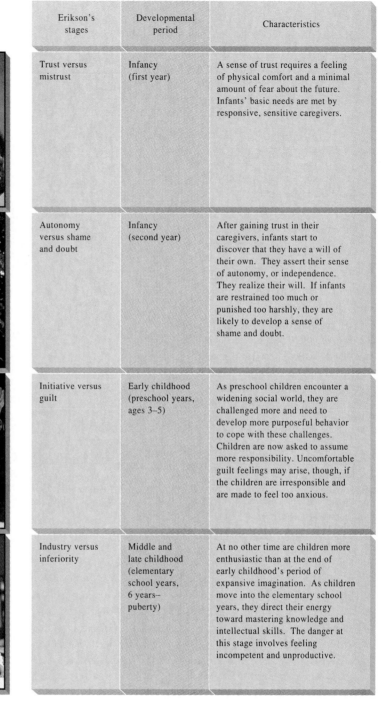

Erikson's stages	Developmental period	Characteristics
Trust versus mistrust	Infancy (first year)	A sense of trust requires a feeling of physical comfort and a minimal amount of fear about the future. Infants' basic needs are met by responsive, sensitive caregivers.
Autonomy versus shame and doubt	Infancy (second year)	After gaining trust in their caregivers, infants start to discover that they have a will of their own. They assert their sense of autonomy, or independence. They realize their will. If infants are restrained too much or punished too harshly, they are likely to develop a sense of shame and doubt.
Initiative versus guilt	Early childhood (preschool years, ages 3–5)	As preschool children encounter a widening social world, they are challenged more and need to develop more purposeful behavior to cope with these challenges. Children are now asked to assume more responsibility. Uncomfortable guilt feelings may arise, though, if the children are irresponsible and are made to feel too anxious.
Industry versus inferiority	Middle and late childhood (elementary school years, 6 years– puberty)	At no other time are children more enthusiastic than at the end of early childhood's period of expansive imagination. As children move into the elementary school years, they direct their energy toward mastering knowledge and intellectual skills. The danger at this stage involves feeling incompetent and unproductive.

FIGURE 3.6

Erikson's Eight Stages of the Human Life Span

Erikson's stages	Developmental period	Characteristics	
Identity versus identity confusion	Adolescence (10 to 20 years)	Individuals are faced with finding out who they are, what they are all about, and where they are going in life. An important dimension is the exploration of alternative solutions to roles. Career exploration is important.	
Intimacy versus isolation	Early adulthood (20s, 30s)	Individuals face the developmental task of forming intimate relationships with others. Erikson described intimacy as finding oneself yet losing oneself in another person.	
Generativity versus stagnation	Middle adulthood (40s, 50s)	A chief concern is to assist the younger generation in developing and leading useful lives.	
Integrity versus despair	Late adulthood (60s –)	Individuals look back and evaluate what they have done with their lives. The retrospective glances can either be positive (integrity) or negative (despair).	

example. Nonetheless, in the healthy solution to a stage crisis, the positive resolution dominates. A summary of Erikson's stages is presented in figure 3.6.

Erikson's Ideas on Identity Development

As we develop through adolescence, we are confronted with the need to develop many new roles, especially in the vocational and romantic realms. A **psychological moratorium** *is Erikson's term for the gap between childhood security and adult autonomy that individuals experience as part of their identity exploration.* As we explore and search our culture's identity files, we often experiment with different roles. Individuals who successfully cope with these conflicting identities emerge with a new sense of self that is both refreshing and acceptable. Those who do not successfully resolve this identity crisis suffer identity confusion. The confusion often takes one of two courses: individuals withdraw, isolating themselves from peers, family, and others, or they immerse themselves in the world of peers and lose their identity in the crowd.

During a psychological moratorium, individuals try out different roles and aspects of their personality before reaching a stable sense of self. They may be argumentative one moment, cooperative the next, or, they may be very close to a particular friend one month, and then despise this "former friend" the next. This type of personality exploration is a deliberate and worthwhile effort on the part of individuals to find out where they fit in the world.

As we come to realize that we will be responsible for ourselves and our own lives, we actively search how to design our personal life course. The process is often unsettling to both the searcher and to others who know the individual. Many parents and other adults, accustomed to having children go along with what they say, are bewildered or incensed by the wise cracks, the rebelliousness, and the rapid mood swings that accompany identity exploration. It is important for adults to remember that youth need the time and the opportunity to explore different roles and personalities. In turn, most youth eventually discard undesirable roles.

of a life well spent, and the person will feel a sense of satisfaction; integrity will be achieved. If the older adult resolved many of the earlier stages negatively, the retrospective glances will likely yield doubt or gloom; this is the despair Erikson talks about.

Erikson does not believe the proper solution to a stage crisis is always completely positive in nature. Some exposure or commitment to the negative end of the person's bipolar conflict is sometimes inevitable—you cannot trust all people under all circumstances and survive, for

Mahatma Gandhi (*center*) was the spiritual leader of India in the middle of the twentieth century. In his book *Gandhi's Truth*, Erikson (1969) described Gandhi's identity development and how it led him to become a spiritual leader.

Literally hundreds of roles exist for young people to try out, with just as many ways to pursue each of these myriad roles. Erikson believes that vocational roles are central to identity development, especially in highly technical societies like the United States. Individuals who have been well trained and educated for appropriate careers have the greatest potential for achieving high self-esteem. They also often experience the least stress in developing their identity.

Some individuals reject jobs offering good pay and traditionally high social status, choosing to form their identity around helping others, such as joining the Peace Corps, working in community psychology clinics, or teaching disadvantaged children. Traditionally, more women have chosen career identities emphasizing nurturance rather than prestige or financial rewards. Other individuals even say they would prefer unemployment to the prospect of working at a job they feel they would be unable to perform well in or at which they would feel useless. To Erikson, this attitude reflects the desire to achieve a meaningful identity by being true to oneself, rather than burying one's identity in that of the larger society.

Erikson's ideas provide rich insights about the development of a personal identity. We recommend that you try to read one or more of his original books. A good starting point is *Identity: Youth and Crisis* (1968). Other books that portray how we develop an identity are *Young Man Luther* (1962) and *Gandhi's Truth* (1969)—the latter won a Pulitzer Prize.

> *In case you're worried about what's going to become of the younger generation, it's going to grow up and start worrying about the younger generation.*
>
> —Roger Allen

Some Contemporary Alternative Views on Identity Development

Contemporary views of identity development suggest several important considerations. First, identity development is a long process, in many instances a more gradual, less cataclysmic transition than Erikson's term *crisis* implies. Second, identity development is enormously complex.

Identity formation neither begins nor ends with adolescence. It begins with the appearance of attachment, the development of a sense of self, and the emergence of independence in infancy. It reaches its final phase with a life review and integration in old age. Identity development in adolescence is important because for the first time physical development, cognitive development, and social development advance to the point at which the individual can begin to sort through and synthesize childhood identities and identifications to construct a viable path toward adult maturity. Resolution of identity as a developmental task does not mean, however, that identity will remain stable through the remainder of life. Decisions are not made once and for all, but have to be made again and again. An individual who develops a healthy identity is flexible, adaptive, and open to changes in society, relationships, and careers. This openness assures numerous reorganizations of identity's contents through the identity-achieved individual's life.

Identity formation does not happen neatly and it usually does not happen cataclysmically. At the bare minimum, it involves commitment to a vocational direction, an ideological stance, an integration with one's culture, and a sexual orientation. Some decisions that seem trivial when we make them may turn out to be major contributions to our identity: whom to date, whether or not to break up, whether or not to have intercourse, whether or not to take drugs, whether or not to go to college or finish high school and get a job, which major to pursue, whether to study or to play, whether or not to be politically active, and so on. Over the years of adolescence and the early part of our adult lives, we make decisions that begin to form a core of what we as human beings are all about—what is called identity.

Two contemporary theorists who have explored identity formation in adolescence are James Marcia and Carol Gilligan. We will examine their ideas in turn.

Marcia's Four Statuses of Identity

Eriksonian researcher James Marcia (1966, 1994) believes that Erikson's theory of identity development involves four possible statuses of identity, or ways of resolving the identity crisis: identity diffusion, identity foreclosure, identity moratorium, and identity achievement. The extent of the crisis and commitment being experienced is used to classify the

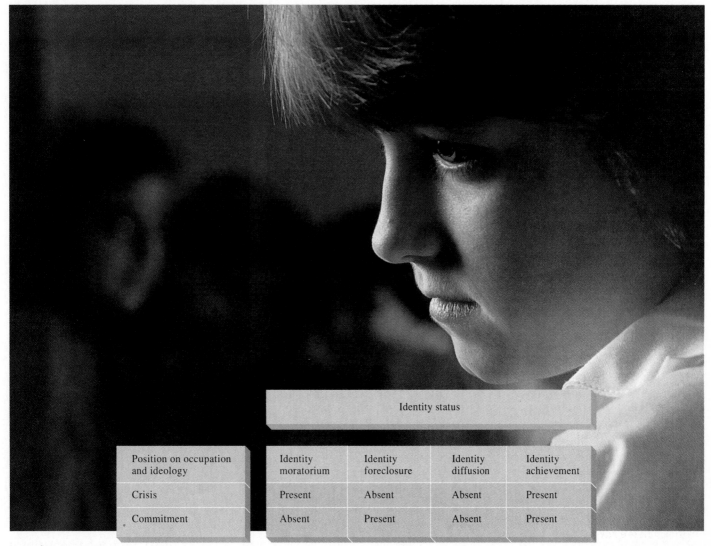

Identity status

Position on occupation and ideology	Identity moratorium	Identity foreclosure	Identity diffusion	Identity achievement
Crisis	Present	Absent	Absent	Present
Commitment	Absent	Present	Absent	Present

FIGURE 3.7

Marcia's Four Statuses of Identity

individual according to one of the four identity statuses. **Crisis** *is defined as a period of identity development during which the person is choosing among meaningful alternatives.* Most researchers prefer the term *exploration* rather than *crisis*, although, in the spirit of Marcia's formulation, we will use the term *crisis*. **Commitment** *is the aspect of identity development in which individuals show a personal investment in what they are going to do.* Let's see how these two aspects occur in each of the four statuses, summarized in figure 3.7.

Identity diffusion *is the term Marcia uses to describe persons who have not yet experienced a crisis (that is, they have not yet explored meaningful alternatives) or*

made any commitments. Not only are they undecided about occupational and ideological choices, they are also likely to show little interest in such matters. For example, 15-year-old Mario is having too much fun right now to decide whether to go to college after high school. He's really not thinking much about future goals at all.

Identity foreclosure *is the term Marcia uses to describe persons who have made a commitment but have not experienced a crisis.* This occurs most often when parents hand down commitments to their adolescents, usually in an authoritarian manner. In such circumstances, adolescents do not experience adequate opportunities to explore different approaches, ideologies, and vocations on

their own. Seventeen-year-old Owana is a good example of identity foreclosure—since she was 6 years old she has known that after high school graduation she will have a career in her family's restaurant business. Owana never really considered any other career possibilities.

Identity moratorium *is the term Marcia uses to describe individuals who are in the midst of a crisis, but their commitments either are absent or are only vaguely defined.* For example, college freshman Peter really wishes he knew what his career path is going to be—he really feels he should have already decided. But Peter has been unable to decide on a college major. So far he has wavered between pre-med, pre-law, and business.

Identity achievement *is Marcia's term for persons who have undergone a crisis and have made a commitment.* During high school, Priscilla extensively discussed career opportunities with several guidance counselors. They helped her become aware of her exceptional abilities in science and math. The counselors also oriented her toward colleges that have strong programs in these areas. Now, at age 20 and a college junior, Priscilla is well on her way to a degree in chemical engineering.

> *You can live a lifetime and, at the end of it, know more about other people than you know about yourself.*
> —**Beryl Markham,**
> ***West with the Night, 1942***

Some experts believe that the most important identity changes take place in the college years. For example, Alan Waterman (1991) found that from the years preceding high school through the last few years of college, there is an increase in the number of individuals who achieve identity, along with a decrease in the number of those who are experiencing identity diffusion. College juniors and seniors are more likely to have achieved identity than are college freshmen or high school students. To further evaluate identity development, see Critical Thinking. This developmental change is especially true in the area of vocational choice. Fewer college students have reached the identity-achieved status in their religious beliefs and political ideologies; in these complex decision-making areas, a substantial number of college students are identity-foreclosed or diffused. Thus, the timing of identity may depend on the particular role involved with many college students still wrestling with ideological commitments.

Many identity status researchers believe it is common for individuals who develop positive identities to follow what are called (MAMA) cycles Moratorium-Achiever-Moratorium-Achiever (Marcia, 1991). These cycles may be repeated throughout life, which suggests periods of inactivity between periods of accomplishment. Personal, family, and societal changes are inevitable and as they occur, the flexibility and skill required to explore new alternatives and develop new commitments likely facilitate an individual's coping skills.

Gilligan's Study of Gender Influence

Erikson believed that the identity was a distinctly different process for females and males. In his classic presentation on identity development, Erikson (1968) described male aspirations as oriented toward career and ideological commitments, while he described female aspirations as being centered around marriage and child rearing. In the 1960s and 1970s, researchers found support for Erikson's assertion about gender differences in identity. For example, vocational concerns were more central to the identity of males, affiliative concerns more important in the identity of females (LaVoie, 1976). In the last decade, however, as women have developed stronger vocational interests and men's friendships have changed, gender differences are diminishing (Archer, 1991).

Carol Gilligan (1992) challenged Erikson's ideas about the sequence of emotional tasks involved in achieving identity. Relationships and emotional bonds are more important concerns for females, but autonomy and achievement are more important for males. One view is that for males identity formation is likely to precede the stage of intimacy, while for females intimacy often precedes identity. In one study, the development of a clear sense of self by adolescent girls was related to their concerns about care and response in relationships (Rogers, 1987). In another study, a strong sense of self in college women was associated with their ability to solve problems of care in relationships while staying connected with both self and others (Skoe & Marcia, 1988).

Gilligan (1992) suggested that the task of identity exploration in adolescence might be more complex for girls than for boys, because girls must establish identities in more domains than boys must. In today's world, the options for

CRITICAL THINKING

Major Decisions and Identity Formation

One checkpoint for identity development in college is the decision to major in a particular area. How are you faring in this important decision, and where does this place you in terms of the "statuses" proposed by Marcia? Your ability to use this framework to understand your decision about what to major in reflects *applying psychological concepts to promote adjustment.*

For example, if you arrived at college in unambiguous pursuit of a teaching degree, your status might be *identity foreclosure* if you never considered any other possibilities. If you are still exploring, you might be experiencing *identity diffusion.* Perhaps you have tried several majors and found your talents best suited to psychology; this reflects *identity achievement* if your commitment has followed a crisis. Some students find the pressures of college overwhelming and stop-out for a period. Their choice of a major is delayed during *identity moratorium.*

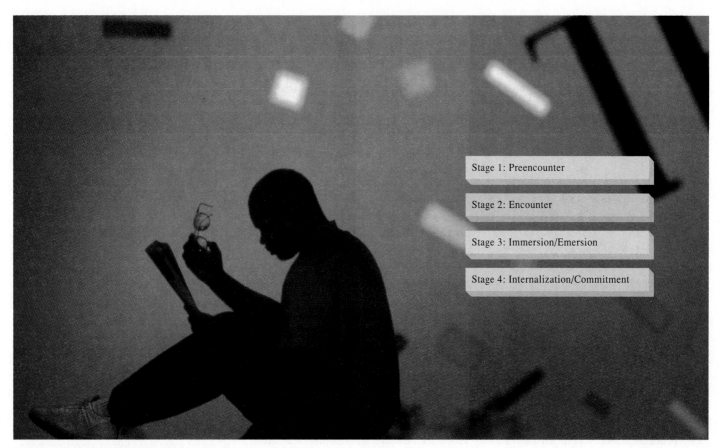

FIGURE 3.8

Helms' Four Stages of Ethnic Minority Identity Development

Stage 1: Preencounter

Stage 2: Encounter

Stage 3: Immersion/Emersion

Stage 4: Internalization/Commitment

women have increased faster than the options for men. Thus, women who hope to integrate family and career roles successfully might be experiencing far more confusion and conflict (Archer, 1991).

The Influence of Culture and Ethnicity

Erikson was especially sensitive to the role of culture in identity development. He pointed out that, throughout the world, ethnic minority groups have struggled to maintain their cultural identities while blending into the dominant culture (Erikson, 1968). Erikson said that this struggle for an inclusive identity, or identity within the larger culture, has been the driving force in the founding of churches, empires, and revolutions throughout history.

African American psychologists Janet Helms (1990) and William Cross (1972), as well as Asian American psychologists Derald Wing Sue and David Sue (1972), believe that a number of stages are involved in the development of ethnic identity, whether for minorities or for Whites. Our resolution of our own ethnic identity will strongly influence how open we are to those whose ethnicity is different from our own.

First we will examine Helms' model of minority identity development, then we will look at her model for White identity development.

Minority Identity Development

Helms' model of minority development has four stages, each of which we will discuss in turn (see figure 3.8).

Stage 1: Preencounter In this first stage, ethnic minority individuals prefer dominant cultural values to those of their own culture. Their role models, lifestyles, and value systems are adopted from the dominant group, while the physical and/or cultural characteristics that single them out as ethnic minority individuals are a source of pain and

stress. For example, African Americans may perceive their own physical features as undesirable and their African American cultural values and ways a handicap to success in the American society.

Stage 2: Encounter Although moving to the encounter stage is usually a gradual process, reaching this stage may occur because of an event that makes ethnic individuals realize they will never be a member of mainstream White America. This might be a monumental event, such as the assassination of Martin Luther King, Jr., or a more personal "identity shattering" event that serves as a trigger. In the encounter stage, ethnic minority individuals begin to break through their denial. Latinos who feel ashamed of their cultural upbringing may have conversations with other Latinos who are proud of their cultural heritage. At this stage, ethnic minority individuals become aware that not all cultural values of the dominant group are beneficial to them. This stage is characterized by conflicting attitudes about the self, minority group culture, and the dominant culture. The person wants to identify with the minority group, but does not know how to develop this identity. The recognition that an identity must be *developed* and not *found* leads to the third stage, immersion/emersion.

Stage 3: Immersion/Emersion   At the beginning of this stage, ethnic minority individuals completely endorse minority views and reject the dominant society. Individuals become strongly motivated to eliminate the oppression of their ethnic minority group. Movement into this stage likely occurs because (1) individuals begin to resolve some conflicts from the previous stage and develop a better understanding of societal forces such as racism, oppression, and discrimination; and (2) individuals begin to ask themselves, "Why should I feel ashamed of who I am?" The answer at this point often elicits both guilt and anger—the guilt of "selling out" in the past, which is perceived as contributing to the ethnic minority group's oppression, and anger at having been oppressed and "brainwashed" by the dominant group.

In the second phase of this stage—emersion—individuals experience feelings of discontent and discomfort with their rigid views of the previous phase and develop notions of greater individual autonomy. Emersion allows them to vent the anger that characterized the beginning of this stage, through rap groups, explorations of their own culture, discussions of racial/ethnic issues, and so on. Education and opportunities to expel hostile feelings allow individuals' emotions to level off, so that they can think more clearly and adaptively. It is no longer necessary to reject everything from the dominant culture and accept everything from one's own culture. People now have the autonomy to decide for themselves what the strengths

and weaknesses of their culture are, and which parts of the culture will become part of their own identity.

Stage 4: Internalization/Commitment   The main theme of this stage of ethnic minority identity development is that individuals experience a sense of fulfillment regarding the integration of their personal and cultural identities. Having resolved the conflicts and discomforts that were experienced in the immersion/emersion stage, individuals now attain greater self-control and flexibility. They also more objectively examine the cultural values of other ethnic minority individuals and groups, as well as those of the dominant group. In this stage, the individual wants to eliminate all forms of oppression. The commitment in this stage refers to the behavioral enactment of the newly realized identity. The individual takes actions, large or small, to reach the goal of eliminating oppression, whether engaging in large-scale political or social activism or performing everyday activities that are consistent with one's ethnic identity.

Helms' White Ethnic Identity Model

Helms (1990) also proposed a model of White ethnic identity, in which White individuals represent a range of experience from a stage of naivete about racial issues to a sophisticated state of multiculturism or racial transcendence. Helms' theory assumes that increased ethnic identity in both minority and majority individuals involves our understanding of success or failure in cross-ethnic interactions. The five stages of White ethnic identity development follow (see figure 3.9).

Stage 1: Contact   White individuals are unconcerned with or oblivious to ethnic/racial/cultural issues. They rarely think of themselves in ethnic or racial terms.

Stage 2: Disintegration   White individuals become aware of the social implications of race and ethnicity on a personal level, caught between having the privileges of the "White culture" and having the humane desire to treat individuals fairly.

Stage 3: Reintegration   White persons idealize anything that is associated with the White culture and denigrate anything that is associated with ethnic minority cultures. Anger is most common at this stage.

Stage 4: Psuedo-Independence   White individuals develop an understanding of the privileges of "Whiteness" and recognize a personal responsibility to combat racism.

Stage 5: Autonomy   White individuals develop a multicultural or transcendent worldview. At this stage, individuals have adopted a positive, nonracist "White identity," feeling a kinship with people regardless of their race and seeking to abolish the oppression of ethnic minority groups.

Although the identity development models include distinct stages, the boundaries between the stages are not always abrupt and clearly defined. In many instances, one stage blends into the next. Also, not all individuals experience the entire range of these stages in their lifetime. Some individuals are born and raised in a family functioning at stage 4 in the White identity development model and may never experience the earlier stages.

The trouble with being tolerant is that people think you don't understand the problem.

—Merle L. Meacham

Next, starting with chapter 4, we will turn our attention to how individuals function under stress. We will examine successful coping methods as well as the consequences of failing to cope.

Stage 1: Contact

Stage 2: Disintegration

Stage 3: Reintegration

Stage 4: Pseudo-independence

Stage 5: Autonomy

FIGURE 3.9

Helms' Five Stages of White Ethnic Identity Development

REVIEW

Identity

By far the most complete portrayal of identity development is Erik Erikson's theory of human development, which consists of eight stages: trust versus mistrust, autonomy versus shame and doubt, initiative versus guilt, industry versus inferiority, identity versus identity confusion, intimacy versus isolation, generativity versus stagnation, and integrity versus despair.

Erikson suggests that individuals experience a psychological moratorium between their childhood security and their adult independence. During this psychological moratorium, individuals try out different roles before reaching a stable sense of self.

Contemporary theorists view identity development as being more gradual and less cataclysmic than Erikson envisioned and as being enormously complex.

Two contemporary theorists who have examined identity development in adolescence are James Marcia and Carol Gilligan. Marcia proposed that by combining the two factors of crisis (exploration) and commitment, individuals can be classified in terms of four identity statuses: diffusion, foreclosure, moratorium, or achievement. Some experts believe that the most important identity changes take place in the college years. Erikson believed that identity development proceeds differently for females and males—with females focused on marriage and child rearing, and males on careers and ideological

commitments. Gilligan argued that relationships and emotional bonds are more central identity concerns of females, and that autonomy and achievement are more important for males.

Erikson is especially sensitive to the role of culture in identity development, understanding how throughout the world ethnic minority groups have struggled to maintain their cultural identities while blending into the majority culture. Helms proposed a model of ethnic minority identity development that consists of four stages: preencounter, encounter, immersion/emersion, and internalization/commitment. She also proposed a five-stage model of ethnic identity development in White individuals: contact, disintegration, reintegration, pseudo-independence, and autonomy.

You need only claim the events of your life to make yourself yours. When you truly possess all you have been and done, which may take some time, you are fierce with reality.

—Florida Scott Maxwell

How can people gain insight into their distinctive identities? Regardless of their orientation, most psychologists would say that the process of understanding yourself is not an easy path. For example, psychoanalysts would suggest that self-understanding is unlikely without the long-term assistance of a good analyst, who would penetrate your resistance and interpret your dreams and reveries in order to unveil your unconscious motives.

Humanists would help you claim yourself by exploring the congruence of different aspects of your self. How coherent are your hopes, your dreams, and your abilities? Do your abilities outstrip your objectives? Are your plans grander than your talents? Humanists especially appreciate the courage that it takes to embark on the challenge of attaining self-knowledge.

As you might guess, behaviorists often turn to data collection to facilitate self-understanding, through a technique referred to as *self-monitoring*. Maintaining a diary of your behaviors and their consequences can provide you with an objective analysis to enhance your problem solving in new and difficult situations. By documenting your patterns of behavior, you can gain insights into what would be more fulfilling courses of action in the future.

Sociocultural psychologists emphasize that our self-understanding is dependent on the contexts in which we grow. For example, some cultures strongly emphasize individual development and endorse activities that strengthen the self-concept. In our culture, we spend enormous sums of money on therapy and other self-help interventions to enhance our personal appearance, our intellectual prowess, our technological abilities, and even our grasp on reality. Other cultures dislike drawing attention to the individual because it might threaten the common good. These cultures would not be sympathetic to our investing so much of our resources in individual development.

Many perspectives converge when we evaluate the impact of *role models* on self-understanding. Behaviorists have shown we are influenced by even our most subtle observations of others. That influence may be enhanced when the role model is someone whom we admire. Humanists would suggest that an inspiring role model offers a version of the *ideal self*. Sociocultural psychologists emphasize that sociocultural factors influence the effectiveness and availability of role models. We tend to be influenced more by people we see as similar to ourselves (Rokeach & Ball-Rokeach, 1989). This finding takes on particular significance when we recognize that not all groups in the culture have access to the same opportunities.

Who have been your role models? In what ways have they influenced your identity? Were your role models very similar to you? How did they become your role models? Do your role models know of their importance to you? Thinking through these questions can help you to *engage in self-reflection to enhance adjustment and growth*. This exercise can bring you one step closer to claiming yourself.

Self is an important concept in human adjustment. Your self is your sense of who you are and what makes you different from others. Psychologists have conceptualized the self in a number of different ways, including in terms of self-understanding and self-concept, conscious and unconscious selves, self-congruence, possible selves, and self-esteem. Several kinds of challenges hinder self-development, such as self-discrepancy, low self-esteem, narcissism, and multiple personality disorder. To fully understand the self, it is important to evaluate the self in sociocultural context. Our coverage of identity development focused on Erikson's eight stages of the life span as well as his ideas about identity development. We also studied some contemporary alternatives to Erikson's views, especially those of James Marcia and Carol Gilligan. Remember that you can obtain an overall summary of the chapter by again studying the two in-chapter reviews on pages 62 and 71.

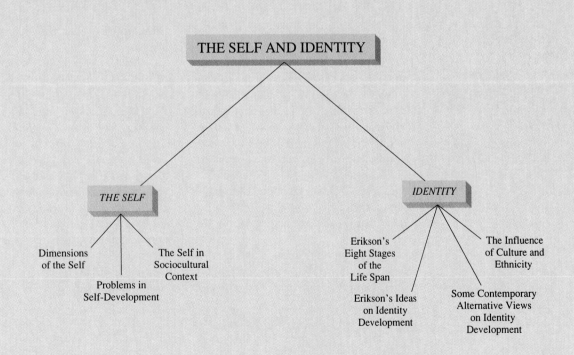

PRACTICAL KNOWLEDGE ABOUT ADJUSTMENT

WOMEN & SELF-ESTEEM

(1984) by Linda Sanford & Mary Donovan. New York: Anchor Doubleday.

Women & Self-Esteem explains why women often have low self-esteem and how they can improve the way they think about themselves. Sanford and Donovan draw on research, interviews, and group workshop information to address a wide range of issues concerning the development and expression of self-esteem in women. They examine the causes of low self-esteem in women and give suggestions for prevention and remediation of this widespread condition. The authors argue that low self-esteem translates into other problems such as depression, negative body image, fear of intimacy, and overinvestment in romantic relationships. They provide readers with exercises that will help them engage in self-evaluation, reduce their negative self-images, and decrease their self-destructive behaviors. This is a good book for women with low self-esteem.

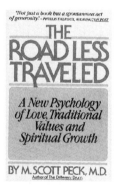

THE ROAD LESS TRAVELED

(1978) by M. Scott Peck. New York: Simon & Schuster.

The Road Less Traveled presents an approach to self-fulfillment based on spirituality and emotions. Peck begins by stating that life is difficult and that we all suffer pain and disappointment. He believes we should face up to life's difficulties and not be lazy. Indeed, Peck equates laziness with the original sin, going on to say that people's tendency to avoid problems and emotional suffering is the root of mental disorders. Peck also believes that people are thirsting for integrity in their lives. They are not happy with a country that has "In God we trust" as one of its main emblems and at the same time still leads the world's arms race. They also can't tolerate being just Sunday morning Christians, he says. To achieve integrity, Peck believes, people need to move spirituality into all phases of their lives.

Peck speaks of four important tools to use in life's journey: delaying gratification, accepting responsibility, dedication to the truth, and balancing. After a thorough analysis of each, Peck explores the will to use them, which he calls love. Then he probes further and analyzes the relation of growth and religion, which leads him to examine the final step of "the road less traveled": grace. By grace, Peck means the whole range of human activities that support the human spirit. Grace operates at the interface between humans and God and at the frontier between unconscious and conscious thought, in Peck's view.

NARCISSISM

Scoring

1. Give yourself one point for every true statement in items 1–9. This is your score on the leadership/authority section.

2. Give yourself one point for every true statement in items 10–18. This is your score on the self-absorption/self-admiration section.

3. Give yourself one point for every true statement in items 19–29. This is your score on the superiority/arrogance section.

4. Give yourself one point for every true statement in items 30–37. This is your score on the exploitiveness/entitlement section.

5. Total your score from (1) through (4) above; this is your score on the narcissistic personality inventory.

Interpretation

Narcissistic personality disorder/pathological narcissism occurs only with extreme manifestations of the above beliefs and behaviors. If you endorsed many of the statements, your narcissistic characteristics reflect a personality style that is characterized by self-absorption, self-serving bias, egocentricism, high sense of self-importance and uniqueness, exhibitionism, entitlement, and preoccupation with grandiose fantasies. Most students will endorse at least a few of these statements. Some of the results of narcissistic beliefs are the denial of personal blame for failed outcomes, increases in racism, sexism, nationalism, or political and religious beliefs, more selfish marital interactions, and self-absorption. Levels of self-esteem may be healthy or pathological.

SELF-ESTEEM

Scoring

For questions 1, 2, 4, 6, and 7, give yourself one point for each answer of a or b. For questions 3, 5, 8, 9, and 10, give yourself one point for each answer of c or d.

Interpretation

If your score is 5 or above, your self-esteem is likely to be high. Scores below 3 are likely to indicate low self-esteem.

John Santrock
In Torment, detail

CHAPTER

4

Stress

*A great many people have come up to me
and asked how I manage to get so much
work done and still keep looking
so dissipated.*

—Robert Benchley

Mort, age 52, has worked as an air traffic controller for the past 15 years. An excitable person, he compares the job to being in a cage. During peak air traffic, the tension is almost unbearable. In these frenzied moments, Mort's emotions are a mixture of rage, fear, and anxiety. Unfortunately, the tension also spills over into his family life. In his own words, "When I go home, my nerves are hopping. I take it out on the nearest person." Two years ago, Mort's wife, Sally, told him that if he could not calm his emotions and handle stress more effectively, she would leave him. She suggested that he change to a less upsetting job, but he ignored her advice. His intense emotional behavior continued, and she left him. Last Sunday evening the roof fell in on Mort—the computer that monitors air traffic temporarily went down, and Mort had a heart attack. Quadruple bypass surgery saved his life.

Yesterday his doctor talked with him about the stress in his life and what could be done to reduce it. Mort rarely gets enough sleep, weighs too much but frequently skips meals, never exercises, smokes two packs of cigarettes a day, and drinks two or three scotches every evening (more on weekends). He professes no religious interests. He rarely dates since his divorce and has no relatives within 50 miles. He has only one friend and does not feel very close to him. Mort says that he never has enough time to do the things he wants to do and rarely has quiet time to himself during the day. He has fun only about once every 2 weeks.

The doctor gave Mort a test, shown in table 4.1, to reveal his vulnerability to stress. Mort's score of 68 on the stress test indicates that he is "seriously vulnerable" to stress and close to the "extremely vulnerable" range. Stress is inevitable in our lives, so it is important to understand what factors are involved in managing stress and in maintaining a healthy lifestyle. How do *you* fare on the stress test?

Stress is inevitable in our lives, so it is important to understand it and cope with it effectively.

TABLE 4.1
Stress Test

Rate yourself on each item, using this scale:

1 = almost always
2 = often
3 = sometimes
4 = seldom
5 = never

1. I eat at least one hot, balanced meal a day.
2. I get 7 to 8 hours of sleep at least four nights a week.
3. I give and receive affection regularly.
4. I have at least one relative within 50 miles whom I can rely on.
5. I exercise to the point of perspiration at least twice a week.
6. I smoke less than half a pack of cigarettes a day.
7. I take fewer than five alcoholic drinks a week.
8. I am the appropriate weight for my height.
9. I have an income adequate to meet my basic expenses.
10. I get strength from my religious beliefs.
11. I regularly attend church.
12. I have a network of friends and acquaintances.
13. I have one or more friends to confide in about personal matters.
14. I am in good health (including eyesight, hearing, teeth).
15. I am able to speak openly about my feelings when angry or worried.
16. I have regular conversations with the people I live with about domestic problems (e.g., chores, money, and daily living issues).
17. I do something for fun at least once a week.
18. I am able to organize my time effectively.
19. I drink fewer than three cups of coffee (or tea or cola drinks) a day.
20. I take quiet time for myself during the day.

Total:

To get your total score, add up the figures and subtract 20. Any number over 30 indicates a vulnerability to stress. You are seriously vulnerable if your score is between 50 and 75 and extremely vulnerable if it is over 75.

"Vulnerability Scale" from the Stress Audit developed by Lyle H. Miller and Alma Dell Smith. Copyright 1987, Biohavioral Associates, Brookline, MA. Reprinted with permission.

PREVIEW

There are too many Morts in the world who do not handle stress effectively. Our coverage of stress begins by exploring the nature of stress, and then turns to a discussion of a number of important facets of stress, including biological and emotional factors, person factors, and contextual factors.

UNDERSTANDING STRESS

We live in a world that includes many stressful circumstances. According to the American Academy of Family Physicians, two-thirds of all office visits to family doctors are for stress-related symptoms. Stress is also believed to be a major contributor to coronary heart disease, cancer, lung problems, accidental injuries, cirrhosis of the liver, and suicide, six of the leading causes of death in the United States. Recently, two of the five best selling drugs in the United States were an antianxiety drug (Xanax) and an ulcer medication (Zantac). No one really knows whether we experience more stress than our parents or grandparents did at our age, but it seems as if we do.

Life is not a spectacle or a feast: it is a predicament.

—**George Santayana**

Stress is not an easy term to define. Psychologists have sometimes debated whether stress is the threatening events in our world or the response we make to those demands. We favor the latter interpretation. **Stress** *is the response of individuals to the circumstances and events that threaten them and tax their coping abilities.* **Stressors** *are threatening aspects of the environment that induce stress reactions.*

Initially the word *stress* was loosely borrowed from physics. Humans, it was thought, are in some ways similar to physical objects, such as metals, that resist moderate outside forces or stressors. At some point of greater pressure, stress becomes **strain,** *a weakened resistance to stressors and diminished resilience.* Like

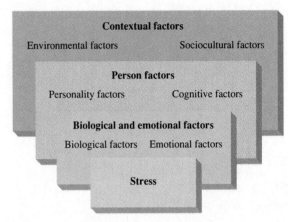

FIGURE 4.1

Factors Involved in Stress

metals under force, humans also experience strain. Unlike metals, human beings can think, reason, and experience a myriad of social and environmental circumstances that make defining stress more complicated in psychology than in physics (Hobfoll, 1989). Understanding human stress requires knowledge about the related biological, emotional, person, and contextual factors (see figure 4.1).

We will examine coping in considerable detail in chapter 5. In this chapter we will discuss each of the other dimensions of stress, beginning with the biological and emotional factors in stress.

BIOLOGICAL AND EMOTIONAL FACTORS IN STRESS

To understand the body's role in stress, we need to examine the nature of the autonomic nervous system, the endocrine system, the general adaptation syndrome, and illness and the immune system. And we need to evaluate the role of emotional factors to further our understanding of stress.

Biological Factors

The key biological factors in stress include the autonomic nervous system, the endocrine system, the general adaptation syndrome, and the immune system.

The Autonomic Nervous System

As you drive down a highway, the fog thickens. Suddenly you see a pile of cars in front of you. Your mind temporarily freezes, your muscles tighten, your stomach becomes queasy, and your heart feels like it is going to pound out of your chest. You immediately slam on the brakes and try to veer away from the pile of cars. Tires screech, windshield glass flies, metal smashes, then all is quiet. After a few seconds, you realize you are alive. You find that you can walk out of the car. Your fear turns to relief as you sense your luck in not being hurt. In a couple of seconds, the relief turns to anger. You loudly ask who caused the accident.

As you moved through this stressful situation, your body changed. The **autonomic nervous system (ANS)** *takes messages to and from the body's internal organs, monitoring such processes as breathing,*

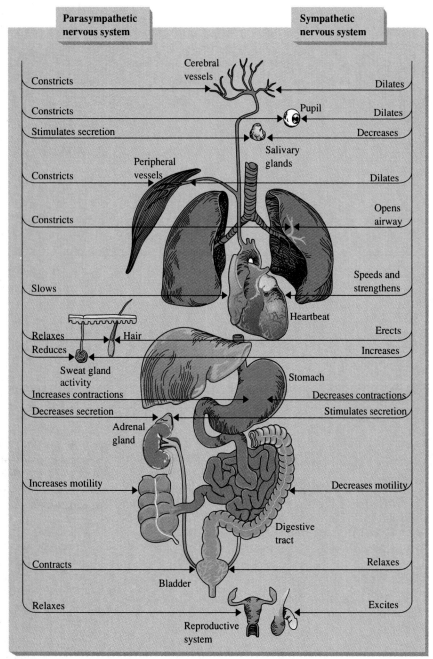

Parasympathetic nervous system | Sympathetic nervous system

Cerebral vessels
Constricts — Dilates
Pupil
Constricts — Dilates
Stimulates secretion — Decreases
Salivary glands
Peripheral vessels
Constricts — Dilates
Constricts — Opens airway
Speeds and strengthens
Heartbeat
Slows
Erects
Hair
Relaxes — Increases
Reduces —
Sweat gland activity
Stomach
Increases contractions — Decreases contractions
Decreases secretion — Stimulates secretion
Adrenal gland
Increases motility — Decreases motility
Digestive tract
Contracts — Relaxes
Bladder
Relaxes — Excites
Reproductive system

FIGURE 4.2

Autonomic Nervous System: Parasympathetic and Sympathetic Divisions
The sympathetic system is at work when we are aroused; the parasympathetic system is at work when we are calm. Both systems influence most organs. For example, the sympathetic system speeds and strengthens heartbeat; the parasympathetic system slows heartbeat.

heart rate, and digestion. The ANS is divided into two parts, the **sympathetic nervous system,** *which arouses the body,* and the **parasympathetic nervous system,** *which calms the body* (see figure 4.2). These two components of the autonomic nervous system function in a complementary way to keep the bodily systems both in balance and responsive to the environment.

The Endocrine System

In addition to regulating such processes as respiration, heart rate, and digestion, the autonomic nervous system acts upon the endocrine glands, producing a number of important bodily reactions.

The **endocrine glands** *release their chemical products directly into the bloodstream. The endocrine glands manufacture*

hormones, *chemical messengers that travel in the bloodstream to all parts of the body.* The endocrine glands consist of the hypothalamus and the pituitary gland at the base of the brain, the thyroid and parathyroid glands at the front of the neck, the adrenal glands just above the kidneys, the pancreas in the abdomen, and the ovaries in the female's pelvis and testes in the male's scotum (see figure 4.3). The action of the endocrine glands is constantly monitored and changed by the neural, hormonal, and chemical information sent to them.

The **adrenal glands,** *located just above the kidneys, play an important role in our ability to cope with stress, in our moods, and in our energy level.* Each adrenal gland secretes epinephrine (also called adrenaline) and norepinephrine (also called noradrenaline). Although most hormones travel rather slowly, epinephrine and norepinephrine work quickly. Epinephrine helps ready an individual for an emergency by acting on the smooth muscles, heart, stomach, intestines, and sweat glands. Norepinephrine alerts the individual for emergency situations by interacting with the pituitary gland and the liver.

The human race's prospects of survival were considerably better when we were defenseless against tigers than they are today when we have become defenseless against ourselves.

—Arnold Toynbee

The General Adaptation Syndrome

According to the Austrian-born founder of stress research, Hans Selye (1974, 1983), stress simply is wear and tear on the body due to the demands placed on it. Any number of environmental events, or stimuli, will produce the same stress response in the body. Selye observed patients with various problems: the death of someone close, a loss of income, arrest for embezzlement. Regardless of which problem the patient had, similar symptoms appeared: loss of appetite, muscular weakness, and decreased interest in the world.

The **general adaptation syndrome (GAS)** *is Selye's concept of the common effects on the body when demands are placed*

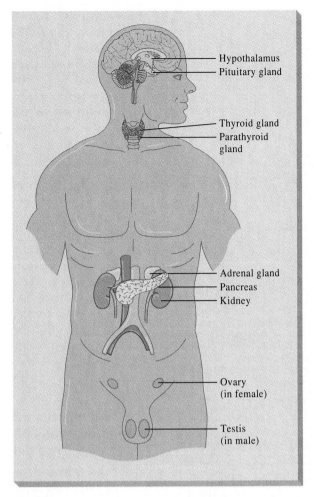

FIGURE 4.3

The Major Endocrine Glands
The pituitary gland releases hormones that regulate the hormone secretions of the other glands. The pituitary gland is itself regulated by the hypothalamus.

on it. The GAS consists of three stages: alarm, resistance, and exhaustion. First, in the *alarm stage,* the body enters a temporary state of shock, a time when resistance to stress is below normal. The body detects the stress and tries to eliminate it. The body loses muscle tone, temperature decreases, and blood pressure drops. Then a rebound called "countershock" occurs, in which resistance to stress begins to pick up; the adrenal cortex enlarges and hormone release increases. Soon after the alarm stage, which is short, the individual moves into the *resistance stage,* a no-holds-barred effort to combat stress. Stress hormones flood the body; blood pressure, heart rate, temperature, and respiration rate all skyrocket. If the all-out effort succeeds, the body returns to a more normal resting state. If

the all-out effort to combat stress fails and the stress persists, the individual moves into the *exhaustion stage.* The wear and tear on the body takes its toll—the person may collapse in a state of exhaustion, and vulnerability to disease increases. Figure 4.4 illustrates Selye's general adaptation syndrome.

Not all stress is bad, though. **Eustress** *is Selye's term for positive stress.* Competing in an athletic event, writing an essay, or pursuing someone who is attractive requires the body to expend energy. Selye does not say we should avoid these fulfilling experiences in life, but he does emphasize that we should minimize their wear and tear on our bodies.

One of the main criticisms of Selye's view is that human beings do not always react to stress in the uniform way

he proposed. There is much more to understanding stress in humans than knowing their physical reactions to it. We also need to know about their physical makeup, their perceptions, their personalities, and the contexts in which the stressors occur (Seiffge-Krenke, 1995).

Illness and the Immune System

Psychoneuroimmunology *is the field that explores connections among psychological factors, such as attitudes and emotions, the nervous system, and the immune system.* The immune system keeps us healthy by recognizing foreign materials such as bacteria, viruses, and tumors, and then destroying them. Its machinery consists of billions of white blood cells located in the lymph system. The number of white blood cells and their effectiveness in killing foreign viruses or bacteria are related to stress levels. When in the alarm or exhaustion stage, for example, the immune system functions poorly. During these stages, viruses and bacteria are more likely to multiply and cause disease.

What are some of the biological pathways that might link stress and illness? What are some of the behavioral pathways? What interventions are effective in breaking down the connection between stress and illness?

Biological Pathways Stress can set in motion biological effects that involve the autonomic, endocrine, and immune systems (Anderson, Kiecolt-Glaser, & Glaser, 1994). The immune system might be one of the more important biological determinants in the control of certain malignant diseases. Are there stress-mediated immune responses and stress-mediated health effects?

There are three lines of support for the view that there are stress-mediated immune responses. First, acute stressors can produce immunological changes in healthy individuals. For example, during a stressful exam period, decreases in interferon production occurred in healthy medical students (Glaser & others, 1987). Also, in relatively healthy HIV-infected individuals, as well as individuals with cancer, the onset of acute stressors was associated with poorer immune system functioning.

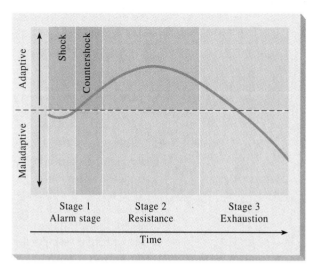

FIGURE 4.4

Selye's General Adaptation Syndrome

The general adaptation syndrome (GAS) is the typical series of responses individuals have to stress. In the first stage (alarm), the body enters a temporary state of shock, a time when resistance to stress is below normal. Then a rebound called "countershock" occurs, in which resistance to stress begins to pick up. Not much later, the individual moves into the second state (resistance), during which resistance to stress is intensified in an all-out effort to combat stress. If the effort fails and stress persists, the individual moves into the third and final stage (exhaustion), when wear and tear on the body worsens, the person may collapse in a state of exhaustion, and vulnerability to disease increases.

From H. Selye, *The Stress of Life*, 2d ed. Copyright © 1978 McGraw-Hill, Inc. Reprinted by permission of McGraw-Hill, Inc.

Second, chronic stressors are associated with an increasing downturn in immune system responsiveness rather than with adaptation. This effect has been documented in a number of contexts, including living next to a damaged nuclear reactor, close relationship failures (such as divorce, separation, and marital distress), and burdensome caregiving for a family member with progressive dementia (Kiecolt-Glaser & others, 1991).

Third, research with cancer patients links quality of life with immunity (Levy & others, 1990).

Two other lines of research reveal the role of stress in health. First, acute stress is related to illness, especially infectious illness in young, healthy individuals. In one study, increased cold infection was associated with increased stress. Second, chronic stressors can affect health as well. In one study, "at risk" Alzheimer's caregivers had more and longer-lasting respiratory infections than their non-at-risk counterparts (Kiecolt-Glaser & others, 1991).

Behavioral Pathways   Health behaviors and compliance are significant factors in stress and illness. Individuals who experience psychological stress from an illness often develop other health-related problems. Distressed individuals often have appetite disturbances, resulting in their eating less often or eating meals of lower nutritional value. Individuals who are depressed, anxious, or both are more likely to self-medicate with alcohol and other drugs. Thus, poor health behaviors can magnify the effects of stress on illness. Both poor nutrition and substance abuse can directly lower the immune system's functioning. On the positive side, there is increasing evidence that physical activity can improve immune system functioning. For example, in one study, exercise and fitness were linked with positive immune system functioning in HIV-infected men (LaPerriere & others, 1990).

Noncompliance is a general health problem involved in the link between stress and illness. For instance, the psychological or behavioral effects of cancer treatments can be so disruptive that patients can become discouraged and might fail to complete, or might even refuse, treatment.

Interventions   Appropriately designed interventions can reduce stress and enhance quality of life as well as improve behavioral responses, such as health behaviors and adherence to treatment regimes. Therapy components that have been effective in reducing stress in cancer patients include emotional support, training in coping strategies, and relaxation training (Fawzy & others, 1993).

Conclusions About Biological Factors   Much of what we know about psychoneuroimmunology needs to be further clarified, verified, and explained. Over the next several decades, research in this field should expand. Researchers hope to tease apart the precise links between psychological factors, the brain, and the immune system. These research findings may provide clues to more successful treatments for some of the most baffling diseases—cancer and AIDS among them. As we see next, more than biological factors are involved in understanding stress.

Emotional Factors

When we experience stress, don't we often react emotionally? Often when we are under stress we display negative emotions such as anger, anxiety, fear, and sadness. For example, individuals who face the stress of an important exam might be angry at themselves for not studying enough (or angry at the professor for making the class so tough), anxious about the possibility of not doing well on the exam, fearful that failing the exam might mean getting kicked out of school, and sad that life isn't more enjoyable.

Defining Emotion

Just as with motivation, there are different kinds and intensities of emotions. A person can be not only motivated to eat rather than have sex, but more or less hungry, or more or less interested in having sex. Similarly, a person can be happy or angry, and can be fairly happy or ecstatic, annoyed or fuming.

Defining emotion is difficult because it is not easy to tell when a person is in an emotional state (Cornelius, 1996). Are you in an emotional state when your heart beats fast, your palms sweat, and your stomach churns? when you think about how much you are in love with someone? when you smile or grimace? The body, the mind, and the face play important roles in understanding emotion. Psychologists debate how critical each is in determining whether we are in an emotional state. For our purposes, we will define **emotion** *as feeling, or affect, that involves a mixture of physiological arousal (fast heartbeat, for example), conscious experience (thinking about being in love with someone, for example), and overt behavior (smiling and grimacing, for example).*

> *Blossoms are scattered by the wind and the wind cares nothing, but the blossoms of the heart no wind can touch.*
>
> —**Yoshida Kenko,**
> ***The Harvest of Leisure,* 1930**

Classifying Emotion

When we think about emotions, a few dramatic feelings, such as rage, fear, and glorious joy, usually spring to mind. But emotions can be subtle as well—the anticipation of seeing good friends, the mild irritation of boredom, the uneasiness of living in the nuclear age. And the kinds of emotions we can experience are legion. There are more than two hundred words for emotions in the English language. How have psychologists handled the complex task of classifying emotions?

A number of psychologists use wheel diagrams to classify the emotions we experience. One such model was proposed by Robert Plutchik (1980), who believes that emotions have four dimensions: (1) they are positive or negative; (2) they are primary or mixed; (3) many are polar opposites; and (4) they vary in intensity. Ecstasy and enthusiasm are positive emotions; grief and anger are negative emotions. For example, think about your ecstasy when you get an unexpected A on a test, or your enthusiasm about the football game this weekend—these are positive emotions. In contrast, think about negative emotions, such as your grief when someone close to you dies or your anger when someone verbally attacks you. Positive emotions enhance our self-esteem; negative emotions lower our self-esteem. Positive emotions improve our relationships with others; negative emotions depress the quality of those relationships.

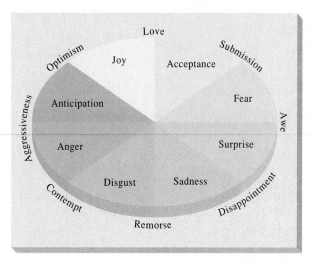

FIGURE 4.5

Plutchik's Wheel of Emotions
This diagram shows the eight primary emotions and "dyads" that result from mixtures of adjacent primaries. For example, a combination of the primary emotions of fear and surprise produces awe. Joy mixed with acceptance leads to love.

REPRINTED WITH PERMISSION FROM *PSYCHOLOGY TODAY* MAGAZINE. Copyright © 1980 (Sussex Publishers, Inc.).

Plutchik also believes that emotions are like colors. Every color of the spectrum can be produced by mixing the primary colors. Possibly some emotions are primary, and, if mixed together, they combine to form all other emotions. Happiness, disgust, surprise, sadness, anger, and fear are candidates for primary emotions. For example, combining sadness and surprise gives disappointment. Jealousy is composed of love and anger. Plutchik developed the emotion wheel (shown in figure 4.5) to show how primary emotions work. Mixtures of primary emotions adjacent to each other combine to produce other emotions. Some emotions are opposites—love and remorse, optimism and disappointment. Plutchik believes we cannot experience emotions that are polar opposites simultaneously. You cannot feel sad at the same time you feel happy, he says. Imagine just getting a test back in this class. As you scan the paper for the grade, your emotional response is happy or sad, not both.

Happiness

It was not until 1973 that *Psychological Abstracts*, the major source of psychological research summaries, included *happiness* as an index term. The recent interest in happiness focuses on positive ways we experience our lives, including cognitive judgments of our well-being (Parducci, 1996). That is,

psychologists want to know what makes you happy and how you perceive your happiness. Many years ago, French philosopher Jean-Jacques Rousseau described the subjective nature of happiness this way: "Happiness is a good bank account, a good cook, and a good digestion."

In a recent review of research on happiness, being a good cook and good digestion were not on the list of factors that contribute to our happiness, but these four factors were (Myers, 1992):

- Self-esteem—happy people like themselves
- Optimism—happy people are hope-filled
- Extroversion—happy people are outgoing
- Personal control—happy people believe that they choose their own destinies

Some factors that many people believe are involved in happiness, such as age and gender, actually are not.

But what about Rousseau's "good bank account"? Can money buy happiness? One study tried to find out if lottery winners are happier than people who have not received a windfall of money (Brickman, Coates, & Janoff-Bulman, 1978). Twenty-two major lottery winners were compared with twenty-two people living in the same area of the city. The general happiness of

CRITICAL THINKING

And the Winner Is . . .

Regardless of your wagering practices, suppose that you won the lottery. What would you do with this enormous amount of money to achieve a happier existence? Make a list of the top five things you would do with the money.

Next, *identify what values underlie your expressed intentions.* For example, if you decide to pass on a portion of your fortune to a charity, one of your key values would be *altruism.* If your list contains only new toys for yourself, your main value is *materialism.* What does your list suggest about your values? How you would realize greater happiness from your good fortune? Just how long would the happiness last?

the two groups did not differ when they were asked about the past, present, and the future. The people who hadn't won a lottery actually were happier doing life's mundane things such as watching television, buying clothes, and talking with a friend.

Winning a lottery does not appear to be the key to happiness. What is important, though, is having enough money to buy life's necessities. Extremely wealthy people are not happier than people who can purchase the necessities. People in wealthy countries are not happier than people in poor countries. The message is clear: If you believe money buys happiness, think again (Diener, 1984). To further evaluate whether there is a relationship between money and happiness, see Critical Thinking.

> *Happiness is not a state to arrive at, but a manner of traveling.*
> —**Margaret Lee Runbeck**

Psychologist Ed Diener (1984) agrees that intense positive emotions—such as we would feel at winning a lottery or getting a date with the person of our dreams—do not add much to a person's general sense of well-being, in part because they are rare, and in part because they can decrease the positive emotion and increase the negative emotion we feel in other circumstances. According to Diener, happiness boils down to the frequency of positive emotions and the infrequency of negative emotions. Diener's view flies in the face of common sense; you would think that frequent, intense positive emotions and minimal nonintense negative emotions produce the most happiness. But the commonsense view fails to consider that intense positive moments can diminish the sensation of future positive events. For example, you will be overwhelmed with happiness the first time you shoot par in a round of golf, but if you play golf a week later and do well but not great, the previous emotional high can diminish your positive experience. It is the rare, if nonexistent, human being who experiences intense positive emotions and infrequent negative emotions week after week after week.

Happiness is also a socially attractive emotion (Lazarus, 1991). We want to be with happy people and avoid being with unhappy people, and these states are often infectious. Positive emotions like happiness also are more likely to increase generosity, eagerness, expansiveness, and free-flowing use of one's resources than negative emotions like sadness. Happiness stands in marked contrast to the constriction and defensiveness associated with the harm, loss, and threat that negative emotions such as sadness and anger produce.

Psychologist Mihaly Csikszentmihalyi (1990) has been studying the optimal experiencing of emotion—those times when people report feelings of deep enjoyment and happiness—for more than two decades. According to Csikszentmihalyi, optimal experiences include what the sailor feels when the wind whips through her hair and the boat lunges through the waves like a colt—sails, hull, wind, and sea harmoniously vibrating in the sailor's body. Optimal experience is what an artist feels when the colors on a canvas begin to establish a magnetic relation with each other, and a *new thing* begins to take shape in front of the astonished creator. Optimal experience of emotion also is the feeling a father has when his child responds to his smile for the first time. Such events do not occur only when external conditions are favorable: People who have survived concentration camps or who have lived through near-fatal dangers often recall that in the midst of their ordeal they experienced extraordinary richness of emotion in response to such simple events as hearing the song of a bird in the forest, completing a difficult task, or sharing a crust of bread with a friend.

Contrary to what we usually believe, says Csikszentmihalyi, moments like these, the best emotional moments of our lives, are not usually passive, relaxing times—although such experiences can also involve enjoyable emotions, if we have worked hard to attain them. The best emotional moments frequently occur when a person's body or mind is stretched to the limits in a voluntary effort to achieve something difficult and worthwhile. Thus, the optimal experience of emotion is something we *make* happen. For a child, it might be using trembling fingers to place a final block on a tower she has built, higher than any she has previously constructed; for a swimmer, it might be training extremely hard and then beating his best record; for a violinist, it might be mastering an intricate musical passage. For each individual, there are thousands of opportunities, thousands of challenges, to expand ourselves and attain optimal emotional experiences.

Such experiences are not necessarily pleasant at the time they occur. The swimmer's muscles might have ached during training and even during his most memorable race; his lungs might have felt like they were exploding, and he might have been dizzy with fatigue—yet these

Psychologists often assess feelings of anger and hostility towards others. Anger is a complex human emotion and plays an important role in many aspects of our relationships with others and ourselves. Below is a sample of items that psychologists have used to assess angry feelings. Read each statement and consider how well each describes you. Think about how your answers may vary depending on what you have been doing or the kind of day you have had.

I feel angry.
I feel like I'm about to explode.
I feel like banging on the table.
I am furious.
I feel like hitting someone.
I am quick tempered.
I am a hotheaded person.
I fly off the handle.
When I get mad, I say nasty things.
When I get frustrated, I feel like hitting someone.

could have been the best moments of his life. Gaining control over life is never easy, and sometimes it can be painful. But in the long run optimal experiences of emotion add up to a sense of mastery—or perhaps better, a sense of *participation* in determining the contents of life—that comes as close to what is usually meant by happiness as anything else we can conceivably imagine.

Flow *is Csikszentmihalyi's concept of optimal experiences in life that are most likely to occur when people develop a sense of mastery. Flow involves a state of concentration in which an individual becomes absorbed while engaging in an activity.* Flow can be controlled and should not be left to chance. We can develop flow by setting challenges for ourselves—tasks that are neither too difficult nor too simple for our abilities. With such goals, we learn to order the information that enters consciousness and thereby the quality of our lives.

Anger

Anger is a powerful emotion. It not only has a strong impact on our social relationships, but also on the person experiencing the emotion (Lazarus, 1991). We can easily recount obvious examples of anger that often not only harm others but affect the angry individual as well—unrestrained and recurrent violence toward others, verbal and physical abuse of

children, perpetual bitterness, the tendency to carry a "chip on the shoulder" in which a person overinterprets others' actions as demeaning, and the inability to inhibit the expression of anger. To assess your anger tendencies, see the Self-Assessment. Using this assessment, you explore your typical amount of anger (trait anger) and your current anger level (state anger).

What makes people get angry? People often get angry when they feel they are not being treated fairly or when their expectations are violated. One researcher asked people to remember or keep records of their anger experiences (Averill, 1983). Most of the people said they became at least mildly angry several times a week; some said they became mildly angry several times a day. In many instances, the people said they got angry because they perceived that a friend or a loved one performed a misdeed. They especially got angry when they perceived the other person's behavior as unjustified, avoidable, and willful.

Doesn't getting angry sometimes make us feel better and possibly help us cope better with our challenging lives? **Catharsis** *is the release of anger or aggressive energy by directly or vicariously engaging in anger or aggression; the catharsis hypothesis states that behaving angrily or watching others behave angrily reduces subsequent anger.*

When angry, count four; when very angry, swear.

—Mark Twain

Psychoanalytic theory promotes catharsis as an important way to reduce anger, arguing that people have a natural, biological tendency to display anger. From this perspective, taking your anger out on a friend or a loved one should reduce your subsequent tendency to display anger; so would heavy doses of anger on television, such as the anger presented in many dramatic shows, television news, and televised sports including football, hockey, and professional wrestling. Why? Because such personally acted out or viewed experiences supposedly release pent-up anger.

On the other hand, social learning theory argues strongly against the catharsis view. Social learning theory states that, by acting angrily, people are often rewarded for their anger and, by watching others display anger, people learn how to be angry themselves. Which view is right? Research findings are more supportive of social learning theory. Indeed, studies on catharsis suggest that acting angrily does not have any long-term power in reducing anger. If the catharsis hypothesis were correct, war would have a cathartic effect in reducing anger and aggression, but a study of wars in 110 countries since 1900 revealed that warfare actually stimulated domestic violence (Archer & Gartner, 1976). Compared with nations that remained at peace, postwar nations had an increase in homicide rates.

As psychologist Carol Tavris (1989) says in her book *Anger: The Misunderstood Emotion,* one of the main results of the ventilation approach to anger is to raise the noise level of our society. It is not a way to reduce anger or solve our problems. When individuals prone to anger express their anger, they get even angrier, not less angry. Thus, ventilating anger often follows this cycle: a precipitating event, an angry outburst, shouted recriminations, screaming or crying, a furious peak (sometimes accompanied by physical assault), exhaustion, and a sullen apology or just sullenness.

Every person gets angry at one time or another. How can we control our anger so it does not become destructive? Tavris (1989) makes the following recommendations:

1. When your anger starts to boil and your body is getting aroused, work on lowering the arousal by waiting. Emotional arousal will usually simmer down if you just wait long enough.

2. Cope with the anger in ways that involve neither being chronically angry over every little bothersome annoyance nor passively sulking, which simply rehearses your reasons for being angry.

3. Form a self-help group with others who have been through similar experiences with anger. The other people will likely know what you are feeling and together you might come up with some good solutions to anger problems.

4. Take action to help others, which can put your own miseries in perspective, as exemplified in the actions of the women who organized Mothers Against Drunk Drivers, or other people who work to change conditions so that others will not suffer what they did.

5. Seek ways of breaking out of your usual perspective. Some people have been rehearsing their "story" for years, repeating over and over the reasons for their anger. Retelling the story from other participants' points of view often helps individuals to find routes to empathy.

Let not the sun go down on your wrath.
—**Ephesians 4:26**

The Nature of Stress, Biological Factors, and Emotional Factors

Stress is the way we respond to circumstances that threaten us and tax our coping abilities. To understand stress we need to know about the following factors: biological and emotional, personality, cognitive, environmental, sociocultural, and coping.

The autonomic nervous system consists of the sympathetic nervous system, which arouses the body, and the parasympathetic nervous system, which calms the body. A number of important bodily reactions result from the action of the autonomic nervous system on the endocrine glands, which release their chemical products into the bloodstream. The endocrine glands manufacture hormones, chemical messengers that travel in the bloodstream to all parts of the body. The adrenal glands, located just above the kidneys, play an important role in our ability to cope with stress, in our moods, and in our energy. Each adrenal gland secretes epinephrine (adrenaline) and norepinephrine (noradrenaline).

Selye's general adaptation syndrome (GAS) is a model of the common effects of stress on the body. Selye describes stress as the wear and tear on the body due to the demands placed on it. The GAS involves three stages—alarm, resistance, and exhaustion. Not all stress is bad—Selye calls good stress eustress. Critics argue that humans do not always respond as uniformly as Selye envisioned and that we also need to know about such factors as the individual's coping strategies.

Psychoneuroimmunology explores the connections among psychological factors, the nervous system, and the immune system. Biological pathways that connect stress and illness include stress-mediated immune responses and stress-mediated health effects. Behavioral pathways that link stress and illness include health behaviors and compliance. A number of interventions have been successful in improving the quality of life of individuals with illnesses, including cancer patients and individuals with AIDS.

When we experience stress, we often react emotionally, especially displaying negative emotions such as fear and anger. Emotions are feelings, or affect, that involve a mixture of physiological arousal, conscious experience, and overt behavior. We experience a wide range of emotions. Plutchik believes that emotions are positive or negative, are primary or mixed, come in bipolar opposites, and vary in intensity. Self-esteem, a good marriage or love relationship, social contacts, regular exercise, the ability to sleep well, and religious faith are related to happiness. Positive emotions like happiness are more likely to increase generosity, eagerness, expansiveness, and free-flowing use of one's resources than are negative emotions like sadness. Anger is a powerful emotion that has a strong influence not only on social relationships, but also on the person experiencing the anger. Most psychologists consider catharsis to be an ineffective way of coping with angry feelings. Tavris suggests the following strategies for controlling anger: waiting, not being chronically angry over every little bothersome annoyance or passively sulking, forming a self-help group with others who have been through similar experiences with anger, taking action to help others, and seeking ways of breaking out of a usual perspective.

PERSON FACTORS IN STRESS

Both personality and cognitive factors influence how we respond to stress. We will consider each of these factors in turn.

Personality Factors

Do you have certain personality characteristics that help you cope effectively with stress? Do other characteristics make you more vulnerable to stress? Three important candidates are the Type A behavior pattern, the Type C personality, and hardiness.

Type A Behavior Pattern

In the late 1950s a secretary for two California cardiologists, Meyer Friedman and Ray Rosenman, observed that the chairs in their waiting rooms were tattered and worn, but only on the front edge. The cardiologists had noticed the impatience of their cardiac patients, who often arrived exactly on time for an appointment and were in a great hurry to leave. Subsequently they conducted a study of 3,000 healthy men between the ages of 35 and 59 over a period of 8 years (Friedman & Rosenman, 1974). During the 8 years, one group of men had twice as many heart attacks or other forms of heart disease as anyone else. Autopsies of the men who died revealed that this same group had coronary arteries that were more obstructed than other men. Friedman and Rosenman described the coronary-disease group as characterized by **Type A behavior pattern,** *a cluster of characteristics—being excessively competitive, hard-driven, impatient, and hostile—thought to be related to the incidence of heart disease.*

However, further research on the link between Type A behavior and coronary disease indicates that the association is not as strong as Friedman and Rosenman believed (Williams, 1995). Researchers have examined the different components of Type A behavior, such as hostility, to determine a more precise link with coronary risk (Dolezal, Davison, & DeQuattro, 1996; Faber & Burns, 1996). People who are hostile or consistently turn anger inward, it turns out, are more likely to develop heart disease (Allan & Scheidt, 1996). Such people have been labeled "hot reactors," meaning they have intense physiological

CRITICAL THINKING

Diagnosing Type A Behavior

You have probably encountered many individuals who could be regarded by psychologists as having a classic Type A personality. When the secretary of cardiologists Meyer Friedman and Ray Rosenman noticed that their waiting room chairs were wearing out quickly, the doctors inferred that there must be some greater significance to this unusual pattern of wear, related to their patients' personality. They described the Type A behavior pattern to explain the damage to their furniture.

See if you can think of other behaviors that might tip you off to the presence of Type A personality. What are some common situations in which "hot reactors" reveal themselves? For example, what behaviors would a Type A college student exhibit? Your ability to diagnose Type A personality patterns demonstrates your ability to *make careful observations and interpretations of behavior.*

reactions to stress—their hearts race, their breathing quickens, and their muscles tense up—which could lead to heart disease. Redford Williams (1995), a leading researcher in charting the behavioral and psychological dimensions of heart disease, believes each of us has the ability to control our anger and develop more trust in others, which he believes will reduce the risk for heart disease. To explore Type A behavior in college settings, see Critical Thinking.

Type C Behavior

Type C behavior *refers to the cancer-prone personality, which consists in being inhibited, uptight, emotionally inexpressive, and otherwise constrained.* Some researchers believe that this type of person is more likely to develop cancer than more expressive people are (Temoshok & Dreher, 1992). The concept of Type C behavior fits with the findings of stress and health researchers that holding in one's problems and being inhibited about talking with others about problems can impair one's health.

Hardiness

Hardiness *is a personality style characterized by a sense of commitment (rather*

than alienation), control (rather than powerlessness), and a perception of problems as challenges (rather than threats). In the Chicago Stress Project, male business managers 32 to 65 years of age were studied over a 5-year period. During the 5 years, most of the managers experienced stressful events, such as divorce, job transfers, the death of a close friend, inferior performance evaluations at work, and working at a job with an unpleasant boss. In one study, managers who developed an illness (ranging from the flu to a heart attack) were compared with those who did not (Kobasa, Maddi, & Kahn, 1982). The latter group was more likely to have a hardy personality. Another study investigated whether or not hardiness along with exercise and social support buffered stress and reduced illness in executives' lives (Kobasa & others, 1985). When all three factors were present in an executive's life, the level of illness dropped dramatically. This suggests the power of multiple buffers of stress, rather than a single buffer, in maintaining health. Still at issue, however, is the significance of the various components of hardiness.

Cognitive Factors

Most of us think of stress as environmental events that place demands on our lives, such as losing one's notes from a class, being yelled at by a friend, failing a test, or being in a car wreck. While there are some common ways we all experience stress, not everyone perceives the same events as stressful. For example, one person may perceive an upcoming job interview as threatening, while another person may perceive it as challenging. One person may perceive a D grade on a paper as threatening, another person may perceive the same grade as challenging. To some degree, then, what is stressful depends on how people cognitively appraise and interpret events. This view has been championed by Richard Lazarus (1991; Lazarus & Folkman, 1984). **Cognitive appraisal** *is Lazarus' term for individuals' interpretation of events in their lives as harmful, threatening, or challenging, and their determination of whether they have the resources to effectively cope with the events.* In Lazarus' view, events are appraised in two steps: primary appraisal and secondary appraisal.

Primary Appraisal

In **primary appraisal,** *individuals interpret whether an event involves harm or loss that has already occurred, a threat of some future danger, or a challenge to be overcome. Harm* is the individual's appraisal of the damage the event has already inflicted. For example, if you overslept yesterday and missed an exam, the harm has already been done.

Threat is the individual's appraisal of potential future damage an event may bring. For example, missing the exam may lower the instructor's opinion of you and increase the probability you will get a low grade in the course at the end of the semester. *Challenge* is the individual's appraisal of the potential to overcome the adverse circumstances of an event and ultimately to profit from it. For example, a student may use missing the exam as an opportunity to become acquainted with the instructor and actually benefit academically from what initially appeared to be a hopelessly bad circumstance.

The ultimate measure of a man is not where he stands in moments of comfort and convenience, but where he stands at times of challenge and controversy.
—**Martin Luther King, Jr.**

Secondary Appraisal

After individuals cognitively appraise an event for its harm, threat, or challenge, Lazarus says that they subsequently engage in secondary appraisal. In **secondary appraisal,** *individuals evaluate their resources and determine how effectively they can be used to cope with the event.* This appraisal is called *secondary* because it comes after primary appraisal and depends on the degree to which the event has been appraised as harmful, threatening, or challenging. Coping involves a wide range of potential strategies, skills, and abilities for effectively

managing stressful events. In the example of missing an exam, if you learn that a makeup will be given 2 days later, you may not experience much stress since you already have studied for the exam and have several additional days to study for it. But if the instructor says that you have to write a lengthy paper for missing the test, you may cognitively appraise your situation and determine that this additional requirement places considerable demands on your time and wonder whether you will be able to meet the requirement. In this case, your secondary appraisal indicates a more stressful situation than simply having to take a makeup test several days later (Sears, Peplau, & Taylor, 1997).

Lazarus believes an individual's experience of stress is a balance of primary and secondary appraisal. When harm and threat are high, and challenge and resources are low, stress is likely to be high; when harm and threat are low, and challenge and resources are high, stress is more likely to be low.

We will discuss cognitive factors in much greater detail in chapter 5 as we examine the nature of coping. Next, we study the important roles that environmental and sociocultural factors play in stress.

CONTEXTUAL FACTORS IN STRESS

The contexts we live in strongly influence how we experience stress. In this section we will examine environmental and sociocultural factors in stress reactions.

REVIEW

Person Factors in Stress

Personality factors that are related to stress include Type A behavior and hardiness. Type A behavior pattern refers to a cluster of characteristics—being excessively competitive, hard-driven, impatient, and hostile—thought to be related to heart disease. The Type A pattern is controversial, with some researchers arguing that only specific components of the cluster, such as hostility, are associated with heart disease. Type C behavior refers to the cancer-prone personality, which consists of being inhibited, uptight, lacking in emotional expressiveness, and otherwise constrained. Hardiness is a personality style characterized by a sense of commitment and control, and a perception of problems as challenges rather than threats. Hardiness buffers stress and is related to reduced illness.

Lazarus believes stress depends on how individuals cognitively appraise and interpret events. Cognitive appraisal is Lazarus' term that describes individuals' interpretation of events in their lives as harmful, threatening, or challenging (primary appraisal), and their determination of whether they have the resources to effectively cope with the event (secondary appraisal).

Stress can exist in dramatically different contexts. For example, life on the farm can be stressful due to economic hardship and social isolation. In one investigation, economic hardship in Iowa brought on by crisis in the agricultural industry was associated with inconsistent parenting, as well as increased drug use by adolescents (Lempers, Clarke-Lempers, & Simons, 1989). Contexts that are geared toward technology can also be stressful. Sometimes stimuli become so intense that we become overloaded and can cope no longer. In today's information age, we are especially faced with information overload. It is easy to develop the overwhelming feeling that we don't know as much about a topic as we should, a circumstance that produces what has been dubbed "information anxiety."

Environmental Factors

Many circumstances, large and small, can produce stress in our lives. In some instances, cataclysmic events such as war, an automobile accident, a fire, or the death of a loved one produce stress. In others, the everyday pounding of being overloaded with work, of being frustrated in an unhappy relationship, or of living in poverty produce stress. What makes some situations stressful and others less so?

Conflict, Frustration, and Overload

Environments often create conflict. Conflict occurs when we must decide between two or more incompatible stimuli. Three major types of conflict are approach/approach, avoidance/avoidance, and approach/avoidance. The **approach/approach conflict** *is a conflict in which the individual must choose between two attractive stimuli or circumstances.* Should you go to a movie or watch a video at home? Do you buy a Probe or a Miata? The approach/approach conflict is the least stressful of the three types of conflict because either choice leads to a positive result, even though choosing one over the other means you miss out on the positive experience of the other.

The **avoidance/avoidance conflict** *is a conflict in which the individual must choose between two unattractive stimuli or circumstances.* Will you go to the dentist to

have a bad tooth pulled or endure the toothache? Do you go through the stress of giving an oral presentation in class or not show up and get a zero? You want to avoid both, but in each case, you must choose one. Obviously these conflicts are more stressful than having the luxury of having two enticing choices. In many instances, we delay our decision about the avoidance/avoidance conflict until the last possible moment, perhaps in hopes that other options will present themselves.

The **approach/avoidance conflict** *is a conflict involving a single stimulus or circumstance that has both positive and negative characteristics.* Let's say you really like the person you are going with and are thinking about getting married. On the one hand, you are attracted by the steady affection and love that marriage might bring, but, on the other hand, marriage is a commitment you might not feel ready to make. You look at a menu and face a dilemma—the double chocolate delight would be sumptuous, but is it worth the extra pound of weight? Our world is full of approach/avoidance conflicts and they can be highly stressful. In these circumstances, we often vacillate before deciding (Miller, 1959).

Frustration is another circumstance that produces stress. **Frustration** *refers to any situation in which a person cannot reach a desired goal.* If we want something and cannot have it, we feel frustrated.

Our world is full of frustrations that build up to make our life more stressful—not having enough money to buy the car we want, not getting promoted at work, not getting an A average, being delayed for an important appointment by traffic, and being rejected by a friend. Failures and losses are especially frustrating—not getting grades that are high enough to get into medical school or losing someone we are closely attached to through death, for example. Sometimes the frustrations we experience are major life events, as in the cases of divorce and death. At other times, the accumulation of daily hassles may make us feel as though we're being nibbled to death by ducks.

Responses to frustration vary. When something blocks you from achieving a desired goal or outcome, you can change your goal and *give up*. You can *devalue* the goal. You can *circumvent* the frustration by reaching the goal using some other path. You can *aggress* against the frustration, which might or might not lead to the desired goal. Finally, you can *persist* on the same path toward your goal, gradually adapting to the frustration or eroding the frustrating elements of the situation. In this light, it is easy to understand the positive aspect of frustration. Learning to cope with frustrating circumstances can help us learn to delay gratification and develop patience. To explore grade frustration, turn to Critical Thinking.

CRITICAL THINKING

Making (or Remaking) the Grade

You studied all night for the exam. You thought you knew the material. The questions seemed a little tricky, but you finished the test and turned it in. When you got back a *D*, you were extremely frustrated. Can you apply the principles involved in frustration to predict some probable outcomes in this frustrating circumstance? Which option would you really choose?

- You could withdraw from the class and abandon the goal.
- You could persist in the course and commit to studying even harder.
- You could devalue the experience by making hostile comments in public about the professor's ability to create valid questions.

- You could physically aggress against the source of the frustration—the professor. (Bad idea.)
- You could attempt to switch sections of the course or ask to do work for extra credit, continuing to pursue the goal, by way of a different path.

Note that some of these responses, which demonstrate your ability to *apply psychological concepts to enhance personal adaptation*, are clearly more adaptive than others.

Overload *happens when stimuli become so intense that we can no longer cope with them.* For example, persistent high levels of noise overload our adaptability. Overload can occur with work as well. How often have you said to yourself, "There are not enough hours in the day to do all I have to do"? In today's computer age, we are especially faced with information overload. It is easy to develop the stressful feeling that we don't know as much about a topic as we should, even if we are a so-called expert.

Today the buzzword for overload is **burnout,** *a hopeless, helpless feeling brought about by relentless work-related stress. Burnout leaves its sufferers in a state of physical and emotional exhaustion that includes chronic fatigue and low energy.* Burnout usually occurs not because of one or two traumatic events but because of a gradual accumulation of heavy, work-related stress. Burnout is most likely to occur among individuals who deal with others in highly emotional situations (such as nurses and social workers) but have only limited control over altering their clients'/patients' outcomes.

On a number of college campuses, burnout (which reaches a rate of 25 percent at some schools) is the most frequent reason students leave school before earning their degrees. Dropping out of college for a semester or two used to be considered a sign of weakness. Now it is more accepted and is sometimes called "stopping out" because the student fully intends to return; counselors may actually encourage some students who feel overwhelmed with stress to take a break from college. Before recommending "stopping out," though, most counselors first suggest that the student examine ways to reduce overload and possible coping strategies that would allow the student to remain in school. The simple strategy of taking a reduced or better-balanced class load sometimes works, for example. Most college counseling services have professionals who can effectively work with students to alleviate the sense of being overloaded and overwhelmed by life.

Life Events and Daily Hassles

Think about your life. What events have created the most stress for you? A change in financial status, getting fired at work, a divorce, the death of someone you loved, a personal injury? And what about the everyday circumstances of your life? What hassles you the most? Not having enough time to study, arguing with your girlfriend or boyfriend, not getting enough credit for the work you do at your job?

Petty ills try the temper worse than great ones.
—Ellen Wood (1813–1887)

Researchers have proposed that significant life events are a major source of stress and loosely have linked such life events with illnesses. The effects of individual life events, such as a tornado or volcanic eruption, can be evaluated, or the effects of *clusters* of events can be studied. Thomas Holmes and Richard Rahe (1967) devised a scale to measure clusters of life events and their possible impact on illness in the context of the United States. Their widely used Social Readjustment Rating Scale includes events ranging from the death of a spouse (100 stress points) to minor violations of the law (11 stress points). To test yourself on Holmes and Rahe's Social Readjustment Rating Scale, see the Self-Assessment box.

People who experience clusters of stressful life events, such as divorce, being fired from a job, or sexual difficulties, are more likely to become ill. However, the ability to predict illness from life events alone is modest. Total scores on life-events scales such as the Social Readjustment Rating Scale are frequently

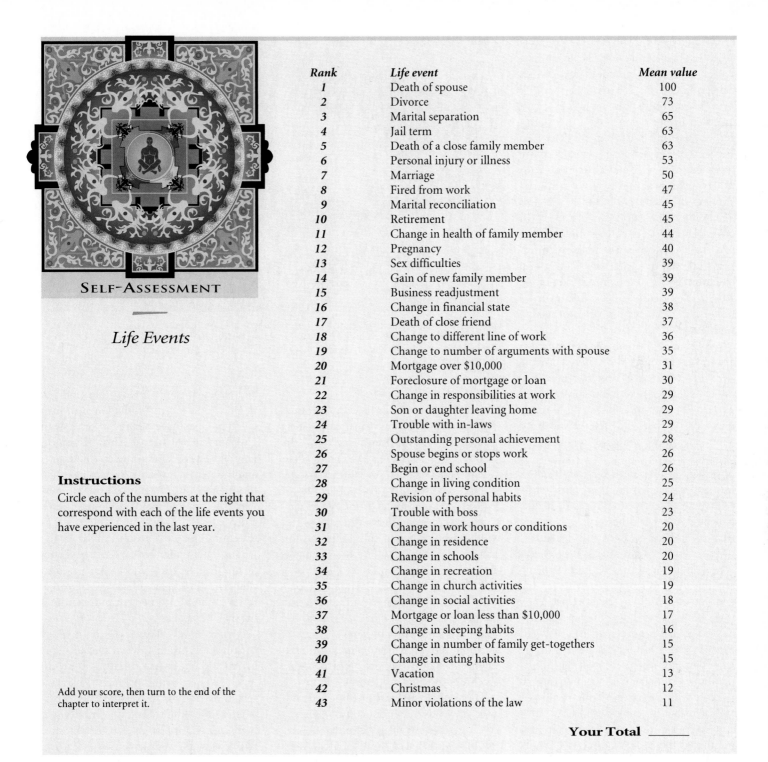

SELF-ASSESSMENT

Life Events

Instructions

Circle each of the numbers at the right that correspond with each of the life events you have experienced in the last year.

Add your score, then turn to the end of the chapter to interpret it.

Rank	Life event	Mean value
1	Death of spouse	100
2	Divorce	73
3	Marital separation	65
4	Jail term	63
5	Death of a close family member	63
6	Personal injury or illness	53
7	Marriage	50
8	Fired from work	47
9	Marital reconciliation	45
10	Retirement	45
11	Change in health of family member	44
12	Pregnancy	40
13	Sex difficulties	39
14	Gain of new family member	39
15	Business readjustment	39
16	Change in financial state	38
17	Death of close friend	37
18	Change to different line of work	36
19	Change to number of arguments with spouse	35
20	Mortgage over $10,000	31
21	Foreclosure of mortgage or loan	30
22	Change in responsibilities at work	29
23	Son or daughter leaving home	29
24	Trouble with in-laws	29
25	Outstanding personal achievement	28
26	Spouse begins or stops work	26
27	Begin or end school	26
28	Change in living condition	25
29	Revision of personal habits	24
30	Trouble with boss	23
31	Change in work hours or conditions	20
32	Change in residence	20
33	Change in schools	20
34	Change in recreation	19
35	Change in church activities	19
36	Change in social activities	18
37	Mortgage or loan less than $10,000	17
38	Change in sleeping habits	16
39	Change in number of family get-togethers	15
40	Change in eating habits	15
41	Vacation	13
42	Christmas	12
43	Minor violations of the law	11

Your Total _____

ineffective at predicting future health problems. A life-events checklist tells us nothing about a person's physiological makeup, constitutional strengths and weaknesses, ability to cope with stressful circumstances, support systems, or the nature of the social relationships involved—all of which are important in understanding how stress is related to illness. A divorce, for example, might be less stressful than a marriage filled with day-to-day tension. In addition the Holmes-Rahe scale includes positive events, such as marital reconciliation and gaining a new family member, which can also create stressors that must be faced. However, the changes that result from positive events are not as difficult to cope with as the changes that result from negative events.

Psychologists increasingly consider the nature of daily hassles and daily uplifts to gain better insight about the nature of stress (Lazarus & Folkman, 1984; Pillow, Zautra, & Sandler, 1996). It might be that the primary sources of stress are not life's major events but, rather, our daily experiences. Enduring a boring but tense job or marriage and living in poverty do not show up on scales of major life events; yet the everyday tension involved in these living conditions adds up to a highly stressful life and in some cases psychological disturbance or illness.

How about your own life? What are the biggest hassles? One study showed that the most frequent daily hassles of college students were wasting time, being lonely, and worrying about meeting high achievement standards (Kanner & others, 1981). In fact, the fear of failing in our success-oriented world often plays a role in college students' depression. College students also found that the small things in life—having fun, laughing, going to movies, getting along well with friends, and completing a task—were their main sources of feeling uplifted.

Critics of the daily-hassles approach argue that some of the same problems with life-events scales occur when assessing daily hassles (Dohrenwend & Shrout, 1985). For example, knowing about a person's daily hassles tells us nothing about the body's resilience to stress, the person's coping ability or strategies, or how that person perceives stress. Further, the hassles scale has not been consistently related to objective measures of health and illness. Yet another criticism is that hassles can be conceived of as dependent measures rather than causes. People who complain about things, who report being anxious and unhappy, and who see the bad side of everything see more hassles in their daily lives. From this perspective, hassles don't predict bad moods; bad moods predict hassles. Supporters of the daily hassles concept contend that information about daily hassles can be used in concert with information about physiological reactions, coping, and how stress is perceived to provide a more complete picture of the causes and consequences of stress.

Sociocultural Factors

Sociocultural factors influence the stressors we are likely to encounter, our perception of events as stressful or not, and our expectations about whether to confront or avoid the stressors (Chang, 1996; Liebkind, 1996). The sociocultural factors that we will explore are acculturative stress, socioeconomic status, and gender.

Vonnie McLoyd (*right*) has conducted a number of important investigations of the roles of poverty, ethnicity, and unemployment in children's and adolescents' development. She has found that economic stressors often diminish children's and adolescents' belief in the utility of education and their achievement strivings.

Acculturative Stress

Cultural subgroups in the United States can find contacts with mainstream society stressful. **Acculturation** *refers to cultural change that results from continuous, first-hand contact between two distinct cultural groups.* **Acculturative stress** *refers to the negative consequences of acculturation.*

Some researchers argue that individuals who belong to cultural subgroups can successfully negotiate the challenge of the subgroup as well as mainstream culture (LaFromboise, Coleman, & Gerton, 1993). They propose an **alternation model,** *according to which individuals can develop bicultural competence without choosing one group over another or diminishing their own subgroup identification.* According to this model, their ability to adapt to different contexts can confer advantages over their monocultural peers.

Cross-cultural psychologists have established that acculturation effects are a factor in the development of coronary problems, emphasizing the role that culture plays in stress and health. As ethnic groups migrate, the health practices dictated by their cultures change while their genetic predisposition to certain disorders remains constant (Ilola, 1990). The Ni-Hon-San Study (Nipon-Honolulu-San Francisco), part of the Honolulu Heart Study, is an ongoing study of approximately 12,000 Japanese men in Hiroshima and Nagasaki (Japan), Honolulu, and San Francisco. In the study, the Japanese men living in Japan have had the lowest rate of coronary heart disease, those living in Honolulu have had an intermediate rate, and those living in San Francisco have had the highest rate. Acculturation explains why the Japanese men's cholesterol level, glucose level, and weight all increased as they migrated and acculturated. As the Japanese men migrated farther away from Japan, their health practices, such as diet, changed. The Japanese men in California, for example, ate 40 percent more fat than the men in Japan.

Conversely, Japanese men in California have much lower rates of cerebrovascular disease (stroke) than do Japanese men living in Japan. Businessmen in Japan tend to consume vast quantities of alcohol and chain-smoke, two high-risk factors for stroke. As a result, stroke was the leading cause of death in Japan until it was surpassed by cancer in 1981. However, death rates from stroke for Japanese American men are the same as for Anglo-American men. Researchers suspect that this level is related to a change in behavior. That is, Japanese American men consume less alcohol and smoke less than do their counterparts in Japan. To read more about stress in ethnic minority individuals, see Sociocultural Worlds of Adjustment.

SOCIOCULTURAL WORLDS OF ADJUSTMENT

The Acculturative Stress of Ethnic Minority Group Individuals

As upwardly mobile ethnic minority families attempt to penetrate historically all-White neighborhoods, interracial tensions often mount (Huang & Gibbs, 1989). While many Americans think of racial tensions and prejudice largely as Black/White issues, this no longer is the case. Racial tensions and hostility often emerge among the various ethnic minorities as each struggles for housing and employment opportunities, seeking a fair share of these limited markets. Clashes become inevitable as Korean stores spring up in African American urban neighborhoods; as Vietnamese extended families displace Puerto Rican apartment dwellers; as the increasing enrollment of Asian students on college campuses is perceived by other ethnic minority students as a threat to affirmative action.

Although the dominant White society has on many occasions tried to enslave or dispossess entire populations, these ethnic minority groups have survived and flourished. In the face of severe stress and oppression, these groups have shown remarkable resilience and adaptation by developing their own communities and social structures such as African American churches, Vietnamese mutual assistance associations, Chinese-American family associations, Japanese-language schools, Indian "bands" and tribal associations, and Mexican American kin systems. In addition, they have learned to negotiate with the dominant White culture. They essentially have mastered two cultures and have developed impressive strategies for adapting to life in America. The resilience and adaptation of ethnic minority groups provide evidence about the value and importance of coping and survival in the face of overwhelming adversity.

To help buffer the stress in their lives, many ethnic minority groups have developed their own social structures, which include Mexican American kin systems, African American churches, Chinese American family associations, and Native American tribal associations. Shown above are members of a Chinese American family association.

Socioeconomic Status

Poverty imposes considerable stress on individuals and families (Hoff-Ginsburg & Tardif, 1995; Huston, 1995). Chronic conditions such as inadequate housing, dangerous neighborhoods, burdensome responsibilities, and economic uncertainties are potent stressors in the lives of the poor (Chase-Lansdale & Brooks-Gunn, 1996). Ethnic minority families are disproportionately among the poor. For example, Puerto Rican families headed by women are 15 times more likely to live in poverty than are families headed by White men. Similarly, families headed by African American women are ten times more likely to live in poverty than are families headed by White men (National Advisory Council on Economic Opportunity, 1980). Many people who become poor during their lives remain so for only 1 or 2 years. However, African Americans and female heads of household are especially at risk for persistent poverty. The average poor African American child experiences poverty that will last almost 20 years (Wilson & Neckerman, 1986).

Poverty is also related to threatening and uncontrollable life events. For example, poor women are more likely to experience crime and violence than middle-class women are (Belle & others, 1981). Poverty undermines sources of social support that play a role in buffering the effects of stress. Poverty is related to marital unhappiness and to having spouses who are unlikely to serve as confidants. Further, poverty means having to depend on many overburdened and often unresponsive bureaucratic systems for financial, housing, and health assistance that may contribute to a poor person's feelings of powerlessness.

No human emotion can transcend the social conditions around it.
—Zhang Jie

Gender

Another sociocultural factor that plays a role in stress is gender. In the United States men and women differ in their longevity. Although men appear to have lower morbidity (fewer illness problems), they die younger than women. Life expectancy for men is 72 years; women can expect to live on the average of 79 years. Men and women tend to succumb to the same illnesses. Heart disease is the primary killer for both sexes.

Women and men have always had multiple roles, but researchers have found that women experience more conflict among roles and overload than men do (McBride, 1990). An important gender difference occurs in family responsibilities, which are detailed in chapter 10. Remember that even when both spouses work, wives perform a disproportionate share of child care and household tasks. Interestingly, in spite of all the strain, the more roles a woman juggles, the healthier she seems to be. Women who take on varied roles benefit from new sources of self-esteem, control, and social support, which, in turn, may improve both their mental and physical health (Rodin & Ickovics, 1990).

The nature and quality of a woman's experiences within a role are also important considerations in understanding stress and health. For example, roles with time constraints, irregular schedules, and little autonomy may jeopardize health. Therefore, women clerical workers, in particular, are more prone to health problems than other working women are. In fact, contrary to the cultural belief that a high-powered career is more stressful to a woman's well-being, it seems that the more authority and autonomy a woman has on the job, the greater her sense of well-being.

Researchers are especially interested in how women's stress and health are affected by working outside of the home in demanding careers. In almost all studies, employed women are healthier than nonemployed women (LaCroix & Haynes, 1987). Researchers have found that women who stay at home and who perceive their lives as stressful and unhappy, who feel extremely vulnerable, and who engage in little physical activity are especially at risk for health problems (Verbrugge, 1989).

Determining why nonemployment is associated with higher stress levels is difficult—much like figuring out the causality in the old chicken-and-egg question. It may be that employment directly promotes health and reduces risk for women. On the other hand, it may be that women in poor health are unable to obtain or keep jobs.

Earlier in our discussion of social class and stress, we found that poverty is associated with increased stress and poorer health. Women are disproportionately among the poor. What's more, poor women face the double jeopardy of poverty and sexism. For example, women are paid less than men and are often denied opportunities to work because of their sex. The term **feminization of poverty** *refers to the fact that far more women than men live in poverty. Women's low incomes, divorce, and the ways divorce cases are resolved by the judicial system are the likely causes of the feminization of poverty.* Approximately one of every two marriages today will end in a divorce, meaning that far more women today than in the past must support themselves and, in many cases, one or more children as well. Further, women today are far less likely to receive alimony, or spousal support, than in the past. Even when alimony or child-support payments are awarded to a woman, they are poorly enforced.

As we saw in our discussion of socioeconomic status, ethnic minority women have especially high rates of poverty. These women face the extremely stressful triple jeopardy of poverty, racism, and sexism. Researchers must turn their attention to the mental health risks that accompany poverty and to ways that poor people, especially women, can cope more effectively with stress.

At this point, we have discussed the biological, cognitive, personality, environmental, and sociocultural factors involved in stress. In the next chapter, we will see that it also is extremely important to understand how to cope with stress.

Contextual Factors in Stress

Conflict, frustration, and overload can lead to stress. Stress can be produced because stimuli become so intense and prolonged we cannot cope. Three types of conflict are approach/approach, avoidance/avoidance, and approach/avoidance. Frustration occurs when we cannot reach our goal. Stress also may be produced by major life events or daily hassles. Life events lists tell us nothing about how individuals cope with stress, their body strengths and weaknesses, and other important dimensions of stress. Daily hassles provide a more focused look, but their evaluation should include information about a person's coping ability and physical characteristics.

Acculturation is cultural change that results from continuous, first-hand contact between two distinct cultural groups. Acculturative stress is the negative consequences of acculturation. The resilience and adaptation of ethnic minority groups can teach us much about coping and survival in the face of overwhelming adversity. Poverty imposes considerable stress on individuals. Chronic conditions such as inadequate housing, dangerous neighborhoods, burdensome responsibilities, and economic uncertainties are potent stressors in the lives of the poor. The incidence of poverty is especially high in ethnic minority families.

Gender is also a sociocultural determinant of stress. Of special interest is how the increased participation by women in the work force has influenced their stress and health. Employment is associated with increased health among women. Even though women experience more conflict between roles and overload than men, women who engage in multiple roles tend to be healthier because multiple roles expand potential resources and rewards. Low-quality roles, such as being a clerical worker, decreases women's health. Special concerns are the feminization of poverty and poverty among ethnic minority women.

CRITICAL THINKING ABOUT ADJUSTMENT

All Stressed Up and Too Many Places to Go

We began this chapter with the story of Mort, whose life was seriously strained by a variety of stressors. Mort's score of 68 on the stress test in table 4.1 diagnosed him as "seriously vulnerable" to stress. How high was your score? How vulnerable are you?

Well-constructed testing devices offer us an effective, systematic way *to make accurate observations, descriptions, and inferences about behavior.* For each test item, you indicated the degree to which the situation addressed by the item could contribute to your overall reactivity to stress; in effect, each item becomes a stress-related observation. The sum of your ratings produced your stress score.

Now what? If your test score suggests that you are vulnerable to stress, what kinds of predictions do you think you can make about your future physical and mental health? Have you already demonstrated particular patterns of "malfunctioning" that could be linked to the high degree of stress that you have reported?

After reading this chapter, you should have a framework for understanding your current stress levels as you work to succeed in college. Many students find that college life is a period of extraordinary, tightly scheduled stressors, and many simply don't survive it. How are you doing?

To what degree do physiological concerns contribute to the stress that you perceive in managing all that you must in order to succeed in college? Which biological systems tend to fall victim to the strains in your life? Have you noticed an increase in your vulnerability to colds and flu, especially around periods when exams and papers become more intense?

How do your personality characteristics and cognitive appraisal skills influence your ability to perform? Have you managed to maintain or to develop a sense of hardiness to sustain you through the taxing times? Can you accurately evaluate substantial threats to your self-esteem and deal with them in positive ways, or do you become preoccupied with any slight or missed goal, making it doubly difficult to be successful in the next challenge?

How does context influence your ability to adapt to increasing challenges? Have you determined reasonable ways to vent your frustration and solve problems early in their development, or have you already flirted with burnout? In what ways is your context supportive of your growth and development, and in what ways could it improve? Is there any way that you could pace your work more effectively, or does attention to scheduling actually interfere with the quality of your life?

This exercise encourages you *to practice self-reflection to enhance adaptation and growth.* You may be intrigued to compare the strategies you have already developed to be successful in a college setting with the ones that are described in the next chapter on coping.

Of course there is no formula for success except, perhaps, an unconditional acceptance of life and what it brings.

—**Arthur Rubinstein**

We began this chapter by exploring the biological and emotional factors involved in stress. The biological factors included the autonomic nervous system, endocrine system, general adaptation syndrome, and immune system. Our discussion of emotional factors focused on defining emotion, classifying emotion, happiness, and anger. Our coverage of person factors emphasized personality factors, such as the Type A behavior pattern, Type C behavior pattern, and hardiness, and cognitive factors, such as primary and secondary appraisal. Contexual factors involved in stress include environmental factors (such as frustration, conflict, and overload) as well as life events and daily hassles, and sociocultural factors (such as acculturative stress, socioeconomic status, and gender). Don't forget that you can obtain an overall summary of the chapter by again studying the in-chapter reviews on pages 86, 88, and 95.

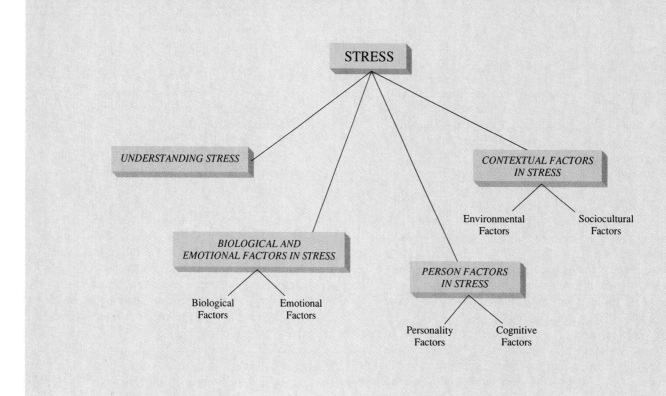

PRACTICAL KNOWLEDGE ABOUT ADJUSTMENT

THE DANCE OF ANGER

(1985) by Harriet Lerner. New York: Harper Perennial.

The Dance of Anger was written mainly for women about the anger in their lives, both theirs and that of the people they live with, especially the men. Lerner believes that women have more difficulty coping with anger than men do. She says that expressions of anger are not only encouraged more in boys and men, but may be glorified to maladaptive extremes. In contrast, girls and women have been denied even the healthy and realistic expression of anger. Lerner argues that to express anger—especially openly, directly, or loudly—has been taken as making a woman unladylike, unfeminine, unmaternal, and sexually unattractive. Society has taught women to be passive and quiet, not angry. Many women fear that if they express anger, they will rock the relationship boat. Lerner not only explains the difficulties women have in getting angry, but how to use their anger to gain a stronger, more independent sense of self. Numerous patterns of anger in intimate relationships are discussed in *The Dance of Anger*.

Rooted in both family systems and psychoanalytic theory, *The Dance of Anger* discusses styles of managing anger that don't work for women in the long run—silent submission, ineffective fighting and blaming, and emotional distancing. She also paints the cultural context of an American society that has created these ineffective styles in women, and she motivates women to develop the courage to change these old, protective ways.

FLOW

(1990) by Mihaly Csikszentmihalyi. New York: Harper & Row.

Flow is about the optimal experiencing of life. Csikszentmihalyi (pronounced "chik-sent-me-high-yee") has been investigating the concept of flow for more than 2 decades. Earlier in the chapter we discussed the author's view of what flow is, namely a deep happiness people feel when they have a sense of mastering something. Flow is a state of concentration in which a person becomes absorbed while engaging in an activity. We can develop flow by setting challenges for ourselves, by stretching ourselves to the limits to achieve something worthwhile, by developing competent coping skills, and by combining life's many experiences into a meaningful pattern. Flow is the antidote of the twin evils of boredom and anxiety, says Csikszentmihalyi.

SELF-ASSESSMENT SCORING AND INTERPRETATION

ANGER

If a majority of the statements describe you, you likely would benefit from working on how you handle stressful circumstances. Think about how a more calm, assertive approach would benefit you better than an angry, aggressive approach.

LIFE EVENTS

In this Social Readjustment Scale developed by Holmes and Rahe, the sum is an index of how much life change related to stress you have experienced in this 1-year period. In their original study, Holmes and Rahe (1967) found that a score in the 200s was associated with about

a 50 percent change of illness and that a score of 300 or above was correlated with about an 80 percent chance of illness. Notice that this scale was developed in 1967; a more contemporary version would feature revised entries, such as an increase in the amount of the loan or mortgage figures. Also, as we indicated in our evaluation of the Social Readjustment Scale, the changes that result from positive events are not separated from the changes that result from negative events. Life-events scales don't tell us anything about how the individual copes with stress, the person's support systems, and the person's physical makeup—all factors that influence how stress is experienced. Thus, a high score on the Social Readjustment Scale does not necessarily mean that you will encounter an illness.

John Santrock
Busy Pleasures, detail

Coping

CHAPTER OUTLINE

CRITICAL THINKING ABOUT ADJUSTMENT

CHAPTER BOXES

SOCIOCULTURAL WORLDS OF ADJUSTMENT

CRITICAL THINKING

SELF-ASSESSMENT

*Adapt or perish, now as ever,
is Nature's inexorable imperative.*

—H. G. Wells,
Mind at the End of Its Tether, 1946

THE STORY OF LEARNING GONE AWRY:
BAD GRADES AND BAD STRATEGIES

hink back to the first weeks of this class. You may remember students who used to sit near you, or in front of you, whom you no longer see in class. Where did they go?

The disappearing student is almost inevitable in college classes. Every semester several students typically stop showing up for classes, often after the first exam. They never talk to their instructors about their performance in class. They don't inquire about how they can do better in the course. They usually don't even go through proper procedures for dropping a class. When they avoid the immediate stress of making adaptive changes to succeed in the course, they virtually guarantee that they will later have to face the stressful circumstance of receiving an F at the end of the semester.

The hostile student also ends up being unsuccessful. Sometimes students strike out aggressively when faced with the stress of poor grades. One student who failed a psychology class came to his professor's office and delivered a few choice epithets after he received his grade. The next day he returned to apologize, saying he deserved the F and that he had also failed two other classes. He recognized that he felt compelled to discharge his anger in the heat of the moment. He apologized and left with a clearer conscience as well as a clear understanding of his failing performance.

Manipulative students also run a risk of being unsuccessful in a course due to the nature of the excuses they offer and the demands they make. They might be asked to disappear. Students who try to manipulate the system are people who develop phony excuses to appeal to the professor for sympathy and for a second chance. Their dogs eat their homework, their grandmothers regularly die, and their health is always poor. They rarely take responsibility for their poor performance, and their chronic appeals for exception make professors appropriately suspicious. Such students fail to realize that their energies would be better spent in doing the required work than in dreaming up bids for sympathy.

All three strategies are ineffective attempts to deal with the stresses and strains of college. Retreating, threatening, and manipulating might provide some short-term relief, but they enhance the likelihood of long-term suffering. Part of the implicit curriculum of college is to help you develop effective strategies for managing complex demands.

PREVIEW

This chapter describes effective and ineffective strategies for coping with stress. We will examine many forms of coping that involve either attitudinal or behavioral changes, including developing self-efficacy, thinking positively and optimistically, seeking social supports, increasing self-control, and improving appropriate risk taking. We will also explore various forms of stress management, including meditation and relaxation, biofeedback, assertiveness training, and time management. Part of this chapter's value is that it offers you practical pointers about how to adjust to the pressures of college life.

THE NATURE OF COPING

Coping is an extremely important part of adjustment. Just what do we mean by coping? **Coping** *is the process of managing taxing circumstances, expending effort to solve personal and interpersonal problems, and seeking to master, minimize, reduce, or tolerate stress and conflict.*

Not everyone responds the same way to stress. Some individuals throw in the towel and give up when even the slightest thing goes wrong in their life. Others are motivated to work hard to seek solutions to personal problems and successfully adjust to even extremely taxing circumstances. A stressful event can be rendered considerably less stressful when a person successfully copes with it.

Cognitive Appraisal

In our discussion of stress in chapter 4, we described Richard Lazarus' (1981, 1993) view that cognitive appraisal—interpreting events as harmful, threatening, or challenging, and determining whether one has the resources to effectively cope with the event—is critical to coping. Lazarus also believes that two general types of coping efforts can be distinguished. **Problem-focused coping** *is Lazarus' term for the cognitive strategy of squarely facing one's troubles and trying to solve them.* For example, if you are having trouble with a class, you might go to the study skills center at your college or university and enter a training program to learn how to study more effectively. You have faced your problem and attempted to do something about it. **Emotion-focused coping** *is Lazarus' term for responding to stress in an emotional manner, especially using defensive appraisal.* Emotion-focused coping involves using the defense mechanisms. In emotion-focused coping, we might avoid something, rationalize what has happened to us, deny it is occurring, laugh it off, or call on our religious faith for support. If you use emotion-focused coping, you might avoid going to the class. You might say the class doesn't matter, deny that you are having a problem, laugh and joke about it with your friends, or pray that you will do better. In one study, depressed people used strategies to avoid facing their problems more than people who were not depressed (Ebata & Moos, 1989).

But there are times when emotion-focused coping is adaptive. For example, denial is one of the main protective psychological mechanisms that enables people to cope with the flood of feelings that occur when the reality of death or dying becomes too great. In other circumstances, emotion-focused coping is maladaptive. Denying that the person you were dating doesn't love you any more when that person has actually become engaged to someone else is not

adaptive. Denial can be used to avoid the destructive impact of shock, however, by postponing the time when you have to deal with stress. Over the long term, though, we are usually better off to use problem-focused more than emotion-focused coping.

Many individuals use both problem-focused and emotion-focused coping when adjusting to a stressful circumstance. For example, in one study, individuals said they used both problem-focused and emotion-focused coping strategies in 98 percent of the stressful encounters they face (Folkman & Lazarus, 1980). But aren't there other ways to cope than just using a combination of problem-focused and emotion-focused strategies?

Types of Strategies

Coping strategies can also be categorized as active-cognitive, active-behavioral, and avoidance (Billings & Moos, 1981). **Active-cognitive strategies** *are coping responses in which individuals actively think about a situation in an effort to adjust more effectively.* For example, if you have had a problem that involved breaking up with a girlfriend or a boyfriend, you may have coped by logically reasoning through why you are better off in the long run without her or him. Or you might analyze why the relationship did not work and use this information to help you develop better dating experiences in the future.

Active-behavioral strategies *are coping responses in which individuals take some type of action to improve their problem situation.* To continue the example with dating, individuals who are having problems in dating may take the action of going to their college or university's counseling center, where they might be "coached" to improve their dating skills.

Stress is so abundant in our society that many of us are confronted with more than one stressor at the same time. An extremely valuable active-behavioral strategy for coping with stress is to try to remove at least one of the stressors from our life. For example, a college student might be taking a very heavy course load, not have enough money to eat regularly, and have problems in a close relationship.

Researchers have found that when several stressors are simultaneously experienced, the effects may be compounded (Rutter & Garmezy, 1983). For example, one study found that people who felt besieged by two chronic life stressors were four times more likely to eventually need psychological services than those who had to cope with only one chronic stressor (Rutter, 1979). The student facing the triple whammy of school, financial, and relationship difficulties probably would benefit from removing one of the stressors—for instance, by dropping one class and taking a normal course load.

Avoidance strategies *are responses that individuals use to keep stressful circumstances out of their awareness so they do not have to deal with them.* Everything we know about coping suggests that avoidance strategies are extremely harmful to individuals' adjustment. In the example of having problems in dating, an avoidance strategy is to simply do nothing about it, with the result of never thinking about better ways to cope with dating problems and never taking any actions either. Examples of active-coping, active-behavioral, and avoidance strategies are shown in figure 5.1.

So far we have described two ways to classify coping responses: (1) problem-focused and emotion-focused, and (2) active-cognitive, active-behavioral, and avoidance. In general, of these different ways to cope, problem-focused coping, active-cognitive coping, and active-behavioral coping are the best strategies. Let's explore some other techniques that enhance the individual's ability to cope.

INDIVIDUAL COPING STRATEGIES

Many strategies for coping with stress are relatively simple. Some involve attitude change. Others require taking some kind of action. However, all of these strategies can be implemented without much fuss.

Developing Self-Efficacy

Self-efficacy—*the belief that one can master a situation and produce positive*

The Nature of Coping

There is individual variation in how people cope, but for everyone, coping is an important part of adjustment. Coping is the process of managing taxing circumstances, expending effort to solve personal and interpersonal problems, and seeking to master, minimize, reduce, or tolerate stress. A stressful event can be rendered considerably less stressful when we cope with it.

According to Lazarus, cognitive appraisal and problem-focused coping are important aspects of effectively coping with stress. Problem-focused coping is the strategy of squarely facing troubles and trying to solve them. Emotion-focused coping occurs when individuals respond to stress in an emotional manner, especially using defensive appraisal. Many individuals use both problem-focused and emotion-focused coping when adjusting to a stressful circumstance. Most of the time it is better to use problem-focused rather than emotion-focused coping.

Coping strategies can also be categorized as active-cognitive, active-behavioral, and avoidance. Active-cognitive strategies occur when individuals think about a situation in an effort to adjust more effectively. Active-behavioral strategies occur when individuals take some type of action to improve their problem situation. An extremely valuable active-behavioral strategy is to try to remove at least one of the stressors from our life. Avoidance strategies occur when individuals keep stressful circumstances out of awareness so they don't have to deal with them. Active-cognitive and active-behavioral strategies are preferred coping strategies; avoidance is not.

Active-cognitive strategies

Pray for guidance and/or strength
Prepare for the worst
Try to see the positive side of the situation
Consider several alternatives for handling the problem
Draw on my past experiences
Take things one day at a time
Try to step back from the situation and be more objective
Go over the situation in my mind to try to understand it
Tell myself things that help me feel better
Promise myself that things will be different next time
Accept it; nothing can be done

Active-behavioral strategies

Try to find out more about the situation
Talk with spouse or other relative about the problem
Talk with friend about the problem
Talk with professional person (e.g., doctor, lawyer, clergy)
Get busy with other things to keep my mind off the problem
Make a plan of action and follow it
Try not to act too hastily or follow my first hunch
Get away from things for a while
Know what has to be done and try harder to make things work
Let my feelings out somehow
Seek help from persons or groups with similar experiences
Bargain or compromise to get something positive from the situation
Exercise more

Avoidance strategies

Take it out on other people when I feel angry or depressed
Keep my feelings to myself
Avoid being with people in general
Refuse to believe that it happened
Drink more to reduce tension
Eat more to reduce tension
Smoke more to reduce tension
Take more tranquilizing drugs to reduce tension

FIGURE 5.1

Examples of Active-Cognitive, Active-Behavioral, and Avoidance Coping Strategies in Response to Stress

outcomes—can be an effective strategy in coping with stress and challenging circumstances. Albert Bandura (1986, 1994) and others have shown that people's self-efficacy affects their behavior in a variety of circumstances, ranging from solving personal problems to going on diets. Self-efficacy influences whether people even try to develop healthy habits, how much effort they expend in coping with stress, how long they persist in the face of obstacles, and how much stress they experience.

Let's look at several examples of how self-efficacy might work in coping. Overweight individuals will likely have more success with their diets if they believe they have the self-control to restrict their eating. Smokers who believe they will not be able to break their habit probably won't try to quit smoking, even though they know that smoking is likely to cause poor health and shorten their life.

How can you increase your sense of self-efficacy? The following steps can be helpful (Watson & Tharp, 1989).

First, select something you expect to be able to do, not something you do not expect to accomplish. Later, as your stronger sense of self-efficacy is developed, you can tackle projects that you previously might not have thought possible. For example, a person who wants to remain sober concentrates on not drinking for "one day at a time." Twenty-four hours of sobriety is easier to accomplish than to start by thinking "I can never, ever have a drink again."

Second, distinguish between your past performance and your present project. You might have learned from past failures that you cannot do certain things. It is important to remind yourself that past failures are just that, *in the past,* and that you now have a new sense of confidence and accomplishment. The only value of looking at past failures is to aid in developing a better strategy for now and the future. For example, a person who has repeatedly failed to lose 80 pounds on a diet should avoid thinking "I'll always fail, this weight is just me." On the other hand, by looking at past attempts, the overweight person might learn that failures came after a few days of starvation diets and decide on a strategy of "sensible diet and a half-hour walk each day."

The third step is to keep good records so you can be concretely aware of your successes. Frustrated with being a poorly organized student, Ichiro is trying to keep to a sensible study schedule. After sticking to the study schedule for four days, Ichiro fails to adhere to it on the fifth day. Ichiro starts to call himself a failure, but his record keeping allows him to notice that he actually is experiencing an 80 percent success rate in improving his studying pattern. This example also reflects the fourth step in building self-efficacy—be sure to pay close attention to your successes. Some individuals have a tendency to remember their failures but not their successes.

The fifth step is to make a list of the specific kinds of situations in which you expect to have the most difficulty and the least difficulty. Whenever possible, begin with the easier situations and tasks and cope with the harder situations and tasks after you have experienced some successes in improving self-efficacy and other coping skills.

In sum, the belief that you can cope does not by itself eliminate all problems you might face. But the self-confidence that self-efficacy brings to challenging situations goes a long way toward overcoming difficult problems and allows you to cope with stress less emotionally (Eden & Aviram, in press; Sadry & Robertson, 1993).

Thinking Positively and Optimistically

> The world is round and the place that may seem like the end may also be the beginning.
>
> —Ivy Baker Priest

Thinking positively and avoiding negative thoughts is generally a good coping strategy when trying to handle stress more effectively. A positive mood improves our ability to process information more efficiently, makes us more altruistic, and gives us higher self-esteem. In most cases, an optimistic attitude is superior to a pessimistic one. It gives us a sense that we are controlling our environment, much like what Bandura talks about when he describes the importance of self-efficacy in coping. For example, in 1989, sports psychologist Jim Loehr pieced together videotaped segments of 17-year-old Michael Chang's most outstanding tennis points in the past year. Chang periodically watched the videotape—he always saw himself winning, he never saw himself make mistakes, and he always saw himself in a positive mood. Several months later Chang became the youngest male to win the French Open Tennis Championship.

Cognitive Restructuring and Positive Self-Talk

Many cognitive therapists believe the process of **cognitive restructuring**—*modifying the thoughts, ideas, and beliefs that maintain an individual's problems*—can be used to get people to think more positively and optimistically. **Self-talk** (also called **self-statements**)—*the soundless, mental speech we use when we think about something, plan, or solve problems*—is often very helpful in cognitive restructuring. Positive self-talk can do a lot to give you the confidence that frees you to use your talents to the fullest. Since self-talk

has a way of becoming a self-fulfilling prophecy, uncountered negative thinking can spell trouble. That's why it's so important to monitor your self-talk.

Several strategies can help you to monitor your self-talk. First, at random times during the day, ask yourself, "What am I saying to myself right now?" Then, if you can, write down your thoughts along with a few notes about the situation you are in and how you're feeling. Your goal is to fine-tune your self-talk to make it as accurate as possible. Before you begin, it is important to record your self-talk without any censorship.

You can also use uncomfortable emotions or moods—such as stress, depression, and anxiety—as cues for listening to your self-talk. When this happens, identify the feeling as accurately as possible. Then ask yourself, "What was I saying to myself right before I started feeling this way?" or, "What have I been saying to myself since I've been feeling this way?"

Situations that you anticipate might be difficult for you also are excellent times to assess your self-talk. Write down a description of the coming event. Then ask yourself, "What am I saying to myself about this event?" If your thoughts are negative, think how you can use your strengths to turn these disruptive feelings into more positive ones and help turn a potentially difficult experience into a success.

It is also useful to compare your self-talk predictions (what you thought would or should happen in a given situation) with what actually took place. If the reality conflicts with your predictions—as it often does when your self-talk is in error—pinpoint where your self-talk needs adjustments to fit reality.

You are likely to have a subjective view of your own thoughts. So it is helpful to enlist the assistance of a sympathetic but objective friend, partner, or therapist who is willing to listen, discuss your self-assessment with you, and help you to identify ways your self-talk is distorted and might be improved. Examples of how positive self-statements can be used to replace negative self-statements in coping with various stressful situations are presented in figure 5.2. To explore the benefits of self-talk, turn to Critical Thinking.

Situation	Negative self-statement	Positive self-statements
Having a long, difficult assignment due the next day	"I'll never get this work done by tomorrow."	"If I work real hard I may be able to get it all done for tomorrow." "This is going to be tough but it is still possible to do it." "Finishing this assignment for tomorrow will be a real challenge." "If I don't get it finished, I'll just have to ask the teacher for an extension."
Losing one's job	"I'll never get another job."	"I'll just have to look harder for another job." "There will be rough times ahead, but I've dealt with rough times before." "Hey, maybe my next job will be a better deal altogether." "There are agencies that can probably help me get some kind of job."
Moving away from friends and family	"My whole life is left behind."	"I'll miss everyone, but it doesn't mean we can't stay in touch." "Just think of all the new people I'm going to meet." "I guess it will be kind of exciting moving to a new home." "Now I'll have two places to call home."
Breaking up with a person you love	"I have nothing to live for. He/she was all I had."	"I really thought our relationship would work, but it's not the end of the world." "Maybe we can try again in the future." "I'll just have to try to keep myself busy and not let it bother me." "If I met him (her), there is no reason I won't meet someone else someday."
Not getting into graduate school	"I guess I'm really dumb. I don't know what I'll do."	"I'll just have to reapply next year." "There are things I can do with my life other than going to grad school." "I guess a lot of good students get turned down. It's just so unbelievably competitive." "Perhaps there are a few other programs that I could apply to."
Having to participate in a class discussion	"Everyone else knows more than I do, so what's the use of saying anything?"	"I have as much to say as anyone else in the class." "My ideas may be different, but they're still valid." "It's OK to be a bit nervous; I'll relax as I start talking." "I might as well say something; how bad could it sound?"

FIGURE 5.2

Examples of How Positive Self-Statements Can Be Used to Replace Negative Self-Statements in Coping with Stressful Situations

CRITICAL THINKING

The Power of Positive Self-Talk

Suppose there existed a simple, brief, nonmedical approach that promised to make you feel better, more competent, or happier. Would you try it? Learning positive self-talk is a good example of *applying psychological concepts to enhance personal adaptation.*

What are some of the effective methods involved in positive self-talk? First, you must be aware of how much you engage in negative self-talk. When you make a mistake, are you unforgiving? Do you chide yourself? Do you refer to yourself as dumb or stupid? By stopping the negative thinking, you will go a long way toward feeling better. Second, you need to identify some things that you like

in your own performance or presentation and focus on these instead. What aspects of the mistake weren't so terrible? What can be learned from the experience? By focusing on the positive features, you will enhance your energy, not drain it. Third: Practice, practice, practice. Find some cues during the day to remind yourself of your better qualities. When you look in a mirror, purposefully admire something you see. When you receive negative feedback, dilute its ego-defeating aspects with positive self-regard. You may want to practice an affirmation as part of your daily ritual for waking up or retiring. Try this approach for a few weeks and see if it makes a difference.

Positive Self-Illusion

For a number of years, mental health professionals believed that seeing reality as accurately as possible was the best path to health. Recently though, researchers have found increasing evidence that maintaining some positive illusions about oneself and the world is healthy. Happy people often have mistakenly high opinions of themselves, give self-serving explanations for events, and have exaggerated beliefs about their ability to control the world around them (Taylor & others, 1988).

> *Humankind cannot bear very much reality.*
>
> —T. S. Eliot

Illusions, whether positive or negative, are related to one's sense of self-esteem. Having too grandiose an idea of yourself or thinking too negatively about yourself both have negative consequences. Rather, the ideal overall orientation may be an optimal margin of illusion in which individuals see themselves as slightly above average (see figure 5.3).

A negative outlook can increase our chances of getting angry, feeling guilty, and magnifying our mistakes. And for some people, seeing things too accurately can lead to depression. Seeing one's suffering as meaningless and random does not help a person cope and move forward, even if the suffering *is* random and meaningless. An absence of illusions may also keep individuals from undertaking the risky and ambitious projects that may yield the greatest rewards (Baumeister, 1989).

For some people, though, a strategy of defensive pessimism may actually work best in handling stress. By imagining negative outcomes, people can prepare for stressful circumstances (Norem & Cantor, 1986). Think about the honors student who is worried that she will flunk the next test, or the nervous host who is afraid his lavish dinner party will fall apart. For these two people, thoughts of failure might not be

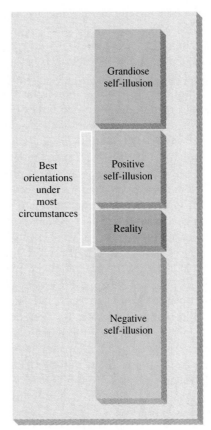

FIGURE 5.3

Reality and Self-illusion
The most healthy individuals often have self-illusions that are slightly above their current level of functioning and ability. Having too grandiose an opinion of yourself or thinking negatively about yourself can have negative consequences. For some individuals, seeing things too accurately can be depressing. Overall, in most contexts, a reality orientation or a slightly above average self-illusion may be the most effective.

paralyzing but instead might motivate them to do everything necessary to ensure that things go smoothly. By imagining potential problems, they may develop relevant strategies for dealing with or preventing negative outcomes. One study found that negative thinking spurred constructive thinking and feelings such as evaluating negative possibilities, wondering what the future held, psyching up for future experiences so they would be positive, feeling good about being prepared to cope with the worst, and forming positive expectations (Showers, 1986).

Developing an Optimistic Outlook

Although some individuals at times use a strategy of defensive pessimism to improve their ability to cope with stress, overall a positive feeling of optimism is the best strategy. Indeed, a number of books have recently promoted the power of optimism in effective coping. *Learned Optimism* by Martin Seligman (1991) and *Positive Illusions: Creative Self-Deception and the Healthy Mind* by Shelley Taylor (1989) both provide excellent recommendations for ways to develop a more optimistic outlook on life that will help you cope more effectively.

How can you develop a more optimistic outlook? Seligman (1991) believes that the best tools for overcoming chronic pessimism lie in cognitive therapy, an approach that emphasizes more positive thinking by challenging self-defeating attitudes. Some cognitive therapists believe that optimistic coping skills can be assembled in six to twelve sessions, although Seligman believes that some individuals can master the techniques on their own. One of cognitive therapy's recommendations is to avoid ruminating and wallowing in self-pity when a bad event occurs. The tendency to think and worry repeatedly about negative circumstances and failures often prevents the development of positive coping strategies. Another recommendation of cognitive therapists is to dispute negative thoughts. Pessimists tend to use absolute, all-encompassing terms to describe defeats. They apply damaging labels to their behavior and pepper their language with words like *never* and *always*. Cognitive therapists advocate talking back to these negative thoughts in an optimistic style that limits self-blame and negative generalizations. According to Christopher Peterson, cognitive therapists are not telling people to be out of touch with reality, but rather to wear rose-colored glasses.

An optimistic outlook also may help individuals resist disease, as evidenced in a series of studies conducted by Peterson and his colleagues (Peterson & Stunkard, 1986).

For example, college students were given the Attributional Style Questionnaire that evaluates an individual's optimistic and pessimistic tendencies. Then, their health was monitored over the next year. The pessimists had twice as many infections and doctors' visits as the optimists.

Increasing Self-Control

Chances are that each of us could benefit from an increase in self-control, at least in some aspects of our lives. Let's begin our study of self-control by outlining a five-step program for improving self-control.

A Five-Step Self-Control Program

What would you like to better control about yourself and your life? Use these five steps to help you accomplish increased self-control.

Step 1 You have to *specify* the problem you want to control more effectively in a concrete way. For Mark, this is easy—he is overweight and wants to lose 30 pounds. Stated even more precisely, he wants to consume about 1,000 fewer calories per day than he needs to maintain his current weight—this caloric intake would then give him a weight loss of about 2 pounds per week.

Some problems are more difficult to specify, such as "wasting time," "having a bad attitude toward school," "having a poor relationship," or "being too nervous and worrying a lot." These types of problems have been referred to as "fuzzies" because of their abstract nature. "Unfuzzifying" these abstract problems and making them more specific and concrete is important. For example, "decreasing wasted time," might translate to "not staying in bed after the alarm clock goes off, spending at least 2 hours each evening studying for courses, and limiting phone conversations to 10 minutes each." Problems can be made more precise by writing out your goal and listing the things that would give you clear evidence that you have reached your goal.

Step 2 A second important step in improving your self-control is to make a *commitment* to change (Martin & Pear, 1988). Both a commitment to change and a knowledge of change techniques have been shown to help college students become more effective self-managers of their smoking, eating, studying, and relationship problems. To build a commitment to change, require yourself to do things that will increase the likelihood of sticking to your project. First, tell others about your commitment to change—they will remind you to stay with your self-control program. Second, rearrange your environment to provide frequent reminders of your goal, making sure that the reminders are associated with the positive benefits of reaching your goal. Third, put a lot of time and energy into planning your self-control program. Make a list of statements about your program, such as "I've put a lot of time into this project; I am certainly not going to waste all of this effort now." Fourth, because you will invariably face temptations to backslide or quit your self-control program, plan ahead for ways you can deal with temptation, tailoring these plans to your problem.

Step 3 A third major step in developing a self-control program is to *collect data* about your behavior. This is especially important if your self-control program involves decreasing excessive behaviors, such as overeating and frequent smoking. Collecting data before you modify your behavior provides a reference point for evaluating your progress once you start your self-control program.

When recording the initial frequency of your problematic behaviors, examine the immediate consequences that help maintain these behaviors (Martin & Pear, 1988). Consider Mark's situation. When first asked why he eats so much, Mark said, "Because I like the taste, and eating makes me feel more comfortable." When Mark began evaluating the circumstances in which he usually snacks, however, he noticed that food is associated with reinforcers: he eats a candy bar while waiting to see his girlfriend, Ann; as he was eating potato chips he watched his favorite basketball star score another basket; after sharing a few beers, his fraternity brothers laugh louder at Mark's jokes. Mark discovers that he eats in many rewarding social situations—no wonder he is having trouble controlling his weight.

1. Define the problem

2. Commit to change

3. Collect data about yourself

4. Design a self-control program

5. Make the program last — maintenance

FIGURE 5.4

Five Steps in Developing a Successful Self-Control Program

Step 4 A fourth important step in improving your self-control is to *design a program* following one of several different strategies. Virtually every self-control program incorporates the modification of self-talk and self-statements mentioned earlier in this chapter (Meichenbaum, 1986). Remember how it is important to replace negative self-statements with positive self-statements about your ability to cope with your problem. Also remember the cognitive traps in self-talk, such as all-or-nothing thinking, overgeneralization, and jumping to conclusions, that need to be cognitively restructured.

Step 5 A fifth important step involves *maintaining* your gains and improvement. One strategy is to establish specific dates for post-checks and to plan a renewed course of action if your post-checks are unfavorable. For example, if, like Mark, your self-control program involves weight reduction, you might want to weigh yourself once a week. If your weight increases more than five pounds, then you immediately go back on your self-control program.

Another strategy is to establish a buddy system in which you and a friend set mutual maintenance goals. Once a month, get together and check each other's behavioral success or self-control problems. If your goals have been maintained, celebrate in an agreed-upon way.

Figure 5.4 summarizes the five steps of improving self-control. For other ideas on how to establish an effective self-control program tailored to your needs, try contacting your college counseling center or community mental

CRITICAL THINKING

Enhancing Study Skills

Nearly all students complain that they don't have sufficient time to study. Even strong students recognize that they could probably study more efficiently, whereas weaker students struggle to carve out meaningful study time in an otherwise busy schedule. In this exercise you will *apply psychology concepts to enhance personal adaptation and growth* using the questions below, which reflect the five steps of self-control, to enhance the quality of your study.

Step 1.   What is the specific problem that makes your study periods less effective than you would like?

Step 2.   What measures should you take to make a strong commitment to improving your study quality?

Step 3.   What is your current study ritual, and what are the consequences that maintain your current practice?

Step 4.   What aspects of self-control (such as avoiding all-or-none thinking, positive self-talk) could be incorporated to improve your study quality?

Step 5.   How will you maintain the gains that your new approach offers?

Does this approach appeal to you in enhancing the quality of your study? You might not feel a need to follow this strategy unless your circumstances are dire. However, the discipline of a successful self-control program can help you feel empowered to take on other problem areas as well.

health center. A good book about self-direction and self-control can also be helpful, such as Brian Yates' (1985) *Self-Management: The Science and Art of Helping Yourself,* and David Watson and Roland Tharp's (1989) *Self-Directed Behavior: Self-Modification for Personal Adjustment.* To evaluate your self-control related to study, see Critical Thinking.

Thought Stopping

Thought stopping *is a specific self-control and cognitive restructuring strategy in which the individual says "Stop!" when an unwanted thought occurs and then replaces it immediately with a more pleasant thought.* When using this technique, as soon as you have an unwanted idea, tell yourself "Stop!" Say it clearly, and if not aloud, say it sharply in your mind. Then, as a second step, immediately substitute another idea—a pleasant one that is the opposite of your original unwanted thought. For example, if you imagine a circumstance in which you feel humiliated, say "Stop!" and then immediately recall or create a mental circumstance in which you feel successful and proud.

One woman used thought stopping to fall out of love with a man who was an exploiting liar. The woman initially made a list of the advantages of being out of love with this man, such as: "I will feel better about myself and won't feel so depressed and worthless," "I will be a better

mother to my children," "I will enjoy spending more time with my friends," and "I will be able to become reinvolved in the community activities I gave up for him." She wrote them on a card that she carried with her and made a tape recording of the statements. She frequently read the list or listened to the tape. When she found herself thinking positively about this man, she would think, "Stop!" and substitute an item from her list. In addition, she kept herself busy doing other things so that her thoughts would focus on pleasant activities more than on this man. It took about 2 months for the thought-stopping strategy to accomplish her goals.

Empowerment

Some individuals, especially those with low-income backgrounds or from ethnic minority backgrounds, may not be able to address and resolve their stressful, taxing circumstances on their own. They often have fewer resources for learning coping strategies—they are less likely to have counseling available for them, and they are less likely to have access to psychological ideas for change. At the same time, they are likely to have above average threatening circumstances or stressors in their daily lives. These disenfranchised individuals need empowerment so that they can lead more productive and happier lives.

Empowerment *is the concept of assisting individuals to develop skills they need to control their own lives.*

One effort to improve empowerment is to develop more community-based services by involving natural caregivers in the community (Halonen & Santrock, 1996). Mental health consultation to teachers, ministers, family physicians, and others who directly interact with community members provides them with intervention skills. This approach allows the delivery of services, such as programs of self-control and adaptive skills training, to increased numbers of individuals in comfortable settings for them rather than in the uncomfortable, alienating mental health center. To read further about how community mental health services are involved in empowering Latinos, turn to Sociocultural Worlds of Adjustment.

Mental health professionals are involved in the development of empowerment for many subgroups in society. In rural America, counselors have formed support groups for farmers who were losing their land during economic crises. Others have helped victims of rape and domestic violence to recover from their ordeal. Civil rights movements, women's movements, and gay liberation groups have used psychological education to improve the lives and self-esteem of their members.

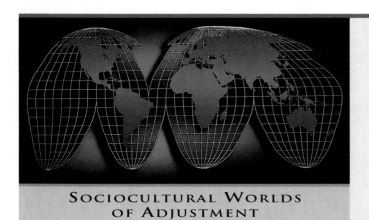

Empowering Latinos Through Community Mental Health Programs

How can community mental health services for Latinos be improved? Following are the recommendations made by Amado Padilla, Rene Ruiz, and Rodolfo Alvarez (1975, 1989). A wide range of innovative programs are needed to improve the lives of Latino Americans and to help them cope with problems. These programs include remedial education, vocational guidance and retraining, drug-abuse and crime prevention programs, and even college counseling. One recommendation is to have the community mental health center serve as a multipurpose center. In addition to providing treatment for a wide range of human problems, the facilities could be used for youth activities, such as sports and dances, for culturally relevant events, such as Spanish-language films and fiestas, or to satisfy many different community needs. Most mental health experts believe it makes sense to involve the community in a center in their neighborhood that is placed there to serve their needs. Community representatives should be involved in the center's administration, and the advertising media, in both Spanish and English, can be used to disseminate information to the target population concerning available facilities, therapeutic services, and other activities.

In one community mental health approach in east Los Angeles, an effort was made to design a mental health service that would attract local Mexican Americans. Major changes in staffing and treatment programs were made. By the end of a 2½ year recruitment program, the director of the facility had attracted 22 full-time professional, paraprofessional (volunteers trained to work with individuals who have problems), and clerical personnel. Of these 22, 15 were completely fluent in Spanish. Ten were natives and/or residents of the area, 12 were of Mexican American descent, and 2 were of Latin descent (Cuban and Peruvian). Service facilities were selected in the heart of the community, convenient to transportation, and were comfortable and inviting. The treatment program was based on a prevention philosophy with an emphasis on mental health consultation to a wide variety of community mental health agencies. As a backup, the center offered short-term crisis-oriented treatment that included individual, family, or chemical therapy. The center seemed to fulfill the objective of providing appropriate treatment for Mexican Americans. More such centers are badly needed in areas in which Latino Americans live.

In another example of a community mental health approach, a group of young Chicanos working in Chicago's west side developed a community-controlled youth center, *El Centro de la Causa*. The original operating budget of $1,800 was raised by a community fiesta. Within months, the group had convinced a church organization to provide $40,000 for staff and services. Within 3 years, the operating budget was more than $400,000. Funding was used to train community residents as paraprofessionals in mental-health-training and reading-improvement programs, English classes, recreation and youth activities, and drug-abuse programs.

Seeking Social Support

Our crowded, polluted, noisy, and achievement-oriented world can make us feel overwhelmed and isolated. Now more than ever, we may need support systems such as family members, friends, and co-workers to buffer stress. **Social support** *is information and feedback from others that we are loved and cared for, esteemed and valued, and part of a network of communication and mutual obligation.*

The benefits of social support can be grouped into three categories: tangible assistance, information, and emotional support (Taylor, 1995). Family and friends can provide *tangible assistance* by giving individuals actual goods and services in stressful circumstances. For example, gifts of food to bereaved family members spares them from cooking for themselves and out-of-town relatives in a time when energy and motivation are low.

Individuals providing support may also give *information* by recommending specific actions and plans to help the stressed person cope more effectively. Offering an overloaded co-worker a suggestion for better time management or how to delegate some assignments is an example of this type of social support.

In stressful situations, individuals often suffer emotionally, develop depression and anxiety, and lose self-esteem. Friends and family can provide *emotional support* by reassuring the stressed person of their value to each other. Knowing that others care allows a person to approach and cope with stress with greater assurance.

Students sometimes form a study group that provides all three kinds of social support. Tangible assistance might involve providing a copy of notes for a student who was ill during one class. Informational support is discussing ideas about possible test questions and answers. Emotional support involves encouraging each other to do well and providing consolation after a poor test grade.

Researchers consistently have found that social support helps individuals cope with stress (Hobfoll, 1996). For example, in one study depressed persons had fewer

*Developing Self-Efficacy,
Thinking Positively and
Optimistically, and Increasing
Self-Control*

Self-efficacy—the belief that one can master problems and produce positive outcomes—can be an effective strategy in coping with stress and challenging circumstances. Self-efficacy provides individuals with self-confidence, influencing whether some people ever even get started in trying to develop better health habits. Judgments about self-efficacy also influence how much effort individuals expend in coping with stress, how long they persist in the face of obstacles, and how much stress they experience.

Many cognitive therapists believe that cognitive restructuring can be used to get people to think more positively and optimistically. Self-talk (also called self-statements) is often helpful in cognitive restructuring. Since self-talk becomes a self-fulfilling prophecy, uncountered negative thinking can spell trouble. That's why it is so important to monitor your self-talk and replace negative self-statements with positive ones. Positive self-illusions can improve some individuals' coping, but it is important to guard against totally unrealistic expectations. While some individuals use a strategy of defensive pessimism to improve their ability to cope with stress, overall a feeling of optimism is the best strategy. An optimistic outlook can even help individuals to resist certain diseases.

Increasing self-control is another important coping strategy. A five-step program to increase self-control involves: defining the problem more specifically and concretely, committing to change, collecting data, designing a self-control program, and making the program last—maintenance. Thought stopping is a specific self-control and cognitive restructuring strategy in which the individual says "Stop!" when an unwanted thought occurs and then replaces it with a thought that is more pleasant. Some individuals may not be powerful enough to address their stressful circumstances on their own, especially individuals from low-income backgrounds and some ethnic minority individuals. Consequently, it is important to empower them so they will be able to develop the skills they need to control their own lives. Empowerment is one of the important goals of many community mental health programs.

---

and less supportive relationships with family members, friends, and co-workers than did nondepressed persons (Billings, Cronkite, & Moos, 1983). In another study, the prognosticators of cancer, mental illness, and suicide included a lack of closeness to one's parents and a negative attitude toward one's own family (Thomas, 1983). Widows die at a rate that is 3 to 13 times higher than married women for every known cause of death. Close, positive attachments to others, both family and friends, consistently show up as important buffers of stress.

Consider Robert, who had been laid off by an automobile manufacturer when it was about to fold, then laid off a decade later by a truck builder, and more recently was laid off by yet another automobile maker. By all accounts, you would expect Robert to be down in the dumps or possibly feel that life had given him a bum deal, yet Robert is one of the most well-adjusted individuals in his community. When asked his secret in dealing with so much adversity, he attributed his ability to cope to having a wonderful family and great friends. The support he receives from others permits him to handle the stress, and is far more important than Robert's trials and tribulations.

In thinking about ways to improve your own coping, consider the potential sources of social support in your own environment and learn how to effectively draw on these resources in times of stress (Taylor, 1995). Sometimes personal coping can also be improved by joining community groups, interest groups, or informal social groups that meet regularly. Many people find individual or group therapy to be a valuable form of social support.

Improving Appropriate Risk Taking

Even though some individuals have a support system of family and friends, they may have difficulty opening up to them and talking about their problems. These individuals would benefit from learning to use coping strategies that enhance their ability to take appropriate risks involving other people. Some of the strategies that can help a person effectively face the taxing circumstances of life are to utilize disinhibition, engage in enjoyable activities, and use humor.

Increasing Disinhibition

Actively inhibiting our emotions and behaviors is associated with a variety of health problems, including heightened physical complaints, such as headaches and colds, chronic health problems such as asthma, and complications related to heart disease. It seems that bottling up problems within yourself and not talking about these problems with others impedes the coping process and negatively affects physical health.

Psychologist James Pennebaker and his colleagues (Pennebaker, 1990; Pennebaker, Colder, & Sharp, 1990) conducted several studies involving the cognitive and health changes that result when individuals either talk about or write about personal problems. In this research study, individuals write about their most traumatic experiences for 15 to 20 minutes per day for 3 or 4 consecutive days. Typically, people feel somewhat anxious or depressed when they initially disclose their traumatic experiences, however, these immediate unpleasant feelings dissipate rather quickly. Interestingly, these college students showed significant drops in physician visits for illness up to 6 months after writing about their most traumatic episodes.

Why would writing about a traumatic experience for 15 minutes a day for just 3 or 4 days increase an individual's health and well-being for months? One possible reason is that silence about traumatic experiences increases the risk for illness; however, other explanations have been suggested. Apparently writing forces people to stand back and reorganize their thoughts and feelings about highly stressful experiences, perhaps leading to an increased sense of survival or self-confidence in ability to cope. Also, putting upsetting experiences into words may stimulate individuals to think about new ways to cope with the stress. Given the success of Pennebaker's studies, you might want to use the writing strategy to help you cognitively restructure and cope more effectively with a traumatic event in your life.

Before concluding our discussion of disinhibition, a caution is in order. Sometimes inhibition is a healthy response to stress. In the overall scheme of an individual's life, inhibition probably contributes more to health than to diminishing health. Throughout our lives, many aspects of self-restraint will promote our health—curbing our drinking of alcohol, giving up drug usage, and inhibiting violent tendencies are examples. So, sometimes inhibition is positive, and, as discussed earlier, sometimes it is negative. Therefore, as with most aspects of life, a balanced approach between inhibition and disinhibition may be best.

Engaging in Enjoyable Activities

When people encounter taxing circumstances and experience traumatic events, inhibition may affect their activity level and their communication pattern. Indeed, some people become immobilized and frozen as they become immersed in their sorrows and anxieties. For some people in stressful circumstances, it is easy to become a virtual hermit and not get out in the world. Individuals who cope with stress in this way rarely engage in any enjoyable activities and do not do anything that makes them feel good. This pattern is obviously not very beneficial.

When stress comes your way, don't let it immobilize you. Don't let it encase you in a cocoon, in an enclosed world that no one can touch. Not only is it helpful to talk with others about your stressful experiences, but you can make your life less miserable by participating in activities that you enjoy. When you are feeling really down in the dumps about a personally stressful experience and a friend suggests that the two of you go bowling, dancing, or shopping, or that it's time to see a movie, eat at a restaurant, or take a weekend trip, go.

Using Humor

Among other benefits, engaging in enjoyable activities not only makes us feel good, it also sometimes makes us laugh. Engaging in enjoyable activities and laughter reduces our inhibition and aids coping with stress. Laughing both releases pent-up emotions and aids redefinition of a stressful circumstance in a less threatening way.

How can you put more humor and laughter into your life? One way is to look for humor in everyday occurrences. If you feel your life needs more humor in it, you might consider keeping an informal log of the ridiculous things that happen at home, school, or work. This 5-minute daily activity allows you to regularly reflect on each day's events that can provide a laugh. You might want to include some of your own laughable mistakes in the informal log—learning to laugh at yourself is considered by some psychologists to be a reflection of self-acceptance.

A cautionary note about using humor. The best way to use humor is to release anxiety about a situation and to allow yourself to be "human rather than perfect." The use of sexist, racist, or ageist humor is not a recommended coping strategy. When, for their own benefit, people tell jokes that put down Italians, or fat people, or blondes, or homosexuals, they are gaining little at a significant cost to others.

Comedy is tragedy—plus time.
—**Carol Burnett**

Using Multiple Coping Strategies

Individuals who face stressful circumstances have many different strategies from which to choose. Often a good strategy is to choose more than one of them. Multiple coping strategies are often better than a single strategy alone. For example, people who have experienced a stressful life event or a cluster of such life events (such as the death of a parent, a divorce, or a significant income reduction) might seek social support, exercise regularly, reduce their drinking, and practice relaxation. These techniques represent adaptive, problem-focused strategies that emphasize changes in thought and action. See figure 5.5 for a summary of the positive methods for coping with stress and enhancing adjustment. These can serve as the basis for adopting some new strategies to manage stress more effectively.

STRESS MANAGEMENT

Because many people have difficulty in managing stress themselves, psychologists have developed a variety of stress-management programs that can be taught to individuals. We will study the nature of these stress-management programs and evaluate some of the techniques that are used in them, such as meditation and relaxation, biofeedback, assertiveness training, and time management.

The Nature of Stress Management

Stress-management programs *teach individuals how to appraise stressful events, how to develop skills for coping with stress, and how to put these skills into use in their everyday lives.* Stress-management programs are often taught through workshops, often held in work settings (Taylor, 1995). Many companies, aware of the high cost of lost productivity to stress-related disorders, have become increasingly motivated to help their workers identify and cope with stressful circumstances in their lives. Some of these programs are broad in scope and teach a variety of techniques while

Strategy	Elaboration
Engage in cognitive appraisal — challenges	Work on interpreting events as challenges to overcome rather than as highly stressful forces that immobilize and emotionally blunt you.
Use cognitive appraisal— coping resources	Evaluate your resources and determine how effectively they can be used to cope with the stressful event.
Engage in problem-focused coping	Use the cognitive strategy of squarely facing your troubles and try to solve your personal and interpersonal problems.
Use emotion-focused coping	Use this strategy sparingly, although such emotion-focused strategies as calling on one's religious faith can be helpful.
Engage in active-cognitive strategies	Develop cognitive actions to cope with stress and adjust more effectively. Use such techniques as trying to see the positive side of situations, drawing on your past experiences, stepping back from the situation to be more objective, and going over the situation in your mind and trying to understand it.
Engage in active-behavioral strategies	Try to take some behavioral action to solve the problem and reduce stress. Use such strategies as finding out more about the situation, enacting a plan, and seeking professional help.
Reduce or eliminate avoidance strategies	Deal with stressful circumstances; don't avoid them. Don't keep your feelings to yourself, don't refuse to believe what happened, and don't try to reduce stress by drinking more, eating more, smoking more, or taking more drugs.
Develop self-efficacy	Develop a sense that your actions will produce favorable outcomes and expect to be able to master situations.
Engage in positive thinking and develop an optimistic outlook	Eliminate self-defeating, pessimistic thinking; develop a positive outlook that your world is going to be better and then make it better.
Engage in self-control	Work on controlling your negative emotions, such as anger and jealousy. Make an effort to keep yourself from getting into a frenzied state in which you can't think clearly about positive ways to cope. Develop patience and don't act too impulsively.
Seek social support	Obtain emotional comfort from others — either friends, your spouse or partner, or a mental health professional.
Follow a disinhibition strategy, engage in some enjoyable activities, and use humor	Open up and talk about your stressful experiences. Engage in some activities you enjoy instead of being immobilized and feeling sorry for yourself. Sometimes humor can help.
Use stress-management techniques or become involved in a stress-management program	Develop a relaxation program, follow a better nutrition regimen, and engage in a more healthy lifestyle, or enroll in a workshop or program that teaches stress management.
Adopt multiple coping strategies	Use more than one coping strategy by examining all of the different coping strategies and analyzing which combination would likely serve you best.

FIGURE 5.5

A Summary of Positive Ways to Cope with Stress and Adjust More Effectively

others teach one specific skill, such as relaxation or assertiveness training (Handelsman & Frielander, 1995). Some stress-management programs are also taught to individuals experiencing similar kinds of problems—such as a group of migraine headache sufferers or individuals who all have high blood pressure. Colleges, too, often offer stress-management programs for their students and staff. If you are finding college to be stressful, you might want to consider enrolling in a college or community stress-management program. Let's now examine some of the techniques used in these programs.

Meditation and Relaxation

At one time, meditation was associated with mysticism rather than science. Its acceptability among scientists has increased, along with its popularity in the United States in recent years. In Asia, meditation has been an important aspect of life for centuries.

Meditation *is the system of thought and practice that is used to attain bodily or mental control and well-being, as well as enlightenment.* The strategies of meditation vary but are generally one of two forms: either cleansing the mind to have new experiences or increasing one's concentration. **Transcendental meditation (TM)** *is the most popular form of meditation in the United States; it is derived from an ancient Indian technique and involves a* **mantra,** *which is a resonant sound or phrase that is repeated mentally or aloud to focus attention.* One widely used TM mantra is the phrase *Om mani padme hum.* By concentrating on this phrase, the individual replaces all other thoughts with the syllables *Om mani padme hum.* In transcendental meditation the person learns to associate a mantra with a special meaning, such as beauty, peace, or tranquility.

Physiologically, the typical meditative state shows qualities of both sleep and wakefulness, yet it is distinct from them. It resembles the hypnagogic state, which is the transition from wakefulness to sleep, but at the very least it is a prolongation of that state.

Early research on meditation's effects on the body revealed that oxygen consumption is lowered, heart rate slows down, blood flow increases in the arms and forehead, and EEG patterns are predominantly of the alpha variety, being regular and rhythmic (Wallace & Benson, 1972). Other research supports these findings but questions whether meditation is more effective than relaxation in reducing bodily arousal. For example, in the research of David Holmes and his colleagues (1983), trained and

SELF-ASSESSMENT

Relaxation

How relaxed are you right now? Would you like to feel more tranquil and peaceful? If so, you can probably reach that feeling state by following some simple instructions. First, you need to find a quiet place to sit. Get a comfortable chair and sit quietly and upright in it. Let your chin rest comfortably on your chest, your arms in your lap. Close your eyes. Then, pay attention to your breathing. Every time you inhale and every time you exhale, notice it and pay attention to the sensations of air flowing through your body, the feeling of your lungs filling and emptying. After you have done this for several breaths, begin to repeat silently to yourself a single word every time you breathe out. The word you choose does not have to mean anything. You can make the word up, you could use the word *one,* or you could try a word that is associated with the emotion you want to produce, such as *trust, love, patience,* or

happy. Try several different words to see which one works best for you. At first, you will find that thoughts intrude and you are no longer attending to your breathing. Just return to your breathing and say the word each time you exhale. After you have practiced this exercise for 10 to 15 minutes, twice a day, every day for 2 weeks, you will be ready for a shortened version. If you notice stressful thoughts or circumstances appearing, simply engage in the relaxation response on the spot for several minutes. If you are in public, you don't have to close your eyes, just fix your gaze on some nearby object, attend to your breathing and say your word silently every time you exhale. Audiotapes that induce the relaxation response are available in most bookstores. They usually include soothing background music and instructions. These audiotapes can especially help induce a more relaxed state before you go to bed at night.

Meditation has been an important dimension of Asians' lives for centuries.

experienced meditators were asked to relax for 5 minutes, then to meditate for 20 minutes, and finally to relax for 5 minutes. Ten other volunteers who had no training or experience in meditation were asked to follow the same regimen with one exception—during the 20 minutes the meditators meditated, the nonmeditators were simply told to rest. Bodily arousal—in the form of heart rate, skin resistance, respiration, and blood pressure—was measured throughout the experiment. Meditation did lower body arousal, but no more than relaxation did. To learn how to put more relaxation into your own life, see the Self-Assessment.

> *The time to relax is when you don't have time for it.*
>
> **—Sydney J. Harris**

Biofeedback

For many years operant conditioning was believed to be the only effective means to deal with voluntary behaviors such as aggression, shyness, and achievement.

Behavior modification helped people to reduce their aggression, to be more assertive and outgoing, and to get better grades, for example. Involuntary behaviors, such as blood pressure, muscle tension, and pulse rate were thought to be outside the boundaries of operant conditioning and more appropriate for classical conditioning. Beginning in the 1960s, though, psychologist Neal Miller (1969) and others began to demonstrate that people can control internal behaviors. **Biofeedback** *is the process in which physical states, such as levels of muscle tension, are monitored by instruments and information from these instruments is given (fed back) to the individuals so they can learn to voluntarily control these states.*

How does biofeedback work? Let's consider the problem of reducing an individual's muscle tension. The individual's muscle tension is monitored and information about the level of tension is fed back, often in the form of an audible tone. As muscle tension rises, the tone becomes louder; as it drops, the tone becomes softer. The reinforcement in biofeedback is the change in the tone (or, in some cases, seeing a dot move up or down on a television screen) as the individual learns to control muscle tension.

When biofeedback was first developed, some overzealous advocates exaggerated its success and potential for helping people with problems such as high blood pressure and migraine headaches. As more carefully designed investigations were conducted, more realistic appraisals of biofeedback's effectiveness replaced the wildly enthusiastic early claims. For example, some success in lowering blood pressure has been achieved, although it is easier to raise blood pressure than to lower it through biofeedback. Relaxation training and more general stress-management programs are often just as effective in reducing blood pressure.

Assertiveness Training

Assertiveness training *involves teaching individuals to act in their own best interests, to stand up for their legitimate rights, and to express their views directly and openly.* Assertiveness training has been especially effective in helping women to stand up for their rights and to express themselves more openly, since many women had been socialized to be passive and dependent. Assertiveness training can benefit virtually anyone who hardly ever says "no" to others' requests and demands.

It is important to distinguish among nonassertive, aggressive, indirectly aggressive, and assertive behaviors. **Nonassertive behavior** *is submissive, self-denying and inhibited, and involves allowing others to choose options for oneself.* **Aggressive behavior** *is hostile, often angry, deprecating of others, and self-enhancing at others' expense; it involves achieving desired goals by hurting and disregarding others.* A variation of aggressive behavior is indirect aggression. **Indirectly aggressive behavior** *involves manipulating others to achieve a particular outcome without being direct or respectful.* **Assertive behavior** *involves acting in your own best interest, standing up for legitimate rights, expressing views directly and openly, being self-enhancing, and making choices without hurting others.* Based on these definitions, assertive behavior is a desirable coping strategy. To assess your assertiveness, turn to the Self-Assessment box.

Behavior therapist Joseph Wolpe (1968) once commented that there are essentially three broad approaches to the conduct of interpersonal relations. The first is to consider yourself only and ride roughshod over others. The second is to always put others before yourself and let others run roughshod over you. The third approach is the golden mean—placing yourself first, but taking others into account. The third approach reflects an assertive orientation to human encounter. To explore the influence of context on assertiveness, turn to Critical Thinking.

In most cultures, women have been more likely to be socialized to be too nonassertive and men to be too aggressive. Assertiveness training can therefore teach a better approach to many women and men.

As part of the changing gender roles in the United States and other Western countries, more women are becoming assertive, and they assert their rights and demand equal recognition/status/pay (Alberti & Emmons, 1986). Assertive women demonstrate that they are capable of choosing their own lifestyle, free of the dictates of tradition, husband, children, and bosses (Phelps & Austin, 1987). They might *choose* to become a homemaker, *elect* to enter a male-dominated occupation, or *opt* to have only one child. In their sexual relationships, women can be more comfortable taking the initiative, or they can say no firmly to sexual contact.

Breaking out of traditionally held patterns can be stressful. Females who were socialized to be the dependent, nurturant, domestic family members but grew up to be independent, decision-making, working adults have had to deal with the conflict and tension involved in changing expected roles. The increased options for women are valuable, but temporarily may increase interpersonal conflict, self-consciousness, and even illness.

Just as an increasing number of women have stepped up their efforts to move from nonassertiveness to assertiveness, more men are making the choice to move away from being aggressive to being assertive. Assertive men feel comfortable with themselves and don't have to put others down to enhance themselves. In contrast, aggressive men often try to demonstrate their manhood by being dominating, showing little concern for others' feelings. Our society would benefit by increasingly valuing assertiveness in both women and men.

If you think that you are either too nonassertive or too aggressive in your relationship with others, you might consider signing up for a stress-management workshop that focuses on assertiveness training, or you might read an assertiveness training book, such as Robert Alberti and Michael Emmons' (1986) *Your Perfect Right* or Stanlee Phelps and Nancy Austin's *The Assertive*

SELF-ASSESSMENT

Assertiveness

Instructions

Use this code to indicate how characteristic or descriptive each of the following statements is of you:

1 = not at all like me
2 = somewhat not like me
3 = neither like me nor unlike me
4 = somewhat like me
5 = like me

Items

1. When someone steps in front of me in line, I do not let them get away with it.
2. I express my opinion without hesitation.
3. Sometimes I just can't say anything.
4. When at a lecture, I never ask questions.
5. I find it tough to say "no" to the needs of others.
6. When I accomplish something important I always let others know about it.
7. I express my feelings openly.
8. I have a hard time saying "no."
9. I usually hold in my emotions.
10. I complain about poor service when I am dissatisfied.
11. I often initiate conversations with strangers.
12. I feel uncomfortable calling business establishments and institutions.
13. If a close friend were annoying me, I would not express my feelings.
14. I don't ask questions because I am afraid I will sound stupid.
15. I avoid arguing over prices with sales people.
16. Most people seem to speak up more than I do.
17. When I am not happy with a service, I complain about it.
18. If someone asks a favor of me, I have a difficult time saying "no."
19. When I am asked to do something, I will usually ask questions about it.
20. It seems that people often take advantage of me.

Turn to the end of the chapter to interpret your responses.

CRITICAL THINKING

Civility in Context

Assertiveness has become an ideal for communication in the late twentieth century. Assertive behavior protects the individual and favors the direct expression of thoughts, needs, and feelings as the most respectful method of interacting with others. The assertiveness model has been widely adopted by therapists as a vehicle for helping people learn communication skills in order to cope more effectively in complex social situations.

There may be some contexts in which assertiveness would not be the most appropriate response. For example, one student who was struggling to learn assertiveness complained that assertiveness "didn't work" on her bowling league when she asked the other team politely to stay quiet while she took aim at the pins. Can you think of some situations in which a more aggressive or a more submissive response might be more adaptive?

In addition, the ideal of assertiveness is culture-bound. Can you speculate about some cultures in which assertiveness might not be seen as a civil response? Which cultures might not support the importance of individual rights or self-expression? Your answers demonstrate the importance of *examining the influence of context and culture on behavior.*

TABLE 5.1

A Bill of Assertive Rights

1. You have the right to be the judge of your own behavior, thoughts, and emotions, and to take the responsibility for their initiation and consequences.

2. You have the right NOT to offer reasons or excuses to justify your behavior, and to judge whether a reason is necessary in a situation.

3. You have the right to judge whether or not to be responsible for finding solutions to other people's problems.

4. You have the right to change your mind.

5. You have the right to be wrong.

6. You have the right to make mistakes, and to be responsible for your mistakes.

7. You have the right to say "I don't know."

8. You have the right to be independent of the good will of others before choosing how to behave with them.

9. You have the right to be illogical.

10. You have the right to say "I don't care."

11. You have the right to say "NO."

From *When I Say No, I Feel Guilty* by Manuel J. Smith. Copyright © 1975 by Manuel J. Smith. Used by permission of Doubleday, a division of Bantam Doubleday Dell Publishing Group, Inc.

Woman. A bill of assertive rights is presented in table 5.1.

Time Management

A popular toast sometimes goes, "We wish you health, wealth, and happiness." Some people who manage to achieve these goals don't have the time to enjoy them. Whether student, parent, or career person, time management can help you cope more effectively with your challenging world. Let's examine time management in more detail.

Time management *involves developing skills for learning how to use time more effectively to accomplish goals.* Most successful individuals have learned how to manage their time effectively. Elizabeth Dole, head of the American Red Cross, says she constantly works on perfecting her time management. She faithfully writes out to-do lists and uses other time management techniques. She periodically turns to an excellent time management book, *The Time Trap* (MacKenzie, 1991).

The daily **to-do list** *is a very effective time management technique that identifies activities, in ranked priority, that you want to accomplish each day.* It is one of the single most important time management tools—some experts say the most important (Kendrick & Kendrick, 1988). If you have never developed such a list, or if you do not make one regularly, you may want to get into the habit of doing so.

The to-do list is best when based on your highest-priority goals and plans. It is important to add to your list activities that are not directly related to your goals but that must be accomplished (such as doing your laundry, paying monthly bills). The to-do list for tomorrow should be completed at the end of today. When forming your list, keep five steps in mind:

1. Review your current goal-accomplishment plans and think about new items that demand your time.

2. Write down the activities you want to accomplish tomorrow, and mark an asterisk (*) by those that *must* be accomplished.

3. Number these activities in order of importance.

4. Estimate the time required to accomplish each activity.

5. Schedule the activities for specific times of the day.

Some individuals keep their lists on a daily calendar or in a special notebook. Others write them on separate pieces of plain white paper. Find a format you like, and stick with it!

Be realistic when estimating the time needed for the tasks on your list. Some individuals take on too many activities because they fail to estimate time required to complete projects accurately. This approach adds to stress, interferes with getting things done efficiently, and increases fears of failure. It is also important to avoid the other extreme and list too few activities. That is, challenge yourself and don't be satisfied with operating below your capabilities.

In addition to making daily to-do lists, you also might want periodically to keep a time log of how you actually spent your time. When first using the time-log tool, a detailed time log is best. If you haven't been accomplishing enough, a time log usually reveals why. For example, people who complete a time log are often amazed to find out how much time they have been spending on low-priority items. It often helps to keep a time log on both a daily and a weekly basis—figure 5.6 shows a cumulative time log of one student's week. For first-time users, a wise strategy is to keep a daily time log for a substantial period of time, usually a month. Also, at the end of each week, make out a cumulative time table like the one in figure 5.6.

> *Time is a great teacher, but unfortunately it kills all its pupils.*
> —**Hector Berlioz**

	Study				In class	Exercise	Naps	Eating, dressing	Social	Sleeping	Misc.	Daily total (awake)
	Course #1	Course #2	Course #3	Course #4								
Sunday	$1\frac{1}{4}$	$1\frac{1}{2}$	5	—	—	1	—	$2\frac{1}{2}$	—	8	—	16
Monday	—	—	2	2	$4\frac{1}{2}$	$\frac{1}{2}$	—	$3\frac{1}{2}$	$1\frac{1}{2}$	$8\frac{1}{2}$	$1\frac{1}{2}$	$15\frac{1}{2}$
Tuesday	2	—	3	—	$4\frac{1}{2}$	—	1	3	1	8	$1\frac{1}{2}$	16
Wednesday	1	4	—	2	3	1	—	$2\frac{1}{2}$	$1\frac{1}{2}$	7	2	17
Thursday	—	2	2	2	$4\frac{1}{2}$	1	2	2	$\frac{1}{2}$	6	2	18
Friday	1	—	—	1	$4\frac{1}{2}$	$\frac{1}{2}$	—	3	3	9	2	15
Saturday	—	2	—	—	—	2	1	4	6	$8\frac{1}{2}$	$4\frac{1}{2}$	$15\frac{1}{2}$
Total hours for week	$5\frac{1}{4}$	$9\frac{1}{2}$	12	7	21	6	4	$20\frac{1}{2}$	$13\frac{1}{2}$	55	$13\frac{1}{2}$	113
Percent of total awake	5%	8%	10%	5%	17%	5%	4%	18%	13%	49%	15%	100%

FIGURE 5.6

Cumulative Time Log for One College Student's Week

REVIEW

Seeking Social Support, Increasing Appropriate Risk Taking, and Stress Management

Social support is information and feedback from others that a person is loved and cared for, esteemed and valued, and included in a network of communication and mutual obligation. Three important benefits of social support are tangible assistance, information, and emotional support. Researchers have consistently found that social support helps individuals to cope more effectively with stress.

Actively inhibiting our emotions and behavior is associated with a variety of health problems. Instead of keeping our troubles bottled up inside of us, we can risk talking about them with others and we can work on cognitively restructuring them ourselves. It is important to remember that some aspects of inhibition are very healthy—such as curbing our drinking, drug taking, and violence. Some

individuals become frozen and immobilized by stress. Engaging in at least some activities you enjoy can be a helpful antidote to the problems you are facing. Another helpful coping strategy is to increase the laughter and humor in your life.

Stress-management programs teach individuals how to appraise stressful events, how to develop skills for coping with stress, and how to put these skills into use in their everyday lives. Stress-management programs are often taught through workshops. Some techniques that are taught in stress-management programs are meditation and relaxation, biofeedback, assertiveness training, and time management.

Meditation is the system of thought and practice used to attain bodily or mental control and well-being, as well as enlightenment. Transcendental meditation is the most popular form of meditation in the United States. Researchers have found that meditation reduces bodily arousal but usually no more than relaxation

does. The "relaxation response" can be especially helpful in reducing arousal and calming a person. Biofeedback is the process in which physical states, such as levels of muscle tension, are monitored by instruments and information from the instruments is given (fed back) to the individuals so they can learn to voluntarily control the physiological activities. Biofeedback has been successful in reducing muscle tension and blood pressure. Assertiveness training involves teaching individuals to act in their own best interests, to stand up for their legitimate rights, and to express their views directly and openly. Distinctions are made between nonassertive behavior, aggressive behavior, and assertive behavior, with assertive behavior favored for superior coping and adjustment. Time management involves developing skills for learning how to use time more effectively to accomplish goals. Most successful individuals have excellent time management skills. Two helpful time management strategies are to make up daily to-do lists and time logs.

Halonen/Santrock: Human Adjustment

Taking the Sting Out of Failure

We began this chapter with a story about the strategies of three kinds of students who were struggling with college life. You might have recognized those three kinds of responses to impending failure in a course. You might even have used one or more of the strategies yourself when facing an unpleasant, ego-damaging outcome.

After reading this chapter, you should have new ideas about how to address stress more effectively. Scan the summary of positive coping strategies in figure 5.7. (You also might want to review the more detailed descriptions of these strategies presented in figure 5.5.) Which of these strategies do you already use to enhance your ability to cope with stress? Why do these strategies appeal to you?

Suppose you were facing the harsh academic prospect of failing a test. Which strategies might be helpful to you in reducing the threat of academic failure? Why are some strategies more appealing than others in addressing academic concerns? What greater lessons could you learn from the failure? Your consideration of this challenge allows you to *practice self-reflection to enhance personal growth.*

Mistakes are a fact of life. It is the response to the error that counts.

—**Nikki Giovanni**

- Engage in cognitive appraisal — challenges
- Use cognitive appraisal— coping resources
- Engage in problem-focused coping
- Use emotion-focused coping
- Engage in active-cognitive strategies
- Engage in active-behavioral strategies
- Reduce or eliminate avoidance strategies
- Develop self-efficacy
- Engage in positive thinking and develop an optimistic outlook
- Engage in self-control
- Seek social support
- Follow a disinhibition strategy, engage in some enjoyable activities, and use humor
- Use stress-management techniques or become involved in a stress-management program
- Adopt multiple coping strategies

FIGURE 5.7

Overview of Positive Ways to Cope with Stress and Adjust More Effectively

We began this chapter by exploring the nature of coping, including the importance of cognitive appraisal and types of strategies. Our coverage of individual coping strategies focused on developing self-efficacy, thinking positively and optimistically, increasing self-control, seeking social support, and using multiple coping strategies. We also studied stress-management skills, including their nature, meditation and relaxation, biofeedback, assertiveness training, and time management. Remember that you can obtain an overall summary of the chapter by again studying the in-chapter reviews on pages 102, 109, and 116.

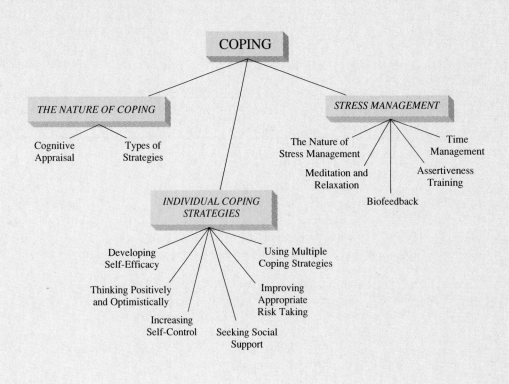

coping   100
problem-focused coping   101
emotion-focused coping   101
active-cognitive strategies   101
active-behavioral strategies   101
avoidance strategies   101
self-efficacy   101
cognitive restructuring   103

self-talk (self-statements)   103
thought stopping   107
empowerment   107
social support   108
stress-management programs   110
meditation   111
transcendental meditation (TM)   111
mantra   111

biofeedback   113
assertiveness training   113
nonassertive behavior   113
aggressive behavior   113
indirectly aggressive behavior   113
assertive behavior   113
time management   115
to-do list   115

PRACTICAL KNOWLEDGE ABOUT ADJUSTMENT

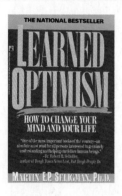

LEARNED OPTIMISM
(1990) by Martin Seligman. New York: Pocket Books.

Learned Optimism is one of the new breed of positive thinking books, a breed that first began to appear in the late 1980s and has increased in number recently. The new breed is based on psychological research and gives specific strategies for optimistic thinking rather than the old breed of cheerleading books that were low on substance.

Seligman argues that optimism and pessimism are not fixed, inborn psychological traits, but rather are explanatory styles—habitual ways we explain things that happen to us. Pessimists, says Seligman, perceive defeat as permanent, catastrophic, and evidence of personal inadequacy; optimists, by contrast, perceive the same mishap as a temporary setback, something that can be controlled, and rooted in circumstances of luck. Seligman's positive message is that since pessimism is learned it can be unlearned. Included are self-tests to determine your levels of optimism, pessimism, and depression.

In the national survey of self-help books, *Learned Optimism* was rated as one of the top 25 books. This is an excellent self-help book that is psychobabble-free and well-documented but not over academic. So, if you are a pessimist and nothing has seemed to work to get you out of your negative-thinking funk, this book is worth a try.

BEYOND THE RELAXATION RESPONSE
(1984) by Herbert Benson. New York: Times Books.

Beyond the Relaxation Response is Herbert Benson's sequel to *The Relaxation Response*. A decade after he coined the term *relaxation response*, Benson concluded that combining the relaxation response with another strategy is even more powerful in combating stress than the relaxation response alone. The other strategy is faith in a healing power either inside or outside of yourself. Benson arrived at this conclusion because of his own clinical observations and studies of Tibetan monks in the Himalayas, which are described in detail in *Beyond the Relaxation Response*. This does not mean you have to believe in a certain dogma or a traditional religion. You can, but you also can achieve the desired result by having faith in yourself, or even in a state while exercising or eliciting the relaxation response. Benson tells you how to harness the power of faith in many different situations—while jogging or walking, swimming, lying in bed, or praying.

Beyond the Relaxation Response was one of the top 25 self-help books in the recent national survey of clinical and counseling psychologists. It is a very practical book that clearly conveys the healing power of relaxation and mental strategies for improving our well-being.

SELF-ASSESSMENT SCORING AND INTERPRETATION

ASSERTIVENESS

Scoring

Before totaling your score, you must change the score for items 3, 4, 8, 9, 12, 13, 14, 15, 16, 18, and 20. Change your score on these items from 1 to 5, 2 to 4, 4 to 2, or 5 to 1. Do not change your score if you indicated a 3. Total your score by adding the numbers. Total scores can range from 20 to 100.

Interpretation

The middle score equals 60. Scores below 60 represent lower levels of assertiveness and scores over 60 represent higher levels of assertiveness. Use your responses to individual items to determine areas in which you could profit from being more assertive.

Monet
Le Genouvillere, detail

CHAPTER

6

Social Thinking and Behavior

> Our concern is not how to worship in the catacombs but how to remain human in the skyscrapers.
>
> —Abraham J. Heschel

THE STORY OF DAVID KORESH:
CHARISMATIC SADIST OR TRUE BELIEVER?

I ronically, *charismatic* and *combustible* were two terms *Time* magazine used to describe cult leader David Koresh in the days before his Waco, Texas, compound exploded on April 19, 1993, killing Koresh and many of his followers. Born Vernon Howell in Houston, Koresh dropped out of the ninth grade but found great comfort in the teachings of an offshoot of the Seventh-Day Adventist Church, the Branch Davidians. He joined an existing congregation in Waco and rose to its leadership, changing his name to David Koresh in 1990. Actively recruiting new members from the United States, Britain, and Australia, he transformed the congregation into a cult based on apocalyptic theology and secular survivalism; they stockpiled food and ammunition to prepare for the end of the world through nuclear or social catastrophe.

According to *Time,* Koresh's charisma allowed him to impose on his followers all manner of sacrifices that he decreed did not apply to him. Members donated their assets and paychecks to cover the expenses of the compound. Men worked at construction while women attended the house and educated the children. Members ate strict rations of vegetables, although Koresh sometimes suddenly instituted dietary changes without explanation. In contrast, Koresh reportedly had access to things that were forbidden to the members, such as meat, beer, and television. Koresh required the men to be celibate and the women to be

David Koresh

available to him as "wives." Although Koresh was charged with sexual child abuse several times, linked to his preferences for young brides, he was never convicted. Those who left the cult described Koresh as a zealous, imaginative preacher, giving sermons that extended long into the night with interpretations that inexplicably varied from one sermon to the next. Former cult members reported that Koresh paddled and humiliated rule breakers; when paddlings didn't produce compliance, Koresh ordered the rule breakers to lie down in raw sewage, refusing to let them bathe afterward. His blend of physical force, psychological strategy, and personal magnetism was described as hard to resist.

Janet Reno had been on her job as Attorney General of the Justice Department for only about a month when the Bureau of Alcohol, Tobacco, and Firearms (ATF) proposed a plan for its second assault on "Ranch Apocalypse,"

Koresh's Waco compound. The ATF believed that Koresh was holding cult members hostage and was converting firearms illegally into weapons of greater efficiency. The ATF's first assault, on February 28, resulted in the deaths of four ATF agents and as many as ten cult members, including one of Koresh's many children. Fifty-one days later, the ATF's second assault began with tear gas, but the compound exploded. Fire raced through the compound, killing an estimated 25 children and 60 adults, including Koresh.

After two congressional hearings and an internal ATF investigation, no one knows for certain what caused the fire—whether it was part of a massive suicide plan on the part of Koresh and his followers, whether the ATF began the fire, or whether the fire had started by accident. One thing that was certain was that the assault had been a mistake. At least for Koresh and his followers, his predictions of a holocaust had come true.

The horrifying story of David Koresh introduces many of the themes that we will explore in this chapter; it shows the power of obedience and conformity and how such power can be abused. The same processes help to determine the latest fashion fads, influence the outcome of political elections, and shape our everyday decisions. In this chapter we will study these processes, beginning with an elaboration of social cognition, that includes social perception, attribution, and attitudes. Next we will turn to persuasion and obedience, the processes of interpersonal social influence. Finally, we will address group relations, including leadership, conformity, and groupthink.

SOCIAL COGNITION

As we interact with our world, we are both actors and spectators, doing and perceiving, acting and thinking. Social psychologists are interested in how we perceive our social world and how we try to make sense of our own behavior and the behavior of others. They are also interested in how we form and change our attitudes. We will begin the study of social cognition by exploring the nature of social perception.

Social Perception

Social perception *is our judgment about the qualities of individuals, which involves how we form impressions of others, how we gain self-knowledge from our perception of others, and how we present ourselves to others to influence their perceptions of us.*

Impression Formation

Our evaluations of people often fall into broad categories—good or bad, happy or sad, introvert or extrovert, for example. If someone asked for your impression of your psychology professor, you might respond, "She is great." Then you might go on to describe your perception of her characteristics—for example, "She is charming, intelligent, witty, and sociable." These opinions represent inferences you make from the samples of her behavior you experience directly. From this description we can also infer that you have a positive impression of her.

As we form impressions of others, we cognitively organize the information in two important ways. First, our impressions are *unified,* and second, our impressions are *integrated.* Traits, actions, appearance, and all of the other information we obtain about a person are closely connected in memory, even though the

information may have been obtained in an interrupted or random fashion. We might obtain some information today, more next week, some more in 2 months. During those 2 months, we interacted with many other people and developed impressions of them as well. Nonetheless, we usually perceive the information about a particular person as unified, as a continuous block of information.

Our first encounter with someone also contributes to the impression we form. First impressions are often enduring. **Primacy effect** *is the term used for the enduring quality of initial impressions.* One reason for the primacy effect is that we pay less attention to subsequent information about the individual (Anderson, 1965). The next time you want to impress someone, a wise strategy is to make sure that you put your best foot forward in your first encounter.

Social Comparison

How many times have you asked yourself questions such as "Am I as smart as Jill?" "Is Bob better looking than I am?" or "Is my taste as good as Carmen's?" We gain self-knowledge from our own behavior; we also gain it from others through **social comparison,** *the process in which individuals evaluate their thoughts, feelings, behaviors, and abilities in relation to other people. Social comparison helps individuals to evaluate themselves, tells them what their distinctive characteristics are, and aids them in building an identity.*

Some years ago Leon Festinger (1954) proposed a theory of social comparison. He stressed that when no objective means is available to evaluate our opinions and abilities, we compare ourselves with others. Festinger believed that we are more likely to compare ourselves

with others who are similar to us than with those who are dissimilar to us. He reasoned that if we compare ourselves with someone who is very different from us, we will not be able to obtain an accurate appraisal of our own behavior and thoughts. This means that we will develop more accurate self-perceptions if we compare ourselves with people in communities similar to where we grew up and live, with people who have similar family backgrounds, and with people of the same sex, for example. Social comparison theory has been extended and modified over the years and continues to provide an important rationale for why we affiliate with others and how we come to know ourselves (Kenrick & others, 1993).

In contrast to Festinger's emphasis on the role of social comparison in evaluating one's abilities, recently researchers have focused more on the self-enhancing properties of downward comparisons (Banaji & Prentice, 1994). Individuals under threat (experiencing negative feedback, low self-esteem, depression, or illness, for example) often try to improve their well-being by comparing themselves with someone less fortunate.

Impression Management

Impression management *(also called self-presentation) involves acting to present an image of oneself as a certain sort of person, which might or might not be who one really is.* In most instances, we try to present ourselves as better than we really are. We spend billions of dollars rearranging our faces, bodies, mind, and social skills to favorably impress others. We especially use self-presentational motives with people we are not familiar with and with persons in whom we have a sexual interest (Leary & others, 1994).

Instructions

These statements concern personal reactions to a number of situations. No two statements are exactly alike, so consider each statement carefully before answering. If a statement is true or mostly true as applied to you, circle the T. If a statement is false or not usually true as applied to you, circle the F.

1. I find it hard to imitate the behavior of other people.   T F
2. I guess I put on a show to impress or entertain people.   T F
3. I would probably make a good actor.   T F
4. I sometimes appear to others to be experiencing deeper emotions than I actually am. T F
5. In a group of people, I am rarely the center of attention.   T F
6. In different situations and with different people, I often act like very different persons. T F
7. I can only argue for ideas I already believe.   T F
8. In order to get along and be liked, I tend to be what people expect me to be. T F
9. I may deceive people by being friendly when I really dislike them.   T F
10. I'm not always the person I appear to be.   T F

To score the items and determine your self-monitoring tendencies, turn to the end of the chapter.

There are five main strategies for influencing the impressions we make on others (Jones & Pittman, 1982). First, **ingratiation** *is a self-presentation technique that involves making yourself likeable, sometimes illicitly, in another person's eyes.* How might you go about doing this? One way is simply to agree with what others say. Another is to praise the other person's accomplishments, personality, and so on. Yet another way is to do favors for the person you want to impress. However, to succeed, the strategies have to be used subtly; if pushed too far, they will often be detected. Knowing how to ingratiate effectively involves knowing how much is too much.

A second impression management strategy is **self-promotion,** *a self-presentation technique in which individuals try to present themselves as competent.* In general, ingratiation is a strategy that involves trying to get other people to like us, while self-promotion involves trying to make other people respect us.

A third impression management strategy is **intimidation,** *a self-presentation technique in which individuals present themselves as dangerous in an effort to coerce others into treating them in a desired way.* Intimidators try to convince others that they can and will cause trouble for others if they don't do what they want.

A fourth impression management strategy is **exemplification,** *a self-presentation technique in which individuals portray themselves as having integrity and being morally worthy.* While self-promoters strive to project that they are competent, exemplifiers strive to project that they are morally pure. Exemplifiers risk being found out and called hypocrites.

A fifth impression management strategy is **supplication,** *a self-presentation technique in which individuals try to make themselves appear weak and dependent.* Supplication may work because it is a norm in our society that we should feel sorry for people who are needy and handicapped.

Keep in mind, though, that impression management techniques that work in one cultural setting may not work in another. In particular, appreciation and flattery are often culture-bound. For example, in some Eastern European countries, if one person expresses great admiration for another's watch, courtesy dictates that the watch should be given to the admirer! In the Native American culture of the Sioux, it's considered courteous to open a conversation with a compliment. Nonverbal cues also vary considerably from culture to culture. For example, in some Middle Eastern countries, it would be deemed offensive and

inappropriate to pass an apple to another using the left hand. These cultures define the left hand as "unclean" and scrupulously avoid interpersonal contact of this type (Axtell, 1991).

Self-Monitoring

Some people are more concerned about and aware of the impressions they make than others are. **Self-monitoring** *is individuals' awareness of the impressions they make on others and the degree to which they fine-tune their performance accordingly.* Lawyers and actors are among the best self-monitors; salespeople, con artists, and politicians are not far behind. Fiorello LaGuardia, a former mayor of New York City, was so good at self-monitoring that observers who watched silent films of his campaign speeches could tell which ethnic group he was courting for votes.

High-self-monitoring individuals seek information about appropriate ways to present themselves and invest considerable time in trying to read and understand others (Simpson, 1995). Social psychologist Mark Snyder (1979) developed a scale to measure the extent to which an individual is a high or low self-monitor. To see how you fare in self-monitoring, see the Self-Assessment, where items from Snyder's scale are presented.

The principle of self-monitoring points out that individuals vary in how much they are tuned in to what is happening in the external world. A theory of psychology that has become prominent in recent years underscores that we seek to explain behavior in terms of internal or external causes; it is called attribution theory.

Attribution

Attribution theorists argue that we want to know why people do the things they do because the knowledge will enable us to cope more effectively with the situations that confront us. **Attribution theory** *states that individuals are motivated to discover the underlying causes of behavior as part of their interest in making sense out of the behavior.* In a way, attribution theorists say people are much like intuitive scientists, seeking the reason something happens.

We can classify the reasons individuals behave the way they do in a number of ways, but one basic distinction stands out above all the others—the distinction between *internal* causes, such as the actor's personality traits or motives, and *external* causes, which are environmental, situational factors (Heider, 1958). If you don't do well on a test, do you attribute it to the professor's having plotted against you and having made the test too difficult (external cause) or to your not having studied hard enough (internal cause)? The answer to such a question influences how we feel about ourselves. If we believe our poor performance is the professor's fault (he gives unfair tests, for example), we don't feel as bad as when we do not spend enough time studying: By using an external attribution, we place the blame somewhere other than on ourselves.

Our attributions are not always accurate (Brehm & Kassin, 1996). In a given situation the person who acts, or the actor, produces the behavior to be explained. Then the onlooker, or the observer, offers a causal explanation of the actor's behavior or experience. Actors often explain their own behavior with external causes, while observers often explain the actor's behavior with internal causes. The **fundamental attribution error** *is that observers overestimate the importance of traits*

Example: The employee left out an entire column of data in his data entry task.

ACTOR (Employee)	OBSERVER (Supervisor)
More likely to give external, situational explanations of own behavior	More likely to give internal, trait explanations of actor's behavior
"It's too noisy in here to concentrate."	"You're really rushing and not being careful."

FIGURE 6.1

The Actor-Observer Hypothesis
In this situation, the supervisor is the observer and the employee is the actor. If the employee has made an error in his work, how are the employee and his supervisor likely to give different explanations of his behavior, based on your knowledge of actor-observer differences and the fundamental attribution error?

and underestimate the importance of situations when they seek explanations of an actor's behavior. On the other hand, actors rely more on situations than they do on traits in explaining their own behavior. Actors often show a self-serving bias in explaining negative outcomes by shifting blame to external forces. Since actors and observers often have different ideas about what causes behavior, many attributions are biased. Behavior is determined by a number of factors, so it is not surprising that our lives are full of squabbling and arguing about the causes of behavior. Attribution theory provides us with a more informed perspective on disagreements in marriages, the courts, the Senate, and many other social arenas (Harvey, 1995). See figure 6.1 for an illustration of how the actor-observer hypothesis works in job-related contexts. To examine the fundamental attribution error in the classroom, turn to Critical Thinking.

Attitudes and Behavior

As Mark Twain said, "It is a difference of opinion that makes horses race." **Attitudes** *are beliefs and opinions that can predispose individuals to behave in certain ways.* We have attitudes about all sorts of things, and we live in a world in which we try to influence each other's attitudes.

Fundamentals of Conflict

The fundamental attribution error is tricky. The concept explains why two individuals can live through one situation and not report the same experience.

For example, suppose the person who sits next to you in class is never on time. He comes in late consistently and makes lots of noise moving to his seat. How would you (the observer) explain his behavior? How would he (the actor) explain his own behavior?

Now suppose you are late to class. How would you, as the *actor*, explain this lapse? What kinds of attributions would your teacher, an *observer*, make about your late arrival? If you are like most people, you will probably notice that your explanations for your own late arrival tend to blame forces outside yourself, while your teacher is more likely to make attributions that emphasize negative aspects of your character and commitment to the class to explain your late arrival.

What value differences are likely to separate the explanations of the actor and the observer? Your conclusions will illustrate your *awareness of underlying values that motivate behavior,* in this case the assignment of a self-protective or dismissive attribution. You might even find yourself hesitating before you judge the motives of others, in order to minimize your own fundamental attribution errors.

In a civilized society we all depend upon each other, and our happiness results from the good opinion of mankind.
—**Samuel Johnson**

Think about your attitudes toward religion, politics, and sex. Now think about your behavior in these areas. Consider sex, for example. How liberal or conservative are your sexual attitudes? Does your behavior match your attitudes? Researchers have found that we have more accepting attitudes toward sexual practices than our behavior actually shows (Dreyer, 1982). As we study the relation of attitudes to behavior, two questions arise: How strongly do attitudes influence behavior? How strongly does behavior influence attitudes?

Predicting Behavior from Attitudes

More than 50 years ago, Richard LaPiere (1934) toured the United States with a Chinese couple. LaPiere expected to encounter prejudice against the Asians. He thought they would be banned from restaurants and hotels, for example. Surprisingly, in more than 10,000 miles of travel, the threesome was rejected only once. It appeared, LaPiere thought, that there were few negative attitudes toward Asians in the United States. To see if this actually was the case, LaPiere wrote a letter to all 251 places he and his Asian friends had visited, asking the proprietors if they would provide food or lodging to Asians. More than half responded; of those, a resounding 90 percent said they absolutely would not allow Asians in their restaurant or motel. LaPiere's study documented a powerful lesson in understanding human behavior: what we *say* may be different from what we *do.*

The connection between attitudes and behaviors may vary with the situation. In the study of attitudes toward Asians in the 1930s, the Chinese who accompanied LaPiere were well dressed and carried expensive luggage; they might have inspired different attitudes if they had appeared in cheaper attire or if they had not been traveling in the company of a European male. To consider further situational influences on attitude-behavior connections, imagine asking someone about his attitude toward people who drive pickup trucks. Let's say he responds, "Totally classless." A month later the guy stops for a cup of coffee in a small West Texas town. A burly man in the next booth is talking with his buddies about the merits of pickup trucks. He turns to our friend and asks, "How do you like that green pickup truck sitting outside?" Needless to say, his response is not "totally classless." This example suggests that the demands of the situation can be powerful even when we hold strong beliefs. This is an important point that social psychologists refer to throughout their work on explaining social behavior.

Behavior's Influence on Attitudes

"The actions of men are the best interpreters of their thoughts" asserted seventeenth-century English philosopher John Locke. Does doing change your believing? If you quit drinking, will you have a more negative attitude toward drinking? If you take up an exercise program, are you more likely to extol the benefits of cardiovascular fitness when someone asks your attitude about exercise?

Changes in behavior can precede changes in attitudes (Bandura, 1991). Social psychologists offer two main explanations of behavior's influence on attitudes. The first is that people have a strong need for cognitive consistency; consequently, they might change their attitudes to make them more consistent with their behavior (Carkenord & Bullington, 1995). The second is that our attitudes often are not completely clear, so we observe our behavior and make inferences about it to determine what our attitudes should be. Let's consider these two views in more detail.

Festinger's Cognitive Dissonance Theory

Cognitive dissonance, *a concept developed by social psychologist Leon Festinger (1957), refers to an individual's motivation*

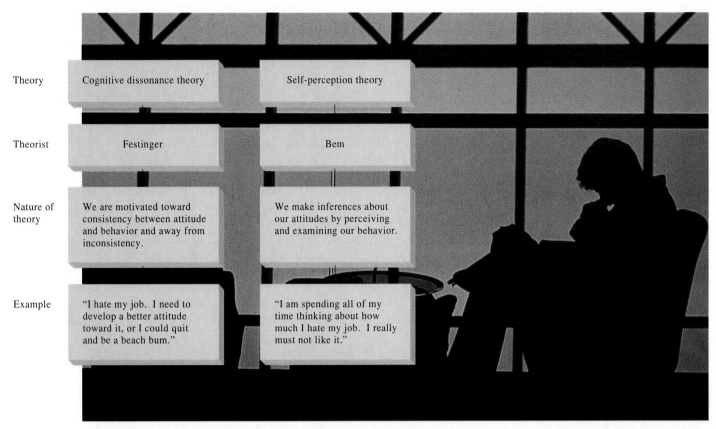

Theory	Cognitive dissonance theory	Self-perception theory
Theorist	Festinger	Bem
Nature of theory	We are motivated toward consistency between attitude and behavior and away from inconsistency.	We make inferences about our attitudes by perceiving and examining our behavior.
Example	"I hate my job. I need to develop a better attitude toward it, or I could quit and be a beach bum."	"I am spending all of my time thinking about how much I hate my job. I really must not like it."

FIGURE 6.2

Two Views of Behavior's Influence on Attitudes

to reduce the discomfort (dissonance) caused by two inconsistent thoughts. For example, we might feel uneasy about a discrepancy that exists between our attitudes and our behavior. The absence of internal justification for the difference between what we believe and what we do creates dissonance. We can engage in a variety of actions to reduce the dissonance. Imagine a circumstance in which you do something you do not feel good about, such as flunking a test. You might reduce the dissonance by devaluing the test or accusing the teacher of unfair testing practices. You might drop the course, deciding it was no longer important for your future. All these actions reduce dissonance. We often justify our behavior, as George Bernard Shaw did with his father's alcoholism: "If you cannot get rid of the family skeleton, you may as well make it dance." Shaw's justification helped him reduce the tension between his father's drinking problem and his attitude about it. Cognitive dissonance is about making our skeletons dance, about

trying to reduce tension by cognitively justifying things that are unpleasant (Aronson, 1995).

Bem's Self-Perception Theory

Not all social psychologists, however, are satisfied with cognitive dissonance as an explanation for the influence of behavior on attitudes. Daryl Bem, for example, believes that the cognitive dissonance view relies too heavily on internal factors, which are difficult to measure. Bem (1967) argues that we should move away from such nebulous concepts as "cognitions" and "psychological discomfort" and replace them with more behavioral terminology. **Self-perception theory** *is Bem's theory of the connection between attitudes and behavior; it stresses that individuals make inferences about their attitudes by perceiving their behavior.* For example, consider the remark "I am spending all of my time thinking about the test I have next week; I must be anxious," or "This is the third time I have gone to the student

union in 2 days; I must be lonely." Bem believes we look to our own behavior when our attitudes are not completely clear. This means that when we have clear ideas about something, we are less likely to look to our behavior for clues about our attitudes; however, if we feel ambivalent about something or someone, our behavior is a good place to look to determine our attitude. Figure 6.2 compares cognitive dissonance and self-perception theories.

We have just explored how social cognitions help us to perceive ourselves and others and to form attitudes. Next we will examine the nature of interpersonal relationships.

INTERPERSONAL SOCIAL INFLUENCE

In the scale of the destinies, brawn will never weigh as much as brain.
—James Russell Lowell (1819–1891)

Social Cognition

Three important dimensions of social perception are developing impressions of others, making social comparisons, and presenting ourselves to others to influence their social perceptions. Our impressions are unified. First impressions are important and influence impressions at a later point. We evaluate ourselves by comparison with others. Festinger stressed that social comparison provides an important source of self-knowledge, especially when no other objective means is available; we are more likely to compare ourselves with others who are similar.

Impression management involves acting to present an image of oneself as a certain sort of person, which might or might not be who one is. Five impression management strategies are ingratiation, self-promotion, intimidation, exemplification, and supplication. Self-monitoring involves individuals' awareness of the impressions they make on others and the degree to which they fine-tune their performance accordingly. Self-monitoring refers to how extensively we are aware of the impressions we make on others and the extent to which we fine-tune our social behavior accordingly.

Attribution focuses on the motivation to infer causes of behavior in order to make sense out of the world. One of the most frequent and important ways we classify the causes of behavior is in terms of internal and external causes. Our attributions are not always accurate; the human mind has a built-in bias in making causal judgments. The fundamental attribution error involves overestimating the importance of traits and internal causes while underestimating the importance of situations and external causes. Actors are more likely to choose external causes, observers internal causes. Attitudes are beliefs and opinions. Social psychologists are interested in how strongly attitudes predict behavior. Today it is believed that, when situational influences are weak, the attitude-behavior connection is strengthened. Cognitive dissonance theory, developed by Festinger, argues that, because we have a strong need for cognitive consistency, we change our attitudes to make them more consistent with our behavior so that dissonance is reduced. Bem developed a more behavioral approach, called self-perception theory; it stresses the importance of making inferences about our own behavior, especially when our attitudes are not clear.

Both brawn and brain have been used to influence others. In this section we will explore the nature of social influence as it occurs between people in relationships and among people in groups.

Social influence between two people comes in many forms. However, influence involves a change in attitude or a change in action that results from the efforts of another. We will examine two kinds of interpersonal influence: persuasion and obedience to authority.

Persuasion

No matter what side of an argument you're on, you always find some people on your side that you wish were on the other side.

—**Jascha Heifetz**

We spend many hours of our lives trying to persuade people to do certain things. A young man might try to persuade a young woman of the intensity of his love for her. Advertisers try to persuade us that their product is superior and life-enhancing. Politicians and corporations are also heavily involved in the persuasion process. Politicians, for example, have full arsenals of speech writers and image consultants to ensure that their words and behavior are as persuasive as possible. Social psychologists believe that persuasion involves four key components: who conveys the message (the source), what the message is (the communication), what medium is used (the channel), and for whom the message is intended (the target).

The Communicator (Source)

Suppose you are running for president of the student body. You tell students you are going to make life at your college better. Would they believe you? That would depend on several different factors.

Two factors involved in whether or not we believe someone are the *expertise* and the *credibility* of the communicator. Expertise depends on qualifications. If you had held other elective offices, students would be more likely to believe you have the expertise to be their president. We attribute competence to experts, believing they are knowledgeable about the topics they address.

In addition to expertise and credibility, *trustworthiness* is an important quality of an effective communicator. This factor depends on whether what you say and how you say it is perceived as honest or dishonest. It was in Abraham Lincoln's best interest, then, to be called "Honest Abe"; being perceived as honest increased the power of his communication.

Social psychologists believe that *power, attractiveness, likableness,* and *similarity* are four important characteristics that add to a communicator's ability to change people's attitudes. In running for student body president, you will probably have more clout with students if you have been on the university president's student issues committee. Power may be an important characteristic for a communicator because it is associated with the ability to impose sanctions or control rewards and punishments (Kelley & Thibaut, 1978). In running for student body president, you are also more likely to get votes if students perceive you as attractive and similar to themselves. That's why you often see presidential candidates putting on miners' helmets in West Virginia, speaking a Spanish phrase in San Antonio, or riding a

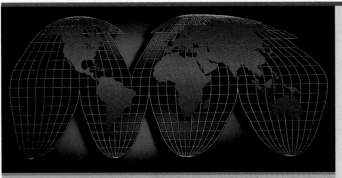

Gender and Politics:
From Ferraro to County Clerk

It is the summer of 1984. The November presidential election is only months away; the Democrats are far behind in the polls. The economy is looking better, and Republican incumbent Ronald Reagan's lead seems insurmountable. What could the Democratic party do to persuade the American population to switch their allegiance? It would have to be something bold, something never tried before in the history of American politics.

One of the areas in which Reagan seemed vulnerable was women's rights; the National Organization for Women (NOW) called Reagan insensitive to women, for example. For the first time in history, a woman—Geraldine Ferraro—was selected to fill the vice-presidential slot on the Democratic ticket. Although the Democrats did not win the 1984 presidential election, Ferraro's selection was an important step for women in their effort to achieve equality.

As more women have sought political office, the issue of gender has assumed a more important role in attitude change. Surveys reveal that, in today's political climate, we are more likely to vote for qualified female candidates, especially if they are running for lower political offices (Gallup, 1984). Discrimination still exists, though, especially in gubernatorial campaigns (Yankelovich, Skelly, & White, 1984).

The challenge is to determine for whom and under what circumstances gender makes the most difference. Social psychologist Carol Sigelman and her colleagues (1986) wanted to find out to what extent voters are influenced by a candidate's gender,

physical attractiveness, and prestige in relation to the responsibility of the office being sought. The researchers gave college students information about six challengers to an incumbent in either a mayoral or county clerk's race. The challengers were men and women of high, moderate, or low physical attractiveness. The researchers found that the male, but not the female, voters discriminated against the female candidates. In addition, the men saw the women as less qualified, fewer of the men voted for the women, and the men rated the women lower overall. The males' antifemale bias was not offset by a preference for the women candidates by the female voters, however. The female voters tended to choose evenly between the male and female candidates. Also, attractiveness was less consistently an asset for the female candidates than it was for the males. Although it appears that less discrimination against female candidates occurs today than in past years, this research suggests that equality has not yet been reached.

Geraldine Ferraro campaigned as a vice-presidential candidate on the Mondale-Ferraro Democratic ticket in 1984. *What is gender's role in political attitudes?*

tractor in Iowa. The candidates are striving to show that they share common interests and an identity with their audience.

Similarity is also widely used in advertising. In commercials we might see a homemaker scrubbing the floor while advertising a new cleaner or a laborer laughing with his buddies at a bar while drinking beer. The creators of these commercials

hope you will relate to these people because you perceive them as similar to yourself. Of course, many products are promoted by appealing to our personal ideals. To do this, attractive or famous individuals are used in advertisements. Elizabeth Taylor tries to persuade us to buy cologne, and Michael Jordan tries to persuade us to buy athletic shoes, for example.

Other factors that influence attitudes are the sex of the communicator and gender roles. To learn more about how gender might be a factor in attitudes about political candidates, see Sociocultural Worlds of Adjustment. As we will see next, the content of the message also is an important factor in influencing attitudes.

Jesse Jackson is shown here campaigning for president in 1988. Whether a candidate is running for president of the United States or for president of a college's student body, expertise, credibility, trust, power, attraction, and similarity are important characteristics.

The Message

What should the content of a message be like to make it more persuasive? Should appeals be more positive than negative? Should a rational or emotional strategy be used?

How often have we seen politicians vow to run a clean campaign but as soon as the bell sounds come out swinging below the belt? In the 1988 presidential campaign, negative advertising became a big issue and proved to be effective. George Bush succeeded in branding Michael Dukakis with the *L* word (liberal) in the campaign. Negative appeals play on our emotions, while positive appeals are directed at our rational, logical thinking. The less informed we are, the more likely we will respond to an emotional appeal. For example, if we do not know anything about nuclear waste, an emotional appeal to keep a hazardous waste dump from being built near our home may influence our attitude about the project more than an appeal based on reasoning. For people who did not know much about Dukakis' political background, Bush's criticism of Dukakis was probably a wise strategy. Bush tried pinning the liberal label on Bill Clinton in the 1992 presidential campaign, but the sociopolitical context had changed.

All other things being equal, the more frightened we are, the more we will change our attitude. The day after the telecast of the vivid nuclear war film *The Day After,* more negative attitudes about the United States' massive nuclear arsenal surfaced (Schofield & Pavelchak, 1989). Advertisers also sometimes take advantage of our fears to stimulate attitude change. For example, you may have seen the Michelin tire ad that shows a baby playing near tires or the life insurance company ad that shows a widow and her young children moving out of their home, which they lost because they did not have enough insurance.

Does persuasion based on fear-inducing strategies change behavior as well as attitudes? In one study, researchers tried to scare smokers into taking chest X rays and becoming nonsmokers by varying the intensity of the fear-producing stimulus (Leventhal, 1970). The low-fear group was advised to get X rays and stop smoking. The moderate-fear group was shown a film in which a young man's cancer was diagnosed from X rays. The high-fear group also was shown the film but viewed a film of a gory operation as well. The researchers concluded that the most frightened were the most likely to show behavior changes. In addition, fear-arousing communication might have limited influence in the absence of clear and specific instructions about taking counter-measures. Four months after the experiment, the subjects who were most frightened and most specifically instructed were smoking less than were subjects who had been in the other groups.

Music is widely used to make us feel good about messages. Think about how few television commercials you have seen without some form of music either in the background or as a prominent part of the message. When we watch such commercials, we may associate the pleasant feelings of the music with the product, even though the music itself does not provide any information about the product.

The Medium

While there are many factors to consider in regard to the message itself, the communicator also needs to be concerned about which medium to use to get the message across. Consider the difference between watching a presidential debate on television and reading about it in the newspaper. Television lets us see how the candidates deliver the message, what their appearance and mannerisms are like, and so on. Because it presents live images, television is considered the most powerful medium for changing attitudes. One study revealed that the winners of various political primaries were predicted by the amount of media exposure they had (Grush, 1980).

Television's power of persuasion is staggering. By the time the average American adolescent graduates from high school, he or she has watched 20,000 hours of television, far more than the number of hours spent in the classroom. Social scientists have studied television's influence on matters such as the impact of commercials on purchases, of mass media political campaigning on voting, of public service announcements on health, of broad-based ideological campaigns on lifestyles, and of television violence on aggression.

Persuasion and the Buddy System

Suppose that you have just taken up running as a good form of exercise and decide to do some research on the best running shoes for your needs. You look at *Consumer Reports*. You go to specialized shoe stores and examine models. After much research and evaluation, you decide on a particular costly pair. But just before you make your purchase, you mention your choice to your favorite running companion, who comprehensively describes all the troubles that she encountered with that brand. She describes poor wear, blisters, and leg aches, all attributed to the bad buy she made, and discourages you from making a similar mistake.

What do you do? Most of us are inclined to abandon all of our painstaking research under the influence of the personal testimony of a friend whose opinion

we prize. A vivid, clear, personal example apparently carries more evaluative weight with us than even our own conclusion derived from more reliable methods. We assume that our friend's experience is typical, when it simply might not be. Can you think of an example in which the power of a personal example may have undermined your confidence in your own more systematic methods? Your awareness of the typicality effect of personal testimony may assist you to *evaluate the validity of your conclusions* as well as save you from acting on testimony about atypical personal experiences.

> *The world is not run by thought, not by imagination, but by opinion.*
>
> —**Elizabeth Drew**

How strong is television's influence on an individual's attitudes and behavior? Some reviews of research conclude that there are few effects (Zeigler & Harmon, 1989). Other reviews conclude television has a more formidable effect (Clifford, Bunter, & McAleer, 1995).

The Target (Audience)

What are some characteristics of the audience that determine whether a message will be effective? Age, gender, and self-esteem are three such factors. Younger people are more likely to change their attitudes than older ones, females appear to be more persuadable than males, and self-esteem is believed to be important but does not have a predictable pattern. Another factor is the strength of the audience's attitude. If the audience is not strongly committed to a particular attitude, change is more likely; if it is strong, the communicator will have more difficulty. To evaluate your own persuasion potential, see the Critical Thinking box.

Obedience

Obedience *is behavior that complies with the explicit demands of an individual in authority.* Although many parents try to instill obedience in their children,

obedience sometimes can be destructive: The disaster in Waco described at the beginning of this chapter, the massacre of Vietnamese civilians at My Lai, and the Nazi crimes against Jews and others in World War II are other examples of destructive obedience. Adolph Eichmann, for example, has been described as an ambitious functionary who believed that it was his duty to obey Hitler's orders. An average middle-class man with no identifiable criminal tendencies, Eichmann ordered the killing of 6 million Jews and others. The following experiment, first performed by Stanley Milgram (1965) at Yale University, provides insight into such obedience.

As part of an experiment in psychology, you are asked to deliver a series of painful electric shocks to another person. You are told that the purpose of the study is to determine the effects of punishment on memory. Your role is to be the "teacher" and punish the mistakes made by a "learner." Each time the learner makes a mistake, your job is to increase the intensity of the shock by a certain amount. You are given a 75-volt shock to show you how it feels. You are then introduced to the "learner," a nice 50-year-old man who mumbles something about having a heart condition.

He is strapped to a chair in the next room and communicates with you through an intercom. As the trials proceed, the "learner" quickly runs into trouble and is unable to give the correct answers. Should you shock him? The apparatus in front of you has thirty switches, ranging from 15 volts (light) to 375 volts (marked "danger") to 450 volts (marked "XXX"). As you raise the intensity of the shock, the "learner" says he's in pain. At 150 volts, he demands to have the experiment stopped. At 180 volts, he cries out that he can't stand it anymore. At 300 volts, he yells about his heart condition and pleads to be released. If you hesitate in shocking the learner, however, the experimenter tells you that you have no choice; the experiment must continue.

As you might imagine, in Milgram's study the "teachers" were uneasy about shocking the "learner." At 240 volts, one "teacher" responded, "Two hundred forty volts delivered: Aw, no. You mean I've got to keep going with that scale? No sir, I'm not going to kill that man—I'm not going to give him 450 volts!" (Milgram, 1965, p. 67). At the very high voltage, the "learner" quit responding. When the "teacher" asked the experimenter what to do, he simply

---

(a)

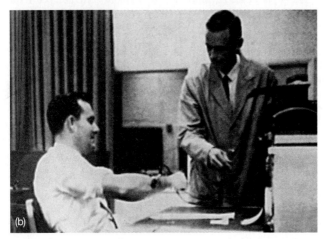

(b)

In 1989 Chinese students led a massive demonstration against the Chinese government in Beijing. The students resisted the government's social influence by putting together resources to challenge the Chinese authorities; however, the government eventually prevailed after ordering the massacre of hundreds of students.

FIGURE 6.3

Milgram Obedience Study
(*a*) A 50-year-old man ("learner") is strapped into a chair. The experimenter makes it look as if a shock generator is being connected to his body through a number of electrodes. (*b*) The subject ("teacher") is given a sample 75-volt shock. *How far do you think you might have taken the shock in order to help science and assist the "learner" to learn?*

Resisting Social Influence

If a man does not keep pace with his companions,
perhaps it is because he hears a different drummer.
Let him step to the music which he hears, however measured or far away.

—**Henry David Thoreau**

instructed the "teacher" to continue the experiment and told him that it was his obligation to complete the job. Figure 6.3 shows the setting of the experiment. The 50-year-old "learner" was a confederate of the experimenter. He was not being shocked at all. Of course, the "teachers" were unaware of this.

Forty psychiatrists were asked how they thought individuals would respond in this situation. The psychiatrists predicted that only 1 in 100 would go further than 150 volts, that fewer than 1 in 25 would go as far as 300 volts, and that only 1 in 1,000 would deliver the full 450 volts. The psychiatrists, it turns out, were way off the mark. Most "teachers" obeyed the experimenter. In fact, almost two of every three delivered the full 450 volts.

In subsequent studies, Milgram set up a storefront in Bridgeport, Connecticut,

and recruited volunteers through newspaper ads. Milgram wanted to create a more natural environment for the experiment and to use a wider cross-section of volunteers. In these additional studies, close to two-thirds of the individuals still selected the highest level of shock for the "learner." In variations of the experiment, Milgram discovered some circumstances that encouraged disobedience: when an opportunity was given to see others disobey, when the authority figure was not perceived to be legitimate and was not close by, and when the victim was made to seem more human. To contemplate the ethics of Milgram's results, see Critical Thinking.

Resistance to interpersonal influence is strongly valued in individualistic cultures. We now turn to ways social influence can be resisted.

Most of us in this culture would prefer to think of ourselves as stepping to our own music, maybe even setting the rhythms for others, rather than trying to keep pace with our companions. However, society requires a certain degree of conformity if society is to function at all. For example, without conformity, traffic patterns in America would be nightmarish. As we go through our lives, we are both conformist and nonconformist. Sometimes conforming can be quite comfortable. For example, chances are good that you wear blue jeans during some part of your week as a result of conforming to some fashion standards. However, sometimes we are overwhelmed by the persuasion and influence of others. In some of those circumstances, we may need to resist and gain personal control over our lives. Our individualistic culture prizes self-direction. It is important to remember that our relation to the social world is reciprocal; when others are

CRITICAL THINKING

Milgram's Results and Standards of Humane Research

We're going to sidetrack for a moment and explore an important point about Milgram's research: How *ethical* was it? The volunteers in Milgram's experience clearly felt anguish, and some were very disturbed about harming another individual. After the experiment was completed, they were told that the "learner" was not actually shocked. Even though they were debriefed and told that they really had not shocked anyone, was it ethical to impose such anguish on them?

Milgram argued that we have learned a great deal about human nature from the experiments. He claimed that they tell us how far individuals will go in their obedience, even if it means being cruel to someone. The volunteers were interviewed later, and more than four of every five said that they were glad they had participated in the study; none said they were sorry they had participated. When Milgram conducted his studies on obedience, the ethical guidelines for research were not as stringent as they are today. The current ethical guidelines of the American Psychological Association stress that researchers should obtain informed consent from their volunteers. Deception should be used only for very important purposes. Individuals are supposed to feel as good about themselves when the experiment is over as they did when it began. Under today's guidelines, it is unlikely that the Milgram experiment would be conducted.

Over three decades have elapsed since Milgram's original study. Many students tend to believe the passing of time is an important variable in understanding how obedient Milgram's volunteers were. They can't imagine being as obedient in the same situation. Suppose we wanted to put this idea to the test. Would finding out how individuals would react to this research challenge be sufficiently valuable to outweigh the level of deception that would be required? Are there other problems in doing research in a contemporary context that Milgram did not have to face? Your consideration of this issue illustrates the importance of *practicing standards of ethical treatment toward individuals and groups.*

REVIEW

Social Influence

Understanding persuasion and attitude focuses on the communicator (source), the message (communication), the medium (channel), and the target (audience). Communicators are most influential when they have expertise and credibility, trustworthiness, and power; attractiveness and similarity also are important. The less informed we are, the better emotional appeals work; the more frightened we are, the more we will be influenced. Positive emotional appeals can be persuasive, especially through the use of music. Because it delivers live images, television may be the most powerful medium; its persuasive capabilities are staggering, given the frequency of viewing. Experts debate television's influence. Younger individuals are more likely to change their attitudes than older individuals and females are more readily persuaded than males. Self-esteem is thought to be important, but a predictable effect for it has not been found. If an audience is not strongly committed to a preexisting attitude, change is more likely. Obedience is behavior that complies with the explicit demands of an authority. Milgram's classic experiment demonstrated the power of obedience. The subjects followed the experimenter's directions even though they perceived they were hurting someone. Milgram's research studies raise the question of ethics in psychological experimentation.

---

attempting to exert undue social influence over us, we can recognize and resist this influence in the tradition espoused by Thoreau. We can also exert personal control over our actions and influence others in turn (Bandura, 1991). If you believe that someone in a position of authority is making an unjust request or asking you to do something wrong, what choice of actions do you have? Your choices include:

- You can comply.
- You also can give the appearance of complying but secretly do otherwise.
- You can publicly dissent by showing doubts and disenchantment but still follow directives.
- You can openly disregard the orders and refuse to comply.
- You can challenge or confront the authority.

- You might get higher authorities to intervene or organize a group of people who agree with you to show the strength of your view.

At this point in our discussion of social psychology, we have examined the interpersonal contexts of our thoughts, behaviors, and activities. Next we will explore group relations.

GROUP RELATIONS

A student joining a fraternity, a jury deciding a criminal case, a company president delegating authority, a family reunion, a prejudiced remark about a minority group, conflicts among nations, arguments in the neighborhood, and attempts to reach peace—all of these circumstances reflect our lives as members of groups. Each of us belongs to many groups. Some we choose; others we do not. We choose to belong to a club, but we are born into a particular ethnic group, for example. Some group participation is very satisfying; other group experiences are frustrating and ineffective.

In this section we will explore social influence in groups and examine the roles that tend to form in groups. We will identify some theories about the development of leaders in groups and how conflicts between participants are resolved. We'll also explore some challenging aspects of social influence, including conformity, groupthink, and deindividuation.

The Nature of Groups

Group membership satisfies our personal needs, rewards us, provides information, raises our self-esteem, and gives us an identity (Davis, 1996; Laughlin, 1996). We might join a group because we think it will be enjoyable and exciting and satisfy our need for affiliation and companionship. We might join a group because we will receive rewards, either material or psychological. By taking a job with a company, we get paid to work for a group, but we also reap prestige and recognition. Groups are an important source of information. For example, as we listen to other members talk in a Weight Watchers group, we learn about their strategies for losing weight. As we sit in the audience at a real estate seminar, we learn how to buy property with no money down. Many of the groups of which you are a member—your family, a college, a club, a team—make you feel good, raise your self-esteem, and provide you with an identity.

Any group to which you belong has certain things in common with all other groups. All groups have their own **norms,** *rules that apply to all members of a group.* The city government requires

Certain individuals in the minority have played important roles in history. (*a*) Martin Luther King, Jr., helped African Americans gain important rights. (*b*) Corazon Aquino, who became president of the Philippines after defeating Ferdinand Marcos, toppled a corrupt political regime and reduced the suffering of many Philippine citizens.

each of its workers to wear socks, Mensa requires individuals to have a high IQ, Polar Bear Club members must complete a 15-minute swim in below-freezing temperatures. These are examples of norms.

Roles *are rules and expectations that govern certain positions in a group. Roles define how people should behave in a particular position in the group.* In a family, parents have certain roles, siblings have other roles, and a grandparent has yet another role. On a football team, many roles must be filled: center, guard, tackle, end, quarterback, halfback, and fullback, for example, and that only covers the offense. Roles and norms, then, tell us what is expected of the members of a group.

One advantage of group participation is that more resources are brought to bear on any given problem. This may enhance the ability to complete tasks on time and accurately, particularly when compared to the efficiency of one individual working alone.

Many factors affect whether a group will be productive or not. The

quality of leadership is one important variable that determines group effectiveness. However, experiences in groups can also lead to some unpleasant outcomes. For example, conflicts can develop between group members. Coalitions can form within a group that can prolong group effort with protracted discussions among the factions. Although it can be an adaptive force in some circumstances, pressures to conform can create some problems for individual group members. In addition, two other problems—groupthink and deindividuation—result in ineffectiveness or poor adaptation.

Leadership

"I am certainly not one of those who need to be prodded. In fact, if anything, I am the prod," British Prime Minister Winston Churchill said of himself. What made Churchill a great leader? Was it a set of personality traits, the situation into which he was thrust, or a combination of the two?

The **great person theory** *says that some individuals have certain traits that make them best suited for leadership*

CRITICAL THINKING

Follow the Leader

You have experienced an enormous number of social interactions in groups of people in which you have been able to observe or exert leadership in a very personal way. Based on these experiences, would you say you believe more in the *great person* or the *situational* theory of leadership? Does it seem to you that leaders tend to be leaders across contexts? If so, you are more inclined to subscribe to the *great person* approach, as you think leadership is a personal trait. Or does it seem to you that most of the leadership you have observed is much more dependent on the characteristics of the context,

which draw out the best leadership qualities in people? You then prefer the *situational theory* as the best way to look at leadership.

What about your own style of leadership? Do people routinely look to you for guidance and motivation about what to do, regardless of the circumstances? Are there certain circumstances in which your flair for leadership emerges? Or are you still waiting to discover situations in which you could exercise true leadership? Your consideration of these questions allows you to *practice self-reflection to enhance personal growth.*

positions. Leaders are commonly thought to be assertive, cooperative, decisive, dominant, energetic, self-confident, tolerant of stress, willing to assume responsibility, diplomatic and tactful, and persuasive. Although we can list traits and skills possessed by leaders, a large number of research studies conclude that we cannot predict who will become a leader solely from an individual's personality characteristics. To explore your leadership style, see Critical Thinking.

Is it the situation, then, that produces leaders? According to the **situational theory of leadership,** *the needs of a group change from time to time, and a person who emerges as a leader in one circumstance will not necessarily be the person who becomes a leader in another circumstance.* Many psychologists believe that a combination of personality characteristics and skills and situational influences determines who will become a leader.

At this point, our discussion of group relations has focused on why we join groups, how groups are structured, and why some individuals are leaders and others are followers. Next we will discuss how groups, especially minority and majority groups, deal with each other.

Majority-Minority Influence

Think about the groups in which you have been a member. Who had the most

influence, the majority or the minority? In most groups—whether a jury, family, or corporate meeting—the majority holds sway over the minority. The majority exerts both normative and informational pressure on the group. Its adherents set the group's norms; those who do not go along may be rejected. The majority also has a greater opportunity to provide information that will influence decision making.

In most cases, the majority wins, but there are occasions when the minority has its day (Latané, 1996). How can the minority swing the majority? The minority cannot win through normative influence because it is outnumbered. It must do its work through *informational pressure.* If the minority presents its views consistently, confidently, and nondefensively, then the majority is more likely to listen to the minority's view. The minority position might have to be repeated several times in order to create sufficient impact.

In group situations, some individuals are able to command the attention of others and thus have a better opportunity to shape and direct subsequent social outcomes. To achieve such a high social impact, they have to distinguish themselves in various ways from the rest of the group. They have to make themselves noticed by others—by the opinions they express, the jokes they tell, or by their nonverbal style. They may be the

first ones to raise a new idea, to disagree with a prevailing point of view, or to propose a creative alternative solution to a problem. People who have a high social impact often are characterized by their willingness to be different. In one recent study, people high in individuation (those who are differentiated from other parts of the physical and social environment) had a stronger social impact on the group than their low individuation counterparts (Whitney, Sagrestano, & Maslach, 1994).

Certain individuals in a minority may play a crucial role. Individuals with a history of taking minority stands may trigger others to dissent, showing them that disagreement is possible, and the minority stand might be the best course. Such is the ground of some of history's greatest moments: When Lincoln spoke out against slavery, racism dominated and tore at the country; when Corazon Aquino became a candidate for president of the Philippines, few people thought Ferdinand Marcos could be beaten. Although the scale is smaller, the triumph might be the same for a gang member who influences the gang's decision not to vandalize, the woman executive who persuades her male colleagues to adopt a less sexist advertising tactic, or the ethnic minority student who expresses his views in a predominantly White classroom.

Conformity

Conformity comes in many forms and affects many areas of our lives. Do you take up jogging because everyone else is doing it? Does fashion dictate that you let your hair grow long this year and cut it short the next? Would you take cocaine if pressured by others or would you resist? **Conformity** *occurs when individuals adopt the attitudes or behavior of others because of real or imagined pressure from others to do so.*

Conformity to rules and regulations result in people engaging in a number of behaviors that make society run more smoothly. For example, consider what would happen if most people did not conform to rules such as these: stopping at red lights, driving on the correct side of the road, not punching others in the face, going to school regularly, and so on. However, in the following experiments, researchers reveal how conformity pressures can sometimes make us act against our better judgment and even have dramatic, unfortunate consequences.

Every society honors its live conformists and its dead troublemakers.
    —**Mignon McLaughlin**

Put yourself in the following situation. You are taken into a room, where you see five other people seated around a table. A person in a white lab coat enters the room and announces that you are about to participate in an experiment on perceptual accuracy. The group is shown two cards, the first having only a single vertical line on it, the second card with three vertical lines of varying length. You are told that the task is to determine which of the three lines on the second card is the same length as the line on the first card. You look at the cards and think, "What a snap. It's so obvious which is longest." The other people in the room are actually associates of the experimenter (researchers often call such persons "confederates" of the experimenter); they've been hired to perform in ways the experimenter dictates (of course, you are not aware of this). On the first several trials, everyone agrees about which line matches the standard. Then, on the

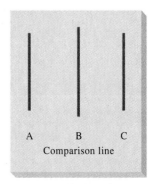

Standard line   A   B   C
                       Comparison line

FIGURE 6.4

Asch's Conformity Experiment
The drawings show the stimulus materials for the Asch conformity experiment on group influence. The photograph shows the dilemma for the subject (*seated in the middle*) after five confederates of the experimenter chose the incorrect line.

fourth trial, each of the others picks an incorrect line; you have a puzzled look on your face. As the last person to make a choice, you're in the dilemma of responding as your eyes tell you or conforming to what the others have said. How do you think you would answer?

Solomon Asch conducted this classic experiment on conformity in 1951 (see figure 6.4). He believed there would be little yielding to group pressure. To find out if this was so, Asch instructed his accomplices to respond incorrectly on 12 of the 18 trials. To Asch's surprise, the volunteer participants conformed to the incorrect answers 35 percent of the time. The pressure to conform is strong. Even in a clear-cut situation, such as in the Asch experiment, we often conform to

what others say and do. We don't want to be laughed at or have others be angry with us.

In a more recent test of group pressure and conformity, college students watched the third Bush-Clinton presidential debate and then rated the candidates' performances (Fein & others, 1993). Students were randomly assigned to three groups: (1) a 30-student group that included 10 confederates of the experimenter who openly supported Bush and criticized Clinton; (2) a 30-student group that included 10 confederates who cheered Clinton and put down Bush; and (3) a 30-student group with no confederates of the experimenter. The effects of the group pressure exerted by the confederates were powerful. For example,

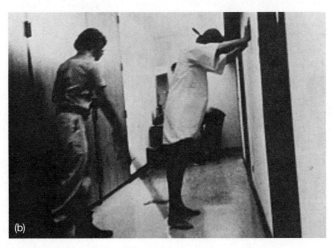

FIGURE 6.5

Zimbardo's Prison Experiment
(*a*) A volunteer for a psychology experiment is picked up on campus—he had lost a coin flip and was designated a prisoner. (*b*) A student conforms to the hostile, abusive role of prison guard.

even Bush supporters rated Clinton's performance more favorably when their group included pro-Clinton confederates of the experimenter.

Put yourself in another situation. You have volunteered to participate in a psychology experiment. By the flip of a coin, half of the volunteers are designated as prisoners and half as guards in a mock prison; you are one of the fortunate ones because you will be a guard. How much would you and your fellow volunteers conform to the social roles of "guard" and "prisoner"? You are instructed to maintain law and order—to do a guard's job. You will make a fine guard, you think, because you are kind and respect the rights and dignity of others. In just a few hours,

however, you find that your behavior, and that of the other "guards" and "prisoners," has changed; each of you has begun to conform to what you think are the expected social roles for guards and prisoners. Over the course of 6 days, you and the other guards begin to make the prisoners obey petty, meaningless rules and force them to perform tedious, useless, and sometimes humiliating tasks. What's more, you find yourself insulting the prisoners and keeping them "in line" with night sticks. Many of the prisoners begin acting like robots. They develop an intense hatred for you and the other guards and constantly think about ways to escape.

You may be thinking that this scenario stretches credibility. No one you

know, and certainly not you, would behave in such an abusive way. However, psychologist Philip Zimbardo and his colleagues (1972) conducted just such an experiment with a group of normal, mature, stable, intelligent young men at Stanford University. In fact, the prison study was scheduled to last 2 weeks, but the behavior of the "guards" and "prisoners" changed so drastically that the experiment had to be stopped after 6 days. Although many of the prisoners resisted the guards and asked questions initially, after a while they gave up and virtually stopped reacting. Five of the prisoners had to be released, four because of severe depression or anxiety and the fifth because he broke out in a rash all over his body; several of the guards became brutal with the prisoners. Figure 6.5 shows some of the circumstances in the prison study.

Cross-cultural psychologists wondered if this tendency to conform in such dramatic ways is an American phenomenon or if the same behavior occurs in other cultures. Using the Asch experiment, researchers have found that research participants in Lebanon, Hong Kong, Brazil, and Fiji conform at about the same rate, 35 percent (Mann, 1980). However, they found conformity lower in Germany (22 percent) and higher among the Bantu of Rhodesia (51 percent). Surprisingly, conformity in Japan was found to be relatively low—25 percent (Frager, 1970). The results of the Japanese study were counterintuitive—that is, contrary to what the researchers expected. Because of strong social pressures to conform in Japan's collectivistic culture, the researchers expected a much higher rate. Perhaps the Japanese feel strong loyalty to their own social groups but not to groups created in the laboratory. In addition, collectivists tend to belong to few in-groups and might be less inclined to feel pressures to conform in contexts that exploit these pressures. As a result, we cannot conclude that the Japanese are nonconforming; it might be that they simply do not conform to the wishes of strangers. Germans also demonstrated less conformity (22 percent). Cross-cultural psychologist Richard Brislin (1993) believes that such results might represent a conscious choice to be perceived as less authoritarian and obedient.

Other cross-cultural research on conformity suggests that people in agricultural societies have a tendency to conform more than people in hunter-gatherer groups (Berry, 1983). Agricultural societies rely on the cooperation of their residents to cultivate, plant, and harvest their food supply. This high degree of interdependence makes it vital that members conform to societal norms. More complex societies sometimes reward nonconformity, encouraging members to exploit the diverse opportunities for career and self-expression offered in the multifaceted dimensions of the societies. Also, in experiments conducted in fourteen countries, conformity rates were lower in individualistic cultures (like the United States) and higher in collectivistic cultures (like China) (Bond & Smith, 1994).

Groupthink

Sometimes groups make rational decisions and come up with the best solution to a problem. Not always. Group members, especially leaders, often want to develop or maintain unanimity among group members. **Groupthink** *is the motivation of group members to maintain harmony and unanimity in decision making, suffocating differences of opinion in the process.* Groupthink evolves because members often boost each other's egos and increase each other's self-esteem by seeking conformity, especially in stressful circumstances. This motivation for harmony and unanimity may result in disastrous decisions and policy recommendations. Examples of groupthink include the United States invasion of Cuba (the Bay of Pigs), the escalation of the Vietnam war, the failure to prepare for the invasion of Pearl Harbor, the Watergate coverup, Irangate, and the launching of the unsafe *Challenger* shuttlecraft.

Leaders often favor a solution and promote it within the group. Members of the group also tend to be cohesive and isolate themselves from qualified outsiders who could influence their decisions. Leaders can avoid groupthink by encouraging dissident opinions, by not presenting a favored plan at the outset, by appointing a "devil's advocate" to argue for unpopular opinions, and by having several independent groups work on the same problem.

Deindividuation

Group membership usually confers many advantages. However, some group processes are not only unpleasant but dangerous. As early as 1895, Gustav LeBon observed that a group can foster uninhibited behavior, ranging from wild celebrations to mob behavior. The brutal activities of the Ku Klux Klan, the wearing of erotic outfits in public during Mardi Gras wild times, and "good ol' boys" rolling a car on spring break in Fort Lauderdale might be due to **deindividuation,** *a state of reduced self-awareness, weakened self-restraints against impulsive actions, and apathy about negative social evaluation.*

One explanation of deindividuation is that the group offers anonymity: We might act in an uninhibited manner because we believe that authority figures and victims are less likely to discover that we are the culprits. Other explanations emphasize that arousal and conformity to the roles emerging in the group can fuel behavior in agitated groups that the individuals involved would not engage in on their own.

We can become deindividuated in groups. Examples of situations in which people can lose their individual identity include (*a*) at Ku Klux Klan rallies, (*b*) at Mardi Gras, and (*c*) in national crowds inflamed with patriotic spirit.

Group Relations

Groups satisfy our personal needs, reward us, provide us with information, raise our self-esteem, and enhance our identity. Every group has norms and roles. Both the great person theory, which emphasizes personality traits and skills, and situational factors have been proposed to explain why certain people become leaders. Personality and situational factors likely combine to determine who will become a leader. The majority usually has the most influence, but at times the minority has its day, being most effective through using informational pressure. Conformity is change in an individual's behavior because of real or imagined pressure to do so. Two experiments demonstrate conformity's power in our lives: Asch's study on judgments of line length and Zimbardo's study of social roles in a mock prison. Groupthink is the motivation of group members to maintain harmony and unanimity in decision making, suffocating differences of opinion in the process. Deindividuation is the loss of identity as an individual and the development of group identity in group situations, which promote arousal and anonymity.

CRITICAL THINKING ABOUT ADJUSTMENT

Jailhouse Rock

When Philip Zimbardo embarked on his prison study in the early 1970s, he truly was shocked by the results he helped to create. The role-playing activities of the college men had to be stopped after 6 days because of the dramatic effects the strain of the activity caused. Zimbardo and his colleagues were astounded at how reasonably normal college men could be transformed into either harassing, brutal officials of a bureaucracy or robotlike wards of that bureaucracy. When mental and physical health concerns mounted, Zimbardo wisely terminated the exercise.

Zimbardo, who participated in the exercise as a warden, was quite shaken by his results. Although he suspected that situations had great power to influence individuals, he had not envisioned the degree to which the participants would enact their roles or the speed with which the strain would become visible. When it was apparent that he had established the power of context to promote harmful and disrespectful behavior, he discontinued the activity. Psychologists often cite his prison study as a cornerstone for understanding the importance of *examining how context and culture influence behavior.*

The American Psychological Association created ethical guidelines for psychological research that would prevent our *replication* (redoing) of Zimbardo's prison study when we are fully aware that such a procedure runs the risk of doing harm to the participants. However, we can speculate about whether Zimbardo's procedure—or variations on the procedure—would produce a similar outcome if such an exercise were to be conducted today. The fundamental question posed here is whether or not we can legitimately generalize Zimbardo's conclusions to others in order to understand something about the power of context and the vulnerability of people to such situations that bring out the worst in them.

Consider the following questions in order to speculate about whether or not we could generalize Zimbardo's conclusions to people today:

- Was there something in particular going on during that era (late 1960s and early 1970s) that would have made Zimbardo's results nonrepresentative of the way human beings really are? Would there be any reason to believe that today's students would somehow be immune to the power of context? Or have we somehow become *more* vulnerable to the effects of inhumane contexts?
- More students during that era were of traditional age for college students. Would the findings have been different if the age range were broader?
- What if Zimbardo had conducted the exercise away from campus, where its being a Stanford enterprise might not have influenced subjects' behavior?
- What if Zimbardo had used both male and female students in his participant group?
- What if he had used only females? Do you think women would have been more compliant and conforming to the assigned roles, or do you think they would have declined circumstances that seemed to be harm-inducing?
- What if we were to conduct the exercise in a culture that was more collectivistic? Would we expect more or less adherence to the requirements of the exercise?

Can you think of other aspects of the design of the exercise that might legitimately limit the degree to which we can generalize Zimbardo's findings? Or is it the unhappy case that, given just the right set of circumstances, we all might exhibit inhumane behaviors?

We began this chapter by studying the nature of social cognition, including social perception, attribution, and attitudes and behavior. Our coverage of social influence emphasized persuasion, conformity, and resisting social influences. We also studied group relations, addressing such topics as persuasion and obedience. Our discussion of group relations addressed the topics of the nature of groups, leadership, majority-minority influence, conformity, groupthink, and deindividuation. Don't forget that you can obtain an overall summary of the chapter by again reading the in-chapter reviews on pages 128, 133, and 139.

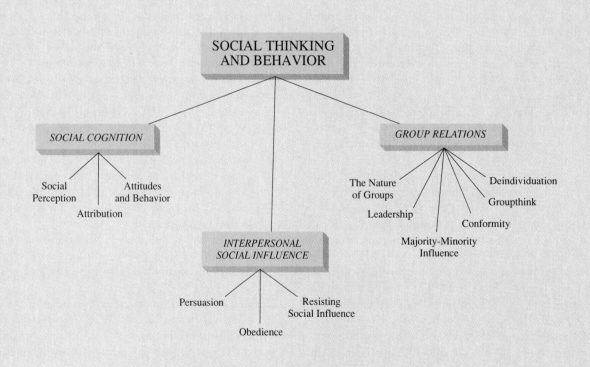

KEY TERMS

PRACTICAL KNOWLEDGE ABOUT ADJUSTMENT

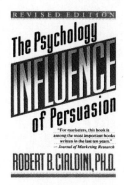

INFLUENCE

(1993, rev. ed.) by Robert Cialdini. New York: Quill.

This highly acclaimed book by a well-known social psychologist explores how influence works in today's marketplace. Cialdini provides valuable suggestions for persuading other people and understanding how others try to persuade us. He also covers how power works, the role of reciprocity in influence, the importance of commitment and consistency, how to say no, scarcity, relationships with others, advertising, sales techniques, and instant influence.

SHYNESS

(1987) by Philip Zimbardo. Reading, MA: Addison-Wesley.

According to Zimbardo, shyness is a widespread social problem that affects as many as four out of every five people at one time or another in their lives. He explores how and why people become shy and examines the roles that parents, teachers, spouses, and culture play in creating shy individuals. What does Zimbardo say shy people can do about their situations? First, you have to analyze your shyness and figure out how you got this way. Possible reasons include negative evaluations, fear of being rejected, fear of intimacy, or lack of adequate social skills. Second, you need to build up your self-esteem. To help you do this, Zimbardo spells out fifteen steps to becoming more confident. And third, you need to improve your social skills. Zimbardo describes several behavior modification strategies, tells you to set realistic goals, and advocates working hard toward achieving these goals. This is an excellent self-help book for shy individuals. It dispenses sound advice, is free of psychobabble, and is easy to read.

SELF-ASSESSMENT SCORING AND INTERPRETATION

SELF-MONITORING

Scoring

Give yourself one point for each of questions 1, 5, and 7 that you answered F. Give yourself one point for each of the remaining questions that you answered T. Add up your points.

Interpretation

If you are a good judge of yourself and scored 7 or above, you are probably a high-self-monitoring individual; 3 or below, you are probably a low-self-monitoring individual.

Rufino Tamayo
Man and Woman, detail

Interpersonal Communication

CHAPTER OUTLINE

CRITICAL THINKING ABOUT ADJUSTMENT

CHAPTER BOXES

SOCIOCULTURAL WORLDS OF ADJUSTMENT

CRITICAL THINKING

SELF-ASSESSMENT

*What you are speaks so loudly
I cannot hear what you say.*

—Ralph Waldo Emerson

E xplaining why his dinner visit to the White House was unsatisfactory, he said, "It was hard to have a conversation with anyone, there were so many people talking." Lorenzo Piero Berra, also known as Yogi Berra, is famous on two fronts (Petras & Petras, 1994). His award-winning baseball career in New York for both the Yankees and the Mets, as both a catcher and a manager, would be sufficient to make Berra a memorable figure. However, it is his unique skills in the creation of **malaprops,** *confused but memorable misuses of language,* that have made him a linguistic legend. His capacity for making language errors is unparalleled. However, his sincerity and commitment somehow transform his errors into sage observations in the ears of the listener.

Yogi Berra, famous baseball player and the "King of Malaprops."

Yogi Berra made the following gaffes regarding his beloved sport baseball:

- "You give a hundred percent in the first half of the game, and if it isn't enough, in the second half you give what's left."
- "We made too many wrong mistakes" (after the Yankees lost the 1960 World series).

- "If you can't imitate him, don't copy him."
- "How can you think and hit at the same time?"
- "If the people don't want to come out to the park, nobody's going to stop 'em."
- "The other team could make trouble for us if they win."
- "Baseball is 90 percent mental. The other half is physical."

Berra's sage advice also extended beyond the confines of baseball:

- "Always go to other people's funerals, otherwise they won't come to yours."
- "A nickel ain't worth a dime anymore."
- "If you come to a fork in the road, take it."
- "Nobody goes there anymore. It's too crowded" (explaining the appeal of a local restaurant).
- "I really didn't say everything I said" (about his linguistic popularity).

PREVIEW

In this chapter, we will study the fascinating landscape of how we communicate with others. This extremely important dimension of our lives can make a big difference in whether other people want to spend time with us or see us as someone to be avoided, and whether they love us or even hate us. In this chapter we will examine the nature of social communication, how we communicate verbally, and how we communicate nonverbally. In several places we will point out how interpersonal communication is influenced by the sociocultural factors of culture, ethnicity, and gender.

THE NATURE OF INTERPERSONAL COMMUNICATION

Good communication is as stimulating as black coffee, and just as hard to sleep after.

—Anne Morrow Lindbergh

It would be hard to do much in this life for very long without communicating with someone. We communicate in every social context—in the heat of intense conflict, in the warmth of an intimate exchange, and even in the chill of a faded relationship. Interpersonal communication can be spontaneous or rehearsed, smooth or jagged, profound or negligible in its impact.

First we will explore the components, or building blocks, of interpersonal communication. We will also examine the dimensions of interpersonal communication, including the content, relationship, transactional, and contextual aspects of communication. This will lead to a definition of interpersonal communication.

What are some of the most important aspects of interpersonal communication?

The Components of Interpersonal Communication

A teacher tells a student, "You just aren't working hard enough." What are the components of interpersonal communication in this example?

First we need to consider how the **message**—*the information being delivered from the sender to the receiver*—is conveyed. The **channel** *is the mode of delivery of communication.* For example, the teacher's message could have been communicated verbally in oral or written form or nonverbally with a furrowed brow or a scowl. Scowling is a nonverbal channel for delivering an unfriendly message.

Second, communication involves **encoding** (*the act of producing messages*) and **decoding** (*the act of understanding messages*). Speakers and writers are encoders; listeners and readers are decoders. For interpersonal communication to take place, messages must be encoded and decoded. Our disappointed teacher could be unsuccessful in communicating her judgment about the student's performance, for two reasons. For example, she could conclude that the student's performance was unsatisfactory but not express this evaluation, failing to encode it as a message. She could also be unsuccessful if she spoke directly to the student but the student was daydreaming, because then neither the verbal nor the nonverbal aspects of the message will be received or decoded (DeVito, 1996).

Another important dimension of interpersonal communication that interferes with decoding is **noise,** *environmental, physiological, and psychological factors that decrease the likelihood that a message will be accurately expressed or understood.* Our environment consists of many sources of noise—such as blaring stereos, the roar of nearby traffic, the yells of a crowd, and even the annoyances of air pollution—that make it difficult to concentrate on what someone is saying.

Our physical makeup can also interfere with the sending and receiving of messages. For instance, a hearing problem, poor vision, or poor health can inhibit how effectively a message is transmitted or received. Numerous psychological factors can also influence the accuracy of message interpretation. For example, a depressed student might have such low self-esteem that even a positive message about her performance might not register as a compliment. Another student might be so anxious about the unwanted attention from the teacher that he jumps to his own defense before the teacher finishes her message.

Communication is far more complex than the message, the channel, and encoding and decoding. Next we will examine the rich influences that enhance or confuse communication.

The Dimensions of Interpersonal Communication

The message "You just aren't working hard enough" includes both a content dimension and a relationship dimension. From the vantage point of content, the sender suggests that someone needs to buckle down. From the vantage point of the relationship, the teacher's higher academic status and power are important in rendering her communication persuasive. She has the formal power over the student to make such judgments. However, imagine this statement being made by the student to the teacher—even if the content is on target, the message violates the power relationship between a student and a teacher.

The relationship dimension of interpersonal communication is especially important because many of the problems people have communicating occur not because of what is said (the content), but because of the implications, especially the power implications of the relationship.

For example, if a student living in a dorm asks his roommate to pick up his socks, the student implies that he has the right to have the roommate do this (no matter how politely couched the request!).

While the roommate might agree that the request is reasonable, he might fail to comply because he doesn't like the unstated implication that he is being given orders in this relationship. Similar situations occur in couple relationships, as when one member buys something, makes plans for the weekend, or invites a guest to dinner without first asking the other member.

Finally, interpersonal communication is **transactional,** *which means that communication is an ongoing process between sender and receiver that unfolds across time, and that it is not unusual for information to be communicated almost simultaneously between the participants.* Much of interpersonal communication is not a one-time, brief interaction that lasts several seconds. Rather, most of our interpersonal communication involves an ongoing volley or parley of verbal and nonverbal actions between the sender and the receiver. Initially person A may be the sender, person B the receiver; then after 15 seconds, person A may become the receiver and person B the sender; and so on, back and forth, over a period of time. At the same time as person A is sending a message verbally, person B may be sending a message nonverbally.

Let's consider an example of how these transactional characteristics of interpersonal communication might work. Jay comes in from work and asks his wife, Jan, "How come dinner isn't ready yet?" Jan responds, "I got home late from work myself. It's going to be about an hour before it is ready." Already, in this brief social communication that has taken only about 10 seconds, both individuals have served as senders and receivers of messages. When Jay got to the word *dinner* in his sentence, Jan had begun to give him a blank stare, and by the time he spoke the word *yet,* the stare had a tone of anger as well. Further, by the time Jan got to the words *an hour before it's ready,* Jay was displaying an angry grimace. Thus, in this interchange, Jay and Jan were sending and receiving messages simultaneously.

Social communication always occurs in a *context,* the environment in which messages are sent and received. The context influences the form and content of social communication. In today's world,

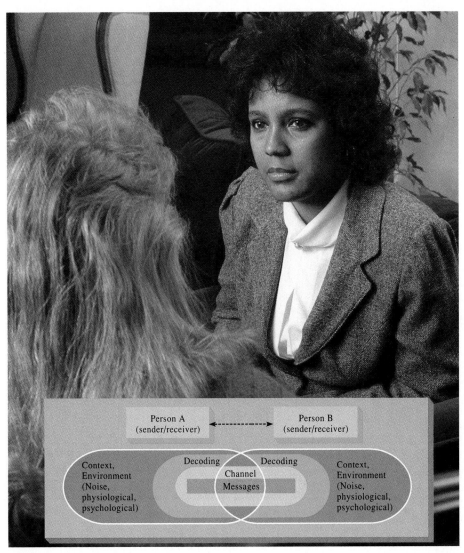

FIGURE 7.1

Some Important Components of Interpersonal Communication

the sociocultural dimensions of context are especially important for understanding interpersonal communication. For example, when people from different cultural and ethnic groups interact, they might follow different rules of communication. This can produce confusion, unintentional insults, inaccurate perceptions, and other miscommunications.

The importance of paying attention to cultural context has sometimes escaped manufacturers trying to capture a world market (Petras & Petras, 1994). For example, the brand name *Coca-Cola* translates to the Chinese consumer as "Bite the wax tadpole." Japanese beverages have been marketed in the West with the names *Kolic, Ucc, Mucos,* and *Pocari*

Sweat. Obviously, successful international marketing requires attention to the rich dimensions of language.

Now that we have examined the main components and characteristics of interpersonal communication, we can define it. **Interpersonal communication** *is a transactional process that is ongoing over time. This process involves at least two individuals, each of whom acts as both sender and receiver, encoding and decoding messages, sometimes simultaneously. These messages are sent through verbal or nonverbal channels. Noise can limit the accuracy of a message. Communication always takes place in a context.* (See figure 7.1 for a visual depiction of these important components of interpersonal communication.)

Interpersonal communication includes both content and relationship dimensions. Communication problems often reside in the relationship dimension. Interpersonal communication is a transactional process that is ongoing over time. This process involves at least two people, each of whom acts as sender and receiver, encoding and decoding messages, sometimes simultaneously. These messages are sent through verbal and nonverbal channels. Noise can limit the accuracy of a message. Communication always takes place in a context.

In discussing the channel of communication in which a message is delivered, we indicated that messages can be transmitted verbally or nonverbally. Let's consider the nature of verbal interpersonal communication first.

VERBAL INTERPERSONAL COMMUNICATION

Virtually every day of our lives we talk to other people, and they to us. To make all of this talk effective, we need to understand the difference between the denotative and the connotative meanings of words and messages. We also need to develop good speaking and listening skills, engage in appropriate self-disclosure, and overcome the barriers to effective verbal communication.

Denotative and Connotative Meanings

When we talk to each other, we use words and send messages that have denotative and connotative meanings. **Denotation** *is the objective meaning of the words and message.* **Connotation** *is the subjective, emotional, or personal meaning of the words and message.* Consider the word *death* (DeVito, 1996). For a doctor, the meaning of *death* might involve the brain's no longer functioning or the heart's no longer beating. For a mother whose son has just died, however, the word *death* takes on more emotional and personal meaning. She might begin reflecting about his childhood, his ambitions, his disease, and what her life is going to be like without him.

Some words—such as *blackboard* or *parallel*—are mainly denotative. Other words—such as *love* and *commitment*—are primarily connotative. A good way to determine whether a word or a message has connotative meaning for you is to ask whether you can apply the label *good* and *bad* to it. If *good* and *bad* don't seem to apply, then the word or message has little connotative meaning for you. However, if you can place the word or message on the *good/bad* continuum, it has connotative meaning for you.

The more concrete our word choices and the messages we deliver, the more people are likely to agree on their meaning. The more abstract the words we use and the messages we send, the less people are likely to agree on their meaning. When we use abstract words too often and deliver too many connotative messages, communication becomes unclear. The result may be breakdowns in communication, misunderstanding, and difficulty in relationships. As we see next, good speaking skills emphasize the use of concrete words.

> *Words, like eyeglasses, blur everything that they do not make clear.*
>
> —**Joseph Joubert**

Speaking Skills

In the flow of conversation we speak and we listen. **Speaking** *involves expressing thoughts and feelings in words and behavior. When speech is clear and accurate, the targeted listener is more likely to understand what the speaker means.* To communicate effectively, speakers need to consider the background, needs, abilities, and other characteristics of their listeners. For example, speakers often must establish context for the listener by providing an explicit introduction to the message that will follow (Smith, 1995).

Messages are conveyed more effectively when spoken in a simple rather than a complex way, a concrete rather than an abstract way, and a specific rather than a general way. When good speakers do want to convey ideas that are abstract, general, or complex, they use appropriate examples to illustrate the ideas. Often the best examples are those that listeners can relate to their own personal experiences. For instance, if Margaret is trying to explain to some friends who do not know what feminism is what it is like to be a feminist, it will help if she gives examples of what she means by feminism—such as favoring equal opportunities regardless of gender—and then has her listeners think of other friends of theirs who are feminists.

Good speakers also make their verbal and nonverbal messages consistent. If you say one thing and nonverbally communicate the opposite, you likely create confusion and distrust on the part of the listener. For example, if you are trying to explain why you didn't get a report in on time to your boss and you look down at the floor while you are talking to her rather than maintain eye contact, the boss might be less likely to believe you, even though you may have had a legitimate reason for being late with the report. Later in the chapter we will discuss a variety of nonverbal behaviors that people use during interpersonal communication.

> *You are what you are.*
> *It is my opinion the trouble in the world comes from people who do not know what they are and pretend to be something they're not.*
>
> —**Lillian Hellman**

Some people try to impress others with how intelligent they are by using big words and talking above the level the listener can understand. Politicians excel in turning regular speech into "fatty, high cholesterol language" (Petras & Petras, 1993). Former secretary of state Alexander Haig set new records for obscurity with comments like "At the moment, we are subsumed in the vortex of criticality."

The intelligent speaker uses words that are clear and whose meaning the listener can readily understand.

Good speakers also don't use a lot of jargon and hackneyed phrases. Television commentator Edwin Newman's (1974) book *Strictly Speaking* is filled with examples of bad usages of language that all too easily can find their way into our messages. For example, Newman describes the butchering of the English language that regularly comes from the mouths of sports announcers and coaches. Consider the following:

- "He moves pretty good for a big man."
- "We stopped them pretty good."
- "They read the papers pretty good for our remarks."
- "The loser might have been able to make up for their deficits except they were hurting pretty good."

Suffice it to say that there are a few too many "pretty goods" on the lips of sportscasters and coaches. To further explore the topic of speaking, see Critical Thinking.

Listening Skills

You listen a lot, more than you probably think. How good a listener are you? Most of us could use some help in this very important dimension of interpersonal communication. First we will describe how much time people usually spend in listening and define what listening really is. Then we will examine different types of listening and see which of these are the most beneficial in interpersonal communication.

How Is Listening Different from Hearing?

Hearing *is a physiological sensory process in which auditory sensations are received by the ears and transmitted to the brain.* On the other hand, **listening** *is the psychological process of interpreting and understanding the significance of what someone says.* In other words, you can hear what another person is saying without really listening to the person (Bolton, 1979). One teenager put it this way: "My friends listen to what I say, but my parents only hear me talk."

CRITICAL THINKING

The Contexts of Public Speaking

Speak the speech, I pray you,
Trippingly on the tongue.
—William Shakespeare

American adults tend to fear public speaking, but we don't have to invoke images of crowds for some people to experience discomfort about speaking. People who are painfully shy struggle with speaking to anyone but their most intimate acquaintances. Consider all the possible contexts in which you speak; some are probably less threatening than others. Think of three contexts in which speaking comes easily for you. What are their common characteristics? Now think of three contexts in which speaking becomes a challenge for you. What features do these contexts have in common? The variation in your own comfort level with speaking *demonstrates the influence of context on behavior.*

How is listening different from hearing?

How Much Time Do We Spend in Listening?

Measuring how much time we spend in listening suggests that listening might be our most important communication activity. By looking at figure 7.2 you can see that, in one study, college students spent more than 50 percent of their communication time in listening (Barker & others, 1981). Of this time spent listening, about 60 percent was spent listening to the communication media (radio and television, for example), while approximately 40 percent was spent in face-to-face listening. Notice, in figure 7.2, that the college students spent more time listening in conversations (21 percent) than they did speaking (16 percent).

We spend a lot of time listening, but whether we listen as effectively as we could is another matter. In actual conversations, most of us probably aren't very good listeners. Given all the time we spend listening, working on our listening skills would seem well worth the effort. Learning to become a better listener does require effort, often a lot of effort.

How Can Someone Become a Better Listener?

Most of us would like to become better listeners but we don't know how. Becoming a better listener requires that you work hard at improving your listening skills and know some basic strategies for good listening. What are some of these strategies?

First, too many of us hog a conversation. We just don't spend enough time listening; we are so busy trying to get our point across that all we do is talk and dominate the conversation. Simply talking less than we usually do can facilitate better listening.

> *The reason we have two ears and only one mouth is so we can listen more and talk less.*
>
> **—Zeno of Citum in 300 B.C.**

Second, good listening means paying *careful attention* to the person who is talking. Effectively attending to the other person is an important dimension of interpersonal communication. It shows the other person that you are interested in what she or he has to say. If during a

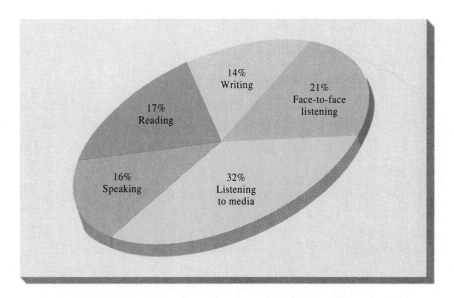

FIGURE 7.2

Percentage of Time Spent by College Students in Different Communication Activities

conversation the listener starts to look at the television set instead of at the speaker's face, chances are good that the listener is not paying careful attention to what the speaker is saying. Better listeners adopt body language that shows respect to the speaker. For example, in Western cultures, better listeners face the speaker squarely, incline the body in a relaxed manner toward the speaker (rather than lean back or slouch in a chair), and maintain eye contact with the speaker. More about these important aspects of nonverbal communication, including the influence of cultural contexts, appears later in this chapter.

Third, being a better listener involves using reflective skills. **Reflective listening** *is an effective communication strategy in which the listener restates the feelings and/or content of what the speaker has communicated and does so in a way that reveals understanding and acceptance.* One technique that can be used in reflective listening is **paraphrasing,** *a concise response to the speaker that states the essence of the speaker's content in the listener's own words.* Following is an example of paraphrasing:

Mary: "I just don't know. Maybe I should have a baby, maybe not. Bill isn't sure either. I like my work, but I think I would like to be a mother too. I

keep feeling pulled back and forth on what to do."

Donna: "You seem like you feel some conflict about what to do—on the one hand you like your work a lot and don't want to quit that, but you also really want a baby too."

Mary: "That's right."

Fourth, better listeners actively synthesize the themes and patterns they hear. The conversational landscape can become strewn with bits and pieces of information that aren't tied together in meaningful ways. A good reflective listener periodically pulls together a *summative reflection* of the main themes and feelings the speaker has expressed over a reasonably long conversation or even several conversations that span several meetings. The summative reflection may tie together a number of comments the speaker has made. The following sentence stems can help you get started in using the communication skill of reflective summation:

- "One theme you seem to keep coming back to is . . ."
- "Let's go over the ground we've been covering so far . . ."
- "I've been thinking about what you have said. Let me see if the following is what you mean . . ."

FIGURE 7.3

The Johari Window

Fifth, good listening means giving feedback in a competent manner. Feedback involves sending a message back to the speaker regarding the listener's reaction to what is said or the effect the message has on the listener. In giving feedback, either verbal or nonverbal, we give the speaker an idea of how much progress the speaker is making in getting an idea across. On the basis of such feedback, the speaker might or might not change the content or form of the messages. Better listeners give feedback to the speaker quickly, honestly, clearly, and informatively.

In sum, listening involves many more skills and strategies than we usually imagine. Listening is an important aspect of interpersonal communication that we often overlook when seeking to become better communicators (Chiasson & Hayes, 1993). Self-disclosure also is an important aspect of interpersonal communication.

Self-Disclosure

Just as some people talk too much in communicating with others, some people don't talk enough. Some people are especially reluctant to engage in **self-disclosure,** *the communication of intimate details about ourselves to someone else.* Self-disclosure involves telling someone about our secrets, our embarrassments, our failures, our desires, our feelings, and all of those things that are personally important to us but we are not willing to share with just anyone (Jourard, 1971).

> *When I am with my friend, it is almost as if I am alone, and as much at liberty to speak anything as to think it.*
>
> **—Seneca, Roman philosopher and playwright first century** A.D.

Self-disclosure is not a simple behavior, according to experts in communication research. Our next topic, the Johari Window, captures the complexity of self-disclosure.

The Johari Window

The **Johari Window** *is a model of self-disclosure that helps us understand the proportion of information about ourselves that we and others are aware of. The Johari Window model of self-disclosure is divided into four basic areas, or quadrants: The open self, the hidden self, the blind self, and the unknown self* (see figure 7.3). The *open self* reflects information about yourself known to you and to others. This might include your name, your sex, your religious affiliation, and where you live. The *hidden self* consists of information you are aware of yourself but you have not shared with others. This might include something you are ashamed about, such as cheating on a test, stealing something, or a private fantasy about

TABLE 7.1

Some Risks of Self-Disclosure

Risk	Reason
Indifference	In some situations when we disclose ourselves, others are indifferent to us and show no interest in getting to know us.
Rejection	When we reveal information about ourselves to others, they might reject us.
Loss of Control	Sometimes others use information we divulge about ourselves to control us.
Betrayal	When we self-disclose, we assume, or sometimes even explicitly request, that the information be treated confidentially. Sometimes our listeners betray our confidence and divulge what we've told them to someone else.

Source: Data from V. J. Derlega, *Communication, Intimacy, and Close Relationships*, 1984.

someone. The *blind self* is made up of information that others know about you but you do not. The blind self might include aspects of your self that are too unpleasant to recognize, such as being self-centered, bragging about your talents, or interrupting others when they talk to you. The *unknown self* includes information that no one—not you or anyone else—knows. Sometimes alcoholics have an unknown self involved in their addiction—they hide their alcoholism from others and are not willing to admit to themselves that they have a drinking problem.

Self-Disclosure in Relationships

Self-disclosure has a special power in deepening relationships. In the early part of relationships, we usually don't engage in self-disclosure as much as when relationships have endured the test of time and trust develops. As relationships deepen, one person will disclose something, then the other person will, and so on, back and forth, until friends and lovers eventually arrive at deeper intimacy (Norton & Brenders, 1995).

A series of simple low-risk self-disclosures may get a friendship or dating relationship going, but deeper close relationships usually demand more vulnerability (Goodman & Esterly, 1988). Getting close to someone usually entails taking some psychological risks. We engage in *risky self-disclosures* when we tell someone about a private thought we have, an embarrassing impulse we possess, a romantic

feeling we harbor, a dream for the future, or an unvarnished truth we have previously concealed. An irony of close relationships is that such risky revelations not only give away power and leave us vulnerable, but at the same time bring us strength and protection because of the intimacy they generate. Special confessions—confessions that are not necessarily about cardinal sins but rather unveil a person's inner life, warts and all—sometimes connect hearts. Some of the possible risks of self-disclosure are listed in table 7.1.

In some instances, mental health problems develop because individuals are unwilling, too fearful, or do not have the ability to disclose psychologically painful facts to friends or family. Self-disclosing psychologically painful information requires that we trust the listener. Privacy, a nonjudgmental ear, empathic understanding, and a common bond all increase the likelihood an individual will engage in self-disclosure. For some people, the feeling of psychological safety needed to self-disclose psychologically painful or embarrassing information never comes. These people might never be able to develop or maintain strong relationships with friends and lovers.

Gender and Self-Disclosure

Gender also plays an important role in self-disclosure (Bruess & Pearson, 1996). These gender differences appear in same-sex friendships and the miscommunications between men and women in close relationships. Women tend to

hone their self-disclosure skills and learn to trust the relationship-enhancing qualities of self-disclosure in their same-sex peer/friendship relationships. In peer/friendship relationships that emphasize competition and challenge, males often avoid revealing weaknesses and at times associate self-disclosure with loss of control and vulnerability. Thus, females and males not only reveal different preferences for and patterns of self-disclosure but also interpret the meaning and purpose of self-disclosure differently (Wood, 1996).

Enhancing Self-Disclosure

If you want to disclose more about yourself to someone, how do you begin? Self-disclosure is not easy for a lot of people—males, in particular, often have a difficult time talking about their innermost feelings. If you want to work on increasing your self-disclosure, you don't want to rush out and unveil all of your darkest life moments to someone, especially someone you do not know very well. Self-disclosure usually proceeds gradually, with one person turning a minimally threatening private thought into a revelation to a friend or lover, then the friend or lover reciprocates with a minor revelation of their own. Eventually, each of you may reach a point at which you feel it is psychologically safe to reveal more painful or embarrassing truths.

> *Some things are better left unsaid. But so many unsaid things can become a burden.*
>
> **—Virginia Axline**

It is important to recognize that each of us often has different levels of intimacy needs. Some people feel a lot more comfortable opening up and divulging private information about themselves than others do. Some people feel very comfortable going beyond the surface in interpersonal communication, others become very nervous about this. There is no absolute level of intimacy we can recommend for everyone. Each individual needs to evaluate what that level is. To explore self-disclosure further, turn to Critical Thinking.

The Limits of Self-Disclosure

Most psychologists believe that self-disclosure is an important feature of meaningful relationships, yet individuals differ with regard to the degree of self-disclosure they routinely participate in. Some are quite selective about their self-disclosure, limiting deep disclosure to only their closest relationships. Others are nonselective, self-disclosing to anyone at nearly any time. What values underlie "close to the vest" self-disclosure styles? What values facilitate broadband self-disclosure? Where do you see yourself along this continuum? What values underlie your own style? Your consideration of these questions will help you *examine the values that underlie behavior.*

What are some barriers to effective communication?

Barriers to Effective Verbal Communication

Mike says, "Well, I blew it again. We took the family to visit my parents last weekend. I resolved beforehand that I wouldn't fall into the trap of letting my parents get to me by criticizing the way I handle my kids. I told myself I would bite my tongue when my mother told me I was too hard on them. We weren't there two hours when my mother started in on me. I told her she hadn't done such a great job with my sister and me. It emotionally exhausted me."

All too often, as in Mike's situation with his parents, we want to communicate better with others but we don't. What are some of the specific barriers to interpersonal communication? They fall into three main categories: judging, proposing solutions, and avoiding the other's concerns (Bolton, 1979).

Judging

Humanistic psychologist Carl Rogers (1961) once commented that the main barrier to interpersonal communication is the tendency to make judgments—to approve or disapprove of the other person's statements. **Judging** *is a barrier to effective communication that includes criticizing, name-calling and labeling, and praising evaluatively.*

Criticizing is one of judging's roadblocks. Many of us believe that if we aren't critical, other people never will improve. Supervisors think they have to criticize their employees' mistakes or production will slip. Marital partners think they have to criticize their spouse's behaviors they don't like or she or he will never learn satisfying courses of action. One wife described her husband as being on a constant fault-finding mission. Among the husband's comments were "You are always leaving stuff out on the counter," "Why aren't you more responsible?" and "You never pick up your clothes." Such negative evaluations of the other person present a serious barrier to effective communication, because the person being judged stays chronically angry or loses self-esteem and withdraws.

Name-calling and *labeling* are other judgmental roadblocks to effective interpersonal communication. Calling someone a "brat," "immature," "sloppy," "dumb," "lazy," "boring," or a "jerk" introduces negative conversational overtones that can damage a relationship. Negative labels put down the other person and should be avoided. One alternative to using labels is to describe specific behaviors that you object to. On the other hand, using positive labels—such as *bright, attractive, responsible, hardworking,* and *dedicated*—usually adds positive overtones to conversation.

However, though we often think that all praise is helpful, sometimes people use praise manipulatively. Some people say only nice things, especially about you, when they are talking with you. It is one thing to think positively and to say nice things to other people; it is quite another *always* to do this and to do it in a manipulative attempt to gain the other person's favor.

Proposing Solutions

Another set of roadblocks involves proposing solutions to other people. **Proposing solutions** *is an ineffective communication pattern in which the proposed solutions are presented caringly as advice, indirectly by questioning, authoritatively as an order, aggressively as a threat, or with a halo as moralizing.*

Advice can be constructive or destructive in relationships. The advice-giving trap is a rather common temptation to most of us. What's wrong with giving advice? Advice too often implies a lack of confidence in the other person or that the person lacks the intelligence to manage the problem independently. Advice can come across as a message like this: "You have been making a big deal out of a problem whose solution is very apparent to me. How stupid you are." It is natural to fall into the trap of giving advice when you feel a need to help others, especially those you care about the most. A safer strategy is first to ask if advice would be helpful. This shows greater respect for the person with the problem.

Orders are sent coercively and forcefully. When coercion and force are used, several outcomes are possible. Under orders, people often become resentful and resistant, or they become submissive and very compliant, which is unhealthy in a relationship. People can also adopt a passive-aggressive response to orders, passively agreeing to comply with the orders but not following through. Orders imply that the other person's judgment is unsound, and they likely lower the other person's self-esteem.

Threats are solutions that are proposed with the message that punishment will be forthcoming if the solution is not implemented. Threats yield the same kind of negative results that are produced by orders.

Too many of us also try to *moralize* in the solutions we offer to others. Moralizing often includes words like *should* and *ought*. Other instances of moralizing include "You don't call me enough," "It's the wrong thing for you to do," "You are not a very moral person when you do that," and "You are a liar." Too often moralizing *demoralizes* by fostering anxiety, arousing resentment, and inviting pretense.

CRITICAL THINKING

Your Own Barriers

As you read about the various obstacles to verbal communication, you probably easily recognized many of the bad habits that emerge in your friends and loved ones when they are not at their best. People tend to fall into bad habits and have difficulty even recognizing the difficulties they create in communication.

But what about you? Chances are that you, too, have developed some bad habits that interfere with your communication. Do you already know how you are inclined to create barriers? Which of the patterns we have described best characterizes your style? Are you most inclined to judge others, to advise others, or to avoid others in conflict situations? What impact does this style have on others? If you don't know which patterns tend to show up most in your own style, how could you find out? Devoting some reflection to this concern demonstrates your ability to *apply psychological concepts to enhance personal adaptation.*

Avoiding the Other's Concerns

Avoiding the other's concerns *is an ineffective communication technique that involves diversion and logical argument, which are especially effective ways to derail a conversation.* A frequent way of switching a conversation from the other person's concerns to your own interests is to use the tactic of *diversion*. The phrase *speaking of . . .* frequently signals the beginning of diverting. Consider the following example of diverting,

Person A: "I've been feeling a lot of stress lately."
Person B: "Speaking of stress, I was talking to someone yesterday and that's all she talked about. She was really stressed."
Person C: "Who was that?"
Person B: "Oh, that was Barbara. Her husband lost his job, you know. And they are having trouble making ends meet."
Person D: "Speaking of someone who lost a job, I know someone who lost her job six months ago and still doesn't have one."

Whoa! Whatever happened to the stressful feelings of Person A? That person got lost in diversions created by the conversation's other participants. To evaluate whether your own style involves barriers to effective communication, see Critical Thinking.

One-upping is a particularly harmful form of diversion. Rather than respond to the speaker's concerns, the one-upper redirects the focus to her or his own concerns. A common one-up response is "You think that is bad, wait till you hear what happened to me!"

Another way of avoiding the other's concerns is to try to solve the communication problem with logical argument. We usually want to use the best logic possible when we think and solve problems. However, too often when one person tries

	Communication spoiler	Its nature	Examples
Judging	Criticizing	Making a negative evaluation of the other person, his or her actions, or attitudes.	"You brought it on yourself — you've got no one else to blame for the mess you're in."
	Name-calling and labeling	"Putting down" or stereotyping the other person.	"What a dope!" "Just like a woman..." "Egghead." "You hardhats are all alike." "You are just another insensitive male."
	Praising evaluatively	Making a positive judgment of the other person, his or her actions, or attitudes with the intent to manipulate.	"You are always such a good girl. I know you will help me with the lawn."
Proposing solutions	Advising	Giving the other person the solution to his or her problem.	"If I were you, I'd sure turn him off." "That's an easy one to solve. First, ..."
	Excessive/ inappropriate questioning	Asking questions that often can be answered in just a few words, usually just "yes" or "no."	"Are you sorry you did it?" "Who is to blame...?"
	Ordering	Commanding the other person to do what you want to have done.	"Do your homework right now." "Why?" "Because I said so."
	Threatening	Trying to control the other person's actions by warning of negative consequences that you will instigate.	"You'll do it or else ..." "Stop that noise right now or else..."
	Moralizing	Telling another person what he or she *should* do. "Preaching" at the other.	"You *shouldn't* get a divorce; think of what will happen to the children." "You *ought* to tell him you are sorry."
Avoiding others' concerns	Diverting	Pushing the other's problems aside through distraction.	"Don't dwell on it. Let's talk about something more pleasant."
	One-upping	Displacing the other's problems with your own concerns.	"Something much worse happened to me."
	Logical argument	Attempting to convince the other with an appeal to facts or logic, usually without considering the emotional factors involved.	"Look at the facts; if you hadn't bought that new car, we could have made the down payment on the house."

FIGURE 7.4

Eleven Conversation Spoilers That Can Undermine Effective Verbal Interpersonal Communication

to foist *logical solutions* to conflict on another person, the second person's feelings are not taken into account. Logic does not deal in feelings. When one person tries to use logic to solve interpersonal problems, the other person's feelings usually get ignored. In one couple's relationship, the husband likes to say, "Well, here is the way to think logically about this. Now listen carefully, and we will go through how to solve this disagreement

logically." Of course, the logic is always according to his way of thinking about the disagreement and does not take into account his wife's feelings.

In sum, there are a lot of ways we can spoil conversations. Further examples of these spoilers are presented in figure 7.4.

Arguments are characterized by many of the conversation spoilers because arguments express oppositional

views rather than open dialogue. Everyone argues now and then, but some people may tend to argue more than others. The Self-Assessment box helps you to evaluate your own argumentativeness.

It is not necessary to understand things in order to argue about them.

—Beaumarchais

Halonen/Santrock: Human Adjustment

SELF-ASSESSMENT

Argumentativeness

Instructions

This questionnaire contains statements about arguing controversial issues. Indicate how often each statement is true for you personally by placing the appropriate number in the blank to the left of the statement:

1 = Almost never true
2 = Rarely true
3 = Occasionally true
4 = Often true
5 = Almost always true

Please turn to the end of the chapter to score and interpret your responses.

Items

_____ 1. While in an argument, I worry that the person I am arguing with will form a negative impression of me.

_____ 2. Arguing over controversial issues improves my intelligence.

_____ 3. I enjoy avoiding arguments.

_____ 4. I am energetic and enthusiastic when I argue.

_____ 5. Once I finish an argument I promise myself that I will not get into another.

_____ 6. Arguing with a person creates more problems for me than it solves.

_____ 7. I have a pleasant, good feeling when I win a point in an argument.

_____ 8. When I finish arguing with someone I feel nervous and upset.

_____ 9. I enjoy a good argument over a controversial issue.

_____ 10. I get an unpleasant feeling when I realize I am about to get into an argument.

_____ 11. I enjoy defending my point of view on an issue.

_____ 12. I am happy when I keep an argument from happening.

_____ 13. I do not like to miss the opportunity to argue a controversial issue.

_____ 14. I prefer being with people who rarely disagree with me.

_____ 15. I consider an argument an exciting intellectual challenge.

_____ 16. I find myself unable to think of effective points during an argument.

_____ 17. I feel refreshed and satisfied after an argument on a controversial issue.

_____ 18. I have the ability to do well in an argument.

_____ 19. I try to avoid getting into arguments.

_____ 20. I feel excitement when I expect that a conversation I am in is leading to an argument.

REVIEW

Verbal Interpersonal Communication

Denotation is the objective meaning of words or a message. Connotation is subjective, personal, or emotional meaning of words or a message. Concrete words and messages are more likely to be denotative, abstract words and messages connotative. Connotative words and messages are often involved in communication problems.

We spend more time in listening than any other communication activity. In actual conversations, however, most of us are not very good listeners.

Learning to become a better listener requires a lot of work and effort. Although hearing is a physiological process, listening is a psychological process that involves interpreting and understanding the significance of what someone says. Most people can improve their listening skills by talking less and listening more; by paying careful attention to the person who is talking; by using reflective listening, including paraphrasing and summative reflection; and by giving feedback in a competent manner.

Self-disclosure is the communication of intimate details about ourselves to someone else. Self-disclosure has a special power in deepening relationships. In some instances, mental health problems develop because individuals do not have the ability to disclose psychologically painful facts to friends or family. Self-disclosure usually proceeds gradually. Gender plays an important role in self-disclosure.

Barriers to effective verbal communication include judging (criticizing, name-calling and labeling, and praising evaluatively), proposing solutions (advising, excessive/inappropriate questioning, ordering, threatening, and moralizing), and avoiding the other's concerns (diverting, using logical argument without considering feelings).

Gender plays a special role in verbal interpersonal communication. Our culture often sends different messages to us about how we should talk to each other, depending on whether the sender and receiver are both males, both females, or male/female, female/male.

NONVERBAL INTERPERSONAL COMMUNICATION

Does how you fold your arms, cast your eyes, move your mouth, cross your legs, and touch someone communicate messages to other people? Many psychologists believe they do. Let's examine what is meant by nonverbal communication and then study more precisely how we use different parts of our body to communicate information.

Defining Nonverbal Communication

Nonverbal communication *refers to messages that are transmitted from one person to another by other than linguistic means. These other means include bodily communication (gestures, facial expressions, eye communication, and touch), spatial communication, silence, and paralanguage (such as the tone of a person's voice).* We might lift an eyebrow for disbelief, rub the nose for puzzlement, clasp our arms to isolate ourselves or to protect ourselves, shrug our shoulders for indifference, wink one eye for intimacy, tap our fingers for impatience, and slap our foreheads for forgetfulness (Fast, 1970). Some communication experts believe that a majority of our interpersonal communication is nonverbal—even a whopping 93 percent in one estimate (Mehrabian & Wiener, 1967).

Dimensions of Nonverbal Communication

Nonverbal communication is complex. It often is spontaneous and sometimes is ambiguous, but it always communicates a message (Costanzo & Archer, 1995). Nonverbal communication tends to be coordinated in clusters, or packages, and might send a different message than verbal communication is sending. Nonverbal communication is strongly influenced by cultural context.

Characteristics of Nonverbal Communication

Even if you are sitting in a corner silently reading a book, your nonverbal behavior is communicating something—perhaps that you want to be left alone or that you are intellectual. Staring out the window when the teacher is lecturing communicates something just as strongly as if you shouted, "I'm very bored!" Experts conclude that you cannot *not* communicate, given the expressiveness of nonverbal behavior. It is difficult to mask or control our nonverbal messages, because nonverbal behavior is spontaneous. True feelings will usually express themselves, no matter how hard we try to conceal them (Hanna, 1995).

Nonverbal behavior can also be ambiguous and difficult to interpret. When a person sits quietly and doesn't say anything about what you have just said, how are you to interpret the silence? It is not easy. When a person smiles, is the smile communicating something positive or something sarcastic? Again, the interpretation may be ambiguous. Because nonverbal behavior is often ambiguous, caution is warranted in interpreting someone's nonverbal behavior. Instead of impulsively jumping to a rash conclusion about a frown, a smile, a raised eyebrow, or a book slammed down on a table, don't consider such nonverbal behaviors in isolation. They must be seen in the context of verbal communication and the ongoing communication that takes place over hours, days, weeks, and even lifetimes.

Paul Ekman and Wallace Frieson (1974) argued that people often attend more to what they are saying than to what they are doing with their bodies. They believe nonverbal leakage permeates our communication. **Nonverbal leakage** *involves the communication of true emotions through nonverbal channels even when the person tries to conceal the truth verbally.* For example, a student might say that he is not nervous about an upcoming test, but as he speaks his voice becomes high-pitched and occasionally cracks, he blinks more than usual, and he bites his lower lip.

How accurately can people tell if someone is being deceptive in their communication? Not very, unless they are trained to detect deceptive expressions

(Costanzo, 1992; DePaulo, 1994). In one study, Paul Ekman and Maureen O'Sullivan (1991) videotaped college students as they watched either an enjoyable film about nature or an emotion-laden gory film. Regardless of which film they saw, the students were asked to describe the film as pleasant and enjoyable. The researchers were able to detect correctly in more than 4 out of 5 cases which students were lying and which were telling the truth by focusing on such cues as a raised voice. Ekman and O'Sullivan asked college students, psychiatrists, court judges, police officers, and polygraph experts if they could detect which students were lying and which were telling the truth. Each of these groups scored at about chance (50 percent). One additional group—secret service agents—did perform above chance, detecting the lies about two-thirds of the time.

How might you become better at detecting nonverbal cues that someone is trying to deceive you? One possibility is to become more knowledgeable about the kinds of behaviors that really do distinguish truths from lies. Researchers have found that, compared to people telling the truth, liars (DePaulo, 1994):

- Blink more and have more dilated pupils
- Show more self-manipulating gestures, such as rubbing and scratching
- Give shorter responses that are more negative, more irrelevant, and more generalized
- Speak in a more distancing way, as if they do not want to commit themselves to what they are saying
- Speak in a higher pitch
- Take more time to plan what they are about to say, but the resulting statements tend to be more internally discrepant and more marred by hesitations, repetitions, grammatical errors, and slips of the tongue

Nonverbal Coordination

Nonverbal behaviors usually don't occur in isolation; they usually come in clusters. For example, it is physically difficult to express an intense emotion with only one part of the body. If you are afraid, your muscles tense up, the pupils of your eyes

Halonen/Santrock: Human Adjustment

As shown in the international examples, context can play a powerful role in the interpretation of gestures. However, we don't need to journey that far to see the influence of context. Think about professional team sports. In the context of competition, men exchange many surprisingly intimate gestures, such as hugging and patting, that most would be loathe to demonstrate in any other context. Can you think of any other examples in which *context influences the acceptability of gestures?* What variables do you think influence such intimate interpersonal expressions in rough-and-tumble settings?

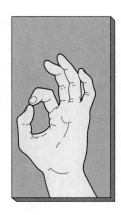

FIGURE 7.5

An Example of a Gesture and Its Meanings
In many cultures, the circle made with the thumb and forefinger means that everything is "OK."

Bodily Communication

We can communicate a nonverbal message through a gesture, a facial expression, a look, or a touch.

Gestures

A **gesture** *is a motion of the limbs or body made to convey a message to someone else.* Examples of gestures include people shaking their fists to convey anger and a circle sign made by forming a ring with the thumb and forefinger of one hand to indicate that everything is "OK" (see figure 7.5). As we talk with our mouths, we often make gestures with our hands—for example, holding our hands a particular distance apart as we describe how wide something is, waving our hands wildly in the air as we talk about how confusing or disturbing something is, and pointing a finger at someone as we are saying something nasty to them.

Gestures are not universal (Cohen & Borsoi, 1996). For instance, the sign shown in figure 7.5, which in our culture usually means "OK," has other meanings in other cultures. In Japan, it can mean "coins." In France, it means "worthless" (as in "zero worth"). In Greece, it is a hostile allusion to body parts. Obviously, tourists should be very careful about their gestures (Axtell, 1991). To explore further the significance of gestures, see Critical Thinking.

Facial Expressions

Facial expressions can communicate important messages. Our faces not only disclose specific emotions, but they can

---

dilate, your heart beats faster, your mouth becomes drier, and your sweat gland activity increases. When you become afraid, you might simultaneously open your mouth wider, grab hold of something in a tense way, clam up and become very quiet, or even begin shaking. These examples illustrate how many aspects of nonverbal communication become coordinated to convey meaning.

Bodies never lie.
—**Agnes de Mille**

Sometimes nonverbal behavior and verbal expression conflict. For example, a husband's face becomes flushed, he clenches his fist, pounds the table, and shouts, "I am *not* angry!" His wife is likely to find her husband's nonverbal behavior more convincing than his verbal behavior. It is not unusual to find a discrepancy between words and body language. When there is a discrepancy, both messages are usually important. People who shout loudly that they are not angry might not want to admit to themselves or others that they are angry.

Self-betrayal oozes from all our pores.
—**Freud**

Sociocultural Influences on Nonverbal Communication

Not only do many cultures have different languages, but they also often have different systems of nonverbal communication (Poyatos, 1988). We will explore some examples of cultural variations in future sections when we examine specific forms of nonverbal communication.

Standards for nonverbal communication often vary across cultural groups and within a culture as well. To read further about nonverbal communication in ethnic minority groups, turn to Sociocultural Worlds of Adjustment.

Gender is another important dimension of the sociocultural contexts that influence nonverbal communication. Females are more likely to sit quietly, males are more likely to be active or even fidgety. Females are more likely to have good posture, males are more likely to have poor posture (Tannen, 1990). The next time you are in a group, observe how the males and females are sitting; females are more likely to sit erect with their legs close together, males are more likely to slouch or sprawl across a chair or sofa, with their legs spread wide apart, claiming a great deal of space.

Next we turn to various forms of communication. For each form we will highlight sociocultural variations.

SOCIOCULTURAL WORLDS OF ADJUSTMENT

The Meanings of Nonverbal Communication in Ethnic Minority Individuals

The nonverbal communication styles of White Americans may differ from that of African Americans, Latinos, Asian Americans, and Native Americans. The ethnic differences captured in the contrasts that follow are based on predominant patterns of each group. Variations within each group are also likely.

During communication, many African Americans may avoid eye contact by looking the other way and may avoid nodding or commenting in the manner that many White Americans do when they want to encourage the speaker and make the speaker feel that he or she is being understood. In such circumstances, White Americans may think that African Americans are not listening, are not interested, or are being presumptuous. The nonverbal behavior of African Americans just described may not mean this at all. It may simply be the result of years of discrimination and prejudice African Americans have experienced in the majority White culture, or it may be a communication style that is more common among African Americans than among White Americans.

An important difference in the nonverbal communication styles of White Americans and Latinos is that Latinos tend to stand close while communicating and to touch one another while communicating; White Americans stand farther apart and tend not to touch one another while communicating. As with African Americans, Latinos may avoid eye contact while they are communicating (Padilla, 1980).

White Americans often use a loud voice and a warm, hearty greeting when they meet each other. By contrast, Asian Americans are more likely to greet each other calmly and quietly. A smile by a White American usually conveys happiness, but a smile by an Asian American, especially of Vietnamese descent, can signify anger, rejection, embarrassment, or other emotions (Brower, 1989). White Americans consider shifty eyes or an unwillingness to make eye contact as suspicious;

however, looking someone in the eye is often perceived as a sign of disrespect or rudeness by many Asian Americans (Baruth & Manning, 1991).

Native Americans speak more softly and at a slower rate than White Americans do. Native Americans also tend to avoid such direct interaction between speaker and listener expressed by signs such as head nods and "uh huh." White Americans view a firm handshake as a sign of strength and power. By contrast, Native Americans view a firm handshake as aggressive and disrespectful (Everett, Proctor, & Cartmell, 1989). As with the other ethnic minority groups we have discussed, many Native Americans consider direct eye contact to be disrespectful so it should not be used when conversing with someone. White Americans expect and maintain more eye contact and may interpret its absence as rude, disrespectful and hostile, as well as conveying disinterest.

In sum, by understanding the cultural meanings of nonverbal behaviors, different ethnic groups can communicate more effectively with each other (Houston & Wood, 1996).

What are some of the meanings of nonverbal behavior in different ethnic minority groups in the United States?

What roles does touch play in our lives?

telegraph what really matters to us. In some situations, a person's face will take on a natural and lively intensity in the midst of a conversation that seems relatively unimportant. When this happens, the listener can zero in on the area of conversation that produced the reaction and converse about topics of high emotional priority to the other person.

Although some facial expressions appear to be universal, the meanings of facial expressions can also vary from culture to culture (Axtell, 1991). For example, shaking the head means no in our culture but means yes in Iran and Bulgaria and in India means that one is listening intently.

Eye Communication

In our culture, eye contact generally serves four functions:

1. To monitor feedback (we often look at someone directly to see how they react to what we have just said)
2. To signal a conversational turn (as when someone speaks in a group and then looks at someone else in the group to convey that it is now his or her turn to speak)
3. To signal the nature of a relationship (when we like someone, we increase eye contact, and when we dislike them we more often avoid eye contact with the person) and
4. To compensate for physical distance (when we catch someone's eye at a party, even though we are some distance from them, we may be able to express psychological closeness to the person)

In addition to eye movements, pupil dilation sends a nonverbal message. In the fifteenth and sixteenth centuries, Italian women put drops of belladonna (which literally means "beautiful woman") into their eyes to dilate the pupils so they would be perceived as more attractive.

Contemporary researchers have found that people are judged as more attractive when their pupils are dilated rather than contracted (DeVito, 1996).

Touch Communication

We experience touch communication very early in our lives. Starting at birth, we are fondled, caressed, patted, and stroked by parents and other adults. All the world seems to want to touch the young infant. Touch is among our first pleasant experiences, not only the rewarding feelings of touch from others, but our own touching. Infants want to pick up just about everything, and their favorite objects (such as a teddy bear or a favorite blanket) often are chosen because of their tactile (touch) properties. Touching not only is an important aspect of nonverbal communication in infancy, but plays powerful roles in the remainder of life as well.

The functions of touch include expressions of sexuality, consolation and support, and power and dominance. Touch is a primary form of sexual interaction, from kissing to foreplay to sexual intercourse. Touch also plays an important role in consoling others, as when we put our arms around people, hold their head in our hands, hold their hands, or hug them. Higher-status people are more often allowed to touch lower-status people than vice versa—it is more permissible for teachers to touch students, doctors to touch patients, managers to touch workers, ministers to touch parishioners, and police officers to touch suspects, than vice versa.

Who touches whom where? It depends to some extent on gender and culture. Generally, women touch more and are touched more than men (Hollender & Mercer, 1976). Touching patterns vary considerably from one culture to another. For example, in one study college students in the United States reported being touched twice as much as their counterparts in Japan did (Barnlund, 1975). There is a strong taboo against strangers' touching in Japan, which is reflected in the sufficient distance maintained by most Japanese in public.

Spatial Communication

In the television show *The Simpsons*, Homer Simpson often gets upset if

CATEGORY	DISTANCE	INTERACTION ACTIVITY	
Intimate			
Close	0–6 inches	Love-making and wrestling	
Far	6–18 inches	Intimate talk in public	
Personal			
Close	1.5–2.5 feet	Peers, friends talk	
Far	2.5–4 feet	Strangers, unequals talk	
Social			
Close	4–7 feet	Impersonal business	
Far	7–12 feet	Formal business	
Public			
Close	12–25 feet	Formal presentation	
Far	25 feet–outward	Famous person presents	

FIGURE 7.6

Personal Space Categories, Distances, and Interactions

anyone sits near him when he is watching television. Most of us don't go into the tirades Homer does when our space is invaded, but most of us do communicate messages about space. Understanding how space communication works requires knowledge about proxemics and territoriality.

Proxemics

Proxemics *is the study of the communicative function of space, especially how people unconsciously structure their space.* The term *proxemics* was coined by anthropologist Edward Hall (1969) to specify the kind of space in which interactions are ordinarily and comfortably conducted. Hall believes that our use of space influences our ability to relate to other people.

Hall says that we have four distinct zones in which we interact:

1. Intimate distance
2. Personal distance
3. Social distance
4. Public distance

For each of these zones, Hall specified what distances are "close" or "far" (see figure 7.6). For example, in the close intimate zone of 0–6 inches, lovemaking and wrestling are examples of activities, while in the far intimate zone of 6–18 inches, intimate talk in public is a representative activity.

Cultures differ in their standards for how close you should stand to a person you are speaking to (individuals of Northern European heritage stand farther apart than their counterparts of Latin

American and Middle Eastern heritage) and how much eye contact is appropriate (direct eye contact is more appropriate for speakers in the Middle East and southern Europe, but more peripheral eye contact or none at all is more appropriate in northern Europe and the Far East) (Hall, 1969).

Territoriality

Territoriality *is the possessive or ownership-like reaction to an area of space or particular objects.* Think for a moment about the space where you live. There probably are certain territories that different people have staked out and where invasions are reason for at least some mild confrontation, if not more—perhaps a specific chair, room, stereo, and so on. Siblings especially are prone to staking out space that their brothers or sisters are not to violate. If you live in a dorm and share a room with someone, it is likely that approximately half of the room is designated as yours and the other half as your roommate's.

How people use space communicates information about power and status. People with higher status usually have more space and more privacy, those with lower status less space and less privacy. Executives of large corporations are often sheltered by an army of outer offices, secretaries, and guards, for example. We can't just barge into the executive's office, but we probably can come into direct contact with the owner of a small single location business.

Territoriality has spawned numerous wars down through history and continues to do so today, as when the invading army of Iraq moved into Kuwait and stimulated the Gulf War. Invasions of territory also involve gangs moving into a rival district, burglars breaking into a house, a rude person breaking into a line waiting to purchase tickets, and stealing a parking space. Most such intrusions will be met with resistance varying from the vigorous to the savagely violent (Morris, 1977).

Chronemics

Chronemics *refers to how time influences behavior.* Practices related to the management of time are influenced by individual lifestyle and status as well as cultural factors. For example, despite the fact that punctuality is highly valued in our culture, some individuals seem to be late for everything—and they seem undisturbed by this violation of cultural values. In contrast, some individuals are punctual to the point of pathology, becoming agitated and distressed if they are only a few minutes late. These individuals regard making others wait as a sign of disrespect.

Status also influences behaviors related to time. We expect lower-status individuals to wait on higher-status individuals. This practice is carried to an extreme in higher education, where the formal wait time for late professors expands according to the professor's rank. In some systems, students wait for lecturers only 10 minutes, while full professors require a 20-minute wait.

Edward Hall (1969) suggested that there are two styles of relating time. People who are **monochronic** *tend to schedule only one thing at a time and become disoriented if they have to do more than one thing at a time.* Monochronic people tend to "take their time" at completing tasks. In contrast, people who are **polychronic** *prefer to juggle multiple tasks at the same time.* Polychronic people tend to be in constant motion, hurrying to get things done, and often report feeling pressured by time.

Hall suggested that cultures tend to have a dominant style. This explains why polychronic people from North America have difficulty when vacationing in monochronic cultures, such as Mexico, South America, or the islands of the Caribbean. Many tourists report that it takes the entire vacation to readjust to the more casual clock and the "no problem" attitude of their host culture. In contrast, some cultures are even more time pressured than ours. For example, even seasoned American tourists report feeling overwhelmed by the intensity of the polychronic culture of Hong Kong.

Instant gratification takes too long.
—**Carrie Fisher**

Silence and Paralanguage

We have seen that we can communicate with words and with nonverbal behaviors such as bodily signals and use of space. We also can communicate nonverbally through the use of silence.

Silence

In our fast-paced modern world we often act as if there is something wrong with anyone who remains silent for more than a second or two after something is said to them. Remarked newscaster Edwin Newman (1974),

> People seem to think there is something wrong with silence. If someone asks you a question and you stop to think before answering, the person thinks there's something wrong with you.

In a word, today we often act as if silence is not golden (Goldin-Meadow, McNeill, & Singleton, 1996). According to Robert Bolton (1979), more than half the people who take communication skills training courses with him are initially uncomfortable with silence. Even a few seconds' pause in a conversation causes many of them to squirm.

By being silent, a good listener engages in certain activities, such as these:

1. Attending to the other person through body posture that indicates that he or she is really there for the other person
2. Observing the other by watching the speaker's eyes, facial expressions, posture, and gestures for communication
3. Thinking about what the other person is communicating, wondering what the other person is feeling, and considering the most appropriate response to make

---

Never forget that when we are silent, we are one. And when we speak, we are two.

—**Indira Gandhi**

Of course, silence can be overdone and sometimes is inappropriate. It is rarely appropriate to listen for an excessive length of time without making at least some verbal response. Interpersonal communication should not be a monologue, but rather a dialogue.

Communication expert Gerald Goodman (1988) believes that silences establish and maintain order between talking people. They constantly regulate the atmosphere of our conversations by controlling the exchange of thoughts and feelings. Silences or lack of silences can change our sense of being allowed to say what we want or of being so rushed we can't get our points across. In Goodman's words, silences or their absence are like traffic talk signals.

Paralanguage

Paralanguage *refers to the nonlinguistic aspects of verbal expression, such as the rapidity of speech, the volume of speech (loudness, softness), and the pitch of speech (based on a sound wave's frequency—a soprano voice is high-pitched, a bass voice is low-pitched).* The effective listener hears far more than the speaker's words. When a person says, "I quit my job," it can mean something different depending on how it is said. The person may say it in a

sad, angry, and fearful way in a low tone of voice that is quivering, or the person may say it in a brighter, bouncier way, suggesting possibly that other opportunities, even better ones, are available. A summary of some of the meanings and

feelings that various paralanguage communications convey is shown in table 7.2.

The voice is a second face.
—**Gerard Bauer**

TABLE 7.2

Different Types of Paralanguage and Their Meanings/Feelings

Paralanguage	Probable Meanings/Feelings
Monotone voice	Boredom
Slow speed, low pitch	Depression
High voice, emphatic pitch	Enthusiasm
Ascending tone	Astonishment
Abrupt speech	Defensiveness
Terse speed, loud tone	Anger
High pitch, drawn-out speech	Disbelief

From L. Sperry, M.D., Ph.D. *Developing Skills in Contact Counseling,* 1975. Reprinted by permission.

REVIEW

Nonverbal Interpersonal Communication

Nonverbal communication refers to messages that are transmitted from one person to another by means other than linguistic. These other means include body communication (gestures, facial expressions, eye communication, and touch), space communication, silence, and paralanguage. Nonverbal communication may occur in clusters or packages, always communicates, is culturally influenced, is often spontaneous and ambiguous, and may be discrepant from verbal communication. Nonverbal leakage often occurs in communication, especially when someone is trying to deceive another person.

A gesture is a motion of the limbs or body to convey a message to someone else. The meaning of some gestures varies across cultures. Most psychologists believe that the facial

expressions of basic emotions are universal across cultures. While facial expressions of emotion are thought to be universal, display rules for emotions often vary from one culture to another. Eye contact serves a number of functions and pupil dilation also sends a nonverbal message—for example, people are perceived as more attractive when their pupils are dilated rather than contracted. Touch communication plays a powerful role in interpersonal communication. Its functions include expressions of sexuality, consolation and support, and power and dominance.

Understanding how space communication works requires knowledge of proxemics and territoriality. Proxemics is the study of the communicative function of space, especially how people unconsciously structure their space. Hall described four distinct zones in which we interact: intimate distance, personal distance, social distance, and public distance. Territoriality

is the possessive or ownership-like reaction to an area of space or particular objects. How people use space communicates information about power and status. *Chronemics* refers to how time influences interpersonal communication.

Silence plays an important role in interpersonal communication, yet many people feel uncomfortable during silence. Being silent during parts of conversation does not mean being inactive during that time. While being silent, the good listener is attending to the other person, observing the other person's behavior, and thinking about what to say next. Paralanguage refers to the nonlinguistic aspects of verbal expression, such as the rapidity of speech, the volume of speech, and the pitch of speech. Different types of paralanguage often have different meanings; for instance, a high voice and emphatic pitch convey enthusiasm, and a monotone voice implies boredom.

Civility in an Electronic Age

As we have moved toward the end of the century, we have witnessed new and powerful forces that appear to be making our culture even more chaotic than it was before. Personal computers have expanded our horizons but also have introduced a whole new terrain of interpersonal communications—and interpersonal communication hazards.

New users of electronic communications report that learning this new communication skill isn't easy. They are startled by how rapidly they can "access" others' electronic mailboxes. Equally startling is how rapidly answers can be returned. They soon discover how "full" an electronic mailbox can become with nonmeaningful messages (electronic junk mail). Most surprising of all, they recognize that the ready access makes communication more challenging rather than less. Electronic communication is a hybrid of speaking (in its casual, spontaneous nature) and writing (in its use of keyboarding). This hybrid status makes it more difficult to learn.

The difficulties are apparent in three areas. First, electronic communications can require a "first-draft" writing mentality. Some software programs for constructing messages on-line discourage the writer from editing the message—unlike most ways of writing in the past. This forces greater thoughtfulness, but sometimes only after the words get away from their author. If the on-line writer cannot edit more than the current line of text, then, inconveniently, the entire message must be rewritten if the writer discovers a mistake when well into the message.

The second problem lies in paralanguage disturbance. Although the medium is casual, the language cues found in speaking are not present in electronic communication. New users quickly discover that language subtleties cannot be communicated easily in e-mail text. Humor and sarcasm, for example, are especially difficult to communicate in this new medium without adding specific clues to the reader to clarify the intent. How have users learned to compensate? In a variety of interesting adaptations. For example, users add emphasis by placing important words in capital letters. This helps the readers see how VERY important some aspect of the message might be. A recent Internet exchange led one user to respond "Stop yelling at me!" to another who used only capitals. Other users have added symbols to provide emotional tone. For instance, punctuation marks carefully arranged alert the reader to a happy or sad tone—:-) or :-(. *Turn the book sideways and read those notations to get the intended effect.*

A third problem has complicated communication in Internet bulletin boards and other chat groups in subscriber services. Many users report distress at how quickly the emotional tone of these forums deteriorates. Some users narcissistically dominate bulletin boards. Others enjoy "flame-baiting" more committed users, hoping to derail the network from the more meaningful exchanges they might have had if they hadn't felt compelled to "flame" the intruder. Critics suggest that such deterioration into hostile communications is due to the absence of human cues in on-line communications.

Whether you are experienced at electronic communications (an "Internaut") or are just beginning your travels on the information highway (a "neubie"), it might be helpful to think about how to succeed at remaining civil in this new medium. Your awareness of the conventions of this new interpersonal communication form will *encourage the practice of civility toward others.*

We began this chapter by exploring what interpersonal communication is and describing its content and relationship dimensions, as well as its components. Our coverage of verbal interpersonal communication focused on the denotative and connotative meanings of words and messages, speaking skills, listening skills, self-disclosure, and barriers to effective verbal communication. We also discussed nonverbal communication—what it is, its dimensions, bodily communication, spatial communication, and silence and paralanguage. Remember that you can obtain an overall summary of the chapter by again studying the in-chapter reviews on pages 147, 155, and 162.

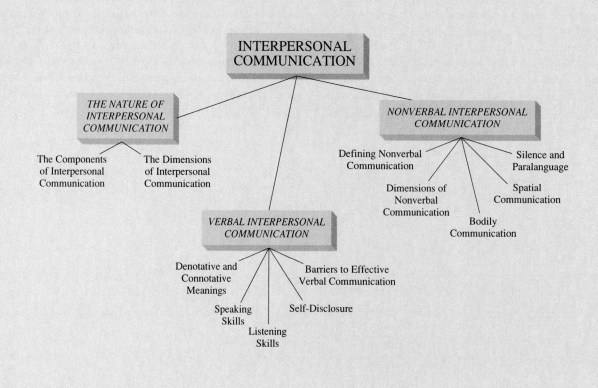

INTERPERSONAL COMMUNICATION

THE NATURE OF INTERPERSONAL COMMUNICATION

The Components of Interpersonal Communication

The Dimensions of Interpersonal Communication

VERBAL INTERPERSONAL COMMUNICATION

Denotative and Connotative Meanings

Speaking Skills

Listening Skills

Self-Disclosure

Barriers to Effective Verbal Communication

NONVERBAL INTERPERSONAL COMMUNICATION

Defining Nonverbal Communication

Dimensions of Nonverbal Communication

Bodily Communication

Silence and Paralanguage

Spatial Communication

PRACTICAL KNOWLEDGE ABOUT ADJUSTMENT

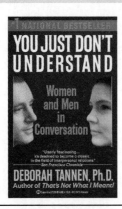

YOU JUST DON'T UNDERSTAND
(1990) by Deborah Tannen. New York: Ballantine.

The subtitle of this book is *Women and Men in Conversation.* This is a book about how women and men communicate—or all too often miscommunicate—with each other. *You Just Don't Understand* reached the status of No. 1 on the *New York Times* bestseller list. Tannen shows that friction between women and men in conversation often develops because boys and girls were brought up in two virtually distinct cultures. Tannen believes that the two distinct gender cultures are rapport talk (women) and report talk (men).

Tannen's book has especially connected with women, who, after reading the book, want their husband, male partner, or other men in their lives to read it. Prior to Tannen's analysis, the common way to explain communication problems between women and men was to resort to blaming men's desire to dominate women. Tannen presents a more balanced approach to communication problems between women and men by focusing on the different ways females and males communicate, and a more positive approach, by emphasizing that women and men can get along better by understanding each other's different styles.

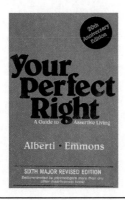

YOUR PERFECT RIGHT (6TH ED.)
(1990) by Robert Alberti and Michael Emmons. San Luis Obispo, CA: Impact.

Your Perfect Right, a national best-seller, emphasizes the importance of developing better communication skills in becoming more assertive. Part 1 speaks to the self-help reader who wants to learn how to become more assertive; Part 2 is a guide for assertiveness-training leaders that teaches them techniques to help others become more assertive.

You learn how to distinguish assertive, aggressive, and nonassertive behavior and why assertive behavior is the best choice. The key components of assertive behavior include self-expression, honesty, directness, self-enhancement, not harming others, being socially responsible, and learned skills. You answer a questionnaire to determine your own level of assertiveness, then you learn about the obstacles you will face in trying to become more assertive. Step-by-step procedures are presented to help you get started and give you the confidence to stand up for your own rights. An excellent chapter on "soft assertions" informs you about how to be more assertive with friends and family members. Some mental health professionals refer to *Your Perfect Right* as the "assertiveness bible," they think so highly of it.

SELF-ASSESSMENT SCORING AND INTERPRETATION

ARGUMENTATIVENESS

The Argumentativeness scale has two separate sections: one that measures a tendency to approach arguments and one that measures the tendency to avoid them.

Scoring

Score each of the two sections separately. Approaching arguments can be scored by adding your answers to questions 2, 4, 7, 9, 11, 13, 15, 17, 18, and 20. Avoiding arguments is scored by adding your answers to questions 1, 3, 5, 6, 8, 10, 12, 14, 16, and 19.

Interpretation

If your score on the approaching section is higher than the avoidance section, you may tend to move toward arguments more than avoid arguments.

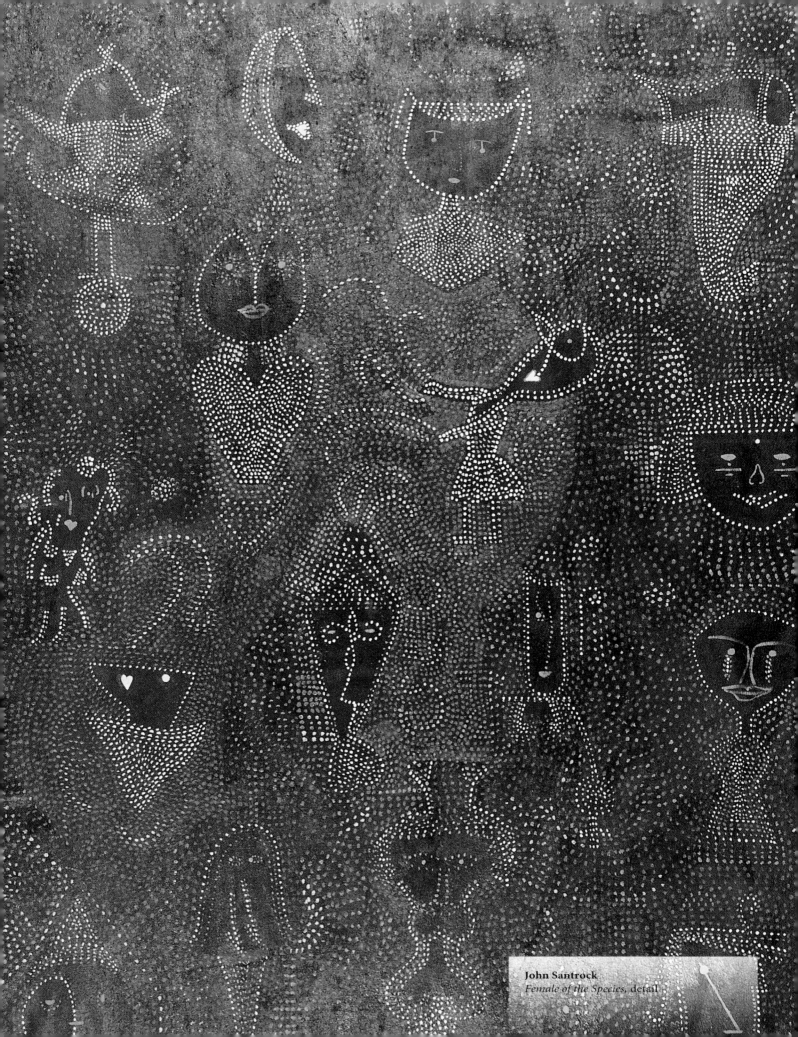

CHAPTER

8

Gender

We are all androgynous, not only because we are all born of a woman impregnated by the seed of a man but because each of us, helplessly and forever, contains the other—male in female, female in male, white in black, and black in white. We are a part of each other.

—James Baldwin

THE STORY OF TITA DE LA GARZA: BOUND BY TRADITION

In her novel *Like Water for Chocolate*, Laura Esquivel shows us the scene of young Tita steeling herself before her mother, Mama Elena. Tita had told her mother that Pedro Muzquiz intended to come and speak with her, and her mother responded vigorously:

> "If he intends to ask for your hand, tell him not to bother. He'll be wasting his time and mine, too. You know perfectly well that being the youngest daughter means you have to take care of me until the day I die."
>
> "But in my opinion . . ."
>
> "You don't have an opinion, and that's all I want to hear about it. For

generations, not a single person in my family has ever questioned this tradition, and no daughter of mine is going to be the one to start."

Tita lowered her head, and the realization of her fate struck her as forcibly as her tears struck the table. . . . Still Tita did not submit. Doubts and anxieties sprang to her mind. For one thing, she wanted to know who started this family tradition. It would be nice if she could let that genius know about one little flaw in this perfect plan for taking care of women in their old age. If Tita couldn't marry and have children, who would take care of her when she got old? . . . Or are daughters who stay home and

take care of their mothers not expected to survive too long after the parent's death? And what about women who marry and can't have children, who will take care of them? And besides, she'd like to know what kind of studies had established that the youngest daughter and not the eldest is best suited to care for their mother. Had the opinion of the daughter affected by the plan ever been taken into account? If she couldn't marry, was she at least allowed to experience love? Or not even that? Tita knew perfectly well that all these questions would have to be buried forever in the archive of questions that have no answers.

PREVIEW

Laura Esquivel's charming tale about Tita in *Like Water for Chocolate* reveals how culture can be a context in which gender and destiny are intertwined. In well-born Mexican families, the youngest daughter was expected to become the careprovider for her aging parents. Tita's reflections and questions reveal a great deal about the role of gender in human development. In some cultures, privilege, responsibility, sacrifice, and restriction are clearly delineated along gender lines; in other cultures, they are less so. In this chapter we will explore the following topics regarding how gender influences adjustment: defining gender, gender comparisons, gender identity, and sociocultural variations.

DEFINING GENDER

Gender *refers to the sociocultural dimension of being female or male.* In her 1993 Senate confirmation hearings for the position of Supreme Court Justice, Ruth Bader Ginsberg distinguished gender as *related to* but *distinct from* sex. She suggested that the term *sex* can be a distraction because it pertains more specifically to biological matters. Use of the term *gender* maintains the focus on the social constructions that distinguish women and men. Her own path through Harvard Law School provided many examples of sex

discrimination that fueled her interest in gender differences. Ultimately, her expertise in equal opportunity influenced her successful appointment as the second woman Supreme Court Justice.

Following are two terms that we will use throughout this chapter. **Gender roles** *are sets of expectations that prescribe how females and males should think, act, and feel.* We will explore how gender roles have been changing in the United States. **Gender identity** *is the sense of being male or female, a part of the self-concept that most children begin to acquire by the age of 2 or 3 years.* Several

theories based on different psychological perspectives have been proposed to explain the process of the development of gender identity.

The Changing American Landscape

Until not too long ago, it was accepted that boys should grow up to be masculine and that girls should grow up to be feminine; boys were said to be made of "frogs and snails and puppy dogs' tails," and girls of "sugar and spice and everything nice." In children's literature, boys were depicted as active and exploring, girls as

Ruth Bader Ginsberg's appointment as the second female Supreme Court Justice was a personal triumph for her. She experienced discrimination throughout law school and in her legal career, based on her being "a female, a mother, and a Jew." This spurred her to develop her expertise in equal-opportunity law, which in turn was an influential factor in her appointment.

passive admirers. The well-adjusted adult male was expected to be independent, aggressive, and power-oriented. The well-adjusted adult female was expected to be dependent, nurturant, and uninterested in power. Further, masculine characteristics were considered to be healthy and good by society; female characteristics were deemed undesirable.

These beliefs and stereotypes have led to *sexism,* the negative treatment of individuals, most commonly of females, because of their sex. Females receive less attention in schools. They are less visible in leading roles on television and continue to be rarely depicted as competent, dominant characters in children's books. They are paid less than males even when they have more education. They are underrepresented in decision-making roles throughout society, from corporate suites to Congress.

Controversy swirls around the question of what are appropriate roles for today's women and men. Although women have gained greater influence in a variety of professional spheres, many continue to find themselves confronted by invisible ceilings that limit access to many of the most powerful positions. Women electing more-traditional roles sometimes feel criticized by other women for "selling out." Men report confusion about the chronic anger they experience from women. Best-sellers emphasize the

differences between women and men, persuading us that there is little likelihood that the genders can reasonably coexist. Social critic Naomi Wolff coined the term *gender-quake* to describe the specific gender-based problems that face individuals in our culture.

> *Women and men. Men and women.*
> *It'll never work.*
> —Erica Jong

In many cultures, well-defined and well-practiced gender roles take the ambiguity out of how women and men relate to each other. However, even where such definitive roles exist, there is likely to be some strain. Anthropologist Florence Kluckhohn (1969) showed that cultures encompass a broad range of experiences, and that very different lives can be lived within one culture. With respect to gender, it is likely that not all members of a culture are content with the gender roles practiced in their culture.

On the other hand, the turmoil currently characterizing gender relations in America offers opportunity to both genders. A girl's mother might promote femininity, the girl might be close friends with a tomboy, and the girl's teachers at school might encourage her assertiveness. Boys might experience fewer restrictions in the goals they set for themselves. For example, Wall Street star Peter Lynch, who headed Fidelity Investment's leading mutual fund, resigned to have more time with his family and to pursue humanitarian projects. And as you might guess, many individuals in this culture are not pleased with the expanded opportunities for women, because they believe this expansion requires undesirable and unwarranted sacrifices by men.

Many contemporary students say they want it all—good careers, good marriages, and two or three children who are not raised by "strangers." Idealistic? Perhaps. Some women will reach these goals, but others will have to make other choices as they move through their adult years. Some women will choose to remain single as they pursue their career goals, others will become married but not have children, some will have children and not marry, and others will somehow balance

the demands of both family and work. In a word, not all women have the same goals; neither do all men.

The History of Psychological Research on Gender

Many feminist scholars believe that, historically, psychology has portrayed human behavior with a "male-dominant theme" (Denmark & Paludi, 1993; Paludi, 1995). Psychologists believed that research with males could be generalized to explain how women would behave. In addition, conducting males-only research permitted experimenters to avoid issues like the variations in behavior that might be caused by menstruation, so they continued these practices in the name of promoting better control procedures in their research. However, such practices did not encourage the examination of the role of gender in human development.

Many psychologists believe that the lack of research on women was also related to how few women were psychologists. Women had a difficult time entering the field of psychology. For example, even though Mary Calkins completed her doctoral work in psychology at Harvard University, that university refused to grant her a degree because she was a woman. Even so, Calkins was able to embark on a career of remarkable achievements. Among her other accomplishments, she was the first woman to be elected president of the American Psychological Association. She also became the president of the American Philosophical Association.

Another outstanding woman in early psychology, Leta Stetter Hollingworth, is instructive not just for her achievement but for her selection of gender-specific research topics. For example, Hollingworth (1914) correlated the quality of task performance with menstruation and found no empirical support for the view that women become incapacitated by the onset of menses, a phenomenon that had been referred to as "functional periodicity."

Another prominent viewpoint about gender early in this century was the "hypothesis of greater male variability." The hypothesis was based on the belief that males had a broader intellectual range than females; they excelled in public, professional activities and were also more often institutionalized for being feeble-minded than women were. Strongly influenced by Darwin's theory of evolution, this doctrine proposed that males were superior because their wider variability had greater adaptive value. Hollingworth (1918) dismissed the supposition that there were many sex differences in mental traits and roundly criticized the psychological research community for reaching subjective conclusions about gender differences without appropriate empirical evidence.

Contemporary feminist scholars are putting greater emphasis on women's life experiences and development, including girls and women as authorities about their own experiences, or, as Harvard psychologist Carol Gilligan (1992) advocates, listening to women's voices: on women's ways of knowing (Belenky & others, 1986); on women's career and family roles (Baruch, Biener, & Barnett, 1987); on the abuse of women and rape (Russo, 1990); and on women's experiences of connectedness and self-determination (Lerner, 1989).

As more women made their way into the field of psychology, gender-related issues became a substantial focus of research. Division 35 of the American Psychological Association supports female and male psychologists in their gender-related research interests. To evaluate your own expectations about gender roles, see Critical Thinking.

The Feminist Perspective

Feminism emerged as a strong force in psychology as the culmination of several forces. First, feminism is humanistic; it supports minimizing the barriers that prevent individuals from achieving their full potential (Freeman, 1995; Ruth, 1995). Second, both the formal research literature and critiques of existing research have underscored the lack of attention to women and to gender issues. Finally, feminist scholars recognize the power of sociocultural factors in creating contexts that define experience—and therefore they continue to be concerned about the degree to which sexism is still rampant in our society and in others worldwide (DeAngelis, 1996). See Sociocultural Worlds of Adjustment for a brief feminist interpretation of the effects of sexism internationally.

CRITICAL THINKING

Gender Roles and the Future

In the last two decades, considerable change in gender roles has taken place in the United States. How much change have you personally experienced? What changes do you think will occur in gender roles in the twenty-first century? Or do you believe that gender roles will stay about the way they are now?

There is a practical side to considering these questions if you are going to have children or have them already. What will your gender expectations be toward your children? Will you try not to promote gender roles? Will you encourage traditional gender roles? Answering such questions allows you to *apply psychological concepts to enhance adaptation and growth.*

Jean Baker Miller (1986), a leading feminist scholar wrote in *Toward a New Psychology of Women,*

> In the last decade it has become clearer that if women are trying to define and create a full personhood, we are engaged in a huge undertaking. We see that this attempt means building a new way of living which encompasses all realms of life, from global economic, social and political levels to the most intimate personal relationships. (p. xi)

Miller has been an important voice in stimulating the examination of psychological issues from a female perspective. She believes that the study of women's psychological development opens up paths to a better understanding of all psychological development, female or male. She also concludes that when researchers examine what women have been doing in life, they find that a large part of it is active participation in the development of others. In Miller's view, women often try to interact with others in ways that foster the others' development along many dimensions—emotionally, intellectually, and socially.

Many feminist thinkers believe that it is important for women not only to maintain their competence in relationships but to be self-motivated too. Miller believes that, through increased

Harriet Lerner has provided insightful analyses about the way females and males have been socialized to handle anger differently. She also has contributed to our understanding of gender differences in intimacy.

self-determination and already developed relationship skills, many women will gain greater power in the American culture. As feminist scholar Harriet Lerner (1989) concludes in her book *The Dance of Intimacy,* it is important for women to bring to their relationships nothing less than a strong, assertive, independent, and authentic self. Lerner

SOCIOCULTURAL WORLDS OF ADJUSTMENT

Women's Struggle for Equality: An International Journey

What are the political, economic, educational and psychosocial conditions of women around the world? Frances Culbertson (1991), as president of the section of the American Psychological Association on the Clinical Psychology of Women, summarized these conditions.

Women and Politics

In politics, women too often are treated as burdens rather than assets. Especially in developing countries, women marry early and have many children quickly, in many cases before their undernourished bodies have an opportunity to mature. These women have little access to education, work, health care, and family planning. Some experts on women's issues believe these needs would have a better chance of being met if women were more strongly represented at the decision-making and managerial levels of governments and international organizations. For example, in 1990, less than 10 percent of the members of national legislatures were women, and for every 100 ministerial level positions around the world, only 5 were filled by women.

Women and Employment

Women's work around the world is more limiting and narrower than that of men. Bank tellers and secretaries are most often women. Domestic workers in North America and in Central and South America are most often women. Around the world, jobs defined as women's work carry low pay, low status, and little security. Two authors described many of these

Around the world women too often are treated as burdens rather than assets in the political process. Few women have leadership positions in government. Some experts on women's issues believe that if women are to gain more access to work, education, health care, and family planning, they need to be more strongly represented at the decision making and managerial levels of government and business.

circumstances as "job ghettos" (Seager & Olson, 1986). In 1990, the only countries in the world that had maternity leave and guaranteed jobs on the basis of national law were Brazil, Chile, Mexico, Finland, Sweden, Switzerland, Germany, Italy, Egypt, Syria, and Russia. Among the major countries without these provisions was the United States.

Women and Education

Canada, the United States, and Russia have the highest percentages of educated women. The countries with the fewest women being educated are in Africa, where in some areas women are given no education at all. In developing countries, 67 percent of women and 50 percent of men over the age of 25 have never been to school. In 1985, 80 million more boys than girls were in primary and secondary educational settings around the world.

Women and Psychosocial Issues

Women around the world experience violence, often from someone close to them. In Canada, 10 percent of women reported they had been beaten by the man they lived with in their home. In the United States almost 2 million women are beaten in their homes each year. In one survey, "The New Woman Ethics Report," wife abuse was listed number one among the 15 most pressing concerns facing society today (Johnson, 1990). Beating women continues to be accepted and expected in too many countries. While most countries around the world now have battered women's shelters, the remedy is still usually too little, too late.

In a study of depression in high-income countries, women were twice as likely as men to be diagnosed as being depressed (Nolen-Hoeksema, 1990). In the United States, from adolescence through adulthood, females are more likely than males to be depressed. Many sociocultural inequities and experiences contribute to the greater incidence of depression in females than in males.

Further inequities that women experience will be discussed in chapter 9—"Human Sexuality." In many cultures, sex is not supposed to be pleasurable for women. For example, in the Near East and Africa, a sizable number of women are given clitorectomies, the surgical removal of the clitoris, to reduce their sexual pleasure. Many women are the victims of date rape and stranger rape. Many people—both men and women—expect women to assume total responsibility for contraception.

believes that competent relationships are those in which the separate "I-ness" of both persons can be appreciated and enhanced while the persons stay emotionally connected to each other.

Not only is a distinct female voice an important dimension of the feminist perspective on gender, so is the effort to reduce and eventually end prejudice and discrimination against women (Paludi, 1995). Although women have broken through many male bastions in the past several decades, feminists argue that much work is left to be done. Feminists today believe that too many people passively accept traditional gender roles and believe that discrimination no longer exists in politics, work, the family, and education. They encourage individuals to question these assumptions, and especially strive to get females to evaluate the gender circumstances of their lives. For example, if you are a female, you may remember situations in which you were discriminated against because of your sex. If derogatory comments are made to you because you are a female, you may ask yourself why you have allowed these comments to go unchallenged or why they made you so angry. Feminists hope that, if you are a male, you will become more conscious of gender issues, of female and male roles, and of fairness and sensitivity in female-male interactions and relationships. You can evaluate your own attitudes toward women by completing the Self-Assessment.

It may be easy to forget how much progress has been made in fostering equality and egalitarianism in this culture. The quotations in table 8.1 from influential males throughout history illustrate the degree to which **misogyny,** *hatred of women,* may have contributed to some ways of thinking that continue to be perpetuated among some men and women even today.

The strain between the sexes also shows up in **misandry,** *hatred of men.* This attitude is expressed by some women who hold males responsible for their harsh and inequitable treatment of females over the years. However, most feminists are not the manhaters they have been portrayed to be by some of the popular press.

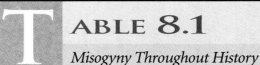

TABLE 8.1
Misogyny Throughout History

There is a good principle which created order, light, and man, and an evil principle which created chaos, darkness, and women.

Attributed to Pythagoras
6th century B.C.E.

Neither earth nor ocean produces a creature as savage and monstrous as woman.

Euripides
Hecuba, c. 425 B.C.E.

As regards the individual nature, woman is defective and misbegotten.

St. Thomas Aquinas
Summa Theologica, c. 1265–1274

Woman is the very root of wickedness, the cause of the bitterest pain, a mine of suffering.

Tulsi Das
Ramayan, 1574

Woman is a pair of ovaries with a human being attached, whereas man is a human being furnished with a pair of testes.

Rudolf Virchow, M.D. (1821–1902)

The most winning woman I ever knew was hanged for poisoning three little children for their insurance money.

Sir Arthur Conan Doyle
The Sign of Four, 1890

Wicked women bother one. Good women bore one. That is the only difference between them.

Oscar Wilde
Lady Windermere's Fan, 1892

You needn't groan when a girl is born—she may in time be the mother of a man!

D. H. Lawrence Letter to Blanche Jennings May 13, 1908

The female of the species is more deadly than the male.

Rudyard Kipling
The Female of the Species, 1911

Woman is at once apple and serpent.

Henrich Heine (1797–1856)

I hate women because they always know where things are.

Attributed to James Thurber (1894–1961)

GENDER COMPARISONS

We will now turn to several topics involving gender comparisons. First we will examine the research on gender roles and gender stereotyping. Next we will explore the similarities and differences that exist between females and males.

Gender Roles

A classic study in the early 1970s summarized the traits and behaviors that college students believed were characteristic of males and those they believed were characteristic of females (Broverman & others, 1972). The traits clustered into two groups that were labeled "instrumental" and "expressive." The instrumental traits paralleled the male's purposeful, competent entry into the outside world to gain goods for his family; the expressive traits paralleled the female's responsibility to be warm and emotional in the home. Such stereotypes were evaluated by the researchers as more harmful to females than to males because the characteristics assigned to males were more valued than those assigned to females.

Halonen/Santrock: Human Adjustment

Attitudes Toward Women

Instructions

The statements listed to the right describe attitudes toward the role of women in society that different people have. There are no right or wrong answers, only opinions. Express your feeling about each statement by indicating whether you (A) agree strongly, (B) agree mildly, (C) disagree mildly, or (D) disagree strongly.

To score and interpret your responses, please turn to the end of this chapter.

Items	Agree Strongly	Agree Mildly	Disagree Mildly	Disagree Strongly
1. Swearing and obscenity are more repulsive in the speech of a woman than of a man.	A	B	C	D
2. Women should take increasing responsibility for leadership in solving the intellectual and social problems of the day.	A	B	C	D
3. Both husband and wife should be allowed the same grounds for divorce.	A	B	C	D
4. Telling dirty jokes should be mostly a masculine prerogative.	A	B	C	D
5. Intoxication among women is worse than intoxication among men.	A	B	C	D
6. Under modern economic conditions with women being active outside the home, men should share in household tasks such as washing dishes and doing the laundry.	A	B	C	D
7. It is insulting to women to have the "obey" clause remain in the marriage service.	A	B	C	D
8. There should be a strict merit system in job appointment and promotion without regard to sex.	A	B	C	D
9. A woman should be as free as a man to propose marriage.	A	B	C	D
10. Women should worry less about their rights and more about becoming good wives and mothers.	A	B	C	D
11. Women earning as much as their dates should bear equally the expense when they go out together.	A	B	C	D
12. Women should assume their rightful place in business and all the professions along with men.	A	B	C	D
13. A woman should not expect to go to exactly the same places or to have quite the same freedom of action as a man.	A	B	C	D
14. Sons in a family should be given more encouragement to go to college than daughters.	A	B	C	D
15. It is ridiculous for a woman to run a locomotive and for a man to darn socks.	A	B	C	D
16. In general, the father should have greater authority than the mother in the bringing up of children.	A	B	C	D
17. Women should be encouraged not to become sexually intimate with anyone before marriage, even their fiancés.	A	B	C	D
18. The husband should not be favored by law over the wife in the disposal of family property or income.	A	B	C	D
19. Women should be concerned with their duties of childbearing and house tending, rather than with desires for professional and business careers.	A	B	C	D
20. The intellectual leadership of a community should be largely in the hands of men.	A	B	C	D
21. Economic and social freedom is worth far more to women than acceptance of the ideal of femininity that has been set up by men.	A	B	C	D
22. On the average, women should be regarded as less capable of contributing to economic production than men.	A	B	C	D
23. There are many jobs in which men should be given preference over women in being hired or promoted.	A	B	C	D
24. Women should be given equal opportunity with men for apprenticeship in the various trades.	A	B	C	D
25. The modern girl is entitled to the same freedom from regulation and control that is given to the modern boy.	A	B	C	D

Defining Gender

Gender is the sociocultural dimension of being female or male. Gender roles are sets of expectations that prescribe how females and males should act, think, and feel. Gender-role identification is the sense of being female or male, a part of self-concept that most children begin to acquire by 2 or 3 years of age. Historically, because of their sex females have often been treated more negatively than males; this is sexism. There is much controversy about what are appropriate roles for today's women and men. Many feminist scholars believe that, historically, psychology has portrayed human behavior with a male-dominant theme. They also believe that sexism is still rampant in society and that women are still discriminated against in the workplace, in politics, and at home, and they argue that too many women have low self-esteem because of these inequities. Jean Baker Miller has been an important voice in stimulating examination of psychological issues from a female perspective. She believes that society should place a stronger emphasis on the importance of connectedness and relationships, which women know how to do. She also argues that women need to increase their self-determination while maintaining their competence at relationship skills.

The 1995 International Women's Conference in Beijing, China, continued the traditions of prior conferences in highlighting women's progress and spotlighting cultures that lag behind in women's rights.

In the 1970s, many females and males began to evaluate the constraints imposed by strict gender stereotypes and to become dissatisfied. Alternatives to masculinity and femininity were explored. Instead of thinking of masculinity and femininity as a continuum, with more of one meaning less of the other, it was proposed that individuals could show both expressive *and* instrumental traits. This thinking led to the development of the concept of **androgyny,** *the presence of desirable masculine and feminine characteristics in the same individual* (Bem, 1977; Spence & Helmreich, 1978). The androgynous individual might be a male who is assertive (masculine) and nurturant (feminine), or a female who is dominant (masculine) and sensitive to others' feelings (feminine).

> *To be meek, patient, tactful, modest, honorable, brave, is not to be either manly or womanly; it is to be humane.*
>
> —**Jane Harrison**

Measures have been developed to assess androgyny. One of the most widely used gender measures, the Bem sex-role inventory, was constructed by a leading early proponent of androgyny, Sandra Bem. To see what the items on Bem's measure are like, turn to the Self-Assessment. Based on their responses to the items in the Bem sex-role inventory, individuals are classified as having one of four gender-role orientations: masculine, feminine, androgynous, or undifferentiated (see figure 8.1). The androgynous individual is simply a female or a male who has a high degree of both feminine (expressive) and masculine (instrumental) traits. Bem invokes no new characteristics to describe the androgynous individual. A feminine individual is high on feminine (expressive) traits and low on masculine (instrumental) traits; a masculine individual shows the reverse of these traits. An undifferentiated person is not high on feminine or masculine traits.

Bem speculated that androgynous individuals are more flexible and mentally healthy than either masculine or feminine individuals. She believes that individuals who are undifferentiated are the least competent. To some degree, though, the context influences which gender role is most adaptive. In close relationships, a feminine or androgynous gender role may be more desirable because of the expressive nature of close relationships. However, a masculine or androgynous gender role may be more desirable in academic and work settings because of the instrumental nature of these settings. The culture in which individuals live also plays an important role in determining what is adaptive. On the one hand, increasing numbers of parents in the United States and other modernized countries such as Sweden are raising their children to behave in androgynous ways. On the other hand, traditional gender roles continue to dominate the cultures of many countries around the world. We will explore more examples of traditional gender roles in other cultures toward the end of this chapter.

Gender-Role Transcendence

Although the concept of androgyny was an improvement over exclusive notions of femininity and masculinity, it has

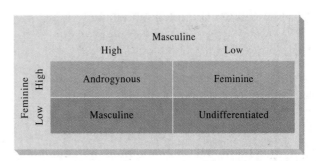

FIGURE 8.1

Gender-Role Classification

turned out to be less of a panacea than many of its early proponents envisioned (Paludi, 1995). Some theorists, such as Joseph Pleck (1981), believe that the idea of androgyny should be replaced with **gender-role transcendence**, *the belief that an individual's competence should be conceptualized not on the basis of masculinity, femininity, or androgyny, but rather on the basis of the person.* Thus, rather than merging gender roles or stereotyping people as "masculine" or "feminine," Pleck believes we should begin to think about people as people. However, both concepts—androgyny and gender-role transcendence—draw attention away from women's unique needs and the power imbalance between women and men in most cultures (Hare-Muston & Maracek, 1988).

Gender Stereotyping

Gender stereotypes *are broad categories that reflect our impressions and beliefs about females and males.* All stereotypes, whether they are based on gender, ethnicity, or something else, are images of the typical member of a particular social category. The world is extremely complex, and using stereotypes is one way individuals simplify complexity so that they are not overwhelmed in their processing of the world. However, simplifications can lead to wrong assumptions and invalid conclusions; they often interfere with seeing other people as the unique individuals that they are. If we simply assign a label, such as *soft,* to someone, we might have much less to consider when we think about that person. However, once labels are assigned, they are remarkably difficult to abandon—even in the face of contradictory evidence.

Inge Broverman and her colleagues (1970) found that professional counselors were also influenced by their attitudes toward men and women. In this study, 33 female and 46 male mental health practitioners were given a list of traits and asked to check off the traits that best describe a mature, healthy, and socially competent adult, adult woman, or adult man. The descriptions they selected of mature and competent adults and adult men were consistent and included characteristics such as being direct, logical, achieving, and active. However, the description they selected of mature and competent adult women was different and included the characteristics of being excitable in minor crises, influenceable, illogical, sneaky, less adventurous, and dependent. For these counselors, a consistent portrait was painted for competent adults and adult men, but competent adult women could not be simultaneously described as competent adults. Although these differences in perceptions are likely to have diminished since 1970, some counselors might still inappropriately hold different standards for their female and male clients.

If you are going to generalize about women, you will find yourself up to here in exceptions.

—Dolores Hitches,
***In a House Unknown* (1973)**

Stereotypes involve diverse behaviors and characteristics. For example, scoring a touchdown and growing facial hair are considered "masculine" behaviors, and playing with dolls and wearing lipstick are considered "feminine" behaviors. Stereotypes often differ in different

Are You Androgynous?

Instructions

The items to the right are from the Bem Sex-Role Inventory. To find out whether you score as androgynous, rate yourself on each item, on a scale from 1 (never or almost never true) to 7 (always or almost always true).

1.	self-reliant	1	2	3	4	5	6	7
2.	yielding	1	2	3	4	5	6	7
3.	helpful	1	2	3	4	5	6	7
4.	defends own beliefs	1	2	3	4	5	6	7
5.	cheerful	1	2	3	4	5	6	7
6.	moody	1	2	3	4	5	6	7
7.	independent	1	2	3	4	5	6	7
8.	shy	1	2	3	4	5	6	7
9.	conscientious	1	2	3	4	5	6	7
10.	athletic	1	2	3	4	5	6	7
11.	affectionate	1	2	3	4	5	6	7
12.	theatrical	1	2	3	4	5	6	7
13.	assertive	1	2	3	4	5	6	7
14.	flatterable	1	2	3	4	5	6	7
15.	happy	1	2	3	4	5	6	7
16.	strong personality	1	2	3	4	5	6	7
17.	loyal	1	2	3	4	5	6	7
18.	unpredictable	1	2	3	4	5	6	7
19.	forceful	1	2	3	4	5	6	7
20.	feminine	1	2	3	4	5	6	7
21.	reliable	1	2	3	4	5	6	7
22.	analytical	1	2	3	4	5	6	7
23.	sympathetic	1	2	3	4	5	6	7
24.	jealous	1	2	3	4	5	6	7
25.	has leadership abilities	1	2	3	4	5	6	7
26.	sensitive to the needs of others	1	2	3	4	5	6	7
27.	truthful	1	2	3	4	5	6	7
28.	willing to take risks	1	2	3	4	5	6	7
29.	understanding	1	2	3	4	5	6	7
30.	secretive	1	2	3	4	5	6	7
31.	makes decisions easily	1	2	3	4	5	6	7
32.	compassionate	1	2	3	4	5	6	7
33.	sincere	1	2	3	4	5	6	7
34.	self-sufficient	1	2	3	4	5	6	7
35.	eager to soothe hurt feelings	1	2	3	4	5	6	7
36.	conceited	1	2	3	4	5	6	7
37.	dominant	1	2	3	4	5	6	7
38.	soft-spoken	1	2	3	4	5	6	7
39.	likable	1	2	3	4	5	6	7
40.	masculine	1	2	3	4	5	6	7
41.	warm	1	2	3	4	5	6	7
42.	solemn	1	2	3	4	5	6	7
43.	willing to take a stand	1	2	3	4	5	6	7
44.	tender	1	2	3	4	5	6	7
45.	friendly	1	2	3	4	5	6	7
46.	aggressive	1	2	3	4	5	6	7
47.	gullible	1	2	3	4	5	6	7
48.	inefficient	1	2	3	4	5	6	7
49.	acts as a leader	1	2	3	4	5	6	7
50.	childlike	1	2	3	4	5	6	7
51.	adaptable	1	2	3	4	5	6	7
52.	individualistic	1	2	3	4	5	6	7
53.	does not use harsh language	1	2	3	4	5	6	7
54.	unsystematic	1	2	3	4	5	6	7
55.	competitive	1	2	3	4	5	6	7
56.	loves children	1	2	3	4	5	6	7
57.	tactful	1	2	3	4	5	6	7
58.	ambitious	1	2	3	4	5	6	7
59.	gentle	1	2	3	4	5	6	7
60.	conventional	1	2	3	4	5	6	7

Turn to the end of the chapter for the Bem Sex-Role Inventory scoring key.

cultures and historical contexts. During the reign of Louis XIV, for example, French noblemen wore satin breeches, cosmetics, and high heels; in contrast, rugged pioneer American males of that time wore dirty, leather clothing. Stereotypes of "femininity" and "masculinity" also vary across the socioeconomic spectrum. For example, lower socioeconomic groups are the most likely to include "rough and tough" as part of the masculine stereotype.

In a study of college students in thirty countries, stereotyping of females and males was pervasive and far-ranging (Williams & Best, 1982). Across the various cultures, the college students described men as dominant, independent, aggressive, achievement-oriented, and enduring, while women were viewed as nurturant, affiliative, less confident, and more helpful in times of distress. Often such beliefs influence our attitudes toward both women and men.

In one study, women and men in developed countries perceived themselves as more similar to one another than did women and men who lived in less-developed countries (Williams & Best, 1989). This makes sense. In the highly developed countries, women are more likely to attend college and have careers. As sexual equality increases, stereotypes of women and men probably diminish. Women are more likely than men to perceive similarity between the sexes.

Stereotypes can often be negative and sometimes involve prejudice and discrimination. **Sexism** *is prejudice and discrimination against an individual because of her or his sex.* A person who believes that women cannot be competent lawyers is expressing sexism; so is a person who says that men cannot be competent nursery school teachers. Prejudice and discrimination against women have a long history, and they continue. Consider a true story about Ann Hopkins, one of only a few female accountants employed by the very large firm, Price Waterhouse (Fiske & others, 1991). Hopkins had performed admirably in her work at Price Waterhouse. She had more billable hours than any of her 87 male co-workers and had brought in $25 million in new business for the firm. However, when a partnership in the firm opened up, Hopkins

was not chosen. The executives at Price Waterhouse said that she had weak interpersonal skills, needed a "charm school" course, and was too "macho." Hopkins filed a lawsuit against Price Waterhouse. After a lengthy trial, the U.S. Supreme Court ruled in Hopkins' favor, stating that gender-based stereotyping had played a significant role in her being denied partnership in the firm.

Sexism can be obvious, as when a chemistry professor tells a female premed student that women belong in the home (Matlin, 1993). Sexism can also be more subtle, as when the word *girl* is used to refer to a mature woman. In one recent analysis, an attempt was made to distinguish between old-fashioned and modern sexism (Swim & others, 1995). *Old-fashioned sexism* is characterized by endorsement of traditional gender roles, differential treatment for men and women, and stereotypes that females are less competent than males. Like modern racism, *modern sexism* is characterized by denial that females are still discriminated against, antagonism toward women's

demands, and lack of support for policies designed to help women attain equity (for instance, in education and work). Table 8.2 shows the types of items that were developed to measure old-fashioned and modern sexism.

Gender Similarities and Differences

Some gender researchers believe that differences between the sexes have often been exaggerated (Hyde & Plant, 1995; Linn & Hyde, 1991). For instance, some analyses of research findings use language that magnifies apparent differences. A researcher might summarize findings by saying that "only 32 percent of women, versus fully 37 percent of men, were. . . ." This difference of 5 percent might, or might not, be statistically significant. The researcher's language, however, implies that the difference is important (Denmark & others, 1988).

A further error is the tendency to think of differences between females and males as always being biologically based. Remember that when differences occur,

ABLE 8.2

Types of Items Developed to Measure Old-Fashioned and Modern Sexism

Old-Fashioned Sexism

Women are generally not as smart as men.

I would not be equally comfortable having a woman as a boss as a man.

It is more important to encourage boys than to encourage girls to participate in athletics.

Women are not as capable as men of thinking logically.

When both parents are employed and their child gets sick at school, the school should call the mother rather than the father.

Modern Sexism

Discrimination against women is no longer a problem in the United States.

Women do not often miss out on good jobs because of sexual discrimination.

It is rare to see women treated in a sexist manner on television.

On the average, people in our society treat husbands and wives equally.

Society has reached the point where women and men have equal opportunities for achievement.

It is not easy to understand why women's groups are still concerned about societal limitations on women's opportunities.

Over the past few years, the government and news media have been showing more concern about the treatment of women than is warranted by women's actual experiences.

Note: Endorsements of the above items reflect old-fashioned sexism and modern sexism, respectively. The wording of the items has been changed from the original research for ease of understanding.

From J. K. Swim, et al., "Sexism and Racism: Old-Fashioned and Modern Prejudices" in *Journal of Personality and Social Psychology,* 68:212. Copyright © 1995 by the American Psychological Association. Adapted with permission.

they might be due mainly to societal or cultural factors. The best assumption to make is that human behavior is always due to a combination of biological and environmental factors (Unger, 1993).

Let's now examine some of the similarities and differences between the sexes, keeping in mind the following: (a) The differences are averages; (b) even when differences are reported, there is considerable overlap between the sexes; (c) differences are due to an interaction between biological and environmental factors; (d) research conducted with other species provides limited, even misleading, information about human males and females. First we will examine physical differences, then we will turn to cognitive and socioemotional differences.

Physical Similarities and Differences

On the average, females live longer than males. Females are also less likely than males to develop physical disorders. A primary reason for this female advantage is estrogen, which strengthens the immune system, making females more resistant to infection. Also, female hormones signal the liver to produce more "good" cholesterol, which makes their blood vessels more "elastic." In males, testosterone triggers the production of low-density lipoproteins, which clog blood vessels. As a result, males have twice the risk of coronary disease as females have. Males also have higher levels of stress hormones, resulting in faster clotting in males but also in higher blood pressure.

Other physical differences are more visible. Adult females have about twice the body fat of adult males. In females, body fat is mostly concentrated around the breasts and hips; in males, fat is more likely to go to the abdomen. Males grow about 10 percent taller than females, on the average, because male hormones promote the growth of long bones while female hormones inhibit such growth at puberty.

Similarity was the rule rather than the exception in a recent study of metabolic activity in the brains of females and males (Gur & others, 1995). The exceptions involved areas of the brain that involve emotional expression and physical expression (which are more active in

females). However, overall, there are many physical differences between females and males. Are there as many cognitive differences?

Cognitive Similarities and Differences

According to a classic review of gender differences in 1974, Eleanor Maccoby and Carol Jacklin (1974) concluded that males have better math skills and better visuospatial ability (the kinds of skills an architect needs to design a building's angles and dimensions), while females have better verbal abilities. More recently, Maccoby (1987) revised her conclusions about several gender dimensions. She said that the accumulation of research evidence now suggests that verbal differences between females and males have virtually disappeared, but that the math and visuospatial differences still exist.

Some experts in the area of gender, such as Janet Shibley Hyde, believe that the cognitive differences between females and males have been exaggerated. For example, Hyde (1994) points out that there is considerable overlap in the distributions of female and male scores on math and visuospatial tasks. Figure 8.2 shows that although the average male score on visuospatial tasks is higher than the average female score, the scores mostly overlap. Thus, although the *average* difference favors males, many females have higher scores on visuospatial tasks than most males do. The comparison statement "Males outperform females in math" does not mean that all males outperform all females. Rather, it means that the average male score is higher than the average female score (Hyde & Plant, 1995).

"So according to the stereotype, you can put two and two together, but I can read the handwriting on the wall."

© 1986 Joel Pett, Phi Delta Kappan.

Socioemotional Similarities and Differences

Most males are more active and aggressive than most females (Maccoby, 1987). The consistent difference in aggression often appears in children's development as early as 2 years of age.

Females and males also differ in their social connectedness. Boys often define themselves apart from their caregivers and peers, while girls emphasize their social ties. As adults, females often become more caring, supporting, and empathic, while males become more independent, self-reliant, and unexpressive.

Unless you've been isolated on a mountaintop away from people, television, magazines, and newspapers, you probably know the master stereotype about gender and emotion: She is emotional, he is not. This stereotype is a powerful and pervasive image in our culture (Shields, 1991).

Is this stereotype confirmed when researchers study the nature of emotional experiences in females and males? Researchers have found that females and males are often more alike in the way they experience emotion than the master stereotype would lead us to believe. Females and males often use the same facial expressions, adopt the same language, and describe their emotional experiences similarly when they keep diaries about their life experiences. Thus, the master stereotype that females are emotional and males are not is simply that—a stereotype. Given the complexity and vast territory of emotion, we should not be surprised that this stereotype is not supported when actual emotional experiences are examined. Thus, for many emotional experiences, researchers do not find differences between females and males—both sexes are equally likely to feel love, jealousy, anxiety in new social situations, anger when they are insulted, grief when close relationships end, and embarrassment when they make mistakes in public (Tavris &

Figure 8.2

Mathematics Performance of Females and Males
Notice that, although the average male mathematics score is higher than the average female score, the overlap between the sexes is substantial. Not all males have better mathematics performance than all females—the substantial overlap indicates that, although the average score of males is higher, many females outperform most males on such tasks.

Wade, 1984). Turn to Critical Thinking to examine how language is involved in gender issues.

For some areas of achievement, gender differences are so large they can best be described as nonoverlapping. For example, no major league baseball players are female, and 96 percent of all registered nurses are female. In contrast, many measures of achievement-related behaviors do not reveal gender differences. For example, females show just as much

persistence at tasks as males do. The question of whether males and females differ in their expectations for success at various achievement tasks is not yet settled.

Gender Controversy

Not all psychologists agree that sex differences between females and males are rare or small. Alice Eagly (1995, 1996) stated that this belief arose from a feminist commitment to gender similarity as a route to political equality and from piecemeal and

inadequate interpretations of relevant empirical research. Many feminists express a fear that differences will be interpreted as deficiencies in females and as biologically based, which would promote the old stereotype of women as being innately inferior to men (Unger & Crawford, 1992). Eagly (1995, 1996) argues that a large body of contemporary psychological research reveals that behavior is sex differentiated to varying extents.

Evolutionary psychologist David Buss (1995, 1996) argues that men and women differ in those domains in which they have faced different adaptive problems across their evolutionary history. In all other domains, predicts Buss, the sexes are psychologically similar. One sex difference Buss cites is males' better performance in the cognitive skill of spatial rotation. This ability is essential for hunting, in which the trajectory of a projectile must anticipate the trajectory of a prey as each moves through space and time. Buss also cites a sex difference in casual sex, with men engaging in this behavior more than women. In one study, men said that ideally they would like to have more than eighteen sex partners in their lifetime; women stated that ideally they would like to have only four or five (Buss & Schmitt, 1993). In another study, 75 percent of the men but none of the women approached by an attractive stranger of the opposite sex consented to a request for sex (Clark & Hatfield, 1989). Such sex differences, says Buss, are exactly the type predicted by evolutionary psychology.

In sum, there is great controversy about whether sex differences are rare and small or frequent and large (Hyde & Plant, 1995; Maracek, 1995). Negotiating the science and politics of gender is not an easy task (Eagly, 1995).

Gender in Context

When thinking about gender similarities and differences, keep in mind that the context in which females and males are thinking, feeling, and behaving should be taken into account (Moskowitz, Suh, & Desaulniers, 1994). To see how context affects gender, let's further explore gender in relation to helping behavior and emotion.

With regard to helping, males are more likely to help in situations in which a perceived danger is present and in which males feel most competent to help (Eagly & Crowley, 1986). For example, males are more likely than females to help a person stranded by the roadside with a flat tire, a context (automobile problems) in which many males feel a sense of competence. By contrast, if the context involves volunteering time to help a child with a personal problem, females are more likely to help because there is little danger present and females feel more competent at nurturing. In many cultures, girls show more caregiving behavior than boys do (Blakemore, 1993). However, in the few cultures where both boys and girls care for younger siblings on a regular basis, they are similar in their tendencies to nurture (Whiting, 1989).

Contexts also are relevant to the display of emotion by males and females (Shields, 1991). Consider anger. Males are more likely to show anger toward strangers, especially other males, when they feel that they have been challenged. Males also are more likely than females to turn their anger into aggressive action (Tavris & Wade, 1984). Differences between females and males in the display of emotion are most evident in contexts that highlight social roles and relationships. For example, females are more likely than males to understand emotions in terms of interpersonal relationships (Saarni, 1988). And females are more likely than males to express fear and sadness, especially when communicating with their friends and family.

CRITICAL THINKING

Rethinking the Words We Use in Gender Worlds

Several decades ago the word *dependency* was used to describe the relational orientation of femininity. Dependency took on negative connotations for females—such as, that females can't take care of themselves but males can. In the 1990s, the term *dependency* is being replaced by the term *relational abilities,* which has a much more positive connotation. Rather than being thought of as dependent, women are now more often described as skilled in forming and maintaining relationships. Make up a list of words that you associate with masculinity and a list of those you associate with femininity. Do the words have any negative connotations for males or females? For the words that do have negative connotations, think about replacements that have more positive connotations. By rethinking the words we use to describe people as masculine or feminine, you are learning to think critically by *making accurate observations and descriptions.*

GENDER IDENTITY

Many different perspectives can be linked to contemporary discussions about gender identity. Some perspectives have produced formal theories explaining how gender identity develops. In this section we will emphasize explanations derived from the neurobiological, psychoanalytic, behavioral, and cognitive perspectives.

REVIEW

Gender Comparisons

In the past the well-adjusted male was supposed to show instrumental traits, the well-adjusted female expressive traits. Masculine traits were more valued by society. Sexism was widespread. In the 1970s, alternatives to traditional masculinity and femininity were explored. It was proposed that individuals could show both expressive and instrumental traits. This thinking led to the development of the concept of androgyny—the presence of desirable feminine and masculine traits in the same individual. Gender-role measures often categorize individuals as masculine, feminine, androgynous, or undifferentiated. Androgynous individuals are often more flexible and mentally healthy, although the particular context and the individual's culture also determine the adaptiveness of a gender-role orientation. Gender-role transcendence is the belief that an individual's competence should be conceptualized not on the basis of masculinity, femininity, or androgyny, but rather on the basis of the person.

Gender stereotypes are broad categories that reflect our impressions and beliefs about males and females. These stereotypes are widespread around the world, especially emphasizing the male's power and the woman's nurturance. In more highly developed countries, however, females and males are more likely to be perceived as more similar.

A number of physical and biological differences exist between females and males. Some experts, such as Hyde, argue that cognitive differences between females and males have been exaggerated. In terms of socioemotional differences, males are more aggressive and active than females, while females emphasize their social ties. Currently there is great controversy over how similar or different females and males are. An important dimension of understanding gender is to consider the contexts of behavior.

The Neurobiological Perspective

Gender identity is fundamentally linked to anatomy and physiology. In order to understand biological contributions, we will look at the influence of genetics and hormones. It was not until the 1920s that researchers confirmed the existence of human sex chromosomes, the genetic material that determines our sex. Humans normally have 46 chromosomes, arranged in pairs. Usually the 23rd pair has either two X-shaped chromosomes, which produces a female, or one X-shaped and one Y-shaped chromosome, which produces a male (see figure 8.3). One gene (called the TDF, or testes determining factor) on the sex chromosomes determines biological sex.

In the first few weeks of gestation, female and male embryos look alike and are identical in development. Male sex organs start to be differentiated from female sex organs when the TDF gene triggers the secretion of **androgens,** *the main class of male sex hormones,* in the male embryo. Low levels of androgens in female embryos allow the normal development of female sex organs.

Although rare, an imbalance in this system of hormone secretion can occur during fetal development. Insufficient androgens in the male embryo or excessive androgens in the female embryo results in an individual with ambiguous genitals—that is, the sex organs appear to be a mix of male and female genitals. This condition is called *pseudohermaphroditism.*

When genetically female infants (with XX chromosomes) are born with masculine-looking genitals, surgery can achieve female-appearing genitals. At puberty, the production of **estrogens,** *the main class of female sex hormones,* influences the physical and behavioral development of these masculinized girls, but prior to puberty they tend to behave more aggressively than other females. Their prepubertal play patterns and clothing preferences are similar to those of boys (Ehrhardt, 1987).

In animal experiments, when male hormones are injected into female embryos, the female animals develop masculine physical traits and behave aggressively (Hines, 1982). However, humans seem to be less controlled by

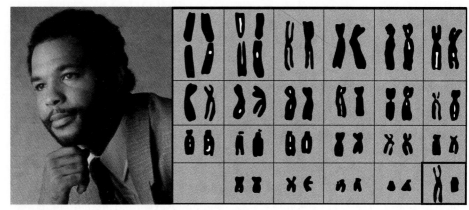

(a)

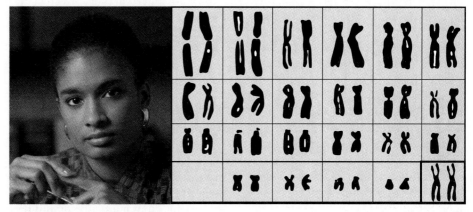

(b)

FIGURE 8.3

The Genetic Difference Between Males and Females
In (*a*) is the chromosome structure of a male, and in (*b*) is the chromosome structure of a female. The 23rd pair is shown in the bottom right box of each figure; notice that the Y chromosome of the male is smaller. To obtain this chromosomal picture, a cell is removed from the individual's body, usually from the inside of the mouth. The chromosomes are magnified extensively and then photographed.

their hormones than other species are. Socializing experiences might exert significant influence. For example, masculinized girls might be more aggressive because they are treated like boys and encouraged to adopt male preferences and behaviors.

Genetic males (with XY chromosomes) with ambiguous genitals pose more-complicated problems than their female counterparts do. Because reconstructive surgery of an infant penis is not possible, most of these infants are reassigned to the female sex. That is, their genitals are surgically reconstructed to be a vagina, clitoris, and labia (the external female genital structures). At puberty, when hormones are normally released, it is necessary to give estrogens and progesterones to these reassigned females so that

they can develop the feminizing effects seen at puberty, such as changes in fatty tissues around the hips and breast development. Despite the complicated procedures involved, these reassigned girls grow up surprisingly well adapted. They look like average females, but they are unable to reproduce.

The Psychoanalytic Perspective

While prenatal hormones might or might not influence gender behavior, psychoanalytic theorists, such as Sigmund Freud and Erik Erikson, have argued that an individual's genitals do play a pivotal role. Freud argued that human behavior and history are directly influenced by sexual drives. He suggested that gender and sexual behavior are essentially unlearned and instinctual.

Freud was the first to develop a theory to explain the mechanism by which children acquire masculine and feminine attitudes and behaviors. Freud's **identification theory** *proposed that the preschool child develops a sexual attraction to the opposite-sex parent. By approximately 5 or 6 years of age, the child renounces this attraction because it generates too much anxiety. The child subsequently identifies with the same-sex parent, unconsciously adopting the same-sex parent's characteristics.* Today many experts do not believe gender development proceeds on the basis of parental identification, at least not on the basis of Freud's hypothesized childhood sexual attraction. Critics suggest that children become gender typed much earlier than 5 years old and that they become attuned to gender roles regardless of the presence of a same-sex parent in the family.

Another controversial psychoanalytic figure who addressed the development of gender identification was Erik Erikson. Erikson argued that genital differences contributed to males' being more intrusive and aggressive and to females' being more inclusive and passive. Critics of Erikson's central ideas contended that he failed to give enough credit to the role of experience in personality development and that women and men are freer to choose their behavior than Erikson allows. In fact, Erikson later modified his original views. He observed that females in today's world are transcending their biological heritage and making contributions to society that go beyond childbearing.

Though researchers acknowledge that biology is an important influence on gender, most believe that social and cultural expectations have a greater influence on gender identity than hormones and sexual anatomy do.

The Behavioral Perspective

In our culture, adults discriminate between the sexes from the moment infants are born. While still in the hospital, many babies are dressed in pink and blue, according to their sex, and this differentiation often continues in obvious differences between male and female hairstyles, clothing, and toys. Both adults and peers reward gendered behavior throughout childhood and adolescence. Moreover, boys and girls also learn gender roles through imitation or observational learning—that is, by watching what others say and do and doing likewise.

The view that parents are the critical agents in gender-role development has come under fire (Huston, 1983), because culture, schools, peers, the media, and other family members have been shown to also influence gender behavior. However, it is important not to disregard parental influence; especially in the early developmental years parents play important roles in gender-role socialization.

The **social learning theory of gender** *emphasizes that children's gender development occurs through observation and imitation of gender-related behaviors, and through rewards and punishments children experience for gender-appropriate and gender-inappropriate behavior.* Unlike identification theory, social learning theory does not emphasize sexual attraction as the major factor in gender development (see figure 8.4). Instead, behavioral consequences shape gender-based behaviors,

As reflected in this tug-of-war battle between boys and girls, the playground in elementary school is like going to "gender school." Elementary school children show a clear preference for being with and liking same-sex peers. Eleanor Maccoby (*inset*) has studied children's gender development for many years. She believes peers play especially strong roles in socializing each other about gender roles.

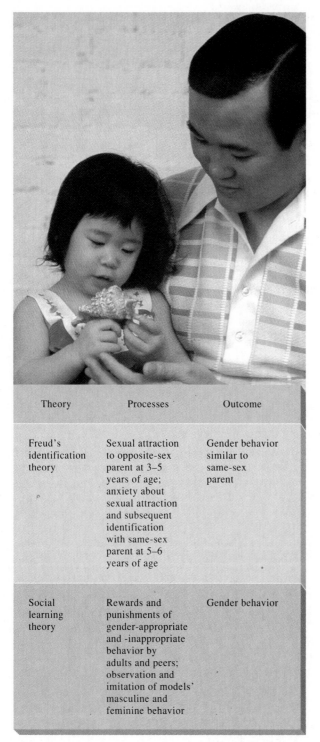

Theory	Processes	Outcome
Freud's identification theory	Sexual attraction to opposite-sex parent at 3–5 years of age; anxiety about sexual attraction and subsequent identification with same-sex parent at 5–6 years of age	Gender behavior similar to same-sex parent
Social learning theory	Rewards and punishments of gender-appropriate and -inappropriate behavior by adults and peers; observation and imitation of models' masculine and feminine behavior	Gender behavior

FIGURE 8.4

A Comparison of Identification Theory and Social Learning Theory Regarding Gender Development

While parents are important models of gender roles, young children also learn gender roles from observing other adults in their neighborhood and characters on television, even Saturday-morning cartoons. As children get older, peers become increasingly important influences. For example, when children play in ways that our culture says are gender-appropriate, they tend to be rewarded by their peers. Those who engage in activities that are considered gender-inappropriate tend to be criticized or even abandoned by their peers. Young Ben loved his Cabbage Patch boy doll, but when boys a year older than him laughed at him for bringing it to his preschool's show-and-tell, Ben immediately stopped playing with the doll. His same-sex peers had quickly taught him that even a male doll is not an appropriate toy for a boy.

Children show a clear preference for same-sex peers (Maccoby, 1993). The segregation of the sexes during play is so evident that researchers who have observed elementary school children playing in all-boy and all-girl groups have characterized playgrounds as "gender school" (Luria & Herzog, 1985). Even when engaging in similar activities, such as riding tricycles and bicycles, these same-sex groups play differently. For example, boys, but not girls for the most part, often ride their vehicles deliberately into each other.

The social learning view is sometimes criticized for its emphasis on the passive acquisition of gender roles via modeling and rewards and punishments. Other approaches regard children as more actively constructing their gender worlds. We will discuss those approaches in the next section.

The Cognitive Perspective

The role of cognitive influence on gender has been addressed by two prominent theories: cognitive developmental theory and gender schema theory.

Cognitive Developmental Theory

According to the **cognitive developmental theory of gender,** *children's gender typing occurs after they have developed a concept of gender constancy. Once children consistently conceive of themselves as male*

according to this theory. For example, parents might reward their daughter's feminine behavior with a compliment (such as "Karen, you are being a good girl when you play gently with your doll!") or punish their son's nonmasculine behavior with a reproach (such as "Keith, a big boy like you is not supposed to cry"). Moreover, parents provide boys with few, if any, dolls while giving them eighteen times as many toy vehicles as they give girls (Unger, 1993).

or female, they often organize their world on the basis of gender. Initially developed by psychologist Lawrence Kohlberg (1966), this theory summarizes typical gender development progression in the following way: "I am a girl, I want to do girl things; therefore, the opportunity to do girl things is rewarding." Kohlberg based his ideas on Piaget's cognitive developmental theory, which emphasizes that once they have acquired the ability to categorize things, children strive toward consistency in their use of categories and behavior. Therefore, as children's cognitive development matures, so does their understanding of gender. Two-year-olds can apply the labels *boy* and *girl* correctly to themselves and others; their concept of gender is simple and concrete. Preschool children rely on physical features such as dress and hairstyle to decide who falls into each gender category. Girls are people with long hair; boys are people who never wear dresses. Some preschool children believe that people can change their gender by getting a haircut or a new outfit. Obviously they do not yet have the cognitive machinery to think of gender as adults do. According to Kohlberg, all the reinforcement in the world won't modify that fact.

However, by the concrete operational stage (Piaget's third stage, which begins around the age of 6 or 7 years), children understand gender constancy. They know, for example, that a male is still a male regardless of whether he is wearing pants or a skirt or an earring, or whether his hair is short or long (Tavris & Wade, 1984). Now that their concept of gender constancy is clearly established, school-age children become motivated to become a competent, or "proper," boy or girl. Consequently, the child finds same-sex activities rewarding and imitates the behavior of same-sex models.

Gender Schema Theory

A **schema** *is a cognitive structure, or network of associations, that organizes and guides an individual's perceptions.* A **gender schema** *organizes the world in terms of female and male.* **Gender schema theory** *states that an individual's attention and behavior are guided by an internal motivation to conform to gender-based sociocultural*

standards and stereotypes (Rose & Martin, 1993). Gender schema theory suggests that "gender typing" occurs when individuals are ready to encode and organize information along the lines of what is considered appropriate or typical for males and females in a society. Whereas Kohlberg's cognitive developmental theory argues that a particular cognitive prerequisite—gender constancy—is necessary for gender typing, gender schema theory states that a general readiness to respond to and categorize information on the basis of culturally defined gender roles fuels children's gender-typing activities. A comparison of the cognitive developmental and gender schema theories is presented in figure 8.5. To explore how the broad perspectives in psychology apply to an issue that involves gender, see Critical Thinking.

SOCIOCULTURAL VARIATIONS

A wide variety of examples reinforce the importance of context in understanding gender. First, we will explore men's issues. Second, we will explore the link between gender and ethnicity. We will conclude by looking at how diverse cultures deal with gender.

CRITICAL THINKING

Tita's Plight and How It Evolved

Men's Issues

The male of the species—what is he really like? What does he really want? As a result of the women's movement and its attack on society's male bias and discrimination against women, some men have developed their own movement (Levant, 1996). The men's movement has not been as political or as activist as the women's movement. Rather, it has been more an emotional, spiritual movement that reasserts the importance of masculinity and urges men to resist women's efforts to turn them into "soft" males. Or it has been a psychological movement that recognizes men's need to be less violent and more nurturant but still retain much of their masculine identity. Many of the men's movement disciples argue that society's changing gender arena has led many men to question what being a man really means.

Herbert Goldberg became a central figure in the early development of the men's movement in the 1970s and early 1980s, mainly as a result of his writings about men's rights in *The Hazards of Being Male* and *The New Male*. Goldberg argues that a critical difference between men and women creates a precipitous gulf between them. That difference: Women can sense and articulate their feelings and problems; men, because of

At the beginning of this chapter you were introduced to a young Mexican woman whose mother refused to speak with the man she wished to marry. Depending on your own traditions, you may have struggled to comprehend how Tita could comply with her mother's wishes or how she could consider defying them. Tita not only complied; she watched her older sister marry her beloved and she embarked on a life of service to the family. As we try to comprehend such adherence to role expectations, the frameworks we have studied might help clarify how she reached her decision. When you reflect on this, you are *pursuing alternative explanations to understand complex behavior.*

How would the psychoanalytic, neurobiological, behavioral, and cognitive perspectives explain Tita's loyalty?

Halonen/Santrock: Human Adjustment

Theory	Processes	Emphasis
Cognitive developmental theory	Development of gender constancy, especially around 6–7 years of age, when conservation skills develop; after children develop the ability to consistently conceive of themselves as male or female, children often organize their world on the basis of gender, such as selecting same-sex models to imitate	Cognitive readiness facilitates gender-typing.
Gender schema theory	Sociocultural emphasis on gender-based standards and stereotypes; children's attention and behavior are guided by an internal motivation to conform to these gender-based standards and stereotypes, allowing children to interpret the world through a network of gender-organized thoughts	Gender schemas reinforce gender-typing.

FIGURE 8.5

The Development of Gender-Typed Behavior According to the Cognitive Developmental and Gender Schema Theories of Gender Development

their masculine conditioning, can't. The result is an armor of masculinity that is defensive and powerful in maintaining self-destructive patterns. Goldberg says that most men have been effective work machines and performers but most else in their lives suffers. Men live about 8 years less than women, on the average, have higher hospitalization rates, and show more behavioral problems. In a word, Goldberg believes millions of men are killing themselves by striving to be "true" men, a heavy price to pay for masculine "privilege" and power.

How can men solve their dilemma and live lives that are healthier physically and psychologically? Goldberg argues that men need to get in touch with their emotions and their bodies. They can't do this by just piggybacking on the changes that are occurring in women's attitudes, he says. Rather, men need to develop their own realization of what is critical for their survival and well-being. Goldberg especially encourages men to

- Recognize the suicidal "success" syndrome and avoid it
- Understand that occasional impotence is nothing serious
- Become aware of their real needs and desires and get in touch with their own bodies
- Elude the binds of masculine role-playing
- Relate to liberated women as their equals rather than serving as their guilty servants or hostile enemies
- Develop male friendships

Goldberg's messages to men that they need to become more attuned to their inner self and emotional makeup and work on developing more positive close relationships are important ones.

One author who helped usher in a renewed interest in the men's movement in the 1990s is Robert Bly, a poet, storyteller, translator, and best-selling author who is a disciple of Carl Jung's ideas. In *Iron John* (1990), Bly says we live in a society that hasn't had fathers around since the Industrial Revolution. With no viable rituals for introducing young boys to manhood, Bly believes, today's men are left confused. Bly thinks that too many of today's males are "soft," having bonded with their mothers because their fathers were unavailable. These "soft" males know how to follow instead of lead, how to be vulnerable, and how to go with the flow, says Bly. He believes that they don't know what it's like to have a deep masculine identity. Iron John, a hairy mythological creature, has

*Gender Identity—
Neurobiological,
Psychoanalytic, Behavioral,
and Cognitive Perspectives*

The 23rd pair of chromosomes determines our sex. Ordinarily females have two X chromosomes; males have an X and a Y. Chromosomes determine anatomical sex differences, but gender behavior is strongly influenced by society and culture. Freud's and Erikson's theories promote the thesis that anatomy determines behavior. Hormones from the testes (androgen) determine whether an organism will have male genitals (if androgen is secreted) or female genitals (if little androgen is secreted). Androgen in males and estrogen in females are the dominant sexual hormones. Hermaphrodites are individuals whose genitals become intermediate between male and female because of a hormonal imbalance.

Adults and peers reward and model gender-appropriate behavior. Parents—as well as culture, schools, peers, the media, and other family members—influence the development of children's gender behavior. Two prominent theories address the way children acquire masculine and feminine attitudes and behavior from their parents—identification theory and social learning theory.

Two theories address cognitive influences on gender—cognitive developmental theory and gender schema theory. In the cognitive developmental theory, children's gender typing occurs after children have developed a concept of gender, which is achieved in concert with the development of conservation skills at about 6 or 7 years of age. Gender schema theory states that an individual's attention and behavior are guided by an internal motivation to conform to gender-based, sociocultural standards and stereotypes. Gender schema theorists point out that very young children have more gender role knowledge than cognitive developmental theory predicts.

Once a year, the giant wooden phallus made during one of Robert Bly's male retreats is raised and used as a centerpiece for a naming ceremony at the Mendocino Men's Conference in California.

a deep masculine identity. He is, he says, spontaneous and sexual, an action taker, a boundary definer, and an earth preserver. He has untamed impulses and thoughtful self-discipline.

The only way women could have equal rights nowadays would be to surrender some.

—Burton Hillis

Bly's views have been criticized heavily by feminists and others. Bly dramatically overstates the separateness of the sexes. Regression to the traditional macho model of masculinity, which excludes sensitivity to others in relationships, is not an orientation that most psychologists believe is wise.

Ethnicity and Gender

Are gender-related attitudes and behavior similar across ethnic groups? All ethnic minority females experience gender expectations for women, just as all ethnic minority males experience gender expectations for men. There are many similarities in the gender-related attitudes of females across ethnic minority groups and of males across ethnic minority groups. Nevertheless, the different experiences of African American, Latino, Asian American, and Native American females and males need to be considered in understanding their gender-related attitudes and behavior. In some instances even small differences can be important. For example, the socialization of males and females in other cultures who subsequently migrate to America often reflects a stronger gap between the status of males and females than is experienced in America. Keeping in mind that there are many similarities between females in all ethnic minority groups and between males in all ethnic minority groups, we examine, first,

information about females from specific ethnic minority groups, followed by a discussion of males from specific ethnic minority groups.

Ethnic Minority Females

Let's now consider the behavior and psychological orientations of females from some ethnic minority groups: specifically, African American, Asian American, Latina, and Native American females.

Researchers in psychology have only begun to focus on the behavior of African American females (Ballentine & Inclan, 1995; Chow, Wilkinson, & Baca Zinn, 1996). For too long, African American females were considered only as a comparison group for White females on selected psychological dimensions, or they were the subjects in studies in which the primary research interest related to poverty, unwed motherhood, and such (Hall, Evans, & Selice, 1989). This narrow research approach could be viewed as attributing no personal characteristics to African American females beyond the labels given to them by society.

The nature and focus of psychological research on African American females has begun to change—to some extent paralleling societal changes. In the 1980s, psychological studies of African American females began to shift away from studies focused only on the problems of African

Fortunately, in the past decade, psychologists have begun to study the positive traits of African American females, such as self-esteem, achievement, motivation, and self-control. As with White women, connectedness in close relationships is an important concern of African American women.

American females and toward research on the positive aspects of African American females in a pluralistic society. In the last decade, psychologists have been studying the more individualized, positive dimensions of African American females, such as self-esteem, achievement, motivation, and self-control.

African American females, like other ethnic minority females, have experienced the double jeopardy of racism and sexism. The ingenuity and perseverance shown by ethnic minority females as they have survived and grown against the odds is remarkable.

> *Of my two "handicaps," being female puts many more obstacles in my path than being black.*
> **—Shirley Chisholm**

Asian American women find significant role changes from the gender traditions of their ancestors. Asian females are often expected to carry on domestic duties, to marry, to become obedient helpers of their mothers-in-law, and to bear children, especially males (Nishio & Bilmes, 1993). In China, the mother's responsibility for the emotional nurturance

and well-being of the family, and for raising children, derives from Confucian ethics (Huang & Ying, 1989). However, as China has become modernized, these roles have become less rigid. Similarly, in acculturated Chinese families in the United States, only derivatives of these rigidly defined roles remain. For example, Chinese American females are not entirely relegated to subservient roles. Author Amy Tan, in works like *The Joy Luck Club* (1989), has eloquently described how Chinese Americans manage bicultural gender expectations.

In traditional Mexican families, women assume the expressive role of homemaker and caretaker of children. This continues to be the norm, although less so than in the past (Comas-Diaz, 1993; Leong, 1996). Historically, the Mexican female's role has been one of self-denial. Her needs were subordinated to those of other family members. Joint decision making and greater equality of males' and females' roles are becoming more characteristic of Mexican American families. Of special significance is the increased frequency of Mexican American women's employment outside the home, which in many instances has enhanced a wife's status in the family and in decision making.

For Native Americans, roles and family configurations involving women and men depend on the tribe (LaFromboise, 1993). For example, in the traditional matriarchal Navajo family, an older woman might live with her husband, her unmarried children, her married daughter, and the daughter's husband and children. In patriarchal tribes, women function as the central "core" of the family, maintaining primary responsibility for the welfare of children. Grandmothers and aunts often provide child care. As with other ethnic minority females, Native American females who have moved to urban areas experience the cultural conflict of traditional ethnic values and the values of mainstream American society (LaFromboise & Trimble, 1996).

Ethnic Minority Males

Just as ethnic minority females have experienced considerable discrimination and have had to develop coping strategies in the face of adversity, so have ethnic minority males. As with ethnic minority females, our order of discussion will be on African American males, Asian American males, Latino males, and Native American males.

Statistics indicate the difficulties many African American males have faced (Parham & McDavis, 1993). African American males of all ages are three times as likely as White males to live in poverty. Of males aged 20 to 44, African Americans are twice as likely to die as Whites. African American male heads of households earn 70 percent of the income of their White male counterparts. Although they make up only 6.3 percent of the U.S. population, African American males constitute 42 percent of jail inmates and more than 50 percent of men executed for any reason in the last 50 years. Murder by gun is the leading cause of death among African American males aged 15 through 19, and rates are getting worse. From 1979 to 1989, the rate of death by guns among this age group of African American males increased 71 percent. One study found that a lack of male role models in African American boys' development was a contributing factor (Browne & others, 1993).

Statistics sometimes do not tell the complete story (Coleman, 1996; Evans & Whitfield, 1988). The sociocultural aspects of historical discrimination against an ethnic minority group must be taken into account to understand these statistics. Just as with African American females, researchers are beginning to focus on some of the more positive dimensions of African American males. For example, researchers are finding that African American males are especially efficient at the use of body language in communication, decoding nonverbal cues, multilingual/multicultural expression, and improvised problem solving.

Asian cultural values are reflected in traditional patriarchal Chinese and Japanese families (Sue & Sue, 1993). The father's behavior in relation to other family members is generally dignified, authoritative, remote, and aloof. Sons are generally valued over daughters. Firstborn sons have an especially high status. As with Asian American females, the acculturation experienced by Asian American males has eroded some of the rigid gender roles that characterized Asian families in the past. Fathers still are often the figurative heads of families, especially when dealing with the public, but in private they have relinquished some of their decision-making powers to their wives.

In Mexican families, men traditionally assume the instrumental role of provider and protector of the family. The concept of machismo continues to influence the role of the male and the patriarchal orientation of Mexican families, though less than in the past. Traditionally, this orientation required men to be forceful and strong, and also to withhold affectionate emotions. Ideally, it involved a strong sense of personal honor, family, loyalty, and care for children. However, it also has involved exaggerated masculinity and aggression. The concepts of machismo and absolute patriarchy are currently diminishing in influence, but adolescent males are still given much more freedom than adolescent females in Mexican American families.

Some Native American tribes are also patriarchal, with the male being the head of the family and primary decision maker. In some tribes, though, child care is shared by men. For example, Mescalero Apache men take responsibility for children when not working away from the family. Autonomy is highly valued among the male children in many Native American tribes, with the males operating semi-independently at an early age. As with Native American females, increased movement to urban areas has led to modifications in the values and traditions of some Native American males.

Culture and Gender

Anthropology studies have provided rich resources for studying the social construction of gender. We will examine examples of cultures that narrowly prescribe gender roles, sometimes in a manner that is alien to our own practices. We will explore examples of cultures that provide unusual gender roles and those that treat gender as a lifelong process rather than a status. We will also examine how gender roles change within culture over time. These examples will illustrate the arbitrary quality of the social construction of gender across and within cultures.

Prescribed Gender Roles

Margaret Mead (1935, 1968) identified three different gender constructions in her studies of the people of New Guinea that illustrate narrow, but divergent definitions of gendered behavior. The Arapesh—both men and women—display cooperative, peaceful, and nurturant behavior, characteristics that we have traditionally associated with women in this culture. Mundugumor women and men display aggressive and competitive behavior, qualities that we have traditionally attributed to men. The Tchambuli demonstrate behavior opposite to the dominant expectations we have for gender in this culture. Women have dominance in this culture from political power to sexual conquest. Men behave in a delicate manner and invest their time making themselves attractive to women. The various social systems of New Guinea underscore the degree to which gender roles are influenced by socialization but can still lead to narrow prescriptions within a culture.

Gender Crossing

Some cultures recognize more than two gender categories (Renzetti & Curran, 1992). In such cultures, individuals who have cross-gender characteristics may achieve special status. For example, traditional Navajo societies have a third category—nadle—that is assigned to those with ambiguous genitals at birth or claimed by some males later in life. Nadles, treated as women, perform both masculine and feminine tasks, mediate problems between women and men, and marry either sex.

The Mohave also offer unusual gender roles that are enacted with the full endorsement of the culture. Mohave women may choose to become hwame; they dress like and conduct themselves like men even if they have had children, but they are restricted from leadership or warrior activities. Boys may become alyha by marrying men and doing female tasks. They may even simulate menstruation, pregnancy, and childbirth without stigma in their culture.

Gender as Process

The Hua of Papua New Guinea believe that gender changes over the lifetime (Gilmore, 1990). Feminine people are seen as invincible, but they have low status because they are "polluted." Women gradually lose their femininity—and their status as polluted—by bearing children. They are no longer polluted after bearing three babies, but they are also no longer invincible. At this point they may share in the higher-status activities of men. As men age, they gradually lose their masculinity to young boys through Hua rituals. They lose authority and status because the loss of masculinity renders them polluted, but in exchange they earn invincibility. For the Hua, gender is not a stable category, but a dynamic process that confers status and stigma.

Gender Redefinition

Gender expectations may change within a culture over time as the cultural context evolves (Wood, 1994). Masculine and feminine attributes are usually defined in relation to each other and the predominant values of the context in which gender differences will be played out.

Anthropologists emphasize that economic arrangements and technology have an impact on the degree to which female and male roles become differentiated. Cultures oriented to gathering or producing food stress cooperation and may promote fewer differences between women and men. Following the Industrial Revolution, task specialization placed greater value on physical power and endurance as an attribute of masculinity. In contrast, femininity involved physical weakness and dependence. As technology becomes more sophisticated, the importance of physical strength diminishes. Economic competence and intelligence become more highly valued than physical strength. These examples illustrate how social constructions of masculine and feminine behavior can change within a culture over time.

In the culture of the Wodaabe, a nomadic group in Niger, Africa, men—not women—compete in beauty contests to enhance their appeal as potential mates. They apply makeup to enhance their features, adopt colorful and appealing attire, and even have talent competitions. The mating rituals involve dancing and eyeball-rolling. The Wodaabe place great value on being able to roll the eyes in and out independently because they link strength of the eye muscles to the ability to make strong marriages. Such contests might sound familiar even if the gender and context are different.

Sociocultural Variations

As a result of the women's movement, men have developed their own movement. Herb Goldberg was a central figure in the men's movement in the 1970s and 1980s. He believes that because of their masculine conditioning men have developed a number of self-destructive behavior patterns. He argues that men need to become more attuned to their inner self and emotional makeup, and work on developing more positive close relationships. A new men's movement in the 1990s, led by Robert Bly, stresses that men are too soft today and that men need to get back to being what a true man really is—deeply masculine. Critics say Bly dramatically overstates the separateness of the sexes, and they don't like his regression to the macho model of masculinity.

There are many similarities between women in different ethnic minority groups and between men in different ethnic minority groups, but even small differences can sometimes be important. Researchers in psychology have only begun to focus on female behavior in specific ethnic groups in a positive way. Many ethnic minority females have experienced the double jeopardy of racism and sexism. In many instances, Asian American, Latina, and Native American females have lived in patriarchal, male-dominated families, although gender roles have become less rigid in these ethnic groups in recent years. Just as ethnic minority females have experienced considerable discrimination and have had to develop coping strategies in the face of adversity, so have ethnic minority males. Researchers are beginning to focus more on the positive dimensions of African American females and males. A patriarchal, male-dominant orientation has characterized many ethnic minority groups, such as Asian Americans, Latinos, and some Native American groups, although women are gaining greater decision making in these cultures, especially women who develop careers and work outside of the home.

CRITICAL THINKING ABOUT ADJUSTMENT

Gender Equality and Imbalance

You have been exposed to many stories about the limitations and opportunities linked to gender. Many might have surprised you, perhaps even shocked you. You may have questioned whether you could have thrived under conditions very different from those in which you were raised. Or you might have wondered whether our own culture would be better off with more clearly delineated expectations on gender.

One challenge cross-cultural researchers face is the need to remain objective in their observations and analyses, especially regarding practices that appear contrary to their own sense of values. For example, feminist scholars find it difficult to study cultures with gender systems based on inequity, especially those that deny women full participation in the culture or cause them physical harm. We may struggle to understand practices that involve mutilation of the female genitalia, that restrict freedom of choice and mobility, and that deprive women of any economic or political influence. The temptation is strong to make judgments about the progressiveness—or lack of it—in such a culture.

As much progress as we have made with regard to equal opportunity in our own culture, systems of privilege—subtle and not so subtle—are still operative in the United States. Any socialization that deprives people of one gender the opportunities that are open to people of the other can be suspected of not promoting equality. Reflect on these examples:

- Who is socialized about proper leg position (e.g., knees together)?
- Who pays for the check?
- Can a woman ask a man for a date without enduring suspicion?
- Whose name changes as a result of the wedding ceremony?
- Who drives?
- Who cleans up during major holiday gatherings?
- Who holds back in some skill so as not to embarrass the partner?
- Who initiates sex?
- Who interrupts and who yields?

If we prize equality, we must recognize that social systems take a long time to change. Such understanding can help us *appreciate individual and group differences* and avoid being judgmental about the adequacy of other cultures. We need to take precautions not to assume that ours is the only or best way of life.

There are very few jobs that actually require a penis or vagina. All other jobs should be open to everybody.

—**Florynce R. Kennedy**

We began this chapter by defining gender, including ideas about the changing American landscape of gender, the history of psychological research on gender, and the feminist perspective. Next we turned our attention to gender comparisons, evaluating the nature of gender roles, gender-role transcendence and stereotyping, and similarities and differences between women and men. Our coverage of gender identity focused on four main perspectives: the neurobiological, psychoanalytic, behavioral, and cognitive. Then we studied sociocultural variations involving gender—men's issues, ethnicity and gender, and culture and gender. Don't forget that you can obtain an overall summary of the chapter by again reading the in-chapter reviews on pages 174, 180, 186, and 190.

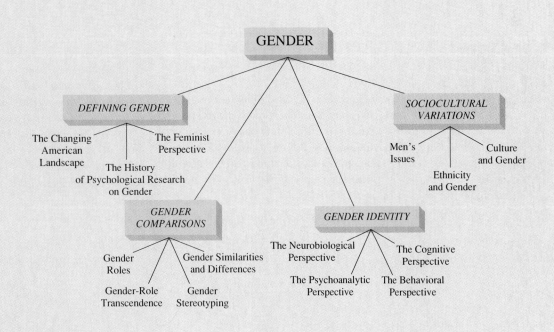

PRACTICAL KNOWLEDGE ABOUT ADJUSTMENT

THE MISMEASURE OF WOMAN

(1992) by Carol Tavris.
New York: Touchstone.

The Mismeasure of Woman explores the stereotyping of women and similarities and differences between women and men. The eight main issues explored in this book are summarized in the chapter subtitles as follows:

- Why women are not inferior to men
- Why women are not superior to men
- Premenstrual syndrome, postmenstrual syndrome, and other normal "diseases"

- Why women are "sick" but men have problems
- Fables of female sexuality
- How women cornered the love market
- Speaking of gender—the darkened eye restored

Tavris believes that no matter how hard women try, they can't measure up. They are criticized for being too female or not female enough, but they are always judged and mismeasured by how well they fit into a male world. *The Mismeasure of Woman* contains a thorough review of research studies that document how women are ignored, misrepresented, and even harmed by the still-male-dominated health professions.

THE NEW MALE

(1980) by Herb Goldberg.
New York: Signet.

This book is subtitled *From Macho to Sensitive but Still Male.* Goldberg's purpose in writing *The New Male* was to explore what the world of the traditional male has been like in the past, including his relationship with females; what the male's world is like

in today's era of changing gender roles; and what the future could hold for males if they examine, reshape, and expand their gender role behavior and self-awareness. Goldberg argues that the way the traditional male role has been defined has made it virtually impossible for males to explore their inner selves, examine their feelings, and show sensitivity toward others.

ATTITUDES TOWARD WOMEN

Scoring

Score the following questions using the scale A = 0, B = 1, C = 2, and D = 3:s 1, 4, 5, 10, 13, 14, 15, 16, 17, 19, 20, 22, and 23. For questions 2, 3, 6, 7, 8, 9, 11, 12, 18, 21, 24, and 25, use the scale A = 3, B = 2, C = 1, D = 0. Add your answers to get your score.

Interpretation

Higher scores indicate more liberal attitudes and lower scores indicate more traditional views. Scores range between 0 and 75. Scores lower than 36 suggest relatively traditional views, with most women scoring more liberal than most men.

ARE YOU ANDROGYNOUS?

Scoring

Add up your ratings for items 1, 4, 7, 10, 13, 16, 19, 22, 25, 28, 31, 34, 37, 40, 43, 46, 49, 55, and 58. Divide the total by 20. That is your masculinity score.

Add up your ratings for items 2, 5, 8, 11, 14, 17, 20, 23, 26, 29, 32, 35, 38, 41, 44, 47, 50, 53, 56, and 59. Divide the total by 20. That is your femininity score.

Interpretation

If your masculinity score is above 4.9 (the approximate median for the masculinity scale) and your femininity score is above 4.9 (the approximate femininity median) then you would be classified as androgynous on Bem's scale.

August Klimt
The Kiss, detail

Human Sexuality

The sexual embrace can only be compared with music and with prayer.

—Havelock Ellis,
On Life and Sex, 1937

THE STORY OF CLELIA MOSHER:
SEX RESEARCHER IN THE VICTORIAN ERA

S exual repression reigned in England and in the United States in the late 1800s during Queen Victoria's rule in England. In this Victorian era, women were not supposed to possess any sexual desires.

A remarkable woman, Dr. Clelia Mosher, emerged in the Victorian context. She attended Wellesley, Stanford, and Johns Hopkins, receiving her M.D. degree at Hopkins in the 1890s. Over a period of three decades, beginning when she was an undergraduate student, Mosher conducted a sex survey of Victorian women, administering her nine-page questionnaire to 47 women. Admittedly, the sample was small and nonrandom—many of the women were faculty wives at universities or women from Mosher's

medical practice. Of the sample, more than four out of five had attended college, a high level of education for women in the 1800s (Jacob, 1981).

Nonetheless, the survey is extremely enlightening because, despite well-known views about Victorian women, Mosher's is the only actual survey about these women known to exist. Following are some intriguing findings from the survey (Hyde, 1994):

- The stereotype about Victorian women is that they experienced no sexual desire. However, in Mosher's survey, 80 percent of the women said they felt a desire for sexual intercourse.
- The Victorian stereotype also includes the belief that Victorian women should not have orgasms.

Yet in Mosher's survey, 72 percent of the Victorian women said that they experienced orgasms.
- Some of the women in Mosher's survey reported that women's longer time to reach orgasm might be a source of marital conflict. One woman said that she achieved orgasm if time is taken. Another complained that men have not been properly trained.
- Almost two-thirds of the women used some form of birth control. Douching was the most popular method, followed by withdrawal and "timing." Several women's husbands used a "male sheath," and two women used a "rubber cap over their uterus."

In sum, Clelia Mosher's survey revealed that many Victorian women managed to enjoy sex despite the sexually repressive Victorian attitudes of the time.

PREVIEW

Clelia Mosher's Victorian sex survey calls attention to the extensive role that stereotypes, myths, and sociohistorical contexts play in human sexuality. Sex is a powerful human motive that influences the quality of human adjustment. Philip Wylie, in *Generation of the Vipers* (1942), labeled sex "one of the three or four prime movers of all we do and are and dream." We will explore many different dimensions of human sexuality in this chapter, including sexual arousal and the human sexual response, sexual knowledge, attitudes, and behavior, psychosexual disorders, and sexuality and harm.

SEXUAL AROUSAL AND THE HUMAN SEXUAL RESPONSE CYCLE

The first time you experienced a tingling sensation in your genital area, you may have been reading a book, thinking about a person to whom you were really attracted, or sleeping and having a pleasurable sensuous dream. If you wondered

what that tingling sensation was about, you were not alone. Most of us become sexual beings before we have any idea what sex is all about. What causes us to get sexually aroused?

Sexual Arousal

Both biological and psychological factors are involved in our sexual arousal. Human sexual behavior is influenced

by the presence of hormones in the blood stream. Hormones are among the most powerful, yet subtle, chemicals in nature. All of the hormones are controlled by the pituitary gland, which is located in the brain. Estrogens are the main class of sex hormones in females, while androgens (of which testosterone is the most important) are the main class in males.

At puberty, males experience a dramatic increase in testosterone levels, with a resultant increase in sexual thoughts and fantasies, masturbation, and nocturnal emissions. Indeed, in male adolescents, the higher the blood levels of testosterone, the more the adolescent is preoccupied with sexual thoughts and engages in sexual activities. Throughout the year, the male's testes secrete androgens in fairly consistent amounts (see figure 9.1 for a diagram of the male reproductive system, including the testes). Because of the consistent levels, males are hormonally ready to be stimulated to engage in sexual behavior at any time. As a man ages, his testosterone level gradually declines; this is usually accompanied by a decline in sexual interest and activity.

At puberty, females' ovaries begin to produce the female sex hormones called estrogen (see figure 9.2 for a diagram of the female reproductive system). Unlike androgen, estrogen is not constantly produced. Rather, estrogen levels vary over an approximately month-long cycle. Estrogen levels are highest when the female is ovulating (releasing an egg from one of her ovaries), which is midway through the menstrual cycle. It is at this time that a female is most likely to become pregnant. In many nonhuman animals, this high-estrogen period is the only time that females are receptive to male initiatives to mate. Although the strength of sexual interest in females varies with estrogen levels, human females are capable of being interested in sexual involvement throughout the menstrual cycle. Indeed, only a minimal level of estrogen seems to be required to sustain sexual desire in women. Thus, as we move from the lower to the higher animals, hormonal control over behavior is less dominant, although still important, in sexual arousal; for humans, both sociocultural and cognitive factors play more-important roles. Still, estrogen does have some influence on women's sexuality. Although postmenopausal

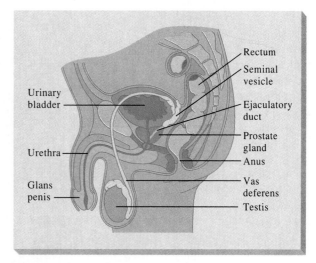

FIGURE 9.1

Male Reproductive Organs
The testes are the male gonads that produce sperm cells and manufacture the male androgen called testosterone. The glans penis is the head of the penis. The vas deferens is the duct through which stored sperm is passed. It is the vas deferens that is cut or blocked in a vasectomy. The seminal vesicles are the two sacs of the male internal genitalia, which secrete nutrients to help sperm become motile. The prostate gland is a structure of the internal male genitalia that secretes a fluid into the semen prior to ejaculation to aid sperm motility and elongate sperm life. The urethra is the tube through which the bladder empties urine outside the body and through which the male sperm exits.

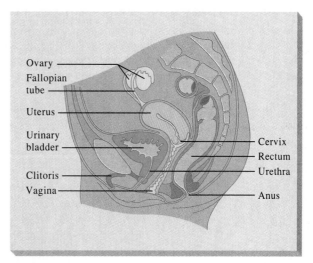

FIGURE 9.2

Female Reproductive Organs
The uterus is a pear-shaped, hollow structure of the female genitalia, in which the embryo and fetus develop prior to birth. The thick, muscular wall of the uterus expands and contracts during pregnancy. The cervix is the mouth of the uterus, through which the vagina extends. The vagina is the hollow, tunneled structure of the female internal genitalia; its reproductive functions are to receive the penis and its ejaculate, to be a route of exit for the newborn, and to provide an exit for menstrual flow. The clitoris is a part of the female genitalia that is very sensitive to stimulation. The ovaries, adjacent to both sides of the uterus, house ova prior to their maturation and discharge; they also produce estrogen. The fallopian tubes are the routes through which eggs leave the ovaries on their way to the uterus. Fertilization usually takes place in the fallopian tubes.

women have a significant drop in estrogen, they are still sexually active; if given estrogen, they experience an increased interest in sex and report that sexual activity is more pleasurable.

Cultural Contexts and Arousal

What "turns people on" is influenced by their sociocultural background, their individual preferences, and their cognitive interpretations. The range in cultural sexual values is considerable. Some cultures consider sexual pleasures as "normal" or "desirable" while other cultures view sexual pleasures as "weird" or "abnormal." Consider the people who live on the small island of Ines Beag off the coast of Ireland. They are among the most sexually repressed people in the world. They know nothing about tongue kissing or hand stimulation of the penis, and nudity is detested. For both females and males, premarital sex is out of the question. Men avoid most sexual experiences because they believe that sexual intercourse reduces their energy level and is bad for their health. Under these repressive conditions, sexual intercourse occurs only at night and takes place as quickly as possible as the husband opens his nightclothes under the covers and the wife raises her nightgown. As you might suspect, female orgasm is rare in this culture (Messinger, 1971).

By contrast, consider the Mangaian culture in the South Pacific. In Mangaia, young boys are taught about masturbation and are encouraged to engage in it as much as they like. At age 13, the boys undergo a ritual that initiates them into sexual manhood. First their elders instruct them about sexual strategies, including how to aid their female partner in having orgasms. Then, 2 weeks later, the boy has intercourse with an experienced woman who helps him hold back ejaculation until she can achieve orgasm with him. By the end of adolescence, Mangaians have sex virtually every day. Mangaian women report a high frequency of orgasm.

Sexuality is the great field of battle between biology and society.

—Nancy Friday,
My Mother/My Self, 1977

Our culture is more liberal than that of the Ines Beag but less tolerant and more conservative than that of the Mangaians. The cultural diversity in sexual behavior around the world is testimony to the importance of environmental experiences in determining sexual arousal. In complex organisms, experience plays a more powerful role in sexuality than hormones do.

Sexual behavior has its magnificent moments throughout the animal kingdom. Insects mate in midair, peacocks display their plumage, and male elephant seals have prolific sex lives. Socioemotional experiences and cognitive interpretation play a more important role in human sexual behavior. We can talk about sex with each other, read about it in magazines, and watch it on television and the movie screen.

Arousal Cues

We cannot mate in midair like bees or give magnificent displays of plumage like peacocks do, but we can talk about sex with each other, read about it in magazines, and watch it on television or at the movies. Touch, visual cues, certain words written or heard, and smells can all be sexually arousing. However, there are individual differences in what turns people on. One woman might thrill to having her ears nibbled; another might find it annoying. Most of us think of kissing as highly stimulating, but in a vast majority of tribal societies kissing is either unheard of or thought to be disgusting.

Whoever named it necking was a poor judge of anatomy.

—**Groucho Marx**

Men and women differ in the role that visual stimulation plays in sexual arousal. Men are more aroused by what they see; perhaps this fact helps to explain why erotic magazines and X-rated movies are more directed toward males than toward females (Money, 1986). More than through visual stimulation, women become sexually aroused through tender, loving touches that are coupled with verbal expressions of love. However, when stimulated effectively, women and men appear to have similar patterns of arousal, including timing (Masters & Johnson, 1966).

The Human Sexual Response Cycle

How do humans respond physiologically during sexual activity? To answer this question, gynecologist William Masters and his colleague Virginia Johnson (1966) carefully observed and measured the physiological responses of 382 female and 312 male volunteers as they masturbated or had sexual intercourse. The **human sexual response cycle** *consists of four phases—excitement, plateau, orgasm, and resolution—as identified by Masters and Johnson* (see figure 9.3). The *excitement phase* begins erotic responsiveness;

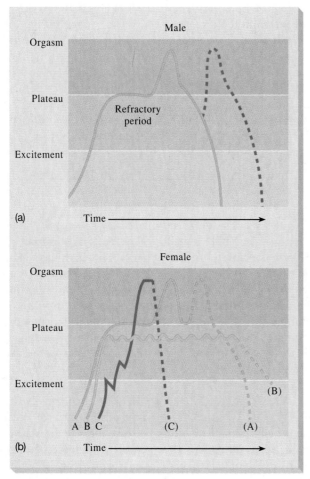

FIGURE 9.3

Male and Female Human Sexual Response Patterns
(*a*) This diagram shows the excitement, plateau, orgasm, and resolution phases of the human male sexual response pattern. Notice that males enter a refractory period, which lasts from several minutes up to a day, in which they cannot have another orgasm. (*b*) This diagram shows the excitement, plateau, orgasm, and resolution phases of the human female sexual response pattern. Notice that female sexual responses follow one of three basic patterns. Pattern *A* somewhat resembles the male pattern, except that pattern *A* includes the possibility of multiple orgasm (the second peak in pattern *A*) without falling below the plateau level. Pattern *B* represents nonorgasmic arousal. Pattern *C* represents intense female orgasm, which resembles the male pattern in its intensity and rapid resolution.

it lasts from several minutes to several hours, depending on the nature of the sex play involved. Engorgement of blood vessels and increased blood flow in genital areas and muscle tension characterize the excitement phase. The most obvious signs of response in this phase are lubrication of the vagina and partial erection of the penis.

> *Whatever else can be said about sex, it cannot be called a dignified performance.*
>
> —**Helen Laurenson**

The second phase of the human sexual response, called the *plateau phase,* is a continuation and heightening of the arousal begun in the excitement phase. The increases in breathing, pulse rate, and blood pressure that occurred during the excitement phase become more intense, penile erection and vaginal lubrication are more complete, and orgasm is closer.

The third phase of the human sexual response cycle is *orgasm.* How long does orgasm last? Some individuals sense that time is standing still when it takes place, but orgasm lasts for only about 3 to

15 seconds. Orgasm involves an explosive discharge of neuromuscular tension and an intense pleasurable feeling. However, not all orgasms are exactly alike. For example, females show three different patterns in the orgasm phase, as shown in figure 9.3: (a) multiple orgasms, (b) no orgasm, and (c) excitement rapidly leading to orgasm, bypassing the plateau phase; the third pattern most clearly corresponds to the male pattern in intensity and resolution.

Following orgasm, the individual enters the *resolution phase,* in which blood vessels return to their normal state. One difference between males and females in this phase is that females can be stimulated to orgasm again without delay. Males enter a refractory period, lasting anywhere from several minutes to an entire day, in which they cannot have another orgasm. The length of the refractory period increases as men age.

We have examined some of the biological aspects of human sexual behavior. Next we will explore how individuals in the United States learn about sexuality and how this influences attitudes about sexual expression.

SEXUAL KNOWLEDGE, ATTITUDES, AND BEHAVIOR

According to sexuality expert Bernie Zilbergeld (1992), our culture has experienced dramatic changes in the sexual landscape in the last decade—from changing expectations of and about women to new definitions of masculinity, from the fear of disease to renewed focus on long-term relationships. Even though scientific knowledge about sexuality has grown substantially, we are unlikely to acquire sexual knowledge in a scientific or systematic fashion. It is not that American adolescents and adults are sheltered from sexual messages; sexual information and imagery are abundant in this culture. However, much that passes for information is misinformation. Our attitudes about sexuality are shaped by education, experience, media, and mythology.

Sexual Knowledge, Myths, and Education

How widespread are sexual myths? What is the nature of sex education?

Sexual Knowledge

How much do we really know about sex? According to June Reinisch (1990), director of the Kinsey Institute for Sex, Gender, and Reproduction, the United States is a nation whose citizens know more about how their automobiles function than about how their bodies function sexually. Reinisch directed a national assessment of basic sexual knowledge that was given to 1,974 adults. For example, 65 percent did not know that most erection difficulties begin with physical problems. Fifty percent did not know that oil-based lubricants should not be used with condoms or diaphragms because some can produce holes in them in less than 60 seconds. There is a great deal that we might not know, but what might be even more problematic are the unfounded myths about sexuality that we believe.

Sexual Myths

Sexuality's many myths have led to unrealistic expectations for our lives. One man commented that he had learned so much misinformation about sex as a child that it was taking him the rest of his life to unlearn it. In middle age, he still can't believe how much stress he caused himself when he was younger and wishes he could apologize to the women who knew him in his earlier years.

Adolescents in the United States believe in a distressing amount of misinformation and mythology. In one investigation, a majority of adolescents believed that pregnancy risk is greatest during menstruation (Zelnick & Kantner, 1977). Additional examples of the myths that complicate sexual understanding are explored in the critical thinking exercise at the end of this chapter. These examples underscore the serious need for improving our sexual awareness and knowledge; this can help reduce unwanted pregnancies and promote self-protection.

Sex Education

We get very little sex education from our parents. A large majority of American adolescents say they cannot talk freely about sex with their parents. Because many parents so inadequately handle sex education, it is not surprising that most of them prefer to let the schools do the job. In a national poll conducted by *Time* magazine, 78 percent of parents wanted schools to teach sex education, including information about birth control (Wallis, 1985).

Despite the majority opinion, sex education remains controversial. On one side are groups like Planned Parenthood who argue that sex education should be more open and birth control more available, like they are in European countries (see Sociocultural Worlds of Adjustment to read about the sex education and attitudes of youth in Holland and Sweden). On the other side are individuals who believe sex education should be provided solely by parents. These persons usually believe that teaching adolescents about birth control is simply giving them a license to have sex and be promiscuous. The controversy has led to clashes at school board meetings throughout the nation. For instance, to combat its runaway adolescent pregnancy problem, New York City initiated a program to, among other things, distribute condoms to students. Religious groups showed up at a school board meeting with a list of over fifty objections. In San Juan Capistrano, California, conservatives appeared at a school board meeting dressed in Revolutionary War clothes to protest liberal sex education practices.

Sex education programs in schools might not by themselves prevent adolescent pregnancy and sexually transmitted diseases. Researchers have found that sex education classes do improve adolescents' knowledge about human sexuality but do not always change their sexual behavior. When sex education classes are combined with readily available contraceptives, teen pregnancy rates are more likely to drop (Wallis, 1985). Such findings have led to the development of *school-linked* rather than *school-based* approaches to sex education and pregnancy prevention. In one program pioneered by some Baltimore public schools in cooperation with Johns Hopkins University, family-planning clinics are located adjacent to the schools. These clinics send a nurse and a social worker into the schools to make formal presentations about sexuality and the services available from the clinics. They also make themselves available to the students for counseling several hours each day. The same personnel conduct after-school sessions at the clinic, consisting of further counseling, films, and family-planning information. The results have been very positive. Students who participated in the school-linked programs delayed their first intercourse longer than students in a control group did.

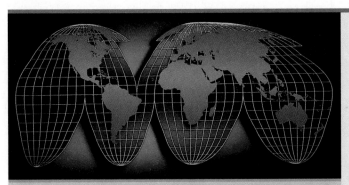

Sex Education and Attitudes Among Youth in Holland and Sweden

In Holland and Sweden, sex does not carry the mystery and conflict it does in American society. Holland does not have a mandated sex education program, but adolescents can obtain contraceptive counseling at government-sponsored clinics for a small fee. The Dutch media also have played an important role in educating the public about sex through frequent broadcasts focused on birth control, abortion, and related matters. Most Dutch adolescents do not consider having sex without birth control.

Swedish adolescents are sexually active at an earlier age than are American adolescents, and they are exposed to even more explicit sex on television. However, the Swedish National Board of Education has developed a curriculum that ensures that every child in the country, beginning at age 7, will experience a thorough grounding in reproductive biology and, by the age of 10 or 12, will have been introduced to information about various forms of contraception. Teachers are expected to handle the subject of sex whenever it become relevant, regardless of the subject they are teaching. The idea is to take some of the drama and mystery out of sex so that familiarity will make students less vulnerable to unwanted pregnancy and sexually transmitted diseases (Wallis, 1985). American society is not nearly so open about sex education.

Sex is much more demystified and less dramatized in Sweden than in the United States, and adolescent pregnancy rates are much lower in Sweden than in the United States.

After 28 months, the pregnancy rate had declined to 30 percent in the school-linked programs, while it rose to 60 percent in the control group. Thus, the support services provided by the community-based, school-linked family-planning clinic were effective in reducing adolescent pregnancy.

Contraception

Most couples in the United States want to be able to control whether and when they will conceive a child. For them it is important to have accurate knowledge about contraception.

Inadequate knowledge about contraception, coupled with inconsistent use of effective contraceptive methods, has resulted in this country's having the dubious distinction of having the highest adolescent pregnancy rate in the industrialized world. Although the rate of use among teenagers is improving, many still do not use contraception. Moreover, a majority of adolescents do not use contraception during their first sexual intercourse experience (Hofferth, 1990). Seventy percent of females who become sexually active before the age of 15 have unprotected first intercourse; the percentage drops to about 50 percent for those who become active around the age of 18 or 19.

Age also influences the choice of contraceptive method. Older adolescents and young adults are more likely to rely on the pill or diaphragm; younger adolescents are more likely to use a condom or withdrawal (Hofferth, 1990). Even adults in stable relationships sometimes do not use adequate contraception, perhaps feeling that some contraceptives, such as condoms, interrupt the spontaneity of sex, or they might overestimate the effectiveness of some of the unreliable methods.

No single method of contraception is best for everyone. When choosing a method of contraception, couples need to consider such factors as their physical and emotional concerns, the method's effectiveness, the nature of their relationship, their values and beliefs, and the method's convenience. Calculations of the effectiveness of a contraceptive method often are based on the failure rates during the first year of use. It is estimated that if

Adolescents are increasing their use of contraceptives, although large numbers of sexually active adolescents still do not use contraceptives, especially at first intercourse.

Think about how you learned the "facts of life." Did most of your information come from well-informed sources? Were you able to talk freely and openly with your own parents about what to expect sexually? Did you acquire some false beliefs through your trial-and-error efforts? Based on your experience in learning about sexuality, how do you think sex education should be addressed as a larger health issue in society? Were some of your beliefs off-target or even blatantly wrong? How significant have the consequences of your sexual misinformation been?

Answering these questions provides you with the opportunity to *practice self-reflection to enhance personal growth.*

no contraceptive method were used, about 90 percent of women would become pregnant in their first year of being (heterosexually) sexually active (Hatcher & others, 1988). Table 9.1 shows the typical failure rate of different contraceptive methods.

Women who miscalculate are called "mothers."

—**Abigail Van Buren**

The knowledge we acquire serves as the foundation of our attitudes about sexuality as well as the behaviors we engage in. To evaluate your own sexual knowledge, see Critical Thinking. In the next section we will explore how knowledge, attitudes, and sexual behavior are interrelated.

Heterosexuality and Homosexuality

Gathering accurate information about sexual attitudes and behavior is a difficult task. Consider how you would respond if someone asked you the following questions: How often do you have sex? How many different sexual partners have you had? How often do you masturbate? The people most likely to respond to surveys about sexual behavior are those with liberal sexual attitudes who engage in liberal sexual behaviors. Thus, what we know is limited by the reluctance of some individuals to answer questions candidly about extremely personal matters, and by our inability to get any answer, candid or otherwise, from individuals who believe that they should not talk about sex with strangers. Researchers refer to this as a "volunteer bias." Imagine how challenging this problem would be with the additional complication of studying sexual practices in other cultures. With these cautions in mind, let's now turn to a discussion of sexual attitudes and behavior, primarily in the United States, beginning with heterosexual relations and then turning to homosexual relations.

Heterosexual Attitudes and Behavior

To explore heterosexual relations, we examine a number of surveys of sexual attitudes and behavior at different points in the twentieth century, the frequency of sexual intercourse, and sexual scripts.

TABLE 9.1

Failure Rates of Birth Control Methods

Method	Typical Failure Rate (%)	Cost (*)	Advantages	Disadvantages
1. Abstinence	0.0	0	No chance of pregnancy	May require much motivation
2. Abortion	0.0	$175-$300	Can terminate a pregnancy after positive tests	Surgical risk; possible medical complications; may reduce cervical competence
3. Tubal ligation	0.4	$800–$1500	Permanent relief from pregnancy worries	Low success of surgical reversal; possible surgical/medical/ psychological complications
4. Vasectomy	0.15	$300	Permanent relief from pregnancy worries	Low success of surgical reversal; possible surgical/medical/ psychological complications
5. Injectable progestin	0.3	$30 per injection/3 mo. coverage	No day-to-day attention required; long-lasting protection	Some risk in regaining fertility; side effects
6. Combined birth control pills	3.0	$14/mo ±	Highly effective; easy to use	Daily use required; continuing cost; slight medical risk; side effects
7. Progestin-only minipill	2.5	$15/mo ±	Highly effective; easy to use	Irregular menses; daily use required
8. IUD	6.0	$80–$90	Needs little attention; no expense after insertion	Side effects; possible expulsion; may perforate uterine wall; some incidence of PID
9. Male condom	12.0	$0.50–$1.50/condom	No side effects; easy to use; easy to obtain; helps prevent disease	Continuing expense; must use every time; may interrupt continuity of lovemaking
10. Female condom	13.0-26.0	$7	No side effects; helps prevent disease	Incorrect use
11. Cervical cap	18.0	$160	Can be left in place for several days; uses no hormones; no side effects	May be dislodged by intercourse; requires skill in insertion; may cause vaginal or cervical trauma
12. Diaphragm (with spermicide)	18.0	$15–$18	Easy to obtain and use; uses no hormones; no side effects; helps prevent disease; no prescription required	Continuing expense; requires high motivation to use correctly and consistently with each intercourse
13. Spermicidal agents (foams, creams, jellies, and vaginal suppositories)	21.0	$5–$10/container	Easy to obtain and use; no prescription required	Continuing expense; requires high motivation to use correctly and consistently with each intercourse
14. Sponge (with spermicide)	21.0	No longer available		
15. Natural family planning (calendar, basal body temperature, cervical mucus, sympto-thermal methods)	20.0	0	No preparation or cost; no hormones or chemicals	May be frustrating to full enjoyment of intercourse; low effectiveness
16. Withdrawal (coitus interruptus)	18.0	0	No hormones or chemicals; acceptable to those who object to devices or hormones/chemicals	Requires much motivation and cooperation between partners
17. Chance (no protection)	89.0	0	No preparation; no hormones/chemicals	High risk of pregnancy; provides little peace of mind

*An approximation, will vary with location; may be less in public clinics.

***Trends in Heterosexual Attitudes
and Behavior in the Twentieth Century*** Had you been a college student in
1940, you probably would have had a
very different attitude toward many aspects of sexuality than you do today,
especially if you are a female. A review of
college students' sexual practices and attitudes from 1900 through the 1990s reveals two important trends (Darling,
Kallon, & Van Duesen, 1984; Robinson
& others, 1991) (see figure 9.4). First,
more young people today are reporting
having had sexual intercourse. Second,
the gap between the proportion of sexually active males and sexually active females is narrowing. Prior to the 1970s,
about twice as many college males as college females reported they had engaged
in sexual intercourse, but since 1970 the
proportion of males and females has become nearly equal. These changes suggest
a major shift away from a double standard of sexual behavior, which held that
it was more acceptable for unmarried
males than for unmarried females to
have sexual intercourse.

Two surveys that included wider
age ranges of adults verified this shift in
trends. In 1974 Morton Hunt surveyed
more than 2,000 adult readers of *Playboy*.
Although the magazine readership's bias
might have led to an overestimation of
sexual permissiveness, the results suggested movement toward increased sexual
permissiveness when compared to the results of Alfred Kinsey's inquiries during
the 1940s (Hunt, 1974; Kinsey, Pomeroy,
& Martin, 1948). Kinsey's earlier survey
found that foreplay consisted of a kiss or
two, but by the 1970s Hunt had discovered that foreplay had lengthened, aver-
aging 15 minutes. Hunt also found that
individuals in the 1970s were using more-
varied sexual techniques in their lovemaking. For example, oral-genital sex,
virtually taboo at the time of Kinsey's survey, was more accepted in the 1970s.

More than 40 years after Kinsey's
famous study, Robert Michael and his
colleagues (1994) conducted a comprehensive survey of American sexual patterns. The findings are based on
face-to-face interviews with nearly 3,500
individuals from 18 to 50 years of age.

FIGURE 9.4

**Percentage of College Women and Men Who Reported Having Sexual Intercourse—
a Summary of Data from Studies Conducted from 1900 to 1980**

The sample generated by Michael and his
colleagues was randomly selected, unlike
the flawed samples of Kinsey, Hunt, and
others, which were based on unrepresentative groups of volunteers.

Among the key findings from the
1994 survey:

- Americans tend to fall into three
  categories: One-third have sex twice
  a week or more, one-third a few
  times a month, and one-third a few
  times a year or not at all.

- Married couples have sex the
  most and also are the most likely
  to have orgasms when they do.
  Figure 9.5 shows the frequency
  of sex for married and
  noncohabiting individuals in
  the past year.

- Most Americans do not engage in
  kinky sexual acts. When asked
  about their favorite sexual acts,
  the vast majority (96 percent) said
  that vaginal sex was "very" or
  "somewhat" appealing. Oral sex

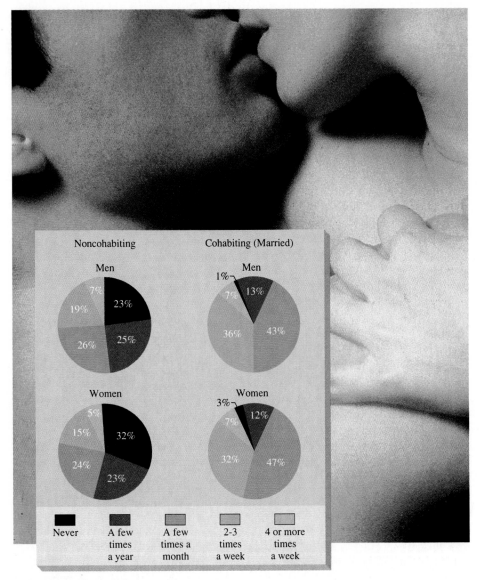

Noncohabiting

Men

- 7%
- 19%
- 26%
- 23%
- 25%

Women

- 5%
- 15%
- 24%
- 32%
- 23%

Cohabiting (Married)

Men

- 1%
- 7%
- 36%
- 13%
- 43%

Women

- 3%
- 7%
- 32%
- 12%
- 47%

| Never | A few times a year | A few times a month | 2-3 times a week | 4 or more times a week |

FIGURE 9.5

The 1994 Sex in America Survey
Shown here are the percentages of noncohabiting and cohabiting (married) males' and females' responses to the question "How often have you had sex in the past year?"

was in third place, after an activity that many have not labeled a sexual act—watching a partner undress.

- Adultery is clearly the exception rather than the rule. Nearly 75 percent of the married men and 85 percent of the married women indicated that they have never been unfaithful.
- Men think about sex far more than women do—54 percent of the men said they think about it every day or several times a day, whereas 67 percent of the women said they think about it only a few times a week or a few times a month.

The findings in the 1994 Sex in America survey contrast sharply with some magazine polls that portray Americans as engaging in virtually unending copulation. The magazine polls are inflated from the start by the individuals who fill them out, such as *Playboy* subscribers who want to brag about their sexual exploits. Even the famous Kinsey studies, which caused such a scandal in the 1940s and 1950s by indicating that half of American men had extramarital affairs, were flawed. Kinsey obtained his subjects where he could find them—in boarding houses, college fraternities, and even mental hospitals. He also quizzed hitchhikers who passed through town. Clearly, Kinsey's subjects were not even close to being a random sample of the population.

In sum, one of the most powerful messages in the 1994 survey was that Americans' sexual lives are more conservative than previously believed. Although 17 percent of the men and 3 percent of the women said they have had sex with at least 21 partners, the overall impression from the survey was that sexual behavior is ruled by marriage and monogamy for most Americans.

Sexual Scripts As we explore our sexual identities, we often follow sexual scripts. A **sexual script** *is a set of stereotyped role prescriptions for how individuals should behave sexually.* Two well-known sexual scripts in the United States are the traditional religious script and the romantic script.

In the **traditional religious script,** *sex is accepted only within marriage. Both premarital and extramarital sex are taboo, especially for women.* In some forms of the religious script, sex is viewed positively only in terms of its reproductive value, and sexual ideas and behaviors are often seen as sin. This religious sexual script was more conservative in earlier times than it is in the twentieth century. Early Christian churches proposed that sexual behavior must accord with "natural law," meaning that the only purpose for sex was procreation; all romantic passion, lust, and masturbation were viewed as sinful. The ideal sexual standard was that intercourse was quick, quiet, and infrequent. Marital sex was to be performed only with the man on top, and it was forbidden on Sundays, Wednesdays, Fridays, and 40 days before and after Easter, and 40 days before and after Christmas. Although the current religious sexual script is still comparatively conservative, it is much more liberal now than in previous centuries.

In the **romantic script,** *sex is synonymous with love. If we develop a relationship with someone and fall in love, it is acceptable to have sex with that person, whether or not we are married.* In the twentieth-century United States, the romantic sexual script has become increasingly influential. However, many people regard the traditional religious sexual script as the ideal. As a result, many individuals find themselves struggling to resolve ethical dilemmas created by the conflicting expectations of these two divergent sexual scripts (Sprecher & McKinney, 1993).

Differences in female and male sexual scripts can cause problems for individuals as they work out their sexual identities and seek sexual fulfillment (King, 1996). Females learn to link sexual intercourse with love more than males do (Cassell, 1984). Therefore females are more likely than males to justify their sexual behavior by telling themselves that they were swept away by love. A number of investigators have found that females, more than males, cite being in love as the main reason for being sexually active. Far more females than males have intercourse only with partners they love and would like to marry. Other reasons females offer for having sexual intercourse include giving in to the male's desire for pleasure, gambling that sex is a way to get a boyfriend or husband, curiosity, and sexual desire unrelated to loving and caring. The male sexual script emphasizes sexual conquest; higher status tends to accrue to males who can claim substantial sexual activity. For males, sex and love might not be as intertwined as they are for females.

Although it has recently become acceptable for females to engage in premarital sex, there is still a **double standard,** *a belief that many sexual activities are acceptable for males but not for females.* The double standard can be hazardous because it encourages women to deny their sexuality and do minimal planning to ensure that their sexual encounters are safe. It can also lead females to think that males are more sexual than females, that males are less in control of their sexual behaviors, and that

females must justify their sexual activity by claiming that they were swept away by the passion of the moment.

The double standard encourages males to dismiss or devalue their female partner's values and feelings, and it puts considerable pressure on males to be as sexually active as possible. As one male adolescent remarked, "I feel a lot of pressure from my buddies to go for the score." Further evidence of physical and emotional exploitation of females was found in a survey of 432 adolescents from 14 to 18 years old (Goodchilds & Zellman, 1984). Of the adolescents surveyed, both females and males accepted the view that the male adolescent had a right to be sexually aggressive and assigned to females the task of setting limits for the male's behavior. Males who accept the double standard might believe that touch and contact are not "manly," and sex with a woman might be the only experience of touch and bodily comfort acceptable to these "real men." The seemingly cold and uncaring concept of "scoring" might be the only option some males think they have to reduce their loneliness, have warmth with another person, and "let their guard down" (Osherson, 1992).

He was one of those men who come in a door and make any woman with them look guilty.

—F. Scott Fitzgerald

Homosexual Attitudes and Behavior

Until the end of the nineteenth century, it was generally believed that people were either heterosexual or homosexual (Byar & Shainberg, 1997). Today, many experts in the field of human sexuality view sexual orientation as a continuum ranging from exclusive heterosexuality to exclusive homosexuality. Pioneering this view were Alfred Kinsey and his associates (Kinsey, Pomeroy, & Martin, 1948), who described sexual orientation as a continuum of a six-point scale, with 0 signifying exclusive heterosexuality and 6 signifying exclusive homosexuality (see figure 9.6). Some individuals are *bisexual,* being sexually attracted to people of both sexes. In Kinsey's research, approximately 1 percent of individuals reported being bisexual (1.2 percent of males and 0.7 percent of females) and from 2 to 5 percent reported being homosexual (4.7 percent of males and 1.8 percent of females). The actual incidence of exclusive homosexuality continues to be debated; estimates range from approximately 1 percent (in a recent national survey, only 1.1 percent said they are exclusively gay) to 10 percent (Billy & others, 1993). In the 1994 Sex in America study, 2.7 percent of men and 1.3 percent of women reported that they had had homosexual sex in the past year (Michael & others, 1994).

Although many people think of heterosexual and homosexual behavior as

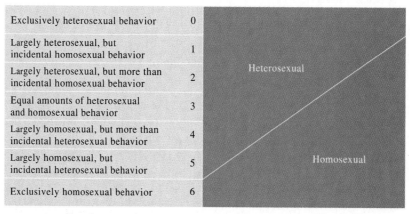

FIGURE 9.6

Continuum of Sexual Orientation
The continuum ranges from exclusive heterosexuality, which Kinsey and associates (1948) rated as 0, to exclusive homosexuality (a rating of 6). People who are about equally attracted to both sexes (ratings 2 to 4) are bisexual.

distinct patterns of behavior that are easy to define and composed of fixed decisions, orientation toward a sexual partner of the same or the opposite sex is not necessarily a fixed decision that is made once in life and adhered to forever. For example, it is not unusual for an individual, especially a male, to engage in homosexual experimentation in adolescence but not as an adult. Homosexual behavior is common among prisoners and others with no alternatives for intimate, enduring relationships. Kinsey's 1948 findings revealed that 37 percent of men and 13 percent of women had participated in some homosexual acts to orgasm between adolescence and old age.

Male and female homosexual experiences reflect different behavioral choices, too. Sexual researchers report that lesbians are more likely to be involved in intimate, enduring relationships, have fewer sexual partners, and have fewer "one-night stands" than homosexual men

(Bell & Weinberg, 1978). Also, just like cohabiting and married heterosexual couples, homosexual couples have sex more frequently in their first 2 years of being together than when they have been together for 2 to 10 years (Blumstein & Schwartz, 1983).

For the last few decades, attitudes toward homosexuality have been becoming more permissive, at least until recently. Beginning in 1986, Gallup polls began to detect a shift in attitudes brought about by increasingly conservative views and by public awareness of acquired immunodeficiency syndrome (AIDS). For example, in 1985 slightly more than 40 percent of Americans believed that "homosexual relations between consenting adults should be legal"; by 1986 the figure had dropped to about 30 percent (Gallup Report, 1987). On the other hand, this increase in "hard-line" attitudes against homosexuals might have been only temporary;

a 1989 Gallup poll once again showed increased acceptance of homosexuality and increased support for civil rights for gays.

Individuals who have negative attitudes toward homosexuality also are likely to favor severe controls for AIDS, such as excluding AIDS carriers from the workplace and schools. Irrational and negative feelings against homosexuals produce a variety of hostile behaviors. Typically hostility is associated with avoidance of homosexuals, false beliefs about homosexuals (such as believing that child molesters are homosexuals), and subtle or overt discrimination in housing, employment, and other areas of life. However, persons who are extremely hostile toward homosexuals have sometimes ridiculed, assaulted, and even murdered homosexuals.

Why are some individuals homosexual and others heterosexual? Speculation about this question has been

What are some similarities and differences between heterosexual and homosexual couples?

extensive, but no firm answers are available. Homosexuals and heterosexuals have similar physiological responses during sexual arousal and seem to be aroused by the same types of tactile stimulation. Investigators find no differences between homosexuals and heterosexuals for a wide range of attitudes, behaviors, and adjustments (Bell, Weinberg, & Mammersmith, 1981). In the 1970s, recognizing that homosexuality is not a form of mental illness, both the American Psychiatric Association and the American Psychological Association discontinued their classification of homosexuality as a mental disorder.

Recently researchers have explored the possible biological basis of homosexuality by examining genetic factors, hormone levels, and differences in anatomical structures. In one study of pairs of identical twins in which one of the twins was homosexual, over 50 percent of the other twins in the pairs were also homosexual. In contrast, only one-fourth of the fraternal twins of homosexuals were homosexual (Bailey & Pillard, 1991). (Fraternal twins are genetically no more similar than ordinary siblings, because they come from different eggs and sperm; identical twins develop from the same fertilized egg.) The results of hormone studies have been inconsistent. If male homosexuals are given male sex hormones (androgens), their sexual orientation does not change; their sexual desire simply increases. A critical period in fetal development might influence sexual orientation. In the second to fifth months after conception, exposure of the fetus to hormone levels characteristic of females might cause the individual (female or male) to become attracted to males (Ellis & Ames, 1987). If this critical-period hypothesis turns out to be correct, it would explain why clinicians have found that sexual orientation is difficult, if not impossible, to modify.

With regard to anatomical structures, neuroscientist Simon LeVay (1991) proposed, based on autopsy evidence, that an area of the hypothalamus that governs sexual behavior is twice as large (about the size of a grain of sand) in heterosexual men as it is in homosexual men. In homosexual men, this part of the

hypothalamus is about the same size as in heterosexual females. Critics of LeVay's work point out that many of the homosexuals in the study had AIDS and suggest that their brains could have been altered by the disease.

An individual's sexual orientation—homosexual, heterosexual, or bisexual—is most likely determined by a combination of genetic, hormonal, cognitive, and environmental factors (Whitman, Diamond, & Martin, 1993). Most experts on homosexuality believe that no one factor alone causes homosexuality and that the relative weight of each factor can vary from one individual to the next. In effect, no one knows exactly what causes an individual to be homosexual. Scientists have a clearer picture of what does not cause homosexuality. For example, children raised by gay or lesbian parents or couples are no more

likely to be homosexual than are children raised by heterosexual parents (Patterson, 1996). There also is no evidence that male homosexuality is caused by a dominant mother or a weak father, or that female homosexuality is caused by girls' choosing male role models.

Although most of us manage to develop a mature sexuality, most of us also have some periods of vulnerability, confusion, and even dysfunction along the way. Many individuals have an almost insatiable curiosity about sexuality. Many people wonder and worry about their sexual attractiveness and their ability to satisfy their sexual partner. Often our worries about our sexuality are fueled by media stereotypes about sexual potency and superhuman sexual exploits. The next section explores how we evaluate sexual satisfaction.

REVIEW

Sexual Knowledge, Attitudes, and Behavior

According to a recent national survey, Americans are not very knowledgeable about sex. Many American adults and adolescents have misconceptions about sex. A majority of parents favor letting schools handle sex education, although school-based sex education has been controversial. School-linked community-based family planning clinics have reduced adolescent pregnancy rates. In many European countries such as Holland and Sweden, sex does not carry the mystery and conflict it does in America. Most couples want to be able to control when they will conceive a child, and for them, it is important to be knowledgeable about contraception. In choosing a method of contraception, such factors as physical and emotional effects, effectiveness, and convenience need to be considered.

Although heterosexual attitudes and behavior have become more liberal in the twentieth century, the 1994 Sex in America survey portrayed Americans' sex lives as more conservative than previously believed. The sample of subjects for the 1994 survey was more random than those of previous

studies. Sexual scripts are stereotyped patterns of role prescriptions about how individuals should behave sexually. Two well-known sexual scripts are the traditional religious script and the romantic script. Females and males have often been socialized to follow different sexual scripts. Sexual scripts often involve a double standard.

Today, it is generally accepted to view sexual orientation along a continuum from exclusively heterosexual to exclusively homosexual rather than as an either-or proposition. Some individuals (approximately 1 percent) are bisexual. About 2 to 5 percent of individuals report being exclusively homosexual. Preference for a sexual partner of the same sex is not always a fixed decision. Until recently, acceptance of homosexuality had been increasing, but in concert with the AIDS epidemic, acceptance of homosexuality temporarily decreased. Acceptance of lesbian and gay lifestyles seems to be increasing again. An individual's sexual orientation—heterosexual, homosexual, or bisexual—is likely determined by a combination of genetic, hormonal, cognitive, and environmental factors. A special concern is sexual satisfaction regardless of a person's sexual orientation.

Sexual Satisfaction

Instructions

This questionnaire is designed to measure your degree of sexual satisfaction with a partner. Answer each item as carefully and as accurately as you can. Place the number that represents your response in the space provided.

Please turn to the end of the chapter to interpret your responses.

1 = Rarely or none of the time
2 = A little of the time
3 = Some of the time
4 = A good part of the time
5 = Most of the time

_____ 1. I think that my partner enjoys our sex life.

_____ 2. My sex life is very exciting.

_____ 3. Sex is fun for my partner and me.

_____ 4. I think that my partner sees little in me except for the sex I can give.

_____ 5. I think that sex is dirty and disgusting.

_____ 6. My sex life is monotonous.

_____ 7. When we have sex, it is too rushed and hurriedly completed.

_____ 8. I think my sex life is lacking in quality.

_____ 9. My partner is sexually very exciting.

_____ 10. I enjoy the sex techniques that my partner likes or uses.

_____ 11. I think that my partner wants too much sex from me.

_____ 12. I think that sex is wonderful.

_____ 13. My partner dwells on sex too much.

_____ 14. I think that sex is something that has to be endured in our relationship.

_____ 15. My partner is too rough or brutal when we have sex.

_____ 16. My partner observes good personal hygiene.

_____ 17. I think that sex is a normal function of our relationship.

_____ 18. My partner does not want sex when I do.

_____ 19. I think that our sex life really adds a lot to our relationship.

_____ 20. I would like to have sexual contact with someone other than my partner.

_____ 21. It is easy for me to get sexually excited by my partner.

_____ 22. I think that my partner is sexually pleased with me.

_____ 23. I think that I should have sex more often.

_____ 24. I think that my sex life is boring.

Sexual Satisfaction

Too often people think of sex as a performance skill like race car driving or swimming. However, sex is best conceptualized as a form of communication within a relationship. Indeed, caring couples with good communication skills can usually survive most sexual problems, but uncaring couples with poor communication skills often do not have lasting relationships even if their sex is adequate or even good. Each of us seeks sexual satisfaction, whether we have a heterosexual, homosexual, or bisexual orientation. To learn about your own personal level of sexual satisfaction, see the Self-Assessment.

> _Sex ought to be a wholly satisfying link between two affectionate people from which they emerge unanxious, rewarded, and ready for more._
> **—Alex Comfort**

Myths about males and females would have us believe that many women are "frigid" and uninterested in sexual pleasure, while most men can hardly get enough. Both myths are challenged by the accumulated observations of sex researchers and sex therapists. Women and men have similar desires for sexual pleasure, but individuals of both sexes can experience psychological problems that interfere with their attaining pleasure. We explore these difficulties in the next section.

PSYCHOSEXUAL AND GENDER IDENTITY DISORDERS

Psychosexual disorders _are sexual problems caused mainly by psychological factors._ Some psychosexual disorders we will discuss are psychosexual dysfunctions and paraphilias. Transsexualism is a disorder of gender identity.

Psychosexual Dysfunctions

Psychosexual dysfunctions *are disorders that involve impairments in the sexual response cycle, either in the desire for gratification or in the ability to achieve it.* In disorders associated with the desire phase, individuals show little or no sexual drive or interest. For women, a common problem in the excitement phase is inhibited orgasm. Many women do not routinely experience orgasm during sex; this pattern is so common that it can hardly be called dysfunctional. Although inhibited male orgasm does occur, it is much less common. Men with excitement-phase disorders are more likely to experience difficulties in achieving or maintaining an erection. In the orgasmic phase, men may experience premature ejaculation, or rapid orgasm, when the time between the beginning of sexual stimulation and ejaculation is unsatisfactorily brief.

Some nights he said that he was tired, and some nights she said that she wanted to read, and other nights no one said anything.

—Joan Didion

The treatment of psychosexual dysfunctions has undergone nothing short of a revolution in recent years. Once thought of as an extremely difficult therapeutic challenge, most cases of psychosexual dysfunction now yield to techniques tailored to improve sexual functioning (Crooks & Bauer, 1996; LaPera & Nicastro, 1996).

Attempts to treat psychosexual dysfunctions through traditional forms of psychotherapy, as if the dysfunctions were personality disorders, have not been successful; however, new treatments that focus directly on each sexual dysfunction have reached success rates of 90 percent or more (McConaghy, 1993). For example, the success rate of a treatment that encourages women to enjoy their bodies and engage in self-stimulation to orgasm, with a vibrator if necessary, approaches 100 percent (Anderson, 1983). Many of these women subsequently transfer their newly developed sexual responsiveness to interactions with partners. Success rates also approach 100 percent in the treatment of premature ejaculation, but considerably lower success rates occur in the treatment of males who cannot maintain an erection.

Over the past two decades, sex researchers and therapists have developed a broad technology for treating sexual problems (Rosen & Leiblum, 1995; Schuetz-Mueller, Tiefer, & Melman, 1996). Since the turn of the century, sex researchers have recognized that many sexual problems are caused by psychological factors. This insight led to attempts to use psychological techniques to treat sexual dysfunctions. Most early psychological interventions resulted in only limited success. More recent work, however, has been highly successful. A major breakthrough occurred in the pioneering work of Masters and Johnson. After detailing the sexual response of human beings, and all of the physical changes that occur in sexual functioning, Masters and Johnson proposed a method of sex therapy. The techniques they suggested formed the basis for modern psychological treatments of sexual problems.

Masters and Johnson based their therapy on several principles. First, they stated that therapy should be focused on the actual problem the person is experiencing, rather than on things that might be unrelated or irrelevant to the problem. They also said that therapy should occur in the context of a sexual relationship. Whenever possible, the therapist should include the partner of the person who is having sexual difficulties in the therapy. Masters and Johnson believed that heterosexual therapy should be conducted by two therapists, a female and a male. They believed that most issues can be dealt with better when the therapists present the perspectives of both sexes and when both partners are present. Finally, they suggested that therapy be kept as brief as possible and include "homework" for couples to try corrective measures on their own and report back to the therapists about their progress.

Following the lead of Masters and Johnson, psychiatrist Helen Kaplan (1974) proposed "the new sex therapy." While accepting and building on Masters and Johnson's work, Kaplan focused even more on relationship issues that might be related to sexual difficulties. She also emphasized the importance of an individual's sexual desires, pointing out that often sexual difficulties are directly related to inhibitions in sexual desires.

Keep in mind that sex therapy is a very specialized field. Not all professional helpers can legitimately call themselves sex therapists. To be qualified as a competent sex therapist, a mental health professional should receive very specific training. Unlike general counseling or psychotherapy, sex therapy is a specialization. This training usually occurs in very specific workshops, professional training seminars, or postgraduate training.

How can you tell if a sex therapist is qualified to be conducting sex therapy? One way is to find out whether she or he has been certified as a sex therapist. The American Association of Sex Educators, Counselors, and Therapists (AASECT) certifies sex therapists to ensure that the professional has received very specific training, has been supervised by qualified professionals, and has satisfied rather strict criteria. These are minimum standards for professionals to be qualified to practice sex therapy. Given the great deal of success seen with today's sex therapy techniques and the availability of qualified sex therapists, people who suffer from sexual difficulties should be encouraged to seek help.

Paraphilias

Paraphilias *are psychosexual disorders in which the source of an individual's sexual satisfaction is an unusual object, ritual, or situation.* Many sexual patterns deviate from what we consider to be "normal." These abnormal patterns of sexual arousal from unusual sources include fetishism, transvestism, exhibitionism, voyeurism, sadism, masochism, and pedophilia.

Fetishism *is a psychosexual disorder in which an individual relies on inanimate objects or a specific body part for sexual gratification.* Even though an individual might have a similar preference—for example, a man's preference for women with long legs or a woman's preference for men with beards, most of us are attracted to another person because of a wide range of personal factors. Some fetishists become obsessed with certain objects—fur, women's underpants, stockings—that arouse them. The objects take on greater importance than the arousing qualities of any one partner. Most fetishists are male.

Transvestism *is a psychosexual disorder in which an individual obtains sexual gratification by dressing up as a member of the opposite sex.* Most transvestites view themselves as heterosexual and lead quiet, conventional lives, cross-dressing only in the privacy of their homes. One pattern of transvestites is to cross-dress only during sexual relations with their partners.

Exhibitionism and voyeurism are the two sex practices that most often come to the attention of the police. **Exhibitionism** *is a psychosexual disorder in which individuals expose their sexual anatomy to others to obtain sexual gratification.* **Voyeurism** *is a psychosexual disorder in which individuals derive sexual gratification from observing the sex organs or sex acts of others, often from a secret vantage point.* Both exhibitionism and voyeurism provide substitute gratification and a sense of power to otherwise sexually anxious individuals, especially males. In many instances, voyeurs are sexually inhibited.

Sadism *is a psychosexual disorder in which individuals derive sexual gratification from inflicting pain on others.* The word *sadism* comes from the novels of the Marquis de Sade (1740–1814), who wrote about erotic scenes in which women were whipped. **Masochism** *is a psychosexual disorder in which individuals derive sexual gratification from being subjected to physical pain, inflicted by others or themselves.* The word *masochism* comes from the novels of Austrian writer Leopold von Sacher-Masoch (1836–1895), whose male characters became sexually excited and gratified when they were physically abused by women. It is not unusual for a sadist and a masochist to pair up to satisfy each other's sexual wishes; such relationships are called sadomasochistic. However, it is rare for a sadist and masochist to match each other's needs and have a stable and lasting relationship.

Pedophilia *is a psychosexual disorder in which the sex object is a child and the intimacy involves manipulation of the child's genitals.* A pedophile covertly or overtly masturbates while talking to children, manipulates the child's sex organs, or engages the child in sexual behavior. Most pedophiles are men, usually in their thirties or forties. Like exhibitionists, pedophiles often have puritanical ideas about sex and see sex with children as being purer, safer, or less embarrassing. Often the target of a male pedophile is a child he knows, such as a child of a relative, neighbor, or family friend.

Gender Identity Disorder

Transsexualism *is a disorder of gender identity in which an individual has an overwhelming desire to become a member of the opposite sex.* The individual's gender identity is at odds with his or her genetic makeup and anatomical features. A transsexual might eventually decide to undergo surgery to change sex. Transsexuals often say that, as far back as they can remember, they have felt uncomfortable

(*Left*) Dr. Richard Raskin is shown playing tennis before he underwent a transsexual operation that transformed him into a woman. (*Right*) Raskin changed his name to Renée Richards following the transsexual operation. Richards caused quite a stir by entering women's professional tennis tournaments. After considerable controversy, Richards was allowed to play on the women's professional tennis tour.

REVIEW

Psychosexual Disorders

Psychosexual dysfunctions involve impairments in the sexual response cycle, either in the desire for sexual gratification or in the ability to achieve it. Significant advances in the treatment of psychosexual dysfunctions have been made in recent years. Paraphilias are psychosexual disorders in which the source of an individual's sexual satisfaction is an unusual object, ritual, or situation. Many sexual patterns deviate from what we consider to be normal. These abnormal patterns of sexual arousal from unusual sources include fetishism, transvestism, exhibitionism, voyeurism, sadism, masochism, and pedophilia. Gender identity disorder or transsexualism is a psychosexual disorder in which the person's gender identity is discordant with his or her anatomical sex and genetic makeup.

---

in their own bodies. They believe that they were born in a body of the wrong sex. Psychologists are uncertain why people are transsexual.

Can transsexuals lead full sex lives? In the female-to-male transsexual transformation, the surgically constructed male sex organs are cosmetic and the clitoris retains its orgasmic sensations; male sex hormones are given to intensify orgasm. Male-to-female transsexuals describe their sexual sensations as diffuse and intense. They report that they enjoy functioning as females, especially in terms of physical closeness, skin responsiveness, and breast sensations.

Next we will explore other behaviors related to sex that have been clearly linked to causing harm, including sexual harassment, sexual assault, incest, pornography, and sexually transmitted diseases.

SEXUALITY AND HARM

Sexuality can be a context in which the participants are harmed. From the psychological harm that results from sexual harassment through the physical and emotional harm that results from rape and incest, we will examine some harsh realities associated with sex. We will also explore the effects of pornography on sexual behavior. We will conclude this chapter with a discussion of the harms engendered by sexually transmitted diseases.

Sexual Harassment

Women encounter sexual harassment in many different forms—from sexist remarks and covert physical contact (patting, brushing against their bodies) to blatant propositions and sexual assaults (Paludi, 1995). Literally millions of women experience such sexual harassment each year in work and educational settings.

Sexual harassment, a manifestation of power and domination of one person over another, can result in serious psychological consequences for the victim (Koss, 1993). The elimination of such exploitation requires the development of work and academic environments that are compatible with the needs of women workers and students, providing them with equal opportunities to develop a career and obtain an education in a climate free of sexual harassment. In addition, social intolerance of sexual harassment will help decrease this pervasive problem.

Forcible Sexual Behavior

Most people choose to engage in sexual intercourse or other sexual activities, but, unfortunately, some people force others to engage in sex. **Rape** *is forcible sex with a person who does not give consent.* Legal definitions of rape differ from state to state. For example, in some states husbands are not prohibited from forcing their wives to have intercourse, because the wife is considered the husband's property. States that still have this antiquated law are being challenged in the courts.

It is difficult to determine the actual incidence of rape because many rape victims do not tell anyone that they have been raped and because disagreement exists about what behaviors and circumstances constitute rape. Rape is more common in large cities. However, rape does exist in every type of community across the nation. Nearly 200,000 rapes are reported annually in the United States. Experts believe the actual number of rapes might be as high as ten times this number.

Why is rape so pervasive in the American culture? Feminist writers believe males are socialized to be sexually aggressive, to regard women as inferior beings, and to view their own pleasure as the most important goal. Rapists share some common characteristics: Rapists use aggression to enhance their sense of power or masculinity; rapists are generally angry at women; and rapists almost always want to hurt their victims (Brown & Williams, 1993).

A recently acknowledged significant problem is **date or acquaintance rape,** *which is coercive sex forced by someone with whom the victim is at least casually acquainted.* Date rape is an increasing problem on college campuses. Almost two-thirds of college men admit that they fondle women against their will, and one-half admit to having forced sexual activity. Men who coerce women into sexual activity tend to endorse a wide range of cultural myths about rape, such as that women want to be raped and that men are unable to control their sexual behavior.

Rape is a traumatic experience for the victim and those close to her. The rape victim initially feels shock and numbness and often is acutely disorganized. Many choose not to report rape because they fear criticism, stigma, and shame. Some women show their distress through words and tears, others show more internalized suffering. As victims strive to get their lives back to normal, they may experience depression, fear, and anxiety for months or years. Sexual dysfunctions, such as reduced sexual desire and the inability to reach orgasm, occur in 50 percent of rape victims (Sprei & Courtois, 1988). Many rape victims make changes in their lifestyle, such as moving to a new apartment or refusing to go out at night. About one-fifth of rape victims have attempted suicide; this rate is eight times higher than that of women who have not been raped.

A woman's recovery after a rape depends on both her coping abilities and her psychological adjustment prior to the assault. Social support from parents, partner, and others close to her are important factors in recovery, as is the availability of professional counseling, which sometimes is obtained through a rape crisis center (Koss, 1993). Many rape victims become empowered by reporting the rape to the police and assisting in the prosecution of the rapist if he is caught. Women who prosecute rapists should be sure they have the aid of supportive counselors throughout the legal ordeal. Because prosecution can magnify feelings of victimization, each woman must be allowed to make her own, individual decision about whether to report the rape or not. To examine the multiple factors contributing to rape, see Critical Thinking.

Although most victims of rape are women, male rape does occur. A review of the victims treated at a sexual assault treatment center found that 6 percent were men (Lipscomb & others, 1992). Of those, 20 percent were assaults in the community and 80 percent were assaults in prison. Men in prisons are

CRITICAL THINKING

*Understanding Rape as a
Complex Phenomenon*

Historically, rape used to be considered a crime of passion. More recently, scholars have established that rape is multidimensional: There are likely to be many factors contributing to rape. How many different factors (variables) can you identify that might contribute to the occurrence of rape? Examine your list of variables: How much responsibility have you placed on the rapist? How much responsibility have you attributed to the victim? How much blame have you placed on societal conditions?

Your reflections on factors that contribute to rape are an example of *pursuing alternative explanations to understand behavior comprehensively.*

Feminists organized campaigns against pornography in the late 1970s. When sexual content is combined with violence, increased male aggression toward females may occur. However, there is no evidence that sexual content without violence stimulates aggression against women.

especially vulnerable to rape, usually by heterosexuals who are using rape to establish their domination and power within the prison. Though it might seem impossible for a man to be raped

by a woman, a man's erection is not completely under his voluntary control; some cases of male rape by women have been reported (Sarrel & Masters, 1982). Although male victims account for

fewer than 5 percent of all rapes, the trauma that males suffer is just as great as that experienced by females.

Incest

Incest *is sex between people who are close relatives; it is virtually universally taboo.* By far the most common form of incest in the United States is brother-sister incest; father-daughter incest is the second most common. Mother-son incest and same-sex incest (usually father-son) are not as common incestuous patterns. Incest is psychologically harmful, not only for immediate family relationships, but also for the future relationships of a child involved in incest. Another misfortune associated with incest is that any resulting offspring have higher than average risks for genetic disorders and mental retardation.

Taboos against incest have developed in virtually all human societies, although a few exceptions have been noted, such as the Incan society and the societies of ancient Iran and ancient Egypt (Murdock, 1949). Possibly the taboos arose because of the harmful physical, psychological, and social effects that incest carries with it.

Pornography and Violence Against Women

Contemporary campaigns against pornography began in the late 1970s. Initial feminist arguments against pornography were of two main sorts: (1) Pornography demeans women (for instance, by depicting them as sex slaves in male fantasies); and (2) much of pornography glorifies violence against women, perpetuating the cultural myth that women who say no to sex really want to be overpowered and raped.

Sex researchers have found that the visual cues in erotic films and pictures influence sexual behavior, but only for a brief period of time. Both men and women show increased sexual activity within 24 hour of exposure to sexually explicit material. Viewing sexual violence and reading sexually violent material increase male acceptance of sexual and other forms of aggression against females. However, sex researcher Edward Donnerstein (1987) argues that it is the violence against women, not the erotic material, that causes negative attitudes toward women.

In one study, Donnerstein (1980) studied college males in a three-part experiment. First the subjects were either provoked or treated neutrally by a male or female accomplice of the experimenter. Next they were shown one of three types of films—neutral, erotic, or aggressive-erotic depicting rape. Third, the subjects were led to believe that they could administer a shock to the accomplice of any intensity they chose. Men who had been provoked by the accomplice and had seen the aggressive-erotic film showed the highest levels of aggression (chose the highest intensity of shock to administer to the accomplice). Other studies by Donnerstein and his colleagues also pinpoint aggression and violence, rather than erotic content, as a contributor to males' aggressive attitudes toward women.

Rapists themselves report less exposure to erotic magazines and movies during their adolescent years than do those who are not sex offenders. Indeed, when Denmark ended its censorship of pornographic materials in the 1960s, sex-related crimes there decreased. In short, it appears that sexual content combined with violence can increase male aggression against females (Malamuth & Donnerstein, 1983), but there is no evidence that sexual content that is not paired with violence stimulates aggression against women.

Erotica is about sexuality, but pornography is about power and sex-as-weapon.

—**Gloria Steinem**

AIDS

A **sexually transmitted disease (STD)** *is a disease that is contracted primarily through sexual intercourse as well as oral-genital and anal-genital sex.* No single STD has had a greater impact on sexual behavior, or created more public fear in the last decade, than AIDS. **AIDS** *is a sexually transmitted disease that is caused by the human immunodeficiency virus (HIV), which destroys the body's immune system.*

The danger of contracting HIV highlights the role our individual choices make in the length and quality of our lives. Daily we make decisions that can affect our health immediately, soon, or even years from now. Still, it becomes hard to deal with the reality of the dangers. Most young people, for example, continue to believe that AIDS is "someone else's disease" and feel secure that their partners are "clean." In reality, 1 college student in 500 tests positive for HIV; 1 in 300 Job Corps participants tests positive. In spite of the growing number of cases among teenagers and young adults, many individuals still have unprotected sex. Only about one-half of all adolescents use condoms during their first intercourse (Kantrowitz & others, 1992). Eighteen-year-old Kaye Brown has HIV, and she blames herself for not insisting on condoms. She says, "It makes me angry that I allowed this to happen. Choices I made have stolen away the choices that I might have had in the future." To explore personal responsibility with regard to STDs further, see Critical Thinking.

The Impact of AIDS

A person who is infected with HIV is vulnerable to germs that a normal immune system could destroy. In 1981, when AIDS was formally recognized in the United States, there were fewer than 60 reported cases. Beginning in 1990, we started losing as many Americans each year to AIDS as the total number of Americans killed in the Vietnam War—

CRITICAL THINKING

Privacy Versus Protection

Caroline contracted genital herpes from her boyfriend, whom she had been dating for the past 3 years. After breaking off that relationship and spending some time on her own, Caroline began dating Charles. Before becoming sexually involved with him, Caroline told Charles about her herpes infection, thinking that it was the right thing to do. Charles seemed accepting of the news, but soon after the discussion he began treating Caroline differently. He became distant and cold toward her, and eventually broke off their relationship saying that it "just wasn't working." Caroline firmly believed it was because she had told him about the herpes.

Caroline later met Jeff, whom she really liked and wanted to start dating. As they became closer to developing a sexual relationship, Caroline felt that she should tell Jeff about the herpes, but she was afraid that he also would abandon her.

She thought that if she arranged it so that they never had sexual contact when she had herpes blisters (the time when infecting someone else is most likely to occur), she could protect him. She also thought that if they used latex condoms for protection, he would be safe, even though condoms can break.

Would Caroline's not telling Jeff be acceptable to you, even if she acted to protect him? If Jeff should know, in what ways would it be best to tell him? If Caroline did tell Jeff, and he did end their relationship, would telling him have been a mistake? Does Jeff have a right to know? Does Caroline have a right to privacy? Your consideration of these questions encourages you to *identify the values that influence behavior* and to *practice ethics and civility toward sexual partners* in an age when sexuality is becoming increasingly more complex.

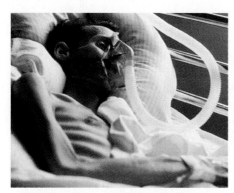

The AIDS virus destroys the body's immune system. The individual with AIDS shown here is one of more than 60,000 Americans who die every year from AIDS.

almost 60,000. According to federal health officials, from 1 to 1.5 million Americans are now asymptomatic carriers of AIDS—they are infected with the virus and capable of infecting others, but they show no clinical symptoms of AIDS. The primary way people are becoming infected with HIV today is through sexual contact and injecting drugs. To evaluate your own knowledge of AIDS, turn to the Self-Assessment.

In the United States the incidence of AIDS is especially high among Latinos and African Americans (Brunswick & Banaszak-Holl, 1996). Latino men are three times more likely than non-Latino White men to be infected with HIV. Much of the AIDS prevention literature, as well as the instructions included with condoms, requires a high school reading proficiency. About 40 percent of adult Latinos lack this proficiency.

In 1989 researchers made the first attempt to assess the rate of AIDS infection in American college students. Tests of 16,861 students found 30 infected with the virus (American College Health Association, 1989). If the 12.5 million students attending college that year were infected in the same proportion, 25,000 students had the AIDS virus.

Transmission

Experts say that AIDS can be transmitted only by sexual contact, the sharing of needles, contaminated blood transfusions (which intensified testing in the last few years has made very unlikely), or other contact with an infected person's blood, semen, or vaginal fluids through cuts in the skin or mucous membranes (Jones, 1996; Kalichman, 1996). Although it continues to be the case that 90 percent of AIDS cases in the United States occur among homosexual males and intravenous drug users, researchers have reported a disproportionate increase among females who are heterosexual partners of bisexual males or intravenous drug users (Squire, 1993). This increase suggests that in the United States the risk of AIDS might be increasing among heterosexuals who have multiple sex partners.

Recently in the United States, many people thought that gay men were the only people who needed to be concerned about HIV and AIDS. This could not be further from the truth. Although in the United States gay men were hit hardest early in the AIDS epidemic, there are no boundaries to AIDS. People of all sexual orientations, ethnic backgrounds, incomes, and geographical locations can be at risk for HIV infection. The things a person *does* are what puts people at risk. The general public came to realize this most vividly when basketball star Earvin "Magic" Johnson announced that he was infected with HIV. Magic Johnson's message was that anyone could get HIV if they engaged in behaviors that put them at risk, such as having sex without using a condom. Although condoms can break and are effective only when used properly, they do substantially decrease the chances of HIV infection. Condoms offer the best protection against the virus during sexual intercourse.

Although the greatest risk for HIV infection comes from sexual behaviors, not all sexual behavior is risky with regard to HIV infection. Some sexual behaviors are high-risk, while others are lower in risk, and still other sexual behaviors have absolutely no risk of infection at all. Those that are highest in risk are those that allow for the exchange of blood (even if in microscopic amounts), semen (the fluid men release that carries sperm), and vaginal fluids. These body fluids can contain HIV and cause infection. Thus, using a condom during sexual intercourse decreases the chance of infection because it prevents the fluids from entering sexual partners' bodies. Also, behaviors like hugging, and caressing, which do not allow for the exchange of body fluids, do not pose any risk for HIV infection. Today, scientists also state that kissing is safe with respect to HIV, as there is no evidence that people can get infected from kissing.

Just asking a date about his or her sexual behavior does not guarantee protection from AIDS and other sexually transmitted diseases. For example, in one investigation, 655 college students were asked to answer questions about lying and sexual behavior (Cochran & Mays, 1990). Of the 422 respondents who said they were sexually active, 34 percent of the men and 10 percent of the women said they had lied so their partner would have sex with them. Much higher percentages—47 percent of the men and 60 percent of the women—said they had been lied to by a potential sexual partner. When asked what aspects of their past they would be most likely to lie about, more than 40 percent of the men and women said they would understate the number of their sexual partners. Twenty percent of the men, but only 4 percent of the women, said they would lie about their results from an AIDS blood test.

Disease Course

Having discussed AIDS transmission, let's now examine the course of AIDS. In the first stage of the disease, referred to as being HIV-positive (HIV+) and asymptomatic, infected individuals do not show the symptoms of AIDS but can transmit the disease to others. Researchers estimate that 20 to 30 percent of those in stage 1 will develop AIDS within 5 years. In stage 2—HIV+ and symptomatic—the infected individual develops symptoms, including swelling of the lymph glands, fatigue, weight loss, diarrhea, fever, and sweats. Many who are HIV+ and symptomatic continue to the final stage—AIDS. With AIDS, a person has the symptoms just mentioned plus at least one disease, such as pneumonia, which is fatal to AIDS patients because of their vulnerable immune systems.

Although there is no known cure for AIDS, scientists continue to work on interventions that alleviate symptoms and lengthen life. According to Project Inform (1996), a nonprofit group devoted to AIDS education, AZT (zidovudine) is the most widely prescribed medication; it appears to reduce the

Knowledge of AIDS Risk Behavior

Instructions

This is a true/false test. Please do not skip any questions. Some of the statements are true and accurate; others are false and inaccurate.

Please turn to the end of the chapter to score and interpret your responses.

Items

1. Most people who transmit the AIDS virus look unhealthy.
2. Anal intercourse is high risk for transmitting the AIDS virus.
3. Oral intercourse carries risk for AIDS virus transmission.
4. A person can be exposed to the AIDS virus in one sexual contact.
5. Keeping in good physical condition is the best way to prevent exposure to the AIDS virus.
6. It is unwise to touch a person with AIDS.
7. Condoms make intercourse completely safe.
8. Showering after sex greatly reduces the transmission of AIDS.
9. When people become sexually exclusive with one another, they no longer need to follow "safe sex" guidelines.
10. Oral sex is safe if the partners "don't swallow."
11. Most people who have been exposed to the AIDS virus quickly show symptoms of serious illness.
12. By reducing the number of different sexual partners, you are effectively protected from AIDS.
13. The AIDS virus does not penetrate unbroken skin.
14. Female-to-male transmission of the AIDS virus has not been documented.
15. Sharing toothbrushes and razors can transmit the AIDS virus.
16. Pre-ejaculatory fluids carry the AIDS virus.
17. Intravenous drug users are at risk for AIDS when they share needles.
18. A person must have many different sexual partners to be at risk from AIDS.
19. People carrying the AIDS virus generally feel quite ill.
20. Vaginal intercourse carries high risk for AIDS virus transmission.
21. Withdrawal immediately before orgasm makes intercourse safe.
22. Persons who are exclusively heterosexual are not at risk from AIDS.
23. Healthy persons in AIDS risk groups should not donate blood.
24. Sharing kitchen utensils or a bathroom with a person with AIDS poses no risk.
25. Intravenous drug users become exposed to the AIDS virus because the virus is often contained in heroin, amphetamines, and the injected drugs.
26. A wholesome diet and plenty of sleep will keep a person from becoming exposed to the AIDS virus.
27. A cure of AIDS is expected within the next two years.
28. It is more important to take precautions against AIDS in large cities than in small cities.
29. A negative result on the AIDS virus antibody test can occur even for people who carry the virus.
30. A positive result on the AIDS virus antibody test can occur even for people who do not carry the virus.
31. Coughing does not spread AIDS.
32. Only receptive (passive) anal intercourse transmits AIDS.
33. Most present cases of AIDS are due to blood transfusions that took place before 1984.
34. Most persons exposed to the AIDS virus know they are exposed.
35. A great deal is now known about how the AIDS virus is transmitted.
36. Donating blood carries no AIDS risk for the donor.
37. No cases of AIDS have ever been linked to social (dry) kissing.
38. Mutual masturbation and body rubbing are low in risk unless the partners have cuts or scratches.
39. People who become exposed to the AIDS virus through needle-sharing can transmit the virus to others during sexual activities.
40. The AIDS virus can be transmitted by mosquitoes or cockroaches.

frequency and severity of opportunistic diseases associated with AIDS and might prolong life by as much as 6 to 21 months. However, resistance to the drug and potential side effects, including liver damage, have prompted physicians to use AZT in combination with other antiviral medications, such as DDI (didanosine) and DDC (zabcitabine). Another area of promise includes the use of growth hormone to address the physical wasting away AIDS causes, although the expense of this procedure might preclude widespread use.

Other Sexually Transmitted Diseases

You might be less familiar with the term *STD* than with the term *venereal disease,* or *VD,* an older term that has been increasingly replaced with the term *STD.* STDs are an increasing health problem in the United States, especially for individuals in their late teens and early twenties (Leukefeld & Haverkos, 1993). For example, in 1988, 720,000 new cases of gonorrhea were reported by the National Center for Health Statistics. At greatest risk are 20- to 24-year-olds (32 percent of cases, compared with their being 8 percent of the population). Those who are 15 to 19 years old have the second highest level of risk (27 percent of reported cases, for 7 percent of the population). We hope the information presented in this section will encourage you to protect yourself and your sexual partner(s) from these highly contagious sexually transmitted diseases. We begin with three STDs caused by bacterial infections—gonorrhea, syphilis, and chlamydia. Each of these STDs is a serious disease, but, fortunately, detected cases can be successfully treated. Then we will discuss an STD that is caused by a virus—genital herpes, which is not curable.

Except for the few years between the invention of the Pill and the discovery of herpes, sex has always been dangerous.
　　　　　　　　　—*Vogue* **magazine**

Gonorrhea

Gonorrhea, *a sexually transmitted disease that is commonly called the "drip" or the* "clap," *is a common STD in the United States.* It is caused by a bacterium from the gonococcus family, which thrives in the moist mucous membranes lining the mouth, throat, vagina, cervix, urethra, and anal tract. The bacterium is spread by contact between the infected moist membranes of one individual and the membranes of another. Thus, virtually all forms of sexual contact can spread the gonococcus, although transfer does not necessarily occur with every contact. Males have a 10 percent chance of becoming infected with each exposure to gonococcus. Females have more than a 40 percent chance of infection with each exposure, because of the large surface area of the vaginal mucous membrane.

Symptoms of gonorrhea appear in males within 3 days to a month after contact. The symptoms include a discharge from the penis, burning during urination, blood in the urine, aching pain or pressure in the genitals, and swollen and tender lymph glands in the groin. Unfortunately, 80 percent of infected females show no symptoms in the early stages of the disease, although pelvic inflammation is common at this early point. Untreated, the disease causes infection in the reproductive area and the pelvic region within 2 months. Scarring of the fallopian tubes and infertility can result. Gonorrhea can be successfully treated in its early stages with penicillin or other antibiotics. Despite reporting laws, many gonorrhea cases go unreported. The incidence of reported gonorrhea cases in 1990 was 690,000, down from 1 million in 1975 but still well above the number of reported cases in other industrialized countries (Billy & others, 1993).

Syphilis

Syphilis *is a sexually transmitted disease caused by the bacterium* Treponema pallidum, *a member of the spirochete family.* The spirochete needs a warm, moist environment to survive. It is transmitted by penile-vaginal, oral-genital, or anal contact. Syphilis can also be transmitted from a pregnant woman to her fetus after the fourth month of pregnancy. If the mother is treated before this time with penicillin, the syphilis will not be transmitted to the fetus.

Syphilis occurs in four stages: primary, secondary, latent, and tertiary. In the primary stage, a sore, or chancre, appears at the site of the infection. The sore heals after 4 to 6 weeks, giving the impression that the problem has gone away, but, untreated, it moves into the secondary stage. A number of symptoms occur at this stage, including a rash, fever, sore throat, headache, swollen glands, joint pain, poor appetite, and hair loss. Treatment with penicillin can be successful if begun at this stage or earlier.

Without treatment, symptoms of the secondary stage go away after 6 weeks, and the disease enters a latent stage. The spirochetes spread throughout the body, and, in 50 to 70 percent of those affected, remain there for years in the same stage. After the first 2 years, the disease can no longer be transmitted through sexual contact, but it can still be passed from a pregnant woman to her fetus. For 30 to 50 percent of those who reach the latent stage, a final, tertiary stage follows. In this advanced stage, syphilis can cause paralysis, insanity, and death. In 1988, the Public Health Service received 103,000 reports of syphilis, and in many areas of the United States syphilis is on the rise.

Chlamydia

Chlamydia, *the most common of all sexually transmitted diseases, is named for* Chlamydia trachomatis, *an organism that spreads by sexual contact and infects the genital organs of both males and females.* Although fewer individuals have heard of chlamydia than of gonorrhea and syphilis, its incidence is much higher. About 4 million Americans are infected with chlamydia each year. In fact, about 10 percent of all college students have chlamydia. This STD is highly infectious; women run a 70 percent risk of contracting it in a single sexual encounter, and the male risk is estimated as being between 25 and 50 percent.

The main symptoms of chlamydia are a thin, usually clear genital discharge and mild discomfort while urinating. The symptoms are somewhat similar to those of gonorrhea in the male, but gonorrhea produces more-painful urination and a more profuse, puslike discharge. Chlamydia is treated with tetracycline or erythromycin; it does not respond to penicillin. Poorly treated or undiagnosed cases can lead to a number of complications, such as urethral damage in females and males and pelvic inflammatory disease in females (Hyde, 1994).

Genital Herpes

Genital herpes *is a sexually transmitted disease in which the symptoms are small, painful bumps or blisters on the genitals.* These sores are caused by the herpes simplex virus type 2 in about 85 percent of the cases; the rest are caused by the type 1 virus. Type 1 is usually characterized by cold sores and fever blisters in nongenital parts of the body. Genital herpes is transmitted by sexual intercourse, and type 1 can be transmitted to the genitals during oral-genital sex.

Three to 5 days after sexual contact, itching and tingling can occur, followed by an eruption of sores and blisters—on the vaginal lips (labia) in women and on the penis in men. The blisters heal on their own in about 3 weeks in the first episode of infection. The virus continues to live in the body, sometimes remaining dormant for the rest of the person's life. However, the symptoms can recur unpredictably so that the person repeatedly experiences 7- to 14-day periods of sores. On the average, individuals with herpes have four recurrences per year. They are most infectious when they are having an active outbreak, although it is not clear that there is any entirely safe period (Hyde, 1994). The disease also can be transmitted from a pregnant woman to her fetus, which can lead to brain damage or even death for the infant. A cesarean section can prevent infection, because infection occurs as the baby moves through the birth canal. Women with herpes are eight times more likely to develop cervical cancer than are uninfected women.

With an estimated 600,000 new cases of herpes per year in the United States, genital herpes approaches gonorrhea and chlamydia in frequency. These figures don't count recurrent cases, which may number 5 to 10 million. In one study, 16 percent of individuals in the United States between the ages of 15 and 74 reported that they were infected with genital herpes (Johnson & others, 1989).

There is no known cure for genital herpes. Researchers are pursuing two solutions—drugs that would cure symptoms in a person who is already infected, and vaccinations that would prevent contracting herpes. The drug acyclovir can prevent or reduce recurring symptoms, but it does not cure the disease.

Reducing Risk Through Improved Communication

Because it is possible, and even probable among high-risk groups, to have more than one STD at a time, efforts to prevent one disease help reduce the prevalence of other diseases (Tafoya, 1993). Given the high rate of sexually transmitted diseases, it's crucial that both teenagers and adults understand these diseases and act in accordance with standards of safety. It is also crucial to be able to communicate effectively about sexually transmitted diseases.

Sensitive issues arise in relationships when sharing information in an open, honest way can have a negative effect on the relationship (Perlmutter-Bowen & Michal-Johnson, 1996). People often must decide how best to be honest and how to share information. Raising the topic of condoms can imply to your partner that you have an "undesirable past" or that you do not trust your partner. On the other hand, starting a discussion about using condoms can be taken as showing concern for your partner's

health and well-being, as well as respect and care for yourself. How can people discuss the use of condoms, as well as other sensitive issues revolving around disease prevention and contraception?

One way to think about these issues is to consider the *way* things are said rather than *what* is said. Too often people approach such topics with great hesitation because they are worried about what the other person will think of them. Their own uncomfortableness is conveyed even before the conversation starts. So, the place to start might be to evaluate your own feelings and beliefs before even considering how to approach another person. Once you are clear on your own values and views, then you can plan how to best initiate the conversation. Where and how such a discussion occurs may be most important. Carefully consider privacy and comfort. Also, the mood should be right. For example, would it be wise to begin discussing the use of condoms or one's sexual past in the middle of an argument, or after watching a comedy act? The mood of this conversation should be serious, though it could also be somewhat light.

How best to start such a sensitive discussion depends on many aspects of yourself, your partner, and your relationship. At the heart of any such discussion is usually a concern over your own welfare, the health of your partner, and doing what is best for your relationship. Perhaps it would be best to express these feelings at the start. In addition, as is true in many situations that require you to be assertive, it is best to express your own needs and to acknowledge the other person's feelings. Through such mutual concern, it is likely that you and your partner can find ways to protect each other and liberate yourselves from the fears and worries you would suffer if you stayed in silence and doubt.

Halonen/Santrock: Human Adjustment

Sexuality and Harm

Unfortunately, some individuals force others to engage in a sexual activity. Rape is forcible sex with a person who does not give consent. Legal definitions of rape sometimes vary from state to state. An increasing concern is date or acquaintance rape. Rape is a traumatic experience, and a woman's recovery depends on her coping resources as well as how well she was adjusted psychologically prior to the assault. Male rape constitutes about 5 percent of all rape cases. Sexual harassment is an expression of one person's power over another. Incest is sex between two close relatives, which is virtually universally taboo. The most common form is brother-sister, followed by father-daughter. Incest can cause extensive psychological harm to children.

Feminists and others organized the first campaigns against pornography in the late 1970s. When sexual content is combined with violence, increased male aggression toward females may occur. However, there is no evidence that sexual content without violence stimulates aggression against women.

Sexually transmitted diseases (STDs) are contracted primarily through sexual contact. AIDS is caused by a virus, HIV (human immunodeficiency virus), that destroys the body's immune system. AIDS can be transmitted only through sexual contact, the sharing of needles, blood transfusions, or other contact with an infected person's blood, semen, or vaginal fluids through cuts in the skin or mucous membranes. There is no known cure for AIDS.

Gonorrhea, commonly called the "drip" or the "clap," is one of the most common STDs in the United States. Gonorrhea is caused by a tiny gonococcus bacterium. It can be treated with penicillin and other antibiotics. Syphilis is caused by the bacterium *Treponema pallidum,* also called a spirochete. Syphilis occurs in four phases—primary, secondary, latent, and tertiary. If detected in the first two phases, it can be successfully treated with penicillin. Chlamydia is the most common of all sexually transmitted diseases. Herpes is caused by a family of viruses with different strains. Herpes simplex has two variations. Type 1 is characterized by cold sores and fever blisters. Type 2 includes sores on the lower body—genitals, thighs, and buttocks. There is no known cure for herpes.

One of the most important skills of good critical thinkers in psychology is *being able to evaluate how truthful claims are.* Because misinformation about sex is so widespread, it is especially important to adopt a skeptical attitude about many claims about sex until evidence confirms or disconfirms them.

Here is a sample of the myths that some psychology students have claimed to believe until they encountered disconfirming evidence:

- You can get pregnant most easily if you make love in water.
- If women don't achieve an orgasm during sex, then they won't get pregnant.
- A woman can prevent pregnancy by jumping up and down after sex.
- You can't get pregnant the first time you have intercourse.
- Women can't achieve orgasm without direct stimulation of the G spot.
- The size of a man's penis determines how satisfying sex will be.
- The size of a man's penis corresponds to the size of his nose (foot, thumb).
- Simultaneous orgasm is the only acceptable form of satisfaction.
- Breast-feeding prevents pregnancy.
- If men can't ejaculate after a certain threshold of stimulation has been reached, they'll become sick.

Some of these myths are abandoned after experience provides (sometimes painful) disconfirmation. How can adolescents and adults learn to navigate the precarious waters of sexuality with a minimum of misinformation to make informed choices about their behavior? The following specific strategies can help protect you.

1. *Regard cause-and-effect claims about sexuality with suspicion.* Nature encourages behavior that will help living organisms reproduce. Pregnancy requires contact of an egg and a sperm. Measures that don't directly prevent that contact are not likely to be effective against pregnancy.

2. *Remember your own mortality.* It is relatively easy, especially in moments of passion, to abandon good judgment about self-protection. In such moments we tend to think of ourselves as immune to the laws of nature ("It won't happen to me"; "Just this once and never again"). Many carefree lovers end up very care-ridden by the biological consequences of impulsive unprotected sex.

3. *Evaluate the risk if the claim appears to be untrue.* Taking risks is part of life. However, sexual risk-taking in the absence of knowledge can result in dramatic life-changing outcomes. Where the risk is too great, restraint is the wiser course.

4. *Assess whether the source of the claims is trustworthy and astute.* Sometimes people promote myths as a strategy for getting a sexual relationship. Claims made by a person in the hopes of achieving intimacy could be manipulative; you need to establish whether you can trust a person you are considering becoming intimate with. People also sometimes pass along misguided sexual lore, with an intention not to take advantage but only to inform—but end up only misinforming. You need to establish whether the person you are discussing sexual lore with is likely to be well informed.

5. *Ask for evidence to support claims about risks.* Always require evidence in support of any claim about a cause-and-effect relationship in behavior. This is imperative regarding claims that are relevant to the risks you might be taking by engaging in sexual activity. Questions to keep in mind include the following: *How did you learn about that? How much confidence do you have in the claim? What if you are wrong?*

Remembering the specific aspects of practicing sexual skepticism can help you make more responsible and reasonable sexual choices in an increasingly challenging world. Developing a skeptical attitude can assist you in *evaluating the validity of claims about behavior.*

Our coverage of human sexuality began with consideration of sexual arousal and the human sexual response cycle. Then we evaluated sexual knowledge, attitudes, and behavior—focusing on heterosexuality and homosexuality. Next we studied psychosexual disorders, including sexual dysfunctions, paraphilias, and gender identity disorder. We concluded the chapter by exploring sexuality and harm—sexual harassment, forcible sexual behavior, incest, pornography and violence against women, AIDS, and other sexually transmitted diseases. Don't forget that you can obtain an overall summary of the chapter by again reading the in-chapter reviews on pages 200, 208, 211, and 219.

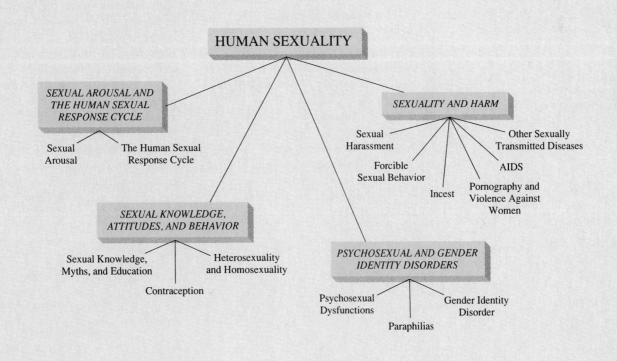

PRACTICAL KNOWLEDGE ABOUT ADJUSTMENT

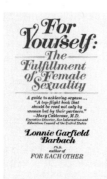

FOR YOURSELF
(1975) by Lonnie Barbach.
New York: Signet.

For Yourself provides advice for women about how to achieve sexual fulfillment. Barbach addresses the worries that often distress nonorgasmic women and tells them how to achieve orgasm. Barbach attacks the negative cultural attitudes that say women should not enjoy sex. Several exercises that will enable women to achieve orgasm are presented—each exercise that is given is accompanied by an explanation of why it can be effective and potential pitfalls to avoid. The book also incudes many examples of the sexual lives of women Barbach has counseled in her sex therapy groups.

A second book by Barbach, *For Each Other,* is also a good choice; it devotes more time to achieving an orgasm with a sexual partner (especially the communication aspects of sexuality with a partner), women who rarely desire sex, and women who find sex painful.

THE NEW MALE SEXUALITY
(1992) by Bernie Zilbergeld.
New York: Bantam.

The New Male Sexuality is a very up-to-date, comprehensive book about male sexuality. (Zilbergeld's *Male Sexuality* is also a very good book, first published in 1978.) Why did Zilbergeld write *The New Male Sexuality?* Because, he says, in the last decade we have seen dramatic changes in the sexual landscape, from the changing expectations of women to new definitions of masculinity, and from the fear of disease to the renewed focus on long-term relationships.

An introductory section in *The New Male Sexuality* tackles male sexual myths and unrealistic expectations, and then the author turns to sexual reality and gives men a brief course in sexual knowledge. The next section explores better sex through topics such as how to be a good lover with your partner, how to be a better listener, touching, arousal, and how to keep the spark alive in long-standing relationships. A final section is devoted to resolving problems and includes discussion of ejaculatory control, erection difficulties, problems of sexual desire, and even advice for fathers on how to communicate more effectively about sex with their sons.

PERMANENT PARTNERS
(1988) by Betty Berzon.
New York: Plume.

Permanent Partners presents the knowledge and understanding that will help gay and lesbian couples make their relationship work and last. Berzon examines the obstacles that same-sex couples face as they try to create a new life together. The author is a lesbian who has counseled same-sex couples for many years. Among the obstacles she explores are the lack of visible long-term couples as role models; the absence of support from society—from employers to landlords to insurers—and too often from a gay or lesbian couple's families of origin; a tradition of failure; and the guidance gap that has not provided adequate advice for how to effectively build a life with another man or woman.

This is an excellent book on gay and lesbian relationships, both for gays and lesbians who are thinking about becoming coupled or are perplexed about their current relationship, and for anyone who wants to improve their understanding of gay and lesbian couples. Two other good books on gay and lesbian relationships are *The New Loving Someone Gay,* by Don Clark, and *Lesbian Couples,* by D. Merilee Clunis and G. Dorsey Green.

SELF-ASSESSMENT SCORING AND INTERPRETATION

SEXUAL SATISFACTION
Scoring
First, be sure you have responded to all the items.

Second, you have to rescore some of the items because they are worded in a different direction than the others. Change the scores for items 1, 2, 3, 9, 10, 12, 17, 19, 21, 22, 23 as follows:

An answer of 5 is changed to a 1
4 is changed to a 2
3 remains a 3
2 is changed to a 4
1 is changed to a 5

Third, after rescoring, add these scores for all 24 items and from the total subtract 20. This is your **total score:** _____ .

Interpretation
Fourth, the possible range of scores is from 0 to 100. This exercise, of course, is not absolutew but only an indication of the magnitude of sexual satisfaction in a two-person relationship. A low score would indicate a very small or no sexual problem existing in your relationship with this person and a high score would indicate the presence of a sexual problem to some degree. Keep in mind that a "sexual problem" will be relative to the personality dynamics of the individuals involved in the relationship. It could be helpful to go back over your responses and look for ways to improve the sexual aspect of your relationship with your partner.

KNOWLEDGE OF AIDS RISK BEHAVIOR
Scoring
Give yourself one point for each correct answer. Any wrong answers should be clarified and corrected.

Interpretation
If you missed more than four questions, you should gather more information about AIDS. Free pamphlets and brochures with up-to-date information are available from your local health department and student health center. The correct answers to the test are:

1 = F, 2 = T, 3 = T, 4 = T, 5 = F, 6 = F, 7 = F, 8 = F, 9 = F,
10 = F, 11 = F, 12 = F, 13 = T, 14 = F, 15 = T, 16 = T, 17 = T,
18 = F, 19 = F, 20 = T, 21 = F, 22 = F, 23 = T, 24 = T, 25 = F,
26 = F, 27 = F, 28 = F, 29 = T, 30 = T, 31 = T, 32 = F, 33 = F,
34 = F, 35 = T, 36 = T, 37 = T, 38 = T, 39 = T, 40 = F.

Paul Klee
Love Song by the New Moon, detail

Caring and Close Relationships

*Love is a canvas furnished by nature
and embroidered by imagination.*

—**Voltaire**

P hil is a lovesick man. On two consecutive days he put expensive ads in New York City newspapers, urging, begging, pleading a woman named Edith to forgive him and continue their relationship. The first ad read as follows:

> **Edith**
> *I was torn two ways.*
> *Too full of child*
> *to relinquish the lesser.*
> *Older now, a balance struck,*
> *that a child forever behind me.*
> *Please forgive me,*
> *reconsider.*
> *Help make a new us;*
> *better now than before.*
> **Phil**

This ad was placed in the *New York Post* at a cost of $3,600. Another full-page ad appeared in the *New York Times* at a cost of $3,408. Phil's ads stirred up quite a bit of interest. Forty-two Ediths responded; Phil said he thought the whole process would be more private. As Phil would attest, relationships are very important to us. Some of us will go to almost any length and spend large sums of money to restore lost relationships (Worschel & Cooper, 1979).

Sherry is not searching for a particular man. She is at the point where she is, well, looking for Mr. Anybody. Sherry is actually more particular than she says, although she is frustrated by what she calls the great man shortage in this country. In the United States, for every 100 men over 15 years of age who have never been married or are widowed or divorced, there are 123 women; for African Americans the ratio is 100 men for every 133 women.

William Novak (1983), author of *The Great Man Shortage,* believes it is the quality of the gap that bothers most women. He says the quality problem stems from the fact that in the last 2 decades, the combination of the feminist movement and women's tendency to seek therapy when their personal relationships do not work out has made women outgrow men emotionally. He points out that many women are saying to men, "You don't have to earn all the money anymore, and I don't want to have to do all the emotional work." Novak observes that the whole issue depresses many women because society has conditioned them to assume that their lack of a marriage partner is their fault. One 37-year-old woman told Novak, "I'm no longer waiting for a man on a white horse. Now I'd settle for the horse."

PREVIEW

Our close relationships can bring us warm and cherished moments. They also can have a chilling side, producing stress and pain. In this chapter, we will explore the ways in which human caring is expressed, the processes that draw us to one another, how we develop intimate relationships, and the negative aspects of close relationships, such as anger and jealousy.

THE DIMENSIONS OF CARING

How can we classify and study the phenomena of caring? One classification of caring distinguishes four forms: altruism, friendship, romantic, and affectionate love (Berscheid, 1988). We will consider each of these important types of love in turn.

Altruism

Altruism *is an unselfish interest in helping someone else.* We often hear or read about acts of generosity and courage, such as rock concerts and fund-raisers to help AIDS victims, the taxi driver who risks his life to save a woman in a dark alley, and volunteers who pull a baby from an abandoned well. You probably have placed some of your hard-earned cash in the palm of a homeless person, or perhaps you have cared for a wounded cat. How do psychologists account for such acts of human altruism?

Psychologists have differentiated between helping behaviors that are unselfish, or altruistic, and those done for some form of personal gain, or egoistic acts. Some psychologists argue that true altruism never occurs, that all helping behaviors are self-serving; others believe that there is a distinction between altruism and egoism (Batson & others, 1986). **Egoism** *is involved when person A gives to person B to ensure reciprocity, to gain self-esteem, to present oneself as powerful, competent, or caring, or to avoid social and self-censure for failing to live up to normative expectations.* By contrast, altruism occurs when

Friends of Ian O'Gorman (*being held aloft*) demonstrated an unusual degree of altruism when eleven of them shaved their heads prior to the chemotherapy that would cause Ian to lose his hair. Ian had non-Hodgkins lymphoma, and his chemotherapy protocol enhanced his chances of survival. The idea was originally Taylor Herber's. He claimed he would shave his head as a joke but then decided to do it because it would be less traumatizing for his best friend, who was likely to lose his hair as a side effect of chemotherapy. Others joined the cause as soon as they heard. His friends were relieved that the girls, who wanted to join in support, never followed through, since they believed Ian wouldn't want to be "followed around by a bunch of bald girls." The boys committed to future shaved heads if Ian's illness required more chemotherapy.

person A gives to person B with the ultimate goal of benefitting person B. Any benefits that come to person A are unintended.

Reciprocity and exchange are important aspects of altruism. Humans everywhere give to and receive from others. Reciprocity is a fundamental tenet of every widely practiced religion in the world—Judaism, Christianity, Hinduism, Buddhism, and Islam, for example. Reciprocity is reflected in Christianity's golden rule, "Do unto others what you would have them do unto you." Regardless of religious background, the same human sentiments are involved in reciprocity, with trust being the most important principle over the long run. Guilt and anger also play important roles; we feel guilty if we do not reciprocate, and we feel angry if someone else does not reciprocate.

One theory from social psychology addresses the reciprocal nature of human interactions. According to **social exchange theory,** *individuals should benefit those who benefit them, and when a benefit*

Examples of human altruism are plentiful. Here a young woman assists a handicapped child.

is received, an equivalent benefit should be returned at some point. In other words, in relationships we try to be fairly even in what we give and what we take. If we exchange birthday presents with our best friend, we try to make our presents about equal in cost or effort. When one family invites us to a barbecue at their place, we

tend to invite them back perhaps for an evening of food and bridge. Sometimes we may decide not to do something nice for another person because we don't expect anything back from that person. For example, after sending Christmas cards to Steven for the past 4 years and never getting a card back, Owana decides to cross Steven off her card list. Perhaps it sounds cold and calculating to describe altruism in terms of costs and benefits, but that is what social exchange theory does. We look at our costs (Owana's costs include the cost of a card and stamp and her effort in writing a note as well as feeling upset that Steven does not keep in touch) and our rewards (Owana can feel like she's spread Christmas cheer to someone who obviously needs some) and then decide if the behavior is worth carrying out. To further explore how social exchange is involved in long-term commitments, turn to Critical Thinking.

Describing individuals as having altruistic or egoistic motives implies that person variables are important in understanding altruistic behavior. Behavior is determined by both person and situational variables. A person's ability to empathize with the needy or to feel a sense of responsibility for another's welfare affects altruistic motivation. The stronger these dispositions, the less we would expect situational variables to influence whether giving, kindness, or helping occur.

As with any human behavior, however, characteristics of the situation influence the strength of altruistic motivation. Some of these characteristics include the degree of need shown by the other individual, the needy person's responsibility for his or her plight, the cost of assisting the needy person, and the extent to which reciprocity is expected.

Why does one person help a stranger in distress while another won't lift a finger? It often depends on the circumstances. More than 20 years ago a young woman named Kitty Genovese cried out repeatedly as she was brutally murdered. Attacking at about 3 A.M. in a respectable area of New York City, the murderer left and returned three times until he finally ended Kitty's life as she crawled to her apartment door and

Social exchange theory is a useful framework for understanding why some long-term relationships end and others continue. For example, no one seems to understand why Debbie stays with Joe. He tends to ignore her and sometimes ridicules her in public. She believes that he might be having an affair, and yet she stays committed to the relationship. Can you *think of some alternative explanations* that would show that Debbie's benefits outweigh the costs of staying with Joe?

In social exchange theory, the individual decides what the costs and rewards are and how much weight goes to each factor. A person might choose to stay in a costly relationship with few rewards because it seems to be the best option available. Another person might leave a rewarding relationship because a new relationship promises even more rewards and fewer costs.

We may rarely be in a position to understand the intricacies of any individual cost-benefit analysis when it comes to others' committed relationships. For this reason it is usually adaptive to avoid making judgments about the motives of others in maintaining or abandoning their long-term relationships.

---

screamed for help. During the 30 minutes it took to kill Kitty, 38 neighbors watched the gory scene and heard Kitty Genovese's screams. No one helped or even phoned the police. When interviewed, the witnesses all saw themselves as good, caring people, but they had seen the other witnesses and decided that the police had already been called. This incident initiated one of the most widely studied aspects of altruism, that of bystander intervention.

The **bystander effect** *is that individuals who observe an emergency help less when someone else is present than when they are alone.* The bystander effect helps to explain the apparent cold-blooded indifference to Kitty Genovese's murder. Social psychologists John Darley and Bibb Latané (1968) documented the bystander effect in a number of criminal and medical emergencies. Most of the bystander intervention studies show that when alone, a person will help 75 percent of the time, but when another bystander is present, the figure drops to 50 percent. **Diffusion of responsibility,** *the tendency to feel less responsible and to act less responsibly in the presence of others,* is one explanation of why bystanders fail to act. When a situation is sufficiently ambiguous, we might tend to look to the behavior of others for clues about what to do. People may think that someone else will call the police or that since no one is helping, possibly the person does not need help.

Many other aspects of the situation influence whether the individual will intervene and come to the aid of the person in distress. Bystander intervention is less likely to occur in the following situations (Shotland, 1985):

- When the intervention might lead to personal harm, retaliation by the criminal, or days in court testifying
- When helping takes time
- When a situation is ambiguous
- When the individuals struggling or fighting are married or related
- When a victim is perceived as being drunk rather than disabled, or of a different ethnic group
- When bystanders have no prior history of victimization themselves, have witnessed few crimes and intervention efforts, or have not had training in first aid, rescue, or police tactics

Helping others improves our ability to get along with others in the world. As we see next, liking others and being liked in return within the close relationship of friendship is an important aspect of our adjustment.

Love is a fruit in season at all times, and in reach of every hand.
—**Mother Teresa**

Friendship

One friend in life is much, two are many, and three hardly possible.
—**Henry Adams**

As suggested by Henry Adams, true friendship is hard to come by. **Friendship** *is a form of close relationship that involves enjoyment, acceptance, trust, intimacy, respect, mutual assistance, understanding, and spontaneity.* We like to spend time with our friends, and we accept their friendship without trying to change them. We assume our friends will act in our best interest and believe that they make good judgments. We help and support our friends and they return the assistance. When we share experiences and deep personal matters with a friend, we believe that the friend will understand our perspective. We feel free to be ourselves

Love scale

1. I feel that I can confide in __________ about virtually everything.
2. If I could never be with __________, I would feel miserable.
3. One of my primary concerns is __________'s welfare.

Liking scale

1. I would highly recommend __________ for a responsible job.
2. Most people would react favorably to __________ after a brief acquaintance.
3. __________ is the sort of person I myself would like to be.

FIGURE 10.1

Sample Items from Rubin's Loving and Liking Scales
Subjects are asked to fill out the questionnaire in terms of their feelings for their boyfriend or girlfriend, and in terms of their feelings for a platonic friend of the opposite sex.

around our friends (Davis, 1985). One study of more than 40,000 individuals revealed that many of these characteristics are considered the qualities of a best friend (Parlee, 1979).

How is friendship different from love? The difference can be seen by looking at the scales of liking and loving developed by Zick Rubin (1970) (see figure 10.1). Rubin says that liking involves our sense that someone else is similar to us; it includes a positive evaluation of the individual. Loving, he believes, involves being close to someone; it includes dependency, a more selfless orientation toward the individual, and qualities of absorption and exclusiveness.

Friends and lovers are also similar in some ways. Keith Davis (1985) has found that friends and romantic partners share the characteristics of acceptance, trust, respect, confidence, understanding, spontaneity, mutual assistance, and happiness. However, he found that relationships with spouses or lovers are also more likely to involve fascination and exclusiveness. Relationships with friends were perceived as more stable, especially more than those among unmarried lovers.

Are the friendships of women and men different? Although it has been proposed that males treat friendships in terms of respect, whereas females emphasize the affection dimension of friendship (Tannen, 1990), tests of this difference have not always held up (Gaines, 1994).

> *No love, no friendship can cross the path of our destiny without leaving some mark on it forever.*
>
> **—François Mauriac**

Romantic Love

> *What is this thing called love?*
>
> **—Cole Porter**

What is this thing called love? This question has intrigued philosophers, poets, and songwriters for centuries. Obviously, romantic love covers a vast and complex territory of human behavior.

Romantic love *is also called passionate love or Eros; it has strong components of sexuality and infatuation, and it often predominates in the early part of a love relationship.* Poets, playwrights, and musicians through the ages have lauded the fiery passion of romantic love—and lamented the searing pain when it fails. Think for a moment about songs and books that hit the top of the charts. Chances are they're about love. Well-known love researcher Ellen Berscheid (1988) says that it is romantic love we mean when we say that we are "in love" with someone. It is romantic love she believes we need to understand if we are to learn what love is all about. To assess your experience with passionate love, turn to the Self-Assessment.

In our culture, romantic love is the main reason we get married. In 1967, a famous study showed that men maintained that they would not get married if they were not "in love." Women either were undecided or said that they would get married even if they did not love their prospective husband (Kephart, 1967). In the 1980s, women and men tended to agree that they would not get married unless they were "in love." And more than half of today's men and women say that not being "in love" is sufficient reason to dissolve a marriage (Berscheid, Snyder, & Omoto, 1989).

> *I flee who chases me, and chase who flees me.*
>
> **—Ovid, *The Loves,* A.D. 8**

Romantic love is especially important among college students. One study of unattached college men and women found that more than half identified a romantic partner, rather than a parent, sibling, or friend, as their closest relationship (Berscheid, Snyder, & Omoto, 1989). We are referring to romantic love when we say, "I am *in love,*" not just "I *love.*"

Romantic love includes a complex intermingling of different emotions—fear, anger, sexual desire, joy, and jealousy, for example. Obviously, some of these emotions are a source of anguish. One study found that romantic loves were more likely than friends to be the cause of depression (Berscheid & Fei, 1977).

Although Berscheid admits this is an inadequate answer, she concluded that romantic love is about 90 percent sexual

Passionate Love

Instructions

The items ask you what it's like when you are passionately in love. Please think of the person you love most passionately *right now*. If you are not in love right now, please think of the person you loved passionately. If you have never been in love, think of the person you came closest to caring for in that way. Keep this person in mind as you complete the items. Try to tell how you felt at the time your feelings were the most intense. Select a number from 1 to 9 that best reflects your feelings for each item.

Not at all true				Moderately true				Definitely true
1	2	3	4	5	6	7	8	9

1. I would feel deep despair if _____ left me.

2. Sometimes I feel I can't control my thoughts; they are obsessively on _____ .

3. I feel happy when I am doing something to make _____ happy.

4. I would rather be with _____ than anyone else.

5. I'd get jealous if I thought _____ were falling in love with someone else.

6. I yearn to know all about _____ .

7. I want _____—physically, emotionally, mentally.

8. I have an endless appetite for affection from _____ .

9. For me, _____ is the perfect romantic partner.

10. I sense my body responding when _____ touches me.

11. _____ always seems to be on my mind.

12. I want _____ to know me—my thoughts, my fears, my hopes.

13. I eagerly look for signs indicating _____'s desire for me.

14. I possess a powerful attraction for _____ .

15. I get extremely depressed when things don't go right in my relationship with _____ .

Turn to the end of the chapter to interpret your passionate love experience.

---

desire. Berscheid (1988) believes sexual desire is vastly neglected in the study of romantic love. As she puts it, "To discuss romantic love without also prominently mentioning the role sexual arousal and desire plays in it is very much like printing a recipe for tiger soup that leaves out the main ingredient."

Love is purely a creation of the human imagination . . . the most important example of how the imagination continually outruns the creature it inhabits.

—Katherine Anne Porter

Affectionate Love

Love is more than just passion. **Affectionate love,** *also called companionate love, is the type of love that occurs when individuals desire to have the other person near and have a deep, caring affection for the person.*

There is a growing belief that the early stages of love have more romantic ingredients, but as love matures, passion tends to give way to affection. Phillip Shaver (1986) describes the initial phase of romantic love as a time that is fueled by a mixture of sexual attraction and gratification, a reduced sense of loneliness, uncertainty about the security of developing another attachment, and

excitement from exploring the novelty of another human being. With time, he says, sexual attraction wanes, attachment anxieties either lessen or produce conflict and withdrawal, novelty is replaced with familiarity, and lovers either find themselves securely attached in a deeply caring relationship or distressed—feeling bored, disappointed, lonely, or hostile, for example. In the latter case, one or both partners may eventually seek another close relationship.

When two lovers go beyond their preoccupation with novelty, unpredictability, and the urgency of sexual attraction, they are more likely to detect

---

Schizophrenia   "split-mind"   o Substance-use disorders.

1) Disorganized
2) Catatonic
3) Paranoid
4) Undifferentiated

o Schizotypal personality disorder
o Borderline personality disorder
o Obsessive-compulsive personality disorder
o Antisocial personality disorder

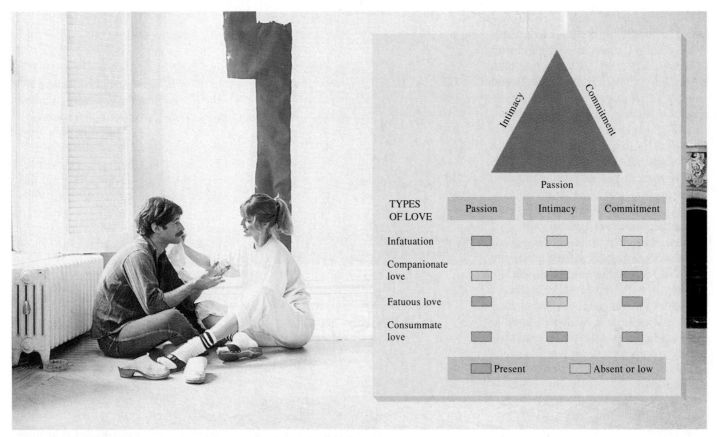

FIGURE 10.2

Sternberg's Triangle of Love

In a study in 1967, the men said they would not get married unless they were in love with a woman, but the women were either undecided or said they would get married even if they did not love the man. However, in the 1980s, women had changed their opinions to the point that theirs were almost identical to men's, no longer maintaining they would get married if they were not in love.

deficiencies in each other's caring. This may be the point in a relationship when women, who often are better caregivers than men, sense that the relationship has problems. Wives are almost twice as likely as husbands to initiate a divorce, for example.

So far we have discussed two forms of love: romantic (or passionate) and affectionate (or companionate). Robert J. Sternberg (1988) described a third form of love, consummate love, which he said is the strongest, fullest type of love. Sternberg proposed the **triangular theory of love:** *that love includes three dimensions—passion, intimacy, and commitment* (see figure 10.2). Couples must share all three dimensions to experience consummate love.

Passion, as described earlier, is physical and sexual attraction to another. Intimacy is the emotional feelings of warmth, closeness, and sharing in a relationship. Commitment is our cognitive appraisal of the relationship and our intent to maintain the relationship even in

the face of problems. If passion is the only ingredient (with intimacy and commitment low or absent), we are merely *infatuated.* This might happen in an affair or a fling in which there is little intimacy and even less commitment. A relationship marked by intimacy and commitment but low or lacking in passion is called *affectionate love,* a pattern often found among couples who have been married for many years. If passion and commitment are present but intimacy is not, Sternberg calls the relationship *fatuous love,* as when one person worships another from a distance. To compare different individuals' experiences of falling in love, turn to Critical Thinking.

We are who we love.

—**Erik Erikson**

Relationship Cognition

Researchers are increasingly interested in the role of cognition in close relationships (Berscheid, 1994). One area that has been fruitful in improving our knowledge of close relationships is the study of attribution—our motivation to seek the causes of behavior (Finchum & Bradbury, 1992). A number of investigators have found that the attributions spouses make for marital events are related to their marital satisfaction (Karney & others, 1994). Specifically, distressed spouses are more likely than nondistressed spouses to attribute marital problems and negative partner behaviors to stable and global characteristics of the partner and to view the partner as behaving intentionally, in a blameworthy manner, and with selfish motivations. For example, an unhappily married, distressed spouse might attribute a sharp-tongued remark to a global trait of the partner ("Why did I marry such a loser"), whereas a happily married, nondistressed spouse might attribute the same caustic remark to a temporary circumstance ("Maybe he had a bad day at work").

Relationship memories are another aspect of relationship cognition that is currently being studied (Jussim, 1991). The accuracy of relationship memories might depend on who is doing the remembering. In one study, women were likely to recall relationship events (such as their first date) more vividly and in greater detail than their male partners were (Ross & Holmberg, 1990). This gender difference might stem from the greater importance of relationships to women and women's tendency to reminisce about relationships. In another study that supports this viewpoint, when talking about a relationship women showed more relationship awareness (such as awareness of the couple's interaction patterns) than men did (Acitelli & Holmberg, 1993). Women might also have more highly developed cognitive schemas for relationships because they spend more time in social interaction than men do (Wong & Csikszentmihalyi, 1991).

The individual difference factor that is currently receiving the most attention is attachment security, which can be viewed as a relationship schema (Shaver & Hazen, 1993). Closely related to attachment security is relationship trust. Highly trusting partners often cope with negative information about their partner without

CRITICAL THINKING

How Do You Know When You Are in Love?

Author Nancy Mitford once said, "To fall in love you have to be in the state of mind for it to take, like a disease." You may have thought you were "afflicted" only to discover with the passing of time and some disappointment that you were wrong. What are your symptoms of falling in love? Once you have in mind your characteristics, interview three other people about their symptoms, and compare your symptoms with theirs. Are there common characteristics? Are there interesting differences? Your interviews will *demonstrate appreciation of individual differences.*

Love conquers all things except poverty and toothache.

—**Mae West**

Having a successful relationship requires developing communication skills to deal with disagreements.

diminishing their trust. According to research on attachment, an important dimension of most relationships is that partners be secure in their feeling that each partner cares about the other. To explore the strength of your relationship with a partner, see the Self-Assessment.

Most people tend to be very selective in choosing romantic and affectionate partners. Next we will explore the characteristics that draw us into intimate relationships with others.

THE NATURE OF ATTRACTION

The forces that draw us to each other often seem mysterious. Psychologists' efforts to

Close Relationships

	Yes	No
1. I expect some of our romantic love will fade.	___	___
2. I am concerned about my partner's drinking/smoking.	___	___
3. I can easily share my positive and negative feelings with my partner.	___	___
4. We have some important disagreements that never seem to get resolved.	___	___
5. We have decided how to handle our finances.	___	___
6. At times I feel pressure to participate in activities my partner enjoys.	___	___
7. I am very satisfied with the amount of affection I receive from my partner.	___	___
8. I have (would have) some concerns about my partner's parenting skills.	___	___
9. We have clearly decided how to share household responsibilities.	___	___
10. We sometimes disagree on religious beliefs.	___	___

Instructions

Answer yes or no to the following items regarding your relationship partner.

Turn to the end of the chapter to interpret your responses.

REVIEW

Dimensions of Caring

One classification system of forms of caring is based on four components of love: altruism, friendship, romantic or passionate love, and affectionate or companionate love. Examples of human altruism are plentiful. Reciprocity and social exchange are often, but not always, involved. Psychologists have studied both person and situation variables in altruism. Extensive research has been conducted on bystander intervention.

Friends and lovers have similar and dissimilar characteristics. Despite some personality and situational variations, females in general engage in more intimate self-disclosure with a friend than males do. Romantic love is involved when we say we are "in love"; it includes passion, sexuality, and a mixture of emotions, some of which may be negative. Affectionate love is more important as relationships mature. Shaver proposed a developmental model of love and Sternberg a triangular model. Sternberg believes that affectionate love is made up of intimacy and commitment, which along with romantic love, comprise the three facets of love in his model.

Researchers are increasingly interested in the role that cognition plays in close relationships. Areas of relationship cognition that are being studied include attribution, memory, attachment security, and trust.

explain attraction have focused on three primary influences on attraction: the role of similarity, the importance of physical attractiveness, and the influence of personality characteristics.

Similarity

Physical proximity does not guarantee that we will develop a positive relationship with an individual. Familiarity can breed contempt, but familiarity is a condition that is necessary for a close relationship to develop. For the most part, friends and lovers have been around each other for a long time; they may have grown up together, gone to high school or college together, worked together, or gone to the same social events. Once we have been exposed to someone for a period of time, what is it that makes the relationship breed friendship and even love?

Birds of a feather do indeed flock together. One of the most powerful lessons generated by the study of close relationships is that we like to associate with people who are similar to us. Our friends, as well as our lovers, are much more like us than unlike us. We have similar attitudes, behavior, characteristics, clothes, intelligence, personality, other friends, values, lifestyle, physical attractiveness, and so on. In some limited cases and on some isolated characteristics, opposites may attract. An introvert may wish to be with an extravert, or someone with little money may wish to associate with someone who has a lot of money, for example. But

Computer Dating Questionnaire

Computer dating is based almost entirely on the idea that people with similar interests and attitudes are compatible. In applying for a date, the person completes a questionnaire, like the one below and is then matched with a person of the opposite sex who has similar interests and attitudes.

Key

A—Yes Definitely!
B—Yes
C—Maybe
D—No
E—No definitely!

1. Do you sometimes look down at others?   A B C D E
2. Do you enjoy being the center of attention in group activities?   A B C D E
3. Do you think it proper for unmarried couples to go on a trip by themselves?   A B C D E
4. Do you think you would be content married to an unaffectionate mate?   A B C D E
5. Do you believe that our schools should teach evolution?   A B C D E
6. Do you find yourself getting angry easily or often?   A B C D E
7. Do you usually prefer being with groups of people to being alone?   A B C D E
8. Do you think that a theft is ever justifiable?   A B C D E
9. Do you think that sex is over-exploited in advertising?   A B C D E
10. Do you believe some religious instruction is necessary for all children?   A B C D E
11. Do you feel that your life as a child was enjoyable?   A B C D E
12. Do you ever go out of your way to avoid someone?   A B C D E
13. Do you think it proper for a schoolteacher to smoke or drink in public?   A B C D E
14. Do you think college campuses are too sexually liberated?   A B C D E
15. Do you believe you could permit your child to choose a different religion?   A B C D E

These are sample items from a dating questionnaire developed by a computer dating firm that matches up people who are interested in meeting someone they think they would like to date. The computer dating firm would take your responses to the items and try to match you with someone with similar characteristics and interests.

overall we are attracted to individuals with similar rather than opposite characteristics. In one study, for example, the old adage "Misery loves company" was supported, as depressed college students preferred to meet unhappy others while nondepressed college students preferred to meet happy others (Wenzlaff & Prohaska, 1989). The fact that individuals are attracted to each other on the basis of similar characteristics and attitudes is reflected in the questions that computer dating services ask their clients (see the Self-Assessment).

Consensual validation *provides an explanation of why people are attracted to others who are similar to them. Our own attitudes and behavior are supported when someone else's attitudes and behavior are similar to ours—their attitudes and behavior validate ours.* People tend to shy away from the unknown. We may tend, instead, to prefer people whose attitudes and behavior we can predict. Similarity also implies that we will enjoy doing things with the other person, which often requires a partner who likes the same things and has similar attitudes.

Physical Attraction

Sex appeal is 50 percent what you've got and 50 percent what people think you've got.

—Sophia Loren

The force of similarity also operates at a physical level. Most of us can't have Cindy Crawford or Denzel Washington as a friend or lover; how do we deal with this limitation? We usually seek out someone at our own level of attractiveness in both physical characteristics and social attributes. Most of us come away with a reasonably good chance of finding a "good match." Research indicates that this **matching hypothesis**—*that although in the abstract we might prefer a more attractive person, in the real world we end up choosing someone who is close to our own level of attractiveness*—holds up (Kalick & Hamilton, 1986).

Several additional points help to clarify the role of physical beauty and attraction in our close relationships. Much of the research has focused on initial or short-term encounters; researchers have not often evaluated attraction over the course of months and years. As relationships endure, physical attraction probably assumes less importance. Rocky Dennis, as portrayed in the movie *Mask,* is a case in point. His peers and even his mother initially wanted to avoid Rocky, whose face was severely distorted, but over the course of his childhood and adolescent years, the avoidance turned into attraction and love as people got to know him. As Rocky's story demonstrates, familiarity can overcome even severe initial negative reactions to a person.

> *Ask a toad what is beauty . . . he will answer that it is a female with two great round eyes coming out of her little head, a large flat mouth, a yellow belly and a brown back.*
>
> —**Voltaire,** *Philosophical Dictionary,* **1764**

Might our criteria for beauty also vary from one culture to another and from one point in history to another? For the answer to this question, turn to Sociocultural Worlds of Adjustment.

Personality Characteristics

When you think of what attracts you to someone else, certain personality characteristics probably come to mind. Wouldn't you rather be around someone who is sincere, honest, understanding, loyal, truthful, trustworthy, intelligent, and dependable than someone who is mean, obnoxious, insulting, greedy, conceited, rude, and

TABLE 10.1

Personality Traits That People Like and Don't Like

Highly Likeable	Highly Unlikeable
sincere	liar
honest	phony
understanding	mean
loyal	cruel
truthful	dishonest
trustworthy	untruthful
intelligent	obnoxious
dependable	malicious
thoughtful	dishonorable
wise	deceitful
considerate	untrustworthy
good-natured	unkind
reliable	insincere
mature	insulting
warm	spiteful
earnest	greedy
kind	conceited
friendly	rude
kind-hearted	thoughtless
happy	insolent

From N. H. Anderson, "Likeableness Ratings of 55 Personality Trait Words" in *Journal of Personality and Social Psychology,* 9:272–279. Copyright © 1968 by the American Psychological Association. Reprinted with permission.

thoughtless? In one study, these and other personality traits were among those we like and do not like, respectively (Anderson, 1968) (see table 10.1).

DEVELOPING INTIMATE RELATIONSHIPS

> *Seven years would be insufficient to make some people acquainted with each other, and seven days are more than enough for others.*
>
> —**Jane Austen**

People differ in their desire for intimacy as well as in how they achieve their goals. In this section, we will examine the relationship between identity development and the balance between independence and intimacy. We will also examine different styles of intimate interactions and forms of relationship maturity.

Intimacy, Independence, and Identity

Determining how connected we want to be with others and negotiating these needs is a major challenge that occupies

SOCIOCULTURAL WORLDS OF ADJUSTMENT

Physical Attraction Around the World

Are there universal criteria for physical attractiveness? Two social psychologists reviewed the research on physical attractiveness and concluded that "today, scholars have admitted defeat in their search for universal beauty. . . . Anthropologists have ended where they began—able to do no more than point to the dazzling array of characteristics that various people in various places at various times have idealized" (Hatfield & Sprecher, 1986, p. 12). Even within a culture, the criteria for beauty may change over time, as shown in the following examples of idealized female beauty (Lamb & others, 1993). In the 1940s, the ideal female beauty was a well-rounded shapely one typified by Marilyn Monroe, who at 135 pounds and only 5 feet 5 inches tall would today be viewed as pudgy. By the late 1960s and the 1970s, women aspired to look more like Twiggy, a model known for her pencil-thinness. In the 1980s and 1990s, the ideal physique is neither pleasingly plump nor extremely slender. As a result of the American preoccupation with health, a well-toned female body has become the ideal physique, as shown by the popularity of exercise videos by Jane Fonda, Cher, and Denise Austin.

Exotic definitions of beauty notwithstanding, some psychologists believe that certain aspects of attractiveness are consistent across cultures (Cunningham & others, 1995). One classic early study found that health, feminine plumpness, and cleanliness were the criteria for attractiveness across a wide range of cultures (Ford & Beach, 1951). Evolutionary psychologists are not surprised by such findings—they argue that men are attracted to healthy women because their genes are more likely to lead to successful reproduction (Buss, 1995). In another investigation, men were most attracted to women with waists that were approximately one-third smaller than their hips, which, say evolutionary psychologists, suggests youthful fertility (Singh, 1993). Indeed, the more youthful the woman's appearance, the more attractive she was rated in thirty-seven different cultures (Buss, 1989). By contrast, women rate men as more attractive if they are mature and dominant, which, according to evolutionary psychologists, signals an ability to support and protect (Buss, 1995). In a recent national study of gender differences in mate preference in the United States, men were attracted to women on the basis of physical attractiveness and youth, while women were attracted to men on the basis of their earning potential (Sprecher, Sullivan, & Hatfield, 1994).

What are the criteria for physical attraction around the world?

much of our adult lives. We must determine what kinds of relationships will be fulfilling. We also need to establish a balance in our relationships between dependence and independence.

Recall from chapter 3 that Erik Erikson (1968) proposed that this challenge—determining who we are, what we are all about, and where we are going in life—emerges as *the* important task of adolescence. If we fail to establish intimate connections during Erikson's sixth developmental stage, we might be left in isolation as adults.

Erikson believed that intimacy pursuits should follow the development of a stable and successful identity. He described intimacy as finding oneself yet losing oneself in another person. An important aspect of this relationship is the commitment of the individuals to each other, but these individuals also show a strong interest in independence and freedom. Development in early

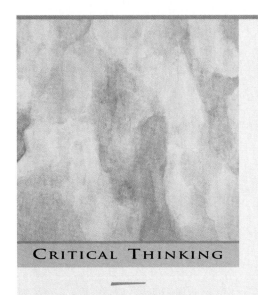

Support and Suffocation

Consider Jeannie. Although her prospects for a successful career seemed bright, her supervisors were puzzled when she turned down a promotion that would have led to more responsibility and relocation in a glamorous new city. Jeannie's father was pleased at Jeannie's decision. He was worried that the new job would be too much stress for Jeannie and offered to buy her a new car to make up for any disappointment she might experience by turning down the promotion. How would Erikson describe the developmental problem posed by Jeannie's dilemma? Your ability to apply Erikson's frameworks *demonstrates sensitivity to the influence of context on behavior.*

Jeannie's failure to achieve autonomy will have long-ranging effects on her ability to survive as an adult. An overprotective parent who continues to support her financially when it is no longer essential probably does not want to let go of her. In early adulthood, the daughter may have difficulty developing mature intimate relationships, and she might have career difficulties. When things do not go well in her adult life, she might go crying to her parents instead of facing the problem in an autonomous manner.

In some cultures, however, Jeannie's decision would not be regarded as ill-directed. Some traditions place higher value on family continuity than on career progress, especially for women.

adulthood often involves this intricate balance (McAdams, 1988). Young adults must learn to increase their independence from their parents and enrich their friendship commitments while also learning to think for themselves and to act without always relying on what others say or do.

The extent to which the young adult has begun to develop autonomy has important implications for early adulthood maturity. The young adult who has not sufficiently moved away from parental ties can have difficulty in both interpersonal relationships and a career. To examine an example of difficulties that can be caused by intense family ties, see Critical Thinking.

Levels of Relationship Maturity

Most psychologists believe that it is desirable to have the goal of developing a mature identity and having close relationships with others. Kathleen White and her colleagues (White & others, 1987) developed a model of relationship maturity that includes this goal at its highest level. In this model, individuals move through three levels of relationship maturity: self-focused, role-focused, and individuated-connected.

The **self-focused level** *is the first level of relationship maturity; from this perspective on another person or a relationship, one is concerned only with the effects on oneself.* At this level, the individual's own wishes and plans overshadow those of others, and the individual shows little concern for others. Intimate communication skills are in the early developing, experimental stages. In terms of sexuality, there is little understanding of mutuality or consideration of another's sexual needs.

The **role-focused level** *is the second or intermediate level of relationship maturity, at which perceiving others as individuals in their own right begins to develop. However, at this level, the perspective is stereotypical and emphasizes social acceptability.* Individuals at this level know that acknowledging and respecting another is part of being a good friend or a romantic partner. Yet commitment to an individual is secondary to the romantic partner role itself. Generalizations about the importance of communication in relationships abound, but underlying this talk is a shallow understanding of commitment.

The **individuated-connected level** *is the highest level of relationship maturity, at which there is evidence of an understanding of oneself and consideration of* others' *motivations and anticipation of their needs. Concern and caring involve emotional support and individualized expression of interest.* Commitment is made to specific individuals with whom they share a relationship. At this level, individuals understand the personal time and investment needed to make a relationship work. In White's view, it is not until adulthood that the individuated-connected level is likely to be reached. She believes most individuals making the transition from adolescence to adulthood are either self-focused or role-focused in their relationship maturity.

Intimate interactions vary not only in their levels of maturity but also in the style of the relationship. Next we will explore distinctive patterns in partner choice.

Styles of Intimate Interaction

Young adults show various styles of intimate interaction. Psychologist Jacob Orlofsky (1976) developed a classification of intimate relationships based on five styles: intimate, preintimate, stereotyped, pseudointimate, and isolated.

In the **intimate style,** *the individual forms and maintains one or more deep and long-lasting love relationships.* Many individuals aspire to this style of interaction

REVIEW

The Nature of Attraction and Developing Intimate Relationships

Familiarity precedes a close relationship. We like to associate with people who are similar to us. The principles of consensual validation and matching provide explanations of why we are attracted to people who are similar to us. Physical attraction and personality characteristics are important aspects of close relationships and attraction. Physical attraction is usually more important in the early part of a relationship, and it varies across cultures and historical time.

Intimacy versus isolation is Erikson's sixth developmental stage, which Erikson believes individuals experience in early adulthood. Orlofsky described five styles of intimate interaction—intimate, preintimate, stereotyped, pseudointimate, and isolated. White proposed a model of relationship maturity in which individuals move through three levels: self-focused, role-focused, and individuated-connected. There is a delicate balance between intimacy and commitment on the one hand, and independence and freedom on the other. These themes are germane to understanding our lives as young adults, but they usually are worked and reworked throughout the adulthood years.

as the most fulfilling. In the **preintimate style,** *the individual shows mixed emotions about commitment, an ambivalence that is reflected in the strategy of offering love without obligations or long-lasting bonds.* These individuals tend to be involved in short-term sequential relationships. In one study, intimate and preintimate individuals were more sensitive to their partners' needs, and were more open in their friendships, than were individuals with other intimacy styles (Orlofsky, Marcia, & Lesser, 1973).

In the **pseudointimate style,** *the individual maintains a long-lasting sexual attachment with little or no depth or closeness.* This intimacy style gives the appearance of closeness but provides little opportunity to meet real intimacy needs. In the **stereotyped style,** *the individual has superficial relationships that tend to be dominated by friendship ties.* These individuals might or might not wish for more intimate relationships with others. People with an **isolated style** *tend to withdraw from social encounters and have few or no significant attachment to others.* Occasionally the isolated person shows signs of developing close interpersonal relationships, but usually the interactions are stressful.

THE DARK SIDE OF CLOSE RELATIONSHIPS

The most destructive elements in close relationships include anger, jealousy, and excessive dependence. Falling out of love also has its harsh side, as does loneliness for those who do not have close relationships.

Anger

Anger is a powerful emotion and can sometimes become an extremely destructive element in close relationships. Psychotherapist Richard Driscoll described three cyclic anger patterns that commonly occur in close relationships. In the "anger justifies itself" pattern, angry expressions are fueled by belief in one's own propaganda. The "passivity and outburst" pattern is common among individuals who fear the expression of any form of anger or conflict. In the "catharsis—perceived injustice" pattern, individuals are all too willing to express angry feelings (Tavris, 1989). Note that when problems are framed as in figure 10.3, they become a circle with no beginning or end, rather than a straight line with a start and a finish. The couple's task is to learn how to make anger less destructive in their relationship by breaking out of the cyclic patterns and controlling their anger more effectively.

In *Anger, the Misunderstood Emotion,* Carol Tavris (1989) described how to break the destructive cycle of anger in close relationships. First, it is necessary to drop the dream of rescuing or changing your partner. Often in the course of an ongoing problem one partner becomes overfocused on the other, and the other is underfocused on himself or herself. Suppose the husband has the problem of being out of work and won't look for a job. His naturally sympathetic wife becomes overfocused on his problem as she tries to help. She may say things like "I talked to my friend and she told me about a counselor you can see," or "I know a book you can read," and so on. The more he resists and the longer he sits and mopes around the house, the angrier she gets. The more she focuses on his problem, the less motivated he is to solve it. Overfocused individuals can be very self-righteous in their efforts to help the other and usually don't see how they are contributing to the continuation of the problem (Lerner, 1985). Ultimately the relationship becomes polarized between the competent helper and the incompetent helpee.

> *Never go to bed mad. Stay up and fight.*
> —**Phyllis Diller**

The second step in breaking the cycle of anger, thus, is to admit that what you are doing to change the other person is not working. In the case of the out-of-work husband, his wife can put her energy into figuring out her own options, given the way he is. If she opts for staying with him, she needs to specify to herself and to him what it is she has to do so she will not feel so angry. She might say that she can tolerate his not working but that she is not going to support him as she has in the past. For example, she could keep a separate bank account, and he could agree to clean the house regularly. Or she might ask him what solutions he has for

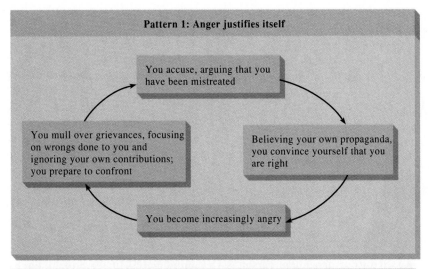

Pattern 1: Anger justifies itself

- You accuse, arguing that you have been mistreated
- Believing your own propaganda, you convince yourself that you are right
- You become increasingly angry
- You mull over grievances, focusing on wrongs done to you and ignoring your own contributions; you prepare to confront

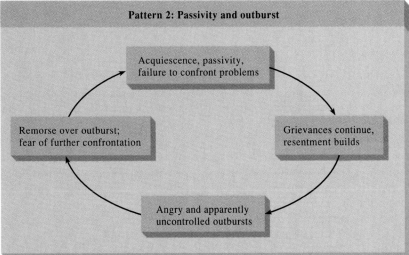

Pattern 2: Passivity and outburst

- Acquiescence, passivity, failure to confront problems
- Grievances continue, resentment builds
- Angry and apparently uncontrolled outbursts
- Remorse over outburst; fear of further confrontation

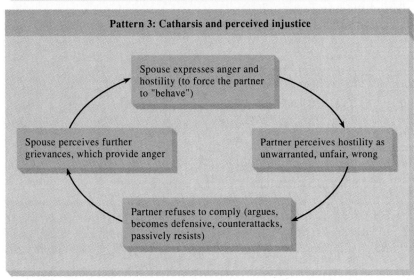

Pattern 3: Catharsis and perceived injustice

- Spouse expresses anger and hostility (to force the partner to "behave")
- Partner perceives hostility as unwarranted, unfair, wrong
- Partner refuses to comply (argues, becomes defensive, counterattacks, passively resists)
- Spouse perceives further grievances, which provide anger

FIGURE 10.3

Three Destructive Patterns of Anger in Close Relationships

their problem. The benefit of seeing your role in the partnership's problem is that you gain options and increased control.

Tavris (1989) also describes the importance of civility in keeping anger controlled. As we indicated in our discussion of anger in chapter 4, catharsis usually is not an effective way to handle anger. Sometimes the best way to control anger is to do nothing at all about it and let it subside. More often than not the anger will be only momentary. After you have cooled down, you might decide that what bothered you an hour ago was trivial. Managing anger depends on assuming responsibility for your emotions and your actions by refusing the temptation to wallow in blaming, in fury, or in silent resentment.

Jealousy

Jealousy can also become a destructive element in close relationships. **Jealousy** *is fear of the perceived possibility of losing someone's exclusive love.* The word *perceived* is an important part of the definition, because the possibility of losing the other's love might or might not be real. Jealousy emerges when there is a challenge to a special relationship we have with someone, or when we think there is. The sexual, affectionate, and contractual relationships we have with partners and lovers are complex. When they are challenged through infidelity or threaten to disintegrate, an intense jealousy can arise.

Jealousy is often stimulated by a specific event or situation. For example, situations that are likely to trigger jealous reactions in a relationship are (Salovey & Rodin, 1989):

- Finding out your lover is having an affair
- Discovering that someone is going out with the person you like
- Observing that someone is getting closer to a person to whom you are attracted
- Hearing your lover tell you how sexy an old girlfriend/boyfriend is
- Learning that your lover has visited a person she or he used to date
- Realizing that your partner would rather be with his or her friends than you

> *Jealousy is no more than feeling alone against smiling enemies.*
> —**Elizabeth Bowen**

Some people are more likely to become jealous than others. Individuals with low self-esteem and feelings of insecurity are especially prone to becoming jealous, sometimes imagining threats to their exclusive love when no threat exists. Jealous individuals often perceive their partner as a highly desirable possession and doubt that their own attractiveness or sexual adequacy is enough to hold onto the other person. Jealous individuals tend to idealize their partner and underestimate their own self-worth.

Even the most secure people may occasionally feel some jealousy, but they don't let the feelings become so intense that they interfere with their productive functioning or threaten their relationship. Healthy relationships are not built on insecure feelings and couples should work to develop trust in each other to increase feelings of security. In some cases, jealousy is irrational and the partner is doing nothing that will threaten the close relationship. The jealous person needs to examine how logical his or her thoughts and feelings of jealousy really are.

Overcoming jealous feelings involves reducing feelings of insecurity and thinking more rationally about the relationship. People who feel good about themselves are less likely to be jealous than are those who feel bad about themselves. Developing stronger self-esteem can reduce your vulnerability in intimate relationships. Discussing your concerns and needs with a partner in subdued and nonaccusing terms can clarify your intentions for your partner.

Dependence

A third destructive element in close relationships is excessive dependence. In some close relationships, one partner has an extreme degree of dependence, dependence that is so great that it is unhealthy for the relationship.

As children, we depended on our parents to satisfy most of our needs. As we grew up, we gradually assumed more independence and responsibility for our own well-being. Some individuals, though, never develop enough responsibility and depend excessively on others, especially their partners in close relationships.

> *If I have to lead another life in any of the planets, I shall take precious good care not to hang myself around any man's neck, either as a locket or a millstone.*
> —**Jane Carlyle**

An excessively dependent person is likely to be perceived as a burden by the partner. Two people in a close relationship normally enjoy doing things for each other, but there is a limit to the amount of time and energy most individuals are willing to devote even to someone they love very much. When the dependent person makes excessive demands, the partner often feels resentment and hostility. Even when the true cause of hostility (the overdependence, in this case) is not communicated to the dependent partner, the hostility will usually appear as frequent arguments, sexual problems, or the termination of the relationship.

Just as most jealous individuals have low self-esteem and feelings of insecurity, so do excessively dependent persons. Their feelings of dependence do nothing to improve their self-esteem, and they might become very jealous of their partner. Three basic steps are important in overcoming excessive dependence. First, we must recognize or admit the nature of the problem, usually stimulated by a partner's complaints of feeling crowded or suffocated by our demands. Second, we need to explore the reasons for such neediness. Third, we need to initiate some strategies that will lead to increased independence. For example, a dependent person might seek to enrich friendships beyond the partnership in order to develop new interests and give the partner some emotional space. As adults, it is important for us not only to have strong, positive relationships but also to develop ourselves as persons in our own right.

Falling Out of Love

The collapse of a close relationship can feel tragic; however, at other times our happiness and personal development can benefit from getting over being in love and ending a close relationship. Some examples of situations in which individuals might be wise to fall out of love include being obsessed with a person who repeatedly betrays our trust; being involved with someone who is draining us emotionally or financially; or being desperately in love with someone who does not return our feelings.

Falling out of love is usually painful and highly emotional. For example, being in love when love is not returned can lead to depression, obsessive thoughts, sexual dysfunction, inability to work effectively, difficulty in making new friends, and self-condemnation. Thinking clearly in such relationships is often difficult, because they are so colored by arousing emotions.

What are some intelligent guidelines for breaking the bonds of love? First, we need to identify the feelings that make it hard to surrender the relationship. Close friends can help us recognize the destructive aspects of the attachment. However, friends can help us only if we tell them openly and honestly what goes on in the relationship and our own conflicting feelings about the relationship.

Second, leaving a destructive relationship requires developing a stronger sense of self-esteem and independence. A main cause of getting into and staying in destructive relationships is feelings of being incomplete and inadequate by oneself. We must realize that we do not need the other person for our identity and self-esteem. Our friends can be invaluable in helping us to rebuild an identity as a competent, independent individual. They can provide ongoing support that we need during the period of adjustment when we are breaking off a relationship.

Ideally, a love relationship should reinforce self-esteem, but being rejected or involved in a destructive relationship may be devastating. One strategy for improving self-esteem is to use individual index cards to record, every day, at least two positive things about ourselves. They

It is important to distinguish being alone from being lonely. Most of us cherish the moments we can be left alone for a while. Aloneness can heal, but loneliness can hurt.

might be some of our basic characteristics or some of the positive behaviors we have engaged in that day or even at some time in the past.

A third recommendation for leaving a destructive relationship is to recognize and then stop the self-defeating thoughts that prevent us from taking effective actions to leave the relationship. Phillips suggests that when we find ourselves thinking negatively about ourselves, we should say, "Stop" and immediately think a good thought about ourselves. If how we think about ourselves has been learned, then we can learn to think about ourselves more positively. We can also use thought stopping (which we discussed in chapter 5 as an effective way of coping with stress) to think progressively less and less about the loved person. The basic idea is that letting a thought return again and again reinforces the thought, making it grow stronger and often more destructive.

A final recommendation for falling out of love is to fall in love with someone else, but only when you are emotionally ready. Too often individuals engage in an immediate rebound romance, which is often as destructive as the relationship it replaced. There does come a time, though, when living in the memory of a past love is also destructive. At that point, we should motivate ourselves, or take the suggestions of well-meaning friends, to get out and meet new people. This might lead to meeting someone with whom we can develop a healthy love relationship.

Some people get taken advantage of in relationships. For example, some relationships evolve into dominant and submissive roles, without either person realizing it. Detecting this pattern in a relationship is an important aspect of learning to reconstruct the relationship in a more emotionally satisfying way, or deciding to end the relationship if the problems cannot be worked out. To evaluate vulnerability in your own close relationship, turn to the Self-Assessment.

Not all of us experience the passion, intimacy, and commitment of love. Many people are lonely. In the final section of this chapter, we will explore the nature of loneliness.

Loneliness

Loneliness, like depression, can be a dark cloud that enfolds a person's day-to-day life. Feeling lonely should not be confused with being alone. Time spent alone can be quite satisfying and meaningful, but when we find ourselves longing to be with others and feeling unconnected, isolated, and alienated, our loneliness can seriously interfere with our sense of life satisfaction. Although most of us may feel lonely from time to time, some people find themselves feeling intensely lonely for long periods of time. Our society's emphasis on self-fulfillment and achievement, the importance we attach to commitment in relationships, and a decline in stable close relationships are among the reasons loneliness is common today (de Jong-Gierveld, 1987).

Loneliness is associated with gender, attachment history, self-esteem, and social skills. Both men and women who lack female companions have a greater risk of being lonely. Lonely people often have a history of poor relationships with their parents. Early experiences of rejection and loss (as

Vulnerability in a Close Relationship

Instructions

Read each question carefully while reflecting on your present or most recent close relationship. Check True or False as either relates to your situation.

Turn to the end of the chapter to interpret your responses.

Items True False

1. Is your partner often unavailable for phone calls at home or at work? ___ ___

2. Does he/she ask about the amount of money you earn or your parents earn, or try to get involved with your financial planning? ___ ___

3. Does your partner ever belittle your efforts and/or ideas? ___ ___

4. Has your partner ever disappeared for any length of time (overnight, several days, a week) and not informed you of his/her whereabouts? ___ ___

5. Does he/she live with you and contribute little or nothing to household maintenance? ___ ___

6. Does your partner borrow money and seldom bother to repay it, or frequently ask you to buy him/her things, or always use your car? ___ ___

7. Has he/she had one or more tragic misfortunes that needed your financial assistance? ___ ___

8. Has your partner told you early in your relationship that he/she would like to be married and described a life of love and luxury for both of you, but made no definite steps in that direction? ___ ___

9. Do you stop your present activity or postpone your plans when he/she calls to do something on the spur of the moment? ___ ___

10. Is he/she the only person in your life? ___ ___

11. Do you allow your partner to take the upper hand in your affairs? ___ ___

12. Have you ever noticed any discrepancies concerning what your partner has told you in regard to his/her name, job, background, family, etc.? ___ ___

13. When you are out does your partner avoid socializing with his/her or your family and friends? ___ ___

14. Do you usually wait for others to introduce you to potential partners instead of taking the initiative to meet new people on your own? ___ ___

15. When your partner describes his/her future goals, does it seem unclear as to where you fit into the future? ___ ___

16. Do you feel that you should be married to be happy? ___ ___

when a parent dies) can cause a lasting feeling of being alone. Lonely people often have low self-esteem and tend to blame themselves more than they deserve for their inadequacies. Also, lonely people usually have poor social skills. For example, they show inappropriate self-disclosure, self-attention at the expense of attention to a partner, or an inability to develop comfortable intimacy.

When students of traditional college age leave the familiar world of their hometown and family to enter college, they may feel especially lonely. Many college freshmen feel anxious about meeting new people and developing a new social life. One student commented:

My first year here at the university has been pretty lonely. I wasn't lonely at all in high school. I lived in a fairly small town—I knew everyone and everyone knew me. I was a member of several clubs and played on the basketball team. It's not that way at the university. It is a big place and I've felt like a stranger on so many occasions. I'm starting to get used to my life here and

in the past few months I've been making myself meet people and get to know them, but it has not been easy.

As this comment illustrates, freshmen rarely take their high school popularity and social standing into the college environment. There may be a dozen high school basketball stars, National Merit scholars, and former student council presidents in a single dormitory wing. Especially if students attend college away from home, they face the task of forming new social relationships.

In one study, 2 weeks after the school year began, 75 percent of 354 college freshmen felt lonely at least part of the time since arriving on campus (Cutrona, 1982). More than 40 percent said their loneliness was moderate to severe in intensity. Students who were the most optimistic and had the highest self-esteem were more likely to overcome their loneliness by the end of their freshman year. Loneliness is not reserved only for traditional-age college freshmen, though. Upperclassmen and nontraditional-age students are often lonely as well.

Males and females attribute their loneliness to different sources. Men are more likely to blame themselves, and women are more likely to blame external factors. Men are socialized to initiate relationships, whereas women are traditionally socialized to wait, then respond. Perhaps men blame themselves because they feel they should do something about their loneliness, whereas women wonder why no one calls.

How do you determine if you are lonely? Scales of loneliness ask you to rate yourself on items like the following:

I don't feel in tune with the people
    around me.
I can find companionship when I want it.

> *Where you used to be, there is a hole in the world, which I find myself constantly walking around in the daytime, and falling into at night.*
> **—Edna St. Vincent Millay**

Loneliness is about an absence of meaningful connections in our lives. One way to prevent loneliness is to become involved with activities that involve interactions with others. For example, many opportunities to meet others and become involved arise through work, school, community announcements, and religious organizations. Sometimes people can join organizations and volunteer time for some cause that they endorse. Spending time with others and developing social networks will have the long term payoff of reducing the chances of being alone and feeling lonely. In addition, people can arrange their lifestyle in such a way as to increase social contacts. For example, one social gathering can

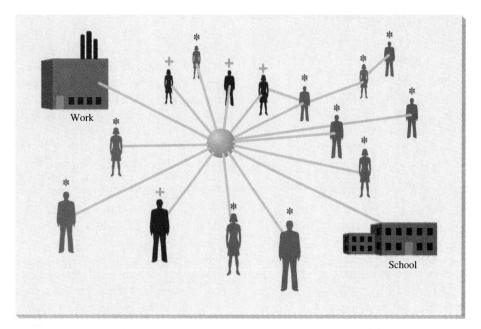

FIGURE 10.4

An Example of a Social Network
The center represents the person, such as yourself, connected to the surrounding persons represented by *s. For this network, there are additional clusters of others in the domains of school and work that the person is connected to. Only four of the persons are close friends, however, represented by a +.

lead to the development of several new social contacts if people take the initiative to introduce themselves to others and start a conversation. Meeting new people and developing social ties always involves taking some personal risks, but the benefits often outweigh these risks.

Loneliness often occurs as a result of the loss of social contacts. Moving to a new community, changing jobs, and breaking-off dating relationships usually decrease the number of social contacts a person has. Thus, when social contacts are lost they need to be replaced. Lost contacts need not be replaced with the same type of relationship. For example, when a dating relationship is broken off, new non-dating friends can fill the social void. Also, social contacts do not necessarily have to be new to meet social needs. Sometimes spending more time with old friends can meet social needs.

As with depression, it is important to recognize the warning signs of loneliness. Knowing what feelings may come about before feeling lonely can allow a person to head off the loneliness by doing something. For example, some people may begin to feel somewhat bored and

alienated before loneliness sinks in. Recognizing these feelings as a warning sign of loneliness can make a big difference in a person being able to prevent themselves from becoming lonely. This is especially important because loneliness can become so intense that it can keep a person from acting. Thus, heading off loneliness, like depression, can be much easier than trying to get out of it.

Over and above most other means of avoiding loneliness is the development of interests and activities that provide the opportunity to develop social contacts. A person's social contacts are referred to as a social network because usually contacts are not isolated from each other, but rather are interconnected. Consider your own social network. You probably know many people, some better than others, and some who know each other. You can examine your own social network by drawing it out in a schematic diagram. Figure 10.4 shows an example of such a diagram, with each star representing a social contact, connected by lines if the contacts know each other. None of the contacts are family and those with a plus are closer friends than those without pluses.

The Dark Side of Close Relationships

Among the most destructive elements in close relationships are anger, jealousy, and excessive dependence. Three anger patterns often appear in destructive relationships: anger justifies itself, passivity and outburst, and catharsis-perceived injustice. Such anger involves a circle with no beginning or end. Recommendations for breaking out of the circle and controlling anger include to stop dreaming of rescuing or changing your partner, to admit that what you are doing to change the other person isn't working, and to be more civil in keeping anger controlled. Jealousy is fear of the perceived possibility of losing someone's exclusive love. Reducing jealousy involves increasing one's own self-esteem, reducing feelings of insecurity, and thinking more rationally. Some individuals never develop enough self-responsibility and excessively depend on a partner—such excessive dependence usually leads to problems in a close relationship. Excessively dependent persons often have low self-esteem and feelings of insecurity. To improve their close relationships, they need to recognize their problem, understand why their problem came about, and start a program that leads to increased independence.

Sometimes the destructive elements in a close relationship become so great that we fall out of love, which is often painful and highly emotional. To adjust successfully to falling out of love, people need to free themselves from the feelings that have prevented them from leaving the relationship, develop their own identity and increase their self-esteem, recognize and then stop the self-defeating thoughts that prevent them from taking effective actions to leave, and fall in love with someone else, but only when emotionally ready.

Loneliness is associated with many factors, including sex, attachment history, self-esteem, and social skills. The social transition to college is a time when loneliness may develop as individuals leave behind the familiar world of hometown and family. It is important to keep in mind the distinction between being lonely and being alone.

CRITICAL THINKING ABOUT ADJUSTMENT

The Power of Love

Love is a fragile creation between two people. It can sometimes feel like a triumph against astronomical odds that two compatible people can find each other in the myriad of people looking for partners. It is even more astounding when a couple survives the forces that could erode their commitment.

Starting a relationship is risky business. It is a painful fact that two people might not have the same level of interest in beginning a relationship. Some individuals avoid forming new relationships with insincere promises to call. Equally lethal to a romantic future is the expressed desire by one partner to become "just friends." Ironically, the person who cares the least about continuing in the relationship has the most power to shape what will happen to the relationship. This principle holds throughout the relationship.

Healthy relationships start from the premise that a reasonably good match has been made. Shared intimacies, endearing gestures, and pleasant memories solidify the commitment. Couples who stay in love manage to find ways to introduce excitement into the relationship. For couples who work at their relationships, a committed and loving partnership can contribute to some of life's peak experiences.

However, love doesn't always wear well. Humans tend to get bored with unchanging stimuli. When partners stop working at maintaining or enhancing their long-term relationship, gnawing boredom can result. This makes it relatively easy to look to new relationships to provide the stimulation we crave. Taking a partner for granted is another way to weaken mutual commitment.

The end of a love relationship can feel especially brutal when one of the partners isn't ready for it to end. The one who wants to stay in the relationship feels abandoned and betrayed. The one who wants to leave feels trapped and sometimes frightened, looking for an escape.

The end of a love relationship provides an important example of a power imbalance and the impact this can have. For example, suppose Nat discovers that Meg has been losing interest in their relationship. He might offer to reform in whatever way she wants if she will promise not to leave. This might be an effective attempt to solve their problems, and it could rekindle the relationship if Meg accepts. Or Meg might withdraw even further because she does not want to exercise the power that Nat is giving her.

How have you managed the emotional roller-coaster of falling in love and staying in love? Have you felt powerless in response to a disinterested beloved who seems beyond your reach? Have you felt trapped by the unwanted affections of someone who seems too devoted to you? Do you recognize the principle that the least interested will be the most powerful in shaping a relationship? Your ability to make these connections demonstrates your ability *to apply psychological concepts to enhance adaptation and growth.*

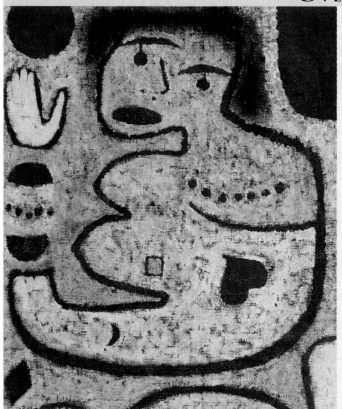

In this chapter we explored the dimensions of caring, which include altruism, friendship, romantic love, affectionate love, and relationship cognition. Our coverage of attraction focused on similarity, physical attraction, and personality characteristics. We also examined intimate relationships, including ideas about intimacy, independence, and identity, levels of relationship maturity, and styles of intimate interaction. We considered the dark side of close relationships—anger, jealousy, dependence, falling out of love, and loneliness. Remember that you can obtain an overall summary of the chapter by again studying the in-chapter reviews on pages 233, 238, and 244.

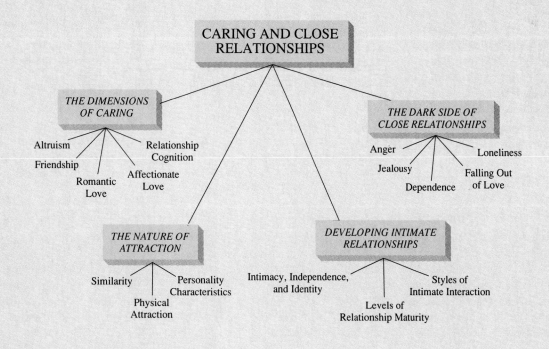

PRACTICAL KNOWLEDGE ABOUT ADJUSTMENT

THE DANCE OF INTIMACY

(1990) by Harriet Lerner. New York: HarperPerennial.

The Dance of Intimacy is written for women and is about women's intimate relationships. The book is subtitled *A Woman's Guide to Courageous Acts of Change in Key Relationships.* Drawing on a combination of psychoanalytic and family systems theories, Lerner weaves together a portrait of a woman's current self and relationships that she believes is derived from longstanding relationships with mothers, fathers, and siblings. Lerner tells women that if they are having problems in intimate relationships with a partner or their family of origin, they need to explore the nature of their family upbringing to produce clues to the current difficulties. Women learn how to distance themselves from their family of origin and how not to overreact to problems. Lerner gives women insights about how to define themselves, how to understand their needs and limits, and how to positively change. The positive change involves moving from being stuck in relationships that are going nowhere or are destructive to intimate connectedness with others and a solid sense of self.

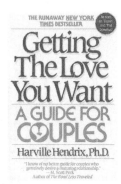

GETTING THE LOVE YOU WANT

(1988) by Harville Hendrix. New York: HarperPerennial.

Getting the Love You Want is a guide for couples to help them improve their relationship. The book is based on Hendrix's couple workshop techniques that are designed to help couples construct a conscious marriage, a relationship based on awareness of unresolved childhood needs and conflicts that cause individuals to select a particular spouse. The author instructs readers how to conduct a 10-week course in marital therapy in the privacy of their home.

PASSIONATE LOVE

Scoring

Total your responses for the 15 items on the passionate love scale.

Interpretation

If your score is 15–45, your passionate love experience has not been a very passionate one; if your score is 60–90, it has been a moderately passionate one; and if your score is 105–135, your passionate love experience has been a very intense one.

CLOSE RELATIONSHIPS

Scoring

Add up the number of "yes" answers to the odd numbered questions (1, 3, 5, 7, 9). Add up the number of "no" answers to the even numbered questions (2, 4, 6, 8, 10). Total the two numbers for your score.

Interpretation

Rated from strongest to weakest, your score shows you have:

8–10: Mostly relationship strengths.
6–7: Many strengths, but some areas that need work.
4–5: Few strengths, many areas that need work.
0–3: A strong need for work on many areas.

COMPUTER DATING QUESTIONNAIRE

No additional scoring is needed. Answers would be matched with those of potential dates.

VULNERABILITY IN A CLOSE RELATIONSHIP

Scoring

Give yourself one point for each true response to the questions.

Interpretation

13–16: You are very vulnerable to being in a lopsided relationship, which may result in hurt feelings in the future. You should seriously examine the contour and direction of your relationship with your partner. For you to continue with your present situation is almost certain to be a waste of time and energy.

9–12: You are vulnerable to being taken advantage of. Stop and ask yourself if you are getting out of this relationship what you are putting into it.

5–8: You are somewhat vulnerable to being hurt. Your relationship probably has potential but needs to be evaluated. You and your partner should discuss your future to determine what type of lifestyle you both desire.

1–4: You do not seem vulnerable to being dominated in your relationship. Keep the statements to which you responded *true* in mind and openly discuss them with your partner.

Adult Lifestyles

CHAPTER OUTLINE

CRITICAL THINKING ABOUT ADJUSTMENT

CHAPTER BOXES

> *When two people are under the influence
> of the most violent, most insane,
> most delusive, and most transient of
> passions, they are required to swear that
> they will remain in that excited,
> abnormal, and exhausting condition
> continuously until death do them part.*
>
> —**George Bernard Shaw**

B urt and Myrna did not know each other until the end of January. After meeting through a mutual friend, they knew that they liked each other. Despite the fact that they had both recently ended long-term relationships, Myrna and Burt felt strongly for each other. They quickly became friends, were engaged within 3 weeks, and married 4 weeks after that. Were they on the rebound? Perhaps. Was their marriage a little hasty? Most likely. Still, Burt and Myrna say they love each other, feel as though they have known each other for years, and feel an honest trust in their relationship.

Jenny and Mark, on the other hand, have been good friends for years. They dated for 2 years before deciding to live together more than a year ago. Jenny sometimes brings up the subject of getting married to "make it official." But after a brief discussion, they usually both agree that they want to keep their relationship the way that it is. They both are happy together and fear that marriage could change things for the worse. Are they avoiding commitment? Maybe. But Jenny and Mark are both satisfied with their life together and say they are very happy.

Steve and Tom are gay and have been in a committed relationship for the past 9 years. They are monogamous and live together. Like the other couples just discussed, they say they love each other and are 100 percent devoted to their relationship. However, in a gay relationship, marriage is not an option. Legally sanctioned marriages are not available to same-sex couples. Steve and Tom have, however, gone to their church and been unofficially joined in a union that, although not legally recognized, is held as marriage in their community.

Valerie has lived alone in her condo with her calico cat for 10 years since graduating from college. Successful in her work as a landscape designer, she has a small circle of friends and feels attached to her neighbors, but she professes no interest in a long-term relationship. She sometimes thinks that she would enjoy having a child, but she isn't confident that she could be successful as a single parent. She reports feeling more anxiety about the decision as her thirty-fifth birthday approaches.

PREVIEW

Adult lifestyles are incredibly diverse. In fact, each adult circumstance almost seems as unique as the individuals making it up. In this chapter we will describe the range of adult relationships, beginning with marriage and then examining alternatives to marriage. We will explore the developmental stages of the family life cycle, along with current trends in family life, and then conclude with an analysis of marital or partner adjustment.

THE DIVERSITY OF ADULT LIFESTYLES

Today's adult lifestyles offer many choices. In the first section of this chapter we will examine marriage, which remains the most popular lifestyle choice. We will focus on the functions of marriage, making the decision to marry, and the processes involved in selecting a mate. We will also explore alternatives to marriage, including cohabitation, lesbian and gay partnerships, and the single life.

Marriage

Marriage—a community consisting of a master, a mistress, and two slaves— making in all two.

—Ambrose Bierce

Despite individuals' getting married at older ages, despite astronomical divorce rates, and despite comedians' relentless attacks regarding its effect on happiness, marriage is still very popular today. Most Americans do get married. **Marriage** *is a legally and socially sanctioned partnership that creates a new family unit.* Clearly, marriage must be fulfilling some important needs and functions in our lives.

The Functions of Marriage

Marriage promotes many functions attributed to the family in general. These include social status, economic enhancement, sex, and reproduction. Marriage also provides emotional support as well as mental and physical health benefits.

Although many of these functions do not require marriage, the formal sanctions for marriage facilitate meeting these needs in a conventional manner.

A review of more than 130 research studies on a wide range of measures of well-being concluded that married women and men are generally happier and less stressed than their unmarried counterparts (Coombs, 1991). Let's examine some of the areas in which marriage benefits individuals.

The main factor that seems to be responsible for the finding that married individuals are happier than nonmarried ones is interpersonal closeness. Without this intimacy, feelings of well-being are diminished, especially for socially isolated persons. No portion of the unmarried population—separated, divorced, widowed, or never married—describes itself as being happy and contented with life as often as married persons do (Campbell, 1981).

Married men report more happiness than married women do (Coombs, 1991). Married men are more likely than married women to receive emotional gratification from their spouse. A substantial number of studies reveal the psychological benefits of an emotionally supportive spouse (Koran & Litt, 1988).

Studies of alcoholism, suicide, longevity (the average age to which individuals can expect to live), and various mental disorders also reveal that married individuals fare better than unmarried ones. Married individuals consistently show less alcoholism and problem drinking than unmarried individuals. Single men are more than three times as likely to die of cirrhosis of the liver (presumably alcohol related) than married men are.

Research that extends back to the nineteenth century (Durkheim, 1897) and continues today (Coombs, 1991) indicates that married individuals, especially men, are less likely to commit suicide than unmarried individuals. Social isolation, more common for unmarried persons, is believed to contribute to suicide. Also consistent from the nineteenth century through today is the finding that the highest incidence of suicide is among divorced men and married women (Durkheim, 1897; Koester & Clark, 1980). Why? Probably

What effect does marriage have on adjustment?

because wives are more likely than husbands to provide emotional support and because husbands are less nurturant and more demanding.

Mental hospital admissions consistently show lower rates for married than for unmarried persons (Robertson, 1974). Again, the provision of interpersonal

support marriage can provide contributes to the lower mental hospital admission rates of married individuals.

Married persons live longer than unmarried persons (Helsing & Szkio, 1981). Marital roles of protection and support, such as the sympathy and services married partners receive from a spouse in times of stress and illness, likely account for this difference. Of course, the mere presence of a spouse does not guarantee a supportive relationship. There is increasing evidence that the quality of interpersonal relationships is associated with physical health (Kennedy, Kiecolt-Glaser, & Glaser, 1988). Women in unhappy, unsupportive marriages have higher cholesterol levels, more illness symptoms, increased levels of depression, and decreased immune system functioning than happily married women (Kiecolt-Glaser & others, 1987).

> *If variety is the spice of life, marriage is the big can of leftover Spam.*
> —Johnny Carson

Marriage, of course, is not for everyone. We all probably know one or more persons who would be better off if they had not gotten married. Marriage and other lifestyles have their advantages and their disadvantages. Next we will outline the process by which people decide to marry.

Deciding to Marry

The decision to get married or remain single is often a complex one, influenced by many personal, interpersonal, and sociocultural factors. For instance, it is influenced by a person's perception of the positive and negative features of being single and being married. Some individuals are well adjusted as single adults and are committed to the development of a career that precludes the time and emotional support needed to make a marriage work. Their decision to remain single for a longer period of time or to never get married may be a wise one. Other individuals are not happy as single adults and perceive an emptiness in their lives that they believe marriage might fill.

Individuals who face the decision of staying single or getting married experience many pulls and pushes from within themselves, from others, and from the society in which they live. In one study of single women and men between the ages of 22 and 45, some factors that pushed them away from being single and pulled them toward being

married were economic security; pressure from parents; fear of independence; loneliness; cultural expectations to be married; a desire for regular sex; a desire for a family; and emotional attachment (Stein, 1976). Some factors that pushed them away from being married and pulled them toward remaining single were the restrictions of marriage (including a suffocating one-to-one relationship and the feeling of being trapped); obstacles to self-development; boredom, unhappiness, and anger; potentially poor communication with a spouse; possible sexual frustration; blocked career opportunities; restrictions on various experiences; the less exciting lifestyle of marriage; and the lack of freedom to change and experiment.

Selecting a Mate

For individuals who do decide to become married, what factors influence their mate selection? Our discussion of love and intimacy in the last chapter provided some clues, especially in terms of the similarities between partners.

Marital researchers and theorists have proposed two labels to illustrate the importance of similarity in marital choice: *homogamy* and *endogamy* (Surra, 1990). **Homogamy** *is a person's tendency to marry someone who has personal characteristics similar to his or her own.* People tend to marry others who are similar in age, education, physical attractiveness, interests, and values. **Endogamy** *is a person's tendency to marry someone in his or her own social group.* Social group factors include such things as ethnicity (for instance, being Latino, African American, White, or Asian), socioeconomic status (such as low-income versus middle-class), and religious convictions (Catholic, Protestant, or Jewish, for example).

To examine how values influence mate selection, see Critical Thinking.

> *People marry most happily their own kind. The trouble lies in the fact that people usually marry at an age when they do not really know what their own kind is.*
> —Robertson Davies

Cohabitation

Living together in nonmarital unions is a lifestyle experienced by many people at some point in their lifetime. Many cohabitors are young adults (68 percent are under the age of 35) and never-marrieds (53 percent), although a sizeable portion have been divorced (34 percent).

An intriguing question in marital relations is whether marital success will be enhanced if the partners have cohabited or lived apart prior to becoming married. An increasing number of studies suggest that living apart prior to marriage predicts greater marital success than cohabiting (Surra, 1990). Why is cohabitation related to less marital stability and higher rates of marital dissolution? Marital researchers suggest that cohabitors may be more committed to personal independence than individuals who do not cohabit. This commitment to independence is reflected in cohabitors' low likelihood of pooling income, jointly owning property, and sharing activities.

Despite the negative findings regarding the potential for cohabitation to improve the success of subsequent marriage, many cohabitors speak highly of the experiences they have had living in a nonmarital union. Most cohabitors plan to marry eventually. However, many others do not. They see cohabitation as an opportunity to experiment with responsibility in a nonmarital union, a union that is less likely to end with the legal entanglements of marriage.

Lesbian and Gay Couples

Homosexuals *are sexually attracted to persons of their own sex. Male homosexuals are often referred to as gays, and female homosexuals are often referred to as lesbians.* **Heterosexuals** *are sexually attracted to persons of the other sex.* In the United States, many churches approve only of sexual acts that can lead to conception within marriage, making homosexual relations unacceptable in their church doctrine. Although some churches have begun to perform marriage ceremonies for homosexual couples, no state yet legally recognizes marriage between partners of the same sex.

In most aspects of relationships, homosexual couples are similar to

Halonen/Santrock: Human Adjustment

Most of us tend to marry people who are similar to us, following the principles of homogamy and endogamy. Yet there are partners who violate these expectations and marry someone dissimilar. For example, "May-December" marriages violate the principle of homogamy because a large age difference exists between the partners. When the woman is substantially older than the man, there is likely to be even more curiosity and disapproval. "Mixed marriages" involving differences in religion or ethnicity violate the principle of endogamy. Romances sometimes fail when the partners attempt to introduce each other to their families.

What *underlying values* might motivate a partner choice that is inconsistent with the principles of homogamy and endogamy? Would you consider such partners to be greater risk-takers? more tolerant than most individuals in our culture? more interested in disturbing the peace in their families of origin? Are there other values that might explain choices that are not homogamous or endogamous?

---

heterosexual couples. However, homosexual couples often do not receive the social sanctions extended to heterosexual couples, including legal recognition, joint property rights, support from family and the community, and rituals such as a marriage ceremony. Because of such deficiencies in support and because lesbian and gay couples face the same intimacy problems as heterosexual couples (such as communication difficulties), lesbian and gay relationships often have an even higher rate of instability than heterosexual marriages do. Nevertheless, many lesbian and gay couples remain together for many years or for life.

Living Single

There is no rehearsal. One day you don't live alone, the next day you do. College ends. Or your wife walks out. Or your husband dies. Suddenly you are in this increasingly modern condition—living alone. Maybe you like it, maybe you don't. Maybe you thrive on the solitude, maybe you ache as if in exile. Either way, chances are you are only half-prepared, if at all, to be sole proprietor of your bed, your toaster, and your time. Most of us were raised in the din and clutter of family life, jockeying for a place in the bathroom in the morning, fighting over the last piece of cake, and obliged to compromise on the simplest of choices—the volume of the stereo, the channel on the TV, for example.

The number of individuals who live alone began to grow in the 1950s, but in the 1970s the pace skyrocketed. In the seventies, the number of men living by themselves increased 97 percent, the number of women, 55 percent. In the eighties, the growth slowed considerably, but it continues and is expected to do so at least through the end of the century. In 1993, 23.6 million individuals lived alone in the United States, accounting for 10 percent of adults. In some respects, the number of individuals living alone is a symptom of other changes: low birth rates, high divorce rates, long lives, and late marriages. But the group of single adults that grew the fastest in the 1970s was young adults, the majority of them young men. In that decade, the number of never-married people under 30 living by themselves more than tripled. For them, marriage was no longer the only way out of the house or the only route to sexual fulfillment.

Myths and stereotypes are associated with being single, ranging from "the swinging single" to "desperately lonely, suicidal single." Most singles, of course, are somewhere between these extremes. Single adults are often challenged by others to get married so they will no longer be regarded as selfish, irresponsible, impotent, frigid, or immature. Clearly, though, being a single adult has some advantages—time to make decisions about one's life course, time to develop personal resources to meet goals, freedom to make autonomous decisions and pursue a schedule and interests, opportunity to explore new places and try out new things, and privacy.

Common problems of single adults focus on intimate relationships with other adults, confronting loneliness, and finding a niche in a society that has traditionally been marriage oriented. Many single adults cite personal freedom as one of the major advantages of being a single adult.

Some adults never marry. Initially, they are perceived as living glamorous, exciting lives. But once we reach the age of 30, there is increasing pressure on us to settle down and get married. If a woman wants to bear children, she may feel a sense of urgency when she reaches 30. This is when many single adults make a conscious decision to marry or to remain single.

Being an old maid is like death by drowning, a really delightful sensation after you cease to struggle.

—**Edna Ferber**

The Diversity of Adult Lifestyles

Marriage is a legally and socially sanctioned relationship within the family system. Marriage fulfills many functions attributed to the family in general, including replacement of members, reproduction, economic enhancement, social status, emotional support, and health benefits. Married persons, especially men, are happier and less stressed than their unmarried counterparts. Interpersonal closeness and emotional support are the factors most likely responsible for the marital advantage in well-being. Married men are happier than married women.

The decision to get married or remain single is a complex one, influenced by many personal, interpersonal, and sociocultural factors. Among the factors that push individuals away from being single and pull them toward marriage are economic security, pressure from parents, loneliness, regular sex, desire for a family, and emotional attachment. Among the factors that push individuals away from marriage and pull them toward staying single are the fear of being suffocated in a one-to-one relationship and feeling of being trapped in a marriage, obstacles to self-development, blocked career opportunities, and the lack of freedom to experiment and change. Homogamy (the tendency to marry someone who has personal characteristics similar to one's own) and endogamy (the tendency to marry someone in his or her own social group) help to predict the person an individual will marry.

Adults can adopt many diverse lifestyles in addition to marriage, three being cohabitation, becoming a lesbian or gay couple, and single adulthood. Many cohabitors are young adults and never-marrieds, although a sizable portion have been divorced. An increasing number of studies reveal that living apart prior to marriage predicts greater marital success than cohabitating. Nonetheless, many cohabitors speak highly of their experiences.

Homosexuals are sexually attracted to persons of their own sex, and they are often identified as either gay (males) or lesbian (females). Heterosexuals are sexually attracted to persons of the other sex. In most aspects of relationships, lesbian and gay couples are similar to heterosexual couples; however, homosexual couples do not receive the social sanctions extended to heterosexual couples.

Being single has become an increasingly popular lifestyle. Myths and stereotypes about singles abound, ranging from "swinging single" to "desperate lonely, suicidal single." There are advantages and disadvantages to being single, one of the advantages being autonomy. Intimacy, loneliness, and a marriage-oriented society are concerns of single adults.

THE FAMILY LIFE CYCLE

As we go through life, we are at different stages in the family life cycle. The stages of the family cycle include these: single young adults, new couples, families with children, families with adolescents, families at midlife, and families in later life. A summary of these stages in the family life cycle is shown in figure 11.1. The summary features aspects of emotional processes involved in the transition from one stage to the next and changes in family status required for developmental change to take place (Carter & McGoldrick, 1989).

Leaving Home

Leaving home *is the first stage in the family life cycle; it involves the concept of launching.* **Launching** *is the process in which the youth moves into adulthood and exits his or her family of origin.* Adequate completion of launching requires that the young adult separate from the family of origin without cutting off ties completely or fleeing in a reactive way to find some form of substitute emotional refuge. The launching period is a time for the youth or young adult to formulate personal life goals, to develop an identity, and to become more independent. This is a time for young people to sort out emotionally what they will take from the family of origin, what they will leave behind, and what they will create themselves. They will also formulate some objectives about the kind of adult lifestyle they hope to achieve.

Complete cut-offs from parents rarely or never resolve emotional problems. The shift to adult-to-adult status between parents and children requires a mutually respectful and personal form of relating, in which young adults can appreciate parents as they are, needing neither to make them into what they are not nor to blame them for what they could not be. Neither do young adults need to comply with parental expectations and wishes at their own expense.

Finding a Partner

Finding a partner *is the second stage in the family life cycle; in this stage two individuals from separate families of origin unite to form a new family system.* This stage involves the development of a new marital system, and a realignment with extended families and friends to include the spouse. Women's changing roles, the increasingly frequent marriage of partners from divergent backgrounds, and the increasing geographical distances between family members are placing a much stronger burden on couples to define their relationship for themselves than in the past.

Marriage is usually described as the union of two individuals, but in reality it is the union of two entire family systems and the development of a new, third system. Some experts on marriage and the family believe that marriage represents such a different phenomenon for women and men that we need to speak of "her"

Family life-cycle stage	Key emotional processes	Changes in family status required to proceed developmentally
1. Leaving home	Accepting emotional and financial responsibility for self	• Differentiating the self in relation to family of origin • Developing intimate peer relationships • Establishing the self in relation to work and financial independence
2. Finding a partner	Commiting to new system	• Creating the marital system • Realigning relationships with extended families and friends to include spouse
3. Becoming parents	Accepting new members into the system	• Adjusting marital system to make space for child(ren) • Joining in child rearing, financial, and household tasks • Realigning relationships with extended family to include parenting and grandparenting roles
4. Parenting adolescents	Increasing flexibility of family boundaries to include children's independence and grandparents' frailties	• Shifting parent-child relationships to permit adolescent to move in and out of system • Refocusing on midlife marital and career issues • Beginning shift toward joint caring for older generation
5. Midlife families	Accepting a multitude of exits from and entries into the family system	• Renegotiating the marital system as a dyad or pair • Developing adult to adult relationships between grown children and their parents • Realigning relationships to include in-laws and grandchildren • Dealing with disabilities and death of parents (grandparents)
6. Families in later life	Accepting the shifting of generational roles	• Maintaining own and/or couple functioning and interests in face of physiological decline; exploring new familial and social role options • Supporting a more central role of middle generation • Making room in the system for the wisdom and experience of the elderly; supporting the older generation without overfunctioning for them • Dealing with the loss of spouse, siblings, and other peers and preparation for own death; life review and integration

FIGURE 11.1

The Stages of the Family Life Cycle

CRITICAL THINKING

The Family Script

Family therapists like to refer to the tendency we have to reproduce patterns in our adult lives from our family of origin as *family scripts*. These scripts can be learned by direct instruction or through imitation. They can be subtle behaviors or major behaviors that define who we are. For example, one young woman couldn't explain why she thought eloping would be the best way to marry until she looked back at her parents' example and recognized that they had eloped. Their ritual descriptions of how they met and married created an expectation that this would be the right way for her to start married life as well. Family scripts involve a wide variety of behaviors, including everything from how we celebrate holidays to what behaviors we expect from our partners.

Think about your own family constellation. Have you found yourself acting out subtle or not-so-subtle scripts that your family has created? Thinking about how behavioral expectations can be passed down through the generations is an example of *engaging in self-reflection to enhance self-knowledge*.

marriage and "his" marriage (Bernard, 1972). In the American society, women have anticipated marriage with greater enthusiasm and more positive expectations than men have, although, statistically, married women report substantial strains, disappointment, and health problems. To explore how family traditions influence expectations about married life, see Critical Thinking.

> When a girl marries, she exchanges the
> attentions of many men for the
> inattention of one.
>
> —Helen Bowland

Becoming Parents

Becoming parents *is the third stage in the family life cycle. Entering this stage requires that adults now move up a generation and become caregivers to the younger generation.* Moving through the lengthy stage successfully requires a commitment of time as a parent, understanding the roles of parents, and adapting to developmental changes in children (Santrock, 1997). Problems that emerge when a couple first assumes the parental role include struggles with each other about taking responsibility and refusal or inability to function as competent parents to children.

The Transition to Parenthood
When people become parents through pregnancy, adoption, or stepparenting, they face disequilibrium and must adapt. Parents want to develop a strong attachment with their infant, but they still want to maintain strong attachments to their spouse and friends, and possibly continue their careers. Parents ask themselves how this new being will change their lives. A baby places new restrictions on partners; no longer will they be able to rush out to a movie on a moment's notice, and money might not be readily available for vacations and other luxuries.

> The value of marriage is not that adults
> produce children but that children
> produce adults.
>
> —Peter DeVries

The excitement and joy that accompany the birth of a healthy baby are often followed by "postpartum blues" in mothers—a depressed state that usually is fleeting but in rare cases can last as long as 9 months after the birth of the baby. The early months of the baby's physical demands may bring not only the joy of intimacy but also the challenge of exhaustion. Pregnancy and childbirth are demanding physical events that require recovery time for the mother.

Becoming a father is both wonderful *and* stressful. In a longitudinal investigation of couples from late pregnancy until 3½ years after the baby was born, Carolyn and Phillip Cowan (Cowan, 1991; Cowan & others, 1995) found that the couples enjoyed more positive marital relations before the baby was born than after. Still, almost one-third showed an increase in marital satisfaction. Some couples said that the baby had both brought them closer together *and* moved them farther apart. They commented that being parents enhanced their sense of themselves and gave them a new, more stable identity as a couple. Babies opened men up to a concern with intimate relationships. The demands of juggling work and family roles stimulated women to manage family tasks more efficiently and pay attention to their personal growth.

> People who say they sleep like a baby
> usually don't have one.
>
> —Leo J. Burke

At some point during the early years of the child's life, parents do face the difficult task of juggling their roles as parents and as self-actualizing adults.

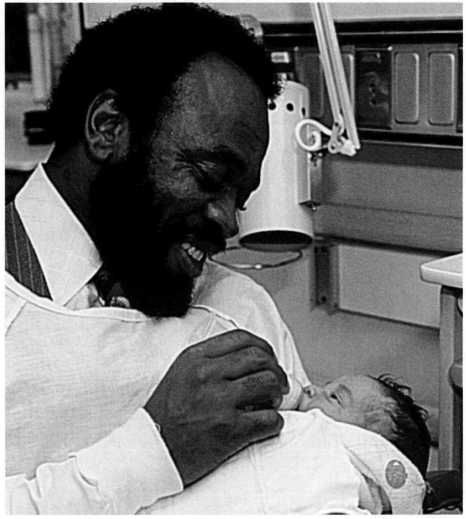

The current image of the father as an active, nurturing, caregiving parent emerged in the 1970s.

- Children will take care of parents in old age.
- Parents can expect respect and get obedience from their children.
- Having a child means that the parents will always have someone who loves them and is their best friend.
- Having a child gives the parents a "second chance" to achieve what they should have achieved.
- If parents learn the right techniques, they can mold their children into what they want.
- It's the parents fault when children fail.
- Mothers are naturally better parents than fathers.
- Parenting is an instinct and requires no training.

> *An ounce of mother is worth a pound of clergy.*
>
> **—Spanish proverb**

Until recently in our culture, nurturing our children and having a career were thought to be incompatible. Fortunately, we now recognize that the balance between caring and achieving, nurturing and working—although difficult to manage—can be accomplished.

The Parental Role

Many adults plan and coordinate the parental role with other roles in life, keeping in mind their economic situation. For others, the discovery that they are about to become parents is a startling surprise. In either event, the prospective parents may have mixed emotions and romantic illusions about having a child. Parenting consists of many interpersonal skills and emotional demands, yet there is little in the way of formal education for this task (Stenhouse, 1996). Most parents learn parenting practices from their own parents—some they accept, some they discard. Husbands and wives may bring different viewpoints of parenting practices to the marriage. Unfortunately, passing the methods of parents on from one generation to the next perpetuates both desirable and undesirable practices.

The needs and expectations of parents have stimulated many myths about parenting (Okun & Rappaport, 1980).

- The birth of a child will save a failing marriage.
- As a possession or extension of the parent, the child will think, feel, and behave like the parents did in their childhood.

In earlier times, women considered being a mother a full-time occupation. Currently, there is a tendency to have fewer children, and as birth control has become common practice, many individuals choose when they will have children and how many children they will raise. The number of one-child families is increasing, for example. Giving birth to fewer children and the reduced demands of child care free a significant portion of a woman's life for other endeavors. Three accompanying changes are these: (1) As a result of working more outside the home, mothers invest less time in their children's development; (2) men are apt to invest a greater amount of time in fathering; and (3) parental care in the home is often supplemented by institutional care (day care, for example).

As more women show an increased interest in developing a career, they are not only marrying later, but also having children later. What are some of the advantages of having children early or late? Some of the advantages of having children early are that parents are likely to have more physical energy (for example, they can cope better with such matters as getting up in the middle of the night with infants, and waiting up until adolescents come home at night); the mother is likely to have fewer medical problems with pregnancy and childbirth; and the parents may be less likely to build up expectations for their children, as do many couples who have waited many years to have children. By contrast, there are also advantages to having children late: Parents will have had more time to consider their goals in life, such as what they want from their family and career roles; parents will be more mature and will be able to benefit from their life experiences to engage in more competent parenting; and parents will be better established in their careers and have more income for child-rearing expenses.

Parenting Styles

Parents want their children to grow into socially mature individuals, and they may feel frustrated in trying to discover the best way to accomplish this. Developmentalists have long searched for the ingredients of parenting that promote competent social development in children. For example, in the 1930s, John Watson argued that parents are too affectionate with their children and recommended strategies to avoid spoiling them. In the 1950s, a distinction was made between physical and psychological discipline, with psychological discipline, especially reasoning, emphasized as the best way to rear a child. In the 1970s and beyond, the dimensions of competent parenting have become more precise.

Especially widespread is the view of Diana Baumrind (1971, 1991), who believes that parents should be neither punitive nor aloof but, instead, should develop rules for their children and be affectionate with them. She emphasizes three types of parenting that are associated with different aspects of a child's social behavior: authoritarian, authoritative, and laissez-faire (permissive). More recently, developmentalists have argued that permissive parenting comes in two forms: indulgent and neglectful. What are these forms of parenting like?

Authoritarian parenting *is a restrictive, punitive style in which parents exhort the child to follow their directions and to respect work and effort. The authoritarian parent places firm limits and controls on the child and allows little verbal exchange. Authoritarian parenting is associated with children's social incompetence.* For example, an authoritarian parent might say, "You do it my way or else. There will be no discussion!" Children of authoritarian parents often tend to be anxious about social comparison, fail to initiate activity, and have poor communication skills.

Authoritative parenting *encourages children to be independent but still places limits and controls on their actions. Extensive verbal give-and-take is allowed and parents are warm and nurturant toward children. Authoritative parenting is associated with children's social competence.* An authoritative parent might put her arm around the child in a comforting way and say, "You know you should not have done that; let's talk about how you can handle the situation better next time." Children whose parents are authoritative tend to be socially competent, self-reliant, and socially responsible.

Permissive parenting comes in two forms: neglectful and indulgent (Maccoby & Martin, 1983). **Neglectful parenting** *is a style in which the parent is very uninvolved in the child's life; it is associated with children's social incompetence, especially a lack of self-control.* This parent cannot answer the question "It is 10 P.M.; do you know where your child is?" Children have a strong need for their parents to care about them; children whose parents are permissive-indifferent develop the sense that other aspects of the parents' lives are more important than they are. Children whose parents are neglectful often appear to be socially incompetent—they show poor self-control and do not handle independence well.

Indulgent parenting *is a style of parenting in which parents are highly involved with their children but place few demands or controls on them. Indulgent parenting is associated with children's social incompetence, especially a lack of self-control.* Indulgent parents let their children do what they want, and the result is that the children never learn to control their own behavior and always expect to get their own way. Some

parents deliberately rear their children in this way because they believe the combination of warm involvement with few restraints will produce a creative, confident child. One boy whose parents deliberately reared him in an indulgent manner moved his parents out of their bedroom suite and took it over for himself. He is 18 years old and has not learned to control his behavior; when he can't get something he wants, he still throws temper tantrums. As you might expect, he is not very popular with his peers. Children whose parents are indulgent have difficulty learning respect for others or controlling their own behavior.

Families with Adolescents

The **family with adolescents** *is the fourth stage of the family life cycle. Adolescence is a period of development in which individuals push for autonomy and seek to develop their own identity.* The development of mature autonomy and identity is a lengthy process, transpiring over at least 10 to 15 years. As adolescents pursue a more autonomous life, many parents perceive them as changing from compliant children to noncompliant adolescents. Parents tend to adopt one of two strategies to handle noncompliance—clamp down and put more pressure on the adolescent to conform to parental values, or become more permissive and let the adolescent have extensive freedom. Neither is a wise overall strategy; rather a more flexible, adaptive approach is best. As adolescents push for autonomy, a wise parent relinquishes control in areas where adolescents make mature decisions. A wise parent also calmly communicates with adolescents and tries to help them make reasonable decisions in areas in which they show less mature behavior.

The old model of parent-adolescent relationships suggested that, as adolescents mature, they detach themselves from parents and move into a world of autonomy apart from parents. The old model also suggested that parent-adolescent conflict is intense and stressful throughout adolescence. The new model emphasizes that parents serve as important attachment figures and support systems as adolescents explore a wider, more complex social world (Holmbeck, 1996). The new model

Halonen/Santrock: Human Adjustment

Old model of parent-adolescent relationships

● Autonomy, detachment from parents; parent and peer worlds isolated

● Intense conflict throughout adolescence; stormy and stressful on a daily basis

New model of parent-adolescent relationships

● Autonomy, but attachment to parents; adolescent-parent and adolescent-peer worlds interconnected

● Moderate conflict promotes growth; conflict greater in early adolescence

FIGURE 11.2

Old and New Models of Parent-Adolescent Relationships

also emphasizes that, in the majority of families, parent-adolescent conflict is moderate rather than severe. Everyday negotiations and minor disputes can serve the positive developmental function of helping adolescents make the transition from childhood dependence to adult independence (see figure 11.2) (Santrock, 1996).

> *Children today are tyrants. They contradict their parents, gobble their food, and tyrannize their teachers.*
>
> **—Socrates**

Families at Midlife

The **family at midlife** *is the fifth stage in the family cycle. It is a time of launching children, playing an important role in linking generations, and adapting to midlife changes in development.* Until about a generation ago, most families were involved in raising their children for much of their adult lives until old age. Because of the lower birth rate and longer life of most adults, parents now launch their children about 20 years before retirement, which frees many midlife parents to pursue other activities.

Empty nest syndrome *is the belief that marital satisfaction will decrease because parents derive considerable satisfaction from their children, and therefore, the children's departure will leave parents with empty feelings.* While the empty nest syndrome may hold true for some parents who live vicariously through their children, the empty nest usually does not lower marital satisfaction. Rather, just the opposite happens; marital satisfaction increases in the post-child-rearing years. Now with children gone, marital partners have more time to pursue career interests and more time for each other.

> *Parenthood; that state of being better chaperoned than you were before marriage.*
>
> **—Marcelene Cox**

In today's uncertain economic climate, the refilling of the empty nest is becoming a common occurrence as adult children return to live at home after an unsuccessful career or a divorce. Some individuals don't leave home at all until their middle to late twenties because they cannot financially support themselves. The middle generation has always provided support for the younger generation, even after the nest is bare. Through loans and monetary gifts for education and through emotional support, the middle generation has helped the younger generation. Adult children appreciate the financial and emotional support their parents provide them at a time when they often feel considerable stress about their career, work, and lifestyle, and parents feel good that they can provide this support.

As with most family living arrangements, however, there are both benefits and drawbacks when adult children return to live at home. Many parents have developed expectations that their adult children would be capable of supporting themselves. Adult children had expectations that they would be on their own as young adults. In one investigation, 42 percent of middle-aged parents said they had serious conflicts with their resident adult children (Clemens & Axelson, 1985). One of the most common complaints voiced by both adult children and their parents is a loss of privacy. The adult children complain that their parents restrict their independence, cramp their sex lives, reduce their rock music listening, and treat them as children rather than adults. Parents often complain that their quiet home has become noisy, that they stay up late worrying when their adult children will come home, that meals are difficult to plan because of conflicting schedules, that their relationship as a married couple has been invaded, and that they have to shoulder too much responsibility for their adult children. In sum, when adult children return home to live, it creates a disequilibrium in family life, which requires considerable adaptation on the part of parents and their adult children. This living arrangement usually works best when there is adequate space, when parents treat their adult children more like adults than like children, and when there is an atmosphere of trust and communication.

Even some marriages that were difficult and rocky during early adulthood turn out to be better adjusted during middle adulthood (Rollins, 1989). Although the partners may have lived through a great deal of turmoil, they eventually discover a deep and solid foundation on which to anchor their relationship. In middle adulthood, the partners may have fewer financial worries, less housework and chores, and more time with each other. Partners who engage in mutual activities usually view their marriage as more positive at this time.

For the most part, family members maintain considerable contact across generations. Parent-child similarity is most noticeable in religious and political areas, least in gender roles, lifestyle, and work orientation. Gender differences also characterize intergenerational relationships. In one study, mothers and their daughters had much closer relationships during their adult years than mothers and sons, fathers and daughters, or fathers and sons (Rossi, 1989). In this same investigation, married men were more involved with their wives' kin than their own. These findings underscore the significance of the woman's role as mother in monitoring access to and feelings toward kin.

In the investigation by Alice Rossi (1989), mothers and their daughters had much closer relationships during their adult years than mothers and sons, fathers and daughters, and fathers and sons. Married men were more involved with their wives' kin than their own. And maternal grandmothers and maternal aunts were cited twice as often as their counterparts on the paternal side of the family as the most important or loved relative.

> One thing they never tell you about child raising is that for the rest of your life, at the drop of a hat, you are expected to know your child's name and how old he or she is.
>
> —Erma Bombeck

Families in Later Life

The **family in later life** *is the sixth and final stage in the family life cycle. Retirement alters a couple's lifestyle, requiring adaptation.* The greatest changes occur in the traditional family, in which the husband works and the wife is a homemaker. The husband might not know what to do with his time, and the wife might feel uneasy having him around the house all of the time. In traditional families, both partners may need to move toward more expressive roles. The husband must adjust from being the good provider to being a helper around the house; the wife must change from being a good homemaker to being even more loving and understanding. Marital happiness as an older adult is also affected by each partner's ability to deal with personal conflicts, including aging, illness, and eventually death.

> Healthy children will not fear life if their elders have integrity enough not to fear death.
>
> —Erik Erikson

Individuals who are married in late adulthood are usually happier than those who are single (Lee, 1978). In this stage, marital satisfaction is greater for women than for men, possibly because women place more emphasis on attaining satisfaction through marriage than men do. However, as more women develop careers, this sex difference may not continue.

We have examined the functions of marriage and selecting a mate, trends and characteristics in marriage and the family, and the family life cycle. Now we turn our attention to current trends in family life.

> When men reach their sixties and retire, they go to pieces. Women just go right on cooking.
>
> —Gail Sheehy

CURRENT FAMILY TRENDS

Many of today's families are far removed from the era of Ozzie and Harriet. Forty years ago, two of three American families consisted of a father who was the bread-winner, a mother who was a full-time homemaker, and the children they were raising. Today, fewer than one in five families fits that description. Let's examine some of the main trends in marriage and the family as we move toward the twenty-first century.

Postponing or Avoiding Marriage

Recently there have been dramatic shifts toward the postponement of marriage, increased cohabitation, and single adulthood. The proportion of men aged 20 to 24 who had not yet wed was 80 percent in 1991, 25 percent higher than it was in 1970. For women in this age group, the proportion never married increased from 36 percent in 1970 to 64 percent in 1990 (U.S. Bureau of the Census, 1990). The increase in never-marrieds has been pervasive across age groups—the proportion never married tripled for women and nearly doubled for men between 1970 and 1991, and for the 30 to 34 age group, the proportion tripled for both genders. The median age of marriage has been rising for the past 30 years—in 1990, the estimated age of first marriage was 23.7 for women and 25.5 for men.

Although it might be argued that the postponement of marriage indicates a general disinterest in close or committed relationships, cohabitation has increased. Today there are more than 3 million unmarried couple households, an increase

of approximately 600 percent since 1970 and an increase of approximately 100 percent since 1980. These figures include not only close relationships but also other living arrangements—such as an elderly woman with a live-in companion.

More precise information about sexually intimate unmarried couples who live together is available. The National Survey of Families and Households provided information about 13,000 persons aged 19 and older (Sweet, Bumpass, & Call, 1988). By their early thirties, almost half of these individuals lived together at some time, and 4 percent were currently cohabiting. Most cohabitors are young adults (68 percent are under the age of 35) and never-marrieds (53 percent), although a sizeable portion have been divorced (34 percent).

Not only has there been a dramatic increase in cohabiting couples, but the percentage of single adults has also increased substantially. Today, more than 20 percent of Americans 18 years and older have never been married, up from 17 percent in 1970. The percentage of single adults who are now divorced also has increased substantially in recent decades.

Changing Gender Roles

Reconceptualization of gender roles has led to the emergence of gender as a pivotal concept in marriage and the family (Duckett & Richards, 1996). Traditional divisions of labor and allocation of resources (especially money) in marriage have been challenged dramatically. For example, many women have postponed motherhood, or in some cases chosen not to have children. They have developed committed, permanent ties to the workplace that resemble the pattern once reserved only for men. When they have had children, they have strived to combine a career and motherhood. There have always been "career" females, but their numbers are growing at an unprecedented rate.

> Some couples go over their budgets very carefully every month; others just go over them.
>
> —Sally Poplin

Dual-career marriages can have advantages and disadvantages. Of course, one of the main advantages is financial. Employment instability and uncertainty, economic deprivation, and economic strain are negatively related to marital and family satisfaction and the quality of family relations. Economic hard times can have severe adverse consequences for families—such as increased risk of marital dissolution, family disorganization, spousal and child abuse, and child neglect. Dual-career marriages offer greater protection for the family during times of economic uncertainty.

One of every three wives earns 30 to 50 percent of the family's total income, which helps to explain why most first-time home buyers are dual-career couples. Other than financial benefits, dual-career marriages can contribute to a more equal relationship between husband and wife and enhanced feelings of self-esteem for women. Among the possible disadvantages or stresses of dual-career marriages are added time and energy demands, conflict between work and family roles, competitive rivalry between husband and wife, and, if the family includes children, concerns about whether the children's needs are being adequately met.

Overall, though, researchers are increasingly finding that women who engage in multiple roles (such as wife, mother, and professional) are better adjusted than women who engage in a single role or fewer roles (such as wife or wife and mother). The psychological benefits of multiple roles include variety, amplification (coming into contact with different people, usually on a daily basis, who can act as audiences), and buffering (dampening the bad—career rewards can buffer the negative events that occur in families and family responsibilities can usually buffer the impact of negative events at work) (Crosby, 1991). Of course, these studies are correlational in nature, so it is possible that better-adjusted women simply select more roles. Still, in recognizing the benefits of multiple roles for women, it is important to not ignore the discrimination women still too often experience at work and the burdens they often still bear at home.

I have yet to hear a man ask for advice on how to combine marriage and a career.

—Gloria Steinem

Not only are there gender differences in intimacy in marriages, but there are also strong gender differences in family work (Crosby & Jasker, 1993). Wives typically do much more family work than husbands. Most women and men agree that women should be responsible for family work and that men should "help out" (Szinovacz, 1984). In one study, only 10 percent of husbands did as much family work as their wives (Berk, 1985). These exceptional men were usually in circumstances with many, usually young, children and wives who worked full time.

The nature of women's involvement in family work is often different from men's. The family work most women do is unrelenting, repetitive, and routine, often involving cleaning, cooking, child care, shopping, laundry, and straightening up. The family work most men do is infrequent, irregular, and nonroutine, often involving household repairs, taking out the garbage, yard work, and gardening. Women often report having to do several tasks at once, which may explain why they find domestic work less relaxing and more stressful than men do.

Because family work is intertwined with love and embedded in family relations, it has complex and contradictory meanings. Most women experience family tasks as mindless but essential work done for the people they love. Most women usually enjoy tending to the needs of their loved ones and keeping the family going, even if they do not find the activities themselves enjoyable and fulfilling. The family work conditions of women are both positive and negative. The women are unsupervised and rarely criticized, they plan their own work, and they have only their own standards to meet; however, women's work is often worrisome, tiresome, menial, repetitive, isolating, unfinished, and unappreciated. Thus, it is not surprising that many women have mixed feelings about family work.

The Decline in Childbearing

A century ago, a large family was considered ideal, but not today. Even as late as the 1940s, 70 percent of Americans thought that three or more children would be the ideal family size. Today, 60 percent of Americans consider two or fewer children the ideal number (Roper Organizations, 1985). One reason for smaller families is increased recognition of the financial strains a large family can cause. This is a reversal from earlier times, when large numbers of children meant more farm hands to help produce family income. Increased use of contraceptive methods and the increased number of women in the work force are two more reasons.

Finally, another reason is the recognition that only children are not necessarily the "spoiled brats" they once were thought to be (Falbo & Polit, 1986). Today researchers present a more positive portrayal of the only child as achievement oriented and adjusted, especially in comparison to children from large families.

Some couples have no children. Until recently, childless couples were pitied because it was assumed that virtually all of them could not have children. After all, it was assumed that all married couples would desire children; therefore not to have any would have to be a big source of disappointment. If a couple said they did not want children, it would be perceived as being selfish because communities and countries wanted their populations to grow. This is no longer the case. There is more concern about overpopulation (some large families have found themselves criticized as being selfish or stupid to have more than two children). Some countries have instituted policies aimed at limiting population growth. The most restrictive country has been China, which punishes families for having more than one child.

Still, childless couples are the minority—about one in five married women will likely remain childless. Couples who remain childless voluntarily are usually highly educated and career oriented. They may have been previously married or have married later in life. Also, some women with demanding careers might perceive that having children will slow their advancement in the labor force. Others simply drift into childlessness, delaying children until they are comfortable in a lifestyle or until the wife is too old to have children. How do childless couples fare? In one study, couples without children reported greater happiness than couples with children, but they also are at a greater risk for divorce, possibly because some married couples with children try to stay together for the sake of the children.

Ethnic Minority Patterns

There has been an increased interest in marriage and the family in ethnic minority groups coinciding with the dramatic increase in ethnic minority individuals in America. African American and Latino families have emerged as special concerns.

Ethnic minority families tend to differ from White American families in their size, structure, and composition, their reliance on kinship networks, and their levels of income and education. Large and extended families are more common among ethnic minority groups than among White Americans. For example, more than 30 percent of Latino families, compared to less than 20 percent of families of the general population, consist of five or more people. African American and Latino children interact more with grandparents, aunts, uncles, cousins, and more distant relatives than do White American children.

Single-parent families are more common among African Americans and Latinos than among White Americans. Compared with couples heading two-parent households, single parents often have less time, money, and energy. This shortage of resources can prompt them to encourage early autonomy in their children. Ethnic minority parents tend to be less educated and to engage in less decision making than White American parents. Ethnic minority children are more likely to come from low-income families than White American children are. Although impoverished families can raise

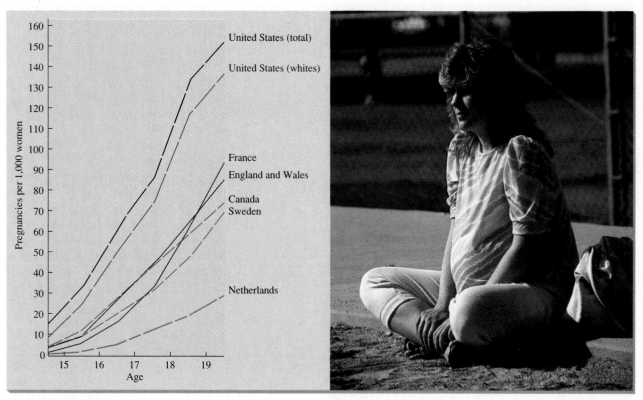

FIGURE 11.3

Pregnancy Rates per 1,000 Women by Women's Age, 1981

competent youth, poor parents may have a diminished capacity for supportive and involved parenting.

Some aspects of home life can help to protect ethnic minority youth from social patterns of injustice. The community and family can filter out destructive racist messages, parents can provide alternate frames of reference than those presented by the majority, and parents can also provide competent role models and encouragement. The extended family system in many ethnic minority families provides an important buffer to stress. To read further about the extended family system in African American and Mexican American families, turn to Sociocultural Worlds of Adjustment.

There is diversity within every ethnic group. For too long virtually any difference between White Americans and ethnic minority Americans was thought of as a deficit on the part of ethnic minority groups. Increasingly, psychologists believe we must examine the

resilience and adaptiveness of ethnic minority families. They caution, however, that to deny the existence of problems among significant numbers of ethnic minority families would be both naive and irresponsible.

Adolescent Parents

Each year more than 1 million American teenagers become pregnant with four of five of them unmarried. Many become pregnant in their early or middle adolescent years—30,000 of them under the age of 15. In all, this means that 1 of every 10 adolescent females in the United States becomes pregnant each year, with 8 of the 10 pregnancies unintended. As one 17-year-old Los Angeles mother of a 1-year-old boy said, "We are children having children."

The adolescent pregnancy rate in the United States is the highest of any in the Western world. It is more than twice the rate in England, France, or Canada; almost three times the rate in

Sweden; and seven times the rate in the Netherlands (Alan Guttmacher Institute, 1981) (see figure 11.3). Although American adolescents are no more sexually active than their counterparts in these other nations, they are many times more likely to become pregnant. To reflect on one proposal for reducing teenage pregnancy, turn to Critical Thinking.

Serious, extensive efforts need to be developed to help pregnant adolescents and young mothers enhance their educational and occupational opportunities (East & Felice, 1996; Murray, 1996). Adolescent mothers also need considerable help in obtaining competent day care and in planning for the future. Experts recommend the following for reducing the high adolescent pregnancy rate in the United States:

- Improved sex-education and family-planning information
- Greater access to contraception
- Broad community involvement and support

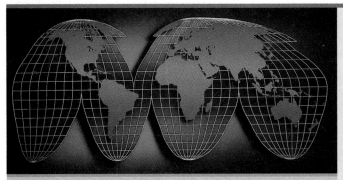

SOCIOCULTURAL WORLDS OF ADJUSTMENT

The Extended Family System in African American and Mexican American Families

In the 1985 Children's Defense Fund study "Black and White Children in America: Key Facts" (Edelman, 1987), African American children were three times as likely as White children to be poor, live with a parent who has separated from a spouse, and die of child abuse; five times as likely to be dependent on welfare; and twelve times as likely to live with a parent who never married. Nonetheless, it is important to keep in mind that millions of African American families are not on welfare; have children who stay in school and out of trouble; and, if they experience difficult times, find a way to cope with and overcome their problems. In 1967 Martin Luther King, Jr., reflected on the African American family and gave the following caution. As public awareness of the predicament of the African American family increases, there will be opportunity and danger. The opportunity will be to deal fully rather than haphazardly with the problem as a whole, as a social catastrophe brought on by many years of oppression. The danger is that the problems will be attributed to innate African American weaknesses and will be used to justify further neglect and to rationalize continued oppression. In today's world, Dr. King's words still ring true.

The African American cultural tradition of an extended family household—in which one or several grandparents, uncles, aunts, siblings, or cousins either live together or provide support—has helped many African American parents cope with adverse social conditions such as economic impoverishment (McAdoo, 1993). African American extended families can be traced to the African heritage of many African Americans, in which a newly married couple does not move away from relatives. Instead, the extended family assists its members with basic family functions. Researchers have found that African American extended families help reduce the stress of poverty and single parenting through emotional support, the sharing of income and economic responsibility, and surrogate parenting (McLoyd & Wilson, 1990; Wakschlag, Chase-Lansdale, & Brooks-Gunn, 1996). The presence of grandmothers in the households of many African American adolescents and their infants has been an important support system for both the teenage mothers and the infants (Stevens, 1984). Active and involved extended family support systems also help a parent or parents from other ethnic minority groups cope with poverty and its related stress.

A basic value in Mexico is represented by the saying "As long as our family stays together, we are strong." Mexican children are brought up to stay close to their families, often playing with siblings rather than with schoolmates or neighborhood children, as American children usually do. Unlike the father in many American families, Mexican fathers are the undisputed authority on all family matters and are usually obeyed without question. Mothers are revered as the primary source of affection and care. This emphasis on family attachment leads the Mexicans to say, "I will achieve mainly because of my family, and for my family, rather than myself." By contrast, a self-reliant American would say, "I will achieve mainly because of my ability and initiative and for myself rather than for my family." Unlike most Americans, families in Mexico tend to stretch out in a network of relatives that often runs to scores of individuals.

Both cultures—Mexican and American—have undergone considerable change in recent decades. It is difficult to predict whether Mexican children will gradually take on the characteristics of American children, or American children will shift closer to Mexican children. The cultures of both countries will probably move to a new order more in keeping with future demands, retaining some common features of the old while establishing new priorities and values.

The extended family plays an important role in the adjustment of ethnic minority individuals.

Mexican American children often grow up in families with a network of relatives that runs into scores of individuals.

In Nathaniel Hawthorne's novel *The Scarlet Letter,* Hester Prynne was required to wear a scarlet letter on her chest as an indication that she had committed adultery. The scarlet letter served as a symbol of her shame. Hester Prynne's neighbors made her feel like an outcast because of her sexuality and her sexual choices.

In recent years, many social critics have proposed that we need to reinstitute some *stigma* (widespread social disapproval) toward adolescent pregnancy. Although they are not proposing the dramatic methods described by Nathaniel Hawthorne, the critics suggest we need to make adolescent pregnancy less desirable by making it socially unacceptable. They point to the collusion of government programs in maintaining high rates of pregnancy by providing child support and sometimes enabling children to escape their own families before they are psychologically or financially ready to be independent.

The contrast of contemporary attitudes with the more repressive atmosphere in which Hester Prynne lived illustrates *the influence of context and culture on behavior.* Do you think the proposed social reform would have an impact on adolescent pregnancy? Can you think of any social reforms that might help reduce this enormous social problem?

REVIEW

The Family Life Cycle and Current Family Trends

As we go through life, we are at different points in the family life cycle. The stages of the family life cycle include: single young adults, new couples, families with children, families with adolescents, families at midlife, and families in later life. The needs and expectations of parents have stimulated many myths about parenting. Authoritarian, authoritative, indulgent, and neglectful are four main categories of parenting. Authoritative parenting is associated with children's social competence more than the other styles.

The new model of parent-adolescent relations suggests that parents serve as important attachment figures for adolescents and that parent-adolescent conflict is usually moderate rather than severe. Today, marital satisfaction usually increases in the post-child-rearing years, which negates the empty nest syndrome. For the most part families maintain considerable contact across generations with women playing a special role in this contact.

Women do much more family work than men, and they experience family work differently than men do. As growing numbers of women pursue careers, they are faced with questions involving career and marriage.

Dual-career marriages can have advantages or disadvantages for individuals. Overall, despite the stress of juggling multiple roles, women are happier and better adjusted when they engage in multiple roles (such as wife, mother, and career) rather than a single or fewer roles (wife only or wife and mother).

Some of the main trends and characteristics of marriage and the family include increased postponement or avoidance of marriage; a decline in childbearing; changes in gender roles that have increased the number of dual-career couples; increased stress in ethnic minority families; and an increase in the number of adolescent pregnancies.

MARITAL ADJUSTMENT

I love being married. It's so great to find that one special person you want to annoy for the rest of your life.
—Rita Rudner

Happy married life is an important goal for many of us, but most of us are likely to be disappointed. Many marriages end in divorce. Many others might not end in a formal or legal way, but might end emotionally. In this section we examine the threats to marital adjustment, including false expectations, communication challenges, family violence, and divorce.

Expectations and Myths

Among the explanations of our nation's high divorce rate and high degree of dissatisfaction in many marriages is that we have such strong expectations of marriage (Rice, 1996). We expect our spouse simultaneously to be a lover, a friend, a confidant, a counselor, a career person, and a parent. In one study, unhappily married couples expressed unrealistic expectations about marriage (Epstein & Eidelson, 1981). Underlying unrealistic expectations about marriage are numerous myths about marriage (Notarius, 1996). A myth is a widely held belief unsupported by facts.

Knowledge of Marital Myths and Realities

Instructions

Take out a sheet of paper and number from 1 to 15. Answer each of the following items true or false. After completing the quiz, turn to the end of the chapter for the correct answers.

Items

1. A husband's marital satisfaction is usually lower if his wife is employed full-time than if she is a full-time homemaker.
2. Today most young, single, never-married people will eventually get married.
3. In most marriages, having a child improves marital satisfaction for both spouses.
4. The best single predictor of overall marital satisfaction is the quality of a couple's sex life.
5. The divorce rate in America increased from 1960 to 1980.
6. A greater percentage of wives are in the workforce today than in 1970.
7. Marital satisfaction for a wife is usually lower if she is employed full-time than if she is a full-time homemaker.
8. If my spouse loves me, he/she should instinctively know what I want and need to be happy.
9. In a marriage in which the wife is employed full-time, the husband usually assumes an equal share of the housekeeping.
10. For most couples, marital satisfaction gradually increases from the first year of marriage through the childbearing years, the teen years, the empty nest period, and retirement.
11. No matter how I behave, my spouse should love me simply because he/she *is* my spouse.
12. One of the most frequent marital problems is poor communication.
13. Husbands usually make more lifestyle adjustments in marriage than wives.
14. Couples who cohabited before marriage usually report greater marital satisfaction than couples who did not.
15. I can change my spouse by pointing out his/her inadequacies, errors, etc.

To study college students' beliefs in the myths of marriage, Jeffry Larson (1988) constructed a marriage quiz to measure college students information about marriage. He compared their responses with what is known about marriage in the research literature. The college students responded incorrectly to almost half of the items. Female students missed fewer items than male students, and students with a less romantic perception of marriage missed fewer items than more romantically inclined students. To evaluate your understanding of the myths of marriage, see the Self-Assessment.

One of the great reasons why so many husbands and wives make shipwreck of their lives together is because a man is always seeking for happiness, while a woman is on a perpetual hunt for trouble.

—Dorothy Dix

Communication and Conflict

Marital satisfaction is a complex topic (Christiansen & Pasch, 1993). Research on marital satisfaction often emphasizes the roles of effective communication and conflict management skills.

Effective Communication

The experiences and implications of marriage can differ for the wife and husband (Thompson & Walker, 1989). This is especially true in the expression of intimacy and in family work. More men than women view their spouses as their best friends (Rubin, 1984).

No one really listens to anyone else, and if you try it for a while you'll see why.

—Mignon McLaughlin

Wives consistently disclose more to their partners than husbands do. Women also tend to express more tenderness, fear, and sadness than their partners. For many men, controlled anger is a common emotional orientation. A common complaint expressed by women in a marriage is that their husbands do not care about their emotional lives and do not express their own feelings and thoughts. Women often point out that they have to pull things out of their husbands and push them to open up. Men frequently respond either that they are open or that they do not understand what their wives want from them. It is not unusual for men to protest that no matter how much they talk it is not enough for their wives. Women also say they want more warmth and openness from their husbands. For example, women are more likely than men to give their partners a spontaneous kiss or hug when something positive happens. Overall, women are more expressive and affectionate than men in marriage, and this difference bothers many women.

Three decades ago, well-known marital researcher Jesse Bernard (1964) described three main dimensions of marital adjustment that most experts in this field still believe are important today:

1. The extent and degree of differences between marital partners
2. The nature of communication between the couple
3. The quality of the relationship between the partners—that is, the positive or negative emotions present, friendliness or hostility, and so on

Differences between partners might be a matter of degree, which makes them easier to negotiate, or they might be categorical, which makes them more difficult to resolve. For example, if one partner says, "We will *never* miss Sunday morning church," "Oral sex is *always* wrong," "The kitchen dishes *never* should be left on the counter," "The baby *has to be* breast-fed for 6 months," "I am going to watch football *every* Sunday," and "We can't afford to *ever* go out to eat on weeknights," then there is no room for flexibility and negotiation to resolve the differences if the other partner does not agree with these dogmatic assertions. Differences of degree, however, allow for more give-and-take, negotiation, and bargaining.

Few of us would doubt the importance of communication in marriage, but communication is a complex concept. As we learned in chapter 7, interpersonal communication can be verbal or nonverbal. Communication can be clear or misleading; it also can draw relationships closer together or rip them apart. To avoid talking completely, to talk constantly, to order, to nag, to scold, to soothe, to praise, and to encourage can each be used to convey certain messages. A review of 20 years of research on marital communication revealed that communication indeed is a very important factor in marital satisfaction (Boland & Follingstad, 1988). Couples with higher rates of self-disclosure and expressions of love, support, and affection experienced greater satisfaction in their

marriage. Positive forms of verbal communication, such as laughter, voice tone, touching spouse, and body position, were found more often in happy couples. Nondistressed couples also were more likely to show better listening skills, clearer speech, and more positive interpretation of their partner's behavior.

The quality of the relationship is a third important factor in marital adjustment. If a spouse is friendly and loving, it does not automatically mean that the marriage will be well-adjusted, but makes accommodations in the marriage easier. Making sacrifices or changes in plans becomes easier when spouses have a love and genuine concern for one another.

Conflict Management

All marriages are confronted with conflicts, and Howard Markman, director of the Center for Marital and Family Studies at the University of Denver, believes that one of the best predictors of marital success is a couple's ability to handle conflict constructively (Markman & Hahlweg, 1993). To strengthen marriages, Markman recommends that couples develop ground rules for discussing marital problems. His suggestions for marital negotiation include these:

Make a date for discussion/negotiation.
Tell your partner you want to talk about such-and-such and ask if this is a good time. Your partner can refuse to discuss it then, but must respond within 24 hours.

Focus on the problem. Talk face-to-face with no distractions. Discuss the problem itself, not the solution at this point. Markman believes that about 70 percent of relationship problems do not need to be solved, but rather people just want their opinions recognized as valid.

Reserve the right to take a break. Either partner can call for a time-out, agreeing to resume the discussion within 24 hours, so that both may leave without resentment if the discussion becomes too heated.

Deal with obstacles. If your partner won't talk, have your partner talk about

the reasons why. Often the partner is afraid that a fight will break out. Assure your partner that will not happen, and don't let it happen.

Go on to problem solving if needed.
Brainstorm solutions, writing them down. Then focus on some form of compromise.

Try out the solution. Renegotiate if necessary.

Try holding a weekly half-hour meeting.
Establish a set time to talk about relationship issues, a time for bringing up subjects that may cause conflict.

The conception of two people living together for 25 years without having a cross word suggests a lack of spirit only to be admired in sheep.

—**Alan Patrick Herbert**

Markman says that if your partner absolutely refuses to talk and the relationship seems very troubled, you probably need to seek counseling to improve the relationship. A common tool used in understanding degrees of marital satisfaction is presented in the Self-Assessment.

Family Violence

Although family members are one's biggest source of love, acceptance, and support, family members can also be one's source of hostility, abuse, and neglect. Indeed, there is an increasing concern about family violence involving various circumstances including child abuse and neglect, courtship aggression, spousal abuse, and elder abuse, yet most family violence remains a secret (Paludi, 1995).

Family violence occurs from adult to adult and from adult to child. With the number of magazine articles, books, and talk shows that cover the topic of battering, domestic violence, or spousal abuse, it may surprise you to know the topic was rarely discussed prior to the 1970s. Indeed, the first book to examine family violence, Erin Pizzey's *Scream Quietly or the Neighbors Will Hear*, was not published until 1974.

Marital Happiness

Instructions

This scale is intended to estimate your *current* happiness with your marriage on each of the ten dimensions listed. You are to circle one of the numbers (1–10) beside each marriage area. Numbers toward the left end of the ten-unit scale indicate some degree of unhappiness and numbers toward the right end of the scale reflect varying degrees of happiness. Ask yourself this question as you rate each marriage area: "If my partner continues to act in the future as he/she is acting *today* with respect to this marriage area, how happy will I be *with this area of our marriage?*" In other words, state according to the numerical scale (1–10) exactly how you feel today. Try to exclude all feelings of yesterday and concentrate only on the feelings of today in each of the marital areas. Also try not to allow one category to influence the results of the other categories.

Items

	Completely unhappy									Completely happy
Household responsibilities	1	2	3	4	5	6	7	8	9	10
Rearing of children	1	2	3	4	5	6	7	8	9	10
Social activities	1	2	3	4	5	6	7	8	9	10
Money	1	2	3	4	5	6	7	8	9	10
Communication	1	2	3	4	5	6	7	8	9	10
Sex	1	2	3	4	5	6	7	8	9	10
Academic (or occupational) progress	1	2	3	4	5	6	7	8	9	10
Personal independence	1	2	3	4	5	6	7	8	9	10
Spouse independence	1	2	3	4	5	6	7	8	9	10
General happiness	1	2	3	4	5	6	7	8	9	10

Please turn to the end of the chapter to interpret your responses.

Spouse Abuse

Since the early 1970s, as people have begun to discuss and try to prevent spousal abuse, the estimate of its prevalence has climbed from "not very common" to the current estimate that it affects at least one in four couples (Paludi, 1995). During the last three decades, growing knowledge of domestic violence has prompted communities to help protect victims by increasing shelters and counseling services, strengthening laws to help prosecute abusers, encouraging victims to leave their abusers and start new lives, and developing counseling programs to help batterers change their behavior. Still, we are in the infancy of trying to amend this national problem.

Lenore Walker (1979) described a three-phase cycle of domestic violence:

1. Tension builds up; the battered person (usually but not always the woman) uses coping skills to avoid abusive situations

2. Tension escalates until the batterer explodes into a violent episode

3. Tension is reduced when the batterer is remorseful, loving, and generous, and the victim chooses to believe that the change is permanent. The tension soon starts to build again, however, and the cycle is repeated.

Batterers are contrite after the violent episode, so why don't they learn to make a permanent change? One obstacle is that batterers minimize and deny the amount of violence that has occurred—both because of loss of memory during the rage and because they use a pattern of blaming the victim for causing the violence (such as "She made me do it; she just wouldn't let up on me"). A second obstacle to permanent change is that men who batter are usually dependent on their spouse as the only source of intimacy, love, and support; in such an isolated, closed system, a natural outgrowth is the development of jealousy, which further poses a barrier to change and increases the amount of violence in a relationship. Often violent episodes are triggered from extreme suspiciousness and accusations of infidelity. To try to stem jealousy-driven rages, women in these relationships may give up all other friendships and outlets, which in the long run makes them very dependent within this violent relationship. Another obstacle to change is that batterers have low self-esteem; they even lack the skills and confidence to ask for what they want from their spouse in a nonthreatening manner. Finally, many batterers were socialized with violence—being physically or sexually abused themselves as children or witnessing violence between their parents. Their family scripts thus involve solving problems by physical force and psychological battering. Counseling programs try to change actual behavioral patterns and alter psychological obstacles to change.

Child Abuse

In addition to spouse abuse, child maltreatment is far too common in our communities. Child maltreatment is one of the great social problems of our time. In 1991 more than 2.5 million children were reported abused or neglected in the United States, a 40 percent increase over 1985. In addition, in 1991 more than 1,200 children died as a result of abuse. These statistics testify to the enormity of the child abuse problem in this country. Child maltreatment takes many forms. Four types of maltreatment are generally identified: sexual abuse, physical abuse, neglect, and emotional maltreatment.

Sexual child abuse of boys and girls is far more common than most people realize; more than 15 percent of maltreated children are victims of sexual abuse. Likewise, physical abuse is rampant, with more than 25 percent of reported abuse involving physical injury. Physical maltreatment results in harm to a child. The physical, developmental, and emotional scars that maltreatment leaves with children are almost always devastating. Frustrations, anger, and rage are often misdirected at children who suffer as a parental outlet. Abused children often remain undetected and the potential for abuse stays a part of family life.

Unfortunately, parental hostility toward children can escalate until one or both parents abuse the children. Although laws in many states now require doctors, teachers, psychologists, and other professionals to report suspected cases of abuse, at least 30 percent of suspected cases are not reported.

> *If our American way of life fails the child, it fails us all.*
> **—Pearl S. Buck**

The origins of child abuse are diverse. Research has implicated individual personality characteristics of parents and the parents' having been abused when they were young (Cicchetti & others, 1991). Cultural attitudes and the extensive violence of American culture also play roles in this country's high rate of child abuse. In China and Sweden, where physical punishment rarely is used to discipline children, the incidence of child abuse is reported to be very low.

Even more common than physical abuse of children is the psychological maltreatment of children. James Garbarino and his colleagues (1986) presented the following examples of psychologically battered children:

- Daily a preschooler is told by his mother, "Maybe today is the day I go away and leave you alone. You'd better be good today, boy, or you'll never see me again."
- A school-age child is daily confined to her room after school by her father, who says, "I don't want you getting involved with other kids; they're not good enough for you."
- Parents respond to their child's report cards with comments such as "No son of ours could be such a dummy. We wish you weren't around all the time reminding us of the mistake we made."
- A mother wants her early-adolescent daughter to earn some money by having sex with one of the mother's boyfriends, so she says, "You're a little slut anyway, and I might as well get something out of being your mother."

As you can see from these examples, psychological maltreatment occurs in a wide variety of ways. All psychological maltreatment is a concerted attack by an adult on a child's development of identity and social competence. Psychological maltreatment can take five forms: rejecting, isolating, terrorizing, ignoring, and corrupting.

In some families, the abuse takes the form of having a family scapegoat, one child who bears the burden for all the problems in the family. In a lifelong pattern of scapegoating, scapegoated children learn to feel responsible for all the family pain. When grown up, they remain emotionally and often physically close to their families, to try to make amends for what they are believed to have done wrong. As adults, scapegoats are often described as loyal, personally rigid, full of anger, cold, emotionally needy, and self-condemning.

Divorce and Remarriage

In the twentieth century America has become a divorcing society. Many divorced persons don't remain single for very long. They remarry. In this section we will examine adjustment issues in divorce and remarriage.

Divorce

Divorce has become epidemic in our culture. Until recently, divorce was increasing at an annual rate of 10 percent, but its rate of increase has now slowed. The probability that a marriage will end in a divorce has increased from approximately 10 percent to more than 50 percent since the beginning of this century (White, 1990). The average duration of a marriage decreased from 17 years in 1971 to just over 9 years in 1990 (U.S. Bureau of the Census, 1990). Increasing numbers of children are growing up in single-parent families. One estimate is that 25 percent of children born between 1910 and 1960 lived in a single-parent family at some time in their childhood, but at least 50 percent of the children who were born in the 1980s will spend part of their childhood in a single-parent family (Glick, 1988).

Although divorce rates have risen for all socioeconomic groups, those in disadvantaged circumstances have a higher incidence of divorce. Youthful marriage, low educational level, and low income are associated with increases in divorce. So too is premarital pregnancy. In one study, half of the women who were pregnant before marriage did not live with the husband for more than 5 years (Sauber & Corrigan, 1970).

Effects on Adults For those who divorce, separation and divorce are complex and emotionally charged (Chase-Lansdale, 1996). In one study, 6 of the 48 divorced couples continued to have sexual intercourse during the 2 years after separation (Hetherington, Cox, & Cox, 1982). Prior social scripts and patterns of interaction are difficult to break. Although divorce is a marker event in the relationship between spouses, it often does not signal the end of a relationship. Attachment to each other might endure regardless of whether the former spouses respect or like each other or are satisfied with the present relationship. Former spouses often alternate between feelings of seductiveness and hostility. They might also have thoughts of reconciliation, and while at times they might express love toward the former mate, most feelings are negative, with hate and anger prominent.

The stress of separation and divorce place both women and men at risk for psychological and physical difficulties (Hetherington & Blechman, 1996; Hetherington & Stanley-Hagen, 1995). Separated and divorced women and men have higher rates of psychiatric disturbances, admission to psychiatric hospitals, clinical depression, alcoholism, and psychosomatic problems, such as sleep disturbances, than do married adults. There is increasing evidence that stressful events of many types—including marital separation—reduce the immune system's capabilities, rendering separated and divorced individuals vulnerable to disease and infection. In one investigation, the most recently separated women (1 year or less) were more likely to show impaired immunological functioning than were women whose separations had occurred several years earlier (1 to 6 years) (Kiecolt-Glaser & Glaser, 1988). Also in this investigation, unhappily married individuals had immune systems that were not functioning as effectively as those of happily married individuals.

Special problems surface for the divorced woman who is a displaced homemaker. She assumed that her work would probably always be in the home. Although her expertise in managing the home may be considerable, future employers do not recognize this experience as work experience. Donna is typical of a divorced, displaced homemaker. She

married young, and at age 18 had her first child. Her work experience consisted of a part-time job as a waitress in high school. Now 32 and with three children—aged 14, 12, and 6—she was recently divorced by her husband, who married someone else. The child support payments are barely enough for rent, clothing, and other necessities. Without any marketable skills, Donna is working as a salesclerk in a local department store. She cannot afford a housekeeper and worries about the children being unsupervised while she works. Creating a positive single identity is essential for divorced adults such as Donna, so they can come to grips with their loneliness, lack of autonomy, and financial hardship (Ahrons & Rodgers, 1987).

Men, however, do not go through a divorce unscathed. They usually have fewer rights to their children, experience a decline in income (though not nearly as great as their ex-wives do), and receive less emotional support. Divorce can also have a negative impact on a man's career.

> *Being divorced is like being hit by a Mack truck. If you live through it, you start looking very carefully to the right and the left.*
>
> **—Jean Kerr**

Effects on Children As we indicated at the beginning of the chapter, the number of children now growing up in single-parent families is staggering. In thinking about how divorce affects children, it is important to remember that family structure (divorce versus an intact, never-divorced family, for example) is only one of many factors that influence children's adjustment. The contemporary approach advocates evaluating the strengths and weaknesses of the child prior to the divorce, the nature of the events surrounding the divorce, and postdivorce family functioning. Support systems (baby-sitters, relatives, day care), an ongoing, positive relationship between the custodial parent and the ex-spouse, authoritative parenting

(a combination of warmth, verbal give-and-take, and some control), financial stability, and the child's competencies at the time of the divorce are related to the child's adjustment (Hetherington, 1995; Santrock & Warshak, 1986).

Developmentalists are especially concerned about single mothers in poverty. More than one-third of single mothers are in poverty, compared to only 10 percent of single fathers. Developmentalist Vonnie McLoyd (1993) states that because poor single mothers are more emotionally distressed than affluent mothers, it is not surprising that single mothers in low-income circumstances might show low levels of support, nurturance, and involvement with their children. Among the reasons for the high poverty rate of single mothers are the low pay of women, infrequent awarding of alimony payments, and poorly enforced child support by fathers. A concern of most divorced mothers, but especially those in poverty, is the unavailability of low-cost, quality day care for children.

Many separations and divorces are highly emotional affairs that immerse the child in conflict. Conflict is a critical aspect of family functioning that seems to outweigh the influence of family structure on the child's development. Children in divorced families that are low in conflict function better than children in never-divorced, intact families that are high in conflict, for example (Wallerstein, Corbin, & Lewis, 1988).

Although escape from conflict may be a positive benefit for children, in the year immediately following the divorce, the conflict does not decline, but instead increases. At this time, children—especially boys—in divorced families show more adjustment problems than children in homes with both parents present. During the first year after the divorce, the child often experiences poor-quality parenting; parents seem preoccupied with their own needs and adjustment—experiencing anger, depression, confusion, and emotional instability—which inhibits their ability to respond sensitively to the child's needs. During the second year after the divorce, parents are more effective in their child-rearing duties, especially with daughters (Hetherington, Cox, & Cox, 1982).

Recent evaluations by Mavis Hetherington and her colleagues (Hetherington, 1993; Hetherington, Hagan, & Anderson, 1989) of children 6 years after the divorce of their parents found that living in nonremarried mother-custody homes had long-term negative effects on boys, with negative outcomes appearing consistently from preschool to adolescence. In contrast, most girls from these families recovered from divorce early in their lives. However, although preadolescent girls in divorced families adapted reasonably well, at the onset of adolescence, a subset of these girls—those who were early maturers—engaged in frequent conflict with their mothers, behaved in noncompliant ways, had lower self-esteem, and experienced more problems in heterosexual relations.

The sex of the child and the sex of the custodial parent are important considerations in evaluating the effects of divorce on children. One research study directly compared children living in father-custody homes with children living in mother-custody homes (Santrock & Warshak, 1986). On a number of measures, including videotaped observations of parent-child interaction, children living with the same-sex parent were more socially competent—happier, more independent, and more mature— and had higher self-esteem than children living with the opposite-sex parent.

Support systems are especially important for low-income divorced families. Extended family and community services play a critical role in the functioning of low-income divorced families. These support systems may be crucial for low-income divorced families with infants and young children, because most of these parents must work full-time but still may not be able to make ends meet.

The age of the child at the time of the divorce also needs to be considered. Young children's responses to divorce are mediated by their limited cognitive and social competencies, their dependence on their parents, and their restriction to the home or inferior day care

(Hetherington & Stanley-Hagen, 1995). During the interval immediately following divorce, young children less accurately appraise the divorce situation. These young children might blame themselves for the divorce, might fear abandonment by both parents, and might misperceive and be confused by what is happening.

Remarriage

The United States has the highest remarriage rate in the world (Coleman & Ganong, 1990). More than 40 percent of marriages are remarriages for one or both partners. We not only remarry at a high rate, we do so soon after divorce. The median interval between divorce and remarriage is just under 3 years. About two-thirds of remarriages are preceded by cohabitation, which means that the median interval between divorce and the establishment of a new close, intimate relationship is even less (Bumpass & Sweet, 1989). Just as with divorce, increasing numbers of children live in stepfamilies—about 4.5 million households contain 6.8 million stepchildren. Approximately 35 percent of children born in the 1980s can expect to live at least part of their childhood in a stepfamily (Glick, 1989).

Younger women tend to remarry more quickly than older women, and childless women divorced prior to the age of 25 have higher remarriage rates than women with children. The more money a divorced male has, the more likely he is to remarry, but for women the opposite is true. Remarriage satisfaction, similar to satisfaction in first marriages, appears to decrease over time (Guisinger, Cowan, & Schuldberg, 1989). In fact, few differences have been found between the factors that predict marital satisfaction in first marriages and those that predict satisfaction in later marriages.

Just like couples who are first-married, remarried individuals often have unrealistic expectations about their step-family. Thus, an important adjustment for remarried persons is to develop realistic expectations. Money and the complexities of family structure in the remarried family often contribute to marital conflict.

Many variations in remarriage have the potential for what is called

boundary ambiguity—*the uncertainty in stepfamilies about who is in or out of the family and who is performing or responsible for certain tasks in the family system.* The uncertainty of boundaries likely increases stress for the family system and the probability of behavior problems in children (Eshleman, 1991).

Research on stepfamilies has lagged behind research on divorced families, but a number of researchers have turned their attention to this increasingly common family structure (Hetherington, 1995). Following remarriage of their parents, children of all ages show a resurgence of behavior problems. Younger children seem eventually to form an attachment to a stepparent and accept the stepparenting role. The developmental tasks facing adolescents, however, make them especially vulnerable to the entrance of a stepparent. At the time they are searching for an identity and exploring sexual and other close relationships outside the family, and a nonbiological parent can increase the stress associated with these important tasks.

Children's relationships with their biological parents are more positive than with their stepparents, regardless of whether a stepmother or a stepfather family is involved. However, stepfathers are often distant and disengaged from their stepchildren. As a rule, the more complex the stepfamily, the more difficult the child's adjustment. Families in which both parents bring children from a previous marriage have the highest level of behavioral problems.

In sum, as with divorce, entrance into a stepfamily involves a disequilibrium in children's lives (Jodl & Dalton, 1996). Most children initially find their parents' remarriage stressful. Remarriage, though, can remove children from stressful single-parent circumstances and provide additional resources for children, such as increased involvement with parents and improved economic circumstances. Many children emerge from their remarried family as competent individuals. As with divorced families, it is important to consider the complexity of stepfamilies, the diversity of possible outcomes for the child, and the factors that facilitate children's adjustment in stepfamilies.

Marital Adjustment

Unrealistic expectations and myths about marriage contribute to marital satisfaction and divorce. Although the landscape of marital satisfaction and conflict is immense and complex, the following factors have often been good predictors of marital success: the extent and degree of differences between marital partners, the nature of communication between the couple, the quality of the relationship between the partners, and the ability to handle conflict constructively. Overall, women are more expressive and affectionate in marriage, and this difference bothers many women. Couples can take steps to improve their ability to manage conflict constructively.

Family violence is a growing problem in this culture, although it has been publicly discussed only since the early 1970s. Many factors conspire to isolate couples involved in spousal abuse. Abused and neglected children suffer long-term effects that influence their adult adjustment.

Divorce has increased dramatically, but its rate has begun to slow. Divorce is complex and emotional. Divorced women and men are at risk for psychological and physical difficulties. Special problems surface for the wife who is a displaced homemaker. Divorce is most stressful for children in the year following the separation or divorce. A host of factors mediate the effects of divorce on children. Remarriage satisfaction is often predicted by factors similar to those that predict marital satisfaction in first marriages. An important adjustment for remarried individuals is to develop realistic expectations. As with divorce, entrance into a stepfamily involves a disequilibrium that requires considerable adjustment, both on the part of the adults and children involved.

CRITICAL THINKING ABOUT ADJUSTMENT

Keeping the Watch

There is nothing harder than the softness of indifference.
—Juan Montalvo

The magnitude of the problems our culture faces regarding family violence can seem overwhelming. Media reports about child neglect and abuse appear all too frequently. They force us to contemplate what depths human beings can sink to, and we might unhappily conclude that the culture as a whole is in serious trouble. Unfortunately, one reaction to relentless stories of violence and abuse is withdrawal. The horror encourages us to develop denial and avoid involvement as a means of maintaining our own equilibrium.

People can do something to assist families who suffer the effects of family violence. For example, every state in the United States has enacted laws to protect children and created social service agencies that specialize in helping families in trouble. All states have created toll-free hotlines for reporting abuse. As an involved citizen, you can help by calling these agencies when you have reason to believe that family members are violent with each other or when there is maltreatment of a child in the family.

How can you learn to recognize domestic violence when it occurs? Physical abuse of family members is usually apparent in signs of physical harm, such as bruises, scratches, and other marks and injuries. Although such injuries can result from other things than abuse, explanations for nonaccidental injuries often do not fit with the evidence. For example, injuries from a beating will look different from injuries resulting from a fall. Victims of family violence may also suffer chronic injury; they might constantly require emergency care and might feel compelled to develop plausible cover stories to allay suspicion. However, explanations of abuse by family members may be presented with fear and tentativeness. Their stories often feel fragile. Although verbal abuse is harder to confirm, statements from children or adults that disclose abuse should always be taken seriously.

Because our social service agencies are often overworked, reports of suspected abuse do not always lead to an intervention. However, imagine how it might feel to suspect abuse, avoid reporting the abuse, and later witness further injury or even the loss of the friend for whom you were concerned. By *practicing ethical sensitivity* when we have these concerns, each of us can play a role in doing something about child abuse and other forms of domestic violence.

In this chapter we explored many different dimensions of adult lifestyles. We began by examining the diversity of adult lifestyles—marriage, cohabitation, lesbian and gay couples, and living single. Our coverage of the family life cycle focused on leaving home, finding a partner, becoming parents, parenting adolescents, families at midlife, and families in later life. The current family trends we read about included marriage postponement, declining childbirth, changing gender roles, ethnic minority patterns, and adolescent parents. We also discussed marital adjustment, including such topics as expectations and myths, communication and conflict, family violence, and divorce and remarriage. Remember that you can obtain an overall summary of the chapter by again studying the in-chapter reviews on pages 254, 265, and 272.

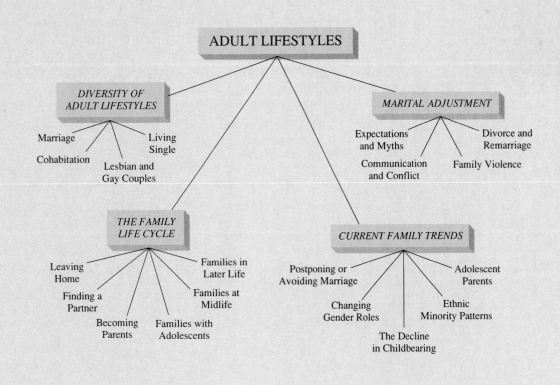

ADULT LIFESTYLES

DIVERSITY OF ADULT LIFESTYLES

Marriage
Cohabitation
Living Single
Lesbian and Gay Couples

MARITAL ADJUSTMENT

Expectations and Myths
Communication and Conflict
Divorce and Remarriage
Family Violence

THE FAMILY LIFE CYCLE

Leaving Home
Finding a Partner
Becoming Parents
Families with Adolescents
Families at Midlife
Families in Later Life

CURRENT FAMILY TRENDS

Postponing or Avoiding Marriage
Changing Gender Roles
The Decline in Childbearing
Ethnic Minority Patterns
Adolescent Parents

PRACTICAL KNOWLEDGE ABOUT ADJUSTMENT

TO LISTEN TO A CHILD

(1984) by T. Berry Brazelton. Reading, MA: Addison-Wesley.

To Listen to a Child addresses parenting throughout the childhood years. The focus is primarily on problematic events that arise in children's lives. Fears, feeding, sleep problems, stomach aches, and asthma are among the normal problems of growing up that Brazelton covers. He assures parents that it is only when parents let their own anxieties interfere that these problems (such as bedwetting) become chronic and guilt-laden. Each chapter closes with practical guidelines for parents. Brazelton deals with common issues parents face, such as discipline, children's search for limits, and the child's emotional well-being.

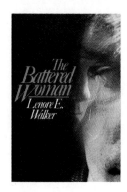

THE BATTERED WOMAN

(1979) by Lenore Walker. New York: Harper & Row.

The Battered Woman is for women who have been or continue to be abused by their husband or romantic partner. Women learn about the myths and realities of abuse, read heart-wrenching stories told by battered women, and find the way out of a battered circumstance. Walker describes how the legal, medical, and psychological fields have not adequately addressed the trauma of battered women. She also outlines the services that battered women say would be more helpful to them.

KNOWLEDGE OF MARITAL MYTHS AND REALITIES

Scoring

1. False	5. True	9. False	13. False
2. True	6. True	10. False	14. False
3. False	7. False	11. False	15. False
4. False	8. False	12. True	

MARITAL HAPPINESS

Scoring

Each of the questions on the scale can be treated as a separate index of specific areas of marital interaction.

Interpretation

Questions rated lower than others indicate areas for possible improvement in the marital relationship, relative to the other areas.

Careers and Work

> *Whatever you can do, or dream you
> can, begin it. Boldness has genius, power,
> and magic in it.*
>
> **—Johann Wolfgang von Goethe**

Robert is in his senior year of college and just had his twenty-first birthday last week. Looking to his future and pondering what life might be like over the next few years, he came up with the following tongue-in-cheek reasons not to take a job:

1. You have to work.
2. It's habit forming. Once you get a job, you'll want another, and then another. . . . It's better not to start at all. Why do you think they call it work?
3. Once you stop being a student, you can never go back. Remember those pathetic people who came back to hang around your high school? You'll look even sillier showing up at mixers, pep rallies, and Sadie Hawkins dances after you have taken a position with some respectable accounting firm.
4. Taking a job means taking on new responsibilities. Before you know it, you will have four sickly brats with crooked teeth and a house in the 'burbs. You will have to take out insurance policies on everything from health care to rodent invasions. Soon you will seriously be considering purchasing a condominium in Fort Lauderdale or Rio Rancho Retirement Village. All this can be avoided by the simple decision not to take a job.
5. Fully employed people can never have sex.
6. You will have to say nice things about the boss's new "flame-thrower red" polyester golf pants, laugh at the boss's jokes about people who mismanage their finances, and carry on endless conversations with your boss about "pennant rallies," "the primaries," and "resort areas." You will have to nod your head with conviction when he refers to his employees as a "team" that works together to "bring home the bacon."
7. If you take a job, you will be an adult (*The Harvard Lampoon Big Book of College Life*).

PREVIEW

In this chapter we will explore what it is like to take a job, as we examine the nature of careers and work. To begin, we will discuss career development across the life span and career planning. Next we will evaluate the impact of work on adult lives. We will conclude by studying the ways the world of work is changing.

CAREER DEVELOPMENT

Said Mary Lyon (1797–1849), "When you choose your fields of labor, go where nobody else is willing to go." Her advice remains valid today, especially in today's intense job competition. In this first section we will explore the nature of career development at different points in the life span, including the processes individuals use to make effective decisions.

Career Development Across the Life Span

Have your thoughts about a career changed as you have developed? Probably so—otherwise the earth would have a tremendous surplus of cowboys, astronauts, ballet dancers, teachers, and firefighters. Let's examine some common changes that take place in career development across the human life span.

Childhood

How far back do you have to go in your own development to come to a point at which you had no conception of what career you wanted to pursue, and, in fact, you actually did not even think about possible careers? You probably have to go back further than when you entered elementary school. Even as a preschooler you probably began to fantasize about some careers you might adopt when you grew up, and you likely continued this fantasy career orientation through most of your childhood years. When asked what they want to be when they grow up, children commonly say they want to be a doctor, an astronaut, a superhero, a teacher, a movie star, a sports hero, and so forth, and many of their aspirations are not very realistic.

Eli Ginzberg (1972) and Donald Super (1976) believe that individuals go through stages in their career development. Ginzberg thinks we go through three stages: fantasy (birth through age 11), tentative (ages 11 through 17), and realistic (from 18 to 25). **Fantasy stage** *is Ginzberg's label for the childhood years during which careers are perceived in an unrealistic manner.* We will discuss his tentative and realistic stages later.

No person has the right to rain on your dreams.

—**Marian Wright Edelman**

Super believes individuals go through the following stages in career development: growth (birth to 14 years of age), exploration (15 through 24), establishment (25 through 44), maintenance (from 45 through 64), and decline (beginning at 65). **Growth stage** *is Super's label for the period of physical and cognitive growth that takes place from birth through early adolescence.* In this stage, children move from having no interest in vocations (birth to 3 years), to extensive fantasies about careers (4 to 10 years), to career interests based on likes and dislikes (10 to 12), to beginning to take ability into account in their career choices (13 and 14).

Anne Roe (1956) believes that parent-child relationships play an important role in occupational selection. For example, she says that individuals who have warm and accepting parents are likely to choose careers that involve work with people, such as sales positions and public relations jobs. By contrast, she says, individuals who have neglecting or rejecting parents are more likely to choose careers that do not require a good "personality" or strong social skills, such as accounting.

Adolescence

During the adolescent years, interest in career exploration increases. During early adolescence, at about 10 to 15 years of age, individuals tone down their wildest, most unrealistic dreams about careers and start to consider their abilities when thinking about vocations they might pursue. Most young adolescents' career thoughts are not completely realistic, though, and often express a dramatic formula that is unlikely to be played out in the adult years.

Tentative stage *is Ginzberg's label for the adolescent period of 11 to 17 years of age, when individuals are in a transition period between the novice fantasy stage of childhood and the more mature realistic stage that will come later.* **Realistic stage** *is Ginzberg's label for the age period of about 18 to 25 years when individuals rid themselves of their fantasies about careers and make more pragmatic decisions.* To explore your own ideas about career development, see Critical Thinking.

Similarly, **exploration stage** *is Super's concept of the late adolescent and young adult years from about 15 to 24 years of age, when individuals explore and evaluate the work world in a general way.* According to Super, needs, interests, capacities, values, and opportunities are more likely to be taken into account when career choices are considered during this stage. More realistic career choices are made, and the individual often makes an initial vocational commitment and might begin a first trial job in the latter part of the stage.

Parents frequently have a strong influence on their children's career development. Some parents pressure their children too strongly in the direction of a particular career and become overinvested in the son's or daughter's career decisions. The mother who did not get into medical school and the father who did not make it as a professional athlete might pressure their children to achieve a career status that is beyond the children's talents. Other parents provide too little guidance and support for their children's career development. For example, a 35-year-old female looks back and describes how her family background restricted her entry into a positive career track. Her parents had expectations that she would graduate from high school,

CRITICAL THINKING

What Do You Want to Be When You Grow Up?

Think about your own childhood in relation to the developmental objectives described so far. Can you recall the kinds of fantasies you had in childhood? How did you respond when people inevitably asked you, "What do you want to be when you grow up?" Was there a pattern of values and interests present in your early career fantasies that still exists in your goals and objectives today?

If you are inclined to people-oriented careers, Anne Roe's work suggests that you probably have warm and accepting parents. If you seek careers that don't require strong people skills, she contends, your parents might be rejecting or neglectful. Are her insights valid in your circumstances? Your ability to answer these questions provides an opportunity *to practice self-reflection in order to enhance personal growth.*

but, at the same time they emphasized that she needed to get a job to help them pay the family's bills. She was never told that she could not go to college, but both parents encouraged her to find someone to marry who could support her financially. This bright woman is now divorced and feels intellectually cheated by her parents, who socialized her in the direction of marriage and away from a college education.

Exploration of many career options is widely recommended by career counselors. Too often, though, individuals approach career exploration with little direction or guidance. In one study of individuals after they left high school, over half the position changes made between leaving high school and the age of 25 involved floundering and unplanned changes (Super, Kowalski, & Gotkin, 1967).

One place where adolescents can get advice about career choices is school. Current educational trends, however, are limiting rather than expanding high school students' access to current, meaningful career advice. First, the back-to-basics movement in educational reform leaves little room for courses or even units on career exploration and

Latino adolescents at a job fair, seeking information about careers. Improving adolescents' awareness of career options and educational requirements is an important agenda for the United States.

development. Further, as budgets of secondary school systems become tighter, the number of guidance counselors tends to decrease. In many schools, students take no career development classes and never come in contact with a career counselor. With a lack of career guidance at home and at school, many adolescents not only do not know what information to seek about careers, but also do not know how to seek it. Many adults also have limited knowledge of this process; later in the chapter we will examine some specific steps in exploring, planning, and making decisions about careers.

The College Board Commission on Precollege Guidance and Counseling (1986) recommended that local school districts develop broad-based planning that actively involves the home, school, and community. Advocating better-trained counselors, the commission strongly supported partnerships between home and school to increase two-way communication about student progress and better collaboration among schools, community agencies, colleges, businesses, and other community resources.

One way teenagers learn about careers is by holding their first jobs. If you

are typical, you held at least one paying job before you graduated from high school, beginning perhaps with yard work or child care and moving on to jobs such as working in a fast-food restaurant or in an office.

Researchers have found that employment is a mixed blessing for teenagers (Greenberger & Steinberg, 1986). On the positive side, teenagers enjoy the status of working and like to have their own spending money. Some adolescents believe that work teaches them how to be responsible and answerable for their actions; however, many teenagers who work place less value on school and get lower grades. In addition, they often give up much of their social life to be able to work. Even the paycheck has some negative features—teenage affluence can lead to financial disappointment when paychecks in adulthood have to be used to pay rent and food as well as clothing and entertainment expenses. Some working adolescents use their money to buy alcohol or drugs. Psychologists find that all the benefits of having a job as a teenager can be acquired by working up to 10 hours a week; at least until the age of 16, more than 10 hours a week is associated with more negative than positive outcomes.

Early Adulthood

Predicting career choices and guiding persons toward rewarding occupations is a complex undertaking. In the first several years of college, most students cannot accurately chart their career path through the adult years. Many students change majors in college, discover that their employment after college is not related to their college major, and change careers during the course of adulthood. To some career counselors, the unpredictability of career pursuit by college students means that students would be wiser to take a broad course of liberal education rather than a narrow path of vocational training. However, other career counselors believe that an intense, focused course of study in a specific discipline is the wiser strategy for increasing the probability of getting a good job.

In the latter part of the exploration stage in Super's theory, individuals often begin their entry into an occupation. Entering into an occupation signals the beginning of new roles and responsibilities for the individual. The career role is different from the role the person might have had as a temporary or part-time worker during high school or college. Career role expectations for competence are high and the demands real for the young adult. When people enter a job for the first time, they may be confronted with unanticipated problems and conditions. They might not anticipate how real the pressures are in this first job, nor understand how important relationships with other employees are, nor expect such extreme demands on their time that interfere with their pleasurable pursuits.

Establishment stage *is Super's term for the period from 25 to 45 years of age, when individuals pursue a permanent career and attain a pattern of stable work in a particular career.* In the first part of this stage, considerable adjustment is still required to adapt to the career path the individual has chosen. Clinical psychologist Daniel Levinson (1978) believes that this is a time when individuals need to develop a distinct occupational identity and establish themselves in the occupational world. Along the way, they might fail, drop out, or begin a new path. They might stay on a single narrow track or try several new directions before settling firmly on one.

Levels of attainment reached by persons in the establishment stage vary considerably. A professional might just be getting started or might have already become well established and widely known. One executive might be on the bottom rung of a corporate ladder; another might be already near the top. An hourly worker might be an unskilled laborer without job security or a highly skilled craftsman earning more than some executives or professionals. Some individuals face unemployment, a circumstance that produces stress whether the job loss is temporary, cyclical, or permanent.

Many of us think of our adult work life as a series of discrete steps, much like the rungs on a ladder. In a factory, a person might move from laborer, to foreman, to superintendent, to production manager, and so on up the ladder. In a business, an individual might move from salesperson, to sales manager, to regional sales manager, to national sales manager, to vice president of the company, and then even possibly to president of the company. Not all occupations have such clearly defined steps, but most jobs involve a hierarchy in which low-level workers and high-level workers are clearly distinguished. How can an individual move up the career ladder?

Having a college education helps. A college degree is associated with earlier and greater career advancement (Golan, 1986). Furthermore, persons who are promoted early tend to move farther up the career ladder than those who are promoted later. Indeed, most career advancement occurs early in our adult lives. By their early forties, many individuals have gone as far as they will go up the career ladder. In one study of a large corporation, this pattern occurred regardless of whether the positions were nonmanagement, lower management, or foreman (Rosenbaum, 1984).

Without work, all life goes rotten.
—**Albert Camus**

Middle Adulthood

When people become middle-aged, many of them have spent from 10 to 25 years in the same occupation, and, in some cases, doing virtually the same job. Also, as we just indicated, by 40 to 45, most people have gone as far as they will up the career ladder. Realizing that they are unlikely to advance much further in their career, many middle-aged adults reflect about what they have done with their career years and what they expect from their future years in their career. Often they show a greater concern for figuring out the meaning of life and determining how their career needs and success fit into the larger picture of their life.

Most middle-aged adults remain in the same career, so for most individuals the label Super gives to this stage is appropriate. According to him, the **maintenance stage** *is a period from about 45 to 64 years of age in which individuals continue in their career and maintain their career status.* Levinson (1978) believes that the midlife career experience is a significant turning point in life for these individuals. Most people have to adjust idealistic hopes to realistic possibilities in light of how much time they have left in an occupation. Focus often turns to how much time remains before retirement and the pace with which occupational goals are being reached (Pines & Aronson, 1988). If people perceive that they are behind schedule or that their goals have been unrealistic, they might reassess and readjust these goals. Levinson (1978) believes this readjustment can result in a sadness or grieving over unfulfilled dreams. In his research, he found that many middle-aged men felt constrained by their bosses, their wives, and their children. Such feelings, he says, can produce rebellion, which can take several forms—extramarital affairs, divorce, alcoholism, suicide, or career change. Although Levinson only studied men's lives in this research, some researchers believe that women experience parallel feelings and can feel constrained by their roles, too.

For about 10 percent of middle-aged Americans, midlife is a time when they change jobs. Why do they change jobs? Some get fired, often as a result of a reorganization, such as a merger, and

have to find other careers. Others may change jobs because of their own motivation. Perhaps they want to redefine their identity through a career change, or perhaps they have lost passion for the current job and feel stuck. Although middle-aged adults can feel thrown off balance by a career shift, most feel rejuvenated by a career transition. Some career shifts require new educational training, and many older adults return to the college classroom to commence a new career direction.

Late Adulthood

When most of us think of late adulthood career development, the two words most likely to come to mind are *decline* and *retirement*. Indeed, this image is reflected in Super's fifth career stage. **Decline stage** *is Super's label for the period of 65 years and older when individuals' career activity declines and retirement takes place.* (Figure 12.1 provides a summary of Super's five stages of career development.) However, some individuals maintain their productivity throughout their adult lives, and some of these older adults may follow a work agenda that exhausts younger workers. Older workers actually have a 20 percent better attendance record than younger workers. Somewhat surprisingly, they also have fewer disabling accidents. Among creative persons, scientists, and writers, many are productive well into their elderly years, with some of their best works produced late in life.

For many workers, retirement is an important event; it can occur at 62 (called early retirement), 65 (standard retirement age), or much earlier to much later. Having a retirement option for older workers is a twentieth-century phenomenon. A much higher percentage of older Americans worked full-time in the early 1900s than today. Indeed, the Social Security system, which establishes benefits for older workers when they retire, was not implemented until 1935. On the average, today's workers will spend 10 to 15 percent of their lives in retirement. Until recently, many workers faced mandatory retirement at age 65. Recent changes in federal laws that allow people over the age of 65 to continue working allow individuals to achieve their own preferences and

	Growth stage
Birth–14 years of age	General physical and cognitive growth
	In this stage, children move from a time when they have no interest in careers (0–3 years), to having extensive fantasies about careers (4–10 years), to career interests based on likes and dislikes (10–12 years), to beginning to take ability into account in their career choices (13–14 years).
	Exploration stage
15–24 years of age	General exploration of the world of work
	In the early part of this stage, individuals begin to take needs, interests, capacities, values, and opportunities into account when career choices are considered. In the latter part of the stage, they often make an initial vocational commitment and may begin a first trial job.
	Establishment stage
25–44 years of age	Entrance into a permanent career and emergence of a stable work pattern.
	In the first part of this stage, considerable adjustment is still required to adapt to the career path that has been chosen. As individuals move through the stage, they establish a distinct occupational identity and a pattern of consistent work.
	Maintenance stage
45–64 years of age	Continuation in a career and maintenance of career status
	A large majority of middle-aged adults remain in the same career; only about 10 percent change careers in middle age.
	Decline stage
65+ years of age	Career activity declines and retirement takes place
	While some individuals maintain a productive life through even the late adulthood years, most people do show a decline in career activity and retire at some point in late adulthood.

FIGURE 12.1

Super's Stages of Career Development

allow productive workers to remain in employment. Another option that is increasingly being chosen by older adults is working part-time.

Of older adults who do retire, who makes the best adjustment? Older adults who adjust best to retirement are healthy, have adequate income, are active, are better educated, have an extended social network that includes both friends and family, and usually were satisfied with their lives before retirement (Palmore & others, 1985). Older adults

with inadequate income, poor health, and who must adjust to other stress that occurs at the same time as retirement, such as the death of a spouse, have the most difficult time adjusting to retirement. Choice and self-determination are also important factors in adjusting to retirement. The fewer choices older adults have regarding their retirement, the less satisfied they are with their lives. Options for control and self-determination are important aspects of the mental health of retired individuals.

Only a person who can live with himself can enjoy the gift of leisure.

—Henry Greber

A typical life course pattern is that the first third emphasizes education, the second third emphasizes work, and the last third emphasizes leisure. It may be that with education becoming more of a lifelong venture and the retirement/leisure years expanding that this formula is becoming more unsatisfactory. Many persons in young adulthood and middle adulthood are engaging in a better mixture of leisure and work and are periodically turning to education. Moreover, as a larger proportion of adults live many years past the traditional retirement age, more adults are choosing to work beyond the age of 65 and to participate in educational opportunities in their later years.

A perpetual holiday is a good working definition of hell.

—George Bernard Shaw

Career Exploration and Planning

Most of you reading this book, regardless of your age, are still in the process of exploring, planning, or making decisions about your career path. Developing a personal, individualized career plan for yourself is an important aspect of your career development. Let's examine how career counselors believe people should go about developing such a plan.

Developing a Career Plan

Developing a good career plan is often perceived as a one-time event, a step toward making a single, major job commitment. Each of us, however, will likely experience changes during our lifetime that will require modifications in our careers, adjustments in our career goals, and often a change of careers. In fact, the average worker now makes five or six job transitions (Hyatt, 1990).

The first job choice is like the first step on a long journey. It is useful to develop the expectation that change cannot be avoided and to have the assumption that change can usually be turned to your advantage. If you look at all the companies that merge, downsize, or even disappear, you can more easily accept the inevitability of change. Furthermore, change is inescapable because, as you have already read, individuals change developmentally as they age through the adult years. Such changes can have profound influences on career development (Michelozzi, 1996).

In the widely popular book on job hunting and careers *What Color Is Your Parachute?*, Richard Bolles (1996) emphasizes that individuals need to use change to become wiser. Our experiences bring about change, so it is useful to understand the two aspects of experiences. The first aspect is the actual event, and the second aspect is the person's interpretation and response to the event. One error in interpretation is to view past mistakes as harmful to career development. Rather, Bolles believes, the most important aspect of career development and adjustment is realizing that you will make mistakes but that positive change comes about by learning from these mistakes.

In addition to learning from our mistakes, it is important to consider three other important components of a successful career plan: (1) goals, wants, and wishes; (2) marketable skills; and (3) personal fit. *Goals, wants, and wishes* are our hopes for the future and the interests we want to pursue. In other words, they are what we would like to do, have, and be. Some people have no problems in articulating goals, but most people don't find it that easy. If articulating goals is difficult, begin with general goals, such as wanting to be happy (which is on everyone's list), and then work toward more specific ones (such as, "I want to retire the December after I am 60 years old," "I want to make enough money by the time I am 30 to buy a Porsche," "I want to get my MBA degree by the age of 25 and work for a large oil company," or "I want to learn foreign languages and travel, the first time by being useful in the Peace Corps").

When thinking about goals, focus on multiple categories, such as health/fitness, mental/intellectual, social interaction, special relationships, work/careers, and so on. For some individuals, geographical location is as important or

more important than the type of career itself. Ardent surfers drive taxis just to be in Honolulu. Aspiring actors wait tables just to live in Hollywood. Some people refuse to live in a large city, others find heaven in Manhattan. For these people, the three most important aspects of a career are identical to the aspects real estate agents give for what is most important to the monetary value of a house: location, location, location!

One person, already a systems analyst, didn't have location on his list of goals, wants, and wishes, but he did have the following: (1) losing 15 pounds and getting in good shape, (2) taking some management courses, (3) spending less time with the people he cared little about and more time with those he loved, and (4) becoming a manager in a computer-oriented department or company. To explore your own career goals, turn to the Self-Assessment. Once listed, a person's goals, wants, and wishes can then become an easy-to-use component of a career-planning system and a tool for finding one's way through the complex, changing world.

To compete successfully in the job market, people must have *marketable skills*. We need to ask ourselves what someone will hire us to do in the current and future workplace. We need to consider current trends of employment and technology, thinking especially hard about the personal talents, abilities, and qualities for which employers are willing to pay good money. Again, it is helpful to make a list that includes abilities, talents, aptitudes, skills, personality characteristics, and attitudes that an employer is likely to find attractive. One way to accumulate items for a marketable skills list is to brainstorm about all of your previous job experiences and talk with others about what abilities, talents, and skills they believe are your strengths. Some career counselors have card sorts that they use for exploring a person's job skills. Two such products are *Motivated Skills Card Sort* and *SkillScan*, each consisting of a deck of cards with different skills on separate cards. The technique can help individuals compile a list of employable skills and can provide good information for a resume.

A third important dimension of a good career plan is *personal fit*. If you have not thought about your personal preferences and characteristics (such as personality traits, geographical preferences, financial requisites, prime interests, values, and natural aptitudes), you should begin to do so. Once you have a handle on what these personal preferences and characteristics are, then it is important to develop a fit between them and various career directions and choices. Next, we examine a vocational theory that emphasizes the importance of matching personality traits and career choices.

Holland's Personality Type Theory

Personality type theory *is vocational theorist John Holland's view that it is important to develop a match or fit between an individual's personality type and the selection of a particular career.* Holland (1973, 1996) believes that when individuals find careers that fit their personality, they are more likely to enjoy the work and stay in their jobs longer than if they worked at jobs not suited for their personality. Holland proposes six basic career-related personality characteristics: realistic, investigative, artistic, social, enterprising, and conventional (see figure 12.2).

Realistic Individuals of the realistic type like the outdoors and enjoy working in manual activities. They are often less social, have difficulty in demanding situations, and prefer to work alone or with other realistic persons. Holland describes the realistic type as physically robust, practical, and often non- or anti-intellectual. A listing of the jobs associated with the realistic type shows a match with mostly blue-collar positions, such as labor, farming, truck driving, and construction, along with a few technical jobs such as engineers and pilots (Lowman, 1991). The realistic type has the lowest prestige level of the six occupational interest types (Lowman, 1987).

Investigative The investigative type is interested in ideas more than people, is rather indifferent to social relationships, is troubled by highly emotional

Career Goal-Setting

Like a long journey, you need markers along your career path to tell you that you are on track. These are your goals, the specific things that you will do and accomplish as you move through your career development. Every dream and vision you might develop about your future career development can be broken down into specific goals and time frames.

Instructions

Keeping your career dreams in focus, write some of the specific work, job, and career goals you have for the next 20, 10, and 5 years. Be as concrete and specific as possible. In making up goals, start from the farthest point—20 years, and work backwards. If you go the other way, you run the risk of adopting goals that are not precisely and clearly related to your dream:

20-Year Goals:

_____
_____
_____
_____
_____

10-Year Goals:

_____
_____
_____
_____
_____

5-Year Goals:

_____
_____
_____
_____
_____
_____

situations, and may be perceived by others as being somewhat aloof and yet highly intelligent. The educational level and the prestige level of tne investigative type are the highest of the six types (Gottfredson, 1980). Most of the scientific, intellectually oriented professions fall into this category.

Artistic The artistic type has a creative orientation. These individuals enjoy working with ideas and materials to express themselves in new ways. Artistic types often have a distaste for conformity, valuing freedom and ambiguity, and sometimes have difficulty in interpersonal relations. They tend to have high educational levels and experience moderate to high prestige. Relatively few artistic

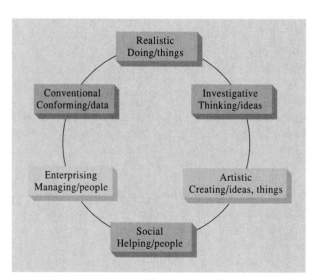

FIGURE 12.2

Holland's Model of Personality Types and Career Choices

occupations exist compared to the relatively large number of individuals who fall into the artistic type. As a result, some artistic types choose careers in their second or third most typical career type and express their artistic tendencies in hobbies and leisure.

Social Oriented toward working through and with other people, social types tend to have a helping orientation. They enjoy nurturing and developing others, perhaps working to assist others in need, especially the less advantaged. Showing a much stronger interest in people than in intellectual pursuits and often having excellent interpersonal skills, they are likely to be best equipped to enter people professions such as teaching, social work, and counseling. The social type also has a high prestige rating.

Enterprising Another type that is more oriented toward people than toward either things or ideas is the enterprising type. These individuals seek to dominate others, especially when they want to reach specific goals. Therefore, enterprising types are good at coordinating the work of others to accomplish a task. Their skills include being able to persuade other people to do something and to adopt their own attitudes and choices. Ranking fourth of the six types in education and prestige, they match up best with such careers as sales, management, and politics.

Conventional The conventional type usually functions best in well-structured circumstances and jobs and is skilled at working with details. Conventional individuals like to work with numbers and perform clerical tasks, as opposed to working with ideas or people. They usually do not aspire to high-level positions in an organization. They are best suited for structured jobs such as bank tellers, secretaries, and file clerks. Of the six types, they show up in fifth place in education and prestige.

If all individuals (and careers) fell conveniently into Holland's personality types, career counselors would have an easy job. However, people are typically more varied and complex than Holland's theory suggests. Even Holland (1987, 1996) states that individuals are rarely pure types, and most persons reflect a combination of two or three types. Still, the basic idea of matching the abilities and attitudes of individuals to particular careers is an important contribution to the career development field (Tay, Ward, & Hill, 1993). Holland's personality types are incorporated into the Strong-Campbell Interest Inventory, a widely used measure in career guidance. In addition, Holland has developed his own career interest inventory called the *Self-Directed Search*. Vocational tests are widely used in career counseling. Let's examine their value and some cautions associated with their use.

> *I'm a great believer in luck, and I find the harder I work the more I have of it.*
> —**Thomas Jefferson**

Vocational Tests

A common strategy of career counselors is to obtain information about the career interests of an individual through the use of tests. Many of you may have taken some type of vocational test at one time or another. Vocational tests can be a valuable part of career guidance, but several cautions about their use are warranted. Some tests, especially those that appear in popular magazines, are often too simple. Other tests, such as the widely used *Myers-Briggs Type Indicator (MBTI)*, have a better research base and track record in successfully predicting good career choices. In addition, even with some of the better-researched tests, career counselors sometimes miss important subtleties in an individual's test profile (Waterman, 1991). For example, on the most widely used career choice measure, the Strong-Campbell Interest Inventory, the person's profile might show that the individual has interests similar to those of a funeral director.

This correspondence does not mean that the person should be advised to enroll in embalming classes or to send a resume to every mortuary in the country. What it could, and often does, mean is that the person enjoys working with people under stress and that the person has entrepreneurial interests, like running a small service business.

Test results also may be inaccurate because the test takers misread or misinterpret some of the questions or answer questions according to how they would like them to be rather than the way they are. Thus, career counselors and the individuals who take vocational tests should interpret test results with considerable care and caution. The individual's career profile should be compared with that produced by other tests the person may have taken. Tests should be used as one part of a larger inquiry process that includes an interview about the person's life interests, goals, and so on. It is important to ask whether the test responses and results confirm or contradict what the person says in a career and life planning interview.

Interests are at the heart of job satisfaction, so career counselors pay special attention to them and rigorously test for them (Subich & Billingsley, 1995). Consider an individual who is now a senior product developer of tests and educational materials. He started off majoring in engineering in college, received his degree in business, and then got his Ph.D. in counseling. He continues to look for some way to integrate his math, business, and psychological interests. Core interests for most people, like those of this person, usually remain rather stable over many years. Thus, it is very important to know what your interests are, and vocational tests, along with a career guidance interview, are a good way to find out what those interests are and what careers would match these interests. If you have not taken a vocational test recently and if you have not had a career development interview, you might want to contact your college's counseling and vocational guidance department to set up an appointment.

THE IMPACT OF WORK

Not only does work provide us with a means of earning a living, but we also hope it will give us a sense of purpose and fulfillment in life. Because work is such a fundamental part of most people's lives, psychologists are becoming increasingly interested in understanding the impact work has on self-definition and quality of life (Aamodt, 1996; Chmiel, 1997).

Working in Groups

Organizations consist of both formal and informal groups (Greenberg, 1996). **Formal groups** *are established by management to do the organization's work.* Formal groups include such departments as quality assurance, electrical engineering, cost accounting, and personnel. Organizations are increasingly using formal groups known as work teams. Work teams are often established for subsections of manufacturing and assembly processes. For example, General Motors reorganized its assembly lines into work teams of 5 to 20 workers. In the work team approach, the team members decide among themselves who will do each task.

Informal groups *are clusters of workers formed by the group's members.* Informal groups develop because of the interests and needs of the individuals who work in the organization. They consist of both friendship groups, arising from relationships that develop among members of the organization, and interest groups, which are organized around a common activity or interest, such as sports, the arts, or politics. Among the interest groups that have developed in recent years are networks of working women. Many of these groups began in male-dominated organizations as informal gatherings of women who wanted the support of other women. Soon, however, they developed far beyond their initial social purposes. The interest groups became sources of counseling, job placement, and management training. Some of the interest groups were established as formal, permanent associations, whereas others remained informal groups.

Informal groups can be as influential as formal groups in determining behavior in an organization. One classic study demonstrated the sensitivity of workers to the behavior of others in their group and the importance of informal norms of behavior at the Hawthorne Plant of the Western Electric Company in Chicago (Roethlisberger & Dickson, 1939). Management set a goal for each worker to wire a certain number of telephone switchboards per day. However, the work group as a whole established an acceptable level of output for its members. Workers who were above or below this informally established norm were criticized by other members of the work group. Workers who failed to meet the acceptable level were called "chiselers," whereas those who exceeded the norm were labeled "rate busters" or "speed

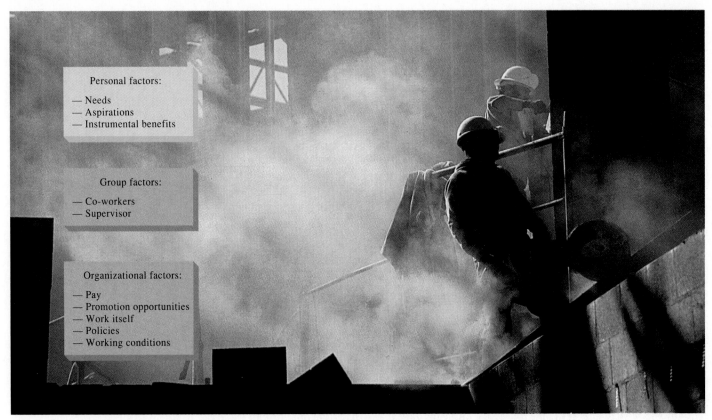

Personal factors:

— Needs
— Aspirations
— Instrumental benefits

Group factors:

— Co-workers
— Supervisor

Organizational factors:

— Pay
— Promotion opportunities
— Work itself
— Policies
— Working conditions

FIGURE 12.3

Factors That Contribute to Job Satisfaction

kings." A worker who wanted to be accepted by the group could not produce at too low or too high a level. Thus, as a worker approached the accepted level for each day, he or she slowed down in order not to overproduce. Even though the individual workers could have made more money by producing more switchboards, they adhered to the informal work group's norm.

> *Working with people is difficult, but not impossible.*
>
> **—Peter Drucker**

Group factors are just one of many influences that determine how satisfying work can be. Next we turn to job satisfaction, including ways that it can be optimized.

Job Satisfaction

Imagine what type of job you hope to be performing 15 years from now. What will it take for this job to be satisfying for you? Let's explore the factors that influence job satisfaction and then turn to some developmental changes in job satisfaction.

Determinants of Satisfaction

Three main kinds of factors contribute to whether individuals are satisfied with their jobs: organizational, group, and personal (see figure 12.3). Organizational factors include pay, opportunities for promotion, the nature of the work, policies and procedures of the organization, and working conditions. Individuals might feel different levels of satisfaction about each of these factors. For example, an employee might feel underpaid but feel positive about the work and working conditions.

The job satisfaction of individuals in a work group may also be influenced by both their co-workers and their supervisor or manager (Robbins, 1995). For example, employees are more likely to be satisfied with their job if they get along well with their co-workers and if they see their boss or supervisor as being warm and understanding and as having a high degree of integrity.

Individuals' needs and aspirations also can influence job satisfaction (Bateman & Snell, 1996). If a person wants to be in a high-status position, gaining such a position will likely enhance the person's job satisfaction. Another important factor is the instrumental benefits of the job, that is, the extent to which the job enables the worker to achieve other ends. A person completing her college degree might take a particular job on a temporary basis because it allows flexible scheduling while paying enough to cover her tuition. She may be quite satisfied with the job as long as she is in college but might become considerably less satisfied with the same job on a permanent basis after she graduates from college.

The extent to which workers are satisfied with their jobs affects turnover and absenteeism. When people are dissatisfied

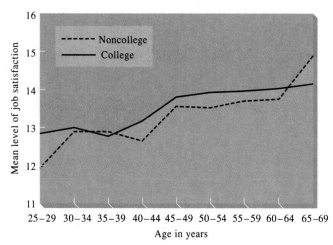

FIGURE 12.4

Age and Job Satisfaction
Job satisfaction increases with age, for both college and noncollege educated adults. Among the reasons for increased satisfaction are more income, higher status jobs, greater job security, and stronger job commitment.

with their jobs, they are more likely to call in sick when they really are not. They may even leave the organization for a more attractive job elsewhere. Conversely, when employees are satisfied, they come to work more regularly and are less likely to seek other employment.

> *By the work one knows the workman.*
> —**Jean de la Fontaine**

As a rule, job satisfaction increases as people grow older. The most common pattern is a steady increase in job satisfaction from the age of 20 to at least 60, for both college-educated and noncollege-educated adults (Rhodes, 1983) (see figure 12.4). This same pattern has been found for both women and men. Satisfaction probably increases because as we get older we get paid more, we are in higher-status positions, and we have more job security. Older adults also show a greater commitment to the job as they get older—they take their jobs more seriously, have lower rates of absenteeism, and are more involved in their work than when they were younger. Younger adults are still experimenting with their work and still sometimes searching for the right occupation, so they may be inclined to seek out what is wrong with their current job instead of focusing on what is right about it.

Optimizing Satisfaction

In his book *Ambition: How We Manage Success and Failure Throughout Our Lives,* Gilbert Brim (1992) describes the role of **just manageable difficulty,** *the optimal level of effort in a person's life, in job satisfaction, and life satisfaction.* The goal becomes to arrange your life so that it is neither overloaded or underloaded—that is, so that you are not just coasting through life or being dragged under the current. An easy job with little or no challenge does not produce job satisfaction; neither does an overwhelming job with extraordinary pressure. Rather, job satisfaction most likely results from positions that entail well-chosen problems that can be solved with a comfortable amount of effort and work (Kristoff, 1996). When problems are resolved successfully, future job satisfaction often rests on an increasing degree of job difficulty. By contrast, following failure, job satisfaction often results when the worker's expectations and the job's difficulty are lowered. According to the concept of just manageable difficulty, the key to job satisfaction is finding the right level of challenge and difficulty.

Work-Related Stress

Work can be the source of considerable stress and strain. We will examine a model of work-related stress and coping. Then we will look at specific sources of

strain, including dysfunctional work sites, family strains, health concerns, and personal doubts.

A Comprehensive Model of Work-Related Stress, Coping, and Adaptation

Figure 12.5 illustrates a comprehensive model of work-related stress, coping, and adaptation (Moos, 1986). The model includes the environmental system (Panel I in the figure), which is made up of organizational and work-related factors and current stressors and social resources that stem from other contexts in the individual's life, such as the family and neighborhood. The personal system (Panel II) involves work-related factors such as the type of job (occupation) and work role, sociodemographic characteristics such as age and social class, and personal factors such as self-esteem, intellectual ability, general problem-solving skills, and needs and value orientations. The personal and environmental systems influence each other, as do work and nonwork factors in both systems.

In this model of work-related stress and coping, the association between the environmental system (Panel I) and adaptation (Panel V) is influenced by the personal system (Panel II), as well as by cognitive appraisal and coping (Panels III and IV). Cognitive appraisal is the outcome of an interplay between the personal and environmental systems. Consider a work group in which employees determine the allocation and sequence of specific tasks, the timing of rest breaks, and the principles underlying variations in pay. Most individuals in such a system are likely to describe it as high in involvement and autonomy. This type of work climate often produces more positive coping and cognitive appraisals than a work climate that is oriented toward external control.

The next step in the model reflects individuals' efforts to manage the environment by selecting a preferred set of coping responses. Such responses are influenced by the personal system (for example, some people are more inclined toward active problem solving and others toward avoidance) and the environmental

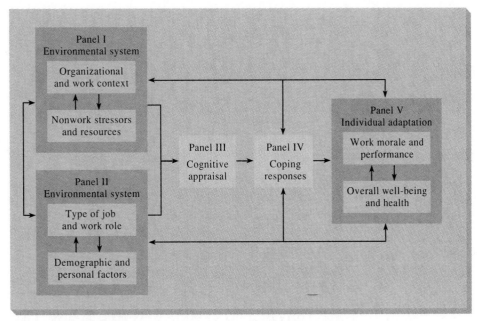

FIGURE 12.5

A Comprehensive Model of Work-Related Stress, Coping, and Adaptation

system (some work settings reward problem solving more than others do). An individual's use of coping skills can also change both systems. For example, a woman who assumes an active role in office decision making may alter her attitudes (a change in the personal system) and help to create a new employee-based decision-making group (a change in the environmental system).

Coping efforts eventually affect the person's standing on work-related criteria such as job morale and performance, as well as life satisfaction and health. In turn, changes in these criteria can alter both personal and environmental factors (such as an increase in job morale may bolster a person's self-concept; more productive employees may create a more cohesive work setting). Additionally, as indicated in figure 12.5, work morale and satisfaction are related to such nonwork factors as family functioning and other life circumstances. Conversely, such outcomes as life satisfaction and overall well-being and health are linked to various dimensions of work and to characteristics of nonwork settings. The bidirectional path of the model suggests that all of these factors can influence each other and that reciprocal feedback can occur at any point.

Dysfunctional Workplaces

Although we have briefly discussed the role of the work-setting characteristics on job dissatisfaction and stress, it is important to acknowledge that many psychologists see problems with workplace structure, organization, and personnel as a major cause of stress in the lives of individuals. Many individuals work in organizations in which there are ambiguous work objectives, work roles, and job responsibilities, as well as a poor organizational structure and climate (such as threatened autonomy, no sense of belonging, lack of effective communications, and office politics). Problems in work organizations and problems with colleagues or supervisors are major concerns of many American workers.

Anne Schaef and Diane Fassel (1988), in their book *The Addictive Organization*, compare dysfunctional workplaces with addictive persons. Some workplaces encourage dysfunctional behaviors such as workaholism, miscommunication, office politics, ambiguous roles and responsibilities, frequent reorganizations, and dishonesty. Persons who work in dysfunctional workplaces often use words like the following to describe their work setting: *confusion, powerlessness,*

distortions, dishonesty, judgmentalism, seduction, manipulation, chaos, crisis-orientation, isolation, vindictiveness, paralysis, forgetfulness, mistrust, and *spiritually bankrupt.*

> *I think that in every company today there is always at least one person who is going crazy slowly.*
>
> **—Joseph Heller**

At times, a dysfunctional workplace is largely attributable to one individual or a few individuals. In *The Success Syndrome*, Steven Berglass (1991), a Harvard Medical School psychologist, discusses the increasing number of narcissists who are in power positions in the workplace. These individuals are often characterized by at least three of the following:

1. Arrogance
2. A sense of aloneness
3. The need to seek adventure
4. Adultery

Although they might appear to have healthy personalities and are able to gather resources, influence, and loyalty, they suffer from a basic mistrust of underlings and a belief that their psychological problems can be resolved by making more money and having more power. In other words, these individuals only have one source of self-esteem—getting ahead at work—and they are willing to achieve this goal by trampling others. Obviously, such an individual can create stress for others who work in the same organization. Berglass suggests that narcissistic bosses can be helped by becoming involved in community or religious activity, thereby learning to build their self-esteem in ways other than overachieving at all costs on the job.

Family Strains

There can be both positive and negative connections between family and work (Durup & Leiter, 1995). Three possible patterns of family-work connections are these:

1. Positive carryover when personal gratification and information from work enrich the family

What issues do women face as they combine a career and family?

In the movie *Baby Boom,* the character played by Diane Keaton (*above*) lost her job when she couldn't find a way to juggle her career and family roles and still give her child adequate care and attention. In her own life, Keaton chose to become a single mother at age 50 by adopting a child; however, her lucrative film career allows her greater choice and flexibility than most women have. Many women are turning down higher-paying jobs in favor of jobs that allow them more flexibility. This increasing trend toward greater flexibility has been documented in *The Corporate Reference Guide to Work-Family Programs,* which was released in 1991—of the 188 Fortune 1,000 companies surveyed, 77 percent reported that they have instituted flexible scheduling, and 48 percent offer job sharing.

2. A more common carryover in which work overload and job-role conflict cause stress in the family
3. Individuals try to conserve their energy and privacy and become less available to family members.

Work and family settings compete for scarce personal resources. As work stressors increase, families often have fewer interpersonal resources available to buffer them. Any person who fulfills both work and family roles may sometimes experience interrole conflict and work overload. In general, though, employment, marriage, and parenthood are associated with good physical health among both women and men (Crosby, 1991).

> Total commitment to family and total commitment to career is possible, but fatiguing.
>
> —**Muriel Fox**

In recent years women have had greater options for working outside the home. Sociocultural Worlds of Adjustment explores a contrast in traditional and work-oriented lifestyles for women.

The Superhuman Syndrome Many persons are worker (some at more than one job), spouse, and parent, and, as some of you reading this well know, student, too. Trying to do several roles well requires people to become like superwomen and supermen; attempts at "superhumanness" have been increasing for the last few decades, especially for women.

In the 1950s, many women worked for a short time, got married and became full-time housewives, and shortly thereafter became full-time stay-at-home mothers. Although there have always been women who balanced career with demands of marriage and possibly parenting, the idealized female adult life did not revolve around a career. Now,

full-time parents may feel like society is not very encouraging of their lifestyle choices even though raising the next generation is crucial to our society's future.

The increasingly favorable attitude toward females' having careers is illustrated in a study from 1972 to 1985 that explored changes in college students' beliefs about women working after marriage (Phillips & Jonston, 1985). Although belief that women's careers are secondary to men's remained the majority position in 1985, there were significant changes in career minimalization for women. About 12 percent of college students in 1972 felt that women should not be employed after marriage; in 1985 this belief had dropped to 2 percent (almost always male students). Belief that women's careers should become and remain minimal after children are part of a family dropped from 38 percent to 9 percent (with this belief more strongly held by men than by women). On the other hand, the view that children create a temporary interruption in women's career climbed from 40 percent to 48 percent (a position held by more females than males). The most dramatic increase was in the belief that women

The Mommy Track Versus the Career Track

The life paths of Joanne and Joan were very different (Gerson, 1986). Joanne grew up in a traditional American family. While her father earned only a modest wage as a repairman, her mother stayed home to rear four children because both parents believed that full-time mothering for the children was more important than additional income. They hoped that Joanne would educate herself for a better life, but Joanne was more interested in dating than in schoolwork or in her part-time job at a fast-food restaurant. When she became pregnant at 17, she was happy to marry her boyfriend and assume the role of a full-time mother. Two children, several brief and disenchanting sales jobs and 10 years later, Joanne still finds satisfaction in full-time mothering. At times she feels financial pressure to give up homemaking for paid work and resents being snubbed when she says her family is her career. Every time she searches the want ads, though, she vividly remembers how much she disliked her temporary jobs. Since her husband earns enough money to make ends meet, the urge to go to work quickly passes. Instead, Joanne is seriously thinking about having another child.

Joanne's life history reflects the traditional model of female development. An adult woman chooses a domestic life for which she was prepared emotionally and practically since childhood. Approximately 20 percent of women from various social classes and family backgrounds are believed to follow this life course (Gerson, 1986). These women are insulated from events that might steer them away from their expected paths. They are neither pushed out of the home by economic necessity or marital instability nor pulled into the workplace by enticing opportunities. Instead, they remain committed to the domestic role that they assume is the woman's proper and natural place in society.

In contrast, consider Joan's path. Like Joanne, Joan believed as a child that when she grew up she would marry, have children, and live happily ever after as a housewife. She harbored a vague wish to go to college, but her father thought women should not go to college, and as a low-paid laborer he could not afford to send her to college anyway. Joan worked after high school as a filing clerk and married Frank, a salesman, 2 years later. Within 6 months of the ceremony, she was pregnant and planning to stay home with her young child, but things changed soon after her daughter was born. Unlike Joanne, she became bored and unhappy as a full-time mother. Taking care of the baby was not the ultimate fulfillment for Joan. Motherhood was a mixture of feelings for her—alternately rewarding and frustrating, joyful and depressive. Despite her reluctance to admit these feelings to anyone but herself, a growing sense of emptiness and the need for additional income spurred Joan to look for paid work. She took a job as a bank teller, perceiving it to be a temporary way to boost family income, but the right time to quit never came. Frank's income consistently fell short of their needs, and as his work frustrations mounted, their marriage began to falter. When Frank pressured Joan to have another child, she began to think more seriously about whether she wanted to remain married to Frank. Just when the marriage seemed unbearable, Joan's boss gave her a chance to advance. She accepted the advance and decided to divorce Frank. Today, more than a decade later, Joan is dedicated to her career, aspires to upper-level management, and does not plan to remarry or expand her family beyond one child.

Joan's life represents an increasingly common pattern among women—one of rising work aspirations and ambivalence toward motherhood. Like their traditional counterparts, these women grew up wanting and preparing for a domestic role, only to find that events stimulated them to move in a different direction. About one-third of women today seem to follow this life pattern (Gerson, 1986). These women are more likely to experience unstable relationships with men, unanticipated opportunities for job advancement, economic squeezes at home, and disappointments with mothering and full-time homemaking. As a consequence, heightened work ambitions replace their earlier home-centered orientation. Although Joanne and Joan experienced similar childhood backgrounds and aspirations, their lives diverged increasingly as they were confronted with the opportunities and restrictions of early adulthood. The career and family paths of women in early adulthood can take many other life trajectories.

would have continuous career involvement, even after having children—an attitude that increased from only 4 percent in 1972 to 33 percent in 1985 (with no gender difference). In other words, one-third of college students had come to embrace the superwoman role—that women can have and do it all.

Several societal factors have allowed women to think about having so many simultaneous roles, with some factors creating dilemmas as well as opening up career possibilities. For example, better contraceptives have allowed women more exact control over when (and if) they have children. Accurate reproductive technology allows women to complete educational and career components without interruption by pregnancy. Conversely, improved reproductive technology produces more concern among childless career women who now must decide whether to continue in their full-time careers or to give birth while their "biological clock" allows this option.

Society has also become more flexible about people's lifestyles—there is no longer an ideal time to marry, have children, and so forth. Even the growing impact of divorce affects women because more want to be economically prepared in case their marriage ends. Gradually, work organizations are providing options that make it easier to be a career woman and mom, such as working at a computer terminal at home, job sharing, part-time careers, and day care at the workplace.

Are multiple roles good for women? Can women survive trying to be a superwoman? Here are some of the conclusions of research studies conducted in the 1980s that might help you decide about the wisdom of having multiple roles (McBride, 1990):

- Women experience significantly more change than men in the transition to parenthood, especially working-class women.
- Role strain is decreased when husbands approve of and support their wives' decisions.
- Role strain is increased when women are dissatisfied with child-care arrangements.
- Mental health seems to be more affected by marital satisfaction than by job satisfaction.
- For women, work often buffers marital stress, but parenthood exacerbates occupational stress.
- Good coping is associated with high income, high job satisfaction, not marrying early, and being able to arrange time for family activities.
- Multiple roles are associated with superior health, an autonomous sense of self, and rating one's own lifestyle positively.

- Problems can accumulate across roles, but participation in multiple roles can cancel some of the negative events generated by a specific role.

One concern of superwomen is that most of them have added career responsibilities and pressures while having about the same amount of caretaking and homemaking responsibilities. Most married couples do not reassign household responsibilities such as shopping, cleaning, cooking, and ironing with equity when both the husband and the wife have outside employment.

Another concern is that superwomen or working mothers at times have been pitted against stay-at-home mothers as women debate who is better off, doing better for their kids, and having more fulfilling lives. Mixed messages to women about what their "proper roles" are and "supermom expectations and anxieties" let the "mommy conflict" be laden with frustration, insecurity, jealousy, and guilt (Darton, 1990). In actuality, both lifestyles can be rewarding and fulfilling.

Interestingly, think about how the media have dealt with supermoms but not superdads, with no corresponding debate between working dads versus stay-at-home dads. This absence reinforces what has already been said—many men are unwilling to take an equal role in child rearing and homemaking even when their wives work at least as many hours outside the home as they do (Denmark, 1992).

The trend for supermen who handle the home, work, and parenting at once began only in the 1980s, and there still are only a few such men. The theme that typified the 1950s was "Why can't a woman be more like a man?" But now some view the ideal man as a "perfected woman," that is, capable of nurturance and intimacy as well as strength and achievement (Goodman, 1992). Still, men are more likely to come in touch with these person-related characteristics in middle-age than in young adulthood, often regretting what they missed in their fathering and marriage in their earlier years (McWilliams, 1992).

Although wives want their husbands to be more active participants in domestic tasks and parenting, women's greater comfort and expertise in these areas sometimes makes it harder for their husbands to take on a bigger role. For example, when a newborn cries and the father picks the child up, trying unsuccessfully to comfort it, the mother might take the infant, soothe it more effectively than he can, and thus defeat her spouse's efforts to learn to be a better nurturer (McWilliams, 1992). Just as many husbands would have to experience emotional stress and be patient for their wives to gain knowledge and skill in auto repair or carpentry, wives may need to tolerate emotional stress if husbands are to learn nurturing and homemaking skills that are unfamiliar to him but routine for her.

Some individuals fail to balance all their obligations, and become completely absorbed in their work. Next we look at workaholism, which many psychologists describe as an addiction. To reflect on whether your daily life has some aspects of superhuman syndrome, see Critical Thinking.

Workaholics Have you ever known someone who seemed to be at work every time you saw them, regardless of the time of day, or day of the week? They most likely go to work early, stay late, take work home with them, and may even work while on vacation, probably even during an airplane flight. You might have noticed that this same person had few if any hobbies or interests outside of work. Such a person might be a **workaholic,** *a person who is seemingly addicted to work.*

They intoxicate themselves with work so they won't see how they really are.
—Aldous Huxley

Although many people view such constant attention to work negatively, this perspective may not always be true. Workaholics do not necessarily experience their work as stressful. In fact, for them, their work may be as enjoyable as other people's hobbies or various forms

The Superhuman Perspective

Many families experience the strain that comes from having too many things to do and too many roles to play. Chances are good that you know this strain personally from balancing the demands of school, family, and possibly work yourself.

In this exercise, your task is to adopt a perspective different from your own in order to think through the impact of superhuman role demands on the family. (If you think of yourself as strained from juggling too many roles, try to adopt the point of view of someone who lives with you. If you think of yourself as strained from living with a juggler, try to think about what life is like from the point of view of the superhuman.) Your responses to the questions that follow give you an opportunity *to adopt a different perspective in solving problems.*

- Why do you adopt your particular pattern of role balancing?
- What values underlie the choices you make in balancing roles?
- What impact does your lifestyle have on your family or roommates?
- What events would need to take place in order for you to change your pattern?
- Are you happy with the balance, or do you wish your life could be different?

---

of recreation. People who work nearly continuously are likely to identify strongly with their career, which in turn is likely to be a source of pride and personal fulfillment. In addition, the amount of satisfaction they have with their job is also likely to be high.

It is important not to confuse a workaholic with a Type A personality. You might recall from chapter 4 that Type A personalities tend to be highly aggressive and impatient with their work. They too may have an obsession with work, but unlike the workaholic, the Type A personality is more likely to experience stress and pressure related to their work. Workaholics, on the other hand, are more likely to have a calmer and more collected obsession with their work and productivity.

How is it possible for a workaholic to find satisfaction in other areas of their life, such as their relationships, family, and friends, when all they seem to be concerned with is work? One way may be involving others in their work. They can share aspects of their jobs with others, or try to balance at least some time with others. Still, a part of being a workaholic is that little else will likely fit into a schedule. This, of course, includes time for the family or leisurely activities. Despite the benefits of leisure

activities for physical and mental health, workaholics rarely take time for relaxation.

Stress and Health Concerns

Four main aspects of work settings are associated with employee stress and health problems:

- High job demands such as heavy work load and time pressure
- Inadequate opportunities to participate in decision making, especially in how work is organized and its pace
- A high level of supervisor control
- Role ambiguity or lack of clarity about the job and criteria for adequate performance (see figure 12.6)

Stress is most likely to occur when job demands (task orientation and work pressure) are high and the individual has little choice in deciding how to meet the demands (low autonomy, high control). When employees are allowed to make decisions about their work, high job demands are often stimulating and can promote active problem solving and innovation. These ideas were explored in a study of groups of working men in the United States and Sweden (Karasek,

1979). Men who held jobs that were demanding and low in autonomy were more likely to report mental exhaustion, depression, and insomnia, to consume more sleeping pills and tranquilizers, and to take more sick leave. These problems declined when workers transferred to less stressful jobs. At every level of job demand, workers who were encouraged and allowed to make decisions experienced less stress. In a 6-year follow-up of the Swedish workers, high work demands and low autonomy predicted new cases of cardiovascular diseases (Karasek, 1981).

All work and no play makes Jack a dull boy—and Jill a wealthy widow.

—Evan Escar

Personal Doubts

One factor that can interfere with job satisfaction is **fear of success,** *a term proposed by Matina Horner (1968) to describe how some individuals sabotage their own performance or avoid success because they expect their success will produce negative consequences.* People may avoid success because they expect that it will place extra demands on them, lead to reduced self-esteem, or make them feel uncomfortably different from their peers. Originally proposed as a

Chapter 12: Careers and Work   293

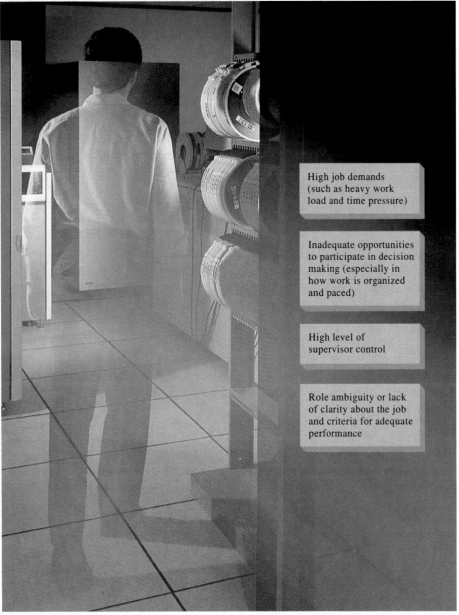

High job demands (such as heavy work load and time pressure)

Inadequate opportunities to participate in decision making (especially in how work is organized and paced)

High level of supervisor control

Role ambiguity or lack of clarity about the job and criteria for adequate performance

FIGURE 12.6

Four Main Dimensions of Work Settings That Increase Stress and Health Problems

"women's phenomenon," fear of success has subsequently been revealed in both women and men, especially in unfamiliar situations. Rather than having a general fear of success most individuals show fear of success in specific situations. For example, a student might do well in college but have some fear of success about making the dean's list because others might expect the student to make the list every semester.

A different type of personal doubting is called the **impostor phenomenon,** *the haunting fear of competent, successful people that their successes will be overturned and they will be revealed as frauds.* The primary cause of the impostor phenomenon is perfectionism in individuals who cannot meet their own extremely high standards of success. Three main characteristics of the impostor

phenomenon are (1) believing that others have been fooled into overestimating your abilities; (2) minimizing your abilities and intelligence, but attributing your well-earned successes to good luck, charm, good looks, or constant effort; and (3) having a constant fear of being uncovered as a fake.

Who experiences the impostor phenomenon? About 70 percent of successful individuals have experienced such feelings at some point in their careers. More than two-thirds of mental health professionals report that they have counseled clients who display the impostor phenomenon. If you experience the impostor phenomenon, remind yourself that your feelings are personal perceptions and do not necessarily reflect objective reality. Try to accept compliments rather than to deny them, and gradually learn to be flexible in your daily routines and more tolerant of your errors. To assess your own tendencies to feel like an impostor, see the Self-Assessment.

Leisure

Former President George Bush found a better balance between work and leisure than many of us—he played golf, fished, jogged, and played tennis even with the job demands and time pressures of being president of the United States. Instead, many American adults view leisure as boring or unnecessary, perhaps partly due to the country's strong, founding work ethic. Despite condescending views of leisure, the importance of leisure has been acknowledged for a long time. Even the ancient Greek philosopher Aristotle emphasized that people need to both work well and use leisure well; he actually described leisure as better because it was the end of work. How can we define leisure? **Leisure** *refers to the pleasant times outside of work when individuals are free to pursue activities and interests of their own choosing—hobbies, sports, or reading, for example.*

Ninety years ago the average work week was 72 hours. Only in the last three to four decades has the work week averaged 40 hours. What do most of us do

The Impostor Test

Instructions

Please answer the questions as honestly as possible using this scale:

1 = *not at all true*
2 = *rarely true*
3 = *sometimes true*
4 = *often true*
5 = *very true*

It is best to give the first response that enters your mind rather than dwelling on each statement and thinking about it over and over.

Please turn to the end of the chapter to interpret your responses.

Items

_____ 1. I have often succeeded on a test or task even though I was afraid that I would not do well before I undertook the task.

_____ 2. I can give the impression that I'm more competent than I really am.

_____ 3. I avoid evaluations if possible and have a dread of others' evaluating me.

_____ 4. When people praise me for something I've accomplished, I'm afraid I won't be able to live up to their expectations of me in the future.

_____ 5. I sometimes think I obtained my present position or gained my present success because I happened to be in the right place at the right time or knew the right people.

_____ 6. I'm afraid people important to me may find out that I'm not as capable as they think I am.

_____ 7. I tend to remember the incidents in which I have not done my best more than those times I have done my best.

_____ 8. I rarely do a project or task as well as I'd like to do it.

_____ 9. Sometimes I feel or believe that my success in my life or in my job has been the result of some kind of error.

_____ 10. It's hard for me to accept compliments or praise about my intelligence or accomplishments.

_____ 11. At times, I feel my success has been due to some kind of luck.

_____ 12. I'm disappointed at times in my present accomplishments and think I should have accomplished much more.

_____ 13. Sometimes I'm afraid others will discover how much knowledge or ability I really lack.

_____ 14. I'm often afraid that I may fail at a new assignment or undertaking even though I generally do well at what I attempt.

_____ 15. When I've succeeded at something and received recognition for my accomplishments, I have doubts that I can keep repeating that success.

_____ 16. If I receive a great deal of praise and recognition for something I've accomplished, I tend to discount the importance of what I have done.

_____ 17. I often compare my ability to those around me and think they may be more intelligent than I am.

_____ 18. I often worry about not succeeding with a project or on an examination, even though others around me have considerable confidence that I will do well.

_____ 19. If I'm going to receive a promotion or gain recognition of some kind, I hesitate to tell others until it is an accomplished fact.

_____ 20. I feel bad and discouraged if I'm not "the best" or at least "very special" in situations that involve achievement.

now that we have more free time than earlier generations? One of the most noticeable factors is our reliance on television over other types of mass media as a form of entertainment. Sports are also an integral part of the nation's leisure activities, both through direct participation and as spectators. The diversity offered by sports allows many individuals to escape the pressures of everyday life, even if only for a few hours a week.

Leisure may be an especially important aspect of life as individuals become middle-aged. For many individuals, middle adulthood is the first time in their lives that they have the opportunity to diversify their interests. Adults in midlife need to begin preparing both financially and psychologically for retirement. Constructive and fulfilling leisure activities are an important part of this preparation. If an adult develops leisure activities that

can be continued into retirement, the transition from work to retirement is likely to be less stressful.

At this point we have discussed many different ideas about careers, work, multiple roles, and leisure. On several occasions we have touched on the importance of gender in careers and work. Next we examine the role of gender in the workplace in greater detail, along with the importance of ethnicity.

The Impact of Work

Three main kinds of factors determine whether individuals are satisfied with their jobs: organizational (pay, promotional opportunities, work itself, policies, working conditions); group (co-workers, supervisor); and personal (needs, aspirations, instrumental benefits). The concept of just manageable difficulty suggests that the key to job satisfaction is finding the right level of challenge and difficulty. Fear of success and the impostor phenomenon can interfere with job satisfaction. A comprehensive view of work-related stress involves the environmental system (organizational and work context, and nonwork stressors and resources), the personal system (type of job and work role, and demographic and personal factors), cognitive appraisal, coping responses, and

individual adaptation (work morale and performance, and overall well-being and health). Many of these factors are interrelated.

Four main aspects of work settings are associated with employee stress and health problems: high job demands, inadequate opportunities to participate in decision making, a high level of supervisor control, and role ambiguity or lack of clarity about the job and criteria for adequate performance. Work-related stress can be due to dysfunctional workplaces.

Three possible patterns of family-work connections are a positive carryover when personal gratification and information from work enrich the family, a more common carryover in which work overload and job-role conflict cause stress in the family, and a pattern in which individuals try to conserve their energy and privacy and become less available to family members.

Multiple roles that compete for an individual's time are one of the main problems related to family strain.

A special concern that has increased in recent years and that is related to the strong work ethic in the American culture is work addiction. Some workaholics have difficulty ever relaxing when they are away from their job or work, not adequately balancing work and leisure in their lives.

Staying healthy in the workplace appears to be related to being able to exercise choice, especially when job demands are high. Good health requires not just effective work habits but also knowing how to relax and enjoy leisure. Leisure refers to the pleasant times outside of work when individuals are free to pursue activities and interests of their own choosing. Leisure might be an especially important aspect of life as individuals become middle-aged.

THE CHANGING WORLD OF WORK

As we move into the twenty-first century, what will the workplace be like? Changes are expected in types of jobs available, the nature of the workplace, and the diversity of the workers. We'll explore each of these aspects in turn.

Tomorrow's Jobs

For almost half a century the U.S. Bureau of Labor Statistics has published the *Occupational Outlook Handbook,* a valuable source for career information. The following information comes from the 1994–1995 edition (the handbook is revised every 2 years). The current long-term shift from goods-producing to service-producing employment will continue. By the year 2000, nearly four out of every five jobs will be in industries that provide services, such as banking, insurance, health care, education, data processing, and management consulting. Continued expansion of the service-producing sector generates a vision of a workforce dominated by

cashiers, retail sales workers, and waiters. In addition to the creation of millions of clerical, sales, and service jobs, the service sector will also be adding jobs for engineers, accountants, lawyers, nurses, and many other managerial, professional, and technical workers. In fact, the fastest growing careers will be those that require the most educational preparation (Ferrell & Hirt, 1996; Ferrett, 1996).

The range of employment growth in various careers will be diverse. As indicated in figure 12.7, the greatest growth in jobs will be for technicians and related support occupations. Workers in this group provide technical assistance to engineers, scientists, and other professional workers as well as operate and program technical equipment. This group also includes the fastest growing occupation—paralegals. Professional specialty occupations are expected to have grown 24 percent from 1988 to 2000. Much of this growth is a result of rising demand for engineers, computer specialists, lawyers, health diagnosing and treating occupations, and preschool, elementary, and secondary

school teachers. The greatest decrease in jobs will be in agriculture, forestry, fishing, and related occupations.

Many jobs are becoming more complex and more cognitively demanding. As knowledge increases exponentially, technically trained workers such as engineers face a half-life of 5 years; that is, half of what engineers know when they graduate is obsolete in 5 years because of rapid technological advances (Goldstein & Gilliam, 1990). Such demands will require considerable continuing education and training programs for workers in the future. Most college students will not finish their education when they get their college degrees; rather, they will participate in workshops, short courses, individualized training packages, and other educational formats to remain employable in their chosen field.

The Changing Workplace

Organizations will also change. Currently, a noticeable number of corporations are failing and others are significantly scaling down the size of their operations. Mergers and acquisitions displace workers with

Halonen/Santrock: Human Adjustment

Occupational group	Percent change in employment, 1990–2005
Total, all occupations	20 37
Technicians and related support occupations	32
Professional specialty occupations	29
Service occupations	27
Executive, administrative, and managerial occupations	24
Marketing and sales occupations	21
Transportation and material moving occupations	20
Construction trades and extractive occupations	16
Mechanics, installers, and repairers	13
Administrative support occupations, including clerical	8
Handlers, equipment cleaners, helpers, and laborers	5
Agriculture, forestry, fishing, and related occupations	
Production occupations	–4

FIGURE 12.7

Projected Growth in Various Occupational Groups

CRITICAL THINKING

Who Is Responsible?

Having fulfilled employees is certainly to the advantage of the employer. Satisfied workers show less absenteeism, so they can produce more, and they are less likely to leave their jobs, so retraining costs are reduced. However, employers differ over how much social responsibility they should assume for their workers. Some provide fitness centers and incentives to adopt a healthy lifestyle. Some offer employee assistance specialists who can help employees by diagnosing reported troubles and making appropriate referrals. Others draw the line at providing decent health insurance; these employers believe that employees should take personal responsibility for their health and fitness and do not necessarily see the connection between work quality and the additional services, or they are unable to pay for them.

How responsible do you think the employer should be for the personal dimension of job satisfaction? What are the *underlying values and assumptions that support your beliefs?*

increasing regularity. Failures, downscaling, and mergers will be part of the workplace of tomorrow, too, one of the major reasons that types of jobs are continuing to shift from the manufacturing sector to the service sector. The service sector accounted for 71 percent of the nation's jobs in 1990, but the percentage will get even larger. In addition, businesses are increasingly becoming international organizations. As a result, success for companies will partly depend on their ability to relate to workers and organizations in other countries (Offermann & Gowing, 1990).

> *It is no longer clear which way is up even if one wants to rise.*
> —Laurence J. Peters

Millions of workers center a great deal of their life on the workplace. As a result, the heads of organizations are increasingly realizing that the workplace is an important setting for promoting health and welfare (Offermann & Gowing, 1990). Many organizations have programs to help workers improve the balance between work and family and promote health through stress management courses and fitness centers. To evaluate the social responsibility of employers, see Critical Thinking.

The Changing Workforce

In the year 2000, workers will be more culturally diverse—one-third of new entrants to the labor force are anticipated to be ethnic minorities. Larger numbers of women will enter the labor force, putting greater pressure on society to help balance the demands between work and family (Ickovics, 1991; Natalle, 1996).

The Impact of Diversity

A study called *Workforce 2000* clearly delineated the dramatic changes we can expect in the workforce of the United States in the twenty-first century. In 1985, White males comprised almost half of the labor force (47 percent), but by the year 2000 they will represent only 15 percent. The remaining 85 percent will consist of women, ethnic minorities, and immigrants.

The dramatic increase in women and ethnic minority individuals into the labor force will require considerable change and adaptation on the part of workers and management. To facilitate employee relations and productivity, employees and management will need to familiarize themselves with the cultures represented in the multiethnic workforce and develop an understanding of how each others' needs and values influence their behavior.

The Glass Ceiling in Management

In the Japanese workplace, most women have inferior roles as temporary workers. Although women and ethnic minorities in the American workplace are considered permanent employees, women and people of color experience a glass ceiling in management. The concept of the **glass ceiling** *was popularized in the 1980s to describe a subtle barrier that is virtually invisible, yet so strong that it prevents women and ethnic minorities from moving up in the management hierarchy.* According to a 1994 report in *Business Week,* women fill 42 percent of management positions but many women complain that they have little authority and are not paid at the same rate as their male counterparts. White males still dominate corporate leadership. Nearly 92 percent of corporate officers are White males; only 6 percent are women and only 2 percent are ethnic minorities.

Several explanations have been proposed for the relative absence of women and ethnic minorities in management (Maupin, 1993; Schein & others, 1996). One explanation alleges inadequacies in women and ethnic minorities. For example, it has been claimed that women are not in management positions because they fear success or are unwilling to take risks. However, female and male managers are much more similar than dissimilar on many different personality, motivational, and intellectual factors. Ethnic minority managers have also shown special strengths in interpersonal relations and stability of performance.

A second explanation is that the dominant group is biased. Many employers, customers, and employees believe that women and people of color are less suited for management positions, even

Among interest groups that have developed in recent years are networks of working women. Many of these groups began as informal gatherings of women in male-dominated organizations who wanted the support of other women.

The corporate board rooms of American businesses are dominated by White males. Although women and ethnic minorities are slowly making gains in management, currently 92 percent of corporate officers are White males.

when they are perfect candidates. Another belief that handicaps women in particular is that the good manager is *masculine* rather than *androgynous* in most organizations.

A third explanation is that the racist, ageist, and sexist underpinnings of society permeate the organization. Intergroup theory states that two types of groups exist in organizations—identity groups (based on ethnicity, family, gender, and age) and organization groups (based on common work tasks, work experience, and positions in the hierarchy). Tension results when organization group membership changes, but identity group membership does not. The demographic profile in an organization often mirrors the pattern in society as a whole, as when Whites fill most of the high-status positions and African Americans the low-status positions. As a result, managers might evaluate women and people of color through the distorted lens of prejudice (Alderfer & Tucker, 1996).

Many organizational psychologists believe that the workplace needs to adjust to better accommodate women and ethnic minorities. Eastman Kodak and Dupont are two companies that have implemented programs designed to help managers work together within a diverse workforce and to reduce discrimination. The value of such programs is that issues are brought out into the open, allowing individuals to discuss their beliefs.

Support groups may increase the number of women and ethnic minority members in management. Security Pacific National Bank developed a program titled Black Officers Support System (BOSS) to recruit African Americans and reduce their turnover (Irons & Moore, 1985). The Executive Leadership Council in Washington, D.C., is made up of fifty African American managers from major industries who recruit and hire ethnic minorities (Leinster, 1988). Such groups provide career guidance and psychological support for women and ethnic minority individuals seeking managerial positions.

The Challenge for White Males

> "White male" is what I call the newest swear word in America.
> —Harris Sussman

Affirmative action initiatives have assumed a central role in U.S. politics. Many White men think they are being personally punished by cultural practices aimed at promoting diversity in the workplace. For instance, a White male who aspired to be a baggage handler for a major airline complained to his career counselor that the only applicants who seemed to be getting hired were women and minorities. He concluded that he was unlikely to be hired because he had "the wrong pigment and the wrong plumbing" (Galen & Palmer, 1994).

Despite the overwhelming predominance of White males in positions of power in corporate America, White males seeking entry-level positions increasingly report diminished opportunities as a result of attempts to create a more level playing field. In periods of corporate downsizing, White men who have established themselves in careers fear being fired first as another corporate strategy for enhancing diversity.

Many people who advocate abandoning affirmative action argue that it promotes "reverse racism" (Fish, 1993). They criticize affirmative action initiatives as undemocratic, penalizing individuals solely on the basis of gender and ethnicity—in this instance, for being male and White. They also believe that affirmative action undercuts the role of merit in employment decisions, and that it can be harmful when unprepared candidates who are destined to fail are hired over more-qualified candidates in order to promote diversity (Sowell, 1994).

Many personnel departments report growing backlash from White males who resent losing opportunity and being blamed for all the prejudices that influenced employment practices in the past. One insidious effect of White male backlash is the supposition that women and ethnic minorities are being hired and promoted solely due to their gender or ethnicity. One experiment demonstrated that attaching an affirmative action label to a list of employee characteristics prompted more negative attributions and competence concerns than were expressed regarding White candidates who had not been given an affirmative action label (Heilman, Block, & Lucas, 1992). These findings support concerns that affirmative action programs might intensify ill feelings based on gender and ethnicity rather than improve the climate of the workplace.

Unfortunately, many strategies used in the corporate world can make matters worse. Some ill-designed diversity training programs simply heap more responsibility for the employment misfortunes of ethnic and female candidates on White men, which fuels anger and resentment (Baker, 1996). A blaming atmosphere obscures the contribution many White males have made toward creating a diverse workplace (Galen & Palmer, 1994). Ironically, destructive diversity initiatives sometimes rely on brief, intense interventions that stir up ill feelings without ongoing support to work such feelings through. Critical to the success of diversity initiatives is a broad-ranging definition of diversity. For example, age, religious traditions, and family structure can also be aspects of diversity in the workplace. Senior managers need to make a substantial,concrete, ongoing effort to stress that enriched diversity can be a corporate asset in global competition.

REVIEW

The Changing World of Work

Tomorrow's jobs will reflect the current expansion in the service sector. Technically trained individuals should also benefit from continuing innovations in technology. Training might have to be a lifelong process. Organizational changes tend to favor downsizing and mergers. Employers seem increasingly disposed to create work environments that promote health and well-being.

By the year 2000, there will be dramatic increases of women and ethnic minorities in the workforce. By the year 2000, only 15 percent of the labor force will be White males, down from 47 percent in 1985. Such substantial changes in the labor force will require considerable adjustment on the part of employees and management. Women and ethnic minority individuals often face many barriers in their efforts to move up in the management hierarchy. The barriers have been referred to as the glass ceiling. Reasons for these low numbers include explanations based on differences that handicap women and ethnic minorities, as well as discrimination. A special concern is tokenism. Affirmative action politics have assumed a central role in the politics of the United States. White men face special challenges in regard to affirmative action.

I am against a homogenized society because I want the cream to rise.

—**Robert Frost**

Careers are getting tougher to break into, and jobs are becoming tougher to get. Having a college degree used to mean career security. Today, job markets in most career areas are far more competitive than in the past. In times of tough competition, it is even more important to use good critical-thinking skills in order to have your application "rise to the top" of the pile of applicants. Not only should *applying psychological concepts enhance your adaptation and growth;* it might even land you a job!

Do Your Homework

Applicants usually fare best when they apply to several potential employers. Most people rely on newspaper classified ads and employment agencies to locate openings. Another option is to do an inventory of the telephone yellow pages to find employers that interest you. Call personnel departments of companies and inquire about potential openings. Asking good questions during your investigation can pay off in getting your résumé placed on file, in preparing you more effectively for an on-site interview, and in landing a position.

Employers are frequently surprised to find that applicants know very little about their company; so well-prepared applicants are at a distinct advantage. Getting information about an employer through the public relations office or other sources might give you just the edge you need. Formulating questions for your employer demonstrates your interest and your problem-solving skills.

Know Yourself Well

Know your own strengths and weaknesses before you seek a position. Employers will want to know the strengths and abilities you have to offer. Being able to describe who you are and what assets you can bring to the company will help an employer determine whether you are right for the position. Being able to describe your abilities with ease and to be candid about areas you have yet to develop (and your willingness to learn them) will also make you a distinctive candidate.

It is especially important to think about whether your own values and aspirations will be well served by the position you seek. Although an employer is selecting you, you must also select your employer. Since your goal should be to find a good match for your talents, you may find it helpful to think of the interviewing process as *mutual* selection.

Present Yourself Well

As you complete your application, avoid overlooking or downplaying your skills (e.g., keyboard skills, computer operating, and being a good team player are all important skills), especially when presenting yourself on paper. Be certain to include any formal training you have received as well as any position you have held that is even remotely related to the job you are applying for. For example, volunteer work will have honed your ability to work with others. Neatness counts. Some employers have been known to dismiss applications that were messy or ungrammatical or didn't follow instructions.

If your written application or phone interviews secure an on-site interview, put your best foot forward. Try to anticipate the kinds of questions an employer would ask of you. Be punctual, and dress appropriately. Show what you have to offer and that you would be pleasant to work with. Interest and enthusiasm, but not overconfidence, are attractive to potential employers.

Don't Give Up

Commitment to a career means that you are willing to go the extra mile. Sometimes this means starting out at an entry-level position. Other times it can mean getting more training and experience. It might even mean searching in other cities and relocating. Particularly when job competition is harsh, it pays in the long run to persist. However, when you have gotten a firm rejection, move on. Don't waste your energies on the ideal position that is no longer realistically available to you. Try to learn something from each job interview, no matter what its outcome.

We began this chapter by exploring the nature of career development, especially focusing on career development across the life span and career exploration and planning. Our coverage of the impact of work involved working in groups, job satisfaction, work-related stress, and leisure. We also read about the changing world of work, evaluating tomorrow's jobs, the changing workplace, and the changing workforce. Don't forget that you can obtain an overall summary of the chapter by again studying the in-chapter reviews on pages 286, 296, and 299.

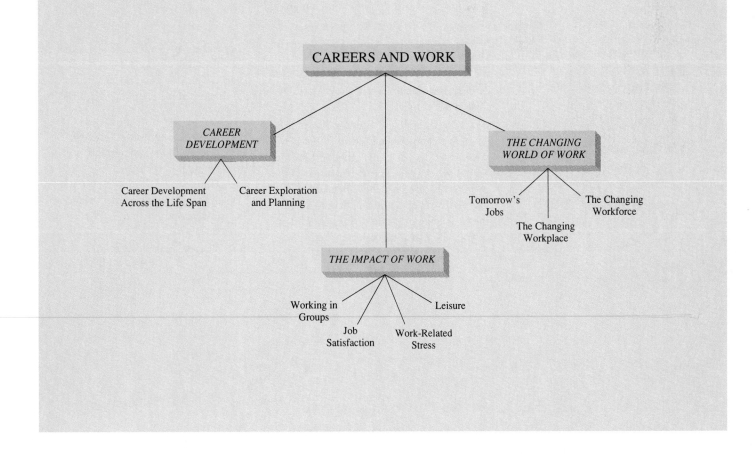

CAREERS AND WORK

CAREER DEVELOPMENT

Career Development Across the Life Span

Career Exploration and Planning

THE IMPACT OF WORK

Working in Groups

Job Satisfaction

Work-Related Stress

Leisure

THE CHANGING WORLD OF WORK

Tomorrow's Jobs

The Changing Workplace

The Changing Workforce

PRACTICAL KNOWLEDGE ABOUT ADJUSTMENT

WHAT COLOR IS YOUR PARACHUTE?

(1996) by Richard Bolles. Berkeley, CA: Ten Speed Press.

What Color Is Your Parachute? is an extremely popular book on job hunting. Author Richard Bolles is an Episcopal priest who changed from pastoral counseling to career counseling. *What Color Is Your Parachute?* was first published in 1970. Since 1975, an annual edition has appeared. This book has become the career seeker's bible. Bolles tries to answer concerns about the job-hunting process and refers readers to many sources that provide valuable information. Unlike many self-help books on job hunting, *What Color Is Your Parachute?* does not necessarily assume that you are a recent college graduate seeking your first job. He also spends considerable time discussing job hunting for people who seek to change careers. Bolles describes many myths about job hunting and successfully combats them. He also provides invaluable advice about where jobs are, what to do to get yourself hired, and how to cut through all of the red tape and confusing hierarchies of the business world to meet with the key people who are most likely to make the decision about whether to hire you or not. The book has remained appreciably the same over the years with updates where appropriate. More recent editions have added material on job hunting for handicapped workers, how to effectively use career counselors to your benefit, and how to find a mission in life.

THE 7 HABITS OF HIGHLY EFFECTIVE PEOPLE

(1989) by Stephen Covey. New York: Simon & Schuster.

The 7 Habits of Highly Effective People tells you how to harness your potential to achieve your goals. Covey argues that to become a quality leader in an organization, you must first become a quality-oriented individual. To reach this status, you have to identify the underlying principles that are important in your life and then evaluate whether you are living up to those standards. He also believes there are seven basic habits that are fundamental to anyone's success and competence. The first three are private victories and the next three are public victories. The seven habits:

- Be proactive instead of reactive
- Begin with the end in mind
- Put first things first
- Think win/win
- Seek first to understand, then to be understood
- Synergize
- Sharpen the saw (renewal)

CAREER GOAL-SETTING
Needs no additional scoring

THE IMPOSTOR TEST
Most people who experience the impostor phenomenon (IP) would not put such a label on themselves, nor would they overtly say, "I feel like an impostor." Yet when they hear or read about the components of the phenomenon, they immediately say, "How did you know exactly how I feel?"

And how do they feel? Someone once said that the ABCs of success are "ability, breaks, and courage." But most IP victims, even though they are often very successful, feel their success has been due to some mysterious fluke or luck, or great effort; they believe their achievements are due only to "breaks and courage" and never the result of their own ability. They're also certain that, unless they go to gargantuan lengths to do so, success can't be repeated again.

Scoring
Add your score for a total between 20 and 100.

Interpretation
The higher your score, the more you may experience the impostor phenomenon.

The Impostor Profile:
1. **The impostor cycle.** Doubts, worrying, remembering what they don't know rather than what they do know. Procrastinating, overworking, overpreparing, panicking.
2. **The need to be special, to be the very best.** Must be the most important, the brightest, the most exceptional. Dismiss good talents unless they are the best.
3. **Superwoman/superman aspects.** Perfectionistic in almost all aspects. Expect to do everything flawlessly and with ease. Left feeling like an overwhelmed failure.
4. **Fear of failure.** Terror that goals will not be met. Extreme anxiety over mistakes.
5. **Denial of competence and discounting praise.** Disclaim objective evidence of intelligence and success. Do not internalize their own competence. Difficulty accepting praise and other positive feedback.
6. **Fear of and guilt about success.** Frightened of the consequences of success, such as interference with relationships or having to set even higher goals and take on more responsibility.

Adult Development and Aging

In youth, we learn, in age we understand.

—Marie Ebner von Eschenbach

J onathan Swift said, "No wise man ever wished to be younger." Without a doubt, a 70-year-old body does not work as well as it once did. It is also true that an individual's fear of aging is often greater than need be. As more individuals live to a ripe *and* active old age, our image of aging is changing. While on the average a 75-year-old's joints should be stiffening, people can practice not to be average. For example, a 75-year-old man might *choose* to train for and run a marathon; an 80-year-old woman whose capacity for work is undiminished might *choose* to continue making and selling children's toys.

Consider 85-year-old Sadie Halperin, who has been working out for 11 months at a rehabilitation center for the aged in Boston, lifting weights and riding a stationary bike. She says that before she started working out, about everything she did—shopping, cooking, walking—was a major struggle. Initially she could lift only 15 pounds with both legs; now she lifts 30 pounds. At first she could bench-press

Eighty-five-year-old Sadie Halperin doubled her strength in exercise after just 11 months. Before developing an exercise routine, she felt wobbly and often had to hold on to a wall when she walked. Now she walks down the middle of hallways and says she feels wonderful.

only 20 pounds; now she bench-presses 50 pounds. Sadie's exercise routine has increased her muscle strength and helps her to battle osteoporosis by slowing the calcium loss from her bones, which can lead to deadly fractures (Ubell, 1992).

PREVIEW

The experiences of 85-year-old Sadie Halperin raise some truly interesting questions about development, among them how much people can continue to change even when they are old. In the 1990s, psychologists have increasingly stressed the importance of successful aging rather than stereotyping older adults as always in decline. Later in this chapter we will explore many different facets of development in older adults, but we will begin by focusing on the nature of development and the transition to adulthood. Then we will move on to the early and middle adulthood years. We will conclude the chapter with a discussion of death and dying.

BECOMING ADULTS

We go through many kinds of changes as we move from adolescence into adulthood. In this section we take an overall look at the developmental processes involved in this transition.

> *You grow up the day you have your first real laugh at yourself.*
>
> —**Ethel Barrymore**

The Nature of Development

Each of us develops in ways that are like all other individuals, like some other individuals, and like no other individuals. Most of the time, our attention is directed to an individual's uniqueness. But psychologists who study development are drawn to our shared as well as our unique characteristics. As humans, each of us has traveled some common paths. Each of us—Leonardo Da Vinci, Joan of Arc, George Washington, Martin Luther King, Jr., you—walked at about 1 year, talked at about 2 years, engaged in fantasy play as a young child, and became more independent as a youth. Each of us, if we live long enough, will experience hearing problems and the death of family and friends.

Just what do psychologists mean when they speak of an individual's development? **Development** *is the pattern of change that begins at conception and continues through the life span.* Most development involves growth, although it also includes decay (as in death and dying). The pattern of movement is complex because it is the product of several processes—biological, cognitive, and socioemotional.

For the purposes of organization and understanding, most psychologists commonly describe development in terms of periods. The most widely used classification of developmental periods involves the following sequence: prenatal period, infancy, early childhood, middle and late childhood, adolescence, early adulthood, middle adulthood, and late adulthood. Our focus here will be on the adult periods and the transition

from adolescence to adulthood. Let's examine what these periods of development are like.

Adolescence *is a developmental period of transition from childhood to early adulthood, entered at approximately 10 to 12 years of age and ending at about 18 to 22 years of age.* Adolescence begins with rapid physical changes—dramatic gains in height and weight, changes in body contour, and the development of sexual characteristics. At this point in development, the pursuit of independence and identity are prominent. More and more time is spent outside the family during this period.

Early adulthood *is a developmental period that begins sometime in the late teens or early twenties and ends sometime in the late thirties to early forties.* It is a time when individuals establish personal and economic independence, intensely pursue a career, and seek intimacy with one or more individuals.

Middle adulthood *is the developmental period beginning at approximately 35 to 45 years of age and extending to the sixties.* It is a time of expanding personal and social involvement and responsibility; of assisting the next generation in becoming competent, mature individuals; and of reaching and maintaining satisfaction in one's career.

Late adulthood *is the developmental period beginning in the sixties or seventies and lasting until death.* It is a time of adjustment to decreasing strength and health, life review, retirement, and adjustment to new social roles.

These brief descriptions of the stages of life raise an interesting question: Is there a best age to be?

When individuals report how happy they are and how satisfied they are with their lives, no particular age group reports greater happiness or satisfaction than any other age group (Stock & others, 1983). In one report of life satisfaction in eight Western European countries, there was no age-related difference in the percentages who reported overall satisfaction with life. For example, 78 percent of 15- to 24-year-olds, 78 percent of 35- to 44-year-olds, and 78 percent of those 65 and older reported satisfaction (Ingelhart &

What is the best age to be? When individuals report how happy they are and how satisfied they are with their lives, no particular age group reports that they are happier or more satisfied than any other age group.

Rabier, 1986). Similarly, slightly fewer than 20 percent of each of the age groups reported that they were "very happy."

Why might older people report just as much happiness and life satisfaction as younger people? Every period of the life cycle has its stresses, its pluses and minuses, its hills and valleys. Adolescents must cope with developing an identity, feelings of insecurity, mood swings, and peer pressure, but the majority of adolescents develop positive perceptions of themselves, feelings of competence about their skills, positive relationships with friends and family, and an optimistic view of their future. Although older adults face a life of reduced income, less energy, decreasing physical skills, and concerns about death, they are also less pressured to achieve and succeed, have more time for leisurely pursuits, and have accumulated many years of experience that help them adapt to their lives with a wisdom they may not have had in their younger years. Growing older is a certain outcome of living, so we can derive considerable pleasure from knowing that we are likely to be just as happy as older adults as when we were younger (Myers, 1995).

The Transition to Adulthood

Mark Twain, reflecting on his youth, commented, "When I was a boy of 14 my father was so ignorant I could hardly stand to have the man around. But when I got to be 21, I was astonished at how much he learnt in seven years." When does an adolescent become an adult? Although no consensus exists as to when adolescence is left behind and adulthood is entered, psychologists have proposed some criteria for the beginning of adulthood.

Faced with a complex world of work, with highly specialized tasks, many post-teenagers spend an extended period of time in technical institutes, colleges, and postgraduate centers to acquire specialized skills, educational experiences, and professional training. Their income generally is low and irregular, and they might change residences frequently. They might shun marriage and starting a family. This period often lasts from 2 to 8 years, although it is not unusual for it to last a decade or longer.

Youth *is sociologist Kenneth Kenniston's (1970) term for the transitional period between adolescence and adulthood, which is a time of extended economic and personal temporariness.* Kenniston argues that youth have not settled the questions whose answers once defined adulthood—questions about one's relation to the existing society, about vocation, and about social roles and lifestyles. Youth differs from adolescence because of youth's struggle between developing an autonomous self and becoming socially involved, in contrast to adolescence's struggle for self-definition.

Psychologists have proposed two criteria as signaling the end of youth and the beginning of early adulthood: economic independence and independent decision making. Probably the most widely recognized marker of the start of adulthood is the occasion when the individual takes a more or less permanent full-time job. This usually occurs when the individual finishes school—high school for some, college for others, and graduate school for still others. For those who finish high school, move away from

home, and assume a career, the transition to adulthood seems to have taken place. But one out of every four individuals does not complete high school, and many individuals who finish college cannot find a job. Further, only a small percentage of graduates settle into jobs that remain permanent throughout their adult lives. Also, attaining economic independence from parents is usually a gradual, rather than an abrupt, process. It is not unusual to find college graduates getting a job and continuing to live, or returning to live, with their parents, especially in today's economic climate.

The second criterion involves the ability to make decisions, another characteristic that does not seem to be fully developed in youth. We refer broadly here to decision making about a career, about values, about family and relationships, and about lifestyle. Youth may still be trying out many different roles, exploring alternative careers, thinking about a variety of lifestyles, and considering the variety of relationships that are available. The individual who enters adulthood usually has made some of these decisions, especially in the areas of lifestyle and career.

Although change characterizes the transition from adolescence to adulthood, keep in mind that there is considerable continuity between these periods (Bachman & others, 1996). Consider the data collected in a longitudinal study of more than 2,000 males from the time they were in the tenth grade until 5 years after high school

(Bachman, O'Malley, & Johnston, 1978). Some of the males dropped out, others graduated from high school; some took jobs after graduating from high school, others went to college; some were employed, others were unemployed. The dominant picture of the males as they went through this 8-year period was stability rather than change. For example, the tenth-graders who had the highest self-esteem were virtually the same individuals who had the highest self-esteem 5 years after high school. The researchers found a similar pattern for achievement orientation—those who were the most achievement oriented in the tenth grade remained the most achievement oriented 8 years later. Some environmental changes produced differences in this transition period. For example, marriage reduced drug use, unemployment increased it. Success in college and career increased achievement orientation; less education and poor occupational performance diminished achievement orientation.

EARLY AND MIDDLE ADULTHOOD

Age is a high price to pay for maturity.
—**Tom Stoppard**

Notice that the approximate age ranges associated with the periods of adult development overlap. Psychologists are more

---

REVIEW

The Nature of Development and the Transition to Adulthood

Development is the pattern of change that begins at conception and continues through the life cycle. For purposes of organization and understanding, psychologists commonly describe development in terms of periods. Our main focus here is on the adult developmental periods of early adulthood, middle adulthood, and late adulthood. Neugarten believes that it is increasingly difficult to describe periods of

development in terms of age; she thinks that most adult themes appear and reappear throughout the adult years, rather than being confined to one age period.

Although no consensus exists as to when adolescence is left behind and adulthood is entered, some criteria have been proposed. Two criteria are economic independence and independent decision making. Kenniston believes that individuals go through youth, a transitional period between adolescence and adulthood that is a time of extended personal and economic temporariness.

Halonen/Santrock: Human Adjustment

certain about the periods of childhood than about the periods of adulthood— most of us would agree that a 1-year-old child is in the period of infancy and that a 4-year-old child is in the period of early childhood. However, the periods of adulthood are much broader; there is less agreement on whether or not a 41-year-old is in middle adulthood. Not only are the criteria and age ranges for adult periods less clear-cut than for childhood, but as prominent life-span theorist Bernice Neugarten (1988) argues, we are rapidly becoming an age-irrelevant society. She points out that we are already familiar with the 28-year-old mayor, the 30-year-old college president, the 35-year-old grandmother, and the 65-year-old father of a preschooler.

Neugarten believes that most adult themes appear and reappear throughout the adult years. Issues of intimacy and freedom that haunt a couple throughout a relationship in early adulthood may be just as salient in later adulthood. The pressure of time, reformulating goals, and coping with success and failure are not the exclusive properties of adults at any particular age. Keeping in mind that the age bands of adult periods are fuzzy, let's now see what physical, cognitive, and social changes take place during the adult years.

Dimensions of Adulthood

Changes continue in adulthood in the physical, cognitive, and socioemotional dimensions. To begin with, we will explore the physical changes that occur in early and middle adulthood.

Physical Development

Athletes keep getting better. Today's athletes run faster, jump higher, and lift more weight than athletes did in earlier years. Despite this steady improvement, the age which athletes are at their best has stayed virtually the same. Richard Schultz and Christine Curnow (1988) analyzed records from track and field, swimming, baseball, and golf to learn at what age athletes truly hit their stride. They found that most athletes reach their peak performance under the age of 30, often between the ages of 19 and 26. Athletes who specialize in strength and speed events peak relatively early. Golf stars peak around the age of 31. In recent years, though, the "biological window" of peak performance has widened, even in the strength and speed events. Weight training, once unthinkable for women, has become standard procedure for star athletes like Florence Griffith Joyner. At age 28, Joyner's ability to lift 320 pounds helped build the strength behind her explosive start and leg drive that won world records in the 100 and 200 meters in the 1988 Olympics.

Not only do we reach our peak performance during early adulthood, but we also are the healthiest then. Few young adults have chronic health problems. They have fewer colds and respiratory problems than they had as children. However, young adults rarely recognize that bad eating habits, heavy drinking, and smoking in early adulthood can impair their health as they age. Despite warnings on packages and in advertisements that cigarettes are hazardous to health, individuals increase their use of cigarettes as they enter early adulthood (Johnston, Bachman, & O'Malley, 1987). They also increase their use of alcohol, marijuana, amphetamines, barbiturates, and hallucinogens.

As we enter middle adulthood, we are more acutely concerned about our health status. We experience a general decline in physical fitness throughout middle adulthood and some deterioration in health. The three greatest health concerns at this age are heart disease, cancer, and weight. Cancer related to smoking often surfaces for the first time in middle adulthood.

The *Harvard Medical School Newsletter* reports that about 20 million Americans are on a "serious" diet at any particular moment. Being overweight is a critical health problem, especially in middle adulthood. For individuals who are 30 percent or more overweight, the probability of dying in middle adulthood increases by 40 percent. Obesity also increases the probability an individual will suffer other ailments, including hypertension and digestive disorders.

Because U.S. culture stresses a youthful appearance, physical deterioration—graying hair, wrinkling skin, and a sagging body—in middle adulthood can be difficult to handle. Many middle-aged adults dye their hair and join weight-loss programs; some even undergo cosmetic surgery to look young. In one study, the middle-aged women focused more attention on their facial attractiveness than did the older or younger women. Middle-aged women also perceived that the signs of aging had a more detrimental effect on their appearance (Novak, 1977).

For women, middle age also means that menopause will occur. **Menopause** *is the time in middle age, usually in the late forties or early fifties, when a woman's menstrual periods cease completely.* The average age at which women have their last period is 52. A small percentage of women— 10 percent—undergo menopause before 40. There is a dramatic decline in the production of estrogen by the ovaries. Estrogen decline produces some uncomfortable symptoms in some menopausal women— "hot flashes," nausea, fatigue, and rapid heartbeat, for example. Some menopausal women report depression and irritability, but in some instances these feelings are related to other circumstances in the women's life, such as becoming divorced, losing a job, caring for a sick parent, and so on (Dickson, 1990).

Research investigations reveal that menopause does not produce psychological problems or physical problems for the majority of women. For example, in a large survey of more than 8,000 randomly selected women, the majority judged menopause to be a positive experience (feeling relief that they no longer had to worry about becoming pregnant or having periods or a neutral experience with no particular feelings at all about it (McKinlay & McKinlay, 1984). Only 3 percent said they regretted reaching menopause. Except for some temporary bothersome symptoms, such as hot flashes, sweating, and menstrual irregularity, most women simply said that menopause was not nearly so negative and painful as a lot of people make it out to be.

Why, then, do so many individuals have the idea that menopause is so negative and painful? Why do we have so many erroneous assumptions—that menopausal women will lose their sexuality and femininity, that they will become deeply depressed, and that they will experience extensive physical pain? Much of the research on menopause is based on small, selective samples of women who go to physicians or therapists because they are having problems associated with menopause. These women are unrepresentative of the large population of women in the United States.

The problem of using a small, selective sample was recently reflected in the popular author Gail Sheehy's book *The Silent Passage* (1991). Sheehy writes about her own difficult experiences and reports the frustrations of a few women she chose to interview. Although Sheehy dramatically overstates the percentage of women who have serious problems with menopause, she does not overstate the stigma attached to menopause or the inadequate attention accorded it by the medical community.

For the minority of menopausal women whose experiences are physically painful and psychologically difficult, estrogen replacement therapy may be beneficial. The painful symptoms are usually related either to low estrogen levels or to hormonal imbalance. Estrogen replacement therapy has been successful in relieving low-estrogen menopausal symptoms like hot flashes and sweating. Medical experts increasingly recommend that, prior to menopause, women have their level of estrogen monitored. In this way, once menopause occurs and estrogen level declines, the physician knows how much estrogen to replace to maintain a woman's normal level.

While estrogen replacement therapy has a lot going for it, some worries about its use have surfaced. According to Veronica Ravnikar (1992), head of the menopause unit at Massachusetts General Hospital, the biggest worry about estrogen replacement is that it might increase the risk of breast cancer. The results of studies usually show no increased risk of breast cancer, but in a few investigations the risk of the disease has increased from 1 case per 1,000 women to 1.2 cases per 1,000 in women taking estrogen. One negative health consequence of estrogen replacement is undisputed: Given by itself, estrogen can increase the risk of cancer of the uterine lining. To combat this effect, most women also take a synthetic form of a second female hormone, progesterone. This second hormone, though, may lessen estrogen's protection against heart attacks, and in about 25 percent of women it causes PMS-like bloating and irritability.

Our portrayal of menopause has been much more positive than its usual portrayals in the past. While menopause overall is not the negative experience for most women it was once thought to be, the loss of fertility is an important marker for women—it means that they have to make final decisions about having children. Women in their thirties who have never had children sometimes speak about being "up against the biological clock" because they cannot much longer postpone decisions about having children.

Cognitive Development

Famous Swiss psychologist Jean Piaget (1960) believed that adults and adolescents think in the same way; however, some developmental psychologists believe that it is not until adulthood that individuals consolidate their ability to think in abstract and logical ways. That is, as adolescents we might plan and hypothesize about problems, but as adults we become more systematic in our approach to problems. Although some adults are more proficient at developing hypotheses and deducing solutions, many adults never develop these formal skills.

Some psychologists believe that the absolute nature of adolescent logic and youth's buoyant optimism diminish in early adulthood (Labouvie-Vief, 1986). They argue that competent young adults are less caught up in idealism than they were in childhood. They tend to think logically and to adapt to life as circumstances demand. Less clear is whether our mental skills, especially memory, decline with age.

Long-term memory appears to decline more than short-term memory. For example, middle-aged individuals can remember a phone number they heard 30 seconds ago, but they probably won't remember the number as efficiently the next day. Memory is also more likely to decline when mnemonic strategies of organization and imagery are not used. In addition, memory tends to decline when the information to be recalled is recently acquired or when the information is not used often. For example, middle-aged adults probably won't remember the rules to a new card game after only a lesson or two, and they are unlikely to know the new fall television schedule after its first week. Finally, memory tends to decline if recall rather than recognition is required. Middle-aged individuals can more efficiently select a phone number they heard yesterday if they are shown a list of phone numbers (recognition) rather than simply recalling the number off the top of their head. Memory in middle adulthood also declines if the individual's health is poor (Rybash, Roodin, & Hoyer, 1995).

Theories of Adult Personality Development

Psychologists have proposed several theories about adult personality development. Most of these theories address the themes of work and love, career and intimacy. One set of theories proposes that adult development unfolds in stages.

Erik Erikson's Life-Span Theory

We initially discussed Erik Erikson's theory of human development in chapter 3. Recall that Erikson's eight stages of the life span include one stage for middle adulthood. Erikson believes that only after identity has been well developed can true intimacy occur. **Intimacy versus isolation** *is Erikson's sixth stage of development, occurring mainly in early adulthood. Intimacy is the ability to develop close, loving relationships.* Intimacy helps us form our identity because, in Erikson's words, "we are what we love." If intimacy does not develop, Erikson argues, a deep sense of isolation and impersonal feelings overcome the individual. **Generativity versus stagnation** *is Erikson's seventh stage of development, occurring mainly in middle adulthood. Middle-aged adults need to assist the younger generation in leading useful lives as well as the older generation of elderly, often frail, parents.* Competent child rearing is one way to achieve generativity. However, adults can also satisfy this need through guardianship or a close relationship with the children of friends and relatives. The positive side of this stage—generativity—reflects an ability to shape the next generation positively. The negative side—stagnation—leaves the individual with a feeling of having done nothing for the next generation. As Erikson (1968) put it, "Generations will depend on the ability of all procreating individuals to face their children."

Daniel Levinson's "Seasons" Theory

In *The Seasons of a Man's Life* (1978), Daniel Levinson also described adult development as a series of stages. He extensively interviewed middle-aged male hourly workers, academic biologists, business executives, and novelists, and concluded that developmental tasks must be mastered at a number of points in adulthood (see figure 13.1).

In early adulthood, the two major tasks are exploring the possibilities for adult living and developing a stable life structure. The twenties represent the novice phase of adult development. By the end of a boy's teens, according to Levinson, a transition from dependence to independence should occur. This transition is marked by a dream—an image of the kind of life the young man wants, especially in terms of marriage and a career. The novice phase is a time of experimenting and testing the dream in the real world.

Men usually determine their goals by the age of 28 to 33. During his thirties, a man usually works to develop his family life and career. In the late thirties, he enters a phase of "becoming one's own man" (BOOM). By age 40, he reaches a stable point in his career, outgrows his earlier, more tenuous status as an adult, and looks forward to the kind of life he will lead as a middle-aged adult.

In Levinson's view, the change to middle adulthood lasts about 5 years and requires that men come to grips with four major conflicts that have existed since adolescence: (1) being young versus being old, (2) being destructive versus being constructive, (3) being masculine versus being feminine, and (4) being attached to others versus being separated from them. The success of the midlife transition depends on how effectively they can reduce these polarities and accept each of them as a part of their being. Levinson's original subjects were all males, but more recently he reported that these midlife

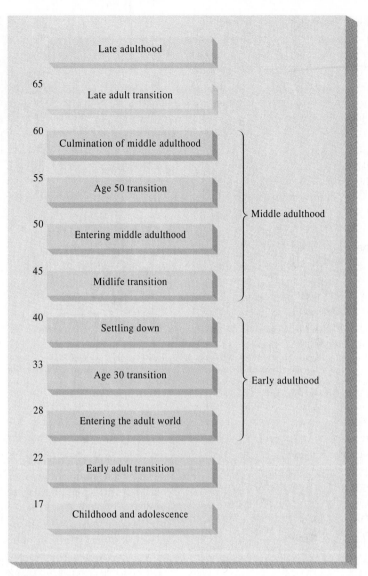

FIGURE 13.1

Levinson's Periods of Adult Development

"Goodbye, Alice, I've got to get this California thing out of my system."

Drawing by Leo Cullum; © 1984 *The New Yorker* Magazine, Inc.

Michaelangelo (1475–1574), the great Renaissance sculptor, painter, architect, and poet, hit a terrifying lull at age 40 after a brilliant earlier career. Free of unworthy patrons, he revived his career with his work on the Medici Chapel.

Julia Child, America's master chef, ate her first bite of French food at 37. It was not until her fifties that her books and TV show gained her fame and fortune.

Action novelist Tom Clancy sold insurance until his early forties, when he thought he might have a book in him. Each of his books, including *The Hunt for Red October,* has been a best-seller, and many have also been made into popular movies.

CRITICAL THINKING

Seasons of a Woman's Life

Levinson argues that his adult stages are basically the same for women as for men. Do you agree or disagree? What kind of evidence would you need to support your position? Thinking about these questions offers an opportunity for you to *challenge assumptions and values* in research and think about whether the results of research are generalizable from one population to another. For instance, can we generalize from theories about men's development to make accurate predictions about women's stages of life?

issues hold for females as well (Levinson, 1987). To speculate about whether Levinson's perspective does a good job of explaining women's experiences, see Critical Thinking.

Gould's Transformations

Psychiatrist Roger Gould (1978) links stage and crisis in his view of developmental transformations. He emphasizes that midlife is every bit as turbulent as adolescence, with the exception that during middle adulthood striving to handle crises will probably produce a happier, healthier life. Gould studied 524 men and women, whom he described as going through seven stages of adult life (see table 13.1). He believes that in our twenties we assume new roles; in our thirties we begin to feel stuck with our responsibilities; and in our forties we begin to feel a sense of urgency that our lives are speeding by. Handling the midlife crisis and realizing that a sense of urgency is a natural reaction to this stage helps to keep us on the path of adult maturity, Gould says. His study has been criticized—not only did his work contain a middle-class bias, but Gould failed to conduct any statistical analyses or evaluations of the reliability of his clinical judgments.

Vaillant's Expansion of Erikson's Stages

Adult developmentalist George Vaillant (1977) believes two additional stages should be added to Erikson's adult stages. **Career consolidation** *is Vaillant's stage that occurs from approximately 23 to 35 years of age. Career consolidation is a period in which an individual's career becomes more stable and coherent.* **Keeping the meaning versus rigidity** *is Vaillant's stage that occurs from approximately 45 to 55 years of age. At this time a more relaxed feeling characterizes adults if they have met their goals, or if they have not, they accept the fact.*

TABLE 13.1

Gould's Transformations in Adult Development

Stage	Approximate Age	Development(s)
1	16 to 18	Desire to escape parental control.
2	18 to 22	Leaving the family: peer group orientation.
3	22 to 28	Developing independence: commitment to a career and to children.
4	29 to 34	Questioning self: role confusion; marriage and career vulnerable to dissatisfaction.
5	35 to 43	Period of urgency to attain life's goals: awareness of time limitation. Realignment of life's goals.
6	43 to 53	Settling down: acceptance of one's life.
7	53 to 60	More tolerance: acceptance of past; less negativism; general mellowing.

Reprinted with the permission of Simon & Schuster from *Transformation: Growth and Change in Adult Life* by Roger L. Gould, M.D. Copyright © 1978 by Roger L. Gould, M.D.

At this time adults become concerned about extracting some meaning from their lives and fight against falling into a rigid orientation.

Conclusions About the Adult Stage Theories

When Vaillant's stages are added to Erikson's stages, there is at least reasonable agreement among Gould, Levinson, and Vaillant about adult stages. All would concur with a general outline of adult development that begins with the change from identity to intimacy, then from career consolidation to generativity, and finally from searching for meaning to some final integration. Thus, although the labels are different, the underlying themes of these adult developmental stage theories are remarkably similar (see figure 13.2).

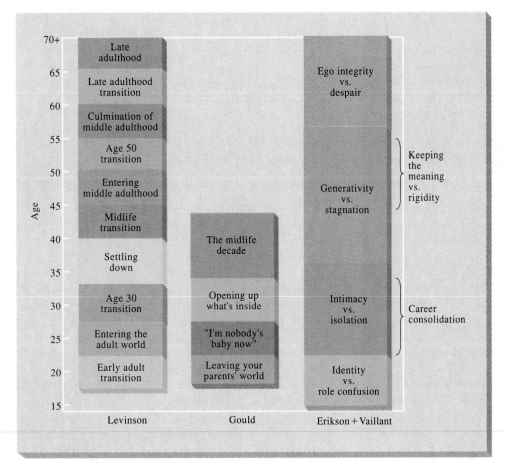

FIGURE 13.2

Comparison of the Adult Developmental Stages Proposed by Levinson, Gould, and Vaillant

When Vaillant's stages are added to Erikson's stages, some agreement between the adult stage theories of Levinson, Gould, and Vaillant is apparent. All would concur with a general outline of adult development that begins with a change from identity to intimacy, then from career consolidation to generativity, and finally from searching for meaning to some final integration.

The adult developmental perspectives of Erikson, Levinson, Gould, and Vaillant emphasize the importance of developmental stages in the life span. Though information about stages can be helpful in pinpointing dominant themes that characterize many individuals at particular points in development, there are several important ideas to keep in mind when considering these perspectives as viable models of adult development. First, the research on which they are based has not been very scientific. Second, there has been a tendency to focus on the stages as crises in development, especially the midlife crisis. Third, there is an alternative perspective that emphasizes the importance of life events rather than stages in development. Fourth, there often is considerable individual variation in the way people experience the stages.

Life Events, Cohort Effects, and Social Clocks

Life events, rather than stages, might be responsible for changes in our adult lives. Such events as marriage, divorce, the death of a spouse, a job promotion, and being fired from a job involve varying degrees of stress and influence our development as adults (Holmes & Rahe, 1967). However, we also need to know about the many factors that mediate the influence of life events on adult development—for example, physical health, intelligence, personality, family support, and income (Hansell, 1991). In addition, we need to know how people perceive the life events and how they cope with the stress involved. For instance, one person might perceive a divorce as highly stressful, whereas another person might perceive the same life event as a challenge. We also need to consider the person's life stage and circumstances. Divorce might be more stressful for an individual in his fifties who has been married for many years, for example, than for someone in her twenties who has been married only a few years (Chiriboga, 1982). Similarly, people might cope with divorce more effectively in the 1990s than in the 1890s because divorce is more commonplace and accepted today.

An increasing number of developmental psychologists believe that changing social expectations influence how different

cohorts—groups of individuals born in the same year or time period—move through the life span. For example, people born during the Depression may have a different outlook on life than those born during the optimistic 1950s (Rossi, 1989).

Bernice Neugarten (1986) believes that the social environment of a particular age group can alter its "social clock"—the timetable according to which individuals are expected to accomplish life's tasks, such as getting married, having children, and establishing themselves in a career. Social clocks act as guides for our lives. People who are somehow out of sync with these social clocks find their lives more stressful than do those who are on schedule, says Neugarten. One study found that, between the late 1950s and the late 1970s, there was a dramatic decline in adults' beliefs that there is a "right age" for major life events and achievements (Passuth, Maines, & Neugarten, 1984) (see figure 13.3).

The first half of our lives is ruined by our parents and the second half by our children.

—**Clarence Darrow**

The Nature of Middle Age

For $8 each, about 2.5 to 3 million Americans who turn 50 each year become members of the American Association for Retired Persons (AARP). There is something incongruous about 50-year-olds joining a retirement group when hardly any of them are retired. Indeed, many of today's 50-year-olds are in better shape, more alert, and more productive than were their 40-year-old counterparts of a generation or two earlier. As more people lead healthier lifestyles and medical discoveries help to stave off the aging process, the boundaries of middle age are being pushed upward. It looks like middle age is starting later and lasting longer for increasing numbers of active, healthy, and productive people. June Reinisch (1992), highly respected researcher and director of the Kinsey Institute for Research in Sex, Gender, and Reproduction at Indiana University, recently said, "I'm 49 this year. I wear clothes that my mother would never thought of wearing when she was this age. When skirts went up, my skirts went up" (p. 52).

Sigmund Freud and Carl Jung studied midlife transitions around the turn of the twentieth century, but "midlife" came much earlier then. In 1900, the average life expectancy was only 47 years of age; only 3 percent of the population lived past 65. Today, the average life expectancy is 75; 12 percent of the U.S. population is older than 65. As a much greater percentage of the population lives to an older age, the midpoint of life and what constitutes middle age or middle adulthood are becoming harder to pin down. In only one century, we have added 30 years to the average life expectancy. Statistically, the middle of life today is about 37 years of age—hardly any 37-year-olds, though, wish to be called middle-aged! What we think of as middle age comes later—anywhere from 40 to about 60 to 65 years of age. And as more people live longer, the upper boundary of 60 to 65 years will likely be nudged upward. When the American Board of Family Practice asked a random sample of 1,200 Americans when middle age begins, 41 percent said it was when you worry about having enough money for health care concerns, 42 percent said it was when your last child moves out, and 46 percent said it was when you don't recognize the names of music groups on the radio anymore (Beck, 1992).

Middle age is such a foggy place.
—**Roger Rosenblatt, 1987**

In sum, middle adulthood is not a crisis for most people. As life-span expert Gilbert Brim (1992) commented recently, middle adulthood is full of changes, twists, and turns; the path is not fixed. People move in and out of states of success and failure.

The concept of a midlife crisis implies that middle adulthood involves considerable change. Let's explore further the issue of change in adult development.

Continuity and Discontinuity

Richard Alpert, an achievement-oriented, hardworking college professor in the 1960s became Ram Dass, a free-spirited guru in search of an expanded state of consciousness in the 1970s. It would seem as though Richard Alpert and Ram Dass

Halonen/Santrock: Human Adjustment

Activity/event	Appropriate age range	% who agree (late '50s study)		% who agree (late '70s study)	
		Men	Women	Men	Women
Best age for a man to marry	20–25	80	90	42	42
Best age for a woman to marry	19–24	85	90	44	36
When most people should become grandparents	45–50	84	79	64	57
Best age for most people to finish school and go to work	20–22	86	82	36	38
When most men should be settled on a career	24–26	74	64	24	26
When most men hold their top jobs	45–50	71	58	38	31
When most people should be ready to retire	60–65	83	86	66	41
When a man has the most responsibilities	35–50	79	75	49	50
When a man accomplishes most	40–50	82	71	46	41
The prime of life for a man	35–50	86	80	59	66
When a woman has the most responsibilities	25–40	93	91	59	53
When a woman accomplishes most	30–45	94	92	57	48

FIGURE 13.3

Individuals' Conceptions of the Right Age for Major Life Events and Achievements: Late 1950s and Late 1970s

REPRINTED WITH PERMISSION FROM *PSYCHOLOGY TODAY* MAGAZINE. Copyright © 1986 (Sussex Publishers, Inc.).

were two very different people. However, Harvard psychologist David McClelland, who knows Ram Dass well, says that he is the same old Richard—still charming, still concerned with inner experience, and still power hungry. Jerry Rubin viewed his own transformation from yippie to Wall Street businessman in a way that underscores continuity in personality. Rubin said that he discovered his identity in a typical Jerry Rubin fashion—trying out anything and everything, behaving in a wild and crazy manner. Whether yippie or Wall Street yuppie, Rubin approached life with enthusiasm and curiosity.

William James (1890) said that our basic personality is like plaster, set by the time we are 30. James believed that our bodies and attitudes may change through the adult years—as did Richard Alpert's and Jerry Rubin's—but the basic core of our personality remains the same. Some modern researchers, such as Paul Costa, also believe that such traits as how extraverted we are, how well adjusted we are, and how open we are to new experiences do not change much during our adult lives (Costa, 1988; Costa & McRae, 1995). Costa says that a person who is shy and quiet at age 25 will be basically that same shy, quiet person at age 50. Still

(a)   (b)

How much does personality change and how much does it stay the same through adulthood? In the early 1970s, Jerry Rubin was a yippie demonstrator (*a*), but, in the 1980s, Rubin became a Wall Street businessman (*b*). Rubin said that his transformation underscored continuity in personality: whether yippie or Wall Street yuppie, he approached life with curiosity and enthusiasm until his untimely death in 1995.

other psychologists are enthusiastic about our capacity for change as adults, arguing that too much importance is attached to personality change in childhood and not enough to change in adulthood.

A more moderate view on the issue of stability versus change comes from the architects of the California Longitudinal Study, which now spans more than 50 years (Eichorn & others, 1981). These researchers believe that some stability exists over the long course of adult development but that adults are more capable of changing than Costa thinks. For example, a person who is shy and introverted at age 25 may not be completely extraverted at

The peak of our physical skills and health usually comes in early adulthood, a time when it is easy to develop bad health habits. In middle adulthood, most individuals experience a decline in physical fitness, and they start to take an interest in health as they notice signs that their health begins to deteriorate. Menopause is a marker that signals the cessation of childbearing capability, arriving usually in the late forties and early fifties. The vast majority of women do not have substantial problems with menopause, although the public perception of menopause has often been negative. Estrogen replacement therapy is effective in reducing the physical pain of menopause.

Some psychologists argue that cognition is more pragmatic in early adulthood. Cognitive skills are strong in early adulthood. In middle adulthood, memory may decline, although such strategies as organization can reduce the decline.

One set of adult personality development theories proposes that adult development unfolds in stages (Erikson, Levinson, Gould). Other theories emphasize life events, social clocks, and cohort effects. The stage theorists have exaggerated the prevalence of midlife crisis. Today midlife comes later and lasts longer. Critics say the adult stage theories have a male bias by emphasizing career choice and achievement. The stage theories do not adequately address women's concerns about relationships. There is both continuity and discontinuity in adult personality development.

age 50, but she may be less introverted than at 25. This person might have married someone who encouraged her to be more outgoing and supported her efforts to socialize; perhaps she changed jobs at age 30 and became a salesperson, placing her in a situation in which she was required to develop her social skills.

Humans are adaptive beings. We are resilient throughout our adult lives, but we do not acquire entirely new personalities. In a sense, we change but remain the same—underlying the change is coherence and stability (Bengtson, 1996).

LATE ADULTHOOD AND AGING

In the words of twentieth-century Italian poet Salvatore Quasimodo, "Each of us stands alone at the heart of the earth pierced through by a ray of sunlight: And suddenly it is evening." Although we may be in the evening of our lives in late adulthood, we are not meant to live out passively our remaining years.

The Nature of Late Adulthood

We are no longer a youthful society. The concept of a late adulthood period is a recent one. Until the twentieth century, most people died before age 65. In 1900 only 1 American in 25 was over 65. Today the figure is 1 in 9. By the middle of the twenty-first century, 1 in 4 Americans will be 65 years of age or older (see figure 13.4).

The life span—the upper boundary of life, the maximum number of years an individual can live—has remained

FIGURE 13.4

Millions of Americans over Age 65 in 1900, 1940, 1980, and Projected for the Year 2040

virtually unchanged since the beginning of recorded history. What has changed is life expectancy—the number of years that will probably be lived by the average person born in a particular year. Even though improvements in medicine, nutrition, exercise, and lifestyle have given us, on the average, 22 additional years of life since 1900, few of us will live to be 100. To evaluate the probability that you will live to be 100, see the Self-Assessment box.

Can You Live to Be 100?

Instructions

The following test gives you a rough guide for predicting your longevity. The basic life expectancy for males is age 71 and for females 78. Write down your basic life expectancy. If you are in your fifties or sixties, you should add 10 years to the basic figure because you have already proved yourself to be a durable individual. If you are over age 60 and active, you can even add another 2 years.

Items

Basic Life Expectancy

Decide how each item below applies to you and add or subtract the appropriate number of years from your basic life expectancy.

1. **Family history**
   Add 5 years if two or more of your grandparents lived to 80 or beyond. ____
   Subtract 4 years if any parent, grandparent, sister, or brother died of heart attack or stroke before 50. ____
   Subtract 2 years if anyone died from these diseases before 60. ____
   Subtract 3 years for each case of diabetes, thyroid disorder, breast cancer, cancer of the digestive system, asthma, or chronic bronchitis among parents or grandparents. ____

2. **Marital status**
   If you are married, add 4 years. ____
   If you are over 25 and not married, subtract 1 year for every unwedded decade. ____

3. **Economic status**
   Add 2 years if your family income is over $40,000 per year. ____
   Subtract 3 years if you have been poor for the greater part of your life. ____

4. **Physique**
   Subtract 1 year for every 10 pounds you are overweight. ____
   For each inch your girth measurement exceeds your chest measurement deduct 2 years. ____
   Add 3 years if you are over 40 and not overweight. ____

5. **Exercise**
   Add 3 years if you exercise regularly and moderately (jogging three times a week). ____
   Add 5 years if you exercise regularly and vigorously (long-distance running three times a week). ____
   Subtract 3 years if your job is sedentary. ____
   Add 3 years if your job is active. ____

6. **Alcohol**
   Add 2 years if you are a light drinker (one to three drinks a day). ____
   Subtract 5 to 10 years if you are a heavy drinker (more than four drinks per day). ____
   Subtract 1 year if you do not drink at all. ____

7. **Smoking**
   Subtract 8 years if you smoke two or more packs of cigarettes per day. ____
   Subtract 2 years if you smoke one to two packs per day. ____
   Subtract 2 years if you smoke less than one pack. ____
   Subtract 2 years if you regularly smoke a pipe or cigars. ____

8. **Disposition**
   Add 2 years if you are a reasoned, practical person. ____
   Subtract 2 years if you are aggressive, intense, and competitive. ____
   Add 1 to 5 years if you are basically happy and content with life. ____
   Subtract 1 to 5 years if you are often unhappy, worried, and often feel guilty. ____

9. **Education**
   Subtract 2 years if you have less than a high school education. ____
   Add 1 year if you attended 4 years of school beyond high school. ____
   Add 3 years if you attended 5 or more years beyond high school. ____

10. **Environment**
    Add 4 years if you have lived most of your life in a rural environment. ____
    Subtract 2 years if you have lived most of your life in an urban environment. ____

11. **Sleep**
    Subtract 5 years if you sleep more than 9 hours a day. ____

12. **Temperature**
    Add 2 years if your home's thermostat is set at no more than 68°F. ____

13. **Health care**
    Add 3 years if you have regular medical checkups and regular dental care. ____
    Subtract 2 years if you are frequently ill. ____

Your Life Expectancy Total ____

Our image of the oldest old (eighties and older) is predominantly of being disabled and frail. The implications of the projected rapid growth of the oldest-old population have often been unremittingly pessimistic—an expensive burden of chronic disability in which the oldest old often require the everyday help of other persons. However, as we discussed earlier in this chapter, the oldest old are a heterogeneous group, and until recently this diversity has not been adequately recognized (Silverstone, 1996). Although almost one-fourth of the oldest old are institutionalized, the majority live in the community and remain independent (Suzman & others, 1992). To speculate about how long you would like to live, see Critical Thinking.

Much attention has been given to the chronic disability of the oldest old, and those who have aged successfully have gone virtually unnoticed and unstudied (Birren & Schaie, 1996). An increased interest in successful aging is giving a more optimistic portrayal of the oldest old than was painted in the past (Whitbourne, 1996). Health service researchers are discovering that a relatively large portion of people in old age are low-cost users of medical services; a small percentage account for a large fraction of expenditures, usually in the last year of life, a period that is expensive at any age (Scitovsky, 1988). A surprisingly large portion of the oldest old do not require personal assistance on a daily basis and are physically robust (Garfein & Herzog, 1995).

In sum, earlier portraits of the oldest old have been stereotypical (Birren & Salthouse, in press). There exists a substantial subgroup of the oldest old who are robust and active, and there is cause for optimism in the development of new regimens of prevention and intervention (Suzman & others, 1992). Strategies for successful aging are discussed later in this chapter. But first let's explore the developmental dimensions of late adulthood.

Dimensions of Late Adulthood

Although we tend to view the period of late adulthood as a period of decline, not all aspects of development deteriorate. Let's begin by looking at physical changes in late adulthood.

CRITICAL THINKING

How Long Would You Like to Live?

In 1726, Jonathan Swift wrote about Gulliver traveling to many lands, including the land of the Struldbrugs, people who never died. Even though they were immortal, the Struldbrugs continued to age, becoming blind, crippled, immobile, in constant pain, and begging for death. Gulliver's world was science fiction, but it raises interesting issues about how long we would like to live and what we want our lives to be like when we become old. How long would you like to live? Why? Describe the oldest person you know. What is he or she like? By thinking about how long you would like to live and what you would like your old age to be like, you are learning to think critically by *applying developmental concepts to enhance adaptation and growth.*

All we know about older adults indicates that they are healthier and happier the more active they are. Several decades ago, it was believed that older adults should be more passive and inactive to be well adjusted and satisfied with life. In today's world, we believe that while older adults may be in the evening of life's human cycle, they were not meant to live out their remaining years passively.

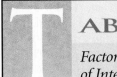

TABLE 13.2

Factors That Reduce the Risk of Intellectual Decline in Older Adults

Absence of cardiovascular and other chronic diseases

Favorable environment mediated by high socioeconomic status

Involvement in complex and intellectually stimulating environment

Flexible personality style at midlife

High cognitive status of spouse

Maintenance of high levels of perceptual processing speed

Source: After K. W. Schaie, *Current Directions in Psychological Science*, 2:171–174, 1994.

Physical Development

Virtually all biological theories of aging and the life span assign an important role to genes. Research demonstrates that the body's cells can divide only a limited number of times; cells from embryonic tissue can divide about 50 times, for example (Hayflick, 1977). Cells extracted from older adults divide fewer times than those taken from younger adults. Although the cells of elderly people are still able to divide, we rarely live to the end of our life-span potential. Based on the rate at which human cells divide, biologists place the upper limit of the human life span at 115 to 120 years.

In old age, arteries become more resistant to the flow of blood, and heart output—about 5 quarts a minute at age 50—drops about 1 percent a year after age 50. The increased resistance of the blood vessels results in elevated heart rate and blood pressure, which are related to heart disease. Even in a healthy older person, blood pressure that was 100/75 at age 25 will probably be 160/90 at age 70.

Cognitive Development

At age 70, Dr. John Rock developed the birth control pill. At age 89, Arthur Rubinstein gave one of his best performances at New York's Carnegie Hall. From 85 to 90 years of age, Pablo Picasso completed three sets of drawings, and at age 76 Anna Mary Robertson Moses took up painting. As Grandma Moses, she became internationally famous and staged fifteen one-woman shows throughout Europe. Are the feats of Grandma Moses and others rare exceptions? As Aeschylus said in the fifth century B.C., "It is always in season for the old to learn."

We have seen that the further we go through the late adulthood years, the more likely it is that we will be physically impaired. Controversy continues about whether our cognitive abilities, such as memory and intelligence, decline as we become older. Intelligence test maker David Wechsler (1972) concluded that intellectual decline is simply part of the general aging process we all go through. The issue seems more complex, however. Although it is true that older adults do not score as high on intelligence tests as young adults do, this is probably because older adults just don't think as fast as young adults. When we consider general knowledge and wisdom, however, older adults often outperform younger adults (Perlmutter, 1994).

In thinking about cognitive development in older adults, an important strategy is to identify the factors that reduce the risk of intellectual decline in older adults. In one recent study of middle-aged and older adults, psychologists identified a number of such factors, ranging from an absence of cardiovascular and other chronic diseases to being married to an intelligent spouse (Schaie, 1994) (see table 13.2).

Socioemotional Development

Enduring loss is an inevitable part of growing older. Losses can encourage retreat, which might be responsible for the image of older adults as sitting in rocking chairs watching the world go by. Now we know that the most well-adjusted and satisfied older adults are active, not passive, in the face of their challenges.

> Senescence begins
> And middle age ends,
> The day your descendants
> Outnumber your friends.
>
> —Ogden Nash

Activity Theory *Activity theory states that the more active and involved older people are, the more satisfied they are and the more likely it is that they will stay healthy.* Researchers have found that older people who go to church, attend meetings, take trips, and exercise are happier than those who simply sit at home. Predictably, the better the health and the higher the income, the more likely it is that an older person will be satisfied with life as well.

Ageism The elderly often face painful discrimination. A new word in our vocabulary is **ageism,** *which is prejudice against people based on their age.* Older adults might be branded by a number of stereotypes—such as being feebleminded, boring, ugly, parasitic. As a result, they might be treated like children and described as cute and adorable. Far worse, they often are not hired for new jobs or are forced out of existing ones, they might be shunned, or they might even be edged out of their own families. The elderly who are poor or from ethnic minority backgrounds face special hardships. To further evaluate stereotypes about the elderly, turn to Critical Thinking.

Ethnicity and Gender Of special concern are the ethnic minority elderly, especially African Americans and Latinos, who are overrepresented in the elderly poor in the United States (Hernandez, 1991; Markides, 1995). Nearly one-third of all elderly African Americans live on less than $5,300 per year. Among African

How are the elderly portrayed on television and in magazines? Are they stereotyped as tired, ugly, helpless, sick, lonely, and ready to die? Sometimes they are portrayed more positively—as wise and kind—which also can be stereotypes. Analyze how elderly are portrayed today in a variety of magazines, such as *Time, Ladies' Home Journal,* and other popular magazines. Then go to the library and find some magazines from earlier decades in this century. Compare the earlier portrayals with today's portrayals. Have images of the elderly become less stereotyped, less negative, or have they remained about the same? By comparing the media images of the elderly in different decades, you are learning to think critically about development by *examining the influence of context and culture on behavior.*

ageism and racism (Tran, Wright, & Chatters, 1991). Both wealth and health decrease more rapidly for the ethnic minority elderly than for elderly White Americans. The ethnic minority elderly are more likely to become ill but less likely to receive treatment. They are also more likely to have a history of less education, unemployment, worse housing conditions, and shorter life expectancies than their elderly White American counterparts. Many ethnic minority workers never enjoy the Social Security and Medicare benefits to which their earnings contribute, because they die before reaching the age of eligibility for benefits.

A possible double jeopardy also faces many women—the burden of *both* ageism and sexism (Harrison, 1991; Kogan & Black, in press; Lopata, 1995). The poverty rate for elderly women is almost double that of elderly men. According to Congresswoman Mary Rose Oakar, the number one priority for midlife and older women should be economic security. She predicts that 25 percent of all women working today can expect to be poor in old age. Only recently has scientific and political interest in aging women developed. For many years, aging women were virtually invisible in aging research and in protests involving rights for the elderly. An important research and political agenda for the 1990s is increased interest in the aging and rights of elderly women (Markson, 1995).

Not only is it important to be concerned about the double jeopardy of ageism and sexism involving older women, but special attention also needs to be devoted to the elderly who are female ethnic minority individuals. They face what could be described as triple jeopardy—ageism, sexism, and racism (Stoller & Gibson, 1994). Income is a special problem for these women. For example, more than one-third of all older African American women have incomes below the poverty level (compared to less than one-fourth of all older African American men and approximately 13 percent of older White American women). One-fourth of all older Latina women have incomes below the poverty level (compared to 19 percent of Latino men) (U.S. Bureau of the Census, 1990). More information about being female, ethnic, and old appears in Sociocultural Worlds of Adjustment.

Because of ageism, older adults might be shunned socially because they are perceived as senile or boring. Their children might edge them out of their lives. In these circumstances, a social network of friendships becomes an important support system for older adults. Researchers have found that close attachment to one or more individuals, whether friends or family, is associated with greater life satisfaction.

American women living alone, the figure is 55 percent. Almost one-fourth of all elderly Latinos are below the poverty line. Only 10 percent of elderly White Americans fall below the poverty line.

Comparative information about African Americans, Latinos, and White Americans indicates a possible double jeopardy for elderly ethnic minority individuals, who face problems related to *both*

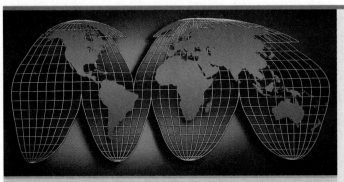

SOCIOCULTURAL WORLDS OF ADJUSTMENT

Being Female, Ethnic, and Old

Part of the unfortunate history of ethnic minority groups in the United States has been the negative stereotypes against members of their groups. Many have also been hampered by their immigrant origins in that they are not fluent or literate in English, might not be aware of the values and norms involved in American social interaction, and might have lifestyles that differ from the mainstream. Often included in these cultural differences is the role of women in the family and in society. Many, but not all, immigrant ethnic groups traditionally have relegated the woman's role to family maintenance. Many important decisions may be made by a woman's husband or parents, and she is often not expected to seek an independent career or enter the workforce except in the case of dire financial need.

Some ethnic minority groups may define an older woman's role as unimportant, especially if she is unable to contribute financially. However, in some ethnic minority groups, an older woman's social status improves. For example, older African American women can express their own needs and can be given status and power in the community. Despite their positive status in the African American family and the African American culture, African American women over the age of 70 are the poorest population group in the United States. Three of five elderly African American women live alone; most of them are widowed. The low incomes of elderly African American women translate into less than adequate access to health care. Substantially lower incomes for African American elderly women are related to the kinds of jobs they hold, which either are not covered by Social Security or, in the case of domestic service, are not reported even when legally required.

A portrayal of older African American women in cities reveals some of their survival strategies. They highly value the family as a system of mutual support and aid, adhere to the American work ethic, and view religion as a source of strength. The use of religion as a way of coping with stress has a long history in the African American culture, with roots in the slave experience. The African American church came to fulfill needs and functions once met by religious-based tribal and community organizations that African Americans brought from Africa. In one study, the elderly African American women valued church organizations more than their male counterparts did, especially valuing the church's group activities and organizations (Taylor, 1982).

In sum, African American elderly women have faced a considerable stress in their lives (Edmonds, 1990). In the face of this stress, they have shown remarkable adaptiveness, resilience, responsibility, and coping skills.

A special concern is the stress faced by elderly African American women, many of whom view religion as a source of strength to help them cope with stress.

Cultural Comparisons For many generations, the elderly in China and Japan experienced higher status than did the elderly in the United States (Ikels, 1989). In Japan the elderly are more integrated into their families than are the elderly in most industrialized countries. More than 75 percent live with their children; few single older adults live alone. Respect for the elderly surfaces in many circumstances: the best seats may be reserved for the elderly, cooking caters to their tastes, and individuals bow to them.

However, the image of elderly Japanese who are spared the heartbreak

As Japan has become more urbanized and Westernized, fewer elderly adults have lived with their children and more elderly adults have returned to work. Today respect for the elderly in Japan is greater than in the United States but not as strong as the idealized images we sometimes have.

associated with aging in the United States by the respect and devotion they receive from children, grandchildren, and society is probably idealized and exaggerated (Tobin, 1987). Americans' images of the elderly in other cultures may be inaccurate, too—we imagine elderly Eskimos adrift on blocks of ice and 120-year-old Russian yogurt eaters, in addition to the honored elders of Japan. For example, Japan has become more urbanized and Westernized; fewer elderly live with their children, and more elderly adults return to work, usually in a lower-status job with lower pay, a loss of fringe benefits, and a loss of union membership. The Japanese culture has acted as a powerful brake in slowing the decline in the respect for the elderly—today respect for the elderly is greater in Japan than in the United States, but not as strong as the idealized images we sometimes have.

Seven factors are most likely to predict high status for the elderly in a culture (Sangree, 1989):

1. Older persons have valuable knowledge.
2. Older persons control key family/community resources.
3. Older persons are permitted to engage in useful and valued functions as long as possible.
4. There is role continuity throughout the life span.
5. Age-related role changes involve greater responsibility, authority, and advisory capacity.
6. The extended family is a common family arrangement in the culture, and the older person is integrated into the extended family.
7. The culture is more collectivistic than individualistic.

Life Review and Integrity "Life is lived forward, but understood backwards," said Danish philosopher Soren Kierkegaard. This is truer of late adulthood than of any other life period. Kierkegaard's words reflect Erikson's final stage of development through the life span. Erikson called this eighth stage **integrity versus despair**; *occurring mainly in late adulthood, it is a time of looking back at what we have done with our lives.* If an older person has developed a positive outlook in each of the preceding periods of development, the retrospective

glances and reminiscences will reveal a life well spent, and the individual will feel satisfied (integrity). However, if the older adult has a negative outlook on life, the retrospective glances may produce doubt, gloom, and despair about the value of one's life. As Erikson (1968) put it, "To whatever abyss ultimate concerns may lead individual men, man as a psychosocial creature will face, toward the end of his life, a new edition of the identity crisis, which we may state in the words, 'I am what survives me.' "

Successful Aging

The good news about aging is that, barring disease, many of our capabilities decline very slowly (Birren & others, 1996). Proper diet, exercise, mental stimulation, and good social relationships and support all play a role in making aging an optimal experience. Throughout our discussion of late adulthood, we have underscored that leading an active rather than passive life will reap physical and psychological benefits. However, successful aging does require effort and coping skills. Adopting these strategies for successful aging can be especially difficult in late adulthood because of declining strength and energy. Nonetheless, older adults who develop a commitment to an active life and who believe that developing coping skills can produce greater life satisfaction are more likely to age successfully than are older adults who don't make this commitment. Let's explore some specific strategies in more detail.

Exercise and Healthful Practices
John Pianfetti, age 70, and Madge Sharples, age 65, recently completed the New York Marathon. Older adults don't have to run marathons to be healthy and happy; even moderate exercise benefits their health. One investigation over an 11-year period of more than 13,000 men and women at the Aerobics Institute in Dallas, Texas, found that the sedentary participants were more than twice as likely to die during that period than were those who were moderately fit (Blair & Kohl, 1988).

In yet another recent study, cigarette smoking and changes in level of physical activity were associated with risk

FIGURE 13.5

The Experimental Setup in Bloor and White's Study of Exercise and Health
Hogs, such as the one shown here, were trained to run approximately 100 miles per week. Then the experimenters narrowed the arteries that supplied blood to the hogs' hearts. The jogging hogs' hearts developed alternative pathways for the blood supply, whereas a group of nonjogging hogs were less likely to recover.

of death during the middle and late adulthood years (Paffenbarger & others, 1993). Beginning moderate vigorous sports activity from the forties through the eighties was associated with a 23 percent lower risk of death; quitting cigarette smoking was associated with a 41 percent lower death risk. Gerontologists are increasingly recommending strength training, in addition to stretching, for older adults (Butler, 1993).

Jogging hogs have even shown the dramatic effects of exercise on health. Colin Bloor and Frank White (1983) trained a group of hogs to run approximately 100 miles per week. Then they narrowed the arteries that supplied blood to the hogs' hearts. The hearts of these jogging hogs developed extensive alternate pathways for the blood supply, and the researchers salvaged 42 percent of the threatened heart tissue, compared to only 17 percent in a control group of hogs (see figure 13.5).

Exercise is an excellent way to maintain health in late adulthood and

possibly increase our longevity. However, coping strategies will also enhance our satisfaction in living longer.

> *It is better to wear out than to rust out.*
> —**George Whitefield**

Coping Strategies

Life-span developmentalist Paul Baltes and his colleagues (Baltes & Baltes, 1990; Marsiske & others, 1995), believe that successful aging is related to three main factors: selection, optimization, and compensation. *Selection* is based on the concept that in old age there is a reduced capacity and loss of functioning, which mandates a reduction of performance in most domains of life. *Optimization* suggests that it is possible to maintain performance in some areas by practice and the use of new technologies. *Compensation* becomes relevant when life tasks require a level of capacity beyond the current level of the older adult's performance potential. Older adults especially need to compensate in circumstances with high mental or physical demands, such as when thinking about and memorizing new material, reacting quickly when driving a car, or when running fast. Illness in old age makes the need for compensation obvious.

Consider the late Arthur Rubinstein, who was interviewed when he was 80 years old. Rubinstein said that three factors were responsible for his ability to maintain his status as an admired concert pianist into old age. First, he mastered the weaknesses of old age by reducing the scope of his repertoire and playing fewer pieces (an example of selection). Second, he spent more time at practice than earlier in his life (an example of optimization). And third, he used special strategies such as slowing down before fast segments, thus creating the image of faster playing than was objectively true (an example of compensation) (Baltes, Smith, & Staudinger, in press).

There is an increasing interest in the roles of selective optimization with compensation as a model for successful aging (Carstensen, Hanson, & Freund, 1995;

Dixon & Backman, 1995). The process of selective optimization with compensation is likely to be effective whenever loss *is* an important component of a person's life. Loss is a common dimension of old age, although there are wide variations in the nature of the losses involved. Thus, while all aging persons are likely to engage in some form of selection, optimization, and compensation, the specific form of adaptation will vary depending on each individual's life history, pattern of interests, values, health, skills, and resources (Abraham & Hansson, 1995).

Mental Health Concerns

Aging entails a great deal of loss, including declining cognitive abilities, and creates significant challenges in adjustment. In this section we will explore the nature of dementia and Alzheimer's disease and also speculate about how to meet the mental health needs of older adults.

> *First you forget names, then you forget faces, then you forget to pull your zipper up, then you forget to pull your zipper down.*
> —**Leo Rosenberg**

Dementia and Alzheimer's Disease

Dementia *is a global term for any neurological disorder in which the primary symptoms involve a deterioration of mental functioning.* Dementias are among the most complex and debilitating of mental disorders in the elderly. More than 20 percent of individuals over 80 years of age may have dementia. Psychologists have identified more than seventy types or causes of dementia (Connolly & Williams, 1993).

Alzheimer's disease *is a progressive, irreversible brain disorder that is characterized by gradual deterioration of memory, reasoning, language, and eventually physical functioning.* Alzheimer's ultimately emerged as by far the most common and possibly the most serious type of dementia. Approximately 2.5 million people over the age of 65 in the United States have this disease. It has been predicted

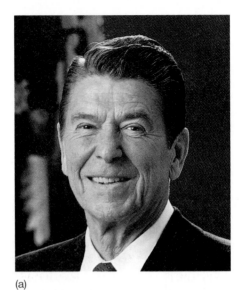

(a)

(b)

(c)

Famous individuals who developed Alzheimer's: (*a*) Former U.S. President Ronald Reagan was diagnosed with the disorder at 83. (*b*) Actress Rita Hayworth died of Alzheimer's at age 68; her struggle focused attention on the disease. (*c*) World champion boxer Sugar Ray Robinson had Alzheimer's when he died at age 67.

that, as increasing numbers of people live to older ages, Alzheimer's disease could triple in the next 50 years. Because of the increasing prevalence of Alzheimer's, researchers have stepped up their efforts to discover the cause of the disease and find more effective ways to treat it (Butters, Delis, & Lucas, 1995).

Trends in the Mental Health Care of Older Adults

According to mental health and aging expert Margaret Gatz (1992), trends in mental health services for older adults in the 1980s included overreliance on inpatient treatment, increased use of general hospitals as treatment sites, inadequate integration with the nursing home industry, and insufficient mental health referrals from general medical providers.

Gatz especially worries about the lack of coordination or cooperation among components of the health and mental health systems. The upshot is that both everyone and no one is responsible for older adults with mental disorders, a situation that borders on being a nonsystem of mental health care.

Three interrelated points are important when evaluating the intersection of health and mental health systems. First, the mental health system reflects and is affected by trends in the health

Margaret Gatz (*right*) has been a crusader for better mental health treatment of the elderly. She believes that mental health professionals need to be encouraged to include more older adults in their client lists and that we need to better educate the elderly about how they can benefit from therapy.

care system, especially government determination of payment allowances. Second, older adults are more likely to consult a physician than a mental health professional about their psychological difficulties. And third, there is often a relation between physical and mental problems in older adults.

Physical problems can lead to mental problems, and mental distress can exacerbate physical symptoms. In the National Nursing Home Survey, of all patients with diagnosable mental disorders, more than 80 percent had at least one area of physical functioning in which they required assistance (National Center for Health Statistics, 1989). In the planning of effective services for older adults, the interaction of physical and mental conditions needs to be taken into account.

As the population of older adults increases, so will the number of those who need mental health services (Knight & others, 1996). One positive trend is that older adults are getting more access to mental health services in the community than in the past because psychologists are now eligible for reimbursement under Medicare. Gatz (1992) speculated about other possible changes that would benefit the mental health needs of the elderly. Among them are caregiving leaves for workers to care for aging family members with mental disorders, elder day centers in the workplace, and an expansion of tax incentives for family caregiving.

A special concern is care for Alzheimer's patients. Psychologists believe that the family can be an important support system for the Alzheimer's patient, but providing this support can be emotionally and physically draining for the family. For example, depression has been reported in 50 percent of Alzheimer's family caregivers (Hirsch & others, 1993). Respite care helps caregivers meet the day-to-day needs of Alzheimer's patients by giving them an important break away from the burden of providing chronic care.

DEATH AND DYING

In the words of clinical psychologist Erich Fromm, "Man is the only animal that finds his own existence a problem he has to solve and from which he cannot escape. In the same sense man is the only animal who knows he must die."

Facing One's Own Death

Knowledge of death's inevitability permits us to establish priorities and structure our time accordingly. As we age, these priorities and structurings change in recognition of diminishing time. Values concerning the most important uses of time also change. For example, when asked how they would spend their time if they had only 6 months to live, younger adults mentioned such activities as traveling and accomplishing things they previously had not done; older adults mentioned more inner-focused activities—contemplation and meditation, for example (Kalish & Reynolds, 1976).

Most dying individuals want an opportunity to make some decisions regarding their own life and death (Petrinovich, 1996). Some individuals want to complete unfinished business; they want to resolve problems and conflicts and to put their affairs in order. Might there be a sequence of stages we go through as we face death?

Elisabeth Kübler-Ross (1969) divided the behavior and thinking of dying persons into five stages: denial and isolation, anger, bargaining, depression, and acceptance. **Denial and isolation** *is Kübler-Ross' first stage of dying, in which the person denies that death is really going to take place.* The person may say, "No, it can't be me. It's not possible." This is a common reaction to terminal illness. However, denial is usually only a temporary defense and is eventually replaced with increased acceptance when the person is confronted with such matters as financial considerations, unfinished business, and worry about surviving family members.

Anger *is Kübler-Ross' second stage of dying, in which the dying person recognizes that denial can no longer be maintained. Denial often gives way to anger, resentment,*

REVIEW

Late Adulthood and Aging

We are no longer a youthful society. Far more people are living to older ages than earlier in the twentieth century. The human life span has remained virtually unchanged since the beginning of recorded history; what has changed is life expectancy. As we age in late adulthood, it becomes more probable that we will have a disease. However, increasingly the emphasis is on successful aging; earlier portraits of the oldest old were stereotypes. Virtually all biological theories of aging assign an important role to genes. The issue of cognitive decline is complex, and a number of factors have been identified that reduce the risk of intellectual decline.

Activity theory states that the more active and involved older people are, the more satisfied they are and the more likely it is that they will stay healthy. One concern is ageism, prejudice against people, especially old people, because of their age. Of special concern are the ethnic minority old. Older women face double jeopardy—ageism and sexism. Cultural comparisons reveal a number of factors that predict whether the elderly will have high status in a society. Erikson's eighth and final life-span stage is integrity versus despair, a time of looking back at what we have done with our lives. There is considerable interest today in the nature of successful aging, including the role of exercise and healthful practices, as well as coping strategies such as selective optimization with compensation.

Dementia is a global term for any neurological disorder in which the primary symptoms involve a deterioration of mental functioning. By far the most common dementia is Alzheimer's disease, a progressive, irreversible brain disorder characterized by gradual deterioration of memory, reasoning, language, and eventually physical functioning. A number of barriers to mental health treatment in older adults exist; older adults receive disproportionately less mental health treatment. There are many different ways to treat the mental health problems of the elderly.

rage, and envy. The dying person's question is, "Why me?" At this point, the person becomes increasingly difficult to care for as anger may become displaced and projected onto physicians, nurses, family members, and even God. The realization of loss is great, and those who symbolize life, energy, and competent functioning are especially salient targets of the dying person's resentment and jealousy.

Bargaining *is Kübler-Ross' third stage of dying, in which the person develops the hope that death can somehow be postponed or delayed.* Some persons enter into a bargaining or negotiation—often with God—as they try to delay their death. Psychologically, the person is saying, "Yes, me, but . . ." In exchange for a few more days, weeks, or months of life, the person promises to lead a reformed life dedicated to God or to the service of others.

Depression *is Kübler-Ross' fourth stage of dying, in which the dying person comes to accept the certainty of death. At this point, a period of depression or preparatory grief may appear.* The dying person may become silent, refuse visitors, and spend much of the time crying or grieving. This behavior should be perceived as normal in this circumstance and is actually an effort to disconnect the self from all love objects. Attempts to cheer up the dying person at this stage should be discouraged, says Kübler-Ross, because the dying person has a need to contemplate impending death.

Acceptance *is Kübler-Ross' fifth stage of dying, in which the person develops a sense of peace; an acceptance of one's fate; and, in many cases, a desire to be left alone.* In this stage the dying person might have virtually no feelings or physical pain. Kübler-Ross describes this fifth stage as the end of the dying struggle, the final resting stage before death. A summary of Kübler-Ross' dying stages is presented in figure 13.6.

No one has been able to confirm that people go through the stages in the order described by Kübler-Ross. Kübler-Ross herself feels that she has been misread, saying that she never intended the stages to be an invariant sequence of steps toward death. Even though Kübler-Ross

FIGURE 13.6

Kübler-Ross' Stages of Dying
According to Elisabeth Kübler-Ross, we go through five stages of dying: denial and isolation, anger, bargaining, depression, and acceptance. Today's interpretation of Kübler-Ross' stages suggests that adaptation does not require us to go through the stages in the order described by Kübler-Ross.

(1974) recognizes the importance of individual variation in how we face death, she still believes that the optimal way to face death is in the sequence she has proposed.

Some individuals, though, struggle until the end, desperately trying to hang onto their lives. Acceptance of death never comes for them. Some psychologists believe that the harder individuals fight to avoid the inevitable death they face and the more they deny

it, the more difficulty they will have in dying peacefully and in a dignified way; other psychologists argue that not confronting death until the end may be adaptive for some individuals (Kalish, 1987). At any one moment, numerous emotions may wax and wane. Hope, disbelief, bewilderment, anger, and acceptance may come and go as individuals try to make sense of what is happening to them.

Death Anxiety

Instructions

If a statement is true or mostly true as applied to you, circle T. If a statement is false or mostly false as applied to you, circle F.

Items

T F **1.** I am very much afraid to die.

T F **2.** The thought of death seldom enters my mind.

T F **3.** It doesn't make me nervous when people talk about death.

T F **4.** I dread to think about having to have an operation.

T F **5.** I am not at all afraid to die.

T F **6.** I am not particularly afraid of getting cancer.

T F **7.** The thought of death never bothers me.

T F **8.** I am often distressed by the way time flies so very rapidly.

T F **9.** I fear dying a painful death.

T F **10.** The subject of life after death troubles me greatly.

T F **11.** I am really scared of having a heart attack.

T F **12.** I often think about how short life really is.

T F **13.** I shudder when I hear people talking about a World War III.

T F **14.** The sight of a dead body is horrifying to me.

T F **15.** I feel that the future holds nothing for me to fear.

Please turn to the end of the chapter to score and interpret your responses.

> *Death is simply a shedding of the physical body, like the butterfly coming out of a cocoon. . . . It's like putting away your winter coat when spring comes.*
>
> **—Elisabeth Kübler-Ross**

In many ways, people in the United States are death avoiders and death deniers. Many of us have a difficult time talking about death and facing death. To evaluate your own anxiety about death, see the Self-Assessment box.

Perceived Control and Denial

Perceived control and denial may work together as an adaptive strategy for some older adults who face death. When individuals are led to believe they can influence and control events—such as prolonging their lives—they may become more alert and cheerful (Baltes & Wahl, 1991).

In one investigation, a group of elderly nursing home residents were encouraged to make more day-to-day choices and thus feel they had more responsibility for and control over their lives (Rodin & Langer, 1977). They began to decide such matters as what they ate, when their visitors could come, what movies they saw, and who could come to their rooms. A similar group in the same nursing home was told by the administrator how caring the nursing home was and how much the staff wanted to help, but these elderly nursing home residents were given no opportunities to take more control over their lives. Eighteen months later, the residents given responsibility and control were more alert and active, and said they were happier, than the residents who were only encouraged to feel that the staff would try to satisfy their needs. And the "responsible" or "self-control" group had significantly better improvement in their health than did the "dependent" group. Even more important was the finding that after 18 months only half as many nursing home residents in the "responsibility" group had died as in the "dependent" group. Perceived control over one's environment, then, may literally be a matter of life or death.

In another investigation, Richard Schulz (1976) gave nursing home residents different amounts of control over visits they received from local college students. Having control over the visits, or at least advance information about them, made the nursing home residents more active, happier, and healthier, probably because control makes life less stressful by making it more predictable. When the experiment ended, so did the visits by the college students. In a follow-up 2 years later, the researchers found that the nursing home residents who had been given control over scheduling of visits, and then had the visits, and the control, taken away, were doing worse psychologically than the others (Schulz & Hanusa, 1978). Loss of control may even be worse than lack of control in some cases.

How can a psychological factor, such as the feeling of control, have such dramatic effects on health? Judith Rodin

(1990) says that individuals who believe they have a high degree of control are more likely to feel their actions can make a difference in their lives, so they are more likely to take better care of themselves by eating healthier foods and exercising. In contrast, those who have reduced feelings of control are likely to feel that what they do will not make a difference, and thus do not even bother to try to make a difference. Rodin also believes the perception of control can have a direct effect on the body. For example, being in control reduces stress and its stress-related hormones. When stress-related hormones remain elevated, there is more wear and tear on the body; high blood pressure, heart disease, arthritis, and certain types of ulcers have all been linked with excessive stress.

Following up on this line of thinking, Rodin (1986) measured stress-related hormones in several groups of nursing-home residents and then taught the residents coping skills to help them deal better with day-to-day problems. She taught the residents how to say no when they did not want something, without worrying whether they would offend someone. She gave them assertiveness training and taught them time management skills. After the training, the nursing home residents had greatly reduced levels of cortisol, a hormone closely related to stress that has been implicated in a number of diseases. The cortisol levels of the "assertive training" residents remained lower, even after 18 months. Further, these nursing home residents were healthier and had a reduced need for medication compared to residents who had not been taught the coping skills. In sum, Rodin's research has shown that simply giving nursing home residents options for control and teaching them coping skills can change their behavior and improve their health.

Denial also may be a fruitful way for some individuals to approach death. It is not unusual for dying individuals to deny death right up until the time they die. Life without hope represents learned helplessness in its most extreme form.

Denial can protect us from the tortuous feeling that we are going to die. Denial may come in different forms. First, we can deny the facts. For example, a woman who has been told by her physician that a scheduled operation is for cancer may believe that the operation is for a benign tumor. Second, we can deny the implications of a disease or life-threatening situation. For example, a man may accept the fact that he has a disease but may deny that it leads to death. Third, some people think that having a belief in spiritual immortality is a form of denial that we die.

Denial can be adaptive or maladaptive. Denial can be used to avoid the destructive impact of shock by delaying the necessity of dealing with one's death. Denial can insulate the individual from having to cope with intense feelings of anger and hurt; however, if denial keeps us from having a life-saving operation, it clearly is maladaptive. Denial is neither good nor bad; its adaptive qualities need to be evaluated on an individual basis.

Coping with Another's Death

Loss can come in many forms in our lives—such as divorce or loss of a job. But no loss is greater than that which comes through the death of someone we love and care for—a parent, sibling, spouse, relative, or friend. In the ratings of life's stresses that require the most adjustment, death of a spouse is given the highest number. How should we communicate with a dying individual? How do we cope with the death of someone we love?

Communicating with the Dying Person

Most psychologists believe that it is best for dying individuals to know that they are dying and for significant others to know this also, so they can interact and communicate with each other on the basis of this mutual knowledge. What are some of the advantages of this open awareness context for the dying individual? Dying individuals can close their life in accord with their own ideas about proper dying. They might be able to complete some plans and projects, can

make arrangements for survivors, and can participate in decisions about a funeral and burial. Dying individuals have the opportunity to reminisce, to converse with others who have been important individuals in their life, and to end life conscious of what life has been like. Finally, dying individuals have more understanding of what is happening within their body and what the medical staff is doing to them.

In addition to an open communication system, what are some other suggestions for conversing with a dying individual? Some experts believe that conversation should not focus on mental pathology or preparation for death but should focus on strengths of the individual and preparation for the remainder of life. Since external accomplishments are not possible, communication should be directed more at cognitive insights. Keep in mind also that caring does not have to come from a mental health professional only; a concerned nurse, an attentive physician, a sensitive spouse, or an intimate friend can provide an important support system for a dying individual.

Coping

Those left behind after the death of a loved one suffer profound grief, often endure financial loss, experience loneliness, and encounter increased physical illness and psychological disorders, including depression (DeSpelder & Strickland, 1996). But how they cope with the crisis varies considerably. Widows outnumber widowers by the ratio of 5 to 1 because women live longer than men, women tend to marry men older than themselves, and a widowed man is more likely to remarry. Widowed women are probably the poorest group in America, despite the myth of huge insurance settlements. Many are also lonely, and the poorer and less educated they are, the lonelier they tend to be. The bereaved are at increased risk for many health problems, including death.

Optimal adjustment depends on several factors. Women do better than men largely because, in our society, women are more responsible for the emotional life of the couple, while men are more responsible for managing finances and material goods. Thus women have better networks of friends, closer relationships with relatives, and experiences in taking care of themselves psychologically. Older widows do better than younger widows, perhaps because the death of a partner is more expected for older women. For their part, widowers usually have more money than widows do. They are much more likely to remarry. For either widows or widowers, social support helps them adjust to the death of a spouse (Bass, Bowman, & Noelker, 1991).

REVIEW

Death and Dying

Kübler-Ross proposed five stages of dying: denial and isolation, anger, bargaining, depression, and acceptance. Not all individuals go through the same sequence. Some individuals may struggle to the end. Perceived control and denial may work together as an adaptive orientation for the dying individual. Simply giving nursing home residents options for control and teaching them coping skills can change their behavior and improve their health. Denial can be adaptive or maladaptive, depending on the circumstance.

Most psychologists recommend an open communication system with a dying person; this system should not dwell on pathology or preparation for death but should emphasize the dying person's strengths. A special concern is the coping skills of the widow or widower.

CRITICAL THINKING ABOUT ADJUSTMENT

Engaging in a Life Review

Frank just turned 45 years old yesterday. As he realizes that he has become middle aged, he recognizes that his life is, almost certainly, at least half over. As he reflects back on his time he begins to consider his goals from when he was younger. In doing so he realizes that some of his aspirations have been met with success, while others with disappointment. Looking back allows Frank the chance to take an assessment of where he has been, where he is now, and where he is headed. Given that he still, at the most, has half of his life to go, he can make some adjustments to reach many of the goals he has not yet achieved.

As you read in this chapter, people frequently engage in a process of life review when they enter their middle years and beyond. This process, often referred to as "life review," can be highly beneficial. Although evaluating the past doesn't always result in greater productivity or progress, taking a look at where we are in life and how we got there can help us work toward the future. Of course, it is not necessary for a person to be in their middle years to engage in a life review; younger and older adults can too.

One way that people can assess their life is to consider each aspect of their life and its history, one segment at a time. For example, think about Frank. As he wonders about his life he is likely to take many aspects into account. He may ponder his career, family life, education, relationships, and many other things. If he is unorganized about his thinking, however, he will probably miss some of the connections between aspects of his life and may not see how he could set a new path. Thus, rather than just thinking about your life, it is possible to actively examine the course of your life. One way to do this is to list several life areas and note how they have gone along throughout life. For example, consider your family. Questions that you could pose to yourself include "What was most important about my childhood?" "What major events have changed my family?" "What aspects of my family life am I most and least satisfied with right now?" "How would I like to see my family life in the future and what can I do to bring it there?" Likewise, consider a career path. Questions such as "How did I get into the work I am currently in?" "How far along have I progressed with respect to my personal goals?" "What can I do to progress along as I have wished?" "Do I need to adjust my goals for the future?"

This life review process requires that you first identify several areas of your life and then write down your perspectives about the past, present, and future prospects of each. Consider the following areas, as well as others that may hold more personal meaning to you. The end result of this process can be a broader view on things that can be put back together into a whole and meaningful picture. Completing a life review *encourages reflection to enhance self-knowledge.*

Example of Life Review Chart

	Past	Present	Future
Family			
Friends			
Education			
Career			
Travel			
Financial Security			
Religious/Spiritual			

In this chapter we learned that development continues through-out the human life span. We began the chapter by studying the nature of development in the transition to adulthood. Then we explored development in early and late adulthood by examining the physical, cognitive, and socioemotional dimensions of development, developmental theories (Erikson's, Levinson's, Gould's, life events, and social clock). Then we continued our journey through development by studying late adulthood and aging—their nature, their dimensions, successful aging, and mental health. The chapter concluded with a discussion of death and dying—facing one's own death, perceived control and denial, and coping with another's death. Don't forget that you can obtain an overall summary of the chapter by again studying the in-chapter reviews on pages 308, 316, 325, and 329.

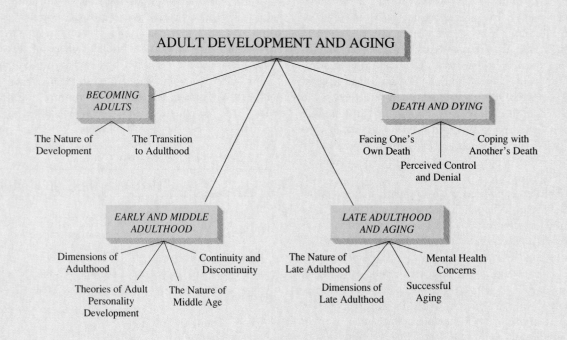

development   307
adolescence   307
early adulthood   307
middle adulthood   307
late adulthood   307
youth   308
menopause   309

intimacy versus isolation   310
generativity versus stagnation   310
career consolidation   312
keeping the meaning versus rigidity   312
activity theory   319
ageism   319
integrity versus despair   322

dementia   323
Alzheimer's disease   323
denial and isolation   325
anger   325
bargaining   326
depression   326
acceptance   326

PRACTICAL KNOWLEDGE ABOUT ADJUSTMENT

HOW TO DEAL WITH YOUR PARENTS

(1992) by Lynn Osterkamp. New York: Berkley Books.

This book was written for adult children who want to understand and improve their relationships with their parents. Osterkamp helps adults answer difficult questions like these:

- Why are so many grown-up people still worrying about what their parents think?

- Why can't you talk to your parents the way you talk to other people?
- Why do you keep having the same arguments with them?
- How can you stop feeling guilty?

Osterkamp's analysis can especially benefit adults in their twenties and thirties who want to get along better with their parents. The book is filled with personal accounts and identifies problems you may be having with your parents. You learn specific ways to communicate more effectively with your parents and reduce the stress in your relationships with them.

MINDFULNESS

(1989) by Ellen Langer. Reading, MA: Addison-Wesley.

Ellen Langer has significantly advanced our knowledge about the importance of choice in our lives. In *Mindfulness,* Langer describes how most people do things out of habit and are not mindful of why they are doing what they are doing.

Langer prescribes some helpful strategies that older adults can follow to change their thinking and make their lives more adaptive and enjoyable. She believes that most older adults have stored mental images of how they are supposed to act old. Langer's goal is to get older adults to understand that they can choose the way they think, and that they do not have to follow the old historical social norms about old people.

SELF-ASSESSMENT SCORING AND INTERPRETATION

CAN YOU LIVE TO BE 100?
No additional scoring is needed.

DEATH ANXIETY

Scoring

Give yourself one point for each question answered as follows:
1 = T, 2 = F, 3 = F, 4 = T, 5 = F, 6 = F, 7 = F, 8 = T, 9 = T, 10 = T, 11 = T, 12 = T, 13 = T, 14 = T, 15 = F. Add up the number of points you have for your total score.

Interpretation

If your score is higher than 11, you might be more anxious about death and dying than most people are.

Paul Klee
Strange Garden, detail

Abnormal Psychology

*They cannot scare me with
their empty spaces
Between stars—on stars where
no human race is.
I have it in me so much nearer home
To scare myself with my
own desert places.*

—Robert Frost

THE STORY OF ERNEST HEMINGWAY: DETERIORATION, DESPAIR, AND DEATH

Even before his father's suicide, American author Ernest Hemingway seemed obsessed by the theme of self-destruction. As a young boy he enjoyed reading Stevenson's "The Suicide Club." At one point in his adult life, Hemingway said he would rather go out in a blaze of light than have his body worn out by age and his illusions shattered.

Hemingway's suicidal thoughts sometimes coincided with his marital crises. Just before marrying his first wife, Hadley, Hemingway became apprehensive about his new responsibilities and alarmed her by the mention of suicide. Five years later, during a crisis with his second wife, Pauline, he calmly told her he would have committed suicide if their love affair had not been resolved happily. Hemingway was strangely comforted by morbid thoughts of death. When he was feeling down and out, Hemingway would think about death and various ways of dying; the best way, he thought, unless he could arrange to die in his sleep, would be to go off an ocean liner at night.

Hemingway committed suicide in his sixties. His suicide made people wonder why a man with such good looks, sporting skills, friends, women, wealth, fame, genius, and a Nobel Prize would kill himself. His actual life did not reflect the glamorous one others assigned to him. Rather, Hemingway had developed a combination of physical and mental disorders. He had neglected his health for some years and suffered from weight loss, skin disease, alcoholism, diabetes, hypertension, and impotence. His body in a shambles, he dreaded becoming an invalid and the slow death this would bring. At this point, the severely depressed Hemingway was losing his memory and no longer could write. One month before his suicide, Hemingway said, "Staying healthy. Working good. Eating and drinking with friends. Enjoying myself in bed. I haven't any of them" (Meyers, 1985, p. 559).

PREVIEW

Mental disorders impair adjustment and know no social and economic boundaries. They find their way into the lives of the rich and famous and the poor and the unknown. In this chapter, we will study several mental disorders, including the depression and suicide that troubled the life of Ernest Hemingway. We begin by examining some basic questions about the nature of abnormal behavior, then turn our attention to the following mental disorders: anxiety, somatoform, dissociative, mood, schizophrenic, personality, and substance-use disorders. We also evaluate the legal aspects of mental disorders.

DIMENSIONS OF ABNORMALITY

Could Hemingway's depression and suicide be considered abnormal behavior? If so, what made them abnormal? What causes abnormal behavior? How can we classify abnormal behavior? How prevalent is abnormal behavior in our culture? We will consider each of these important questions about abnormal behavior.

Defining Abnormality

Distinguishing what is abnormal behavior from what is normal behavior is not an easy task. Many scholars have suggested that a variety of factors can define abnormality, including statistical prevalence, maladaptiveness and harmfulness, personal discomfort, and cultural norms.

Statistical Prevalence

Consider Albert Einstein, Charles Barkley, and Barbara Walters. We think of each of them as atypical. However, we don't think Einstein was abnormal because he was a genius, that Barkley is abnormal because of his mastery of basketball (although some might consider his temperamental outbursts abnormal behavior), or that Walters is abnormal because she is one of television's most talented and highly paid interviewers.

However, many forms of mental disorder are *statistically unusual occurrences* for the vast majority of individuals in a culture who do not experience the problem. Most of us, unlike Hemingway, do not commit suicide as a way of solving problems. Most of us do not engage in extensive hand-washing rituals or hear relentless self-critical voices inside our heads. Thus, one way psychologists categorize behaviors as abnormal is by how infrequently they occur among the general population.

Maladaptiveness and Harmfulness

Statistical rarity alone may be an insufficient criterion of abnormality. However, the second category—*maladaptiveness and harmfulness*—adds another dimension. Maladaptive behavior fails to promote the well-being, growth, and fulfillment of the person and might contribute to the misery or harm of others. Maladaptive and harmful behavior takes many forms, including depression, suicide, bizarre irrational beliefs, assaults on others, and drug addiction. These abnormal behaviors interfere with the ability to function effectively in the world.

At first glance, Hemingway's suicide appears to be maladaptive and harmful because it ended a brilliant writing career. However, we could challenge this inference. Hemingway's declining health and writing obstacles may have prevented him from living a fulfilling life. His depression may have impeded his ability to see other solutions to the problems he experienced.

Personal Discomfort

Hemingway's actions clearly fit the third criterion of abnormal behavior—*personal discomfort*. He communicated his despair in many ways throughout his life. As a criterion of abnormal behavior, personal discomfort need not be as severe as that experienced by Hemingway. Guilt, grief, strain, frustration, disappointment, anger, and fear can all serve as the foundation for experiences that become so intense that they no longer feel "within normal limits" of human experience.

Cultural Influences

Cultures develop *norms* about what behavior is acceptable and what behavior is not. We might consider the same behavior

A depressed Hemingway shortly before his suicide.

abnormal in one context and thoroughly acceptable in another. For example, many people in Western cultures believe that suicide is an unacceptable behavior. Thus, the norm or social custom is avoidance of suicide. In contrast, *hara-kiri* is a form of suicide that the Japanese culture encourages as an honorable alternative to shaming the family.

In some cultures, people go about their daily activities with few or no clothes on. If we were to see someone walking naked down a city street in the United States, we probably would consider such behavior inappropriate; we also might think that such norm-violating behavior signaled that the person was in mental distress.

Sometimes the definition of abnormality changes from one historical period to another. For example, early in this century, many Americans believed that masturbation was sinful and caused everything from warts to insanity. Today only a few people think of masturbation as wicked, and most people accept the practice as a part of normal sexuality.

A final contextual example also poignantly demonstrates the fact that some individuals are empowered with the authority to label behaviors as "abnormal" and that other individuals are likely to be labeled. Prior to the Civil War, authorities diagnosed slaves who attempted to escape as having drapetomania ("excitability and bad judgment"). This diagnosis

categorized as mental illness a behavior that more likely was an adaptive response to severe life circumstances. To reflect further on the topic of abnormality in context, turn to Critical Thinking.

In sum, **abnormal behavior** *is behavior that is maladaptive, harmful, statistically unusual, personally distressing, and/or designated abnormal by the culture.*

> *Madness reveals the ungluing we all secretly fear: the mind taking off from the body, the possibility that that magnet that attaches us to a context in the world can lose its grip.*
> —**Molly Haskell,** ***Love and Other Infectious Diseases,*** **1990**

The Origins of Abnormal Behavior

What causes people to behave abnormally? Psychologists typically sort the causes of abnormal behavior into three categories: biological factors, psychological factors, and sociocultural factors.

The Biological Approach

Proponents of the biological approach believe that abnormal behavior is due to a physical malfunction in the body, especially the brain. If an individual behaves in an uncontrollable manner, is out of touch with reality, or is severely depressed, biological factors are the primary culprits. Today scientists and researchers who adopt the biological approach often focus on brain processes and genetic factors as the causes of abnormal behavior. In the biological approach, drug therapy is frequently used to treat abnormal behavior.

The **medical model,** *also called the disease model, was the forerunner of the biological approach; the medical model states that abnormality is a disease or illness precipitated by internal physical causes.* Within this perspective, abnormalities are called mental *illnesses* and the individuals afflicted are *patients* in *hospitals,* who are treated by psychiatrists and, to a lesser extent, psychologists.

Psychological Approaches

Although the biological approach provides an important perspective for understanding abnormal behavior, many

CRITICAL THINKING

Judging Abnormality in Context

We have studied the four hallmarks of abnormality. Now apply these characteristics to some behaviors observable in our culture:

Example 1. Living on the streets: Are the homeless statistically unusual? Are their behaviors maladaptive or harmful? Do they seem to be in personal distress? Does life on the street violate cultural norms?

Example 2. Making obscene phone calls: Are such phone calls statistically rare? Are they maladaptive? Do the phone callers seem to be in personal distress or do they cause distress to others? Are there cultural norms against making obscene phone calls?

Example 3. Shoplifting: How statistically rare is this behavior? Is shoplifting maladaptive? Who gets distressed by shoplifting? Does shoplifting violate cultural norms?

As you can see, each example behavior might be considered abnormal according to a different criterion. Some behaviors clearly meet all criteria. Others meet only a few. However, we are likely to regard all the examples as abnormal during this historical period in our culture. By applying these characteristics to observable behavior, you are *examining the influence of context and cultures on behavior* by using criteria derived in this culture.

Living in the street, making obscene phone calls, and shoplifting all qualify as abnormal behavior, although these examples vary in how they meet criteria for abnormality.

psychologists believe that the medical model underestimates the importance of psychological factors, such as emotional turmoil, inappropriate learning, distorted thoughts, and inadequate relationships (Gardner, 1995). The theories of personality described in chapter 2—psychoanalytic, behavioral and social learning, and humanistic theories—provide insight into the nature of abnormal as well as normal behavior. Much more about the approaches to the treatment of abnormal behavior appears in the next chapter.

The Sociocultural Approach

As you might expect, the sociocultural approach emphasizes how culture, ethnicity, gender, age, and other sociocultural elements influence abnormal behavior (Broman, 1996). Most experts on abnormal behavior agree that many psychological disorders are universal, appearing in most cultures (Al-Issa, 1982a). However, the frequency and intensity of abnormal behavior vary across cultures. Variations in disorders are related to social, economic, technological,

religious, and other features of cultures (Costin & Draguns, 1989).

Some disorders appear to be especially culture-bound. Al-Issa (1982a) described specific patterns illustrating how cultures influence abnormal behaviors. Certain exceptional patterns are *culturally approved* as opportunities to express expected but unusual behavior. Some cultures provide certain opportunities in which inebriation and sexual excesses are expected. The Mardi Gras celebrations of New Orleans are an example; another is the Greenland Eskimos' *Schimpfduelle*—ritualized insulting with song and drumming. Some abnormal patterns are *culturally tolerated.* For example, in the Highlands of New Guinea, young men under severe stress enact the "wild man" syndrome. The wild man shows agitation, destroys property, and threatens attack. Others in the culture subdue, sometimes pamper, and ultimately reintegrate the wild man into the culture. Finally, some patterns are *culturally suppressed* through adherence to strong cultural prohibitions. Abnormal behavior can surface in direct contrast to the cultural norm. According to Al-Issa (1982a), the severe aggression found among mentally ill Japanese is due to the suppression promoted by Japanese culture's nonviolent norms. To learn more about several of the more unusual culture-bound disorders, see table 14.1.

An Interactionist Approach

When considering an individual's behavior, whether abnormal or normal, it is important to remember the complexity of human nature and the multiple influences on behavior. Neither the biological nor the psychological nor the sociocultural approach independently captures this complexity. Abnormal behavior is influenced by biological factors (brain processes and heredity, for example), by psychological factors (emotional turmoil and distorted thoughts, for example), and by sociocultural factors (poverty and gender, for example). These factors often interact to produce abnormal behavior. We need to examine all approaches in order to produce a full explanation of abnormality.

Prevalence Estimates

How prevalent are mental disorders in the United States today? In a recent survey of 18,571 people randomly selected from five U.S. cities—New Haven, Connecticut; Baltimore, Maryland; St. Louis, Missouri; Piedmont, North Carolina; and Los Angeles, California—more than 15 percent of the respondents had suffered from a mental disorder during the previous month (Robins & Regier, 1990). Only one-third of the individuals reporting mental disorders had received treatment in the previous 6 months.

Prevalence by Gender

For the 1-month incidence of mental disorders, the data were also analyzed separately for men and women. The women had a slightly higher overall rate of mental disorders than the men (16.6 percent versus 15.4 percent). The women had higher rates of mood disorders (for example, depression) (9.7 percent versus 4.7 percent); the men had higher rates of substance-use disorders (6.3 percent versus 1.6 percent) and antisocial personality disorders (0.8 percent versus 0.2 percent).

Women tend to be diagnosed as having disorders that typify traditional stereotypes of females. In particular, women are more likely than men to suffer from anxiety disorders and depression, disorders with symptoms that are internalized, or turned inward. Conversely, men are socialized to direct their energy toward the outside world—that

TABLE 14.1

Unusual Culture-Bound Disorders

Amok	Malaysia, Philippines, Africa	This disorder involves sudden, uncontrolled outbursts of anger in which the person may injure or kill someone. Amok is often found in males who are withdrawn before the onset of the disorder. After an attack on someone, the individual feels exhausted and depressed and does not remember the rage and attack.
Anorexia nervosa	Western cultures, especially the United States	This eating disorder involves a relentless pursuit of thinness through starvation and can eventually lead to death. More about this disorder appears in chapter 15.
Windigo	Algonquin Indian hunters	This disorder involves a fear of being bewitched. The hunter becomes anxious and agitated, worrying he will be turned into a cannibal, with a craving for human flesh.
Nuptial psychosis	North Africa, India	This disorder occurs among very young women whose lives are disrupted by arranged marriage. Sexual trauma, separation from parents, and unfamiliar surroundings contribute to symptoms of confusion, hysteria, and suicide.
Kayak angst	Eskimos of Western Greenland	This occupational disorder strikes seal hunters who experience extreme anxiety after hours of solitary hunting in unfavorable and unstimulating environments.
Malgri	Australia	Severe abdominal pain caused by entering forbidden territory without purification rituals.
Berdache	Prairie Indians	This gender-role rejection allows men to avoid assuming aggressive roles by opting for the role of women.
Latah	Asia, Africa	This syndrome is found among low-status women who exhibit altered states of consciousness, including exaggerated obedience or impulsivity.
Koro	China	Sweating and severe anxiety mark this disorder, which represents a belief that the penis is retracting. The afflicted individual believes that, if the penis disappears, he will die.

Nancy Felipe Russo has been instrumental in calling attention to the sociocultural factors involved in women's depression. She has chaired the National Coalition of Women's Mental Health.

is, to externalize their feelings and thoughts—and are more likely to show disorders involving aggression and substance abuse.

Several explanations have been given as to why women are diagnosed and treated for mental disorders at a higher rate than men (Paludi, 1995). One possibility is that women do not have more mental disorders than men do, but that women are simply more likely to behave in ways that others label as mental disorders. For example, women have been taught to express their emotions, whereas men have been trained to control them. If women express feelings of sorrow and sadness, some individuals may conclude that women are more mentally disturbed than men are. Thus, the difference between the rates of mental disorders could involve the possibility that women more freely display and discuss their problems than men do.

A second explanation of the gender difference in the diagnosis of mental disorders focuses on women's inferior social position and the greater discrimination against women. Women are also more likely to experience certain trauma-inducing circumstances, such as incest, sexual harassment, rape, and marital abuse. Such abuse can increase women's emotional problems.

A third explanation of the gender difference in the diagnosis of mental disorders is that women are often placed in a "double-bind" situation in our society. For example, women can be labeled as mentally disturbed for either overconforming or underconforming to feminine gender-role stereotypes. That is, a woman who is overdependent, excessively emotional, and irrational is overconforming to the traditional feminine gender-role stereotype. On the other hand, a woman who is independent, who values her career as much as or more than her family, who doesn't express emotions, and who acts in a worldly and self-confident manner is underconforming to feminine gender-role stereotypes. In either case, the woman might be labeled emotionally disturbed. In sum, even though statistics show that women are more likely than men to have mental disorders, this gender difference may be the result of antifemale bias in American society.

Ethnicity and Socioeconomic Factors

In the United States, variations in mental disorders involve not only gender, but such factors as socioeconomic status, urbanization, neighborhood, and ethnicity. For example, people who live closest to the center of a city have the greatest risk of developing a mental disturbance (Suinn, 1984). Ethnic minority status also

heightens the risk of mental distress (Huang & Gibbs, 1989). In one study on hospitalization rates, persons with Spanish surnames were more likely to be admitted for mental health problems when they were in the minority than when they were the majority (Bloom, 1975). In another study, conducted in New York City, this finding was supported: The fewer the number of ethnic members in one area—whether they were White, African American, or Puerto Rican—the higher their rate of mental health hospitalization (Rabkin, 1979). In yet another study, Whites living in African American areas had more than a 300 percent higher rate of severe mental disturbance than Whites living in White neighborhoods. Similarly, African Americans living in predominantly White areas have a 32 percent higher rate than African Americans living in African American neighborhoods (Mintz & Schwartz, 1964). All of these studies, however, are correlational; they do not determine cause and effect. It is possible that people who are mentally disturbed, or those predisposed to mental disorders, tend to choose communities in which they are the minority, or it may be that minority-group status produces stress and its related disorders.

Many ethnic minority individuals with a mental disorder live in low-income neighborhoods. However, knowing that people from poor minority neighborhoods

(a)

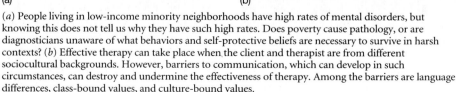
(b)

(*a*) People living in low-income minority neighborhoods have high rates of mental disorders, but knowing this does not tell us why they have such high rates. Does poverty cause pathology, or are diagnosticians unaware of what behaviors and self-protective beliefs are necessary to survive in harsh contexts? (*b*) Effective therapy can take place when the client and therapist are from different sociocultural backgrounds. However, barriers to communication, which can develop in such circumstances, can destroy and undermine the effectiveness of therapy. Among the barriers are language differences, class-bound values, and culture-bound values.

Halonen/Santrock: Human Adjustment

have high rates of disorder does not reveal *why* they have such rates. Does poverty cause pathology, or is poverty a form of pathology for narrowly trained diagnosticians who are unaware of what behaviors and self-protective beliefs are necessary to survive in harsh circumstances? Researchers who are sensitive to, and comfortable with, these cultural dynamics are vital to the search for answers to these questions.

Classifying Abnormal Behavior

Ever since human history began, people have suffered from diseases, sadness, and bizarre behavior. For almost as long, healers have tried to treat and cure them. The classification of mental disorders goes back to the ancient Egyptians and Greeks and has its roots in biology and medicine.

The first classification of mental disorders in the United States, based on the census data of 1840, used one category for all mental disorders. This one inclusive category included both the mentally retarded and the insane.

In the twentieth century, the American Psychiatric Association developed the major classification of mental disturbances in the United States. The *Diagnostic and Statistical Manual of Mental Disorders (DSM),* published in 1952, included better definitions of mental disorders than previous classification efforts. A revised edition, the DSM-II, produced with more systematic assistance from expert diagnosticians, appeared in 1968. A third edition, the DSM-III, was published in 1980, and a revision of that manual, the DSM-III-R, in 1987. Published in 1994, the current manual, the DSM-IV, emphasizes refined empirical support of diagnostic categories.

Advantages of Diagnosis

Before we discuss the most widely used system to classify mental disorders, we will explore the many benefits of classifying mental disorders. First, a classification system provides professionals with a shorthand system for communicating with each other. For example, if one psychologist mentions in a case review that her client has a panic disorder and another psychologist says that her client has a generalized anxiety disorder, the two psychologists understand what the labels communicate about the disturbances. Second, a classification system permits psychologists to construct theories about the causes of particular disorders and design treatments for them. Third, a classification system can help psychologists to make predictions about disorders; it provides information about the likelihood that a disorder will occur, which individuals are most susceptible to the disorder, the progress of the disorder once it appears, and the prognosis for effective treatment (Meehl, 1986).

Disadvantages of Diagnosis

Advocates of the psychological and sociocultural approaches sometimes criticize the medical model and diagnostic practices because they believe that it encourages labeling processes that may be harmful. Some psychologists and psychiatrists believe that labeling individuals as "mentally ill" encourages them to perceive themselves as "sick" and to avoid assuming responsibility for coping with their problems (Szasz, 1977).

Using diagnostic procedures with members of ethnic minority groups may be especially problematic. In particular, studies have found that a client's ethnicity may adversely influence the assessment and diagnosis of mental disorders (Ramirez, 1989). For example, during diagnostic interviews, Native Americans may behave in ways that signal mental distress to a clinician unfamiliar with the Native American culture: Native Americans might be nonassertive, hesitant, and soft-spoken; they might exchange only limited eye contact; they might show discomfort and decreased performance on timed tasks; they might be reluctant to provide details about their personal lives; and they might have a group orientation rather than a self orientation. In addition, the historical difficulties between ethnic groups make it extremely difficult for many Native American, Latino, and African American individuals to trust a White person, or even a middle-class member of their own ethnic group, in the course of psychological assessment. For example, one study revealed that African American clients tend to defend themselves by uttering essentially meaningless phrases or by telling clinicians what they want to hear (Jones & Seagull, 1977).

Cultural misunderstanding can work the other way too. Clinicians who are unfamiliar with their clients' cultural background might fail to pick up on cues that signal mental distress. Japanese Americans, for instance, often view mental disorders as inappropriate behavior or malingering (pretending to be mentally disordered to avoid work or responsibility). Consequently, even when Japanese Americans are in the throes of mental problems, they may be unwilling to acknowledge them. When Japanese Americans do admit to having a problem, they often recast it as a physical ailment rather than as a psychological problem. Thus, it is especially important for clinicians with Japanese American clients to assess both psychological *and* physical factors thoroughly.

Assessing mental disorders in ethnic minority individuals is further complicated by the well-documented findings of ethnic and social class biases in diagnosis. One study revealed that clinicians find fewer psychological disorders among people from affluent backgrounds than among poor people; in fact, people from the lowest socioeconomic backgrounds are diagnosed as having mental disorders at twice the expected rate and are labeled with the most severe diagnoses (Hollingshead & Redlich, 1958). And another study found that the highest rate of mental disorders is in poor African American urban communities (Gould, Wunsch-Hitzig, & Dohrenwend, 1981).

Using the DSM-IV

Continuing revisions of the DSM reflect advancements in knowledge about the classification of mental disorders. On the basis of research and clinical experience, the DSM-IV added, dropped, or revised categories, sometimes generating controversy among the diagnosticians who rely on the classification system.

For example, the DSM-III dropped two important categories that have some historic importance: neurosis and psychosis. **Neurotic disorders** *are relatively mild mental disorders in which the individual has not lost contact with reality.* Individuals who are extremely anxious, troubled, and unhappy may still be able to carry out their everyday functions and have a clear perception of reality; these individuals would be classified as neurotic.

Psychotic disorders *are severe mental disorders in which the individual has lost contact with reality.* Psychotic individuals have such distorted thinking and perception that they live in a very different world from that of others. Psychotic individuals might hear voices that are not present or think they are famous individuals, such as Jesus Christ or Napoleon. The DSM classification system dropped the terms *neurotic* and *psychotic* because they were too broad and ill-defined to be diagnostic labels. Although the DSM system dropped the labels, clinicians still sometimes use them as a convenient way of referring to relatively mild or relatively severe mental disorders, respectively.

> *Neurotic means that he is not as sensible as I am, and psychotic means that he is even worse than my brother-in-law.*
> —**Karl Menninger**

The **DSM-IV** *(Diagnostic and Statistical Manual of Mental Disorders, fourth edition) is the most recent major classification of mental disorders; it contains eighteen major classifications and descriptions of more than two hundred specific disorders.*

One of the features of the DSM-IV is its **multiaxial system,** *which classifies individuals on the basis of five dimensions, or "axes," that include the individual's history and highest level of competent functioning in the last year. This system ensures that the individual will not merely be assigned to a mental disorder category but instead will be characterized in terms of a number of clinical factors.* Following is a description of each of the axes:

Axis I. Clinical Disorders: The primary classification or diagnosis of the disorder (for example, fear of people). This axis includes all disorders except for the personality disorders.

Axis II. Personality Disorders/ Developmental Problems: Personality disorders, long-standing problems in relating to others (for example, long-standing antisocial personality disorder), or developmental problems affecting the adjustment of children and adolescents.

Axis III. General Medical Conditions: General medical conditions that might be relevant in understanding the mental disorder (for example, an individual's history of disease, such as a cardiovascular problem).

Axis IV. Psychosocial and Environmental Problems: Stressors in the individual's recent past that might have contributed to the mental problem (for example, divorce, death of parent, or loss of a job).

Axis V. Global Assessment of Functioning: The individual's current level of functioning, on a scale of 100 (superior) to 1 (inability to maintain safety). The scale takes into account chronicity of symptoms and overall adjustment.

What are some of the changes in the DSM-IV? More than two hundred mental health professionals contributed to the development of DSM-IV. They were a much more diverse group than their predecessors, who were mainly White male psychiatrists. More women, ethnic minorities, and nonpsychiatrists, such as clinical psychologists, were involved in the construction of the DSM-IV (Nathan, 1994). This led to greater attention to the context of gender- and ethnicity-related diagnosis. For example, DSM-IV contains an appendix entitled "Guideline for Cultural Formation and Glossary of Culture-Related Syndromes." Also, the DSM-IV's publication is accompanied by a number of sourcebooks that present the empirical base of the DSM-IV (Frances & Ross, 1996). Thus, the DSM-IV is based more on empirical data than its predecessors were. In previous versions of the DSM, the reasons for diagnostic changes were not always explicit, so the evidence that led to their formulation was never available for public evaluation.

The Controversy Surrounding the DSM-IV

The most controversial aspect of the DSM-IV continues an issue that has been present since publication of the first DSM in 1952. Although more nonpsychiatrists were responsible for drafting the DSM-IV than in previous editions, the DSM-IV still reflects a medical or disease model

(Clark, Watson, & Reynolds, 1995). Classifying individuals based on their symptoms and using medical terminology continues the dominance of the psychiatric tradition of thinking about mental disorders in terms of illness and disease. This strategy implies an internal cause of disorders that is more or less independent of external or environmental factors (Adams & Cassidy, 1993). Thus, even though researchers have begun to illuminate the complex interaction of genetic, neurobiological, cognitive, and environmental factors in the DSM disorders, the DSM-IV continues to espouse a medical or disease model of mental disorders (First, Frances, & Pincus, 1995; Frances, First, & Fincus, 1995). However, many therapists rely on wide-ranging questions to help develop a clear picture of the clinical problem. See Critical Thinking for an example of this kind of questioning.

The DSM-IV also is controversial because it continues to label as mental disorders what are often thought of as everyday problems. For example, under learning or academic skills disorders, the DSM-IV includes the categories of reading disorder, mathematics disorder, and disorder of written expression. Under substance-related disorders, the DSM-IV includes the category of caffeine-use disorders. We don't usually think of these problems as mental disorders. Including them as mental disorders implies that such "normal behavior" should be treated as a mental disorder. But the developers of the DSM system argue that mental health providers have been treating many problems not included in earlier editions of DSM and that the classification system should be more comprehensive. One practical reason that everyday problems in living were included in the DSM-III-R and the DSM-IV is so that more individuals can get their health insurance companies to pay for professional help. Most health insurance companies reimburse their clients only for disorders listed in the DSM-IV system.

Another issue frequently raised by its critics is that the DSM is too responsive to changing political issues. One example is the decision by the DSM-III Task Force to endorse an earlier vote of the American Psychiatric Association to

CRITICAL THINKING

Asking Questions to Create a Complete Picture of Mental Distress

Each time a diagnostician sits across from a new client, she encounters a virtual blank slate that must be filled in by her skilled questioning and the client's responses. A comprehensive diagnostic interview would involve questions that reflect all the perspectives you have studied. Suppose you are introduced to a new client named Ben. What you know about him is that he is White, age 16, unhappy, and failing in school. What questions would you want to ask that would produce answers consistent with the focus of the following perspectives?

A psychoanalytic question: The psychoanalytic focus would lead to questions about Ben's early childhood, his experiences of anxiety, perhaps even his dream life. Any of these areas would be fair game.

A learning question: The learning focus would examine Ben's history of punishment and reward, the role models whom he admires, and the reliable patterns of behavior he exhibits in different settings.

A cognitive question: The cognitive focus would examine Ben's thinking patterns and level of self-regard. Does he think of himself as a loser? Are there consistent negative evaluations that interfere with his functioning?

A neurobiological question: The neurobiologist would ask questions about his physiological experiences.

Is he sleeping well? Eating properly? Is he related to anyone who has experienced the same problems? Does he have a learning difference? Is he abusing alcohol?

A humanistic question: The humanist focus might examine Ben's values and his goals. The humanist would want to know what strivings might motivate his activity as well as the events or outcomes that make him feel unfulfilled.

A sociocultural question: The sociocultural interviewer would identify other demographic aspects that might contribute to the picture. What type of high school does he attend? With whom, if anyone, does he align in friendship? How are his experiences influenced by his family's resources or lack of them?

As you can see, a comprehensive picture of Ben's life will address many elements of his experience. This practice encourages *pursuing alternative explanations to explain behavior comprehensively.*

---

remove homosexuality from the nomenclature and replace it with a limited diagnosis covering only persons who are distressed by their homosexual orientation. Another example is the decision by the DSM-IV Task Force to rename late luteal phase dysphoric disorder, which corresponds to premenstrual syndrome, and retain it in an appendix rather than incorporate it into the regular nomenclature.

Another criticism of the DSM-IV, and indeed of this type of classification system in general, is that the system focuses strictly on pathology and problems, with a bias toward finding something wrong with anyone who becomes the object of diagnostic study. A classic study by David Rosenhan (1973) demonstrated how strong the bias is toward attaching a label of mental disorder to someone. Rosenhan asked eight "normal" individuals to go to the admissions desk of a psychiatric hospital and complain that they

heard an unidentified voice saying, "empty," "thud," and "hollow." The psychiatric staff interviewed the eight individuals, who were honest about their life histories. All eight of these individuals were immediately admitted to the hospitals. They behaved normally while in the psychiatric ward. Seven of the eight were diagnosed as schizophrenic, listed as such on their records, and labeled as schizophrenics in remission when they were discharged. Rosenhan concluded that normal people are not noticeably sane. This "blind spot" is likely due to the absence of a satisfying "sane" option in current mental health classification systems, which define sanity only as the absence of insanity.

Because labels can become self-fulfilling prophecies, emphasizing strengths as well as weaknesses might help to destigmatize labels such as *borderline schizophrenic* or *ex-mental patient.* It would also help to provide clues to treatment that

promote mental competence rather than working only to reduce mental distress.

The DSM-IV was developed by American mental health professionals. Most mental health professionals in other countries adopt the International Classification of Disease (ICD) guidelines established by the World Health Organization. The tenth edition of the ICD (ICD-10) was published in 1993. An effort was made to bring the DSM-IV into closer correspondence with ICD-10, but substantial differences in categories still persist (Frances, Pincus, & Widiger, in press). Such differences ensure that American and non-American mental health professionals will continue to have problems communicating with each other.

Psychologists usually go along with the DSM-IV, but psychiatrists are more satisfied with it. Even though the DSM-IV has its critics, it still is the most comprehensive classification system available.

Dimensions of Abnormality

Abnormal behavior can be statistically unusual within a culture, maladaptive and harmful, personally distressful, and/or designated as abnormal by the culture. A number of views have been proposed about the origins of abnormal behavior. Proponents of the biological approach believe that abnormal behavior is due to a physical malfunction in the body, especially in the brain. The disease model, also called the medical model, was the forerunner of the biological approach; the medical model states that abnormality is a disease or illness precipitated by internal physical causes. Many psychologists believe that the medical model underestimates the importance of psychological factors in abnormal behavior. The sociocultural approach emphasizes how culture, ethnicity, gender, age, and other sociocultural elements influence abnormal behavior. Some disorders are especially culture-bound. Psychologists have made prevalence estimates, including estimates for gender, ethnicity, and economic status, of mental disorders. Many psychologists believe that an interactionist approach to mental disorders is a wise strategy.

DSM stands for Diagnostic and Statistical Manual of Mental Disorders. The DSM-II included the categories of neurotic and psychotic behavior. Though some mental health professionals still use the terms neurotic and psychotic, they have been dropped from the DSM classification. Mental disorder classification systems have both advantages and disadvantages. The most recent version of the DSM (DSM-IV) was published in 1994. One of the DSM-IV's features is its multiaxial system. The DSM-IV Task Force was made up of a much more diverse group of individuals than its predecessors were and the DSM-IV is more empirically based than earlier editions. The most controversial aspects of the DSM-IV continue to be the classification of individuals based on their symptoms and the use of medical terminology that perpetuates the medical or disease model of mental disorders. Critics also point out that some everyday problems should not be included as disorders. Another issue raised by its critics is that the DSM-IV is too responsive to changing political times. Critics suggest that competent mental health categories should reflect positive as well as negative characteristics. The DSM-IV and the ICD-10 (International Classification of Disease) are still not completely compatible.

DIAGNOSTIC CATEGORIES OF MENTAL DISORDERS

Let's now examine the major categories of diagnosis featured in the DSM-IV. Although this is not an exhaustive exploration of the multitude of categories, the review will suggest the general qualities of the most prominent mental disorders, which we will illustrate by mentioning case studies.

Anxiety Disorders

Anxiety is a diffuse, vague, highly unpleasant feeling of fear and apprehension. People with high levels of anxiety worry a lot. **Anxiety disorders** are psychological disorders that include the following main features: motor tension (jumpiness, trembling, inability to relax), hyperactivity (dizziness, a racing heart, or perspiration), and apprehensive expectations and thoughts. Five important types of anxiety disorders are reviewed in this section.

Generalized Anxiety Disorder

Anna, who is 27 years old, had just arrived for her visit with the psychologist. She seemed very nervous and was wringing her hands, crossing and uncrossing her legs, and playing nervously with strands of her hair. She said her stomach felt like it was in knots, that her hands were cold, and that her neck muscles were so tight they hurt. She said that, lately, arguments with her husband had escalated. In recent weeks, Anna indicated, she had felt more and more nervous throughout the day, as if something bad were about to happen. If the doorbell sounded or the phone rang, her heart beat rapidly and her breathing quickened. When she was around people, she had a difficult time speaking. She began to isolate herself. Her husband became impatient with her, so she decided to see a psychologist (Goodstein & Calhoun, 1982).

Anna has a **generalized anxiety disorder,** an anxiety disorder that consists of persistent anxiety for at least 1 month; an individual with a generalized anxiety disorder is unable to specify the reasons for the anxiety. These individuals often say they have been tense and anxious for over half their lives.

Panic Disorder

Panic disorder is a recurrent anxiety disorder marked by the sudden onset of intense apprehension or terror. The individual often has a feeling of impending doom but might not feel anxious all the time. Anxiety attacks often strike without warning and produce severe palpitations, extreme shortness of breath, chest pains, trembling, sweating, dizziness, and a feeling of helplessness. Victims are seized by the fear that they will die, go crazy, or do something they cannot control (Asnis & van Praag, 1995).

What are some of the psychosocial and biological factors involved in panic disorder? As shown in figure 14.1, most panic attacks are spontaneous; those that are not spontaneous are triggered by a variety of events. In many instances, a stressful life event has occurred in the past 6 months, most often a threatened or actual separation from a loved one or a change in job.

Phobic Disorders

Agnes is a withdrawn 30-year-old who has been unable to go higher than the second floor of any building for more than a year. When she tries to overcome her fear of heights by going up to the third, fourth, or fifth floor, she becomes overwhelmed by anxiety. She remembers how it all began. One evening she was

Onset of attack	No. (%) of patients
Spontaneous	47 (78%)
Nonspontaneous, precipitated by	13 (22%)
Public speaking	3
Stimulant drug use	3
Family argument	2
Leaving home	2
Exercise (while pregnant)	1
Being frightened by a stranger	1
Fear of fainting	1

Stressful life events associated with attack	No. (%) of patients
No stressful life event within 6 months	22 (37%)
Stressful life event within 6 months*	38 (63%)
Threatened or actual separation from important person	11
Change in job, causing increased pressure	8
Pregnancy	7
Move	5
Marriage	3
Graduation	3
Death of close person	3
Physical illness	2

*Four patients had two concomitant stressful life events.

FIGURE 14.1

The Nature of First Panic Attack and Associated Life Events
At the bottom is the nature of first panic attack and associated life events, and at the top is Edvard Munch's painting *The Scream*. Experts often interpret Munch's painting as reflecting the terror brought on by a panic attack.

working alone and was seized by an urge to jump out of an eighth-story window. She was so frightened by her impulse that she hid behind a file cabinet for more than 2 hours until she calmed down enough to gather her belongings and go home. As she reached the first floor of the building, her heart was pounding and she was perspiring heavily. After several months, she gave up her position and became a lower-paid salesperson so she could work on the bottom floor of the store (Cameron, 1963).

A **phobic disorder,** *commonly called a phobia, is an anxiety disorder in which an individual has an irrational, overwhelming, persistent fear of a particular object or situation.* Individuals with generalized anxiety disorder cannot pinpoint the cause of their nervous feelings; individuals with phobias can. A fear becomes a phobia when a situation is so dreaded that an individual goes to almost any length to avoid it; for example, Agnes quit her job to avoid being in high places. Some phobias are more debilitating than others. An individual with a fear of automobiles has a more difficult time functioning in our society than a person with a fear of snakes, for example.

Phobias come in many forms. Some of the most common phobias involve heights, open spaces, people, close spaces, dogs, dirt, the dark, and snakes. (Turn to the Self-Assessment box to evaluate your own fears.) Simple phobias are relatively common and are easier to treat through psychotherapy than complex phobias, such as agoraphobia, are. **Agoraphobia,** *the fear of entering unfamiliar situations, especially open or public spaces, is the most common type of phobic disorder.* It accounts for 50 to 80 percent of the phobic population, according to some estimates (Foa, Steketze, & Young, 1984). Women are far more likely than men to suffer from agoraphobia (Magee, 1996). One study found that 84 percent of the individuals being treated for agoraphobia are women, and almost 90 percent of those women are married (Al-Issa, 1982b).

Psychologists have become increasingly interested in *social phobia,* the fear of social situations (Stein, 1995; Stemberger & others, 1995). Bashful or timid people often suffer from this phobia. Social

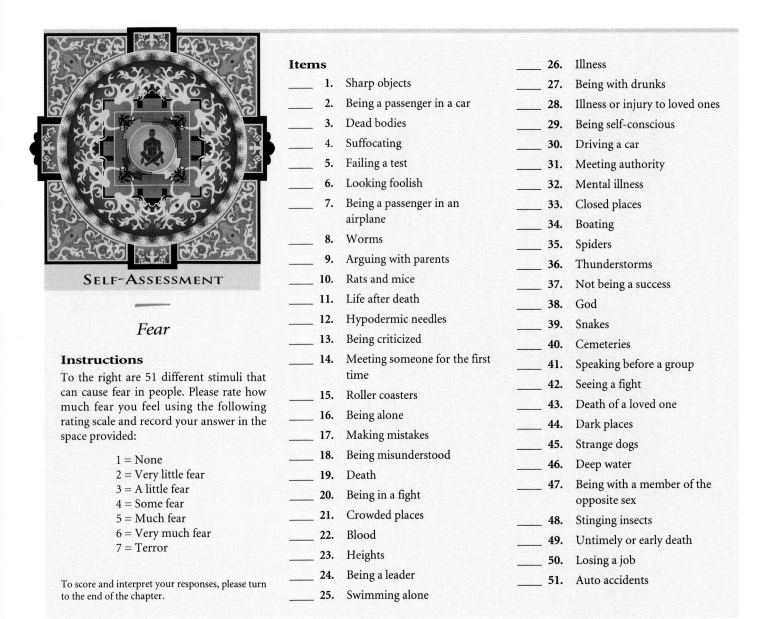

SELF-ASSESSMENT

Fear

Instructions

To the right are 51 different stimuli that can cause fear in people. Please rate how much fear you feel using the following rating scale and record your answer in the space provided:

1 = None
2 = Very little fear
3 = A little fear
4 = Some fear
5 = Much fear
6 = Very much fear
7 = Terror

To score and interpret your responses, please turn to the end of the chapter.

Items

_____ 1. Sharp objects
_____ 2. Being a passenger in a car
_____ 3. Dead bodies
_____ 4. Suffocating
_____ 5. Failing a test
_____ 6. Looking foolish
_____ 7. Being a passenger in an airplane
_____ 8. Worms
_____ 9. Arguing with parents
_____ 10. Rats and mice
_____ 11. Life after death
_____ 12. Hypodermic needles
_____ 13. Being criticized
_____ 14. Meeting someone for the first time
_____ 15. Roller coasters
_____ 16. Being alone
_____ 17. Making mistakes
_____ 18. Being misunderstood
_____ 19. Death
_____ 20. Being in a fight
_____ 21. Crowded places
_____ 22. Blood
_____ 23. Heights
_____ 24. Being a leader
_____ 25. Swimming alone
_____ 26. Illness
_____ 27. Being with drunks
_____ 28. Illness or injury to loved ones
_____ 29. Being self-conscious
_____ 30. Driving a car
_____ 31. Meeting authority
_____ 32. Mental illness
_____ 33. Closed places
_____ 34. Boating
_____ 35. Spiders
_____ 36. Thunderstorms
_____ 37. Not being a success
_____ 38. God
_____ 39. Snakes
_____ 40. Cemeteries
_____ 41. Speaking before a group
_____ 42. Seeing a fight
_____ 43. Death of a loved one
_____ 44. Dark places
_____ 45. Strange dogs
_____ 46. Deep water
_____ 47. Being with a member of the opposite sex
_____ 48. Stinging insects
_____ 49. Untimely or early death
_____ 50. Losing a job
_____ 51. Auto accidents

---

phobia affects as many as 2 of every 100 Americans and tends to be evenly distributed between the sexes.

Why do people develop phobias? The answer often depends on the researcher's perspective. Psychoanalytic theorists, for example, say phobias develop as defense mechanisms to ward off threatening or unacceptable impulses—Agnes, for instance, hid behind a file cabinet because she feared she would jump out of an eighth-story window. Learning theorists, however, explain phobias differently; they say phobias are learned fears. In Agnes's case, she might have fallen out of a window when she was a little girl and, as a result, now associates falling with pain and fears high places.

On the other hand, she may have heard about or seen other people who were afraid of high places. These last two examples are conditioning and observational learning explanations for Agnes's phobia. Cross-cultural psychologists point out that phobias also are influenced by cultural factors. Agoraphobia, for example, is much more common in the United States and Europe than in other areas of the world.

Neuroscientists are finding that biological factors, such as greater blood flow and metabolism in the right hemisphere of the brain than in the left, may also be involved in phobias. First-generation relatives of individuals suffering from agoraphobia and panic attacks

have high rates of these disorders themselves, suggesting a possible genetic predisposition for phobias (d'Ansia, 1989). Others have found that identical twins reared apart sometimes develop the same phobias; one pair independently became claustrophobic, for example (Eckert, Heston, & Bouchard, 1981).

Obsessive-Compulsive Disorders

Bob is 27 years old and lives in a well-kept apartment. He has few friends and little social life. He was raised by a demanding mother and an aloof father. Bob is an accountant who spends long hours at work. He is a perfectionist. His demanding mother always nagged at him to improve himself, to keep the house

---

Agoraphobia is the fear of entering unfamiliar situations, especially open or public places. Individuals with agoraphobia try to avoid crowded situations. They fear that escape would be difficult or impossible if they become highly anxious in such crowded situations. Agoraphobic individuals also usually avoid standing in line and riding in vehicles, activities that intensify their feelings of vulnerability.

spotless, and to be clean and neat, and she made Bob wash his hands whenever he touched his genitals. As a young adult, Bob finds himself ensnared in an exacting ritual in which he removes his clothes in a prearranged sequence and then endlessly scrubs every inch of his body from head to toe. He dresses himself in precisely the opposite way from which he takes off his clothes. If he deviates from this order, he *has* to start the sequence all over again. Sometimes Bob performs the cleansing ritual four or five times an evening. Even though he is aware that this ritual is absurd, he simply cannot stop (Meyer & Osborne, 1982).

Obsessive-compulsive disorder (OCD) *is an anxiety disorder in which an individual has anxiety-provoking thoughts that will not go away (obsession) and/or urges to perform repetitive, ritualistic behaviors to prevent or produce a future situation (compulsion).* Individuals with obsessive-compulsive disorder repeat and rehearse doubts and daily routines, sometimes hundreds of times a day. The basic difference between obsession and compulsion is the difference between thought and action. Obsessions can immobilize the person with horrifying yet irresistible thoughts of killing someone in a traffic accident, for instance, whereas compulsions can result in bloody hands from hours of washing away imaginary germs.

Although obsessions and compulsions are different, a person afflicted with OCD might be caught in the relentless grip of both problems.

> There is nothing worse than taking something into your head that is a revolving wheel you can't control.
> —Ugo Betti, *Struggle Till Dawn,* 1949

The most common compulsions are excessive checking, cleansing, and counting. For example, Wesley believes that he has to check his apartment for gas leaks and make sure the windows are locked. His behavior is not compulsive if he does this once, but, if he goes back to check five or six times and then constantly worries that he may not have checked carefully enough once he has left the house, his behavior is compulsive. Most individuals do not enjoy their ritualistic behavior but feel anxious when they do not carry it out (Oldham, Hollander, & Skodol, 1996).

Positron emission tomography (PET) and other brain-imaging techniques indicate a neurological basis for OCD. Irregularities in neurotransmitter systems, especially serotonin and dopamine, seem to be involved. There also may be a genetic basis for the disorder; OCD runs in families.

Post-Traumatic Stress Disorder

Bernice sought help in therapy because she thought she was "losing her grip." Her boss was continually complaining that she wasn't paying attention to her work as a cashier. She feared that she would lose her job. She was having trouble sleeping. Whenever she would lie down, she had a strange feeling that she wasn't alone. Occasionally, she smelled disturbing smells. All of these problems seemed to intensify following the death of her uncle, a man she hadn't spoken to in decades and had disliked for as long as she could remember. Her therapist considered that Bernice might be a victim of post-traumatic stress disorder.

Post-traumatic stress disorder *is a mental disturbance that develops through exposure to a traumatic event (such as war), a severely oppressive situation (such as the Holocaust), severe abuse (as in rape), a natural disaster (such as a flood or tornado), or an accidental disaster (such as a plane crash). The disorder is characterized by anxiety symptoms that either immediately follow the trauma or are delayed by months or even years.* The symptoms vary but can include the following:

- "Flashbacks" in which the individual relives the event in nightmares, or in an awake but dissociative-like state
- Constricted ability to feel emotions, often reported as feeling numb, resulting in an inability to experience happiness, sexual desire, enjoyable interpersonal relationships
- Excessive arousal, resulting in an exaggerated startle response or an inability to sleep
- Difficulties with memory and concentration
- Feelings of apprehension, including nervous tremors
- Impulsive outbursts of behavior such as aggressiveness, or sudden changes in lifestyle

Not every individual exposed to the same disaster develops post-traumatic stress disorder, which occurs when the individual's usual coping abilities are overloaded (Boudewyns, 1996; Marsella & others, 1996). For example, it is estimated that 15 to 20 percent of Vietnam veterans experienced post-traumatic stress disorder. Vietnam veterans who had some autonomy and decision-making authority, such as Green Berets, were less likely to develop the disorder than soldiers who had no control over where they would be sent or when, and who had no option but to follow orders.

Preparation for a trauma also makes a difference in whether an individual will develop the disorder. For example, emergency workers who are trained to cope with traumatic circumstances usually do not develop post-traumatic stress disorder.

Some experts consider female sexual abuse and assault victims to be the single largest group of post-traumatic stress disorder sufferers (Koss, 1993). This is not very surprising, since these victims had no autonomy nor decision making in the situation. Few women are prepared to deal with the traumatic circumstances and consequences of rape. Many victims of sexual assault receive mixed societal messages after the trauma about the degree of their responsibility, and many victims remain secretive about having been raped. All these factors increase their risk for post-traumatic stress disorder.

Somatoform Disorders

"Look, I am having trouble breathing. You don't believe me. Nobody believes me. There are times when I can't stop coughing. I'm losing weight. I know I have cancer. My father died of cancer when I was twelve." Herb has been to six cancer specialists in the last 2 years; none can find anything wrong with him. Each doctor has taken X rays and conducted excessive laboratory tests, but Herb's test results do not indicate any illnesses. Might some psychological factors be responsible for Herb's sense that he is physically ailing?

Somatoform disorders *are mental disorders in which psychological symptoms take a physical, or somatic, form, even though no physical causes can be found.* Although these symptoms are not caused physically, they are highly distressing for the individual; the symptoms are real, not faked. Two types of somatoform disorders are hypochondriasis and conversion disorder.

Hypochondriasis

Carly seemed to be a classic hypochondriac. She always seemed to overreact to a missed heartbeat, shortness of breath, or a slight chest pain, fearing that something was wrong with her. **Hypochondriasis** *is a somatoform disorder in which the individual has a pervasive fear of illness and disease.* At the first indication of something's being amiss in her body, Carly calls the doctor. When a physical examination reveals no problems, she usually does not believe the doctor. She often changes doctors, moving from one to another searching for a diagnosis that matches her own. Most hypochondriacs are pill enthusiasts; their medicine chests spill over with bottles of drugs they hope will cure their imagined maladies. Carly's pill collection was spectacular.

Hypochondriasis is a difficult category to diagnose accurately. It often occurs with other mental disorders, such as depression.

Conversion Disorder

Conversion disorder *is a somatoform disorder in which an individual experiences genuine physical symptoms, even though no physiological problems can be found.* Conversion disorder received its name from psychoanalytic theory, which stressed that anxiety is "converted" into a physical symptom. A hypochondriac has no physical disability; an individual with a conversion disorder does have some loss of motor or sensory ability. Individuals with a conversion disorder may be unable to speak, may faint, or may even be deaf or blind.

Conversion disorder was more common in Freud's time than today. Freud was especially interested in this disorder, in which physical symptoms made no neurological sense. For example, individuals with *glove anesthesia* report that their entire hand is numb from the tip of their fingers to a cutoff point at the wrist. As shown in figure 14.2, if these individuals were experiencing true physiological numbness, their symptoms would be very different. Like hypochondriasis, conversion disorder often appears in conjunction with other mental disturbances. During long-term evaluation, conversion disorder often becomes displaced by another mental or physical disorder.

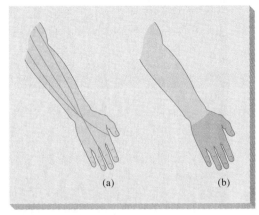

(a)   (b)

FIGURE 14.2

Glove Anesthesia
A patient who complains of numbness in the hand might be diagnosed as suffering from conversion disorder if the area of the hand affected showed that a disorder of the nervous system was not responsible. The skin areas served by nerves in the arm are shown in (a). Therefore, damage to a nerve in the arm tends to make only a portion of the hand numb (for example, the thumb and forefinger). The glove anesthesia shown in (b) could not result from damage to these nerves.

From Bootzin et al., *Abnormal Psychology.* Copyright © 1972 McGraw-Hill, Inc. Reprinted by permission of McGraw-Hill, Inc.

Dissociative Disorders

Dissociative disorders *are psychological disorders that involve a sudden loss of memory or change in identity. Under extreme stress or shock, an individual's conscious awareness becomes dissociated (separated or split) from previous memories and thoughts.* Three kinds of dissociative disorders are amnesia, fugue, and multiple personality.

Amnesia and Fugue

Amnesia is the inability to recall important events. Amnesia can be caused by an injury to the head, for example. However, **psychogenic amnesia** *is a dissociative disorder involving memory loss caused by extensive psychological stress.* For example, a man showed up at a hospital and said he did not know who he was. After several days in the hospital, he awoke one morning and demanded to be released. Eventually he remembered that he had been involved in an automobile accident in which a pedestrian had been killed. The extreme stress of the accident and the fear that he might be held responsible had triggered the amnesia.

Fugue, *which means "flight," is a dissociative disorder in which an individual not only develops amnesia but also unexpectedly travels away from home and assumes a new identity.* For example, one day a woman named Barbara vanished without a trace. Two weeks later, looking more like a teenager than a 31-year-old woman, with her hair in a ponytail and wearing bobby socks, Barbara was picked up by police in a nearby city. When her husband came to see her, Barbara asked, "Who are you?" She could not remember anything about the past 2 weeks of her life. During psychotherapy, she gradually began to recall her past. She had left home with enough money to buy a bus ticket to the town where she grew up as a child. She had spent days walking the streets and standing near a building where her father had worked. Later she had gone to a motel with a man; according to the motel manager, she had entertained a series of men over a 3-day period (Goldstein & Palmer, 1975).

Multiple Personality

Multiple personality *is the most dramatic but least common dissociative disorder; individuals suffering from this disorder have two or more distinct personalities, or selves,* like the fictional Dr. Jekyll and Mr. Hyde of Robert Louis Stevenson's short story. Each personality has its own memories, behaviors, and relationships; one personality dominates the individual at one point; another personality takes over at another time. The personalities might not be aware of each other, and the shift from one to the other can occur suddenly during distress.

The most famous case of multiple personality involves the "three faces of Eve," which in reality is only a portion of the dramatic life history of Chris Sizemore. Sizemore recalls that she had her first experience with dissociation when she was 2. For the next 44 years, she experienced a life filled with severe headaches and periods of amnesia. Around age 25 she was diagnosed with multiple personality disorder. Her psychiatrists identified three alters functioning in her life and named them Eve Black, Eve White, and Jane (Thigpen & Cleckley, 1957).

Eve White was the original, dominant personality. She had no knowledge of her second personality, Eve Black, although Eve Black had been alternating with Eve White for a number of years. Eve White was bland, quiet, and serious—a rather dull personality. Eve Black, by contrast, was carefree, mischievous, and uninhibited. She "came out" at the most inappropriate times, leaving Eve White with hangovers, bills, and a reputation in local bars that she could not explain. During treatment, a third personality, Jane, emerged. More mature than the other two, Jane seemed to have developed as a result of therapy (see figure 14.3 for a portrayal of the three faces of Eve). However, Sizemore's personality didn't stabilize at that point. Alters continued to show up in trios, with one alter demonstrating characteristics of the wife

FIGURE 14.3

Multiple Personality: The Three Faces of Eve
Chris Sizemore, the subject of the book *Three Faces of Eve,* is shown with the work she painted and entitled *Three Faces in One.*

Anxiety Disorders, Somatoform Disorders, and Dissociative Disorders

Anxiety is a diffuse, vague, highly unpleasant feeling of fear and apprehension. The main features of anxiety disorders are motor tension, hyperactivity, and apprehensive expectations and thoughts. Generalized anxiety disorder consists of persistent anxiety for at least 1 month without being able to pinpoint the cause of the anxiety. Panic disorder involves recurrent panic attacks marked by a sudden onset of intense apprehension or terror. Phobic disorders, commonly called phobias, involve an irrational, overwhelming, persistent fear of an object or a situation. Phobias come in many forms; the most common is agoraphobia. Psychoanalytic and learning explanations of phobias have been given; sociocultural and biological factors also are involved. Obsessive-compulsive disorders consist of recurrent obsessions or compulsions. Obsessions are anxiety-provoking thoughts that won't go away. Compulsions are urges to perform repetitive, ritualistic behaviors that usually occur to prevent or produce a future situation. Post-traumatic stress disorder is a mental disorder that develops through exposure to a traumatic event, a severely oppressive situation, severe abuse, a natural disaster, or an accidental disaster. Anxiety symptoms may immediately follow the trauma or may be delayed months or even years.

Somatoform disorders develop when psychological symptoms take a physical, or somatic, form, even though no physical cause can be found. Two somatoform disorders are hypochondriasis and conversion disorder. Hypochondriasis is a pervasive fear of illness and disease. It rarely occurs alone; depression often accompanies hypochondriasis. Conversion disorder develops when an individual experiences genuine symptoms, even though no physiological problems can be found. Conversion disorder received its name from psychoanalytic theory, which stressed that anxiety is "converted" into a physical symptom. Some loss of motor or sensory ability occurs. The disorder was more common in Freud's time than today.

The dissociative disorders involve a sudden loss of memory or a change in identity. Under extreme stress or shock, the individual's conscious awareness becomes dissociated (separated or split) from previous memories and thoughts. Psychogenic amnesia involves memory loss caused by extensive psychological stress. Fugue involves a loss of memory, but individuals unexpectedly travel away from home or work, assume a new identity, and do not remember their old one. Multiple personality involves the presence of two or more distinct personalities in the same individual. The disorder is rare.

---

and mother, another the party girl, and the third an intellectual. Of the twenty-two alters that appeared, ten were poets, seven artists, and one a tailor. According to Sizemore (1989), when her integrated personality emerged at age 47, she could paint and write but she couldn't sew.

A summary of the research literature on multiple personality suggests that the most striking feature related to the disorder is an inordinately high rate of sexual or physical abuse during early childhood (Ludolph, 1982). Sexual abuse occurred in 56 percent of the reported cases, for example. Their mothers had been rejecting and depressed and their fathers distant, alcoholic, and abusive. Remember that, although fascinating, multiple personality disorder is rare. Until the 1980s, only about 300 cases had been reported (Suinn, 1984). In the past decade, however, hundreds more cases have been labeled "multiple personality disorder." Some argue that the increase represents a diagnostic fad. Others believe that it is not so rare but has been frequently misdiagnosed as schizophrenia.

Improved techniques for assessing the physiological changes that occur when individuals change personalities increase the likelihood that more accurate rates can be determined.

Now that we have considered three major types of mental disorders—anxiety, somatoform, and dissociative—we will turn to a set of widespread disorders, the mood disorders.

Mood Disorders

The **mood disorders** *are psychological disorders characterized by wide emotional swings, ranging from being deeply depressed to being highly euphoric and agitated.* Depression can occur alone, as in major depression, or it can alternate with mania, as in bipolar disorder. Depression is linked to the increasing rate of suicide. We will consider each of these disturbances in turn and then examine the causes of the mood disorders.

Major Depression

Major depression *is a mood disorder in which the individual is deeply unhappy,* *demoralized, self-derogatory, and bored. An individual with major depression shows changes in appetite and sleep patterns, decreased energy, feelings of worthlessness, problems concentrating, and guilt feelings that might prompt thoughts of suicide.* For example, Peter had been depressed for several months. Nothing cheered him up. His depression began when the girl he wanted to marry decided marriage was not for her, at least not with Peter. Peter's emotional state deteriorated to the point where he didn't leave his room for days at a time, he kept the shades drawn and the room dark, and he could hardly get out of bed in the morning. When he managed to leave his room, he had trouble maintaining a conversation and he usually felt exhausted. By the time Peter finally contacted his college counseling center, he had gone from being mildly depressed to being in the grips of major depression.

Although most people don't spiral into major depression, as Peter did, everyone feels "blue" sometimes. In our stress-filled world, people often use the term *depression* to describe brief bouts of normal sadness or discontent over life's problems. Perhaps you haven't done well in a class or things aren't working out in your love life. You feel down in the dumps and say you are depressed. In most instances, though, your depression won't last as long or be as intense as Peter's; after a few hours, days, or weeks, you snap out of your gloomy state and begin to cope more effectively with depression.

For many individuals, however, depression is a lingering, exhausting experience that can sometimes be severe enough to weaken ties with reality. Depression is so widespread that it has been called the "common cold" of mental disorders; more than 250,000 individuals are hospitalized every year for the disorder. Students, professors, corporate executives, laborers—no one is immune to depression, not even writers Anne Sexton, Sylvia Plath, or F. Scott Fitzgerald, Abraham Lincoln, or Winston Churchill, each of whom experienced major depression.

---

*I was much too far out all my life
And not waving but drowning.*
—**Stevie Smith,**
Not Waving but Drowning, 1957

A man's lifetime risk of developing major depression is approximately 10 percent. The risk is much greater for a woman—almost 25 percent. In fact, depression is the most common psychiatric diagnosis for African American and White women. To read further about women's depression, turn to Sociocultural Worlds of Adjustment.

In May 1988, the National Institute of Mental Health (NIMH) launched the public education phase of the first major program to communicate information about mood disorders (Regier & others, 1988). The inadequate care that results from a lack of understanding or a misunderstanding of depression is expensive and tragic. The annual cost of major depression to the nation is more than $16 billion. Given the existing range of psychological and pharmacological treatments, many individuals who go untreated suffer needlessly.

Bipolar Disorder

Bipolar disorder *is a mood disorder characterized by extreme mood swings; an individual with this disorder might be depressed, manic, or both.* We have described the symptoms of depression. In contrast, someone who is manic experiences elation, exuberance, and tireless stamina. He or she may be humorous, scheming, restless, and irritable; have a tendency for excess; and be in almost constant motion.

Consider Charlene. She was alternately agitated and euphoric. She had experienced extreme mood swings since she was a child. At age 43, her family wanted to have her hospitalized. She claimed that she had discovered the "secret to life" and laughed heartily when anyone asked her to reveal the secret. Her energy seemed boundless. She often woke at 3 A.M. to do the daily vacuuming. Her family really started worrying when she could no longer control her spending. They found twenty-eight sets of coordinated towels and washcloths stashed under her bed. When she attempted to purchase three cars on the same day, her loan requests were rejected. She threatened suicide, and her family knew they needed help.

The lifetime risk of bipolar disorder is estimated at approximately 1 percent for both men and women. It is more common among divorced persons, although, in such cases, bipolar disorder may be a cause rather than a consequence of the divorce. Bipolar disorder also occurs more frequently in the close relatives of individuals with bipolar disorder than in the close relatives of depressed but non-bipolar-disordered individuals.

Suicide

The rate of suicide has tripled since the 1950s in the United States. Each year about 25,000 people take their own lives. At about the age of 15, the suicide rate begins to rise rapidly. Suicide accounts for 12 percent of the mortality in the adolescent and young adult age group. Men are about three times more likely than women to succeed at committing suicide. This may be due to their choice of method for attempting it—shooting themselves, for example. By contrast, females more often select methods, such as sleeping pills,

which do not immediately cause death. Although males successfully commit suicide more frequently, females attempt it more often (Meyer & others, 1996).

Estimates indicate that 6 to 10 suicide attempts occur for every successful suicide in the general population. For adolescents, the figure is as high as 50 attempts for every life taken. As many as 2 in every 3 college students have thought about suicide on at least one occasion. Their methods range from using drugs to crashing into the White House in an airplane.

There is no simple answer to why people commit suicide. Biological factors appear to be involved. Suicide, as with major depression, tends to run in families. Immediate and highly stressful circumstances, such as the loss of a spouse or a job, flunking out of school, or an unwanted pregnancy, can lead people, especially those who are genetically predisposed, to attempt suicide. Also, drug-related suicide attempts are more common now than in the past.

However, earlier experiences, such as a long-standing history of family instability and unhappiness, can also play a role in attempted suicides. Studies of gifted men and women found several predictors of suicide, such as anxiety, conspicuous instability in work and relationships, depression, and alcoholism (Tomlinson-Keasey, Warren, & Elliot, 1986).

Not all individuals who attempt suicide are clinically depressed. For example, most suicides are committed by older white males who are divorced, in poor health, and unemployed. Substance abuse and having a terminal illness also are related to suicidal thoughts and behavior. In high-pressure cultures, such as Japan and the United States, suicide rates are much higher than in less achievement oriented cultures. Also, as we will see next, in some cultures religion plays an important role in deterring suicide.

Over many centuries, most Latinos have maintained their spiritual belief in Catholicism. However, Latino subcultures interpret Catholicism differently from one another. A comparison of Mexican Americans with Puerto Ricans illustrates how different beliefs in Catholicism affect the suicide rates of

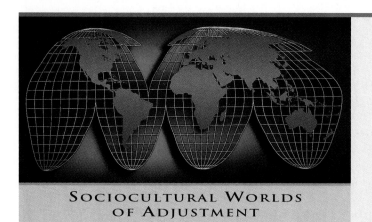

SOCIOCULTURAL WORLDS
OF ADJUSTMENT

Women and Depression

Around the world, depression occurs more frequently among women than among men. The female-male ratio ranges from 2:1 to 3:1 in most industrialized countries (Nolen-Hoeksema, 1990). Three explanations of the sex difference in depression are the following: (1) women are more willing to seek help and, therefore, are more likely to be categorized as having depression; (2) biological differences may exist between females and males that predispose females to become more depressed than males; and (3) psychosocial factors—different rearing environments, different social roles, and less favorable economic and achievement opportunities, for example—may produce greater depression in women than men. Some psychologists also believe that alcoholism may mask, or act as a cover for, depression in men (Culbertson, 1991).

Among the psychosocial factors in women's depression that were proposed by the American Psychological Association's National Task Force on Women and Depression (McGrath & others, 1990) were the following:

- Women's depression is related to avoidant, passive, dependent behavior patterns; it is also related to focusing too much on depressed feelings instead of on action and mastery strategies.

- The rate of sexual and physical abuse of women is much higher than previously thought and is a major factor in women's depression. Depressive symptoms may be long-standing effects of post-traumatic stress syndrome for many women.
- Marriage often confers a greater protective buffer against stress for men than for women. In unhappy marriages, women are three times as likely as men to be depressed. Mothers of young children are especially vulnerable to stress and depression; the more children in the house, the more depression women report.
- Poverty is a pathway to depression and three out of every four people in poverty in the United States are women and children. Minority women, elderly women, chemically-dependent women, lesbians, and professional women are also high-risk groups for depression and merit special attention and support.

Careful diagnosis is critical in the treatment of women's depression. Diagnostic assessment for women, in particular, should include taking a history of sexual and physical violence; exploring prescription drug use; discovering past and current medical conditions; and doing a reproductive life history to determine how menstruation, birth control, pregnancy, childbirth, abortion, and menopause may have contributed to women's depression. According to the Women's Task Force, depression is misdiagnosed at least 30 to 50 percent of the time in women. Approximately 70 percent of the prescriptions for antidepressants are given to women, often with improper diagnosis and monitoring. Prescription drug misuse is a danger for many women.

Understanding the nature of women's depression is a complex undertaking and merits more attention. Perhaps the current effort to better understand women's depression will be successful and reduce women's pain and suffering from depression.

various Latino subcultures. For example, one study found that many depressed Mexican Americans control their suicidal impulses because Catholicism asserts that suicide is an unpardonable sin that carries church sanctions against those who attempt suicide, as well as eternal damnation in hell for those who succeed.

Even though Puerto Ricans tend to be Catholic, they also integrate Indian folk beliefs with their Catholicism. Overall, Puerto Ricans do not adopt organized religion, only minimally adhering to the

Catholic doctrine. Many Puerto Ricans believe that spirits communicate with people through mediums, or people who act as channels of communication between the earthly world and a world of spirits. This belief, combined with the conviction that "unsolvable" conflicts can be handled by committing suicide, promotes a much higher rate of suicide among Puerto Ricans than among Mexican Americans.

Clinicians who have Latino clients need to be aware of such cultural differences. If a clinician erroneously thinks of

Latinos as a homogeneous group, he or she might incorrectly evaluate the client's risk of suicide. For example, if the clinician reasons that Latinos are Catholics and Catholics do not believe in suicide because it is an unpardonable sin against God, the clinician may assess the risk of suicide for a Puerto Rican client as low, in which case the clinician might be very wrong.

Psychologists do not have the complete answers for detecting suicide impulses or for preventing them. However, psychologists believe that the most

Over many centuries, most Latinos have maintained their spiritual belief in Catholicism. However, Catholicism does not always mean the same thing to all Latinos. *What are some variations in the meaning of Catholicism to Latinos from different ethnic backgrounds?*

effective intervention for preventing suicide comes from those who have had special training. The advice offered in table 14.2 provides some valuable suggestions for communicating with someone you think may be contemplating suicide.

Causes of Mood Disorders

Explanations for mood disorders, such as Peter's depression and Charlene's bipolar disorder, come from psychoanalytic theory, cognitive and learning theories, biogenetic theories, and sociocultural theories.

Psychoanalytic Explanations Sigmund Freud (1917) believed that depression is a turning inward of aggressive instincts. He theorized that a child's early attachment to a love object (usually the mother) contains a mixture of love and hate. When the child loses the love object or her dependency needs are frustrated, feelings of loss coexist with anger. Since the child cannot openly accept such angry feelings toward the individual she loves, the hostility is turned inward and experienced as depression. The unresolved mixture of anger and love is carried forward to adolescence and adulthood, where

loss can bring back those early feelings of abandonment.

British psychiatrist John Bowlby (1980) agrees with Freud that childhood experiences are an important determinant of depression in adulthood. He believes that a combination of an insecure attachment to the mother, a lack of love and affection as a child, and the actual loss of a parent during childhood give rise to a negative cognitive set, or schema. The schema built up during childhood causes the individual to interpret later losses as yet other failures in one's effort to establish enduring and close positive relationships.

One longitudinal study of depression found that parents' lack of affection, high control, and aggressive achievement orientation in their children's early childhood are associated with depression among adolescent girls but not boys (Gjerde, 1985). This difference may be because depression generally occurs more often in girls than boys.

Cognitive and Learning Explanations Individuals who are depressed rarely think positive thoughts. They interpret their lives in self-defeating ways and have negative expectations about the future (Bradley, 1996). Psychotherapist

Aaron Beck (1967) believes that such negative thoughts reflect schemas that shape the depressed individual's experiences (Teasdale & others, 1995). These habitual negative thoughts magnify and expand a depressed person's negative experiences. The depressed person may overgeneralize about a minor occurrence and think that he is worthless because a work assignment was turned in late, his son was arrested for shoplifting, or a friend made a negative comment about his hair. Beck believes that depressed people blame themselves far more than is warranted. For example, an athlete may accept complete blame for a team's loss when five or six other teammates, the opposing team, and other factors were involved.

Self-defeating and sad thoughts fit the clinical picture of the depressed individual. Whether these thoughts are the cause or the consequence of the depression, however, is controversial. Critics say that self-defeating thoughts are an outgrowth of biological and environmental conditions that produce depression.

Some years ago, in the interest of science, a researcher drowned two rats (Richter, 1957). The first rat was dropped into a tank of warm water; it swam around for 60 hours before it drowned.

T ABLE 14.2

What to Do and What Not to Do When You Suspect Someone Is Likely to Commit Suicide

What to Do

1. Ask direct, straightforward questions in a calm manner: "Are you thinking about hurting yourself?"
2. Assess the seriousness of the suicidal intent by asking questions about feelings, important relationships, who else the person has talked with, and the amount of thought given to the means to be used. If a gun, pills, rope, or other means has been obtained and a precise plan developed, clearly the situation is dangerous. Stay with the person until help arrives.
3. Be a good listener and be very supportive without being falsely reassuring.
4. Try to persuade the person to obtain professional help and assist him or her in getting this help.

What Not to Do

1. Do not ignore the warning signs.
2. Do not refuse to talk about suicide if a person approaches you about it.
3. Do not react with horror, disapproval, or repulsion.
4. Do not give false reassurances by saying such things as "Everything is going to be OK." Also do not give out simple answers or platitudes, such as "You have everything to be thankful for."
5. Do not abandon the individual after the crisis has passed or after professional counseling has commenced.

Adapted with permission from *Living with 10- to 15-Year-Olds: A Parent Education Curriculum.* Copyright 1992 by The Center for Early Adolescence, University of North Carolina at Chapel Hill, Carrboro, NC.

The second rat was handled differently. The researcher held the rat tightly in his hand until it quit struggling to get loose. Then the rat was dropped into the tank; it swam around for several minutes before it drowned. The researcher concluded that the second rat drowned more quickly because its previous experiences told it to give up hope; the rat had developed a sense of helplessness.

Learned helplessness *occurs when animals or humans are exposed to aversive stimulation, such as prolonged stress or pain, over which they have no control. The inability to avoid such aversive stimulation produces an apathetic state of helplessness.* Martin Seligman (1975) argued that learned helplessness is one reason many individuals become depressed. When individuals encounter stress and pain over which they have no control, they eventually feel helpless and depressed. Some researchers believe that the hopelessness characteristic of learned helplessness is often the result of a person's extremely negative, self-blaming attributions (Metalsky & others, 1993).

Biogenetic Explanations Biological explanations of depression involve genetic inheritance and chemical changes in the brain (McGuffin, 1996; Miller, 1996). In a large twin study conducted in Denmark, the identical twins were more likely to suffer from mood disorders than were the fraternal twins (Bertelson, 1979). If one identical twin developed a mood disorder, the other had a 70 percent chance of developing the disorder; a fraternal twin ran only a 13 percent risk. Another study revealed that biological relatives of an individual with a mood disorder are more likely to suffer from the disorder than are adopted relatives (Wender & others, 1986).

Neurotransmitters are chemical messengers that carry information from one neuron to the next. Two neurotransmitters involved in depression are norepinephrine and serotonin (Mann & others, 1996). Depressed individuals have decreased levels of norepinephrine, whereas individuals in a manic state have increased levels. Patients with unusually low serotonin levels are 10 times as likely to commit suicide than individuals with normal levels (Stanley & Stanley, 1989).

The endocrine system also may be involved in depression—excessive secretion of cortisol from the adrenal gland occurs in depressed individuals, for example. More about the biological aspects of depression appears in the next chapter, where we will discuss the use of drugs to alleviate depression.

Sociocultural Explanations Seligman (1989) speculated that the reason so many young American adults are prone to depression is that our society's emphasis on self, independence, and individualism, coupled with an erosion of connectedness to others, family, and religion, has spawned a widespread sense of hopelessness. Depressive disorders are found in virtually all cultures in the world, but their incidence, intensity, and components vary across cultures. A major difference in depression between Western and many non-Western cultures is the absence of guilt and self-deprecation in the non-Western cultures (Draguns, 1990).

Some cross-cultural psychologists believe that mourning rituals in many non-Western cultures reduce the risks of depression. For example, low depression rates in Taiwan may be related to the overt expression of grief that occurs in Chinese funeral celebrations. Ancestor worship in Japan also may act against depression because love objects are not considered to be lost through death. The mourning practices of African Americans also may reduce depression by providing an opportunity for adequate grieving and by providing the bereaved with support rather than having to cope with death in isolation.

Earlier in this chapter, you learned that women run a far greater risk of depression than men—at a ratio of 2 to 1. Researchers have shown that depression is especially high among single women who are the head of household and among young married women who work at unsatisfying, dead-end jobs (Russo, 1990). Such stressful circumstances, as well as others involving sexual abuse, sexual harassment, unwanted pregnancy, and powerlessness disproportionately affect women. These sociocultural factors may interact with biological and cognitive factors to increase women's rate of de-

pression. A second possibility may be that men in mainstream American society obscure their depression with aggressive behavior that "acts out," or externalizes, their sad feelings. In cultures where alcohol abuse and aggression are rare, such as the culturally homogeneous Amish community (a religious sect in Pennsylvania), the rates of depression for women and men are virtually equal.

Separating the environmental, cognitive, biological, and sociocultural causes of depression is not easy (Beckman & Leber, 1995). Whether neurotransmitters, cognitive factors, environmental factors, or cross-cultural factors are cause or effect is still unknown. Like most behaviors we have discussed, depression is best viewed as complex and multiply determined.

Becoming Educated About Depression

As we saw earlier in this chapter, depression is one of the most pervasive mental disorders. In the last several decades, important advances have been made in the treatment of depression. Different medications, several forms of psychotherapy, and the combination of medication and therapy have been successful in alleviating the debilitating symptoms of depression. As many as 80 percent of persons with depression are likely to show improvement if they are diagnosed and treated properly (Leshner, 1992).

Unfortunately, a survey by the National Institute of Mental Health revealed that only one-third of individuals with depression in the United States receive any professional help for their disorder. Approximately three-fourths of the depressed individuals said they would just live with their depression until the disorder passes. Some people with depression take the unwise course of self-treating their symptoms by abusing drugs or alcohol.

Why do so many people with depression go untreated? The reasons include the public's poor understanding of depression's nature and the probability of successful treatment; stigmatization of the disorder, which makes many depressed individuals unwilling to seek treatment and makes family members and associates perceive depressed individuals as lazy or having a flawed character;

Depression

Instructions

To the right is a list of the ways you might have felt or behaved in the *last week*. Indicate what you felt by putting an X in the appropriate box for each item.

Turn to the end of the chapter to interpret your responses.

Items	Rarely or None of the Time (Less Than 1 Day)	Some or a Little of the Time (1–2 Days)	Occasionally or a Moderate Amount of the Time (3–4 Days)	Most or All of the Time (5–7 Days)
During the past week:				
1. I was bothered by things that usually don't bother me.	☐	☐	☐	☐
2. I did not feel like eating; my appetite was poor.	☐	☐	☐	☐
3. I felt that I could not shake off the blues even with help from my family and friends.	☐	☐	☐	☐
4. I felt that I was just as good as other people.	☐	☐	☐	☐
5. I had trouble keeping my mind on what I was doing.	☐	☐	☐	☐
6. I felt depressed.	☐	☐	☐	☐
7. I felt that everything I did was an effort.	☐	☐	☐	☐
8. I felt hopeful about the future.	☐	☐	☐	☐
9. I thought my life had been a failure.	☐	☐	☐	☐
10. I felt fearful.	☐	☐	☐	☐
11. My sleep was restless.	☐	☐	☐	☐
12. I was happy.	☐	☐	☐	☐
13. I talked less than usual.	☐	☐	☐	☐
14. I felt lonely.	☐	☐	☐	☐
15. People were unfriendly.	☐	☐	☐	☐
16. I enjoyed life.	☐	☐	☐	☐
17. I had crying spells.	☐	☐	☐	☐
18. I felt sad.	☐	☐	☐	☐
19. I felt that people disliked me.	☐	☐	☐	☐
20. I could not get going.	☐	☐	☐	☐

and the failure of many health professionals and physicians to recognize and diagnose depression in clients, which is an essential step for appropriate referral or treatment.

To help remedy the dilemma of so many depressed individuals going undiagnosed and untreated, in 1986 the National Institute of Mental Health began a national campaign to educate the general public, as well as health professionals, about the nature of depression and its treatment. The campaign is called the NIMH Depression Awareness, Recognition, and Treatment (D/ART) program. As part of this campaign, NIMH has developed and distributed a wide array of educational materials and has worked with local and national groups to encourage better public and professional understanding of depression.

A recent thrust of the D/ART campaign is to focus on the workplace as a key site for recognizing depression and providing referral and treatment through employee assistance plans. Employers have been receptive to the D/ART workplace program because they recognize the extensive toll that depression takes in absenteeism and reduced productivity.

You can obtain more information about the nature, diagnosis, and treatment of depression by writing:

Depression/USA
Rockville, MD 20857

How at risk are you for depression? The Self-Assessment box provides a screening experience to estimate how severe your mood has been in the last week.

Schizophrenic Disorders

Schizophrenia produces a bizarre set of symptoms and wreaks havoc on an individual's personality. **Schizophrenic disorders** *are severe psychological disorders characterized by distorted thoughts and perceptions, odd communication, inappropriate emotion, abnormal motor behavior, and social withdrawal. The term* schizophrenia *comes from the Latin words* schizo, *meaning "split," and* phrenia, *meaning "mind." The individual's mind is split from reality, and his or her personality loses its unity.* Schizophrenia is not the same as multiple personality, which sometimes is called a "split personality." Schizophrenia involves the split of *one* personality from reality, not the coexistence of several personalities within one individual.

Characteristics of Schizophrenic Disorders

Bob began to miss work. He spent his time watching his house from a rental car parked inconspicuously down the street and following his fellow employees as they left work to see where they went and what they did. He kept a little black book, in which he scribbled cryptic notes. When he went to the water cooler at work, he pretended to drink but, instead, looked carefully around the room to observe if anyone seemed guilty or frightened.

Bob's world seemed to be closing in on him. After an explosive scene at the office one day, he became very agitated. He left and never returned. By the time Bob arrived at home, he was in a rage. He could not sleep that night, and the next day he kept his children home from school; all day he kept the shades pulled on every window. The next night, he maintained his vigil. At 4 A.M., he armed himself and burst out of the house, firing shots in the air while daring his enemies to come out (McNeil, 1967).

Bob is a paranoid schizophrenic. About 1 in every 100 Americans will be classified as schizophrenic in their lifetime. Schizophrenic disorders are serious, debilitating mental disorders. About one-half of all mental hospital patients in the United States are schizophrenics. More now than in the past, schizophrenics live in society and periodically return for treatment at mental hospitals (Kane & Barnes, 1995). Drug therapy, which will be discussed in the next chapter, is primarily responsible for fewer schizophrenics being hospitalized. About one-third of all schizophrenics get better, about one-third get worse, and another third stay about the same once they develop this severe mental disorder.

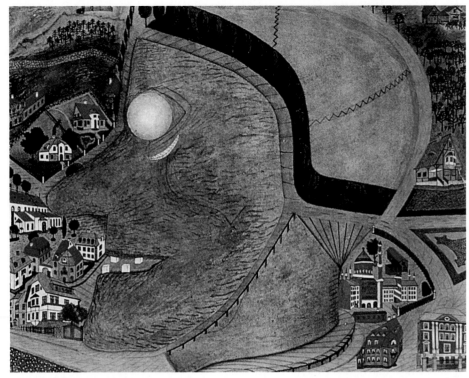

FIGURE 14.4

A Painting by a Schizophrenic
This painting is named *Landscape* and it is by August Neter. He was a successful nineteenth-century electrical engineer until he became schizophrenic in 1907. He lost interest in his work as an engineer as his mind deteriorated.

What symptoms do these individuals have? Many schizophrenics have *delusions,* or false beliefs—one individual may think he is Jesus Christ, another Napoleon, for example. The delusions are utterly implausible. One individual may think her thoughts are being broadcast over the radio; another may think that a double agent is controlling her every move. Schizophrenics also may hear, see, feel, smell, and taste things that are not there. These *hallucinations* often take the form of voices. The schizophrenic might think he hears two people talking about him, for example. On another occasion, he might say, "Hear that rumbling in the pipe? That is one of my men in there watching out for me."

Often schizophrenics do not make sense when they talk or write. Their language does not follow any rules. For example, one schizophrenic might say, "Well, Rocky, babe, help is out, happening, but where, when, up, top, side, over, you know, out of the way, that's it. Sign off." Such speech has no meaning to the listener. These incoherent, loose word associations are called *word salad.* As shown in figure 14.4, schizophrenics' paintings also have a bizarre quality.

A schizophrenic's motor behavior may be bizarre, sometimes taking the form of an odd appearance, pacing, statuelike postures, or strange mannerisms. Some schizophrenics withdraw from their social world; they become so insulated from others that they seem totally absorbed in interior images and thoughts.

He raves; his words are loose as heaps of sand, and scattered from sense. So high he's mounted on his airy throne, that now the wind has got into his head, and turns his brain to frenzy.

—John Dryden

FIGURE 14.5

A Catatonic Schizophrenic
Disturbances in motor behavior are prominent symptoms in catatonic schizophrenia. Individuals may cease to move altogether, sometimes taking on bizarre postures.

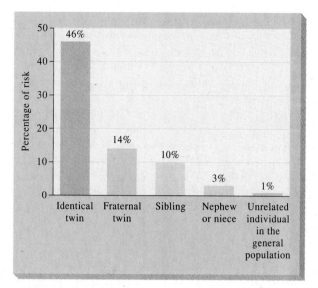

FIGURE 14.6

Lifetime Risk of Becoming Schizophrenic According to Genetic Relatedness
As your genetic relatedness to an individual with schizophrenia increases, so does your risk of becoming schizophrenic.

Forms of Schizophrenic Disorders

Schizophrenic disorders appear in four main forms: disorganized, catatonic, paranoid, and undifferentiated schizophrenia.

Disorganized schizophrenia *is a schizophrenic disorder in which an individual has delusions and hallucinations that have little or no recognizable meaning—hence, the label* disorganized. A disorganized schizophrenic withdraws from human contact and might regress to silly, childlike gestures and behavior. Many of these individuals were isolated or maladjusted during adolescence.

Catatonic schizophrenia *is a schizophrenic disorder characterized by bizarre motor behavior, which sometimes takes the form of a completely immobile stupor* (see figure 14.5). Even in this stupor, catatonic schizophrenics are completely conscious of what is happening around them. An individual in a catatonic state sometimes shows *waxy flexibility;* for example, if the person's arm is raised and then allowed to fall, the arm stays in the new position.

Paranoid schizophrenia *is a schizophrenic disorder characterized by delusions of reference, grandeur, and persecution.* The delusions usually form a complex, elaborate system based on a complete misinterpretation of actual events. It is not unusual for schizophrenics to develop all three delusions in the following order. First, they sense they are special and have been singled out for attention (delusions of reference). Individuals with delusions of reference misinterpret chance events as being directly relevant to their own lives—a thunderstorm, for example, might be perceived as a personal message from God. Second, they believe that this special attention is the result of their admirable and special characteristics (delusions of grandeur). Individuals with delusions of grandeur think of themselves as exalted beings—the pope or the president, for example. Third, they think that others are so jealous and threatened by these characteristics that they spy and plot against them (delusions of persecution). Individuals with delusions of persecution feel they are the target of a conspiracy—for example, recall Bob's situation described earlier.

Undifferentiated schizophrenia *is a schizophrenic disorder characterized by disorganized behavior, hallucinations, delusions, and incoherence.* This category of schizophrenia is used when an individual's symptoms either don't meet the criteria for the other types or they meet the criteria for more than one of the other types.

Causes of Schizophrenia

Schizophrenic disorders may be caused by genetic and biological factors, as well as environmental and sociocultural factors.

Genetic Factors If you have a relative with schizophrenia, what are the chances you will develop schizophrenia? It depends on how closely you are related. As genetic similarity increases, so does your risk of becoming schizophrenic (Pritchard, 1996; Sasaki & Kennedy, 1995). As shown in figure 14.6, an identical twin of a schizophrenic has a 46 percent chance of developing the disorder, a fraternal twin 14 percent, a sibling 10 percent, a nephew or niece 3 percent, and an unrelated individual in the general population 1 percent (Gottesman & Shields, 1982). Such data strongly suggest that genetic factors are involved in schizophrenia, although the precise nature of the genetic influence is unknown.

Neurobiological Factors Many neuro-scientists believe that imbalances in brain chemistry, including deficits in brain metabolism, a malfunctioning dopamine system, and distorted cerebral blood flow, cause schizophrenia (Goldberg, Berman, & Weinberger, 1995). Imaging techniques, such as the PET scan, clearly show deficits in brain metabolism. Do these deficits cause the disorder or are they simply symptoms of a disorder whose true origin lies deeper in the brain, in the genes, or in the environment? Whether the neurobiological factors are the cause or the effect, information about them improves our knowledge of schizophrenia's nature. We do know that schizophrenics produce too much of the neurotransmitter dopamine. More about the dopamine system appears in the next chapter, where we will discuss the use of drugs to block excess dopamine production.

This wretched brain gave way,
And I became a wreck,
At random driven,
Without one glimpse of reason.
— **Thomas Moore**

Environmental Factors As scientists learn about schizophrenia's neurobiological basis, they must remember that schizophrenia, like all other behavior, does not occur in an environmental vacuum. Some researchers believe that environmental factors are important in schizophrenia; others believe that genetic factors outweigh environmental factors.

Stress is the environmental factor given the most attention in understanding schizophrenia. The **diathesis-stress view** *argues that a combination of environmental stress and biogenetic disposition causes schizophrenia.* A defective gene makeup may produce schizophrenia only when an individual lives in a stressful environment. Advocates of the diathesis-stress view emphasize the importance of stress reduction and family support in treating schizophrenia.

Sociocultural Factors Disorders of thought and emotion are common to schizophrenia in all cultures, but the type and incidence of schizophrenic disorders may vary from culture to culture. For example, one of the more puzzling results is that the admission rates to mental health facilities for schizophrenia are very high for Irish Catholics in the Republic of Ireland but not for Irish Catholics living elsewhere. One reason for this difference could be that the diagnostic criteria used in the Republic of Ireland are different from those used elsewhere, but this is not likely to be the complete answer. There are many areas of the world where the incidence of schizophrenia is considerably higher or lower than the worldwide incidence of just under 1 percent.

Rates of schizophrenia may also vary for different groups within a culture. For example, one study revealed that Blacks have higher rates of schizophrenia than Whites in both the United States and Great Britain (Bagley, 1984). In that study, Blacks had a significantly greater number of life crises that may have precipitated schizophrenic episodes. Also, the African Americans and African Britons who became schizophrenic had higher aspirations than those who did not. One explanation may be that their efforts to become assimilated into, and to achieve parity within, a mainstream society that is oppressively racist created considerable stress for them.

R E V I E W

Mood Disorders and Schizophrenic Disorders

The mood disorders are characterized by wide emotional swings, ranging from deeply depressed to highly euphoric and agitated. Depression can occur alone, as in major depression, or it can alternate with mania, as in bipolar disorder. Individuals with major depression are sad, demoralized, bored, and self-derogatory. They often do not feel well, lose stamina easily, have a poor appetite, and are listless and unmotivated. Depression is so widespread that it is called the "common cold" of mental disturbances.

Bipolar disorder is characterized by extreme mood swings; an individual with this disorder might be depressed, manic, or both. In the manic phase, individuals are exuberant, have tireless stamina, and have a tendency for excess. They also are restless, irritable, and in almost constant motion. The rate of suicide has increased dramatically in the United States. There is no simple answer to why individuals attempt suicide—immediate, earlier, biological, and cultural factors may be involved. Explanations of mood disorders come from psychoanalytic theory, cognitive and learning theories, biogenetic theories, and sociocultural theories.

Schizophrenic disorders are severe mental disorders characterized by distorted thoughts and perceptions, odd communication, inappropriate emotion, abnormal motor behavior, and social withdrawal. The individual's mind splits from reality, and the personality loses its unity. About 1 in 100 Americans becomes schizophrenic, and schizophrenia accounts for approximately one-half of all individuals in mental hospitals. Many schizophrenics have delusions, or false beliefs, and hallucinations. They often do not make sense when they talk or write. The schizophrenic's motor behavior may be bizarre, and the schizophrenic may withdraw from social relationships.

Schizophrenia appears in four main forms: disorganized, catatonic, paranoid, and undifferentiated. Proposed causes of schizophrenia include genetic and biological factors, as well as environmental factors. Many neuroscientists believe that imbalances in brain chemistry cause schizophrenia. The diathesis-stress model emphasizes both biogenetic and environmental stress. Cognitive and emotional disorders of thought are common in schizophrenia in all cultures, but the type and incidence of schizophrenic disorders may vary cross-culturally and across social classes.

We have seen that the mood disorders and the schizophrenic disorders are complex and often debilitating. Next you will read about an intriguing set of disorders involving personality.

Personality Disorders

Personality disorders *are psychological disorders that develop when personality traits become inflexible and, thus, maladaptive.* Individuals with these maladaptive traits often do not recognize that they have a problem and might show little interest in changing. Personality disorders are notoriously difficult to treat therapeutically (Livesley, 1995).

Although there are eleven distinct personality disorder diagnoses described in the DSM-IV, clinicians think of the disorders as "clustered" around dominant characteristics. One cluster of personality disorders involves odd or eccentric behaviors. A second cluster emphasizes fear and anxiety. And a third cluster stresses dramatic, emotional, or erratic behaviors. We will describe one or more representative disorders from each of the clusters to illustrate their features. The complete list of personality disorders appears in table 14.3.

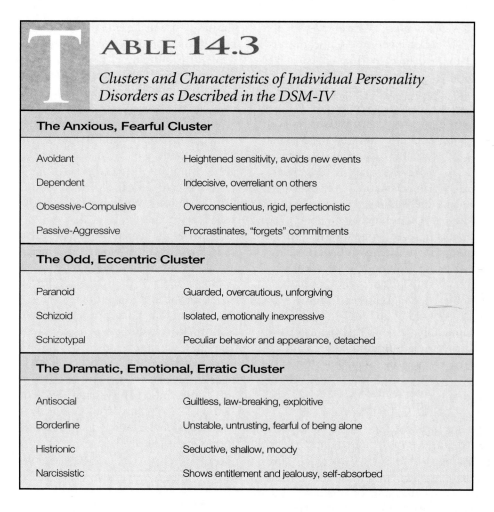

TABLE 14.3

Clusters and Characteristics of Individual Personality Disorders as Described in the DSM-IV

The Anxious, Fearful Cluster

Avoidant	Heightened sensitivity, avoids new events
Dependent	Indecisive, overreliant on others
Obsessive-Compulsive	Overconscientious, rigid, perfectionistic
Passive-Aggressive	Procrastinates, "forgets" commitments

The Odd, Eccentric Cluster

Paranoid	Guarded, overcautious, unforgiving
Schizoid	Isolated, emotionally inexpressive
Schizotypal	Peculiar behavior and appearance, detached

The Dramatic, Emotional, Erratic Cluster

Antisocial	Guiltless, law-breaking, exploitive
Borderline	Unstable, untrusting, fearful of being alone
Histrionic	Seductive, shallow, moody
Narcissistic	Shows entitlement and jealousy, self-absorbed

The Schizotypal Personality Disorder

Schizotypal personality disorder *is a personality disorder in the odd/eccentric cluster. Individuals with this disorder appear to be in contact with reality but many aspects of their behavior are distasteful, which leads others to reject or withdraw from them.* Individuals are likely to be diagnosed with this label based on their eccentric patterns. Consider Bruce. Although he was able to hold a job, he associated little with his co-workers. He strongly preferred to spend his breaks and time away from work with a sketchpad designing new flags for countries of the world. His geographic and political knowledge was impressive, but it was painful for him to engage in conversations with others. In contrast, when constructing new flags, he hummed and talked to himself.

Obsessive-Compulsive Personality Disorder

Obsessive-compulsive personality disorder *is in the anxious, fearful cluster of personality disorders. Anxious adjustment is*

its primary feature. Individuals with this personality disorder tend to be exacting, precise, and orderly. They generate discomfort in others by requiring the same precision from others. They pay attention to each detail as a means of warding off anxiety. Individuals who show obsessive-compulsive style often are successfully adjusted to positions that require careful execution of details. For instance, Alex is a policeman in charge of preparing and maintaining evidence for trials. He repeatedly checks his files for completeness and order. Although well respected for the quality of his work by his fellow officers, he becomes enraged when they alter his meticulous organization.

Borderline Personality Disorder

Borderline personality disorder *is in the dramatic, emotional, erratic cluster of personality disorders.* Consider Pam, who never could manage to keep a college roommate. Each relationship would start off with a promise. Pam spoke enthusiastically about each new prospect as being

"different from all the others." She bought them presents and almost courted their friendship. However, within a few weeks she would wildly criticize a new roommate for her poor hygiene, her preference for "low-life" acquaintances, and her impossible housekeeping skills. In desperation, she would threaten to kill herself if someone more caring and sensitive were not assigned to her immediately. Individuals with borderline tendencies often view the world as neatly divided into good and bad features. Their tolerance of frustration is very limited, as is their capacity to trust others (Goldstein, 1995). These individuals use dramatic, attention-seeking acts as a means of controlling others (Horwitz & others, 1996).

Antisocial Personality Disorder

Antisocial personality disorder *is also in the dramatic, emotional, erratic cluster of personality disorders. It is the most problematic personality disorder for society. These individuals (who used to be called psychopaths or sociopaths) regularly violate* *the rights of others.* Individuals with antisocial personality disorder often resort to crime, violence, and delinquency. This disorder begins before the age of 15 and continues into adulthood; it is much more typical of males than of females. Consider Martin, who shows many of the behaviors typical of adults with antisocial personality. He cannot maintain a consistent work record. He steals, harasses others, rarely plans ahead, and fails to meet his financial obligations. He repeatedly gets into fights and shows little remorse when he has harmed someone. Tiffany also demonstrates many antisocial characteristics already in high school: truancy, school suspension, running away from home, stealing, vandalism, drug use, sexual acting-out, and violation of rules at home and school. Such behaviors are commonplace among young adults afflicted with antisocial personality disorder.

The Controversy About Personality Disorders

The general category of personality disorders is perhaps the most controversial of the diagnostic areas in the DSM-IV. Many scholars believe that we should not regard challenging personality styles as equivalent to other diagnostic categories that may have a clearer medical origin. Some have suggested that personality disorders represent a "wastebasket diagnosis": any individual whose problems do not fit into a more precise diagnosis may end up labeled with a personality disorder. Finally, some scholars (Landrine, 1989) believe that personality disorders might serve as political conveniences to dismiss those whose behavior is troublesome, confusing, or irritating.

Substance-Use Disorders

A problem associated with drug use is called a **substance-use disorder,** *which is characterized by one or more of the following features: (1) a pattern of pathological use that involves frequent intoxication, a need for daily use, and an inability to control use—in a sense, psychological dependence; (2) a significant impairment of social or occupational functioning attributed to the drug use; and (3) physical dependence that involves serious withdrawal problems.*

The use of drugs, which will be described in chapter 16, can lead to a substance-use disorder. Alcohol, barbiturates, and opium derivatives all are capable of producing either physical or psychological dependence. Alcoholism is an especially widespread substance-use disorder; it has been estimated that 6 to 8 million Americans are alcoholics. Although substantial numbers of women abuse alcohol, more men than women are alcoholics. Among African Americans, the male-female alcoholic ratio is 3 to 2; among White Americans, the ratio is approximately 4 to 1.

Many individuals are surprised to learn that substantial numbers of women are alcoholics or abusers of other drugs. Although most of the research on drug abuse has been directed toward males, studies have found that females are just as likely to be treated for drug-related problems in emergency rooms. Without a more intense research effort directed at female drug abusers, the unique facets of their drug abuse will go uncharted. For both male and female drug abusers, biogenetic, psychological, and sociocultural factors may all be involved.

LEGAL ASPECTS OF MENTAL DISORDERS

The legal status of individuals with mental disorders raises a number of controversial issues: What is involved in committing disordered and dangerous individuals to mental institutions? What is the status of using the insanity defense for capital crimes? How does "guilty but insane" differ from competence to stand trial? We will consider each of these issues in turn.

Commitment and Dangerousness

Having a mental disorder in itself is not adequate grounds for placing individuals in mental institutions against their will. However, the behavior of some mentally disordered individuals is so severe that they are a threat to themselves and/or to others, and they may need protective confinement. Although procedures vary somewhat from state to state, certain conditions usually must be present before the state can formally commit persons to a mental institution: The persons must have a mental disorder and must be

dangerous either to themselves or to other people. Dangerousness judgments in the absence of criminal involvement may depend on a demonstrated inability to take care of one's daily physical needs.

Commitment, *the process by which an individual becomes institutionalized in a mental hospital,* can be voluntary or involuntary. Some individuals commit themselves, recognizing that their behavior is potentially dangerous or incompetent. However, the state commits others on an involuntary basis through judicial proceedings. **Civil commitment** *transpires when a judge deems an individual to be a risk to self or others as a function of mental disorder.* A civic commitment proceeding often involves psychiatric evaluation and a formal judicial hearing. The judge must conclude that the evidence is "clear and convincing," based on a 1979 precedent (*Addington v. Texas*), or they cannot order hospitalization.

Determining whether a mentally disordered individual is dangerous is not easy, even for mental health professionals. Nonetheless, there are times when professionals have to make dangerousness judgments (Slobogian, 1996). Recent court decisions have held mental health professionals liable when unconfined clients they were treating have caused harm to others. Legal precedents require therapists to warn potential victims if their patients threaten to kill someone.

Criminal Responsibility

Criminal commitment *occurs when a mental disorder is implicated in the commission of a crime.* Procedures may ensure that the individual receives mental health care as an inpatient in a mental health hospital rather than imprisonment. Two areas in which psychologists make decisions about criminal responsibility include the insanity defense and the determination of competence to stand trial. We will examine each of these challenges in turn.

The Insanity Defense

Insanity is a legal term, not a psychological term. A legally insane person is considered mentally disordered and incapable of being responsible for his or her actions. The **insanity defense** is a plea of "innocent by reason of insanity" used as a legal defense

Two famous cases involving the insanity plea resulted in different outcomes. Before his murder in 1994, Jeffrey Dahmer's insanity defense for murder and cannibalism was unsuccessful. In contrast, a jury found Lorena Bobbitt "innocent by reason of insanity" in her sexual assault on her husband.

in criminal trials. In our culture, guilt implies responsibility and intent—to be guilty of a crime, an individual has to have knowingly and intentionally committed it. The jury determines whether the defendant is guilty, based on such legally defined criteria. Controversy swirls about the concept of insanity because of concerns that criminals will unfairly use this plea to avoid prosecution.

In recent years, two publicized cases employing the insanity defense have led to different outcomes. Jeffrey Dahmer's attorneys were unable to persuade the jury in 1992 that his murdering and ritualized cannibalism of fifteen young men resulted from insanity. The prosecution pointed to his skilled execution and coverup of the crimes as evidence that he was rational and should be held responsible. The jury found Dahmer guilty and sane at the time he committed the crimes and ordered him to serve fifteen life terms without parole. In 1994, Dahmer was murdered by another inmate.

In a contrasting example from 1994, Lorena Bobbitt's attorneys were successful in employing the insanity plea. Lorena Bobbitt claimed that she had suffered years of physical and sexual abuse from her husband, John. According to her defense attorneys, after one particularly abusive episode with her husband, she experienced an irresistible impulse.

She waited for her husband to fall asleep. Then she cut off his penis, drove away from the house, and threw his penis out of the car window. Although her trial was controversial, the jury found her "guilty, but insane" at the time she committed the crime. After several weeks of confinement in a mental hospital, Lorena Bobbitt was able to return to the community.

The appropriateness of the insanity plea remains highly controversial (Perlin, 1996; Slovenko, 1995). Successful insanity defense is relatively rare because juries struggle with applying the legal criteria to complex situations. Some experts recommend changes in the defense, arguing that the courts should establish whether or not the defendant committed the crime, independently of establishing the defendant's sanity status. Many states have moved to adopt this approach. In addition, the Supreme Court reviewed a case in 1994 that opened the opportunity for states to revisit their insanity plea practices.

Determining Competency

Competency *is an individual's ability to understand and participate in a judicial proceeding.* Competent individuals can consult with a lawyer and ask questions about the proceedings. Individuals whom the courts deem competent to stand trial may still plead that they were "guilty, but insane" at the time they committed the offenses. Individuals deemed incompetent to stand trial may be remanded to institutional care at the discretion of a judge who has evaluated the testimony of expert witnesses and other evidence pertinent to the individual's current state of mind. To reflect on your own position regarding the insanity plea, see Critical Thinking.

CRITICAL THINKING

Evaluating the Insanity Plea

Where do your sympathies lie on the appropriateness of the insanity plea? Is the insanity plea a helpful legal procedure to insure mental health care for those who clearly need the help? Or is the insanity plea an insurance policy for those who can neatly sidestep imprisonment through skillful legal defense? Which side do you favor? How energetically would you advocate for changes in the insanity plea defense? What values underlie your position?

Your exploration of this controversial issue encourages you to *identify underlying values that motivate behavior* and challenge assumptions that influence behavior.

*Personality Disorders,
Substance-Use Disorders,
and the Legal Aspects
of Mental Disorders*

Personality disorders are psychological disorders that develop when personality traits become inflexible and, thus, maladaptive. Individuals with a personality disorder often do not recognize that they have a problem and show little interest in changing their behavior. Three clusters of personality disorders are the anxious, fearful cluster; the odd, eccentric cluster; and the dramatic, emotional, erratic cluster. The schizotypal personality is in the odd, eccentric cluster; obsessive-compulsive personality disorder is in the anxious, fearful cluster; borderline personality disorder and antisocial personality disorder are in the dramatic, emotional, erratic cluster. Personality disorders are a controversial category of mental disorders.

A substance-use disorder is characterized by one or more of the following features: (1) a pattern of pathological use that involves frequent intoxication, a need for daily use, and an inability to control use—in the sense of psychological dependence; (2) a significant impairment of social or occupational functioning, attributed to the drug use; and (3) physical dependence that involves serious withdrawal problems.

The legal status of individuals with mental disorders raises a number of controversial issues: commitment and dangerousness, criminal responsibility, the insanity defense, and determining competence.

CRITICAL THINKING ABOUT ADJUSTMENT

Mental Disorders, Biology, and Social Class

A classic study in the 1950s showed that schizophrenia appears to have a "downward drift" according to socioeconomic class (Hollingshead & Redlich, 1958). Studying institutionalization patterns across multiple hospitals, the researchers suggested that being a member of a lower socioeconomic class enhances your risk of schizophrenia in your lifetime.

The usual degree of risk cited for schizophrenia is close to 1 percent, meaning that 1 out of every 100 individuals in the culture will become schizophrenic. However, a number of factors appear to be related to increasing the risk for schizophrenia. Although the presence of these factors does not guarantee the development of schizophrenia, they enhance the risk for the individual with these characteristics.

We can find a good example of increased risk in genetic studies (Gottesman & Shields, 1982). Blood relation to a diagnosed schizophrenic increases risk. Your risk of schizophrenia increases from 1.0 percent to 4.4 percent if you have a schizophrenic parent, to 13.7 percent if your fraternal twin has schizophrenia, and to 46.0 percent if your identical twin has schizophrenia. Thus, biological factors contribute to risk in substantial ways but do not completely account for the development of schizophrenia. If they did, we would expect that identical twins would virtually always avoid or succumb to schizophrenia together.

If living in lower socioeconomic classes does seem to enhance risk, can you identify possible variables that could account for this explanation? What specific factors might account for risk that can be more directly linked to the limited resources families have in lower socioeconomic existence?

One longitudinal study identified many "markers" for increased schizophrenic risk (Watt, 1984). These included

- low birthweight and challenging birth conditions
- absence of a close relationship with the mother early in life
- underdeveloped infant motor coordination
- being raised in an institution or foster home
- underdeveloped intelligence skills, particularly verbal skills
- distractibility and attention problems
- aggressiveness and anger
- confusing parent-child communication

Did you think of other variables that could be associated with lower socioeconomic conditions?

Despite the restrictions that lower-class existence can impose on a person's ability to cope with life's stressors, there are, nonetheless, some individuals from lower-class backgrounds who develop considerable resourcefulness and resilience.

When supposed ethnic differences in schizophrenia are examined in the context of socioeconomic status—comparing African Americans, Latinos, and Whites, for example—the ethnic differences tend to vanish. Thus, it seems that poverty and the living conditions poverty engenders are much more likely to be associated with schizophrenia than is ethnicity. This research serves as a powerful reminder to *pursue alternative explanations to explain behavior comprehensively.*

In this chapter we explored the nature of abnormal psychology, beginning with an evaluation of the dimensions of abnormality. We defined abnormality, studied the origins of abnormal behavior, read about prevalence estimates of disorders, and learned about how mental disorders are classified. Then we spent considerable time exploring the diagnostic categories of mental disorders: anxiety, somatoform, dissociative, mood, schizophrenic, personality, and substance-use. Next, we read about the legal aspects of mental disorders, especially the concepts of commitment and dangerousness, as well as criminal responsibility. Don't forget that you can obtain an overall summary of the chapter by again reading the in-chapter reviews on pages 342, 348, 356, and 360.

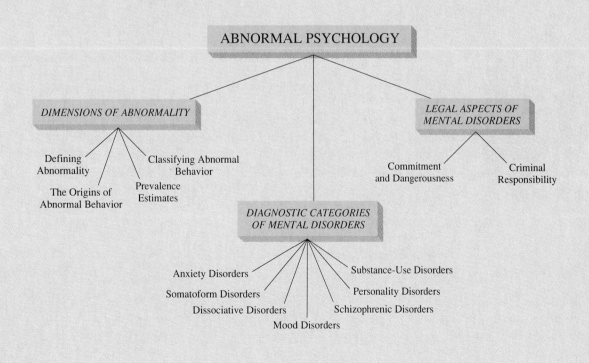

ABNORMAL PSYCHOLOGY

DIMENSIONS OF ABNORMALITY

Defining Abnormality

The Origins of Abnormal Behavior

Classifying Abnormal Behavior

Prevalence Estimates

DIAGNOSTIC CATEGORIES OF MENTAL DISORDERS

Anxiety Disorders

Somatoform Disorders

Dissociative Disorders

Mood Disorders

Schizophrenic Disorders

Personality Disorders

Substance-Use Disorders

LEGAL ASPECTS OF MENTAL DISORDERS

Commitment and Dangerousness

Criminal Responsibility

KEY TERMS

PRACTICAL KNOWLEDGE ABOUT ADJUSTMENT

DON'T PANIC

(1986) by Reid Wilson. New York: Harper-Perennial.

Wilson describes a self-help program for coping with panic attacks. The book describes what panic attacks are like, how it feels when you are undergoing one, and what type of people are prone to having panic attacks. It gives advice on how to sort through the physical and psychological aspects of panic attacks. You also learn how to conquer panic attacks, especially through self-monitoring. Specific recommendations are made about the effective use of breathing exercises, focused thinking, mental imagery, and deep muscle relaxation.

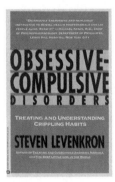

OBSESSIVE-COMPULSIVE DISORDERS

(1991) by Steven Levenkron. New York: Warner Books.

Levenkron believes that obsessive-compulsive disorder is the personality's attempt to reduce anxiety, which may stem from a painful childhood or a genetic tendency toward anxiety. Levenkron developed therapy techniques to help people who suffer from this disorder that include the help and support of parents, teachers, physicians, and friends. The book includes many case histories to illustrate the problems people who have obsessive-compulsive disorder encounter and how they can overcome their problem. Levenkron argues that people can reduce or eliminate their obsessions and compulsions if they follow four basic steps: (1) Rely on a family member or a therapist for support and comfort, (2) unmask their rituals, (3) talk in depth to trusted family members or a therapist, and (4) control their anxiety.

SELF-ASSESSMENT SCORING AND INTERPRETATION

FEAR

Scoring

To score the test, add up your answers to each of the questions. Scores range from 51 to 357.

Interpretation

Higher scores indicate higher levels of fear. The average college student scores slightly more than 100 on the test, with women scoring slightly higher than men.

DEPRESSION

Scoring

After completing the Depression Scale, use the chart below to assign points to your answers. Add up all the points.

Interpretation

If your score is around 7, then you are like the average male in terms of how much depression you experienced in the last week. If your score is around 8–9, then your score is similar to how much depression the average female experienced in the last week. If your score is 16 or more, you might benefit from professional help for the depression you have been experiencing.

During the past week:		Rarely or None of the Time (Less Than 1 Day)	Some or a Little of the Time (1–2 Days)	Occasionally or a Moderate Amount of the Time (3–4 Days)	Most or All of the Time (5–7 Days)
1.	I was bothered by things that usually don't bother me.	1.	0	1	2	3
2.	I did not feel like eating; my appetite was poor.	2.	0	1	2	3
3.	I felt that I could not shake off the blues even with help from my family and friends.	3.	0	1	2	3
4.	I felt that I was just as good as other people.	4.	3	2	1	0
5.	I had trouble keeping my mind on what I was doing.	5.	0	1	3	3
6.	I felt depressed.	6.	0	1	2	3
7.	I felt that everything I did was an effort.	7.	0	1	2	3
8.	I felt hopeful about the future.	8.	3	2	1	0
9.	I thought my life had been a failure.	9.	0	1	2	3
10.	I felt fearful.	10.	0	1	2	3
11.	My sleep was restless.	11.	0	1	2	3
12.	I was happy.	12.	3	2	1	0
13.	I talked less than usual.	13.	0	1	2	3
14.	I felt lonely.	14.	0	1	2	3
15.	People were unfriendly.	15.	0	1	2	3
16.	I enjoyed life.	16.	3	2	1	0
17.	I had crying spells.	17.	0	1	2	3
18.	I felt sad.	18.	0	1	2	3
19.	I felt that people disliked me.	19.	0	1	2	3
20.	I could not "get going."	20.	0	1	2	3

Total Number of Points: _____

John Santrock
In Search of More Insight, detail

Therapies

Nothing can be changed until it is faced.

—James Baldwin

THE STORY OF SUSANNA KAYSEN: A PERILOUS JOURNEY

Etiology

This person is (pick one):

1. on a perilous journey from which we can learn much when he or she returns;
2. possessed by (pick one):
   a) the gods,
   b) God (that is, a prophet)
   c) some bad spirits, demons, or devils,
   d) the Devil;
3. a witch;
4. bewitched (variant of 2);
5. bad, and must be isolated and punished;

6. ill, and must be isolated and treated by (pick one):
   a) purging and leeches,
   b) removing the uterus if the person has one,
   c) electric shock to the brain,
   d) cold stress sheets wrapped tight around the body,
   e) Thorazine or Stelazine;
7. ill, and must spend the next seven years talking about it;
8. a victim of society's low tolerance for deviant behavior;
9. sane in an insane world;
10. on a perilous journey from which he or she may never return. (Susanna Kaysen, *Girl, Interrupted*, p. 15)

Susanna Kaysen's autobiography about her own struggle with disordered behavior offers some provocative insights about the challenge of treating mental disorder. Diagnosed as having a borderline personality disorder with major depression, Kaysen chronicled her journey through a maze of psychotherapeutic treatments. Ultimately she achieved a greater sense of independence and stability, although she herself was uncertain about what aspects of her care helped her improve.

PREVIEW

Many people today seek therapy as a natural part of adjustment. Some, like Susanna Kaysen, find themselves in the immobilizing grip of depression and fear. Others may need help in overcoming trauma, such as physical or sexual abuse in childhood. And others simply want to gain insight about themselves and improve their lives. Whatever the reasons why people seek therapy, there are many different therapies to help them—one count listed more than 450 variations. In this chapter, we begin by exploring the nature of psychotherapy in its earliest recorded forms and in current practice. We will examine both individual therapies and therapies for systems, including groups, families, and even communities. Next, we evaluate the important question of whether psychotherapy is effective, especially from the sociocultural perspective. We conclude with an overview of biomedical therapies.

THE NATURE OF THERAPY

It would be difficult to pinpoint exactly when, historically, some people were first designated as healers to help others with disordered thoughts, emotions, and behavior. However, it is clear today that not only is therapy an acceptable avenue for resolving personal challenges and mental problems, it has become a thriving enterprise. Contemporary practitioners come from a variety of backgrounds and work with an astonishing array of problems with individuals, groups, and communities (Humphreys, 1996). We will first examine the historical underpinnings of modern psychotherapeutic interventions.

As we study the origins of modern therapy, keep in mind that our knowledge about the causes and treatment of disorder is far more sophisticated than that of our ancestors. By the same token, our descendants' knowledge may show many of our own beliefs and practices to be foolish or harmful. The shifts in perspective through the years regarding dysfunction, as well as the durability of some beliefs, underscore the importance of context in influencing judgments about what constitutes normal and disordered behavior.

Historical Viewpoint

In ancient societies it was believed that abnormal behavior had both mystical and organic origins. In many cultures, disordered behavior represented possession by a spirit residing in the afflicted person. When evil spirits were deemed responsible, the authorities imposed **trephining,** *a procedure that involved chipping a hole in the skull to allow the evil spirit to escape* (see figure 15.1). In some other cultures, behavior disorder was interpreted as a sign that nature was out of balance. Such individuals might be granted special privilege, rather than treatment designed to bring them back within the bounds of expected behavior.

In the fourth century B.C., Hippocrates, a Greek physician, proposed that mental problems and disordered

FIGURE 15.1

Trephining

The technique of trephining involved chipping a hole in the skull through which an evil spirit, believed to be the source of the person's abnormal behavior, might escape. The fact that some people actually survived the operation is shown by this skull. The bone had had time to heal considerably before the individual died.

behavior resulted from brain damage or an imbalance of body chemicals. He prescribed rest, exercise, a bland diet, and abstinence from sex and alcohol as cures for depressed mood. Unfortunately, Hippocrates' theories lost their influence.

In the Middle Ages there was a resurgence of the belief that spiritual possession was the cause of disorder. Many of those who were identified as "different" probably suffered from neurological disorders, such as epilepsy or Tourette's syndrome, a disease that involves repetitive motor and vocal tics. Many of the unfortunates, whom the authorities deemed possessed by evil spirits, were labeled as witches. **Exorcism,** *a religious rite that involved prayer, starvation, beatings, and various forms of torture,* became a popular intervention to cast out the evil spirits. Exorcisms that involved particularly harsh practices were intended to

make the disordered individuals so physically uncomfortable that no evil spirit would remain in their bodies. If that didn't work, the only "cure" left was to destroy the body. From the fourteenth through the seventeenth century, 200,000 to 500,000 people thought to be witches were hanged or burned at the stake. Some historians have pointed out that women were usually the victims and that the pursuit of witches seemed to intensify during periods of economic turmoil. To explore why trephining was so widely used, turn to Critical Thinking.

During the Renaissance, the authorities built *asylums* ("sanctuaries") to house the mentally disordered. They probably intended both to provide protection for those who were incapable and to create some clear physical boundaries between normally functioning persons and those who were disordered. However, the

asylums were not much better than exorcisms; the inmates often were chained to walls, caged, or fed sparingly.

Fortunately, Philippe Pinel (1745–1826), the head physician at a large asylum in Paris, initiated a significant change in the treatment of the mentally disordered, whom Pinel described as ordinary people who could not reason well because of their serious personal problems. He believed that treating the mentally disabled like animals not only was inhumane but also hindered their recovery. Pinel convinced the French government to unchain large numbers of patients, some of whom had not been outside of the asylum for 30 to 40 years (see figure 15.2). He replaced the dungeons with bright rooms and spent long hours talking with patients, listening to their problems, and giving advice.

Although Pinel's efforts led to reform, it was slow. Even as late as the nineteenth century in the United States, the mentally disordered were kept alongside criminals in prisons. Dorothea Dix, a nurse who had taken a position at a prison in the middle of the nineteenth century, was instrumental in getting the mentally disabled separated from criminals. She embarked on a state-to-state campaign to upgrade prisons and persuaded officials to use better judgment in deciding which individuals should be placed in prisons. State governments began building large asylums for the mentally disabled because of Dix's efforts, although the conditions in the asylums often were no better than in the prisons.

Although we have made significant advances in the twentieth century in the ways that we view and treat the mentally disordered, we are far from resolving all the problems associated with their care. As you will read later in this chapter, our prevailing attitudes in the United States toward mental disorder have contributed substantially to the problem of homelessness. Our technological sophistication has also rendered us more resistant to non-Western explanations of behavior disorder. For example, many cultural and ethnic traditions maintain beliefs that possession can be a source of disorder, which most Western therapists reject.

You may have been repulsed when you examined the image of the trephined skull in figure 15.1. Imagine having to undergo such an invasive procedure in technologically primitive conditions to resolve your disordered thoughts and feelings. Yet there are many possibilities for how the procedure of trephining could have successfully reduced disordered behavior. Can you develop any plausible psychological explanations based on reasoning to identify why trephining could have been successful in reducing disordered behavior?

The threat of undergoing such a severe procedure (without anesthetic) might have reduced disordered behavior through negative reinforcement. The attention one gained by undergoing this procedure might also have addressed some needs underlying the disorder. The recipient's own expectation that the procedure would help might have produced different behavior. Some individuals in particular cultural traditions believed that the procedure might release the individual from the grip of spirits. Of course, many trephined patients were unlikely to survive the operation, so disordered behavior was automatically reduced when the patient died. Were you able to identify any of these explanations? On-target explanations demonstrate your ability to *make careful interpretations from evidence about behavior.*

FIGURE 15.2

Pinel Unchaining Mentally Disabled Individuals
In this painting, Pinel is shown unchaining the inmates at La Bicetre Hospital. Pinel's efforts led to widespread reform and more humane treatment of mentally disabled individuals.

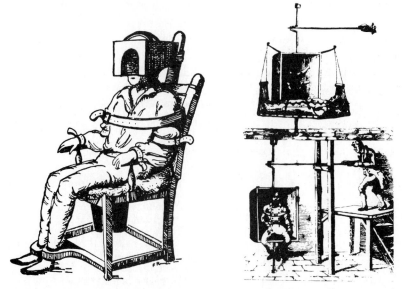

Even after Pinel and others reformed mental institutions, some rather strange techniques were invented to control the most difficult mentally disabled individuals. The tranquilizing chair (*left*) and circulating swing (*right*) were used to calm mentally disabled individuals at the beginning of the nineteenth century. Fortunately, their use soon diminished.

The quest for improved methods, the concern for preventing mental disorder, and the recognition of the importance of humane treatment is not just the province of Western psychology. In our discussion of the nature of psychotherapy, we will emphasize practices in the United States, but we will also examine some therapeutic practices in other cultures (which we will return to later in the chapter).

Current Practice

Psychotherapy *is the process of working with individuals to reduce their emotional problems and improve their adjustment.* Mental health professionals help individuals recognize, define, and overcome personal and interpersonal difficulties. Psychotherapists use a number of strategies to accomplish these goals: talking, interpreting, listening, rewarding, and modeling, for example. Psychotherapy *does not* include biomedical treatment, such as drugs or surgery.

Orientations

The theories of personality discussed in chapter 2 are the basis for a number of important approaches to psychotherapy, which can generally be distinguished as *insight* or *action* therapies. **Insight therapy** *encourages insight into and awareness of oneself as the critical focus of therapy.*

Action therapy *promotes direct changes in behavior; insight is not essential for change to occur.* Psychodynamic therapies, based on the psychoanalytic theories of Freud and those in his tradition, and humanistic therapies, based on the humanistic theories of Rogers and Maslow, among others, are considered to be insight therapies. Therapeutic applications of Skinner's behavioral principles constitute action therapies. Cognitive therapies have both insight-oriented and action-oriented components.

Most contemporary therapists do not use one form of therapy exclusively with their clients. The majority of today's therapists are **eclectic**—*they use a variety of approaches to therapy.* Often therapists tailor the therapeutic approach to their clients' needs. Even a therapist with a psychodynamic orientation might use humanistic approaches or a family therapist might use behavioral techniques, for example.

Therapists also orient themselves toward intervention at a particular level. Some therapists tend to view client needs as a matter of symptoms or problems without particular regard to the context in which the problems are experienced; psychoanalytic and behavioral approaches usually focus on specific *problems.* Humanistic therapists see the

problem as having a wider scope and try to get at the involvement of the whole *person.* Cognitive therapists view adaptation as an interaction between the person and the *situation.* Other therapists like to work at the level of a *system* in which the individual functions. This includes couple and family therapy, group therapy, and community interventions. The expansion of systems therapy has prompted therapists to consider sociocultural factors as important components that influence the success or failure of any intervention.

Practitioners and Settings

A variety of mental health professionals, including clinical psychologists, psychiatrists, and counselors, practice psychotherapy. Remember from chapter 1 that psychiatrists have a medical degree and can prescribe drugs for mental disabilities. Clinical psychologists, by contrast, are trained in graduate programs of psychology and use psychotherapy rather than drugs to treat mental problems, although many psychologists are beginning to advocate granting prescription privileges to appropriately trained psychologists. Table 15.1 describes the main types of mental health professionals, their degrees, the years of education required for the degrees, and the nature of the training.

Just as there is a variety of mental health professionals, there is a variety of settings in which therapy takes place. During the first half of this century, psychotherapists primarily practiced in mental hospitals, where individuals remained for months, even years. During the past several decades, psychologists have recognized that psychotherapy is not just for those who are so mentally disordered that they cannot live in society. Today people who seek counseling and psychotherapy may go to a community health center, to the outpatient facility of a hospital, or to the private office of a mental health practitioner.

Access to Services

Psychotherapy usually is an expensive proposition. Even though reduced fees, and occasionally free services, can be arranged in public hospitals for those who are poor, many of the people who

TABLE 15.1

The Main Types of Mental Health Professionals

Professional Type	Degree	Experience Beyond Bachelor's Degree	Nature of Training
Clinical psychologist and counseling psychologist	Ph.D., ED.d., or Psy.D.	5–7 years	Includes both clinical and research training. Involves a 1-year internship in a psychiatric hospital or mental health facility. Recently some universities have developed Psy.D. programs, which lead to a professional degree with stronger clinical than research emphasis. The Psy.D. training program takes about the same number of years as the clinical psychology Ph.D. program and also requires a 1-year internship.
Psychiatrist	M.D.	7–9 years	Four years of medical school, plus an internship and residency in psychiatry, are required. A psychiatry residency involves supervision in therapies, including psychotherapy and biomedical therapy.
Social worker	M.S.W., D.S.W., or Ph.D.	2–5 years	Graduate work in a school of social work that includes specialized clinical training in mental health facilities.
Psychiatric nurse	R.N., M.A., or Ph.D.	0–5 years	Graduate work in school of nursing, with special emphasis on care of mentally disabled individuals in hospital settings and mental health facilities.
Occupational therapist	B.S., M.A., or Ph.D.	0–5 years	Emphasis on occupational training, with focus on physically or psychologically handicapped individuals. Stresses getting individuals back into the mainstream of work.
Pastoral counselor	None to Ph.D. or D.D. (Doctor of Divinity)	0–5 years	Requires ministerial background and training in psychology. An internship in a mental health facility as a chaplain is recommended.
Counselor	M.A.	2 years	Graduate work in department of psychology or department of education, with specialized training in counseling techniques.

Note: The above listing refers to the mental health professionals who go through formal training at recognized academic and medical institutions. The government commonly licenses these professionals and certifies their skills. Professional organizations regulate their activities.

are most in need of psychotherapy do not get it. Psychotherapists have been criticized for preferring to work with "young, attractive, verbal, intelligent, and successful" clients (called YAVISes) rather than "quiet, ugly, old, institutionalized, and different" clients (called QUOIDs). A national sample of clinical psychologists established that psychologists appear to be less willing to work with poorer and less-educated clients than with people from higher socioeconomic classes (Sutton & Kessler, 1986). This preference is attributed in part to the fact that disenfranchised individuals tend to have a poor *prognosis* (likelihood of improving from treatment). Such individuals might have difficulties keeping to

the rigid appointment schedules required by most therapists, perhaps because their lives are chaotic. These problems hinder the development of a strong working alliance between client and therapist, which has adverse effects on prognosis.

Financial factors also promote a preference for working with clients from higher socioeconomic classes. YAVIS clients tend to seek mental health care from private practitioners in mental health agencies and use health insurance to pay for their care when their therapists can provide a diagnosis consistent with the DSM-IV. QUOID clients usually must rely on reduced-fee or cost-free programs provided by public agencies supported through private grants or

government funding. Clinicians generally earn higher incomes by concentrating services with YAVIS clients rather than QUOID clients.

The challenge involved in paying for psychotherapeutic services has led to dramatic changes in mental health care delivery in recent years. Concerned by mounting mental health care costs that seemed to derive from protracted psychotherapy with questionable gains, health insurance companies began to seek new delivery systems. **Managed health care,** *a system in which external reviewers approve the type and length of treatment to justify insurance reimbursement,* has grown rapidly. Therapists whose clients participate in managed

Halonen/Santrock: Human Adjustment

health care must confer with an external agent about their treatment goals and make systematic reports about client progress to secure continued insurance funding.

Many problems have surfaced with this practice (Broskowski, 1995; Fox, 1995; Glueckauf & others, 1996). Although managed health care has promoted the development of more explicit and measurable treatment plans, the emphasis on cost management clearly favors short-term over long-term therapy methods. This emphasis can inappropriately shift some treatment to superficial interventions when the clinical problem requires more depth and more time than the health care managers allow. Both clients and therapists report discomfort with the potential violation of confidentiality and privacy when reporting therapy details to a third party. Some research suggests that the bureaucracy involved in setting up the watchdog system may absorb the savings that were supposed to be gained through the implementation of the system. Insurance reimbursement and managed health care will both be significantly affected by implementation of national health care mandates (Hersch, 1995).

Ethical Standards

Those who seek treatment from qualified mental health care practitioners can feel some reassurance that their problems will be addressed professionally and ethically, based on the systems used in certifying practitioners. Licensing and certification practices require mental health care providers to know relevant state and professional ethical codes before their credentials are granted. Most of these codes require ethical practice as well as vigilance about unethical practice by others in the field. The codes typically address the importance of doing no harm to clients, protecting the privacy of clients, avoiding dual relationships with clients, and staying updated in contemporary practices. Violations of ethical codes can result in the loss of one's license to practice.

So far we have glimpsed the history and basic nature of psychotherapy as it is practiced today. Contemporary psychotherapies include a number of diverse approaches to working with people to reduce their problems and improve their adjustment. We begin our survey by discussing forms of individual psychotherapy.

INDIVIDUAL THERAPIES

Your prototype of individual therapy might be the stereotyped image of the client lying down on a couch while the therapist makes notes about the client's day-to-day experiences. In fact, few individual therapists follow this strategy. Most individual therapies take place face to face and are more conversational. We will explore four orientations of individual therapy: psychoanalytic, humanistic, behavioral, and cognitive.

Psychodynamic Therapies

The **psychodynamic therapies** *stress the importance of the unconscious mind, extensive interpretation by the therapist, and the role of infant and early childhood experiences.* Many psychodynamic approaches have grown out of Freud's psychoanalytic theory of personality. Today some therapists with a psychodynamic perspective show allegiance to Freud; others do not.

Freud's Psychoanalysis

Psychoanalysis *is Freud's therapeutic technique for analyzing an individual's unconscious thought.* Freud believed that clients' current problems could be traced to childhood experiences, many of which involved conflicts about sexuality. He also recognized that the early experiences were not readily available to the individual's conscious mind. Only through extensive questioning, probing, and analyzing was Freud able to put the pieces of the individual's personality together and help the individual become aware of how these early experiences were affecting present adult behavior. To reach the shadowy world of the unconscious, psychoanalytic therapists often use the therapeutic techniques of free association, catharsis, interpretation, dream analysis, transference, and resistance.

In psychoanalysis the therapist uses **free association,** *the technique of encouraging individuals to say aloud whatever comes to mind, no matter how trivial or*

R E V I E W

The Nature of Therapy

Historically, some of the first forms of therapy derived from the belief, in ancient societies, that abnormal behavior had both mystical and organic origins. Many early treatments of mental disabilities were inhumane. Asylums were built during the Renaissance. Pinel's efforts led to extensive reform. Dix's efforts helped to separate the mentally disabled from prisoners.

In contemporary practice, psychotherapy is the process of working with individuals to reduce their emotional problems and improve their adjustment. Among the orientations of therapists are insight therapy, which encourages insight into and awareness of oneself (both psychoanalytic and humanistic therapies are insight therapies), and action therapy, which promotes direct changes in behavior for which insight is not essential (Skinner's behaviorism is an action therapy). Cognitive therapies have both insight and action components. Many therapists take an eclectic approach to therapy. Therapists also operate at different levels, such as at the level of the individual or at the level of a system—family, group, or community.

Practitioners include clinical psychologists, counseling psychologists, psychiatrists, and social workers. Psychotherapy takes place in a greater variety of settings today than in the past. Individuals of lower socioeconomic status are less likely to receive therapy than are individuals of higher socioeconomic status. Managed health care has increased dramatically in recent years, although not without problems. Psychotherapists are supposed to adhere to certain ethical standards.

To encourage his patients to relax, Freud had them recline on the couch while he sat in the chair on the left, out of their view.

embarrassing. When Freud detected that a client was resisting the spontaneous flow of thoughts, he probed further. He believed that the crux of the person's emotional problem probably lurked below this point of resistance. Freud thought that, when clients talked freely, their emotional feelings emerged. **Catharsis** *is the psychoanalytic term for clients' release of emotional tension when they relive an emotionally charged and conflicted experience.*

Interpretation plays an important role in psychoanalysis. As the therapist interprets free associations and dreams, the client's statements and behavior are not taken at face value. To understand what is truly causing the client's conflicts, the therapist constantly searches for symbolic, hidden meanings in what the individual says and does. From time to time, the therapist suggests possible meanings of the client's statements and behavior.

> The aim in analysis is to bring the magnificent energy of the wild horse under the control of the rider, without using a whip that will kill its spirit.
> —**Marion Woodman**

Dream analysis *is the psychotherapeutic technique psychoanalysts use to interpret a client's dreams. Psychoanalysts believe that dreams contain information about the individual's unconscious thoughts and conflicts.* Freud distinguished between the dream's manifest and latent content. **Manifest content** *is the psychoanalytic term for the conscious, remembered aspects of a dream.* **Latent content** *is the psychoanalytic term for the unconscious, unremembered, symbolic aspects of a dream.* A psychoanalyst interprets a dream by analyzing its manifest content for disguised unconscious wishes and needs, especially those that are sexual and aggressive. For some examples of the sexual symbols psychoanalysts use to interpret dreams, see figure 15.3. Freud cautioned against overinterpreting, however. Once Freud was challenged about possibly having an oral fixation himself, symbolized by his relentless cigar smoking. In response, he quipped, "Sometimes a cigar is just a cigar."

Freud also believed that transference was an inevitable and essential aspect of the analyst-client relationship. **Transference** *is the psychoanalytic term for the client's relating to the analyst in ways that reproduce or relive important relationships in the client's life.* A client might interact with an analyst as if the analyst were a parent or lover, for example. When transference dominates therapy, the client's comments may become directed toward the analyst's personal life. Transference is often difficult to overcome in psychotherapy. However, transference can be used therapeutically as a model of how clients relate to important people in their lives.

Resistance *is the psychoanalytic term for a client's unconscious defense strategies that prevent the analyst from understanding the client's problems.* Resistance occurs because it is painful to bring conflicts into conscious awareness. By resisting therapy, individuals do not have to face their problems. Showing up late or missing sessions, arguing with the psychoanalyst, or faking free associations are examples of resistance. Some clients go on endlessly about a trivial matter to avoid facing their conflicts. A major goal of the analyst is to break through this resistance (Rosenthal, 1996; Strean, 1996).

> Psychotherapy, unlike castor oil which will work no matter how you get it down, is useless when forced on an uncooperative patient.
> —**Abigail Van Buren**

Contemporary Psychodynamic Therapies

Although the face of psychodynamic therapy has changed extensively since its inception almost a century ago, many contemporary psychodynamic therapists still probe clients' unconscious thoughts about their earliest childhood experiences to provide clues to their clients' current problems. Many contemporary psychodynamic therapists also try to help clients gain insight into their emotionally laden, repressed conflicts.

However, only a small percentage of contemporary psychodynamic therapists rigorously follow Freud's guidelines. Many psychodynamic therapists still emphasize the importance of unconscious thought and early family experiences, but they also accord more power to the conscious mind and current relationships in understanding a client's problems. Clients rarely see their therapist several times a week. Now clients usually have weekly appointments.

Sexual theme	Objects or activities in dreams that symbolize sexual themes
Male genitals, especially penis	Umbrellas, knives, poles, swords, airplanes, guns, serpents, neckties, tree trunks, hoses
Female genitals, especially vagina	Boxes, caves, pockets, pouches, the mouth, jewel cases, ovens, closets
Sexual intercourse	Climbing, swimming, flying, riding (a horse, an elevator, a roller coaster)
Parents	King, queen, emperor, empress
Siblings	Little animals

Figure 15.3

The Psychoanalyst's Interpretation of Sexual Symbolism in Dreams
The painting shown is Hieronymous Bosch's *The Garden of Delights.*

Contemporary psychodynamic approaches emphasize the development of the self in social contexts (Erikson, 1968; Kohut, 1977; St. Clair, 1996). In Heinz Kohut's view, early relationships with attachment figures, such as one's parents, are critical. As we develop, we do not relinquish these attachments; we continue to need them. Kohut's prescription for therapy involves getting the patient to identify and seek out appropriate relationships with others. He also wants patients to develop more realistic appraisals of relationships. Kohut believes that therapists need to interact with their clients in ways that are empathic and understanding. As we will see next, empathy and understanding are absolute cornerstones for humanistic therapists as they encourage their clients to further their sense of self.

Humanistic Therapies

In the **humanistic psychotherapies,** *clients are encouraged to understand themselves and to grow personally.* In contrast to psychodynamic therapies, humanistic therapies emphasize conscious thoughts rather than unconscious thoughts, the present rather than the past, and growth and fulfillment rather than curing illness. Two main forms of the humanistic psychotherapies are person-centered therapy and Gestalt therapy.

Person-Centered Therapy

Person-centered therapy *is a form of humanistic therapy developed by Carl Rogers in which the therapist provides a warm, supportive atmosphere to improve the client's self-concept and encourage the client to gain insight about problems.* Rogers' (1961) therapy was initially called client-centered therapy, but he rechristened it person-centered therapy to underscore his deep belief that everyone has the ability to grow. The relationship between the therapist and the person is an important aspect of Rogers' therapy. The therapist must enter into an intensely personal relationship with the client, not as a physician diagnosing a disease but as one human being to another. Notice that Rogers referred to the "client" and then the "person" rather than the "patient." Rogers' approach demonstrates a strong individualistic bias that would fare best in cultures that stress the value of the individual.

Recall from chapter 2 that Rogers believed that each of us grows up in a world filled with *conditions of worth;* the positive regard we receive from others has strings attached. We usually do not receive love and praise unless we conform to the standards and demands of others. This causes us to be unhappy and have low self-esteem as adults; rarely do we feel that we measure up to such standards or feel that we are as good as others expect us to be.

To free the person from worry about the demands of society, the therapist creates a warm and caring environment (Cain, 1996). A Rogerian therapist tries to avoid disapproving of what a client says or does. Recall from chapter 2 that Rogers believed this *unconditional positive regard* improved the person's self-esteem. The therapist's role is "nondirective"—that is, he or she does not try to lead the client to any particular revelation. The therapist is there to listen sympathetically to the client's problems and to encourage greater self-regard, independent self-appraisal, and decision making.

Rogers advocated other techniques in addition to using unconditional positive regard. **Genuineness** *is the Rogerian concept of the importance of the therapist's being genuine and not hiding behind a facade. Therapists must let clients know their feelings.* **Accurate empathy** *is Rogers' term for the therapist's ability to identify with the client.* Rogers believed that therapists must sense what it is like to be the client at any moment in the client-therapist relationship. **Active listening** *is Rogers' term for the ability to listen to another person with total attention to what that person says and means.* One way therapists improve active listening is by restating or paraphrasing what the client said. Clients report that this practice helps them feel supported in order to gain the courage to make changes they wish to make.

Fritz Perls was the founder of Gestalt therapy.

Gestalt Therapy

Gestalt therapy *is a humanistic therapy, developed by Frederick (Fritz) Perls (1893–1970), in which the therapist questions and challenges clients to help them become more aware of their feelings and face their problems.* Perls was trained in Europe as a Freudian psychoanalyst, but as his career developed his ideas became noticeably different from Freud's. Perls agreed with Freud that psychological problems originate in unresolved past conflicts and that these conflicts need to be acknowledged and worked through. Also like Freud, Perls (1969) stressed that interpretation of dreams is an important aspect of therapy.

In other ways, however, Perls and Freud were miles apart. Perls believed that unresolved conflicts should be brought to bear on the here and now of the individual's life. The therapist *pushes* clients into deciding whether they will continue to allow the past to control their future or whether they will choose *right now* what they want to be in the future. To this end, Perls *confronted* individuals and encouraged them to actively control their lives and to be open about their feelings.

Gestalt therapists use a number of techniques to encourage individuals to

be open about their feelings, to develop self-awareness, and to actively control their lives. The therapist sets examples, encourages congruence between verbal and nonverbal behavior, and uses role playing. To demonstrate an important point to a client, a Gestalt therapist might exaggerate a client's characteristic. To stimulate change, the therapist might openly confront the client.

Another technique of Gestalt therapy is role playing, by either the client, the therapist, or both. For example, if an individual is bothered by conflict with her mother, the therapist might play the role of the mother and reopen the quarrel. The therapist may encourage the individual to act out her hostile feelings toward her mother by yelling, swearing, or kicking the couch, for example. In this way, Gestalt therapists hope to help individuals better manage their feelings instead of letting their feelings control them.

As you probably noticed, a Gestalt therapist is much more directive than a person-centered therapist. By being more directive, the Gestalt therapist provides more interpretation and feedback. Nonetheless, both of these humanistic therapies encourage individuals to take responsibility for their feelings and actions,

Psychodynamic and Humanistic Therapies

Psychodynamic therapies stress the importance of the unconscious mind, early family experiences, and extensive interpretation by the therapist. Psychoanalysis is Freud's technique for analyzing an individual's unconscious thought. Free association, catharsis, interpretation, dream analysis, transference, and resistance are techniques used in psychoanalytic therapy. Although psychodynamic therapy has changed, many contemporary psychodynamic therapists still probe the unconscious mind for early family experiences that might provide clues to the client's current problems. The development of the self in social contexts is an important theme in Kohut's contemporary approach.

In the humanistic therapies, clients are encouraged to understand themselves and to grow personally. The humanistic therapies emphasize conscious thoughts, the present, and growth and fulfillment. Person-centered therapy, developed by Rogers, emphasizes that the therapist should provide a warm and supportive atmosphere to improve the client's self-image and to encourage the client to gain insight into problems. The therapist replaces conditions of worth with unconditional positive regard and uses genuineness, accurate empathy, and active listening to raise the client's self-esteem. Gestalt therapy, developed by Fritz Perls, emphasizes that the therapist should question and challenge clients in order to help them become more aware of their feelings and face their problems. Gestalt therapy is more directive than is the nondirective approach of person-centered therapy.

---

to understand their true selves, to develop a sense of freedom, and to look at what they are doing with their lives.

Now that we have studied the insight therapies, we will turn our attention to therapies that take a very different approach to working with individuals to reduce their problems and improve their adjustment—the behavior therapies.

> *Every new adjustment is a crisis in self-esteem.*
>
> **—Eric Hoffer**

Behavior Therapies

Behavior therapies *use principles of learning to reduce or eliminate maladaptive behavior.* Behavior therapies are based on the behavioral theory of learning and personality described in chapter 2. Behavior therapists do not search for unconscious conflicts, like psychodynamic therapists, or encourage individuals to develop accurate perceptions of their feelings and self, like humanistic therapists. Insight and self-awareness are not the keys to helping individuals develop more adaptive behavior patterns, say the behavior therapists. The insight therapies—psychodynamic and humanistic—treat maladaptive symptoms as signs of underlying, internal problems. Behavior therapists, however, assume that the overt maladaptive symptoms are the problem. Individuals can become aware of why they are depressed and still be depressed, say the behavior therapists. A behavior therapist tries to eliminate the depressed symptoms or behaviors themselves rather than try to get individuals to gain insight or awareness about why they are depressed (O'Donahue & Krasner, 1995).

Behavior therapists initially based their interventions almost exclusively on the learning principles of classical and operant conditioning, but behavior therapies have become more diverse in recent years. As cognitive social learning theory grew in popularity and the cognitive approach became more prominent in psychology, behavior therapists increasingly included cognitive factors in their therapy. First we will discuss the classical and operant conditioning approaches; then we will turn to the cognitive therapies.

Classical Conditioning Approaches

We acquire, or learn, some behaviors, especially fears, through classical conditioning. These behaviors can be unlearned, or extinguished. If an individual has learned to fear snakes or heights through classical conditioning, perhaps the individual could unlearn the fear. Two procedures based on classical conditioning that are used in behavior therapy are systematic desensitization and aversive conditioning.

Systematic Desensitization Systematic desensitization *is a method of behavior therapy that treats anxiety by associating deep relaxation with successive visualizations of increasingly intense anxiety-producing situations; this technique is based on classical conditioning* (Wolpe, 1963). Consider the common fear of taking a test. Using systematic desensitization, a behavior therapist first asks the client which aspects of the fearful situation—in this case, taking a test—are the most and least frightening. Then, the behavior therapist arranges these circumstances in order from most to least frightening. An example of this type of desensitization hierarchy is shown in figure 15.4.

The next step is to teach individuals to relax. Behavior therapists teach clients to recognize the presence of muscular contractions, or tensions, in various parts of their bodies and then to contract and relax different muscles. Once individuals are relaxed, the therapist asks them to imagine the least fearful stimulus in the hierarchy. Subsequently the therapist moves up the list of items from least to most fearful while the clients remain relaxed. Eventually individuals are able to imagine the most fearful circumstance without being afraid—in our example, on the way to the university the day of an exam. In this manner, individuals learn to relax while thinking about the exam instead of feeling anxious.

1. On the way to the university on the day of an examination
2. In the process of answering an examination paper
3. Before the unopened doors of the examination room
4. Awaiting the distribution of examination papers
5. The examination paper lies face down before her
6. The night before an examination
7. One day before an examination
8. Two days before an examination
9. Three days before an examination
10. Four days before an examination
11. Five days before an examination
12. A week before an examination
13. Two weeks before an examination
14. A month before an examination

FIGURE 15.4

A Desensitization Hierarchy from Most to Least Fearsome Circumstances

Researchers have found that systematic desensitization is often an effective treatment for a number of phobias, such as fear of giving a speech, fear of heights, fear of flying, fear of dogs, and fear of snakes (Martin & Pear, 1996). If you were afraid of snakes, for instance, the therapist might initially have you watch someone handle a snake. Then the therapist would ask you to engage in increasingly more feared behaviors—you might first just go into the same room with the snake, next you would approach the snake, subsequently you would touch the snake, and eventually you would play with the snake (Bandura, Blanchard, & Ritter, 1969).

Aversive Conditioning Aversive **conditioning** *is an approach to behavior therapy that involves repeated pairings of an undesirable behavior with aversive stimuli to decrease the behavior's rewards so the individual will stop doing it; this technique is based on classical conditioning.* Aversive conditioning is used to teach people to avoid such behaviors as smoking, overeating, and drinking. Electric shocks, nausea-inducing substances, and verbal insults are some of the noxious stimuli used in aversive conditioning.

How would aversive conditioning be used to reduce a person's alcohol consumption? Every time a person drank an alcoholic beverage, he or she also would consume a mixture that induced nausea. In classical conditioning terminology, the alcoholic beverage is the conditioned stimulus and the nausea-inducing agent is the unconditioned stimulus. By repeatedly pairing alcohol with the nausea-inducing agent, alcohol becomes the conditioned stimulus that elicits nausea, the conditioned response. As a consequence, alcohol is no longer associated with something pleasant but, rather, is associated with something highly unpleasant.

Operant Conditioning Approaches

Andy is a college student who has difficulty studying. He complains that he always starts to fall asleep when he goes to his desk to study. He has decided to see a therapist about how he might improve his studying because his grades are deteriorating. The behavior therapist's first recommendation is to replace his desk lamp's 40-watt bulb with a brighter one. The second recommendation is to turn his desk away from his bed. The third recommendation is to do only schoolwork at his desk; he is not allowed to write a letter, read a magazine, or daydream while at the desk. If he wants to do any of these other things, he must leave his desk.

To help Andy improve his study habits, the behavior therapist first evaluated Andy's responses to the stimuli in his room. Then the therapist gave Andy direct and precise suggestions about what to do. The therapist did not spend time analyzing his unconscious conflicts or encouraging him to "get in touch with his feelings." Rather, the therapist wanted to change Andy's responses to the environmental stimuli that were causing the problem.

When we discussed operant conditioning in chapter 2, we examined how an individual's behavior is controlled by its consequences. We also discussed *behavior modification,* which is often used by behavior therapists. The idea behind behavior modification is to replace unacceptable, maladaptive responses with acceptable, adaptive ones. Consequences are set up to ensure that acceptable responses are reinforced and unacceptable ones are not (Bergin & Garfield, 1994; Kohlenberg, Tsai, & Kohlenberg, 1996).

A **token economy** *is a behavior modification system in which behaviors are reinforced with tokens (such as poker chips) that can be exchanged later for desired rewards (such as candy, money, or going to a movie).* Behavior therapists have implemented token economies in a number of classrooms, institutions for the mentally retarded, homes for delinquents, and mental hospitals with schizophrenics.

In some instances, behavior modification works; in others it does not. One person might become so wedded to the tokens that, when they are removed, the positive behavior associated with the tokens disappears. Yet another person might continue the positive behavior after the tokens are removed. Some critics object to behavior modification because they believe such extensive control of another person's behavior unethically infringes on the individual's rights. However, as with the college student who could not study, maladaptive responses can be turned into adaptive ones through behavior modification.

The behavior therapies you have just read about do not include cognitive processes in their effort to modify the behavior of individuals with problems. As we will see next, cognitive therapy gives thought processes a more prominent role in helping individuals reduce their problems and improve their adjustment.

Cognitive Therapies

Derek, a 21-year-old single undergraduate student, has delusions that he is evil. He perceives himself as a failure in school and a failure to his parents. He is preoccupied with negative thoughts, dwells on his problems, and exaggerates his faults. Such thinking is common among depressed individuals and suggests that cognitive therapy might be a viable approach to treating Derek's depression.

The **cognitive therapies** *emphasize that an individual's cognitions, or thoughts, are the main source of abnormal behavior. Cognitive therapies attempt to change the individual's feelings and behaviors by changing cognitions.* Cognitive therapies differ from psychoanalytic therapies by focusing more on overt symptoms instead of deep-seated unconscious thoughts, by providing more structure to an individual's thoughts, and by being less concerned about the origin of the problem (Beck & Haaga, 1992). Cognitive therapies vary in the use of unstructured training sessions that require individuals to practice prescribed exercises. Many cognitive therapies are more likely to adhere to a conversational format. Cognitive therapists also vary in their emphasis on manipulating the environment to increase adaptive behavior.

Cognitive Behavior Therapies

The earliest form of cognitive therapy stemmed from both cognitive psychology, with its emphasis on the effect of thoughts on behavior, and behaviorism, with its emphasis on behavior-change techniques. Cognitive behavior therapists strive to change clients' misconceptions, strengthen their coping skills, increase their self-control, and encourage constructive self-reflection (Meichenbaum, 1993).

Self-efficacy Self-efficacy—*the belief that one can master a situation and produce positive outcomes*—is especially important in developing adaptive behavior, according to social learning theorist Albert Bandura. Moreover, Bandura (1989, 1994) believes that self-efficacy is the key to successful therapy. At each step of the therapy process, people need to bolster their confidence by telling themselves, "I can do this," "I'm going to make it," "I'm getting very good," and so on. As people gain confidence and engage in more adaptive behavior, the successes become intrinsically rewarding. Before long individuals will persist with considerable effort in solving their problems because of the pleasurable outcomes that were set in motion by self-efficacy.

Self-instructional Methods Self-instructional methods *are cognitive behavior techniques aimed at teaching individuals to modify their own behavior.* Using self-instructional methods, cognitive behavior therapists try to get clients to change what they say to themselves. The therapist gives the client examples of constructive statements, known as "reinforcing self-statements," that the client can repeat in order to take positive steps to handle stress or meet a goal. The therapist also encourages the client to practice the statements through role playing and strengthens the client's newly acquired skills through reinforcements. A series of examples of constructive statements that can be used to cope with stressful situations is shown in table 15.2.

In recent years, many therapists have focused less on the structured training session format of cognitive behavior therapy. Two of the most important contemporary cognitive therapies are Albert Ellis' rational-emotive therapy and Aaron Beck's cognitive therapy.

Rational-Emotive Therapy

Rational-emotive therapy *is based on Albert Ellis' view that individuals become psychologically disordered because of their beliefs, especially those that are irrational and self-defeating* (Ellis, 1962, 1993, 1996). Ellis says that we usually talk to ourselves when we experience stress; too often the statements are irrational, making them more harmful than helpful.

Ellis abbreviated the therapy process into the letters *A, B, C, D,* and *E.* Therapy usually starts at *C,* the individual's upsetting emotional *Consequence;* this might involve depression, anxiety, or a feeling of worthlessness. The individual usually says that *C* was caused by *A,* the *Activating Experience,* such as a blowup in marital relations, the loss of a job, or failure in school. The therapist works with the individual to show that an intervening factor, *B,* the individual's *Belief System,* is actually responsible for why she moved from *A* to *C.* Then the therapist goes on to *D,* which stands for *Disputation;* at this point, the individual's irrational beliefs are disputed, or contested, by the therapist. Finally, *E* is reached, which stands for *Effects,* or outcomes, of the rational-emotive therapy, as when individuals put their changed

TABLE 15.2

Statements That Promote Coping in Self-Instructional Methods

Preparing for Anxiety or Stress

What do I have to do?

I'm going to map out a plan to deal with it.

I'll just think about what I have to do.

I won't worry; doesn't help anything.

I have a lot of different strategies to call on.

Confronting and Handling the Anxiety or Stress

I can meet the challenge.

I'll keep on taking just one step at a time.

I can handle it. I'll just relax, breathe deeply, and use one of the strategies.

I won't think about the pain; I'll think about what I have to do.

Coping with Feelings at Critical Moments

What is it I have to do?

I was supposed to expect the pain to increase; I just have to keep myself in control.

When the pain comes, I'll just pause and keep focusing on what I have to do.

Reinforcing Self-Statements

Good, I did it.

I handled it well.

I knew I could do it.

Wait until I tell other people how I did it!

---

beliefs to work. An example of Ellis' rational-emotive therapy approach can be found in the Self-Assessment.

Beck's Cognitive Therapy

Aaron Beck (1976) developed a form of cognitive therapy to treat psychological dysfunctions, especially depression. He believes that the most effective therapy with depressed individuals involves four phases: (1) the depressed clients are shown how to identify self-labels—that is, how they view themselves, (2) they are taught to notice when they are thinking distorted or irrational thoughts, (3) they learn how to substitute appropriate thoughts for inappropriate ones, and (4) they are given feedback and motivating comments from the therapist to stimulate their use of these techniques.

Results from a large-scale study by the National Institute of Mental Health (NIMH) support the belief that Beck's cognitive therapy is an effective treatment for depression (Mervis, 1986). Beck and his colleagues conducted this therapy with moderately to severely depressed individuals for 16 weeks at three sites. The symptoms of depression were eliminated completely in more than 50 percent of the individuals receiving Beck's cognitive therapy, as compared to only 29 percent in a comparison group (Clark & Beck, 1989).

A comparison group is an important feature in most psychological research. Without a comparison group, the researchers in the NIMH study would have had no way of knowing if the symptoms of depression in the experimental group would have disappeared even without therapy. That is, it is possible that, in any random sample of depressed individuals, more than 50 percent show a remission of symptoms over a 16-week period, regardless of whether or not they receive therapy. Because only 29 percent of the depressed individuals in the comparison group became free of their symptoms, the researchers had good reason to believe that the cognitive therapy—which produced more than a 50 percent remission of symptoms—was effective.

Now the real beginnings of the "freedom" which we have discussed for many years—and a heady freedom it is, coming after so many years of reaching outward for it—to finally discover all I had to do was reach inward, and it was there waiting all the time for me!

—Alisa Wells

At this point, we have discussed four major approaches to individual therapy—psychodynamic, humanistic, behavior, and cognitive. Figure 15.5 will help you keep the approaches straight.

SYSTEMS INTERVENTIONS

A major issue in therapy is how it can be structured to reach more people and at less cost. One way to address this problem is for therapists to see clients in a group rather than individually. A second way is through community psychology approaches. These approaches have the advantage of working with individuals in the context of a larger system.

Group Therapies

Nine people make their way into a room, each looking tentatively at the others. Although each person has met the therapist during a diagnostic interview, no one knows any of the other clients. Some of the people seem reluctant, others enthusiastic. All are willing to follow the therapist's recommendation that group therapy might help each of them learn to cope better with their problems. As they sit down and wait for the session to begin,

Irrational Values

People have different opinions. We are interested in knowing your opinions concerning the following issues. There are no right or wrong answers for the items; we are interested in opinions only. Please indicate your own opinion by circling a number from one to nine on the scale provided for each statement. In case of doubt, circle the number that comes closest to representing your true opinion.

Please turn to the end of the chapter to score and interpret your responses.

1. It is essential that one be loved or approved by virtually everyone in one's community.

   Completely disagree   *Completely agree*
   1   2   3   4   5   6   7   8   9

2. One must be perfectly competent, adequate, and achieving to consider oneself worthwhile.

   Completely disagree   *Completely agree*
   1   2   3   4   5   6   7   8   9

3. Some people are bad, wicked, or villainous and therefore should be blamed and punished.

   Completely disagree   *Completely agree*
   1   2   3   4   5   6   7   8   9

4. It is a terrible catastrophe when things are not as one wants them to be.

   Completely disagree   *Completely agree*
   1   2   3   4   5   6   7   8   9

5. Unhappiness is caused by outside circumstances and the individual has no control over it.

   Completely disagree   *Completely agree*
   1   2   3   4   5   6   7   8   9

6. Dangerous or fearsome things are causes for great concern, and their possibility must be continually dwelt upon.

   Completely disagree   *Completely agree*
   1   2   3   4   5   6   7   8   9

7. One should be dependent on others and must have someone stronger on whom to rely.

   Completely disagree   *Completely agree*
   1   2   3   4   5   6   7   8   9

8. One should be quite upset over people's problems and disturbances.

   Completely disagree   *Completely agree*
   1   2   3   4   5   6   7   8   9

9. There is always a right or perfect solution to every problem, and it must be found or the results will be catastrophic.

   Completely disagree   *Completely agree*
   1   2   3   4   5   6   7   8   9

---

one thinks, "Will they really understand me?" Another wonders, "Do the others have problems like mine?" Yet another thinks, "Can I stick my neck out with these people?"

Individual therapy is often expensive and time consuming. Freud believed that therapy is a long process and saw clients as often as three to five times a week for a number of years. Advocates of group therapy stress that individual therapy is limited because the client is seen outside the normal context of relationships, relationships that may hold the key to successful therapy (Gladding, 1995). Many psychological problems develop in the context of interpersonal relationships—within one's family, marriage, or peer group, for example. By seeing individuals in the context of these important groups, therapy may be more successful (Fuhrman & Burlingame, 1995).

Group therapy is diversified (O'Neil, 1996). Some therapists practice psychodynamic, humanistic, behavior, or cognitive therapy. Others use group approaches that are not based on the major psychotherapeutic perspectives. Six features make group therapy an attractive format (Yalom, 1975, 1995):

1. *Information.* Individuals receive information about their problems from either the group leader or other group members.
2. *Universality.* Many individuals develop the sense that they are the only persons who have such frightening and unacceptable impulses. In the group, individuals observe that others also feel anguish and suffering.

Dimension of therapy	Psychodynamic orientation	Humanistic orientation	Behavioral orientation	Cognitive orientation
Focus of treatment	Problem focus; symptoms represent deep-seated unresolved unconscious conflicts	Person focus; individuals fail to function at an optimal level of development	Problem focus; challenges come from maladaptive behavior patterns	Situation focus; difficulties arise from inappropriate cognitions
Therapy objective	Insight into underlying unconscious conflicts	Insight into inherent potential for growth	Action by learning more adaptive behavior	Insight and action geared toward changing cognitions
Nature of therapy and techniques	Psychoanalysis, including free association, dream analysis, resistance, and transference; therapist interprets heavily	Person-centered therapy, including unconditional positive regard, genuineness, accurate empathy, and active listening; Gestalt therapy including confrontation to encourage honest expression of feelings; self-appreciation emphasized	Observation of behavior and its controlling conditions; specific advice given about what should be done; therapies based on classical conditioning, operant conditioning	Conversation with client designed to get him or her to change irrational and self-defeating beliefs; therapies emphasizing self-efficacy and self-instruction

FIGURE 15.5

A Comparison of Psychotherapies

REVIEW

Behavior and Cognitive Therapies

Behavior therapies use principles of learning to reduce or eliminate maladaptive behavior. Behavior therapies are based on behavioral theories of learning and personality. Behavior therapists try to eliminate symptoms or behaviors rather than trying to get individuals to gain insight into their problems. Two classical conditioning procedures used in behavior therapy are systematic desensitization and aversive conditioning. Operant conditioning approaches emphasize modifying an individual's maladaptive responses to the environment. The idea behind behavior modification is to replace unacceptable, maladaptive responses with acceptable, adaptive ones. Consequences are set up to ensure that acceptable responses are reinforced; unacceptable ones are not. A token economy is an example of behavior modification.

Cognitive therapies include cognitive behavior therapy, Ellis' rational-emotive therapy, and Beck's cognitive therapy. Cognitive therapies emphasize that an individual's thoughts, or cognitions, are the main source of abnormal behavior. Cognitive therapies attempt to change the individual's feelings and behaviors by changing cognitions. Cognitive behavior therapy tries to help individuals behave more adaptively by modifying their thoughts. Cognitive behavior therapists strive to change misconceptions, strengthen coping skills, increase self-control, and encourage constructive self-talk. Rational-emotive therapy is a cognitive therapy developed by Albert Ellis. It is based on the idea that individuals become psychologically disabled because of their beliefs, especially those that are irrational and self-defeating; therapy is designed to change these beliefs. Aaron Beck developed a form of cognitive therapy to treat psychological disorders, especially depression. The therapy involves identifying self-labels, detecting irrational thoughts, substituting appropriate for inappropriate thoughts, and receiving feedback from the therapist to stimulate these cognitive changes.

3. *Altruism.* Group members support one another with advice and sympathy and learn that they have something to offer others.
4. *Corrective recapitulation of the family group.* A therapy group often resembles a family (and, in family therapy, the group *is* a family), with the leaders representing parents and the other members siblings. In this "new" family, old wounds may be healed and new, more positive "family" ties made.
5. *Development of social skills.* Corrective feedback from peers may correct flaws in an individual's interpersonal skills. A self-centered individual may see that he is self-centered if five other group members inform him about his

self-centeredness; in individual therapy, he may not believe the therapist.

6. *Interpersonal learning.* The group can serve as a training ground for practicing new behaviors and relationships. For example, a hostile woman may learn that she can get along better with others by not behaving so aggressively.

Family and Couple Therapy

"A friend loves you for your intelligence, a mistress for your charm, but your family's love is unreasoning; you were born into it and are of its flesh and blood. Nevertheless, it can irritate you more than any group of people in the world," commented French biographer André Maurois. His statement suggests that the family may be the source of an individual's problems. **Family therapy** *is group therapy with family members.* **Couple therapy** *is group therapy with married or unmarried couples whose major problem is their relationship.* These approaches stress that, although one person may have some abnormal symptoms, the symptoms are a function of family or couple relationships (Davis, 1996; Lebow & Gurman, 1995; Nichols & Schwartz, 1995). Psychodynamic, humanistic, or behavior therapies may be used in family or couple therapy, but the main form of family therapy is family systems therapy.

> *Woe, woe, woe, and again woe to you if you do not change.*
> —**Elisabeth of Braunschweiger (1510–1558) in a letter to her son**

Family systems therapy *is a form of therapy based on the assumption that psychological adjustment is related to patterns of interaction within the family unit.* Families who do not function well foster abnormal behavior on the part of one or more of their members (Minuchin, 1985; Satir, 1964). Four of the most widely used family systems therapy techniques are these:

1. *Validation.* The therapist expresses an understanding and acceptance of each family member's feelings and beliefs and, thus, validates the

Family systems therapy has become increasingly popular in recent years. In family systems therapy, the assumption is that psychological adjustment is related to patterns of interaction within the family unit.

person. When the therapist talks with each family member, she finds something positive to say.

2. *Reframing.* The therapist teaches families to reframe problems; problems are cast as a family problem, not an individual's problem. For example, the family therapist reframes the problems of a delinquent adolescent in terms of how each family member contributed to the situation. The father's lack of attention to his son and marital conflict may be involved.

3. *Structural change.* The family systems therapist tries to *restructure* the coalitions in a family. In a mother-son coalition, the therapist might suggest that the father take a stronger disciplinarian role to relieve the mother of some of the burden. Restructuring might be as simple as suggesting that parents explore satisfying ways to be together; the therapist may recommend that, once a week, the parents go out for a quiet dinner together, for example.

4. *Detriangulation.* In some families, one member is the scapegoat for two other members who are in conflict but pretend not to be. For example, in the triangle of two

parents and one child, the parents may insist that their marriage is fine but find themselves in subtle conflict over how to handle the child. The therapist tries to disentangle, or *detriangulate,* this situation by shifting attention away from the child and toward the conflict between the parents.

Although many of the principles of family therapy can be applied to most families, cross-cultural psychologists caution against transferring a Western view of family dynamics to other cultures. Unique sociohistorical, cultural circumstances experienced by different ethnic minority groups also require certain considerations. To read about some of the considerations regarding family therapy in African American families, turn to Sociocultural Worlds of Adjustment.

Couple therapy proceeds in much the same way as family therapy. Conflict in marriages and in relationships between unmarried individuals frequently involves poor communication. In some instances, communication has broken down entirely. The therapist tries to improve the communication between the partners. In some cases, she will focus on the roles partners play: One might be "strong," the other "weak"; one might be "responsible," the other "spoiled," for example.

SOCIOCULTURAL WORLDS OF ADJUSTMENT

Therapy with African American Families

Family therapists who work with African American families are often called on to fulfill various roles, such as educator, director, advocate, problem solver, and role model. As a therapist takes on these roles, he or she must recognize that the clients are members of a community, as well as individuals or members of families. The following case study illustrates some of the multiple roles and the community orientation that a therapist must be aware of in working with African American families (Grevious, 1985).

Mrs. B. entered family therapy because her 11-year-old son Todd was disruptive in school and falling behind in his work. She complained of feeling overwhelmed and not being able to cope with the situation. The therapist conducted a home visit and observed that the family lived in a run-down building in a poor neighborhood. Even so, the therapist found that Mrs. B.'s apartment was immaculate, work and sleep space had been set aside for Todd, and it was obvious from the well-worn Bible on the coffee table and the religious paintings and calendars on the walls

that Mrs. B. had strong religious convictions. The therapist discovered that Mrs. B.'s strong-willed mother recently had moved into the apartment after an incapacitating leg operation. The grandmother's diabetes created additional stress in the home. Despite her illness, the grandmother tried to exercise considerable control over Mrs. B. and Todd, causing a power struggle in the family. The therapist also learned that Mrs. B. had recently stopped attending church. After the therapist encouraged her to attend church again, Mrs. B.'s spirits improved considerably. In addition, the grandmother joined a senior citizens program, which transported her to the center three times a week and to church two Sundays a month. These increased community activities for the grandmother had a positive impact on the family.

Family therapists who see African American clients also believe that it is important to provide concrete advice or assistance. If the problem is a parent-child relationship, for example, a family therapist might recommend that the parents participate in a parent training program, rather than conduct insight therapy. Also, therapists may occasionally need to educate African American families about social service programs and the difficulties they might encounter in gaining access to those programs.

A family therapist who works with African American families also needs to emphasize their strengths, such as pride in being African American, the extended family, and religion, as well as take into consideration their vulnerabilities, such as the impact of racism, discrimination, and victimization (Boyd-Franklin, 1993, 1996). Therapists might need to advocate for African American clients whose strain lies in trying to adjust to demands that might be unfair or discriminatory. In addition, therapists need to recognize that there will be diversity of experience among African American families. More about therapy with African Americans and other ethnic minorities appears later in the chapter.

Couple therapy addresses diverse problems such as jealousy, sexual messages, delayed childbearing, infidelity, gender roles, two-career families, divorce, and remarriage. Now we turn our attention to other forms of group therapy—personal growth and self-help groups.

Personal Growth Groups

A number of group therapies in recent years have focused on people whose lives are lacking in intimacy, intensity, and accomplishment. **Personal growth groups** *have their roots in the humanistic therapies; they emphasize personal growth and increased openness and honesty in interpersonal relations.*

An **encounter group** *is a personal growth group designed to promote self-understanding through candid group interaction.* For example, one member of an assembled group thinks he is better than everyone else. After several minutes of listening to the guy's insufferable bragging, one group member says, "Look, jerk, nobody here likes you; I would like to sell you for what you think you are worth and buy you for what you are actually worth!" Other members of the group might also criticize the braggart. Outside of an encounter group, most people probably would not confront someone about bragging; in an encounter group, they may feel free to express their true feelings about each other.

Encounter groups improve the psychological adjustment of some individuals, but not others. For example, in one study, the majority of college students who were members of an encounter group felt better about themselves and got along better with others than did their counterparts, who were not involved in an encounter group (Lieberman, Yalom, & Miles, 1973). However, 8 percent of the participants in the encounter group felt that the experience was harmful. For the most part, they blamed the group leader for intensifying their problems; they said the leader's remarks were so personally devastating that they could not handle them.

Self-Help Groups

Although encounter groups are not as popular today as they were in the 1970s, they were the forerunners of today's self-help groups. **Self-help groups** *are voluntary organizations of individuals who get together on a regular basis to discuss topics of common interest. The group leader and members give support to help individuals with their problems.* Self-help groups are so-called because they are conducted without a professional therapist. Self-help groups play an important role in our nation's mental health—approximately 6.25 million people participate in such groups each year.

In addition to reaching so many people in need of help, these groups are important because they use community resources and are relatively inexpensive. They also serve people who are less likely to receive help otherwise, such as less-educated middle-aged adults, homemakers, and blue-collar workers.

Founded in 1930 by a reformed alcoholic, Alcoholics Anonymous (AA) is one of the best-known self-help groups. Mental health professionals often recommend AA for their alcoholic clients. Weight Watchers and TOPS (Take Off Pounds Sensibly) are also self-help groups. There are myriad self-help groups, such as Parents Without Partners, lesbian and gay support groups, cocaine-abuse support groups, and child-abuse support groups. Table 15.3 provides a sampling of the wide variety of self-help groups available in one city.

You may be wondering how a group of people with the same problem can come together and do one another any good. You might be asking yourself why they don't just help themselves and eliminate the need for the group. In fact, seeing that others share the same burden makes people feel less isolated, less like freaks of nature; it increases a psychological sense of community or belonging; and it can give hope where there might have been none before.

Self-help groups also provide an ideology, or set of beliefs, that members can use as a guide. These groups provide members with a sympathetic audience for confession, sharing, and emotional release. The social support, role modeling,

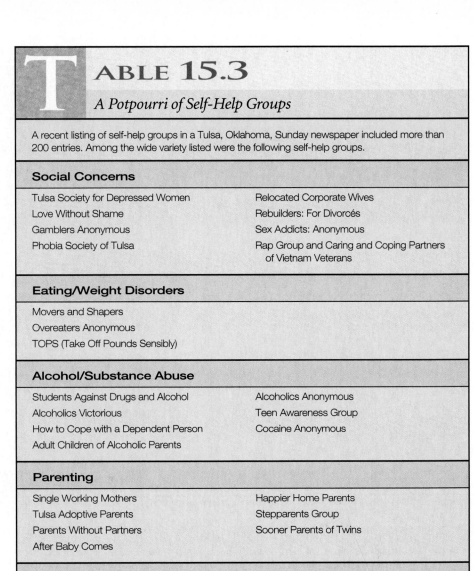

TABLE 15.3

A Potpourri of Self-Help Groups

A recent listing of self-help groups in a Tulsa, Oklahoma, Sunday newspaper included more than 200 entries. Among the wide variety listed were the following self-help groups.

Social Concerns

Tulsa Society for Depressed Women	Relocated Corporate Wives
Love Without Shame	Rebuilders: For Divorcés
Gamblers Anonymous	Sex Addicts: Anonymous
Phobia Society of Tulsa	Rap Group and Caring and Coping Partners of Vietnam Veterans

Eating/Weight Disorders

Movers and Shapers
Overeaters Anonymous
TOPS (Take Off Pounds Sensibly)

Alcohol/Substance Abuse

Students Against Drugs and Alcohol	Alcoholics Anonymous
Alcoholics Victorious	Teen Awareness Group
How to Cope with a Dependent Person	Cocaine Anonymous
Adult Children of Alcoholic Parents	

Parenting

Single Working Mothers	Happier Home Parents
Tulsa Adoptive Parents	Stepparents Group
Parents Without Partners	Sooner Parents of Twins
After Baby Comes	

Health

Resolve of Tulsa (an infertility group)	SHHH (Self-Help for the Hard of Hearing)
Group for Alzheimer's Caregivers	LITHIUM Group (for those with bipolar disorder)
AIDS Support Program	Families of Children with Diabetes
ENCORE (for breast cancer patients)	Indian Health Care Resource Center
Mended Hearts (for those who have had open-heart surgery)	Families of Nursing Home Residents

and sharing of concrete strategies for solving problems that unfold in self-help groups add to their effectiveness. For instance, a woman who has been raped may not believe a male counselor who tells her that, with time, she will be able to put back together the pieces of her life and work through much of the psychological pain. However, the same message from another rape survivor—someone who has had to work through the same feelings of rage, fear, and violation—may be more believable.

> *Life is either a daring adventure or nothing. Security does not exist in nature, nor do the children of men as a whole experience it. Avoiding danger is no safer in the long run than exposure.*
> —**Helen Keller**

Many individuals feel uncomfortable with formal methods of therapy or support. Instead, they might turn to friends, relatives, religious leaders, or

The increased use of drug therapy in mental institutions facilitated the transfer of many mental patients back to the community. The architects of deinstitutionalization believed that these individuals could be given medication to keep them stabilized until they could find continuing care. However, many residents of mental health institutions have no families or homes to go to and community mental health facilities are not adequately equipped to deal with the severe cases. Many individuals who are discharged from state mental hospitals join the ranks of "the homeless." Of course, though, not all homeless people are former mental patients. Controversy continues about whether individuals should be discharged so readily from state mental institutions, which usually struggle with underfunding and staff shortages.

designated officials of the community to assist them in solving problems.

Community Psychology

The community psychology movement was born in the early 1960s, when it became apparent to mental health practitioners, including clinical psychologists, that our mental health care system was woefully inadequate. The system was not reaching the poor. Many of those who could afford help often did not seek therapy because of its social stigma. As a result, deinstitutionalization became a major thrust of the community psychology movement. **Deinstitutionalization** *is the movement to transfer the treatment of mental disabilities from inpatient mental institutions to community-based facilities*

that stress outpatient care. New drugs for treating the severely mentally disabled, such as schizophrenics, meant that large numbers of people could be released from mental institutions and treated in community-based centers.

In 1963 Congress passed the Community Mental Health Center Act, which provided funds for establishing one facility for every 50,000 individuals in the nation. The centers were designed to meet two basic goals—to provide community-based mental health services and to commit resources that help *prevent* disorders as well as treat them. Outpatient care is one of the important services that community mental health centers provide. Individuals can attend therapy sessions at a center and still

keep their jobs and live with their families. Another important innovation that grew out of the community psychology movement is called outreach services. Rather than expecting people with mental or emotional problems to make an appointment at a mental health center, mental health care workers in this program go to community locations, such as storefront clinics, where they are accessible and needed most. Many community-based mental health services stay open 24 hours a day, often handling such emergencies as suicide attempts and drug overdoses.

The philosophy of community-based services also includes training teachers, ministers, family physicians, and others who directly interact with community members to offer lay counseling and various workshops, such as assertive training or coping with stress. This broadens mental health resources, allowing more people to receive help in settings where they are more likely to be comfortable than in traditional mental health centers.

In principle, community-based mental health systems should work well. In practice, the systems are severely underfunded, overenrolled, and sometimes hopelessly bureaucratic. Despite these problems, community psychologists continue to work on many levels to improve community systems.

Primary Prevention

Primary prevention *is a community psychology concept, borrowed from the public health field; primary prevention involves efforts to reduce the number of new cases of mental disorders.* By definition, primary prevention programs are offered to populations completely free of a disorder. Like immunization in public health, primary prevention programs try to identify and "inoculate" people against the development of mental disorders. Primary prevention programs tend to follow one of three strategies: community-wide, milestone, or high-risk.

In the *community-wide* approach, programs are available to everyone in a given geographic area. In Washington, D.C., the program "Beautiful Babies Right from the Start," for example, provides free prenatal care and well-baby care for the baby's first 18 months to women and their infants in the poorest communities. This program attempts to prevent pregnant women from engaging in harmful behaviors, such as substance abuse or poor nutrition, that put infants at risk for premature birth, low birthweight, and such disorders as hyperactivity, impaired memory, and disorganized thinking. In the *milestone* approach, the target group is every person in a population who reaches a certain hurdle, or critical life transition, such as being fired, becoming a parent for the first time, or going away to college. Counseling for fired employees and orientation programs for college students are two examples of milestone programs. In a *high-risk* program, the focus is on specific groups of people whose chances of developing mental disorders are extremely high, such as children of alcoholics, children with chronic illnesses, and ethnic minority children.

Secondary Prevention

Secondary prevention *is a community psychology concept; secondary prevention involves screening for early detection of problems, as well as early intervention.* A major goal of secondary prevention programs is to reach large numbers of potential clients (Yee, 1996). These programs often use *paraprofessionals*, volunteers without formal mental health training who work closely with psychologists, to meet this goal. One approach to secondary prevention involves teaching coping skills to people under high levels of stress, the bereaved, the newly employed, and prospective parents. Another type involves screening groups of individuals, such as schoolchildren, to find those who show early signs of problems and provide them with mental health services.

Tertiary Prevention

Tertiary prevention *is a community psychology concept; tertiary prevention involves efforts to reduce the long-term consequences of mental health disorders that were not prevented or arrested early in the course of the disorders.* Tertiary prevention programs are geared toward people who once required long-term care or hospitalization and provide services that can reduce the probability they will become so debilitated again. Halfway houses (community residences for individuals who no longer require institutionalization but who still need some support in readjusting to the community) are an example of tertiary prevention. Such programs seek to increase individuals' coping skills by reducing their social isolation, by increasing their social skills, and by developing educational strategies tailored to their needs.

Community psychology has successfully reached large numbers of mentally and emotionally distressed people, not only through prevention but also through intervention. Unfortunately, strong cutbacks in federal funding of community mental health centers in the 1980s have diminished their effectiveness and stalled their expansion.

Because programs such as outreach services may be the only mental health care available to those who are poor or who are from ethnic minority backgrounds, community psychology approaches are especially important (Perkins & Zimmerman, 1995). Remember from our earlier comments that psychotherapy has been more available to the wealthy. An explicit value of community psychology is to assist

---

people who are disenfranchised from society to gain access to comparable forms of support. **Empowerment** *refers to helping individuals develop skills they need to improve their adaptation and circumstances.*

IS PSYCHOTHERAPY EFFECTIVE?

Do individuals who go through therapy get better? Are some approaches more effective than others, or is the situation similar to that of the Dodo in *Alice's Adventures in Wonderland?* Dodo was asked to judge the winner of a race; he decided, "Everybody has won and all must have prizes." How would we evaluate the effectiveness of psychotherapy? Would we take the client's word, or the therapist's word? What would be our criteria for effectiveness? Would it be "feeling good," "adaptive behavior," "improved interpersonal relationships," "autonomous decision making," or "more positive self-concept," for example? During the past several decades, an extensive amount of thought and research has addressed these questions.

Outcome Research on the Effectiveness of Psychotherapy

Four decades ago, Hans Eysenck (1952) shocked the pundits in the field of psychotherapy by concluding that treatment is ineffective. Eysenck analyzed 24 studies of psychotherapy and found that approximately two-thirds of the individuals with neurotic symptoms improved. Sounds impressive so far. But Eysenck also found that a similar percentage of neurotic individuals on waiting lists to see a psychotherapist also showed marked improvement even though they were not given any psychotherapy at all.

Critics of Eysenck's findings suggested that there were many irregularities in how he analyzed his data and drew conclusions. Even so, Eysenck's pronouncement prompted a flurry of research on psychotherapy's effectiveness. Hundreds of studies on the outcome of psychotherapy have now been conducted (Sanderson, 1995; Whiston & Sexton, 1993). One strategy for analyzing these diverse studies is called **meta-analysis,** *in*

which the researcher statistically combines the results of many different studies. In one meta-analysis of psychotherapy research, 475 studies were statistically combined (Smith, Glass, & Miller, 1980). Only those studies in which a therapy group had been compared with an untreated control group were compared. The results were much kinder to psychotherapy effectiveness than Eysenck's earlier results: On 88 percent of the measures, individuals who received therapy improved more than those who did not. This meta-analysis documents that psychotherapy is effective in general, but it does not inform us about the specific ways in which different therapies might be effective.

People who are thinking about seeing a psychotherapist not only want to know whether psychotherapy in general is effective, but they would especially like to know which form of psychotherapy is effective for their particular problem. In the meta-analysis conducted by Mary Lee Smith and her colleagues (Smith, Glass, & Miller, 1980) comparisons of different types of psychotherapy were also made. For example, behavior therapies were compared with insight therapies (psychodynamic, humanistic). Both the behavior and insight therapies were superior to no treatment at all, but they did not differ from each other in effectiveness. While no particular therapy was the best in the study by Smith and her colleagues, some therapies do seem to be more effective in treating some disorders than others. The behavior therapies have been most successful in treating specific behavioral problems, such as phobias and sexual dysfunctions. The cognitive therapies have been most successful in treating depression. Also, many therapies have their maximum benefit early in treatment with less improvement occurring as the individual remains in therapy.

The informed consumer also needs to be aware of some evidence that in certain cases psychotherapy can actually be harmful. For example, people who have a low tolerance of anxiety, low motivation, and strong signs of psychological deterioration may worsen as therapy progresses. Characteristics of the therapist also have

been related to a worsening of the client's status as therapy progresses. Therapists who are aggressive, who try to get clients to disclose personal information too quickly, and who are impatient with the process of change may exacerbate their clients' problems. Therapist bias can be harmful when the therapist does not understand ethnic, religious, gender, or other cultural differences, but instead pressures such clients to conform to White, middle-class norms. Finally, therapists who engage in sex with a client harm the client; such behavior is absolutely unethical.

While incompetent and unethical therapists do exist, there are many impeccable therapists who successfully help their clients. Like jazz musicians, psychotherapists must be capable of improvising, gracefully. As psychologist Jerome Frank put it, "Successful therapy is not just a scientific process, it is a healing art as well."

Common Themes and Specificity in Psychotherapy

After carefully studying the nature of psychotherapy for more than 25 years, Jerome Frank (1982) concluded that effective psychotherapies have the common elements of expectations, mastery, and emotional arousal. By inspiring an expectation of help, the therapist motivates the client to continue coming to therapy. These expectations are powerful morale builders and symptom relievers in themselves. The therapist also increases the client's sense of mastery and competence. For example, clients begin to feel that they can cope effectively with their world. Therapy also arouses the individual's emotions, essential to motivating behavioral change, according to Frank.

The therapeutic relationship is another important ingredient in successful psychotherapy (Garfield, 1995; Strupp, 1993). A relationship in which the client has confidence and trust in the therapist is essential to effective psychotherapy (Walborn, 1996). In one study, the most common ingredient in the success of different psychotherapies was the therapist's supportiveness of the client (Wallerstein, 1989). The client and therapist engage in a "healing ritual," which requires the active participation of both the client and the therapist. As part of this ritual, the client gains hope and becomes less alienated.

But while psychotherapies have common themes, some critics worry about carrying this commonality too far. Specificity in psychotherapy still needs careful attention—we need to understand "*what* treatment is most effective for *this* individual with *that* specific problem, and under *which* set of circumstances" within the cultural context (Paul, 1967). At this time, however, we do not know which approach works best in which situation with which therapist. Some therapists are better trained than others, some are more sensitive to a person's feelings, some are more introverted, and some are more conservative. Because of the myriad ways we differ as human beings, the ideal "fit" of therapist and client is difficult to pinpoint scientifically.

Guidelines for Seeking Professional Help

When trying to find a therapist, you could consider a psychologist, psychiatrist, social worker, counselor, or any number of other helping professionals. Each of these mental health professionals is qualified to provide psychotherapeutic services. They all practice from any one or combination of the therapeutic orientations discussed in this chapter. They might also see people on an individual, one-to-one basis, or in small groups, as in group therapy. The critical question is, of course, how does someone go about selecting a therapist to help them? This is not as easy a question as it may appear at first glance. We may face many of the same problems when we try to find a "good" medical doctor, accountant, or dentist; however, the way that most people go about finding these other professional services may not be the best way of selecting a therapist. Asking a friend for a good therapist ignores the fact that some approaches to therapy work better with some problems than others. Also, every therapeutic relationship is different, so one person's experience in therapy is not translatable to another person's. We offer the following general suggestions when looking for a therapist.

1. Identify the professional's credentials. Although all different types of mental health professionals may be competent, psychologists, psychiatrists, and social workers all differ in their approach to therapy, based on differences in training: Psychologists tend to be focused on the person's emotions and behaviors; psychiatrists are trained as medical doctors, so their perspective is likely to involve physical aspects of psychological problems; and social workers will be inclined to take a person's entire family and social situation into account. Regardless of the exact profession, some minimal credentials should be considered important. All states have licensing regulations for professionals who provide public services. Thus, a therapist should be licensed or certified by a state in order to practice. In addition, in some cases it may be important for a professional to have some advanced, specialized training in a certain area. For example, if a person is seeking help with a specific problem, like drug abuse, alcohol abuse, or a sexual problem, the therapist should have some training in that area. You should ask about the professional's credentials either before or during a first visit.

2. When starting therapy, give it some time before making a judgment of how useful it is. Making changes is very difficult. Expecting too much too soon can result in premature dissatisfaction and disappointment. Because a large part of therapy involves the development of a relationship with the therapist, it may take several meetings to really know if things are going well. One suggestion is to give it four to six weekly meetings. If it does not seem like things are going the way you would like, it is a good idea to discuss your progress with the therapist and ask what you should expect with regard to making progress. Setting specific goals with specific time expectations can be helpful. If your goals are not being met, you might consider a new therapist.

3. Be a thoughtful and careful consumer of mental health services. With any services, the more informed you are about the services provided, the better decision you can make about whether or not they are the right services for you. Calling around and asking specific questions about approaches and specializations is one way to become informed about the services offered by therapists. Consider how important it may be that the therapist is of your same or opposite sex, whether it is important that they have experience with your specific difficulty, as well as other specific characteristics. You may also want to learn more about their theoretical orientation to therapy as described in this chapter. Most professionals are quite comfortable talking about their background and training. Your confidence and trust in the professional is an important part of how well therapy will work for you.

These general guidelines should be used when first looking for a therapist. Remember that people should continually evaluate their own progress throughout therapy and when they feel dissatisfied with how it is going, they should discuss this with their therapist. Remember that therapy is like other services: when dissatisfied you can always look for another therapist. Don't think that just because one therapist has not been helpful none will be. All therapists and therapeutic relationships are different. Finding the right therapist is one of the most important factors in therapy success.

Only in the last two decades have psychologists become sensitive to the sociocultural aspects of therapy that are particularly important for making a good match between a therapist and a client. Let's examine how gender, ethnicity and social class, and culture influence treatment effectiveness.

Gender Issues in Treatment Effectiveness

One of the by-products of changing gender roles for women and men is a rethinking of approaches to psychotherapy. In some instances, the development of abnormal behavior and lack of effective psychotherapy may be due to traditional gender conditioning (Worell & Robinson, 1993). Our discussion of gender and therapy focuses on three areas: autonomy and relatedness in therapy, consciousness-raising groups, and feminist therapies, each of which we examine in turn.

Autonomy and Relatedness in Therapy

Autonomy and relatedness are central issues to an understanding of gender conditioning. For many years autonomy was championed as an important characteristic for maturity. As a result, autonomy was the unquestioned goal of many psychotherapies, relatedness was not. Thomas Szasz (1965), for example, claimed that the basic goal of psychotherapy is to foster autonomy, independence, and freedom. The humanistic theorists—Rogers, Maslow, and Perls—argued that to become psychologically healthy, an individual has to become self-actualized through self-determination and fulfillment of needs, independent of social constraints or personal commitments.

But therapists are taking a new look at autonomy as the ideal goal of therapy for females. Should therapy with females focus more on the way most females have been socialized and place more emphasis on relationships? Can females, even with psychotherapy, achieve autonomy in a male-dominated society? Are conventional ways of thinking about autonomy and relatedness appropriate for capturing the complexity of human experience? Would psychotherapy for females, as well as for males, be improved if its goals were more androgynous in nature, stressing better psychological functioning in *both* autonomy and relatedness?

Because traditional therapy often has not adequately addressed the specific concerns of women in a sexist society, several nontraditional approaches have arisen. These nontraditional therapies emphasize the importance of helping people break free from traditional gender roles and stereotypes. The nontraditional therapies avoid language that labels one sex as more socially desirable or valuable than the other. Let's now consider two such nontraditional therapies: Consciousness-raising groups and feminist therapy.

Increased interest has focused on gender roles in psychotherapy. Might female psychotherapists be more likely to encourage autonomy and relatedness, rather than autonomy alone, as psychotherapy goals?

Consciousness-Raising Groups

Consciousness-raising groups *are believed by some feminists to be important alternatives or adjuncts to traditional therapies; they often involve several people meeting in a member's home, are frequently leaderless (or members take turns facilitating discussion), and focus on the members' feelings and self-perceptions.* Instead of seeking and accepting male-biased therapy, women may meet in consciousness-raising groups to define their own experiences with their own criteria.

Some men followed suit and formed all-male consciousness-raising groups in which they discuss what it means to be male in our society (Rabinowitz & Cochran, 1987). Several colleges and universities have rape-awareness programs, a form of consciousness-raising groups for men. Going even further, the University of Wisconsin group Men Stopping Rape offers a version of their program to junior high and high school students (Paludi, 1995).

Feminist Therapies

Feminist therapies *are usually based on a critique of society wherein women are perceived to have less political and economic power than men have. Also, feminist therapies assume that the reasons for women's problems are principally social, not personal.* Many individuals assume that feminist therapies and nonsexist therapies are identical. However, some feminists distinguish between the two. For example, **nonsexist therapy** *occurs when the therapist has become aware of and primarily overcome his or her own sexist attitudes and behavior.* Thus, a nonsexist therapist would not perceive a dependent man or an independent woman to be showing emotional problems just because they are acting in counterstereotypic ways. Nonsexist therapists do not view marriage as any better for women or men. And these therapists also encourage women and men to adopt androgynous gender roles rather than stereotypic masculine or feminine ones (Paludi, 1995). Feminist therapy represents a sociocultural perspective that can be interwoven with other approaches to enhance their effectiveness.

Feminist therapists, both male and female, believe that traditional psychotherapy continues to carry considerable gender bias, and that women clients cannot realize their full potential without becoming aware of society's sexism (Mays, Caldwell, & Jackson, 1996). The goals of feminist therapists are no different from other therapists' goals. Feminist therapists make no effort to turn clients into feminists, but want the female client to be fully aware of how the nature of the female role in the American society can contribute to the development of a mental disorder. Feminist therapists believe women must become aware of the effects of social oppression on their own lives if they are to achieve their mental health goals.

In one feminist approach to therapy, women go through three phases en route to mental health (Williams, 1987). First, in *harmful adaptation,* women accept dependency and the rules of a patriarchal society. In this phase, women harm themselves because they subordinate their own desires and needs to the values of the system. Second, in *corrective action,* when women realize what harmful adaptation has done to them, they begin to develop their own identity and to articulate personal goals. Third, in *health maintenance,* women develop pride in their new identity and form alliances with other women to work toward better conditions for all women. In this model of feminist therapy, women move from acceptance of an oppressive society to taking pride in a new, positive status and helping other women achieve the same.

Ethnicity and Social Class Issues in Treatment Effectiveness

For much too long, psychotherapists were concerned almost exclusively with helping middle- and upper-class individuals cope with their problems while ignoring the needs of people who were poor or from ethnic minority backgrounds (Atkinson, Morten, & Sue, 1993; Ponterotto & others, 1995; Reid & Bing, 1996; Sue, 1996). Although having financial resources does not guarantee happiness, functionality, or a stress-free existence, psychology has been remiss in the seriousness with which it has undertaken to provide improved services to ethnic minority individuals and members of the lower class (Aponte, Rivers, & Wohl, 1995).

Most people, regardless of their ethnicity, prefer to discuss problems with their parents, friends, and relatives rather than with mental health professionals.

(a)

(b)

(c)

(d)

How might therapy proceed differently in the following contexts: (*a*) an ethnic minority client with a White, middle-class therapist, (*b*) a White male client from impoverished circumstances in rural Appalachia, (*c*) an Asian American client who is a recent immigrant to the United States, and (*d*) an African American female client with an African American female therapist?

However, other factors complicate the delivery of health care services to the underserved. One reason is that there are so few ethnic minority psychotherapists (Sue, Ivey, & Pedersen, 1996). For example, one study found that African American college students were more likely to use the college's mental health facilities if an African American clinician or counselor were available than if only White counselors were available (Thompson & Cimbolic, 1978).

Therapy can be effective when the therapist and client are from different cultural backgrounds if the therapist has excellent clinical skills and is culturally sensitive (Gim, Atkinson, & Kim, 1991). Researchers have also found that Asian Americans, African Americans, Latinos, and Native Americans terminate psychotherapy after an initial session at a much higher rate than do Anglo-Americans (Sue, Allen, & Conaway, 1978). The social stigma of being a "mental patient," fear of hospitalization, conflict between their own belief system and the beliefs of modern mental health practitioners, and the availability of an alternate healer are additional reasons ethnic minority individuals terminate therapy early.

Barriers to Therapeutic Effectiveness

Psychotherapy involves interpersonal interaction and communication. Verbal and nonverbal messages need to be accurately sent and received. Very effective therapy can take place when the client and therapist are from different sociocultural backgrounds. However, when the psychotherapist and client come from different cultural backgrounds, barriers to communication can develop, which can lead to misunderstandings that destroy rapport and undermine the effectiveness of psychotherapy (Atkinson, Morten, & Sue, 1993; Parham, 1996). Among the barriers that can impede psychotherapy's effectiveness with individuals from ethnic minority groups are (1) language differences, (2) class-bound values, and (3) culture-bound values.

Language Differences   A psychotherapist's reliance on verbal interaction to establish rapport with a client presupposes that the psychotherapist and the client can understand each other. However, many psychotherapists fail to recognize that there may be a language barrier between them and ethnic minority individuals that restricts the development of rapport. Also, many educationally and economically impoverished clients might not have the verbal skills required to benefit from the psychotherapist's advice, interpretation, and counseling, especially if the psychotherapist communicates complex concepts to the client. Psychotherapists may also misinterpret the body language—gestures and postures, for example—of individuals from ethnic minority groups. For example, African American clients often avoid eye contact in conversation, whereas White clients usually maintain eye contact. A psychotherapist may inappropriately interpret an African American client's lack of eye contact as inattentiveness, lack of interest, or anger.

Class-Bound Values   One of the most frequently encountered issues involving middle-class psychotherapists and lower-class clients is the willingness to make and keep psychotherapy appointments. Lower-class clients may be concerned with "survival" or "making it through the day." Appointments made for 2 weeks in the future or 50-minute sessions might not be appropriate for the needs of a lower-class client who requires immediate help. One clinician described poor Appalachian Whites as refusing to live by the clock and not only refusing to adhere to the values of promptness, planning, and protocol but also suspecting people who do adhere to these values (Vontress, 1973). The clients' socioeconomic status also affects the kind of treatment they receive. For example, one study revealed that students from upper socioeconomic backgrounds are given more exploratory counseling interviews than students from lower socioeconomic backgrounds (Ryan & Gaier, 1968).

Culture-Bound Values   Psychotherapists often impose their own values on clients from a different cultural background. Referring to clients from other cultures, especially those from ethnic minority groups, as "culturally deprived" exemplifies this imposition. Cultural misunderstandings can lead to difficulties in communication, expectations, the quality of care given, and the client's motivation to continue psychotherapy. For instance, many psychotherapists believe that self-disclosure is an important condition for effective psychotherapy. However, clients are less likely to disclose private, sensitive information about themselves to someone who has a different cultural background. Also, self-disclosure may be contrary to the basic cultural values of individuals from some cultures. For example, Chinese Americans are taught at an early age to refrain from emotional expression; they may find psychotherapists' demands to disclose personal information as threatening. Similar conflicts have been reported for Chicanos and Native Americans.

Not all cultures share the Western mainstream views about the causes and appropriate treatment of disorders. In one investigation, six ethnic minority groups viewed maladaptive behavior more broadly than did the mainstream mental health professionals (Flaskerud, 1984). For example, the ethnic minority groups described maladaptive behavior in spiritual, moral, somatic (bodily), psychological, and metaphysical terms. The ethnic minority groups also had different ideas about therapy than the mental health professionals. The ethnic groups said the management of abnormal behavior could include social, spiritual, economic, vocational, recreational, personal, physical, and psychological strategies, whereas the mental health professionals said it should involve traditional psychotherapy and psychopharmaceutical approaches.

Ethnically Responsive Therapy

An example of a broad, culturally sensitive approach to therapy is the recent interest in integrating folk healers into Western therapy when certain ethnic groups are involved. For example, in Florida, the University of Miami's Community Mental Health Center uses folk healers, including Afrocuban *santeros,* Haitian *houngans* or *mambos,* Hispanic *espiritistas,* and African American root doctors as consultants, trainers, and referral sources. Such collaboration allows clients in need of therapy to derive whatever benefit they can from Western methods without turning their backs on the methods of their culture.

In response to demands for more concrete recommendations on how to conduct therapy, some clinicians have attempted to devise ethnically responsive treatments (Casas & San Miguel, 1993). For example, in working with Asian Americans, a number of therapists recommend a directive and structured approach because Asian Americans prefer the concrete direction provided in this format. In working with Latinos, some therapists recommend a reframing of problems as medical rather than psychological to reduce resistance. The assumption is that Latinos will be more receptive to a combined medical and psychological orientation, due to their health concept of an integrated mind and body (Padilla, 1994). In working with African Americans, some therapists recommend externally focused, action-oriented therapy, rather than internally focused, intrapsychic therapy.

> Nobody, as long as he moves about among the chaotic currents of life, is without trouble.
>
> —Carl Jung

Such recommendations, however, raise some important questions. For example, isn't it impossible for therapists to change their therapy orientation to work with ethnic minority groups effectively? Thus, a psychoanalytic therapist might find it difficult to use the externally focused, action-oriented therapy recommended for African Americans. By using a specific approach, supposedly based on the client's cultural background, how does the therapist deal with diversity and individual differences in an ethnic or cultural group? Because of the problems raised by such questions, we cannot just say, "Know the cultural background of the client or use this approach with that particular ethnic or cultural group."

According to Stanley Sue (1990), what we can say is that when they see ethnic minority clients, therapists should emphasize two processes, at least in initial therapy sessions: (1) credibility and (2) giving. **Credibility** *is the therapist's believability.* **Giving** *refers to the client's receiving some kind of benefit from treatment early in the therapy process.* Two factors are important in increasing credibility: ascribed status and achieved status. Ascribed status is one's position or role defined by others or cultural norms. In some cultures, the young are subordinate to the old, those who are naive abide by those in authority, and females have less power than males. Credibility must also be achieved. The therapist can achieve credibility by doing something that the client perceives as being helpful or competent. Lack of ascribed credibility may be the main reason ethnic minority individuals tend to steer clear of therapy; lack of achieved credibility may be the main reason ethnic minority individuals terminate therapy once it has begun as well as problems with rapport.

In terms of giving, clients may wonder how talking to a therapist will alleviate their problems. Therapists need to help ethnic minority clients see the relationship between therapy and why it will help a person get better (Caldwell, 1996). It is important for the therapist to make this association in the first session. Many ethnic minority clients do not understand Western psychotherapy. The first session should not be just an assessment session, but rather the therapist should find out about the client, give some recommendations for treatment, and say something concrete to the client so the client will leave the first session saying, "I got something out of it that I think will help me and I want to come back again." Many therapists believe this approach produces a stronger therapeutic alliance regardless of the ethnicity of the client and therapist. How important would it be for you to find a therapist whose background is similar to your own? This question is the focus of Critical Thinking.

So far we have discussed a variety of psychotherapies that can help individuals cope more effectively with stress and develop more adaptive, less harmful behavior. In recent years considerable progress has also been made in biomedical therapies, which we now discuss.

BIOMEDICAL THERAPIES

Biomedical therapies *are treatments to reduce or eliminate the symptoms of psychological disorders by altering the way an individual's body functions. Drug therapy is the most common form of biomedical therapy.* Psychologists and other mental health professionals may provide

CRITICAL THINKING

The Match Game

How critical is it to the success of psychotherapy for the therapist to have the same demographic characteristics as the client (such as ethnicity, gender, socioeconomic class, religion, and sexual orientation)? How important would it be for you personally to have a therapist with a similar background and characteristics comparable to your own? What justifications can you offer to support your point of view?

Thinking through how to create the best match provides you with *practice in self-reflection to enhance personal growth.*

psychotherapy in conjunction with the biomedical therapy administered by psychiatrists and other medical doctors.

Drug Therapy

Psychotherapeutic drugs are used to treat many mental disorders—anxiety, depression, and schizophrenia, for example. In some instances, these drugs are effective when other forms of therapy are not. Drug therapy has substantially reduced the amount of time schizophrenics must spend in hospitals, for example (Smith & Darlington, 1996). Three main types of psychotherapeutic drugs are antianxiety drugs, antipsychotic drugs, and antidepressant drugs.

Antianxiety Drugs

Antianxiety drugs *are commonly known as tranquilizers; these drugs reduce anxiety by making individuals less excitable and more tranquil.* Why are antianxiety drugs so widely used? Many individuals experience stress, anxiety, or an inability to sleep well; family physicians and psychiatrists prescribe these drugs to improve our abilities to cope with these situations more effectively. The most widely used antianxiety drugs are Xanax and Valium.

The relaxed feelings brought on by antianxiety drugs are a welcome relief to individuals experiencing anxiety and stress in their lives. However, these drugs often cause fatigue and drowsiness; motor abilities can be impaired and work productivity reduced; and extended use can produce dependence. In some instances, the combination of antianxiety drugs and alcohol has caused death. When an individual feels anxious, it may be best to face the problems creating the anxiety rather than relying on antianxiety drugs to avoid the problems.

Antipsychotic Drugs

Antipsychotic drugs *are powerful drugs that diminish agitated behavior, reduce tension, decrease hallucinations and delusions, improve social behavior, and produce better sleep patterns in severely mentally disabled individuals, especially schizophrenics.* Neuroleptics are the most widely used antipsychotic drugs.

The main value of antipsychotic drugs is their ability to block the dopamine system's action in the brain (Breier, 1996; Holcomb & others, 1996). For example, schizophrenics have too much of the neurochemical messenger dopamine. Numerous well-controlled investigations have revealed that, when used in sufficient doses, the neuroleptics reduce a variety of schizophrenic symptoms, at least in the short term (Kirkpatrick & others, 1989). The neuroleptics do not cure schizophrenia, however, and they can have severe side effects. The neuroleptics treat the symptoms of schizophrenia, not its causes. If an individual stops taking the drugs, the symptoms return (Rebec, 1996).

Neuroleptic drugs have substantially reduced the lengths of hospital stays for schizophrenics. Although schizophrenics often are able to return to the community because drug therapy keeps their symptoms from reappearing, most have difficulty coping with the demands of society and most are chronically unemployed.

Tardive dyskinesia *is a major side effect of the neuroleptic drugs; it is a neurological disorder characterized by grotesque, involuntary movements of the facial muscles and mouth, as well as extensive twitching of the neck, arms, and legs.* As many as 20 percent of all schizophrenics taking neuroleptics develop this disorder; elderly women are especially vulnerable.

Long-term neuroleptic therapy also is associated with increased depression and anxiety. For example, schizophrenics who have taken neuroleptics for many years report that they feel miserable most of the time. Nonetheless, for the majority of schizophrenics, the benefits of neuroleptic treatment outweigh its risks and discomforts, even if a cure for schizophrenia remains elusive.

Lithium *is a drug that is widely used to treat bipolar disorder* (recall that this disorder involves wide mood swings of depression and mania). The amount of lithium that circulates in the bloodstream needs to be monitored carefully because its effective dosage is precariously close to toxic levels. Memory impairment is also associated with lithium use.

As with schizophrenia, the treatment of affective disorders might also involve a combination of drug therapy and psychotherapy. In one study, the combination of tricyclics and interpersonal psychotherapy produced a lower than normal relapse rate for depressed clients (10 percent versus 22 percent) (Frank & Kupfer, 1986). The interpersonal therapy focused on the clients' ability to develop and maintain positive interpersonal relationships and included an educational workshop for the clients and their families.

Some strategies for increasing the effectiveness of the neuroleptics involve (1) administering lower dosages over time rather than giving a large initial dose and (2) combining drug therapy with psychotherapy. The small percentage of schizophrenics who are able to hold jobs suggests that drugs alone will not make them contributing members of society. Vocational, family, and social skills training are needed in conjunction with drug therapy to facilitate improved psychological functioning and adaptation to society.

Antidepressant Drugs

Antidepressant drugs *regulate mood. The three main classes of antidepressant drugs are tricyclics, such as Elavil; MAO inhibitors, such as Nardil; and SSRI inhibitors, such as Prozac. The tricyclics,* so-called because of their three-ring molecular structure, probably work because they increase the level of certain neurotransmitters, especially norepinephrine and serotonin. The tricyclics reduce the symptoms of depression in approximately 60 to 70 percent of all cases. The tricyclics are not effective in improving mood until 2 to 4 weeks after the individual begins taking them, and they sometimes have adverse side effects—such as restlessness, faintness, and trembling. The MAO inhibitors are not as widely used as the tricyclics because they are more toxic, they require more dietary restrictions, and they usually have less potent therapeutic effects. Nonetheless, some severely depressed individuals who do not respond to the tricyclics do respond to the MAO inhibitors.

The third category of antidepressant drugs caused such a flurry of attention in recent years that their prescription was the topic of a cover story in both *Time* and *Newsweek*. The most prominent of the selective serotonin reuptake inhibiting (SSRI) type is Prozac (followed by Nardil and Paxil). SSRI drugs work by interfering with the reabsorption of serotonin in the brain. Prozac is most frequently prescribed for dysthymia, a mild to moderate form of clinical depression, but has also successfully treated anxiety, obsession, and shyness. Prozac, approved by the FDA in 1987, is a "clean" drug, meaning that side effects are few and unlikely (they include risk of nausea, diarrhea, and loss of sexual function) and there is no risk of addiction. Although many individuals report that they feel fully themselves when taking Prozac (Kramer, 1993), the drug also can be disinhibiting and dangerous for some individuals, who report an increase in suicidal feelings and aggressive impulses. The popularity of Prozac has prompted social critics to question whether we may be on the brink of a "designer drug culture" in which personal eccentricities of normal personality are seen as warranting correction through medication.

Phototherapy

Can you imagine setting aside several hours every morning during the fall and winter to sit in front of a bright white light in order to avoid disturbing feelings (see figure 15.6)? Phototherapy, the use of full-spectrum light (containing all the colors naturally present in daylight), has received anecdotal support as an effective treatment for those suffering the form of depression called **seasonal affective disorder (SAD)**, *depression that appears to be caused by a decrease in exposure to sunlight.* Those who suffer this problem invariably report greater emotional challenges in the winter months. The creators of the therapy believe that the artificial light compensates SAD sufferers to alleviate the symptoms of depression.

Electroconvulsive Therapy

"Then something bent down and took hold of me and shook me like the end of the world. Wee-ee-ee-ee-ee, it shrilled, through an air crackling with blue light, and with each flash a great jolt drubbed

FIGURE 15.6

Phototherapy
Seasonal affective disorder is often treated with a bank of high-intensity, full-spectrum lights for several hours each morning before daybreak during the fall and winter months when the disorder is most debilitating.

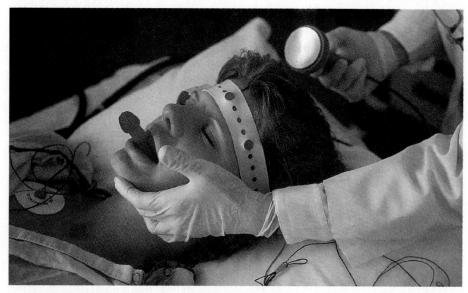

Electroconvulsive therapy (ECT), commonly called "shock therapy," causes a seizure in the brain. ECT is still given to as many as 60,000 people a year, mainly to treat major depression.

me until I thought my bones would break and the sap fly out of me like a split plant." Such images as this description from Sylvia Plath's (1971) autobiographic novel, *The Bell Jar*, have shaped the public's view of **electroconvulsive therapy (ECT).** *Commonly called "shock treatment," ECT is sometimes used to treat severely depressed individuals.* The

goal of ECT is to cause a seizure in the brain much like what happens spontaneously in some forms of epilepsy. A small electric current, lasting for 1 second or less, passes through two electrodes placed on the individual's head. The current excites neural tissue, stimulating a seizure that lasts for approximately 1 minute.

ECT has been used for more than 40 years. In earlier years, it often was used indiscriminately, sometimes even as a punishment for patients. ECT is still used on as many as 60,000 individuals a year, mainly to treat major depression. Adverse side effects may include memory loss or other cognitive impairment. Today ECT is given mainly to individuals who have not responded to drug therapy or psychotherapy.

ECT sounds as if it would entail intolerable pain, but the manner in which it is administered today involves little discomfort. The patient is given anesthesia and muscle relaxants before the current is applied; this allows the individual to sleep through the procedure, it minimizes convulsions, and it reduces the risk of physical injury. The individual awakens shortly afterward with no conscious memory of the treatment.

The following example reveals how ECT, used as a last resort, can be effective in reducing depression (Sackheim, 1985). Clara is a 36-year-old teacher and mother. She has been in psychotherapy for several years. Prior to entering the hospital, she had taken tricyclics with unsuccessful results. In the first 6 months of her hospital stay, doctors tried various drugs to reduce her depression; none worked. She slept poorly, lost her appetite, and showed no interest even in reading newspaper headlines. Obsessed with the idea that she had ruined her children's lives, she repeatedly threatened suicide. With her consent, doctors began ECT; after five treatments, Clara returned to her family and job. Not all cases of ECT turn out as positively, however; and even when ECT works, no one knows why it works (Kramer, 1987).

Psychosurgery

One biomedical treatment is even more extreme than ECT. **Psychosurgery** *is a biomedical therapy that involves the removal or destruction of brain tissue to improve the individual's psychological adjustment.* The effects of psychosurgery are irreversible.

In the 1930s, Portuguese physician Egas Moniz developed a procedure known as a *prefrontal lobotomy*. In this procedure, a surgical instrument is inserted into the brain and rotated, severing fibers that connect the frontal lobe, important in higher thought processes, and the thalamus, important in emotion. Moniz theorized that, by severing the connections between these brain structures, the symptoms of severe mental disorders could be alleviated. Prefrontal lobotomies were conducted on thousands of patients from the 1930s through the 1950s. Moniz was even awarded the Nobel Prize for his work. However, although some patients may have benefited from the lobotomies, many were left in vegetablelike states because of the massive assaults on their brains.

These crude lobotomies are no longer performed. Since the 1960s, psychosurgery has become more precise. When psychosurgery is now performed, a small lesion is made in the amygdala or another part of the limbic system. Today only several hundred patients per year undergo psychosurgery; it is used as a last resort and with extreme caution.

REVIEW

The Effectiveness of Psychotherapy and Biomedical Therapies

Psychotherapy in general is effective, but no single treatment is more effective than others. Behavioral therapies are often most successful in treating specific behavioral problems, such as phobias; cognitive therapy is often most successful in treating depression. Common themes in successful therapies include expectations, a sense of mastery, emotional arousal, and a confiding relationship. We still need to examine further which therapy works best with which individual in which setting with which therapist.

Historically the goal of therapy has been autonomy, but questions are raised about this as an ideal goal of therapy, especially for females. The goals of psychotherapy should include more attention to relatedness. Two nontraditional, gender-related forms of therapy are consciousness-raising groups and feminist therapy. Some feminist therapists distinguish between feminist therapy and nonsexist therapy. For too long, the needs of people from poor and ethnic minority backgrounds were ignored by psychotherapists. Among the barriers that impede psychotherapy's effectiveness with ethnic minority individuals are language differences, class-bound values, and culture-bound values. Credibility and giving are two important therapy processes with ethnic minority clients.

Biomedical therapies are designed to reduce or eliminate the symptoms of psychological disorders by altering the way an individual's body functions. Drug therapy is the most common biomedical therapy. Drug therapy may be effective when other therapies have failed, as in reducing the symptoms of schizophrenia. Three major classes of psychotherapeutic drugs are antianxiety, antipsychotic, and antidepressant. Phototherapy is often used with individuals who have seasonal affective disorder. Electroconvulsive therapy, commonly called "shock treatment," creates a seizure in the brain; its most common use is as a last resort in treating severe depression. Psychosurgery is an irreversible procedure; brain tissue is destroyed in an effort to improve psychological adjustment. Today's psychosurgery is more precise than the early prefrontal lobotomies. Psychosurgery is used only as a last resort.

CRITICAL THINKING ABOUT ADJUSTMENT

The Designer Brain and Enhanced Abilities

One pill makes you larger,
And one pill makes you small.

—Grace Slick

Lewis Carroll's *Alice in Wonderland* is often read as a whimsical metaphorical account of the adaptability that drugs can provide. When Alice was not tall enough to reach an opening, she drank a potion and magically grew to the required height. When she came upon another entrance that was too small for her giant frame, she drank another potion to shrink herself sufficiently.

Although science cannot produce the physical transformations described in Lewis Carroll's tale, many believe we are on the brink of a revolution in pharmacology that will produce mental health "designer drugs" not just to medicate the mentally disordered but to enhance the capacities of people with "normal" personalities. Once again, science may have made technological progress in areas where we have not fully considered the ethical and moral implications of implementing the technology.

Peter Kramer's depressed and anxious patients in *Listening to Prozac* (1993) are persuasive. They speak of feeling liberated from the edginess and depression that confused and confined them. They proclaim that they have discovered their true selves. They regret the span of their lives when they were without Prozac and wonder who they could have become if they had been able to be at their best throughout their lives.

However, the use of medication to enhance normal functioning is decidedly controversial. Many argue against the use of drugs to enhance normal function on religious grounds or because such interventions are "unnatural." Many believe philosophically that lives were meant to be lived fully, including feeling pain without the blunting caused by medication, in order to experience the full range of what life has to offer. Still others object on practical grounds. They express concern that we do not fully understand the long-term implications of using these drugs; they worry that there may be some serious bodily harms from long-term use that we simply have not had time to discover.

Those who advocate the development of mental health designer drugs view this technology as another step in helping humans adapt more effectively to their environments. For example, individuals who are born near-sighted use the technology of eyeglasses and contact lenses to compensate for their deficiencies and to adapt visually to their environments. People with chronic disease in our culture use any available technology to sustain life and promote a better quality of life. Advocates argue that designer drugs are a similar use of technology to adapt to ever worsening stress in contemporary life. They are optimistic that science will continue to produce cleaner and safer drugs for a variety of problems. They also suggest that society as a whole would benefit from citizens who are functioning closer to their maximum potential.

Where do you stand on the use of drugs to enhance normal functioning? If you had the opportunity legally to take a drug that would enhance your performance, would you? Or would you pass this opportunity by, regarding it as an example of human foolishness in trying to attain perfection using artificial methods? What personality characteristics or values undergird your position on designer drugs? Your position should reveal your ability to *identify values and challenge assumptions that influence behavior.*

The desire to take medicine is perhaps the greatest feature which distinguishes man from animals.

—William Osler

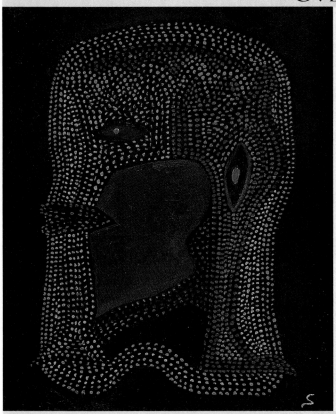

We began this chapter by exploring the nature of psychotherapy, both historically and in terms of current practice. We spent considerable time examining the individual therapies—psychodynamic, humanistic, behavioral, and cognitive. Then we studied systems interventions—group therapies and community psychology. We read about whether therapy is effective, considering outcome research, themes and specificity, guidelines for seeking professional help, and gender, ethnicity, and social class issues. Our coverage of biomedical therapies focused on drug therapy, phototherapy, electroconvulsive therapy, and psychosurgery. Don't forget that you can obtain an overall summary of this chapter by again reading the in-chapter reviews on pages 371, 375, 380, 385, and 394.

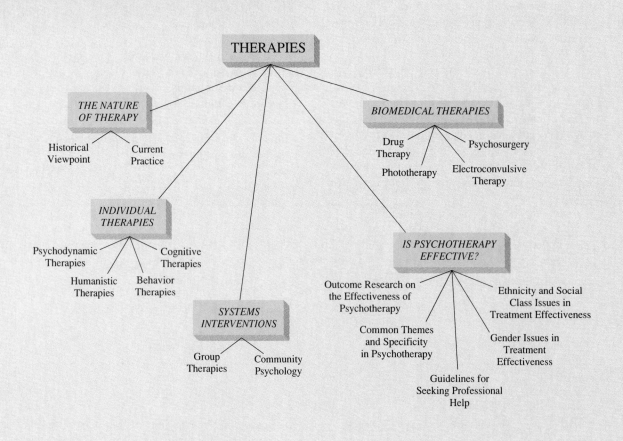

PRACTICAL KNOWLEDGE ABOUT ADJUSTMENT

THE CONSUMER'S GUIDE TO PSYCHOTHERAPY

(1992) by Jack Engler and Daniel Goleman. New York: Simon & Schuster.

This is a comprehensive manual on psychotherapy for consumers. Among the questions the authors ask and evaluate are these:

- How do I decide if I need therapy?
- Which therapy approach is best for me?
- How do I find the right therapist?

- What questions should I ask during the first session?
- How can I afford therapy?
- How can I tell if therapy is really working?
- How do I know when to end therapy?

The book is based on the clinical opinions of almost a thousand therapists nationwide. Included are case studies and listings of mental health organizations, as well as therapist referral sources.

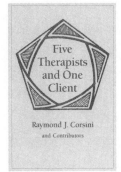

FIVE THERAPISTS AND ONE CLIENT

(1991) by Raymond Corsini and Contributors. Itasca, IL: Peacock.

Therapists with five distinctive approaches to helping clients describe their conceptual orientation and therapy techniques and demonstrate how they would likely work with the same fictitious client. The imaginary client is a relatively normal individual with unusual and persistent problems—a common client for psychotherapists in

private practice. Four clear-cut systems of psychotherapy were selected: Alfred Adler's individual therapy, Carl Rogers' person-centered therapy, Albert Ellis' rational-emotive therapy, and behavior therapy. Finally, a fifth therapy approach—eclectic therapy—was chosen. How therapists from these five different approaches would handle the same client serves as the core of the book, helping you to see distinctive ways therapists with different orientations conduct psychotherapy.

SELF-ASSESSMENT SCORING AND INTERPRETATION

IRRATIONAL VALUES

Scoring

This test is scored by adding up your answers. Scores range from 9 to 81.

Interpretation

Higher scores indicate a greater degree of irrational belief systems. The middle range on the test is in the mid 40s.

Monet
Sunrise, detail

Health

CHAPTER OUTLINE

CHAPTER BOXES

Look to your health and if you
have it value it next to good
conscience. . . . Health is a blessing
we mortals can achieve.

—Izaak Walton

When he died in 1995 at the age of 63, Mickey Mantle had been no stranger to heroism. Born in 1931 in Commerce, Oklahoma, Mickey Mantle may have been destined for a career in baseball. His father, Mutt, was a zinc miner who hoped Mickey would use sports as a path to a different life. He often played catch with Mickey after work until dark.

The practice worked. Mickey's center-field play for the New York Yankees was a thing of beauty. But his monster home runs were what secured his spot in baseball records and fans' hearts. He hit a total of eighteen home runs in a record twelve World Series. He was eighth on the total career home-run list, with one home run that went 650 feet—or, as one sportscaster put it, the equivalent of a $4 cab ride (which was quite a distance in those days). He was named World Series MVP three times. But Mantle's achievements were all the more remarkable when you realize that he performed under the burden of chronic knee problems, alcohol abuse, and the nagging fear that he, like so many of his male relatives, would die from cancer.

His fear was realized. Mantle died from one of the most aggressive liver tumors his doctors had ever seen. In a controversial move, Mantle's physicians had bumped him to the top of the liver transplant list, but their interventions were too late. After the transplant, it was discovered that his cancer had already spread too far for a transplant to save him.

In his eulogy for Mantle, sportscaster Bob Costas said that many Americans' emotional attachment to Mantle was so strong and lasting that it defied logic. Evidence for that attachment surfaced in the controversy that ensued following the public disclosure of Mantle's illness. Some avid fans even volunteered their own livers for transplant to save "the Mick."

Mantle's heroism surfaced in his response to his illness. In making his regrets public by publishing his autobiography, he apologized to his family and fans for his life of alcoholism and self-indulgence and suggested that others learn from his fate the deterioration and turmoil caused by alcohol. He even transcended the controversy over whether he had stolen a liver from someone more deserving or more likely to survive by launching a nonprofit group to increase organ donor registrations, bringing renewed national attention to the urgency of this problem. A newspaper cartoonist in Dallas suggested that, in facing his imminent death, Mickey Mantle played his most courageous ninth inning ever.

PREVIEW

This chapter is about making choices, and how today's choices expand or limit our choices tomorrow. Health psychologists study the relations between lifestyles and diseases. In this chapter we focus on these relations and other aspects of the relationship between adjustment and health. We begin by examining the scope of health psychology and the nature of health habits and lifestyles. Then we turn our attention to coping with illness and psychoactive drugs. We will conclude with a discussion of how we can live healthier lives.

RELATING HEALTH AND PSYCHOLOGY

The link between health and psychological factors is easy to make. You may have noticed in your own life that when you are feeling healthy, life is great. When you are "under the weather" from illness or "under the gun" from stress, other aspects of your life—the quality of your work, the smoothness of your relationships, your ability to study—are all likely to suffer. This connection was first observed many centuries ago.

Healing is a matter of time, but it is sometimes also a matter of opportunity.
—**Hippocrates** (460–357 B.C.)

Historical Background

Good health requires good habits. This was recognized as early as 2600 B.C. by Asian physicians and around 500 B.C. by Greek physicians. Unlike other early cultures, these cultures did not blame the gods for illness. Nor did they think that magic would cure illness. Instead, they realized that people have some control over their health. In these two cultures, the physician's role was to guide and assist the patient in restoring a natural and emotional balance in life.

Despite the wisdom of this integrated viewpoint, this belief did not persist during much of the history that followed. Later ideas about health and illness were based more on superstition and folklore, and old treatment methods seem primitive and foolish by today's standards.

For example, it used to be common to apply leeches for a variety of illnesses—a treatment that might have hastened many a sick person's demise.

As we approach the twenty-first century, once again we recognize the power of lifestyles and psychological states in promoting health. We are returning to the ancient view that the ultimate responsibility for influencing health rests with the individuals themselves. Without negating the importance of our genetic predispositions and the power of viruses and bacteria, we have come to believe that our daily behavioral choices and our general attitude about life play a significant role in the quality of our health. In addition, we affirm this belief using extensive research strategies in a variety of contexts. Psychologists and

other health-related scientists generate evidence to support many of the relationships that the ancient Asians and early Greeks originally suspected.

Current Approaches

Several specialized fields have emerged, primarily in the disciplines of psychology and biology, to explore how health and psychology are related.

Health psychology *is a multidimensional approach to health that emphasizes psychological factors, lifestyle, and the nature of the health-care delivery system.* To underscore the increasing interest in health, the American Psychological Association created a new division, Health Psychology, in 1978. **Behavioral medicine,** *a field closely related to health psychology, attempts to combine medical and*

The pursuit of healthy habits varies greatly across and within different cultures. (*a*) Members of the Masai tribe in Kenya, Africa, can stay on a treadmill for a long time because of their very active life. Heart disease is extremely low in the Masai tribe, which also can be attributed to the energetic lifestyle of the members of the tribe. In contrast, (*b*) Americans show a greater incidence of heart disease. Unfortunately, many Americans are inactive. However, many Americans are increasingly recognizing the health benefits of exercise and an active lifestyle and are working hard to make these habitual. The role of exercise in health is one of health psychology's many interests.

behavioral knowledge to reduce illness and promote health. The interests of health psychologists and behavioral medicine researchers are broad: They include examining decisions about adherence to medical recommendations, evaluating the effectiveness of media campaigns in reducing smoking, identifyng the psychological factors that affect weight loss, and exploring the role of exercise in reducing stress (Turpin & Slade, 1997).

PROMOTING HEALTH

We can do a great deal to promote better health by establishing healthy habits and evaluating and changing our behaviors that interfere with good health. Regular exercise and good nutrition are essential ingredients to a healthier lifestyle (Thayer & others, 1996). Avoiding overeating and smoking are also important in improving the quality of health.

> *Little with health is better than much with sickness.*
> —**Berber proverb**

Regular Exercise

In 1961, President John F. Kennedy offered the following message: "We are underexercised as a nation. We look instead of play. We ride instead of walk. Our existence deprives us of the minimum of physical activity essential for healthy living." Without question, people are jogging, cycling, and aerobically exercising more today than in 1961, but far too many of us are still couch potatoes. **Aerobic exercise** *is sustained exercise—jogging, swimming, or cycling, for example—that stimulates heart and lung activity* (Cooper, 1970).

Preventing Heart Disease

The main focus of research on the effects of exercise on health has involved preventing heart disease. Most health experts recommend that you should try to raise your heart rate to 60 percent of your maximum heart rate. Your maximum heart rate is calculated as 220 minus your age divided by 0.6, so if you are 20, you should aim for an exercise heart rate of 120 ($220 - 20 = 200 \times 0.6 = 120$).

If you are 45, you should aim for an exercise heart rate of 105 ($220 - 45 = 175 \times 0.6 = 105$).

People in some occupations get more vigorous exercise than those in others. For example, longshoremen have about half the risk of fatal heart attacks as co-workers like crane drivers and clerks who have physically less demanding jobs. Further, elaborate studies of 17,000 male alumni of Harvard University found that those who exercised strenuously on a regular basis had a lower risk of heart disease and were more likely to still be alive in their middle adulthood years (Lee, Hsieh, & Paffenbarger, 1995; Paffenbarger & others, 1986). Based on such findings, some health experts conclude that, regardless of other risk factors (smoking, high blood pressure, overweight, heredity), if you exercise enough to burn more than 2,000 calories a week, you can cut your risk of heart attack by an impressive two-thirds (Sherwood, Light, & Bluementhal, 1989). Burning up 2,000 calories a week through exercise requires a lot of effort, far more than most of us are willing to expend. To burn 300 calories a day, through exercise, you would have to do one of the following: swim or run for about 25 minutes, walk for 45 minutes at about 4 miles an hour, participate in aerobic dancing for 30 minutes.

The risk of heart attack can also be cut by as much as one-third over a 7-year period with such moderate exercise as rapid walking and gardening. The catch is that you have to spend an hour a day in these activities to get them to pay off. Going against the popular "no pain, no gain" philosophy, Robert Ornstein and David Sobel (1989) believe that exercise should be pleasurable, not painful. They point out that 20 percent of joggers running 10 miles a week suffer significant injuries, such as torn knee cartilage and pulled hamstring muscles. Ornstein and Sobel argue that most people can stay healthy by participating in exercise that burns up only 500 calories a week. They believe it is overkill to run 8-minute miles, 3 miles at a time, 5 days a week, for example. Not only are fast walking and gardening on their recommended list of exercises, so are 20 minutes of sex (110 calories), 20 minutes of playing with

children (106 calories), and 45 minutes of dancing (324 calories). Remember, regardless of your ultimate exercise program, health experts uniformly recommend that if you are unaccustomed to exercise, always start any exercise program slowly.

Improving Mental Health

Researchers have found that exercise benefits not only physical health, but mental health as well. In particular, exercise improves self-concept and reduces anxiety and depression (Ossip-Klein & others, 1989). In one study, 109 nonexercising volunteers were randomly assigned to one of four conditions: high-intensity aerobic training, moderate-intensity aerobic training, low-intensity nonaerobic training, and waiting list (Moses & others, 1989). In the high-intensity aerobic group, participants engaged in a continuous walk-jog program that elevated their heart rate to 70 to 75 percent of maximum. In the moderate-intensity aerobic group, participants engaged in walking or jogging that elevated their heart rate to 60 percent of maximum. In the low-intensity nonaerobic group, participants engaged in strength, mobility, and flexibility exercises in a slow, discontinuous manner for approximately 30 minutes. Those who were assigned to exercise programs worked out three to five times a week. Those who were on the waiting list did not exercise.

The programs lasted for 10 weeks. As expected, the group assigned to the high-intensity aerobic program showed the greatest aerobic fitness on a 12-minute walk-run. Fitness also improved for those assigned to moderate- and low-exercise programs; however, only the people assigned to the moderate-intensity aerobic training programs showed psychological benefits. These benefits appeared immediately in the form of reduced tension and anxiety. And after 3 months, the moderate-intensity group showed improved aerobic conditioning. The superiority of the moderate aerobic training program over the nonaerobic low-exercise program suggests that a minimum level of aerobic conditioning may be required to obtain important psychological benefits. To speculate about why the results of this study turned out the way they did, see Critical Thinking.

Research on the benefits of exercise suggests that both moderate and intense activities produce important physical and psychological gains. Some people enjoy rigorous, intense exercise. Others enjoy more moderate exercise routines. The enjoyment and pleasure we derive from exercise cooperate with its aerobic benefits to make exercise one of life's most important activities.

Activity Disorder

Is regular exercise always good for a person? No. Some individuals engage in compulsive exercise that is extreme and unhealthy (Polivy & Clendenen, 1993). **Activity disorder** *is an intense, driven, compulsive exercise pattern often combined with rigid dietary restriction that can damage the person's body.* Persons prone to this disorder tend to be high-achieving, independent, and high in self-control and perfectionism. Men and women with activity disorder think they must maintain a high level of activity and are uncomfortable with periods of relaxation. High levels of physical activity are maintained even at the cost of physical and social damage. One common pattern is that of obligatory running, which occurs over a wide age span but is most typical among middle-aged males. Other athletes, such as gymnasts and bodybuilders are also at risk for this pattern.

Several factors make activity disorder resistant to change. They include the following:

1. There is strong cultural support for both diet and exercise, with a built-in bias that more is better.
2. Pleasure is derived from improvements in body functioning and appearance, with narcissism increasing the importance of these feelings.
3. Activity is used to control appetite and weight.
4. There is a cyclic pattern to egocentricity, depression, seclusiveness, hostility, and

CRITICAL THINKING

Explaining Counterintuitive Results

The results of the research study by Moses and others (1989) were somewhat surprising. It would be easy to assume that the group that became the most fit would also be the most psychologically satisfied with their experience. Yet the researchers discovered that only the moderate exercisers demonstrated psychological benefits. Can you provide some explanations for this counterintuitive finding?

It helps to remember that all of the individuals in the study were nonexercisers at the outset. Therefore, the high-intensity training program might have been quite taxing, and the subjects in that group, although they became more fit, might have found the new demands more stressful. This explanation highlights the importance of *identifying underlying values that influence behavior.*

physical deprivation that centers around activity patterns.
5. Physiological effects, such as pleasure from endorphins, are triggered by activity.

In resolving activity disorder, the individual needs to learn how to reduce the level of activity and yet remain active and independent. Through balance, the individual can take better care of the body and injure it less.

Health nuts are going to feel stupid some day, lying in hospitals dying of nothing.

—Redd Foxx

Body Image and Lifestyle Choices

Even after a challenging workout, a tall, slender woman goes into the locker room of the fitness center, hurls her towel across the bench, looks squarely in the mirror, and says, "You fat pig. You are nothing but a fat pig." The alarm goes off, and 35-year-old Robert jumps out of bed, throws on his jogging shorts, and begins his daily predawn 3-mile run.

Returning to shower and dress, he too observes his body in the mirror, tugging at the flabby overhang and commenting, "Why did you eat that bowl of ice cream last night?" Sixteen-year-old Alisha begs her parents to let her have plastic surgery so that her larger-than-average nose won't continue to "destroy her entire life." Indeed, we are a nation obsessed with our looks and how food, activity, and surgical and behavioral alterations can change our looks. Sometimes appearance affects our physical health and our psychological well-being.

Body image *is the way that people perceive themselves and the way they think others see them.* Body image can have a stronger effect on our lifestyle habits and our self-esteem than facts about how to be healthier and live longer. There is a strong "beautiful is good" bias that influences many realms of our lives. For example, as early as kindergarten, both chubby and thin children receive fewer positive peer evaluations than do other children, and obesity has been shown to affect vocational and educational opportunities. Attractive people receive the least workplace discrimination and are more likely to receive favorable jury decisions (Cash, 1990).

In one experiment, the self-concept of depressed women was improved by either weight lifting or running (Ossip-Klein & others, 1989).

Every culture engages in aesthetic self-management, but the tasks involved and the desired goal varies. Americans use dieting, exercise, tanning (even though it increases risk for skin cancers), clothing, facial cosmetics, liposuction, and breast alterations as common tools for improving body image. In earlier times, girdles and corsets were widely used. The Karen women of Burma use brass neck rings to elongate their necks into their cultural ideal. Young girls start with five rings around their neck and as adults wear 24 rings; these rings so stretch the neck vertebrae apart that the brass rings must be permanent because the neck becomes too weak to support the head. From A.D. 900 until the twentieth century, Chinese women were subjected to foot-binding procedures that reduced the foot to one-third its normal size, making it painful, or even impossible, to walk.

Neck rings and foot-binding practices illustrate that feminine aesthetics sometimes involve pain and impracticality. Each practice takes a feminine quality (slender neck, small foot) and alters it in a way that interferes with normal functioning, as if feminine beauty involves a diminishment of a female's competence and independence. Although you might not find such extreme examples in American society, you might consider whether the appeal of such things as high-heel shoes is due to similar factors.

How do you feel about your own body? Do you approve of your own body image? Are there aspects of your body with which you are dissatisfied? If so, you have lots of company. A 1985 survey found that one in five Americans is dissatisfied with his or her face. Even more striking is that 41 percent of men and 51 percent of women are dissatisfied with their weight. Men and women are most likely to be dissatisfied with their mid torso (50 percent and 57 percent, respectively). Men (21 percent) are less likely than women (50 percent) to be dissatisfied with their lower torso. Upper-torso dissatisfaction for men is 20 percent and 32 percent for women (Cash, 1990). This dissatisfaction can lead people to make changes in their behavior that lead to healthier lives, or, this dissatisfaction can result in poorer attitudes, lower self-esteem, and worse behavior choices. Therefore, body image is relevant to the other topics in this section.

Body image also plays a major role in three types of disorders: body dysmorphic disorder, self-mutilation, and eating disorders.

Body dysmorphic disorder (BDD) *is a preoccupation with some imagined deficit in a normal-appearing person.* Alisha, mentioned earlier in this section, has BDD because she is preoccupied by the "disastrous" effect her nose is having on her appearance and life even though her nose is just a bit larger than average. Like others with BDD, she is obsessed with her nose and her personality comes off as a mixture of depression and narcissism. A facial feature is the most likely target of BDD, but other areas of the body can be involved, such as one's thighs or one's hands. Some persons who have plastic surgery done have this disorder.

In some areas of the world both fashion and superstition dictate that young girls apply brass rings around the neck. The weight of the rings not only stretches the woman's neck but can crush the collarbone and ribs. Some people of Thailand believe this practice wards off demonic spirits. *Can you think of fashionable practices in our culture that put women's overall health and well-being at risk?*

Self-mutilation is more common among adolescents than among other age groups. It involves an attitude of "I hate my body," which is thought to be a subset of a more generalized self-condemnation. Self-mutilators experience a sense of body alienation, or a belief that their bodies are somehow separate from their true selves. Alienation often starts through childhood experiences such as physical or sexual abuse, family violence, physical illness, or parental loss. Treatment needs include working on altering self-statements, changing behaviors toward the body, teaching better social skills, and sometimes using plastic surgery to remove the scars from self-mutilation attempts.

Body image distortions play a major role in eating disorders which will be covered later in this chapter. Body image is one of several factors involved in our nation's obsession with food, eating, and dieting. What are the guidelines for good nutrition?

Proper Nutrition

We are a nation obsessed with food, spending an extraordinary amount of time thinking about, gobbling up, and avoiding food. In this chapter, we will focus on the problem of obesity, weight-loss programs, and eating disorders, and on the cultural factors in nutrition.

Obesity

Understanding obesity is complex because body weight involves a number of factors—genetic inheritance, physiological mechanisms, cognitive factors, and environmental influences (Brownell, 1993; Brownell & Fairburn, 1995).

Heredity Until recently, the genetic component in obesity had been underestimated by scientists. Some individuals do inherit a tendency to be overweight. Only 10 percent of children who do not have obese parents become obese themselves, whereas 40 percent of children who become obese have one obese parent and 70 percent of children who become obese have two obese parents. The actual extent to which this is due to genes rather than experience cannot be determined in research with humans, but research documents that animals can be inbred to develop a propensity for obesity (Blundell, 1984). Further, identical human twins have similar weights, even when they are reared apart. Estimates of variance in body mass that can be explained by heredity range from 25 percent to 70 percent.

Set Point and BMR The amount of stored fat in your body is an important factor in your **set point,** *the weight maintained when no effort is made to gain or lose weight.* Fat is stored in adipose cells. When these cells are filled, you do not get hungry. When people gain weight—because of genetic predisposition, early childhood eating patterns, or adult overeating—the number of fat cells increases, and they might not be able to get rid of them. A

normal-weight individual has 30 to 40 billion fat cells. An obese individual has 80 to 120 billion fat cells. When individuals go on a diet, their fat cells might shrink but they do not go away.

Another factor in weight is **basal metabolism rate (BMR),** *the amount of energy an individual uses in a resting state.* BMR varies with age and sex. Rates decline precipitously during adolescence and then more gradually during adulthood; they also are slightly higher for males than for females. Many individuals gradually increase their weight over a period of many years. To some degree the weight gain may be due to a declining basal metabolism rate. The declining BMR underscores the importance of reducing our food intake as we grow older if we want to maintain our weight. Figure 16.1 illustrates how BMR varies with age and sex.

Sociocultural Factors In addition to hereditary and biological factors, environmental factors are involved in weight and shape in important ways (Capaldi, 1996). The human gustatory system and taste preferences developed at a time when reliable sources of food were scarce. Our earliest ancestors probably developed a preference for sweets, since ripe fruit, which is a concentrated source of sugar (and thus calories), was so accessible. Today many people still have a "sweet tooth," but unlike our ancestors' ripe fruit, which contained sugar *plus* vitamins

and minerals, the soft drinks and candy bars we snack on today too often fill us with empty calories.

Strong evidence of the environment's influence is the doubling of the rate of obesity in the United States since 1900, likely due to greater availability of food (especially food high in fat), energy-saving devices, and declining physical activity. The obesity rate also increased more than 50 percent from the 1960s to 1980. Obesity is six times more frequent among low-income women than among upper-income women, and more common among Americans than among Europeans.

The Costs Estimates indicate that 31 percent of men and 24 percent of women in the United States are overweight, with 12 percent of both sexes severely overweight (National Academy of Sciences Research Council, 1989). The economic costs of obesity are estimated at $39 billion per year, or more than 5 percent of all health costs. The staggering cost figures stem from obesity's association with diabetes, hypertension, cardiovascular diseases, and some cancers (Thompson, 1996).

Dieting

Many divergent interests are involved in the topic of dieting—the public, health professionals, policy makers, the media, and the powerful diet and food industries.

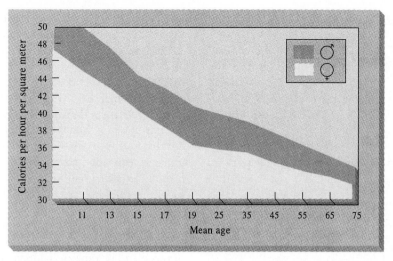

FIGURE 16.1

Basal Metabolism Rate
BMR varies with age and sex. Rates are usually higher for males and decline proportionately with age for both sexes.

On the one side are societal norms that promote a very lean, aesthetic ideal, supported by an industry valued at more than $30 billion per year that provides diet books, programs, videos, foods, pills, and the like. On the other side are health professionals and a growing minority of the press and the public who, although recognizing the alarmingly high incidence of obesity, are frustrated by high relapse rates and are increasingly concerned that chronic dieting may have negative effects on health and well-being (Brownell & Rodin, 1994).

> *Eat, drink, and be merry, for tomorrow ye shall diet.*
> —**Lewis C. Henry**

Dieting is a pervasive concern of many individuals in the United States. In a large-scale national survey, 52 percent of women and 37 percent of men believed that they were overweight (Horm & Anderson, 1993).

Following are some fundamental issues in the dieting debate and the current status of their empirical evaluation (Brownell & Rodin, 1994).

Does Weight Loss Reduce or Increase Health Risks?
Few studies have explored the effects of weight loss on disease and death. The most common type of data comes from population studies in which some individuals lose weight and others do not, and then their mortality is compared. However, the subjects who lose weight are self-selected; possible mediating factors such as body fat distribution and dieting history are not considered. Subjects might be gaining or losing weight because of factors that are related to disease, such as starting and stopping smoking. The type of study required to directly address the relation between dieting and mortality—a longitudinal study with random assignment to weight-loss and no-weight-loss groups, and with a sufficient sample size to evaluate mortality—has not been conducted. Such a study would be costly and difficult to undertake. Possibly because of such limitations, studies on weight loss and mortality are striking in the inconsistency of their results. In sum, the available data

present a mixed picture of whether weight loss is related to mortality.

Do Diets Work?
Some critics argue that all diets fail (Wooley & Garner, 1991). Although there are reports of poor long-term results (Wilson, 1994), some recent studies revealed that programs that combine very-low-calorie diets with intensive education and behavior modification produce good long-term results. In one such study, participants lost an average of 55 pounds, with more than half of this weight kept off 2½ years later (Nunn, Newton, & Faucher, 1992). Thus, it appears that some individuals do lose weight and maintain the loss. How often this occurs and whether some programs produce this outcome better than others are open questions (Brownell & Cohen, 1995).

Are Diets Harmful?
One main concern about diets being harmful focuses on weight cycling ("yo-yo dieting" involving a recurring cycle of dieting and regaining the weight) (Wadden & others, 1996). The empirical evidence does suggest a link between frequent changes in weight and chronic disease (Brownell & Rodin, in press). Another important concern about dieting is that it might lead to eating disorders. Dieting often does precede the development of eating disorders, but no causal link has been documented (Wilson, 1994). Also, overweight individuals who diet and then maintain their weight do become less depressed and reduce their risk for a number of health-impairing disorders (Cristensen, 1996). See the Self-Assessment to evaluate your own eating behavior.

Does Exercise Benefit Individuals Who Want to Lose Weight?
Exercise not only burns up calories but continues to raise the metabolic rate for several hours *after* the exercise. Exercise actually lowers your body's set point for weight, making it much easier to maintain a lower weight (Bennett & Gurin, 1982). Nonetheless, it is difficult to convince obese individuals to exercise. One problem is that moderate exercise does not reduce calorie consumption, and in many cases individuals who exercise take in more calories than their sedentary

counterparts. Still, exercise combined with conscious self-control of eating habits can produce a viable weight-loss program. When exercise is a component of weight-loss programs, individuals keep weight off longer than when calorie reduction alone is followed.

Who Should Diet?
The population is not uniform, and clearly not everyone should go on a diet. A 10 percent reduction in body weight may produce striking benefits in an older, obese, hypertensive man but be unhealthy in an adolescent female who is not overweight. The pressure to be thin, and thus diet, is greatest among young women, yet they are not the group in which the greatest risk of obesity exists or in which the benefits of dieting outweigh the risks.

Researchers have not adequately investigated the question of who should lose weight. This question will likely be best answered by consideration of the medical and psychosocial consequences of weight loss, which may be a highly individualized matter.

Eating Disorders
Eighteen-year-old Jane gradually eliminated foods from her diet to the point at which she subsisted by eating *only* applesauce and eggnog. She spent hours observing her body, wrapping her fingers around her waist to see if it was getting any thinner. She fantasized about becoming a beautiful fashion model and wearing designer bathing suits. However, even when she dropped to 85 pounds, Jane still felt fat. She continued to lose weight, eventually emaciating herself. She was hospitalized and treated for **anorexia nervosa,** *an eating disorder that involves the relentless pursuit of thinness through starvation.* Anorexia nervosa can eventually lead to death, as it did for popular singer Karen Carpenter.

Anorexia nervosa primarily afflicts females during adolescence and the early adulthood years (only about 5 percent of all anorexics are male). Most adolescents with this disorder are White and from well-educated, middle- and upper-income families. Although anorexics avoid eating, they have an intense interest in food. They cook for others, they talk about food, and they insist on watching

Monitoring Your Eating Behavior

Improving health through behavior change is a common goal related to many health concerns, such as smoking, drinking, eating, and exercise. People may try to keep track of their progress, but it is usually best to keep a specific diary of change. Recording changes of behaviors on a daily basis is one form of self-monitoring. To the right is an example of such a diary using dieting as the behavior change, as tracked by caloric intake. Set a daily goal and then look up the calories for each food eaten. Keeping a daily record not only helps you chart your progress, but can also act as a reminder to keep up the changes.

Date _____

	Foods	Where eaten and with whom	Calories
Breakfast			
Lunch			
Dinner			
Outside of meals			

Total calories for day _____

Track your intake everyday and subtract your daily calories from your daily goal. Keep track of how much you deviate from your goal each day. You can keep a log or make a graph of your progress. For days that you take in more calories than your goal, see if there is a pattern of where you are or who you are with. This information allows for further adjustments to your plan.

---

others eat. Anorexics have a distorted body image, perceiving themselves as overweight even when they become skeletal. As self-starvation continues and the fat content of their body drops to a bare minimum, menstruation usually stops and their behavior often becomes hyperactive.

Numerous causes of anorexia nervosa have been proposed, including societal, psychological, and physiological factors (Lam, Goldner, & Grewal, 1996; Pomeroy, 1996). The societal factor most often held responsible is the current fashion image of thinness, reflected in the saying "You can't be too rich or too thin." Psychological factors include motivation for attention, desire for individuality, denial of sexuality, and a need to cope with overcontrolling parents. Some anorexics have parents that place high demands for achievement on them. Unable to meet their parents' high standards, they feel unable to control their own lives. By limiting their food intake, anorexics gain some sense of self-control. Physiological causes involve the hypothalamus, which becomes abnormal in a number of ways when an adolescent becomes anorexic. Unfortunately, we are uncertain of the exact causes of anorexia at this time.

Bulimia *is an eating disorder in which the individual consistently follows a binge-and-purge eating pattern.* The bulimic goes on an eating binge and then purges by self-induced vomiting or using a laxative. Sometimes the binges alternate with fasting, at other times with normal eating. Like anorexia nervosa, bulimia is primarily a female disorder. Bulimia has become prevalent among traditional-age college women. Some estimates suggest that one in every two college women binges and purges at least some of the time. Recent estimates, however, suggest that true bulimics—those who binge and purge on a regular basis—make up less than 2 percent of the college female population (Stunkard, 1987). Another survey of 1,500 high school and university students found that 4 percent of the high school students and 5 percent of the university students were bulimic (Howat & Saxton, 1988). Anorexics can control their eating, but bulimics cannot. Depression is a common characteristic of bulimics. Bulimia can produce gastric and chemical imbalance in the body. Many of the causes proposed for anorexia nervosa are also offered for bulimia (Fairburn, 1995).

Eating disorders are especially common among female gymnasts, who have the lowest body-fat percentage of all women athletes. Perhaps one of every four gymnasts is bulimic in order to control weight. In a study of college gymnasts, about three in four had some bulimic behaviors (such as vomiting more than twice a week; using laxatives, diuretics, and diet pills; starving themselves). Other female sports with high rates of bulimia include field hockey, distance track, and skating, while low rates are found in basketball, golf, and swimming. In addition, some male wrestlers are bulimic.

Cultural Factors in Nutrition

Current food preferences in the United States reflect problematic relationships with food. Many people eat too much fast food, which increases fat and cholesterol intake, both of which are implicated in heart disease and high blood pressure. Some individuals have adopted more rigorous nutritional habits to limit or avoid foods associated with poor health. For example, vegetarians exclude meat but plan their diets carefully to ensure that they get the proper amounts and kinds of proteins. Proper nutrition is ensured not just by limiting calorie intake but by carefully selecting foods that provide plenty of nutrients with their calories. Researchers have found that mice fed a high-fat diet are more likely to develop breast cancer than mice fed on a low-fat diet, and a cross-national study involving women also found a strong positive correlation between fat consumption and death rates from breast cancer (Cohen, 1987) (see figure 16.2).

One of the most telling comparisons to link fat intake and cancer is between the United States and Japan. Both

countries have similar levels of industrialization and education, as well as high medical standards. Although the overall cancer rates of the two countries are similar, cancers of the breast, colon, and prostate are common in the United States but rare in Japan. By contrast, cancer of the stomach is common in Japan but rare in the United States. Within two generations, Japanese immigrants to Hawaii and California have developed breast cancer rates that are significantly higher than those in Japan and that approach those of Americans. Many researchers believe that the high fat intake of Americans and the low fat intake of the Japanese are implicated in the countries' different cancer rates.

The general good health, low cancer rates, and longevity of Seventh-Day Adventists, an evangelical Protestant faith, further support the link between cultural factors, especially diet, and cancer. Strict Seventh-Day Adventists adhere to biblical precepts that determine diet and other lifestyle behaviors. Their well-balanced diet includes generous portions of unrefined foods, grains, vegetable protein,

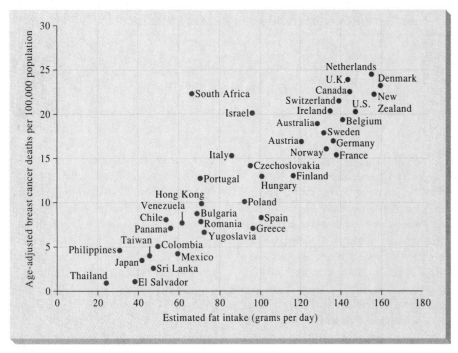

FIGURE 16.2

Cross-Cultural Comparisons of Diet and Cancer
In countries in which individuals have a low daily intake of fat, the rate of breast cancer is low (in Thailand, for example). In countries in which individuals have a high daily intake of fat, the rate of breast cancer is high (in the Netherlands, for example).

fruits, and vegetables. Smoking is prohibited. As a result, there is a very low incidence of lung cancer among Seventh-Day Adventists. In addition, Seventh-Day Adventists have less cancer of any type—including breast, pancreas, and colorectal cancer—than other cultural groups in the United States.

As is the case with any cultural group, some Seventh-Day Adventists adhere more strictly to the sect's lifestyle than do others. In one study of religiously inactive Norwegian Seventh-Day Adventists, their risk of disease was similar to that of Norwegians who were not Seventh-Day Adventists (Fonnebo, 1985). Similarly, Seventh-Day Adventists in the United States who marginally adhere to the sect's guidelines for physical, mental, and spiritual health have an increased risk of disease.

Freedom from Smoking

The year 1988 marked the 75th anniversary of the introduction of Camel cigarettes. Some magazines surprised readers with elaborate pop-up advertisements for Camels. Camel's ad theme was "75 years and still smokin'." Coincidentally 1988 was also the 75th anniversary of the American Cancer Society.

In 1989 the surgeon general and his advisory committee issued a report, *Reducing the Health Consequences of Smoking: 25 Years of Progress.* It was released 25 years after the original warnings that cigarettes are responsible for major health problems, especially lung cancer. New evidence was presented to show that smoking is even more harmful that previously thought. For example, the report indicated that in 1985 cigarette smoking accounted for more than one-fifth of all deaths in the United States—20 percent more than previously believed. Thirty percent of all cancer deaths were attributed to smoking, as were 21 percent of all coronary heart disease deaths and 82 percent of chronic pulmonary disease deaths.

Researchers are also increasingly finding that passive smoke (environmental smoke inhaled by nonsmokers who live or work around smokers) carries health risks (Sandler & others, 1989). Passive smoke is estimated to be

THE FAR SIDE   By GARY LARSON

The real reason dinosaurs became extinct

the culprit in as many as 8,000 lung cancer deaths a year in the United States. Children of smokers are at special risk for respiratory and middle-ear diseases. For children under the age of 5, the risk of upper respiratory tract infection is doubled if their mothers smoke. And in one recent study, the greater the number of cigarettes the infant was passively exposed to after birth from all adults, the higher was the infant's risk of sudden infant death syndrome, a condition that occurs when the infant stops breathing and suddenly dies (Klonoff-Cohen & others, 1995).

The surgeon general's 1989 report contains some good news, however. Fewer people smoke today, and almost half of all living adults who ever smoked have quit. In particular the prevalence of smoking among men fell from over 50 percent in 1965 to about 30 percent in 1989. Current estimates place smoking prevalence at just over 25 percent (National Institutes of Health, 1994). As a consequence, a half-century's uninterrupted escalation in the rate of death due to lung cancer among males has ceased, and the incidence of lung cancer among White males has fallen. Although approximately 56 million Americans 15 to 84 years of age were smokers in 1985, the surgeon general's report estimates that 91 million would have been smoking had there been no changes in smoking and

health knowledge, norms, and policy over the past quarter century.

However, the bad news is that over 50 million Americans *continue* to smoke, most having failed at attempts to quit. No single voluntary behavior would do more to prevent death than stopping smoking. Why, in the face of the damaging figure that more than one-fifth of all deaths are due to smoking, do so many people still smoke?

Smoking as an Addiction

Most adult smokers would like to quit, but their addiction to nicotine often turns their efforts into dismal failure. Nicotine, the active drug in cigarettes, is a stimulant that increases a smoker's energy and alertness, a pleasurable experience that is positively reinforcing (Payne & others, 1996). Nicotine also causes the release of acetylcholine and endorphin neurotransmitters, which have a calming and pain-reducing effect. However, smoking not only works as a positive reinforcer; it also works as a negative reinforcer by ending a smoker's painful craving for nicotine. A smoker gets relief from this painful aversive state simply by smoking another cigarette.

Smoking is costly in more ways than physical health. A two-packs-per-day habit costs $1,500 per year.

We are rational cognitive beings. Can't we develop enough self-control to overcome the pleasurable, immediate, reinforcing circumstances by thinking about the delayed, long-term, damaging consequences of smoking? As indicated earlier, many adults have quit smoking because they recognize that it is "suicide in slow motion," but the immediate pleasurable effects of smoking are extremely difficult to overcome.

Smoking Is Preventable

Smoking usually begins during childhood and adolescence. A 1992 survey of eighth-graders in Michigan found that 45 percent had already tried cigarettes (Institute for Health Policy, 1993). Adolescent smoking reached its peak in the mid-1970s, when 29 percent of high school seniors smoked on a daily basis. In 1994, the rate had dropped to 17 percent (Johnston, O'Malley, & Bachman, 1994). Among adolescents, females are now

Many adolescents who smoke know the health risks associated with smoking, but they smoke anyway. *Given this information, what might be the best strategy for reducing teenage smoking?*

more likely to be smokers than males are. The smoking rate is still at a level that will cut short the lives of many adolescents. Despite the growing awareness that it is important to keep children from starting to smoke, there are fewer restrictions on children's access to cigarettes today than there were in 1964, and the existing restrictions are rarely enforced.

Traditional school health programs appear to have succeeded in educating adolescents about the long-term health consequences of smoking but have had little effect on adolescent smoking *behavior.* That is, adolescents who smoke know the facts about the health risks, such as their chances of getting lung cancer and emphysema, but they go ahead and smoke just as much anyway (Miller & Slap, 1989). Few teenagers think that the serious unpleasant effects of smoking will affect their own lives, because rationalizations such as "Yes, but it won't happen to me" are typical of adolescent thinking.

As a result of this gap between what teens *know* and what they *do* in regard to smoking, researchers are focusing on the factors that place teens at high risk for future smoking, especially social pressures from peers, family members, and the media. The tobacco industry preys on young peoples' desire to feel grown up by including "cool" people who smoke in their advertisements—successful young women smoking Virginia Slims cigarettes and rugged, handsome men smoking Marlboros, for example. The advertisements encourage adolescents to associate cigarette smoking with a successful and, ironically, athletic and active lifestyle. Legislators are trying to introduce more stringent laws to further regulate the tobacco industry and the media. In one recent study, a combination of school and mass media interventions reduced cigarette smoking through adolescence (Flynn & others, 1995).

> *I'm glad I don't have to explain to a man from Mars why each day I set fire to dozens of little pieces of paper, and then put them in my mouth.*
> —**Mignon McLaughlin**

One comprehensive health program that includes an attempt to curb cigarette smoking by adolescents was developed by clinical psychologist Cheryl Perry and her colleagues (1988). Three programs were developed based on peer group norms, healthy role models, and social skills training. Elected peer leaders were trained as instructors. In grade 7, adolescents were offered *Keep It Clean,* a six-session course emphasizing the negative effects of smoking. In grade 8, students were

---

R E V I E W

Relating Health and Psychology

Health psychology is a multidimensional approach to health that emphasizes psychological factors, lifestyle, and the nature of the health-care delivery system. Closely aligned with health psychology is behavioral medicine, which combines medical and behavioral knowledge to reduce illness and promote health. Psychoneuroimmunology explores the connections among psychological factors, the nervous system, and the immune system. Exploratory research suggests that our emotions and attitudes are connected to our immune system.

Both moderate and intense exercise produce important physical and psychological gains, such as lowered risk of heart disease and reduced anxiety. Experts increasingly recommend that the level of exercise you participate in should be pleasurable. Every indication suggests our nation's children are not getting enough exercise. Activity disorder is a problem that some people who are driven to reach a high level of fitness develop.

Understanding obesity is complex because body weight involves a number of factors. Estimates of body mass that can be explained by heredity range from 25 to 70 percent. Set point and BMR are other biological processes involved in weight. Environmental factors also play a role in obesity—obesity rates have doubled in the United States since 1900. Obesity has high costs. Dieting is a pervasive concern of many individuals in the United States and raises many questions, such as whether weight loss reduces or increases health risks, whether diets work (some do, many don't), whether diets are harmful, whether exercise benefits individuals who want to lose weight, and who should diet. Two increasingly common eating disorders are anorexia nervosa and bulimia. Cultural factors also are involved in nutrition.

In 1989 the surgeon general released extensive new evidence that smoking is more harmful than previously believed, accounting for one-fifth of all deaths in the United States. Researchers are increasingly finding that passive smoke also carries health risks. Smoking is both addictive and reinforcing. Stronger educational and policy efforts regarding smoking are needed. Current prevention programs with young people focus on social pressures from family, peers, and the media.

No matter how much evidence appears from medical research about the hazardous effects of smoking, many individuals remain unconvinced. These skeptics point to examples of people who regularly smoke and who have managed to live very long lives.

George Burns was a good example. Even after reaching his hundredth birthday, Burns was rarely seen without a cigar. If smoking is so awful, then how could George Burns have lived so long?

Can you use this example to propose *some alternative explanations* for both George Burns' longevity and the hazards of smoking?

Why might someone like George Burns be able to live so long even though he was a heavy cigar smoker?

involved in *Health Olympics,* an approach that included exchanging greeting cards on smoking and health with peers in other countries. In grade 9, students participated in *Shifting Gears,* which included six sessions focused on social skills. In the social skills program, students critiqued media messages and created their own positive health videotapes. At the same time the school intervention occurred, a community-wide smoking cessation program, as well as a diet and health awareness campaign, were initiated. After 5 years, students who were involved in the smoking and health program were much less likely to smoke cigarettes, use marijuana, or drink alcohol than were their counterparts who were not involved in the program. To explore why people continue to smoke despite the risks, see Critical Thinking.

COPING WITH ILLNESS

Even if we manage stress effectively and practice good health habits, we cannot always prevent illness. How do we recognize, interpret, and seek treatment for the symptoms of an illness? What is a patient's role? How good are we at adhering to medical advice and treatment? We will consider each of these questions in turn.

Recognizing and Interpreting Symptoms

How do you know if you are sick? Each of us diagnoses how we feel and interprets the meaning of symptoms to decide whether we have a cold, the flu, a sexually transmitted disease, an ulcer, heart disease, and so on. However, many of us are not very accurate at recognizing the symptoms of an illness. For example, most people believe that they can tell when their blood pressure is elevated. The facts say otherwise. Most heart attack victims have never sought medical attention for cardiac problems. Many of us do not go to the doctor when the early warning signs of cancers, such as a lump or cyst, appear. Also, we are better at recognizing the symptoms of illnesses we are more familiar with, such as a cold or the flu, than of illnesses we are less familiar with, such as diabetes.

We use schemas, organized ways of looking at things that influence our expectations, to interpret information about ourselves in our world. Our prior experiences with a particular symptom may lead us to interpret it based on the schema we have for that symptom. For example, an individual with a long record of sprained ankles might dismiss a swollen ankle as simply another sprain,

not recognizing that she has a more serious injury—a fracture. By contrast, an individual who has never had a sprained ankle might perceive the swelling as serious and pursue medical intervention.

> *Symptoms, then, are in reality nothing but the cry from suffering organs.*
> —**Jean-Martin Charcot**

Seeking Treatment

Whether or not we seek treatment for symptoms depends on our perception of their severity and of the likelihood that medical treatment will relieve or eliminate them. If a person's ankle is fractured so badly he cannot walk without assistance, he is more likely to seek treatment than if the fracture produces only a slight limp. Also, someone may not seek treatment for a viral infection if she believes that no drug is available to combat it effectively. By contrast, a person is more likely to seek treatment if she believes that a fungus infection on her foot can be remedied by antibiotics.

When people direct their attention outward, they are less likely to notice symptoms than when they direct their attention inward. For example, a woman whose life is extremely busy and full of distracting activities is less likely to notice a lump on her breast than is a woman who has a much less active life. People who have boring jobs, who are socially inactive, and who live alone are more likely to report symptoms than people who have interesting jobs, who have active social lives, and who live with others (Pennebaker, 1983). Perhaps people who lead more active lives have more distractions and focus their attention less on themselves than do people with quieter lives. Even for people who have active lives, situational factors influence whether they will be attentive to symptoms. In one experiment, joggers were more likely to experience fatigue and be aware of their running-related aches and pains when they ran on a boring course than when they ran on a more interesting and varied course (Pennebaker & Lightner, 1980). The boring course likely increased the joggers' tendency to turn their attention inward and, thus, recognize their fatigue and pain.

Belief systems are also a factor in responding to symptoms. For example, Western people generally maintain a very positive, confident attitude about their health care. That attitude has only strengthened with advances in technological interventions. Many critics suggest that overconfidence in technological prowess may encourage more use of medical intervention than is really necessary. In addition, physicians in the United States are trained to regard illness and death as enemies to be fought. Our "medicalization" of many of life's processes may prevent us from seeing them as natural parts of the cycle of life. For contrasting experiences in other ethnic traditions, see Sociocultural Worlds of Adjustment.

The Patient's Role

Shelley Taylor (1979) identified two general types of patient roles. According to her analysis, some hospitalized individuals take on a "good patient" role, others a "bad patient" role. In the **"good patient" role,** *a patient is passive and unquestioning and behaves "properly."* The positive consequences of this role include being well-

liked by the hospital staff, who in turn respond quickly to the "good patient's" emergencies. Like many roles, however, the "good patient" is somewhat superficial, and Taylor believes that, behind the facade, the patient may feel helpless, powerless, anxious, and depressed. In the **"bad patient" role,** *a patient complains to the staff, demands attention, disobeys staff orders, and generally misbehaves.* The refusal to become helpless, and the accompanying anger, might actually have some positive consequences, because "bad patients" take an active role in their own health care. The negative side of "bad patient" behavior, however, is that it might aggravate such conditions as hypertension and angina, and it might stimulate staff members to ignore, overmedicate, or prematurely discharge the "bad patient."

How can the stress of hospitalization be relieved? Realistic expectations about the experience, predictable events, and social support reduce the stress of hospitalization. When doctors communicate clearly to their patients about the nature of the treatment procedures and what to expect when they are hospitalized, patients' confidence in the medical treatment also increases, and, as we learned in the earlier discussion of stress,

the social network of individuals who deeply care about us goes a long way toward reducing stress. Visits, phone calls, cards, and flowers from family members and friends lift patients' spirits and improve their recovery from illness.

Adherence to Medical Advice and Treatment

An estimated one-third of patients fail to follow recommended treatments. Adherence depends on the disorder and the recommendation. Only about 15 percent of patients do not follow doctors' orders for tablets and ointments, but more than 90 percent of patients do not heed lifestyle advice, such as to stop smoking, to lose weight, or to stop drinking (DiNicola & DiMatteo, 1984).

Why do we pay money to doctors and then not follow their advice? We might not adhere to a doctor's recommendations because we are not satisfied with the quality of the care we are receiving and because we have our own theories about our health and do not completely trust the doctor's advice. This mistrust is exacerbated when doctors use jargon and highly technical descriptions to inform patients about a treatment. Sometimes doctors do not give patients clear information or fully

R E V I E W

Coping with Illness

Many of us are not very accurate at diagnosing the symptoms of illness. When our attention is directed outward, we are less likely to detect symptoms than when our attention is directed inward. We use schemas developed through prior experience to interpret symptoms. Seeking treatment depends on our perception of the severity of the symptoms and the likelihood that medical treatment will reduce or eliminate the symptoms.

In the "good patient" role, individuals are passive, unquestioning, and

behave properly. In the "bad patient" role, individuals complain to the staff, demand attention, disobey staff orders, and generally misbehave. Realistic prior expectations, predictable events, and social support reduce the stress of hospitalization.

Approximately one-third of patients do not follow treatment recommendations. Compliance varies with the disorder and the treatment recommendation, whether we are satisfied with the quality of care we are receiving, and our own theories about why we are sick and how we can get well. Clearer doctor-patient communication is needed for improved compliance.

Health Care for African, Latino, Asian, and Native Americans

As mentioned before, there are differences within ethnic groups as well as among them. This is just as true of health among ethnic groups as it is of, say, family structure. The spectrum of living conditions and lifestyles within an ethnic group are influenced by social class, immigrant status, social and language skills, occupational opportunities, and such social resources as the availability of meaningful support networks. All of these can play a role in an ethnic minority member's health. Psychologists Felipe Castro and Delia Magaña (1988) developed a course in health promotion in ethnic minority communities, which they teach at UCLA. A summary of some of the issues they discuss in the course follows.

Prejudice and racial segregation are the historical underpinnings for the chronic stress of discrimination and poverty that adversely affects the health of many African Americans. Support systems, such as an extended family network, may be especially important resources to improve the health of African Americans and help them cope with stress.

Some of the same stressors mentioned for African Americans are associated with migration to the United States by Puerto Ricans, Mexicans, and Latin Americans. Language is often a barrier for unacculturated Latinos in doctor-patient communications. In addition, there is increasing evidence that diabetes occurs at an above-average rate in Latinos, making this disease a major health problem that parallels the above-average rate of high blood pressure among African Americans.

Asian Americans have a broad diversity of national backgrounds and lifestyles. They range from highly acculturated Japanese Americans, who may be better educated than many Anglo-Americans and have excellent access to health care, to the many Indochinese refugees who have few economic resources and may be in poor health.

Cultural barriers to adequate health care include a lack of financial resources and poor language skills. In addition, members of ethnic minority groups are often unfamiliar with how the medical system operates, confused about the need to see numerous people, and uncertain about why they have to wait so long for service (Snowden & Cheung, 1990).

Other barriers may be specific to certain cultures, reflecting differing ideas regarding what causes disease and how it should be treated. For example, there are Chinese herbalists and folk healers in every Chinatown in the United States. Depending on their degree of acculturation to Western society, Chinese Americans might go to either a folk healer or a Western doctor first, but generally they will consult a folk healer for follow-up care. Chinese medicines are usually used for home care. These include ginseng tea, boiled centipede soup for cancer, and eucalyptus oil for dizziness resulting from hypertension.

Native Americans sometimes view Western medicine as a source of crisis intervention, quick fixes for broken legs, or cures for other symptoms; but they might not rely on Western medicine as a source for treating the causes of disease or for preventing disease. They also are reluctant to become involved in care that requires long-term hospitalization or surgery.

Both Navajo Indians and Mexican Americans rely on family members to make decisions about treatment. Doctors who expect such patients to decide on the spot whether or not to undergo treatment will likely embarrass the patient or force the patient to give an answer that may lead to canceled appointments. Mexican Americans also believe that some illnesses are due to natural causes whereas others are due to supernatural causes. Depending on their level of acculturation, Mexican Americans may be disappointed and confused by doctors who do not show an awareness of how to treat diseases with supposed supernatural origins.

Health care professionals can increase their effectiveness with ethnic minority patients by improving their knowledge of patients' attitudes, beliefs, and folk practices regarding health and disease. By integrating such information into Western medical treatments, health care professionals can avoid alienating patients.

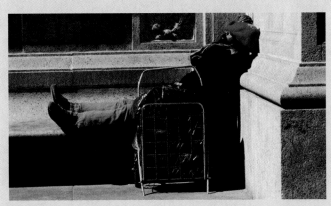

Prejudice and racial segregation can intensify the chronic stress of discrimination and poverty that adversely affect the health of many African Americans.

Herbalists and folk healers continue to play an important role in the health care of Chinese Americans. For example, there are Chinese herbalists and folk healers in every Chinatown in the United States.

explain the risks of ignoring their orders. Sometimes patients might not communicate their concerns as clearly as they could, leaving doctors with an incomplete profile of the patient's concerns. To be motivated to stop smoking, to eat more nutritionally, or to stop drinking, patients need a clear understanding of the dangers involved in failure to adhere to the doctor's recommendation. Success or failure in treatment may depend on whether the doctor can convince patients that a valid, believable danger exists and can offer an effective, concrete strategy for coping with the problem.

PSYCHOACTIVE DRUGS AND ADDICTION

When Sigmund Freud began to experiment with cocaine, he was searching for possible medical applications, such as a painkiller for eye surgery. He soon found that the drug induced ecstasy. He even wrote to his fiancée and told her how just a small dose of cocaine produced lofty, wonderful sensations. As it became apparent that some people become psychologically addicted to cocaine, and after several died from overdoses, Freud quit using the drug. Just what are psychoactive drugs?

Psychoactive Drugs

Psychoactive drugs *act on the nervous system to alter our state of consciousness, modify our perceptions, and change our moods.* Ever since our ancient ancestors first sat entranced in front of a communal fire, humans have searched for substances that would produce pleasurable sensations and alter their states of consciousness. Among the substances that alter consciousness are alcohol, hemp and cactus plants, mushrooms, poppies, and tobacco, an herb that has been smoked and sniffed for more than 400 centuries.

Human beings are attracted to psychoactive substances because they help them adapt to or escape from an ever-changing environment. Smoking, drinking, and taking drugs reduce tension and frustration, relieve boredom and fatigue, and in some cases help us to escape from the harsh realities of the world. Psychoactive drugs provide us with pleasure by giving us tranquility, joy, relaxation, kaleidoscopic perceptions, surges of exhilaration, and prolonged heightened sensation. They sometimes have practical uses, like the use of amphetamines to stay awake all night to study for an exam. We might also take drugs because we are curious about their effects, in some cases because of sensational accounts in the media. We may wonder if drugs can provide us with unique, profound experiences. We also take drugs for social reasons, hoping they will make us feel more at ease and happier in our interactions and relationships with others.

In our culture, however, the use of psychoactive drugs for such personal gratification and temporary adaptation carries a high price tag: drug dependence, personal and social disorganization, and a predisposition to serious and sometimes fatal diseases. What might initially have been intended as enjoyment and adaptation can eventually turn into sorrow and maladaptation. For example, drinking might initially help people relax and forget about their worries. But then they might begin to drink more and more, until the drinking becomes an addiction that destroys relationships and careers and leads to physical and psychological damage, including permanent liver damage, major depression, and other effects on the body and brain.

Addiction

What is addiction? Are addictions diseases?

The Nature of Addiction

As a person continues to take a psychoactive drug, the body develops a **tolerance,** *which means that a greater amount of the drug is needed to produce the same effect.* The first time someone takes 5 milligrams of Valium, for example, the drug will make them feel very relaxed. But after taking the pill every day for 6 months, the person might need to take 10 milligrams to achieve the same calming effect.

Addiction *is a physical dependence on a drug.* **Withdrawal** *is the undesirable intense pain and craving that an addicted person feels when the addicting drug is withdrawn.* **Psychological dependence** *is the need to take a drug to cope with problems and stress.* In both physical addiction and psychological dependence, the psychoactive drug plays a powerful role in the user's life.

Are Addictions Diseases?

There is great controversy over the question of whether addictions are diseases. The **disease model of addiction** *describes addictions as biologically based, lifelong diseases that involve a loss of control over behavior and require medical and/or spiritual treatment for recovery.* According to the disease model, addiction is either inherited or taught to a person early in life. As such, alcohol might have more far-reaching and damaging effects on the addiction-prone individual whose genetic vulnerabilities induce severe reactions to addicting substances. Current or recent problems or relationships do not cause the disease. Addiction is a progressive, irreversible disease from which there is never complete recovery. People with the disease cannot control their addiction themselves; they require help from others and from a higher power or spiritual redemption. Denial characterizes addicted people—they resist perceiving that they have an addiction. And relapse is viewed as a reemergence of the disease. The disease model has been strongly promoted and supported by the medical profession and Alcoholics Anonymous.

Critics of the disease approach offer several arguments against it: The biological mechanisms that might account for addictive behavior have not been identified. Addiction is not necessarily a lifelong process. The disease model discourages people from developing self-control and stigmatizes people with labels like *addict* and *alcoholic,* in some cases for life. The disease approach prescribes a rigid program of therapy rather than advocating more flexible approaches.

Two critics of the disease model, Stanton Peele and Archie Brodsky (1991), believe that addiction is a habitual response and a source of gratification or security. They say that an

We live in a society in which alcohol use is widely accepted. Drinking is often portrayed as sophisticated and glamorous. Alcohol use also helps many people "loosen up" and become more relaxed. However, the use of alcohol for such personal gratification and adaptation carries a high price for individuals who cannot adequately control their drinking and therefore develop alcohol dependence.

addiction can involve *any* attachment or desire for sensations that grows to such proportions that it impairs the person's life; such attachments can include attachments to drugs, food, gambling, shopping, love, and sex. In this view, the "hook" of the addiction—what keeps people coming back to it—is that it provides people with feelings and gratifying sensations that they are not able to get in other ways. Peele and Brodsky believe that understanding addiction requires placing it in the proper context, as part of people's lives, their personalities, their relationships, their environments, and their perspectives. They call their model the "life-process" model. In sum, according to the **life-process model,** *addiction is not a disease but rather a habitual response and a source of gratification or security that can be understood only in the context of social relationships*

and experiences. Each of these views of addiction—the disease model and the nondisease, life-process model—has its supporters.

Alcohol

We do not always think of alcohol as a drug, but it is an extremely powerful one. Alcohol acts upon the body primarily as a depressant and slows down the brain's activities. This might seem surprising, since people who normally tend to be inhibited might begin to talk, dance, or socialize after a few drinks, but people "loosen up" after one or two drinks because the areas in the brain involved in controlling inhibition and judgment *slow down.* As people drink more, their inhibitions become even further reduced and their judgments become increasingly impaired. Activities requiring intellectual functioning and

skill, such as driving, become impaired as more alcohol is consumed. Eventually the drinker becomes drowsy and falls asleep. With extreme intoxication, a person may even lapse into a coma and die. Each of these effects varies with how the person's body metabolizes alcohol, body weight, the amount of alcohol consumed, and whether previous drinking has led to tolerance.

> *Maybe it picks you up a little, but it sure lets you down in a hurry.*
>
> **—Betty Ford,**
> ***The Time of My Life,* 1978**

Alcohol Use in America

Alcohol is the most widely used drug in our society. A 1992 Gallup poll revealed that 64 percent of American adults drank beer, wine, or liquor at least occasionally—down from 71 percent in the late 1970s. More than 13 million people in the United States call themselves alcoholics. Alcoholism is the third leading killer in the United States. Each year approximately 25,000 people are killed, and 1.5 million injured, by drunk drivers. More than 60 percent of homicides involve the use of alcohol by either the offender or the victim, while 65 percent of aggressive sexual acts against women involve the use of alcohol by the offender. Alcohol costs the United States more than $40 billion each year in health costs, lost productivity, accidents, and crimes.

> *Alcohol is a good preservative for everything but brains.*
> —**Mary Pettibone Poole,**
> ***A Glass Eye at a Keyhole,* 1938**

A special concern is the high rate of alcohol use and abuse by adolescents and college students. Alcohol is the substance most abused by adolescents and college students. According to national surveys of more than 15,000 high school seniors taken every year since 1975, approximately one-third have consumed 5 or more drinks in a row in the past 2-week interval (Johnston, O'Malley, & Bachman, 1994). Alcohol use by high school students has gradually declined since the early 1980s; for example, the percentage of high school seniors who use alcohol monthly has declined from 72 percent in the early 1980s to 50 percent in 1994. However, the drinking habits of college students have shown little drop—almost half of all college students say they drink heavily (Johnston, O'Malley, & Bachman, 1994).

The assumption among many college students that "everyone" is getting drunk, or wishes they were, might increase alcohol abuse. In one recent series of studies, students systematically overestimated their fellow students' support for heavy drinking (Prentice & Miller, 1993). Thus, many college students are under the false impression that everyone else approves of heavy drinking, and they don't want to appear "uncool." See table 16.1 for some questions that often identify young adult substance abusers.

It is often difficult to distinguish between alcoholism and problem drinking. Even professionals have difficulty determining whether an individual, such as a binge-drinking college student, is an alcoholic or just has a drinking problem.

In the recent national study on college drinking patterns that surveyed 17,592 college students on 140 campuses, 47 percent of the binge drinkers reported problems such as missing classes, injuries, troubles with police, or having unprotected sex. For example, the binge drinkers were eleven times more likely to fall behind in school, ten times more likely to drive after drinking, and several times more likely to have unprotected sex than were the students who did not binge drink.

A special concern that has surfaced recently is an increase in drug use, including alcohol consumption, by young adolescents. While the gradual decline in drinking by high school seniors continued, the decline did not occur for eighth-graders; in fact, they showed a slight increase in drinking (Johnston, O'Malley, & Bachman, 1994).

People in many other countries actually drink more than Americans do.

TABLE 16.1

Items on the Rutgers Collegiate Substance Abuse Screening Test That Were Most Likely to Identify Young Adult Substance Abusers

1. Have you gotten into financial difficulties as a result of drinking or using other drugs?
2. Is alcohol or other drug use making your college life unhappy?
3. Has drinking alcohol or using other drugs ever been behind your losing a job?
4. Has alcohol ever interfered with your preparation for exams?
5. Has your efficiency decreased since drinking &/or using other drugs?
6. Is your drinking &/or drug use jeopardizing your academic performance?
7. Has your ambition decreased since drinking &/or drug using?
8. Does drinking or using other drugs cause you to have difficulty sleeping?
9. Have you ever felt remorse after drinking &/or using other drugs?
10. Do you crave a drink or other drug at a definite time daily?
11. Do you want a drink or other drug the next morning?
12. Have you ever had a complete or partial loss of memory as a result of drinking or using other drugs?
13. Is drinking or using other drugs affecting your reputation?
14. Does drinking &/or using other drugs make you careless of your family's welfare?
15. Have you ever been to a hospital or institution on account of drinking or other drug use?

Note: Young adults who answered yes to these questions were more likely to be substance abusers than were those who answered no.
The RCSAST is to be used only as part of a complete assessment battery since more research needs to be done with this instrument.
Reprinted with permission from *Journal of Studies on Alcohol,* 54:522–527, 1993. Copyright by Alcohol Research Documentation, Inc., Rutgers Center of Alcohol Studies, Piscataway, NJ 08855.

More than 90 percent of the adults in Belgium, England, the Czech Republic, and Hungary drink, and more than 85 percent of the adults in Australia, Norway, and Spain drink (compared to 64 percent of adults in the United States). Some ethnic groups have higher rates of alcoholism than others. Irish and Native Americans, as well as people in many European countries, such as France, have high rates of alcoholism. Jews, Greeks, and Chinese have low rates of alcoholism.

The Role of Heredity in Alcoholism

Some experts conclude that heredity plays an important role in some forms of alcoholism. However, the precise mechanism for inheritance has not yet been identified. Family studies consistently find a high frequency of alcoholism in the first-degree relatives of alcoholics (Cotton, 1979). In one review of research on family alcoholism, when the father was an alcoholic, both sons and daughters had increased rates of alcoholism; when the mother was an alcoholic, increased rates of alcoholism occurred only for daughters (Pollock & others, 1987). Twin studies of alcoholism have revealed a modest influence of heredity, while adoption studies document the contribution of biological relatives' alcoholism to alcoholism in male adoptees (Sher, 1993).

Although the family, twin, and adoption studies reveal a genetic influence on alcoholism, they also indicate that environmental factors play an important role. For example, family studies indicate that many alcoholics do not have close relatives who are alcoholics (Sher, 1993). Adoption studies suggest that heredity and environment interact for at least one form of alcoholism (environmentally dependent susceptibility), and some alcoholics do not have alcoholic biological parents. The large cultural variations in alcohol use also underscore that the environment plays an important role in alcoholism. Like other behaviors and problems, alcoholism is multiply determined, has multiple pathways, and can be effectively treated in multiple ways.

Many characteristics of addictive behavior seem to be involved in other choices that harm individuals' health. See Critical Thinking to get some practice in taking different perspectives on whether it is legitimate to describe problems of self-control in terms of addiction.

Treatment of Alcoholism

Treatments for alcoholism include twelve-step programs such as Alcoholics Anonymous; codependency, cognitive therapy, and life-skills training programs; marital and family therapy; and training in drinking moderately.

Twelve-Step Programs and Alcoholics Anonymous Twelve-step programs, *such as Alcoholics Anonymous (AA), emphasize the importance of confession, group support, and spiritual commitment to God to help individuals cope with alcoholism.* The twelve steps represent the heart of AA principles, providing a precise guide for members to use in their recovery. An overview of the twelve steps is presented in table 16.2.

Alcoholics Anonymous groups are open and free to anyone, alcoholics as well as nonalcoholics. Twenty-nine percent of AA members stay sober for more than 5 years. AA members range in age from teenagers to the elderly. AA meetings often involve extensive personal testimonies by AA members. Revised versions of the AA principles have been adopted by other self-help groups, such as Narcotics Anonymous, Gamblers Anonymous, and Al-Anon.

Codependence A decade or two ago the term *codependence* did not exist. In just a few short years, it has become a household word. It seems that everyone is talking or writing about it—in magazines, on TV talk shows, in self-help groups, and in self-help books. Many bookstores now even have codependence sections.

Just what is codependence? *Codependence* originally referred to the problems of people married to alcoholics,

CRITICAL THINKING

The Addicted Society

Is it possible to be addicted to behaviors that don't involve drug use? Many therapists have identified a whole range of behaviors, such as gambling and abusive relationships, that appear to have addictive qualities. For instance, compulsive gamblers seem to have little self-control when they are in the grip of gambling—winning or losing, compulsive gamblers cannot resist the lure of the possibility of easy money. They demonstrate denial about the significance of their problem. The pattern tends to be progressive and irreversible.

Critics of the expansive use of the term *addiction* suggest that it is inappropriate to compare drug-related behaviors that have a strong physiological component with behaviors that do not have such a clear link to physiology. They argue that such a sweeping use of the term *addiction* trivializes the problems involved in substance abuse.

What arguments support the use of the term *addiction* for problems unrelated to substance use? What arguments support using the term only for problems of substance abuse? Your consideration of this controversy allows you to *solve problems actively by developing the perspectives of both sides.*

TABLE 16.2

AA's Twelve-Step Recovery Program

Following are the twelve steps as they were originally presented in the *Big Book, Alcoholics Anonymous.*

1. We admitted we were powerless over alcohol, that our lives had become unmanageable.
2. Came to believe that a Power greater than ourselves could restore us to sanity.
3. Made a decision to turn our will and our lives over to the care of God as we understood Him.
4. Made a searching and fearless moral inventory of ourselves.
5. Admitted to God, to ourselves, and to another human being the exact nature of our wrongs.
6. Were entirely ready to have God remove all these defects of character.
7. Humbly asked Him to remove our shortcomings.
8. Made a list of all persons we had harmed, and became willing to make amends to them all.
9. Made direct amends to such people wherever possible, except when to do so would injure them or others.
10. Continued to take personal inventory and when we were wrong promptly admitted it.
11. Sought through prayer and meditation to improve our conscious contact with God as we understood Him, praying only for knowledge of His will for us and the power to carry that out.
12. Having had a spiritual awakening as the result of these steps, we tried to carry this message to alcoholics, and to practice these principles in all our affairs.

The Twelve Steps are reprinted with permission of Alcoholics Anonymous World Services, Inc. Permission to reprint the Twelve Steps does not mean that A.A. has reviewed or approved the contents of this publication, nor that A.A. agrees with the views expressed herein. A.A. is a program of recovery from alcoholism *only*—use of the Twelve Steps in connection with programs and activities which are patterned after A.A., but which address other problems, or in any other non-A.A. context, does not imply otherwise.

especially wives of alcoholic men, but its meaning expanded rapidly to include a host of other circumstances. Agreement on a precise definition of codependence has not been forthcoming, although Melodie Beattie, one of the leaders of the codependence movement, says that a codependent person is someone who has let another person's behavior affect him or her, and who is obsessed with controlling that person's behavior. Lots of people fit this definition. Beattie agrees, saying that codependence is virtually *anything* and that *everyone* is codependent.

What most disciples of codependence do agree on is that the number of women who are codependent is staggering. And they agree that women who are codependent have low self-esteem, grew up in a dysfunctional family, and need to focus more on their own inner feelings instead of catering to someone else's needs, especially those of an alcoholic husband. In the language of codependence, many women stay with an unreliable partner, usually a male, because they are addicted to the relationship dynamics of being subservient to a male. Recommended therapy strategies for codependent people usually include a spiritually based twelve-step

program similar to that developed by Alcoholics Anonymous.

Codependence is a highly controversial concept in psychology. It has its enthusiastic supporters and its highly critical detractors. Codependency Anonymous is one of the most rapidly growing self-help support groups in the United States. Advocates of this self-help group approach believe that codependence helps to explain women's emotional problems better than any other approach. Until they learn about the nature of codependence, say the codependency endorsers, codependents are not aware of why they got into their troubled relationships in the first place or why they are still in them.

Not long after the codependence concept emerged, critics began attacking it. The criticisms included these (Tavris, 1989):

Codependence's emphasis on inner feelings and a higher power underestimates the importance of social influences on people's lives. For example, children and finances influence women's lives, but codependence does not deal with them.

Codependence describes people as sick and diseased without evaluating the larger sociocultural world in which people are embedded.

Codependence places too much blame on the woman for her male partner's problems; the husband is usually not considered to be responsible for his abusive, violent, and rotten behavior in the codependence framework.

The vagueness of codependence concepts makes it easy for just about anyone to have its symptoms, which is a perfect formula for selling self-help books but does not necessarily make a good self-help book or a good psychological theory.

Codependence does not address the individual perturbations that punctuate every person's life, but rather fits every person's unique woes under a label—codependence—that supposedly names a problem that is common to just about everyone.

The many supporters of the concept of codependence believe it calls attention to serious problems in human relationships, especially in terms of family dysfunction, and provides an excellent framework for counseling individuals who have let other people control them. The many detractors argue that the concept of codependence underestimates social influences, relies on an inappropriate disease model, places too much blame on women, is too vague, and does not adequately address individual differences.

Cognitive and Behavior Therapy

Cognitive and behavior therapists have developed several strategies for treating alcoholism and other substance-abuse disorders.

Cognitive therapists believe that the best way to treat alcoholism is to replace maladaptive thought patterns with adaptive ones. In contrast to AA's emphasis on spiritual commitment and powerlessness, cognitive therapists argue that the development of self-control and personal responsibility, rather than control by a higher power, will help alcoholics increase their sobriety (Ellis & Velton, 1992).

Rational Recovery (RR) is one of the increasing number of nonreligious self-help groups for recovering alcoholics and their relatives that have been formed in recent years. RR traces its roots directly to cognitive therapist Albert Ellis. It teaches that problem drinking results from people's beliefs that they are powerless and incompetent. Using Ellis' approach, a moderator (usually a recovered RR member) helps guide group discussion and get members to think more rationally and act more responsibly. Unlike AA, which stresses that alcoholics can never recover but are always in some phase of recovery, RR tells its members not only that recovery is possible, but that their methods can help them kick their drinking problem in a year or so. Two other self-help groups (unrelated to Ellis' approach) that have sprung up in recent years as alternatives to AA are the Secular Organization for Sobriety (SOS) and Women for Sobriety (WFS). Turned off by AA's religious emphasis, the new groups rely more on willpower and self-control than on a higher power.

Stanton Peele and Archie Brodsky (1991) developed a life-skills training program for combating alcoholism. They train people to develop skills for taking control of their lives. Like Ellis, they believe that an emphasis on responsibility and self-control is better than AA's emphasis on abdication of power and helplessness. In the life-skills training approach, people learn how to assess their values and what is really important to them, how to carry out plans of change, and how to establish community ties.

Behavior therapists use techniques like aversion therapy to treat alcoholism. **Aversion therapy** *is based on classical conditioning procedures; it is the process in which the sight, smell, or taste of alcohol is paired with a noxious stimulus.* For example, alcoholics might be given painful electrical shocks while drinking alcohol, or they might be given substances that induce vomiting when they drink, smell, or taste alcohol. After several sessions of taking the vomit-inducing substance, alcoholics might vomit or feel nauseated without the presence of the noxious substance, whenever they smell, taste, or think about alcohol.

Marital and Family Therapy The basic concept of marital and family therapy is that outcomes can be improved for both alcoholics and their family members when the entire family is involved in understanding and preventing relapse (Marlatt & Barrett, 1995). Instead of blaming family members for participating in an alcoholic's drinking problems, or assuming codependence, marital and family therapy offer an active approach to teaching family members about relapse and how to prevent it. This includes learning to recognize the behavioral indicators that signal the beginning of relapse and practicing new adaptive behaviors to cope with high-risk situations. For example, negative emotional states, such as anger and conflict in relationships, are triggers for relapse. Family members can learn assertiveness, communication, and negotiation skills to minimize conflict and anger, and thus prevent relapse.

Developing a Moderate Drinking Pattern Mark and Linda Sobel (1993) believe that abstinence is not necessarily the best way to overcome alcoholism (AA says it is). They taught a number of moderate drinking skills to help individuals learn to drink in moderation rather than abuse alcohol. In their study, moderate drinking led to better long-term results in reducing problem drinking than complete abstinence did. Their study has been controversial, but other researchers have also found that many alcoholics can be trained to drink in moderation. Moderate drinking is a goal of many behaviorally oriented alcoholism treatment programs.

Multimodal Approach In view of the many factors that maintain drug-related disorders like alcoholism, some treatment programs use combinations of approaches. For example, alcoholics might be detoxified through treatment with Antabuse (a chemical substance that produces an aversion to alcohol) and simultaneously be given behavioral treatment, such as stress management. Other therapies might include a combination of Alcoholics Anonymous, educational training, family therapy, and individual therapy. Proponents of multimodal therapy believe that no single treatment is likely to be completely successful and that effective outcomes often require major changes in alcoholics' lives.

Other Psychoactive Drugs

Now that we have discussed alcohol, let's explore the nature of a number of other psychoactive drugs.

Barbiturates and Tranquilizers

Barbiturates, *such as Nembutal and Seconal, are depressant drugs that induce sleep or reduce anxiety.* In heavy dosages, they can lead to impaired memory and decision making. When combined with alcohol (for instance, sleeping pills taken after a night of binge drinking), the result can be lethal. Barbiturates by themselves also can produce death in heavy dosages, which makes them the drug most often chosen in suicide attempts. Abrupt withdrawal from barbiturates can produce seizures.

Tranquilizers, *such as Valium and Xanax, are depressant drugs that reduce anxiety and induce relaxation.* They are among the most widely used drugs in the United States and can produce withdrawal symptoms when a person stops taking them.

Opiates

Opiates, *which consist of opium and its derivatives, depress the central nervous system's activity.* The most common opiate drugs—morphine and heroin—affect synapses in the brain that use endorphins as their neurotransmitter. When these drugs leave the brain, the affected synapses become understimulated. For several hours after taking an opiate, a person feels euphoric and relieved of pain and has an increased appetite for food and sex. But the opiates are among the most physically addictive drugs, leading to craving and painful withdrawal when the drug becomes unavailable. Morphine is sometimes used medically as a painkiller.

Recently, another hazardous consequence of opiate addiction has surfaced: AIDS. Most heroin addicts inject the drug intravenously. When they share their needles, blood from the needles can be passed on. When this blood comes from someone with AIDS, the virus can spread from the infected user to the uninfected user.

In 1969, huge crowds attended Woodstock. Sometimes called the "Woodstock Generation," many of these individuals smoked marijuana and took hallucinogens. The use of particular substances is sometimes linked with cultural subgroups or even to particular periods of time. Recently, though, LSD use began to increase.

Stimulants

Stimulants *are psychoactive drugs that increase the central nervous system's activity.* The most widely used stimulants are caffeine, nicotine (in cigarettes), amphetamines, and cocaine. Coffee, tea, and caffeinated soft drinks are mild stimulants. Amphetamines and cocaine are much stronger stimulants.

Amphetamines are widely prescribed, often in the form of diet pills. They are also called "pep pills" and "uppers." Amphetamines increase the release of the neurotransmitter dopamine, which increases the user's activity level and pleasurable feelings.

Cocaine comes from the coca plant, native to Bolivia and Peru. For centuries Bolivians and Peruvians have chewed on the plant to increase their stamina. Today cocaine is either snorted or injected in the form of crystals or powder. The effect is a rush of euphoria, which eventually wears off, followed by depression, lethargy, insomnia, and irritability. Cocaine can even trigger a heart attack, stroke, or brain seizure.

When animals and humans chew coca leaves, small amounts of cocaine gradually enter the bloodstream, without any apparent adverse effects. However, when extracted cocaine is sniffed, smoked, or injected, it enters the bloodstream very rapidly, producing a rush of euphoric feelings that lasts for about 15 to 30 minutes. Because the rush depletes the supply of the neurotransmitters dopamine and norepinephrine in the brain, an agitated, depressed mood usually follows as the drug's euphoric effects decline.

Crack *is an intensified form of cocaine, consisting of chips of pure cocaine that are usually smoked.* Crack is believed to be one of the most addictive substances known, being much more addictive than heroin, barbiturates, and alcohol. Emergency-room admissions related to crack soared from less than 600 cases in 1985 to more than 15,000 cases a year in the early 1990s.

Treatments for cocaine addiction have not been very successful. Cocaine's addictive properties are so strong that 6 months after treatment, more than 50 percent of cocaine abusers return to the drug. Researchers have found that monkeys will press a lever more than 12,000 times to obtain a single injection of cocaine, a testimony to cocaine's addictive qualities (Siegel, 1990). Experts on drug abuse believe the best approach to reduce cocaine addiction is through prevention programs.

Marijuana

Marijuana is the dried leaves and flowers of the hemp plant, *Cannibas sativa*, which originated in central Asia but is now grown in most parts of the world.

The plant's dried resin is known as hashish. The active ingredient in marijuana is THC, which stands for the chemical delta-9-tetrahydrocannabinol. This ingredient does not resemble the chemicals of other psychoactive drugs and does not affect a specific neurotransmitter. Rather, marijuana disrupts the membranes of neurons and affects the functioning of a variety of neurotransmitters and hormones.

The physical effects of marijuana include increases in pulse rate and blood pressure, reddening of the eyes, coughing, and dryness of the mouth. Psychological effects include a mixture of excitatory, depressive, and mildly hallucinatory characteristics, making it difficult to classify the drug. Marijuana can trigger spontaneous unrelated ideas, distorted perceptions of time and place, increased sensitivity to sounds and colors, and erratic verbal behavior. Marijuana can also impair attention and memory. When used daily in large amounts, marijuana can also alter sperm count and change hormonal cycles; it might be involved in some birth defects. Marijuana use declined during the 1980s, but an upsurge in its use has occurred in the 1990s (Johnston, O'Malley, & Bachman, 1994).

Hallucinogens

Hallucinogens *are psychoactive drugs that modify a person's perceptual experiences and produce visual images that are not real. Hallucinogens are also called psychedelic drugs, which means "mind altering."* LSD, PCP, and mescaline are examples of hallucinogens.

LSD (lysergic acid diethylamide) is a hallucinogen that even in low doses produces striking perceptual changes. Objects change their shape and glow. Colors become kaleidoscopic, fabulous images unfold as users close their eyes. Designs swirl, colors shimmer, bizarre scenes appear. Sometimes the images are pleasurable; sometimes they are grotesque. Figure 16.3 shows one kind of perceptual experience that a number of LSD users have reported. LSD can influence the user's perception of time as well. Time often seems to slow down dramatically, so that brief glances at objects are experienced as deep, penetrating, and

FIGURE 16.3

LSD-Induced Hallucination
Under the influence of hallucinogenic drugs, such as LSD, several users have reported seeing images that have a tunnel effect like the one shown here.

lengthy examinations, and minutes often seem to be hours or days.

LSD's effects on the body can include dizziness, nausea, and tremors. LSD acts primarily on the neurotransmitter serotonin in the brain, though it can affect dopamine as well. Emotional and cognitive effects can include rapid mood swings and impaired attention and memory. LSD was popular in the late 1960s and early 1970s, but its popularity dropped after its unpredictable effects became well publicized. However, a recent increase in LSD use by high school and college students has been reported (Johnston, O'Malley, & Bachman, 1994). LSD may be a prime example of generational forgetting. Today's youth don't

hear what an earlier generation heard—that LSD can cause bad trips and undesirable flashbacks.

TOWARD HEALTHIER LIVES

In this chapter we have seen that being healthy involves far more than simply going to a doctor when you get sick and being treated for disease. We are becoming increasingly aware that our behavior determines whether we will develop a serious illness and when we will die.

Seven of the ten leading causes of death in the United States are associated with the *absence* of health behaviors. Diseases such as influenza, polio, and rubella no longer are major causes of death.

More deaths are now caused by heart disease and stroke (33.5 percent of all deaths in 1990) and cancer (23.4 percent).

Personal habits and lifestyle play key roles in resisting disease and thriving under stress. These findings lead health psychologists, behavioral medicine specialists, and public health professionals to predict that the next major step in improving the general health of the American population will be primarily behavioral, not medical. The federal government and the Society for Public Health Education have set health objectives for the year 2000 (Schwartz & Eriksen, 1989). Among them are the following:

- To develop preventive services targeting diseases and such problems as cancer, heart disease, stroke, unintended pregnancy (especially among adolescents), and AIDS.
- To promote health, including behavior modification and health education; stronger programs are urged for dealing with smoking, alcohol and drug abuse, nutrition, physical fitness, and mental health.
- To work toward cleaner air and water.
- To improve workplace safety, including reducing exposure to toxic chemicals.
- To meet the health needs of special populations, such as gaining a better understanding of disease prevention in African American and Latino populations (ethnic minority groups suffer disproportionately from cancer, heart disease, diabetes, and other major diseases).

America's health care costs have soared and are moving toward the $1 trillion mark annually. Health experts hope to make a dent in these costs by encouraging people to live healthier lives. Many corporations have begun to recognize that health promotion for their employees is cost effective. Businesses are increasingly examining their employees' health behavior and the workplace environment as they recognize the role health

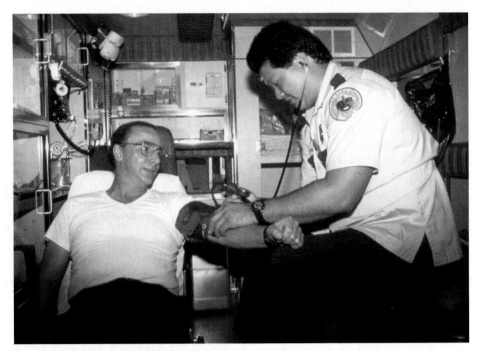

Cross-cultural psychologists, such as Richard Brislin, believe that, to ensure the success of social service programs, the people who introduce or maintain them should be highly respected members of the community. In Hawaii, for example, firefighters—highly respected and visible in Hawaiian communities—have been successful in getting Hawaiian residents to have their blood pressure checked.

plays in productive work. Smoke-free work environments, onsite exercise programs, bonuses to quit smoking and lose weight, and company-sponsored athletic events are increasingly found in American businesses.

You only live once—but if you work it right, once is enough.

—Joe E. Lewis

Government Interventions and Preventive Health Care

Seventh-Day Adventists have strong convictions about behavior and health. Could a government be as successful as the Seventh-Day Adventists are in promoting behavior that ensures the health of its citizens? Several governments have tried various measures, with mixed success. The government of Finland, for example, has placed more restrictions on tobacco advertisements and liquor sales than most countries, which many believe has resulted in improved health for Finnish citizens. However, in the United States, both citizen and industry lobbying

groups have made it difficult for health-related legislation to be approved. Cross-cultural psychologist Lisa Ilola (1990) points to seat belt use and mandatory helmets for motorcycle riders as examples of how many Americans, instead of accepting these reasonable protections for health and safety, bridle at what they believe is government intrusion into freedom of choice. The degree of respect for the government and the appropriateness of the government's action, it appears, are important factors in whether or not people will abide by legal constraints to promote their health and safety.

Cross-cultural psychologist Richard Brislin (1990) emphasizes that, to ensure the success of a social service program, the people who introduce or maintain it should be highly respected members of the community. For example, Hawaii has a highly successful program to encourage citizens to receive free blood pressure checkups. Firefighters volunteer to oversee the program. Anyone in Hawaii can have their blood pressure checked free of charge simply by going to a fire station. Residents take advantage of this program in large part because firefighters are highly respected and visible in Hawaiian communities—they have an active program in presenting safety information to schools, they entertain schoolchildren on field trips to fire stations, they are active in community service, and many are members of native Hawaiian families that go back five or six generations.

Prevention Related to Gender and Ethnicity

Gender and ethnicity play roles in life expectancy and health. According to psychologist Bonnie Strickland (1989), males are at greater risk than females for death at every age in the life span. The cause of death also varies for men and women. For example, four times more men than women die as a result of homicide, and twice as many men as women die as a result of respiratory cancer, suicide, pulmonary disease, accidents, cirrhosis of the liver, and heart disease.

In general, African Americans have a higher mortality rate than Whites for thirteen of the fifteen leading causes of death. Also, of all ethnic minority women, African American women are the most vulnerable to health problems. For example, African American women, compared with White American women, are three times more likely to have high blood pressure, are twice as likely to die from cardiovascular disease, have a 35 percent higher death rate for diabetes, and are four times more likely to be a victim of homicide.

Not only are there cross-cultural and ethnic variations in health, but women and men experience health and the health care system differently (Stanton & Gallant, 1995). Special concerns about women's health today focus on unintended and unwanted pregnancy, abuse and violence, AIDS, the role of poverty in women's health, eating disorders, drug abuse, breast diseases, reproductive health, and the medical establishment's discrimination against women (Anderson, 1996; O'Hara & others, 1995).

The women's health movement in the United States rejected an assumption that was all too often made by the male medical profession: that women lose control of their bodies out of ignorance. Consciousness-raising groups and self-help groups formed throughout the country in the 1960s and 1970s to instruct women about their bodies, reproductive rights, nutrition, and health care. Information was also given on how to conduct breast and pelvic examinations. The Boston Women's Health Book Collective, which was formed in 1969, has, as one of its goals, to teach women about their physical and mental health. It published *The New Our Bodies, Ourselves* (1992) and *Ourselves Getting Older* (1987), which are excellent resources for information about women's health.

Although females are increasingly becoming physicians, medicine continues to be a male-dominated profession. Women's physical complaints often are devalued, interpreted as "emotional"

rather than physical in origin, and dismissed as trivial. In one investigation, physicians described their men and women patients differently: The men were characterized as very direct, very logical, good decision makers, and rarely emotional, whereas the women were characterized as very excitable in minor crises, more easily influenced, less adventurous, less independent, very illogical, and even very sneaky (Broverman & others, 1970).

The issue of sex and gender bias has also recently been raised in selecting participants in medical research studies (Rabinowitz & Sechzur, 1993). Most medical research has been conducted with men, and frequently the results are generalized to women without apparent justification. For example, in a large-scale study involving 22,000 physicians that demonstrated the beneficial effect of an aspirin every other day on coronary heart disease, not a single woman was included in the study. Women's health advocates continue to press for greater inclusion of women in medical studies to reduce the bias that has characterized research on health, and they hope that the medical establishment will give increased attention to women's health concerns and treat women in less prejudiced, less biased ways (Strickland, 1988).

In this chapter and many others we have seen that cultural factors are important determinants of behavior and adjustment. Culture provides a *context* for the way in which health and the treatment of illness are perceived.

Psychoactive Drugs, Addiction, and Toward Healthier Lives

Psychoactive drugs act on the central nervous system to alter states of consciousness, modify perceptions, and alter mood. Psychoactive substances have been used since the beginning of recorded history for pleasure, utility, curiosity, and social reasons. Tolerance for a psychoactive drug develops when a greater amount of the drug is needed to produce the same effect. Physical withdrawal is the intense pain and craving that arise when an addicted person stops taking the addictive drug. Psychological dependence is the need to take a drug to cope with problems and stress.

The disease model of addiction describes addictions as biologically based, lifelong diseases that involve a loss of control over behavior and require medical and/or spiritual treatment for recovery. Critics of the disease model argue that the biological mechanisms of alcoholism have not been identified, that alcoholism is not necessarily lifelong, that the disease model stigmatizes people with labels like *addict* and *alcoholic*, and that it advocates a rigid program of therapy. In the life-process model, addiction is not a disease, but rather a habitual response and a source of gratification or security that can be understood and treated only in the context of social relationships and experience.

Alcohol is an extremely powerful drug that acts on the body primarily as a depressant. Drinking makes people less inhibited and impairs their judgment, motor skills, and intellectual functioning. With extreme intoxication, the drinker may lapse into a coma and even die. Effects of alcohol vary according to a number of factors. Alcohol is the most widely used drug in America and the third leading killer. A special concern is the high rate of alcohol consumption by high school and college students. People in many countries drink more than people in the United States do.

Treatments for alcoholism include twelve-step programs such as Alcoholics Anonymous; codependency, cognitive, and behavior therapy; marital and family therapy; and multimodal approaches. Twelve-step programs emphasize the importance of confession, group support, and spiritual commitment to God to help individuals combat alcoholism. The concept of codependence has its enthusiastic supporters and its highly critical detractors. Cognitive therapists, such as Ellis, advocate replacing maladaptive with adaptive thought patterns. Behavior therapies include aversion therapy and covert sensitization. Marital and family therapy approaches involve the entire family in learning how to prevent relapse. Yet another strategy for reducing problem drinking is to emphasize moderate drinking rather than complete abstinence. Some treatment programs follow a multimodal approach that involves the use of several different types of therapies.

Barbiturates are depressant drugs that induce sleep or reduce anxiety. Tranquilizers are depressant drugs that reduce anxiety and induce relaxation. Opiates (opium and its derivatives) depress the central nervous system's activity. Stimulants are psychoactive drugs that increase central nervous system activity. The most widely used stimulants are caffeine, nicotine, amphetamines and cocaine. Cocaine provides a euphoric rush that is followed by depression, lethargy, insomnia, and irritability. Cocaine can trigger a heart attack, stroke, or brain seizure. Crack is an intensified form of cocaine and is believed to be one of the most addictive drugs. Treatments for cocaine addiction have not been very successful. Marijuana's psychological effects include a mixture of excitatory, depressive, and mildly hallucinatory characteristics, making the drug difficult to classify. Marijuana affects a number of neurotransmitters and hormones, and can impair attention and memory. Hallucinogens are psychoactive drugs that modify a person's perceptual experiences and produce visual images that are not real. Hallucinogens are also called psychedelic ("mind altering") drugs. LSD, PCP, and mescaline are examples of hallucinogens. There has been a recent increase in use of LSD.

Seven of the ten leading causes of death—heart disease, cancer, and stroke, for example—are associated with the absence of healthy behaviors. The next major improvements in general health may be behavioral, not medical. Several health goals for the year 2000 have been proposed and businesses are increasingly interested in improving the health of their employees. Government interventions and preventions in health care require consideration of the degree people respect the government and the appropriateness of the intervention and prevention.

A special concern is the manner in which women have been treated in the medical domain. A greater concern about women's issues needs to become a part of the medical arena, which historically has been male-dominated.

An Alcohol Detour

Whiskey drowns some troubles and floats a lot more.
—**Robert C. Edwards**

The amount of alcohol consumed by high school and college students in the United States is nothing short of staggering. In spite of many public education initiatives, there has been little success in reducing the trend. Such early alcohol abuse greatly enhances the risk for life-threatening car accidents and lifelong struggles with alcoholism.

What would it take to have a successful intervention to reduce under-age alcohol use? There are no easy answers to this, but success would rest with *identifying the values that influence behavior* and building a campaign to persuade drinkers about the negative effects of alcohol abuse. Which of the following strategies do you think would be successful, and what values does each appeal to?

- A heartfelt plea from the president
- Staging, in full view of school, a bloody accident in which lives are lost and a drunk driver is hauled off to jail
- Testimony from a star on *Melrose Place*
- Statistics and graphs about the long-range damage alcohol abuse causes
- Speeches from members of Alcoholics Anonymous
- Calculating how much potential income is lost to alcohol purchases

Can you think of any other strategies that might influence under-age drinkers to rethink their alcohol consumption?

We began this chapter by discussing the relation between health and psychology, exploring the historical background and current approaches. Our coverage of promoting health focused on regular exercise, body image and lifestyle choices, proper nutrition, and freedom from smoking. We also read about coping with illness—recognizing and interpreting symptoms, seeking treatment, the patient's role, and adherence to medical advice and treatment. We discussed psychoactive drugs and addiction, including the nature of psychoactive drugs, addiction, alcohol, and other psychoactive drugs. We concluded the chapter by examining how we can develop healthier lives, touching on issues involving government interventions and preventive health care, as well as prevention related to gender and ethnicity. Remember that you can obtain an overall summary of the chapter by again studying the in-chapter reviews on pages 410, 412, and 424.

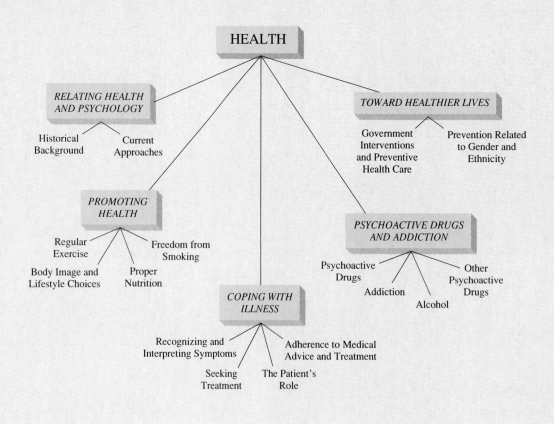

PRACTICAL KNOWLEDGE ABOUT ADJUSTMENT

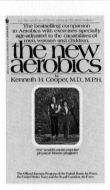

THE NEW AEROBICS

(1970) by Kenneth Cooper. New York: Bantam.

The New Aerobics lays out Cooper's age-adjusted recommendations for aerobic exercise. The aerobic exercise program recommended by Cooper has been adopted by the United States Air Force, the United States Navy, and the Royal Canadian Air Force. The aerobics system is carefully planned to condition the heart, lungs, and body tissues of people who are either in fairly good health or poor health (the latter should especially have a physical exam before embarking on any exercise program).

The aerobic program uses common forms of exercise—walking, running, swimming, cycling, handball, squash, and basketball—to achieve the desired results.

Cooper's recommended program will reap physical and psychological benefits for you. More than any other individual, Kenneth Cooper is responsible for getting a lot of people off their couches and out on the walking or jogging track. His positive influence is even international. In Brazil, when people go out to run they call it "doing the Cooper." Another Cooper book we recommend is *The Aerobics Program for Well-Being.*

THE NEW FIT OR FAT (REVISED ED.)

(1991) by Covert Bailey. Boston, MA: Houghton Mifflin.

The New Fit or Fat describes ways to become healthy by developing better diet and exercise routines. Bailey argues that the basic problem for overweight people is not losing weight, which fat people do periodically, but in gaining weight, which fat people do more easily than those with a different body chemistry. He explores ways our body stores fat and analyzes why crash diets don't work. He explains the relation between fat metabolism and weight, concluding that the ultimate cure for obesity is aerobic exercise coupled with a sensible low-fat diet.

Originally published in 1977 as *Fit or Fat,* the 1991 edition is greatly expanded with new information on fitness lifestyles and recent scientific advances. A new chapter also answers readers' most frequently asked questions about Bailey's views on diet and exercise. This book offers solid, no-nonsense advice on how to lose weight and become more physically fit.

SELF-ASSESSMENT SCORING AND INTERPRETATION

MONITORING YOUR EATING BEHAVIOR

Needs no additional scoring.

John Santrock
The Crusader, detail

Values and Religion

with Raymond Paloutzian

*A belief is not merely an idea
the mind possesses; it is an idea
that possesses the mind.*

—Robert Bolton

THE STORY OF MARTIN LUTHER KING, JR.:
A MAN OF CONVICTION

One of the most important figures in the United States this century was the Reverend Martin Luther King, Jr. (1929–1968). The son of a preacher, he received religious training himself, including a doctorate in theology from Boston University. As an African American minister in the South during the 1960s, King became actively involved in efforts to ease the plight of African Americans in housing, jobs, equal access to voting and education, and other civil rights issues. Earlier, in the 1950s, he organized a bus boycott in Montgomery, Alabama, as a way of protesting forced racial segregation in the city's bus system. The boycott lasted 381 days, during which time King's home was bombed and King received death threats and was

Martin Luther King, Jr.

jailed. King's boycott efforts made an important difference: The United States Supreme Court ruled that it was illegal to have forced segregation in public transportation in the city.

King became a renowned civil rights leader who led marches, rallies, and legal actions to promote racial

equality. He won the Nobel Peace Prize in 1964 for these efforts. Among the most important of his teachings was the concept that people should be judged not by the color of their skin but rather by the content of their character. In 1968, at the height of social upheaval in the 1960s, King was shot and killed in Memphis, Tennessee. His funeral in Atlanta, Georgia, was attended by 100,000 people. King's birthday is now a U.S. national holiday.

Martin Luther King, Jr., was a religiously motivated man. His values, moral reasoning, and religion served as his motivational springboard for working to change society toward greater equality between people from diverse ethnic backgrounds.

PREVIEW

Throughout human history, morals, values, and religion have played powerful roles in people's lives, as they did in the life of Martin Luther King, Jr. Great acts of love and great acts of hate have both been committed in the name of religion and defending morals and values. On the positive side, religion has seen to the construction of hospitals, the feeding of starving people, and the comforting of those whose lives have been damaged. But the harsh side of religion has also emerged at various times in history. Many cruelties have taken place in the name of religion, including military conquests and the Inquisition. At various times throughout history, people have been forced to practice a religion against their wills.

In this chapter, we will explore the nature of values and morals. We will also explore a number of topics in the psychology of religion, including the history of religion and the nature of religion and religious experience.

VALUES

Values *are standards that we maintain about the things we prefer or the ideas that capture our allegiance.* Values not only influence our perceptions and judgment,

but also predispose us toward taking particular actions or believing new ideas. For our purposes in this chapter, an important subset of values is **morals,** *behavioral ideals regarding right and wrong behavior.*

Values are abstractions. We infer values based on people's behavior. For example, when you observe a person waving a flag at a Fourth of July parade, you would be reasonable to infer that the person is expressing patriotism.

Values can be obvious (as with the flag waver) or subtle. For instance, others at the parade might feel a more fervent patriotism than the flag waver but not reveal this by clear observable signs. Perhaps the subtle patriots wear a small flag pin on their shirts. Perhaps they give no outward sign at all of their patriotism. Perhaps only a serious conversation about their ideals would reveal their patriotism.

Individuals vary in the intensity with which they hold values (Seligman, Olson, & Zanna, 1996). Some values become the basis of individual identity. Political values, religious values, and sexual values are examples of values that exert strong influence on individual behavior and identity. Other values might inspire only mild allegiance. The Self-Assessment encourages you to identify the values that tend to dominate your own ideals.

> *When you know you're right, you don't care what others think. You know sooner or later it will come out in the wash.*
>
> **—Barbara McClintock**

Sometimes individuals might not be aware of their values until they find themselves in a situation that exposes their beliefs. They might be unaware of the depth of their feeling and conviction until they are forced to take some action. For example, you might be surprised to find yourself reacting strongly if you see the student next to you cheating on an exam. In such a situation you might experience a **value conflict,** *a conflict between two competing values that encourage opposing actions.* Perhaps the value *integrity* prompts you to turn in the cheater, while the value *noninvolvement* encourages you to mind your own business.

Another reason we might not be conscious of our values is that they come to us from our experience within our own culture. When a value is very widespread within a culture, the power of that value might be difficult to recognize for the members of that culture. For example, an American tourist in England was startled to hear his English host call Americans "charmingly practical." It had

not occurred to the tourist that Americans share the value of **pragmatism,** *being inclined to practical solutions,* because practical solutions were so commonplace to him in daily life. The Englishman gave him a viewpoint from outside his own (American) culture. Sometimes we make our values easier to see and understand by writing them down. For instance, the Declaration of Independence is a formal statement of the values on which American culture is built. To reflect on other American values, turn to Critical Thinking.

Psychologists have not always recognized the important influence of values on behavior. It was not until the 1950s that social psychologist Gordon Allport undertook the first formal study of values. He created descriptions of value types and conducted normative studies to determine how frequently those value profiles were likely to show up in the culture. Largely due to the rise of behaviorism, the study of values fell into disfavor as a research area. With the upsurge in cognitive psychology, psychologists have

SELF-ASSESSMENT

Dominant Personal Values

This list is not exhaustive, but it captures the types of values that serve as the cornerstones of identity. Place a checkmark next to the values that seem to be the strongest in the personal and social identity you have developed.

_____ achievement	_____ self-worth
_____ religion	_____ physical health
_____ tradition	_____ personal authority
_____ awe	_____ service
_____ family belonging	_____ wisdom
_____ family responsibility	_____ materialism
_____ justice	_____ care/nurturance
_____ altruism	_____ creativity
_____ self-regard	_____ order & discipline
_____ sensory stimulation	_____ fidelity
_____ loyalty	_____ productivity
_____ patriotism	_____ play
_____ approval	_____ interdependence
_____ self-preservation	_____ certainty
_____ sensory pleasure	_____ security
_____ efficiency	_____ control
_____ peace	_____ thrift
_____ environment	_____ noninvolvement
_____ independence	_____ self-expression
_____ self-fulfillment	_____ novelty

CRITICAL THINKING

Value Billboards

Over the last two decades or so, Americans have popularized a style of dress that provides a great opportunity for interpreting the values that individuals hold: decorated T-shirts. By observing and interpreting others' wardrobes, you can often determine where they have vacationed, what musical groups they prefer, what sports teams they root for, and a host of other information. Such data can imply values. For example, if you encounter someone with a T-shirt that proclaims recent participation in a bowling tournament, you can reasonably infer that the person values competition.

Carefully observe the next ten decorated T-shirts that you encounter. What preferences are they advertising? What can you infer from them about the wearer's values? How confident can you be regarding your interpretation? This exercise encourages you to *observe and interpret behavior carefully in order to identify underlying values.*

shown more interest in researching values, including how values are expressed by college students (Reed, 1996; Reed, Turiel, & Brown, 1996).

Values in College

Over the past two decades, college students have shown an increased concern for their own personal well-being and a decreased concern for the well-being of others, especially the disadvantaged (Astin & others, 1994). As shown in figure 17.1, today's college freshmen are more strongly motivated to be well off financially and less motivated to develop a meaningful philosophy of life than college students were 20 or even 10 years ago. Becoming very well off financially was a "very important" reason for attending college for a record high percentage of college students (73 percent) in the 1990 survey. The percentage declined only slightly (to 71 percent) in 1994. In 1971, only 50 percent of college students

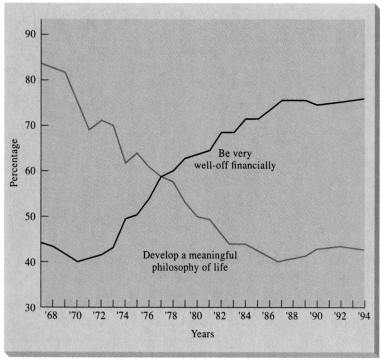

FIGURE 17.1

Changing Freshman Life Goals, 1968–1994.
The percentages indicated are in response to the question of identifying a life goal as "essential" or "very important." There has been a significant reversal in freshman life goals in the last two decades, with a far greater percentage of today's college freshmen stating that a "very important" life goal is to be well-off financially, and far fewer stating that developing a meaningful philosophy of life is a "very important" life goal.

There are some signs that today's college students are shifting toward a stronger interest in the welfare of society, as evidenced by the volunteer work these college students are doing on Earth Day.

cited financial well-being as a very important reason for attending college.

However, two aspects of values that increased during the 1960s continue to characterize many of today's youth: self-fulfillment and self-expression (Conger, 1988). As part of their motivation for self-fulfillment, many adolescents show great interest in their physical health and well-being. Greater self-fulfillment and self-expression can be laudable goals, but if they become the only goals, self-destruction, loneliness, or alienation may result. Young people also need to develop a corresponding sense of commitment to others' welfare. Encouraging adolescents to have a strong commitment to others, in concert with an interest in self-fulfillment, is an important task for America at the close of the twentieth century.

Some signs indicate that today's students are shifting toward a stronger

interest in the welfare of society (National and Community Service Coalition, 1995; Yates, 1996). For example, between 1986 and 1994 there was an increase in the percentage of freshmen who said that they were strongly interested in participating in community action programs (28 percent in 1994, compared to 18 percent in 1986) and in helping to promote racial understanding (40 percent in 1994, compared to 27 percent in 1986). One recent study reported that students' participation in community service stimulated them to reflect on society's political organization and moral order (Yates, 1995). More students are showing an active interest in the problems of homelessness, child abuse, hunger, and poverty (Conger, 1988). The percentage of students who believe that it is desirable to work for a social service organization rose from 11 percent in 1980 to 17 percent in 1989

(Johnston, Bachman, & O'Malley, 1990). Whether concern for the community and society will continue to increase, even in such small increments, in the remainder of the 1990s, is difficult to predict.

> *Without civic morality communities perish; without personal morality their survival has no value.*
>
> **—Bertrand Russell**

Values in Psychology and Adjustment

Controversy swirls about the issue of whether psychology is value free (Schwartz, 1990). As a science, psychology is dedicated to discovering facts about behavior and creating theories to explain those facts. In this abstract description, values do not crop up. The scientific system requires only that psychology discover the most dependable facts and generate the best theories possible (Kimble, 1989). Conducting research that is value-free is complex, because psychology deals with living organisms.

Researchers' values influence their choice of research questions. For example, a divorced single parent might decide to study the inadequate involvement of male noncustodial parents in their children's development rather than the increased role of males in caring for children.

Each of us also has preconceived ideas about behavior. Consider the values involved in such questions as the right to own guns versus handgun control, bans on sexually explicit books versus freedom of literary expression, the public's right to know versus an individual's right to privacy, retribution versus rehabilitation as the goal of criminal codes, a verdict of "not guilty by reason of insanity" versus "guilty but insane," and "freedom of choice" versus "right to life." Our personal values related to these questions may influence the way we perceive and label behavior. One individual might call a sexual act "a sexual variation"; another individual might label the same act "sick." One individual might label a female's assertive behavior "too aggressive"; another individual might label the same behavior "competent." One individual might observe a male's long hours of work and label the behavior "overachieving" or "workaholic," whereas another individual might call the same behavior "maximizing potential."

When psychologists are called on as experts, they often make statements and recommendations that are laden with values. The therapist you consult about your problems might have certain personal values about sexual conduct that influence the advice she gives. The professor in your class might have certain personal values about moral behavior, child rearing, and how to get ahead in life that she communicates to you. A psychologist interviewed by Ted Koppel on *Nightline* might have certain values about government's responsibility in caring for the homeless, an adolescent's level of responsibility in dealing cocaine, and a mentally disordered individual's responsibility in committing mass murder. In sum, although psychology often strives to reduce the role of values as it seeks the truths of human behavior, in the court of life, which is psychology's setting, values and psychology are difficult to disentangle.

MORAL DEVELOPMENT

Our values are the basis of our moral reasoning and judgment. We are often confronted with choices that reveal our values. And we are also often in a position—whether we like it or not—to judge the morality of others' actions.

Let's turn now to the theory and research that have dominated the study of moral development in recent years, the cognitive developmental approach of Lawrence Kohlberg.

There is no moral precept that does not have something inconvenient about it.

—Diderot

Kohlberg's Stages of Moral Reasoning

Lawrence Kohlberg (1976, 1986) devised eleven stories to investigate the nature of moral thought. One of them was this:

> In Europe a woman was near death from a rare form of cancer. There was one drug that the doctors thought might save her: a form of radium that a druggist in the same town had recently discovered. The drug was expensive to make, but the druggist was charging ten times what the drug cost him to make it. He paid $200 for the radium and charged $2,000 for a small dose of the drug. The sick woman's husband, Heinz, went to everyone he knew to borrow the money, but he could get together only $1,000. He told the druggist that his wife was dying and asked him to sell it cheaper or let him pay later. However, the druggist said, "No. I discovered the drug, and I am going to make money from it." Desperate, Heinz broke into the man's store to steal the drug for his wife. (Kohlberg, 1969, p. 379)

After reading this story, interviewees answer a series of questions about the moral dilemma. Should Heinz have stolen the drug? Was it right or wrong? Why? Is it a husband's duty to steal the drug for his wife if he can get it in no other way? Would a good husband do it? Did the druggist have the right to charge that much when there was no law setting a limit on the price? Why?

Based on the answers that individuals have given to questions about this and other moral dilemmas, Kohlberg believed that there are three levels of moral development, each of which is characterized by two stages. A key concept in understanding moral development, especially Kohlberg's theory, is **internalization,** *the developmental change from behavior that is externally controlled to behavior that is controlled by internal, self-generated standards and principles.*

1. The **preconventional level** *is Kohlberg's lowest level of moral thinking, in which an individual shows no internalization of moral values—moral thinking is based on punishments (stage 1) or rewards (stage 2) that come from the external world.* In regard to the story about Heinz and the druggist, at stage 1 an individual might say that Heinz should not steal the drug because it is a big crime; at stage 2, an individual might say he shouldn't steal the drug because the druggist needs to make a profit.

2. The **conventional level** *is Kohlberg's second level of moral thinking, in which an individual has an intermediate level of internalization. The individual abides by certain standards (internal), but they are the standards of others (external), such as the standards of parents (stage 3) or the laws of society (stage 4).* At stage 3, an individual might say that Heinz should steal the drug for his wife because that is what a good husband would do; at stage 4, an individual might say that it is natural to want to save his wife but that it is always wrong to steal.

3. The **postconventional level** *is Kohlberg's highest level of moral thinking; moral development is completely internalized and not based on others' standards. An individual recognizes alternative moral courses, explores the options, and then develops a personal moral code. The code is among the principles generally accepted by the community (stage 5) or it is more individualized (stage 6).* At stage 5, an individual might say that the law was not set up for these circumstances so Heinz can steal the drug; it is not really right, but he is justified in doing it. At stage 6, the individual is faced with the decision of whether to consider the other people who need the drug just as badly as Heinz's wife. Heinz should consider the value of all lives involved.

Kohlberg believed that these levels and stages occur in a sequence and are age-related. Some evidence to support Kohlberg's theory has been found, although few people reach stages 5 and 6 (Colby & others, 1983). Kohlberg stated that moral development occurs through maturation of thought, the mutual give-and-take of peer relations, and opportunities for role taking. Parent-child relationships contribute very little to moral thought, in Kohlberg's view, because they are too dominated by parents' moral values, with little opportunity for the youths to experiment with alternative moral choices.

Criticisms of Kohlberg's Theory

Kohlberg's provocative view continues to generate considerable research on moral development. However, critics challenge his theory (Kurtines & Gewirtz, 1991). One criticism of Kohlberg's view is that moral reasons are often a shelter for immoral behavior. When bank embezzlers and presidents are asked about their moral reasoning, they might appear to be at an advanced level, even at Kohlberg's postconventional level, but when their behavior is examined it might be filled with cheating, lying, and stealing. The cheaters, liars, and thieves might know what is right and what is wrong but still do what is wrong.

A second major criticism of Kohlberg's view is that it does not adequately reflect relationships and concerns for others (Day & Tappan, 1996; Lapsley, 1996). The **justice perspective** *is a theory of moral development that focuses on the rights of the individual; individuals independently make moral decisions. Kohlberg's theory is a justice perspective.* By contrast, the **care perspective** *is Carol Gilligan's theory of moral development, which sees people in terms of their connectedness with others and focuses on interpersonal communication, relationships with others, and concern for others.* According to Gilligan (1982, 1996), Kohlberg greatly underplayed the care perspective in moral development. She believes that this may have happened because he was a male, most of his research was with males rather than females, and he used male responses as a model for his theory.

Recently Gilligan conducted extensive interviews with girls from 6 to 18 years of age (Gilligan, 1992). She found that girls consistently reveal reported, detailed knowledge about human relationships, based on listening and watching what happens between people. According to Gilligan, girls have the ability to pick up different rhythms in relationships and are often able to follow the pathways of feelings.

Gilligan also believes that girls reach a critical juncture in their development when they reach adolescence. Gilligan says that at the beginning of adolescence, at about 11 to 12 years of age, girls become aware that their intense interest in intimacy is not prized by the

Carol Gilligan (*center*) is shown with some of the students she has interviewed about the importance of relationships in a female's development. According to Gilligan, the sense of relationships and connectedness is at the heart of female development.

male-dominated culture, even though society values females as caring and altruistic. The dilemma, says Gilligan, is that girls are presented with a choice that makes them appear either selfish (if they become independent and self-sufficient) or selfless (if they remain responsive to others). Gilligan states that, as young adolescent girls experience this dilemma, they increasingly "silence" their own distinctive voices. They become less

confident and more tentative in offering their opinions, and this often persists into adulthood. Some researchers believe that this self-doubt and ambivalence too often translates into depression and eating disorders among adolescent girls.

Some critics argue that Gilligan overemphasizes differences between genders. One of those critics is developmentalist Eleanor Maccoby, who says that Gilligan exaggerates the differences in intimacy and connectedness between males and females. Other critics fault Gilligan's research strategy, which rarely includes a comparison group of boys and rarely includes statistical analysis. Instead, Gilligan conducts extensive interviews with girls and then provides excerpts from the girls' narratives to buttress her ideas. Other critics fear that Gilligan's findings reinforce stereotypes—females as nurturing and sacrificing, for example—that might undermine females' struggle for equality. These critics say that Gilligan's different voice should perhaps be called "the voice of the victim."

In reply, revisionists, such as Gilligan, say that their work provides a way to liberate females and transform a society that has far too long discriminated against females. If females' approach to life is acknowledged as authentic, they will no longer have to act like males. The revisionists state that females' sensitivity in relationships is a special gift in our culture. Influenced by Gilligan's and other feminists' thinking, some schools are beginning to incorporate the feminine voice into their curriculum. For example, at the Emma Willard School in Troy, New York, the entire curriculum has been revamped to emphasize cooperation rather than competition and to encourage girls to analyze and express ideas from their own perspectives rather than responding in stereotyped or conformist ways.

A third criticism of Kohlberg's view is that it is culturally biased (Banks, 1993; Miller, 1995). Kohlberg's scoring system was strongly influenced by the individualistic biases of his own culture. Therefore his stage theory might fit his own cultural context better than it fits other cultures. One review of research on moral development in 27 countries found that moral reasoning appears to be more culture-specific than Kohlberg envisioned and that Kohlberg's scoring system does not recognize higher-level moral reasoning in certain cultural groups (Snarey, 1987). Kohlberg did not recognize such values as communal equity and collective happiness in Israel, the unity and sacredness of all life forms in India, or the relation of an individual to the community in New Guinea as examples of higher-level moral reasoning. Kohlberg's system would not

score these values at the highest level of moral reasoning because they do not emphasize an individual's rights and abstract principles of justice. In summary, moral reasoning is shaped more by the values and beliefs of a culture than Kohlberg acknowledged.

Character Education

Character education, or moral education, has become a widely discussed topic (Rest, 1995). Many parents worry that their offspring are growing up without traditional values. Teachers complain that many of their students are unethical. Among the questions about moral education we examine are these: What is the hidden curriculum? What is the nature of direct moral education versus indirect moral education? What is values clarification? What is cognitive moral education?

The Hidden Curriculum

The **hidden curriculum** *is the pervasive moral atmosphere that characterizes schools.* This atmosphere includes school and classroom rules, attitudes toward academics and extracurricular activities, the moral orientation of teachers and school administrators, and text materials. More than half a century ago, educator John Dewey (1933) recognized that, whether or not they offer specific programs in moral education, schools provide moral education through the hidden curriculum. Schools, like families, are settings for moral development. Teachers serve as models of ethical or unethical behavior. Classroom rules and peer relations at school transmit attitudes about cheating, lying, stealing, and consideration of others. The school administration, through its rules and regulations, represents a value system to students.

Character building begins in our infancy, and continues until death.
—**Eleanor Roosevelt**

Direct and Indirect Moral Education

Approaches to moral education can be classified as either direct or indirect. **Direct moral education** *involves either emphasizing values or character traits*

during specified time slots or integrating those values or traits throughout the curriculum. **Indirect moral education** *involves encouraging students to define their own and others' values and helping them to define the moral perspectives that support those values.*

In the direct moral education approach, instruction in specified moral concepts can assume the form of example and definition, class discussions and role-playing, or rewarding students for proper behavior. The use of McGuffey Readers during the early part of the twentieth century exemplifies the direct approach. The stories and poems in the readers taught moral behavior and character in addition to academics. Some contemporary educators advocate a direct approach to moral education. Former U.S. Secretary of Education William Bennett (1986) wrote:

> If a college is really interested in teaching its students a clear lesson in moral responsibility, it should tell the truth about drugs in a straightforward way. This summer, our college presidents should send every student a letter saying they will not tolerate drugs on campus—period. The letter should then spell out precisely what the college's policy will be toward students who use drugs. Being simple and straightforward about moral responsibility is not the same as being simplistic and unsophisticated.

Bennett also believes that every elementary and secondary school should have a discipline code, making clear to students and parents what the school expects of them. Then the school should enforce the code.

The most widely adopted indirect approaches to moral education are values clarification and cognitive moral education, each of which we consider in turn.

Values Clarification Values clarification *is an indirect moral education approach that focuses on helping students to clarify what their lives are for and what is worth working for.* In values clarification, students are asked questions or presented with dilemmas and expected to respond, either individually or in small groups.

The intent is to help students to define their own values and to become aware of others' values.

In the following values clarification example, students are asked to select from among ten people the six who will be admitted to a fallout shelter during World War III:

A fallout shelter under your administration in a remote Montana highland contains only enough space, air, food, and water for six people for three months, but ten people wish to be admitted. The ten have agreed by radio contact that, for the survival of the human race, you must decide which six of them shall be saved. You have exactly 30 minutes to make up your mind before Washington goes up in smoke. These are your choices:

1. A 16-year-old girl of questionable IQ, a high school dropout, pregnant.

2. A policeman with a gun (which cannot be taken from him), thrown off the force recently for brutality.
3. A clergyman, 75.
4. A woman physician, 36, known to be a confirmed racist.
5. A male violinist, 46, who served seven years for pushing narcotics.
6. A 20-year-old Black militant, no special skills.
7. A former prostitute, female, 39.
8. An architect, a male homosexual.
9. A 26-year-old law student.
10. The law student's 25-year-old wife who spent the last nine months in a mental hospital, still heavily sedated. They refuse to be separated.

In this exercise, no answers are considered right or wrong. The clarification of values is left up to the individual student. Advocates of the values clarification approach argue that it is value-free. Critics

argue that, because of its controversial content, it offends community standards. Critics also say that, because of its relativistic nature, values clarification undermines accepted values and fails to stress truth and what is right behavior.

Cognitive Moral Education Like values clarification, cognitive moral education also challenges direct moral instruction. **Cognitive moral education** *is an indirect moral education approach that emphasizes that students adopt such values as democracy and justice as their moral reasoning is developed.* In this approach, students' moral standards are allowed to develop through their attention to environmental settings and exercises that encourage more advanced moral thinking. Thus, in contrast to values clarification, cognitive moral education is not value-free. Such values as democracy and justice are emphasized. The advocates of cognitive moral education argue that, when moral standards are imposed—as in the

R E V I E W

Values and Moral Development

Values are characteristics of belief or ideals that influence behavior and judgment. Values orient individuals toward particular actions. The dominance of behaviorism in American psychology meant there was little interest in research on values for many years. However, with the rise of cognitive psychology there has been a resurgence of interest in values. Of special interest is character education.

Values are abstractions, so we must infer their presence by observing people's behavior. Values can be held with varying intensities. Political, religious, and sexual values are examples of values that can strongly influence people's behavior and identity.

Over the past two decades, college students have increasingly valued personal well-being and decreasingly valued the well-being of others. However, today's college students might be

shifting back toward a stronger interest in the welfare of society.

Our values serve as the basis of our moral reasoning and judgment. The cognitive developmental approach of Lawrence Kohlberg has dominated recent theorizing and research on moral development. Kohlberg proposed three levels (each with two stages) of moral development: preconventional, conventional, and postconventional. The three levels vary in the degree to which moral development is internalized, with complete internalization occurring only at the highest level. Kohlberg's critics include Carol Gilligan, who believes his theory is biased against females and underrepresents the care perspective. Other criticisms of Kohlberg's theory include its overemphasis on cognition and underemphasis on behavior, as well as evidence for greater cultural variability in the sequence of stages than Kohlberg proposed.

The hidden curriculum is the pervasive moral atmosphere that

characterizes any school, regardless of whether there is a specific moral curriculum. Direct moral education involves either emphasizing values or character traits during specified time slots or integrating those values or traits throughout the curriculum. Indirect moral education involves encouraging adolescents to define their own and others' values and helping them to define the moral perspectives that support those values.

The two main approaches to indirect moral education are values clarification and cognitive moral education. Values clarification focuses on helping students to clarify what their lives are for and what is worth working for. Cognitive moral education emphasizes that such values as democracy and justice are adopted through the development of students' moral reasoning. Kohlberg's theory has extensively influenced the cognitive moral education approach.

direct moral education approach—students can never completely integrate and fully understand moral principles, and that only through participation and discussion can students learn to apply the rules and principles of cooperation, trust, community, and self-reliance.

Lawrence Kohlberg's theory of moral development has extensively influenced the cognitive moral education approach. Contrary to what some critics say, Kohlberg's theory is not completely morally neutral. Higher-level moral thinking is clearly preferred to lower-level moral thinking. And Kohlberg's theory stresses that higher-level thinking can be stimulated through focused discussion of dilemmas. Also, in the 1980s, Kohlberg (1986) revised his views on moral education by placing more emphasis on the school's moral atmosphere, not unlike John Dewey did many years ago.

RELIGION

Values and morals are embedded in religion. In this section we will explore the history of the psychology of religion and the nature of religion and religious experience.

> Religion enlightens, terrifies, subdues; it gives faith, inflicts remorse, inspires resolutions, and inflames devotion.
> —Henry Newman, 1853

The History of the Psychology of Religion

The psychology of religion is both one of the oldest and one of the newest research areas in psychology. The psychology of religion was part of the field of psychology at its beginning. The famous psychologist William James wrote *The Varieties of Religious Experience* in 1902. One of the first journals in psychology was *The American Journal of Religious Psychology and Education*, and books were written early in this century about adolescent religious awakening and conversion.

The psychology of religion flourished until the 1930s but then fell dormant for about three decades. In the last several decades, there has been a renewed interest in it. A number of books and many research studies suggest that once

again the psychology of religion is an important and vital area in the discipline of psychology (Batson, Schoenrade, & Ventis, 1993; Hood & others, 1996; Paloutzian, 1996; Wulff, 1991).

Today, psychologists involved in the psychology of religion work in a variety of settings. These include colleges and universities, hospitals, clinics, counseling centers, churches and synagogues, schools, research institutes, and private practice.

> The religious need of the human mind remains alive, never more so.
> —Charlotte Perkins Gilman, 1935

The Nature of Religion

Although you probably think you know what religion is, scholars have had an extraordinarily difficult time agreeing on a definition of religion. The task is complicated by the wide range of religions in the world, their complex histories, and their cultural meanings.

Defining Religion

One way to define religion is by defining its function. For example, Daniel Batson and his colleagues (Batson, Schoenrade, & Ventis, 1993) state that religion is what a person does to answer the basic existential questions of life. The term *existential* means having to do with the nature of human beings' existence and life's meaning. Such questions include these:

- Why am I here?
- What does life mean in general?
- What does my particular life amount to?
- What happens when I die?

Another way to define religion is through its emphasis on a person's conscious dependence on a deity or God. However, not all religions stress belief in a deity. In addition, some psychologists emphasize the *unconscious* rather than the *conscious* underpinnings of religion. Finally, no one has yet come up with a definition of religion that adequately covers all of its psychological and emotional functions.

The Scope of Religion

How extensively does religion touch our lives? One psychologist commented that religion is gradually disappearing from the face of the earth, and even where it exists it exerts little influence (Beit-Hallahmi, 1989). How accurate is this belief? Probably not very. In a recent national poll, approximately 95 percent of Americans said that they believe in God or a universal spirit, and about 60 percent said they attend religious services—figures that have not changed much since the 1950s ("Spiritual America," 1994). In this recent poll, only 9 percent professed to having no religion at all. Approximately three-fourths of Americans say that they pray or engage in some spiritual practice (Religion in America, 1993). Religion is also an important aspect of people's lives around the world—98 percent of the population in India, 88 percent in Italy, 72 percent in France, and 63 percent in Scandinavia say that they believe in God (Gallup, 1987). Of the world's 5.5 billion people, approximately two-thirds either are involved in religion or are affected by religion in important ways.

> Prayer is not asking. It is a longing of the soul.
> —Mohandas Gandhi

Religion and Adjustment

A common stereotype is that religion is a crutch for weak people and that unconscious feelings of guilt are the reasons that people become religious. William James (1902) commented about how many historical figures are known to have suffered from their visions and rapt conditions. Augustine of Hippo (A.D. 354–430), who after his conversion became one of the most influential Christian writers of all times, had his vision of God after experiencing profound guilt and remorse. Moses had his vision of God after murdering a man and tending to sheep for 40 years in the desert. Apostle Paul was highly aggressive prior to his conversion. These vivid illustrations foster the stereotype that religious leaders, of necessity, suffer from some type of mental disorder.

Religious interest is widespread around the world. Of the world's 5.5 billion people, approximately two-thirds either are involved in a religion or have been affected by religion in important ways. The large photograph shows worshipers at the Makka (Mecca) mosque in Saudi Arabia. (*top left inset*) A Jewish rabbi reads prayer. (*bottom left inset*) Temple of the Thousand Buddhas in Bangkok, Thailand. (*top right inset*) Children at the San Fernando Catholic Christmas service in San Antonio, Texas. (*bottom right inset*) A congregation singing at an American Protestant church.

However, if some famous religious individuals have shown signs of a mental disorder, this does not mean that their religious beliefs caused the disorder or that they adopted their beliefs because of the disorder. Similarly, if individuals with severe mental disorders, such as schizophrenia, have delusions that they are "Jesus," this does not mean that their religion caused the mental disorder. Nor does it mean that they became religious to try to cure themselves. All that such illustrations do is inform us that aspects of religion and mental disorder co-occur in a small number of individuals. They tell us nothing about a causal relationship between the two.

> *Religious awe is the same organic thrill which we feel in a forest at twilight or in a mountain gorge.*
>
> **—William James**

Coping What is the relation between religion and the ability to cope with stress? Some psychologists have categorized prayer and religious commitment as defensive coping strategies, sometimes arguing that they are less effective in helping individuals cope than are life-skills, problem-solving strategies. However, recently researchers have found that some styles of religious coping are associated

with high levels of personal initiative and competence. Even when defensive religious strategies are initially adopted, they sometimes set the stage for the later appearance of more active religious coping (Pargament & Park, in press).

In John Clausen's (1993) analysis of subjects in the Berkeley longitudinal study, competent women and men in middle age were more likely to have a religious affiliation and involvement than were their less competent counterparts. In sum, various dimensions of religiousness can help some individuals cope more effectively in their lives. To read about an exemplary religious life, turn to Sociocultural Worlds of Adjustment.

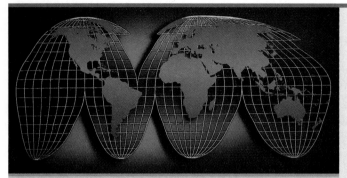

SOCIOCULTURAL WORLDS
OF ADJUSTMENT

The Exemplary Religious
Life of Mother Teresa

Occasionally someone progresses to a stage of religious existence that serves as a superior example for others. One such example of highly developed religiousness is Mother Teresa of Calcutta, India.

Mother Teresa was born Agnes Gonxha Bojaxhiu, in Albania in 1910. She became a Roman Catholic nun and founded the Missionaries of Charity after having entered the order of the Sisters of Our Lady of Loreto at the age of 18 while in Ireland. After taking her vows in 1937, she served in Calcutta in a Roman Catholic high school. While in Calcutta, she became grieved by seeing so many people sick and dying on the city's streets. She began to minister to these impoverished people and opened a home for them in 1952. Mother Teresa's home and

Mother Teresa

ministry continue today. In addition, she has expanded her work so that, in various forms, it is conducted on five continents. In 1979, Mother Teresa was awarded the Nobel Peace Prize.

Happiness Are people who have a meaningful faith happier than those who do not? Reviews of psychological studies about happiness suggest that happy people do tend to have a meaningful religious faith (Diener, 1984; Meyers, 1993). Remember, though, that a correlation between two factors does not imply that one causes the other. Although some researchers have found that religiously active individuals report greater happiness than those who are inactive, it is still unclear whether faith enhances a person's happiness, or whether happiness makes a person turn to religious faith. Gender might be a factor in religious commitment. To speculate about gender-based differences in religious behavior, see Critical Thinking.

CRITICAL THINKING

Faith and Evidence

Faith is the substance of things hoped for, the evidence of things not seen.

—St. Paul

Religion appears to be much more prominent in the lives of women than in the lives of men. Women practice religion more, believe more in the presence of a higher power, and describe religion as more important to them. How many explanations can you think of for this important gender difference in religious behavior and experience? Generating more than one explanation gives you an opportunity to *develop alternative explanations to explain a behavior comprehensively.*

The History of the Psychology of Religion, and the Nature of Religion

The psychology of religion was part of the field of psychology from the beginning. William James wrote *The Varieties of Religious Experience* in 1902. The psychology of religion flourished until the 1930s, then was dormant for about three decades. In the last several decades, interest in the psychology of religion has revived.

Scholars have had a difficult time agreeing on a definition of religion. One strategy is to define religion functionally—as what a person does to answer the basic existential questions of life. Another strategy is to define religion in terms of a conscious dependence on a deity or God.

There is extensive interest in religion worldwide. Over 75 percent of Americans engage in some form of spiritual practice. A common stereotype of religion is that religion is a crutch for weak people and that guilt feelings are the main reason people become religious. However, probably very few people associate religion with mental disorders. For some individuals, religion can play an important role in coping. Happy people tend to have a meaningful religious faith, but it is important to remember that the link is correlational, not causal.

> *I have never yet met a healthy person who worries very much about his health, or a really good person who worries much about his own soul.*
>
> —J. B. S. Haldane

Religious Experience

As you study the psychology of religion in this chapter, it is helpful to remember that psychology can neither prove nor disprove the truth of religion in general or any particular religion. However, the psychology of religion can tell us much about how religion works in people's lives.

To study religious experience, researchers evaluate behaviors, beliefs, and attitudes such as church attendance, degree of belief in religious doctrines (such as those involving the virgin birth, the resurrection of Jesus, the ascendance of Mohammed, and the literal truth of Exodus), and spiritual well-being. To evaluate your own spiritual well-being, turn to the Self-Assessment. In the rest of this section, we will explore specific aspects of religious experience.

Religious Orientation

One of the most important concepts to guide research in the psychology of religion since the 1960s is the concept of intrinsic and extrinsic religious orientation. **Intrinsic religious orientation** *involves internal religious motives that lie within the person.* By contrast, **extrinsic religious orientation** *involves external religious motives that lie outside the person.* To understand better the distinction, consider the following two physicians. As a consequence of her religion's teachings about helping needy people in Third World countries, physician Jones becomes a medical missionary. She receives little money for doing so; indeed, even the small amount she does receive has to be raised from individual supporters. In contrast, physician Smith practices medicine in Hollywood for movie stars and receives large fees for doing so. To which physician would we attribute an intrinsic, altruistic motive (her only desire is to help someone)? To which would we attribute an extrinsic (monetary) motive? In this situation, we would infer that physician Jones's behavior is intrinsically motivated and that physician Smith's behavior is extrinsically motivated.

Looking at the kinds of statements that are used on questionnaires to measure intrinsic and extrinsic religious motivation can help to clarify the meanings of these concepts. Intrinsically motivated individuals are more likely to agree with statements like these:

- I try hard to carry my religion over into all my other dealings in life.
- My religious beliefs are what really lie behind my whole approach to life.

Extrinsically motivated individuals are more likely to agree with statements like these:

- Although I believe in my religion, I think there are many more important things in life.
- The primary reason for interest in religion is that my church provides social activities that I enjoy.

Social psychologist Gordon Allport (1966) said that intrinsics *live* their religion while extrinsics *use* it. Overall, an intrinsic religious orientation tends to be associated with a sense of competence and control, freedom from worry and guilt, and an absence of illness. An extrinsic orientation tends to be associated with the opposite characteristics (Ventis, in press). It might seem that having an intrinsic religious orientation is good and having an extrinsic religious motivation is bad. In actuality, religious orientation is not so simple.

Some experts on the psychology of religion, such as Ken Pargament (1992), argue against this kind of simplistic interpretation of orientation. For example, he says that a person using religion blatantly for social gain is likely to be the exception rather than the rule. More often, it can be a sign of maturity for an individual to both live *and* use their religion. After all, much of life is a matter of combining means and ends to reach a goal. According to Pargament, mature religion

Spiritual Well-Being

For each of the following statements, assign a score from 1 to 6 according to how strongly you agree or disagree with it.

		Strongly Agree					Strongly Disagree
1.	I don't find much satisfaction in private prayer with God.	1	2	3	4	5	6
2.	I don't know who I am, where I came from, or where I am going.	1	2	3	4	5	6
3.	I believe that God loves me and cares about me.	1	2	3	4	5	6
4.	I feel that life is a positive experience.	1	2	3	4	5	6
5.	I believe that God is impersonal and not interested in my daily situations.	1	2	3	4	5	6
6.	I feel unsettled about my future.	1	2	3	4	5	6
7.	I have a personally meaningful relationship with God.	1	2	3	4	5	6
8.	I feel very fulfilled and satisfied with life.	1	2	3	4	5	6
9.	I don't get much personal strength and support from my God.	1	2	3	4	5	6
10.	I feel a sense of well-being about the direction my life is headed in.	1	2	3	4	5	6
11.	I believe that God is concerned about my problems.	1	2	3	4	5	6
12.	I don't enjoy much about life.	1	2	3	4	5	6
13.	I don't have a personally satisfying relationship with God.	1	2	3	4	5	6
14.	I feel good about my future.	1	2	3	4	5	6
15.	My relationship with God helps me not to feel lonely.	1	2	3	4	5	6
16.	I feel that life is full of conflict and unhappiness.	1	2	3	4	5	6
17.	I feel most fulfilled when I'm in close communion with God.	1	2	3	4	5	6
18.	Life doesn't have much meaning.	1	2	3	4	5	6
19.	My relationship with God contributes to my sense of well-being.	1	2	3	4	5	6
20.	I believe there is some real purpose for my life.	1	2	3	4	5	6

Please turn to the end of the chapter for scoring and interpretation.

---

involves combining intrinsic and extrinsic motivation, pathways and destinations, means and ends. A mature religious life involves blending the two types of motivation. For example, mature intrinsic-extrinsic religiously oriented individuals might use religious means (such as church resources) to accomplish a goal important to their own spiritual values (such as feeding the poor).

Perspectives on Religious Beliefs

The psychology of religion draws on a number of psychological models to explain religious thought and behavior. Four such models are the behavioral model, the psychoanalytic model, the humanistic model, and the sociocultural model (see figure 17.2). The **behavioral model of religion** *emphasizes the*

importance of analyzing a person's learning history to determine the extent to which her or his religious behavior has been, and is being, rewarded or punished and the extent to which it is imitative. By evaluating a person's learning history, we can identify the pattern of rewards and punishments the person has experienced for various aspects of religiousness. For example, children

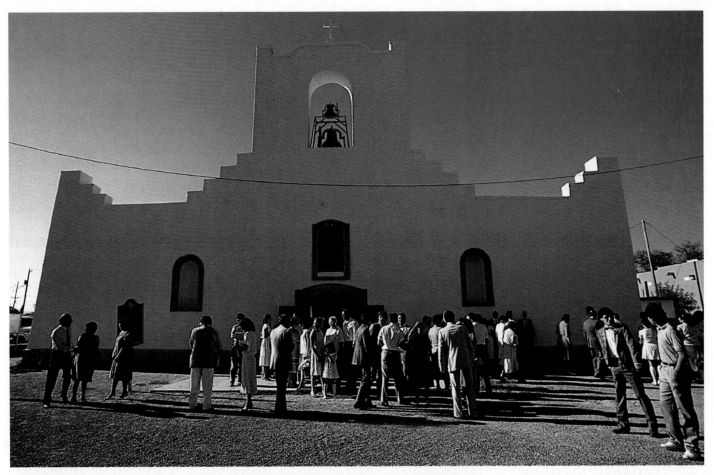

What are intrinsic and extrinsic religious orientations like? How might the two orientations be blended together in a religiously mature individual?

Behavioral

Psychoanalytic

Humanistic

Sociocultural

FIGURE 17.2

Psychological Models and Religion

would be more likely to attend church in the future if they have been rewarded for attending than if they have been punished for attending. Similarly, children are more likely to pray as adults if their parents pray and the children imitate the parents' prayer behavior and the parents approve of this imitation.

The **psychoanalytic model of religion** *emphasizes that the key to understanding religiousness resides deep in the unconscious mind. According to this model, individuals have instinctual needs that they are not aware of (such as needs for safety and security) and that can be met by relating to a higher power.* For example, individuals who as children were not nurtured in a secure, loving way by their parents might have an unconscious insecurity as adults. This insecurity could lead the individual to identify with God as a protector and provider; in ways like this, religious practice could meet such unconscious human needs.

The **humanistic model of religion** *emphasizes that a person's most important needs include needs related to growth, purpose, and self-actualization.* According to this model, we have innate tendencies to want to fulfill our potential and express our values, and religion is an important vehicle for doing this.

The **sociocultural model of religion** *emphasizes that individuals adopt a particular religious stance because of the experiences they have in the culture in which they live.* Most people learn religion from the cultural group into which they are born. For example, someone who grows up in Rome is likely to be Catholic, while someone who grows up in Iran is likely to be Muslim.

Is any of these four models a better model for the psychology of religion than the others? Not necessarily. Like most areas of psychology, the psychology of religion involves many useful approaches, all of which, in combination, can help us better understand the nature of religious life. To examine how these approaches explain your own religious beliefs, see Critical Thinking.

The Development of Religious Belief

Psychologists have shown significant interest in how religious beliefs develop. In this section we will look at the religious socialization of children and adolescents.

Many children show an interest in religion. Religious institutions created by adults are designed to introduce children to certain beliefs and ensure that they will carry on a religious tradition. For example, societies have invented Sunday schools, parochial education, tribal transmission of religious traditions, and parental teaching of children at home to promote religious traditions.

Does this teaching work? In many cases it does. In general, adults tend to adopt the religious teachings of their upbringing. For instance, individuals who are raised as Catholics and still consider themselves Catholic at age 25 likely will continue to be Catholic throughout their adult years. A religious change or reawakening is most likely to take place during adolescence (Argyle & Beit-Hallahmi, 1975).

Religious issues are important to adolescents. In one recent survey, 95 percent of 13- to 18-year-olds said that they believe in God or a universal spirit (Gallup & Bezilla, 1992). Almost three-fourths of adolescents said that they pray, and about one-half indicated that they

Many children and adolescents show an interest in religion, and many religious institutions created by adults are designed to introduce children to certain beliefs and ensure that they will carry on a religious tradition. In the large photograph, girls are shown in a Muslim school in Malaysia. In the left inset, a child participates in a Greek Orthodox religious service in South Australia. In the right inset, an African child carries a Bible during an emancipation parade.

CRITICAL THINKING

Your Own Journey

You have studied how psychologists have used four perspectives in psychology to explain how religious belief develops. As you examine the development of your own religious beliefs, which of the perspectives tends to best explain what you believe and what you reject? Which of the perspectives is least helpful in shedding light on your choices?

Your analysis allows you to *practice self-reflection to enhance adjustment* as you gain practice in applying the perspectives of psychology.

had attended religious services within the past week. Almost one-half of the youth said that it is very important for a young person to learn religious faith.

Don't be agnostic—be something.
—Robert Frost

Adolescence might be an especially important juncture in religious development. Even if children have been taught a religion by their parents, because of advances in their cognitive development they might begin to question what their own religious beliefs truly are.

During adolescence, especially in late adolescence and the college years, identity development becomes a central focus (Erikson, 1968). Youth want to answer questions like these: "Who am I?" "What am I all about as a person?" "What kind of life do I want to lead?" As part of their search for identity, adolescents begin to grapple in more sophisticated, logical ways with questions like these: "Why am I on this planet?" "Is there really a God or higher spiritual being, or have I just been believing what my parents and the church imprinted in my mind?" "What really are my religious views?"

One area of religion's influence on adolescent development involves sexual activity. Although variability and change in church teachings make it difficult to characterize religious doctrines simply, most churches discourage premarital sex. Thus, the degree of adolescents' participation in religious organizations may be more important than religious affiliation as a determinant of premarital sexual attitudes and behavior. Adolescents who attend religious services frequently may hear messages about abstaining from sex. Involvement of adolescents in religious organizations also enhances the probability that they will become friends with adolescents who have restrictive attitudes toward premarital sex. In one recent study, adolescents who attended church frequently and valued religion in their lives were less experienced sexually and had less permissive attitudes toward premarital sex than their counterparts who attended church infrequently and said that religion did not play a strong role in their lives (Thornton & Camburn, 1989). However, while religious involvement is associated with a lower incidence of sexual activity among adolescents, adolescents who are religiously involved and sexually active are less likely to use medical methods of contraception (especially the pill) than their sexually active counterparts with low religious involvement (Studer & Thornton, 1987, 1989).

Religious Conversion

Religious conversion is one of the most profound and perplexing phenomena that can happen in a person's life. The individual might never be the same because of it. How can such events be explained psychologically?

Conversion means "change." **Religious conversion** *is the change from having no religious belief to accepting a religious belief system as one's own, or from one religious belief system to another.*

Two types of conversion are usually distinguished—sudden conversion and gradual conversion. **Sudden conversion** *is a religious change that occurs all at once with no prior warning.* When asked if they remember how their conversion experience occurred, sudden converts can point to a specific place and set of life circumstances involved in the conversion. By contrast, **gradual conversion** *is a religious change that takes place over a reasonably long period of time, ranging from several weeks or months to years.* In gradual conversion, people think through and evaluate issues and options before arriving at a religious choice. There might be a decision point similar to that in sudden conversion, but the slower evaluative process is the defining feature that distinguishes the two types.

Both of these types of conversion contrast with **religious socialization,** *a lifelong process in which individuals cannot remember not having a religious faith.* In lifelong religious socialization, the individual is brought up with the religion and never deviates from it.

Psychological efforts at explaining conversion have evolved from fairly simplistic accounts to more complex models. Religious conversion used to be explained as something that happened to someone more or less against the person's will. In this view, conversion can be explained in two ways. It can be the result of a psychological need of which the person is unaware (such as a need for safety or security, or a need to reduce guilt feelings); the person is unconsciously driven to accept God and forgiveness, even though at the conscious level the person might fight against this (Richardson, 1989). The second explanation emphasizes social pressures operating within the person that are so strong that the person is unable to resist them; for instance, the person might not be able to say no to a recruiting religious group. In other words, in the old model the person undergoing conversion was viewed as passively subject to forces, whether the forces were unconscious or social.

A more recent view is that individuals who undergo conversion are active and religion-seeking rather than buffeted by forces beyond their control (Richardson, 1989). In this view, whether the beliefs they adopt are traditional or nontraditional, individuals choose the beliefs in a self-aware and purposeful manner.

The best-known model of religious conversion adopts this view of individuals as active, religion-seeking, and self-aware (Lofland & Stark, 1965). The following personal and social factors are likely to be involved:

1. The individuals experience tension—a discrepancy between an actual and an ideal state of affairs.
2. The individuals adopt a religious problem-solving strategy.
3. The individuals see themselves as religion seekers.
4. The individuals are at a turning point in their lives and encounter the religious group.
5. Affective bonds develop between the religion seekers and the religious group.
6. Attachments to those who are not in the religious group decrease.
7. Intensive interaction occurs between the religion seeker and the members of the new religious group.

Note the emphasis on both personal factors (descriptions 1–3) and social factors (descriptions 4–7).

Different motives can lead different persons to seek out different kinds of religious teachings or groups to satisfy their different needs (Glock & Stark, 1965). For example, someone who is suffering from a physical or mental illness might be attracted to a religious healing group. Someone who perceives or personally suffers from ethical deprivation (such as differences between ideal values and actual performance) might gravitate toward social reform movements. Someone suffering from a lack of meaning in life might adopt a religion that teaches a new value system.

Psychologists have offered more cognitively oriented explanations of conversion. One such view links conversion with the mental processes involved in creative thinking, in which the person reorganizes information and sees it in a new way (Batson, Schoenrade, & Ventis, 1993). Similarly, conversion has been described as a cognitive restructuring in which the individual's portrayal of self and the world undergoes a major shift (Brown & Caetano, 1992).

Cults

Barb is 18 years old. She grew up in an affluent family and was given all of the material things she wanted. When she was 15, her parents paid her way to Europe, and for the last 3 years she has been attending a private boarding school. Her parents attended a Protestant church on a regular basis, and when Barb was home, they took her with them. Six months ago, Barb joined the "Moonies."

In all, there are more than 2,500 cults in the United States. Two to 3 million youth and young adults are cult members (Levine, 1984). Among the more specific religious cults that have attracted the attention of youth are the Unification Church of Sun Myung Moon (the "Moonies"), the Divine Light Mission of Maharaj Ji, the Institute of Krishna Consciousness, the Children of God, and the Church of Scientology.

One concern about cults focuses on satanism, or devil worship. The nightmarish tale of human sacrifice that unfolded in the spring of 1989 in Matamoros, Mexico, brought national attention to the increasing prevalence of devil worship. Some of the bodies in the mass grave had been decapitated. Investigation of the satanism cult revealed its ties to drugs. The cult's ringleader, Adolpho de Jesus Constanzo, controlled members' lives, getting them to believe that the devil has supernatural, occultlike powers.

Critics of the cults argue that cult leaders are hypocritical, exploit members to gain wealth, brainwash youth, and develop an almost hypnotic spell over members' lives. In some cases, cults have been accused of kidnapping youth and

Hare Krishna is one of several religious cults that have attracted youth. Members of the religious cult are shown worshiping in Los Angeles.

subjecting them to deprivation to gain control over their minds. Most cults have elaborate training programs in which the cult's preachings are memorized. Cult members are usually required to turn over their wealth to cult leaders. And cult members are often told that they can associate with or marry only other members of the cult (Galanter, 1989).

Why do some young people join cults? Some experts believe that the inadequacies of organized religion and the church, as well as a weakening of family life, are causes (Spilka, 1991). What kinds of youth are most vulnerable to the appeal of cults? Six characteristics have been identified (Swope, 1980):

1. *Idealistic.* Due to the teachings and examples of family, religious leaders, peers, educators, and others, young people have developed a desire to help others, to improve society, and often to know God better. The cults manipulate this idealism, convincing members that only within their specialized groups can such inclinations be actualized.

2. *Innocent.* Because relationships with religious leaders in the past have been wholesome, the potential recruit naively believes that all who claim to speak in the name of God are sincere and trustworthy. The trappings of religion are a powerful lure here.

3. *Inquisitive.* On college and high school campuses around the country, intelligent young people, looking for interesting groups to join, are approached by enthusiastic, "together" recruiters who invite them to meetings where, they are told, they will meet other fine young people. It sounds exciting. Discussion, they are assured, will focus on ecology, world problems, religion, ethics, education— anything in which the recruit has shown some interest.

4. *Independent.* Many young people are recruited into cults when they are away from home—independent for the first time. Parents of such students are not always aware of how their children spend evenings

and weekends, and often do not learn that they have left college until several weeks or months after they drop out. Backpackers are particular targets for cult recruiters. These young people are often lonely and susceptible to invitations for free meals and fellowship.

5. *Identity-seeking.* Young adults in every generation experience identity crises as they seek to determine their strengths and weaknesses, value systems, goals, and religious and social beliefs.

6. *Insecure.* Inquisitive young people—looking for new experiences, seeking to clarify their own identities, away from the influence of family, friends, and mentors—develop uneasy feelings of insecurity. Lacking trusted counselors to whom they can turn when upset or disturbed, they are especially vulnerable to smiling, friendly people who show great interest in them and manipulate them through what one cult calls "love bombing."

R E V I E W

Religious Experience

To study the psychology of religion, researchers evaluate a number of behaviors, beliefs, and attitudes ranging from church attendance to spiritual well-being. Research on the topic of the psychology of religion covers a wide array of topics.

One of the most important concepts to have guided the psychology of religion since the 1960s is the concept of intrinsic religious orientation (internal religious motives within the person) and extrinsic religious orientation (external religious motives outside the person). Allport said that intrinsically religious persons live their religion, while their extrinsic counterparts use it. Although intrinsic religious motivation

has been portrayed more positively than extrinsic religious motivation, Pargament believes that all religion involves the simultaneous interaction of intrinsic and extrinsic motivation.

The psychology of religion draws on a number of psychological perspectives to explain religious concepts. Four such models are the behavioral, psychoanalytic, humanistic, and sociocultural.

Many children show an interest in religion, and religious institutions are designed to introduce children to religious beliefs. In many cases, the teaching works. Religious issues are important to adolescents, and adolescence can be a special juncture in religious development. Many adolescents incorporate a religious view into their identity development. Linkages

between religiousness and sexuality occur during adolescence.

The types of religious conversion include sudden conversion, gradual conversion, and lifelong religious socialization. The old view was that religious conversion occurs against a person's will. The new view is that converts are active and religion-seeking. More cognitively oriented versions of conversion have also been offered.

A special concern focuses on cults. At least 2 to 3 million youth and young adults are members of cults in the United States. Critics of cults argue that cult leaders are hypocritical, exploit members, and brainwash youth. Some experts believe that the inadequacies of the organized church and the weakening of families contribute to the allure of cults.

It is a good thing that we don't regularly have to face decisions as difficult as Heinz's about whether or not to steal a drug to save his wife's life. However, decisions about right and wrong regularly confront us on a much smaller scale. Examine the everyday moral dilemmas described below, decide on your likely course of action, and think about the reasons why you would act in that manner.

- Do you tell the waitress who has charged you an insufficient amount about her error, or do you pocket the difference?
- Do you comment to Don that his new hairstyle, which you find unflattering, is "different" or "awful"?
- Have you ever found your eyes wandering to your neighbor's test paper to compare your answer, when the teacher is out of the room?
- At tax time are you scrupulous about reporting to the Internal Revenue Service every earned penny, or do you look for opportunities to misrepresent your income?
- Do you invite people to parties because you wish to be in their company or do you sometimes ask people you don't like because you might lose some social status?
- When you sell a car, do you identify every aspect of the car that will need repair?

Kohlberg was less interested in establishing moral absolutes in relation to the dilemmas he created than he was in the justifications or reasons that his interviewees provided to justify their actions. As you examine your responses to the small moral dilemmas described above, do any patterns emerge in your answers? Would you have been scrupulously honest in those circumstances? Or would you have acted according to self-protection or personal gain? Was there any variation in your responses?

Let's examine just one moral dilemma from Kohlberg's point of view to sort out the levels of moral reasoning that apply to the situation. This exercise will encourage *the practice of ethical treatment toward individuals and groups.* Suppose we examine the moral challenge of properly paying income taxes. Are you ever tempted to cheat or do you consistently pay what the government says you owe? What is your justification?

You could pay your taxes out of fear of getting caught, or you could decide to take some inappropriate write-offs because you'd be willing to pay the penalty if you get caught. Both of these answers reflect a *preconventional* level of reasoning because a concern with the rewards and punishments is at the heart of your decision. At the *conventional* level, you might pay your taxes because everyone else does. You would not like to risk the disapproval of other good citizens. On the other hand, you might decide to misrepresent your tax debt, justifying your actions with your belief that most taxpayers engage in the same sort of tactics. You might even believe that you would lose others' approval by paying your appropriate amount. Finally, *postconventional* reasoning can also be present in justifying either course of action. You might choose fair payment because you believe democratic governments need to be well funded to function well and serve the citizenry effectively. You might even be proud to pay your fair share. On the other hand, the postconventional reasoner might justify nonpayment as withholding support from government activities that aren't humane. As you can see, the specific decision does not dictate whether an act is evaluated as moral or immoral. The complexity of the justification is what determines the level of reasoning, according to Kohlberg.

We began this chapter by exploring values—what they are like during the college years, and values in psychology and adjustment. Our coverage of moral development focused on Kohlberg's cognitive developmental theory, criticisms of his view, and character education. We also examined many dimensions of religion, including the history of the psychology of religion, the nature of religion, and religious experience. Don't forget that you can obtain an overall summary of the chapter by again studying the in-chapter reviews on pages 437, 441, and 447.

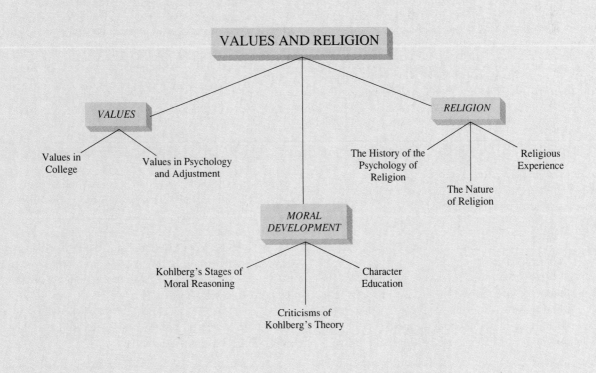

KEY TERMS

values   430
morals   430
value conflict   431
pragmatism   431
internalization   434
preconventional level   434
conventional level   434
postconventional level   434
justice perspective   435

care perspective   435
hidden curriculum   436
direct moral education   436
indirect moral education   436
values clarification   436
cognitive moral education   437
intrinsic religious orientation   441
extrinsic religious orientation   441

behavioral model of religion   442
psychoanalytic model of religion   443
humanistic model of religion   444
sociocultural model of religion   444
religious conversion   445
sudden conversion   445
gradual conversion   445
religious socialization   445

PRACTICAL KNOWLEDGE ABOUT ADJUSTMENT

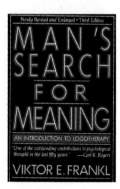

MAN'S SEARCH FOR MEANING

(1984) by Viktor Frankl. New York: Pocket.

Man's Search for Meaning presents an existentialist approach to the pursuit of self-fulfillment. The word existentialist refers to attempts to explain human beings' existence and an emphasis on each person's uniqueness, freedom of choice, and responsibility. After Viktor Frankl survived the German concentration camp at Auschwitz, he founded a school of psychotherapy known as logotherapy, which maintains that the desire to find a meaning in life is the primary human motive. Frankl's mother, father, brother, and wife died in the concentration camps or gas chambers. Frankl emphasizes each person's uniqueness and

finiteness of life. He thinks that examining the finiteness of your existence and certainty of your death adds meaning to the remaining days of your life. If life were not finite, says Frankl, you could spend your time doing just about whatever you please because time would last forever for you.

Frankl believes the three most distinct human qualities are spirituality, freedom, and responsibility. Logotherapists often ask clients questions such as why they exist, what they want from life, and what the meaning of their life is. This book tells the incredible story of a man who became a number who became a person. It will challenge you to think deeply about what the meaning of your life is all about. This was one of the top 25 books in the recently completed national survey of self-help books.

SELF-ASSESSMENT SCORING AND INTERPRETATION

DOMINANT PERSONAL VALUES

No further scoring or interpretation is needed.

SPIRITUAL WELL-BEING

The spiritual well-being scales measure two main areas: (1) religious well-being and (2) existential well-being. The religious scale refers to religion and one's relationship with God, the existential scale to meaning in life and questions about the nature of one's existence. To obtain your spiritual well-being score, add up your

responses to items 1, 5, 9, and 13; reverse the scores for items 3, 7, 11, 15, 17, and 19 (that is change the 1 to a 6, the 2 to a 5, the 3 to a 4, and so on). Combine these two subtotals to get your overall spiritual well-being score.

To obtain your existential well-being score, add up your responses to items 2, 6, 12, 16, and 18; reverse the scores for items 4, 8, 10, 14, and 20. Combine these two subtotals to obtain your overall existential well-being score.

Your overall scores on each of these two scales can range from 10 to 60. On each of the scales, a score of 40 or higher reflects well-being (religious or existential).

EPILOGUE

Critical Thinking About Sociocultural Issues

Consider the flowers of a garden: though differing in kind, colour, form and shape, yet, inasmuch as they are refreshed by the waters of one spring, revived by the breath of one wind, invigorated by the rays of one sun, this diversity increaseth their charm, and addeth unto their beauty. . . .
How unpleasing to the eye if all the flowers and plants, the leaves and blossoms, the fruits, the branches and the trees of that garden were all of the same shape and colour! Diversity of hues, form and shape, enricheth and adorneth the garden, and heighteneth the effect thereof.

—*'Abdu'l-Bahá*

THE STORY OF ROSA PARKS: A DIGNIFIED CHALLENGE

While riding home on the bus from her job as an assistant tailor in a department store in downtown Montgomery, Alabama, 42-year-old Rosa Parks resisted her way into history. On December 1, 1955, she chose a seat next to an African American man in the front of the area in the bus that the bus line set aside for African Americans. The front of the bus, which was reserved for Whites, was already full. When a White man got on in search of a seat, the driver asked the four African Americans in the front row of their section to move, which was the established practice of the bus line. Parks refused to move, even though the others complied. The driver called the police, who arrested Parks and sent her to jail. Released on a $100 bond, she moved quickly to help in the organization of the Montgomery Improvement Association (MIA) to address the problem of segregation, electing Martin Luther King, Jr., as the organization's first president. They initiated a bus boycott to protest practices that discriminated against African Americans, who constituted 75 percent of the ridership of the bus line. At her trial, the jury found Parks guilty and fined her $10. She refused to pay, and the authorities sent her back to jail. The MIA targeted Alabama segregation laws by filing suit against the state for discriminatory treatment of Parks and others on the bus line. Nearly a year later, after much litigation, the U.S. Supreme Court ordered the integration of the Montgomery bus lines. The costly boycott of the bus line ended after 381 days.

Parks had learned about prejudice and slavery from the stories that her maternal grandparents told. She had joined the NAACP in 1943, serving as the secretary for 13 years. She also had been active in recruiting African Americans to vote. Despite her activism, she might not have foreseen what events would follow her resistance that day on the Montgomery bus. In an interview later in her life, she explained her action by saying, "I felt just resigned to give what I could to protest against the way I was treated."

After Parks served her jail term, her circumstances worsened. She and her husband lost their jobs and suffered significant harassment from the community. Finding life in Montgomery no longer tolerable, they eventually moved to Detroit, where she continued her community-organizing activities. Her refusal to give up her seat in the face of tremendous social pressure and well-established discriminatory practices has made her widely recognized as "the mother of the civil rights movement." As a result of her courage and her commitment, the United States began to change, setting the stage for new opportunities to understand and celebrate the diversity of the American people (Smith, 1991).

AN IMPORTANT CONNECTION: CULTURE/ETHNICITY AND CRITICAL THINKING

Throughout this book we have emphasized the importance of contexts in understanding human behavior. In that regard, we have especially underscored that culture and ethnicity are becoming increasingly important contexts. Throughout this book we have also emphasized the importance of critical thinking in understanding human behavior. In every chapter you have engaged in activities to improve your critical thinking about psychological matters. Let's explore the importance of engaging in critical thinking about culture and ethnicity.

If we want to make something really superb of this planet, there is nothing whatever that can stop us.
—**Shepherd Mead**

Part of the excitement that the future holds is the promise of continuing extensive contact between people from quite different cultural and ethnic backgrounds. However, we will also continue to face significant challenges in developing a stable social and political structure that treats individuals with differing backgrounds in an equitable manner. Although the standards, practices, and traditions of White Americans have dominated our society, immigrants, refugees, and ethnic minority individuals are requesting that the nation's schools, employers, and governments honor many of their cultural customs. On a practical basis, our institutions cannot accommodate every aspect of every culture represented in our nation. One unfortunate consequence is that many children learn attitudes in school that are inconsistent with the attitudes they learn at home (Brislin, 1993). This is just one example of the serious decisions that we face about shaping a fair and harmonious future during an era of increasing complication.

Most ethnic minorities want to participate fully in society, but they don't necessarily agree on how to accomplish that goal. People are often caught between conflicting values of assimilation and cultural pluralism (Sue, 1990). You will recall that assimilation refers to the absorption of an ethnic minority group into the dominant group. This often entails the loss of some or all of the behavior and values of the ethnic minority group. Those who advocate assimilation as the dominant outcome of cultural contact usually exhort ethnic minority groups to become more "American." In contrast, *pluralism* is the coexistence of distinct ethnic and cultural groups in the same society. Those who advocate pluralism usually promote respect for cultural differences, urging that those differences be maintained and appreciated. Although assimilation still has many supporters, many people now believe that pluralism offers the greatest hope for strengthening our nation and improving our ability to function effectively with other cultures who share the planet with us.

Intimate personal contact that involves sharing doubts, hopes, problems, ambitions, and much more is one way to improve interethnic relations.

> It is well to remember that the entire population of the universe, with one trifling exception, is composed of others.
> —John Andrew Holmes

CRITICAL THINKING SKILLS FOR PROMOTING CULTURAL PLURALISM

In the first chapter of this book we highlighted a number of important critical-thinking skills that can help you better understand human behavior. To conclude this chapter, we return to those critical-thinking skills and apply them to an important agenda for the remainder of this decade and the approaching twenty-first century: promoting cultural pluralism.

Describe and Interpret Behavior Carefully

Accurate observation, description, and inference are essential to understanding behavior. Psychologists practice careful observation and precise description to reduce misunderstanding. They recognize that inferences leave a great deal of room for personal interpretation and error. Obviously, these abilities are especially important in being able to understand sociocultural issues.

You have experienced how easy it can be to make inappropriate inferences about behavior. In fact, you might have found it helpful sometimes to think about your own personal experiences instead of the examples we have given. In sociocultural contexts, incautious inferences can lead to conclusions that are not just wrong but harmful to ourselves and others.

> You can observe a lot just by watching.
> —Yogi Berra

One fact that should enhance our abilities as interpreters of reality is that there is diversity within every group. No cultural characteristic or value is common to all or nearly all members of a particular ethnic group, whether Russians, Italians, or Indonesians. Failure to assume individual variation is likely to result in stereotyping and ineffective social interaction with individuals from other ethnic and cultural traditions (Triandis, 1994). We may need to develop some generalizations in order to guide our actions, to make accurate predictions, and to adapt to the challenges in the environment, but we should be ready to modify or abandon these schemas if they don't explain the variations we encounter or if they harm others.

Stereotypes are based on inferences. We often attribute negative characteristics to members of groups based on a negative experience we have had with a member of that group, in part because we predict that what is true of one person will be true of others. It is also important to recognize how easy it is to make generalizations. As we discovered in the chapters on learning and thinking, some experiences produce "one-trial learning." That is, we can usually learn the components of unpleasant or painful situations readily. Unfortunately, this suggests that we can rapidly generalize a bad experience with one representative of a group to unfavorable and rejecting evaluations of the group itself. We need to restrain our natural pattern-finding abilities in order to honor the true variation that exists in any group.

Identify Values and Challenge Assumptions About Behavior

As you have seen in many exercises throughout the text, two individuals can experience the same situation and come away from the experience with entirely different versions, based on values that can serve as perceptual filters. Value conflicts in sociocultural contexts have been a source of considerable controversy. According to Stanley Sue (1990), without properly identifying the assumptions and effects of the conflicting values, it may be difficult to resolve ethnic minority issues.

We have explored some of the more common value differences that can influence sociocultural conflict resolution. The fact that some groups are collectivistic and some are individualistic can help you to predict the kind of values that most group members might hold. Harry Triandis (1994) identified security, obedience, duty, harmony, hierarchy, and personalized relationships as characteristic of collectivists. Individualists emphasize the values of pleasure seeking, winning, achievement, freedom, autonomy, and fair exchange. For example, suppose governmental agencies create incentive programs to lure businesses into urban areas. Collectivists might see such incentives as a great idea because a thriving business offers new opportunities to the community, particularly to ethnic minority workers. Individualists might evaluate such incentives in terms of the profits and risks involved in such a move at an individual level. Both perspectives have relevance to the issue, but they will produce different justifications for action and may lead to different preferred outcomes.

Examine the Influence of Context and Culture on Behavior

Cross-cultural psychologists Walter Lonner and Roy Malpass (1994) describe psychology as not just culture-blind but also culture-bound. They point out that over 90 percent of all psychologists *who have ever lived* have been reared in Western contexts. Obviously, most of their research reflects the Western contexts that are familiar to them, which means that much of psychology is culture-bound to Western ways of thinking.

To understand the various explanations that have been put forward by psychologists to understand behavior, we

must accept that these scientists' creations reflect the times in which they were developed. For example, Freud's claims that women are morally inferior must be understood as a reflection of the general prejudice against women in Viennese culture at the turn of the century. Similarly, the kinds of theories being proposed by contemporary psychologists will need to be judged in the context of the late twentieth century.

Historical and cultural contexts become especially important as we struggle to determine whether the explanations we have come up with to explain behavior are culture-bound. Attention to context helps establish what aspects of behavior are universal and which are specific to the context in which they were observed.

Many human beings are inclined to make ethnocentric judgments—that is, they tend to see their own culture as inherently superior and cultures with unfamiliar practices as inherently backward or confused. Our awareness of the potential limitations of psychological explanations that neglect context provides us with critical tools that enhance our ability to develop more comprehensive explanations. Conscientiousness about contextual factors also encourages attention to unique aspects of other cultures without necessarily judging the cultural practices as abnormal or eccentric when compared to our own traditions.

Evaluate the Validity of Claims About Behavior

Psychologists have long endorsed the standard of using objective evidence in creating and defending arguments about behavior. The dominance of experimental research methods attests to the widespread belief among psychologists in the importance of manipulation and control as elements of developing sound arguments. Science seeks to explain why things work the way they do. Social science tries to bring that sense of orderliness to the explanation of behavior. Some culture experts suggest that psychologists avoid abstract and complicated ideas such as culture because they don't want to

sacrifice the possibility of establishing order (Lonner & Malpass, 1994).

> *Technological man can't believe in anything that can't be measured, taped, or put into a computer.*
> —**Clare Boothe Luce**

Contemporary criticisms of research methods suggest that even with careful attention to details of control and objectivity, bias can still contaminate the results of research in ways that may be difficult to detect. A researcher can define constructs in ways that may reflect bias. Subject selection, operational definitions, and interpretation of results are all arenas in which bias can hinder objective analysis. Researchers need to be especially sensitive to the assumptions they make when they interpret their results with regard to the larger sociocultural context.

Psychology itself tends to demonstrate a bias that predisposes attention to the different or deviant rather than the normal. For example, we study aggression rather than peaceful behavior. We publish research studies in which groups demonstrate differences rather than similarities. Some research journals might not even publish findings unless a difference between groups has been discovered. Many researchers suggest that the search for significant differences may create some artificial emphases in our understanding of behavior and hinder our ability to find similarities among different kinds of people.

Adherence to objective standards remains an important feature of psychological argumentation. However, as we seek to understand the realities of diverse peoples, we will need to expand the methods we use to explore those realities. Qualitative research methods, which do not insist upon manipulation and control as part of the research protocol, are gaining acceptance among many psychologists.

In the past the influence of behaviorism and the importance of observable evidence have also placed some topics of human behavior beyond the bounds of acceptable research. For example, many psychologists have traditionally struggled with spiritual issues. With the growing acceptance of the cognitive perspective, however, matters of spirit may also find new opportunities for attention using psychological methods. This inclusiveness may be especially important in exploring ethnic traditions, such as those of Latino and Native Americans, in which matters of spirit are prominent and compelling. Some culture experts describe as culture-blindness the tendency to overlook characteristics that are not part of Western culture (Lonner & Malpass, 1994).

Seek Multiple Points of View and Alternative Explanations

Psychologists actively look for alternative explanations to explain behavior. You have studied various perspectives (such as the psychoanalytic and neurobiological) presented in this text that foster comprehensive explanations. Using these perspectives is especially important when we are forming conclusions about behaviors or behavioral differences.

Incorrect assumptions about the differences between White Americans and ethnic minority Americans proliferate and take on a power all their own (for example, stereotypes that all Jews are ambitious and all African Americans are naturally athletic). Belief in these stereotypes can keep us from recognizing the many ways in which people, regardless of ethnicity or culture, are similar. As members of ethnic minorities begin to have a stronger voice in society, more similarities will emerge. Understanding these similarities between people, regardless of ethnicity, will help break down the stereotypes that lead to prejudice.

> *Natives who beat drums to drive off evil spirits are the objects of scorn to smart Americans who blow horns to break up traffic jams.*
>
> —**Mary Ellen Kelly**

When we think about what causes a person's behavior and adaptation, we tend to think in terms of a single cause.

However, human behavior and adaptation are not simple matters. For example, consider 19-year-old Tom, a Native American high school dropout. It's possible he quit school because his family did not adequately appreciate the importance of education. Even if that were true, it is likely that other factors were involved. For example, it is possible that Tom comes from a low-income family that he helps to support. The school Tom attended may have had a poor history of helping Native Americans adapt to school; perhaps it has no multicultural programs or no Native Americans within the school administration who can serve as role models. It may also turn out that the town in which Tom lives devotes few resources to programs for youths, regardless of their ethnicity. And there undoubtedly are more factors that contributed to Tom's decision to leave school. Because it is the result of many factors, behavior is said to be multiply determined.

Appreciate Individual and Group Differences

Ours is a diverse, multicultural world teeming with different languages, family structures, and customs. A cascade of historical, economic, and social experiences have produced these differences among ethnic and cultural groups (Albert, 1988; Triandis, 1994). We need to recognize and respect legitimate differences to appreciate the common ground we share with people whose ethnicity and cultural heritage differ from our own. Respecting others with different traditions will facilitate communication and cooperation in our increasingly interdependent world.

While this sounds reasonable to many of us now, for too long legitimate ethnic differences were overlooked. Virtually any difference from middle-class White characteristics and lifestyles—ranging from the way people looked to the kind of music they listened to—was thought of as a deficit. Too often, these differences have been seized upon by some segments of society, seeking to justify their own biases, to exploit, to humiliate, and to oppress people from

ethnic minority backgrounds (Jones, 1991, 1994). Many psychologists now seek to discover the psychological assets and strengths of ethnic groups. This new trend is long overdue.

Practice Ethical Sensitivity and Civility Toward Others

Psychologists maintain rigorous ethical standards with regard to the care of clients and the treatment of participants in research. Their concerns about confidentiality and disclosure, among other ethics practices, attest to the importance of treating people with fairness and dignity. As you have seen in exploring research studies through history, the discipline of psychology has not always abided by such high standards. Formal codes of ethics, licensure proceedings, and research review processes help to facilitate the higher standards that have evolved in the field of psychology. Concerns for humane and ethical treatment remain strong among psychologists as the borders of psychology appropriately expand into new sociocultural territories.

In one Gallup poll, Americans said they believe that the United States is tolerant of ethnic differences and that overt racism is basically unacceptable ("Poll Finds Racial Tension Decreasing," 1990). However, many ethnic minority members experience persistent forms of discrimination and prejudice in many domains of life—in the media, in interpersonal interactions, and in daily conversations (Sue, 1990). However, prejudice and racism are often expressed in more subtle and indirect ways than they once were (Sears & others, 1997). As an expression of high ethical standards, we need to be vigilant about subtle racist expectations and behaviors we may have acquired.

In today's world, most people agree that children from different ethnic groups should attend the same school. However, despite more accepting attitudes about many dimensions of ethnicity, a substantial portion of individuals say that they don't feel comfortable with people from ethnic groups other than their own. For example, in a recent survey of students at 390 colleges

Interacting with People from Other Cultures

Even when people don't have any prejudices and don't intend to discriminate against people from other cultures and ethnic groups, problems in intercultural communication can develop. Some of the reasons problems surface are subtle and difficult to understand. For example, no convenient language has developed to help people discuss many unintended intercultural difficulties.

How can people improve their interaction with people from other cultures? Developing certain skills and personality traits can help. For many years, cross-cultural psychologist Richard Brislin has been studying ways to improve the communication of people from different cultures. A summary of his recently proposed suggestions follows (Brislin, 1993).

Brislin believes that people who are *culturally flexible* can make changes in their behavior that meet the challenges of various sociocultural contexts. For example, the Japanese want to know their business associates as *people*. Casual conversations about people's backgrounds and interests give them the opportunity to get to know each other better. The lengthy time spent chatting with business associates gives the Japanese a way of determining whether or not the individuals can be trusted in future negotiations. Culturally flexible American businesspeople might find themselves in Japan and be willing to engage in more "small talk" than if they were doing business in their own country.

Intercultural interaction is improved when the participants are *enthusiastic* about developing intercultural relationships. Many individuals merely tolerate such interactions as necessary for completing a task. Instead, individuals who are enthusiastic actually look forward to the diversity and stimulation that intercultural relationships can produce.

Enthusiasm also increases the likelihood that people from different cultures *will use a variety of effective ways of communicating with each other*. Enthusiastic individuals will make the effort to learn another language and explore the nonverbal behaviors that will improve their communication with people from another culture. Enthusiasm can also help people overcome the discomfort that results from making mistakes, such as when they struggle to speak the foreign language they are learning and make a number of errors.

People who are competent in intercultural interaction *have methods to resolve conflicts effectively*. Effective conflict resolution involves addressing difficulties in a collaborative manner, focusing on issues instead of personalities, and working toward mutual understanding. Focusing on cultural differences can actually be a part of effective conflict management. For example, one person might suggest to another that the fact that they are from different cultures and have different ways of doing things could contribute to their disagreement on a particular issue. Highlighting cultural differences can draw attention away from the more threatening emphasis on personalities.

Being willing to modify one's behavior to meet the expectations of people in other cultures is the final dimension in improving intercultural interaction. By trying new approaches, an individual can not only communicate that there are many ways to behave and think, but demonstrate tolerance for that which may be unfamiliar or different. The pattern of socialization most familiar to you might not be the best for a person in another part of the world. The need for tolerance toward differences in ethnic heritage, cultural background, religion, gender, sexual orientation, and medical history is becoming an increasingly important issue in many parts of the world.

---

and universities, more than half of the African Americans and almost one-fourth of the Asian Americans, but only 6 percent of the Anglo Americans, said that they felt excluded from school activities (Hurtado, Dey, & Trevino, 1994). We still have a long way to go in reducing discrimination and prejudice.

Prejudice is the reason of fools.
—**Voltaire**

Apply Psychological Concepts to Enhance Adaptation and Growth

Throughout the text, you have had an opportunity to apply psychological concepts to improve your understanding of many aspects of your personal life. Part of improving the quality of your personal adaptation involves coming to terms with a changing world. Global interdependence is no longer a matter of preference or choice. It is an inescapable reality. We are not just citizens of the United States or Canada or Puerto Rico. We are citizens of the world, a world that through modern communication and transport has become increasingly intertwined. By improving our understanding of the behavior and values of cultures around the world, we hope that we can interact more effectively with each other and make this a more hospitable, peaceful planet. To read further about interacting with people from different cultures, see Sociocultural Worlds of Adjustment.

People who develop the habit of thinking of themselves as world citizens are fulfilling the first requirement of sanity in our time.

—**Norman Cousins**

Conclusions

The knowledge base of information about sociocultural issues in psychology is increasing, but a lot of blank spaces remain in the study of ethnicity and culture. It is very important for psychologists to devote increased effort toward expanding the knowledge base of information about ethnicity and culture (Graham, 1992). We need to know more about how diverse socialization experiences and adaptations to changing environments, especially those that present competing demands, can be integrated to produce a more competent human being (Jones, 1991, 1994). We need to know more about why Latino and Native American children leave school at such high rates. We especially need to know more about ways to prevent such high dropout rates, or how to intervene to help high school dropouts lead more competent, satisfying lives. Also, ethnicity and culture should be systematically included on the agendas at all levels of education—from preschool through graduate school—to help us construct a culture with greater tolerance and improved communication.

Through much of its history, the field of psychology has not had an admirable record on the topics of ethnicity and culture or in helping to create environments in which ethnic minority students can thrive. This decade represents a precious opportunity for individuals to make important contributions to our understanding of sociocultural concerns. Psychology not only needs to improve its knowledge base about sociocultural issues but also needs more well-trained psychologists who can deal effectively with sociocultural concerns. Consider a career in psychology in which you can help improve the lives of all human beings through education, teaching, research, intervention, or prevention. If your career interests do not lie with psychology, remember to use psychology to enhance your personal adaptation and to improve your quality of life. Figure E.1 summarizes critical-thinking skills for a pluralistic society.

Describe and interpret behavior carefully
by limiting generalizations about individuals

Identify values and challenge assumptions about behavior
involved in sociocultural conflicts

Examine the influence of context and culture on behavior
to avoid making ethnocentric judgments

Evaluate the validity of claims about behavior
through vigilance about bias in arguments

Pursue alternative explanations to explain behavior comprehensively
to challenge incorrect assumptions that are motivated by prejudice

Actively take the perspective of others in solving problems
by considering different sides of sensitive issues

Appreciate individual and group differences
by recognizing and respecting legitimate differences within groups

Practice ethical sensitivity and civility toward others
by discouraging discrimination and prejudice

Apply psychology concepts to enhance adaptation and growth
in a world that is increasing in global interdependence

Practice self-reflection to enhance self-growth
and to contribute to society

FIGURE E.1

Critical-Thinking Skills for a Pluralistic Society

We are not just citizens of the United States or Canada. We are citizens of the world. By increasing our understanding of the behavior and values of cultures around the world, we hope that we can interact with people from other cultures more effectively and make this planet a more hospitable, peaceful place in which to live.

GLOSSARY

A

abnormal behavior   Behavior that is maladaptive, harmful, statistically unusual, personally distressing, and/or designated abnormal by the culture.   335

acceptance   Kübler-Ross' fifth stage of dying, in which the dying person develops a sense of peace, an acceptance of fate, and, in many cases, a desire to be left alone.   326

acculturation   Cultural change that results from continuous, firsthand contact between two distinct cultural groups.   92

acculturative stress   The negative consequences of acculturation.   92

accurate empathy   Rogers' term for the therapist's ability to identify with the client.   374

action therapy   Therapy that promotes direct changes in behavior; insight is not essential for change to occur.   369

active listening   Rogers' term for the ability to listen to another person with total attention to what the person says and means.   374

active-behavioral strategies   Coping responses in which individuals take some type of action to improve their problem situation.   101

active-cognitive strategies   Coping responses in which individuals actively think about a situation in an effort to adjust more effectively.   101

activity disorder   An intense, driven, compulsive exercise pattern often combined with rigid dietary restrictions that can damage a person's body.   403

activity theory   The theory that the more active and involved older people are, the more satisfied they will be with their lives and the more likely it is that they will stay healthy.   319

actor-observer hypothesis   The hypothesis that differences in interpretations of motives are based on points of view.   125

actual self   An individual's representation of the attributes she or he believes her- or himself to actually possess.   55

addiction   Physical dependence on a drug.   414

adjustment   The psychological process of adapting to, coping with, and managing the problems, challenges, and demands of everyday life.   6

adolescence   The developmental period of transition from childhood to early adulthood, entered at approximately 10 to 12 and ending at about 18 to 22 years of age.   307

adrenal glands   Glands located just above the kidneys that play an important role in our moods, energy levels, and ability to cope with stress.   80

aerobic exercise   Sustained exercise—jogging, swimming, or cycling, for example—that stimulates heart and lung activity.   402

affectionate love   Also called companionate love, this type of love occurs when individuals desire to have the other person near and have a deep, caring affection for the person.   230

ageism   Prejudice against people based on their age.   319

aggressive behavior   Hostile, often angry, behavior that involves deprecating others, and enhancing oneself at the expense of others.   113

agoraphobia   The fear of entering unfamiliar situations, especially open or public spaces; the most common phobic disorder.   343

AIDS   A sexually transmitted disease that is caused by the human immuno-deficiency virus (HIV), which destroys the body's immune system.   214

alternation model   The model according to which individuals can develop bicultural competence without choosing one culture over another or diminishing their own subgroup identification.   92

altruism   An unselfish interest in helping someone else.   226

Alzheimer's disease   A progressive, irreversible brain disorder involving gradual deterioration of memory, reasoning, language, and eventually physical function.   323

anal stage   Freud's second stage of development, occurring between 1½ and 3 years of age, in which the child's greatest pleasure involves the anus or the eliminative functions associated with it.   28

androgens   The main class of male sex hormones.   181

androgyny   The presence of desirable masculine and feminine characteristics in the same individual.   174

anger   Kübler-Ross' second stage of dying, in which the dying person realizes that denial can no longer be maintained; the dying person often then feels anger, resentment, rage, and envy.   325

anorexia nervosa   An eating disorder that involves the relentless pursuit of thinness through starvation.   406

antianxiety drugs   Drugs that are commonly known as tranquilizers and reduce anxiety by making individuals less excitable and more tranquil.   392

antidepressant drugs   Drugs that regulate mood. The three main classes of antidepressant drugs are tricyclics, such as Elavil; MAO inhibitors, such as Nardil; and SSRI inhibitors, such as Prozac.   392

antipsychotic drugs Powerful drugs that diminish agitated behavior, reduce tension, decrease hallucinations and delusions, improve social behavior, and produce better sleep patterns in severely mentally disabled individuals, especially schizophrenics. 392

antisocial personality disorder A personality disorder in the dramatic, emotional, and erratic cluster; the most problematic personality disorder for society. Individuals with this disorder often resort to crime, violence, and delinquency. 357

anxiety disorders Psychological disorders that include the following main features: motor tension (jumpiness, trembling, inability to relax), hyperactivity (dizziness, racing heart, or perspiration), and apprehensive expectations and thoughts. 342

approach/approach conflict A conflict in which the individual must choose between two attractive stimuli or circumstances. 89

approach/avoidance conflict A conflict involving a single stimulus or circumstance that has both positive and negative characteristics. 89

archetypes Primordial influences in every individual's collective unconscious that filter our perceptions and experiences. 31

assertive behavior Acting in one's own best interest, standing up for one's legitimate rights, expressing one's views directly and openly, being self-enhancing, and making choices, but doing these things without hurting others. 113

assertiveness training Teaching individuals to act in their own best interests, to stand up for their legitimate rights, and to express their views directly and openly. 113

astrology The pseudopsychology that uses the positions of the stars and planets at the time of a person's birth to describe, explain, and predict their behavior. Scientific researchers have repeatedly demonstrated that astrology has no scientific merit. 12

attitudes Beliefs and opinions that can predispose individuals to behave in certain ways. 125

attribution theory The theory that individuals are motivated to discover the underlying causes of behavior as part of their interest in making sense out of the behavior. 125

authoritarian parenting A restrictive, punitive parenting style in which the parents exhort the child to follow their directions and to respect work and effort. The authoritarian parent places firm limits and controls on the child and allows little verbal exchange. Authoritarian parenting is associated with children's social incompetence. 258

authoritative parenting A parenting style in which parents encourage children to be independent but still place limits and controls on their actions. Extensive give-and-take is allowed, and parents are warm and nurturant toward their children. Authoritative parenting is associated with children's social competence. 258

autonomic nervous system (ANS) The part of the nervous system that monitors processes such as breathing, heart rate, and digestion by taking messages to and from the body's internal organs. 79

autonomy versus shame and doubt Erikson's second psychosocial stage, which is experienced in late infancy and toddlerhood (1 to 3 years of age). After gaining trust in their caregivers, infants and toddlers begin to discover that their behavior is their own. 63

aversion therapy Therapy in which the sight, smell, or taste of alcohol is paired with a noxious stimulus in order to establish an aversion to alcohol; based on classical conditioning procedures. 419

aversive conditioning An approach to behavior therapy that involves repeated pairings of an undesirable behavior with aversive stimuli to decrease the behavior's rewards so that the individual will stop doing it; this technique is based on classical conditioning. 376

avoidance/avoidance conflict A conflict in which the individual must choose between two unattractive stimuli or circumstances. 89

avoidance strategies Responses that individuals use to keep stressful circumstances out of their awareness so they do not have to deal with them. 101

avoiding the other's concerns An ineffective communication pattern that involves diversion and logical argument, which are especially effective means for derailing conversations. 153

B

"bad patient" role The role of complaining to the staff, demanding attention, disobeying staff orders, and generally misbehaving. 412

barbiturates Depressant drugs, such as Nembutal and Seconal, that induce sleep or reduce anxiety. 419

bargaining Kübler-Ross' third stage of dying, in which the dying person develops the hope that death can somehow be postponed or delayed. 326

basal metabolism rate (BMR) The amount of energy an individual uses in a resting state. 405

becoming parents The third stage of the family life cycle, in which adults move up a generation and become caregivers to the younger generation. 256

behavior Everything we do that can be directly observed. 5

behavior therapies Therapies that use principles of learning to reduce or eliminate maladaptive behavior. 375

behavioral medicine A field closely related to health psychology that attempts to combine medical and behavioral knowledge to reduce illness and promote health. 401

behavioral model of religion A model that emphasizes the importance of analyzing a person's learning history to determine the extent to which religious behavior has been, and is being, rewarded or punished, and the extent to which it is imitative. 442

biofeedback The process in which physical states, such as levels of muscle tension, are monitored by instruments and information is given (fed back) to the individuals so they can learn to voluntarily control these states. 113

biomedical therapies Treatments to reduce or eliminate the symptoms of psychological disorders by altering the way an individual's body functions. Drug therapy is the most common form. 391

bipolar disorder A mood disorder characterized by extreme mood swings; an individual with this disorder might be depressed, manic, or both. 349

body dysmorphic disorder (BDD) A preoccupation with some imagined deficit in a normal-appearing person. 404

body image The way that people perceive themselves and the way they think others see them. 403

borderline personality disorder A personality disorder in the dramatic, emotional, and erratic cluster; the person's behavior exhibits these characteristics. 357

boundary ambiguity The uncertainty in stepfamilies about who is in or out of the family and who is responsible for certain tasks in the family system. 271

bulimia An eating disorder in which the individual consistently follows a binge-and-purge eating pattern. 407

burnout A hopeless, helpless feeling brought on by relentless work-related stress that leaves the individual in a state of physical and emotional exhaustion that includes chronic fatigue and low energy. 90

bystander effect The tendency for individuals who witness an emergency to help less when someone else is present than when they are alone. 228

C

care perspective A moral perspective that views people in terms of their connectedness with others and emphasizes interpersonal communication, relationships with others, and concern for others. 435

career consolidation Vaillant's stage, which occurs from about 23 to 35 years of age, in which an individual's career becomes more stable and coherent. 312

catatonic schizophrenia A schizophrenic disorder characterized by bizarre motor behavior, which sometimes takes the form of an immobile stupor. 355

catharsis The psychoanalytic term for clients' release of emotional tension when they relive an emotionally charged and conflicted experience. 85, 372

channel The mode of delivery of communication. 145

chlamydia The most common of all sexually transmitted diseases, named for *Chlamydia trachomatis,* an organism that spreads by sexual contact and infects the genital organs of both males and females. 217

chronemics The influences of time on behavior. 161

civil commitment Commitment that transpires when a judge deems an individual to be a risk to self or others due to a mental disorder. 358

civility The practice of respectful behavior toward others. 1

classical conditioning The process in which a neutral stimulus becomes associated with a meaningful stimulus and acquires the capacity to elicit a similar response. 34

clinical and counseling psychology The most widely practiced specialty in psychology, which involves evaluating and treating people with psychological problems. 5

cognitive appraisal Lazarus' term for individuals' interpretation of events in their lives as harmful, threatening, or challenging, and their determination of whether they have the resources to effectively cope with the events. 88

cognitive developmental theory of gender The view that children's gender typing occurs after they have developed a concept of gender. Once they begin to consistently conceive themselves as male or female, children often organize their world on the basis of gender. 183

cognitive dissonance A concept developed by social psychologist Leon Festinger; an individual's motivation to reduce the discomfort (dissonance) caused by two inconsistent thoughts. 126

cognitive moral education An indirect moral education approach that emphasizes that students adopt such values as democracy and justice as their moral reasoning is developed. 437

cognitive restructuring Modifying the thoughts, ideas, and beliefs that maintain an individual's problems. 103

cognitive social learning theory The contemporary version of social learning theory that stresses the importance of cognition, behavior, and environment in determining personality. 36

cognitive therapies Therapies that emphasize that an individual's cognitions, or thoughts, are the main source of abnormal behavior; cognitive therapies attempt to change the individual's feelings and behaviors by changing her or his cognitions. 377

collective unconscious In Jung's theory, the impersonal, deepest layer of the unconscious mind, which is shared by all human beings because of their common ancestral past. 31

collectivism An emphasis on values that serve the group by subordinating personal goals to preserve group integrity, interdependence of members, and harmonious relationships. 45

commitment The aspect of identity development in which individuals show a personal investment in what they are going to do. 67

commitment The process by which an individual becomes institutionalized in a mental hospital. 358

compensation Adler's term for the individual's attempt to overcome imagined or real inferiorities or weaknesses by developing her or his abilities. 31

competency An individual's ability to understand and participate in a judicial proceeding. 359

conditional positive regard Rogers' term for making the bestowal of love or praise conditional on the individual's conforming to parental or social standards. 38

conditioned response (CR) The learned response to the conditioned stimulus that occurs after CS-US pairing. 34

conditioned stimulus (CS) A previously neutral stimulus that elicits the conditioned response after being paired with the unconditioned stimulus. 34

conformity Adopting the attitudes or behavior of others because of real or imagined pressure from others to do so. 136

connotation The subjective, emotional, or personal meaning of words and messages. 147

consciousness-raising groups Groups that are believed by some feminists to be an important alternative or adjunct to traditional therapy. They often involve several people meeting in a member's home, are frequently leaderless, and focus on members' feelings and self-perceptions. Instead of seeking and accepting male-biased therapy, women may meet in consciousness-raising groups to define their own experiences with their own criteria. 388

consensual validation An explanation of why people are attracted to others who are similar to them. Our own attitudes and behavior are supported when someone else's attitudes and behaviors are similar to ours—their attitudes and behaviors validate ours. 234

contexts The historical, economic, social, and cultural factors that influence mental processes and behavior. 6

conventional level The second, or intermediate, level of moral thinking in Kohlberg's theory, in which internalization is immediate and individuals abide by the standards of others, such as parents or the laws of society.   434

conversion disorder A somatoform disorder in which an individual experiences genuine physical symptoms, even though no physiological problems can be found.   346

coping The process of managing taxing circumstances, expending effort to solve personal and interpersonal problems, and seeking to master, minimize, reduce, or tolerate stress and conflict.   100

couple therapy Group therapy with married or unmarried couples whose major problem is their relationship.   381

crack An intensified form of cocaine; chips of pure cocaine that are usually smoked.   420

credibility A therapist's believability.   391

criminal commitment Commitment that occurs when a mental disorder is implicated in the commission of a crime.   358

crisis A period of identity development during which an individual is choosing among meaningful alternatives.   67

critical thinking In the context of adjustment, making appropriate decisions and developing competent strategies that promote your own or other people's well-being.   8

culture The behavior patterns, beliefs, and other products of a particular group of people—including their values, work patterns, music, dress, diet, and ceremonies—that are passed on from generation to generation.   7

D

date or acquaintance rape Coercive sex forced by someone with whom the victim is at least casually acquainted.   212

decline stage Super's label for the period of 65 and older when individuals' career activity declines and retirement takes place.   281

decoding The act of understanding messages.   145

defense mechanisms The psychoanalytic term for unconscious methods of dealing with conflict, by which the ego distorts reality, thereby protecting itself from anxiety.   26

deficiency needs Maslow's term for essential requirements—physiological needs (for food, shelter, comfort, and so on) and psychological needs (for affection, security, self-esteem, and so on)—that must be met or else individuals will try to make up for their absence.   39

deindividuation A state of reduced self-awareness, weakened self-restraints against impulsive actions, and apathy about negative social evaluation.   138

deinstitutionalization The movement to transfer the treatment of mental disabilities from inpatient medical institutions to community-based facilities that stress outpatient care.   384

dementia A global term for any neurological disorder in which the primary symptoms involve a deterioration of mental function.   323

denial and isolation Kübler-Ross' first stage of dying, in which the person denies that death is really going to take place.   325

denotation The objective meaning of words and messages.   147

depression Kübler-Ross' fourth stage of dying, in which the dying person comes to accept the certainty of death and may experience depression or preparatory guilt.   326

development The pattern of change that begins at conception and continues throughout the life span.   307

diathesis-stress view The view that a combination of environmental stress and biogenetic disposition causes schizophrenia.   356

diffusion of responsibility The tendency to feel less responsible and to act less responsibly in the presence of others.   228

direct moral education Education that involves either emphasizing values or character traits during specified time slots or integrating those values or traits throughout the curriculum.   436

disease model of addiction A model according to which addictions are biologically based, lifelong diseases that involve a loss of control over behavior and require medical and/or spiritual treatment for recovery.   414

disorganized schizophrenia A schizophrenic disorder in which an individual has delusions and hallucinations that have little or no recognizable meaning—hence the label *disorganized*.   355

displacement The psychoanalytic defense mechanism that occurs when an individual shifts unacceptable feelings from one object to another, more acceptable object.   27

dissociative disorders Psychological disorders that involve a sudden loss of memory or change in identity. Under extreme stress or shock, an individual's conscious awareness becomes dissociated (separated or split) from previous memories and thoughts.   346

double standard The belief that many sexual activities are acceptable for males but not for females.   206

dream analysis The psychotherapeutic technique psychoanalysts use to interpret a client's dream. Psychoanalysts believe that dreams contain information about the individual's unconscious thoughts and conflicts.   372

DSM-IV *Diagnostic and Statistical Manual of Mental Disorders,* fourth edition. The DSM-IV is the most recent major classification of mental disorders and contains eighteen major classifications and describes more than 200 specific disorders.   340

E

early adulthood The developmental period that begins sometime in the late teens or early twenties and ends in the late thirties to early forties.   307

eclectic Using a variety of approaches.   369

ectomorph Sheldon's term for a tall, thin, fragile person who is fearful, introverted, and restrained.   42

ego The Freudian structure of personality that deals with the demands of reality; the ego is called the executive branch of personality because it makes decisions based on rationality.   26

egoism Being motivated by the desire to ensure reciprocity, to gain self-esteem, to appear powerful, competent, or caring, or to avoid social- and self-censure for failing to live up to normative expectations.   226

electroconvulsive therapy (ECT) Commonly called shock treatment, a type of therapy sometimes used to treat severely depressed individuals by causing brain seizures similar to those caused by epilepsy.   393

emotion Feeling, or affect, that involves a mixture of physiological arousal (such as fast heartbeat), conscious experience (such as thinking about being in love with someone), and overt behavior (such as smiling or grimacing).   83

emotion-focused coping   Lazarus' term for responding to stress in an emotional manner, especially using defensive appraisal.   101

empowerment   Assisting individuals to develop skills they need to control their own lives.   107, 386

empty nest syndrome   The belief that marital satisfaction will decrease when the children are launched because parents derive considerable satisfaction from their children (the opposite actually happens, marital satisfaction tends to increase in the post-child rearing years).   259

encoding   The act of producing messages.   145

encounter group   A personal-growth group designed to promote self-understanding through candid group interaction.   382

endocrine glands   Glands that manufacture hormones and release them directly into the bloodstream.   80

endogamy   An individual's tendency to marry someone in his or her own social group.   252

endomorph   Sheldon's term for a soft, round, large-stomached person who is relaxed, gregarious, and food loving.   42

epigenetic principle   Erikson's term for the process that guides development throughout the life span. Anything that grows has a blueprint, each part having its special time of ascendancy, until all of the parts have arisen to form a functioning whole.   63

erogenous zones   Those parts of the body at each stage of development that, according to Freud's theory, have especially strong pleasure-giving qualities.   28

establishment stage   Super's term for the period from 25–45 when individuals pursue a permanent career and attain a pattern of stable work in a particular career.   280

estrogens   The main class of female sex hormones.   181

ethnic identity   A sense of membership in an ethnic group, on shared language, religion, customs, values, history, and race.   7

ethnicity   A characteristic that is based on cultural heritage, nationality characteristics, race, religion, and language, as well as descent from common ancestors.   7

eustress   Selye's term for positive stress.   81

exemplification   A self-presentation technique in which individuals try to portray themselves as having integrity and being morally worthy.   124

exhibitionism   A psychosexual disorder in which individuals expose their sexual anatomy to others to obtain sexual gratification.   211

exorcism   A religious rite used during the Middle Ages that was designed to remove evil spirits from a person; it involved prayer, starvation, beatings, and various forms of torture.   367

exploration stage   Super's concept of the late adolescent and young adult years from about 15–24 when individuals explore and evaluate the work world in a general way.   279

extrinsic religious orientation   External religious motives that lie outside the person.   441

F

family at midlife   The fifth stage of the family life cycle, a time of launching children, which plays an important role in linking generations.   259

family in later life   The sixth and final stage of the family life cycle, in which retirement alters the lifestyle, requiring adaptation.   260

family systems therapy   A form of therapy based on the assumption that psychological adjustment is related to patterns of interaction within the family unit.   381

family therapy   Group therapy with family members.   381

family with adolescents   The fourth stage of the family life cycle, when adolescents push for autonomy and seek to develop their own identity.   258

fantasy stage   Ginzberg's label for the childhood years during which careers are perceived in an unrealistic manner.   278

fear of success   In Horner's theory, a person's expectation that success will produce negative consequences; this can lead the person to sabotage her own performance or avoid success.   293

feminist therapies   Therapies that usually are based on a critique of society wherein women are perceived to have less political and economic power than men have. Also, feminist therapies assume that the reasons for women's problems are principally social, not personal.   388

feminization of poverty   The fact that far more women than men live in poverty today. Likely causes of the feminization of poverty include the low incomes paid to women, divorce, and the ways the judicial system resolves divorce cases.   94

fetishism   A psychosexual disorder in which an individual relies on inanimate objects or a specific part of the body for sexual gratification.   210

finding a partner   The second stage of the family life cycle, during which two individuals from separate families of origin unite to form a new family system.   254

fixation   The psychoanalytic defense mechanism that occurs when the individual remains locked in an earlier developmental stage because her or his needs are under- or overgratified.   28

flow   Csikszentmihalyi's concept of optimal experiences in life that are most likely to occur when people develop a sense of mastery. Flow involves a state of concentration in which an individual becomes absorbed while engaging in an activity.   85

formal groups   Groups established by management to do the organization's work.   286

free association   The technique of encouraging individuals to say aloud whatever comes to mind, no matter how trivial or embarrassing.   371

friendship   A form of close relationship that involves enjoyment, acceptance, trust, intimacy, respect, mutual assistance, understanding, and spontaneity.   228

frustration   Any situation in which a person cannot reach a desired goal.   89

fugue   A dissociative disorder in which an individual not only develops amnesia but also unexpectedly travels away from home and establishes a new identity (*fugue* means "flight").   347

fundamental attribution error   Observers' tendency to overestimate the importance of traits and underestimate the importance of situations when they seek explanations of an actor's behavior.   125

G

gender   The sociocultural dimension of being female or male.   7, 168

gender identity   The sense of being male or female, which most children begin to acquire by the time they are 3 years old.   168

gender role A set of expectations that prescribes how females or males should think, act, or feel. 168

gender-role transcendence The belief that an individual's competence should be conceptualized not on the basis of masculinity, femininity, or androgyny but, rather, on the basis of the person. 175

gender schema A cognitive structure that organizes the world in terms of female and male. 184

gender schema theory The theory that children's attention and behavior are guided by an internal motivation to conform to gender-based sociocultural standards and stereotypes. 184

gender stereotypes Broad categories that reflect our impressions and beliefs about females and males. 175

general adaptation syndrome (GAS) Selye's conception of the common effects on the body when demands are placed on it. The GAS consists of three stages: alarm, resistance, and exhaustion. 80

generalized anxiety disorder An anxiety disorder that consists of persistent anxiety for at least 1 month. An individual with this disorder is unable to specify the reasons for the anxiety. 342

generativity versus stagnation Erikson's seventh developmental stage, which occurs during middle adulthood. A chief concern is assisting the next generation in developing and leading useful lives. 64, 310

genital herpes A sexually transmitted disease in which the symptoms are small, painful bumps or blisters on the genitals. 218

genital stage The fifth Freudian stage of development, occurring from puberty on; the time of sexual reawakening; the source of sexual pleasure now becomes someone outside of the family. 29

genuineness The Rogerian concept of the importance of the therapist's being genuine and not hiding behind a facade. 374

Gestalt therapy A humanistic therapy developed by Fritz Perls, in which the therapist questions and challenges clients to help them become more aware of their feelings and face their problems. 374

gesture A motion of the limbs or body made to convey a message to someone else. 157

giving The client's receiving some kind of benefit from treatment early in the therapy process. 391

glass ceiling A concept from the 1980s. A subtle barrier that is virtually invisible, yet so strong that it prevents women and ethnic minorities from moving up in the management hierarchy. 298

gonorrhea A sexually transmitted disease that is commonly called the "drip" or the "clap"; a common STD in the United States. 217

"good patient" role The role of being passive and unquestioning and behaving properly. 412

gradual conversion A religious change that takes place over a reasonably long period of time, ranging from several weeks or months to even years. 445

graphology The pseudopsychology of using handwriting analysis to describe, explain, and predict a person's behavior. 12

great person theory The theory that individuals with certain traits are best suited for leadership positions. 134

groupthink The motivation of group members to maintain harmony and unanimity in decision making, suffocating differences of opinion in the process. 138

growth stage Super's label for the period of physical and cognitive growth that takes place from birth through early adolescence. 279

H

hallucinogens Psychoactive drugs that modify a person's perceptual experiences and produce hallucinatory visual images; hallucinogens are called psychedelic ("mind altering") drugs. 421

hardiness A personality style characterized by a sense of commitment (rather than alienation), control (rather than powerlessness), and a perception of problems as challenges (rather than threats). 87

health psychology A multidimensional approach to health that emphasizes psychological factors, lifestyle, and the nature of the health-care delivery system. 401

hearing A physiological sensory process in which auditory sensations are received by the ears and transmitted to the brain. 148

heterosexual An individual who is sexually oriented toward persons of the other sex. 252

hidden curriculum The pervasive moral atmosphere that characterizes schools. 436

hierarchy of needs According to Maslow, the main kinds of needs that each individual must satisfy, in this sequence: physiological needs, safety needs, the need for love and belongingness, the need for esteem, cognitive needs, aesthetic needs, and the need for self-actualization. 39

homogamy An individual's tendency to marry someone who has personal characteristics similar to his or her own. 252

homosexual An individual who is sexually oriented toward persons of the same sex. 252

hormones Chemical messengers that travel through the bloodstream to all parts of the body. 80

human sexual response cycle The four phases of human sexual response—excitement, plateau, orgasm, and resolution—as identified by Masters and Johnson. 198

humanistic model of religion A model that emphasizes that a person's most important needs include needs for growth, purpose, and self-actualization. Humans have innate tendencies to fulfill their potential and express their values. Religion is an important vehicle for fulfilling potential and expressing values. 444

humanistic perspective The most widely adopted phenomenological approach to personality, stressing a person's capacity for personal growth, freedom to choose one's own destiny, and positive qualities. 37

humanistic psychotherapies Therapies that encourage clients to understand themselves and to grow personally. In contrast to psychodynamic therapies, humanistic therapies emphasize conscious thoughts rather than unconscious thoughts, the present rather than the past, and growth and fulfillment rather than curing illness. 373

hypochondriasis A somatoform disorder in which the individual has a pervasive fear of illness and disease. 346

I

id The Freudian structure of personality that consists of instincts, which are the person's reservoir of psychic energy. 26

ideal self An individual's representation of the attributes she or he would ideally like to possess—that is, a representation of the person's hopes, aspirations, or wishes. 55

identification theory The Freudian theory that preschool children develop a sexual attraction to the opposite-sex parent and then, at 5 to 6 years of age, renounce the attraction, due to anxiety, subsequently identifying with the same-sex parent and unconsciously adopting the same-sex parent's characteristics. 182

identity achievement Marcia's term for people who have both experienced a crisis and made a commitment. 68

identity diffusion Marcia's term for people who have not experienced a crisis or made a commitment. 67

identity foreclosure Marcia's term for people who have not experienced a crisis but have made a commitment. 67

identity moratorium Marcia's term for people who are in the midst of a crisis but have not yet made a commitment. 67

identity versus identity confusion Erikson's fifth developmental stage, which occurs during adolescence. Individuals are faced with finding out who they are, what they are all about, and where they are going in life. 64

impostor phenomenon A haunting fear felt by some successful people that their success will be overturned and that they will be shown to be frauds. 294

impression management (self-presentation) Acting to present an image of oneself as being a certain sort of person, which might or might not be who one really is. 123

incest Sex between two close relatives; virtually universally taboo. 213

indirect moral education Education that involves encouraging students to define their own and others' values and helping them define the moral perspectives that support those values. 436

indirectly aggressive behavior Manipulating others to achieve a particular outcome without being direct or respectful. 113

individual psychology The name Adler gave to his theory of psychology to emphasize the uniqueness of every individual. 31

individualism Giving priority to personal goals rather than group goals; an emphasis on values that serve the self, such as feeling good, personal achievement and distinction, and independence. 45

individuated-connected level At this highest level of relationship maturity, individuals have both an understanding of themselves and a consideration of others' motivation, along with an anticipation of others' needs (there is concern and caring which involves emotional support and individualized expression of interest). 237

indulgent parenting A parenting style in which the parents are highly involved with their children but place few demands or controls on them. Indulgent parenting is associated with children's social incompetence, especially a lack of self-control. 258

industry versus inferiority Erikson's fourth developmental stage, which occurs in the elementary school years (6–11 years of age). Children's initiative brings them into contact with a wealth of new experiences. They now direct their energy toward mastering knowledge and intellectual skills. 63

inferences Conclusions we draw from observing behavior. 5

inferiority complex The name Adler gave to exaggerated feelings of inadequacy. 31

informal groups Clusters of workers formed by the group's members. 286

ingratiation A self-presentation technique that involves illicitly making yourself likable to another person. 124

initiative versus guilt Erikson's third stage, which occurs during the preschool years (3–5 years of age). As preschool children encounter a widening social world, they are challenged more than they were as infants. Active, purposeful behavior is needed to cope with these challenges. 63

insanity A legal term, not a psychological one. A legally insane person is considered mentally disordered and incapable of being responsible for his or her actions. 358

insanity defense A plea of "innocent by reason of insanity," used as a legal defense in criminal trials. 358

insight therapy Therapy that encourages insight into and awareness of oneself as the critical focus of therapy. 369

integrity versus despair Erikson's eighth and final stage, which occurs in late adulthood. Individuals review their life and evaluate how positive or negative it has been. 64, 322

internalization Developmental change from behavior that is externally controlled to behavior that is controlled by internal standards and principles. 434

interpersonal communication A transactional process that is ongoing over time. This process involves at least two individuals, each of whom acts as both sender and receiver, encoding and decoding messages, sometimes simultaneously. These messages are sent through verbal and nonverbal channels. Noise can limit the accuracy of a message. Communication always takes place in a context. 146

intimacy versus isolation Erikson's sixth developmental stage, which occurs in early adulthood. Individuals face the developmental task of forming intimate relationships with others. 64, 310

intimate style Orlofsky's term for the style of interpersonal interaction in which the individual forms and maintains one or more deep and long-lasting love relationships. 237

intimidation A self-presentation technique in which individuals try to present themselves as dangerous in an effort to coerce others into treating them in a desired way. 124

intrinsic religious orientation Internal religious motives that lie within the person. 441

isolated style Orlofsky's term for the style of interpersonal interaction in which the individual withdraws from social encounters and has little or no attachment to individuals of either sex. 238

J

jealousy Fear of the perceived possibility of losing someone's exclusive love. 239

Johari Window A model of self-disclosure, divided into four quadrants (open self, blind self, hidden self, and unknown self), that helps us understand the proportion of information about ourselves that we and others are aware of. 150

judging A barrier to effective communication that includes criticizing, name-calling and labeling, and praising evaluatively. 152

just manageable difficulty Difficulty that requires the optimal level of effort in a person's life, in job satisfaction and in life satisfaction. 288

justice perspective A moral perspective that focuses on the rights of the individual; individuals stand alone and independently make moral decisions. 435

K

keeping the meaning versus rigidity
Vaillant's stage, occurring from about 45 to 55 years of age, in which individuals experience a more relaxed feeling if they have met their goals, and an acceptance if they have not. Adults at this stage become interested in extracting some meaning from their lives and fight against falling into a rigid orientation.   312

L

late adulthood   The developmental period beginning from the sixties or seventies and lasting until death.   307

latency stage   The fourth Freudian stage of development, occurring approximately between 6 years of age and puberty; the child represses all interest in sexuality and develops social and intellectual skills.   28

latent content   The psychoanalytic term for the unconscious, unremembered, symbolic aspects of a dream.   372

launching   The process in which youths move into adulthood and exit their family of origin.   254

learned helplessness   A response that occurs when animals or humans are exposed to aversive stimulation, such as prolonged stress or pain, over which they have no control. The inability to avoid such aversive stimulation produces an apathetic state of helplessness.   352

leaving home   The first stage in the family life cycle, which involves the concept of launching.   254

leisure   The pleasant times outside of work when individuals are free to pursue activities and interests of their own choosing—hobbies, sports, or reading, for example.   294

life-process model of addiction   A model according to which addiction is not a disease but rather a habitual response and a source of gratification and security that can be understood only in the context of the addict's social relationships and experiences.   415

listening   The psychological process of interpreting and understanding the significance of what someone says.   148

lithium   A drug that is widely used to treat bipolar disorder.   392

M

maintenance stage   Super's term for the period from 45–64 when individuals continue in their careers and maintain their career status.   281

major depression   A mood disorder in which the individual is deeply unhappy, demoralized, self-derogatory, and bored. An individual with major depression shows changes in appetite and sleep patterns, decreased energy, feelings of worthlessness, concentration problems, and guilt feelings that might prompt thoughts of suicide.   348

malaprops   Confused but memorable misuses of language.   144

managed health care   A system in which external reviewers approve the type and length of treatment to justify insurance reimbursement.   370

manifest content   The psychoanalytic term for the conscious, remembered aspects of a dream.   372

mantra   A resonant sound or phrase that is repeated mentally or aloud to focus attention.   111

marriage   A legally and socially sanctioned relationship that creates a new family.   250

masochism   A psychosexual disorder in which individuals derive sexual gratification from being subjected to physical pain, inflicted by others or themselves.   211

matching hypothesis   The hypothesis that although in the abstract we might prefer a more attractive person, in the real world we end up choosing someone who is close to our own level of attractiveness.   235

medical model   Also called the disease model; the forerunner of the biological approach. This model states that abnormal behavior is a disease or illness precipitated by internal physical causes.   335

meditation   The system of thought and practice that is used to attain bodily or mental control and well-being, as well as enlightenment.   111

menopause   The time in middle age, usually in the late forties or early fifties, when a woman's menstrual periods cease completely.   309

mental processes   Thoughts, feelings, and motives that each of us experiences privately but that cannot be observed directly.   5

mentoring   A system in which an experienced person serves as a competent role model by developing a one-to-one relationship with a less experienced person.   37

mesomorph   Sheldon's term for a strong, athletic, and muscular person who is energetic, assertive, and courageous.   42

message   The information being delivered from the sender to the receiver.   145

meta-analysis   A research strategy that involves statistically combining the results of many different studies.   386

metaneeds   In Maslow's theory the higher needs involved in self-actualization; these include needs for truth, goodness, beauty, wholeness, vitality, uniqueness, perfection, justice, inner wealth, and playfulness; also called growth needs.   39

middle adulthood   The developmental period beginning at 35 to 45 and extending to the sixties.   307

misandry   Hatred of men.   172

misogyny   Hatred of women.   172

monochronic   People who tend to schedule only one thing at a time and become disoriented if they must do more than one thing at a time.   161

mood disorders   Psychological disorders characterized by wide emotional swings, ranging from deeply depressed to highly euphoric and agitated. Depression can occur alone, as in major depression, or it can alternate with mania, as in bipolar disorder.   348

morals   Behavioral ideals regarding right and wrong behavior.   430

morita therapy   A therapy, based on Japanese Zen Buddhism, that emphasizes accepting feelings, knowing one's purposes, and, most importantly, doing what needs to be done.   61

multiaxial system   A feature of the DSM-IV in which individuals are classified on the basis of five dimensions, or "axes," that include the individual's history and highest level of functioning in the last year. This system ensures that the individual will not merely be assigned to a mental disorder category, but instead will be characterized by a number of clinical factors.   340

multiple personality   The most dramatic but least common dissociative disorder; individuals with this disorder have two or more distinct personalities.   347

multiple personality disorder   A personality that feels divided into separate entities or selves.   61

N

narcissism   A self-centered approach in dealing with others.   59

neglectful parenting   A parenting style in which the parents are very uninvolved in the child's life. Neglectful parenting is associated with children's social incompetence, especially a lack of self-control.   258

neurotic disorders   Relatively mild mental disorders in which the individual has not lost contact with reality.   339

New Age movement   A popular culture that expresses a distrust of science while engaging in a search for new levels of spiritual awareness. Proponents of the New Age movement maintain that there are hidden "spiritual dimensions" to reality that cannot be discovered by science's experimental strategies.   12

noise   Environmental, physiological, and psychological factors that decrease the likelihood that a message will be accurately expressed or understood.   145

nonassertive behavior   Submissive, self-denying, and inhibited behavior that involves allowing others to choose options for oneself.   113

nonsexist therapy   Therapy that occurs when the therapist has become aware of and primarily overcome his or her sexist attitudes and behavior.   388

nonverbal communication   Messages that are transmitted from one person to another by nonlinguistic means, including bodily communication (gestures, facial expressions, eye communication, and touch), spatial communication, silence, and paralanguage (such as tone of voice).   156

nonverbal leakage   The communication of true emotions through nonverbal channels even when the person tries to conceal the truth verbally.   156

norms   Rules that apply to the members of a group.   134

O

obedience   Behavior that complies with the explicit demands of an individual in authority.   131

observational learning   Learning that occurs when a person observes and then repeats someone else's behavior; also called modeling.   36

obsessive-compulsive disorder (OCD)   An anxiety disorder in which the individual has anxiety-provoking thoughts that will not go away (obsession) and/or urges to perform repetitive, ritualistic behaviors to prevent or produce a future situation (compulsion).   345

obsessive-compulsive personality disorder   A personality disorder in the anxious, fearful cluster; anxious adjustment is the primary feature.   357

Oedipus complex   In Freud's theory, the young child's developing an intense desire to replace the parent of the same sex and to enjoy the affections of the opposite-sex parent.   28

operant conditioning (instrumental conditioning)   A form of learning in which the consequences of behavior produce changes in the probability of that behavior's occurrence.   36

opiates   Opium and its derivatives; these depress the central nervous system's activity.   419

oral stage   The term Freud used to describe development during the first 18 months of life, when the infant's pleasure centers on the mouth.   28

ought self   An individual's representation of the attributes he or she believes he or she should possess—that is a representation of the person's duties, obligations, and responsibilities.   55

overcompensation   Adler's term for the individual's attempt to deny rather than acknowledge a real situation, or the individual's exaggerated efforts to conceal a weakness.   31

overload   What we experience when stimuli becomes so intense that we no longer can cope with them.   90

P

panic disorder   A recurrent anxiety disorder that is marked by the sudden onset of apprehension or terror.   342

paralanguage   The nonlinguistic aspects of verbal expression, such as the rapidity of speech, the volume of speech (loudness, softness), and the pitch of speech (based on a sound wave's frequency—a soprano voice is high-pitched, a bass voice low-pitched).   162

paranoid schizophrenia   A schizophrenic disorder characterized by delusions of reference, grandeur, and persecution.   355

paraphilias   Psychosexual disorders in which the source of an individual's sexual satisfaction is an unusual object, ritual, or situation.   210

paraphrasing   A concise response to a speaker that states the essence of the speaker's content in the listener's own words.   149

parasympathetic nervous system   The part of the autonomic nervous system that calms the body.   80

pedophilia   A psychosexual disorder in which the sex object is a child and the intimacy usually involves manipulation of a child's genitals.   211

person-centered therapy   A form of humanistic therapy developed by Carl Rogers, in which the therapist provides a warm, supportive atmosphere to improve the client's self-concept and encourage the client to gain insight about problems.   373

personal growth groups   Groups that have their roots in the humanistic therapies; they emphasize personal growth and increased openness and honesty in interpersonal relations.   382

personality   Enduring, distinctive thoughts, emotions, and behaviors that characterize the way an individual adapts to the world.   24

personality disorders   Psychological disorders that develop when personality traits become inflexible and, thus, maladaptive.   357

personality type theory   Holland's view that it is important to develop a match or fit between an individual's personality type and the selection of a particular career.   283

phallic stage   Freud's third stage of development, which occurs between the ages of 3 and 6; its name comes from the Latin word *phallus,* which means "penis." During the phallic stage, pleasure focuses on the genitals as the child discovers that self-stimulation is enjoyable.   28

phenomenological worldview   A worldview that stresses the importance of our perceptions of ourselves and our world in understanding personality. This view emphasizes that, for each individual, reality is what that person perceives.   37

phobic disorder   An anxiety disorder that occurs when an individual has an irrational, overwhelming, persistent fear of a particular object or situation; commonly called a phobia.   343

pleasure principle The Freudian concept that the id always seeks pleasure and avoids pain. 26

polychronic People who prefer to juggle several tasks at the same time. 161

possible selves What individuals might become, including what they would like to become and what they are afraid of becoming. 55

post-traumatic stress disorder A mental disorder that develops through exposure to any of several traumatic events, such as war, the Holocaust, severe abuse as in rape, natural disasters such as floods and tornados, and accidental disasters such as plane crashes. The disorder is characterized by anxiety symptoms that may be apparent 1 month after the trauma or be delayed by months or even years until onset. 345

postconventional level The highest level of moral thinking in Kohlberg's theory, in which morality is completely internalized and not based on others' standards. 434

pragmatism Being inclined to practical solutions. 431

preconventional level The lowest level of moral thinking in Kohlberg's theory, in which the individual shows no internalization of moral values—moral reasoning is controlled by external rewards and punishments. 434

preintimate style Orlofsky's term for the style of interpersonal interaction in which the individual shows mixed emotions about commitment, which is reflected in the strategy of offering love without obligations or long-lasting bonds. 238

primacy effect The enduring quality of initial impressions. 123

primary appraisal Individuals' interpretations of whether an event involves harm or loss that has already occurred, a threat to some future danger, or a challenge to be overcome. 88

primary prevention A community psychology concept, borrowed from the public health field, denoting efforts to reduce the number of new cases of mental disorders. 385

problem-focused coping Lazarus' term for the cognitive strategy of squarely facing one's own troubles and trying to solve them. 101

projection The psychoanalytic defense mechanism that occurs when we attribute our own shortcomings, problems, and faults to others. 27

proposing solutions An ineffective communication pattern in which the proposed solutions are presented caringly as advice, indirectly by questioning, authoritatively as an order, aggressively as a threat, or with a halo as moralizing. 153

proxemics The study of the communicative function of space, especially how people unconsciously structure their space. 160

pseudointimate style Orlofsky's term for the style of interpersonal interaction in which the individual maintains a long-lasting sexual attachment with little or no depth or closeness. 238

pseudopsychology A nonscientific system that only superficially resembles psychology. Pseudopsychologies lack a scientific base. Their descriptions, explanations, and predictions either cannot be directly tested or, when tested, turn out to be unfounded. 12

psychiatry A branch of medicine practiced by physicians who have specialized in abnormal behavior and psychotherapy. 6

psychoactive drugs Drugs that act on the nervous system to alter our state of consciousness, modify our perceptions, and change our moods. 414

psychoanalysis Freud's therapeutic technique for analyzing an individual's unconscious thought. 371

psychoanalytic model of religion A model that emphasizes that the key to understanding religiousness resides deep within the unconscious mind. Individuals are believed to have instinctual needs they are not aware of, such as needs for safety and security, which can be met by relating to a higher power. 443

psychodynamic therapies Therapies that stress the importance of the unconscious mind, extensive therapist interpretation, and the role of infant and early childhood experiences. 371

psychogenic amnesia A dissociative disorder involving memory loss caused by extensive psychological stress. 346

psychological dependence The felt need to take a drug to cope with problems and stress. 414

psychological moratorium Erikson's term for the gap between childhood security and adult independence experienced as part of identity exploration. 65

psychology The scientific study of behavior and mental processes in contexts. 5

psychoneuroimmunology The field that explores the connections among psychological factors (such as attitudes and emotions), the nervous system, and the immune system. 81

psychosexual disorders Sexual problems caused mainly by psychological factors. 209

psychosexual dysfunctions Disorders that involve impairments in the sexual response cycle, either in the desire for gratification or in the ability to achieve it. 210

psychosurgery A biomedical therapy that involves the removal or destruction of brain tissue to improve the person's psychological adjustment. 394

psychotherapy The process of working with individuals to reduce their emotional problems and improve their adjustment. 369

psychotic disorders Severe mental disorders in which the individual has lost contact with reality. 340

punishment A consequence that decreases the probability that a behavior will occur. 36

R

radical behaviorists Psychologists who emphasize only observable behavior and reject its cognitive dimensions. 36

rape Forcible sex with a person who does not give consent. 212

rational-emotive therapy Therapy based on Albert Ellis's assertion that people become psychologically disordered because of their beliefs, especially those that are irrational and self-defeating. 377

rationalization The psychoanalytic defense mechanism that occurs when the ego does not accept the real motive for the individual's behavior and replaces it with a sort of cover motive. 27

reaction formation The psychoanalytic defense mechanism that occurs when we express an unacceptable impulse by transforming it into its opposite. 27

realistic stage Ginzberg's description of the age period of about 18–25 when individuals rid themselves of their fantasies about careers and make more pragmatic decisions. 279

reality principle The Freudian concept that the ego tries to make the pursuit of individual pleasure conform to the norms of society. 26

reciprocal determinism Bandura's social learning model in which behavior, cognitive and other personal factors, and environmental influences interact to cause social learning. 36

reflective listening An effective communication strategy in which the listener restates the feelings and/or content of what the speaker has communicated and does so in a way that reveals understanding and acceptance. 149

reflexes Automatic stimulus-response connections that are "hardwired" into the brain. 34

regression The psychoanalytic defense mechanism that occurs when we behave in a way that is characteristic of a previous developmental level. 27

reinforcement (reward) A consequence that increases the probability that a behavior will occur. 36

religious conversion The change from having no religious belief to accepting a religious belief system as one's own, or from one religious belief system to another. 445

religious socialization A lifelong process in which individuals cannot remember not having a religious faith. 445

repression The most powerful and pervasive defense mechanism, according to Freud; it works to push unacceptable id impulses and traumatic memories out of awareness and back into the unconscious mind. 26

resistance The psychoanalytic term for a client's unconscious defense strategies that prevent the analyst from understanding the client's problems. 372

role-focused level At the second level of relationship maturity, perceiving others as individuals in their own right begins to develop. The perspective is still stereotypical and emphasizes social acceptability. 237

roles Rules and expectations that govern certain positions in a group. Roles define how people should behave in a particular position in the group. 134

romantic love A type of love that has strong components of sexuality and infatuation and often predominates in the early part of a love relationship; also called passionate love or eros. 229

romantic script The behavioral script according to which sex is synonymous with love; in this script, it is acceptable to have sex with a person, whether we are married or not, if we are in love with that person. 206

S

sadism A psychosexual disorder in which an individual derives sexual gratification from inflicting pain on others. 211

schema A cognitive structure, or network of associations, that organizes and guides an individual's perception. 184

schizophrenic disorders Severe psychological disorders characterized by distorted thoughts and perceptions, odd communication, inappropriate emotion, abnormal motor behavior, and social withdrawal. The term *schizophrenia* comes from the Latin words *schizo,* meaning "split," and *phrenia,* meaning "mind." The individual's mind is split from reality, and his or her personality loses its unity. 353

schizotypal personality disorder A personality disorder in the odd, eccentric cluster. Individuals with this disorder appear to be in contact with reality, but many aspects of their behavior are distasteful, which leads to rejection, retreat or withdrawal from others. 357

science of psychology The use of systematic methods to observe, describe, explain, and predict behavior and mental processes. 5

scientology A pseudopsychology developed by L. Ron Hubbard in the 1950s. Scientology states that people become socially programmed and respond too automatically to their world. Scientology offers to free people from the shackles of their conditioning and deliver wondrous insights. 12

seasonal affective disorder (SAD) Depression that appears to be caused by seasonally shorter exposure to sunlight. 393

secondary appraisal Individuals' evaluations of their resources to determine how effectively they can be used to cope with an event. 88

secondary prevention A prevention method involving screening for early detection problems and early intervention; a community psychology concept. 385

self Your sense of who you are and what makes you different from others. 54

self-actualization The highest and most elusive human need, according to Maslow; the motivation to develop to one's full potential as a human being. 39

self-concept Our overall thoughts and feelings about ourselves; sometimes called self-understanding. 38, 55

self-disclosure The communication of intimate details about ourselves to someone else. 150

self-discrepancy theory The theory that problems occur when various selves in different domains or from different views are inconsistent, or discrepant, with each other. 57

self-efficacy The belief that one can master a situation and produce positive outcomes; an effective coping strategy. 37, 101, 377

self-esteem The evaluative and affective dimension of self-concept; also referred to as self-worth or self-image. 56

self-focused level At this first level of relationship maturity, individuals are only concerned with how another (or the relationship with another) will affect themselves. 237

self-help groups Voluntary organizations of individuals who get together on a regular basis to discuss topics of common interest. The group leader and members give support to help individuals with their problems. Self-help groups are so-called because they are conducted without a professional therapist. 383

self-instructional methods Cognitive behavioral techniques aimed at teaching individuals to modify their own behavior. 377

self-monitoring Individuals' awareness of the impressions they make on others and the degree to which they fine-tune their performance accordingly. 124

self-perception theory Bem's theory of connections between attitudes and behavior; it stresses that individuals make inferences about their attitudes by perceiving their behavior. 127

self-promotion A self-presentation technique in which individuals try to present themselves as competent. 124

self-talk (self-statements) The soundless mental speech people use when they think about something, plan, or solve problems; often helpful in cognitive restructuring. 103

self-understanding The individual's cognitive representation of the self, the substance and content of the person's beliefs about the self and its operation. 54

set point The weight maintained when no effort is made to gain or lose weight. 405

sex The biological dimension of being female or male. 7

sexism Prejudice and discrimination against a person because of her or his sex. 177

sexual script A set of stereotyped role prescriptions for how individuals should behave sexually. 205

sexually transmitted diseases (STDs) Diseases that are contracted primarily through sex. 213

situational theory of leadership The theory that the needs of a group change from time to time and that a person who emerges as leader in one circumstance will not necessarily be the person who becomes a leader in another circumstance. 135

situationism Mischel's view that a person's personality often varies from one context to another. 43

skepticism A reluctance to believe expressed in a questioning stance. 11

social comparison The process in which individuals evaluate their thoughts, feelings, behaviors, and abilities in relation to other people. 123

social exchange theory The theory that individuals should benefit those who benefit them, and that when a benefit is received, equivalent benefit should be returned at some point. 227

social learning theory of gender The theory that children's gender development occurs through observation and imitation of gender-related behavior, as well as through the rewards and punishments children experience for gender-appropriate and gender-inappropriate behaviors. 182

social perception Our judgment about the qualities of individuals, which involves how we form impressions of others, how we gain self-knowledge from perception of others, and how we present ourselves to others to influence their perceptions of us. 123

social support Information and feedback from others that we are loved and cared for, esteemed and valued, and part of a network of communication and mutual obligation. 108

sociocultural approach An approach that emphasizes that culture, ethnicity, and gender are essential to understanding adjustment and behavior. 7

sociocultural model of religion A model according to which individuals adopt a particular religious stance because of the experiences they have in the culture they live in. 444

somatoform disorders Mental disorders in which the psychological symptoms take a physical, or somatic, form, even though no physical causes can be found. 346

somatotype theory Sheldon's theory that precise charts reveal distinct body types, which in turn are associated with certain personality characteristics. 42

speaking Expressing thoughts and feelings in words and behavior with accuracy and clarity so that the targeted listener understands what you mean. 147

stereotyped style Orlofsky's term for the style of interpersonal interaction in which the individual has superficial relationships that tend to be dominated by friendship ties. 238

stimulants Psychoactive drugs that increase the central nervous system's activity. 420

strain A weakened resistance to stressors and diminished resilience. 79

stress Individuals' response to the circumstances and events, called stressors, that threaten them and tax their coping abilities. 79

stress-management programs Programs that teach individuals how to appraise stressful events, how to develop skills for coping with stress, and how to put these skills to use. 110

stressors Threatening aspects of the environment that induce stress reactions. 79

striving for superiority The human motivation to adapt to, improve, and master the environment. 31

sublimation The psychoanalytic defense mechanism that occurs when the ego replaces an unacceptable impulse with a socially approved course of action. 27

substance-use disorder A disorder characterized by one or more of the following features: (1) a pattern of pathological use that involves frequent intoxication, a need for daily use, and an inability to control use—in the sense of psychological dependence; (2) a significant impairment of social or occupational functioning attributed to drug use; and (3) physical dependence that involves serious withdrawal problems. 358

sudden conversion A religious change that occurs all at once with no prior warning. 445

superego The Freudian structure of personality that is the moral branch of personality. The superego takes into account whether something is right or wrong. 26

superiority complex Adler's concept of exaggerated self-importance that is designed to mask feelings of inferiority. 31

supplication A self-presentation technique in which individuals try to make themselves appear weak and dependent. 124

sympathetic nervous system The part of the autonomic nervous system that arouses the body. 80

syphilis A sexually transmitted disease caused by the bacterium *Treponema pallidum,* a member of the spirochete family. 217

systematic desensitization A method of behavior therapy that treats anxiety by associating deep relaxation with successive visualizations of increasingly intense anxiety-producing situations; this technique is based on classical conditioning. 375

T

tardive dyskinesia A major side effect of the neuroleptic drugs; a neurological disorder characterized by grotesque, involuntary movements of the facial muscles and mouth, as well as extensive twitching of the neck, arms, and legs. 392

tentative stage Ginzberg's label for the adolescent period of 11–17 when individuals are in transition between the novice fantasy stage of childhood and the more mature, realistic stage that will come later. 279

territoriality A possessive or ownership-like reaction to an area of space or particular objects. 161

tertiary prevention A community psychology concept denoting efforts to reduce the long-term consequences of mental health disorders that were not prevented or arrested early in the course of the disorders. 385

thought stopping A specific self-control and cognitive restructuring strategy in which the individual says "Stop!" when unwanted thought occurs and then replaces it immediately with a more pleasant thought. 107

time management Using one's time effectively to accomplish one's goals. 115

to-do list A time management technique that identifies activities, in ranked priority, that you want to accomplish each day. 115

token economy A behavior modification system in which behaviors are reinforced with tokens (such as poker chips) that can be exchanged later for desired rewards (such as candy, money, or going to a movie). 377

tolerance   The physical state that has developed when a greater amount of a drug is needed to produce the same effect as a smaller amount previously produced.   414

traditional religious script   The behavioral script according to which sex is acceptable only within marriage; both premarital and extramarital sex are taboo, especially for women.   205

trait theories   Theories that propose that people have broad dispositions that are reflected in the basic ways they behave, such as whether they are outgoing and friendly and whether they are dominant and assertive.   42

traits   Broad dispositions that lead to characteristic responses.   41

tranquilizers   Depressant drugs, such as Valium and Xanax, that reduce anxiety and induce relaxation.   419

transactional   Being an ongoing process between sender and receiver that unfolds across time. Information often is communicated simultaneously between the participants.   146

transcendental meditation (TM)   The most popular form of meditation in the United States. It is derived from an ancient Indian technique and involves a mantra, which is a resonant sound or phrase that is repeated mentally or aloud to focus attention.   111

transference   The psychoanalytic term for a client's relating to an analyst in ways that reproduce or relive important relationships in the client's life.   372

transsexualism   A gender identity disorder in which an individual has an overwhelming desire to become a member of the opposite sex.   211

transvestism   A psychosexual disorder in which an individual obtains sexual gratification by dressing as a member of the opposite sex.   211

trephining   A procedure, no longer used, that involved chipping a hole in the skull to allow evil spirits to escape.   366

triangular theory of love   Sternberg's view that love involves three main dimensions: passion, intimacy, and commitment.   231

trust versus mistrust   Erikson's first psychological stage, which is experienced in the first year of life. A sense of trust requires a feeling of physical comfort and a minimal amount of fear and apprehension about the future.   63

twelve-step programs   Programs, like Alcoholics Anonymous, that emphasize confession, group support, and spiritual commitment to a higher power to help individuals cope with alcoholism or other behavioral problems.   417

Type A behavior pattern   A cluster of characteristics (being excessively competitive, hard-driven, impatient, and hostile) thought to be related to the incidence of heart disease.   87

Type C behavior   The cancer-prone personality, which consists of being inhibited, uptight, lacking in emotional expression, and being otherwise constrained. This type of person is more likely to develop cancer than more expressive persons are.   87

U

unconditional positive regard   Rogers' term for accepting, valuing, and being positive toward another person regardless of the person's behavior.   38

unconditioned response (UR)   An unlearned response that is automatically associated with the US.   34

unconditioned stimulus (US)   A stimulus that produces a response without prior learning.   34

undifferentiated schizophrenia   A schizophrenic disorder characterized by disorganized behavior, hallucinations, delusions, and incoherence.   355

V

values   Standards about the things we prefer or the ideas we are loyal to.   8, 430

values clarification   An indirect moral education approach that focuses on helping students clarify what their lives are for and what is worth working for.   436

value conflict   A conflict between two competing values that encourage opposing actions.   10, 431

voyeurism   A psychosexual disorder in which individuals derive sexual gratification by observing the sex organs or sex acts of others, often from a secret vantage point.   211

W

withdrawal   The undesirable intense pain and craving that an addicted person feels when the addicting drug is withdrawn.   414

workaholic   A person who seemingly is addicted to work.   292

Y

youth   Kenniston's term for the transitional period between adolescence and adulthood, a time of extended economic and personal temporariness.   308

REFERENCES

A

Aamodt, M. G. (1996). *Applied industrial/organizational psychology* (2nd ed.). Pacific Grove, CA: Brooks/Cole.

Abraham, J. D., & Hansson, R. O. (1995). Successful aging at work: An applied study of selection, optimization, and compensation through impression management. *Journal of Gerontology, 50B*, P94–P103.

Acitelli, L. K., & Holmberg, D. (1993). Reflecting on relationships: The role of thoughts and memories. In D. Perlman & W. H. Jones (Eds.), *Advances in personal relationships* (Vol. 4). London: Kingsley.

Adams, H. E., & Cassidy, J. F. (1993). The classification of abnormal behavior: An overview. In P. B. Sutker & H. E. Adams (Eds.), *Comprehensive textbook of psychopathology* (2nd ed.). New York: Plenum Press.

Adler, A. (1927). *The theory and practice of individual psychology.* New York: Harcourt, Brace, & World.

Ahrons, C. R., & Rodgers, R. H. (1987). *Divorced families.* New York: W. W. Norton.

Alan Guttmacher Institute. (1981). *Teenage pregnancy: The problem that has not gone away.* New York: Author.

Albert, R. D. (1988). The place of culture in modern psychology. In P. A. Bronstein & K. Quina (Eds.), *Teaching a psychology of people: Resources for gender and sociocultural awareness.* Washington, DC: American Psychological Association.

Alberti, R. E., & Emmons, M. L. (1986). *Your perfect right: A guide to assertive behavior* (5th ed.). San Luis Obispo, CA: Impact.

Alderfer, C. P., & Tucker, R. C. (1996). A field experiment for studying race relations embedded in organizations. *Journal of Organizational Behavior, 17*, 43–58.

Al-Issa, I. (1982a). Does culture make a difference in psychopathology? In I. Al-Issa (Ed.), *Culture and psychopathology.* Baltimore: University Park Press.

Al-Issa, I. (1982b). Sex differences in psychopathology. In I. Al-Issa (Ed.), *Culture and psychopathology.* Baltimore: University Park Press.

Allan, R., & Scheidt, S. (Eds.). (1996). *Heart and mind.* Washington, DC: American Psychological Association.

Allen, L., & Majidi-Ahi, S. (1989). Black American children. In T. T. Gibbs & L. N. Huang (Eds.), *Children of color.* San Francisco: Jossey-Bass.

Allport, G. W. (1966). The religious context of prejudice. *Journal for the Scientific Study of Religion, 5*, 447–457.

Allport, G. W., & Odbert, H. S. (1936). Trait names: A psycholexical study. *Psychological Monographs, 47* (whole no.211).

American College Health Association. (1989, May). *Survey of AIDS on American college and university campuses.* Washington, DC: Author.

Anderson, B. L. (1983). Primary orgasmic dysfunction: Diagnostic considerations and a review of treatment. *Psychological Bulletin, 93*, 105–136.

Anderson, B. L., Kiecolt-Glaser, J. K., & Glaser, R. (1994). A biobehavioral model of cancer stress and disease course. *American Psychologist, 49*, 389–404.

Anderson, N. (1996, June). *Socio-economic status and health.* Paper presented at the meeting of the American Psychological Society, San Francisco.

Anderson, N. H. (1965). Primacy effects in personality impression formation using a generalized order effect paradigm. *Journal of Personality and Social Psychology, 2*, 1–9.

Anderson, N. H. (1968). Likableness ratings of 55 personality trait words. *Journal of Personality and Social Psychology, 9*, 272–279.

Aponte, J. F., Rivers, R. R., & Wohl, J. (1995). *Psychological interventions with ethnically diverse groups.* Needham Heights, MA: Allyn & Bacon.

Archer, D., & Gartner, R. (1976). Violent acts and violent times: A comparative approach in postwar homicide. *American Sociological Review, 41*, 937–963.

Archer, S. L. (1991). Identity development, gender differences. In R. M. Lerner, A. C. Petersen, & J. Brooks-Gunn (Eds.), *Encyclopedia of adolescence* (Vol. 1). New York: Garland.

Argyle, M., & Beit-Hallahmi, B. (1975). *The social psychology of religion.* London & Boston: Routledge & Kegan Paul.

Aronson, E. (1995). *The social animal* (7th ed.). New York: W. H. Freeman.

Asch, S. E. (1951). Effects of group pressure on the modification and distortion of judgments. In H. S. Guetzkow (Ed.), *Groups, leadership and men.* Pittsburgh: Carnegie University Press.

Asnis, G. M., & van Praag, H. M. (1995). *Panic disorder.* New York: Wiley.

Astin, A. W., Korn, W. S., Sax, L. J., & Mahoney, K. M. (1994). *The American freshman.* Los Angeles: University of California, Higher Education Research Institute.

Atkinson, D., Morten, G., & Sue, D. (1993). *Counseling American minorities* (4th ed.). Madison, WI: Brown & Benchmark.

Averill, J. R. (1983). Studies on anger and aggression: Implications for theories of emotions. *American Psychologist, 38*, 1145–1160.

Axtell, R. (1991). *Gestures!: The do's and taboos of body language around the world.* New York: Wiley.

B

Bachman, J., O'Malley, P., & Johnston, L. (1978). *Youth in transition: Vol. 6. Adolescence to adulthood—Change and stability of the lives of young men.* Ann Arbor: University of Michigan, Institute of Social Research.

Bachman, J. G., Johnston, L. D., O'Malley, P. M., & Schulenberg, J. (1996). Transitions in drug use during late adolescence and early adulthood. In J. A. Graber, J. Brooks-Gunn, & A. C. Petersen (Eds.), *Transitions through adolescence.* Hillsdale, NJ: Erlbaum.

Bagley, C. (1984). The social aetiology of schizophrenia in immigrant groups. In J. E. Mezzich & C. E. Berganza (Eds.), *Culture and psychopathology.* New York: Columbia University Press.

Bailey, J. M., & Pillard, R. C. (1991). A genetic study of male sexual orientation. *Archives of General Psychiatry, 48*, 1089–1096.

Baker, O. (1996). Managing diversity: Implications for White managers. In B. P. Bowser & R. G. Hunt (Eds.), *Impacts of racism on White Americans.* Newbury Park, CA: Sage.

Ballentine, S. F., & Inclan, J. B. (Eds.). (1995). *Diverse voices of women.* Mountain View, CA: Mayfield.

Baltes, M. M., & Wahl, H. W. (1991). The behavior system of dependency in long-term care institutions. In M. G. Ory, R. P. Abeles, & P. D. Lipman (Eds.), *Aging, health, and behavior.* Newbury Park, CA: Sage.

Baltes, P. B., & Baltes, M. M. (1990). Psychological perspectives on successful aging: The model of selective optimization with compensation. In P. B. Baltes & M. M. Baltes (Eds.), *Successful aging: Perspectives from the behavioral sciences.* New York: Cambridge University Press.

Baltes, P. B., Smith, J., Staudinger, U. M., & Sowarka, D. (in press). Wisdom: One facet of successful aging? In M. Perlmutter (Ed.), *Late-life potential.* Washington, DC: Gerontological Association of America.

Banaji, M., & Prentice, D. A. (1994). The self in social contexts. *Annual Review of Psychology, 45,* 297–332.

Bandura, A. (1977). *Social learning theory.* Englewood Cliffs, NJ: Prentice Hall.

Bandura, A. (1986). *Social foundations of thought and action.* Englewood Cliffs, NJ: Prentice Hall.

Bandura, A. (1989). Social cognitive theory. In R. Vasta (Ed.), *Six theories of child development.* Greenwich, CT: JAI.

Bandura, A. (1991). Social cognitive theory of moral thought and action. In W. M. Kurtines & J. Gewirtz (Eds.), *Handbook of moral behavior and development: Advances in theory, research, and application.* Hillsdale, NJ: Erlbaum.

Bandura, A. (1991). Self-efficacy: Impact of self-beliefs on adolescent life paths. In R. M. Lerner, A. C. Petersen, & J. Brooks-Gunn (Eds.), *Encyclopedia of adolescence* (Vol. 2). New York: Garland.

Bandura, A. (1994). Social cognitive theory of mass communication. In J. Bryant & D. Zillman (Eds.), *Media effects.* Hillsdale, NJ: Erlbaum.

Bandura, A., Blanchard, E. B., & Ritter, B. (1969). Relative efficacy of desensitization and modeling approaches for inducing behavioral, affective, and attitudinal changes. *Journal of Personality and Social Psychology, 13,* 173–199.

Banks, E. C. (1993, March). *Moral education curriculum in a multicultural context: The Malaysian primary curriculum.* Paper presented at the biennial meeting of the Society for Research in Child Development, New Orleans.

Barker, L., Edwards, R., Gaines, C., Gladney, K., & Holley, F. (1981). An investigation of proportional time spent in various communication activities by college students. *Journal of Applied Communication Research, 8,* 101–109.

Barnlund, D. C. (1975). Communicative styles in two cultures: Japan and the United States. In A. Kendon, R. M. Harris, & M. R. Key (Eds.), *Organization of behavior in face-to-face interaction.* The Hague: Mouton.

Baruch, G. K., Biener, L., & Barnett, R. C. (1987). Women and gender in research on work and family. *American Psychologist, 42,* 130–136.

Baruth, L. G., & Manning, M. L. (1991). *Multicultural counseling and psychotherapy: A lifespan perspective.* New York: Macmillan.

Bass, D. M., Bowman, K., & Noelker, L. S. (1991). The influence of caregiving and bereavement support on adjusting to an older relative's death. *Gerontologist, 31*(31), 32–41.

Bateman, T., & Snell, S. (1996). *Management* (3rd ed.). Burr Ridge, IL: Irwin.

Batson, C. D., Bolen, M. H., Cross, J. A., & Jeuringer-Benefiel, H. E. (1986). Where is the altruism in the altruistic personality? *Journal of Personality and Social Psychology, 50,* 212–220.

Batson, C. D., Schoenrade, P., & Ventis, W. L. (1993). *Religion and the individual.* New York: Oxford University Press.

Baumeister, R. F. (1989). *Masochism and the self.* Hillsdale, NJ: Erlbaum.

Baumeister, R. F. (1991). The self against the self: Escape or defeat. In R. C. Curtis (Ed.), *The relational self.* New York: Guilford.

Baumrind, D. (1971). Current patterns of parental authority. *Developmental Psychology Monographs, 4* (1, Pt. 2).

Baumrind, D. (1991). Effective parenting during the early adolescent transition. In P. A. Cowan & E. M. Hetherington (Eds.), *Advances in family research* (Vol. 2). Hillsdale, NJ: Erlbaum.

Beck, A. (1976). *Cognitive therapies and the emotional disorders.* New York: International Universities Press.

Beck, A. T. (1967). *Depression.* New York: Harper & Row.

Beck, A. T., & Haaga, D. A. F. (1992). The future of cognitive therapy. *Psychotherapy, 29,* 34–38.

Beck, M. (1992, December 7). Middle Age. *Newsweek,* pp. 50–56.

Beckham, E. E., & Leber, W. R. (Eds.). (1995). *Handbook of depression* (2nd ed.). New York: Guilford Press.

Bednar, R. L., & Peterson, S. R. (1995). *Self-esteem: Paradoxes and innovations in clinical theory and practice* (2nd ed.). Washington, DC: American Psychological Association.

Beit-Hallahmi, B. (1989). *Prologue to the psychological study of religion.* Toronto: Associated University Presses.

Belenky, M. F., Clinchy, B. M., Goldberger, N. R., & Tarule, J. M. (1986). *Women's ways of knowing.* New York: Basic Books.

Bell, A. P., & Weinberg, M. S. (1978). *Homosexualities.* New York: Simon & Schuster.

Bell, A. P., Weinberg, M. S., & Mammersmith, S. K. (1981). *Sexual preference: Its development in men and women.* New York: Simon & Schuster.

Belle, D., Longfellow, C., Makosky, V., Saunder, E., & Zelkowitz, P. (1981). Income, mothers' mental health, and family functioning in a low-income population. In American Academy of Nursing (Ed.), *The impact of changing resources on health policy.* Kansas City: American Nurses Association.

Bem, D. J. (1967). Self-perception. An alternative interpretation of cognitive dissonance phenomena. *Psychological Review, 74,* 183–200.

Bem, S. L. (1977). On the utility of alternative procedures for assessing psychological androgyny. *Journal of Consulting and Clinical Psychology, 45,* 196–205.

Bengtson, V. L. (Ed.). (1996). *Adulthood and aging.* New York: Springer.

Bennett, W. I., & Gurin, J. (1982). *The dieter's dilemma: Eating less and weighing more.* New York: Basic Books.

Bennett, W. J. (1986). *First lessons: A report on elementary education in America.* Washington, DC: U.S. Government Printing Office.

Bergin, A. E., & Garfield, S. L. (1994). *Handbook of psychotherapy and behavior change.* New York: Wiley.

Berglass, S. (1991). *The success syndrome.* New York: Plenum.

Berk, S. F. (1985). *The gender factory: The apportionment of work in American households.* New York: Plenum.

Bernard, J. (1964). The adjustment of married mates. In H. T. Christensen (Ed.), *Handbook of marriage and the family.* Chicago: Rand McNally.

Bernard, J. (1972). *The future of marriage.* New York: Bantam.

Berry, J. W. (1983). Textured contexts: Systems and situations in cross-cultural psychology. In S. H. Irvine & J. W. Berry (Eds.), *Human assessment and cultural factors.* New York: Plenum.

Bersheid, E. (1988). Some comments on love's anatomy: Or, whatever happened to an old-fashioned lust? In R. J. Sternberg & M. L. Barnes (Eds.), *Anatomy of love.* New Haven, CT: Yale University Press.

Berscheid, E. (1994). Interpersonal relationships. *Annual Review of Psychology, 45,* 79–129.

Berscheid, E., & Fei, J. (1977). Sexual jealousy and romantic love. In G. Clinton & G. Smith (Eds.), *Sexual jealousy.* Englewood Cliffs, NJ: Prentice Hall.

Berscheid, E., Snyder, M., & Omoto, A. M. (1989). Issues in studying close relationships: Conceptualizing and measuring closeness. In C. Hendrick (Ed.), *Close relationships.* Newbury Park, CA: Sage.

Bertelson, A. (1979). A Danish twin study of manic-depressive disorders. In M. Schous & E. Stromgren (Eds.), *Origin, prevention, and treatment of affective disorders.* Orlando, FL: Academic Press.

Billings, A. G., Cronkite, R. C., & Moos, R. H. (1983). Social-environmental factors in unipolar depression. *Journal of Abnormal Psychology, 92,* 119–133.

Billings, A. G., & Moos, R. H. (1981). The role of coping responses and social resources in attenuating the stress of life events. *Journal of Behavioral Medicine, 4,* 157–189.

Billy, J. O. G., Tanfer, K., Grady, W. R., & Klepinger, D. H. (1993). The sexual behavior of men in the United States. *Family Planning Perspectives, 25,* 52–60.

Birren, J. E. (Ed.). (1996). *Encyclopedia of gerontology.* San Diego, CA: Academic Press.

Birren, J. E., & Salthouse, T. A. (in press). *The psychology of aging.* Cambridge, MA: Blackwell.

Birren, J. E., & Schaie, K. W. (Eds.). (1996). *Handbook of the psychology of aging* (4th ed.). Orlando, FL: Academic Press.

Birren, J. E., Schaie, K. W., Abeles, R. P., & Salthouse, T. S. (Eds.). (1996). *Handbook of the psychology of aging* (4th ed.). San Diego, CA: Academic Press.

Blair, S. N., & Kohl, H. W. (1988). Physical activity: Which is more important for health? *Medicine and Science and Sports and Exercise, 20,* (2 Suppl.), 5–7.

Blakemore, J. E. O. (1993, March). *Preschool children's interest in babies: Observations in naturally occurring situations.* Paper presented at the biennial meeting of the Society for Research in Child Development, New Orleans.

Bloom, B. (1975). *Changing patterns of psychiatric care.* New York: Human Science Press.

Bloor, C., & White, F. (1983). Unpublished manuscript, University of California at San Diego.

Blumstein, P. W., & Schwartz, P. (1983). *American couples.* New York: William Morrow.

Blundell, J. E. (1984). Systems and interactions: An approach to the pharmacology of feeding. In A. J. Stunkard & E. Stellar (Eds.), *Eating and its disorders.* New York: Raven Press.

Bly, R. (1990). *Iron John.* New York: Vantage.

Boland, J. P., & Follingstad, D. R. (1988). The relationship between communication and marital satisfaction: A review. *Journal of Sex and Marital Therapy, 13,* 286–313.

Bolles, R. N. (1996). *What color is your parachute? A practical manual for job hunters and career-changers.* Berkeley, CA: Ten Speed Press.

Bolton, R. (1979). *People skills.* New York: Touchstone.

Bond, R., & Smith, P. B. (1994). Culture and conformity: A meta-analysis of studies using the Asch-type perceptual judgment task. *British Psychological Society 1994 Proceedings,* p. 41.

Boston Women's Health Book Collective. (1987). *Ourselves Getting Older.* New York: Simon & Schuster.

Boston Women's Health Book Collective. (1992). *The New Our Bodies, Ourselves.* New York: Simon & Schuster.

Boudewyns, P. A. (1996). Post-traumatic stress disorder. In M. Hersen, R. M. Eisler, & P. M. Miller (Eds.), *Progress in behavior modification* (Vol. 30). Pacific Grove, CA: Brooks/Cole.

Bower, G. H., & Gilligan, S. G. (1979). Remembering information related to one's self. *Journal of Research in Personality, 13,* 404–419.

Bowlby, J. (1980). *Attachment and loss: Vol. 3. Loss, sadness, and depression.* New York: Basic Books.

Bowser, B. P., & Hunt, R. G. (Eds.). (1996). *Impacts of racism on White Americans.* Newbury Park, CA: Sage.

Boyd-Franklin, N. (1993, August). *Psychotherapy with African-American women and men.* Paper presented at the meeting of the American Psychological Association. Toronto.

Boyd-Franklin, N. (1996, August). *Home and community based family intervention with African Americans.* Paper presented at the meeting of the American Psychological Association, Toronto.

Bradley, M. M. (1996). Gonna change my way of thinking. *Contemporary Psychology, 41,* 258–259.

Braun, B. G. (1988). *The treatment of multiple personality disorder.* Washington, DC: American Psychiatric Press.

Brehm, S. S., & Kassin, S. M. (1996). *Social psychology* (3rd ed.). Boston: Houghton Mifflin.

Breier, A. (Ed.). (1996). *The new pharmacotherapy of schizophrenia.* Washington, DC: American Psychiatric Association.

Brickman, P., Coates, D., & Janoff-Bulman, R. J. (1978). Lottery winners and accident victims: Is happiness relative? *Journal of Personality and Social Psychology, 36,* 917–927.

Brim, G. (1992, December 7). Commentary, *Newsweek,* p. 52.

Brim, G. (1992). *Ambition: How we manage success and failure throughout our lives.* New York: Basic Books.

Brislin, R. W. (Ed.). (1990). Applied cross-cultural psychology. An introduction. *Applied cross-cultural psychology.* Newbury Park, CA: Sage.

Broman, C. L. (1996). Coping with personal problems. In H. W. Neighbors & J. S. Jackson (Eds.), *Mental health in Black America.* Newbury Park, CA: Sage.

Broskowski, A. T. (1995). The evolution of health care: Implications for the training and careers of psychologists. *Professional Psychology, 26,* 156–162.

Broverman, I., Broverman, D., Clarkson, F., Rosenkrantz, P., & Vogel, S. (1970). Sex-role stereotypes and clinical judgments of mental health. *Journal of Consulting and Clinical Psychology, 34,* 1–7.

Broverman, I., Vogel, S., Boverman, D., Clarkson, F., & Rosenkranz, P. (1972). Sex-role stereotypes: A current appraisal. *Journal of Social Issues, 28,* 59–78.

Brower, I. O. (1989). Counseling Vietnamese. In D. R. Atkinson, G. Morten, & D. W. Sue (Eds.), *Counseling American minorities.* Dubuque, IA: Wm. C. Brown.

Brown, A., & Williams, K. R. (1993). Gender, intimacy, and lethal violence: Trends from 1976 through 1987. *Gender and Society, 7,* 78–98.

Brown, W. S., & Caetano, C. (1992). Conversion, cognition, and neuropsychology. In H. Newton Malony & S. Southard (Eds.), *Handbook of religious conversion.* Birmingham, AL: Religious Education Press.

Browne, C. R., Brown, J. V., Blumenthal, J., Anderson, L., & Johnson, P. (1993, March). *African-American fathering: The perception of mothers and sons.* Paper presented at the biennial meeting of the Society for Research in Child Development, New Orleans.

Brownell, K. D. (1993). Whether obesity should be treated. *Health Psychology, 10,* 303–310.

Brownell, K. D., & Cohen, L. R. (1995). Adherence to dietary regimens. *Behavioral Medicine, 20,* 226–242.

Brownell, K. D., & Fairburn, C. G. (Eds.). (1995). *Eating disorders and obesity.* New York: Guilford.

Brownell, K. D., & Rodin, J. (1994). The dieting maelstrom: Is it possible and advisable to lose weight? *American Psychologist, 9,* 781–791.

Brownell, K. D., & Rodin, J. (in press). Medical, metabolic, and psychological effects of weight cycling and weight variability. *Archives of Internal Medicine.*

Bruess, C. J., & Pearson, J. C. (1996). Gendered patterns in family communication. In J. T. Wood (Ed.), *Gendered relationships.* Mountain View, CA: Mayfield.

Brunswick, A. F., & Banaszak-Holl, J. (1996). HIV risk behavior and the health belief model. *Journal of Community Psychology, 24,* 44–65.

Bumpass, L., Sweet, J., & Martin, T. C. (1990). Changing patterns of remarriage. *Journal of Marriage and the Family, 52,* 747–756.

Buss, D. M. (1989). Sex differences in human mate preferences: Evolutionary hypotheses tested in 37 cultures. *Behavioral and Brain Sciences, 12,* 1–49.

Buss, D. M. (1995). Evolutionary psychology: A new paradigm for psychological science. *Psychological Inquiry, 6,* 1–30.

Buss, D. M. (1995). Psychological sex differences: Origins through sexual selection. *American Psychologist, 50,* 164–168.

Buss, D. M. (1996). Paternity uncertainty and the complex repertoire of human mating strategies. *American Psychologist, 51,* 161–162.

Buss, D. M., & Schmitt, D. P. (1993). Sexual strategies theory: An evolutionary perspective on human mating. *Psychological Review, 100,* 204–232.

Butler, R. N. (1993). Did you say 'sarcopenia'? *Geriatrics, 48,* 11–12.

Butters, N., Delis, D., & Lucas, J. (1995). Clinical assessment of memory disorders in amnesia and dementia. *Annual Review of Psychology, 46.* Palo Alto, CA: Annual Reviews.

Byar, C. O., & Shainberg, L. W. (1997). *Dimensions of human sexuality* (5th ed.). Madison, WI: Brown & Benchmark.

C

Cain, D. J. (1996). A person-centered therapist's perspective on Ruth. In G. Corey (Ed.), *Case approach to counseling and psychotherapy* (4th ed.). Pacific Grove, CA: Brooks/Cole.

Caldwell, C. H. (1996). Predisposing, enabling, and need factors related to help-seeking in Black women. In H. W. Neighbors & J. S. Jackson (Eds.), *Mental health in Black America.* Newbury Park, CA: Sage.

Cameron, N. (1963). *Personality development and psychopathology.* Boston: Houghton Mifflin.

Campbell, A. (1981). *The sense of well-being in America: Recent patterns and trends.* New York: McGraw-Hill.

Capaldi, E. (Ed.). (1996). *Why we eat what we eat.* Washington, DC: American Psychological Association.

Carkenord, D. M., & Bullington, J. (1995). Bringing cognitive dissonance to the classroom. In M. E. Ware & D. E. Johnson (Eds.), *Demonstrations and activities in teaching of psychology* (Vol. 3). Hillsdale, NJ: Erlbaum.

Carroll, L. (1916). *Alice's adventures in Wonderland.* New York: Bantam.

Carstensen, L. L., Hanson, K. A., & Freund, A. M. (1995). Selection and compensation in adulthood. In R. A. Dixon & L. Backman (Eds.), *Compensating for psychological deficits and declines.* Hillsdale, NJ: Erlbaum.

Carter, B., & McGoldrick, M. (1989). Overview: The changing family life cycle—A framework for family therapy. In B. Carter & M. McGoldrick (Eds.), *The changing family life cycle* (2nd ed.). Boston: Allyn & Bacon.

Casas, J. M., & San Miguel, S. (1993). Beyond questions and discussion: There is a need for action. *Counseling Psychologist, 21,* 233–239.

Cash, T. F. (1990). The psychology of physical appearance: Aesthetics, attributes, and images. In T. F. Cash & T. Pruzinsky (Eds.), *Body images: Development, deviance, and change.* New York: Guilford.

Cassell, C. (1984). *Swept away: Why women fear their own sexuality.* New York: Simon & Schuster.

Castro, F. G., & Magaña, D. (1988). A course in health promotion in ethnic minority populations. In P. A. Bronstein & K. Quina (Eds.), *Teaching a psychology of people.* Washington, DC: American Psychological Association.

Cauce, A. M. (1996, June). *Culture and ethnicity: Between or within—Which is it?* Informal talk at the Family Research Summer Consortium, San Diego.

Chance, P. (1979). *Learning and behavior.* Belmont, CA: Wadsworth.

Chang, E. C. (1996). Cultural differences in optimism, pessimism, and coping. *Journal of Counseling Psychology, 43,* 113–123.

Chase-Lansdale, P. L. (1996, June). *Effects of divorce on mental health through the life span.* Informal talk at the Family Research Summer Consortium, San Diego.

Chase-Lansdale, P. L., & Brooks-Gunn, J. (Eds.). (1996). *Escape from poverty.* New York: Cambridge University Press.

Chiasson, C. A., & Hayes, L. (1993). The effects of subtle differences between listeners and speakers on the referential speech of college freshmen. *Psychological Record, 43,* 13–24.

Chiriboga, D. A. (1982). Adaptation to marital separation in later and earlier life. *Journal of Gerontology, 37,* 109–114.

Chmiel, N. (1997). Psychology in the workplace. In P. Scott & C. Spencer (Eds.), *Psychology.* Cambridge, MA: Blackwell.

Chodorow, N. J. (1989). *Feminism and psychoanalytic theory.* New Haven, CT: Yale University Press.

Chow, E. N., Wilkinson, D., & Baca Zinn, M. (1996). *Race, class, and gender: Common bonds, different voices.* Newbury Park, CA: Sage.

Christensen, L. (1996). *Diet-behavior relationships.* Washington, DC: American Psychological Association.

Christiansen, A., & Pasch, L. (1993). The sequence of marital conflict. *Clinical Psychology Review, 13,* 3–14.

Cicchetti, D., Beeghly, M., Carlson, V., Coster, W., Gersten, M., Rieder, C., & Kegan, R. (1991). Development and psychopathology: Lessons from the study of maltreated children. In D. P. Keating & H. G. Rosen (Eds.), *Constructivist perspectives on atypical development.* Hillsdale, NJ: Erlbaum.

Clark, D. A., & Beck, A. T. (1989). Cognitive theory and therapy of anxiety and depression. In P. C. Kendall & D. Watson (Eds.), *Anxiety and depression.* San Diego: Academic Press.

Clark, K. B., & Clark, M. P. (1939). The development of self and the emergence of racial identification in Negro preschool children. *Journal of Social Psychology, 10,* 591–599.

Clark, L. A., Watson, D., & Reynolds, S. (1995). Diagnosis and classification in psychopathology. *Annual Review of Psychology, 46.* Palo Alto, CA: Annual Reviews.

Clark, R. D., & Hatfield, E. (1989). Gender differences in receptivity to sexual offers. *Journal of Psychology and Human Sexuality, 2,* 39–55.

Clausen, J. A. (1993). *American lives.* New York: Free Press.

Clemens, A. W., & Axelson, L. J. (1985). The not-so-empty nest: The return of the fledgling adult. *Family Relations, 34,* 259–264.

Clifford, B. R., Bunter, B., & McAleer, J. L. (1995). *Television and children.* Hillsdale, NJ: Erlbaum.

Cloninger, S. C. (1996). *Theories of personality* (2nd ed.). Upper Saddle River, NJ: Prentice Hall.

Cochran, S. D., & Mays, V. M. (1990). Sex, lies, and HIV. *New England Journal of Medicine, 322* (11), 774–775.

Cohen, L. A. (1987, November). Diet and cancer. *Scientific American,* pp. 128–137.

Cohen, R. L., & Borsoi, D. (1996). The role of gestures in description-communication: A cross-sectional study of aging. *Journal of Nonverbal Behavior, 20,* 45–64.

Colby, A., Kohlberg, L., Gibbs, J., & Lieberman, M. (1983). A longitudinal study of moral judgment. *Monographs of the Society for Research in Child Development, 48*(21, Serial No. 201).

Coleman, L. (1996, March). *What does it mean to be a Black man or a Black woman?* Paper presented at the meeting of the Society for Research on Adolescence, Boston.

Coleman, M., & Ganong, L. H. (1990). Remarriage and stepfamily research in the 1980s: Increased interest in an old form. *Journal of Marriage and the Family, 52,* 925–939.

College Board Commission on Precollege Guidance and Counseling. (1986). *Keeping the options open.* New York: College Entrance Examination Board.

Comas-Diaz, L. (1993). Hispanic/Latino communities: Psychological implications. In D. R. Atkinson, G. Morten, & D. W. Sue (Eds.), *Counseling American minorities.* Madison, WI: Brown & Benchmark.

Conger, J. J. (1988). Hostages to the future: Youth, values, and the public interest. *American Psychologist, 43,* 291–300.

Connolly, N. K., & Williams, M. E. (1993). Plagues and tangles in approaching dementia. *Journal of Gerontology, 33,* 133–136.

Coombs, R. H. (1991). Marital status and personal well-being: A literature review. *Family Relations, 40,* 97–102.

Cooper, K. (1970). *The new aerobics.* New York: Bantam.

Coopersmith, S. (1967). *The antecedents of self-esteem.* New York: W. H. Freeman.

Cornelius, R. R. (1996). *The science of emotion.* Upper Saddle River, NJ: Prentice Hall.

Cortes, J. B., & Gatti, F. M. (1970, April). Physique and propensity. *Psychology Today,* pp. 42–44.

Costa, P. T. (1988, August). *Personality continuity and the changes of adult life.* Paper presented at the American Psychological Association, Atlanta.

Costa, P. T., & McRae, R. R. (1995). Solid ground in the wetlands of personality: A reply to Block. *Psychological Bulletin, 117,* 216–220.

Costanzo, M., & Archer, D. (1995). A method for teaching about verbal and nonverbal communication. In M. E. Ware & D. E. Johnson (Eds.), *Demonstrations and activities in teaching of psychology* (Vol. 3). Hillsdale, NJ: Erlbaum.

Cotton, N. (1979). The familial incidence of alcoholism: A review. *Journal of Studies on Alcohol, 40,* 89–116.

Cowan, C. P., Cowan, P. A., Heming, G., & Boxer, C. (1995, March). *Preventive interventions with parents of preschoolers.* Paper presented at the biennial meeting of the Society for Research in Child Development, Indianapolis.

Cowan, P. A. (1991). Individual and family life transitions: A proposal for a new definition. In P. A. Cowan & E. M. Hetherington (Eds.), *Family transitions.* Hillsdale, NJ: Erlbaum.

Crooks, R., & Bauer, K. (1996). *Our sexuality* (6th ed.). Pacific Grove, CA: Brooks/Cole.

Crosby, F. J. (1991). *Juggling.* New York: Free Press.

Crosby, F. J., & Jasker, K. L. (1993). Women and men at home and at work: Realities and illusions. In S. Oskamp & M. Costanzo (Eds.), *Gender issues in contemporary society.* Newbury Park, CA: Sage.

Cross, W. E. (1972). The Negro-to-Black conversion experience. *Black World, 20,* 13–27.

Csikszentmihalyi, M. (1990). *Flow.* New York: Harper & Row.

Culbertson, F. M. (1991, August). *Mental health of women: An international journey.* Paper presented at the meeting of the American Psychological Association, San Francisco.

Cunningham, M. R., Roberts, A. R., Barbee, A. P., Druen, P. B., & Wu, C. (1995). "Their ideas of beauty are, on the whole, the same as ours": Consistency and variability in the cross-cultural perception of female physical attractiveness. *Journal of Personality and Social Psychology, 68,* 261–279.

Cutrona, C. E. (1982). Transition to college: Loneliness and the process of social adjustment. In L. A. Peplau & D. Perlman (Eds.), *Loneliness: A sourcebook of current theory, research and therapy.* New York: Wiley.

D

Damon, W., & Hart, D. (1988). *Self-understanding in childhood and adolescence.* New York: Cambridge University Press.

d'Ansia, G. I. D. (1989). Familial analysis of panic disorder and agoraphobia. *Journal of Affective Disorders, 17,* 1–8.

Darley, J. M., & Latané, B. (1968). Bystander intervention in emergencies: Diffusion of responsibility. *Journal of Personality and Social Psychology, 8,* 337–383.

Darling, C. A., Kallon, D. J., & Van Duesen, J. E. (1984). Sex in transition, 1900–1984. *Journal of Youth and Adolescence, 13,* 385–399.

Darton, N. (1990, June 4). Mommy vs. Mommy. *Newsweek,* pp. 64–67.

Davis, J. H. (1996). Group decision making and quantitative judgments: A consensus model. In E. H. Witte & J. H. Davis (Eds.), *Understanding group behavior* (Vol. 1). Hillsdale, NJ: Erlbaum.

Davis, K. (1996). *Families.* Pacific Grove, CA: Brooks/Cole.

Davis, K. E. (1985, February). Near and dear: Friendship and love compared. *Psychology Today,* pp. 22–29.

Day, J. M., & Tappan, M. (1996). The narrative approach to moral development: From the epistemic subject to dialogical selves. *Human Development, 32,* 67–82.

de Jong-Gierveld, J. (1987). Developing and testing a model of loneliness. *Journal of Personality and Social Psychology, 53,* 119–128.

DeAngelis, T. (1996, March). Women's contributions large; recognition isn't. *APA Monitor, 27,* 12–13.

Denmark, F. L. (1992). The thirty-something woman: To career or not to career. In B. R. Wainrib (Ed.), *Gender issues across the life cycle.* New York: Springer.

Denmark, F. L. (1994). Engendering psychology. *American Psychologist, 49,* 329–334.

Denmark, F. L., & Paludi, M. A. (Eds.). (1993). *Handbook on the psychology of women.* Westport, CT: Greenwood Press.

Denmark, F. L., Russo, N. F., Frieze, I. H., Sechzur, J. (1988). Guidelines for avoiding sexism in psychological research: A report of the ad hoc committee on nonsexist research. *American Psychologist, 43,* 582–585.

DePaulo, B. M. (1994). Spotting lies: Can humans learn to do better? *Current Directions in Psychological Science, 3,* 83–86.

DeSpelder, L. A., & Strickland, A. L. (1996). *The last dance* (4th ed.). Mountain View, CA: Mayfield.

DeVito, J. A. (1996). *The interpersonal communication book* (7th ed.). New York: Harper Collins.

Dewey, J. (1933). *How we think: A restatement of the relation of reflective thinking to the educative process.* Lexington, MA: D. C. Heath.

Dickson, G. L. (1990). A feminist post-structuralist analysis of the knowledge of menopause. *Advances in Nursing Science, 12,* 15–31.

Diener, E. (1984). Subjective well-being. *Psychological Bulletin, 95,* 542–575.

Diener, E. (1984). Subjective well-being. *Psychological Bulletin, 109,* 125–129.

DiNicola, D. D., & DiMatteo, M. R. (1984). Practitioners, patients, and compliance with medical regimens: A social psychological perspective. In A. Baum, S. E. Taylor, & J. E. Singer (Eds.), *Handbook of psychology and health* (Vol. 4). Hillsdale, NJ: Erlbaum.

Dixon, R. A., & Backman, L. (1995). Concept of compensation. In R. A. Dixon & L. Backman (Eds.), *Compensating for psychological deficits and declines.* Hillsdale, NJ: Erlbaum.

Dohrenwend, B. S., & Shrout, P. E. (1985). "Hassles" in the conceptualization and measurement of life stress variables. *American Psychologist, 40,* 780–785.

Dolezal, S. L., Davison, G. C., & DeQuattro, V. (1996, March). *Hostile behavior, Type A, cardiac damage and neuroendocrine response in hostility-provoking social interactions.* Paper presented at the meeting of the American Psychosomatic Society, Williamsburg, VA.

Donnerstein, E. (1980). Aggressive erotica and violence against women. *Journal of Personality and Social Psychology, 39*, 269–277.

Donnerstein, E. (1987, May). *Pornography, sex, and violence.* Invited presentation, University of Texas at Dallas.

Draguns, J. G. (1990). Applications of cross-cultural psychology in the field of mental health. In R. W. Brislin (Ed.), *Applied cross-cultural psychology.* Newbury Park, CA: Sage.

Dryer, P. H. (1982). Sexuality during adolescence. In B. B. Wolman (Ed.), *Handbook of developmental psychology.* Englewood Cliffs, NJ: Prentice Hall.

Duckett, E., & Richards, M. H. (1996, March). *Fathers' time in child care and the father-child relationship.* Paper presented at the meeting of the Society for Research on Adolescence, Boston.

Durkeim, E. (1897). *Le suicide: Etude sociologie.* Paris: Alcan.

Durup, M. J., & Leiter, M. P. (1995, August). *Role of environmental resources in managing family and work.* Paper presented at the meeting of the American Psychological Association, New York City.

E

Eagly, A. H. (1995). The science and politics of comparing men and women. *American Psychologist, 50*, 145–158.

Eagly, A. H. (1996). Differences between women and men. *American Psychologist, 51*, 158–159.

Eagly, A. H., & Crowley, M. (1986). Gender and helping behavior: A meta-analytic review of the social psychological literature. *Psychological Bulletin, 100*, 283–308.

East, P., & Felice, M. E. (1996). *Adolescent pregnancy and parenting.* Hillsdale, NJ: Erlbaum.

Ebata, A. T., & Moos, R. H. (1989, April). *Coping and adjustment in four groups of adolescents.* Paper presented at the biennial meeting of the Society for Research in Child Development, Kansas City.

Eckert, E. D., Heston, L. L., & Bouchard, T. J. (1981). MZ twins reared apart. Preliminary findings of psychiatric disturbances and trait. In L. Gedda, P. Paris, & W. D. Nance (Eds.), *Twin research* (Vol. 1). New York: Alan Liss.

Edelman, M. W. (1987). *Families in peril: An agenda for social change.* New York: Alan Guttmacher Institute.

Eden, D., & Aviram, A. (in press). Self-efficacy training to speed reemployment: Helping people to help themselves. *Journal of Applied Psychology.*

Edmonds, M. Mc. (1990). The health of the black aged female. In Z. Harel, E. A. KcKinney, & M. Williams (Eds.), *Black aged.* Newbury Park, CA: Sage.

Ehrhardt, A. A. (1987). A transactional perspective on the development of gender differences. In J. M. Reinisch, L. A. Rosenblum, & S. A. Sanders (Eds.), *Masculinity/femininity: Basic perspectives.* New York: Oxford University Press.

Eichorn, D. H., Clausen, J. A., Haan, N., Honzik, M. P., & Mussen, P. H. (Eds.). (1981). *Present and past in middle life.* New York: Academic Press.

Ekman, P., & Friesen, W. (1974). Detecting deception from the body or face. *Journal of Personality and Social Psychology, 29*, 288–298.

Ekman, P., & O'Sullivan, M. (1991). Who can catch a liar? *American Psychologist, 46*, 913–920.

Ellis, A. (1962). *Reason and emotion in psychotherapy.* New York: Lyle Stuart.

Ellis, A. (1993). Reflections on rational-emotive therapy. *Journal of Consulting and Clinical Psychology, 61*, 199–201.

Ellis, A. (1996). A rational emotive behavior therapist's perspective on Ruth. In G. Corey (Ed.), *Case approach to counseling and psychotherapy.* (4th ed.). Pacific Grove, CA: Brooks/Cole.

Ellis, A., & Velton, E. (1992). *When AA doesn't work for you: Rational steps to quitting alcohol.* Fort Lee, NJ: Barricade Books.

Ellis, L., & Ames, M. A. (1987). Neurohormonal functioning and sexual orientation: A theory of homosexuality-heterosexuality. *Psychological Bulletin, 101*, 233–258.

Engler, B. (1995). *Personality theories* (4th ed.). Boston: Houghton Mifflin.

Epstein, N., & Eidelson, R. J. (1981). Unrealistic beliefs of clinical couples: Their relationship to expectations, goals, and satisfaction. *American Journal of Family Therapy, 9*, 13–21.

Epstein, S. (1973). The self-concept revisited: Or a theory of a theory. *American Psychologist, 28*, 404–416.

Erikson, E. H. (1962). *Young man Luther.* New York: W. W. Norton.

Erikson, E. H. (1968). *Identity: Youth and crisis.* New York: W. W. Norton.

Erikson, E. H. (1969). *Gandhi's truth.* New York: W. W. Norton.

Eshleman, J. R. (1991). *The family* (6th ed.). Boston: Allyn & Bacon.

Evans, B. J., & Whitfield, J. R. (Eds.). (1988). *Black males in the United States: An annotated bibliography from 1967 to 1987.* Washington, DC: American Psychological Association.

Everett, F., Proctor, N., & Cartmela, B. (1989). Providing psychological services to American Indian children and families. In D. R. Atkinson, G. Morten, & D. W. Sue (Eds.), *Counseling American minorities.* Dubuque, IA: Wm. C. Brown.

Eysenck, H. J. (1952). The effects of psychotherapy. An evaluation. *Journal of Consulting Psychology, 16*, 319–324.

Eysenck, H. J. (1967). *The biological basis of personality.* Springfield, IL: Charles C Thomas.

F

Faber, S. D., & Burns, J. W. (1996). Anger management style, degree of expressed anger, and gender influence cardiovascular recovery from interpersonal harassment. *Journal of Behavioral Medicine, 19*, 55–72.

Fairburn, C. G. (1995). *Overcoming binge eating.* New York: Guilford.

Falbo, T., & Polit, D. F. (1986). A quantitative review of the only-child literature. Research evidence and theory development. *Psychological Bulletin, 100*, 176–189.

Fast, J. (1970). *Body language.* New York: Pocket Books.

Fawzy, F. I., Fawzy, N. W., Hyun, C. S., Gutherie, D., Fahey, J. L., & Morton, D. (1993). Malignant melanoma: Effects of an early structured psychiatric intervention, coping, and affective state on recurrence and survival six years later. *Archives of General Psychiatry, 50*, 681–689.

Fein, S., Goethals, G. R., Kassin, S. M., & Cross, J. (1993, August). *Social influence and presidential debates.* Paper presented at the meeting of the American Psychological Association, Toronto.

Ferrell, O. C., & Hirt, G. (1996). *Business: A changing world* (2nd ed.). Burr Ridge, IL: Irwin.

Ferrett, S. K. (1996). *Strategies: Getting and keeping the job you want.* Burr Ridge, IL: Irwin.

Festinger, L. (1954). A theory of social comparison processes. *Human Relations, 7*, 117–140.

Festinger, L. (1957). *A theory of cognitive dissonance.* Evanston, IL: Row Peterson.

Finchum, F. D., & Bradbury, T. N. (1992). Attributions and behavior in marital interaction. *Journal of Personality and Social Psychology, 63*, 613–628.

First, M. B., Frances, A., & Pincus, H. A. (1995). *DSM-IV handbook for differential diagnosis.* Washington, DC: American Psychiatric Press.

Fish, S. (1993). Reverse racism of how the pot got to call the kettle black. *Atlantic Monthly, 272*, 128–136.

Fiske, S. T., Bersoff, D. N., Borgida, E., Deaux, K., & Heilman, M. E. (1991). Social science research on trial: Use of sex stereotyping research in *Price Waterhouse v. Hopkins. American Psychologist, 23*, 399–427.

Flaskerud, J. (1984). A comparison of perceptions of problematic behavior by six minority groups and mental health professionals. *Nursing Research, 33*, 190–228.

Flynn, B. S., Worden, J. K., Secker-Walker, R. H., Badger, G. J., & Geller, B. M. (1995). Cigarette smoking prevention effects of mass media and school interventions targeted to gender and age groups. *Journal of Health Education, 26*, S45–S51.

Foa, E. B., Steketze, G., & Young, M. C. (1984). Agoraphobia. *Clinical Psychology Review, 4*, 431–457.

Folkman, S., & Lazarus, R. S. (1980). An analysis of coping in a middle-aged community sample. *Journal of Health and Social Behavior, 21*, 219–239.

Fonnebo, V. (1985). The Tormso heart study: Coronary risk factors in Seventh-Day Adventists. *American Journal of Epidemiology, 112*, 789–793.

Ford, C., & Beach, F. (1951). *Patterns of sexual behavior.* New York: Harper.

Fox, R. E. (1995). The rape of psychotherapy. *Professional Psychology, 26*, 147–155.

Frager, R. (1970). Conformity and anticonformity in Japan. *Journal of Personality and Social Psychology, 15*, 203–210.

Frances, A., First, M. B., & Pincus, H. A. (1995). *DSM-IV guidebook.* Washington, DC: American Psychiatric Press.

Frances, A., & Ross, R. (1996). *DSM-IV case studies.* Washington, DC: American Psychiatric Association.

Frances, A. J., Pincus, H. A., & Widiger, T. A. (in press). DSM-IV and international communication in psychiatric diagnosis. In Y. Honda, M. Kastrup, & J. E. Mezzich (Eds.), *Psychiatric diagnosis: A world perspective.* New York: Springer.

Frank, E., & Kupfer, D. J. (1986). Psychotherapeutic approaches to treatment of recurrent unipolar depression. Work in progress. *Psychopharmacology Bulletin, 22*, 558–565.

Frank, J. D. (1982). Therapeutic components shared by all psychotherapies. In J. H. Harvey & M. M. Parks (Eds.), *Psychotherapy research and behavior change.* Washington, DC: American Psychological Association.

Freeman, J. (Ed.). (1995). *Women: A feminist perspective* (5th ed.). Mountain View, CA: Mayfield.

Freud, S. (1917). *A general introduction to psychoanalysis.* New York: Washington Square Press.

Friedman, M., & Rosenman, R. (1974). *Type A behavior and your heart.* New York: Knopf.

Fromm, E. (1947). *Man for himself.* New York: Holt Rinehart.

Fuhrman, A., & Burlingame, G. M. (1995). *Handbook of group psychotherapy.* New York: Wiley.

G

Gaines, S. O., Jr. (1994). Reciprocity of respect-denying behavior in male-female friendships. *Journal of Social and Personal Relationships, 11,* 5–24.

Galanter, M. (1989). *Cults: Faith, healing, and coercion.* New York: Oxford University Press.

Galen, M., & Palmer, A. T. (1994, January 31). White, male, and worried. *Business Week,* pp. 50–55.

Gallup, G. (1984, August–September). *Gallup Report,* Nos. 228 and 229, 2–9.

Gallup, G. H., & Newport, F. (1991). Belief in paranormal phenomena among adult Americans. *Skeptical Inquirer, 15,* 137–146.

Gallup, G. H., Jr., & Bezilla, R. (1992). *The religious young Americans.* Princeton, NJ: Gallup Institute.

Gallup Report. (1987). Legalized gay relations. *Gallup Report,* No. 254, p. 25.

Garbarino, J. (1985). *Adolescent development: An ecological perspective.* Columbus, OH: Merrill.

Garbarino, J., Guttman, E., & Seeley, J. W. (1986). *The psychologically battered child.* San Francisco: Jossey-Bass.

Gardner, J. M. (1995). The myth of the mental illness game: Sick is just a four letter word. In M. E. Ware & D. E. Johnson (Eds.), *Demonstrations and activities in psychology* (Vol. 3). Hillsdale, NJ: Erlbaum.

Garfein, A. J., & Herzog, A. R. (1995). Robust aging among the young-old, old-old, and oldest-old. *Journal of Gerontology, 50B,* S77–S87.

Garfield, S. L. (1995). *Psychotherapy* (2nd ed.). New York: Wiley.

Gatz, M. (1992). The mental health system and older adults. *American Psychologist, 47,* 741–751.

Gerson, K. (1986). *Hard choices: How women decide about work, career, and motherhood.* Berkeley, CA: University of California Press.

Gilligan, C. (1982). *In a different voice.* Cambridge, MA: Harvard University Press.

Gilligan, C. (1992, May). *Joining the resistance: Girls' development in adolescence.* Paper presented at the symposium on development and vulnerability in close relationships, Montreal.

Gilligan, C. (1996). The centrality of relationships in human development: A puzzle, some evidence, and a theory. In G. G. Noam & K. W. Fischer (Eds.), *Development and vulnerability in close relationships.* Hillsdale, NJ: Erlbaum.

Gilmore, D. O. (1990). *Manhood in the making.* New Haven, CT: Yale University Press.

Gim, R. H., Atkinson, D. R., & Kim, S. J. (1991). Asian-American acculturation, counselor ethnicity and cultural sensitivity, and ratings of counselors. *Journal of Counseling Psychology, 38,* 57–62.

Ginzberg, E. (1972). Toward a theory of occupational choice: A restatement. *Vocational Guidance Quarterly, 20,* 169–176.

Gjerde, P. (1985, April). *Adolescent depression and parental socialization patterns. A prospective study.* Paper presented at the biennial meeting of the Society for Research in Child Development, Toronto.

Gladding, S. T. (1995). *Group work* (2nd ed.). Upper Saddle River, NJ: Prentice Hall.

Glaser, R., Rice, J., Sheridan, J., Fertel, R., Stout, J. C., Speicher, C. E., Pinsky, D., Kotur, M., Post, A., Beck, M., & Kiecolt-Glaser, J. K. (1987). Stress-related immune suppression: Health implications. *Brain, Behavior, and Immunity, 1,* 7–20.

Glick, P. (1989). Remarried families, stepfamilies, and stepchildren: A brief demographic analysis. *Family Relations, 38,* 24–27.

Glick, P. C. (1988). The role of divorce in the changing family structure: Trends and variations. In S. A. Wolchick & P. Karoly (Eds.), *Children of divorce: Empirical perspectives on divorce.* New York: Gardner.

Glock, C. Y., & Stark, R. (1965). *Religion and society in tension.* Chicago: Rand McNally.

Glueckauf, R. L., Frank, R. G., Bond, G. R., & McGrew, J. H. (Eds.). (1996). *Psychological practice in a changing health care system.* New York: Springer.

Golan, N. (1986). *The perilous bridge.* New York: Free Press.

Goldberg, T. E., Berman, K. F., & Weinberger, D. R. (1995). Neuropsychology and neurophysiology of schizophrenia. *Current Opinion in Psychiatry, 8,* 34–40.

Goldin-Meadow, S., McNeill, D., & Singleton, J. (1996). Silence is liberating: Removing the handcuffs on grammatical expression in the manual modality. *Psychological Review, 103,* 34–55.

Goldstein, I. R., & Gilliam, P. (1990). Training system issues in the year 2000. *American Psychologist, 45,* 134–143.

Goldstein, M. J., & Palmer, J. O. (1975). *The experience of anxiety.* New York: Oxford University Press.

Goldstein, W. N. (1995). The borderline patient. *American Journal of Psychotherapy, 49,* 317–337.

Goodchilds, J. D., & Zellman, G. L. (1984). Sexual signaling and sexual aggression in adolescent relationships. In N. M. Malamuth & E. D. Donnerstein (Eds.), *Pornography and sexual aggression.* New York: Academic Press.

Goodman, G. (1988). Silences. In G. Goodman & G. Esterly (Eds.), *The talk book.* New York: Ballantine.

Goodman, G., & Esterly, G. (1988). *The talk book.* New York: Ballantine.

Goodman, M. (1992). Gender issues of the young adult male. In B. R. Wainrib (Ed.), *Gender issues across the life cycle.* New York: Springer.

Goodstein, L. D., & Calhoun, J. F. (1982). *Understanding abnormal behavior.* Reading, MA: Addison-Wesley.

Gottesman, K. I., & Shields, J. (1982). *The schizophrenic puzzle.* New York: Cambridge University Press.

Gottfredson, L. (1980). Construct validity of Holland's occupational typology in terms of prestige, census, Department of Labor, and other classification systems. *Journal of Applied Psychology, 651,* 697–714.

Gould, M., Wunsch-Hitzig, R., & Dohrenwend, B. S. (1981). Estimating the prevalence of childhood psychopathology. *Journal of American Academy of Child Psychiatry, 20,* 462–476.

Gould, R. L. (1978). *Transformations: Growth and change in adult life.* New York: Simon & Schuster.

Greenberg, J. (1996). *Managing behavior in organizations.* Upper Saddle River, NJ: Prentice Hall.

Greenberger, E., & Steinberg, L. (1986). *When teenagers work: The psychological and social costs of adolescent employment.* New York: Basic Books.

Grevious, C. (1985). The role of the family therapist with low-income black families. *Family Therapy, 12,* 115–122.

Grush, J. E. (1980). Impact of candidate expenditures, regionality, and prior outcomes on the 1976 Democratic presidential primaries. *Journal of Personality and Social Psychology, 38,* 337–347.

Guisinger, S., Cowan, P., & Schuldberg, D. (1989). Changing parent and spouse relations in the first years of remarriage of divorced fathers. *Journal of Marriage and the Family, 51,* 445–456.

Gur, R. C., Mozley, L. H., Mozley, P. D., Resnick, S. M., Karp, J. S., Alavi, A., Arnold, S. E., & Gur, R. E. (1995). Sex differences in regional cerebral glucose metabolism during a resting state. *Science, 267,* 528–531.

H

Hall, C. C. I., Evans, B. J., & Selice, S. (Eds.). (1989). *Black females in the United States.* Washington, DC: American Psychological Association.

Hall, E. (1969). *The hidden dimension.* Garden City, NY: Anchor.

Halonen, J. (1995). Demystifying critical thinking. *Teaching of Psychology, 22,* 75–81.

Halonen, J., & Santrock, J. W. (1996). *Psychology: The contexts of behavior* (2nd ed.). Madison, WI: Brown & Benchmark.

Handelsman, M. M., & Frielander, B. L. (1995). The use of an experiential exercise to teach about assertiveness. In M. E. Ware & D. E. Johnson (Eds.), *Demonstrations and activities in teaching of psychology* (Vol. 3). Hillsdale, NJ: Erlbaum.

Hanna, S. L. (1995). *Person to person* (2nd ed.). Upper Saddle River, NJ: Prentice Hall.

Hansell, S. (1991). The meaning of stress. *Contemporary Psychology, 36,* 112–114.

Hare-Muston, R., & Marecek, J. (1988). The meaning of difference: Gender theory, postmodernism, and psychology. *American Psychologist, 43,* 455–464.

Harris, A. S. (1996). *Living with paradox: An introduction to Jungian psychology.* Pacific Grove, CA: Brooks/Cole.

Harrison, C. A. (1991). Older women in our society: America's silent, invisible majority. *Educational Gerontology, 17,* 111–122.

Harter, S. (1990). Self and identity development. In S. S. Feldman & G. R. Elliott (Eds.), *At the threshold: The developing adolescent.* Cambridge, MA: Harvard University Press.

Harvey, J. H. (1995). *Odyssey of the heart.* New York: W. H. Freeman.

Hatcher, R., & others. (1988). *Contraceptive technology, 1988–1989* (14th ed.). New York: Irvington.

Hatfield, E., & Sprecher, S. (1986). *Mirror, mirror . . . : The importance of looks in everyday life.* Albany: State University of New York Press.

Hayflick, L. (1977). The cellular basis for biological aging. In C. E. Finch & L. Hayflick (Eds.), *Handbook of the biology of aging.* New York: Van Nostrand.

Heider, F. (1958). *The psychology of interpersonal relations.* New York: Wiley.

Heilman, M. E., Block, C. J., & Lucas, J. A. (1992). Presumed incompetent? Stigmatization and affirmative action efforts. *Journal of Applied Psychology, 77,* 536–544.

Helms, J. E. (1990, August). *Black and White racial identity theory and professional interracial collaboration.* Paper presented at the meeting of the American Psychological Association, Boston.

Helsing, K., & Szklo, M. (1981). Mortality after bereavement. *American Journal of Epidemiology, 114,* 41–52.

Hernandez, G. G. (1991). Not so benign neglect: Researchers ignore ethnicity in defining family caregiver burden and recommending services. *Gerontologist, 31,* 271.

Hersch, L. (1995). Adapting to health care reform and managed care: Three strategies for survival and growth. *Professional Psychology, 26,* 16–26.

Hetherington, E. M. (1993, March). *An overview of the Virginia Longitudinal Study of divorce and remarriage with a focus on early adolescence.* Paper presented at the biennial meeting of the Society for Research in Child Development, New Orleans.

Hetherington, E. M. (1995, March). *The changing American family and the well-being of children.* Paper presented at the meeting of the Society for Research in Child Development, Indianapolis.

Hetherington, E. M., & Blechman, E. A. (Eds.). (1996). *Stress, coping, and resiliency in children and families.* Hillsdale, NJ: Erlbaum.

Hetherington, E. M., Cox, M., & Cox, R. (1982). Effects of divorce on children and parents. In M. E. Lamb (Ed.), *Nontraditional families.* Hillsdale, NJ: Erlbaum.

Hetherington, E. M., & Stanley-Hagan, M. M. (1995). Parenting in divorced and remarried families. In M. H. Bornstein (Ed.), *Children and parenting* (Vol. 4). Hillsdale, NJ: Erlbaum.

Higgins, E. T. (1984). *Self-discrepancy: A theory relating self and affect.* Unpublished manuscript, New York University.

Higgins, E. T. (1987). Self-discrepancy: A theory relating self and affect. *Psychological Review, 94,* 319–340.

Hines, M. (1982). Prenatal gonadal hormones and sex differences in human behavior. *Psychological Bulletin, 92,* 56–80.

Hines, T. (1988). *Pseudoscience and the paranormal.* Buffalo, NY: Prometheus Books.

Hirsch, C. H., Davies, H. D., Boatwright, F., & Ochango, G. (1993). Effects of a nursing-home respite admission on veterans with advanced dementia. *Gerontologist, 33,* 532–528.

Hobfall, S. E. (1996). Social support. In N. Vanzetti & S. Duck (Eds.), *A lifetime of relationships.* Pacific Grove, CA: Brooks/Cole.

Hobfoll, S. E. (1989). Conversation of resources: A new attempt at conceptualizing stress. *American Psychologist, 44,* 513–524.

Hofferth, S. L. (1990). Trends in adolescent sexual activity, contraception, and pregnancy in the United States. In J. Bancroft & J. M. Reinisch (Eds.), *Adolescence and puberty.* New York: Oxford University Press.

Hoff-Ginsberg, E., & Tardif, T. (1995). Socioeconomic status and parenting. In M. H. Bornstein (Ed.), *Children and parenting* (Vol. 2). Hillsdale, NJ: Erlbaum.

Hogan, R. (1987, August). *Conceptions of personality and the prediction of job performance.* Paper presented at the meeting of the American Psychological Association, New York.

Holcomb, H. H., Cascella, N. G., Thaker, G. K., Medoff, D. R., Dannals, R. F., & Tamminga, C. A. (1996). Functional sites of neuroleptic drug action in the human brain. *The American Journal of Psychiatry, 153,* 41–49.

Holland, J. L. (1973). *Making vocational choices: A theory of careers.* Englewood Cliffs, NJ: Prentice Hall.

Holland, J. L. (1987). Current status of Holland's theory of careers: Another perspective. *Career Development Quarterly, 36,* 24–30.

Holland, J. L. (1996). Exploring careers with a typology: What we have learned and some new directions. *American Psychologist, 51,* 397–406.

Hollender, M., & Mercer, A. (1976). Wish to be held and wish to hold in men and women. *Archives of General Psychiatry, 33,* 49–51.

Hollingshead, A. B., & Redlich, F. C. (1958). *Social class and mental illness.* New York: Wiley.

Hollingworth, L. S. (1914). Functional periodicity: An experimental study of the mental and motor abilities of women during menstruation. *Teachers College Contributions to Education,* No. 69.

Hollingworth, L. S. (1918). Sex differences in mental traits. *Psychological Bulletin, 13,* 377–384.

Holmbeck, G. N. (1996). A model of family relational transformations during the transition to adolescence: Parent-adolescent conflict and adaptation. In J. A. Graber, J. Brooks-Gunn, & A. C. Petersen (Eds.), *Transitions through adolescence.* Hillsdale, NJ: Erlbaum.

Holmes, D. S., Solomon, S., Cappo, B. M., & Greenberg, J. L. (1983). Effects of transcendental meditation versus resting on physiological and subjective arousal. *Journal of Personality and Social Psychology, 44,* 1244–1252.

Holmes, T. H., & Rahe, R. H. (1967). The social readjustment rating scale. *Journal of Psychosomatic Research, 11,* 214–218.

Hood, R. W., Jr., Spilka, B., Hunsberger, B., & Gorsuch, R. (1996). *Psychology of religion: An empirical approach* (2nd ed.). New York: Guilford.

Horm, J., & Anderson, K. (1993). Who in America is trying to lose weight? *Annals of Internal Medicine, 119,* 672–676.

Horner, M. (1968). *Sex differences in achievement motivation and performance in competitive and non-competitive situations.* Unpublished dissertation, University of Michigan.

Horney, K. (1945). *Our inner conflicts.* New York: Norton.

Horwitz, L., Gabbard, G. O., Allen, J. G., Frieswyk, S. H., Colson, D. B., Newsom, G. E., & Coyne, L. (1996). *Borderline personality disorder.* Washington, DC: American Psychiatric Press.

Houston, M., & Wood, J. T. (1996). Difficult dialogues—Communicating across race and class. In J. T. Wood (Ed.), *Gendered relationships.* Mountain View, CA: Mayfield.

Howat, P. M., & Saxton, A. M. (1988). The incidence of bulimic behavior in a secondary and university school population. *Journal of Youth and Adolescence, 17,* 221–231.

Huang, L. N., & Gibbs, J. T. (1989). Future directions: Implications for research, training, and practice. In J. T. Gibbs & L. N. Huang (Eds.), *Children of color.* San Francisco: Jossey-Bass.

Huang, L. N., & Ying, Y. (1989). Chinese American children and adolescents. In J. T. Gibbs & L. N. Huang (Eds.), *Children of color.* San Francisco: Jossey-Bass.

Hubbard, L. R. (1989). *Scientology: The fundamentals of thought.* Los Angeles: Bridge.

Humphreys, K. (1996). Clinical psychologists as psychotherapists. *American Psychologist, 51,* 190–197.

Hunt, M. (1974). *Sexual behavior in the 1970s.* Chicago: Playboy.

Hurtado, S., Dey, E. L., & Trevino, J. G. (1994). *Exclusion or self-segregation? Interaction across racial/ethnic groups on college campuses.* Paper presented at the American Educational Research Association annual meeting.

Huston, A. (1995, August). *Children in poverty and public policy.* Paper presented at the meeting of the American Psychological Association, New York City.

Huston, A. C. (1983). Sex-typing. In P. H. Mussen (Ed.), *Handbook of child psychology* (4th ed., Vol. 4). New York: Wiley.

Hyatt, C. (1990). *Shifting gears: How to master career change and find the work that's right for you.* New York: Simon & Schuster.

Hyde, J. S. (1994). Meta-analysis and the psychology of women. In F. L. Denmark & M. A. Paludi (Eds.), *Handbook on the psychology of women.* Westport, CT: Greenwood.

Hyde, J. S. (1994). *Understanding human sexuality.* New York: McGraw-Hill.

Hyde, J. S., & Plant, E. A. (1995). Magnitude of psychological gender differences: Another side of the story. *American Psychologist, 50,* 159–161.

I

Ickovics, J. R. (1991, August). *Labor force diversity: A challenge to psychology.* Paper presented at the meeting of the American Psychological Association, San Francisco.

Ikels, C. (1989). Becoming a human being in theory and practice: Chinese views of human development. In D. I. Kertzer & K. W. Schaie (Eds.), *Age structuring in comparative perspective.* Hillsdale, NJ: Erlbaum.

Ilola, L. M. (1990). Culture and health. In R. W. Brislin (Ed.), *Applied cross-cultural psychology.* Newbury Park, CA: Sage.

Ingelhart, R., & Rabier, J. (1986). Aspirations adapt to situations—But why are the Belgians so much happier than the French? A cross-cultural analysis of the subjective quality of life. In F. M. Andrews (Ed.), *Research on the quality of life.* Ann Arbor: University of Michigan, Institute of Social Research.

Institute for Health Policy. (1993). *Substance abuse: Key indicators for policy.* Princeton, NJ: Robert Wood Johnson Foundation.

Irons, E. E., & Moore, G. W. (1985). *Black managers: The case of the banking industry.* New York: Praeger.

J

Jacob, K. A. (1981). The Mosher report. *American Heritage,* pp. 57–64.

James, W. (1890). *The principles of psychology.* New York: Dover.

James, W. (1902). *Varieties of religious experience.* New York: Longmans.

Jodl, K. M., & Dalton, R. (1996, March). *Longitudinal predictors of competence-at-a-cost in adolescents growing up in stepfamilies.* Paper presented at the meeting of the Society for Research on Adolescence, Boston.

Johnson, C. (1990, May). The new woman's ethics report. *New Woman, 6.*

Johnson, R. E., & others (1989). A seroepidemiologic survey of the prevalence of herpes simplex virus type 2 infection in the United States. *New England Journal of Medicine, 321,* 7–12.

Johnston, L., Bachman, J. G., & O'Malley, P. M. (1990). *Monitoring the future.* Ann Arbor: University of Michigan, Institute of Social Research.

Johnston, L. D., O'Malley, P. M., & Bachman, J. G. (1987). *National trends in drug use and related factors among American high school students and young adults, 1975–1986.* Ann Arbor: University of Michigan, Institute of Social Research.

Johnston, L. D., O'Malley, P. M., & Bachman, J. G. (1994). *National survey results on drug use from the Monitoring the Future study, 1975–1994.* Rockville, MD: National Institute on Drug Abuse.

Jones, A., & Seagull, A. (1977). Dimensions of the relationship between the Black client and the white therapist. *American Psychologist, 32,* 850–856.

Jones, E. E., & Pittman, T. S. (1982). Toward a general theory of strategic self-presentation. In J. Suls (Ed.), *Psychological perspectives on the self* (Vol. 1). Hillsdale, NJ: Erlbaum.

Jones, J. M. (1991). Psychological models of race: What have they been and what should they be? In J. D. Goodchilds (Ed.), *Psychological perspectives on human diversity in America.* Washington, DC: American Psychological Association.

Jones, J. M. (1994). The African American: A duality dilemma? In W. J. Lonner & R. Malpass (Eds.), *Psychology and culture.* Needham Heights, MA: Allyn & Bacon.

Jones, L. (1996). *HIV/AIDS: What to do about it.* Pacific Grove, CA: Brooks/Cole.

Jourard, S. M. (1971). *The transparent self.* New York: Van Nostrand Reinhold.

Jung, C. G. (1917). *Analytic psychology.* New York: Moffat, Yard.

Jussim, L. (1991). Social perception and social reality: A reflection-construction model. *Psychological Review, 98,* 54–73.

K

Kagitcibasi, C. (1995). Is psychology relevant to global human development issues? *American Psychologist, 50,* 293–300.

Kagitcibasi, C. (1996). *Family and human development across cultures.* Hillsdale, NJ: Erlbaum.

Kalichman, S. C. (1996). *Answering your questions about AIDS.* Washington, DC: American Psychological Association.

Kalick, S. M., & Hamilton, T. E. (1986). The matching hypothesis reexamined. *Journal of Personality and Social Psychology, 51,* 673–682.

Kalish, R. A. (1987). Death. In G. L. Maddox (Ed.), *Encyclopedia of aging.* New York: Springer.

Kalish, R. A., & Reynolds, D. K. (1976). *An overview of death and ethnicity.* Farmingdale, NY: Baywood.

Kandel, D. B. (1991). Drug use, epidemiology and developmental stages of involvement. In R. M. Lerner, A. C. Petersen, & J. Brooks-Gunn (Eds.), *Encyclopedia of adolescence* (Vol. 1). New York: Garland.

Kane, J. M., & Barnes, T. R. E. (1995). Schizophrenia research: Challenges and opportunities. *Current Opinion in Psychiatry, 8,* 19–20.

Kanner, A. D., Coyne, J. C., Schaefer, C., & Lazarus, R. S. (1981). Comparisons of two modes of stress measurement. Daily hassles and uplifts versus major life event. *Journal of Behavioral Medicine, 4,* 1–39.

Kantrowitz and others (1992). Teens and AIDS. *Time.*

Kaplan, H. (1974). *The new sex therapy.* New York: Times Books.

Karasek, R. (1979). Job demands, job decision latitude, and mental strain: Implications for job redesign. *Administrative Science Quarterly, 24,* 285–307.

Karasek, R. (1981). Job socialization and job strain: The implication of two related psychosocial mechanisms for job design. In B. Gardell & G. Johansson (Eds.), *Working life.* New York: Wiley.

Karney, B. R., Bradbury, T. N., Fincham, F. D., & Sullivan, K. T. (1994). The role of negative affectivity in the association between attributions and marital satisfaction. *Journal of Personality and Social Psychology, 66,* 413–424.

Katigbak, M. S., Church, A. T., & Akamine, T. X. (1996). Cross-cultural generalizability of personality dimensions: Relating indigenous and imported dimensions in two cultures. *Journal of Personality and Social Psychology, 70,* 99–114.

Keating, C. F. (1994). World without words: Messages from face and body. In W. J. Lonner & R. Malpass, *Psychology and culture.* Needham Heights, MA: Allyn & Bacon.

Kelley, H. H., & Thibaut, J. (1978). *Interpersonal relations: A theory of interdependence.* New York: Wiley.

Kendrick, J. W., & Kendrick, J. B. (1988). *Personal productivity.* Armonk, NY: M. E. Sharpe.

Kennedy, S., Kiecolt-Glaser, J. K., & Glaser, R. (1988). Immunological consequences of acute and chronic stressors: Mediating role of interpersonal relationships. *British Journal of Psychiatry, 61,* 77–85.

Kenniston, K. (1970). Youth: A "new" stage of life. *American Scholar, 39,* 631–654.

Kenrick, D. T., Montello, D. R., Gutierres, S. E., & Trost, M. R. (1993). Effects of physical attractiveness on affect and perceptual judgments: When social comparison overrides social reinforcement. *Personality and Social Psychology Bulletin, 19,* 195–199.

Kephart, W. M. (1967). Some correlates of romantic love. *Journal of Marriage and the Family, 29,* 470–474.

Kiecolt-Glaser, J. K., Dura, J. R., Speicher, C. E., Trask, O. J., & Glaser, R. (1991). Spousal caregivers of dementia victims: Longitudinal changes in immunity and health. *Psychosomatic Medicine, 53,* 345–362.

Kiecolt-Glaser, J. K., Fisher, L. D., Ogrocki, P., Stout, J. C., Speicher, C. E., & Glaser, R. (1987). Marital quality, marital disruption, and immune function. *Psychosomatic Medicine, 49,* 13–34.

Kiecolt-Glaser, J. K., & Glaser, R. (1988). Behavioral influences on immune function. In T. Field, P. McCabe, & N. Schneiderman (Eds.), *Stress and coping across development.* Hillsdale, NJ: Erlbaum.

Kimble, G. A. (1989). Psychology from the standpoint of a generalist. *American Psychologist, 44,* 491–499.

King, B. M. (1996). *Human sexuality today* (2nd ed.). Upper Saddle River, NJ: Prentice Hall.

Kinsey, A. C., Pomeroy, W. B., & Martin, E. E. (1948). *Sexual behavior in the human male.* Philadelphia: Saunders.

Kirkpatrick, B., Buchanan, R. W., Waltrip, R. W., Jauch, D., & Carpenter, W. T. (1989). Diazepam treatment of early symptoms of schizophrenic relapse. *Journal of Nervous and Mental Disease, 177,* 52–53.

Kirschenbaum, H. (1995). *100 ways to enhance values and morality in schools and youth settings.* Boston: Allyn & Bacon.

Klonoff-Cohen, H. S., Edelstein, S. L., Lefkowitz, E. S., Srinivasan, I. P., Kaegi, D., Chang, J. C., and Wiley, K. J. (1995). The effect of passive smoke and tobacco exposure through breast milk on sudden infant death syndrome. *Journal of the American Medical Association, 293,* 795–798.

Knight, B. G., Teri, L., Wohlford, P., & Santos, J. (Eds.). (1996). *Mental health services for older adults.* Washington, DC: American Psychological Association.

Kobasa, N., Maddi, S., & Kahn, S. (1982). Hardiness and health. A prospective study. *Journal of Personality and Social Psychology, 42,* 168–177.

Kobasa, S. C., Maddi, S. R., Puccetti, M. C., & Zola, M. (1985). Relative effectiveness of hardiness, exercise, and social support as resources against illness. *Journal of Psychosomatic Research, 29,* 525–533.

Koester, L. S., & Clark, C. H. (1980, September). *Academic job satisfaction: Differences related to sex and marital status.* Paper presented at 88th annual meeting of the American Psychological Association, Montreal.

Kogan, N., & Black, K. (in press). *Gender and aging.* Cambridge, MA: Blackwell.

Kohlberg, L. (1966). A cognitive-developmental analysis of children's sex-role concepts and attitudes. In E. E. Maccoby (Ed.), *The development of sex differences.* Palo Alto, CA: Stanford University Press.

Kohlberg, L. (1969). Stage and sequence: The cognitive-developmental approach to socialization. In D. A. Goslin (Ed.), *Handbook of socialization theory and research.* Chicago: Rand McNally.

Kohlberg, L. (1976). Moral stages and moralization: The cognitive-developmental approach. In T. Lickona (Ed.), *Moral development and behavior.* New York: Holt, Rinehart & Winston.

Kohlberg, L. (1986). A current statement on some theoretical issues. In S. Modgil & C. Modgil (Eds.), *Lawrence Kohlberg.* Philadelphia: Falmer.

Kohlenberg, R. J., Tsai, M., & Kohlenberg, B. S. (1996). Functional analysis in behavior therapy. In M. Hersen & P. M. Miller (Eds.), *Progress in behavior modification* (Vol. 30). Pacific Grove, CA: Brooks/Cole.

Kohut, H. (1977). *The restoration of the self.* New York: International Universities Press.

Koran, L. M., & Litt, I. F. (1988). Housestaff well-being. *Western Journal of Medicine, 148*, 97–101.

Koss, M. P. (1993, August). *Sex gone wrong: Current perspectives on rape and sexual harassment.* Paper presented at the meeting of the American Psychological Association, Toronto.

Kramer, B. A. (1987). Electroconvulsive therapy use in geriatric depression. *Journal of Nervous and Mental Disease, 175*, 233–235.

Kramer, P. D. (1993). *Listening to Prózac.* New York: Penguin.

Kristof, A. L. (1996). Person-organization fit: An integrative review of its conceptualization, measurement, and implications. *Personnel Psychology, 49*, 1–51.

Kübler-Ross, E. (1969). *On death and dying.* New York: Macmillan.

Kübler-Ross, E. (1974). *Questions and answers on death and dying.* New York: Macmillan.

Kurtines, W. M., & Gewirtz, J. (Eds.). (1991). *Moral behavior and development: Advances in theory, research, and application.* Hillsdale, NJ: Erlbaum.

L

Labouvie-Vief, G. (1986, August). *Modes of knowing and life-span cognition.* Paper presented at the meeting of the American Psychological Association, Washington, DC.

LaCroix, A. Z., & Haynes, S. G. (1987). Gender differences in the health effects of workplace roles. In R. C. Barnett, L. Biener, & G. K. Baruch (Eds.), *Gender and stress.* New York: Free Press.

LaFromboise, T., Coleman, H. L. K., & Gerton, J. (1993). Psychological impact of biculturalism: Evidence and theory. *Psychological Bulletin, 114*, 395–412.

LaFromboise, T., & Trimble, J. (1996). Multicultural counseling theory and American-Indian populations. In D. W. Sue (Ed.), *Theory of multicultural counseling and therapy.* Pacific Grove, CA: Brooks/Cole.

LaFromboise, T. D. (1993). American Indian mental health policy. In D. R. Atkinson, G. Morten, & D. W. Sue (Eds.), *Counseling American minorities.* Madison, WI: Brown & Benchmark.

Lam, R. W., Goldner, E. M., & Grewal, A. (1996). Seasonality of symptoms in anorexia and bulimia nervosa. *Eating Disorders, 19*, 35–44.

Lamb, C. S., Jackson, L. A., Cassiday, P. B., & Priest, D. J. (1993). Body figure preferences of men and women: A comparison of two generations. *Sex Roles, 28*, 345–358.

Landrine, H. (1989). The politics of personality disorder. *Psychology of Women Quarterly, 13*, 325–339.

La Pera, G., & Nicastro, A. (1996). A new treatment for premature ejaculation: The rehabilitation of the pelvic floor. *Journal of Sex & Marital Therapy, 22*, 22–26.

LaPerriere, A. R., Antoni, M. H., Schneiderman, N., Ironson, G., Klimas, N., Caralis, P., & Fletcher, M. A. (1990). Exercise intervention attenuates emotional distress and natural killer cell decrements following notification of positive serologic status for HIV-A. *Biofeedback and Self-Regulation, 15*, 229–242.

LaPiere, R. (1934). Attitudes versus actions. *Social Forces, 13*, 230–237.

Lapsley, D. K. (1996). Commentary on the narrative approach to moral development. *Human Development, 32*, 100–107.

Large, P. (1984). *The micro revolution revisited.* New Jersey: Rowman & Allanheld.

Larson, J. H. (1988). The Marriage Quiz: College students' beliefs in selected myths about marriage. *Family Relations, 37*, 3–11.

Latané, B. (1996). Strength from weakness: The fate of opinion minorities in spatially distributed groups. In E. H. Witte & J. H. Davis (Eds.), *Understanding group behavior* (Vol. 1). Hillsdale, NJ: Erlbaum.

Laughlin, P. L. (1996). Group decision making and quantitative judgments. In E. H. Witte & J. H. Davis (Eds.), *Understanding group behavior* (Vol. 1). Hillsdale, NJ: Erlbaum.

LaVoie, J. (1976). Ego identity formation in middle adolescence. *Journal of Youth and Adolescence, 5*, 371–385.

Lazarus, R. S. (1981). The stress and coping paradigm. In C. Eisdorfer, D. Cohen, A. Kleinman, & P. Maxim (Eds.), *Models for clinical psychopathology.* New York: Spectrum.

Lazarus, R. S. (1991). *Emotion and adaptation.* New York: Oxford University Press.

Lazarus, R. S. (1993). From psychological stress to the emotions: A history of a changing outlook. *Annual Review of Psychology, 44*, 1–21.

Lazarus, R. S., & Folkman, S. (1984). *Stress appraisal and coping.* New York: Springer.

Leary, M. R., Nezlek, J. B., Downs, D., Radford-Davenport, J., Martin, J., & McMullen, A. (1994). Self-presentation in everyday interactions: Effects of target familiarity and gender composition. *Journal of Personality and Social Psychology, 67*, 664–673.

Lebow, J. L., & Gurman, A. S. (1995). Research assessing couple and family therapy. *Annual Review of Psychology, 46.* Palo Alto, CA: Annual Reviews.

Lee, D. J., & Hall, C. C. I. (1994). Being Asian in North America. In W. J. Lonner & R. Malpass (Eds.), *Psychology and culture.* Needham Heights, MA: Allyn & Bacon.

Lee, G. R. (1978). Marriage and morale in late life. *Journal of Marriage and the Family, 40*, 131–139.

Lee, I., Hsieh, C., & Paffenbarger, R. S. (1995). Exercise intensity and longevity in men. *Journal of the American Medical Association, 273*, 1179–1184.

Leinster, C. (1988, January 18). Black executives: How they're doing. *Fortune,* pp. 109–120.

Leong, F. (1996). Multicultural counseling theory and Asian-American populations. In D. W. Sue (Ed.), *Theory of multicultural counseling and therapy.* Pacific Grove, CA: Brooks/Cole.

Lerner, H. G. (1985). *The dance of anger.* New York: Harper & Row.

Lerner, H. G. (1989). *The dance of intimacy.* New York: HarperCollins.

Leshner, A. I. (1992, July). Winning the war against clinical depression. *USA Today,* pp. 86–87.

Leukefeld, C. G., & Haverkos, H. W. (1993). Sexually transmitted diseases. In T. P. Gulotta, G. R. Adams, & R. Montemayor (Eds.), *Adolescent sexuality,* Newbury Park, CA: Sage.

Levant, R. (1996). The male code and parenting: A psychoeducational approach. In M. P. Andronico (Ed.), *Men in groups.* Washington, DC: American Psychological Association.

LeVay, S. (1991). A difference in hypothalamic structure between heterosexual and homosexual men. *Science, 253*, 1034–1037.

Leventhal, H. (1970). Findings and theory in the study of fear communications. *Advances in Experimental Social Psychology, 5*, 119–186.

Levine, S. V. (1984, August). Radical departures. *Psychology Today,* pp. 18–27.

Levinson, D. J. (1978). *The seasons of a man's life.* New York: Knopf.

Levinson, D. J. (1987, August). *The seasons of a woman's life.* Paper presented at the meeting of the American Psychological Association, New York City.

Levy, S. M., Herberman, R. B., Lee, J., Whiteside, T., Kirkwood, J., & McFeeley, S. (1990). Estrogen receptor concentration and social factors as predictors of natural killer cell activity in early-stage breast cancer patients. *Natural Immunity and Cell Growth Regulation, 9*, 313–324.

Lieberman, M. A., Yalom, I. D., & Miles, M. B. (1973). *Encounter groups: First facts.* New York: Basic Books.

Liebkind, K. (1996). Acculturation and stress: Vietnamese refugees in Finland. *Journal of Cross-Cultural Psychology, 27*, 161–180.

Linn, M. C., & Hyde, J. S. (1991). Cognitive and psychosocial gender differences, trends in. In R. M. Lerner, A. C. Petersen, & J. Brooks-Gunn (Eds.), *Encyclopedia of adolescence* (Vol. 1). New York: Garland.

Lipscomb, G. H., Muram, D., Speck, P. M., & Mercer, B. M. (1992, June). Male victims of sexual assault. *Journal of the American Medical Association, 267*, 3064.

Livesley, W. J. (Ed.). (1995). *The DSM-IV personality disorders.* New York: Guilford.

Lofland, J., & Stark, R. (1965). Becoming a world-saver: A theory of conversion to a deviant perspective. *American Sociological Review, 30*, 862–875.

Lonner, W. J. (1988, October). *The introductory psychology text and cross-cultural psychology: A survey of cross-cultural psychologists.* Bellingham, WA: Western Washington University, Center for Cross-cultural Research.

Lonner, W. J., & Malpass, R. (Eds.). (1994). *Psychology and culture.* Boston: Allyn & Bacon.

Lopata, H. Z. (1995). *Circles and settings: Role changes of American women.* Albany, NY: State University of New York Press.

Lowman, R. L. (1987). Occupational choice as a moderator of psychotherapeutic choice. *Psychotherapy, 24*, 801–808.

Lowman, R. L. (1991). *The clinical practice of career assessment.* Washington, DC: American Psychological Association.

Ludolph, P. (1982, August). *A reanalysis of the literature on multiple personality.* Paper presented at the American Psychological Association, Washington, DC.

Luria, A., & Herzog, E. (1985, April). *Gender segregation across and within settings.* Paper presented at the biennial meeting of the Society for Research in Child Development, Toronto.

M

Maccoby, E. E. (1987, November). Interview with Elizabeth Hall: All in the family. *Psychology Today,* pp. 54–60.

Maccoby, E. E. (1993, March). *Trends and issues in the study of gender role development.* Paper presented at the biennial meeting of the Society for Research in Child Development, New Orleans.

Maccoby, E. E., & Jacklin, C. N. (1974). *The psychology of sex differences.* Palo Alto, CA: Stanford University Press.

Maccoby, E. E., & Martin, J. A. (1983). Socialization in the context of the family: Parent-child interaction. In P. H. Mussen (Ed.), *Handbook of child psychology* (4th ed., Vol. 4). New York: Wiley.

MacKenzie, A. (1991). *The time trap.* New York: AMA Com.

Maddi, S. (1996). *Personality theories* (6th ed.). Pacific Grove, CA: Brooks/Cole.

Magee, W. J. (1996). Agoraphobia, simple phobia, and social phobia in the national comorbidity survey. *Archives of General Psychiatry, 68,* 87–99.

Malamuth, N. M., & Donnerstein, E. (Eds.). (1983). *Pornography and sexual aggression.* New York: Academic Press.

Mann, J. J., Malone, K. M., Diehl, D. J., Perel, J., Cooper, T. B., & Mintun, M. A. (1996). Demonstration of in vivo reduced serotonin responsivity in the brain of untreated depressed patients. *The American Journal of Psychiatry, 153,* 174–182.

Mann, L. (1980). Cross-cultural study of small groups. In H. C. Triandis & R. W. Brislin (Eds.), *Handbook of cross-cultural psychology* (Vol. 5). Boston: Allyn & Bacon.

Maracek, J. (1995). Gender, politics, and psychology's ways of knowing. *American Psychologist, 50,* 162–163.

Marcia, J. (1966). Identity six years after: A follow-up study. *Journal of Youth and Adolescence, 5,* 145–160.

Marcia, J. (1991). Identity and self-development. In R. M. Lerner, A. C. Petersen, & J. Brooks-Gunn (Eds.), *Encyclopedia of Adolescence* (Vol. 1). New York: Garland.

Marcia, J. E. (1994). The empirical study of ego identity. In H. A. Bosma, T. L. G. Graafsma, H. D. Grotevant, & D. J. DeLevita (Eds.), *Identity and development.* Newbury Park, CA: Sage.

Marin, G. (1994). The experience of being a Hispanic in the United States. In W. J. Lonner & R. Malpass (Eds.), *Psychology and culture.* Needham Heights, MA: Allyn & Bacon.

Markides, K. S. (1995). Aging and ethnicity. *Gerontologist, 35,* 276–277.

Markman, H. J., & Hahlwag, K. (1993). The prediction and prevention of marital distress: An international perspective. *Clinical Psychology Review, 13,* 29–44.

Markson, E. W. (1995). Older women: The silent majority? *Gerontologist, 35,* 278–281.

Markus, H., & Nurius, P. (1986). Possible selves. *American Psychologist, 41,* 954–969.

Markus, H. R., & Kitayama, S. (1991). Culture and the self: Implications for cognition, emotion, and motivation. *Psychological Review, 98,* 224–253.

Marlatt, G. A., & Barrett, K. (1995). Relapse prevention in the treatment of substance abuse. In M. Galanter & H. D. Kleber (Eds.), *The treatment of substance abuse.* New York: American Psychiatric Press.

Marsella, A. J., Friedman, M. J., Gerrity, E. T., & Scurfield, R. M. (Eds.). (1996). *Ethnocultural aspects of posttraumatic stress disorder.* Washington, DC: American Psychological Association.

Marsiske, M., Lang, F. R., Baltes, P. B., & Baltes, M. M. (1995). Selective optimization with compensation. In R. A. Dixon & L. Backman (Eds.), *Compensating for psychological deficits and declines.* Hillsdale, NJ: Erlbaum.

Martin, G., & Pear, J. (1988). *Behavior modification: What it is and how to do it* (3rd ed.). Englewood Cliffs, NJ: Prentice Hall.

Martin, G. L., & Pear, J. (1996). *Behavior modification* (5th ed.). Upper Saddle River, NJ: Prentice Hall.

Maslow, A. H. (1954). *Motivation and personality.* New York: Harper & Row.

Maslow, A. H. (1971). *The farther reaches of human nature.* New York: Viking.

Masters, W. H., & Johnson, V. E. (1966). *Human sexual response.* Boston: Little, Brown.

Matlin, M. W. (1993). *The psychology of women* (2nd ed.). Fort Worth, TX: Harcourt Brace.

Matsumoto, D. (1996). *Culture and psychology.* Pacific Grove, CA: Brooks/Cole.

Maupin, R. J. (1993). How can women's lack of upward mobility in accounting organizations be explained? Male and female accountants respond. *Group and Organization Management, 18,* 132–152.

Mayer, F. S., & Sutton, K. (1996). *Theories of personality* (2nd ed.). Upper Saddle River, NJ: Prentice Hall.

Mays, V., Caldwell, C. H., & Jackson, J. S. (1996). Mental health symptoms and service utilization patterns of help-seeking among Black women. In H. W. Neighbors & J. S. Jackson (Eds.), *Mental health in Black America.* Newbury Park, CA: Sage.

McAdams, D. P. (1988). *Power, intimacy, and the life story.* New York: Guilford.

McAdams, D. P. (1990). *The person.* San Diego: Harcourt Brace Jovanovich.

McAdoo, H. P. (Ed.). (1993). *Family ethnicity.* Newbury Park, CA: Sage.

McBride, A. B. (1990, March). Mental health effects of women's multiple roles. *American Psychologist, 45,* 381–384.

McBurney, D. H. (1996). *How to think like a psychologist.* Upper Saddle River, NJ: Prentice Hall.

McConaghy, N. (1993). *Sexual behavior: Problems and management.* New York: Plenum.

McGrath, E., Keita, G. P., Strickland, B., & Russo, N. F. (1990). *Women and depression: Risk factors and treatment issues.* Washington, DC: American Psychological Association.

McGuffin, P. (1996). A hospital-based twin registry study of the heritability of DSM-IV unipolar depression. *Archives of General Psychiatry, 68,* 55–64.

McKinlay, S. M., & McKinlay, J. B. (1984). *Health status and health care utilization by menopausal women.* Unpublished manuscript, Cambridge Research Center, American Institutes for Research, Cambridge, MA.

McLoyd, V. (1996). The impact of poverty and low socioeconomic status on socioemotional functioning of African-American children and adolescents: Mediating effects. In R. D. Taylor & M. C. Wang (Eds.), *Social and emotional adjustment and family relations in ethnic minority families.* Hillsdale, NJ: Erlbaum.

McLoyd, V. C. (1993, March). *Sizing up the future: Economic stress, expectations, and adolescents' achievement motivation.* Paper presented at the biennial meeting of the Society for Research in Child Development, New Orleans.

McLoyd, V. C., & Ceballo, R. (1995, March). *Conceptualizing economic context.* Paper presented at the meeting of the Society for Research in Child Development, Indianapolis.

McLoyd, V. C., & Wilson, L. (1990). Maternal behavior, social support, and economic conditions as predictors of distress in children. In V. C. McLoyd & C. A. Flanagan (Eds.), *Economic stress: Effects on family life and child development.* San Francisco: Jossey-Bass.

McNeil, E. B. (1967). *The quiet furies.* Englewood Cliffs, NJ: Prentice Hall.

McWilliams, N. (1992). The worst of both worlds: Dilemmas of contemporary young women. In B. R. Wainrib (Ed.), *Gender issues across the life cycle.* New York: Springer.

Mead, M. (1935/1968). *Sex and temperament in three primitive societies.* New York: Dell.

Meehl, P. E. (1986). Diagnostic taxa as open concepts. In T. Millon & G. I. Klerman (Eds.), *Contemporary directions in psychopathology.* New York: Guilford Press.

Mehrabian, A., & Wiener, M. (1967). Decoding of inconsistent communications. *Journal of Personality and Social Psychology, 6,* 109–114.

Meichenbaum, D. (1986). Cognitive behavior modification. In F. H. Kanfer & A. P. Goldstein (Eds.), *Helping people change: A textbook of methods.* New York: Pergamon.

Meichenbaum, D. (1993). Changing conceptions of cognitive behavior modification: Retrospect and prospect. *Journal of Consulting and Clinical Psychology, 61,* 202–204.

Mervis, J. (1986, July). NIMH data point way to effective treatment. *APA Monitor, 17,* 1, 13.

Messinger, J. C. (1971). Sex and repression in an Irish folk community. In D. S. Marshall & R. C. Suggs (Eds.), *Human sexual behavior: Variations in the ethnic spectrum.* New York: Basic Books.

Metalsky, G. I., Joiner, T. E., Hardin, T. S., & Abramson, L. Y. (1993). Depressive reactions to failure in a naturalistic setting. *Journal of Abnormal Psychology, 102,* 101–109.

Meyer, K. A., Borgealt, D. A., Zurazesei, R. M., & Forshaun, S. (1996, March). *Attributions concerning adolescent suicide: The impact of gender, method, and outcome.* Paper presented at the meeting of the Society for Research on Adolescence, Boston.

Meyer, R. G., & Osborne, Y. V. H. (1982). *Case studies in abnormal behavior.* Boston: Allyn & Bacon.

Meyers, J. (1985). *Hemingway.* New York: Harper & Row.

Michael, R. T., Gagnon, J. H., Laumann, E. O., & Kolata, G. (1994). *Sex in America.* Boston: Little, Brown.

Michelozzi, B. N. (1996). *Coming alive from nine to five: The career search handbook.* Mountain View, CA: Mayfield.

Milgram, S. (1965). Some conditions of obedience and disobedience to authority. *Human Relations, 18,* 56–76.

Miller, H. L. (1996). Clinical and biochemical effects of catecholamine depletion on antidepressant-induced remission of depression. *Archives of General Psychiatry, 68,* 38–54.

Miller, J. B. (1986). *Toward a new psychology of women* (2nd ed.). Boston: Beacon Press.

Miller, J. G. (1995, March). *Culture, context, and personal agency: The cultural grounding of self and morality.* Paper presented at the meeting of the Society for Research in Child Development, Indianapolis.

Miller, N. E. (1959). Liberalization of basic S-R concepts. Extension to conflict behavior, motivation, and social learning. In S. Koch (Ed.), *Psychology: A study of science.* New York: McGraw-Hill.

Miller, N. E. (1969). Learning of visceral glandular responses. *Science, 163,* 434–445.

Miller, S. K., & Slap, G. B. (1989). Adolescent smoking: A review of prevalence and prevention. *Journal of Adolescent Health Care, 10,* 129–135.

Mintz, N., & Schwartz, D. (1964). Urban ecology and psychosis: Community factors in the incidence of schizophrenia and manic-depression among Italians in Greater Boston. *International Journal of Social Psychiatry, 10,* 101–118.

Minuchin, P. (1985). Families and individual development. Provocations from the field of family therapy. *Child Development, 56,* 289–302.

Mischel, W. (1968). *Personality and assessment.* New York: Wiley.

Mischel, W. (1973). Toward a cognitive social learning reconceptualization of personality. *Psychological Review, 80,* 252–283.

Mischel, W. (1995, August). *Cognitive-affective theory of person-environment psychology.* Paper presented at the meeting of the American Psychological Association, New York City.

Money, J. (1986). *Lovemaps: Clinical concepts of sexual/erotic health and pathology, paraphilia, and gender transposition in childhood, adolescence, and maturity.* New York: Irvington.

Moos, R. H. (1986). Work as a human context. In M. S. Pallack & R. Perloff (Eds.), *Psychology and work: Productivity, change, and employment.* Washington, DC: American Psychological Association.

Morris, D. (1977). *Manwatching.* New York: Abrams.

Moses, J., Steptoe, A., Mathews, A., & Edwards, S. (1989). The effects of exercise training on mental well-being in the normal population: A controlled trial. *Journal of Psychosomatic Research, 33,* 47–61.

Moskowitz, D. S., Suh, E. J., & Desaulniers, J. (1994). Situational influences on gender differences in agency and communion. *Journal of Personality and Social Psychology, 66,* 753–761.

Munroe, R. L., & Munroe, R. H. (1975). *Cross-cultural human development.* Monterey, CA: Brooks/Cole.

Murdock, G. P. (1949). *Social structure.* New York: Macmillan.

Murray, V. M. (1996, March). *Sexual and motherhood statuses: Subsequent life experiences of African-American high school graduates.* Paper presented at the meeting of the Society for Research on Adolescence, Boston.

Myers, D. G. (1992). *The pursuit of happiness.* New York: William Morrow.

Myers, D. G. (1993). *The pursuit of happiness.* New York: William Morrow.

Myers, D. G. (1995). *Psychology* (4th ed.). New York: Worth.

N

Natalle, E. J. (1996). Gendered issues in the workplace. In J. T. Wood (Ed.), *Gendered relationships.* Mountain View, CA: Mayfield.

Nathan, P. E. (1994). DSM-IV: Empirical, accessible, not yet ideal. *Journal of Clinical Psychology, 50,* 103–109.

National Academy of Sciences, National Research Council. (1989). *Diet and health: Implications for reducing chronic disease risk.* Washington, DC: National Academy Press.

National Advisory Council on Economic Opportunity. (1980). *Critical choices for the '80s.* Washington, DC: U.S. Government Printing Office.

National and Community Service Coalition. (1995). *Youth volunteerism: Here's what the surveys say.* Washington, DC: Author.

National Center for Health Statistics (1989). *National nursing home survey* (DHHS Publication No. PHS 89-1758, Series 13, No. 97). Washington, DC: U.S. Government Printing Office.

National Institutes of Health. (1994). Cigarette smoking among adults, United States, 1992, and changes in definition of current cigarette smoking. *Mortality and Morbidity 43,* 342–346.

Neugarten, B. L. (1986). The aging society. In A. Pifer & L. Bronte (Eds.), *Our aging society: Paradox and promise.* New York: W. W. Norton.

Neugarten, B. L. (1988, August). *Policy issues for an aging society.* Paper presented at the meeting of the American Psychological Association, Atlanta.

Newman, E. (1974). *Strictly speaking.* Indianapolis: Bobbs-Merrill.

Nichols, M. P., & Schwartz, R. C. (1995). *Family therapy.* Needham Heights, MA: Allyn & Bacon.

Nisbett, R. E., & Wilson, T. D. (1977). Telling more than we can know: Verbal reports on mental processes. *Psychological Review, 84,* 231–259.

Nishio, K., & Bilmes, M. (1993). Psychotherapy with Southeast Asian clients. In D. R. Atkinson, G. Morten, & D. W. Sue (Eds.), *Counseling American minorities.* Madison, WI: Brown & Benchmark.

Nolen-Hoeksema, S. (1990). *Sex differences in depression.* Stanford, CA: Stanford University Press.

Norem, J. K., & Cantor, N. (1986). Anticipatory and post-hoc cushioning strategies: Optimism and defensive pessimism in a "risky" situation. *Cognitive Therapy Research, 10,* 347–362.

Norton, R., & Brenders, D. (1995). *Communication and consequences.* Hillsdale, NJ: Erlbaum.

Notarius, C. I. (1996). Marriage: Will I be happy or sad? In N. Vanzetti & S. Duck (Eds.), *A lifetime of relationships.* Pacific Grove, CA: Brooks/Cole.

Novak, C. A. (1977). Does youthfulness equal attractiveness? In L. E. Troll, J. Israel, & K. Israel (Eds.), *Looking ahead: A woman's guide to the problems and joys of growing older.* Englewood Cliffs, NJ: Prentice Hall.

Novak, W. (1983). *The great man shortage.* New York: Rawson.

Nunn, R. G., Newton, K. S., & Faucher, P. (1992). 2.5 years follow-up of weight and body mass index values in the Weight Control for Life! program: A descriptive analysis. *Addictive Behaviors, 17,* 579–585.

O

O'Donahue, W., & Krasner, L. (Eds.). (1995). *Theories of behavior therapy.* Washington, DC: American Psychological Association.

O'Hara, M. W., Reiter, R. C., Johnson, S. R., & Engeltinger, J. (1995). *Psychological aspects of women's reproductive health.* Bristol, PA: Taylor & Francis.

O'Neil, J. M. (1996). The gender role journey workshop. In M. P. Andronico (Ed.), *Men in groups.* Washington, DC: American Psychological Association.

Okun, B. F., & Rappaport, L. J. (1980). *Working with families: An introduction to family therapy.* North Scituate, MA: Duxbury Press.

Oldham, J. M., Hollander, E., & Skodol, A. E. (Eds.). (1996). *Impulsivity and compulsivity.* Washington, DC: American Psychiatric Association.

Orlofsky, J. (1976). Intimacy status: Relationship to interpersonal perception. *Journal of Youth and Adolescence, 5,* 73–88.

Orlofsky, J., Marcia, J., & Lesser, I. (1973). Ego identity status and the intimacy vs. isolation crisis of young adulthood. *Journal of Personality and Social Psychology, 27,* 211–219.

Ornstein, R., & Sobel, D. (1989). *Healthy pleasures.* Reading, MA: Addison-Wesley.

Osherson, S. (1992). *Wrestling with love: How men struggle with intimacy, with women, children, parents, and each other.* New York: Fawcett Columbine.

Ossip-Klein, D. J., Doyne, E. J., Bowman, E. D., Osborn, K. M., McDougall-Wilson, I. B., & Neimeyer, R. A. (1989). Effects of running or weight lifting on self-concept in clinically depressed women. *Journal of Consulting and Clinical Psychology, 57,* 158–161.

P

Padilla, A. M. (1980). The role of cultural awareness and ethnic loyalty in acculturation. In A. M. Padilla (Ed.), *Acculturation.* Boulder, CO: Westview.

Padilla, A. M. (Ed.). (1994). *Hispanic psychology.* Newbury Park, CA: Sage.

Padilla, A. M., & Ruiz, R. A. (1975). Community mental health services for the Spanish speaking/surnamed population. *American Psychologist, 30,* 392–405.

Padilla, A. M., Ruiz, R. A., & Alvarez, R. (1989). Community mental health services for the Spanish speaking/surnamed population. In D. R. Atkinson, G. Morten, & D. W. Sue (Eds.), *Counseling American minorities.* Dubuque, IA: Wm. C. Brown.

Paffenbarger, R. S., Hyde, R. T., Wing, A. L., Lee, I., Jung, D. L., & Kampter, J. B. (1993). The association of changes in physical-activity level and other life-style characteristics with morality among men. *New England Journal of Medicine, 328,* 538–545.

Paffenbarger, R. S., Hyde, R. T., Wing, A. L., & Hsieh, C. (1986). Physical activity, all-cause mortality, and longevity of college alumni. *New England Journal of Medicine, 314,* 605–612.

Palmore, E. B., Burchett, B. M., Fillenbaum, C. G., George, L. K., & Wallman, L. M. (1985). *Retirement: Causes and consequences.* New York: Springer.

Paloutzian, R. F. (1996). *Invitation to the psychology of religion* (2nd ed.). Needham Heights, MA: Allyn & Bacon.

Paludi, M. A. (1995). *The psychology of women* (2nd ed.). Madison, WI: Brown & Benchmark.

Parducci, A. (1996). *Happiness, pleasure, and judgment.* Hillsdale, NJ: Erlbaum.

Pargament, K. E., & Park, C. L. (in press). Merely a defense? Examining psychologists' stereotype of religion. *Journal of Social Issues.*

Pargament, K. I. (1992). Of means and ends: Religion and the search for significance. *International Journal for the Psychology of Religion, 2*(4), 201–229.

Parham, T. (1996). Multicultural counseling theory and African-American populations. In D. W. Sue (Ed.), *Theory of multicultural counseling and therapy.* Pacific Grove, CA: Brooks/Cole.

Parham, T. A., & McDavis, R. J. (1993). Black men, an endangered species: Who's really pulling the trigger. In D. R. Atkinson, G. Morten, & D. W. Sue (Eds.), *Counseling American minorities.* Madison, WI: Brown & Benchmark.

Parlee, M. B. (1979, April). The friendship bond: PT's survey report on friendship in America. *Psychology Today*, pp. 43–54, 113.

Passuth, P. M., Maines, D. R., & Neugarten, B. L. (1984). *Age norms and age constraints twenty years later.* Paper presented at the annual meeting of the Midwest Sociological Society, Chicago.

Patterson, C. J. (1996, August). *Children of lesbian and gay parents: Research, law, and policy.* Paper presented at the meeting of the American Psychological Association, Toronto.

Paul, G. L. (1967). Strategy of outcome research in psychotherapy. *Journal of Consulting Psychology, 31,* 109–119.

Pavlov, I. P. (1927). *Conditioned reflexes.* (F. V. Anrep, Trans. and Ed.). New York: Dover.

Payne, T. J., Smith, P. O., Sturges, L. V., & Holleran, S. A. (1996). Reactivity to smoking cues: Mediating roles of nicotine and duration of deprivation. *Addictive Behaviors, 21,* 139–154.

Peele, S., & Brodsky, A. (1991). *The truth about addiction and recovery.* New York: Simon & Schuster.

Pennebaker, J. W. (1983). Accuracy of symptom perception. In A. Baum, S. E. Taylor, & J. Singer (Eds.), *Handbook of psychology and health* (Vol. 4). Hillsdale, NJ: Erlbaum.

Pennebaker, J. W. (1990). *Opening up: The healing power of confiding in others.* New York: Morrow.

Pennebaker, J. W., Colder, M., & Sharp, L. K. (1990). Accelerating the coping process. *Journal of Personality and Social Psychology, 58,* 528–537.

Pennebaker, J. W., & Lightner, J. M. (1980). Competition of internal and external information in an exercise setting. *Journal of Personality and Social Psychology, 39,* 165–174.

Perkins, D. D., & Zimmerman, M. A. (1995). Empowerment theory, research, and application. *American Journal of Community Psychology, 23,* 569–580.

Perlin, M. L. (1996). The insanity defense. In B. D. Sales and D. W. Shuman (Eds.), *Law, mental health, and mental disorder.* Pacific Grove, CA: Brooks/Cole.

Perlmutter, M. (1994). Cognitive skills within the context of adult development and old age. In C. Fisher & R. Lerner (Eds.), *Applied developmental psychology.* New York: McGraw-Hill.

Perlmutter-Bowen, S., & Michal-Johnson, P. (1996). Being sexual in the shadow of AIDS. In J. T. Wood (Ed.), *Gendered relationships.* Mountain View, CA: Mayfield.

Perls, F. (1969). *Gestalt therapy verbatim.* Lafayette, CA: Real People Press.

Perry, C., Hearn, M., Murray, D., & Klepp, K. (1988). *The etiology and prevention of adolescent alcohol and drug abuse.* Unpublished manuscript, University of Minnesota.

Pervin, L. A. (1993). *Personality* (6th ed.). New York: Wiley.

Peterson, C. (1988). *Personality.* San Diego: Harcourt Brace Jovanovich.

Peterson, C., & Stunkard, A. J. (1986). *Personal control and health promotion.* Unpublished manuscript, Department of Psychology, University of Michigan, Ann Arbor.

Petras, R., & Petras, K. (1993). *The 776 stupidest things ever said.* New York: Doubleday.

Petras, R., & Petras, K. (1994). *The 776 even stupider things ever said.* New York: Doubleday.

Petrinovich, L. (1996). *Living and dying well.* New York: Plenum.

Phares, E. S. (1984). *Personality.* Columbus, OH: Merrill.

Phelps, S., & Austin, N. (1987). *The assertive woman.* San Luis Obispo, CA: Impact.

Phillips, S. D., & Jonston, S. L. (1985). Attitudes toward work roles for women. *Journal of College Student Personnel, 26,* 334–338.

Piaget, J. (1960). *The child's conception of the world.* Totowa, NJ: Littlefield.

Pillow, D. R., Zautra, A. J., & Sandler, I. (1996). Major life events and minor stressors: Identifying mediational links in the stress process. *Journal of Personality and Social Psychology, 70,* 381–394.

Pines, A., & Aronson, E. (1988). *Career burnout: Causes and cures.* New York: The Free Press.

Pizzey, E. (1974). *Scream quietly or the neighbors will hear you.* Baltimore: Penguin.

Plath, S. (1971). *The bell jar.* New York: Harper & Row.

Pleck, J. (1981). *Three conceptual issues in research on male roles.* Working paper no. 98, Wellesley College Center for Research on Women, Wellesley, MA.

Plutchik, R. (1980). *Emotion: A psychoevolutionary synthesis.* New York: Harper & Row.

Polivy, J., & Clendenden, V. J. (1993, August). *Exercise and compulsive behavior.* Paper presented at the meeting of the American Psychological Association, Toronto.

Poll finds racial tension decreasing. (1990, June 29). *Asian Week,* p. 4.

Pollock, V. E., Schneider, L. S., Gabrielli, W. F., & Goodwin, D. W. (1987). Sex of parent and sex of offspring in the transmission of alcoholism: A meta-analysis. *Journal of Nervous and Mental Disease, 173,* 668–673.

Pomeroy, C. (1996). Anorexia nervosa, bulimia nervosa, and binge eating disorder. In J. K. Thompson (Ed.), *Body image, eating disorders, and obesity.* Washington, DC: American Psychological Association.

Ponterotto, J. G., Casas, J. M., Suzuki, L. A., & Alexander, C. M. (Eds.). (1995). *Handbook of multicultural counseling.* Newbury Park, CA: Sage.

Powell, G. J., & Fuller, M. (1972). The variables for positive self-concept among young Southern Black adolescents. *Journal of the National Medical Association, 43,* 72–79.

Poyatos, F. (Ed.). (1988). *Cross-cultural perspectives in nonverbal communication.* Toronto: Hogrefe.

Prentice, D. A., & Miller, D. T. (1993). Pluralistic ignorance and alcohol use on campus: Some consequences of misperceiving the social norm. *Journal of Personality and Social Psychology, 64,* 243–256.

Pritchard, D. J. (1996). Genetic analysis of schizophrenia as an example of a putative multifactorial trait. *Annals of Human Genetics, 60,* 105–123.

Project Inform. (1966, January). "Antiviral medications fact sheet." Project Inform web site.

R

Rabinowitz, F. E., & Cochran, S. V. (1987). Counseling men in groups. In M. Scher, M. Stevens, G. Good, & G. A. Eichenfield (Eds.), *Handbook of counseling and psychotherapy with men.* Newbury Park, CA: Sage.

Rabinowitz, V. C., & Sechzur, J. (1993). Feminist methodologies. In F. L. Denmark & M. A. Paludi (Eds.), *Handbook on the psychology of women.* Westport, CT: Greenwood.

Rabkin, J. (1979). Ethnic density and psychiatric hospitalization: Hazards of minority status. *American Journal of Psychiatry, 136,* 1562–1566.

Ramirez, O. (1989). Mexican American children and adolescents. In J. T. Gibbs & L. N. Huang (Eds.), *Children of color.* San Francisco: Jossey-Bass.

Ravnikar, V. (1992, May 25). Commentary, *Newsweek,* p. 82.

Rebec, G. V. (1996, June). *Neurochemical and behavioral insights into the mechanisms of action of stimulant drugs.* Paper presented at the meeting of the American Psychological Society, San Francisco.

Reed, E. S. (1996). Selves, values, cultures. In E. S. Reed, E. Turiel, & T. Brown (Eds.), *Values and knowledge.* Hillsdale, NJ: Erlbaum.

Reed, E. S., Turiel, E., & Brown, T. (Eds.). (1996). *Values and knowledge.* Hillsdale, NJ: Erlbaum.

Regier, D. A., Hirschfeld, R. M. A., Goodwin, F. K., Burke, J. D., Lazar, J. B., & Judd, L. L. (1988). The NIMH depression awareness, recognition, and treatment program: Structure, aims, and scientific basis. *American Journal of Psychiatry, 145,* 1351–1357.

Reid, P. T. (1996, August). *Urban children: Great expectations or limited opportunities.* Paper presented at the meeting of the American Psychological Association, Toronto.

Reid, P. T., & Bing, V. (1996). Women and the psychotherapeutic "color line." *Contemporary Psychology, 41,* 19–20.

Reinisch, J. (1992, December 7). Commentary, *Newsweek,* p. 54.

Reinisch, J. M. (1990). *The Kinsey Institute new report on sex: What you must know to be sexually literate.* New York: St. Martin's Press.

Religion in America. (1993). Princeton, NJ: Princeton Religious Research Center.

Renzetti, C. M., & Curran, D. J. (1992). *Women, men, and society.* Boston: Allyn & Bacon.

Rest, J. (1995). *Concerns for the social-psychological development of youth and educational strategies; Report for the Kaufmann Foundation.* Minneapolis, MN: University of Minnesota, Dept. of Educational Psychology.

Reynolds, D. (1984). *Playing ball on running water.* New York: Quill.

Reynolds, D. K. (1976). *Morita therapy.* Berkeley: University of California Press.

Rhodes, S. R. (1983). Age-related differences in work attitudes and behavior: A review and conceptual analysis. *Psychological Bulletin, 93,* 329–367.

Rice, F. P. (1996). *Intimate relationships, marriages, and families* (3rd ed.). Mountain View, CA: Mayfield.

Richardson, J. T. (1989). The psychology of induction: A review and interpretation. In M. Galanter (Ed.), *Cults and new religious movements: A report of the American Psychiatric Association.* Washington, DC: American Psychiatric Association.

Richer, C. P. (1957). On the phenomenon of sudden death in animals and man. *Psychosomatic Medicine, 19,* 191–198.

Robbins, S. P. (1995). *Organizational behavior* (7th ed.). Upper Saddle River, NJ: Prentice Hall.

Robertson, N. C. (1974). The relationship between marital status and the risk of psychiatric referral. *British Journal of Psychiatry, 124,* 191–202.

Robins, L., & Regier, D. A. (Eds.). (1990). *Psychiatric disorders in America.* New York: Macmillan.

Robinson, I., Ziss, K., Ganza, B., Katz, S., & Robinson, E. (1991). Twenty years of the sexual revolution, 1965–1985: An update. *Journal of Marriage and the Family, 53,* 216–220.

Robinson, N. S. (1995). Evaluating the nature of perceived support and its relation to perceived self-worth in adolescents. *Journal of Research in Adolescence, 5,* 253–280.

Rodin, J. (1986). Health, control, and aging. In M. M. Baltes & P. B. Baltes (Eds.), *The psychology of control and aging.* Hillsdale, NJ: Erlbaum.

Rodin, J. (1990, January). Conversation with Robert Trotter. *Longevity,* pp. 60–67.

Rodin, J., & Ickovics, J. R. (1990). Women's health: Review and research agenda as we approach the 21st century. *American Psychologist, 45,* 1018–1034.

Rodin, J., & Langer, E. J. (1977). Long-term effects of a control-relevant intervention with the institutionalized aged. *Journal of Personality and Social Psychology, 35,* 397–402.

Roe, A. (1956). *The psychology of occupations.* New York: Wiley.

Roethlisberger, F., & Dickson, W. J. (1939). *Management and the worker.* Cambridge, MA: Harvard University Press.

Rogers, A. (1987). *Questions of gender differences: Ego development and moral voice in adolescence.* Unpublished manuscript, Dept. of Education, Harvard University.

Rogers, C. R. (1961). *On becoming a person.* Boston: Houghton-Mifflin.

Rogers, C. R. (1963). The actualizing tendency in relation to "motives" and consciousness. In M. R. Jones (Ed.), *Nebraska symposium on motivation.* Lincoln, NE: University of Nebraska Press.

Rogers, C. R. (1974). In retrospect: Forty-six years. *American Psychologist, 29,* 115–123.

Rokeach, M., & Ball-Rokeach, S. J. (1989). Stability and change in American value priorities. *American Psychologist, 44,* 775–784.

Rollins, B. C. (1989). Marital quality at mid-life. In S. Hunter & M. Sundel (Eds.), *Midlife myths.* Newbury Park, CA: Sage.

Rollins, J. H. (1996). *Women's minds/women's bodies.* Upper Saddle River, NJ: Prentice Hall.

Roper Organizations. (1985). *Virginia Slims poll.* New York: Richard Weiner.

Rose, H. A., & Martin, C. L. (1993, March). *Children's gender-based inferences about others' activities, emotions, and occupations.* Paper presented at the biennial meeting of the Society for Research in Child Development, New Orleans.

Rosen, R. C., & Leiblum, S. R. (1995). Treatment of sexual disorders in the 1990s: An integrated approach. *Journal of Consulting and Clinical Psychology, 63,* 877–890.

Rosen, R. D. (1977). *Psychobabble.* New York: Atheneum.

Rosenbaum, J. E. (1984). *Career mobility in a corporate hierarchy.* New York: Academic Press.

Rosenberg, M. (1965). *Society and the adolescent self-image.* Princeton, NJ: Princeton University Press.

Rosenhan, D. L. (1973). On being sane in insane places. *Science, 179,* 250–258.

Rosenthal, L. (1996). Phenomena of resistance in modern group analysis. *American Journal of Psychotherapy, 50,* 75–89.

Ross, M., & Holmberg, D. (1990). Recounting the past: Gender differences in the recall of events in the history of a close relationship. In J. M. Olson & M. P. Zanna (Eds.), *Self-inference processes: The Ontario Symposium.* Hillsdale, NJ: Erlbaum.

Rossi, A. (1989). A life course approach to gender, aging, and intergenerational relations. In K. W. Schaie & C. Schooler (Eds.), *Social structures and aging.* Hillsdale, NJ: Erlbaum.

Rubin, L. B. (1984). *Intimate strangers: Men and women working together.* New York: Harper.

Rubin, Z. (1970). Measurement of romantic love. *Journal of Personality and Social Psychology, 16,* 265–273.

Russo, N. F. (1990). Overview: Forging research priorities for women's mental health. *American Psychologist, 45,* 368–374.

Ruth, S. (Ed.). (1995). *Issues in feminism.* Mountain View, CA: Mayfield.

Rutter, M. (1979). Protective factors in children's response to stress and disadvantage. In M. W. Kent & J. E. Rolf (Eds.), *Primary prevention in psychopathology* (Vol. 3). Hanover, NH: University Press of New England.

Rutter, M., & Garmezy, N. (1983). Developmental psychopathology. In P. H. Mussen (Ed.), *Handbook of child psychology* (4th ed., Vol. 4). New York: Wiley.

Ryan, D. W., & Gaier, E. L. (1968). Student socio-economic status and counselor contact in junior high school. *Personnel and Guidance Journal, 46,* 466–472.

Rybash, J. W., Roodin, P. A., & Hoyer, E. (1995). *Adult development and aging* (2nd ed.). Madison, WI: Brown & Benchmark.

S

Saarni, C. (1988). Children's understanding of the interpersonal consequences of dissemblance of nonverbal emotional-expressive behavior. *Journal of Nonverbal Behavior, 12,* 275–294.

Sackheim, H. A. (1985, June). The case for ECT. *Psychology Today,* pp. 37–40.

Sadry, G., & Robertson, I. T. (1993). Self-efficacy and work-related behavior: A review and meta-analysis. *Applied Psychology, 42,* 139–152.

St. Clair, M. (1996). *Object relations and self psychology.* Pacific Grove, CA: Brooks/Cole.

Salovey, P., & Rodin, J. (1989). Envy and jealousy in close relationships. In C. Hendrick (Ed.), *Close relationships.* Newbury Park, CA: Sage.

Sanderson, W. C. (1995, March). Which therapies are proven effective? *APA Monitor,* p. 4.

Sandler, D. P., Comstock, G. W., Helsing, K. J., & Shore, D. L. (1989). Deaths from all causes in non-smokers who lived with smokers. *American Journal of Public Health, 79,* 163–167.

Sangree, W. H. (1989). Age and power: Life-course trajectories and age structuring of power relations in East and West Africa. In D. I. Kertzer & K. W. Schaie (Eds.), *Age structuring in comparative perspective.* Hillsdale, NJ: Erlbaum.

Santrock, J. W. (1996). *Adolescence* (6th ed.). Madison, WI: Brown & Benchmark.

Santrock, J. W. (1997). *Children* (5th ed.). Madison, WI: Brown & Benchmark.

Santrock, J. W., Minnett, A. M., & Campbell, B. D. (1994). *The authoritative guide to self-help books.* New York: Guilford.

Santrock, J. W., & Warshak, R. A. (1986). Development, relationships, and legal/clinical considerations in father-custody families. In M. E. Lamb (Ed.), *The father's role: Applied perspectives.* New York: Wiley.

Sarrel, P., & Masters, W. (1982). Sexual molestation of men by women. *Archives of Human Sexuality, 11,* 117–131.

Sasaki, T., & Kennedy, J. L. (1995). Genetics of psychosis. *Current Opinion in Psychiatry, 8,* 25–28.

Satir, V. (1964). *Conjoint family therapy.* Palo Alto, CA: Science and Behavior Books.

Sauber, M., & Corrigan, E. M. (1970). *The six year experience of unwed mothers as parents.* New York: Community Council of Greater New York.

Schaef, A. W., & Fassel, D. (1988). *The addictive organization.* New York: Harper & Row.

Schaie, K. W. (1994). The Seattle longitudinal studies of adult intelligence. *Current Directions in Psychological Science, 21,* 171–174.

Schein, V. E., Mueller, R., Lituchy, T., & Liu, J. (1996). Think manager—Think male? A global phenomenon? *Journal of Organizational Behavior, 17,* 33–42.

Schofield, J. W., & Pavelchak, M. A. (1989). Fallout from The Day After: Impact of a TV film on attitudes related to nuclear war. *Journal of Applied Social Psychology, 19,* 433–448.

Schuetz-Mueller, D., Tiefer, L., & Melman, A. (1996). Follow-up of vacuum and nonvacuum constriction devices as treatment of erectile dysfunction. *Journal of Sex & Marital Therapy, 21,* 229–238.

Schulz, R. (1976). Effects of control and predictability on the physical and psychological well-being of the institutionalized aged. *Journal of Personality and Social Psychology, 33,* 563–573.

Schultz, R., & Curnow, C. (1988). Peak performance and age among super athletes: Track and field, swimming, baseball, tennis, and golf. *Journal of Gerontology, 43,* pp. 113–120.

Schulz, R., & Hanusa, B. H. (1978). Long-term effects of control and predictability-enhancing interventions. Findings and ethical issues. *Journal of Personality and Social Psychology, 11,* 1194–1201.

Schwartz, R., & Eriksen, M. (1989). Statement of the Society for Public Health Education on the national health promotion disease prevention objectives for the year 2000. *Health Education Quarterly, 16,* 3–7.

Schwartz, S. H. (1990). Individualism-collectivism. *Journal of Cross-Cultural Psychology, 21,* 139–157.

Scitovsky, A. A. (1988). Medical care in the last twelve months of life: Relation between age, functional status, and medical care expenditures. *Milbank Quarterly, 66,* 640–660.

Scott-Jones, D. (1996, August). *Urban children in family contexts: Ethnic variations.* Paper presented at the meeting of the American Psychological Association, Toronto.

Seager, J., & Olson, A. (Eds.). (1986). *Women of the world: An international atlas.* New York: Simon & Schuster.

Sears, D. O., Peplau, L. A., & Taylor, S. E. (1997). *Social psychology* (9th ed.). Englewood Cliffs, NJ: Prentice Hall.

Seffge-Krenke, I. (1995). *Stress, coping, and relationships in adolescence.* Hillsdale, NJ: Erlbaum.

Seligman, C., Olson, J. M., & Zanna, M. P. (Eds.). (1996). *The psychology of values.* Hillsdale, NJ: Erlbaum.

Seligman, M. E. P. (1978). *Helplessness: On depression, development, and death.* San Francisco: W. H. Freeman.

Seligman, M. E. P. (1989). Why is there so much depression today? The waxing of the individual and the waning of the common. In *The G. Stanley Hall Lecture Series.* American Psychological Association.

Seligman, M. E. P. (1991). *Learned optimism.* New York: Knopf.

Selye, H. (1974). *Stress without distress.* Philadelphia: W. B. Saunders.

Selye, H. (1983). The stress concept. Past, present, and future. In C. I. Cooper (Ed.), *Stress research.* New York: Wiley.

Shaver, P. (1986, August). *Being lonely, falling in love: Perspectives from attachment theory.* Paper presented at the meeting of the American Psychological Association, Washington, DC.

Shaver, P. R., & Hazan, C. (1993). Adult romantic attachment: Theory and evidence. In D. Perlman & W. H. Jones (Eds.), *Advances in personal relationships* (Vol. 4). London: Kingsley.

Sheehy, G. (1991). *The silent passage.* New York: Random House.

Sheldon, W. H. (1954). *Atlas of men.* New York: Harper & Brothers.

Sher, K. J. (1993). Children of alcoholics and the intergenerational transmission of alcoholism: A biopsychosocial perspective. In J. S. Baer, G. A. Marlatt, & R. J. McMahon (Eds.), *Addictive behaviors across the life span.* Newbury Park, CA: Sage.

Sherwood, A., Light, K. C., & Bluementhal, J. A. (1989). Effects of aerobic exercise training on hemodynamic responses during psychosocial stress in normotensive and borderline hypertensive Type A men: A preliminary report. *Psychosomatic Medicine, 51,* 123–136.

Shields, S. A. (1991, August). *Doing emotion/doing gender.* Paper presented at the meeting of the American Psychological Association, San Francisco.

Shotland, R. L. (1985, June). When bystanders just stand by. *Psychology Today,* pp. 50–55.

Showers, C. (1986, August). *The motivational consequences of negative thinking: Those who imagine the worst try harder.* Paper presented at the meeting of the American Psychological Association, Washington, DC.

Siegel, R. K. (1990). *Intoxification.* New York: Pocket Books.

Sigelman, C. K., Thomas, D. B., Sigelman, L., & Ribich, F. D. (1986). Gender, physical attractiveness, and electability: An experimental investigation of vote biases. *Journal of Applied Social Psychology, 16,* 229–248.

Silverstone, B. (1996). Older people of tomorrow: A psychosocial profile. *The Gerontologist, 36,* 27–32.

Simpson, J. A. (1995). Self-monitoring and commitment to dating relationships: A classroom demonstration. In M. E. Ware & D. E. Johnson (Eds.), *Demonstrations and activities in teaching of psychology.* Hillsdale, NJ: Erlbaum.

Singer, J. L. (1984). *The human personality.* San Diego: Harcourt Brace Jovanovich.

Singh, D. (1993). Adaptive significance of female physical attractiveness: Role of waist-to-hip ratio. *Journal of Personality and Social Psychology, 65,* 293–307.

Sizemore, C. C. (1989). *A mind of my own.* New York: William Morrow.

Skinner, B. F. (1938). *The behavior of organisms: An experimental analysis.* New York: Appleton-Century-Crofts.

Skoe, E. E., & Marcia, J. E. (1988). *Ego identity and care-based moral reasoning in college women.* Unpublished manuscript, Acadia University.

Slobogian, C. (1996). A jurisprudence of dangerousness as a criterion in the criminal process. In B. D. Sales & D. W. Shuman (Eds.), *Law, mental health, and mental disorder.* Pacific Grove, CA: Brooks/Cole.

Slovenko, R. (1995). *Psychiatry and criminal culpability.* New York: Wiley.

Smith, J. C. (Ed.). (1991). *Notable Black American women.* Detroit: Gale Research.

Smith, M. L., Glass, G. N., & Miller, R. L. (1980). *The benefit of psychotherapy.* Baltimore: Johns Hopkins University Press.

Smith, P. C. (1995). Assessing writing and statistical competence in probability and statistics. *Teaching of Psychology, 22,* 49–50.

Smith, P. F., & Darlington, C. L. (1996). *Clinical psychopharmacology.* Hillsdale, NJ: Erlbaum.

Snarey, J. (1987, June). A question of morality. *Psychology Today,* pp. 6–8.

Snowden, L. R., & Cheung, F. K. (1990). Use of inpatient mental health services by members of ethnic minority groups. *American Psychologist, 45,* 347–355.

Snyder, M. (1979). Self-monitoring processes. In L. Berkowitz (Ed.), *Advances in experimental social psychology* (Vol. 12). New York: Academic Press.

Sobell, M. B., & Sobell, L. C. (1993). Treatment for problem drinkers: A public health priority. In J. S. Baer, G. A. Marlatt, & R. J. McMahon (Eds.), *Addictive behaviors across the life span.* Newbury Park, CA: Sage.

Sowell, T. (1994). *Race and culture: A world view.* New York: Basic Books.

Spence, J. T., & Helmreich, R. (1978). *Masculinity and femininity: Their psychological dimensions.* Austin: University of Texas Press.

Spilka, B. (1991). Cults, adolescence and. In R. M. Lerner, A. C. Petersen, & J. Brooks-Gunn (Eds.), *Encyclopedia of adolescence* (Vol. 1). New York: Garland.

Spiritual America. (1994, April 4). *U.S. News and World Report,* pp. 48–59.

Sprecher, S., & McKinney, K. (1993). *Sexuality.* Newbury Park, CA: Sage.

Sprecher, S., Sullivan, Q., & Hatfield, E. (1994). Mate selection preferences: Gender differences examined in a national sample. *Journal of Personality and Social Psychology, 66,* 1074–1080.

Sprei, J. E., & Courtois, C. A. (1988). The treatment of women's sexual dysfunctions arising from sexual assault. In R. A. Brown & J. R. Fields (Eds.), *Treatment of sexual problems in individual and couples therapy.* Great Neck, NY: PMA.

Squire, C. (1993). *Women and AIDS.* Newbury Park, CA: Sage.

Staats, A. W. (1996). *Psychological behaviorism and personality.* New York: Springer.

Stanley, M., & Stanley, B. (1989). Biochemical studies in suicide victims: Current findings and future implications. *Suicide and Life-Threatening Behavior, 19,* 30–42.

Stanton, A. L., & Gallant, S. J. (Eds.). (1995). *The psychology of women's health.* Washington, DC: American Psychological Association.

Stark, E. (1989, July). Off-the-shelf salvation. *Health,* pp. 28–30.

Steers, R. M. (1988). *Introduction to organizational behavior* (2nd ed.). Glenview, IL: Scott, Foresman.

Stein, M. B. (Ed.). (1995). *Social phobia.* Washington, DC: American Psychiatric Association.

Stein, P. J. (1976). *Single.* Englewood Cliffs, NJ: Prentice Hall.

Stemberger, R. T., Turner, S. M., Beidel, D. C., & Calhoun, K. S. (1995). Social phobia: An analysis of possible developmental factors. *Journal of Abnormal Psychology, 104,* 526–531.

Stenhouse, G. (1996). *Practical parenting.* New York: Oxford.

Sternberg, R. J. (1988). *The triangle of love.* New York: Basic Books.

Stock, W. A., Okum, M. A., Haring, M. J., & Witter, R. A. (1983). Age and subjective well-being: A meta-analysis. In R. J. Light (Ed.), *Evaluation studies: Review annual* (Vol. 8). Newbury Park, CA: Sage.

Stoller, E. P., & Gibson, R. C. (1994). *Worlds of difference: Inequality in the aging experience.* Thousand Oaks, CA: Pine Forge Press.

Strean, H. S. (1996). Resistance viewed from different perspectives. *American Journal of Psychotherapy, 50,* 29–31.

Strickland, B. (1988). Sex-related differences in health and illness. *Psychology of Women Quarterly, 12,* 381–399.

Strupp, H. H. (1993, August). *Lessons from psychotherapy practice and research.* Paper presented at the meeting of the American Psychological Association, Toronto.

Studer, M., & Thornton, A. (1987). Adolescent religiosity and contraceptive usage. *Journal of Marriage and the Family, 49,* 117–128.

Studer, M., & Thornton, A. (1989). The multifaceted impact of religiosity on adolescent sexual experience and contraceptive usage: A reply to Shornack and Ahmed. *Journal of Marriage and the Family, 51,* 1085–1089.

Stunkard, A. J. (1987). The regulation of body weight and the treatment of obesity. In H. Weiner & A. Baum (Eds.), *Eating regulation and discontrol.* Hillsdale, NJ: Erlbaum.

Subich, L. M., & Billingsley, K. D. (1995). Integrating career assessment into counseling. In W. B. Walsh & S. H. Osipow (Eds.), *Handbook of vocational psychology* (2nd ed.). Hillsdale, NJ: Erlbaum.

Sue, D., & Sue, D. W. (1993). Ethnic identity: Cultural factors in the psychological development of Asians in America. In D. R. Atkinson, G. Morten, & D. W. Sue (Eds.), *Counseling American minorities.* Madison, WI: Brown & Benchmark.

Sue, D. W. (1996). Multicultural counseling: Models, methods, and actions. *The Counseling Psychologist, 24,* 279–284.

Sue, D. W., Ivey, A. E., & Pedersen, P. B. (1996). Research, practice, and training implications of multicultural counseling theory. In D. W. Sue (Ed.), *Theory of multicultural counseling and therapy.* Pacific Grove, CA: Brooks/Cole.

Sue, D. W., & Sue, S. (1972). Counseling Chinese-Americans. *Personnel and Guidance Journal, 50,* 637–644.

Sue, S. (1990, August). *Ethnicity and culture in psychological research and practice.* Paper presented at the meeting of the American Psychological Association, Boston.

Sue, S., Allen, D., & Conaway, L. (1978). The responsiveness and equality of mental health care to Chicanos and Native Americans. *American Journal of Community Psychology, 6,* 137–146.

Suinn, R. M. (1984). *Fundamentals of abnormal psychology.* Chicago: Nelson-Hall.

Sullivan, H. S. (1953). *The interpersonal theory of psychiatry.* New York: W. W. Norton.

Super, D. E. (1976). *Career education and the meanings of work.* Washington, DC: U.S. Office of Education.

Super, D. E., Kowalski, R., & Gotkin, E. (1967). *Floundering and trial after high school.* Unpublished manuscript, Columbia University.

Surra, C. A. (1990). Research and theory on mate selection and premarital relationships in the 1980s. *Journal of Marriage and the Family, 52,* 844–865.

Sutton, R. G., & Kessler, M. (1986). National study of the effects of clients' socioeconomic status on clinical psychologists' professional judgments. *Journal of Consulting and Clinical Psychology, 54,* 275–276.

Suzman, R. M., Harris, T., Hadley, E. C., Kovar, M. G., & Weindruch, R. (1992). The robust oldest old: Optimistic perspectives for increasing healthy life expectancy. In R. M. Suzman, D. P. Willis, & K. G. Manton (Eds.), *The oldest old.* New York: Oxford University Press.

Sweet, J. A., Bumpass, L. L., & Call, V. A. R. (1988). *The design and content of the National Survey of Families and Households* (NSFH Working Paper No. 1). Madison: University of Wisconsin, Center for Demography and Ecology.

Swim, J. K., Aikin, K. J., Hall, W. S., & Hunter, B. A. (1995). Sexism and racism: Old-fashioned and modern prejudices. *Journal of Personality and Social Psychology, 67,* 199–214.

Swope, G. W. (1980). Kids and cults: Who joins and why? *Media and Methods, 16,* 18–21.

Szasz, T. (1965). *The ethics of psychoanalysis.* New York: Basic Books.

Szasz, T. (1977). *Psychiatric slavers: When confinement and coercion masquerade as cure.* New York: Free Press.

Szinovacz, M. E. (1984). Changing family roles and interactions. In B. B. Hess & M. B. Sussman (Eds.), *Women and the family: Two decades of change.* New York: Hayworth Press.

T

Tafoya, T. (1993, August). *Who's parenting the parents? Shattered scripts, missing models, and AIDS.* Paper presented at the meeting of the American Psychological Association, Toronto.

Tan, Amy. (1989). *The joy luck club.* New York: Putnam.

Tannen, D. (1990). *You just don't understand: Women and men in conversation.* New York: Ballantine.

Tavris, C. (1989, December). Do codependency theories explain women's unhappiness—or exploit their own insecurities? *Vogue,* pp. 220–226.

Tavris, C. (1989). *Anger: The misunderstood emotion* (2nd ed.). New York: Touchstone.

Tavris, C., & Wade, C. (1984). *The longest war: Sex differences in perspective* (2nd ed.). San Diego: Harcourt Brace Jovanovich.

Tay, K. H., Ward, C. M., & Hill, J. A. (1993, August). *Holland's congruence and certainty of career aspirations in Asian graduate students.* Paper presented at the meeting of the American Psychological Association, Toronto.

Taylor, R. D. (1996). The effects of economic and social stressors on parenting and adolescent adjustment in African-American families. In R. D. Taylor & M. C. Wang (Eds.), *Social and emotional adjustment and family relations in ethnic minority families.* Hillsdale, NJ: Erlbaum.

Taylor, R. D., & Wang, M. C. (Eds.). (1996). *Social and emotional adjustment and family relations in ethnic minority families.* Hillsdale, NJ: Erlbaum.

Taylor, S. E. (1979). Hospital patient behavior: Reactance, helplessness, or control? *Journal of Social Issues, 35,* 156–184.

Taylor, S. E. (1989). *Positive illusions: Creative self-deception and the healthy mind.* New York: Basic Books.

Taylor, S. E. (1995). *Health psychology* (2nd ed.). New York: McGraw-Hill.

Taylor, S. E., Collins, R., Skokan, L., & Aspinwall, L. (1988, August). *Illusion, reality, and adjustment in coping with victimizing events.* Paper presented at the meeting of the American Psychological Association, Atlanta.

Taylor, S. P. (1982). Mental health and successful coping among aged Black women. In R. C. Manuel (Ed.), *Minority aging.* Westport, CT: Greenwood.

Teachman, J. D., & Polonko, K. A. (1990). Cohabitation and marital stability in the United States. *Social Forces, 69,* 207–220.

Teasdale, J. D., Taylor, M. J., Cooper, Z., Hayhurst, H., & Paykel, E. S. (1995). Depressive thinking: Shifts in construct accessibility or in schematic mental models? *Journal of Abnormal Psychology, 104,* 500–507.

Temoshok, L., & Dreher, H. (1992). *The Type C syndrome.* New York: Random House.

Thayer, J. F., Rossy, L., Sollers, J., Friedman, B. H., & Allen, M. T. (1996, March). *Relationships among heart period variability and cardiodynamic measures vary as a function of fitness.* Paper presented at the meeting of the American Psychosomatic Society, Williamsburg, VA.

Thigpen, C. H., & Cleckley, H. M. (1957). *The Three Faces of Eve.* New York: McGraw-Hill.

Thomas, C. B. (1983). Unpublished manuscript. Baltimore: Johns Hopkins University.

Thompson, J. K. (Ed.). (1996). *Body image, eating disorders, and obesity.* Washington, DC: American Psychological Association.

Thompson, L., & Walker, A. J. (1989). Gender in families: Women and men in marriage, work, and parenthood. *Journal of Marriage and the Family, 51,* 845–871.

Thompson, R. A., & Cimbolic, P. (1978). Black students' counselor preference and attitudes toward counseling center use. *Journal of Counseling Psychology, 25,* 570–575.

Thornton, A., & Camburn, D. (1989). Religious participation and sexual behavior and attitudes. *Journal of Marriage and the Family, 51,* 641–653.

Tobin, J. J. (1987). The American idealization of old age in Japan. *Gerontologist, 27,* 53–58.

Tomlinson-Keasey, C., Warren, L. W., & Elliott, J. E. (1986). Suicide among gifted women prospective study. *Journal of Abnormal Psychology, 95,* 123–130.

Tran, T. V., Wright, R., & Chatters, L. (1991). Health, stress, psychological resources, and subjective well-being among older Blacks. *Psychology and Aging, 6,* 100–108.

Triandis, H. C. (1994). *Culture and social behavior.* New York: McGraw-Hill.

Triandis, H. C. (1996). The psychological measurement of cultural syndromes. *American Psychologist, 51,* 407–415.

Triandis, H. C., Brislin, R., & Hui, C. H. (1988). Cross-cultural training across the individualism divide. *International Journal of Intercultural Relations, 12,* 269–288.

Trimble, J. E., & Fleming, C. (1989). Client, counselor, and community characteristics. In P. Pedersen, J. Draguns, W. Lonner, & J. Trimble (Eds.), *Counseling across cultures* (3rd ed.). Honolulu: University of Hawaii Press.

Turpin, G., & Slade, P. (1997). Psychology and health. In P. Scott & C. Spencer (Eds.), *Psychology.* Cambridge, MA: Blackwell.

U

U.S. Bureau of the Census. (1990). *Statistical abstracts of the United States, 1990.* Washington, DC: U.S. Department of Commerce.

Ubell, C. (1992, December 6). We can age successfully. *Parade,* pp. 14–15.

Unger, R., & Crawford, M. (1992). *Women and gender* (2nd ed.). New York: McGraw-Hill.

Unger, R. K. (1993, August). *Social construction of biological sex.* Paper presented at the meeting of the American Psychological Association, Toronto.

Unger, R. K., & Crawford, M. (1992). *The psychology of sex and gender.* New York: McGraw-Hill.

V

Vaillant, G. E. (1977). *Adaptation to life.* Boston: Little, Brown.

Ventis, W. L. (in press). The relationships between religion and mental health. *Journal of Social Issues.*

Verbrugge, L. M. (1989). The twain meet: Empirical explanations of sex differences in health and mortality. *Journal of Health and Social Behavior, 30,* 282–304.

Vontress, C. E. (1973). Counseling: Racial and ethnic factors. *Focus on Guidance, 5,* 1–10.

W

Wadden, T. A., Foster, G. D., Stunkard, A. J., & Conill, A. M. (1996). Effects of weight cycling on the resting energy expenditure and body composition of obese women. *Eating Disorders, 19,* 5–12.

Wakschlag, L. S., Chase-Lansdale, P. L., & Brooks-Gunn, J. (1996, March). *Not just "ghosts in the nursery": Contemporaneous intergenerational relationships and parenting in young African American families.* Paper presented at the meeting of the Society for Research on Adolescent Development, Boston.

Walborn, F. S. (1996). *Process variables.* Pacific Grove, CA: Brooks/Cole.

Walker, L. E. (1979). *The battered woman.* New York: Harper & Row.

Wallace, R. R., & Benson, H. (1972). The physiology of meditation. *Scientific American, 226,* 85–90.

Wallerstein, J., Corbin, S. B., & Lewis, J. M. (1988). Children of divorce: A ten-year study. In E. M. Hetherington & J. Arasteh (Eds.), *Impact of divorce, single-parenting, and stepparenting on children.* Hillsdale, NJ: Erlbaum.

Wallerstein, R. S. (1989). The psychotherapy research project of the Menninger Foundation: An overview. *Journal of Consulting and Clinical Psychology, 57,* 195–205.

Wallis, C. (1985, December 9). Children having children. *Time,* pp. 78–88.

Ward, R. A., & Grashai, A. F. (1995). Using astrology to teach research methods to introductory psychology students. In M. E. Ware & D. E. Johnson (Eds.), *Demonstrations and activities in teaching of psychology* (Vol. 1). Hillsdale, NJ: Erlbaum.

Waterman, J. A. (1991). Career and life planning: A personal gyroscope in times of change. In J. M. Hummerow (Ed.), *New directions in career planning and the workplace*. Palo Alto, CA: Consulting Psychologists Press.

Watson, D. L., & Tharp, R. G. (1989). *Self-directed behavior* (5th ed.). Pacific Grove, CA: Brooks/Cole.

Watts, A. (1973). *This is it*. New York: Random House.

Wechsler, D. (1972). "Hold" and "Don't Hold" test. In S. M. Chown (Ed.), *Human aging*. New York: Penguin.

Wender, P. H., Kety, S. S., Rosenthal, D., Schulsinger, E., Ortmann, J., & Lunde, I. (1986). Psychiatric disorders in the biological and adoptive families of adopted individuals with affective disorders. *Archives of General Psychiatry, 43*, 923–939.

Wenzlaff, R. M., & Prohaska, M. L. (1989). When misery loves company: Depression, attributions, and responses to others' moods. *Journal of Experimental Social Psychology, 25*, 220–223.

Weskott, M. (1986). *The feminist legacy of Karen Horney*. New Haven, CT: Yale University Press.

Westin, D. (1991). Cultural, emotional, and unconscious aspects of self. In R. C. Curtis (Ed.), *The relational self*. New York: Guilford.

Whiston, S. C., & Sexton, T. L. (1993). An overview of psychotherapy outcome research: Implications for practice. *Professional Psychology, 24*, 43–51.

Whitbourne, S. K. (1996). *The aging individual*. New York: Springer.

White, K. M., Speisman, J. C., Costos, D., & Smith, A. (1987). Relationship maturity: A conceptual and empirical approach. In J. Meacham (Ed.), *Interpersonal relations: Family, peers, friends*. Basel, Switzerland: Karger.

White, L. K. (1990). Determinants of divorce: A review of research in the eighties. *Journal of Marriage and the Family, 52*, 904–912.

Whiting, B. B. (1989, April). *Culture and interpersonal behavior*. Paper presented at the biennial meeting of the Society for Research in Child Development, Kansas City.

Whitman, F. L., Diamond, M., & Martin, J. (1993). Homosexual orientation in twins: A report of 61 pairs and three triplet sets. *Archives of Sexual Behavior, 22*, 187–198.

Whitney, K., Sagrestano, L. M., & Maslach, C. (1994). Establishing the social impact of individuation. *Journal of Personality and Social Psychology, 66*, 1140–1153.

Williams, J. (1987). *Psychology of women: Behavior in a biosocial context* (3rd ed.). New York: W. W. Norton.

Williams, J. E., & Best, D. L. (1982). *Measuring sex stereotypes: A thirty-nation study*. Newbury Park, CA: Sage.

Williams, J. E., & Best, D. L. (1989). *Sex and psyche: Self-concept viewed cross-culturally*. Newbury Park, CA: Sage.

Williams, R. B. (1995). Coronary prone behaviors, hostility, and cardiovascular health: Implications for behavioral and pharmacological interventions. In K. Orth-Gomer & N. Schneiderman (Eds.), *Behavioral medicine approaches to cardiovascular disease prevention*. Hillsdale, NJ: Erlbaum.

Wilson, G. T. (1994). Behavioral treatment of obesity: Thirty years and counting. *Advances in Behaviour Research and Therapy, 16*, 31–75.

Wilson, W. J., & Neckerman, K. M. (1986). Poverty and family structure: The widening gap between evidence and public policy issues. In S. Danziger & D. Weinberg (Eds.), *Fighting poverty*. Cambridge, MA: Harvard University Press.

Wolpe, J. (1963). Behavior therapy in complex neurotic states. *British Journal of Psychiatry, 110*, 28–34.

Wolpe, J. (1968). *Psychotherapy by reciprocal inhibition*. Stanford, CA: Stanford University Press.

Wong, H. Z. (1982). Asian and Pacific Americans. In L. Snowden (Ed.), *Reaching the underserved: Mental health needs of neglected populations*. Beverly Hills, CA: Sage.

Wong, M. M., & Csikszentmihalyi, M. (1991). Affiliation motivation and daily experience: Some issues on gender differences. *Journal of Personality and Social Psychology, 609*, 154–164.

Wood, J. T. (1994). *Gendered lives: Communication, gender, and culture*. Belmont, CA: Wadsworth.

Wood, J. T. (1996). Gender, relationships, and communication. In J. T. Wood (Ed.), *Gendered relationships*. Mountain View, CA: Mayfield.

Wooley, S. C., & Garner, D. M. (1991). Obesity treatment: The high cost of false hope. *Journal of the American Dietetic Association, 91*, 1248–1251.

Worell, J., & Robinson, D. (1993). Feminist counseling therapy for the 21st century. *Counseling Psychologist, 21*, 92–96.

Worschel, S., & Cooper, J. (1979). *Understanding social psychology*. Homewood, IL: Dorsey.

Wulff, D. M. (1991). *Psychology of religion: Classic and contemporary views*. New York: Wiley.

Y

Yalom, I. D. (Ed.). (1995). *The theory and practice of group psychotherapy* (4th ed.). New York: Basic Books.

Yankelovich, D., Skelly, F., & White, A. (1984). *Sex stereotypes and candidacy for high level political office*. New York: Author.

Yates, B. (1985). *Self-management: The science and art of helping yourself*. Belmont, CA: Wadsworth.

Yates, M. (1996, March). *Community service and political-moral discussions among Black-urban adolescents*. Paper presented at the meeting of the Society for Research on Adolescence, Boston.

Yates, M. J. (1995, March). *Political socialization as a function of volunteerism*. Paper presented at the meeting of the Society for Research in Child Development, Indianapolis.

Yee, B. W. K. (1996, August). *Breaking bamboo barriers: Prevention in Southeast Asian immigrant communities*. Paper presented at the meeting of the American Psychological Association, Toronto.

Z

Zeigler, L. H., & Harmon, W. (1989). More bad news about the news. *Public Opinion, 12*, 50–52.

Zelnik, M., & Kantner, J. F. (1977). Sexual and contraceptive experiences of young unmarried women in the United States, 1976 and 1971. *Family Planning Perspectives, 9*, 55–71.

Zilbergeld, B. (1992). *The new male sexuality*. New York: Bantam Books.

Zimbardo, P., Haney, C., Banks, W., & Jaffe, D. (1972). *The psychology of imprisonment: Privation, power, and pathology*. Unpublished manuscript, Stanford University, Stanford, CA.

CREDITS

Image Bank-Chicago; 11.1f: © K. Kasmauski/ Woodfin Camp & Associates; 11.1g: After: Carter, B., & McGoldrick, M. Overview: The changing life cycle—A framework for family therapy.; p. 257: © Peter Menzel/Stock Boston; 11.2: © Michael Melford/The Image Bank-Texas; p. 260: © William Hubbell/ Woodfin Camp and Associates; 11.3: © William Hopkins; p. 264 left: © Jim Whitmer Photography; p. 264 right: © Bob Daemmrich/Image Works

Chapter 12

Opener: © Art Resource/Erich Lessing; p. 280: © Bob Daemmrich/Image Works; 12.3: © Gill G. Kenny/The Image Bank-Chicago; p. 290 left: © Shooting Star; p. 290 right: © Kenneth Jarecke/Contact Press; 12.6: © Weinberg Clark/The Image Bank-Chicago; p. 298 top: © David Frazier Photolibrary; p. 298 bottom: © Brett Froomer/The Image Bank-Chicago

Chapter 13

Opener: © SuperStock; p. 306: © John Goodman; p. 307: © Henley & Savage/The Stock Market; p. 312 all: © Bettmann; 13.3a: © Bettmann Archive; 13.3b: © Andy Caulfield/The Image Bank-Texas; p. 315a: © Owen Franken/Stock Boston; p. 315b: © Bettman Archives; 13.4: © Nilo Lima/Photo Researchers, Inc.; p. 318: © Bob Daemmrich/ Stock Boston; p. 318 left: © Bruce Kliewe/ Jeroboam; p. 320: © Elyse Lewin/The Image Bank-Texas; p. 321: © Wayne Floyd/Unicorn Photos; p. 322: © Comstock, Inc.; 13.5: Courtesy of University of California; p. 324 left: © Julie Markes/AP/Wide World Photos; p. 324 middle: Neal Peters Collection; p. 324 right: © Bettmann/UPI; p. 324 bottom: Courtesy of Margaret Gatz; 13.6: © Eastrath/Momatwick/Image Works

Chapter 14

Opener: The Metropolitan Museum of Art, The Berggruen Klee Collection, 1984; p. 335: © Bettmann Archives; p. 336 left: © Robert Brenner/PhotoEdit; p. 336 middle: © David Young Wolff/PhotoEdit; p. 336 right: © Richard Hutchings/PhotoEdit; p. 338 top: Courtesy of Nancy Felipe Russo; p. 338a: © Adam Tannen/Comstock; p. 338b: © Stephen Marks/The Image Bank-Chicago; 14.1: © MUSEUM; p. 345: © Richard Laird/FPG; 14.3: © Gerald Martineau/The Washington Post; p. 351: © Bob Daemmrich/Stock Boston; 14.4: August Natterer, Inv. Nr. 184, "Hexenkopf", date unknown, Prinhorn-Collection of the Psychiatric Clinic, University of Heidelberg, Jugeborg Klinger; 14.5: © Grunnitus/ Monkmeyer Press; p. 359 left: © AP Wide World Photos; p. 359 right: © Bettmann

Chapter 15

Opener: Courtesy of John W. Santrock; 15.1: © National Museum of Denmark; 15.2: © Stock Montage; p. 372: © Stock Montage;

15.3: © Bosch/Art Resource; p. 374: Courtesy of Deke Simen; 15.4: David Frazier Photolibrary; p. 381: © Bob Daemmrich/Stock Boston; p. 384: © Jay Lurie Photography; p. 388: © Russ Kinne/Comstock; p. 389a: © Comstock; p. 389b: © J. Y. Rabeuf/Image Works; p. 389c: © Peter Menzel/Stock Boston; p. 389d: © Robert Houser/Comstock; p. 393: © Will McIntyre/Photo Researchers, Inc.

Chapter 16

Opener: © Scala/Art Resource; p. 401 left: © George V. Mann, M.D.; p. 401 right: © David Stoecklein/The Stock Market; p. 404 top left: © Douglas Fisher/The Image Bank-Chicago; p. 404 bottom left: © W. Woodworth/SuperStock; p. 404 right: © David Ball/Tony Stone; 16.2: © John Elk; p. 410: © Tony Freeman/PhotoEdit; p. 411: © Wide World Photos; p. 413 left: Roy Morsch/The Stock Market; p. 413 right: © Comstock; p. 415: © James Wilson/ Woodfin Camp; p. 420: © Uzzle/Actuality; p. 422: © John Bowen (photographer) and Richard Brislin

Chapter 17

Opener: Courtesy of John W. Santrock; p. 430: AP/Wide World Photos; 17.1: © D. W. Productions/The Image Bank-Texas; p. 433: © Randall Hyman/Stock Boston; p. 435: © Keith Carter; p. 439 top left: © Nabeel Turner/Tony Stone Images; p. 439 top right: © Don Smetzer/Tony Stone Images; p. 439 bottom left: © David Austen/Tony Stone Images; p. 439 bottom right: © Bob Daemmrich/Tony Stone Images; p. 439 middle: © Jim Pickeral/Tony Stone Images; p. 440: UPI/Bettmann; p. 443 top: © Bob Daemmrich/Tony Stone Images; 17.2: © Tony Arruza/Tony Stone Images; p. 444 top: © Paul Chesley/Tony Stone Images; p. 444 left: © David Austen/Tony Stone Images; p. 444 right: © Bob Daemmrich/Tony Stone Images; p. 446: © Lawrence Manning/Tony Stone Images

Epilogue

Opener: © SuperStock; p. 460 top left: Connie Coleman/Tony Stone Images; p. 460 middle left: © Carlos Navajos/The Image Bank-Chicago; p. 460 bottom left: © David Frazier; p. 460 top right: © Marvin Neuman/The Image Bank-Chicago; p. 460 bottom right: © Phil Borgen/Tony Stone Images

---

LINE ART AND TEXT

Chapter 1

p. 21: From John W. Santrock, et al., *The Authoritative Guide to Self-Help Books.* Copyright © 1994 The Guilford Press. Reprinted by permission. p. 21: Hines, Terence, *Pseudoscience and the Paranormal: A Critical Examination of the Evidence* (1988: Buffalo: Prometheus Books). Reprinted by permission.

Chapter 2

Figure 2.1: From *Psychology: A Scientific Study of Human Behavior* by L. S. Wrightsman, C. K. Sigelman, and F. H. Sanford. Copyright © 1979, 1975, 1970, 1965, 1961 Brooks/Cole Publishing Company, Pacific Grove, CA 93950, a division of International Thomson Publishing Inc. By permission of the publisher. Self-Assessment, p. 32: From C. R. Snyder and H. L. Fromkin, *Uniqueness: The Human Pursuit of Difference.* Copyright © 1980 Plenum Publishing Corporation. Reprinted by permission. Figure 2.8: Courtesy of Dr. Hans J. Eysenck. Poem, p. 43: Excerpted from a poem entitled "Self-Improvement Program"—Copyright © 1973, 1974, 1976 by Judith Viorst. Appears in her book entitled *How did I get to be 40 & other atrocities,* published by Simon & Schuster. Reprinted by permission. p. 50: Reprinted with the permission of Simon & Schuster from *Control Your Depression* by Peter M. Lewinsohn, Ricardo F. Muñoz, Mary Ann Youngren, and Antonette M. Zeiss. Cover copyright © 1992 by Simon & Schuster, Inc. p. 50: Published by Aslan Publishing, PO Box 108, Lower Lake, CA 95457, (800)275–2606. Reprinted by permission.

Chapter 3

Self-Assessment, p. 57: Source: M. Rosenberg, *Society and the Adolescent Self-Image,* Princeton University Press, 1965. Self-Assessment, p. 62: From R. A. Emmons, "Narcissism: Theory and Measurement" in *Journal of Personality and Social Psychology,* 52:11–17. Copyright © 1987 by the American Psychological Association. Reprinted with permission. p. 74: From Linda Tschirhart Sanford and Mary Ellen Donovan, *Women and Self-Esteem,* 1984. Reprinted by permission of Bantam Books, a division of Bantam Doubleday Dell Publishing Group, Inc. p. 74: Reprinted with the permission of Simon & Schuster from *The Road Less Traveled* by M. Scott Peck. Copyright © 1979 by Robert Anthony, Inc.

Chapter 4

Figure 4.2: From: *Brain, Mind, and Behavior* by Bloom, Lazerson, and Hofstadter. Copyright © 1985 by the Educational Broadcasting Corporation. Used with permission of W. H. Freeman and Company. Figure 4.3: From Schmitt and Worden (Eds.), *The Neurosciences: A Third Study Program.* Copyright © 1974 The MIT Press. Reprinted by permission. Self-Assessment, p. 85: Adapted and reproduced by special permission of the publisher, Psychological Assessment Resources, Inc., 16204 North Florida Avenue, Lutz, FL 33549, from the STAXI by Charles D. Spielberger, Ph.D., Copyright 1979, 1986, 1988, by Psychological Assessment Resources, Inc. Reproduced by special permission from PAR, Inc. Self-Assessment, p. 91: Reprinted by permission of the publisher from T. H. Holmes and

R. H. Rahe, "The Social Readjustment Rating Scale" in *Journal of Psychosomatic Research,* 11:203–218. Copyright 1967 by Elsevier Science Inc. p. 97: From Harriet Lerner, *The Dance of Anger.* Copyright © 1985 Harper Perennial, New York, NY. Reprinted by permission. p. 97: From Mihaly Csikszentmihalyi, *Flow.* Copyright © 1990 Harper & Row, New York, NY. Reprinted by permission.

Chapter 5

Figure 5.1: From C. J. Holahan and R. H. Moos, "Personal & Contextual Determinants of Coping Strategies" in *Journal of Personality and Social Psychology,* 52:946–955. Copyright © 1987 by the American Psychological Association. Reprinted with permission. Figure 5.2: From *Contemporary Behavior Therapy,* by M. D. Spiegler and D. C. Guevremont. Copyright © 1993 Brooks/Cole Publishing Company, Pacific Grove, CA 93950, a division of International Thomson Publishing Inc. By permission of the publisher. Figure 5.6: Reprinted from J. W. Kendrick & J. B. Kendrick, *Personal Productivity,* © 1988 by permission of M. E. Sharpe, Inc. p. 119: Reprinted with the permission of Pocket Books, a division of Simon & Schuster from *Learned Optimism* by Martin E. P. Seligman. Copyright © 1990 by Bob Silverman. p. 119: From Herbert Benson, *Beyond the Relaxation Response.* Copyright © 1984 Times Books. Reprinted by permission of Times Books, a division of Random House, Inc.

Chapter 6

Self-Assessment, p. 124: From M. Snyder, *Journal of Personality and Social Psychology,* 30:526–537. Copyright © 1974 by the American Psychological Association. Reprinted with permission. Figure 6.4: Source: S. E. Asch, "Studies of Independence and Conformity: A Minority of One Against a Unanimous Majority" in *Psychological Monographs,* 90 (whole no. 416), American Psychological Association, 1956. p. 141: Cover of *Influence* by Robert Cialdini. Cover design by Tom McKeveny. By permission of Quill Trade Paperbacks, an imprint of William Morrow & Company, Inc. p. 141: P. Zimbardo, *Shyness,* © 1977 Philip Zimbardo, Inc. Reprinted by permission of Addison-Wesley Publishing Company, Inc.

Chapter 7

Figure 7.2: Source: Data from L. Barker, et al., "An Investigation of Proportional Time Spent in Various Communication Activities by College Students" in *Journal of Applied Communication Research,* Vol. 8, Speech Communication Association, 1981. Figure 7.3: From Joseph Luft, *Group Processes: An Introduction to Group Dynamics.* Copyright © 1984 Mayfield Publishing Company. Reprinted by permission. Figure 7.4: From

Parent Effectiveness Training by Thomas Gordon. Copyright © 1970 by Thomas Gordon. Reprinted by permission of David McKay Co., a division of Random House, Inc. Self-Assessment, p. 155: From D. A. Infants and A. S. Rancer, "A Conceptualization of Argumentativeness" in *Journal of Personality Assessment* 46:72–80. Copyright © 1982 Lawrence Erlbaum Associates, Inc. Reprinted by permission. p. 165: From Deborah Tannen, *You Just Don't Understand.* Copyright © 1990 Ballantine, a division of Random House, Inc. Reprinted by permission. p. 165: From *Your Perfect Right: A Guide to Assertive Living* (Sixth Edition) © 1990 by Robert E. Alberti and Michael L. Emmons. Reproduced by permission of Impact Publishers, Inc., PO Box 1094, San Luis Obispo, CA 93406. Further reproduction prohibited.

Chapter 8

Excerpt, p. 168: From *Like Water for Chocolate* by Laura Esquivel. Copyright Translation © 1992 by Doubleday, a div. of Bantam, Doubleday, Dell Publishing Group, Inc. Used by permission of Doubleday, a division of Bantam Doubleday Dell Publishing Group, Inc. Self-Assessment, p. 173: From *Bulletin of the Psychonomic Society* 2:219–220, 1973, reprinted by permission of Psychonomic Society, Inc. Self-Assessment, p. 176: From Janet S. Hyde, *Half the Human Experience: The Psychology of Women,* 5th ed. Copyright © 1995 by D. C. Heath and Company, Lexington, MA. Used by permission of Houghton Mifflin Company. Figure 8.2: From Janet S. Hyde, et al., "Gender Differences in Mathematics Performance" in *Psychological Bulletin,* 107:139–155. Copyright © 1990 by the American Psychological Association. Reprinted with permission. p. 192: Reprinted with the permission of Simon & Schuster from *The Mismeasure of Woman* by Carol Tavris. Copyright © 1992 by Carol Tavris. p. 192: From *The New Male* by Herb Goldberg. Used by permission of Dutton Signet, a division of Penguin Books USA Inc.

Chapter 9

Figure 9.3: From W. H. Masters and V. E. Johnson, *Human Sexual Response,* 1966. Reprinted by permission. Figure 9.4: From C. A. Darling, et al., "Sex in Transition, 1900–1984" in *Journal of Youth and Adolescence,* 13:385–399. Copyright © 1984 Plenum Publishing Corporation. Reprinted by permission. Figure 9.5: From *Sex in America* by Robert Michael, et al. Copyright © 1994 by CSG Enterprises, Inc., Edward O. Laumann, Robert T. Michael, and Gina Kolata. By permission of Little, Brown and Company. Figure 9.6: From Alfred C. Kinsey, *Sexual Behavior in the Human Female.* Copyright © 1953 The Kinsey Institute for Research in Sex, Gender, and Reproduction. Reprinted by permission of The Kinsey Institute for Research in Sex, Gender, and Reproduction,

Inc. Self-Assessment, p. 209: Reprinted from *The Journal of Sex Research,* a publication of The Society for the Scientific Study of Sex; PO Box 208, Mount Vernon, IA 52314, USA. Self-Assessment, p. 216: Reprinted from *Journal of Behavior Therapy and Experimental Psychiatry,* 20, J. Kelly, et al., "An Objective Test of AIDS Risk Behavior Knowledge: Scale Development, Validation, and Norms," pages 227–234, Copyright 1989, with permission from Pergamon Press Ltd, Headington Hill Hall, Oxford 0X3 0BW, UK. p. 222: From *For Yourself: The Fulfillment of Female Sexuality* by Lonnie Garfield Barbach. Copyright © 1975 by Lonnie Garfield Barbach. Used by permission of Dutton Signet, a division of Penguin Books USA Inc. p. 222: From Bernie Zilbergeld, *The New Male Sexuality.* Copyright © 1992 Bantam Books. Reprinted by permission of Bantam Doubleday Dell Publishing Group, Inc. p. 223: From *Permanent Partners* by Betty Berzon, Ph.D. Copyright © 1988 by Betty Berzon, Ph.D. Used by permission of Dutton Signet, a division of Penguin Books USA Inc.

Chapter 10

Figure 10.1: © Zick Rubin, 1969. Reprinted by permission of the author. Self-Assessment, p. 230: From E. Hatfield, "Passionate and Companionate Love" in R. J. Sternberg and M. L. Barnes (Eds.), *The Psychology of Love.* Copyright © Yale University Press. Reprinted by permission. Figure 10.2: Source: Data from R. J. Sternberg, *The Triangle of Love,* Basic Books, Inc., 1988. Self-Assessment, p. 233: From David H. Olson, Ph.D., University of Minnesota. Reprinted with permission. Figure 10.3: Reprinted with the permission of Simon & Schuster from *Anger: The Misunderstood Emotion* by Carol Tavris. Copyright © 1989 by Carol Tavris. p. 246: From Harriet Lerner, *The Dance of Intimacy.* Copyright © 1990 Harper Perennial, New York, NY. Reprinted by permission. p. 246: From Harville Hendrix, *Getting the Love You Want.* Copyright © 1988 Harper Perennial, New York, NY. Reprinted by permission.

Chapter 11

Figure 11.1: From Betty Carter and Monica McGoldrick, *The Changing Family Life Cycle: A Framework for Family Therapy,* 2d ed. Copyright © by Allyn & Bacon. Reprinted by permission. Figure 11.3: Reproduced with the permission of The Alan Guttmacher Institute from: Elise F. Jones, et al., "Teenage Pregnancy in Developed Countries: Determinants and Policy Implications," *Family Planning Perspectives,* Volume 17, Number 2, March/April 1985. Self-Assessment, p. 266: From Jeffry H. Larson, "The Marriage Quiz: College Students' Beliefs in Selected Myths about Marriage" in *Family Relations,* 37:1. Copyright © 1988 by the National Council on Family Relations, 3989 Central Ave. NE, Suite 550, Minneapolis, MN

55421. Reprinted by permission. Self-Assessment, p. 268: Reprinted from *Behavior Research and Therapy,* 11, N. H. Azrin, et al., "Reciprocity Counseling: A Learning Based Procedure for Marital Counseling," pages 365–382, Copyright 1973, with kind permission from Pergamon Press Ltd, Headington Hill Hall, Oxford 0X3 0BW, UK. p. 274: T. Berry Brazelton, *To Listen to a Child,* © 1984 T. Berry Brazelton. Reprinted by permission of Addison-Wesley Publishing Company, Inc. Photo © Hornick/Rivlin. Reprinted by permission. p. 274: From Lenore Walker, *The Battered Woman.* Copyright © 1979 Harper & Row, New York, NY. Reprinted by permission.

Chapter 12

Excerpt, p. 278: From *The Harvard Lampoon Big Book of College Life.* Copyright © The Harvard Lampoon. Reprinted by permission. Figure 12.2: Holland, J. L. (1973, 1985, 1992) *Making Vocational Choices: A Theory of Vocational Choices and Work Environments* (Second edition), Psychological Assessment Resources, Inc., Odessa, FL. Figure 12.3: Gregory Moorhead and Ricky Griffin: *Organizational Behavior,* Third Edition. Copyright © 1992 by Houghton Mifflin Company. Adapted with permission. Figure 12.4: From Lois M. Tamir, *Men in their Forties.* Copyright © 1982 Springer Publishing Company, Inc., New York 10012. Used by permission. Figure 12.5: From R. H. Moos, "Work as a Human Context" in M. S. Pollack and R. Perloff (Eds.), *Psychology and Work.* Copyright © 1986 by the American Psychological Association. Reprinted with permission. Self-Assessment, p. 295: Pauline Rose Clance, *The Imposter Phenomenon: When Success Makes You Feel Like a Fake.* Atlanta: Peachtree Publishers, 1985. Reprinted with permission. Figure 12.7: Source: Data from the Bureau of Labor Statistics; chart from Occupational Outlook Handbook. p. 302: *What Color Is Your Parachute?* by Richard Nelson Bolles. Copyright © 1996 by Richard Nelson Bolles. Reprinted by permission of Ten Speed Press, PO Box 7123, Berkeley, CA 94707. p. 302: Reprinted with the permission of Simon & Schuster from *The Seven Habits of Highly Effective People* by Stephen R. Covey. Copyright © 1989 by Stephen R. Covey.

Chapter 13

Figure 13.1: From *The Seasons of a Man's Life* by Daniel J. Levinson, et al. Copyright © 1978 by Daniel J. Levinson. Reprinted by permission of Alfred A. Knopf, Inc. Figure 13.4: Source: U.S. Bureau of the Census, *The Statistical History of the United States,* 1976, Social Security Administration. Poem, p. 319: From *Verses From 1929 On* by Ogden Nash. Copyright © 1956 by Ogden Nash. Copyright © renewed 1984 by Frances Nash, Isabel Nash Eberstadt and Linnell Nash Smith. First appeared in *The New Yorker.* By permission of Little, Brown and Company. Self-Assessment, p. 327: From R. Lonetto and D. Templer, "The Nature of Death Anxiety" in *Advances in Personality Assessment,* Vol. 3, C. D. Speiberger and J. Buther (Eds.). Copyright © 1983 Lawrence Erlbaum Associates, Inc. Reprinted by permission. p. 331: From *How to Deal with Your Parents When They Still Treat You Like a Child* by Lynn Osterkamp, Ph.D. Copyright © 1992 by Lynn Osterkamp, Ph.D. Reprinted by permission of The Berkley Publishing Group. p. 331: E. Langer, *Mindfulness,* © 1989 Ellen J. Langer. Reprinted by permission of Addison-Wesley Publishing Company, Inc.

Chapter 14

Poem, p. 333: From *The Poetry of Robert Frost* edited by Edward Connery Lathem. Copyright 1936 by Robert Frost. Copyright © 1964 by Lesley Frost Ballantine. Copyright © 1969 by Henry Holt and Co., Inc. Reprinted by permission of Henry Holt and Co., Inc. Self-Assessment, p. 344: Reprinted from *Behavioral Research and Therapy,* 3, J. Geer, "The Development of a Scale to Measure Fear," pages 45–53, Copyright 1965, with kind permission from Pergamon Press Ltd, Headington Hill Hall, Oxford 0X3 0BW, UK. Self-Assessment, p. 353: Source: L. Radloff, "The CES-D Scale: A Self-Report of Depression Scale for Research in the General Population" in *Journal of Applied Psychological Measurement,* 1:385–401, 1977. Figure 14.6: From I. I. Gottesman and J. Shields, *Schizophrenia: The Epigenetic Puzzle.* Copyright © 1992 Cambridge University Press. Reprinted with the permission of Cambridge University Press. p. 362: From R. Reid Wilson, *Don't Panic.* Copyright © 1986 HarperCollins Publishers, Inc. Reprinted by permission. p. 362: From Steven Levenkron, *Obsessive-Compulsive Disorders,* 1991. Reprinted by permission of Warner Books, Inc., New York.

Chapter 15

Drawings, p. 369: Source: National Library of Medicine. Self-Assessment, p. 379: From A. MacDonald and R. Games, "Ellis' Irrational Values" in *Rational Living,* 7:25–28. Copyright © 1972 Human Sciences Press, Inc. Reprinted by permission. p. 397: Reprinted with the permission of Simon & Schuster from *The Consumer's Guide to Psychotherapy* by Jack Engler and Daniel Golemann. Cover copyright © 1992 by Simon & Schuster, Inc. p. 397: Reproduced by permission of the publisher F. E. Peacock Publishers Inc., Itasca, Illinois. From Raymond J. Corsini, *Five Therapists and One Client,* 1991, cover.

Chapter 16

Figure 16.1: From L. L. Langley, *Physiology of Man.* Copyright © 1971 Van Nostrand Reinhold. Reprinted by permission of the author. p. 427: From Kenneth Cooper, *The New Aerobics,* 1970. Used by permission of Bantam, a division of Bantam Doubleday Dell Publishing Group. p. 427: Copyright © 1977, 1978, 1991 by Covert Bailey. Used by permission of Houghton Mifflin Co. All rights reserved.

Chapter 17

Figure 17.1: Reprinted by permission of the Higher Education Research Institute, University of California, Los Angeles. Self-Assessment, p. 442: From Craig W. Ellison and Raymond F. Paloutzian, The Spiritual Well-Being Scale. Copyright © Craig W. Ellison and Raymond F. Paloutzian. Reprinted by permission. p. 450: Reprinted with the permission of Simon & Schuster from *Man's Search for Meaning* by Viktor E. Frankl. Copyright © 1984 by Viktor E. Frankl.

Epilogue

Display quotation on page 453 reprinted by permission from 'Abdu'l-Baha, *Selections from The Writings of 'Abdu'l-Baha,* comp. Research Department of the Universal House of Justice, trans. Committee at the Baha'i World Center and Marzieh Gail, Copyright © 1978 by the Universal House of Justice.

Illustrators

Illustrious, Inc.

2.1, 2.5, 2.8, 2.9, 4.3, 4.4, 4.5, 6.2B, 6.4B, 8.1, 8.4B, 9.1, 9.2, 10.2A, 10.4, 11.3A, 13.1A, 13.3C, 13.4B, 14.1B, 14.2, 14.6, 15.3A, 15.4A, 15.5; text art, page 245

Hans & Cassady:

4.2

PC&F:

13.6A

Precision Graphics:

7.5

Wilderness Graphics:

2.4, 2.6H, 3.1, 3.2, 3.3, 3.4B, 3.5, 3.8B, 3.9B, 4.1, 5.1, 5.2, 5.3, 5.4, 5.5, 5.6, 5.7, 6.1B, 7.1, 7.2, 7.3B, 7.4, 7.6E, 9.4B, 12.2, 12.5, 12.7, 13.2, 16.2B, 17.1B, E.1; text art, pages 20, 49, 54, 73, 96, 118, 140, 164, 191, 221, 273, 302, 330, 361, 396, 426, 449

Name Index

Laughlin, P. L., 134
LaVoie, J., 68
Lazar, J. B., 349
Lazarus, R. S., 84, 85, 88, 91, 92, 101
Leary, M. R., 123
Leber, W. R., 352
Lebow, J. L., 381
Lee, D. J., 9
Lee, G. R., 260
Lee, I., 402
Lee, J., 82
Lefkowitz, E. S., 409
Leiblum, S. R., 210
Leinster, C., 299
Leiter, M. P., 289
Lerner, H. G., 170, 238
Leshner, A. I., 352
Lesser, I., 238
Leukefeld, C. G., 217
Levant, R., 184
LeVay, S., 208
Leventhal, H., 130
Levine, S. V., 446
Levinson, D., 280, 281, 311
Levinson, D. J., 312
Levy, S. M., 82
Lewis, J. M., 270
Lieberman, M., 434
Lieberman, M. A., 382
Liebkind, K., 92
Light, K. C., 402
Lightner, J. M., 412
Linn, M. C., 177
Lipscomb, G. H., 212
Litt, I. F., 251
Lituchy, T., 298
Liu, J., 298
Livesley, W. J., 357
Lofland, J., 446
Longfellow, C., 94
Lonner, W. J., 45, 456, 457
Lopata, H. Z., 320
Lowman, R. L., 283
Lucas, J., 324
Lucas, J. A., 299
Ludolph, P., 61, 348
Lunde, I., 352
Luria, A., 183
Lyon, M., 278

M

Maccoby, E. E., 178, 183, 258
MacKenzie, A., 115
Maddi, S., 25, 87
Magana, D., 413
Magee, W. J., 343
Mahoney, K. M., 432
Maines, D. R., 314
Majidi-Ahi, S., 60
Makosky, V., 94
Malamuth, N. M., 214
Malone, K. M., 352
Malpass, R., 456, 457
Mammersmith, S. K., 208
Mann, J. J., 352
Mann, L., 137

Manning, M. L., 157
Mantle, M., 400
Maracek, J., 175, 179
Marcia, J., 66, 68, 238
Marcia, J. E., 66, 68
Marin, G., 9
Markides, K., 318
Markman, H. J., 267
Markson, E. W., 320
Markus, H., 44, 55
Marlatt, G. A., 419
Marsella, A. J., 345
Marsiske, M., 323
Martin, C. L., 184
Martin, E. E., 204, 206
Martin, G., 106
Martin, G. L., 376
Martin, J., 123, 208
Martin, J. A., 258
Maslach, C., 135
Maslow, A. H., 37, 39
Masters, W., 213
Masters, W. H., 198
Mathews, A., 402, 403
Matlin, M. W., 177
Maupin, R. J., 7, 298
Mayer, F. S., 25
Mays, V., 388
Mays, V. M., 215
McAdams, D. P., 55, 237
McAdoo, H. P., 264
McAleer, J. L., 131
McBride, A. B., 94, 292
McBurney, D. H., 15
McConahy, N., 210
McDavis, R. J., 187
McFeeley, S., 82
McGoldrick, M., 254
McGuffin, P., 350, 352
McKinlay, J. B., 309
McKinlay, S. M., 309
McKinney, K., 206
McLoyd, V. C., 8, 9, 264, 270
McMullen, A., 123
McNeil, E. B., 354
McNeill, D., 162
McRae, R. R., 315
McWilliams, N., 292
Meacham, M. L., 70
Medoff, D. R., 392
Meehl, P. E., 339
Mehrabian, A., 156
Meichenbaum, D., 106, 377
Melman, A., 210
Mercer, A., 159
Mercer, B. M., 212
Mervis, J., 378
Messinger, J. C., 198
Metalsky, G. I., 352
Meyer, K. A., 349
Meyer, R. G., 345
Meyers, D. G., 440
Meyers, J., 334
Michael, R. T., 204, 206
Michal-Johnson, P., 218
Michelozzi, B. N., 283

Miles, M. B., 382
Milgram, S., 131
Miller, D. T., 416
Miller, H. L., 352
Miller, J. G., 436
Miller, N. E., 89, 113
Miller, R. L., 386
Miller, S. K., 410
Minnett, A. M., 18
Mintun, M. A., 352
Mintz, N., 338
Minuchin, P., 381
Mischel, W., 36, 43, 44
Money, J., 198
Montello, D. R., 123
Moore, G. W., 299
Moos, R., 101
Moos, R. H., 101, 109, 288
Morris, D., 161
Morten, G., 389, 390
Morton, D., 82
Moses, J., 402, 403
Moskowitz, D. S., 179
Mozley, L. H., 178
Mozley, P. D., 178
Mueller, R., 298
Munroe, R. H., 45
Munroe, R. L., 45
Muram, D., 212
Murdock, G. P., 213
Murray, D., 410
Murray, V. M., 263
Mussen, P. H., 315
Myers, D. G., 83, 308

N

Natalle, E. J., 297
Nathan, P. E., 340
National Academy of Sciences, National
    Research Council, 405
National Advisory Council on Economic
    Opportunity, 94
National and Community Service
    Coalition, 433
National Center for Health Statistics, 325
National Institutes of Health, 409
Neckerman, K. M., 94
Neugarten, B. L., 309, 314
Newman, E., 148, 161, 162
Newport, F., 21
Newsom, G. E., 357
Nezlek, J. B., 123
Nicastro, A., 210
Nichols, M. P., 381
Nisbett, R. E., 55
Nishio, K., 187
Noelker, L. S., 329
Nolen-Hoeksema, S., 171, 350, 352
Norem, J. K., 105
Norton, R., 151
Notarius, C. I., 265
Novak, C. A., 309
Novak, W., 226
Nunn, R. G., 406
Nurius, P., 55

Sasaki, T., 355
Satir, V., 381
Sauber, M., 269
Saunder, E., 94
Sax, L. J., 432
Saxton, A. M., 408
Schaef, A. W., 289
Schaefer, C., 92
Schaie, K. W., 318, 319, 322
Scheidt, S., 87
Schein, V. E., 298
Schmitt, D. P., 179
Schneider, L. S., 417
Schneiderman, N., 82
Schoenrade, P., 438, 446
Schofield, J. W., 130
Schuetz-Mueller, D., 210
Schuldberg, D., 271
Schulenberg, J., 308
Schulsinger, E., 352
Schulz, R., 309, 327
Schwartz, D., 338
Schwartz, P., 207
Schwartz, R., 422
Schwartz, R. C., 381
Schwartz, S. H., 45, 433
Scitovsky, A. A., 318
Scott-Jones, D., 9
Scurfield, R. M., 345
Seager, J., 171
Seagull, A., 339
Sears, D. O., 457
Sechzur, J., 177, 423
Secker-Walker, R. H., 410
Seeley, J. W., 269
Seffge-Krenke, I., 81
Selice, S., 186
Seligman, C., 431
Seligman, M. E. P., 105, 352
Selye, H., 80
Sexton, T. L., 386
Shainberg, L. W., 206
Sharp, L. K., 109
Shaver, P., 230
Shaver, P. R., 232
Sheehy, G., 310
Sheldon, W. H., 42
Sher, K. J., 417
Sheridan, J., 81
Sherwood, A., 402
Shields, J., 355, 360
Shields, S. A., 178, 180
Shore, D. L., 409
Shotland, R. L., 228
Showers, C., 105
Shrout, P. E., 92
Siegel, R. K., 420
Sigelman, C. K., 129
Sigelman, L., 129
Silverstone, B., 318
Simpson, J. A., 124
Singer, J. L., 25
Singh, D., 236
Singleton, J., 162
Sizemore, C. C., 348
Skelly, F., 129

Skinner, B. F., 34–36
Skodol, A. E., 345
Skoe, E. E., 68
Skokan, L., 105
Slade, P., 402
Slap, G. B., 410
Slobogian, C., 358
Slovenko, R., 359
Smith, J., 322
Smith, J. C., 454
Smith, M. L., 386
Smith, P. B., 138
Smith, P. C., 147
Smith, P. F., 392
Smith, P. O., 409
Snarey, J., 436
Snell, S., 287
Snowden, L. R., 413
Snyder, M., 124, 229
Sobel, D., 402
Sobell, L. C., 419
Sobell, M. B., 419
Solomon, S., 111
Sowarka, D., 322
Sowell, T., 299
Speck, P. M., 212
Speicher, C. E., 81, 82, 252
Speisman, J. C., 237
Spence, J. T., 174
Spilka, B., 438, 447
Sprei, J. E., 212
Squire, C., 215
Srinivasan, I. P., 409
Staats, A. W., 34
Stanley, B., 352
Stanley, M., 352
Stanley-Hagan, M. M., 270, 271
Stanton, A. L., 423
Stark, E., 15
Stark, R., 446
Staudinger, U. M., 322
Stein, M. B., 343
Stein, P. J., 252
Steinberg, L., 280
Steketze, G., 343
Stemberger, R. T., 343
Steptoe, A., 402, 403
Sternberg, R. J., 231
Stock, W. A., 307
Stoller, E. P., 320
Stout, J. C., 81, 252
Strean, H. S., 372
Strickland, A. L., 328
Strickland, B., 423
Strupp, H. H., 386
Studer, M., 445
Stunkard, A. J., 105, 407
Sturges, L. V., 409
Subich, L. M., 285
Sue, D., 188, 389, 390
Sue, D. W., 69, 188, 389, 390
Sue, S., 8, 69, 390, 391, 455, 456, 457
Suh, E. J., 179
Suinn, R. M., 61, 338, 348
Sullivan, H. S., 30

Sullivan, K. T., 232
Sullivan, Q., 236
Super, D. E., 278, 279
Surra, C. A., 252
Sutton, K., 25
Suzman, R. M., 318
Sweet, J. A., 261
Swift, J., 306, 318
Swim, J. K., 177
Swope, G. W., 447
Szasz, T., 339, 388
Szinovacz, M. E., 262
Szkio, M., 251

SUBJECT INDEX

A

Abnormal behavior
  diagnosis, advantages/disadvantages of, 339
  DSM-IV classification, 339–341
  and ethnic minorities, 338–339
  gender differences, 337–338
  interactionist approach, 337
  and maladaptive behavior, 335
  medical model, 335
  and poverty, 338–339
  psychological approach, 335–336
  sociocultural view, 335, 336–337
  statistical prevalence, 334–335
  See also Mental disorders
Acceptance, stage of dying, 326
Acculturation
  alternation model, 92
  meaning of, 92
Acculturative stress, 92–93
Accurate empathy, 374
Achievement, and self-esteem, 59
Action therapy, 369
Active-behavioral strategies, coping, 101, 102
Active-cognitive strategies, coping, 101, 102
Active listening, 374
Activity disorder, 403
Activity theory, late adulthood, 319
Actual self, 55
Addiction, 414–415
  cigarette smoking, 409
  disease model, 414–415
  life-process model, 415
  meaning of, 414
  withdrawal, 414
Adjustment
  challenges to process, 4–5
  definition of, 6–7
  meaning of, 11
  sociocultural approach, 7–8
Adolescence, stage of, 307
Adolescents
  in family life cycle, 258–259
  teenage pregnancy, 263
Adrenal glands, and stress, 80
Adulthood
  career consolidation in, 312
  cognitive development, 310
  continuity/discontinuity in, 314–316
  developmental transformations theory, 312
  early adulthood, 307
  Erikson's theory, 310–311
  keeping the meaning versus rigidity, 312
  late adulthood, 307, 316, 318–325

life events, 314
life-span theory, 310–311
middle adulthood, 307
middle age, 314
physical development, 309–310
seasons theory, 311–312
and social clock, 314
Advice, as communication barrier, 153
Aerobic exercise, 402
Affectionate love, 230–231
Affirmative action, 299
African Americans, 9
  family, 262–263, 264
  and family therapy, 382
  gender roles, 186–188
  and nonverbal communication, 158
  older women, profile of, 321
  and schizophrenia, 356
Ageism
  meaning of, 319
  and women, 320
Aggressive behavior, meaning of, 113
Agoraphobia, 343
AIDS, 214–216
  course of disease, 215, 217
  impact of, 214–215
  transmission of, 215
Alcoholics Anonymous (AA), 417–418
  twelve steps in, 418
Alcoholism, 415–419
  and codependence, 417–418
  genetic factors, 417
  incidence of, 416–417
  sociocultural view, 416–417
Alcoholism treatment
  Alcoholics Anonymous (AA), 417–418
  aversion therapy, 419
  behavior therapy, 419
  cognitive therapy, 418–419
  family therapy, 419
  moderation approach, 419
  multimodal approach, 419
Alternation model, acculturation, 92
Altruism, 226–228
Alzheimer's disease, nature of, 323–324
American culture, diversity of, 9
Amnesia, psychogenic, 346
Amphetamines, 420
Anal stage, 28
Androgens, 181
Androgyny, 174–175
  meaning of, 174
  measurement of, 175, 176

Anger
  and catharsis, 85
  causes of, 85
  control of, 86
  in relationships, 85–86
  stage of dying, 325–326
Anima/animus, 31
Anorexia nervosa, 406–407
Antianxiety drugs, 392
Antidepressant drugs, 392–393
  types of, 392–393
Antipsychotic drugs, 392
Antisocial personality disorder, 357–358
Anxiety disorders, 342–346
  and antianxiety drugs, 392
  generalized anxiety disorder, 342
  obsessive-compulsive disorder, 344–345
  panic disorder, 342
  phobic disorders, 342–344
  post-traumatic stress disorder, 345–346
Approach/approach conflict, 89
Approach/avoidance conflict, 89
Archetypes, 31
Arguments, as communication barrier, 154
Asian Americans, gender roles, 187, 188
Assertive behavior, meaning of, 113
Assertiveness training, 113–115
  bill of assertive rights, 115
  and women, 113
Astrology, nature of, 12
Attitudes, 125–127
  behavior influence on, 126
  and cognitive dissonance, 126–127
  prediction of behavior from, 126
  self-perception theory, 127
Attraction, 232–235
  and consensual validation, 234
  matching hypothesis, 235
  and personality characteristics, 235
  physical attraction, 234–235
  and similarity, 233–234
  sociocultural view, 236
Attribution theory, 125
  fundamental attribution error, 125
  internal and external attributions, 125
Audience, and persuasion, 131
Authoritarian parenting, 258
Authoritative parenting, 258
Autonomic nervous system
  divisions of, 80
  and stress, 79–80
Autonomy versus shame and doubt, 63
Aversion therapy, alcoholism treatment, 419

Aversive conditioning, 376
Avoidance/avoidance conflict, 89
Avoidance strategies, coping, 101, 102

B

Bad patient role, 412
Barbiturates, 419
Bargaining, stage of dying, 326
Basal metabolism rate (BMR), and obesity, 405
Behavior, definition of, 5
Behavioral medicine, 401–402
Behaviorism, 33–36
    classical conditioning, 34–35
    operant conditioning, 35–36
    radical behaviorists, 36
Behavior modification, 376–377
    token economy, 377
Behavior therapy, 375–377
    alcoholism treatment, 419
    aversive conditioning, 376
    behavior modification, 376–377
    systematic desensitization, 375–376
Biofeedback, 112–113
Biomedical therapy, 391–394
    drug therapy, 392–393
    electroconvulsive therapy, 393–394
    phototherapy, 393
    psychosurgery, 394
Bipolar disorder, 349
    lithium treatment, 392
Body dysmorphic disorder (BDD), 404
Body image, 403–404
    body dysmorphic disorder (BDD), 404
    meaning of, 403
    sociocultural view, 404
Body language, 157–159
    eye communication, 159
    facial expressions, 157, 159
    gestures, 157
    touch communication, 159
Borderline personality disorder, 357
Boundary ambiguity, in stepfamilies, 271
Bulimia, 407–408
Burnout, meaning of, 90
Bystander intervention, 227–228
    bystander effect, 228
    diffusion of responsibility, 228

C

Career consolidation, in adulthood, 312
Career development
    and adolescence, 279–280
    career plan, development of, 282–283
    and childhood, 278–279
    decline stage, 281–282
    and early adulthood, 280–281
    establishment stage, 280–281
    exploration stage, 279
    fantasy stage, 278
    growth stage, 279
    and late adulthood, 281–282
    maintenance stage, 281
    and middle adulthood, 281
    and personality type theory, 283–285
    realistic stage, 279
    tentative stage, 279
    vocational tests, 285
    See also Work
Care perspective, moral development, 435–436

Caring, altruism, 226–228
Catatonic schizophrenia, 355
Catharsis
    meaning of, 85
    in psychoanalysis, 372
Character education, 436–438
    cognitive moral education, 437–438
    direct and indirect education, 436
    and hidden curriculum, 436
    values clarification, 436–437
Child abuse, 269
    psychological abuse, 269
    sexual abuse, 269
Chlamydia, 217–218
Chronemics, 161
Cigarette smoking, 409–411
    as addiction, 409
    passive smoke, 409
    prevention of, 409–411
Civility, meaning of, 11
Class-bound values, 390
Classical conditioning, 34–35
    in animals, 34
    conditioned response (CR), 34
    conditioned stimulus (CS), 34
    in humans, 34–35
    reflexes, 34
    unconditioned response (UR), 34
    unconditioned stimulus (US), 34
Clinical psychology, 5–6
Cocaine, 420
Codependence, and alcoholism, 417–418
Cognitive appraisal
    primary appraisal, 88
    secondary appraisal, 88
Cognitive development
    adulthood, 310
    late adulthood, 319
Cognitive developmental theory, gender
    identity, 183–184
Cognitive moral education, 437–438
Cognitive restructuring, 103–104
    self-talk, 103–104
    thought stopping, 107
Cognitive social learning theory, 36–37
    observational learning, 36–37
    reciprocal determinism, 36
    self-efficacy, 37
Cognitive theories
    of coping, 101–110
    of depression, 351–352
    of gender identity, 183–184
    of stress, 88
Cognitive therapy, 377–378
    alcoholism treatment, 418–419
    Beck's approach, 378
    rational-emotive therapy, 377–378
    self-instruction methods, 377
Cohabitation, 252
    increase in, 261
Collective unconscious, 31
Collectivism
    versus individualism, 44–46
    meaning of, 45
Commitment
    civil commitment, 358
    criminal commitment, 358
    and identity, 67
    to mental hospital, 358
Communicator, in message, 128–129

Community psychology, 384–386
    development of, 384–385
    primary prevention, 385
    secondary prevention, 385
    tertiary prevention, 385–386
Compensation, 31
Competency, of criminal, 359
Conditional positive regard, 38
Conditioned response (CR), 34
Conditioned stimulus (CS), 34
Conflict, 89
    approach/approach conflict, 89
    approach/avoidance conflict, 89
    avoidance/avoidance conflict, 89
Conformity, 136–138
    cross-cultural view, 137–138
    experiments on, 136–137
Congruence, Rogers' theory, 55
Connotation, 147
Consciousness-raising groups, 388
Conscious self, 55
Consensual validation, and attraction, 234
Contexts
    critical thinking about, 456
    meaning of, 6, 8
Contraception, 201–202
    age and choice of, 201
    failure rates of, 203
Conventional level, of moral development, 434
Conversion disorder, 346
Coping
    active-behavioral strategies, 101, 102
    active-cognitive strategies, 101, 102
    avoidance strategies, 101, 102
    cognitive restructuring, 103–104
    with death/dying, 328–329
    emotion-focused coping, 101
    and empowerment, 107–108
    and humor, 110
    increasing disinhibition, 109–110
    and increasing self-control, 106–107
    in late adulthood, 323
    meaning of, 100
    multiple strategies, 110
    and optimism, 103, 105–106
    and positive self-illusion, 105
    problem-focused coping, 101
    and religion, 439
    and self-efficacy, 101–102
    and social support, 108–109
Counseling psychology, 5–6
Couple therapy, 381–382
Crack, 420
Criminal behavior, 358–359
    competency, 359
    criminal commitment, 358
    insanity defense, 358–359
Crisis, identity, 67
Critical thinking
    alternative explanations, exploring, 11
    on careers, 300
    about cultural pluralism, 455–458
    on domestic violence, 272
    about drug therapy, 395
    about electronic communication, 163
    about ethnic minorities, 454–455
    on gender equality, 190
    on labeling, 48
    on life review, 329
    about love, 244
    meaning of, 8

about mental disorders and social class, 360
about moral behavior, 448
on prison study, 139
scope of, 10
on self/identity, 72
on sexual risk-taking, 220
about stress, 95, 117
Criticizing, as communication barrier, 152
Cults, 446–447
reasons for joining, 447
Cultural pluralism, critical thinking about, 455–458
Culture, definition of, 7
Culture-bound values, 390

D

Daily hassles, and stress, 90–92
Date rape, 212
Death/dying, 325–329
communication with dying, 328
perceived control/denial adaptive strategy, 327–328
stages of, 325–326
survivor coping with, 328–329
Decline stage, career development, 281–282
Decoding, in communication, 145
Defense mechanisms, 26–28
displacement, 27
projection, 27
rationalization, 27
reaction formation, 27, 28
regression, 27–28
repression, 26
sublimation, 27, 28
Deficiency needs, 39
Deindividuation, 138
Deinstitutionalization, 384
Delusions, 354
Dementia, nature of, 323
Denial, stage of dying, 325, 327–328
Denotation, 147
Dependence, in relationships, 240
Depression
antidepressant drugs, 392–393
biological view, 352
cognitive/learning theory views, 351–352
electroconvusive therapy (ECT), 393–394
psychoanalytic theory of, 351
seasonal affective disorder, 393
sociocultural view, 352
stage of dying, 326
treatment of, 352
undiagnosed/untreated cases, 352–353
and women, 350, 352
Development
adolescence, 307
definition of, 307
early adulthood, 307
late adulthood, 307
middle adulthood, 307
transition to adulthood, 308
youth, 308
Developmental transformations theory, adulthood, 312
Diagnostic and Statistical Manual of Mental Disorders (DSM-IV), 339–341
issues related to, 340–341
multiaxial system, 340
neurotic disorders, 340
psychotic disorders, 340

Diathesis-stress view, 356
Diets, 405–406
effectiveness of, 406
and health, 406
Diffusion of responsibility, 228
Direct moral education, 436
Disease model, addiction, 414–415
Disorganized schizophrenia, 355
Displacement, 27
Dissociative disorders, 346–348
fugue, 347
multiple personality, 347–348
psychogenic amnesia, 346–347
Diversion, as communication barrier, 153–154
Divorce, 269–271
effects on adults, 269–270
effects on children, 270–271
increase in, 269
Double standard, meaning of, 206
Dream analysis, 372
Drug therapy, 392–393
antianxiety drugs, 392
antidepressant drugs, 392–393
antipsychotic drugs, 392

E

Early adulthood, stage of, 307
Eating disorders, 406–407
anorexia nervosa, 406–407
bulimia, 407–408
Eclectic approach, therapy, 369
Ectomorph, 42
Ego, 25–26
Egoism, 126–127
Electroconvulsive therapy (ECT), 393–394
Emotion-focused coping, 101
Emotions, 82–86
anger, 85–86, 238–239
classification of, 83
definition of, 82
disinhibition, increasing of, 109–110
gender differences, 180
happiness, 83–85
loneliness, 241–243
Empathy, Rogers' theory, 38
Empowerment, 107–108
of ethnic minorities, 108
meaning of, 107, 386
Empty nest syndrome, 259
Encoding, in communication, 145
Encounter group, 382
Endocrine system
hormones, 80
and stress, 80
Endogamy, mate selection, 252
Endomorph, 42
Environmental factors
obesity, 405
schizophrenic disorders, 356
Epigenetic principle, 63
Epinephrine, 80
Erikson's theory, 63–66
autonomy versus shame and doubt, 63
epigenetic principle, 63
generativity versus stagnation, 64, 310–311
identity development, 65–66
identity versus identity diffusion, 64
industry versus inferiority, 63–64
initiative versus guilt, 63

integrity versus despair, 64–65, 322
intimacy versus isolation, 64, 310
psychological moratorium, 65
trust versus mistrust, 63
Erogenous zones, 28
Establishment stage, career development, 280–281
Estrogen replacement therapy, 310
Estrogens, 181, 197
Ethical standards, and therapy, 371
Ethnic identity, definition of, 7
Ethnicity, definition of, 7
Ethnic minorities
and abnormal behavior, 338–339
acculturative stress, 92–93
critical thinking about, 454–455
and depression, 349–350
empowerment of, 108
and family, 262–263
and gender roles, 186–188
and health, 423
and health care, 413
identity development, 69–70
and late adulthood, 319–321
and nonverbal communication, 158
and psychotherapy, 389–391
self-esteem in, 60
Ethnocentrism, 456
Eustress, 81
Exemplification, impression management, 124
Exercise, 402–404
and activity disorder, 403
aerobic exercise, 402
and heart disease, 402
in late adulthood, 322–323
mental health benefits, 402–403
and weight loss, 406
Exhibitionism, 211
Exorcism, 367
Exploration stage, career development, 279
Extrinsic religious orientation, 441
Extroversion, and happiness, 83
Eye communication, 159

F

Facial expressions, 157, 159
Family, 254–264
empty nest syndrome, 259
and ethnic minorities, 262–263
family with adolescents, 258–259
gender role changes in, 261–262
in later life, 260–261
launching stage, 254
marriage stage, 254, 256
at midlife, 259–260
parenthood, 256–258
small family size trend, 257, 262
women and family work, 262
Family therapy, 381
alcoholism treatment, 419
family systems therapy, 381
Family violence, 267–269
child abuse, 269
spouse abuse, 268
Fantasy stage, career development, 278
Fear of success, 293–294
Female reproductive organs, 197
Feminist psychology, 170–172
Feminization of poverty, 94

Fetishism, 210–211
Fixation, 28
Flow, meaning of, 85
Formal groups, 286
Free association, 371–372
Freudian slip, 25
Freudian theory, 25–30
   anal stage, 28
   criticisms of, 30
   defense mechanisms, 26–28
   erogenous zones, 28
   fixation, 28
   genital stage, 29
   id/ego/superego in, 25–26
   identification theory, 182
   latency stage, 28–29
   neo-Freudians, 29–30
   Oedipus complex, 28
   oral stage, 28
   phallic stage, 28
   pleasure principle, 26
   psychoanalysis, 371–372
   reality principle, 26
   revisionism related to, 30
Friendship, 228–229
   compared to love, 229
Frustration
   meaning of, 89
   responses to, 89
   and stress, 89
Fugue, 347
Fully functioning person, 38–39

G

Gender, definition of, 7, 168
Gender differences
   abnormal behavior, 337–338
   cognitive differences, 178
   controversy over, 179
   emotions, 180
   in family work, 262
   identity development, 68–69
   nonverbal communication, 157
   physiological differences, 178
   self-disclosure, 151
   socioemotional differences, 178–179, 180
   stress, 94
Gender identity, 180–184
   cognitive developmental theory, 183–184
   definition of, 168
   gender schema theory, 184
   learning theory, 182–183
   neurobiological view, 181
   psychoanalytic theory, 181–182
Gender identity disorder, transsexualism,
   211–212
Gender roles, 172, 174–175
   androgyny, 174–175
   changing in families, 261–262
   definition of, 168
   and ethnic minorities, 186–188
   gender crossing, 188
   gender redefinition, 188–189
   gender-role transcendence, 175
   men's issues, 184–186
   prescribed gender roles, 188
   as process, 188
   sociocultural view, 188–189
Gender-role transcendence, 175

Gender schema, meaning of, 184
Gender schema theory, 184
Gender stereotyping, 175, 177
   sexism, 177
General adaptation syndrome, 80–81
   stages in, 81
Generalized anxiety disorder, 342
Generativity versus stagnation, 64, 310–311
Genetic factors
   alcoholism, 417
   obesity, 405
   schizophrenic disorders, 355
Genital herpes, 218
Genital stage, 29
Genuineness, 374
Gestalt therapy, 374–375
Gestures, 157
Gilligan's moral development theory, 434–435
Glass ceiling, 298
Gonorrhea, 217
Good patient role, 412
Gradual conversion, religious, 445
Graphology, 14
   nature of, 12
Great person theory, 134–135
Groups
   conformity, 136–138
   deindividuation, 138
   groupthink, 138
   leadership, 134–135
   majority-minority influence, 135
   nature of, 134
   norms, 134
   roles, 134
   work groups, 286
Group therapy, 378–384
   consciousness-raising groups, 388
   couple therapy, 381–382
   encounter group, 382
   family systems therapy, 381
   family therapy, 381
   features of, 379–381
   personal growth groups, 382–383
   self-help groups, 383–384
Groupthink, 138
Growth stage, career development, 279

H

Hallucinations, 354
Hallucinogens, 421
Happiness, 83–85
   factors contributing to, 83
   and flow, 85
   and optimal experiences, 84–85
   and religion, 440
Hardiness, characteristics of, 87
Health
   and cigarette smoking, 409–411
   and eating disorders, 406–407
   and ethnic minorities, 423
   and exercise, 402–404
   and nutrition, 408–409
   and obesity, 405–406
   preventive health care, 422–423
   women's health movement, 423
Health care
   and ethnic minorities, 413
   rising costs, 422

Health psychology, 401
Hearing, meaning of, 148
Heart disease, and exercise, 402
Heterosexuality, 202, 204–206
   attitudes/behaviors in, 202, 204–205
   meaning of, 252
Hidden curriculum, and character
   education, 436
Hierarchy of needs theory, 39, 40
   deficiency needs, 39
   metaneeds (growth needs), 39
   self-actualization, 39, 41
   types of needs in, 40
Homogamy, mate selection, 252
Homosexuality, 206–208
   attitudes toward, 207
   causation possibilities, 208
   homosexual relationships, 252–253
   meaning of, 252
Hormones
   functions of, 80
   and gender development, 181
   and sexual arousal, 196–197
Horney's theory, 30
Humanistic theories
   basic concepts in, 37
   evaluation of, 39, 41
   hierarchy of needs theory, 39, 40
   of religion, 444
   Rogers' theory, 38–39
Human sexual response cycle, 198–199
   phases of, 198–199
Humor, and coping, 110
Hypochondriasis, 346

I

Id, 25–26
Ideal self, 55, 72
Identification theory, 182
Identity
   commitment, 67
   crisis, 67
   Erikson's theory, 65–66
   and ethnic minorities, 69–70
   gender differences, 68–69
   identity achievement, 68
   identity diffusion, 67
   identity foreclosure, 67
   identity moratorium, 67
   identity statuses theory, 66–68
   and life span, 66
   white identity model, 70
Identity development, Erikson's theory, 65–66
Identity versus identity diffusion, 64
Illness, 411–414
   and patient compliance, 412, 414
   role of patient, 412
   seeking treatment, 411–412
   and stress, 81, 82, 293
Immune system, psychoneuroimmunology, 81
Impostor phenomenon, 294
Impression formation, 123
   primacy effect, 123
Impression management, 123–124
   strategies for, 124
Incest, 213
Indirectly aggressive behavior, meaning of, 113
Indirect moral education, 436

Individualism
    versus collectivism, 44–46
    meaning of, 45
Individual psychology, 31
    compensation, 31
    inferiority complex, 31
    overcompensation, 31
    striving for superiority, 31
    superiority complex, 31
Individuated-connected level, relationship
        maturity, 237
Indulgent parenting, 258
Industry versus inferiority, 63–64
Inferiority complex, 31
Informal groups, 286
Ingratiation, impression management, 124
Initiative versus guilt, 63
Insanity, legal definition, 358
Insanity defense, 358–359
Insight therapy, 369
Integrity versus despair, 64–65, 322
Interactionist approach, abnormal
        behavior, 337
Internalization, and moral development, 434
Interpersonal communication
    barriers to, 152–153
    components of, 145
    dimensions of, 145–146
    listening, 148–150
    in marriage, 266–267
    meaning of, 146
    nonverbal communication, 156–162
    self-disclosure, 150–151
    transactional nature of, 146
    verbal communication, 147–148
Interpretation, in psychoanalysis, 372
Intimacy, 235–238
    Erikson's view, 236
    intimate interaction, levels of, 237–238
Intimacy versus isolation, 64, 310
Intimate style, of intimate interaction, 237
Intimidation, impression management, 124
Intrinsic religious orientation, 441
Isolated style, of intimate interaction, 238

J

Jealousy, 239–240
Job satisfaction, 287–294
    determinants of, 287–288
    and fear of success, 293–294
    optimization of, 288
    and work-related stress, 288–293
Johari window, 150–151
Judging, as communication barrier, 152, 154
Jungian theory, 30–31
    anima/animus, 31
    archetypes, 31
    collective unconscious, 31
Justice perspective, moral development, 435
Just manageable difficulty, 288

K

Kohlberg's moral development theory,
        434–435
    criticisms of, 435
    stages in, 434

L

Labeling, as communication barrier, 152
Late adulthood, 316, 318–325
    activity theory, 319
    ageism, 319
    cognitive development, 319
    coping in, 323
    death/dying, 325–329
    Erikson's theory, 322
    and ethnic minorities, 319–321
    exercise effects, 322–323
    and increased life expectancy, 316
    life review, 322
    mental health problems in, 323–325
    oldest old, 318
    physical development, 319
    sociocultural view, 321–322
    stage of, 307
Latency stage, 28–29
Latent content, dreams, 372
Later life, family in, 260–261
Latinos, 9
    family, 262–263, 264
    gender roles, 187, 188
    and nonverbal communication, 158
Launching stage, family life cycle, 254
Leadership, 134–135
    great person theory, 134–135
    situational theory, 135
Learned helplessness, and depression, 352
Learning theories
    basic concepts in, 34
    behaviorism, 33–36
    cognitive social learning theory, 36–37
    of depression, 351–352
    evaluation of, 37
    gender identity, 182–183
    of phobia, 344
    of religion, 442
Leisure, 294–295
Life events, 314
    and stress, 90–92
Life-process model, addiction, 415
Life review, 329
    late adulthood, 322
Life-span theory, 310–311
Lifestyles
    cohabitation, 252
    family life, 254–264
    homosexual couples, 252–253
    marriage, 250–252, 265–271
    singlehood, 253
Listening, 148–150
    improvement of, 149–150
    meaning of, 148
    and paraphrasing, 149
    reflective listening, 149
    and silence, 161
Lithium, 392
Lobotomy, 394
Loneliness, 241–243
    and college students, 242–243
    factors related to, 241–242
    remedies for, 243
Love, 229–231
    affectionate love, 230–231
    falling out of, 240–241
    compared to friendship, 229

versus infatuation, 231
    romantic love, 229–230
    triangular theory of, 231
LSD, 421
Lying, signs of, 156

M

Maintenance stage, career development, 281
Major depression, 348–349
Majority-minority influence, 135
Male rape, 212–213
Male reproductive organs, 197
Managed health care, effects on cost of
        therapy, 370–371
Mania, in bipolar disorder, 349
Manifest content, dreams, 372
Mantra, 111
Marijuana, 420–421
Marriage, 250–252, 265–271
    communication in, 266–267
    conflict management, 267
    decision making about, 252
    divorce, 269–271
    dual-career marriage, 261
    expectations/myths about, 265–266
    in family life cycle, 254, 256
    functions of, 250–252
    mate selection, 252
    postponement/avoidance of, 261
    remarriage, 271
Masochism, 211
Matching hypothesis, attraction, 235
Mate selection, 252
Medical model, abnormal behavior, 335
Meditation, 111–112
    physiological effects, 111–112
Medium, and persuasion, 130–131
Men, female hatred of, 172
Menopause, 309–310
    and estrogen replacement therapy, 310
Men's movement, 184–186
Mental disorders
    anxiety disorders, 342–346
    commitment, 358
    and criminal behavior, 358–359
    dissociative disorders, 346–348
    mood disorders, 348–353
    personality disorders, 357–358
    schizophrenic disorders, 353–357
    somatoform disorders, 346
    substance-use disorders, 358
Mental hospitals, historical view, 367
Mental processes, definition of, 5
Mentoring, meaning of, 37
Mesomorph, 42
Message
    in interpersonal communication, 145
    and persuasion, 130
Metaneeds (growth needs), 39
Middle adulthood, stage of, 307
Midlife, family at, 259–260
Midlife transition, 314
Minority groups. *See* Ethnic minorities
Misandry, 172
Misogyny, 172
Modeling, observational learning, 36–37
Monochronic, 161

Psychobabble, 16–17
Psychodynamic therapy
  Gestalt therapy, 374–375
  person-centered therapy, 373–374
  psychoanalysis, 371–373
Psychogenic amnesia, 346–347
Psychological information
  being consumer of, 14–15
  self-help books, 15–18
Psychological moratorium, 65
Psychology
  clinical and counseling psychology, 5–6
  definition of, 5
  as science, 5
Psychoneuroimmunology, study of, 81
Psychosexual disorders, 209–212
  exhibitionism, 211
  fetishism, 210–211
  masochism, 211
  paraphilias, 210–211
  pedophilia, 211
  psychosexual dysfunction, 210
  sadism, 211
  transvestism, 211
  voyeurism, 211
Psychosurgery, 394
Psychotherapy, 369–371
  barriers to effectiveness, 390–391
  and ethnic minorities, 389–390, 391
  finding a therapist, 387
  gender issues, 387–388
  outcome research, 386
  themes/specificity in, 386–387
Psychotic disorders, 340
  antipsychotic drugs, 392
Punishment, operant conditioning, 36

R

Radical behaviorists, 36
Rape, 212–213
  date rape, 212
  male rape, 212–213
  recovery after, 212
Rational-emotive therapy, 377–378
Rationalization, 27
Rational Recovery, 419
Reaction formation, 27, 28
Realistic stage, career development, 279
Reality principle, 26
Reciprocal determinism, 36
Reflective listening, 149
Reflexes, in classical conditioning, 34
Regression, 27–28
Reinforcement, operant conditioning, 36
Relationships
  anger in, 238–239
  attraction, 232–235
  cognition in, 231–232
  dependence in, 240
  friendship, 228–229
  intimacy, 235–238
  jealousy in, 239–240
  love, 229–231
  relationship maturity, levels of, 237
  self-disclosure in, 151
  social exchange theory of, 227
Relaxation, process of, 112
Religion
  and adjustment, 438–440
  behavioral model of, 442

and coping, 439
cults, 446–447
definition of, 438
development of religious belief, 444–445
and happiness, 440
humanistic model of, 444
psychoanalytic model of, 443
psychology of, 438
religious conversion, 445–446
religious orientation, intrinsic and extrinsic,
  441–442
religious socialization, 445–446
scope of, 438
sociocultural model of, 444
Repression, 26
Resistance, in psychoanalysis, 372
Rogers' theory
  conditional and unconditional positive
    regard, 38
  congruence, 55
  fully functioning person, 38–39
  person-centered therapy, 373–374
  self-concept, 38, 55
Role-focused level, relationship maturity, 237
Role models, 72
Role overload, and women, 94, 291–292
Roles, groups, 134
Romantic love, 229–230
Romantic script, 206

S

Sadism, 211
Schema, meaning of, 184
Schizophrenic disorders, 353–357
  catatonic schizophrenia, 355
  characteristics of, 354
  diathesis-stress view, 356
  disorganized schizophrenia, 355
  environmental factors, 356
  genetic factors, 355
  neurobiological factors, 356
  paranoid schizophrenia, 354, 355
  and social class, 360
  sociocultural view, 356–357
  undifferentiated schizophrenia, 355
Schizotypal personality disorder, 357
Science, psychology as, 5
Scientology, nature of, 12
Seasonal affective disorder (SAD), 393
Seasons theory, adulthood, 311–312
Secondary appraisal, 88
Secondary prevention, 385
Self
  actual self, 55
  conscious and unconscious selves, 55
  definition of, 54
  diminished self, 58–59
  ideal self, 55
  multiple selves, 61
  narcissism, 59, 61
  ought self, 55
  possible selves, 55–56
  self-concept, 55
  self-congruence, 55
  self-discrepancy theory, 57
  self-esteem, 56–57
  self-evaluation, 55–56
  self-understanding, 54–55
  sociocultural view, 61
Self-actualization, 39, 41
  characteristics of, 41

Self-concept
  meaning of, 55
  Rogers' theory, 38
Self-control, method for increasing,
  106–107
Self-disclosure, 150–151
  gender differences, 151
  Johari window, 150–151
  meaning of, 150
  process of, 151
  in relationships, 151
Self-efficacy, 37, 59
  increasing of, 102–103
  meaning of, 101–102, 377
Self-esteem, 56–57
  in ethnic minorities, 60
  factors in increase of, 59
  and happiness, 83
  and jealous feelings, 240
  low self-esteem, 58–59
Self-focused level, relationship maturity, 237
Self-help books
  best books, listing of, 18
  evaluation of, 15–18
Self-help groups, 383–384
  types of, 383
Self-instruction methods, 377
Self-monitoring, 72, 124–125
Self-perception theory, 127
Self-promotion, impression management, 124
Self-talk, 103–104
Self-understanding, meaning of, 54–55
Serotonin, 352
Set point, and obesity, 405
Sex, meaning of, 7
Sex education, 200–201
  sociocultural view, 201
Sexism
  ageism/sexism double jeopardy, 320
  examples of, 177
  meaning of, 169, 177
  modern type, 177
  old-fashioned type, 177
Sex therapy, forms of, 210
Sexual abuse
  of children, 269
  and multiple personality disorder, 348
Sexual arousal, 196–198
  arousal cues, 198
  hormonal influences, 196–197
  sociocultural view, 197–198
Sexual harassment, 212
Sexuality
  contraception, 201–202
  heterosexuality, 202, 204–206
  homosexuality, 206–208
  human sexual response cycle, 198–199
  incest, 213
  pornography, 213–214
  psychosexual disorders, 209–212
  rape, 212–213
  sexual arousal, 196–198
  sexual harassment, 212
  sexual knowledge, 200–210
  sexually transmitted disease, 214–218
  sexual satisfaction, 209
  sexual scripts, 205–206
Sexual knowledge, 200
  sex education, 200–201
  sexual myths, 200

Sexually transmitted disease, 214–218
    AIDS, 214–216
    chlamydia, 217–218
    genital herpes, 218
    gonorrhea, 217
    risk reduction, 218
    syphilis, 217
Sexual scripts, 205–206
    double standard, 206
    romantic script, 206
    traditional religious script, 205–206
Silence, as nonverbal communication,
        161–162
Similarity, and attraction, 233–234
Singlehood, 253
    increase in, 261
Situational theory, leadership, 135
Skepticism, meaning of, 11
Social clock, 314
Social cognition
    attitudes, 125–127
    attribution theory, 125
    social perception, 123–125
Social comparison, 123
Social exchange theory, 227
Social influence
    obedience, 131–133
    persuasion, 128–131
    resistance to, 132–133
Socialization, religious socialization, 445–446
Social learning theory, gender identity,
        182–183
Social perception, 123–125
    impression formation, 123
    impression management, 123–124
    meaning of, 123
    self-monitoring, 124–125
    social comparison, 123
Social phobia, 343–344
Social Readjustment Rating Scale, 90, 91
Social support
    and coping, 108–109
    meaning of, 108
Sociocultural view
    abnormal behavior, 335, 336–337
    of adjustment, 7–8
    alcoholism, 416–417
    American culture, diversity of, 9
    attraction, 236
    body image, 404
    conformity, 137–138
    depression, 352
    emphasis in, 7
    gender roles, 188–189
    individualism versus collectivism, 44–46
    late adulthood, 321–322
    nonverbal communication, 157
    nutrition, 408–409
    of personality, 44–46
    proxemics, 160–161
    of religion, 444
    schizophrenic disorders, 356–357
    self, 61
    sex education, 201
    sexual arousal, 197–198
    stress, 92–93
Somatoform disorders, 346
    conversion disorder, 346
    hypochondriasis, 346
Somatotype theory, 42

Spatial communication, 159–161
    chronemics, 161
    proxemics, 160–161
    territoriality, 161
Speaking skills, 147–148
Spouse abuse, 268
Stepfamilies, 271
    boundary ambiguity in, 271
Stereotyped style, of intimate interaction, 238
Stereotyping, gender stereotyping, 175, 177
Stimulant drugs, 420
Strain, definition of, 79
Stress
    acculturative stress, 92–93
    and autonomic nervous system, 79–80
    behavioral manifestations, 82
    cognitive view, 88
    and conflict, 89
    definition of, 79
    emotional factors, 82–86
    and endocrine system, 80
    and frustration, 89
    gender differences, 94
    general adaptation syndrome, 80–81
    and illness, 81, 82
    and life events/daily hassles, 90–92
    and overload, 90
    personality factors, 87
    positive stress, 81
    and poverty, 94
    and schizophrenia, 356
    sociocultural view, 92–93
    work-related stress, 288–293
    See also Coping
Stress management
    assertiveness training, 113–115
    biofeedback, 112–113
    goals of, 110
    meditation, 111–112
    time management, 115
Stressors, definition of, 79
Striving for superiority, 31
Sublimation, 27, 28
Substance-use disorders, 358
Sudden conversion, religious, 445
Suicide, 349–351
    and ethnic minorities, 349–350
    interventions for, 351
    predictors of, 349
Superego, 25–26
Superhuman syndrome, 290–292
Superiority complex, 31
Supplication, impression management, 124
Sympathetic nervous system, 80
Syphilis, 217
Systematic desensitization, 375–376

T

Tardive dyskinesia, 392
Teenage pregnancy, 263
Tentative stage, career development, 279
Territoriality, 161
Testosterone, 197
Therapy
    access to services, 369–371
    action therapy, 369
    behavior therapy, 375–377
    biomedical therapy, 391–394

cognitive therapy, 377–378
community psychology, 384–386
eclectic approach, 369
economic factors, 370–371
ethical standards, 371
feminist therapy, 388–389
Gestalt therapy, 374–375
group therapy, 378–384
historical view, 366–367
insight therapy, 369
person-centered therapy, 373–374
practitioners, types of, 369, 370
psychoanalysis, 371–372
psychotherapy, 369–371
Thought stopping, 107
Threats, as communication barrier, 153
Time management, 115
To-do list, 115
Token economy, 377
Tolerance, meaning of, 414
Touch communication, 159
Traditional religious script, 205–206
Traits, definition of, 41
Trait theories, 42–43
    core personality factors, 43
    early theories, 43
    trait-situation interaction, 43–44
Tranquilizers, 419
Transaction, in interpersonal
        communication, 146
Transcendental meditation, 111
Transference, in psychoanalysis, 372
Transsexualism, 211–212
Transvestism, 211
Trephining, 366–367
Triangular theory of love, 231
Trust versus mistrust, 63
Twelve-step programs, 417
    Alcoholics Anonymous (AA), 417–418
Type A behavior pattern, 87, 293
Type C behavior pattern, 87

U

Unconditional positive regard, 38, 374
Unconditioned response (UR), 34
Unconditioned stimulus (US), 34
Unconscious self, 55
Undifferentiated schizophrenia, 355

V

Values
    and college students, 432–433
    and culture, 431
    meaning of, 8, 10, 430
    moral development, 434–438
    in psychology, 433–434
    and psychotherapy, 390
    value conflict, 431
Values clarification, 436–437
Verbal communication, 147–148
    barriers to, 152–154
    connotation, 147
    denotation, 147
    speaking skills, 147–148
Violence, in family, 267–269
Vocational tests, 285
Voyeurism, 211

W

Withdrawal, meaning of, 414
Women
    ageism/sexism double jeopardy, 320
    career versus domestic life, 291
    and depression, 350, 352
    and education, 171
    and employment, 171
    feminist psychology, 170–172
    male hatred of, 172
    and politics, 129, 171
    and poverty, 94
    psychological research on, 169–170
    and psychosocial issues, 171
    sexual violence against, 212–214
    superhuman syndrome, 290–292
    women's health movement, 423
    See also Gender differences
Word salad, 354
Work
    affirmative action, 299
    glass ceiling, 298
    job satisfaction, 287–294
    and leisure, 294–295
    workforce changes, 297–299
    work groups, 286–287
    workplace changes, 296–297
    work-related stress, 288–293
    See also Career development
Workaholics, 292–293
Workforce 2000, 297

Work-related stress
    comprehensive model for, 288–289
    and dysfunctional workplaces, 289
    and family strains, 289–299
    and health problems, 293
    superhuman syndrome, 290–292
    workaholics, 292–293

Y

Youth
    stage of, 308
    values of, 432–433

Z

Zen Buddhism, on self, 61